THE WOMEN'S ARMY CORPS

COLONEL OVETA CULP HOBBY

UNITED STATES ARMY IN WORLD WAR II

Special Studies

THE WOMEN'S ARMY CORPS

by

Mattie E. Treadwell

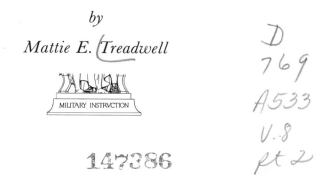

MILITARY INSTRVCTION

147386

OFFICE OF THE CHIEF OF MILITARY HISTORY

DEPARTMENT OF THE ARMY

WASHINGTON, D. C., 1954

Library of Congress Catalog Card Number 53–61563

Reprinted 1968

UNITED STATES ARMY IN WORLD WAR II
Kent Roberts Greenfield, General Editor

Advisory Committee
(As of 1 May 1953)

James P. Baxter
President, Williams College

Brig. Gen. Verdi B. Barnes
Army War College

John D. Hicks
University of California

Brig. Gen. Leonard J. Greeley
Industrial College of the Armed Forces

William T. Hutchinson
University of Chicago

Brig. Gen. Elwyn D. Post
Army Field Forces

S. L. A. Marshall
Detroit News

Col. Thomas D. Stamps
United States Military Academy

Charles S. Sydnor
Duke University

Col. C. E. Beauchamp
Command and General Staff College

Charles H. Taylor
Harvard University

Office of the Chief of Military History
Maj. Gen. Albert C. Smith, Chief*

Chief Historian	Kent Roberts Greenfield
Chief, War Histories Division	Col. G. G. O'Connor
Chief, Editorial and Publication Division	Col. B. A. Day
Chief, Editorial Branch	Joseph R. Friedman
Chief, Cartographic Branch	Wsevolod Aglaimoff
Chief, Photographic Branch	Maj. Arthur T. Lawry

*Maj. Gen. Orlando Ward was succeeded by General Smith on 1 February 1953.

v

... to Those Who Served

Foreword

This history of the WAC is comprehensive and detailed. The author has written it not only from available records but also out of personal experience. She was a WAC staff officer, who, together with all the other Wacs, found herself in a man's army that was somewhat shocked by the advent of a women's corps in its midst.

It is usual for both newcomer and old resident to have suspicions of each other, but after the characteristic period of false starts prejudices disappear and confidence is established. So it was with the WAC and the Army.

This book stresses the misunderstanding, appropriately enough, since it affected many decisions reached at the policy-making level. The WAC did not always understand the Army—its customs and traditions, its organization and necessary chain of command. The Army did not always understand the WAC—its needs and temperament, and the many other things that man, being the son of woman, should have known but did not, much to his continued embarrassment.

Washington, D. C.
30 January 1953

ORLANDO WARD
Maj. Gen., U.S.A.
Chief of Military History

The Author

Mattie E. Treadwell, a native of Texas, holds a B.A. and an M.A. degree from the University of Texas. During World War II she was an officer, first in the WAAC and later in the WAC, holding such assignments as assistant to the Director WAC, assistant to the Air WAC Officer, and assistant to the Commandant, School of WAC Personnel Administration. She had the additional distinction of having been a member of the first class of women sent to the Command and General Staff School. While on active duty she attained the rank of lieutenant colonel.

From September 1947 to March 1952 Miss Treadwell was a historian in the Office of the Chief of Military History. Upon her departure she became Assistant Director, Dallas Regional Office, Federal Civil Defense Administration, in charge of women's activities and volunteer manpower, an office that she currently holds. Her present military status is that of a lieutenant colonel in the U.S. Air Force Reserve.

Washington, D. C.
30 January 1953

LEO J. MEYER
Colonel, Reserve Corps
Deputy Chief Historian

Preface

Soon after the end of hostilities, the decision was made to devote to the Women's Army Corps one volume of the Army's major historical series, U.S. ARMY IN WORLD WAR II. Although small by comparison with the size of the Army, the WAC at its peak strength of 100,000 constituted an enviably large group for study. Because of its 24-hour-a-day control of its personnel, the Army had access to information not easily obtainable by business or industry, concerning not only the women's job efficiency but their clothing and housing needs, and the effects of their employment upon their health, conduct, morale, and recreation.

For most of the war months, the potential importance of this material was not recognized, and little systematic effort was made to collect it. A number of Army commands had rulings against the collection of separate statistics for women, while others lacked either the time or the means to compile such material.

In postwar days, with renewed emphasis upon future planning, the present study was authorized in an attempt to pull together such evidence as remained. It was recognized that the experience of the relatively small group in World War II might provide a guide to any later and more extensive national mobilization of womanpower that might be necessary. Although no one possessed sufficient clairvoyance to predict the course of history, it was plainly evident that, in any future emergencies, the proper mobilization and employment of womanpower reserves might become a primary national issue.

The preservation of the wartime discoveries made in this field assumed added importance in view of the fact that no other American or British service has yet published a full official history of its women's corps. Significantly, comparison of the records of these groups reveals that the problems and achievements of each fall into a pattern so similar as to suggest a strong measure of predictability of the course of future groups. The Navy Department's draft narrative of the WAVES remains under classification, as do those of the Women Marines and the Army Nurse Corps. The story of the Air Forces women is included in the present volume, since the wartime Air Wacs were a part of the WAC.

The Army's discoveries in general appear valid and reliable, not only for militarized groups, but for most nonmilitary institutions or businesses which train or employ women. The observations on health, fatigue, accident rates, and psychological patterns should be a useful addition to current industrial studies. The discoveries in the fields of training, housing, clothing, feeding, and disciplining groups of women may present a fresh viewpoint to educational institutions. In particular, the conclusions on the leadership of women offer a clue to an explanation of the current misunderstandings and contradictory impressions on the subject.

It must be recognized at the outset that the problem of integrating women into an army was merely a part of the larger problem of their evolving status in civil life, accelerated by the industrial revolution and affecting every phase of modern society. Although the scope of this volume does not permit frequent comment upon the general place of women in society, few of the developments were without precedent. This was particularly true of the public skepticism and masculine hostility into which the WAC ran headlong in its first year. Admittedly, the Army had its share of a conservative element that had scarcely recovered from the shock of the mechanized horse when confronted with the militarized woman.

It should also be noted that the development and integration into the Army of a women's corps was at every turn a part of the larger development of the Army, and that few problems of the smaller group were unique. The Women's Army Corps, like this volume, must be viewed in perspective as one small facet of the larger entity.

While parallel, the problems of the employment of men and women were by no means identical in nature or solution. At the time of the organization of the Women's Army Auxiliary Corps early in World War II, the misapprehension was general that women could be treated exactly like men and that little research would therefore be required for the successful incorporation of womanpower into the Army. Some believed that the WAC, as a minor group within the Army, was in the same general category as other groups dubbed minorities by reason of race, creed, or color, for whom differences of treatment would be improper. In practice it was soon discovered, however, that while a soldier might wear the same design of clothing regardless of race or creed, the same could not be said regardless of sex. The same principle was shortly found true in the fields of medicine, conduct, recreation, recruiting, physical capacity, and others. While all authorities were agreed that equal treatment must be given to men and women in the Army, it was soon apparent that *equal* did not mean *identical* in every case. The Army was thus faced with the problem of what styles of garments, though not identical with those of men, gave equal comfort, fit, and military appearance; what medications and surgery, although not identical, promoted equally good health; what standards of conduct, well-being, recreation, and training would enable the military service to answer to the American public for the women in its keeping as conscientiously as it customarily did for the men. In most cases, by the end of the war, these problems were successfully solved or the key to the solution was known.

As the following pages will reveal, the final conclusions of the wartime heads of the women's services were far from optimistic concerning the dangers of employing women in the armed forces if their special needs were not constantly understood and dealt with by trained specialists and well-informed commanders.

Several major decisions concerning the scope and nature of this volume were dictated by the wide range of subjects it must cover, by the fact that its material was scattered through world-wide Army commands, and by the fact that only one writer-researcher could be assigned to the task. One such decision was that the approach must generally be on the level of policy and planning, rather than upon that of individual unit histories and statistics. Army commands employing Wacs activated and inactivated hundreds of companies, and sent thousands of women back and forth among them individually and in small groups, to an extent that would have required another volume to record. Even could statistics be included upon the locations and movements of such personnel, the significance for future planning would be small.

However, in the interests of proper emphasis and perspective, it should be noted that an account at this high level is not necessarily a complete picture of the Corps. The efficiency of a WAC unit in the field was often relatively untouched by the struggles concerning the nation's womanpower which raged over its head. A WAC unit could, and often did, exist happily for months without proper uniforms, training, or other advantages, no matter how distressing to the War Department such deficiencies might be.

A generally more unworried tone could be given this volume only if it were possible to place in a row, beside the headaches of headquarters, the approximately five hundred separate stories of field achievement, which by sheer weight would reduce the policy and planning problems to their proper proportion.

Another decision which affected the nature of the history was that it should include all possible material of assistance to future planners. A considerably shorter volume could have been produced by a rapid account of the Corps' formation, strength, employment, and achievements, with no indication of its problems, the private controversies they engendered, or the means by which they were surmounted. However, for those specialists whose assigned mission is the efficient employment of womanpower, or even for the general Army reader, such a surface analysis would have been of small value.

In preparing this volume, I have had the advice of almost all of the wartime leaders, men and women, of the Women's Army Corps. Col. Oveta Culp Hobby has not only commented upon the manuscript, but has answered specific questions and has given me generously of her time in discussing puzzling references. Lt. Col. Helen Hamilton Woods, WAAC preplanner and later Deputy Director, read and reread various drafts, and opened her Washington home to me for interviews with prominent participants including Congresswoman Edith Nourse Rogers. Dr. Betty Bandel has submitted a detailed commentary on each chapter in its draft form, and has answered innumerable questions concerning the 40,000 Air Forces women, whom she represented, and the Corps as a whole, of which she was Acting Deputy. Lt. Col. Katherine R. Goodwin has clarified many points regarding the Army Service Forces Wacs, for which she was advisor. Before her death, Dr. Jess Rice, the wartime Deputy Director, commented upon early parts of the manuscript and gave me many admonitions concerning historical technique, which I have endeavored to follow, as well as strictures against making her a heroine of the story, which I have endeavored to ignore in the interests of historical accuracy.

Gen. George C. Marshall has read and commented upon various passages, appealing on one occasion to the former Director to know if she had actually encountered all of the recruiting difficulties described.* Maj. Gen. Miller G. White, the Army man who, as G–1 of the War Department, worked most closely with WAC policy, has read all of the manuscript and added comments and excerpts from his diary. The Auxiliary Corps portion has been commented upon by, among others, Maj. Gen. John H. Hilldring, Brig. Gens. Don C. Faith and Thomas B. Catron, and Cols. Harold Tasker and Gilman Mudgett.

To the hundreds of other Army men and women—from general officer to private—who have given me their opinions—each chapter will make proper acknowledgment.

Within the Office of the Chief of Military History, I have received great assistance from the Chief Historian, Dr. Kent R. Greenfield, the Deputy Chief Historian, Lt. Col. Leo J. Meyer, and their entire staff, whose aid will be particularly acknowledged in the chapters concerned. Dr. Mae Link has contributed valuable research on the Army Service Forces, and Maj. Margaret Bacchus on the British services. For typing and preparing the manuscript I am indebted to Sgt. Amelia Madrak, Mrs. Lorraine Bonifant, Mrs. Lois Riley, and Mrs. Elizabeth Phillips and her staff.

My particular aid and counsel has been Miss Ruth Stout, the editor of this volume, who has provided much-needed help and encouragement as well as perspective, advice, and good judgment. We are both grateful to the Chief Editor, Mr. Joseph R. Friedman, for his sympathetic interest and advice, and to Mr. Allen R. Clark for care and precision in copy editing. I am also indebted to Mr. Clark for the comprehensive index. The work of selecting illustrations has been performed by Miss Margaret E. Tackley, who lent the project not only her technical skill but her experience as a wartime officer of the WAC, thereby avoiding the errors common to inexperienced judges of WAC photographs.

Credit for the successful planning and launching of the project belongs to the early staff of the Army's Historical Division, especially Col. Allen F. Clark, Col. John M. Kemper, Col. Allison R. Hartman, and the first Chief Historian of the Army, the late Dr. Walter L. Wright, Jr. And finally, the broad and constructive criticism, based on years of military experience, offered by Maj. Gen. Orlando Ward, Chief of Military History during the last months of the volume's preparation, was of great assistance in completing the work.

Washington, D. C.   MATTIE E. TREADWELL
15 April 1953

---

*Her answer: "No, more."

Contents

PART ONE

Organization and Growth of a Women's Corps

PART TWO

World-Wide Employment

PART THREE

War Department Policy Concerning the Women's Army Corps

PART FOUR

Last Days of the Wartime WAC

Charts

Illustrations

Illustrations—*Continued*

Photographs are from the Department of Defense files.

PART ONE

ORGANIZATION AND GROWTH OF A
WOMEN'S CORPS

CHAPTER I

From 1776 to World War II

On the hot and sticky morning of Monday, 20 July 1942, the green parade ground at Fort Des Moines, Iowa, was lush with grass, daisies, gnats, and members of the press. The photographers required the most supervision because of their tendencies toward photographing female underwear or latrine scenes. There were representatives of four press associations, nineteen newspapers, four foreign news organizations, six motion picture companies, and two photographic services, plus many well-known writers. The occasion was the opening of the United States Army's first training center for women.

Centuries of evolution in warfare and in society had been required to make possible this unprecedented event. From the days of the American Revolution to the early twentieth century, there could be found little serious consideration of a women's corps in the United States Army. For the pioneer woman, home defense was a readily acceptable activity, but it had no connection in the public mind with an organized military corps of women.

However, from the earliest days there were innumerable popular stories of females who had disguised themselves well enough to enlist in the Army as individuals. None of these stories could be verified from Army files, and they apparently occurred more often in legend than in fact, but there was evidence that not all were fictional. The American Congress went so far as to recognize the claims of one Revolutionary soldier, Deborah Sampson Gannett, by granting her husband a widow's pension.

Every succeeding war had its Molly Pitchers, most of whom made good copy for the young American press. Nineteenth century newspapers reveled in such headlines as SERVED BY HER LOVER'S SIDE, or THE DEAD SOLDIER WAS A WOMAN. According to these accounts, the Union Army inadvertently awarded some women the Kearny Cross and the Confederacy placed others on a Roll of Honor. One Confederate wife, declaring that she was "perfectly wild about war," was said to have donned a false mustache and successfully raised and commanded a regiment of recruits. Such stories were legion, but scarcely of help to later Army planners.[1]

Of more significance for the future were scattered cases in which, because of an actual need for women's skills, the Army employed groups of civilian women as nurses, laundresses, clerks, and emergency aides of many types, sometimes in uniforms of their own devising. It was not unusual, for example, that each regiment of the Braddock expedition was allowed some forty women employees, one ration

---

[1] (1) *Magazine of History*, Vol. XXV, pp. 33–34 (July 1917). (2) Ltr, TAG to Editor, *Rural New Yorker*, May 12, 1915. WD Rec AGO, Enl Br 7275–C, with 3132–C–1884, 2285035 National Archives. (See Bibliographical Note.) (3) Francis Henry Gribble, *Women in War* (London: Sampson Low, Marston & Co., Ltd., 1916).

per woman. In 1775 General Washington sponsored a bill that created a hospital department for the Army and allowed it to pay civilian nurses approximately twenty-five cents a day. In time of emergency, civilian women of prominence and reputation continued to nurse the sick, sew, operate canteens, and lend what assistance their skills permitted. However, for a reputable woman to accept such employment was often considered daring in view of the danger of confusion with the more numerous women camp followers, whose ill repute was apt to attach itself to any female employee. In later wars, the employment of women became more common; drill, mascot, and social groups were also organized, complete with uniforms and sometimes rifles.[2]

There was a very clear distinction in the Army's and the public's minds between such groups and a corps of women with soldiers' legal status, rights, and discipline. Just before the nation's entry into the first World War, the Army stated positively:

No official record has been found in the War Department showing specifically that any woman was ever enlisted in the military service of the United States as a member of any organization of the Regular or Volunteer Army. It is possible, however, that there may have been a few instances of women having served as soldiers for a short time without their sex having been detected, but no record of such cases is known to exist in the official files. Women were often employed as laundresses and as nurses, but they were merely civilians while so engaged and were in no sense in the *military* service of the United States.[3]

Total War and the Industrial Revolution

Serious consideration of an official women's corps was scarcely possible before the twentieth century. Until then, war was not organized and mechanized to an extent that required more manpower than a nation could provide from among its men; the great supply systems and fixed headquarters of total war were yet to come. Also, women were skilled in few duties that would have been useful to an army even had it needed manpower, and few women felt it proper to practice even their traditional tasks of cooking and nursing outside the home.

Both reasons were swept away in the nineteenth and early twentieth centuries, when the industrial revolution that mechanized men's wars also taught women to work outside the home. Long before the Army began to consider the admittance of women, businesses and factories had employed them and had trained them as clerks, typists, telephone operators, and technicians. Some such fields were in fact taken over by women so completely that by the time of the first World War it was already difficult for the Army to find any number of competent male typists and telephone operators.

Nevertheless, there remained considerable room for doubt as to the value of woman as a military employee. Industry's experience had produced the general impression that women were suited only for work of limited responsibility; that "women won't work for women" and certainly that men would not; that a woman employee was handicapped by a weaker constitution and more frequent ailments. Business surveys as late as 1942 confirmed the fact that women supervisors were unpopular with employees because of alleged

---

[2] (1) Sir John William Fortescue, *History of the British Army* (London and New York: Macmillan and Co., 1890–1930), Vol. I. (2) Rapid City, S. D., *Daily Journal,* October 21, 1944.

[3] Ltr cited n. 1(2).

deficiencies in leadership. Army planners also noted delicately that a woman had a "physiological handicap which renders her abnormal, unstable, etc., at certain times." [4] Medical statistics indicated that women were in general smaller than men in stature, lighter in weight, less in average weight of skeletal muscles and heart, lower in basal metabolism, and with only about 60 percent the strength to lift, grip, or pull loads. [5]

It therefore was a matter for grave consideration whether an Army would be justified in accepting women into military positions where unreliability would be not merely uneconomical but disastrous, even though farm and factory were thereby stripped of their last man. In the relatively flexible civilian economy, a woman might soften in many ways her adjustment to difficult work, but in the rigid military framework, adaptation would be an all-or-nothing affair. There would be no easy absenteeism, home privacy and comforts, or choice of working conditions, nor yet the privilege of quitting a demanding job.

Even if these handicaps proved exaggerated, there was one obstacle that was not—the opposition of the American public. The Army did not operate in the vacuum of a dictatorship, but in a nation, society, and culture whose traditions must be considered. The course of public opinion regarding woman's place had by no means kept pace with her economic progress. The saying was still frequently heard that "woman's place is in the home," and it appeared certain that there would be great public opposition to placing women in soldier's jobs and in positions of rank and command. Army psychiatrists later noted that "in order for women to gain an active participation in military activities it was necessary for man

to change his basic concept of the feminine role, to overcome his fear of 'women generals.' " [6] Army planners realized that such an obstacle existed, but it was not until after the establishment of a women's corps that its full extent was to be revealed.

The Army Nurse Corps

First to take the field against these obstacles was the Army Nurse Corps, whose development provided a close parallel to later WAC events. The admitted superiority of female nursing first caused acceptance of nurses as civilian employees, but in war after war it was found extremely difficult to maintain a civilian group within a military organization. Much inefficiency in Civil War medical care was believed due to "the lack of a single unified Nurse Corps with official status." In the Spanish-American War, it was noted that "unified direction and control within the Army framework itself was the only way to avoid administrative confusion and to assure maximum efficiency." [7]

Such full admission was delayed chiefly by popular opposition to military status for females, which led one early organizer to remark, "The nurse question is the women question; we shall have to run the

---

[4] Ltr, Maj L. W. McIntosh, Exec, Office Chief of Air Corps, to Maj Everett S. Hughes, G-1, 17 Apr 30. G-1/19835.

[5] Anna M. Baetjer, *Women in Industry; Their Health and Efficiency* (Philadelphia: W. B. Saunders Co., 1946). Prepared in the Army Industrial Hygiene Laboratory under auspices of the National Research Council.

[6] Maj Albert Preston, Jr., History of Psychiatry in the Women's Army Corps, 1946. SGO. Hereafter cited as Preston, Hist of Psychiatry in WAC.

[7] All references to the Army Nurse Corps, and to nursing, unless otherwise stated, are from a pamphlet published by the ANC, *The Army Nurse.* Copy in War College Library.

gantlet of those historic rotten eggs." [8] In 1901 Congress established the Army Nurse Corps, with somewhat the same status as the later Women's Army Auxiliary Corps (WAAC)—a military organization, but without Army rank, officer status, equal pay, or Army benefits such as retirement and veteran's rights. After the first World War its members were given relative rank and some retirement benefits, although pay and allowances still were not those of the men. Full military rank was not to be granted to nurses until 1944, a year after the WAAC had been legally admitted to full Army status and rank as the Women's Army Corps (WAC).[9]

Nevertheless, in placing nurses in a militarized and uniformed corps, the nation had taken one long step toward admission of women to full membership in the armed forces. Neither the public nor the Army was prepared to take further steps; the serious proposal for the establishment of the Women's Army Corps waited for the day when some great war that would almost drain the pool of American manpower should coincide with an availability of women workers trained in the modern skills an army required.

World War I

The first World War narrowly missed being that occasion. The first pinch of manpower shortage was felt chiefly by American industry and business, but by the end of 1918 the military services were also seriously concerned. The British, whose war effort was more nearly total, had already established women's auxiliaries in several of their services, and there was considerable evidence that had the war lasted a few months longer the United States might have done likewise. At the moment of the Armistice, the War Department General Staff was beset by serious proposals to this effect from both within and without the Army.[10]

One of the first of these proposals was initiated by the American Expeditionary Force in France. On 8 October 1917, General Pershing cabled a request for one hundred women telephone operators who could speak French and recommended that they be uniformed. This request was approved and the women were sent as civilian contract employees with privileges very similar to those of the Army Nurse Corps. Subsequently other groups were sent overseas, under varying contracts, by The Quartermaster General, the Ordnance Department, and the Medical Corps, but none had military status. In spite of extensive use of these groups, and of French women for unskilled work, the labor shortage of the AEF continued.[11]

At the same time, numerous civilian volunteer welfare groups, using over 5,000 American women, thrived and multiplied overseas in an un-co-ordinated manner, and appeared to the Army to be striving through competitive publicity to show what they had done for "the boys." While Army reports recorded almost no criticism of the conduct of these women, they did

[8] Statement attributed to Mrs. Bedford Fenwick, about 1887. Lucy Ridgely (Buckler) Seymer, *A General History of Nursing* (London: Faber and Faber, Ltd., 1933).

[9] The use of the abbreviations WAAC (later WAC) for the Corps and of Waacs (later Wacs) for its members was authorized, provided the full title of the Corps was used first, by Office Memorandum 21, 11 September 1942. SPWA 300, 1942 WAAC files. (See Bibliographical Note.)

[10] D. Colett Wadge, ed., *Women in Uniform* (London: Sampson Low, Marston & Co., Ltd., 1946).

[11] (1) Cablegram 276, par 15*b*, 8 Nov 17; (2) Memo, Dir of Women's Relations for G-1, 6 Aug 26, sub: Utilization of Women in Mil Serv. G-1/7000-2.

criticize the lack of orderly administration, the overlapping of duties, and the absence of any Army control. The confusion in the welfare groups was in striking contrast to the organized service given by members of the British Women's Auxiliary Army Corps, the largest of the British auxiliaries, whose services were lent to the AEF when the need for women's skills grew desperate. American Army officers in later years remembered favorably the discipline, efficiency, and *esprit de corps* of the British women's services.[12]

In still further attempts to solve the AEF's labor shortages, the commanding general of the AEF's Services of Supply, Maj. Gen. James G. Harbord, cabled repeatedly to the War Department in August of 1918 for authority to send a representative to the United States to recruit and organize a group of 5,000 women clerical workers to replace enlisted men. The representative was sent, followed by a proposal from the AEF that a women's service corps be organized as a part of the Army Service Corps. After considerable War Department debate as to whether the women should be enlisted, Civil Service, or uniformed contract employees, General Harbord was informed that, because of the change in draft age, 5,000 limited service men would be sent instead of the women. Concerning a women's corps, the War Department stated that it was not yet convinced of "the desirability or feasibility of making this most radical departure in the conduct of our military affairs." [13]

Meanwhile, strong supporting action for the AEF's effort came from posts and camps and from headquarters agencies in the United States. All Army and National Guard cantonments and camps had previously been forbidden to employ civilian women in any capacity except as nurses.[14]

In the face of pleas from station commanders, this ruling was soon modified to authorize civilian employment of women "in essential work for which men employees cannot be obtained . . . taking only those of mature age and high moral character." [15] The War Department noted, "With careful supervision, women employees may be permitted in camps without moral injury either to themselves or to the soldiers." [16] Even with this concession, enough employees could not be procured, especially in isolated and uncomfortable stations, to perform all necessary duties. The Washington headquarters offices also found it difficult to obtain and hold an adequate number of female Civil Service employees.[17]

Therefore, the conclusion was reached almost simultaneously by several Army agencies, both in Washington and in the field, that a corps of women under military control would be the solution to these problems. As The Quartermaster General pointed out concerning laundresses:

Every effort in the past of this office to provide a hired force of women at camps and cantonments has been unsatisfactory . . .

---

[12] (1) Memo cited n. 11(2), Table G, Rpts on Welfare Work, AEF; Tables A, B. (2) Senate Com on Mil Affairs, 77th Cong, 2d sess, *Hearings on S 2240*, 6 Feb 42, pp. 10–14.

[13] (1) Memo cited n. 11(2). Also: (2) Memo, CofS for TAG, Oct 18, sub: Enlmt of Women for Serv in France. WD Rec OCofS, 10730–19, National Archives. (3) Memo, TAG for CofS, 2 May 18, AG 011.2; approved by ACofS, 11 May 18, in Memo for TAG, 11 May 18. WD Rec AGO, WPD 10730–7, National Archives.

[14] Stf Memo, 8 Oct 17, in 1st Ind OQMG, 16 Oct 17. G–1/7000–2.

[15] Ltr, TAG to CGs of all National Guard and National Army Divs, 11 Dec 17. AG 230.2211 (Misc Div). See Memo cited n. 11(2).

[16] Memo, Lt Col Robert I. Rees, GSC, for CofS, 7 Dec 17. Copy in Memo cited n. 11(2).

[17] Memo 62, Col Ira L. Reeves, IGD, for ASW, 24 Aug 18. Copy in Memo cited n. 11(2).

only women of doubtful character show any inclination to remain as long as the voluntary system of employment is in vogue.[18]

The Quartermaster General thereupon recommended that legislation be secured to authorize the enlistment of women, ages 21–45, to be organized as the Women's Auxiliary Quartermaster Corps. Similar requests, giving similar reasons, were also made by the Inspector General's Department, the Chief of Engineers, the Operations Branch of the General Staff, and the Chief of Ordnance. The Chief of Ordnance estimated that the yearly turnover of civilian employees in his branch was approaching 84 percent. Ordnance and other branches went so far as to devise the uniform to be worn by enlisted women. At a meeting with representatives of The Quartermaster General, The Surgeon General, Signal Corps, Military Aeronautics, and the Corps of Engineers, it was decided that the uniform should be of "soft silver brown wool material," with a tan pongee blouse and brown Windsor tie, and that "no furs shall be worn with the uniform." [19]

These pleas did not receive favorable consideration by the War Department. Legislation to enlist "effective and able-bodied women" had in fact already been introduced in Congress in December of 1917, but had been returned to the House Military Affairs Committee by the Secretary of War with an expression of his disapproval. The memorandum upon which this opinion was based stated in unmistakable terms:

The enlistment of women in the military forces of the United States has never been seriously contemplated and such enlistment is considered unwise and highly undesirable . . . the action provided for in this bill is not only unwise, but exceedingly ill-advised.

War Plans Division noted in May of 1918:

Industrial conditions in the United States are not yet in such shape that it is necessary to undertake a line of action that would be fraught with so many difficulties.[20]

The War Department was equally unfavorable to an attempt by The Surgeon General to commission women doctors in the Medical Corps. The Judge Advocate General was unable to discover in the terminology of the National Defense Act any legal barrier to the appointment of women under that act. Nevertheless, the War Department's opinion was upheld on the grounds that only persons "physically, mentally, and morally qualified" could be appointed and that women doctors were obviously not physically qualified.[21]

The dismay of certain Army agencies at the lack of Army authority to enlist women was heightened by the Navy's action in placing the opposite interpretation upon its legislative authority and enlisting all the women it needed without further ceremony. As one Army planner later complained, "By enlisting Yeomen (F) the Navy Department ignored the Civil Service Commission and satisfied its needs regardless of the needs of others. They

---

[18] Memo, OQMG for TAG, 24 Apr 18, sub: Legislation Authorizing Enlmt of Women. WD Rec, OCofS, War College Div, 10730–7, 400.6 General, National Archives.

[19] (1) Memo cited n. 11(2), Tab F. (2) Series of five studies by Dr. Kristine Mann, Civilian Workers' Br, OCofOrd, 19 Sep to 28 Sep 18. (3) Memo, CofOrd for WPD, 26 Sep 18. WD Rec, OCofS, War College Div 10730–16 and 17, 342/8, National Archives.

[20] (1) HR 7112, 6 Dec 17. (2) Memo, Actg Chief, War College Div, for CofS, 22 Dec 17, sub: Bill Introduced in House of Representatives. Rejection was by Ltr, Newton D. Baker, SW, to Chmn, House Com on Mil Affairs, 26 Dec 17. WD Rec, OCofS, War College Div, 10730–1, National Archives. (3) Memo, Dir WPD for CofS, 8 May 18. WD Rec, OCofS, War College Div, 10730–7, AG 011.2, National Archives.

[21] Operations JAG 1917, I, 126. National Archives.

WOMEN DURING WORLD WAR I *served in France as telephone operators in a civilian capacity, and with the Navy and Marine Corps in the same status as men.*

wanted clerks and they got them." [22] Nearly 13,000 women enlisted in the Navy and Marine Corps on the same status as men and wore a uniform blouse with insignia. These women were the first in the United States to be admitted to full military rank and status. [23]

In addition to the pressure on the War Department from military advocates of the enlistment of women, there was undoubtedly some activity by organized women's groups. Prominent women in various sections of the country went so far as to organize semimilitary groups. In New York the Women's League for Self-Defense, five hundred strong and dressed in bloomers and puttees, drilled with rifles in the 66th Regimental Armory, and informed reporters that they had written Secretary of War Newton D. Baker and Maj. Gen. Leonard Wood "offering our service as the only strictly military women's organization in America." [24] The YWCA proposed that any more women sent to France be placed in a women's army corps like the British WAAC, with strict discipline and no individual billeting. [25] A similar proposal came from the American Council on Education, which concluded that military status would make for fewer resignations among trainees for war jobs. [26]

All such proposals came to an abrupt end with the cessation of hostilities on 11 November 1918. With a one-page sigh of relief the General Staff shelved the bulky documents that had set forth the arguments pro and con, and declared:

In view of the present military situation it is believed no longer desirable that arrangements be made to form military organizations composed of women. . . . A continuance of the war would have required the United States in completing its program for the year 1919 to make a much more extended use of women . . . to replace men sent overseas or men shifted to heavy work which men alone can do. [27]

With this, the serious consideration of the establishment of a women's military group was relinquished to another generation of planners and to another war.

Twenty-three Years of Peace

The nation had hardly settled itself into postwar routine when it became evident that considerable political power was being wielded by the newly enfranchised female sex and its many well-organized national groups. It soon began to appear to the Army, as well as to many female leaders, that the mass of American women was dangerously susceptible to the charms of pacifism and other doctrines that advocated the abolition of the military as the best means of insuring peace. [28]

To stem this tide of opinion the Army sought to teach women voters more about

---

[22] Memo, Hughes for G–1, 21 Sep 28, sub: Participation of Women in War. G–1/8604–1.

[23] Memo cited n. 11(2). The legality of the Navy's action was held in "grave doubt" in a later decision of the Comptroller of the Treasury, but payment of the women was permitted in order not to interfere with naval efficiency. The Navy thereupon ceased enlisting women, but those already enlisted retained rights of service personnel and later of veterans. Memo, Maj Briant H. Wells, GS, for CofS, 22 Jun 17. WD Rec, OCofS, War College Div, 8196–7, National Archives.

[24] New York *American*, February 9, 1917.

[25] Memo, Dir WPD for CofS, 21 Oct 18, sub: Enlmt of Women for Serv in France. WD Rec, OCofS 10730–19, National Archives.

[26] Memo, Chmn, Com on War Serv Tng for College Women, American Council on Education, 18 Sep 18. WD Rec, OCofS 10730–16, National Archives.

[27] Memo, CofOpns Div GS for CofS,—Nov 18, sub: Orgn of WAAC and Equivalent Orgn in U.S. WD Rec, OCofS, War College Div, 10730–23, National Archives. Copy in Memo cited n. 11(2).

[28] Proceedings of Fifth Women's Patriotic Conference on National Defense, 29–31 Jan 30, Constitution Hall, Washington, D. C. Copy in G–1/9835.

its own nature and purpose. To this end, Secretary Baker in 1920 created a new position under the comprehensive title of Director of Women's Relations, United States Army, with an office in G–1 Division of the General Staff. The director was to maintain liaison between the War Department and the women of the country and to secure their co-operation by explaining to them that the Army was "a progressive, socially minded human institution" and that women voters should not "fanatically demand the dissolution of a ruthless military machine." [29] There was some consideration as to whether the director should have military status, but the Army decided to await developments.

The first incumbent of the position resigned after one year, for personal reasons and for what her successor believed to be "dissatisfaction with the lack of support given her." [30] The next appointee, Miss Anita Phipps, the daughter of an Army family, was also dissatisfied. There ensued a decade-long battle as to whether her position should degenerate into that of a supervisor of the Army's thirty-odd hostesses, or should be expanded into that of planner-in-chief for a women's Army corps, and first director.

Miss Phipps' difficulties, as set forth in periodic lengthy memoranda to the Secretary of War, centered around War Department failure to support her commitments and to give her military status. She thus, in her opinion, lost prestige in the eyes of powerful women's groups. She was embarrassed in the presence of Army and Navy nurses by her "undignified makeshift" of a uniform. Headquarters divisions and offices often failed to consult her when corresponding with women's organizations. General officers, when asked to speak before women's groups, ignored the careful tip sheets Miss Phipps had prepared for their guidance, and often alienated those whom she had cultivated with care. Her recommendations and staff studies were frequently filed without further action. One of her chiefs in G–1 Division went so far as to state baldly that her position should be abolished, since the male members of the General Staff were competent to plan the future utilization of women by the military service. [31]

In 1929, after almost ten years of work, Miss Phipps had nevertheless secured tentative approval of a plan that would unite the support of the most powerful women's groups behind the Secretary of War by means of a system of civilian aides to the Secretary—one chief aide, one in each corps area, and one in each state. Secretary of War Dwight F. Davis on 25 February 1929 publicly announced this plan to the press after a conference with women members of the League of Women Voters, American War Mothers, Daughters of the American Revolution, National Federation of Business and Professional Women's Clubs, and other such groups.

There at once arose a storm of letters from Senators and clergymen and from male civilian aides threatening to resign if women were also made civilian aides. Only fifteen days later a new Secretary of War, James W. Good, was in office and promptly sent telegrams to the women representatives, canceling the meeting of the nominating committee. This action, which in Miss Phipps' opinion greatly alienated the powerful women's groups,

---

[29] Memo, Dir Women's Relations for SW, 8 Jan 27. G–1/9562. Copy, with history of the office attached, in G–1/9835.

[30] *Ibid.*

[31] Memo, Brig Gen Campbell King, G–1, for CofS, 29 Sep 27, sub: Duty of Dir Women's Relations for U.S. Army. G–1/9835.

was followed in October by a final letter from Mr. Good to the women concerned, regretting that "the present is not a propitious time for appointing women civilian aides." [32]

Discouraged and in ill health, Miss Phipps in 1930 made a last appeal to the Secretary of War to define her duties and authority or to abolish her position. Nothing definite was done, and in 1931 her work was terminated by illness and by a new Chief of Staff, Gen. Douglas MacArthur, who overrode a favorable G–1 opinion and informed the Secretary of War that he considered her duties to be of no military value. [33]

Plans for a Women's Service Corps

The Director of Women's Relations left behind her the first complete and workable plan for a women's corps. Over a period of several years she compiled all evidence concerning the utilization of women during World War I, including the opinions of the British, the Congress, the Navy, and various Army commands. The heart of the plan was that the proposed women's service corps should be *in* the Army and not an auxiliary. She rejected the then-popular idea of enlisting women and giving them a uniform and a job but no military training, organization, discipline, housing, or required courtesies. This idea, she noted, had been tried and proved undesirable by both the Navy and the British. Instead, she proposed that women be fully trained and assigned only in units under the command of women officers, with not less than a squad at any station and no individual billeting allowed. All Army Regulations were to apply, plus special regulations for women as needed. [34]

By sending questionnaires to eight corps areas, three territorial departments, and eighteen chiefs of branches or similar services, Miss Phipps discovered that about 170,000 women would be wanted in wartime, although only six agencies favored giving them immediate military status.

In view of later debate about the proper jobs for women in the Army, it was significant that at this time the concept of a menial type of corps of low-grade personnel still loomed large in Army thinking. Not quite half of the requests were for clerks and stenographers; a few others were for small numbers of skilled workers such as draftsmen, dietitians, and telephone operators. The rest were chiefly for large numbers for relatively unskilled work: approximately 5,800 laundry workers, 7,000 cooks, 1,300 charwomen and janitors, 5,000 chauffeurs, 2,000 messengers, 11,000 laborers, 8,000 seamstresses, and so on.

The whole idea was rejected by the General Staff in August of 1926, although most divisions called it a "very splendid" study. [35] G–2 Division objected to the cost of housing, G–3 to difficulties in transportation and toilet facilities, and G–4 to the personnel policy involved. War Plans

[32] (1) Copies of ltrs and telgs are in G–1/9835 (1927). (2) Ltr, SW to Mrs. John Sippel, President, Gen Federation of Women's Clubs, 19 Oct 29. G–1/8604–3.

[33] (1) Memo, Miss Phipps for SW, 21 Oct 30; (2) Memos, G–1 for CofS, 13, 14 Nov 30; (3) Memos, OCofS, 5–6 Mar 31; (4) Ltr, CofS to SW, 10 Mar 31. All in G–1/9835 (1931).

[34] (1) Her voluminous preliminary notes and studies are still on file in several roughly bound volumes in G–1/7000. (2) Memo, Dir Women's Relations for G–1, 6 Aug 26. G–1/7000–2. For Navy and British experiences see: (3) Memo, OCofOrd for 3d ASW. WD Rec, OCofS, War College Div, 10730–16, National Archives. (4) Memo cited n. 25.

[35] Memo, G–1 for G–2, G–3, G–4, and WPD, 14 Aug 26, sub: Utilization of Women in Mil Serv, and atchd replies. G–1/7000–3.

Division suggested that the study be used only as a basis for further study and planning.

Throughout the comments of the entire General Staff ran the conviction that the mobilization of the United States would be a leisurely affair. G–4 Division noted: "To consider the development of a training organization for women workers in the beginning of a major emergency appears unthinkable.' [36]

A more powerful reason for private opposition among officers of the General Staff was noted by the Assistant Chief of Staff, G–1, Brig. Gen. Campbell King. General King wrote personally to the Chief of Staff that Miss Phipps seemed to wish to perfect within the Army an organization of women, headed by a woman, with a hierarchy of subheads plus influential civilian advisers, which would constitute "a powerful machine difficult to control and endowed with possibilities of hampering and embarrassing the War Department." [37]

Oddly enough, during a decade when neither a military corps nor a civilian advisory group could receive approval, a few women somewhat accidentally fell heir to the full blessings of Army status. When, in a more or less routine order, the supposedly all-male category of Army field clerks was blanketed into military service, it was found to include a handful of women employees. While this occurrence was scarcely noted on the planning level and was never considered a precedent for an organized women's corps, the few individuals concerned were later held by the Comptroller General to have been full-fledged members of the military service, with the same status as the Navy yeomanettes. Later, Congress amended the armed forces' legislation to place the word *male* before *persons*, thus effectually guaranteeing that neither the yeomanette nor the field clerk episode would be repeated without its sanction. [38]

The Hughes Plan

Male planners up to this time had not come to very close grips with the problem of planning for a women's corps. While students at the Army War College had studied a course entitled "Conservation by Utilization of Women in Industry, in Military Service, and in Welfare Work," it was ordinarily assumed that such "Conservation" would be most appropriately left to industry. The chief Army planner for a women's corps was appointed in 1928; he was Maj. Everett S. Hughes of G–1 Division, General Staff. [39]

Pointing out that nothing but fruitless conflict had resulted from previous arguments between extreme feminists on the one side and male die-hards on the other, all disagreeing endlessly over minor details, Major Hughes proposed acceptance of the fact that women would inevitably play a part in the next war—the more nearly total the war, the greater the part. No amount of wishful thinking could avert that necessity, powered as it was by social and economic trends beyond the nation's powers to reverse.

On the other hand, he stated, the Army should not attempt a detailed solution until the situation was known; it would be futile to waste time debating minor points,

[36] Memo, G–4 for G–1, 13 Sep 26. G–4/20390.
[37] (1) Memo, G–1 for CofS, 6 Jul 27. G–1/9835. (2) Memo, Lt Col George Grunert for G–1, 3 Feb 27. G–1/7000–2.
[38] The Comptroller General's decision is discussed in Ch. XII, below.
[39] Discussion of Hughes plan, unless otherwise indicated, is from Memo, Hughes for G–1, 21 Sep 28, sub: Participation of Women in War. G–1/8604–1.

such as whether women should enter the combat zone, until it was known what the combat zone of the next war might include. Before the time arrived to make these specific decisions, the women who were to help make them must be trained not merely in drill but in an understanding of Army thinking, a process that could not be achieved overnight. And the men who were to make the decisions must also be trained in understanding the problems of militarization of women. If the women who were to lead the new corps were ignorant, said Hughes, *"this ignorance, coupled with man's intolerance, may be fatal."* [40]

The Hughes plan contemplated that only women overseas or in danger zones would be militarized. The only advantage to the Army in militarizing other women would be that of being able to order them to perform certain unpopular duties such as laundry work, and the plan noted the fallacy of supposing that women of a higher type would enlist after they knew that only menial work was in store for them.

The need for military status in danger zones was strongly indicated by current arguments then before Congress concerning women who had worked in France and who were seeking compensation for the loss of their health. The War Department had already decided that such women were not entitled to veterans' gratuities, ruling in one case:

Female telephone operators have no military status whatever . . . those serving with the American Expeditionary Forces [were] not even under civil service regulations. . . . It is not believed that Congress intended that a gratuity should be paid to any person not actually a member of the military establishment. [41]

Nevertheless, the sentiment in Congress favored those women whose disabilities were directly due to war service, and financial relief to prevent their destitution was voted in certain cases. At this time Congresswoman Edith Nourse Rogers of Massachusetts developed an interest in the problem which was to lead ultimately to her sponsorship, fifteen years later, of the WAAC bill. [42]

Major Hughes also stated that it was uneconomical and confusing to have separate organizations of men and women, and that qualified women could be integrated into the men's army, with a similar uniform and privileges. He argued against camouflaging rank by odd titles such as Deputy Controller, which spared the male ego but confused the employing agencies. "Why not take the whole step and do the thing right?" he wrote.

Major Hughes' prophetic efforts were embalmed with indorsements, laid out for observation for a period, and then buried so deep in the files that they were recovered only after the WAAC was six months old and War Department planners had already made most of the mistakes he predicted. [43] His study was sent to the Chief of

---

[40] Author's italics.

[41] Memo, Dir WPD for CofS, 18 Mar 19. WD Rec, OCofS, War College Div, 10730-26, National Archives.

[42] (1) House Com on Veterans Legislation, 69th Cong, 1st sess, *Hearings,* 6 Aug 26. (2) Interv with Mrs. Rogers, 14 Dec 45. (This form of citation is used throughout the volume for interviews conducted by the author.)

[43] The study was recovered then only when Mrs. Oveta Culp Hobby, Director, WAAC, on temporary duty in England, was introduced to Maj. Gen. Everett S. Hughes, who demanded to know what G-1 had done with his masterpiece. Returning to Washington, she unearthed it but found no evidence that it had been known to the G-1 planners. Interv with Lt Col Helen Hamilton Woods, Deputy Dir WAC, 22 Oct 45.

Throughout the volume, the rank held by the officer at the time of the interview or of the discussion in the text is given. Since this is not a completely chronological account, an officer who appears in an early

Staff in 1928 and again, refurbished, in 1930.[44] At this time the new G–1, Brig. Gen. Albert J. Bowley, also distinguished himself in the field of prophecy by proposing an immediate campaign of education for Regular Army officers, since

Successful co-operation between men and women during the next war will depend to a great extent on the attitude of the officers of the Regular Army toward the women of the country. To influence this attitude will require much time and discussion.[45]

A dejected-looking sheaf of handwritten scraps of paper indicated that the studies were carried back and forth from G–1 to the Chief of Staff to the Secretary of War to G–1, bearing notations of diminishing intensity, such as "Hold until Secretary of War decides"; "Hold until fall when women return to their homes after summer activities"; and, finally, merely "Hold." The last one in the series, dated 5 January 1931, stated: "General B. says may as well suspend; no one seems willing to do anything about it."

So ended the peacetime planning for a women's corps.

The Approach of World War II

On 1 September 1939, under the shadow of imminent hostilities, Gen. George C. Marshall was appointed Chief of Staff, and a month later planning for a women's corps was resumed. A staff study of the problem was shortly prepared by G–1 Division. The study did not reflect its predecessors in any way; planners were evidently not aware of the Phipps and Hughes studies.[46]

The most important idea in the new plan was that women must under no circumstances be given full military status. The Civilian Conservation Corps was hit upon as the model. The plan stated:

The CCC has shown how persons may be grouped in units with a military form of organization, uniformed, given grades of rank, paid and cared for, employed under orders of Army Officers, administered by the Army's chain of command, and governed by War Department Regulations, without being members of the Army.

WAAC leaders were later to consider this analogy extremely unfortunate, since the CCC had been a peacetime organization employed in separate camps, whereas the WAAC was to be used in Army camps and overseas where a legal distinction in status would be far more difficult. The plan likewise proposed that some women would be set up in "quasi-military female organizations" similar to companies, while others would move about individually or in small groups. It was stated that women's probable jobs would include those of "hostesses, librarians, canteen clerks, cooks and waitresses, chauffeurs, messengers, and strolling minstrels." The plan was held in abeyance, and for another eighteen months the War Department did not commit itself.[47]

---

chapter as a lieutenant colonel subsequently may be referred to as a major or a captain. It should also be noted that, just as brigadier, major, and lieutenant generals are customarily referred to, after their initial mention, simply as General ———, lieutenant colonels are referred to similarly as Colonel ———. Colonel Hobby was the only full colonel in the wartime WAC.

[44] (1) Memo, Gen King, G–1, for CofS, 24 Aug 28. G–1/8604–1. (2) Memo, Brig Gen Albert J. Bowley, G–1, 28 Feb 30. G–1/8604–4.

[45] Memo, G–1 for CofS, 4 Jun 29, sub: Participation of Women in War. G–1/8604–2.

[46] Memo, Capt Williston B. Palmer for G–1, 2 Oct 39, sub: Women with the Army (Emergency). G–1/15839.

[47] (1) *Ibid.* (2) Personal Ltr, Col William Rose, AGO, to Col Lawrence Whiting, 11 Jun 40, forwarded to Hist Div WDSS, 11 Apr 45, sub: Compilation of WAC History. OCMH.

Meanwhile, numerous letters and telegrams began to be received from women's organizations and from individuals offering their services. G–1 Division now expressed mild anxiety lest any of these women arrive in a theater of operations before they could be organized in some civilian corps under military control. With the collapse of France in May and June of 1940 and the subsequent Battle of Britain, the offers of help redoubled. When in September of 1940 the first peacetime Selective Service Act became law, women's groups increased their demands that they be allowed to contribute to the nation's defense. By March of 1941 a change in tone could be noted in official statements. In a letter to an inquirer General Marshall stated:

> While the United States is not faced with an acute shortage of manpower such as has forced England to make such an extensive use of its women, it is realized that we must plan for every possible contingency, and certainly must provide some outlet for the patriotic desires of our women.[48]

The pressure of these patriotic desires was soon considerable. In Chicago, the Women's League of Defense, 17,000 strong, set itself up as an agency for the enrollment and classification of "women who can do anything helpful to replace a man in the event of war." In Los Angeles, the Women's Ambulance and Defense Corps trained women in military skills and persistently sought recognition as an Army-sponsored agency for training women officers. In Pittsburgh, the Memorial Gold Cross First Aid and Ambulance Corps enrolled 2,000 members. In Washington, D. C., the Green Guards stated that they had "contended, urged, and pleaded with the powers that be to include women in the national defense plan in some ca-

pacity." In Ohio, the Toledo Unit of the Willys-Overland Women's Motor Defense Corps proposed to train women for duties with the Army.

Many other such private organizations arose, most of them genuine, but a few spurious. G–2 Division was obliged to discontinue replies from the Chief of Staff to organizations that had previously tried to convince the public that they had Army sponsorship. During these months, private citizens without number also wrote to the Army and to Congress offering their services.[49]

More significant than this sporadic activity was evidence that Congress or national groups might act to set up women's units outside Army control, or with full military status. Congresswoman Edith Nourse Rogers reported herself ready to introduce a bill for full military status. The Air Corps requested a woman's volunteer defense corps for duty with its Aircraft Warning Service; as the War Department delayed, the Air Corps decided that a separate women's corps under its own control might be preferable. U.S. Army representatives in England also advised that a women's auxiliary would be necessary in the event that larger forces were sent overseas, since members of the British Women's Auxiliary Air Force and Auxiliary Territorial Services could not be borrowed by the U.S. forces in sufficient numbers because of the British manpower shortage.

From the White House came two infor-

---

[48] See entire file G–1/15839 (5–11–42), especially Memo, G–1 for CofS, 13 Aug 40; and Ltr, CofS to Dr. John W. Colbert, 19 Mar 41.

[49] Examples are from: (1) Collection of ltrs and documents in G–1/15839–1 (5–11–42); and (2) Rupert Hughes, "Shall We Have a Women's National Guard?" *Liberty*, March 8, 1941.

mal proposals. Mrs. Eleanor Roosevelt suggested that American women, like the British, be used in antiaircraft barrage work, a duty that was considered by some military planners as dangerously close to combat work. In a separate proposal she suggested a pool of women for service with the Army, Navy, and Marine Corps, as needed, but under the command of none of them; instead, it would possibly be under the Office of Civilian Defense, although members of Congress protested such action from the House floor because of the "miserable record of mismanagement" of that organization.[50]

Immediate impetus was supplied by Congresswoman Rogers, for many years an authority on legislation concerning women. Mrs. Rogers stated later, when asked her motives:

My motives? In the first World War, I was there and *saw*. I saw the women in France, and how they had no suitable quarters and no Army discipline. Many dietitians and physiotherapists who served then are still sick in the hospital, and I was never able to get any veterans' compensation for them, although I secured passage of one bill aiding telephone operators. I was resolved that our women would not again serve with the Army without the protection men got.[51]

Mrs. Rogers later informed the House: "I have been nursing this measure along through the years."[52]

In the spring of 1941 Mrs. Rogers called upon the Chief of Staff and informed him that she intended to introduce a bill to establish a women's corps. General Marshall replied, "Give me a week to consider it," and afterwards asked that the week be extended to a month.[53]

During this month the War Department plunged into furious planning for a bill that the Army could safely sponsor.

The planners' motives were made clear in a staff memorandum from the Assistant Chief of Staff, G-1, who wrote:

Congresswoman Edith Nourse Rogers has been determined for some time to introduce a bill to provide a women's organization in the Army. We have succeeded in stopping her on the promise that we are studying the same thing, and will permit her to introduce a bill which will meet with War Department approval.

Mrs. Roosevelt also seems to have a plan.

The sole purpose of this study is to permit the organization of a women's force along lines which meet with War Department approval, so that when it is forced upon us, as it undoubtedly will be, we shall be able to run it our way.[54]

The resulting plan was the work of Col. James Taylor of G-1 Division and, later, of Maj. Robert W. Berry. It provided for a Women's Army Auxiliary Force (WAAF), definitely a civilian auxiliary and not part of the Army. The plan's authors believed that it would avoid the errors made during World War I. They stated:

The War Department initially made no provision for the use of women in the last war with the exception of the Army Nurse Corps.

---

[50] (1) Ltr, AC to TAG, 19 Mar 41. AG 324.4 (3-19-41). (2) D/F, G-1 for AC, 8 May 41. G-1/15839-10, Pt 1. (3) Ltr, GHQ AF to CofAAF, 27 Dec 41, and subsequent documents. ACC 324.5 AWS (Women). AG 291.9 WAAC Sec 1, Pt 1. (4) [Henry G. Elliott] The Predecessor Commands, SPOBS and USAFBI, Pt I of The Administrative and Logistical History of the ETO, Hist Div USFET, 1946, MS, p. 255, OCMH. (5) Memos, Chief, Women's Interest Sec, WDBPR, for CofS, 14 Nov 41, and 9 Dec 41, sub: HR 4906. AG 291.9 WAAC Sec 1 Pt 1 (6-2-41). (6) *Congressional Record*, Vol. 88, No. 55, p. 2657, 17 Mar 42.

[51] Interv cited n. 42(2); also *Congressional Record*, Vol. 87, No. 100, p. 4639, 28 May 41.

[52] *Congressional Record* entry cited n. 50(6).

[53] Interv cited n. 42(2).

[54] Memo, Brig Gen Wade H. Haislip, G-1, for CofS, 29 Apr 41. G-1/15839-10. Also in WA 320 (5-29-41) DRB AGO.

. . . However, the services of women were found to be so necessary overseas and in posts, camps, and bureaus in the United States that before the World War was over, a large group of women were serving with the Army in unorganized and uncoordinated groups, hastily and inefficiently recruited, under little if any discipline, and with no military status or recognition.[55]

Cited advantages of the plan included not only its greater controls but the fact that "it will tend to avert the pressure to admit women to actual membership in the Army." Cited disadvantages included not only the many special arrangements necessary for women's care but the fact that the corps would "inject many other unpredictable problems into military administration."

Most of the General and Special Staff Divisions, when the plan was submitted to them for comment, agreed with G–1's reasoning. The name was changed from WAAF to WAAC, at the suggestion of The Adjutant General, because a parallel with the earlier British name was believed desirable, although Mrs. Rogers and other women advisers objected because of the sound and the similarity to the word *wacky*. G–4 Division concurred "in time of war only." [56]

Although The Surgeon General concurred, the Director of the Army Nurse Corps, Maj. Julia Flikke, did not favor the bill, saying, "It is my opinion that the disadvantages outweigh the advantages . . . complications would arise between that organization and other existing organizations." She feared that it would inconvenience citizens by causing "a dearth of domestic help" during the war and that "this organization necessarily would be composed largely of married women who would find it difficult to comply with

regulations because of home ties, and would always need special consideration and no doubt there would be many who would object to regimentation." [57] Only the Judge Advocate General proposed full military status, fearing—all too accurately, as it later proved—legal complications in an auxiliary.[58]

The Secretary of War rejected the plan at first sight, declaring it "premature," but upon learning the alternatives he acceded, being reassured by G–1 Division that "if the organization of this force is authorized by law, it is the intention of the War Department to develop it slowly and by trial and error. It is not the purpose of the War Department to rush into this matter on a large scale." [59]

H.R. 4906

On 28 May 1941 Mrs. Rogers introduced in the House of Representatives "A Bill to establish a Women's Army Auxiliary Corps for Service with the Army of the United States." [60] She accepted auxiliary status for the corps, saying:

In the beginning, I wanted very much to have these women taken in as a part of the Army. . . . I wanted them to have the same rate of pension and disability allowance. I . . . realized that I could not secure that. The War Department was very unwilling to have these women as a part of the Army.[61]

[55] Memo, G–1 for CofS, 31 Mar 41. G–1/15839–10.

[56] Comments and concurrences are all in two bound files, G–1/15839–10, Pts 1 and 2.

[57] Memo, Supt ANC for Col Howard T. Wickert, 9 Apr 41, atchd to Memo, SGO for G–1, 12 Apr 41. SGO 322.5–1 WAAF.

[58] Bound files cited n. 56.

[59] Memo cited n. 54.

[60] HR 4906, 77th Cong, 1st sess, 28 May 41.

[61] *Congressional Record* entry cited n. 50(6).

She also correctly estimated Congressional temper as being at this time much opposed to any idea of full military status for women.

H.R. 4906, as prepared by Major Berry and other officers of G–1 Division, took fourteen printed pages to outline the ways in which the Corps did and did not differ from the Army. The WAAC was to be a corps of 25,000 women for noncombatant service; it was "not a part of the Army but it shall be the only women's organization authorized to serve *with* the Army, exclusive of the Army Nurse Corps." There followed a statement of its mission that was extremely significant, for it indicated a decision which was perhaps the most basic and vital of the Corps' history: the WAAC was established "for the purpose of making available to the national defense the knowledge, skill, and special training of the women of the nation." Deliberate emphasis was placed on the utilization of a small number of skilled high-grade workers, instead of large numbers of unskilled low-grade personnel, as contemplated in earlier plans. Planners noted:

> The problem in the United States is not primarily one of utilizing women in the military service for the purpose of releasing manpower, but is one of utilizing women to increase the efficiency of the Army.[62]
>
> Both educational and technical qualifications should be set exceptionally high to make of the projected organization an elite corps, in order that it may quickly attain the highest reputation for both character and professional excellence.[63]

Later developments were to make it appear that no one yet fully understood the tremendous implications which this decision would have in necessitating procedures different from those for men, who were of course enlisted without any such selectivity as to skills and character. In fact, the same planners in a list of possible duties included jobs manifestly unfit for recruits of skill and education, such as charwoman and laundry worker.

The bill neglected to spell out a point that had been clearly stated in earlier plans: the WAAC was to operate under Army command channels above the company level. Instead, command responsibility was publicly placed on a woman entitled Director, who was to "operate and administer the Corps in accordance with the normal military procedure of command." The Director was also to "advise the War Department" and "make recommendations as to plans and policies."

Endless legal distinctions were also attempted. Waacs were to receive medical service from the Army, but no medical or other benefits after discharge except those provided by the Employees Compensation Commission. They were considered military personnel for benefits of the Soldiers and Sailors Relief Act but not for benefits of the act granting re-employment rights, except for those who left Civil Service jobs. Most important, the extent to which Waacs could be disciplined was not clear. It was stated that Waacs were to be subject to the Articles of War "when applicable," but it was to develop that no one then or later ever knew when they were applicable except in overseas areas.

The bill was obliged to be specific on matters such as pay, allowances, grades and the numbers in each grade, travel pay, leave, and other points that were to be quickly outmoded by subsequent Army

---

[62] Memo cited n. 55.
[63] Memo, Morale Br for G–1, 7 Apr 41. MB 320.2 (3–31–41) WR. Copy with G–1/15839.

legislation, thereupon requiring additional WAAC legislation.

Still worse, the camouflaged grades were not strictly comparable to Army grades in either rank or pay and were to cause great confusion in finance and personnel offices when the attempt was made to replace men on Army Tables of Organization. Instead of lieutenants and captains, the WAAC had third, second, and first officers. A first officer was comparable to a captain in duties and insignia but drew the pay of a first lieutenant; a second officer drew pay somewhere between a first and second lieutenant's; and a third officer was comparable to a second lieutenant, with pay of $1,500.

Enlisted grades were still more confusing, with three grades of auxiliaries comparable to the Army's two grades of privates and three grades of leaders in place of the Army's five grades of noncommissioned officers. In addition there was to be a director, who was authorized the salary of $3,000, comparable to a major's, and a few assistant directors, who were to receive a captain's pay of $2,400.

This bill after its introduction immediately sank from sight; it was not to become law for a full year. It was referred routinely to the Bureau of the Budget, which did not reply for four months. Meanwhile, G-1 Division had reversed its previous stand and ventured the hope that the Chief of Staff would withdraw his support or at least not commit himself until the Bureau of the Budget was heard from.[64]

Nevertheless, the Chief of Staff, almost alone in the War Department, made it clear in the fall of 1941 that he had come to look on the bill with more than official approval. Mrs. Rogers noted that "General Marshall now became very enthusiastic about the bill."[65] Col. John H. Hilldring, soon to assume office as G-1, stated later:

By the summer of 1941, General Marshall was intensely interested in the WAAC business. He foresaw a cycle of shortages; that of the moment was the supply shortage, in which the scarcity of supplies hindered mobilization, but he now became convinced that the bottleneck of the future would be that of manpower. He also considered the fact that war had become a complicated business which needed many civilian techniques, and that many of these were almost completely in the control of women. General Marshall asked me why we should try to train men in a specialty such as typing or telephone work which in civilian life has been taken over completely by women; this, he felt, was uneconomical and a waste of time which we didn't have. For example, the Army's telephone service had always had a reputation for being bad in spite of our superior equipment, and women operators could and did end all that.

The Chief of Staff was also influenced by the fact that the ladies wanted in; he literally has a passionate regard for democratic ideals.[66]

General Marshall at this time told several of his staff members that, while he did not see any immediate need for large numbers of women in the Army, he would like to have authorization for a women's corps on his books so that, if the need for quick action should arise, the point of debate would be past.[67] This agreed with what he later wrote to Congress:

---

[64] Memo, Budget and Leg Plng Br for G-1, 18 Jun 41, sub: Rpt on HR 4906. AG 291.9 WAAC sec 1 pt 1 (6-2-41).

[65] Interv cited n. 42(2).

[66] Interv with Gen Hilldring, 17 Jan 46.

[67] *Ibid.;* also, statement was made to Mrs. Hobby and repeated by her later to a Congressional committee. House Com on Mil Affairs, 77th Cong, 2d sess, *Hearings on HR 6293,* 20-21 Jan 42, p. 33.

I regard the passage of this bill at an early date as of considerable importance. In general, we have secured most of the legislation required for the complete mobilization of the Army so that we can go ahead with its development and definitely plan for the future. However, we lack Congressional authority for the establishment of a Women's Army Auxiliary Corps, and as a result can make no definite plans. Also, I am under continued pressure from many directions regarding this phase of our preparations.

It is important that as quickly as possible we have a declared national policy in this matter. Women certainly must be employed in the overall effort of this nation. . . . We consider it essential that their status, their relationship to the military authority, should be clearly established.[68]

The Chief of Staff therefore took personal action to needle the agencies still brooding on the WAAC bill. Although the U.S. Civil Service Commission and the Employees Compensation Commission both had been persuaded by Mrs. Rogers to render favorable reports, the Bureau of the Budget informed the War Department on 7 October: "It is not believed that the enactment of the proposed legislation, at least at the present time, should be considered as being in accord with the program of the President."[69] The Bureau of the Budget stated, "There appears to be no need for a WAAC inasmuch as there will never be a shortage of manpower in the limited service field."[70]

In his attempts to get the measure past the Bureau of the Budget, the Chief of Staff employed a newcomer to the War Department, one of its civilian consultants, Mrs. Oveta Culp Hobby. Mrs. Hobby had, in the summer of 1941, been "virtually drafted" to come to Washington to set up the new Women's Interests Section of the War Department Bureau of Public Relations, a section designed to furnish soldiers' wives and mothers with information that would reassure them about the living conditions of their drafted relatives. She had agreed to stay for not more than four months, or until the agency was functioning properly; any longer absence from home she considered undesirable in view of the fact that she had a husband and two children and was coeditor and publisher of a newspaper.[71]

General Marshall reported himself impressed with Mrs. Hobby's work in organizing a meeting, at which he spoke, of the national presidents of the twenty-one largest women's organizations, designed to secure their good will and assistance to the Army.[72] He therefore asked her to give the G–1 planners any assistance on the public relations aspect of the WAAC bill that they might need. At the time of certain discussions with the President's wife, General Marshall himself sent a handwritten note to G–1: "Please utilize Mrs. Hobby as your agent to smooth the way in this matter through Mrs. Roosevelt."[73] As a result, Mrs. Hobby was thoroughly familiar with the legislation and was appointed

[68] Ltr, CofS to Hon. John W. McCormack, 6 Feb 42. CofS personal files.

[69] Ltr, Bur of Budget to SW, 7 Oct 41. AG 291.9 WAAC sec 1 pt 1 (6–2–41).

[70] Quotation from Memo, Maj Berry for Gen Haislip, 2 Dec 41. WA 042.2 (12–2–41), DRB AGO. See also Memo, Mrs. Hobby for CofS, 2 Dec 41, sub: HR 4906. CofS personal files.

[71] Senate Com on Mil Affairs, 77th Cong, 2d sess, *Hearings on S 2240*, 6 Feb 42, p. 23. The Senate suspected that the office had been set up to lobby for the WAAC, with which it actually had no connection. See also Ltr, CG, Pacific Ocean Area (Lt Gen Robert C. Richardson, Jr., formerly with WDBPR) to Col Hobby, 12 Oct 44. WDWAC 320.2. Also see undated MS draft, The Mission That Grew. WDWAC 314.7 (1945–46).

[72] Memo, Brig Gen Alexander D. Surles, Chief, WDBPR, for CofS, 13 Oct 41. CofS personal files.

[73] Memo, Chief, Women's Interests Sec for CofS, 14 Nov 41, sub: HR 4906. AG 291.9 WAAC sec 1 pt 1.

GEN. GEORGE C. MARSHALL *speaking to a meeting of the national presidents of the twenty-one largest women's organizations, 13 October 1941.*

the only female representative of the War Department in negotiations with the Bureau of the Budget and in later Congressional hearings.

In further efforts to get the WAAC bill past the Bureau of the Budget, General Marshall made a personal call and sent a highly favorable written report to the effect that "this legislation has great merit." Already overshadowed by the coming events at Pearl Harbor, the report on 25 November 1941 spoke of gaining "valuable time while time is available" in order to develop a small corps in an orderly and efficient fashion.[74]

On Thanksgiving eve General Marshall checked over with Colonel Hilldring the measures now completed to make the War Department ready for the gathering storm and, noting that WAAC legislation was still among the missing, directed him to omit no step to ensure its immediate passage. Colonel Hilldring recounted later: "General Marshall shook his finger at me and said, 'I want a women's corps right away and I don't want any excuses!' At that, I displayed considerable energy."[75]

Colonel Hilldring's energy was shortly reinforced by that of the Japanese at Pearl Harbor. On 11 December, four days after Pearl Harbor, the Bureau of the Budget withdrew its objections.[76] The way was now clear to ask Congress for the orderly

[74] Memo, DCofS for Dir Bur of Budget, 25 Nov 41, sub: Proposed Revised Rpt on HR 4906. G–1/15839–10.

[75] Interv cited n. 66.

[76] Ltr, Bur of Budget to SW, 11 Dec 41. G–1/15839–10. Also in AG 291.9 WAAC sec 1 pt 1.

and efficient development of a small women's corps capable of expansion in wartime.

When later criticism came to be leveled against the agencies and individuals who failed, in the five months now left before the passage of the bill, to anticipate and prevent every problem of the new organization's development, they were able to note in reply that they were attempting in one hundred and fifty days, and in the midst of events that dwarfed the WAAC in importance, to settle problems which twenty-three years of leisurely planning had not succeeded in solving. "Woman's ignorance" and "man's intolerance" had now come together in the fatal combination of Major Hughes' prophecy.

CHAPTER II

Establishment of the WAAC

From the date of Pearl Harbor onward, plans for a women's corps moved with a speed unequaled in the past decades. The Secretary of War sent his approval of the WAAC bill to Congress on Christmas Eve. By the last day of 1941 Mrs. Rogers had incorporated the War Department's proposed amendments into the bill and reintroduced it as H.R. 6293. The Navy Department occasioned some delay while it tried to persuade the War Department not to sponsor the corps. Finally the Assistant Secretary of War in person succeeded in persuading the Navy to withdraw "their objections to our endorsing it." Navy personnel chiefs flatly refused to make the project a joint one, informing Colonel Hilldring, "You are going to take a beating and we'll wait to see what happens." [1]

Congressional consideration was rapid but rough. "It was a battle," said General Hilldring later. "In my time I have got some one hundred bills through Congress, but this was more difficult than the rest of the hundred combined." [2] Opposition was felt more on the floor of the House, and in the cloakrooms, than in the Committees on Military Affairs. At the committee hearings Mrs. Rogers emphasized the protective and disciplinary aspects of the measure.

The only real issue at these hearings was that of militarization versus civil service.

Army spokesmen offered reassurance that Waacs would be used only where civilians were unobtainable, or where security required military personnel, and would never under any conditions displace a Civil Service employee. One powerful argument was advanced by the Air Corps, which asserted that twenty-four-hour daily security in the Aircraft Warning Service could not be achieved with civilian volunteers and that, unless Waacs could be obtained, there would be actual danger to the east coast, especially the capital. [3]

Much of the work of steering the bill was personally handled by Col. Ira P. Swift of the War Department. The committees moved with what Mrs. Rogers felt was unprecedented speed. The House hearing on 20 January was followed by the committee's approval on 28 January, by

---

[1] (1) Ltr, SW to Chmn, House Com on Mil Affairs 24 Dec 41. AG 291.9 WAAC sec 1 pt 1. (2) Memo, ASW for Hilldring, 21 Dec 41. G–1/15839–10. (3) Interv with Maj Gen John H. Hilldring, 17 Jan 46. Confirmed by interv with Mrs. Rogers, 14 Dec 45, and by First Draft Narrative, U.S. Naval Administration in World War II: Bureau of Naval Personnel, Women's Reserve, 18 January 1946. Dir of Naval History. (Hereafter cited as WAVES Hist.)

[2] Interv with Gen Hilldring cited n. 1(3).

[3] All refs to com hearings are from: (1) House Com on Mil Affairs, 77th Cong, 2d sess, *Hearings on HR 6293*, 20–21 Jan 42; (2) House Rpt 1705, 77th Cong, 2d sess, 28 Jan 42; (3) Senate Com on Mil Affairs, 77th Cong, 2d sess, *Hearings on S 2240*, 6 Feb 42; (4) Senate Rpt 1051, Calendar 1086, 77th Cong, 2d sess, 9 Feb 42.

Senate hearings on 6 February, and committee approval on 9 February. There were no really angry remarks, although there were a few such as "You are going to have a few generals, aren't you? . . ." "No, the women 'generals' will remain at home"; or "Are you going to start a matrimonial agency?" Eventually the hearings ended in a blaze of gallantry on the part of the Southern senators.

Next, the bill stuck in the House Rules Committee for some days. General Hilldring said later: "In all my experience with legislation, I had never before had a bill stick in the Rules Committee, but they refused to report it out. I spent three hours talking to them; I never confronted a colder audience." Mrs. Rogers added, "The Rules Committee was rough." Its members eventually yielded, stating that they dared not oppose their opinions to the Chief of Staff's on the matter of measures required for the national defense.[4]

When the measure finally reached the House floor the real opposition developed. Members argued that a soldier would go forward in battle even if his buddy was shot down beside him, but if his buddy was a woman he would stop and render first aid. Others declaimed, variously:

I think it is a reflection upon the courageous manhood of the country to pass a law inviting women to join the armed forces in order to win a battle.

Take the women into the armed service, who then will do the cooking, the washing, the mending, the humble homey tasks to which every woman has devoted herself?

Think of the humiliation! What has become of the manhood of America?[5]

It was General Hilldring's opinion that the bill was saved from immediate defeat at this time only by the personal support and prestige of the Chief of Staff. The Secretary of War likewise threw his support behind the measure. Nevertheless, it eventually became clear that, at best, passage would be delayed for some weeks while other more important war measures took precedence.[6]

The Appointment of WAAC Pre-Planners

Meanwhile, War Department planning was racing to keep ahead of the bill's estimated rate of progress. Forty-five days were lost in December and January before it was decided to secure an officer with wide experience and acquaintance in the War Department to establish and guide the new corps. He was to have the title of Pre-Planner, WAAC, and was to operate from a floating position in G–1 Division in order to secure necessary action from all other agencies. Such an officer was not immediately available in the War Department, and G–1 brought in from the field and temporarily assigned Lt. Col. Gilman C. Mudgett, ordering him to "build a fire under WAAC planning."[7] Colonel Mudgett was a Cavalry officer with twenty years' experience in the Regular Army, and an expert in Advanced Equitation. Most of his experience had been as a squadron officer with mounted units and as an instructor at the Cavalry School; he

---

[4] Intervs cited n. 1(3); also Memos, Chief, Budget and Leg Plng Br, for Secy, WDGS: (1) 11 Feb 42, sub: HR 6293; (2) 19 Feb 42, sub: WAAC; (3) 26 Feb 42, sub: Leg Proceedings. G–1/15839–10 (7-8-42).

[5] All from *Congressional Record*, Vol. 88, No. 55, 17 Mar 42.

[6] House Rpt cited n. 3(2).

[7] (1) Ltr, Col Mudgett to Miss Faustine Dennis, 11 Feb 42; (2) Ltr Orders, AG 210, G–1 Gen Stf (1–13–42). Both in Col Mudgett's Staybacks, 1942 WAAC files. (Hereafter cited as Mudgett Staybacks.) (3) Interv with Lt Col Harold P. Tasker, 20 Nov 42.

had never been assigned to the War Department until two weeks before he became WAAC Pre-Planner.[8]

Colonel Mudgett found that very little information could be furnished him by the War Department, most of that outdated.[9] Except for copies of the legislation, he was provided with little more than a statement that civilian employees were hard to get in such places as Pig Point, Va., and Matagorda Island, Tex.[10]

The problem at the time looked deceptively simple: The WAAC was to be a small organization, developed slowly. A director, and perhaps five assistant directors, and one hundred officer candidates would be appointed. Colonel Mudgett called the local YWCA to locate one hundred rooms for the officer candidates, who would attend a leisurely three months' course before enlisted women—called enrolled women or auxiliaries—were admitted. The War Department proposed to get its first enrolled women from among volunteers already working at Aircraft Warning Service stations, placing them in uniform and paying them for their rations and quarters so that they could continue to live at home—thus, incidentally, repeating the first mistake that British services had made. After the Aircraft Warning Service companies were filled, it was thought there would be ample time to consider the ten other companies which were to go to corps areas.[11]

Colonel Mudgett had one assistant, Mrs. Marjorie Fling, selected by Civilian Personnel Division because of her familiarity with War Department procedure and her desire to join the WAAC when it was established. Mrs. Fling set to work at once to compile WAAC Regulations, based on CCC Regulations and Canadian and British WAAC Regulations.[12]

On his first day of operation, the WAAC Pre-Planner, as directed by the War Department, distributed WAAC planning among the various staff agencies of the War Department, informing each of its responsibility:

To The Adjutant General's Office: WAAC recruiting. All administrative functions performed for the Army.

To The Quartermaster General: WAAC uniform, design, and procurement. WAAC insignia. WAAC equipment.

To the Judge Advocate General: Disciplinary regulations.

To The Surgeon General: Medical treatment for women.

To the Chief of Finance: Fiscal responsibility.

To G–3: WAAC training and training regulations. WAAC organization.

To G–4: Housing and supply policy. Tables of Basic Allowances. Burial.

To the Air Forces: Organization and training of Aircraft Warning Service units.

Each of these agencies was asked to designate a representative for WAAC planning. The instructions to these agencies did not specify their relationship to any future WAAC headquarters or who would have the final word in disputes.[13]

On the same day corps areas were asked

---

[8] Personnel Abstracts, WAC files, OCMH.

[9] He later noted, "As I look back, I would have given a great deal to have had access to the background material that you [Military History] have collected. . . . The widely scattered data were apparently on file, but unfortunately . . . not made available to me." Ltr, Mudgett to author, 19 Aug 49. OCMH.

[10] Pencil note, Swift to Mudgett. WA 600.9 (1–20–42), 1942 WAAC files.

[11] All statements unless otherwise specified are from Mudgett Staybacks. Original copies of most documents are in G–1/15839–10. See references to specific documents in following pages.

[12] (1) Memo, G–1 for Dir of Pers, 28 Jan 42. G–1/15839–10. (2) Interv with Mrs. Marjorie Fling Onthank, 16 Jan 46.

[13] Memos, G–1 for [each office], 4 Feb 42, sub: WAAC. G–1/15839. Replies are in G–1/15839–10 (7–8–42).

to plan for the use of one WAAC company each, and chiefs of branches were asked to comment on the possible later use of Waacs at their service schools. Letters to these commands included a statement on which the War Department was later to reverse itself: Waacs could be assigned to replace not only enlisted men but "civilian employees not in the Civil Service now used for purely administrative or house-keeping duties." [14]

It was not yet decided whether Waacs counted against a station's Troop Basis, or its civilian allotment, or both; most stations understandably assumed that Waacs constituted some sort of happy bonus. Also, the previous decision that the Army needed a small elite corps with high clerical skills was nullified by the authorization to use Waacs to replace non-Civil Service civilians, most of whom were unskilled. Consequently, corps area requisitions later that month asked for Waacs not only for skilled clerical and technical work but also for work that it was difficult to get civilians to accept: jobs as maids, charwomen, janitresses, cooks, mess attendants, messengers, hostesses, mail orderlies, housekeepers, and hospital attendants.

As a result of the double misunderstanding—that Waacs would be recruited for unskilled menial duties and that they would not count against personnel allotments—not too much significance could be attached to the corps areas' enthusiasm in at once requesting not ten but twenty-four WAAC companies. On the other hand, all of the chiefs of branches, including infantry, cavalry, and artillery, replied that they wanted none: "Strongly advise that they not be assigned." The Chief of Engineers asked to be excused from taking a unit. The Surgeon General refused to use Waacs in hospitals, saying,

"Can see no use for a WAAC unit without displacing Civil Service employees." [15] No attempt was made to force a unit upon any reluctant command, since there would obviously not be enough Waacs to fill even the current requisitions.

In only a few days WAAC preplanning had the requisite fire under it. Uniform designs were being prepared by The Quartermaster General; The Adjutant General was converting Army blank forms and records for WAAC use; the Judge Advocate General was preparing tentative disciplinary regulations; the Signal Corps and the Air Corps were planning Aircraft Warning Service companies. Colonel Mudgett suggested that a female director and staff of three male officers be appointed at once, and action to secure these was begun by G–1. Within another ten days Colonel Mudgett had obtained rough drafts of WAAC Regulations, was working with G–4 on barracks plans, had consulted the Office of The Surgeon General on the enlistment physical examination, and had planned recruiting with The Adjutant General. In four more days he had made plans for press releases on the appointment of the Director and had secured G–3 approval of a training center Table of Organization.[16]

---

[14] D/F, G–1 to TAG, 5 Feb 42, sub: WAAC. G–1/15839–10. Branches included were Infantry, Cavalry, Field Artillery, Coast Artillery, Engineers, Air Corps, Armored Forces, Quartermaster Corps, and Medical Department.

[15] Tally of replies is preserved in Folder U, (Utilization), Col Tasker's files, in 1942 WAAC files. (Hereafter cited at Tasker files.)

[16] (1) Memo, Preplanner for Col Oscar B. Abbott, 6 Feb 42; (2) Memo, Preplanner for Maj Gen James A. Ulio, 11 Feb 42; (3) Memo, Preplanner for Lt Col Lester D. Flory, G–4, 11 Feb 42; (4) Memo, Preplanner for Col Harry D. Offutt, SGO, 13 Feb 42; (5) M/R, Conf with Col Harold N. Gilbert, AGO, 13 Feb 42; (6) Memo for Col Abbott, 19 Feb 42. All in Mudgett personal or stayback files, 1942 WAAC files.

Planning could not await the appointment of the Director, WAAC, and in fact planners deemed it wise "to be able to present [completed plans] to the Director, when appointed, in order to avoid the initiation of plans based entirely on the viewpoint of one individual." By 23 February 1942, when the future Director was added to the preplanning group, many plans were too far advanced for much change without controversy with the planning agency. By this date the WAAC Regulations were already written and approved by G–3 Division, as was the outline of instruction for the officer candidate school. Budget estimates had already been forwarded to the War Department, and the Finance Department had virtually completed all fiscal rules. A Table of Organization had been drawn up for WAAC Headquarters, showing the numbers and grades of persons required, as had similar tables for WAAC companies and platoons. The Army Recruiting Service believed itself prepared to conduct recruiting. G–4 Division was convinced that WAAC housing would present no great problem. Finally, a request had been submitted for the assignment of an experienced Regular Army officer to act as school commandant.[17]

Other matters awaited the Director's action. No location had been found for a training center; no uniforms or other clothing had been procured; no actual recruiting machinery was set up, although it was suggested that the Director make a transcontinental tour and personally select the first one hundred officer candidates. The future WAAC Headquarters had not been organized, although a major and two lieutenants had been ordered in for immediate assistance.[18]

All of the Pre-Planner's work, complete or incomplete, suffered from being based on the War Department's assumption as to the WAAC's future size, which was to be discarded later in the summer when manpower problems began to appear. It was supposed that the Corps would, during its first year, train only 10,600 auxiliaries and 340 officers—a miscalculation of some 600 percent. Most of the plans, therefore, shortly had to be revised or abandoned, but, as General Hilldring later noted, they were not without value, being in the same category as all military "anticipatory planning." [19]

Selection of a Director

G–1 Division demanded that all candidates for the position of WAAC Director be healthy, of an active temperament, between the ages of 30 and 50, with executive experience involving the successful management of both men and women assistants, and, most important, they must have had no previous affiliation with any "pressure group."

Mrs. Hobby, then of the Bureau of Public Relations, was asked to recommend women who met these requirements. She submitted a list of nine that included some of the nation's most successful career women—an advertising executive, a business manager, a bank president, several educators. Social and political leaders were not included. Congresswoman Rogers was also asked to recommend

[17] (1) Quotation from Memo for Col Flory, G–4, 11 Feb 42. Mudgett Staybacks. (2) Memo, Preplanner for Dir WAAC, 23 Feb 42. 1942 WAAC file, unnumbered. (3) Memo, CofS for G–1, 26 Feb 42. CofS/ 19481–60.

[18] Earlier draft of Memo cited n. 17(2).

[19] Ltr, Hilldring to Maj Gen Orlando Ward, Chief, Mil Hist, 5 Jan 51. OCMH.

candidates; she submitted only one name—Mrs. Hobby's. G–1 Division likewise submitted its own list of candidates to the Chief of Staff, and this included three names, headed by Mrs. Hobby's. Colonel Mudgett also approved of the recommendation, commenting later: "I have never known a finer executive, man or woman." [20]

Biographical data compiled by G–1 added that Mrs. Oveta Culp Hobby was at this time 37 years old, the wife of former Governor William P. Hobby of Texas, and the mother of two children. She had served for several years as parliamentarian of the Texas legislature, and, after her marriage, as newspaper and radio executive, publisher, lawyer, writer, president of the Texas League of Women Voters, and civic worker in numerous state and city organizations of both men and women. As of this date she had been for almost a year the chief of the Bureau of Public Relations' Women's Interests Section, which she had initiated and organized.

For a number of reasons the War Department's final choice fell upon Mrs. Hobby. She had the advantage over all other recommended candidates of already being familiar with WAAC plans and with War Department organization. Officers of G–1 Division wrote: "She has ability, vision, and is broad-minded enough to assemble a staff of capable assistants around her. [She is] already known to most of the key people in government and War Department circles." [21]

All acquaintances noted her personal energy, magnetism, sincerity, and idealism, and observed that a very considerable diplomatic ability on all matters was combined with a certain stubborn determination in pursuing major issues. Another asset, from the Army viewpoint, was that Mrs. Hobby was not a representative of any pressure group, as it was deemed essential that the Director owe allegiance only to the War Department. The Chief of Staff informed the Secretary of War that Mrs. Hobby was his choice for the position of Director solely because of her brilliant work in the Bureau of Public Relations and in negotiations for the WAAC bill, and that "I had never seen, or even heard of, Mrs. Hobby prior to this time, and she had no prior knowledge of the bill." He added:

In all of these duties she displayed sound judgment and carried out her mission in a manner to be expected of a highly trained staff officer. She has won the complete confidence of the members of the War Department Staff with whom she has come into contact, and she made a most favorable impression before the Committee of Congress.

. . . This Corps can be of great assistance to our military effort, and it can easily be a great embarrassment to the War Department. I therefore urge the appointment of Mrs. Hobby, with the request that the decision be made in advance of the completion of the legislation in order that the War Department can anticipate the burdens of organization so far as possible. [22]

Mrs. Hobby was not considered disqualified by the fact that she had children, since women with children were to be accepted for immobile units like the Aircraft Warning Service, where they could live at home. [23]

---

[20] (1) Memo, G–1 for CofS, 3 Feb 42, sub: Dir WAAC. G–1/15838. Three lists are Tables A, B, and C. (2) Ltr, Col Mudgett to author, 19 Aug 48. OCMH.

[21] Memo, Chief, Misc Div G–1, for Gen Hilldring, 29 Jan 42, sub: Suggested Candidates for Position of Dir WAAC. Mudgett Staybacks.

[22] Memo, CofS for SW, 18 Mar 42, sub: Chief of WAAC. WDCSA 291.9 (3–18–42).

[23] Interv with Mrs. Hobby, 29 Jun 48. Also see Ch. XXXV, below.

Meanwhile, a number of prominent political figures, including members of Congress, had acquired their own candidates,[24] and G–1 Division urged speed in the appointment of a director, since "efforts will be made by certain pressure groups to influence the Secretary of War in his appointment of the Director." [25]

At the end of February, when no announcement from the Secretary of War was forthcoming, the Chief of Staff took upon himself the responsibility of moving Mrs. Hobby from the Bureau of Public Relations to join the WAAC Pre-Planners, although in view of her lack of official status all planning done by her was subject to reversal later if another candidate was selected by the Secretary of War.[26]

Organization of Director's Headquarters

Mrs. Hobby now found herself in a strange status; she was the unannounced head of a nonexistent office which could not become WAAC Headquarters until passage of legislation at an uncertain future date, but which meanwhile must perfect very complete plans requiring the formal co-ordination of many War Department agencies. Her "staff" was one Cavalry lieutenant colonel and one civilian woman assistant. This little group began meeting in a corner of the Miscellaneous Branch of G–1 Division, but later in March acquired several rooms and a telephone in the wooden Temporary M Building.

On 27 February, a few days after Mrs. Hobby's arrival, the man who had been intended to be WAAC Pre-Planner, Lt. Col. Harold P. Tasker, arrived. Colonel Tasker was a Regular Army officer, with fifteen years' service in the Coast Artillery Corps and as instructor in mathematics at West Point. He had been retired for disability in 1939 but later recalled on limited service. Although he had never previously served in the War Department, all members of the new group stated that his outstanding ability quickly rendered him invaluable.[27]

With Colonel Tasker came two young Reserve lieutenants, just called to active duty, who had no Army experience.[28] For almost a month these six constituted the headquarters. About the middle of March the office acquired its senior member, Col. William Pearson, who was selected by The Adjutant General to be WAAC adjutant general. Colonel Pearson was the only member of the staff who had previously served in Washington. His service was not recent; he had been retired in 1936, after more than thirty-four years in the Regular Army, and had just been recalled to active duty. Shortly, four more officers arrived to complete the military staff. Two of these were lieutenant colonels who were intended to be school commandant and quartermaster, respectively, but both were replaced within a few months.[29] The third was Maj. J. Noel Macy of the Bureau of Public Relations, on temporary loan to handle publicity, and the fourth was another young Reserve lieutenant.[30]

Mrs. Hobby also secured the services of two women advisers. Mrs. Genevieve Forbes Herrick, a prominent writer and newspaperwoman, was designated adviser

---

[24] Ltrs, G–1/15839–10 (1942).
[25] Memo cited n. 20(1).
[26] Memo cited n. 22.
[27] Intervs with members of the group: Mrs. Hobby, Mrs. Woods, Mrs. Fling, Mrs. Genevieve Forbes Herrick.
[28] Lts. Charles L. Fleming and Henry Lee Munson.
[29] Interv with Col Tasker, 20 Nov 45.
[30] Lt. William W. Foulkes.

on public relations and the press. Mrs. Helen Hamilton Woods was named adviser on legislative matters, recruiting, and administration in general. Mrs. Woods, who was later to enroll in the WAAC, was the widow of New York Police Commissioner Arthur Woods, and the mother of three sons in the service. A civic leader and political worker, and a descendant of the first Secretary of the Treasury, she had had much experience with volunteer groups and had been employed by the Treasury in connection with the information program for defense bond sales.[31]

Assignment to Services of Supply

Planning was somewhat hampered when the little group of WAAC preplanners was immediately dropped two echelons in the War Department during the reorganization of 9 March 1942, one of the major upheavals of War Department history. At this time the entire General Staff was reduced in size and bereft of operating functions, and the many organizations reporting directly to it were swept away, leaving direct access to the General Staff a privilege of three new major commands—the Army Air Forces, the Army Ground Forces, and the Services of Supply (later renamed the Army Service Forces). Many of the chiefs of services who had formerly reported directly to the Chief of Staff—such as The Adjutant General, the Judge Advocate General, and The Quartermaster General—now were grouped under the command of the Services of Supply (SOS), which was to be the operating agency for the General Staff.

The WAAC was similarly transferred from G–1 Division to Personnel Division of the Services of Supply, and directives drafted by WAAC preplanners henceforth had to be signed by that office rather than by Brig. Gen. John H. Hilldring in G–1. Few of the transferred agencies were very happy about the change. WAAC planners in particular realized its disadvantages, since they no longer had the close guidance of the General Staff during the Corps' formative period, and could not reach it with any ideas that were disapproved by the Services of Supply. The move made it particularly difficult to work directly with the Army Air Forces or the Army Ground Forces.

The legality of the Director's assignment to this lower echelon was somewhat doubtful, since the wording of the WAAC bill made her adviser to the War Department. At the time of the move the Chief of Staff therefore directed Mrs. Hobby to come to him personally if she had any difficulty that she could not iron out by herself. This privilege Mrs. Hobby used infrequently, since she understood that the Services of Supply would scarcely be a comfortable location if she bypassed its channels whenever her proposals were disapproved.

From this time onward General Marshall was consulted only when crucial decisions were required. The new and smaller General Staff also obviously had less time to advise the planners. At one of its meetings, the WAAC was dismissed with the brief and overoptimistic note that its administration would be the same whether it was *in* or *with* the Army; the same meeting was devoted to dozens of more important matters involved in the world-wide combat situation. Nevertheless, WAAC planners united in giving great personal credit to the Assistant Chief

---

[31] Intervs with Mrs. Herrick, 9 Jan 46, and with Mrs. Woods, 14 Dec 45.

of Staff, G–1, General Hilldring, for the fact that in the following hectic weeks they actually did complete full plans, workable if not perfect. General Hilldring repeatedly stepped down from his echelon to give planners more of his personal time and advice than the small WAAC organization could have expected from its current importance to the war effort.[32]

The Services of Supply immediately delegated WAAC planning to the various SOS divisions, in much the same way that this once had been divided among War Department staff sections. For example, the SOS's Training Division received authority to establish policies for the training of all WAAC officers, auxiliaries, and units. In actual practice, the general nature of the subsequent WAAC plans was worked out in joint conferences, put in writing by the preplanners, and approved by various SOS Divisions.[33] It was not made clear what procedure would be followed if disagreements occurred.

The British Parallel

Mrs. Hobby's first step was to pause and assess the experience of the British and Canadian women's services, already well established.[34] During the first days of March she visited Canada, accompanied by Colonel Tasker and the commandant-elect, and was afforded the opportunity to talk to leaders of the Canadian WAC and of the Women's Division, Royal Canadian Air Force, as well as to British women officers then visiting Canada. She also later dispatched Major Macy to England to collect references and histories.

The visit did much to restore Mrs. Hobby's morale, which had been depressed by the opinion of many of her friends among older U.S. Army officers

that a women's corps could not succeed. Every Canadian staff officer and post commander to whom she talked told her that he had experienced initial doubts but was now enthusiastic about employment of women in his command. British officers likewise reported the success of their women's services in spite of extensive early hardships.[35]

The histories of the several British and Canadian women's services presented patterns so nearly identical as to suggest a certain amount of inevitability, with the British, of course, one or two wars ahead. Before and during World War I, the British had set up a few tentative women's corps, on a civilian auxiliary basis. Manpower problems had proved so great, and the women such efficient workers, that by 1918 such groups were to be found in every branch of service. The only handicap had been the very considerable public gossip concerning the alleged immorality of women in France, which hampered recruiting and alarmed parents, although a Royal Commission of Enquiry reported after investigation that the charges were "mischievous and false."

Nevertheless, when the British women's services were revived in World War II, they repeated the whole unhappy pattern

---

[32] (1) Interv cited n. 29, and from study of whole series of documents and orders cited. (2) Min, Gen Council, 4 May 42.

[33] 1st Ind, Dir Tng SOS to WAAC Preplanners, 25 Apr 42, to Memo, Preplanners for Dir Tng SOS, 15 Apr 42, sub: Preliminary OCS. SPTRS 353 WAAC (4–15–42).

[34] Unless otherwise indicated this section is based upon, and quotations are from: (1) *Report of the Committee on Amenities and Welfare Conditions in the Three Women's Services, Presented to Parliament by Command of His Majesty, August, 1942,* (London: *HM Stationery Office, 1942*). Hereafter cited as *Conditions in the Three Women's Services.* Copy in 1942 WAAC files. (2) Wadge, *Women in Uniform.*

[35] Interv cited n. 29.

as far as public opposition was concerned. "Vague and discreditable allegations" were spread to such an extent that a Parliamentary committee investigation was ordered. Gossip alleged a high rate of illegitimate pregnancy, excessive drinking, and general promiscuity among servicewomen. The committee upon investigation found that the women's morality was actually better than that of the comparable civilian population, and deplored the "malicious and careless talk" that had again damaged recruiting and discouraged women members and their parents.

The British Auxiliary Territorial Services (ATS) and the Women's Auxiliary Air Force (WAAF) had also suffered in the first days of World War II from difficulties caused by rapid mobilization—shortage of uniforms, inadequacy of housing, improper medical attention, all intensified by the lack of trained and experienced women officers to care for the units. By 1942 many difficulties had been overcome, supply shortages had eased, gossip had been partially quelled, and the women's work had proved so valuable that their numbers had been tremendously increased and their jobs expanded from five or six to several hundred. Finally, when manpower conditions became more desperate and recruiting failed to fill needs, the British National Service Act was applied to women and female draftees were directed to fill the vacancies in the armed forces.

At the time of Mrs. Hobby's visit to Canada in March of 1942 the British services were thus well established and offered a valuable precedent to the WAAC in the United States. WAAC planners might have regarded their history with even more interest had they known that it could, without alteration, have been a summary of the WAAC's future, in all except the matter of eventual recourse to Selective Service.

One major effect of the Canadian visit upon the headquarters was that it became what its members called "public-relations conscious." All future plans came to be scrutinized in the light of their possible effect upon public sentiment, and extreme care was used to avoid any measure that might provoke an outburst of slander and gossip of the type that had hindered British recruiting and necessitated the drafting of women. This tendency was deplored by some Regular Army members of the staff, since it frequently raised the issue of whether certain established Army practices were adaptable to the WAAC.

Another conspicuous lesson in the history of the British services was that the civilian auxiliary organization was notably inefficient and friction provoking. Already two of the three major British women's services had been admitted to full military status. In Canada Mrs. Hobby noted that the Women's Division of the Royal Canadian Air Force, which was actually *in* the Air Force, had fewer administrative difficulties than the Canadian WAC, which was only an auxiliary *with* the Army. Most commanders heartily disliked separate command channels, separate rules, and separate status for any members of their station complements and, in fact, the Canadian WAC was to be admitted to full Army status within a few months, and the Women's Royal Canadian Naval Service, just being organized, never attempted to operate without full Navy membership.[36]

Mrs. Hobby therefore proposed that an amendment immediately be added to the

---

[36] *Ibid.*

WAAC bill before its passage, placing the WAAC *in* the Army and giving its members full military status and discipline. The War Department was not enthusiastic about this change and Mrs. Rogers objected also, on the assumption, which proved quite correct, that the attempt would merely delay the bill's passage and would not be accepted by Congress even after the delay.[37] Nevertheless, Mrs. Hobby insisted that the amendment at least be considered by the committee, and consideration was finally agreed upon, a step that was to delay passage of the bill until May.[38]

Recruiting Plans

The British precedent was also quickly reflected in other plans, primarily those for the selection of officers. Mrs. Hobby and Colonel Mudgett at once discarded previous plans for her to appoint assistant directors and to select one hundred officer candidates. The number of applications now on file from individuals with prominent social, political, or military figures for sponsors indicated that, were appointments direct, the WAAC might be forced to repeat the British ATS mistake of commissioning these women in such numbers that forced retirements would later be necessary. The ATS had come to the conclusion that selection by means of officer candidate boards and schools was the best way to produce women officers able and willing to care for their troops effectively. Accordingly, Mrs. Hobby formed a basic policy from which she was never thereafter to swerve[39]—that of Corps democracy: all officers, even assistant directors, were to be graduates of the officer candidate school and not direct appointees. After the first class, all officers would come from the

ranks. Mrs. Hobby also decided at the same time that selection of the initial class should be by impartial Army recruiting machinery, and not by herself or any other individual. Negroes were to be included in the same proportion as in the Army.[40]

Preplanners hastily prepared and sent to the printers detailed instructions for corps areas to follow in selecting officer candidates. Mrs. Hobby secured the advice of a conference of eight prominent psychiatrists, as well as that of The Adjutant General's battery of test construction experts, to determine qualifications and to help devise a method of screening. All corps areas were alerted to expect instructions and application blanks by air mail, immediately upon passage of the bill, and were given a military schedule whereby date of passage was designated D Day. The first officer candidates were to be selected and at the school by D plus 47.[41]

The WAAC D Day now bore down upon the pre-planners. The WAAC bill passed the House of Representatives on 17 March by a vote of 249 to 86, authorizing an auxiliary corps only, and was sent to the Senate, which had promised to consider full Army status.[42]

Public interest mounted daily. Planners hid themselves away and answered the

---

[37] Interv with Mrs. Rogers cited n. 1(3).

[38] See text below for full discussion of War Department and other views in May committee hearings.

[39] See later chapters for discussion.

[40] (1) Interv cited n. 29. (2) *Conditions in the Three Women's Services*. (3) Memo, G–1 for CofS, 22 Mar 42. G–1/15839, in CofS 291.9.

[41] (1) Ltr, TAG to all Corps Areas, 16 Mar 42. AG 291.9 (3–16–42) E–R. (2) Memos, SOS for TAG, 17 Mar 42. G–1/15839–10. (3) Rough notes of conf of psychiatrists. 1942 WAAC files, unnumbered. (4) Interv cited n. 29. (5) See Ch. III, below.

[42] *Congressional Record*, Vol. 88, No. 55, p. 2657, 17 Mar 42.

telephone with a vague "Personnel Division," but were nevertheless plagued with telephone calls, visitors, letters, and unsolicited offers. Candidates sought guarantees of commissions because of their acquaintance with prominent people, or their dubious experience in bossing women; individuals sought to interest the WAAC in mobile laundry units or fur-lined overcoats.[43] Prospective recruits wrote, variously: "My husband is already drafted and my mother cannot afford to have me staying on . . ."; "My brother was killed on December 7"; "I have always wished that I were a man"; "I am a widow, with no dependents"; "At present I am working as a warder at the Women's Reformatory."[44]

This was only a foretaste of the merciless publicity that was to haunt the WAAC from its inception. In desperation the planners ordered thousands of acknowledgment cards thanking applicants for their offers and telling them that, if the bill became law, full details would be released through local recruiting stations.[45] Considerable embarrassment appeared in store if the WAAC D Day arrived before the War Department was ready with plans for it.

Search for a Training Center

For several frantic weeks it appeared impossible to find a training center. The idea of a CCC camp was considered and abandoned, since extensive additional construction and repair would have been necessary. Premature rejoicing was general early in March when the Tome School, a private institution in nearby Maryland, was found to be available. Unfortunately, G–3 Division ruled that no contract could legally be signed until the

bill became law. The Army's complicated machinery of approval moved as far as it dared—budget estimates were made, an engineer survey for barracks space was authorized, acquisition of property was approved. After serious study of the relative fame of American heroines it was recommended that the school be named the Molly Pitcher School. Detailed grades were even allotted to the Third Service Command and personnel was being selected. All of these plans collapsed suddenly in the last week of March when the Navy acquired the Tome School.[46]

Immediate passage of the bill was now believed possible, with April occupancy of some school a necessity. Army engineers hastily surveyed Northwestern University and found it full of naval trainees; Lake Forest College had a capacity of only 400; the University of Chicago was filled by the Navy and the Signal Corps, and Ohio State by the Air Corps; Eastern Kentucky State Teachers College would not take Negroes.

As the search continued through other areas, it was found in general that all large universities were training so many Army and Navy technical specialists that even their gymnasiums and classrooms were converted to barracks; all small colleges

---

[43] Ltrs of application. 1942 WAAC files, unnumbered.

[44] *Congressional Record*, Vol. 88, No. 53, pp. 1078–81, Mar 42.

[45] Memo, Preplanners for TAG, 31 Mar 42, sub: Acknowledgment Cards for WAAC Applicants. Mudgett Staybacks.

[46] (1) Memo, G–3 for CofS, 19 Apr 42. WDGCT 291.9 (4–15–42). Copy in CofS 291.9. (2) Memo, G–1 for G–4, 7 Mar 42. G–1/15839–10. (3) D/F, Pers Div SOS to CofEngrs, 11 Mar 42. Same file. (4) Memo, Pers Div SOS for CofS, 13 Mar 42. Same file. (5) Memo, SOS for TAG, 28 Mar 42. Mudgett Staybacks. (6) Corps areas became service commands in the reorganization of 1942.

could accommodate only a few trainees; and most suitable resort hotels either had been taken over by the Air Forces or would have had to be condemned at a prohibitive price. Engineers as a last resort surveyed even state fair grounds, but found them either leased for government storage or not convertible. For a time the National Chautauqua Circuit at Jamestown seemed the best possibility, although isolated and in a cold climate.[47]

At last, in late April, the mechanization of the U.S. Cavalry made possible the use for Waacs of an old mounted Cavalry post, Fort Des Moines in Iowa. Fort Des Moines was near the geographical center of the United States, had no major defense projects in the area, would present no race and color difficulties, had suitable utilities to handle expansion to 5,000 population, and already had room for 1,000 and suitable administration, supply, and recreation buildings. Its solid red-brick barracks, needing only converted toilet facilities, surrounded an impressively large green parade ground. In addition, said the delighted planners, there were "nine large stables suitable for conversion to barracks."[48] Time was short and there was no inclination to quibble about the distance from WAAC Headquarters, the climate, or the previous equine occupants.

Immediate authority to start alterations at the post was sought, but could not be obtained until passage of the bill.[49] It was at least possible to bring into the planning group nine Army officers to be indoctrinated before they went to Fort Des Moines as a nucleus of the staff. To replace the officer previously selected as commandant, G–1 Division chose Col. Don C. Faith, a Regular Army officer of twenty-five years' service. He had been a National Guard instructor and a staff officer, and

later a member of the War Department's G–4 and G–1 Divisions.[50]

The Uniform

The most troublesome problem remaining to the planners was that of the WAAC uniform, which soon assumed a difficulty out of all proportion to its importance. Procurement could not be undertaken until passage of the bill, but it was essential to have agreement on design and number of articles so that contracts could be signed with manufacturers at the moment the bill became law. At first, the problem of clothing only 12,000 Waacs appeared fairly simple, and The Quartermaster General, in one of the greater understatements of recorded military history, anticipated "no unusual difficulties."[51]

Three agencies sent representatives to planning sessions: The Quartermaster General's Office, the Philadelphia Quartermaster Depot, and WAAC Headquarters, although The Quartermaster General later decided that this last was a mistake, since "neither she [Mrs. Hobby] nor anyone on her immediate staff was qualified to make decisions."[52] As a matter of fact,

[47] (1) Personal ltr, Tasker to Lt C. M. Carr, Cooks and Bakers School, Ft Meade, Md., 21 Mar 42. Col Tasker's personal file, 1942 WAAC files. (2) M/R, 9 Apr 42, sub: Inspection of Available Sites. WA 600.9 (4–9–42). (3) M/R, 11 Apr 42, sub: Facilities. WA 600.9.

[48] Memo, G–1 for CofS, 22 Apr 42. G–1/15839. Colonel Mudgett successfully persuaded Des Moines newspapermen to ignore the conversion of stables to barracks for fear of the possible effect upon recruiting.

[49] Memo, G–1 for CofS, 13 May 42, sub: Estab of WAAC Tng Cen at Ft Des Moines, Iowa. WDGAP 352.01 WAAC. Approved by DCofS, 15 May 42.

[50] Personnel Abstracts, WAC file, OCMH.

[51] All references to WAAC clothing and equipment, unless otherwise noted, are from Erna Risch, *A Wardrobe for the Women of the Army* (QMC Historical Studies 12, October 1945).

[52] *Ibid.*, Chs. II and III.

none of the planning agencies included any specialists in women's clothing. The Quartermaster General had been responsible for the design and procurement of nurses' uniforms since World War I, but no great quantity had been involved, and the products, although they photographed well on a dress form (male), had admittedly always looked peculiar on the female figure.

Responsibility for the WAAC uniform program was delegated by The Quartermaster General, as a part-time duty, to Col. Letcher O. Grice of the Standardization Branch. Before Mrs. Hobby's arrival, Colonel Grice had secured some sketches by famous designers, and had suggested that the uniform be in two shades of blue. Because of the word *distinctive* in legislative authorization for a WAAC uniform, Colonel Grice was of the opinion that the uniform must be different in color and design from that of the Army or any other organization; even the two shades of blue must be different from that of the Army Nurse Corps. Blue was selected because New York designers informed him that blue dyestuffs would be most readily available; gray was rejected as too hard to match.

The representative of the Philadelphia Depot was not summoned by The Quartermaster General until some three months of planning were past and, upon arrival, expressed some annoyance in view of the depot's opinion that research and development was its rightful province. This officer also was not a specialist in women's clothing, and expressed a strong belief in "nothing fancier for Wacs than for combat soldiers," which threatened to leave the women equipped for office work in boots and coveralls.

The WAAC representatives at this time likewise included no clothing specialists

and in any case had no authority to take action in the matter. Female members of Mrs. Hobby's staff faithfully wore sample undergarments while carrying on preplanning; male planners offered their best guesses in the matter, and the staff became accustomed, as one member noted, "to seeing Lt. F. stalk through the office with a cigar in one hand and a pair of pink panties in the other."

Mrs. Hobby at once announced her conviction that the WAAC uniform should be identical in color with that of the Army and as much like it in design as possible, especially in view of her pending attempt to place the WAAC in the Army. The battle of blue versus olive drab continued for some time and was finally resolved by the Philadelphia Depot, which wished to use olive drab and khaki material already procured, and deemed it madness to start procuring two more shades of blue. The materials, covert and barathea for winter and 8.2 khaki for summer, were also determined by depot stocks, although some, especially the khaki, were to prove too heavy for the proper fit of women's garments.

Sketches from well-known designers were considered—Mangone, Maria Krum, Russell Patterson, Helen Cookman, Mary Sampson. The jacket could be called a group product, since it incorporated desirable features from all designs—a lapel from one, a pocket from another. A belt for the jacket was on, off, and on again: it would help faulty female figures, said Mangone; it would rub holes in the jacket, said The Quartermaster General; it should be leather, said Maria Krum; cotton was cheaper, said The Quartermaster General. A rather narrow six-gore skirt was adopted after War Production Board restrictions on the use of material made pleats impossible, although all agreed that pleats would have looked better.

Slacks had originally been a part of the outfit, but they were eliminated as too troublesome to fit; culottes were considered and rejected by Mrs. Hobby as unsuitable for mechanics. Since at this time it was believed that the only outdoor work that Waacs could perform was in motor transport, no trousers except coveralls were believed necessary. Mrs. Hobby also desired that women wear skirts instead of slacks wherever possible, in order to avoid a rough or masculine appearance which would cause unfavorable public comment.

All agreed that a shirt with tie would be more military and dignified than one with an open collar, and the regulation khaki tie was chosen, although some designers favored an ascot.

The choice of WAAC headgear involved most controversy then and later. The Quartermaster General had suggested a stiff service cap like the men's cap for WAAC officers and an overseas cap for enlisted women, with a brimmed khaki summer hat, but Mrs. Hobby called for identical hats for officers and enlisted women, as being more democratic. The overseas cap was becoming, but was then being adopted by many women's volunteer groups and private service organizations. Mrs. Hobby believed that it was essential to have a WAAC cap that could not be mistaken for that of any civilian group or, more precisely, that it was essential that the Waacs not be blamed for any misconduct on the part of the thousands of civilian women soon to be wearing overseas caps. The firms of Knox and Stetson therefore submitted designs of "miner" hats, visor caps, and berets. A majority vote of the conference selected the visor cap as one that would shield the eyes, not blow off in pa-

rades, and be both distinctive and military.

A heavy topcoat was designed by Mangone, very similar in cut to the men's overcoat. In place of the men's field jacket, a light utility coat was designed by Maria Krum, resembling a hooded raincoat with button-in lining. A handbag with shoulder strap was authorized, since women's uniforms obviously had no pants pockets, and experiments with carrying necessities in breast pockets quickly produced a rule against even so much as a pack of cigarettes in that location.

Tan oxfords, tennis shoes, galoshes, and bedroom slippers were selected. Mrs. Hobby recommended plain pumps for dress shoes, but was outvoted on grounds of economy. She also desired lisle stockings for dress, but only rayons were available; and plain cotton stockings for work were chosen instead of the novelty-ribbed cotton she preferred.

There began to be apparent at this time a significant difference of opinion as to the number and type of garments to be issued. By accepted practice, the Army was obligated to furnish its members any articles it required them to wear. This clothing, in the Director's opinion, had to be judged according to accepted civilian custom for females, but in the opinion of most quartermaster representatives could most fairly be based on the amount and type of clothing received by men. Thus, concerning what were called "foundation garments," it was noted that some women required these in order to present a "neat and military appearance," yet could not be directed to wear them unless the garment was issued—an action without military precedent. Similarly, it appeared to be discrimination against men to issue free pajamas and bathrobes, yet it was also not desired to authorize nude female appearances in the various military installations that did not have connecting latrines. As for the required physical training, men received nothing similar to the seersucker exercise dress, yet it appeared undesirable for women to assemble on the drill field in nothing but panties. In this last case, it was luckily noted that Waacs, except for a few women drivers, did not receive the fatigue coveralls that men did; thus, the seersucker dress could be accepted as a non-discrimatory substitute for men's coveralls. On most of the other items, authorization was not made until June and was withdrawn again in a few months.

The Quartermaster General reduced some of the requested allowances to the number authorized for men; the WAAC request for eight shirts was reduced to four. The request for six cotton dresses and six cotton aprons for cooks, and four coveralls for drivers, was reduced by The Quartermaster General to three, three, and two. In requesting two uniform jackets, pre-planners pointed out that men received heavy wool shirts to be worn without a jacket, but that the WAAC's thin cotton shirts were designed for wear with the whole suit, and that "cleanliness, good health, and appearance" required two suit jackets. However, only one jacket was finally authorized, since men got only one.[53]

The Heraldic Section of The Quartermaster General's Office meanwhile had submitted designs for insignia. Designers were initially somewhat at a loss, since insignia usually portrayed the function of the corps concerned and no one knew exactly what the Waacs were to do, except that they would perform several Army jobs. A first attempt produced only a busy-bee-like insect, which Mrs. Hobby pronounced a bug, adding that she had no

desire to be called the Queen Bee.

Designers then hit upon the idea of a head of Pallas Athene, a goddess associated with an impressive variety of womanly virtues and no vices either womanly or godlike. She was the goddess of handicrafts, wise in industries of peace and arts of war, also the goddess of storms and battle, who led through victory to peace and prosperity.[54] Accordingly, the head of Pallas Athene, together with the traditional *U.S.*, was selected for lapel insignia, cut out for officers and on discs for enlisted women.

An eagle for the cap was also designed, less intricate than the Army eagle and later to be familiarly known to Waacs, for reasons closely connected with its appearance, as "the buzzard." Since Army buttons could not be used for an auxiliary corps, the WAAC eagle was also to be imprinted on plastic buttons. Only the insignia of grade required no planning; it was to be the same as the Army's, with a tab lettered *WAAC* sewed under the chevrons.[55]

Housing Plans

Plans for housing were less urgent, since field companies would not be ready for assignment for several months. On the basis of British experience and of her conferences with psychiatrists, Mrs. Hobby

---

[53] All from: (1) Memo, OQMG for G-1, 3 Jun 42. SPQRR 421. Copy in SPWA 421. (2) Memo, Dir WAAC for OQMG, 5 Jun 42. SPWA 400.34 (3-21-42)(1) sec 1 (1943). (3) Memo, Lt. W. W. Foulkes for Dir WAAC, 20 Jun 42. Same file. (4) Memo, OQMG for USW, 16 Sep 42. Folder, WAC Recruiting, ASF Sp Coll DRB AGO.

[54] Personal ltr, Brig Gen Clarence Weems to *Field Artillery Journal,* January 1943. 1942 WAAC files WA 600.9.

[55] Memo, Dir Mil Pers SOS for G-1, 23 May 42. G-1/15839-10, in SPWA 421 (5-16-42) sec 1.

OFFICERS

RIGHT LAPEL

LEFT LAPEL

ENLISTED

WAAC INSIGNIA

feared that women might not react to communal living exactly as did men. While men were accustomed from childhood to the tribal living of scout camps, gangs, teams, and clubs, no one could predict the results of the deprivation of privacy on women who were at all inclined to be nervous—particularly since most men's units remained only temporarily at any camp before overseas shipment, whereas a WAAC unit would settle down in its barracks for several years.

Mrs. Hobby therefore proposed that Waacs have dormitories of the type used to house civilian women workers, with two persons to a room. She was quickly overruled on this point on the grounds of economy and feasibility; housing plans had already been made that would use existing barracks, with minor modifications, or new construction like the old.

Allocation of Units

Only one major phase of planning remained: that of the composition of units and their allocation. It was decided that post headquarters companies would consist of 147 auxiliaries and 3 officers, and that Aircraft Warning Service companies would be somewhat smaller. Any unit under 50 members was deemed uneconomical. The problem was how to devise a fixed company with one Table of Organization that would suit all stations, since not all could use the same number of typists, drivers, or other workers.

Already the Army had realized that the fixed Table of Organization Company, while excellent for combat units, was not the proper means for allotting men to stations in the United States, where no two stations had exactly the same needs. Colonel Mudgett later noted, "The bulk allot-

ment system would have saved us many a headache on this problem." Unfortunately for the WAAC, the bulk allotment system was not yet adopted by the Army, and preplanners were forced to try to set up an inflexible T/O unit that would meet the needs of all stations using Waacs. One table for filter companies and one for operation companies was set up. For the more difficult post headquarters unit, planners hit upon the idea of having five types of platoons: clerical, communications, service, machine records, and miscellaneous. It was believed that almost any station, large or small, could meet its needs by requesting the proper assortment of platoons in its WAAC company.[56]

Concerning the disadvantages of this system in eventual use, Colonel Faith said later:

Post commanders didn't have the remotest idea as to what they wanted to use women for. . . . Their recommendations were studied, integrated into a type WAC company. . . . I am amazed that we did as well as we did. We set up a semi-rigid organization based upon ideas from the field, which in turn were based on poor guess-work, which the field accepted from us as being authoritative and scientific, which it was not. These

---

[56] (1) Ltr, Mudgett to author, 19 Aug 48. OCMH. (2) T/O 35–37, WAAC Filter Co, AWS, 4 Jul 42; T/O 35–67, WAAC Opns Co, AWS, Regional, 4 Jul 42; and T/O 35–12. WAAC Post Hq Co, 26 Aug 42. The Clerical Platoon had 10 stenographers, 30 typists, 15 postal clerks, etc.; the Communications Platoon included 18 switchboard operators; Service included 16 chauffers; Machine Records had various machine operators; Miscellaneous had housekeepers, motion picture projectionists, etc. For later modifications, see M/T 35–2018, 14 Dec 42, WAAC Post Hq Co; M/T 35–2026, 26 Nov 42, WAAC Bn; M/T 35–2137, WMC Photo Lab Co, Aerial; M/T 35–2022, 26 Nov 42, and change 1, 9 Jan 43, WAAC Hq Co; M/T 35–2122, 10 Dec 42, WAAC Post Hq Co, AAF. (3) D/F, G–3 to CG SOS, 11 Apr 42. WDGCT 291.9 (4–11–42). (4) D/F, G–1 to TAG, 6 May 42. WDGAP 320 WAAC.

tables provided for relatively few jobs for women—overhead, clerical, motor transport, service.[57]

Corps areas that had asked for Waacs were now requested to specify the assortment of platoons desired in a T/O unit, and planners optimistically proposed to recruit skills exactly to specification, since a woman with no skill or with some odd skill would not fit into any platoon and so could not be assigned. Only skilled women were sought; it was not proposed to waste time by taking women who needed technical training—except a brief course in army driving, army cooking, or army clerical work to help adapt civilian skills to the military.

Although supposedly soothed by the assurance that no WAAC post headquarters units would arrive for some time, or until further warning, many station commanders now became extremely nervous, and it was decided that Colonel Tasker or some other representative of the group must visit each designated station to prepare it for Waacs. In carrying out this indoctrination, Colonel Tasker later found many stations in a state of virtual siege, throwing up barbed-wire entanglements around WAAC areas and setting aside separate nights for Waacs to use post theaters and service clubs, so that men and women could be kept isolated from each other. Many post commanders were found to be much opposed to having Waacs on the post, and none of course had as yet any information as to the proper employment of such a unit.[58]

WAAC Regulations

The WAAC Regulations, which had been prepared in G–1 Division before Mrs. Hobby's arrival, were ready for publication as soon as the bill became law. As provided in the Rogers bill, the WAAC was set up as a separate command entity headed by the Director. The Corps was to be assigned to the Services of Supply, in which its headquarters was located, with its units only attached for duty to the Air Forces and other stations where they were employed.

The Director would at first command all of these units directly, requesting The Adjutant General to issue her orders for assignment, transfer, discharge, or other change in status. As soon as they could be trained, regional directors would be sent out to form an intermediate command echelon. It was decided that the regional directors would be nine in number and would be located in the headquarters of the nine corps areas in order that they might use the area facilities.

For a unit in the field, the station where it was located was responsible only for furnishing supplies, housing, and medical and dental care. As for the authority of Army section chiefs, the Regulations stated:

Officers and noncommissioned officers of the Army under whom individuals or groups or units of the WAAC are assigned for work tasks have supervisory authority as they would with civilian employees generally, but have no disciplinary authority. Derelictions of duty will be reported to the WAAC officer commanding.[59]

The WAAC company commander and higher WAAC officers were specified as responsible for discipline, promotion, discharge, and other command matters.

---

[57] Speech to Meeting of Classification Offs. Min in SPWA 201.6 (9–18–43).

[58] Interv cited n. 35.

[59] WAAC Regulations (Tentative), 1942.

For a time there was consideration of removing these powers from WAAC Headquarters and delegating them to the regional directors or even to the company commanders, since for Army men powers such as discharge were already held at the station level. However, for men the correct procedures were set forth in detail in Army Regulations, thus insuring uniform action and individual justice Army-wide.

Because of the Waacs' civilian status, these Army Regulations could not always be applied, particularly in matters of discipline—in which court-martial was not possible except overseas—and of discharge—since certain types of discharge could be given only by courts-martial. Neither was it possible to make the first WAAC Regulations as full as Army Regulations, which had been built up over a period of years.

The first WAAC Regulations were therefore marked Tentative and were scheduled for amplification as soon as experience permitted. To permit such amplification, it was directed that all discharge cases and other personnel actions be sent to WAAC Headquarters for decision, until a sufficient body of experience existed to permit publication of detailed regulations. Until this time, Mrs. Hobby noted that it would be unsafe to allow action at the station level, since one woman officer would be made both accuser and judge, contrary to the American system.[60]

In the exercise of its command prerogatives, WAAC Headquarters proposed to be extremely cautious. It was directed that women be sent only to stations where housing and other arrangements had been checked upon by Colonel Tasker or another staff member; that no unit of less than fifty women be assigned, in order that supply and inspection would not be unduly difficult; and that no enlisted woman be sent to any station unless a WAAC officer was located there.[61]

By April several agencies had already begun to question this system. G–3 Division, which had previously approved the regulations, now declared in conference that Army commanders should have complete control of WAAC units on their stations, transferring them in the United States or overseas without informing the Director, and discharging, disciplining, or promoting, presumably under Army Regulations, since no other detailed ones existed. Also, G–3 proposed that the command of a company be divided among the different Army section chiefs for whom the women worked, rather than vested in the WAAC company commander.[62]

The Signal Corps concurred, fearing that the Director might use her command powers arbitrarily to remove women from vital communications work; it was asserted that the British Signal Corps had experienced many difficulties in employing servicewomen who were *with* and not *in* the Army. Air Forces representatives supported these views and also objected to the Corps' location in the Services of Supply.[63] If command authority was given to them, the Signal Corps proposed to place women at once in mixed tactical groups overseas, without a WAAC company com-

---

[60] These principles were incorporated in all subsequent WAAC Regulations. First ref to them seems to be Memo, Tasker for Dir WAAC, 21 May 42. Tasker Staybacks.

[61] (1) Senate Com on Mil Affairs, 77th Cong, 2d sess, *Hearings on HR 6293,* 1 and 4 May 42. (2) *Congressional Record,* Vol. 88, No. 81, p. 3821.

[62] Memo, G–3 for G–1, atchd to Memo, G–1 for Mil Pers Div SOS, G–3, G–4, WAAC, TAG, CofFin, JAG, SG, 29 Apr 42. WDGAP 320 WAAC (4–29–42).

[63] Memo, SigC for Dir Pers SOS, 4 Jun 42. G–1/15839–10 (7–8–42) WAAC. (2) Memo cited n. 60.

mander, and the Air Forces announced plans to assign an additional 10,000 women in mobile units of its Terrestrial Service.

It soon became clear that the heart of the difficulty was the auxiliary system itself. As predicted, it was plainly about to prove most objectionable to Army commanders if they could not at once exercise as full authority over women as over men, or if they were obliged to apply different regulations to men and women. On the other hand, to apply Army Regulations to a civilian auxiliary corps was clearly illegal. As for her own position as Director, Army advisers informed Mrs. Hobby that it would be unsafe to accept that office if G–3's plan prevailed, since she would be in the militarily impossible situation of having responsibility without authority. Thus, the WAAC's auxiliary status made her legally responsible for the women's command and well-being, yet she would actually be ignorant of where they had been transferred or what financial, supply, disciplinary, or other measures were being taken by station commanders.[64]

By 3 April the WAAC preplanners considered the situation so confused that they appealed directly to the Chief of Staff, stating: "Confusion exists as to the interpretation of the Bill which says: 'The Director shall operate and administer the Corps in accordance with normal military channels of command and administration.'"[65] The Chief of Staff upheld the WAAC preplanners by signing their draft of the WAAC Regulations and approving it for publication if the bill giving the WAAC auxiliary status should pass.

This verdict had the effect of uniting the Services of Supply with Mrs. Hobby in supporting the amendment to place the WAAC in the Army. The WAAC's immediate superiors in the Services of Supply in fact opposed the separate command system so strongly that they neglected to prepare the necessary War Department circulars that would make the WAAC Regulations binding upon the Army in the event that the amendment failed.[66]

Passage of WAAC Bill

In their drive to complete plans before passage of the legislation, all echelons were seriously handicapped by uncertainty as to the type of bill that would pass Congress. After the WAAC bill had passed all committees and the House, thus virtually assuring it of passage in some form, the Navy had introduced a bill to establish the WAVES *in* the Navy and not as an auxiliary.

True to prediction, the brunt of argument had been borne by the WAAC, and the WAVES bill passed the House without difficulty. It seemed only reasonable that Congress would approve the amendment to place women in the Army. The unhappy planners were therefore forced to make two sets of plans: one for an auxiliary and one for an Army corps. Two versions of regulations were prepared and approved by nine interested agencies. Fourteen different agencies were asked to reconsider their plans in the light of the possible adoption of the amendment, and some, like the Judge Advocate General,

---

[64] *Ibid.* (1) M/R, sub: Conf Concerning WAAC Admin, 24 Jun 42. Col Tasker's file of rough drafts, under "WAAC Hqs Org," 1942. (2) Memo, AG WAAC for CofAdm Serv SOS, 27 Jun 42. WA 210.31 (6–4–42).

[65] Memo, Preplanners for CofS, 3 Apr 42, sub: Responsibility for Opn of WAAC. G–1/15839–10.

[66] Memo, Dir Mil Pers SOS for G–1, 20 Apr 42, sub: Amendment to HR 6293. G–1/15839–10 WAAC (7–8–42).

replied despairingly that none of their previous plans would apply.[67]

In spite of support from the Services of Supply and Mrs. Hobby, the War Department was unable to push the amendment for equal status. Comment on the floor of the House of Representatives was unrestrained and caustic. Members objected strenuously to placing women in the Army because this would give them the disability benefits and pensions that men received. Some also feared that women generals would rush about the country dictating orders to male personnel and telling the commanding officers of posts how to run their business.

This opposition was not tempered in the least by the fact that the House had just passed and sent to the Senate the bill placing the WAVES in the Navy with all of these possible benefits. As members pointed out, Congress was now in the incongruous position of giving Waves the full protection of military status while forbidding them, in their bill, to go overseas, whereas the WAAC bill allowed women to go overseas without the protection of military status. Opinion in the Senate committee was divided, but members finally became convinced that great delay would result from any attempt to change the Rogers bill.

There was one last flurry when it seemed that the Director of Selective Service would secure Presidential approval to a plan to request the voluntary registration of all women. This step would have made little change in the WAAC plan, but might have considerably increased the prospect of recruits if women had believed the registration a prelude to forced service in farms and factories. However, on 4 May 1942 the President decided against the plan.[68]

It was shortly apparent that Congress would pass the Rogers bill immediately without any of the proposed amendments. The War Department and the WAAC planners waited, braced for the outburst of publicity and the need for furious action, which they knew must accompany the bill's passage. Their plans were complete, as far as human guesswork could foretell the future. Men who had never seen an enlisted woman and women who had never been one had together planned for the future welfare and efficiency of women who were to be enlisted to work for the Army.

On 14 May 1942, the Rogers bill was approved by the Senate, 38 to 27, and when signed the next day by the President became Public Law 554, An Act to Establish a Women's Army Auxiliary Corps for Service with the Army of the United States.

---

[67] (1) The nine: G-3, G-4, TAG, JAG, SGO, Fin, Mil Pers Div SOS, G-1, SW. See D/F, G-1 to [above], 20 Apr 42. Copy in Mudgett Staybacks. (2) The fourteen: G-4, Budget and Leg Plng Br, Fin, JAG, Req Div SOS, SGO, CofAdm Serv SOS, Tng Div SOS, TAG Enl Br, TAG, G-3, G-1, OQMG. See Memo for each, 24 Apr 42. G-1/15839-10. (3) Memo, JAG for Dir Pers SOS, 5 May 42. SPJGA 354.01.

[68] (1) D/F, G-1, 27 Apr 42, sub: Voluntary Registration of Women. G-1/15839-27; (2) Ltr, SW to Dir SS, 27 Apr 42, and reply, SS to SW, 8 May 42. G-1/15839-1 (5-11-42).

CHAPTER III

The WAAC's First Summer

On the rainy morning of 16 May 1942, Mrs. Oveta Culp Hobby took the oath of office as Director, WAAC. This event represented a neatly executed *coup d'etat* on the part of the Army, which, on the night of 14 May, had sent Col. Robert N. Young of the General Staff hurrying to the home of the Secretary of War with the letter of appointment in his hand. The Secretary demurred at the haste but was persuaded that this was the only way to avoid irresistible political pressure the next morning to appoint other candidates who would be disastrously unfamiliar with the Army's plans. Competition for the position was by now so open that newspaper columnists were speculating on various candidates' qualifications, or lack of them.[1]

Thus on 15 May there was simultaneous announcement of the President's signature and of the appointment of the Director. The appointment ceremony the next morning was witnessed by the Secretary of War, the Chief of Staff, Congresswoman Rogers, Governor Hobby, and a few others. Mrs. Hobby accepted, saying, "You have said that the Army needs the Corps. That is enough for me." The occasion was not particularly inspiring for participants: klieg lights blazed; the speeches had to be given over and over for cameramen; Mrs. Hobby was asked to raise her hand and repeat the oath several times. Furthermore, her wide-brimmed hat proved unreasonably difficult to photograph. Thus the first Waac was sworn in.[2]

From this moment forward, Director Hobby was faithfully credited by some millions of Americans with having personally initiated the Corps and dictated its every move. Although she had neither originated the idea, written the legislation, nor determined the Regulations, her office repeatedly had to answer inquirers such as an Army private, who wrote: "From whom or whence did she derive the idea of organizing such a unit?"[3]

The Press

There followed immediately a well-attended press conference, the first of many to come. The War Department realized the importance of the initial reac-

[1] Interv with Brig Gen Robert N. Young, CG MDW, 14 Dec 45. The syndicated column, "The National Whirligig," May 20, 1942. WDBPR Newspaper Clippings, WAC, DRB AGO.

[2] Letter of appointment was dated 15 May 1942. Memo, WAAC Hq for TAG, 18 May 42. WA 314.7 (6–2–41) sec 1, DRB AGO. Director Hobby's assigned serial number was OA–1. For others, the letter A was prefixed for auxiliaries, and L for officers. It was never specified what the L represented—presumably "Lady." The numbers from 100,000 to 199,999 were assigned to the First Service Command, 200,000 to 299,999 to the Second, and so on. Memos, TAG for Dir WAAC, 16 and 20 May 42. SPWA 341.

[3] Ltr, Pvt Frank Wetrich to OWI, 22 Feb 44, forwarded to Dir WAC. SPWA 095.

MRS. OVETA CULP HOBBY *is sworn in as the first Waac by Maj. Gen. Myron C. Cramer. General Marshall, second from left, and Secretary of War Henry L. Stimson were among witnesses of the ceremony.*

tion, and General Hilldring said, "This whole thing stands or falls on the next 60 days." [4]

The basic idea of the Corps which the Director and the Chief of Staff wished to impress upon the public was that of a sober, hard-working organization, composed of dignified and sensible women. Their work must be shown as real, just as the war was real and the nation's danger was real. Although there might be problems of feminine adjustment, the War Department did not intend to encourage frivolity.

This excellent but somewhat staid approach was not expected by even the most sanguine to offer any great appeal to the press. The Director's staff noted that "news" about women had long been patterned on three stereotypes of the American woman: (1) she was a giddy featherbrain frequently engaged in powder-puff wars and with no interest beyond clothes, cosmetics, and dates; (2) she was a henpecking old battle-ax who loved to boss

---

[4] Details, unless otherwise indicated, are from intervs with Mrs. Herrick, 9 Jan 46, Mrs. Eric Knight, 27 Feb 46, and Gen Hilldring, 17 Jan 46.

the male species; or (3) she was a sainted wife and mother until she left her kitchen, whereupon she became a potentially scarlet woman. Director Hobby had already taken issue with these views, saying, "Waacs will be neither Amazons rushing to battle, nor butterflies fluttering about." [5] One idea which she was particularly anxious to avoid was the familiar "morale purposes" accusation—that Waacs were not wanted to fill Army jobs so much as to provide companionship for soldiers. General Marshall had been deliberately careful, in urging Congress to pass the bill, to use solely the arguments concerning the usefulness of Waacs as workers, and never those that treated them chiefly as women. [6]

Here at this first conference was to begin a never-finished battle as to which idea of woman in the Army would prevail— whether the public would get stories mainly of her real work and useful jobs, or of her underwear, cosmetics, dates with soldiers, her rank-pulling, sex life, and misconduct. Certain sections of the press were expected to co-operate, in the interest of the war effort, by playing down sensational angles that might hinder recruiting. Since not all could be expected to do so, the Director and her public relations consultant, Mrs. Herrick, sat up the night before the conference listing all possible embarrassing questions that reporters might ask, and rehearsing and polishing the Director's replies so as to minimize frivolous matters and emphasize the serious purpose of the Corps. A comparison of their list with the questions asked the next day showed that they did not miss even one, and in fact thought of a few that the reporters overlooked.

At the press conference, the Director was supported by the Chief of Staff himself, General Marshall, and the head of the Bureau of Public Relations, Maj. Gen. Alexander D. Surles. A routine handout was devoted to recruiting and training plans, enlistment requirements, and other statistics. A description of the uniform, especially the underwear, for which reporters were eager, was tactfully withheld a few days because its procurement was not yet finally approved. Frustrated here, the reporters opened up the expected barrage of questions directed at Mrs. Hobby: [7]

Q. How about girdles?
A. If you mean, will they be issued, I can't tell you yet. If they are required, they will be supplied.

Q. Will Waacs be allowed to use make-up?
A. Yes, if it is inconspicuous.

Q. What do you consider that to be?
A. I hope their own good taste will decide.

Q. Nail polish?
A. If inconspicuous, yes.

Q. Will the women salute?
A. Yes, they will salute.

Q. Will they march and carry arms?
A. They will learn to march well enough to parade, but they will carry no guns.

Q. Will they be put in guardhouses?
A. No, no guardhouses.

Q. This is a burning question. Will officer Waacs permitted to have dates with privates?
A. [Here Mrs. Hobby turned to one of the generals [8] for a description of Army tradition. He explained that Army policy was that officers when not with troops, and enlisted men when off duty, might associate, but that he

---

[5] MS history of First WAAC Training Center. Folder, Supplementary Hist Material Sent to Washington Nov 1945. WD Library. (Hereafter cited as Hist of 1st WAAC Tng Cen.)

[6] Interv with Gen Hilldring, 17 Jan 46

[7] Compiled from Associated Press and United Press releases as well as syndicated columns for May 16, 1942. WDBPR Newspaper Clippings, WAC, DRB AGO.

[8] Associated Press said it was General Marshall; United Press said General Surles.

hadn't been to the field lately and didn't know how it worked for nurses.]

Some questions became even more pointed. "There was one male reporter in particular," reported a spectator, "who kept prodding the woman reporter next to him to ask more and more about illegitimate babies." To this query, Mrs. Hobby replied briefly that pregnant women, married or unmarried, would be discharged.

"The Director handled herself excellently," reported another observer. "She was very direct, forthright, composed, and as candid as could be. She made a good impression." The next day's newspaper stories confirmed this, although a few women columnists [9] pointed out that Mrs. Hobby's previous "unavailability" had not made her popular with newspaperwomen who wanted intimate details, and the Negro press attacked the appointment of a woman from Texas.[10] In general, the hundreds of clippings collected by the Bureau of Public Relations showed widespread praise for the Corps and the Director. A few spiced up the story with headlines such as "Petticoat Army" or "Doughgirl Generalissimo,"[11] and some punsters were obviously unable to resist such opportunities as "Wackies," "Powder-magazines," "Fort Lipstick," and (concerning girdles), "It wouldn't do to let the fighting lassies get out of shape."[12] Male columnists were the worst offenders, in spite of Damon Runyon's remark, "A lady in the uniform of her country will scarcely be an object of jesting on the part of a gentleman not in the same garb."[13] Some of the attacks contained savage comparisons to "the naked Amazons . . . and the queer damozels of the Isle of Lesbos."[14] Others, as expected, had a field day with the idea that woman's place is in the maternity ward. Said

one: "Women's prime function with relation to war is to produce children so that the supply of men for fighting purposes can be kept up to par." Another: "Give the rejected 4-F men a chance to be in the Army and give the girls a chance to be mothers." Others became emotional over their assumption that all Waac recruits would be married women who had deserted infants.[15]

Thus began the fight to hold the line on public relations, which had wrecked recruiting for British women's services. Prematurely hopeful that the worst was over, the Director and her staff began their first day as a recognized and operating headquarters.

Establishment of WAAC Headquarters

"The next month was chaos," said a staff member later. "Every newspaper and magazine writer came down to see us. Important people of all sorts were also now willing to advise us."[16] The open bays of the office at Temporary M swarmed with new clerks, insistent visitors, and hurrying staff members; telephones buzzed and boxes of supplies were stacked in corners.

On the day after the Director's appoint-

[9] Columns mentioned n. 7.
[10] *Pittsburgh Courier,* May 23, 1942, and others. WDBPR Newspaper Clippings, WAC, DRB AGO.
[11] *Fargo* (N. D.) *Morning Forum,* May 17, 1942, and Niles (Mich.) *Star,* May 20, 1942, respectively.
[12] First three in Little Rock *Arkansas Democrat,* May 23, 1942. The last in the column "The Totem Pole," *Seattle Star,* May 20, 1942.
[13] The column, "The Brighter Side," May 22, 1942. WDBPR Newspaper Clippings, WAC, DRB AGO.
[14] The column, "Miami Story," Miami (Fla.) *News,* May 20, 1942.
[15] Editorials in New York *Daily News* and *Augusta* (Ga.) *Herald,* and a column in Oklahoma City *Daily Oklahoman,* May 1942, respectively. WDBPR Newspaper Clippings, WAC, DRB AGO.
[16] Interv with Mrs. Herrick, 9 Jan 46.

ment, the little headquarters pulled itself together and began to issue numbered memoranda. Now that there legally was a WAAC, the long-delayed funds could at last be allotted for a training center; the tentative Regulations could be published; the items of uniform could be approved for procurement and details released to the underwear-conscious press. More important, the still-nebulous group of preplanners could now be solidified into a real WAAC Headquarters, complete with charts and ready for rapid expansion. Thirty-seven civilians were also allotted, including another woman consultant, Mrs. Gruber, wife of Brig. Gen. William R. Gruber, to advise on military protocol and manage the Director's schedule. The office now totaled some fifty people.[17]

By any military standards this was hardly an impressive headquarters, scarcely the equal of that of a respectable Army regiment; and in spite of the exaggerated power that was attributed to it by the press and general public, its members by this time entertained few delusions of grandeur. As an insignificant civilian group, which included no general officer, they expected and got a low priority of attention as compared with the more vital phases of the combat effort, particularly in such matters as office space, cafeteria hours, entertainment allowances, and transportation.[18]

The office had at least a military-looking chief when, in June, there arrived the first WAAC uniform, especially made for Director Hobby. She promptly put it on, reported formally to the Chief of Staff, and came back wearing a colonel's silver eagles, which he had pinned on and directed her to wear. The relative rank of Director was thus established at that of colonel, although Congress had author-

ized pay equal only to that of a major. Both relative rank and pay were thus established as the same as that recently given to the Superintendent, Army Nurse Corps. The relative rank of full colonel was also necessitated by the grades of the Army officers on her staff, since Director Hobby would be superior in the WAAC chain of command to the commandant of the training center, Colonel Faith, as well as to her own staff, which now included Col. William Pearson as adjutant general and Col. Bickford Sawyer as finance officer.

No later Waacs ever suffered from uniform shortages as did Director Hobby at this time; there was in existence only one WAAC shirt, and in her travels her luggage contained little but an electric fan and an iron, which enabled her to wash, dry, and iron the shirt nightly.

Location in the Services of Supply

Meanwhile, the Services of Supply was considering a more important matter: the proper place in the headquarters chart to insert the square labeled WAAC. Competition for the honor of supervising the WAAC was not exactly brisk; it might be said that each agency outdid the other in striving to bestow this gift on its neighbor.[19]

---

[17] (1) Various Hq Memos in WA 300 (5–20–42) Office Memos, sec 1. (2) Memo, G–1 for CofS, 13 May 42. WDGAP 352.01 WAAC. (3) Memo, TAG for Dir WAAC, 26 May 42. AG 291.9 (5–15–42). (4) Memo, OQMG for G–1, 16 May 42, and Inds. SPQRE 420 WAAC. Copy in SPWA 421 (5–16–42) sec 1. (5) WD SO 129, 17 May 42; Memo, WAAC Ln Off for Pers Div SOS, 15 May 42. Tasker Staybacks.

[18] (1) Memo, W. Pearson for TAG, 19 Mar 42, and atchd answer. WA 029.21 (3–19–42). (2) Memo, Dir WAAC for SOS, 16 May 42, and atchd reply from TAG. WA 451 (5–16–42).

[19] Intervs with Lt Col Woods, 14 Dec 45, and Lt Col Betty Bandel, 15 Dec 45. (Both former Deputy Directors.)

At one time it seemed that Civilian Personnel Division would be forced to assume control, although this was obviously inappropriate, since WAAC administration would be conducted along military lines. Military Personnel Division, from whence the preplanners had operated, was also inappropriate, as it was strictly a policy-making agency and did not operate, while WAAC Headquarters would operate a training center and various units. The loser in this unique contest was eventually the Chief of Administrative Services, at that time Maj. Gen. John P. Smith. General Smith was shortly to be succeeded by Maj. Gen. George Grunert, who, as a lieutenant colonel, had in 1927 been one of the War Department staff officers to recommend postponement of plans for a women's service corps. The Administrative Services, a large subdivision of the Services of Supply, included many comparable operating agencies, such as the Army Specialist Corps, the Army Exchange Service, and the National Guard Bureau. WAAC Headquarters would now be removed from the Chief of Staff by three echelons: first, the Chief of Administrative Services; over him the Commanding General, Services of Supply; and over both on personnel matters the Assistant Chief of Staff, G–1. The new position was not advantageous in many ways, but it appeared to the Director's advisers that there was at the moment no alternative.[20]

The WAAC's new status as one of the Administrative Services was set forth to the field by the first important War Department Circular governing the WAAC— Circular 169 of 1 June 1942—which, after two weeks of the Corps' existence, at last made the WAAC legitimate. The circular was so brief that a second circular was clearly needed at once, although it did in-form the Army that (1) the Director would command the Corps and (2) other Services of Supply offices would set WAAC policy. It gave no details either of command channels or of interoffice co-ordination; neither did it refer to the tentative WAAC Regulations. All WAAC plans and recommended policies were required to be sent to the Chief of Administrative Services "for reference to the appropriate staff division of the Services of Supply." The Chief of Administrative Services wrote: "While the WAAC is not a part of the Army, yet the entire administration of the Corps, including its organization and development, must be supervised and assisted by the Services of Supply." [21]

Director's Schedule

As the new Corps began the selection of officer candidates and the establishment of its training center, the work load upon the headquarters, never light, suddenly became so great as seriously to threaten its efficiency.[22] A fourteen-hour day and a seven-day week became standard in the Director's office, a schedule of course not uncommon throughout the War Department at this date. Even this was often exceeded; staff members reported that for days at a time Mrs. Hobby and her assistants worked every night until three, five, and sometimes seven in the morning, averaging only two or three hours of sleep each night, or merely going home for a shower and coffee before returning to work. Staff members worked under condi-

---

[20] Memo, Dir Mil Pers SOS for CofAdm Serv, 21 May 42. SPGAP/1619-49, in AG 291.9 WAAC (5-15-42).

[21] Ibid.

[22] This section from interviews, already cited, with staff members; or from Hq Memos cited n. 17(1).

tions of what they called "awful confusion" and pointed out that the developments of the following months could be seen in perspective only if it was understood that they occurred, not separately and in order, but simultaneously and in the midst of wildly growing national publicity that was in itself a full-time problem.

Director Hobby attempted to cope with the confusion by rigorously budgeting her time. To Mrs. Gruber was given the task of scheduling all persons wishing to see the Director, in the belief that "more speed can be made if she finishes one subject without interruption." Staff members prepared summaries of staff papers and kept a chart for the Director's daily briefing; Colonel Pearson also directed that the Director be left free for "formulation of basic policies." Unfortunately, at this stage everything was new and policy was inseparable from detail; the situation resolved itself into a struggle to meet the daily crises without crushing the Director with decisions. The War Department Bureau of Public Relations required the Director to hold a full two-hour press conference twice weekly. Also, interviews with the public were scheduled four times a week, thus leaving only a few days entirely free for military problems. Even this amount of time was highly unsatisfactory to members of the press and Congress and other citizens who now came to call, and some criticism resulted. One Congressman complained, "I can get to the President in five minutes, but I can't get to Mrs. Hobby at all."

The Director was aware of the problem and stated in an office memorandum:

The successful launching of the WAAC is a public relations problem to probably a greater extent than any other War Depart-ment activity. We must establish a reputation for not giving the "brush-off" or "run-around" to those calling.

However, she felt little sympathy toward those who wanted merely a sight of her or some personal favor. She said later:

Many of them were just curiosity-seekers; they could have got accurate information from any Army officer in our headquarters, but they wanted to sit and chat with that new curiosity, a woman in Army uniform.

More important than seeing such people, she felt, were her military responsibilities to the Army and to the women about to join the WAAC.

Operating Duties

These military duties, and not the public pressure, constituted the real problem of the heavy work load. The Director realized from the beginning that her duties were exactly the reverse of what they should have been; she said later: "We had foreseen this problem in Canada, and it was one of the reasons why we wanted Army status. Now, we were an Auxiliary and it was none of Army offices' legal business."

For example, the office set out to prepare Tables of Basic Allowances for the WAAC Training Center and for units, and was at once struggling with terms such as "T-Square, Maple, Plastic lined, one per publications section"; "Chart, Anatomical, Blood System, one per training center"; "Can, corrugated, with cover, 32 gal, one per 20 mbrs." Realizing that the WAAC's staff of eleven officers did not possess the necessary specialist training to prepare accurate tables of chemical, signal, medical, and other equipment and that the tables could be done quickly by the Army specialists who prepared tables for men, Colonel Pearson attempted to send the work to the Chief of Administrative Services for distribution to other Services of Supply offices. It was promptly returned to him with the statement that the only thing wanted for distribution to the SOS offices was the final plan or policy for approval.[23] Director Hobby noted further:

We had to prepare our own budget for presentation to Congress—a complicated statistical matter—because the people who prepared Army budgets said it wasn't their responsibility. Then, three of us worked all one night until 9 the next morning writing the recruiting circulars which I had to present for approval to The Adjutant General; TAG wouldn't write them. We had to check all the blueprints for housing at every station—endless, bewildering blueprints.[24]

In every field of military responsibility, it was the same story. The technical work of the WAAC was done by an office that knew little of the method, and the policy approval was given to agencies that knew nothing of WAAC over-all needs. Staff members realized that, had Army status made it possible, just the opposite organization would have been most efficient. Under the circumstances, most of the summer's tasks were accomplished, if at all, only by a process of mutual irritation.

Colonel Pearson, the office's oldest and most experienced adviser, was likewise unable to obtain from the Services of Supply any clear-cut decision that would enable him to distinguish between policy matters which he must refer to other offices and routine decisions which he could make and put into effect without delay. Colonel Pearson finally forced the issue by sending direct to The Adjutant General for publication a minor decision which he considered routine—that of raising the age limit for the first officer candi-

date class from 45 to the legal limit of 50. Refusing to publish it, The Adjutant General sent it to Control Branch, SOS, for clearance; Control Branch sent it for comment to Military Personnel Division, which commented and sent it back to Control Branch, which a week later returned it to the WAAC, with directions to draft the circular instead of asking The Adjutant General to do it, and a brief verbal spanking: "In the future, please transmit all matters of this nature to the Chief of Administrative Services."

It was thus established that even simple WAAC decisions would probably be considered policy matters and thus require approval by several SOS branches before they could be put into operation. While such a procedure proved useful in avoiding errors, it became impossible for WAAC Headquarters to act with anything like speed and decisiveness in the emergencies bearing down upon it.[25]

Drastic expedients were suggested to the Director by her Army advisers, some involving the disbandment of WAAC Headquarters. The most plausible of these—although probably not legal—was to dismember the office and give the various pieces to the SOS divisions that handled the same matters for men, while the Director and a small office for control and inspection would soar upward for several SOS echelons and attach themselves to the office of the Commanding General, Services of Supply, Lt. Gen. Brehon B. Somervell. From this vantage point the Director could then heckle other offices when dif-

---

[23] Memo, Chief, Sup Div WAAC for CofAdm Serv, 1 Sep 42. SPWA 400.34 (3–21–43)(1) sec 1.

[24] Interv with Mrs. Hobby, 23 Aug 48.

[25] Correspondence cited is a series of papers under dates of 25 and 27 May, 11, 12, 13, 15, and 16 Jun 1942. AG 291.9 (6–2–41). Staff comments are from interv with Mrs. Onthank, 4 Sep 46.

ficulties occurred. "As it is now," the Army advisers wrote mournfully, "we have to ask help from all of these branches, and maybe get it and maybe don't, and get bounced all around unless we want to go to the top to help us out, and that is a bad system." [26] This plan, although eminently workable, was not be adopted until the WAAC became part of the Army.

In spite of the unresolved confusion and the demands upon them, staff members remained enthusiastic and optimistic; Director Hobby publicly thanked them for their loyalty and for putting so much into the struggle. [27]

Selection of the First Officer Candidates

From the public viewpoint, selection of the WAAC officer candidates was the only important matter that the WAAC now had on its hands. From the moment of passage of the bill, WAAC Headquarters had been besieged, to the detriment of its other duties, by long-distance telephone calls, telegrams, visitors, and letters of application, all asking commissions. Congressmen, Army heads, and public officials were swamped by demands from friends and constituents. Officers of all the armed forces sought to get commissions for their friends and relatives, while powerful pressure groups sought to name assistant directors. "Every important person had a candidate," said a woman staff member, "and they all wanted guarantees of commissions and important positions." [28]

Under its legislation, the WAAC could have commissioned many of its officers direct from civil life with appropriate rank, as the Army did and as the WAVES and other women's services were later to do. Mrs. Hobby's previous decision to grant no direct commissions was severely tested.

Mrs. Rogers, the Corps' sponsor, urged her to commission several lieutenant colonels at once, as she feared that otherwise the WAAC leaders would have no prestige in their dealings with ranking Army officers. [29] However, it appeared that if even two or three women were commissioned directly, it would be impossible to refuse hundreds of others with prominent sponsors, and Director Hobby believed that Mrs. Rogers' objection concerning rank could be overcome by rapid promotion as soon as the women had demonstrated their ability.

It was General Hilldring's belief that the Director was strengthened in her original decision by the opinions of General Marshall.

The Chief of Staff was a great democrat [said General Hilldring]. I told Mrs. Hobby how, at his direction, I had made a fight to get more officers from the ranks of enlisted men. I told her that he might not object to appointing a few civilian women for the top jobs, but the rest of the officers must come from the ranks. They must be the best women in the ranks even if this was not necessarily the best in the nation. [30]

Also, staff members in their discussions of this point gave some weight to what they called "the man-woman element," a factor which did not ordinarily operate in the selection of male officers for commissions, but which now made it difficult to judge with entire accuracy the motives behind demands for the commissioning of female friends and secretaries. [31]

The experiences of other nations indi-

---

[26] (1) Min, Stf Mtg, 24 Aug 42. (2) Memo, PRO for Dir WAAC, 9 Sep 42. SPWA 300.4.
[27] Unnumbered Memo, 1 Jun 42. WA 300 (5–20–42).
[28] List of some applicants in SPWA 029 (1942).
[29] Interv with Mrs. Rogers, 14 Dec 45.
[30] Interv with Gen Hilldring, 17 Jan 46.
[31] All interviews confirm this.

cated that, by its initial choice of officers, the entire future course of a women's corps might be determined. In England initial limitation of commissioned rank to socially or politically prominent women had left a corps without adequate troop officers. In some Continental countries commissions had been awarded chiefly to enable certain personnel to travel with ranking officers. It was recognized that, without firm leadership at this moment, the first American auxiliary might set out on a similar course. Finally, a General Staff decision was obtained that confirmed the Director's original policy of limiting the future WAAC leadership to those women who would enlist without guarantees, and making it possible to refuse all requests from high authorities without incurring charges of discrimination.[32] All applicants who stormed WAAC Headquarters were therefore told to apply at their local Army recruiting stations. Director Hobby's own civilian advisers, Mrs. Woods and Mrs. Fling, had to follow this procedure when they desired to enlist.

By 27 May, Army recruiting stations all over the United States were supplied with application blanks, and newspapers carried the story that the doors were now open for officer candidate applications.[33] The response was a rush that swamped recruiting stations and startled recruiters. The Adjutant General had optimistically sent each corps area 10,000 application blanks, a total of 90,000, although only 360 candidates were to be selected. Three days later, urgent calls had already come from the Second, Third, Fourth, and Sixth Corps Areas for 10,000 more each, and from the Fifth and Ninth for 5,000. Of the 140,000 blanks given out, it was assumed that many would not be returned, as the 4 June deadline gave little leeway on delayed applications. Some recruiting officers attempted to weed out the obviously unqualified and to give the scarce blanks only to eligibles.

In New York City, 1,400 women stormed the Whitehall Street office on the first day and stood in line from 8:30 to 5:00 o'clock. In five days over 5,200 had received application blanks in New York City alone, although only 30 women could be picked from the whole of New York State, New Jersey, and Delaware. In Washington 1,700 applied for the eight positions open to the District of Columbia. Numbers as reported by newspapers varied in different cities: Sheboygan—20; Lowell—65; Richmond—65; Baltimore—500; Portland—380; Sacramento—135; Minneapolis—600 given out, but only 50 returned; Butte—"a few cautious inquiries." Nothing could be told as yet of the type of woman who had applied. Newspapers featured an Indian woman in full tribal regalia, a sixteen-year-old who wanted to get away from home, a wild-eyed mother brandishing a pistol and demanding to get to the front. It was hoped that these were not typical applicants.[34]

Screening of Applicants

It had been decided that Army induction facilities could be used for women, with of course the necessary segregation

---

[32] Document not positively identified; possibly Memo, G–1 for CofS, 22 Mar 42, sub: WAAC. G–1/15839, in CofS 291.9.

[33] WDBPR Press Release, 26 May 42. All WDBPR Press Releases are in WDBPR file, DRB AGO.

[34] *New London Day* (Conn.), *New York World-Telegram, Washington Post, Sheboygan Press* (Wisc.), *Lowell Sun,* (Mass.), *Richmond Times-Dispatch,* Baltimore *Evening Sun, Portland Morning Oregonian, Sacramento Daily Union, Minneapolis Tribune,* all of June 2, 1942; Butte *Montana Standard,* May 24, 1942.

for physical examination.[35] This decision provided an extra and unscheduled screening device, for only women of some valor dared approach the Army offices. Members of the first class commented: "The recruiting station was the dirtiest place I ever saw." "It was in the post office basement next to the men's toilets." "I was whistled at by the selectees." "Everyone in the room turned to look as the Captain bawled out 'Are you one of them Wackies?' "[36] WAC recruiters were later to find the location and nature of Army recruiting facilities a major handicap in recruiting women.

Some 30,000 women braved this obstacle and filed applications. Their papers were reviewed by the stations, and those who were not obviously disqualified for age, citizenship, or other causes were summoned for an aptitude test. This test had been prepared by the Personnel Procedures Section of The Adjutant General's Office to eliminate 55 percent of all applicants.[37] It was attempted to make standard questions more appropriate for females, but some were not easily converted, and women were confronted by such problems as, "You are a first baseman, and after putting the batter out by catching the ball (not a fly) with your foot on the bag, you . . ."[38]

Those who passed the aptitude test were further screened by a preliminary local interviewing board of two women and an Army officer selected by the corps area. To avoid appointment of unqualified women to these boards, the preplanners had sent out instructions that members were to be local personnel directors, business executives, YWCA supervisors, and women of like standing. These local boards weeded out those applicants who were visibly unsuited by reason of char-

acter, bearing, or instability. Members were asked to consider the question: "Would I want my daughter to come under the influence of this woman?"[39]

The numbers passing both the test and the first board still hopelessly overcrowded Army medical facilities for the examination of women. It was therefore directed that only the top five hundred applicants in each corps area be given physical examinations. The examination was not entirely consistent throughout the corps area and it was evident that the Army still had far to go in working out a satisfactory physical examination for women, but it did eliminate those with the more obvious physical disqualifications.

There then arrived at each corps area headquarters an especially selected woman to be the Director's representative on the final screening board. Among the women selected were Dean Dorothy C. Stratton of Purdue, later head of the SPARS, and Dean Sarah Blanding of Cornell, later President of Vassar.[40] In spite of the pres-

---

[35] (1) M/R 1-7, Oct 40, sub: Reception of SS EM. (2) Folder, Selection Processing, Hobby files.

[36] Related to author by members of first officers' candidate class.

[37] (1) WDAGO Mental Alertness-1, X-Z, Mar 42, called MAT-1. (2) Speech, Col Tasker to Corps Area G-1 Cong, 12 Jun 42. WAAC Hist File, 1942 WAAC Files. (3) D/F, SOS to TAG, 11 Mar 42, sub: WAAC. G-1/15839-10.

[38] It proved very difficult to discover the correlation between the WAAC Mental Alertness Test (MAT) and the Army General Classification Test (AGCT). For details of testing, see Folder, Tests, in WAAC Planning files (unnumbered files now with Staff Rec Sec, DRB AGO), containing: (1) Memo, Dir WAC for TAG, 10 Aug 43, SPWA 201.6; (2) M/R, undated, 2d Lt Ruth W. Brainerd, sub: AGCT and MAT; (3) Memo, Opns and Tng Div AGO for Dir WAC, 16 Dec 43, AG 220.01 (12-16-43)OC-L.

[39] Memo, Hq SOS for TAG, 17 Mar 42, sub: WAAC. G-1/15839-10.

[40] All members listed in WDBPR Press Release, 30 Jun 42.

SCREENING OF APPLICANT *for first officer candidate class by local interviewing board at Fort McPherson, Georgia, 20 June 1942.*

sure of time, the final personal interviews were more extensive, and delved thoroughly into each candidate's record in school, college, and business to see if signs of leadership were evident.[41] The Director's representatives then returned immediately to Washington bearing the candidates' complete papers, pictures, and interview records. Their private comments varied with the corps areas. One said, "Decidedly disappointed in both number and general type of applicants"; another, "A complete cross-section from young things to professional women"; and a third, "I was impressed with the common denominator shared by the extremes in types—wanting to do organized effective war work."[42]

The final selection process was of unequaled intensity. An evaluating board of eleven prominent psychiatrists[43] searched the work histories for evidences of mental instability, choosing women who showed steady progress and acceptance of responsibility rather than frequent unexplained changes of jobs. Application forms also revealed data on parents and family life,

[41] Memo, Dir WAAC for Pers Div SOS, 2 Jun 42. G–1/15839–10 (7–8–42).

[42] Off-the-record comments, Folder, Selection Processing, Hobby files.

[43] Named in WDBPR Press Release, 30 Jun 42.

whether applicants had ever lived in clubs or dormitories, their travel, sports interests, and health. Answers to the essay question on "Why I Desire Service" were believed to be particularly revealing. There followed what Director Hobby called "four days of careful, almost prayerful, work of making the final selections."[44] The Director personally read each of the final papers. The 30,000 applicants had been reduced to the 4,500 who appeared before the final boards, and in the midst of selection procedure, word came from the Chief of Staff to pick not 360, but 1,300, the papers of the extra candidates to be kept for call to later classes as needed.[45]

The work was finally completed late on the night of 30 June. Within a week, corps areas had notified the 360 top-rated applicants, who thus had less than two weeks to close out their jobs, take the oath, and get to Fort Des Moines for the opening on 20 July.

The selected candidates had one characteristic in common: 99 percent had been successfully employed in civil life. Although there was no such educational requirement, 90 percent had college training and some had several degrees. Most fell in the age group of 25 to 39, although 16 percent were under 25 and 10 percent were 40 and over. About 20 percent were married, most of them to men in service, and there were some mothers, especially mothers of servicemen, though none with small children.[46] The candidates included many women who had held responsible jobs: a dean of women, a school owner and director, a personnel director, a Red Cross official, a former sales manager, and several editors, and there were many more who had been reporters, office executives, lawyers, social workers, Army employees,

and teachers. In compliance with promises made to Congress, it had been necessary to choose a certain number from each corps area and from each state, regardless of density of population, with the result that many highly qualified women in certain crowded areas had to be turned down, while in certain sparsely settled states it was necessary to take almost every woman who applied.[47]

Special Groups of Candidates

Two other problems complicated the task of the selecting authorities: the selection of Negro officer candidates and the selection of Aircraft Warning Service candidates. The Negro problem was particularly delicate, for the Negro press had immediately attacked the choice of a Director, and the National Negro Council had written President Roosevelt protesting the appointment of a Southern woman.[48]

The opposition was unexpected, since the War Department had early informed Congress that it would train Negro WAAC officers and auxiliaries up to 10 percent of the Corps and Mrs. Hobby had declared her support of the plan; while the Navy Department's WAVES, although not headed by a Southerner, did not accept any Negroes at all for almost three years.

The real cause of the objections came out in later news stories, which revealed that Negro leaders had hoped to use the

[44] Speech at Howard University, 6 Jul 42. WDBPR Press Release, 6 Jul 42.
[45] Memo, Preplanners for G–1, 7 May 42. Tasker Staybacks.
[46] Some of the Aircraft Warning Service candidates later added to this group had young children, as it was supposed that they would live at home.
[47] (1) Figures given to Senate Com on Mil Affairs. (2) List in WDBPR Press Memo, 3 Sep 42.
[48] *Atlanta Daily World*, May 17, 1942.

new Corps to break the "traditional and undemocratic policy of the Army and Navy" of placing Negro personnel in separate units.[49] Their demand that the WAAC place Negro and white women in the same unit was rejected because the WAAC had been directed to follow the Army policy. Now the National Negro Council recommended to the Secretary of War that Dr. Mary McLeod Bethune and one other Negro leader be commissioned assistant directors, which was of course impossible under the no-direct-appointment policy. To make relations more precarious, it soon became apparent that not enough qualified Negro women had presented themselves as applicants for officer candidate school, and it was feared that WAAC failure to fill the quota of 10 percent would be interpreted by the Negro press as discrimination. Accordingly, Army officers made hurried trips to Negro colleges to attempt to recruit qualified women. Mrs. Bethune assisted in the selection of these candidates, not being within the age limit to attend the school herself.[50]

For the Aircraft Warning Service the Army Air Forces asked that it be allowed to put women in uniform without sending them to school, but after long consideration it was decided that AWS officers must graduate from the regular officer candidate school before donning the WAAC uniform. On the matter of selection the Director felt unable to offer opposition, since the women to be selected were already running the operations and filter boards. The Air Forces were therefore allotted eighty vacancies for the first officer candidate class, which brought that class to a total of 440. WAAC Headquarters suffered some misgivings about the absence of the usual tests. However, while

choices were later found to include some women without responsible paid experience and with test scores in the lowest aptitude category, Group V, the majority made successful officers.[51]

There was one applicant for attendance at the school who gave the War Department more trouble than all others combined. This was Director Hobby herself, who had made up her mind to attend the school as an ordinary student in order to understand through her own experience the problems of a woman's adjustment to military training. She stood firm in this decision for some time while the expostulations of shocked advisers raged around her.[52] The Director carried this determination unaltered up through several strata of general officers and was stopped at last only by General Marshall himself, who told her sympathetically but with finality that the thing was impossible under the Army system of rank.

The First WAAC Training Center

Meanwhile, the situation at Fort Des Moines could scarcely have been termed tranquil. Immediately upon passage of the WAAC bill, Colonel Faith and his staff of ten Army officers shot out of Washington in the race to have the training center ready when the women arrived.[53] They reached Des Moines with less than two months to spare before opening date.

[49] *Chicago Defender*, May 23, 1942.
[50] (1) *Ibid.* (2) Copy of plan in Folder Recruiting, Tasker files, 1942 WAAC files. (3) Interv with Lt Col Woods, 21 Mar 46.
[51] Memo, AG WAAC for Dir WAAC, 3 Jun 42. Tasker Staybacks. Also from intervs.
[52] This incident related separately by former staff members present at the time: Mrs. Herrick, Mrs. Knight, and Mrs. Woods.
[53] Memo, G-1 for CofS, 13 May 42. WDGAP 352.01 WAAC. Approved 15 May 42.

Colonel Faith's basic plan in beginning the undertaking was to make the course so military that Army skeptics could find little to criticize. Reporters who interviewed him came away stating, "It will be no glamour girls' playhouse." They gathered that few concessions would be made to "feminine vanity and civilian frippery." [54] Colonel Faith deplored the press phrasing of the matter, and stated later:

It was obvious to all of us that a considerable percentage of the Army was either opposed to the WAAC idea or very doubtful of its potential success. The best way to combat this attitude was to train the new soldiers in those qualities which the Army values most highly: neatness in dress, punctiliousness in military courtesy, smartness and precision in drill and ceremonies, and willingness and ability to do the job. [55]

The students were, however, to be taught the Army's reasons for the things they were required to do. "The American woman is the most co-operative human being on earth if she fully understands an order," Faith declared hopefully. [56]

Remodeling and new construction at Fort Des Moines began as soon as the induction station and reception center could be moved. Classrooms were erected, stables and plumbing converted, and separate housing provided for the male cadre. The rest of the staff, forty-one officers and 192 enlisted men, arrived about 30 May. [57] The director of training was especially selected by Colonel Tasker; he was Lt. Gordon C. Jones, a former instructor at The Citadel.

Direct communication had been authorized between Colonel Faith and the Director, and this proved indeed fortunate for the training center, which began to send by telephone, wire, and mail a steady stream of requests. [58] Dayroom furniture was needed, also a Special Services officer,

two women doctors, a post utilities officer, pictures of uniforms for the local press, instruments for the band, and money for everything. Boxes of training literature had not arrived, nor had test forms.

A hostess and a librarian were needed for the service club, also a Red Cross field director. Highly skilled classification teams had to be found to interview and classify the women, who might be expected to have job experience not ordinarily encountered by the Army. The Chief of Finance "strenuously objected" to furnishing a fiscal officer. The Corps of Engineers had no capable post utilities officer to offer. The $20,000 already allotted to the Seventh Corps Area was so restricted that Colonel Faith could not use it to purchase many of the miscellaneous items needed. There was no money for entertaining the scores of prominent people who desired to view the school.

These assorted requests, coming as they did during the period when WAAC Headquarters was struggling to establish its own organization and policies and to select officer candidates, quickly began to reveal still more of the difficulties which the Director's office must face as an operating headquarters. Most of the fairly minor matters discussed with Colonel Faith could easily have been decentralized to the Seventh Corps Area had the WAAC been in the Army, but since it was a separate organization, all of its funds and

[54] (1) AP Release, June 1, 1942, quoted in *New York Times*, June 2, 1942. (2) Lee Carson, INS Release, May 19, 1942, in Los Angeles *Examiner*, May 20, 1942.

[55] Ltr, Faith to Ward, 18 May 50. OCMH.

[56] Press Releases cited n. 54.

[57] Memo cited n. 53.

[58] Personal ltrs, memos, and transcripts of tp convs in: (1) Folder T, Tasker files, 1942 WAAC files, dated 3, 8, 22, 25, 26, 27, 29 June, 3, 6, 20, 21, 28 July. (2) Tasker Staybacks, dated 3, 10 June, 6 July.

personnel allotments had to be handled separately and justified by the Director's office.

The Adjutant General had meanwhile directed various Army commands to select and send to Des Moines the men who would serve as instructors and cadre until Waacs could take over.[59] This personnel had no sooner reported than it was discovered that few if any of the instructors were qualified for the exacting and unprecedented task ahead. The director of training wrote:

Out of 41 officers which we requested originally, we got one man who is fitted for the job at hand. The others are all doing their best to fill jobs far beyond their former experience. The new officers are all fine fellows (we are fortunate to have gotten no duds) but professionally. . . .[60]

As the time grew shorter, it became apparent that some deficiencies were inevitable. Requisitions for field and technical manuals, circulars, forms, and Army Regulations were only partially filled or back-ordered, with no assurance from harassed supply depots that they could be filled within the next six months. The post's two mimeograph machines ran continuously to duplicate missing material.[61] Funds for certain equipment did not arrive on time, and neither did some of the faculty. Colonel Tasker wrote, "The lieutenant who was to join your force cannot be located. Please let me know if others are missing."[62] Even ahead of these difficulties came the greatest problem of all, and an unexpected one—expansion.

Expansion Plans, Summer of 1942

In the midst of the WAAC's hurried preparations there occurred an event which was to bring far-reaching changes to all plans. On 13 June 1942 the Chief of Staff called into his office three Army officers representing the Chief of Administrative Services, the Office of the Director, WAAC, and Aircraft Warning Service.[63] General Marshall informed these men that in view of the approaching Army personnel shortage it was his desire that every effort be made to organize and train personnel of the Women's Army Auxiliary Corps at the earliest possible date. He felt it would be possible to have considerable numbers in active service a great deal sooner than existing plans provided. The staff officers were directed to formulate the necessary speed-up plans.

All British precedent indicated that such a move meant great difficulty for the WAAC. British observers had commented, "It is difficult for the general public to realize the strain created by the great expansion of the women's services, built up as they have been . . . from almost non-existent foundations."[64] Director Hobby and the preplanners had fervently hoped for at least "time for trial and error before going into an assembly-line type of production."[65]

Nevertheless, WAAC expansion was a calculated risk that the Army's current situation made necessary. In spite of earlier optimistic estimates, the armed forces were now experiencing what historians called "the manpower crisis of the summer of

[59] Telg, TAG to CG Second Army at Memphis, Tenn., 22 May 42. AG 220.31 (5–23–42)EA, in G–1/15839–10 (7–8–42).

[60] Personal ltr, Jones to Tasker, 27 Jun 42. Folder T, Tasker files, 1942 WAAC files.

[61] Ltr, Faith to Dir WAAC, 24 Aug 42. SPWA 400.311 (8–24–42).

[62] Ltr, Tasker to Faith, 28 Jul 42. Tasker files, 1942 WAAC files.

[63] Memo, Lt Col James L. Tarr to CofAdm Serv, 13 Jun 42. G–1/15839–10 (7–8–42).

[64] *Conditions in the Three Women's Services.*

[65] Ltr, Mudgett to author, 19 Aug 48. OCMH.

1942." [66] The Army Ground Forces was already short more than 160,000 men. Only two days before General Marshall's decision the War Department had admitted the necessity either to train units understrength or to slow down the activation of new units, thus jeopardizing invasion plans. It was also being forced toward unpopular measures such as drafting eighteen-year-olds and fathers and cutting more deeply into defense industry and agriculture.[67]

On the other hand, the WAAC was concurrently rocking along with its modest prewar plan for about 12,000 women in the first year. Meanwhile, thousands of women were clamoring for admittance, and requisitions for over 80,000 of them had by this time been received from Army commands, of which at least 63,000 seemed suitable for employment. This did not include the needs of overseas theaters and many other domestic commands which had also shown interest.[68]

Thus, WAAC expansion seemed logical in spite of its practical difficulties. The Army itself was faced with the same expansion problems, and men were training with wooden guns, sleeping in tent camps, and wearing clothing often inappropriate to the climate, all with greater success than might have been expected. The WAAC move was nevertheless the greater risk, since men could be drafted to face these hardships while women would have to volunteer.

Plans for expansion were drawn up by the Services of Supply at hasty conferences on 14 and 15 June and submitted to the Chief of Staff on 17 June. The WAAC's ultimate strength was to be increased at least fivefold, from 12,000 to more than 63,000. Within a year, by May of 1943, there would be in the field 25,000 instead

of the 12,000 previously planned for that date. Within two years, or by April of 1944, the entire 63,000 would be trained and at work. The divisions of the Services of Supply concerned believed it would be possible to manage this expansion successfully, and gave it their written concurrence.[69]

The plan was approved by the Chief of Staff, although within three months it, too, was to be discarded by the General Staff in favor of still greater expansion. This moment marked an important turning point in Corps history: up to this date, it was obvious that the WAAC had been forced upon an unwilling Army by a combination of circumstances; from this time forward, its employment was not only voluntary but was extended more rapidly than its original sponsors had contemplated.

As the first result of the plan, construction at Fort Des Moines was stepped up by 20 percent, and action was taken by condemnation to lease Des Moines hotels, garages, office buildings, college dormi-

---

[66] Kent Roberts Greenfield, Robert R. Palmer, and Bell I. Wiley, *The Organization of Ground Combat Troops,* in UNITED STATES ARMY IN WORLD WAR II (Washington, 1947), pp. 206–08.

[67] Remarks of Lt Gen Joseph T. McNarney, Min, Gen Council, 12 Oct 42.

[68] Memo, Brig Gen James E. Wharton, Dir Mil Pers SOS, for CofS, Attn: G–1, 17 Jun 42. G–1/15839–10.

Command	Requisitioned	Approved
Total	80,750	63,750
AAF, AWS	31,600	31,600
AAF, airfields	19,300	19,300
AAF, ferrying commands	1,100	1,100
Service Commands	6,450	6,450
Signal Corps	7,500	[a] 2,500
Antiaircraft commands	750	750
Weather Bureau	2,050	2,050
Post Exchanges	12,000	0

[a] Disapproved 5,000 intended for overseas.

[69] *Ibid.* Concurrences: SOS Tng Div, Reqmts Div, Pers Div, Opns Div, CofAdm Serv, and Dir WAAC; also Rctg Div AGO.

tories and classrooms, and even the local coliseum, so that specialist training might be given in the city, leaving more room for basic trainees at the post.[70] A tent camp was set up at Fort Des Moines for an additional 634 male cadre, who were intended to stay only four months, until Waacs could graduate and replace them. Action was not taken until 3 July to order these men in, and most arrived at Des Moines scarcely one jump ahead of the women whom they were to instruct.

It was now determined that the first officer candidate class of 440, which began on 20 July, would be followed by classes of 125 women weekly until at least 1,300 officers had been trained. Officer training time had already been cut from three months to six weeks. It had also been decided to start the first class of enrolled women soon after the first officer candidate class, without waiting for WAAC officers to graduate and assist in their training. Enrolled women would have only a brief four weeks of basic training, instead of the originally planned three months.[71]

Specialist schools—for cooks, clerks, and drivers—would be ready to function in August when the first enrolled women graduated from basic training. Thus it was believed that it would be possible as early as 9 November 1942 to begin sending three fully trained headquarters companies, with officers and cadre, to field stations each week, and to train and return to their station 300 Aircraft Warning Service Waacs weekly, beginning in September.[72]

The First WAAC Officer Candidate Class, 20 July–29 August 1942

By 20 July 1942, with the opening of the first officer candidate class,[73] the mounting interest of press and public reached a

point of near-hysteria. The old post at Fort Des Moines swarmed with dignitaries, invited and uninvited, who braved the steamy midsummer Iowa weather in order to view history in the making. Every angle of the new scene was well documented by the press, while photographers invaded the barracks in search of the still-elusive WAAC underwear. Authorities were particularly alarmed to discover that a number of women reporters had resolved to participate in the first week of processing in order to reveal to the waiting public a woman's every sensation as she was converted into a soldier. Because it was not yet known whether the women's sensations would be printable, this request was refused, and the press was informed that the post was theirs for one day only. After that, a two-week news blackout was to be enforced while the Army and the women became acquainted in comparative privacy. This step seemed necessary to avoid complete disruption of training, but was later believed by some staff officers to have alienated certain writers and news agencies.[74]

Before crowds of interested Des Moines citizens the arriving Waacs were whisked

---

[70] Memo cited n. 63. Also Folder, Lease of Real Estate, 27 Jun 42, SPWA 481 (6–7–42).

[71] Memo, Preplanners for G-1, 2 Apr 42. Tasker Staybacks.

[72] (1) Memo, Brig Gen Idwal H. Edwards, G-3, for CofS, 3 Jul 42. WDGCT 291.9 WAAC, in CofS 291.9 WAAC. (2) 1st Ind, AG WAAC for Dir Mil Pers SOS through CofAdm Serv, 29 Jun 42. WA 320.2 (6–25–42). Copy in Tasker Staybacks.

[73] Dir WAAC for CofS, 4 Aug 42, 1st Ind, Exec Off CofAdm Serv, for Dir WAAC, 10 Aug 42. SPAAI 320 WAAC, in Dir Adm Serv ASF Sp Coll DRB AGO.

[74] If no other source is stated, descriptions of this first class are based upon: (1) accounts given by women participants to the author, and upon her own impressions as a member of Company 1. Other accounts differ only as to whether Company 1, 2, 3, or 4 was the best company. (2) Hist of 1st WAAC Tng Cen.

WAAC STAFF AND MEMBERS OF THE PRESS *at Fort Des Moines, Iowa, 20 July 1942.*

from incoming trains to waiting Army trucks. At the fort processing moved efficiently and included a brief physical check, an immediate meal, and assignment to one of the four companies. Each woman was assigned a bed, a wall locker, a footlocker, and a metal chair, and soon discovered that the Army had no bathrooms, only something two flights of stairs away called a latrine. Male company officers and cadre clung to their orderly and supply rooms, designating the first arrivals as barracks guides for the rest and hastily, if inaccurately, informing all comers that only married men with children had been given this assignment.

The issuance of uniforms was the main interest. Mobilized at the clothing warehouse were almost all of the saleswomen and fitters from department stores in Des Moines, and the Waacs were passed down an assembly line from one curtained booth to another. The underwear and foundation garments proved to be of excellent quality, although the rich mud-brown color of slips and panties was slightly disconcerting.

The morning was not an hour old before more was learned about women's uniforms than had been discovered in the past six months of research. It was immediately apparent that the articles shipped to Des Moines by the Philadelphia Quartermaster Depot bore little resemblance to the model that had been approved by the preplanners. The heavy cotton khaki skirts were cut as if to fit men's hips, and buckled and wrinkled across the stomach, so that even the slimmest Waac presented a potbellied appearance after she had sat down once. When Waacs walked or marched the skirts climbed well above the knee, unless a desperate grip on the skirt was substituted for the required arm swing. The hot, stiff cotton jackets, made of men's materials, draped as becomingly as a strait jacket and were of much the same texture. Shrieks of dismay arose as women tried on the WAAC caps, uncharitably christened "Hobby hats," which were not only unbecoming to many women but also cut the forehead and were easily warped, crushed, or soiled.

Furthermore, the Quartermaster size range had apparently been set up for a race of giants, and there were not enough small sizes in outer garments. As extensive alterations were necessary to cut down larger sizes, most of the women emerged with nothing to wear for a day or two except the brown-striped seersucker exercise suits—short button-front dresses worn over matching bloomers. However, the cameramen were diverted to a few women whose uniforms fitted without alteration; these were placed in the front row for platoon pictures or posed beside the post's one cannon.

The rest of the processing, carried on intermittently during the week, closely followed the Army pattern for men. There were simultaneous tetanus, typhoid, and smallpox shots; outside the dispensary stood an embarrassed Army sergeant with smelling salts, which actually proved little needed. The Articles of War were solemnly explained, although they applied to a Waac only in the improbable event that she should find herself "in the field." Lessons were given in bedmaking, care of clothing and equipment, the difference between *fall out* and *fall in,* the beginnings of close order drill, and the other Army orientation that for men was usually given at reception centers. Women were given the standard Army General Classification Test (AGCT), and their skills were classified.

On the fourth day, with processing completed and the women at last neatly uniformed in khaki skirts and shirts, Director Hobby addressed the group for the first time. She had been at the Fort since the first day, observing somewhat wistfully. Now she spoke words calculated to remove the military trees and reveal the forest, to give the women perspective on history and where they now stood in it:

May fourteenth is a date already written into the history books of tomorrow. . . . Long-established precedents of military tradition have given way to pressing need. Total war is, by definition, endlessly expansive. . . . You are the first women to serve. . . . Never forget it. . . .
You have just made the change from peacetime pursuits to wartime tasks—from the individualism of civilian life to the anonymity of mass military life. You have given up comfortable homes, highly paid positions, leisure. You have taken off silk and put on khaki. And all for essentially the same reason—you have a debt and a date. A debt to democracy, a date with destiny. . . .
You do not come into a Corps that has an established tradition. You must make your own. But in making your own, you do have one tradition—the integrity of all the brave American women of all time who have loved their country. You, as you gather here, are living history. On your shoulders will rest the military reputation and the civilian recognition of this Corps. I have no fear that any woman here will fail the standards of the Corps.
From now on you are soldiers, defending a free way of life. Your performance will set the standards of the Corps. You will live in the spotlight. Even though the lamps of experience are dim, few if any mistakes will be permitted you.
You are no longer individuals. You wear the uniform of the Army of the United States. Respect that uniform. Respect all that it stands for. Then the world will respect all that the Corps stands for. . . . Make the adjustment from civilian to military life without faltering and without complaint. . . .

In the final analysis, the only testament free people can give to the quality of freedom is the way in which they resist the forces that peril freedom.[75]

As one of the women later said, "It was only then that I really knew what I had done in enlisting. I looked around the roomful of women and suddenly had no more doubts that it was right. My feet stopped hurting, and the war and my place in it became very real."

The Training Course

From this time on the work began in earnest. The women were up at five-thirty or before in order to be neatly dressed for six o'clock reveille, a process that took most women somewhat longer than men. After making beds, cleaning, and picking up cigarette butts and photographers' flash bulbs in the area, the women marched to breakfast and then began classes, which lasted until five in the afternoon, with an intermission for lunch. After supper there was a required study hour and then a session devoted to the washing and pressing of uniforms and the shining of shoes.

The WAAC basic and officer candidate courses were identical with corresponding courses for men, except for the omission of combat subjects. Women studied military sanitation and first aid, military customs and courtesy, map reading, defense against chemical attack, defense against air attack, interior guard, company administration, supply, mess management, and other familiar subjects. A few courses were more or less adapted to women. The hygiene course was designed by the local hospital

---

[75] WDBPR Press Release, 23 Jul 42, revised copy, Remarks by Mrs. Hobby, Dir WAAC, to Students at WAAC Tng Cen.

personnel to apply to women's hygiene. The Army organization course contained vague references to WAAC organization, which no one even in Washington understood too well. Drill was without arms, and the physical training course was devised and conducted by a civilian consultant.[76]

The military courtesies course, which set out to permit no deviations for women, soon ran into the inescapable fact that there were socially accepted differences for women to which the Army must perforce conform. For example, women of some faiths could not remove their hats in church as was proper for men, and most women felt self-conscious about removing hats in such places as dining rooms and lobbies. Endless commotion was also caused when women attempted to open doors and show other required courtesies for men who outranked them. Army officers were, for the first time, confronted with a situation in which a man might be either an officer or a gentleman, but not both; there resulted much sprinting for doorways and leaping out of the wrong side of vehicles to avoid the eager assistance of a nearby Waac.

As the women learned about the Army, the Army also began to learn the many minor yet important items about the administration of women that could be learned only by experience. Oddly enough, these were not the expected difficulties that the planners had feared, for the women were agreeable about inspections and did not have hysterics in the barracks or faint at the discomforts of latrine ablutions. Instead, unique specific needs arose, more practical than psychological.

For example, a few laundry tubs and ironing boards had been provided, although men's barracks ordinarily did not have them. On the first day, the Waacs as one woman headed for these—a true WAAC pattern which was not to vary through hundreds of stations in the field— and it was discovered that the women considered the number of laundry tubs, drying racks, and irons inadequate. Women stood in line until late at night for a turn at the irons. Many Waacs were found to have brought their own irons, in numbers which so frequently blew out barracks fuses that their use had to be limited. The allowance of four khaki shirts and four skirts did not permit use of local laundries, which took a week, for the women considered that neat appearance in the sticky hot climate required at least one and often two clean shirts daily.

Lack of opportunity to launder and iron her shirt for the next day was to prove a greater morale hazard to a woman soldier than any lack of movies, camp shows, and pinball machines. The women's anxiety about the matter gave strong support to a fact which civilian psychologists had already suspected, and which was to prove a new problem to station commanders: that a woman's grooming was vitally connected not only with her morale but with her health and actually with her conduct.[77]

Similarly, the women felt that the Army provided too few brooms, too little scrubbing powder, and not enough dustcloths. The women also suffered somewhat, as did male recruits, from sleeplessness, sore feet, heat and humidity, and— somewhat more than men did—from the general lack of privacy.

Other expected difficulties with wom-

---

[76] For a full discussion of physical training and all other courses, see below, Ch. XXXII.

[77] See later chapters, particularly XXII and XXXI.

FIRST OFFICER CANDIDATE CLASS, *20 July–29 August 1942. Left page, top, reveille; middle, instruction in Military Customs and Courtesy; bottom, close order drill. Right page, top, classroom instruction; middle, physical training; bottom, chow line.*

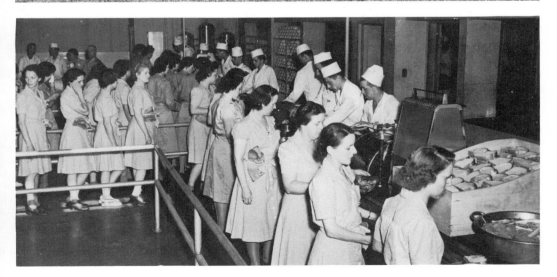

en's administration did not arise. Most Waacs were entranced with parades and bands and ceremonies of all sorts. They took well to drill, and after an exhausting day enthusiastic squads could be seen in the summer twilight, giving themselves extra drill practice. One company officer alleged, "They learn more in a day than my squads of men used to learn in a week." They were not disconcerted by the necessity for discipline and regimentation; their shoes were shined, uniforms spotless, beds tightly made, footlockers neat. Neither did they prove especially subject to quarrels, but appeared to be as good comrades as were the members of men's units.

On the other hand, the exciting publicity about the Corps and the steep competition for places had prepared women very little for the fact that the Army lacked wings and a halo. One disappointment was the caliber of the instruction at the training center. Ninety percent college women, the Waacs expected classes of challenging difficulty. Realizing this, WAAC Headquarters had sent Military Personnel Division a long account of the qualifications desired in the instructors assigned, saying, "The results to be obtained at the WAAC Training Center will depend in a large measure on the type of instructors which are detailed. . . . Time is too short to permit training these individuals after their arrival at Fort Des Moines." [78]

Colonel Faith felt that the resulting selection had been good, since the instructors were a "group of fine and sincere young men" who, although with little Army experience, were for the most part graduates of The Adjutant General's School or others of similar level. [79] Never-

theless, it became apparent to the students on the first day of classes that most of the instructors were not teachers, not public speakers, not college men, and sometimes without Army experience in the subjects they were teaching. It was a lucky young instructor who did not confront in every class some students with college training or years of teaching experience. The situation was similar to that which the WAVES were to encounter a few months later, of which the Navy noted, "The early indoctrination was largely farcical, with youthful male Reservists parroting material they had just received, to women their seniors . . . especially in teaching experience. Politeness and good humor on both sides made the situation tolerable." [80] The Waacs' most respected instructors were often the teachers of company administration, newly commissioned former sergeants who really knew the peculiarities of the morning report, although one of them startled his first class by welcoming them with, "Put dem hats on dose tables." [81]

There were other situations that the women solemnly noted for correction in the days when they would be running the Corps. All companies habitually marched out to mess at the same time, so that the last of the 440 stood in line for an hour. The aptitude tests were given at 7:00 P.M. of a stifling summer evening, immediately after a heavy meal. The summer uniforms were like nothing ever before worn by woman, with five sweat-soaked layers of cloth around the waist and three around

---

[78] 1st Ind, WAAC Hq for Dir Mil Pers SOS, 29 Jun 42. WA 320.2 (6–25–42), Tasker Staybacks.

[79] Ltr cited n. 55.

[80] WAVES Hist.

[81] Vol., General Information, SPWA 314.7, WAAC Hist File.

the neck.[82] The young officers did not seem to know how to put in their places the female apple polishers and classroom show-offs whose tactics were transparent to other women. The food was good and abundant but not always attractively prepared. These and similar occurrences gave the first hint of what was repeatedly demonstrated: that Waacs were often less tolerant of imperfection than men—a trait which some Army psychologists believed was due less to their sex than to the fact that all were volunteers, since male volunteers also frequently showed greater impatience than did draftees.[83]

This first class was nevertheless still too uncertain as to correct procedure, and too eager to please, to be very critical. General morale was at unprecedented heights. Women stood retreat with real appreciation of the ceremony. They trembled lest their company officers give them a gig. They crossed streets and ran out of doorways to practice their salute on everything that glistened, until the outnumbered male officers were forced to flee the front walks. No imperfection seemed of much importance when weighed against the general desire to justify the Army's admission of women to its ranks.

Graduation

On the eve of graduation there occurred one further test of the new soldiers' soldierliness: the release of the roster of class standing. Herein, it was discovered that young women who had dated their company officers had mysteriously soared in rating to outrank the older women who had led their classes in training.[84]

Since many of the company officers were ex-college boys of 19, any woman

over 30 had evidently appeared antique. Katherine R. Goodwin, who later headed some 50,000 Army Service Forces Wacs, recalled: "Captain B. called me in and told me I was so old he didn't see how I could have made the journey to Des Moines, and that he couldn't imagine what use the Army could ever make of me, and perhaps I had better go home before I got any older."

Angry members rose in class to ask an explanation of the mathematics involved in rating, and an inquiry was launched by WAAC Headquarters. In general it was found that the honest tendency of the male officer was to consider a glamorous young woman, or a mannish loud-voiced one, the best material for leadership of women, whereas the women themselves had given highest ratings to women of mature judgment, and to those with a faculty for sweeping and polishing their share of the area. It was concluded that the problem would correct itself in later classes where women company officers had replaced men. However, the same situation was later to cause some difficulty in the field where men ordinarily selected and promoted WAC officers.

Graduation day, on 29 August, saw 436 new WAAC third officers, all with shining new gold bars but no WAAC insignia,

---

[82] Around waist: (1) heavy jersey panties, (2) sturdy girdle, (3) heavy jersey slip, (4) cotton shirt, (5) double 8.2 chino waistband of skirt; plus for dress uniform: (6) heavy cotton jacket, (7) double jacket belt. Around neck: (1) neckband of shirt (about four layers of cotton), (2) mohair tie; and for dress (3) jacket collar.

[83] Opinion of Maj Albert Preston, Jr., MC, head of Consultation Serv at Ft Des Moines. See below, Ch. XXXI.

[84] Rating was based one third each on grades, platoon rating, and company officer rating, but in the final results the last item was found to have outweighed the other two.

which The Quartermaster General was late in procuring. Mrs. Hobby spoke to the women, and Congresswoman Rogers told them: "You are soldiers and belong to America. Every hour must be your finest hour." [85] The Army was represented by Maj. Gen. James A. Ulio, The Adjutant General, and Maj. Gen. Frederick E. Uhl, Commanding General, Seventh Corps Area. General Marshall personally wrote out a congratulatory telegram for Director Hobby, saying, "Please act for me in welcoming them into the Army. This is only the beginning of a magnificent war service by the women of America." [86]

---

[85] *Congressional Record*, Vol. 88, No. 151, p. 7242, August 1942.
[86] (1) WDBPR Press Release, 8 Sep 42. (2) TWX, CofS for Mrs. Hobby at Ft Des Moines. WDCSA 291.2 (8–29–42).

CHAPTER IV

September–October 1942: Beginnings of Field Duties

Among the more important officer assignments were those of the eighteen carefully selected members of the first graduating class who arrived in WAAC Headquarters on 17 September 1942. They reported with a formality that delighted Regular Army staff members, having been particularly trained by Colonel Faith in how to knock, enter, and salute.[1] Third Officer proving unwieldy for direct address, the use of Lieutenant and Ma'am—instead of Sir, as WAVES officers were addressed—was adopted.[2]

For their own guidance, the Director and her advisers decided that WAAC Headquarters should be irreproachably military, with salutes rendered when entering the office of a superior, and with a command-type organization wherein no junior member of one section conferred with a junior member of another except through their respective Army section chiefs. The Director observed, "War Department officials will have to get used to the idea of treating Waacs as officers rather than as women."

The impeccably formal behavior of the Waacs did cause comment, not to say consternation, in War Department offices; it also was to impose considerable handicaps on staff operation, which did not reach maximum efficiency for many months, until the WAAC was part of the Army and could stop being military. The very junior WAAC members reported that few of them ever at this time saw the Director or had opportunity to influence Army policy. However, they grasped their assignments with rapidity and covered the scheduled three-month indoctrination course in three weeks.

Prominent among the eighteen members were Third Officers Helen H. Woods and Marjorie D. Fling, the former civilian assistants, who were now assigned, respectively, to Control Division and to Office Management. Third Officer Emily E. Davis, a former insurance company employee, was assigned to a position in the Executive Office. An especial point was made of securing a Negro Waac, Third Officer Harriet West, as one of those assigned to Personnel Division, in order that minority needs might not be overlooked in planning. Other offices receiving Waacs included Public Relations, Supply, and Plans and Training.

Possibly the most important assignment

---

[1] All references to staff opinions or meetings, unless otherwise specified, are from the WAAC Daily Journal. (See Bibliographical Note.)

[2] Office Memo 22, 15 Sep 42. SPWA 300. This directs that they not be called Third Officer except in correspondence, and never Miss nor Mrs.

WAAC OFFICERS ASSIGNED FOR DUTY IN WASHINGTON *sign the register, above, and receive explanation of Tables of Organization in Temporary M Building, below.*

was that of the Director's first WAAC aide, Third Officer Betty Bandel, formerly a reporter, music and drama critic, and woman's page editor for an Arizona newspaper. Her duties at once tended to expand beyond those of aide, for which in her own opinion she was the world's least qualified. She recalled later a moment in a London hotel when "the Director came to herself to find that *she* was sewing a button on *my* uniform; she pointed a finger at me and screamed, 'You're fired!' " Lieutenant Bandel came to be employed chiefly as a traveling deputy; on visits to field stations the two officers developed tactics whereby, if the Director was hopelessly immobilized by local dignitaries, the aide unobtrusively detached herself and explored the enlisted women's viewpoints.

New Graduating Classes

Meanwhile, a steady stream of new members, officer and enrolled, graduated weekly at Fort Des Moines. Most initial assignments were naturally to the training center. Enrolled women were shortly doing most of Fort Des Moines' office work, driving its vehicles, and staffing its messes. There was even a Waac bugler, and a band was being organized. WAAC officers at once took over much of the instruction: a former aircraft spotter taught the course in Identification of Enemy Aircraft; home economics teachers revised the mess management courses; a graduate chemist taught the course in Defense Against Chemical Attack. WAAC officers were also assigned to staff the incoming training companies, with the aid of Army "tactical advisers." No major responsibilities were turned over to women, but they were assigned as understudies to various section chiefs.

During these weeks Colonel Faith reported himself as harassed by all the ills known to similar growing institutions, and a few previously unknown. With thousands of new students scattered through officer candidate school, basic training, administrative school, motor transport school, and cooks and bakers school, the training center was still lacking in training manuals, film strips, balopticons, photographic equipment, and instructional materials of all kinds. For lack of typewriters, the administrative school could not train typists in Army methods; it was to be almost a year before a typing school could be opened. The motor transport school, unable to obtain vehicles, graduated women drivers who had driven an Army vehicle only once, and built its own demonstration engines from junk salvaged from nearby Army posts. The burden of cutting orders for hundreds of graduates was a heavy one, but teletypewriter service to Washington was not to be obtainable for eight months.

Colonel Faith's increasingly urgent reports of these matters were necessarily referred to the Services of Supply's Military Training Division, which delayed action while making further inquiry into the basis of his estimates and whether he had properly staggered schedules in order to reduce requirements.[3]

The most alarming shortage, however, was that of winter uniforms. For reasons unknown to the training center, The

---

[3] (1) Ltr, Comdt to Dir WAAC, 24 Aug 42, and Inds. SPWA 400.312 (8–24–42). (2) Min, Stf Conf, 14 Nov 42, WAAC Daily Journal. (3) Ltr, 1st WAAC Tng Cen to Dir WAAC, 15 Feb 43. SPWA 400.34 (3–21–42) (1) sec 3. (4) M/R, Stf Conf, 6 Jan 43. Folder, Memos Prior to 7 Jan 43 in WAC Planning, WAAC Planning files. (5) Memo, WAAC Hq for CofAdm Serv, 18 Jul 42. WA 483 (7–18–42).

Quartermaster General's specified ship-ment schedules were not being met. The supply of summer uniforms became er-ratic, while almost no winter clothing of any sort—underwear, coats, or uniforms—had been received. The Iowa weather proved un-co-operative, and an unseason-able cold spell struck in September, blank-eting Fort Des Moines in snow. Tempera-tures stood near the freezing mark inside the newly constructed barracks and class-rooms, known informally as Boomtown, where heating equipment had not yet been installed.

Within a few days the training center was plunged into a crisis of health—and, it was feared, of public relations—as re-spiratory disorders swept the student body. Hospitals filled suddenly, while continued instruction was made difficult by coughing and sneezing in the unheated classrooms.

At this point Director Hobby herself hastened to the training center. Putting on the summer raincoat the women were wearing, she immediately caught a bad cold, and, more practically, telephoned to higher headquarters in Washington in a manner that evoked a promise to expedite clothing shipments without delay. She also took the precaution of demanding several thousand enlisted men's overcoats from a neighboring station's surplus stock, and these were on their way before nightfall. They were to be worn all winter while ac-tion was being expedited in Washington.[4]

The men's overcoats proved excellent substitutes not only for WAAC coats but also for mittens and leggings, since they covered hands and feet and trailed on the ground. Unfortunately, Waacs found them so amusing in appearance that they could not forbear taking pictures, which they sent indiscriminately to friends and relatives, to the dismay of recruiters.

Close behind the Director came the Deputy Chief of Staff, Lt. Gen. Joseph T. McNarney, who verified her comments and immediately wrote to the Services of Supply: "Although the weather was cold, the Waacs were still wearing summer uni-forms. They had been issued enlisted men's coats as an expedient. Please look into the matter of expediting winter uniforms."[5] Meanwhile, a brief Indian summer inter-vened to make summer uniforms again adequate.

In spite of supply difficulties, officers who inspected the training center in late September and early October reported that an excellent state of training had been attained. The WAAC graduates, both officer and enrolled, won unanimous praise. What seemed most remarkable to reviewing officers was the somewhat unre-markable fact that women could march and drill, a sight which melted the sternest critics. WAAC Headquarters' superior, General Grunert, Chief of Administrative Services, reported upon his return from Des Moines in early October:

I was received at the entrance to the post by the band and an escort of honor which I complimented on its smart appearance, cor-rect procedure, and excellent marching. . . . I was particularly impressed by the uniform smart appearance of all personnel, with the instructional setup, with the orderliness and arrangement of quarters, and with the punc-tilious saluting. . . . A late afternoon review was a gratifying sight to behold. The forma-tions, evolutions, marching, and saluting compared favorably with the best I have seen anywhere. . . .
I feel assured that the WAAC is off to an excellent start and that the commands re-

---

[4] From: (1) Persons at Des Moines at the time, including the author; (2) the Waac aide to the Direc-tor, 3d O Betty Bandel.

[5] Memo, DCofS for Somervell, 11 Oct 42. WDCSA 291.9 (9–11–42).

ceiving WAAC units will be agreeably surprised to find how much these units can contribute to the war effort.[6]

Also, in spite of the inconveniences of supply and climate, the women's morale remained high. Psychiatrists later remarked that the women seemed pleased with the idea that they were approximating the hardships of Army men. Whatever the cause, the trainees joked through their sniffles, laughed at their own appearance, and felt great pride in their new status and enthusiasm for the Corps' future. At night, wrapped in blankets, they sat on the floor in freezing unfurnished dayrooms to sing Army songs, including one written by a member of an early class which soon swept the training center:

All you fighting men, keep on fighting to win,
For the WAAC is in back of you;
If a plane you fly, keep it flying high
For the WAAC is in back of you.
Spread the news around that we're victory
    bound,
And our hearts we pledge anew
That our flag shall wave o'er the home of the
    brave,
And the WAAC is in back of you.[7]

The character and ability of the incoming recruits also continued to receive approval. By the end of September there were more than 3,000 Waacs at Des Moines, including 792 officers, with more arriving daily. Some 3,300 more had also been enrolled but could not yet be called to active duty for lack of training space.[8] The average ability of these recruits remained surprisingly higher than that of the Army or the civilian population. In the month of September, some 60 percent were found to be in the first two AGCT groups, I and II, having scores ordinarily required only of officers, and only 0.8 percent were in the fifth or lowest group.[9]

Furthermore, every recruit possessed a civilian skill expected to be readily useful to the Army.

The Second WAAC Training Center

It had been known since summer that a second WAAC training center would be required to meet the expansion program directed by the General Staff. The only site offered the WAAC was that of Daytona Beach, Florida, where it was proposed to train women in leased city buildings, rather than to dispossess the occupants of any established military post. It was also believed that the climate would prevent suffering from the current lack of winter clothing for women.

However, soon after Colonel Faith first inspected the proposed facilities, Director Hobby appealed to the Services of Supply for any other location, stating that a military atmosphere and reasonable discipline could not be inculcated at any such establishment. The town itself was a resort area, with streets perpetually crowded with sail-

---

[6] Ltr, CofAdm Serv to Dir WAAC, 6 Oct 42. SPAAE 333.1. Such favorable impressions of Des Moines do not appear to have been exactly accidental. A staff note concerning other important visitors observes privately: "Des Moines will be prepared to . . . put on the same sort of show which has been arranged for General Grunert." Min, Stf Mtg, 6 Oct 42.

[7] By Ruby Jane Douglass. *WAAC Parodies*, pamphlet published by WAAC Publications Office, Ft. Des Moines, May 1943. Copy in OCMH.

[8] (1) Memo, Stat Br GS for CofS, 6 Oct 42. WDGSA 291.9. (2) Memo, Dir WAAC for CofAdm Serv, 28 Sep 42. SPWA 291.9 (9–28–42) E. Copy in SPWA 314.7 sec 3.

[9] Table III, in History of Military Training: WAAC/WAC Training, Army Service Forces, prepared by Maj. Lavinia L. Redd, WAC, 5 Feb 46. OCMH. Hereafter cited as ASF Hist of WAC Tng. An even higher average score in July was due to the relatively large number of officer candidates, but by September there were only 350 in this group.

ors, soldiers, and coastguardmen from nearby military stations. For barracks, it was proposed to house the Waac trainees in a number of scattered hotels and apartment houses, ranging in capacity from 37 to 600, as well as auto courts, inns, and villas; and a 6,000-woman tent camp was to be built in a cantonment area. For classrooms there were to be provided the Methodist, Baptist, and Presbyterian churches, a golf course, several garages and storerooms, the city auditorium, the Fifth Avenue Gown Shop, a theater, and other business houses. There were no recreation facilities other than the resort nightspots plentifully sprinkled among the buildings to be leased.[10]

In her appeal to the Services of Supply, Director Hobby asked instead for any regular Army post, preferably part of Fort Benjamin Harrison, which currently had vacant space.[11] This request was refused by the Services of Supply, the various facilities at Daytona were leased by the Army, and Colonel Faith was ordered to divide his staff and to activate the Second WAAC Training Center on 10 October, with recruits to arrive 1 December.

Both Army and WAAC cadre at Des Moines were divided as equally as possible, and efforts were made to duplicate courses of study, instructional materials, and the operation of staff sections. Over his written protest, Colonel Faith was assigned as commandant of the Second WAAC Training Center, with the promise that he could return to Des Moines in six months. A member of the Des Moines staff was promoted to be commandant at the First WAAC Training Center, but lasted only a few days after planning a series of measures considered discriminatory by the National Association for the Advancement of Colored People. A third

commandant was then selected—Col. John Hoag, Field Artillery, who was to remain at the First and Fifth WAAC Training Centers for the next seven months.[12]

Aircraft Warning Service Units

The first enrolled women to reach the field were those of the Aircraft Warning Service, to which shipment of units began in early September. These units went out complete with officers and formally activated under Tables of Organization for operations and filter companies.[13] Within less than two months, nine operations companies and eighteen filter companies were in the field, located at First Fighter Command stations along the east coast—New York, Norfolk, Boston, Philadelphia, Portland, Albany, Harrisburg, Baltimore, Syracuse, Wilmington, Charleston, Jacksonville, and Miami.[14]

In preparing these units for the field, there became apparent in rapid succession the unexpected problems that these early WAAC field units were to face. Although a number of the units went to northern and eastern stations where winter clothing was already required for men, winter uniforms were not available at the training center, and the first units went

---

[10] (1) Min, Stf Mtg, 24 Aug 42. WAAC Daily Journal. (2) Ltr, Faith to Chief of Mil Hist, 18 May 50. OCMH.

[11] (1) Memo cited n. 8(2). (2) Min, Stf Mtgs, 24 Aug and 29 Sep 42. (3) Rpt, Daytona Beach, WAAC Housing files; (4) Memo, CG SOS for CofEngrs, 30 Nov 42. SPWA 600.1 (7–2–42) sec 1.

[12] (1) Memo, CofS for G–1, 15 Oct 42. WDCSA 291.9. (2) Interv with Actg Dir WAAC who received NAACP in Dir Hobby's absence, 9 Oct 48.

[13] T/O 35–37, WAAC Opns Co, AWS, 4 Jul 42; T/O 35–57, WAAC Filter Co, AWS, 4 Jul 42; Also series of Memos in AG 320.2 (6–15–42)(14) Const and Activ of WAAC Units.

[14] WDBPR Press Release, 26 Nov 42.

out in summer khaki. By October the supply of even this was exhausted, and whole units trained, graduated, and crossed the country by public carrier, costumed only in the short seersucker exercise dresses and bloomers. The long-curious citizens who lined the streets to see a Waac in uniform were reportedly thrown into a state which wavered between panic and hilarity. The problem soon became one of health as well as publicity, as Waacs in short-sleeved seersucker marched to work through the October weather of Maine and Massachusetts.[15]

It had been planned to have WAAC regional directors on hand to complete advance arrangements for the women, but this had not been possible because of the Services of Supply's continued delay in publishing authorization for these positions. In the total absence of published Army Regulations on the subject, the Air Forces' station commanders fended for the women as best they could in the unfamiliar matters of auxiliary supply, finance, and discipline. Luckily, few discharges, promotions, or other personnel actions were yet required. It was supposedly understood that the companies were assigned to the Services of Supply and attached to the Air Forces for duty; it became clear at any rate that the Air Forces were firmly attached to the units.

The women were assigned at once, a few as clerical help in the wing headquarters offices, but the majority to staff the filter boards and operations centers on which they had worked before enlistment. Here they received telephone calls from civilian spotters as to aircraft sighted, plotted the information on the boards, and traced the path of every aircraft to cross the area, for the benefit of liaison officers from the various services who identified

them or sent up interceptors. Some filter boards had as many as fifteen or twenty positions, each filled by a woman wearing headphones and enduring endless boredom while waiting for the scarce telephone calls. Company commanders argued ceaselessly to keep the women assured of the importance of the work, since an unfilled position meant an uncovered area of several square miles into which an enemy plane might penetrate before detection.

The Air Forces soon reported that the boards and centers showed a marked increase in efficiency when freed from reliance upon the uncertain attendance of part-time volunteers. It also appeared that the use of Waacs might be more efficient than the use of soldiers in duties of such a monotonous, sedentary nature. Therefore, the Air Forces announced that Waacs would be requested to staff literally hundreds more Aircraft Warning Service stations to be established on both coasts and eventually inland. Other units were requested for regular air bases, and a new type of company, the WAAC Headquarters Company, AAF, was devised to fit the need. After less than three months' experience with the employment of Waacs, the Air Forces in November approached WAAC Headquarters with a discussion of the possibility of obtaining 540,000 more and of giving them full Army status.[16]

In spite of their efficiency, the units encountered a series of difficulties which em-

---

[15] Unless otherwise specified, statements in this section are from interviews with former Staff Directors, First and Third Service Commands, who had many of the units and who were charged with correcting the conditions described, which had occurred before their arrival.

[16] Memo, CofS for Gen Stratemeyer, 27 Nov 42. WDCSA 291.9.

FILTER BOARD, MITCHEL FIELD, NEW YORK. *The Waacs, wearing head-phones, plotted the path of every aircraft that was called in by civilian aircraft spotters.*

phasized the need for regional directors to get to the field. Problems began when the Air Forces found themselves unable to recruit sufficient local women to fill the enlisted vacancies, although officers had been easily obtainable. To fill out the units, WAAC Headquarters was obliged to divert to the Aircraft Warning Service many women who had been recruited elsewhere for general service, although such women were seldom very happy about loss of the expected work on a military post. Since these nonlocal recruits could not live at home, government quarters had to be hastily provided. No sooner was this action under way than it was found that Army Regulations forbade any

member of a unit to live at home if government quarters were provided. Many local women with husbands and young children had been enlisted on the promise of being able to live at home; the only solution in such cases was to offer immediate honorable discharge, which a number of newly trained women accepted.[17] Enlistment regulations were amended to prevent the acceptance of any more women with dependent children.

Since many of these centers were located in the poorer areas of large cities, the

---

[17] Ltr, WAAC Opns Co, Wilmington, N. C., to Wilmington Air Def Region, 19 Dec 42, and Inds. SPWA 620.

leased hotels sometimes proved to be, in the best phrasing of the matter, third-rate. Women living in such quarters were not only frequently insulted and accosted, but were at times endangered by drunken invaders who pounded on hotel doors or crawled up fire escapes and into windows. At several stations the surrounding slum areas were so dangerous that women were advised not to leave their quarters except in groups. The effect of such housing upon the women themselves was not serious, since they proved far from helpless to meet their own problems. One commander later recalled with pleasure, "When a man climbed the fire escape at the ———— hotel, he was bopped by a Waac at the top."

The effect upon civilian opinion was a different matter; combined with the appearance of the women's clothing, it appeared sufficient to bring the whole WAAC recruiting program to a halt in the cities concerned. Director Hobby eventually besought the Engineers to avoid acquiring WAAC housing previously used for "questionable purposes."[18] In a few cities, hotel accommodations were excellent. In Philadelphia, one of the best hotels was secured for WAAC housing, but was lost at once to the WAVES, since the Navy was able to pay more per enlisted person.[19]

At all stations proper food for the women was frequently lacking, since members had been expected to eat at home and units contained no mess personnel. On moving to government quarters, women were therefore given the Army ration allowance of about $1.25 a day—a sum that might have been adequate in some localities, but was found by those stationed in large cities to be scarcely enough to purchase one nutritious meal in city restaurants.[20]

The impact of enlisted men's opinion was another problem that had not been fully anticipated. One company commander reported:

My women came of good local families, and as civilian volunteers had all been respectfully treated . . . now every man assumed that their uniform gave him the right to insult them. They were actually afraid to ride up in the elevators with the enlisted men because of the language they heard. . . . I went to the commanding officer but he didn't do anything; I heard that the men's actions were only reflections of his private remarks to his staff.[21]

Also, because of the Air Forces' inability to recruit women to staff the stations completely, it was necessary temporarily to retain part of the volunteer civilian workers. Many of these, although for various reasons not desiring to enlist, wished to take part in some form of patriotic activity, and were not pleased at the prospect of being eventually ousted by Waacs. Prominent women in several communities caused Congressional pressure to be placed upon the Air Forces to withdraw the Waacs. Where working groups were mixed, it quickly became clear that Waacs were in no position to compete with "free" labor which could quit at any time. Waacs were almost invariably given the

---

[18] Memo, WAAC Hq for Reqmts Div ASF, 18 Jul 43. SPWA 600.12 (1942).

[19] Passages on AWS, except as otherwise documented, are based on: (1) The WAC Program in the Army Air Forces, by Lt Col Betty Bandel, hereafter cited as AAF WAC Hist. (See Bibliographical Note.) (2) Intervs with WAAC Stf Dirs, 1st and 3d SvCs, and with company officers of Jacksonville, Philadelphia, Charleston, and Norfolk.

[20] Ltr, Stf Dir 1st SvC to Lt Betty Bandel, 2 Dec 42. SPWA 319.2 WAAC Stf Mtg, WAAC Planning files.

[21] Intervs with Maj Caroline Essex, formerly of Norfolk unit, Capt Caroline Varn and Maj Madge Williams, formerly of Jacksonville company, and Maj Mary Anderson, formerly in Charleston and Philadelphia.

graveyard shift, or the least desirable hours, while supervisory positions usually went to civilians and the least interesting work to the Waacs. A few civilian women were as insulting in their remarks as had been the enlisted men.

Under the circumstances, it was considered remarkable that few applications for discharge were received. The women remained in generally high spirits, although expressing considerable indignation against a vague WAAC Headquarters, which they regarded as all-powerful, because of the absence of published regulations, regional directors, necessary supplies, and attention to other obvious needs.

Appeals for Publication of Command Channels

The same months of September and October had seen a final struggle waged in WAAC Headquarters to get WAAC command channels published and WAAC regional directors sent out. In the months since the passage of the WAAC bill in May, the Services of Supply had repeatedly refused to take any such action. Its reasons for this stand were never to be made entirely clear. Only what staff members called "mysterious silence" had met their repeated attempts, throughout the summer, to clarify the power and responsibilities of WAAC Headquarters.

The Director's appeals had begun in July, even before the first Waacs had reached Des Moines. At this time she first began to be apprehensive about the forthcoming winter clothing shortage, as a result of the action of Requirements Division, Services of Supply, in refusing to approve signing of contracts for winter clothing. Although General Marshall himself had personally approved every item on the list, the Services of Supply took issue

with some of his decisions. Appeals from both the Director and The Quartermaster General failed to get approval of contracts until winter was at hand and the September supply scandal unavoidable.

The Director believed this problem to be only one facet of the larger issue: the need for publication of some directive on the powers of her office and its relation to other Services of Supply staff sections. A parallel problem that she cited was the action of The Surgeon General in calling a meeting of civilian doctors, at which the WAAC was not represented, which formulated and came close to announcing to the public a plan for issuance of prophylactics and contraceptives to the women to be enlisted. This plan was suppressed only when Mrs. Hobby went directly to the Deputy Chief of Staff, General McNarney.

In August, after a series of such incidents, the Director appealed in writing to General Marshall to clarify her responsibility in relation to Services of Supply offices, alleging that the current lack of co-ordination was resulting in "serious jeopardy of the military and civilian acceptance of the whole idea of the Corps." [22] She recommended that:

(a) all papers dealing directly and specifically with WAAC matters be routed through the Director WAAC for comment or concurrence.
(b) . . . clarification [be made] as to final authority for decision in cases of non-concurrence. . . .
(c) no meeting of civilian agencies or individuals be called . . . without prior approval of the Director. [23]

General Marshall did not receive the appeal addressed to him. The Services of

---

[22] Memo, Dir WAAC for CofS, 4 Aug 42. Copy (partial) in SGO files, SPMC 322.5–1 (Wash, D.C.)F; Copy in Adm Serv ASF Sp Coll DRB AGO.
[23] *Ibid.*

Supply returned it to Director Hobby in August with the statement that there would be no change in "established practice."[24]

The same reception was given to the Director's request that the Services of Supply approve publication of the WAAC command system with its authorization for regional directors. The necessary circular was prepared by WAAC Headquarters and forwarded for approval in midsummer, but no publication resulted. It was rumored that the Services of Supply was not in accord with either the circular or the WAAC Regulations on which it was based, although previously these had been approved by General Marshall. In August, without notice to WAAC Headquarters, the Services of Supply published a directive that contradicted these regulations. In a section of its new Organization Manual, it gave the commanding generals of service commands the authority, vested in the Director by WAAC Regulations, to transfer and assign WAAC personnel; this action could be taken without reference to WAAC Headquarters. The Manual also, without advance notice, removed the training center at Des Moines from under the Director's command and placed it under the Seventh Service Command.

This publication thoroughly puzzled the Director's staff, since by removing command from the Director it contradicted, but did not rescind, Circular 169 and WAAC Regulations. It came as a surprise to the Air Forces and Signal Corps, who liked SOS control even less than the system of command by WAAC regional directors. The Director's staff appealed to General Grunert for clarification, but was informed only that the Manual meant what it said.[25]

Director Hobby therefore requested her

Army staff officers to explain the situation to her and to formulate some plan of operation that would comply with all directives. The senior staff member, Colonel William Pearson, had just been removed from the office after a dispute with The Adjutant General over the custody of WAAC files, which were also removed from the office, over its protests.[26] The new Executive, Colonel Tasker, stated that he was unable to devise any military method of reconciling the directives, since it appeared impossible for the Director to exercise those remaining portions of her command responsibility concerning discipline, discharge, and promotion while lacking that portion concerning assignment and transfer. Even to locate the women, if they were transferred by other agencies, it would be necessary to go through some four echelons to reach post headquarters companies and possibly seven to reach certain Air Forces units. The time factor rendered this system impossible, since evidently more than a month would elapse before any action could be secured through so many echelons. On the other hand, unless the cases were sent to WAAC Headquarters, it would never be possible to expand the Tentative Regulations, as had been intended, on the basis of experience.

The staff therefore informed the Direc-

---

[24] 1st Ind, SGO for CofAdm Serv, 8 Aug 42, to Memo cited n. 22. SPMCR.

[25] (1) SOS Orgn Manual, Aug 42, sec 405.04. (2) Memo, Dir WAAC for CofAdm Serv, 4 Aug 42. SPWA 300.3 (4–29–42) sec 2. (3) Memo, CofAdm Serv for Dir WAAC, 11 Aug 42. SPWA 300 (8–8–42).

[26] (1) Office Memo, 8 Aug 42. SPWA 300. (2) AGO Memo 111, 7 Aug 42. SPWA 314.7 (6–2–41)(1) sec 3. This states that all file papers on the WAAC, regardless of where prepared, will be sent to file in AGO Civilian Components Branch. Col Pearson had maintained that the WAAC needed its files in the same building for planning purposes.

tor that in coping with current emergencies it was still "violating all the above" by writing and telephoning directly to Colonel Faith. Staff members warned her that she was now in the position, feared since passage of the Rogers bill, of bearing legal responsibility without authority; the Services of Supply had evidently removed not only policy but command powers, while leaving her legally designated as the women's commander.[27]

New Expansion Plans

The WAAC staff's alarm over the Director's position was increased by the fact that, meanwhile, a series of directives from the General Staff had made the June expansion plans obsolete and posed problems of administration that would have been difficult to solve under even the clearest command system.

The first such directive called for overseas shipment. The Director had intended that no units be sent overseas for "the experimental period of a year," since supply and supervision would be proportionately more difficult overseas.[28] However, in August word was received from Europe that General Marshall, on tour, had promised an allotment of Waacs to General Eisenhower. The Joint Chiefs of Staff informed the Director briefly that "Eisenhower's headquarters is badly in need of clerical help and Waacs seem to be the best answer."[29] The Director at once dispatched Major Macy to England to discover how WAAC supply and its vague administration could be stretched so far. As the first few classes graduated at Des Moines, the training center was charged with organizing and equipping two overseas units, and much of the scarce winter equipment so far received was held for

their use in case the momentarily expected shipment call should come from the General Staff. The Director was informed that dozens more overseas units would be wanted shortly.[30]

The problem of expansion overseas paled into insignificance when, on 15 September 1942, G–3 Division dropped a veritable blockbuster on WAAC Headquarters—a directive that immediate steps be taken to plan for an expansion of the Corps to a strength of well over a million members.

As the Chief of Staff had predicted a year earlier, the nation was now in the grip of a manpower shortage. Industry had already turned to womanpower as a supplement; in one aircraft company the employment of women had increased by 2,575 percent.[31] Not to be left behind in the developing competition, G–3 Division stated:

1. Tentative mobilization plans projected through 1946 indicate a necessity for a materially increased use of the Women's Army Auxiliary Corps in the overall structure of the Army.

2. The widespread character of current and projected operations is well known. One major and very serious effect of such a scheme of operations has been to force the design of an Army in which the ratio of personnel in service and overhead installations to personnel in combat units is undesirably high. As the Army further increases in size, it is evident that unless this ratio is reduced, and unless sources other than the able-bodied manpower of this nation are used to provide

---

[27] (1) Min cited n. 10(1). (2) Memo, PRO for Dir WAAC, 9 Sep 42. SPWA 300.4.

[28] Memo, Tasker for Dir WAAC, 21 May 42. Tasker Staybacks.

[29] Memo, Secy JCS for Somervell, 3 Aug 42. Dir Adm Serv ASF, Sp Coll, DRB AGO.

[30] Memo, CofOpns SOS for TAG, 20 Sep 42. SPOPU 320.2 (9–20–42).

[31] "The Margin is Womanpower," *Fortune,* January 1943.

a major portion of this service and overhead, we face a situation where we have mobilized a tremendous force which is strong everywhere except on the battlefield.

3. It is requested that your Division [G–1] cause a study to be initiated to determine all the occupations in the Army which can satisfactorily be filled by members of the WAAC. Such study should contemplate their use at home and abroad in practically every field except the actual handling of weapons. They should constitute the bulk of personnel assigned to overhead installations in the Zone of the Interior. Extensive use in defense command installations appears logical.

4. As a basis for an approach to the solution of the problem, it is recommended that an expansion of the Corps from its present authorized strength to an ultimate strength of 1,500,000 be contemplated.[32]

The earlier June plans for an increase of 500 percent—to an ultimate 63,000 members—were thus obliterated after only three months of existence. Complete new plans were obviously required: new schools, new recruiting quotas, new clothing procurement, and new legislation. Director Hobby was convinced that the new quota could not be filled by voluntary recruiting but would require the drafting of women.[33] Such plans, and such an expansion in size, were clearly impossible without immediate agreement upon, and publication of, a system of command for the WAAC.

General Marshall's Intervention

Simultaneously with the arrival of G–3's directive, General Marshall sent his staff officers to confer with the Director's staff, at which time they learned of the contradictory existing instructions on Corps administration and command.[34] On 17 September the Chief of Staff intervened to direct General Somervell to restore the Director's command powers. Even had

the WAAC been legally subject to military law, General Marshall was of the opinion that it would be dangerous to assume that no new Army-wide policies would have to be set. He stated:

I find that the WAAC has been fitted into the SOS somewhat on the same basis as the Military Police. For a new organization, particularly one composed entirely of women, I think that this is not an effective arrangement. While units assigned to various localities and theaters must come under the local commanders, yet it would seem to be important for some time to maintain a rather direct relationship between the Director and these highly special organizations. There is too much that is entirely new and that demands a woman's point of view to decentralize to the extent that we do with Infantry, Cavalry, and Field Artillery, as well as other special units.[35]

For his guidance in publishing necessary instructions, General Marshall sent General Somervell a copy of the regulations that had been prepared earlier by the Director's staff.

At the same time, General Marshall informed General Somervell that WAAC Headquarters must be furnished with more assistance to carry the new planning load. He noted that Mrs. Hobby looked "rather overworked" and that, while her assistants "are doing a good job," she needed a high-ranking officer with experience and prestige in the War Depart-

---

[32] (1) Memo, G–3 for G–1, 15 Sep 42. WDGCT 291.9 WAAC (9–15–42). (2) Memo, Opns Div SOS for Dir Mil Pers SOS, 19 Sep 43. SPAOG 201, copy in AG 320.2 (6–15–42)(14) Const and Activ of WAAC Units, with Incl G–3 Memo, G–1 paper, and request for study.

[33] WAAC Daily Journal, Vol. I, particularly Min, Mtg, 14 Jan 43.

[34] (1) Memo, Tasker for Dir WAAC, 31 Aug 42, sub: Results of Confs with Col Faith, 29 and 30 Aug 42. SPWA 334.8 Conf (8–21–42). (2) Memo, Tasker for Young, 17 Sep 42. SPWA 300.

[35] Memo, CofS for Somervell, 17 Sep 42. WDCSA 291.9 (9–17–42).

ment "to get things going on the most efficient basis and to relieve her of many time-consuming details and also to obviate many delays." Such an officer, he stated, "might make an important contribution as a sort of military secretary during the formative period of the Corps." [36]

This second portion of the Chief of Staff's instructions was the first on which General Somervell took action. Directing that "immediate action be initiated to assist and aid the WAAC in the execution of its duties," [37] he sent inspectors from his Control Division to repeat the inspection they had just made in August, at which time little had been reported out of place except the furniture. [38] Control Division now noted that "the WAAC occupies an unusual and peculiar position . . . it is both within and without the military framework." However, they vetoed the Chief of Staff's suggestion for a "military secretary" and proposed instead an executive, who would be in the chain of command instead of an adviser, for which "a Regular U.S. Army Officer is essential . . . to guide the Director in Army methods." [39]

General Marshall had called for an officer "conversant with War Department procedure," but such an officer was not found available and the Director was assigned a retired Regular Army officer, Col. Thomas B. Catron, who had not served in the War Department in twelve years. Colonel Catron had, however, thirty-seven years' experience in the Regular Army, and was personally known to General Grunert's deputy, Brig. Gen. Madison Pearson, WAAC Headquarters' immediate superior. [40] The Services of Supply also regrouped the six major divisions of the Director's office into two—Personnel and Operations-Training. Both divisions were to be headed by newly assigned Regular

Army officers since, Control Division noted, "The War Department and the Services of Supply must rely on the data furnished . . . so it should be reliable." [41] WAAC Headquarters' Supply Division was abolished, since "it is apparent that the functions of a supply division are not of sufficient importance to justify a separate division." [42]

General Somervell approved the reorganization pattern, saying, "This is splendid. . . . With General Grunert personally assisting, I think you are on the right track for future progress." [43] Colonel Catron replaced Colonel Tasker as Executive; Colonel Tasker and other senior members of the former staff remained for a few more months, while new Regular Army officers gradually arrived. The junior Army members had already begun to depart as new contingents of WAAC officers reported to take over routine duties. [44]

Under Colonel Catron's direction, the office adopted the motto: "Simplify, Qualify, Consolidate." Colonel Catron also directed that the staff begin to use

---

[36] *Ibid.*

[37] Rpt, Col Betters, Contl Div SOS, 7 Oct 42. SPWA 020 (1943).

[38] Memo, Chief, Contl Div SOS for CofAdm Serv, 1 Aug 42. SPWA 317.7 (6–2–42) sec 3. The Director's Office then had 14 Army officers and 50 civilians. There were four divisions, corresponding to G–1, G–3, G–4, and OPD of a general staff.

[39] Rpt cited n. 37.

[40] Personnel Abstracts, WAC file, OCMH.

[41] There were also three small branches: Office Management, Control and Inspection, and Technical Information.

[42] Rpt cited n. 37.

[43] Memo, CG ASF for Dir WAAC, 7 Oct 42. File SPICY, in Folder, WAC Recruiting, ASF, Sp Coll, DRB AGO.

[44] (1) Intervs with members of the group. (2) Min, 24 Aug, 17 and 21 Sep 42. WAAC Daily Journal. (3) Memo, Macy for Dir WAAC, 24 Sep 42. SPWA 352.0. (4) Mimeographed Tng Program, 11 Sep 42. SPWA 352.0 (8–24–42).

both sides of the stationery, and that they write or wire the training center instead of telephoning.[45] The training center was restored, by General Somervell's direction, to WAAC command, under which it had in fact operated all summer.

Some four weeks elapsed before the publication of the system of WAAC command prescribed by General Marshall. Meanwhile, Director Hobby was not informed that the Chief of Staff had already decided the issue, and her staff continued in some confusion, attempting to devise another system which would be acceptable to General Somervell, for the command of the WAAC units, now already in the field. In one paper the Director offered to use a British system of command, in which the Director retained assignment authority only over company officers and cadre, thus allowing Army commanders to transfer other women, yet insuring that transfer would not be made to stations where barracks and cadre were not located. When this suggestion received no response, she proposed an alternate command system wherein she would gradually give up all command power to commanding generals of service commands, provided that they refrained from exercising this power until civilian auxiliary rules could be published on the basis of cases sent directly to WAAC Headquarters.[46] This proposal also received no reply. The Director begged General Grunert's office for some published system, stating, "If the War Department and the public are to hold the Director of the WAAC responsible for the proper administration of the Corps, the proper authority to accompany this responsibility is a natural and automatic requirement."[47]

By the second week in October, there were already a dozen Aircraft Warning Service companies in the field and some two hundred officers in recruiting stations and Army specialist schools. On 11 October General McNarney, General Marshall's Deputy, sent a second message to General Somervell:

On a recent trip to the West Coast, including a stop at Des Moines, I gained the distinct impression that there exists no basic plan or schedule for the use of the WAAC. At two stations, Randolph Field and Fort Huachuca, they had been informed that they would receive WAAC companies, but they seemed very hazy as to the trades, skills, qualifications to be expected, where they should and could be used, together with a distinct lack of any indication that the use of Waacs should result in a nearly corresponding decrease in the number of men assigned to an activity. Station commanders scheduled to receive Waacs should be furnished, without delay, sufficient information to permit effective utilization, and directives for a corresponding decrease in men assigned. . . .[48]

It was not until 13 October 1942 that the Services of Supply published an explanatory statement to the field—Circular 344, the second important War Department publication in WAAC history. The circular at last made WAAC command channels clear to the field, although the channels themselves were complicated.

---

[45] Min, Stf Conf, 27 Oct 42.

[46] (1) Memo, Civ Components Br AGO for AG WAAC, 18 Jul 42, and reply, 10 Aug 42, office notes atchd. WA 300.3 (4–29–42) sec 2. (2) Memo, Tasker for Dir WAAC, 5 Oct 42. SPWA 314.7 (6–2–41)(1) sec 3. (3) WAAC Cirs 4 (10 Jul 42), 13 (14 Oct 42), and 16 (11 Dec 42). Cases are cited in Memo, Dir WAAC for CofAdm Serv, 3 Oct 42. SPWA 300 (10–3–42).

[47] (1) Memo cited n. 8(2). (2) Memo, WAAC Hq for CofAdm Serv, 29 Sep 42. SPWA 300.3 (4–29–42) sec 2. (3) Memo cited n. 46(3). (4) These were all recalled on 5 October 1942, when the Director first learned of General Marshall's action, by Memo, Dir WAAC for Contl Div SOS, 5 Oct 42, sub: Revision of WD Cir 169. SPWA 300.3 (4–29–42).

[48] Memo cited n. 5.

Three sets of channels were required in order to maintain the Corps' legal auxiliary status while allowing it to work for, and be supplied by, the Army.

Job performance was rated through the same normal channels of command as for soldiers and civilians at a station, and so offered no problems or causes of complaint from any station—Air Forces, Signal Corps, service command, or other. *Supply and routine post administration* were also the responsibility of the post commander, just as they were for men. However, above post level only service command stations could follow normal channels of supply, since WAAC clothing was stocked only at a few service command depots. Non-service command stations had to follow unfamiliar channels of requisitioning through the service command to get WAAC supplies. Finally, in *personnel matters,* the short WAAC command channel would operate, from the WAAC company commander to the WAAC regional director to Director Hobby. Personnel channels were specifically defined as including the disputed right of assignment and transfer, as well as promotion, discipline, and discharge, plus "all policies involving the welfare of members of the WAAC which, by virtue of the fact that they are women, differ from those prescribed for men."

Assignment of Regional Directors

Upon the moment of publication of Circular 344, nine WAAC regional directors departed for their posts in a race to remedy the Corps' field situation. These nine women had been chosen in early October and brought into WAAC Headquarters for assignment to the nine service commands as soon as the Services of Supply published authority for them. Of necessity

the choice was made in ignorance of military aptitude although, as Director Hobby later noted, "Every one [service commander] said, 'You must put your very best officer on this.' " [49] The women chosen were all required to be over 35 years of age. They included two former business administration supervisors, a college teacher and a dean of women, a sales director, a government executive, a lawyer, and a housewife. In spite of the haste, the selection proved generally good, and included four women who were later to play a leading part in world-wide WAC administration—Third Officers Katherine R. Goodwin of the First Service Command, Jessie P. Rice of the Third, Westray B. Boyce of the Fourth, and Mary-Agnes Brown of the Eighth.[50]

The ten-day indoctrination of these women in WAAC Headquarters understandably proved something of a farce. Detailed auxiliary regulations and guides to WAAC needs had not yet been worked out, and could not be until more Waacs reached the field and until the regional directors themselves discovered their needs. Members of the group related that Colonel Catron told them, "No one can tell you what to do, because there's never been a job like this. No one knows what you're going to encounter when you get there." [51]

Circular 344 gave the job a difficult dual status: when handling matters pertaining to the "Personnel Channel" the regional director was responsible only to Director Hobby and signed herself "Director's Representative" (later, "WAAC Service Command Director"); but in all

---

[49] Speech at WAAC Stf Dirs Conf, 15–17 Jun 43. SPWA 337 (6–1–43).
[50] WDBPR Press Release, 28 Oct 42.
[51] Related to author by Lt. Col. Jessie P. Rice and other members of the group.

other matters such as supply she was only a staff adviser to the commanding general of the service command and could take action only through military channels, signing herself "Chief, WAAC Branch." [52] The latter position was roughly comparable to that of service command special staff officers such as the surgeon, finance officer, or quartermaster. However, these officers were chiefly colonels and were expected to be experts in one field only, while the Waac was a second lieutenant and was supposed to be an adviser in all fields—health, supply, housing, personnel, discipline, finance, public relations, and all others. If there were no WAAC Regulations to cover a situation, she must determine whether Army Regulations could legally apply, or whether it would be necessary to recommend new WAAC Regulations. In addition to her work in headquarters, she must visit every service command station where Waacs were assigned or expected, as a traveling trouble shooter to resolve difficulties and promote efficiency. She was also responsible for the command and well-being of Waacs at airfields, ports, Signal Corps stations, and all other exempted activities within the service command, most of which were already bristling at the thought of control through alien channels.

Because of the alarming responsibilities of the positions, some thought was given to the possibility of promoting all service command directors at once to the rank that was allotted to the position: assistant director or lieutenant colonel. After much debate, Director Hobby decided to postpone promotions until each woman's efficiency on the job was proven. However, Acting Director Helen H. Woods some days later secured permission to send an explanatory letter to each commanding general, noting: "We were conscious of the fact that we were sending out second lieutenants to the field to break ground, and to confer with major generals concerning their relative command powers." [53]

Only one major policy was fully impressed upon the regional directors before their departure: they must as far as possible act as if the Corps were a part of the Army; they must demonstrate that women needed no extra frills and comforts such as Army commanders might feel a gallant desire to provide. [54]

Field Action

The initial reception accorded these women upon their arrival at service commands varied from "all the co-operation a person could ask or need" down through various degrees of lesser warmth to "standoffish." [55] One fact became abundantly clear the moment each staff officer reported, and that was that most of the service commands—in fact, eight of the nine—had no intention whatever of complying with War Department Circular 344 insofar as it pertained to a WAAC command channel. Said one director, "When I arrived at this station and was presented to the Commanding General, he informed me, with some emphasis, that he was in charge of the Service Command and did not propose to tolerate any dual channels; that my loyalty was to him and to no one else." Others told much the same story.

---

[52] AGO Memo S635, 4 Dec 45. SPWA 314.7 (6–2–41) sec 3.

[53] Interv with Mrs. Woods, 9 Oct 48.

[54] Undated Draft of Dir WAAC speech to SvC mtg, Dec 42, in personal papers of Col Rice.

[55] Ltrs from SvC Dir, 30 Nov–9 Dec 42. SPWA 319.2 (12–2–42) WAAC Stf Mtg, WAAC Planning files.

LT. COL. HELEN H. WOODS (*then Third Officer*).

The four service command directors on the Atlantic seaboard plunged at once into the work of aiding the Aircraft Warning Service units to obtain supplies, warm uniforms, three meals a day, and safer quarters, as well as of providing a legal means for the personnel actions that began to be necessary. Particular difficulty was experienced in persuading non-service command stations to permit such efforts. Some measure of success was eventually obtained. For example, after repeated telephone calls and correspondence had failed to convince the Norfolk Air Defense Wing, Third Officer Jessie P. Rice of the Third Service Command paid a personal visit and reported a "long and pleasant" conversation with the commanding officer, during which he alleged that he had never seen War Department Circular 344, but

agreed to abide by it and WAAC Regulations in the future.[56]

In stations at which units had not yet arrived, service command directors set themselves to prevent the hardships and poor publicity that unpreparedness had brought to the Aircraft Warning Service units. One surviving memorandum on "How to Visit the Field" offered strenuous advice:

1. Visit the commanding officer and explain the WAAC's status.

2. Visit the quartermaster and check with him methods of requisitioning WAAC uniforms and other supplies and equipment peculiar to females; where stocked, and so on.

3. Visit the post engineer and verify safety and proper construction of WAAC barracks, including plumbing, fire escapes, shades, and distance from men's barracks.

4. Visit the post surgeon and arrange for separate sick call and separate wards for women, different medical supplies, and the like.

5. Visit the finance officer and explain how the Auxiliary is paid.

6. Visit the post exchange officer and suggest toilet articles, sanitary supplies and other items to be stocked for women purchasers.

7. Visit the athletic and recreation officer and arrange for recreation suitable for women, and for admission to post theater, service club, and other activities.

8. Visit the provost marshal and discuss the Auxiliary disciplinary system and its wide difference from the Army system, the power of military police over Waacs, and related matters.

---

[56] (1) Ltr, Stf Dir 3d SvC to 3d O Betty Bandel, 1 Dec 42. SPWA 319.12. (2) Ltr, Stf Dir 3d SvC to Dir WAAC, 1 Jan 43, sub: Rpt on Trip to Norfolk, Va., 27 Dec 42. Same file.

9. Visit the post chaplain and discuss the special problems of a woman's adjustment to the Army.

10. Visit the post adjutant and advise that WAAC officers be allowed to use the officers' mess and club, and discuss other matters of administration.

11. Visit any other staff officers who might have special problems caused by the arrival of female personnel, such as the public relations officer, or those who might employ Waacs, such as the signal officer.[57]

Director Overseas

A few days before the regional directors went out, Director Hobby was obliged to entrust their further indoctrination and guidance to her staff, having received orders to accompany Mrs. Eleanor Roosevelt on an observation tour of the British women's services. Third Officer Helen Woods was left as Acting Director. On 19 October the Director and her aide, Third Officer Bandel, left for the British Isles, not to return until 11 November.[58]

At this time it appeared that the Corps was in fair condition to meet the strain of the oncoming expansion. As a result of General McNarney's intervention to expedite WAAC supply, every Waac at Fort Des Moines at last had a winter uniform and an overcoat, and supplies had been forwarded to those women who had left the training center without uniforms. As for the Second WAAC Training Center at Daytona Beach, a full conference of Services of Supply agencies assured Director Hobby before her departure that all necessary supplies and uniforms would reach it before the 1 December opening date. Also encouraging was the office's move to the newly completed Pentagon, where co-ordination with other Army offices was greatly simplified.[59]

The expansion program that had been mastered was, however, merely that which had originated in June. Still to be reckoned with was G–3's September plan for 1,500,000 Waacs.

---

[57] Table V–2, Vol. Gen Information, WAAC Hist files.

[58] Memo cited n. 5.

[59] (1) Min, Stf Conf, 27 Oct 42. (2) Weekly Rpt, WAAC Hq for CofAdm Serv, 1–7 Nov 42. SPWA 319.12. (3) Admin Memo 56, Hq SOS, 14 Oct 42. SPWA 310.2.

CHAPTER V

November 1942–January 1943: Plans for a Million Waacs

While Director Hobby was overseas, the necessary steps were taken by the Services of Supply to carry out the September expansion plan. To verify G–3's estimate of a need for 1,500,000 Waacs, The Adjutant General's Office was asked to make a list of all the Army jobs suitable for women. A committee of classification experts at once began the project, the most comprehensive study ever made of the outer limits to which replacement of men in the United States Army could theoretically be pushed.

The Adjutant General's Estimates

After pondering over each of the 628 military occupations listed by the Army, The Adjutant General's committee came to the conclusion that 406 were suitable for women and only 222 unsuitable. A job was deemed unsuitable if it involved combat, if it required considerable physical strength, or if the working conditions or environment were improper for women. Jobs requiring long training time were also eliminated. Typical of the jobs ruled unsuitable were brake inspector and railway operator (too heavy and requiring too much training time), switchboard installer (too heavy), laborer (too heavy), intelligence specialties (improper environment),

and so on. All supervisory jobs were automatically declared unsuitable for women. The committee likewise, after some disagreement, ruled that for psychological reasons women should not be used in such jobs as classification specialist, personnel consultant, or psychological assistant, since in these jobs they might be called upon to classify recruits for combat duty, and it was felt that men would resent being classified as suitable for combat by individuals who were themselves noncombatants. The committee nevertheless admitted that, in an acute manpower shortage, women could actually be used in many of the 222 jobs thus ruled unsuitable.

The Adjutant General, using these lists, determined that in 1943 there would be 3,972,498 men in Army jobs appropriate for women—over half of the Army's strength at that date. In the interests of caution, this number was reduced to allow for the fact that some jobs, although of a suitable type, might be rendered unsuitable by their location or for some other reason. For instance, it would not be economical to maintain women at small stations where only a few could be used; it would not be wise to replace all of the supply clerks at any station, since work too heavy for women might occasionally occur; women could not conveniently do the office work in men's units. With such deductions, it was decided that women could fill 450,000 of the Army's 665,256 administrative and clerical jobs; 100,000 of the 834,600 motor transport jobs; 25,000 of the 121,000 radio operators' positions; 30,000 of 96,755 supply jobs. The total of women who could be used immediately was 750,000, and by the end of 1943 it was estimated that at least 1,323,400 could be used. Thus it was discovered that G–3 Division had, if anything, been conservative in estimating that 1,500,000 Waacs could be used by 1946.[1]

Estimates Based on Field Requisitions

Simultaneously with its request for The Adjutant General's theoretical estimates, the Services of Supply conducted a field survey to provide a practical check on the numbers usable by the Army. On 22 October, a few days after Director Hobby's departure, the Services of Supply informed its subordinate commands that further use of Waacs was contemplated, and asked for recommendations as to which jobs under their jurisdiction could be filled by WAAC personnel.[2]

Requisitions prompted by this letter were soon pouring into WAAC Headquarters, increasing those already arriving as a result of the earlier June expansion plans. They were listed in order of receipt, except for urgent cases, and forwarded for final approval in turn to the Chief of Administrative Services, the Chief of Operations, and G–3 Division of the War Department.

In order to determine which requests merited final approval, it was necessary to devise a number of new policies concerning the types of work and places of em-

ployment which would be authorized for Waacs. The number and variety of the requests went far beyond the four simple types of jobs originally authorized. The Air Forces requested Waacs for some thirty-one different technical and mechanical duties; the Signal Corps, Transportation Corps, Corps of Engineers, Ordnance Department, Chemical Warfare Service, and other agencies listed dozens of new types of work, many of which could not be filled by women except after Army technical training. There were also requests for new types of companies: Machine Records Units, Finance Department Companies, Base Post Offices, Mess Companies, and others for which no WAAC Table of Organization as yet existed. There were many requests for Waacs to replace civilians: as clerks in post exchanges, as laundresses, and in other non-Civil Service work. Several commands wanted mobile units for combat theaters, and the Signal Corps wanted these units mixed, with men and women in the same company.[3]

As a guide for determining which of these requests to honor, a most important policy had been recommended by Director Hobby before her departure: that Waacs not be allowed to replace civilians and that they be considered only for the 406 Army jobs included in The Adjutant

---

[1] (1) Memo, Classif & Repl Br AGO for Col Catron, 31 Oct 42; (2) Rpt, Classif & Repl Br AGO for WAAC Hqs, 25 Nov 42. SPWA 201.6 (10–2–42) (1) secs 1, 2.

[2] Memo, TAG for Chiefs of Servs SOS, 22 Oct 42. SPX 320.2 (10–17–42) PR–W–SPAAE. Also AGO Memo W635–2–42, 22 Oct 42.

[3] (1) Min of Stf Confs, Aug–Nov 42. Folder, Stf Confs, Hobby files. (2) Memo, MPD SOS for G–1, 4 Nov 42. SPGAM 320.2 WAAC (9–15–42). (3) Ltr, FA Sch to Dir WAAC, 25 Sep 42, and reply. AGF 320.2 WAAC, Binder 1, DRB AGO.

General's study. The Director stated that she had understood from the beginning that Waacs were to replace only enlisted men, except in the Aircraft Warning Service. General Grunert disagreed, recommending that stations be allowed to use Waacs in civilian jobs that they could not get civilians to accept.[4] G–1 Division upheld the Director, and the policy was established that *"First priority will be given to requests which result in WAAC personnel relieving enlisted men of the Army for combat duty."*[5] This was a policy of enormous importance to the Corps' entire future employment.

It was also decided that first priority was to be given to fixed installations in the United States and second priority to fixed installations in foreign theaters of operations. Mobile units were not, however, ruled out of consideration at some future date when all other needs were filled.[6]

No requests for Waacs to perform new or unusual military duties were disapproved, but it was obvious that actual provision of Waacs for such work would depend upon the establishment of new training schools and of types of units other than the standard Table of Organization company. Research was authorized to find some more flexible means of allotment which would permit Finance, Hospital, Mess, and other units.

The number of Waacs that could be used was greatly limited by a decision not to employ them in Washington, D. C., where as much as one third of the Navy women were eventually to be employed. This prohibition had originally applied to the Services of Supply only, having been announced by General Somervell at a staff meeting as an off-the-record policy for his Chiefs of Services, one of whom accidentally recorded it:

Our policy can be only the policy that he has announced to us. That policy he particularly does not want committed to writing, because the minute that anybody gets ahold of it and puts it in the paper, there will be a mess. This is the policy . . . he does not want any of them here, except in the Office of the Headquarters of the WAAC, and certain ones in G–2, whom for some reason they prevailed upon him to have. Do you get it? We don't want anything said about it.[7]

However, a few weeks later, when it became clear that the War Department and the Air Forces were planning to bring Waacs into their headquarters, General Somervell recommended the policy in writing to the Chief of Staff, "in order that field agencies may have full benefit of the services of members of the WAAC." This policy was approved by the Chief of Staff and put into effect, with exceptions to be granted only by his own office for important secret work.[8] It was also generally agreeable to WAAC Headquarters, since assignments to Washington were not popular with enlisted women who wished to work on a military post. However, the policy caused added confusion in current planning, since agencies such as the Signal Corps, which had attempted to get WAAC officers to aid in planning for enlisted

[4] Memo, Dir WAAC for CofAdm Serv, 16 Sep 42, and Inds. SPWA 320.2 (9–5–42).

[5] D/F, G–1 to Dir WAAC through Adm Serv SOS, 1 Oct 42. AG/WDGAP 212.31 WAAC; 1st Ind, 2 Oct 42, Adm Serv SOS for Dir WAAC. SPAAE 320 (9–16–42).

[6] Memo cited n. 2.

[7] Tp Conv, Col H. L. P. King and Brig Gen James A. Code, Jr., OCSigO, 25 Sep 42, 11:05 A. M. SigC 320.2 WAC, 1942–45.

[8] (1) Memo, Somervell for CofS, 4 Oct 42, with approval 7 Oct 42. CofS 291.9. Also AGO Memo W635–1–42, 12 Oct 42. (2) Memo, Opns WAAC for CofAdm Serv, 28 Oct 42. SPWA 320.2 (10–28–42) O, in Dir Adm Serv ASF Sp Coll DRB AGO. (3) Memo, G–1 for CG AAF, 9 Dec 42. WDGAP 320.2 WAAC (12–9–42), in WDCSA 291.9 WAAC.

women, were obliged to relinquish them when informed that, "by order of General Somervell, no WAAC officers will be placed on duty in the space occupied by the Office of the Chief Signal Officer." [9]

Even with the various limitations, the results of the field survey generally upheld The Adjutant General's estimates. It was difficult to make an exact calculation of the constantly shifting requests, but the total, which had been 63,000 in midsummer and about 82,000 at the beginning of October, jumped to 386,267 toward the end of November and to 526,423 in December. These figures included only "actual requests . . . based on present tentative plans as to how and where Waacs can be used." [10] Thus, if more than 500,000 women could be assigned immediately, before overseas theaters and many other commands were heard from, it was clear that the G–3 estimate of 1,500,000 by 1946 had not been in excess of probable field requirements.

Proposals To Draft Women

Considerable change in planners' thinking resulted from the somewhat amazing revelation that, in a modern Army, possibly half of all "soldiers' " jobs were appropriate for women. With little natural limit thus existing upon the use of womanpower, major decisions were clearly required as to the Army's future policy: the number of women that it would attempt to employ in World War II, the rate at which it would take these, and the means by which it would attempt to get them.

The first and easiest solution to occur to most planners was that of drafting women. Although Director Hobby was not available for consultation, the Services of Supply on 4 November 1942 recommended

to the War Department that, in furtherance of G–3's plans, legislation be sought to draft some 500,000 women yearly through regular induction facilities. According to SOS estimates, there were 25,605,179 women of ages 20 through 44 in the United States, of whom about 13,000,000 should be available for the war effort. Even if the WAAC required the present maximum Adjutant General's estimate of 1,300,000, this would constitute only 10 percent of the pool, leaving 90 percent for industry, farm, and other armed services. In recommending that the Army draft women, the Services of Supply noted:

The nation is obligated to see that women will be placed to best advantage, not only from the standpoint of economical use, but to avoid any disastrous aftermath due to misplacement in the war effort, or by the employment of women who have definite obligation in other fields. . . . It is to the advantage of the nation that the best use be made of this pool of labor, and it certainly should not be frittered away in useless competition between competing agencies in our country. [11]

Unfortunately for the speed of WAAC planning, this proposal was so serious as to require extended War Department consideration and high-level negotiation with other agencies. It was realized that any such proposal from the Army would provoke considerable public outcry and Congressional opposition, and therefore could

---

[9] R&W Sheet, Col King to Aux C Sec through Deputy Chief and Exec Off, 24 Nov 42. SigC 320.2 WAC, 1942–45.

[10] (1) Memo, Dir WAAC for CofAdm Serv, 28 Sep 42. SPWA 291.9 (9–28–42) E, in SPWA 314.7 (6–2–41) sec 3. (2) Outline for speech "Role of the WAAC in the Service Command," December 1942; given to author by Lt Col Jess Rice.

[11] Stf Study, Dir Mil Pers SOS for G–1, 4 Nov 42. SPGAM 320.2 WAAC (9–15–42).

be publicly made, if at all, only with the full co-ordination of the sponsoring agencies. For this reason, as the winter of 1942 continued, no War Department reply as to the possibility of drafting women was received by either General Somervell or WAAC Headquarters.

The Weakness of the Auxiliary System

A second possibility which presented itself to planners was that of seeking legislation to give Waacs full military status. If a draft was later to be sought, such status was essential; even if it was not sought, there was already considerable evidence that no greatly expanded employment of womanpower was possible on an Auxiliary status.

In particular, it became clear during the autumn that most plans for overseas service must be canceled if the Auxiliary status continued. This was a serious blow, for the whole idea of the Corps had originally been thought of by the War Department as a means of preventing the confusion of civilian overseas service that occurred in World War I. During her visit to England, Director Hobby received from Lt. Gen. Dwight D. Eisenhower a request for immediate shipment of the two overseas companies then in training and for quick organization of a number of others. She also discovered—at that time top secret information—that the invasion of North Africa was imminent and that it was General Eisenhower's intent to take Waacs with him.

Director Hobby returned to the United States on 11 November, much impressed by the need for Waacs in General Eisenhower's headquarters, where she had observed a colonel typing a letter by the one-finger method. However, after con-

ferring with her staff about current Comptroller General and Judge Advocate General decisions on the WAAC's legal status, her enthusiasm abated. It had recently been decided that Waacs were not eligible for the various benefits that protected men overseas—they could not, like the men, receive extra overseas pay; they were not eligible for government life insurance as men were, and would probably invalidate their civilian insurance by entering a war area; if sick or wounded they would not be entitled to veterans' hospitalization; if they were killed their parents could not collect the death gratuity; if captured by the enemy they could be treated as the enemy pleased instead of being entitled to the rights of prisoners of war. Under the circumstances, it appeared impossible for the Army to assume the responsibility of ordering women overseas; nor did the military situation yet require it, as the Director pointed out to the Chief of Staff:

One of the primary reasons for the establishment of the WAAC was to replace men. Until necessity dictates otherwise, conditions in the theaters of operation indicate replacement in the United States.

The Army classification system should be able to find among men the skills needed by the Army in the European Theater of Operations. Members of the WAAC can thus properly replace men found in the United States and release them for essential Army service overseas. . . .[12]

General Marshall therefore somewhat reluctantly postponed any consideration of immediate shipment overseas except for the two all-volunteer units already trained, saying: "They do not enjoy the same privileges that members of the Army do who

---

[12] Memo, Dir WAAC for CofS, 14 Nov 42. SPWA 320.2 sec 1.

become a prey to the hazards of ocean transport or bombing." [13]

In addition to negating plans for overseas shipment, it appeared possible that continued Auxiliary status would cause a rift with the Army Air Forces, which had been expected to employ more than 500,-000 of the projected million-plus Waacs. Shortly after the Director's return from Europe, representatives of the Air Forces informed her that they could not employ Waacs on an Auxiliary status and would prefer to seek legislation for their own corps. General Marshall temporarily squelched this effort with a note to the Air Forces on 27 November:

I believe Colonel Moore this morning took up with Mrs. Hobby the question of her attitude toward a separate women's organization for the Air Corps. I don't like the tone of this at all. I want to be told why they cannot train these women, why the present legal auxiliary status prevents such training. [14]

The attitude of the Signal Corps and other employing agencies continued to be very similar to that of the AAF.

It also began to appear that the Army would have difficulty in obtaining any large corps of women on an Auxiliary status in competition with the newly organized WAVES, who could offer women all military benefits—free mailing, government insurance, allotments to dependents, reinstatement rights to jobs, veterans' bonuses, and other advantages, none of which the Waacs were entitled to.

However, the granting of full Army status to women still appeared to many Army men as a drastic step, particularly in view of the fact that only a few units had as yet left the training centers. In late November it was finally decided to delay decision on both draft legislation and on Army status for the WAAC. The head of

the Army's Legislative and Liaison Division, Brig. Gen. Wilton B. Persons, advised the General Council to postpone consideration of further legislation of any sort "until the Waacs have taken the field and demonstrated their usability." [15]

A few days later, Director Hobby submitted a substitute proposal believed to be more palatable to Congress: that of merely registering women in order to obtain accurate knowledge of the manpower potential of the nation according to numbers, skills, and other data. This recommendation was also approved by General Somervell and sent to the Chief of Staff on the first anniversary of Pearl Harbor.[16] However, it also was known to have small chance of immediate approval.

Proposals for Expansion on Auxiliary Status

There remained to planners the least desirable of the possible means of Corps expansion: to attempt to undertake G–3's directed program by voluntary recruiting and on an Auxiliary basis. A certain amount of action could be taken under existing legislation. It was therefore decided that, as a preliminary measure, the full 25,000 authorized by executive order should if possible be enrolled by the end of December 1942 instead of by the following June. Next, the Secretary of War petitioned the President to change the executive limitation from 25,000 to the full 150,000 authorized by Congress. The

[13] Memo, CofS for G–1, 3 Dec 42. CofS 291.9 WAAC.

[14] Memo, "G.C.M." for Gen Stratemeyer, 27 Nov 42. WDCSA 291.9 (11–27–42). Reference is to Col. Aubrey Moore, head of AAF's Allocations and Programs Division.

[15] Min, Gen Council, 23 Nov 42.

[16] Memo, Dir WAAC for CG SOS, 26 Nov 42. SPWA 324.71 (11–26–42) D, and Ind. Folder, WAC Recruiting, ASF Sp Coll DRB AGO.

President agreed and on 19 November 1942 raised the WAAC strength limit to 150,000. The Secretary of War indicated that the 150,000 women would be enrolled as fast as training facilities permitted, after which further legislation would probably be recommended.[17]

Meanwhile, recruiting quotas were opened as wide as training capacity would permit. From a beginning of 1,259 in July and 2,019 in August, the number of reported recruits had increased to 3,536 in September. In October and November, as Des Moines neared its maximum capacity, slightly over 4,000 women a month were enrolled. For December, estimated training capacity permitted advance quotas of approximately 6,000.[18]

In order to determine how fast the rest of the 150,000 could be enrolled, the General Staff called upon WAAC Headquarters for estimates as to the recruiting and training facilities that would be required to train 150,000 women by various possible dates, as well as greater numbers by later dates. The two WAAC training centers' combined peak capacity would plainly be insufficient to supply such numbers except over a period of years. The General Staff's desire was to take as many women as possible as rapidly as possible, since Army jobs were already waiting and since applicants might accept other war work if required to wait. Against this desire had to be balanced the practical question of where to get basic and specialist schools, of which the Army currently had none to spare. Compilation of a list of suitable schools was begun. It was also necessary to work out large flow charts to govern intake and output of proposed training centers and specialist schools, so that on a given date each would simultaneously produce exactly the required

number of basics and specialists to make up exactly the number of WAAC companies departing for the field on that day, and for whom exactly the right amounts of housing and clothing were ready. Such charts had to be worked out for every possible total strength that the War Department desired to consider for every possible date.[19]

Opinions differed widely as to how quickly the WAAC should attempt to reach the 150,000 mark. Maj. Gen. Miller G. White, the new G–1 of the War Department, recommended to the General Staff in November that the Corps reach this number by July 1943—a deadline that would require at least 20,000 recruits a month for the intervening months, as well as several new training centers. An even more optimistic recommendation came from the new head of WAAC Headquarters' Recruiting Section, Capt. Harold A. Edlund, who advised a target of 50,000 a month, or 750,000 in 1943. Captain Edlund stated: "It may be that the goal outlined will appear to some as outside the realm of reason or possibility . . . but the reaching of a more modest goal is doubly assured if we bend every effort for the greater enrollment figure." On the contrary, General Surles, chief of the War Department Bureau of Public Relations, gave his opinion that not even 150,000

[17] (1) Ltr, SW to Bur of Budget, 12 Nov 42. WDGAP 320 WAAC (11–7–42), in WDCSA 291.9 WAAC. (2) Exec Order 9274, 19 Nov 42, in WD Bull 58, 28 Nov 42.

[18] (1) Weekly Rpt, WAAC Hq to CofAdm Serv, 8–16 Nov 42. SPWA 319.12 (11–9–42) sec 1. (2) Memo cited n. 10(1). (3) Table III, ASF Hist of WAC Tng. OCMH. (4) Although not reported fully at the time, actual nationwide enrollments as finally credited by The Adjutant General were: 1,259, July; 2,019, August; and 3,536, September.

[19] (1) Min, Stf Mtgs, 25 Sep, 6 Oct 42. (2) Flow Charts, WAAC Planning files, 1943.

could be obtained, and added: "We have about exhausted that group of women who are willing to volunteer to leave their homes." [20] This was also Director Hobby's opinion; after her return from Europe she expressed the opinion that not even 150,000 women could be recruited by voluntary means. [21]

The somewhat unfortunate effect of this division of opinion was that, for the remainder of 1942, the War Department was no more communicative upon the subject of WAAC 1943 goals than it had been upon the questions of legislation. As a staff member later observed:

> The Corps was placed in the position of a small businessman who overnight was told he must increase his business more than eight times, and to do it at once even before he knew what he was to produce, out of what materials, when or how the product was to be made, and with practically no organization to assist. [22]

The Winter Months

While it was realized that major decisions concerning womanpower could not be made easily in these, the darkest months of the war, their absence caused continued confusion in the new headquarters. At the same time, developments in the two training centers gave grounds for grave doubt as to whether any sort of expansion program could be supported.

In the second week of November, just before Director Hobby's return from England, urgent telegrams were received from the commandant at Fort Des Moines, pointing out that clothing shipments had again failed just as recruits were increased. The improvement caused by General McNarney's intervention in October had lasted scarcely a month.

Immediate investigation by WAAC Headquarters drew an alarming reply from The Quartermaster General: clothing promised to Fort Des Moines could not be delivered as scheduled. Also, no clothing could be sent to Daytona Beach by its opening date, as previously agreed by the Services of Supply. The Quartermaster General stated that his previous commitments had been contingent upon immediate letting of contracts and, for unexplained reasons, Requirements Division, Services of Supply, had again held up approval of the contracts for more than six weeks. [23]

On 11 November Director Hobby returned from England to find a recurrence of the September crisis at Des Moines: hundreds of recruits without winter clothing, and sickness rates again high. Colonel Hoag reported the entire supply of clothing now exhausted except for a little summer-weight underwear. The civilian clothing in which recruits arrived was far from adequate protection for four weeks of winter training in snow-covered Fort Des Moines. Most women had been instructed to bring only one outfit, and this, particularly in the case of women from the southern and southwestern states, frequently included nothing warmer than a dress, a light topcoat, and open-toed shoes.

[20] (1) Memo, CofS SOS for CofAdm Serv, 26 Nov 42. SPEX, in SPAA 320.2 WAAC, CofAdm Serv file, Sp Coll DRB AGO. (2) Surles statement in Min, Gen Council, 23 Nov 42. (3) Memo, Capt Edlund, Chief, WAAC Rctg Sec, for Dir WAAC, 22 Dec 42. Folder, Memos Prior to 7 Jan 43 in WAAC Planning, WAAC Planning files.

[21] Min of Speech, 31 Mar 43. SPWA 334.8 Conf, 1943.

[22] Miss B. Eugenia Lies, Civilian Consultant to Dir WAAC, The Overall WAAC Picture, (first draft), 28 Mar 43. Folder, Planning Serv Notes, WAAC Planning files, 1943 in SPWA 291.9.

[23] Weekly Rpts, WAAC Hq to CofAdm Serv, 1–7 Nov and 8–16 Nov 42. SPWA 319.12 (10–19–42) and (11–9–42) sec 1.

Units were now being shipped to the Aircraft Warning Service in the same civilian clothing in which the women had reported for training. It was known that trainees had written of these conditions to friends and relatives.[24]

Director Hobby's attempts at remedial action were somewhat delayed by the fact that, upon her return, she was immediately ordered to Fort Leavenworth, Kansas, to lecture to the Command and General Staff School on the proper administration of Waacs. She had brought back from England much valuable material on this subject, none of which had any effect on the situation. The fact was that the American WAAC was helplessly repeating every one of the British WAAC's mistakes, not because the WAAC did not know them and how to avoid them, but because their occurrence hinged on outside factors over which it had no control.[25] Nevertheless, three days after her return from England, the Director called in the two training center commandants, Colonels Faith and Hoag, for a meeting with Colonel Catron, Colonel Tasker, and herself. Here, in a stormy session, Colonel Faith alleged that the Services of Supply were neglecting the Waacs because they were not military personnel. He had particular reference to his experiences in trying to open the Second Training Center; for example:

Colonel Faith: I feel it is the function of this department [WAAC Headquarters] to get the War Department to understand that the Waacs are soldiers. It looks like I am going to have to open a training center at Daytona without anything. . . . I am not going to lie down because I do not have clothing, but I do sense the feeling that the War Department believes they have an Army, and some Waacs. . . .

Colonel Catron: No, the War Department feels that the Waacs ought to have what they need, but the clothing is not available. . . .

I do not believe there is a tendency to say there is an Army and some Waacs; not in the Services of Supply. . . .

Lt. Colonel Tasker: I think there was that condition. . . .

[Colonel Faith goes on to describe how The Services of Supply refused him other equipment normally furnished to Army schools.]

Director Hobby: . . . Let me straighten out the position of this headquarters. You are given a job to do and a time schedule to do it on, and when your equipment does not come through I want to know about it. I will say another thing: you will find a lot of people with a bureaucratic frame of mind that would kill anything new unless you fought for it. It is my job to fight for it.[26]

A number of events therefore occurred on 21 November. On that day the Director stopped all further shipments of uniformless units to the Aircraft Warning Service. She simultaneously directed recruiters to warn recruits to bring enough warm civilian clothing to last for several months. She also requested and received from her Army staff a report on the action they had taken to date. This report showed not only that all Services of Supply staff divisions had concurred before expansion plans had been put into effect, but also that the Quartermaster General's Office had been informed by telephone in June and again in September as soon as WAAC Headquarters had itself learned of the plans. With this report in her office, and also General Madison Pearson, she therefore telephoned General Somervell's Chief of Staff, Maj. Gen. Wilhelm D. Styer.[27]

---

[24] (1) *Ibid.,* and Rpt of 15–21 Nov 42. (2) Account in the possession of Capt. Charlotte Dyer, made available to the author, 31 January 1946.

[25] Folder of British materials in 1942 WAAC files.

[26] Min, Tng Cen Comdts Conf, 14 Nov 42. Folder, Stf Confs, Hobby files.

[27] (1) Ltr, WAAC Hq to all SvCs, 21 Nov 42. SPWA 421 (11–19–42). Also Rpt, 15–21 Nov 42, cited n. 24(1). (2) Memo, Tasker for Dir WAAC, 21 Nov 42. WA 421 (11–20–42).

What was said was not recorded, but observers reported that it was sufficient to bring General Styer down the hall to WAAC Headquarters. Staff members were under the impression that Director Hobby mentioned that her own resignation would be necessary if the Services of Supply did not intend to give the WAAC the equipment for survival in the coming winter. In any event, General Styer was found to be not in agreement with the previous management of the WAAC supply program by his subordinates, which he attempted to correct by personal telephone calls on the spot. Emergency procurement of any available kind of cold-weather garments was authorized.[28]

The situation at Daytona Beach also was found to be critical. Before Director Hobby's return, a meeting had been held in General Grunert's office to consider whether to cancel the scheduled opening of the second training center, since it could not be supplied with uniforms. Lieutenant Woods personally made the decision that the Army's stated needs must be met, in spite of the inconveniences to trainees. The Second WAAC Training Center therefore opened on 1 December 1942 as scheduled. It was virtually without equipment; shoes had been sent, and 600 utility coats—scarcely enough for one week's trainees.[29]

Colonel Faith forwarded requests for improvement in the scattered housing and other facilities at Daytona Beach. A British report brought back by Director Hobby noted that to house women in scattered billets usually damaged health, administration, and the "amenities," and that "for young recruits undergoing basic training it is generally very unsuitable." [30] It was obvious that Waacs in Daytona Beach must either do without recreation or attend civilian night spots of doubtful respectability. Since a tent camp was being built

to house some 6,000 of the trainees, Director Hobby asked in early December that it include the recreational facilities normally provided for an Army camp of 6,000 men—one theater, one service club, one library, and one post exchange. However, the Chief of Engineers objected on the grounds that critical building material would have been required, and the request was rejected by Requirements Division, Services of Supply. Colonel Faith also believed the commercial laundry facilities inadequate, but his requests for military supplements were refused by the Services of Supply.[31]

Colonel Faith's most serious concern, however, was not the lack of material facilities so much as the difficulty in getting competent Army cadre to augment the staff, which remained inadequate even after the original Army cadre was divided and the newly graduated Waacs assigned to all possible duties.[32] The greatest need was for highly competent key Army offi-

---

[28] (1) Interv with Col Woods, 9 Oct 48. (2) Rpt, 15–21 Nov 42, cited n. 24(1). (3) Memo, ACofS, Opns Div SOS, for QMG, 27 Nov 42. SPDDQ 420 Clothing, in SPWA 421 (11–27–42) 1942. (4) 1st Ind, Reqmts Div SOS to QMG, 3 Dec 42. SPRMD 421 (11–26–42), in WA 400.34.

[29] (1) Memo, OQMG for CG SOS, 10 Nov 42, with 1st Ind, 13 Nov 42. SPQXA 420 WAAC, in SPWA 400.34 (3–2–42) sec 1. (2) Ltr, WAAC Hq to Ft Des Moines, 19 Nov 42; and Ltr, WAAC Hq to 2d Tng Cen, 20 Nov 42. SPWA 421.

[30] *Conditions in the Three Women's Services.*

[31] (1) Memo, WAAC Hq for Chief, Reqmts Div SOS, 17 Dec 42; refused by 1st Ind, 6 Jan 43. WA 600.1 (1942). (2) Memo, WAAC Hq for OQMG, 2 Nov 42, and Inds. WA 486.3.

[32] Waacs were made chiefs of sections (Motor Transport, Officers Candidate, Basic, and Administrative) on 6 February 1943 at Fort Des Moines; dates for other centers not preserved. On 23 April 1943 at Fort Des Moines, Waacs became commanders of training regiments, chiefs of training sections, mess officers, public relations officers, and the like. On 24 April 1943 Waacs were designated Chief of Plans and Training, Assistant Commandant, and Chief Public Relations Officer at Fort Des Moines. MS Hist of 1st WAAC Tng Cen.

cers. The Director's requests for certain individuals by name had been refused, and General Grunert informed her that the WAAC would be assigned only officers unfit for duty with male troops. At the November commandants' meeting, Colonel Faith and Colonel Catron came to open dispute over this decision, with Colonel Faith stating: "I absolutely refuse any reduction in the quality of material. We cannot go any lower. We cannot allow any more culls. . . . I don't want a one of them. I cannot make it any stronger." To this Colonel Catron replied, "You will find lots of good material in the over troop age group. I think you are going to have to take it." Director Hobby added, "My own limited service in the War Department has taught me that it is difficult to get quality for the WAAC. It seems to be against the theory." [33]

The seriousness of the objections to the Daytona site was not to become fully evident for several months, but it was sufficiently clear to Director Hobby, when she saw the center for the first time in December, to cause her to demand that the already scheduled Third WAAC Training Center be located on an Army post. Accordingly, she requested assignment of Fort Oglethorpe, Georgia, just outside of Chattanooga, Tennessee. Fort Oglethorpe was in a central location, which would make it convenient to draw trainees from most of the United States; it was also in a temperate climate. Nonconcurrences on its use for Waacs were offered by the Provost Marshal General, who maintained an internment camp there, and by the Commanding General, Army Ground Forces, one of whose mechanized regiments would also be forced to move. These objections were overridden by the Chief of Staff himself and Fort Oglethorpe was designated

the Third WAAC Training Center. Col. Hobart Brown was selected to command it, and its activation date was set for 1 January 1943, with recruits to report in February. [34]

In order to co-ordinate the work of the three training centers and the others that might be expected, it was decided to group them into a WAAC Training Command, which would form an intermediate echelon between the training centers and WAAC Headquarters. [35] Colonel Faith was chosen to command the new agency, and was promoted to the rank of brigadier general—an action that created a somewhat peculiar military situation, since the head of the WAAC Training Command was himself immediately under the command of Director Hobby, who wore colonel's eagles. Nevertheless, the rank of brigadier general was obviously quite modest for the commander of three large posts. General Grunert accordingly proposed that action be taken to change the Director's relative rank to that of brigadier general, and the Director immediately asked that equal rank be given Colonel Catron. General Somervell shelved both proposals and directed that no action be taken, pending decision on his proposal to draft women, which would necessarily place the WAAC in the Army. If the Corps should be given Army status, its Director and regional directors would become staff advisers instead of commanders, and an upward adjustment of

---

[33] Min, Stf Conf, 14 Nov 42. Folder, Stf Confs, Hobby files.

[34] (1) Memo, G-3 for CofS, 15 Dec 42. WDGCT 291.2 WAAC (12-8-42), in OCS 291.9 WAAC. (2) Weekly Rpts, WAAC Hq for CofAdm Serv, 7-12 Dec and 14-19 Dec 42. SPWA 319.12 (11-9-42) sec 1.

[35] Request for establishment approved 17 Nov 42 by CofAdm Serv, according to notes for speech, "Role of WAAC in the SvC."

BRIG. GEN. DON C. FAITH *shortly after his promotion and assignment to command the WAAC Training Command.*

the allotted grades of female leaders as the Corps expanded would not be obligatory.[36]

Shipment of the First Post Headquarters Companies

For some time disgruntled station commanders had complained about the repeated postponement of arrival dates originally given them for WAAC post headquarters companies. Many, ignorant of the fact that all available Waacs had gone to staff the Daytona Beach training center, began to repeat the rumor that the Corps was a failure and would never materialize in the field. One WAAC service command director noted, "I spent most of my time apologizing to my General for the peculiar behavior of WAAC Headquarters."[37]

The necessity for staffing the Third

WAAC Training Center with cadre again set back the shipment schedule of post headquarters companies. By Christmas of 1942 only two Army stations had received their promised shipment—Fort Sam Houston, Texas, and Fort Huachuca, Arizona.[38] These units went out well equipped with winter uniforms at the expense of those remaining in training centers, in compliance with the Director's ban on shipment in civilian clothing. They were also more fortunate than the pioneer Aircraft Warning Service companies, in that careful preparations had been made for them by the WAAC service command directors.

The women as a whole were consumed with eagerness to reach genuine Army stations, and both morale and discipline were good. Mrs. Woods noted later, "In spite of the difficulties topside, the spirit of the women was remarkable, especially the fervor with which they accepted all sorts of unexplained difficulties. There sprang up among them an unexcelled *esprit de corps*." [39]

The arrival of the first Waacs at Fort Sam Houston on 17 December was described by a WAAC spectator, who wrote:

The consensus of opinion at Fort Sam Houston was that it would be unfair and unwise to parade a company upon the day of its arrival by troop train. In fact the remark was made: "They will not make a good impression while disheveled." You would have been

---

[36] (1) Memo, ACofS Pers Div SOS for CofAdm Serv, 23 Jan 43, SPAP 322.5 WAAC (1–18–43), ref to Memo, CofAdm Serv for Gen Dalton, 13 Jan 43; (2) Memo, Dir WAAC for MPD SOS, 14 Jan 43, and Inds, SPWA 210. All in ASF Sp Coll DRB AGO.

[37] Intervs with Stf Dirs, 1st and 3d SvCs.

[38] Date of shipment given as 2 Dec 42 for Ft Huachuca units, in MS Hist of 1st WAAC Tng Cen; WDBPR Press Release, 19 Dec 43, gives 15 Dec as date of shipment and 17 Dec as date of arrival.

[39] Interv with Mrs. Woods, 9 Oct 48.

proud, however, if you had been standing there when they got off the train—their noses were powdered, their shoes were shined, they showed that they were well-trained and well-disciplined. Before the last ones had got off the train, the cannon was fired for retreat. Like one woman they came to attention and saluted. . . . The salutes so impressed the photographers that they stopped taking pictures and faced the flag. . . . I am sorry that no pictures were taken at that time.[40]

The other unit, composed of Negro enrolled women with Negro officers, was likewise well received at Fort Huachuca, and housed in new barracks with hairdressing facilities, recreation room, and athletic area. Upon arrival the women found their bunks already made up and their first meal prepared.[41]

Shipment of post headquarters companies to the seven other service commands was postponed indefinitely to permit the opening of new training centers, but the defrauded commands set up such protest that certain exceptions had to be made. Just before Christmas Director Hobby called a meeting at New Orleans of WAAC directors from the service commands, to explain the situation and to point out that delay at this stage would result in tremendously greater supply when all training centers came into full production. Nevertheless, all appealed so earnestly for at least one unit per command that Director Hobby promised to send it, as token to the service commands that Waacs really did exist. This was done, and during the last of December 1942 companies were placed on orders for shipment to stations in the remaining seven service commands. Very little could yet be told of what their assignments or job performance would be, although WAAC Headquarters eagerly awaited such news.[42]

In December also two experimental

antiaircraft units reached the field, their "secret" station being actually Bolling Field, within sight of the Pentagon. The Antiaircraft Artillery, as directed by General Marshall, began the task of determining which of its duties could be performed by women and with what degree of success.[43]

First Overseas Shipment

Considerably more complications attended efforts to get the first two units overseas in December. These units had been ready for shipment since September, and were by this date trained to a hairtrigger state of tension while waiting for a shipment priority from England, which had not arrived. To ease the crowding at Des Moines, they were shipped to Daytona Beach, as soon as its cadre arrived, for another period of training.[44] Their morale was scarcely improved by the constant turnover of officers. Since no one yet knew what qualities a women leader needed, there was a process of trial and error by which several officers were successively relieved from duty because of in-

[40] Ltr, Lt Charlee Kelly, Rctg Off, to Capt Mary-Agnes Brown, WAAC Stf Dir 8th SvC, as quoted in Ltr, Capt Brown to Dir WAAC, 9 Jan 43. SPWA 319.1.

[41] (1) Ft Huachuca file, SPWA 291.21. For difficulties experienced by the first Negro Wac units, see Ch. XXX, below. (2) WAAC Daily Journal, Vol. I, 30 Jan 43.

[42] (1) Notes of Dir's speech to CGs of SvCs, New Orleans, La., 17–18 Dec 42. SPWA 334.8 Conf (11–18–42). (2) Weekly Rpts, WAAC Hq for CofAdm Serv, 14–19 Dec 42 and 27 Dec 42–1 Jan 43. SPWA 319.12 (1942).

[43] AG Ltr, WD 320.2 WAAC (12–23–42) PR–W–WPOPU, 24 Dec 42, sub: Activation of 150th and 151st WAAC Tech Cos, and 1st Ind from MDW, 17 May 43. AG 320.2 WAAC (5–10–43).

[44] Ltr, WAAC Hq to Comdt 2d WAAC Tng Cen, 31 Oct 42, sub: 75th and 76th Cos, and two Inds. SPWA 320.2 sec 1.

ON THE JOB AT FORT SAM HOUSTON, TEXAS. *Motor pool attendant, above; dental assistant in the post dental school, below.*

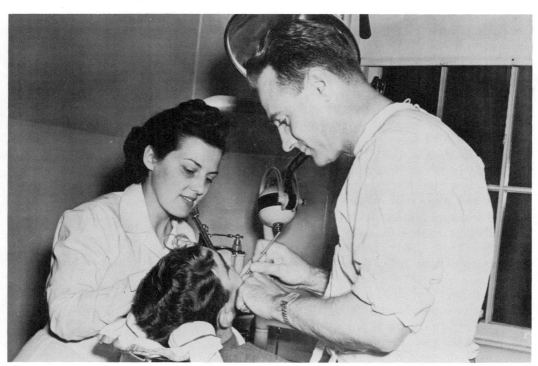

sufficient experience, lack of outstanding ability, or domineering traits and a habit of "treating adult women like high school freshmen." [45]

The prolonged delay could not be explained to the women, since even their destination, like all troop movements, was classified; in general, they attributed it to vacillation and bungling in WAAC Headquarters. Actually, shipment waited upon authority from the European theater, which had requested activation of the units but had not yet furnished shipment priority. At the same time, Operations Division of the General Staff informed WAAC Headquarters that shipment without a priority was impossible because of the shipping jams resulting from the invasion of North Africa in November. [46]

Disbandment of the units was being considered when, a few days after the invasion, General Eisenhower cabled for a company of WAAC typists and telephone operators for North Africa, and provided a high shipment priority. However, although the units earmarked for London contained the necessary specialists, Director Hobby felt unable to assume the responsibility of ordering them into the more active North African area without the protection of military status.

The danger was graphically demonstrated a few days later when, in answer to a cabled request from the European theater setting high air priority, the first five of the Waacs were flown to England—five officers qualified to act as executive secretaries. These officers were immediately placed by the theater on a ship for North Africa; General Eisenhower had in fact cabled for them on the fifth day of invasion. Nearing the coast, the ship carrying the Waacs was sunk by enemy action, with loss of all equipment. The five Waacs

were fortunate enough to be rescued by a lifeboat and a British destroyer, but the scare was sufficient to emphasize the War Department's untenable position had the issue of hospitalization, capture, or death gratuity arisen publicly.

At this, Director Hobby herself flew to Daytona Beach and told the assembled women that their shipment must be either canceled or diverted to an unnamed but dangerous combat theater to which she would not order them against their wishes. She noted later that she reminded them of their lack of military status and its protection and "that I wanted them to appreciate the full significance of what I was saying." Then, in a speech which spectators called reminiscent of another Texan's at the Alamo, she called for volunteers to step forward to fill the unit. There were 300 women in the room, of whom 298 volunteered upon the instant. At this, Director Hobby was unable to continue speaking and hastily sought privacy in a broom closet. [47]

Half of this number were chosen, processed, and ordered to the staging area in December. The remainder were held until the European theater had three times more postponed its shipping priority, when they were disbanded and sent to other duties. [48]

[45] Documents dated 23 Oct 42 and 27 Nov 42. SPWA 320.2 sec 1.

[46] (1) D/F, OPD to G-1, 24 Nov 42. OPD 322.999 WAAC (11-14-42); (2) Cbls, London to AGWAR, 4416, 3 Nov 42, London to WAR, 5057, 19 Nov 42, and London to AGWAR, 5445, 4 Dec 42. All in SPWA 320.2 secs 1 and 4a.

[47] The two nonvolunteers had invalid parents. (1) Senate Com on Mil Affairs, 78th Cong, 1st sess, *Hearings on S 495*, 3 Feb 43. (2) Interv with Col Bandel.

[48] (1) Hist of WAAC–WAC in ETO, 1942–44, by Hist Sec, ETO. (Hereafter cited as ETO WAC Hist.) OCMH. (2) Ltr, WAAC Hq to Col Abbott, Hq ETO. 27 Jan 43. SPWA 320.2 sec 2.

FIRST AMERICAN WAACS EN ROUTE TO NORTH AFRICA. (*Photograph was taken in London, 30 November 1942.*)

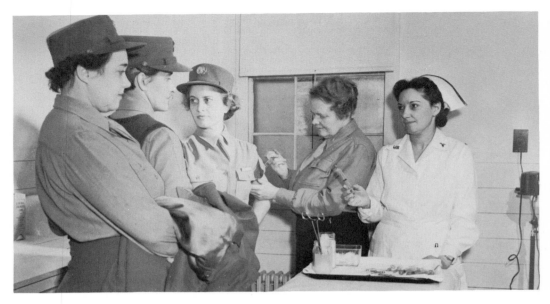

PROCESSING FOR OVERSEAS. *Members of the first WAAC unit to go overseas receive their immunization shots, above, and are inspected by the WAAC director, below.*

PROCESSING FOR OVERSEAS. *Waacs give each other a lift to waiting trucks, above, and, below, are helped over the rail and onto the ship's deck.*

End of 1942

Thus, by the end of 1942, the WAAC could boast two training centers open and a third being readied, twenty-seven Aircraft Warning Service units, nine service command companies shipped or ready to ship, two secret units with the Antiaircraft Artillery, and one on its way overseas. In late December Director Hobby reminded her staff that, in spite of the uncertainties and hardships of rapid expansion, "Our six months' achievement is really something to boast about." [49] Whereas she had originally promised the War Department 12,000 Waacs by July of 1943, the Corps had achieved that strength by December of 1942, with 12,767 enrolled. The year had witnessed a complete revolution in military thinking on the use of womanpower: in January, 12,000 Waacs had seemed too many; but in December, 1,200,000 seemed too few. [50]

The WAAC's first Christmas brought added praise from the Chief of Staff, in the name of the Army, for the Corps' spirit and contributions. [51] At Christmas also, anticipating the greater effort that would be required by the impending General Staff decision, the Director telegraphed her staff, "May God bless you and give you strength for the task ahead." [52]

Indecision as to Planning Goals

Strength of some sort was needed, for by January of 1943, planners feared that the WAAC could not survive unless the General Staff's decision as to its size and future status came quickly. It had now been almost five months since G-3 had called for 1,500,000 Waacs without setting definite goals. When these were not an-

nounced by the beginning of 1943, it was necessary to set an interim recruiting quota for January of about 10,000, based on existing training capacity. Reports indicated that this was being met, and that training centers were seriously overcrowded, yet by all evidence the Corps was still far from approaching the peak of General Staff expectations. It was learned informally that it was the General Staff's intent to authorize at once still another training center, the fourth. Again field shipment schedules were outdated and previous plans held up. [53]

At a meeting on 6 January, staff officers noted that, until it was known how big the Corps would be and how many new training centers would be required, it was impossible to set up shipping schedules or to tell Army stations when Waacs would arrive. The Quartermaster General and the Chief of Engineers were frantic for estimates on clothing and housing requirements which could not be given them. [54] Neither was it possible to publish detailed discharge and other regulations—to remove the burden of cases still coming to the office—since the Judge Advocate General desired to wait for a decision on the Corps' future status. [55] Staff members, in-

[49] Note on Memo, Mrs. Knight for Dir WAAC, 2 Dec 42. SPWA 300.6 (3–30–42) sec 2.
[50] M/R, Stf Conf, 6 Jan 43. Folder, Memos Prior to 7 Jan 43 in WAAC Planning, WAAC Planning files.
[51] Ltr, CofS to Mrs. Hobby, 19 Dec 42, in CofS personal file, made available to author in December 1945 by his secretary.
[52] Telg, Dir WAAC to Stf, 24 Dec 42. SPWA 335.15.
[53] Memo, Tasker for Exec WAAC, 1 Feb 43. SPWA 600.914 (2–1–43).
[54] Comment 2, WAAC Hq to CofAdm Serv, 5 Dec 42, to Memo, Dir Reqmts Div SOS for CofAdm Serv, 26 Nov 42. SPRMP 291.9 WAAC, DRB AGO.
[55] (1) ETO WAC Hist. (2) Ltr, WAAC Hq to Col Oscar B. Abbott, Hq ETO, 27 Jan 43. SPWA 320.2 sec 2.

terviewed later, commented, "No one seemed to know what he was doing." One of the ablest of the early staff members, Colonel Tasker, who had been replaced as Executive by Colonel Catron, now gave up in despair and transferred to the General Staff in spite of Director Hobby's protest that "his knowledge concerning the creation and growth of this activity is such that his reassignment would be a very real loss." [56] Similarly, First Officer Helen Woods, the first woman to serve as Acting Director, applied for transfer to a regional directorship as far from Washington as possible.[57]

By the end of the year it was obvious that the October office reorganization directed by General Somervell's inspectors was a failure, and Colonel Catron again reorganized the headquarters. Previous divisions were abolished and two new main halves were set up—Operating and Planning. It was thus hoped that the daily crises and emergencies of operation could be kept from disturbing the calmer atmosphere necessary to finely calculated schemes and schedules, while at the same time action on urgent field needs would not be delayed because staff members were busy preparing estimates for the General Staff. The Planning Service was headed for a few weeks by Colonel Tasker and later by a new arrival, Lt. Col. Robert F. Branch; the Operating Service was headed by another new arrival, Col. Howard F. Clark, a regular Army officer of many years' experience. For the more technical aspects of personnel planning and statistics, a civilian woman consultant, Miss B. Eugenia Lies, was also employed. The employment of a civilian appeared to be the Director's first move to overcome the rigid channelization which

prevented her contact with junior staff members, since Miss Lies was given authority to ignore all office channels in securing information for the Director.[58]

This reorganization also was a failure almost from the beginning. Colonel Branch soon recommended that his large Planning Service be dissolved, saying, "It is a good deal like having a Diesel engine connected with a sewing machine." [59] With Planning and Operating Divisions both the same size and considering the same subjects, it proved virtually impossible for planners not to operate, or for operators not to plan; overlapping and disagreement resulted. Also, as Colonel Branch pointed out, it was useless for the WAAC to make any plans at all in the face of its dependence on other un-co-operative or dilatory agencies. He said:

The opportunity scarcely exists for original or creative planning, since the problems of the Corps have been principally composed of situations after the fact. Action is therefore remedial in nature and choices are limited. Congressional action, War Department policy, and the attitude of other agencies are limitations which, regardless of their propriety or necessity, reduce the scope of planning work.[60]

Many badly needed improvements, which were never made or which were delayed, were ordered by Director Hobby during this period. Finer adjustments and accurate research were to be impossible until

[56] Personnel Abstracts. WAC files, OCMH.
[57] AAF Western Flying Tng Comd, Santa Ana, Calif.
[58] Memo, Plng Serv for Dir WAAC, 18 Mar 43, sub: Progress Rpt, 16 Feb–15 Mar 43. SPWA 319.1.
[59] Memo, Chief, WAAC Plng Serv, for Dir WAAC, 10 Apr 43. SPWA 020.
[60] Memo, Chief, WAAC Plng Serv for Dir WAAC, 15 Apr 43, sub: Progress Rpt, 16 Mar–15 Apr 43. SPWA 600.914.

a solution could be found to the basic problems of survival.[61]

By the end of January, when no directives were forthcoming from the General Staff, the WAAC planners, milling about helplessly among their schedules and flow charts, were in dispair. The office's Daily Journal for 1 February indicated: "Director asked General Grunert to obtain from the General Staff a definitive directive governing recruitment, training, and use of Waacs, particularly within remainder of fiscal year." As a result, General Grunert's office wrote the General Staff asking a quick decision on: "(1) how many Waacs we are to recruit and train by July, (2) where we can get training capacity, and (3) how we are to slow down recruiting if we do not [get the above]." [62]

---

[61] (1) WAAC Office Memo, 23 Feb 43. SPWA 300.6 (3–30–42) sec 2. (2) Folder, Stf Confs (1942), and WAAC Daily Journal, Vol. I (1943), in Hobby files. See also list of 24 Planning Service projects in WAAC Planning files, 1942.

[62] WAAC Daily Journal, dates cited.

CHAPTER VI

The Need for Military Status

The delay in the decision to launch the expansion program was partially attributable to debate on a controversial matter: whether to give full Army status and rank to women. The War Department's decision in this matter was never to be fully understood by many outside its planning group, representing as it did a complete reversal of the opinion of the previous year. For those inside the War Department, and for many station commanders employing WAAC companies, there actually was no room for question in the matter: the General Staff in fact was obliged to make the decision to grant Army status before it could authorize the expansion program. The evidence at hand overwhelmingly indicated that no great employment of woman power was even remotely possible under the Auxiliary system.

Administrative Handicaps of an Auxiliary

Almost from the moment the first Waacs reached them, Army field agencies had begun to bombard WAAC Headquarters with questions concerning which Army administrative procedures were applicable to the WAAC and which were illegal. This had once been considered a simple matter; it was now discovered that in almost all legal and technical matters it was far from simple, and that the problem was far more than that of dispensing information.

The questions were such that it was frequently necessary to consult authorities ranging as high as the Secretary of War, the Comptroller General, and the Bureau of the Budget before a legal answer might be obtained.

Thus, on the universal question of whether Waacs might use the franking privilege when mailing their letters, The Adjutant General ruled that Waacs were "persons in the military service" for this purpose, but the Judge Advocate General ruled that they were not, and the privilege was rescinded after being widely used—a situation that distressed Waacs and caused many to realize for the first time that they were not soldiers or members of the military team.[1] As time passed, almost no two authorities agreed upon the occasions when Waacs could be considered "persons in the military service." To permit WAAC units to shop at post exchanges and share dividends, the Secretary of War was forced to declare them persons in the military service.[2] On the other hand, General Grunert, the Judge Advocate General, and the Veterans' Administration united to overrule Director Hobby's request for Na-

---

[1] (1) Memo, WAAC Hq for TAG, 21 May 42, and Ind. Published in WAAC Cir 2, 6 Jun 42. (2) Ltr, Postmaster Gen to SW, 17 Aug 42, and atchd decisions. WAAC Cir 9, 16 Sep 42, rescinded Cir 2.

[2] Ltr, Tng Cen to Dir WAAC, 31 Jul 42, and Inds. SPWA 331.3 (7–31–42). AR 30–2290 amended 24 Oct 42.

tional Service Life Insurance for Waacs, declaring:

Such persons are not in the active service in the land or naval forces of the United States. . . . The WAAC as constituted under existing law is essentially a civilian group. The principle upon which war risk insurance is founded . . . has no application to those in civilian occupations.

G–1 Division believed this decision unfair, and attempted to process new legislation, but this was vetoed by the Bureau of the Budget.[3]

Likewise, the Judge Advocate General, General Grunert, and the Comptroller General agreed that Waacs were not "persons in the military service" for purposes of making allotments under the Servicemen's Dependents Allowance Act, nor could they even allot money from their own pay, since the act granted this privilege only to "members of the Army, Army Nurse Corps, contract surgeons, and civilians overseas." [4] On the other hand, Congress itself indicated that Waacs were "persons in the military service" under the Soldiers and Sailors Relief Act, so that The Adjutant General was able to issue Certificates of Military Service to protect members from litigation.[5] As for re-employment rights, Congress indicated that Waacs who left Civil Service jobs had soldiers' rights to reinstatement, but that those who left other jobs had not. When queried concerning state bonuses and other state benefits, The Judge Advocate General decided that each state would have to determine for itself whether Waacs were "persons in the military service" as interpreted by its laws.[6] In some matters of finance, the Chief of Finance ruled that Waacs were "members of the military forces of the United States," but the Chief of Transportation was unable to find similar authority to pay for mileage or for transportation of dependents.[7]

Such administrative annoyances were endless and apparently would continue to be so while the WAAC remained an auxiliary. It was necessary to refuse Army station commanders' requests to award Waacs the Good Conduct Medal, to issue them the command's sleeve patch, to appoint them as warrant officers; even the chaplains were obliged to secure a special amendment before they could give each Waac a free New Testament.[8] The final

[3] (1) Ltr, WAAC Tng Cen to WAAC Hq, 19 Jun 42, and Inds; (2) Memo, Dir WAAC for Adm Serv SOS, 14 Jul 42, WA 291.9; (3) D/F, CofAdm Serv to WAAC Hq 29 Jul 42, SPAAS 243 (7–6–42); (4) Ltr, VA to SW, 21 Jul 42; (5) Min, Gen Council, 28 Jul 42; (6) Ltr, Bur of Budget to SW, 1 Oct 42, and incl ltr, AG 291.9 (6–2–41). All in SPWA 314.7 (6–2–41)(1) sec 4.

[4] (1) TWX, WAAC Tng Cen to Dir WAAC, 3 Jul 42; (2) Memo, Dir WAAC for Adm Serv SOS, 6 Jul 42, with Ind, SPJGA 354.01; (3) WAAC Cir 4, 10 Jul 42; (4) Memo cited n. 30(3); (5) Ltr, Compt Gen to SW, 6 Aug 42, B–27558; (6) WAAC Cir 7, 29 Aug 42; (7) Min, Gen Council, 28 Jul 42; (8) Decision, JAG to CofAdm Serv, 4 Aug 42, SPJGA 354.01, 2d Ind. All in SPWA 314.7 (6–2–41)(1) sec 4.

[5] Memo, JAG for CofAdm Serv, 6 Aug 42. SPJGA 354.01, in WA 014.3.

[6] (1) Ltr, State of N. J. to TAG, 11 Jul 42, and reply; (2) Ltr, Los Angeles to JAG, 5 Oct 42; (3) Ltr, Induction Station, Portland, Ore., to Hq 9th SvC, 19 Apr 43; (4) Ltr, Pittsburgh to WAAC, 17 Oct 42, and Ind, SPJGA 354.01, in SPWA 315.7 (8–2–41)(1) sec 4. All in SPWA 230.57 (6–15–42).

[7] (1) 2d Ind, CofFin to San Antonio Avn Cadet Cen, 8 Dec 42. SPWA 012.33. (2) Memo, TC for Dir WAAC through CofFin, 4 Sep 42. SPTOT 531.2 (AR 30–925), in SPWA 300.3 (4–29–42) sec 2.

[8] (1) Memo, WAAC Hq for G–1, 24 May 43, sub: Good Conduct Medal. SPWA 200.6. Eventually granted. (2) Memo, Dir WAAC for CofAdm Serv, 21 Apr 43. SPWA 400.34 (3–21–42)(1) sec 3. T/E amended to permit sleeve patches. (3) Ltr, Ft Oglethorpe to O Dir WAAC, 8 Jul 43, sub: Appointment of Bandleaders as WOs, and Inds. SPWA 211 (11–13–43). (4) Ltr, Dir WAAC to CofChaplains, 20 Jul 43. SPWA 300.5, 1943. (5) Compilation for ready reference to all points made by 3d Officer Bernice Keplinger, WAAC Hq, 23 Nov 42. SPWA 314.8 (6–2–41)(1) sec 4.

word came from The Quartermaster General, who ruled that Waacs were not eligible for burial with a flag, military honors, or an escort to accompany the remains home. After conducting a Waac's funeral, an indignant American Legion post protested: "It would probably interest you to know that, at this particular Waac's funeral, she was given full military honors regardless of what her status is, even though she has passed on into another world." To this a harassed War Department made no reply, probably believing that it was difficult enough to determine a Waac's status in the present world without pursuing the matter further.[9]

There were minor points without number in which Waacs did not receive all of a soldier's privileges. Under the new military pay scale, the WAVES were able to offer recruits $50 a month, whereas, the Auxiliary legislation limited the WAAC to $21 a month. A particularly serious discrepancy was the matter of disability benefits and retirement. Soldiers and Waves who suffered disabling injuries or illnesses were entitled to lifetime pensions and hospitalization, but Waacs, under the Federal Employees' Compensation Act, were entitled only to a few dollars' compensation. Under the law, the Army could give a Waac hospitalization only until her disability was pronounced permanent, at which time she must be discharged and ordered to leave the military reservation. She had no right to a pension or to veterans' hospitalization.[10]

The Auxiliary Disciplinary System

Even had these lesser administrative difficulties not existed, there was another, important enough in itself to have invalidated the Auxiliary system, and not capable of solution by any course short of full Army status; this was the question of establishing a legally sound and equitable WAAC disciplinary system.

It had been known since passage of the legislation that Waacs, like other civilians, could not legally be made subject to court-martial and to the Articles of War unless they were "in the field." This was not even a matter of discretion; no citizen of the United States could legally be tried by military courts unless he had military status or unless he accompanied an army in the field. When not "in the field," the WAAC had its own code of conduct, which was extremely strict but which was limited to civilian punishments for infractions—fines, reprimands, restrictions, or discharge (white or blue); it could not legally subject members to court-martial, imprisonment, or dishonorable (yellow) discharge.[11]

During the autumn of 1943, Judge Advocate General decisions began to make it clear that Waacs could almost never be considered "in the field" unless they were overseas or in the unlikely event that they should accompany an army on maneuvers.[12] One station commander did actually try a Waac by court-martial on the grounds that his station on the Eastern seaboard was subject to attack and therefore "in the field," but by the time the

---

[9] Ltr, OQMG to 6th SvC, 21 Dec 42; also Ltr, N. J. American Legion Post 16 to WAAC Hq. SPWA 293 (12–10–42).

[10] Senate Com on Mil Affairs, 78 Cong, 1st sess, *Hearings on S 495*, 3 Feb 43, p. 18. For six months after discharge, pay and allowances continued if dischargee was hospitalized; no provision was made for hospital expenses in excess of WAAC pay scales. WD Memo 35–46, 24 Jan 46. WDWAC 705. Also Min, mtgs, Jun–Jul 42. WA 300.3 (4–29–42) sec 2.

[11] WAAC Regs, 1942 (Tentative), sec 47.

[12] Memo, M. C. M., N. K. B., C. E. F. for Dir WAAC, 15 Dec 42, sub: Interpretation of "In the Field." SPWA 016.2.

Judge Advocate General had considered the legality of the proceedings, the Waac had served her sentence and been discharged.[13] The Judge Advocate General decided that other stations, if they wished to take court-martial action against a Waac, must first get a legal decision as to whether the post was currently subject to attack, and that "military police would be liable for suit if restraint was found improper."[14]

At first there appeared to be little need for military discipline to hold Waacs in their jobs, but when recruiting quotas were raised standards fell somewhat and several WAAC "Awols" occurred. The military police occasionally apprehended a few and began to ask the correct procedure to follow in returning them. One service command inquired: Could the procedure in Army Regulations and the Articles of War be followed? Or were only members of the WAAC qualified to arrest a Waac? Was it legal to confine them until they could be returned?[15]

WAAC Headquarters at first replied that the regular procedure should be followed, except that the women should not be confined in the same guardhouses with men and should have WAAC escorts on the return trip. As WAAC Headquarters attempted to revise the regulations to this effect, it became evident that there was no legal way to provide for the return of a Waac to WAAC control; in the few cases shipped back so far, the expenditure of government funds had been illegal.[16]

Army staff members surmised that nothing could be done except to let the woman go and to mail her a blue discharge. To this the Judge Advocate General added that there was probably no legal foundation to the whole WAAC disciplinary system: any punishment meted out by WAAC company commanders might be unconstitutional, since it was not done by court-martial and therefore deprived the individual of civil rights without due process of law. Only admonition or reprimand would be safe. Restriction to quarters would be legal if it was not considered "confinement." Summary (blue) discharge, said the Judge Advocate General in an informal conference, was also probably "legal" although "without due process of law." This so startled WAAC Headquarters that it hastily drew up a directive to the field forbidding any further company discipline until the matter was settled. After consideration, this was not sent out; the Corps had gone too far to retreat, and since the Office of the Judge Advocate General itself had written the WAAC disciplinary regulations only a few months before, it was believed that some legal basis must exist.[17]

Accordingly, steps were taken to set up an exact procedure for trying offenses, so as to protect the individual. Also, after considerable debate, the authority of the military police was extended to apply to Waacs. This was somewhat risky in view of representations previously made to Congress that the women would be under virtually no more restraint than civilian employees except when "in the field." Therefore, to ward off Congressional criti-

---

[13] Folder, Discipline, files of Air WAC Div, Hq AAF, 1943.

[14] Memo cited n. 12.

[15] Memo, 7th SvC Internal Security Div for Gen Faith, 18 Dec 42, and Inds. SPWA 300.3 (4–29–42) sec 2.

[16] WD Memo W635–6–43, 1 May 43, sub: Apprehension of WAAC Absentees.

[17] (1) Memo, Maj James R. Gifford for Exec WAAC, 6 Jan 43. SPWA 300.3 (4–29–42) sec 2. (2) Memo, JAG for G–1, 7 Mar 42. JAG 354.01, in WA 300.3 (4–29–42) sec 1. (3) Two Memos, Stf for Dir, 15 Dec 42. SPWA 300.3 sec 1. (4) Weekly Rpt, WAAC Hq to CofAdm Serv, 14–19 Dec 42. SPWA 319.12.

cism, the provision was made that Waacs would not be placed in guardhouses. Such official extension of authority was needed quickly if WAAC Awols were to be returned at all, since some service commands had already forbidden their military police to take any responsibility in effecting apprehension of absentees.[18]

Even if absentees were returned to their company, there was no way of holding them. "Restriction to quarters" could obviously not be enforced on a determined absentee unless several shifts of guards were placed in the barracks.[19] As time went on, the situation became more than faintly ridiculous. Two young sisters named Lydia and Elvira wired Director Hobby:

HAVE BEEN IN WAACS 3½ MONTHS. NOW AT HOME ON EMERGENCY FURLOUGH. HAVE NO INTENTION TO RETURN. CANNOT TAKE BEING IN CORPS. NERVOUS WRECK AND WILL LOSE OUR MIND IF NOT RELEASED. MA NEEDS US BOTH AT HOME AND CANNOT RETURN UNDER ANY CIRCUMSTANCES. PLEASE TAKE IMMEDIATE ACTION AND REPLY.[20]

This was probably the only occasion in history when a deserter directed a commanding officer to "take immediate action and reply." There were other cases even more annoying; for instance, four women who were picked up in Washington after repeated absences without leave. The report said: "The girls claim they know Regulations and nothing can be done to them to hold them if they want to go AWOL except discharge, which is what they want most."[21] In another case, a Waac from a large city alighted from the train at the dreary and isolated station which was to be her first assignment. Upon being informed that there were 149 Waacs at a nearby station behind sand dunes and brush, she remarked, "Well,

there won't be 150"; she climbed back on the train and was never seen again.[22] Some new recruits even refused to comply with initial orders to active duty if they had changed their minds since taking the oath of enlistment.[23]

In other words, it was now clear that the Army had little more hold over Waacs than over civilian workers. The women could obviously leave the service at any time they desired, just as a civilian employee could. Under such conditions it would be risky to replace thousands of trained men on any very vital or secret work with an equal number of Waacs who might depart as readily as other civilians. The large women's corps which the War Department planned could scarcely be built on such shaky foundations.

Remedial Legislation

Long before the examples cited had come to light, the War Department had perceived that remedial legislation would be necessary. Some three months before, General Marshall had directed preparation of such legislation to give the WAAC the new pay scale beginning at $50 a month. Noting that the Services of Supply had taken no action on it in this period, the Chief of Staff expressed some annoy-

[18] (1) Memo, Dir WAAC for CofAdm Serv, 27 Mar 43; (2) Memo, WAAC Hq for JAG, 15 May 43, and Inds. SPWA 300.3 (1–7–43) sec 1. (3) Ltr, 2d SvC to WAAC Tng Cen, 16 Apr 43. SPWA 251.1.

[19] Ltr, SFPOE to WAAC Hq, sub: AWOL—WAAC. SPWA 251.1.

[20] Telg, Lydia and Elvira B. to Mrs. Hobby, 15 Jun 43. SPWA 251.1.

[21] Memo, Stf to 1st O Kerins, Field Insp Div, 23 Jun 43. SPWA 251.5.

[22] Remarks of WAAC Stf Dir, 9th SvC. Min, Stf Dirs Conf, Chicago, 15–17 Jun 43, SPWA 337 (6–1–43).

[23] Ltr, 7th SvC to Dir WAAC, 20 May 43. SPWA 300.3 (1–7–43) sec 2.

ance, in view of the WAVES' competition, and wrote: "It should be pressed to the limit." [24] In the same bill, it was asked that the confusing WAAC grades, officer and enlisted, be changed to correspond exactly to the Army's, except that general officer grades would not be open to women. Considerable Congressional objection resulted. The House first voted to leave the Director's and assistant directors' pay at the equivalent of major and captain, respectively, on the grounds that "the duties and responsibilities of these officers" did not merit higher pay. After some delay, the pay bill was finally approved intact on 26 October 1942.[25]

Other piecemeal legislation followed. On 23 July Congresswoman Edith Rogers had introduced a bill to give Waacs the benefits of National Service Life Insurance, but this got nowhere.[26] On 8 October Mrs. Rogers introduced a bill to grant Waacs hospitalization and domicilary care by the Veterans' Administration. Five months later, after numerous vicissitudes, this provision, plus burial benefits, was enacted into law.[27] In October, November, and again in January, bills were introduced to give free postage to Waacs, but these also got nowhere.[28] In October Mrs. Rogers introduced a bill to place the WAAC in the Army Reserve Corps.[29] This was intended to supplant the pay bill and other partial legislation by making pay and everything else equivalent. It did not pass, because General Marshall informally sent word to Congress that he believed the pay bill urgent and did not wish to delay it with a more controversial measure. General White reported:

He [General Marshall] said that at that time the Corps was still in a formative period, we had no units actually organized and functioning with the Army [as distinguished from

the Aircraft Warning Service], and under the circumstances he preferred that we go ahead as we were until we had gone far enough to know just how valuable this Corps was going to be to the Army.[30]

Introduction of WAC Bill

By the beginning of 1943 General Marshall had changed his mind. He informed the Director:

Although the Corps is still in the formative period of organization, its members have convincingly demonstrated their ability to render a vital military service. The standards of discipline, training, and general efficiency are on the highest level and are a complete reassurance to the officials of the War Department as to the outstanding services which will be rendered by this organization.[31]

In January Mrs. Rogers worked with the Director's Office to draft a bill for Army status. This she introduced on 14 January 1943. The bill very simply stated that women might be enlisted and com-

[24] Memo, "G. C. M." to G–1. WDCSA 291.9 (8–31–42), in AG 291.9 (6–2–41).
[25] (1) Memo, G–1 through CofS to MPD SOS, 24 May 42. WDGAP 421 WAC, in CofS 291.9 WAAC. (2) Memo, Dir WAAC for Col Abbott, 20 May 42; (3) Ltr, Bur of Budget to SW, 2 Sep 42; (4) Memo, G–1 for CofS, 2 Sep 42; (5) Ltr, SW to Chmn Senate Com on Mil Affairs, 3 Sep 42; (6) S 2751, 77th Cong; (7) Senate Com on Mil Affairs, 77th Cong, 2d sess, *Hearings on S 2751*, 4 Sep 42; (8) Senate Calendar No. 1655, Rpt 1603; (9) HR 7539, 77th Cong, 10 Sep 42; (10) HR Rpt 2475, 21 Sep 42; (11) HR Rpt 2524, 12 Oct 42; (12) PL 761, 77th Cong, 26 Oct 42. All except (1) in AG 291.9 (6–2–41).
[26] HR 7435, 77th Cong, 2d sess, 23 Jul 42.
[27] (1) HR 7673, 77th Cong, 2d sess, 8 Oct 42. (2) HR 665, 78th Cong, 1st sess, 6 Jan 43. (3) Subcom of Senate Fin Com, 78th Cong, 1st sess, *Hearings on S 230*, 25 Feb–1 Mar 43. (4) HR 1749, 78th Cong, 1st sess. (5) PL 10, 78th Cong, 2d sess, 17 Mar 46.
[28] HR 7748 (27 Oct 42) and HR 7812 (24 Nov 42), 77th Cong, 2d sess; HR 844, 78th Cong, 1st sess, 7 Jan 43.
[29] HR 7718, 77th Cong, 2d sess, 16 Oct 42.
[30] Senate Com on Mil Affairs, 78th Cong, 1st sess, *Hearings on S 495*, 3 Feb 43, p. 4.
[31] Memo, 16 Dec 42. WDCSA 291.9 WAAC.

missioned in the Women's Army Auxiliary Corps, Army of the United States. A later version changed the proposed name to Women's Army Corps. No limitations were placed upon the Secretary of War's authority over the size of the Corps, rank, pay, or any other matter.[32]

The War Department's official attitude toward the new bill was not at once made clear, but on 1 February the Secretary of War announced his support, stating: "Although in the past the War Department has not advocated the establishment of the Corps as a part of the Army, experience has proved that the present arrangement will not be satisfactory."[33] On 3 February General White of G-1 Division told a Senate committee:

We are now in the position of favoring that which we have heretofore in a sense opposed—not that we did not want it in the beginning. . . . We have more than 10,000 now actually organized into units and on duty in the field. . . . Wherever we have put them they have proved highly valuable.[34]

However, General White informed the committee that in his opinion a WAAC unit would not be able to replace an equal number of men, stating concerning the replacement: "Well, I do not think it will run quite one for one. I have always estimated that three women would release two men."[35]

By the date of the next hearings in early March, War Department support was considerably more enthusiastic. Reports from the first unit at Fort Sam Houston indicated that three women had replaced, not two men, but four. It was indicated that one woman could not replace one man in heavy work such as motor transport, but that women stenographers, typists, and switchboard operators could often replace two or more men apiece.

Equally good reports also began to arrive from the North African unit and the anti-aircraft experiment, accompanied by requisitions for more Waacs. Thereafter the War Department without hesitation directed every station receiving 150 Waacs to effect replacement of 150 enlisted men— a rate which was actually better than one for one, since part of the women had to be used for unit housekeeping and were not available to replace men.[36]

In an effort to secure speedy enactment of military status for women, General Marshall informed Congress in early March:

In recent months great strides have been made in the organization. Sufficient numbers have now been trained, organized into appropriate units, and placed on duty in various activities to enable us to know that we are moving in the right direction. I am now certain that the women's organization will be of great value to the military service. . . .

It is evident also that the operation of the women's organization will be simplified and its efficiency vastly improved if it is made an actual component of the Army. The personnel of the Army have definite, defined duties, are subjected to prescribed disciplines, and have clear-cut relations to each other and to the civilian population. These have been found necessary to the effective functioning of military establishments the world over. They are equally important in the WAAC, which in its present half-civilian, half-military status will be seriously handicapped. . . .

Having the Corps with the Army, but not

---

[32] (1) Weekly Rpt, WAAC Hq for CofAdm Serv, 10–16 Jan 43. SPWA 319.12 (11–9–42) sec 1. (2) Identical bills HR 1188, 14 Jan 43, and S 495, 21 Jan 43, and later version, HR 1751, 8 Feb 43; 78th Cong, 1st sess.

[33] Ltr to Hon. Robert Rice Reynolds, Chmn, Senate Com on Mil Affairs, 1 Feb 42.

[34] Senate Com on Mil Affairs, 78th Cong, 1st sess, *Hearings on S 495*, 3 Feb 43, p. 4.

[35] *Ibid.*

[36] House Com on Mil Affairs, 78th Cong, 1st sess, *Hearings on S 495*, 9 Mar 43. Statement by Gen White.

in it, also results in inequalities and injustices to its members. . . . There is, finally, the important element of morale. Membership in the Army carries with it a natural and proper pride . . . for which service in an adjunct of the Army provides no satisfactory substitute.[37]

General White in his testimony was even more specific on the administrative annoyances of an auxiliary system. He said:

We have found that we run into administrative, disciplinary,[38] and command difficulties. . . . The Army Regulations are not applicable to the Waacs. The Army Regulations are contained in a set of books as long as this table. It took years to develop them. Now we are faced with having to develop almost a parallel set of regulations to govern another part of the Army. . . . There are little things that are constant irritants. They are the same difficulties we had in trying to operate the Army Specialists Corps—people not in the Army working with and doing the same thing people in the Army were doing, on a different basis and in a different status. There are questions of relative rank, command, administrative records, and so forth. It just simplifies the whole operation of the Corps to have them all alike. In other words, in the Army we want one category of people.[39]

No difficulty was encountered in the Senate, which passed the bill on 15 February 1943. The House of Representatives was another matter; its Committee on Military Affairs appeared hopelessly divided into two factions, which at public hearings fell to quarreling so vigorously that their chairman was obliged to remind them that such discussions should be taken up in executive session and not in the presence of Army witnesses.

One faction held with the congressman from Texas who said, "I spoke against it [putting the WAAC in the Army the previous year] four times from the floor. . . .

Then we went ahead and organized the other women's auxiliaries as integral parts of the other services; I feel that we are going to have to do this now, no matter how good my argument was before." However, a representative from Indiana argued that draftees should receive soldiers' benefits, but Waacs and men who volunteered should not because they were not "forced into the Army." He also maintained that Waacs should not get soldiers' benefits because they did not go into front lines; this provoked an argument over whether General Eisenhower and the men in his fixed headquarters were entitled to military status. A congressman from Ohio joined in objecting to compensation for both husband and wife if both were in the Army and both were injured.

It was also feared that a Waac's husband would get a government allotment whether he needed it or not, since the law provided this for a soldier's wife whether she needed it or not. On this General White observed, "I am inclined to believe that the Comptroller General, who at one time recently ruled, in effect, that women were not persons, would rule that husbands are not wives." The representative from Ohio also failed to understand why the Secretary of War could not legally make the authority of military courts applicable to civilian women without giving them military status and benefits; this brought on another futile discussion of what "in the field" meant.[40]

It very shortly became clear that the

---

[37] Ltr to Hon. Andrew Jackson May, Chmn, House Com on Mil Affairs, 1 Mar 43.
[38] At the word *disciplinary*, Congressmen interrupted to inquire details, and discovered that General White was referring not to Waac misbehavior but to the legal and technical questions discussed above.
[39] *Hearings* cited n. 36.
[40] *Ibid.*

House of Representatives would not pass the bill without any number of hampering amendments concerning the size of the Corps, the top rank attainable, the types of duty permitted, and the benefits to be allowed. These amendments would have to be fought out with the Senate and a compromise reached, and when, if ever, the legislation would pass now became uncertain.

The first six months of 1943 were therefore, from the Corps' viewpoint, to be much like the uncertain period of the previous spring, when passage of the first WAAC bill was not sure and all plans had to be made subject to change without notice. However, in this case, the Corps was not merely a plan on paper; it was a living organization which grew from 12,767 women in December 1942 to 60,243 in June 1943, and which required detailed administration. Passage of the bill was to be expected in March, in April, in May. Director Hobby said, when it did not pass in April, "I am sure it will come in May as a birthday present to the Corps.[41] But it was not to come in May, or in early June.

Meanwhile, from January of 1943 onward, the War Department, insofar as legally possible, proceeded with plans for the expansion program, both in the United States and overseas, as if it were an assured fact that the Corps would be given military status.

---

[41] (1) Lecture by Comdt, Sch of WAC Pers Adm. OCMH. (2) Min, Gen Council, 5 and 26 Apr 43.

CHAPTER VII

Spring, 1943: Expansion and Decentralization

A few weeks after the decision to seek military status, the General Staff on 30 January and 6 February 1943 announced the long-awaited series of further decisions on the Corps' future—perhaps the most important staff action in the WAAC's existence.

The first was that a draft of women would not yet be sought: "Plans for the procurement of personnel will be based on the continuance of voluntary enlistment." [1] The proposal to draft women was still highly shocking to many individuals, and clearly would stand no chance of approval by Congress unless the military successes in North Africa should unexpectedly turn to disaster and the situation should approach that of Britain, which had perforce adopted national service laws. Events of a year later, when national service was finally proposed by other agencies, confirmed the present surmise that a draft proposal would merely have involved the Army in a bitter and ultimately futile legislative battle, without providing womanpower in time to aid in the current war. [2]

After making this decision the War Department faced a choice between attempting to secure a large Corps by other means, or abandoning G–3's idea and increasing the draft call on men. In a preliminary conference with G–1 and G–3 Divisions

on 29 January, Director Hobby again informed them that in her opinion the WAAC could not recruit anything like a million women. Her frequently expressed view was: "I don't believe we are going to get even 150,000 volunteer women unless there is some move by the Federal Government requiring national registration or compulsory service." [3]

Expansion Program Decided

The important 6 February conference of General Staff representatives, which decided upon the expansion rate to be attempted, was headed by Maj. Gen. Idwal H. Edwards of G–3 Division, and included General Madison Pearson and other Services of Supply representatives, and both Director Hobby and Colonel Catron from WAAC Headquarters. There resulted a decision that appeared a moderate compromise to all concerned, although actu-

---

[1] (1) Memo, G–3 for TAG, 30 Jan 43. WDGCT 291.9 WAAC (1–30–43). (2) Ltr, TAG to CG SOS, 10 Feb 43. AG 320.2 WAAC (1–30–43) PR–W–WDGCT.

[2] See Austin-Wadsworth bill, HR 1742 and S 666, 78th Cong, 1st sess, 8 Feb 43; *Congressional Record*, Vol. 89.

[3] (1) WAAC Daily Journal, Vol. I, 29 Jan 43. (2) Speech, in Min, Conf of Tng Cen Comdts, Washington, D. C., 31 Mar 43. SPWA 334.8 Conf (3–29–43).

ally it was to have calamitous effects upon every phase of the Corps' future program.

To the conferees it was obvious that G–3's earlier optimistic calls for 1,500,000 Waacs could not be met by voluntary recruiting and that it would be necessary to set a far lower figure, while simultaneously increasing draft calls for men to make up the deficit. Director Hobby outlined the various recruiting difficulties that were closing in upon the WAAC, particularly the competition shortly to be expected from the Navy and the War Manpower Commission. The date at which these factors would be felt was uncertain, but she expressed the view that by June they would have cut off most if not all of the WAAC's intake.

On the other hand, it was evident that they had not yet had serious effect. Instead, the Army Recruiting Service had overrecruited every quota to date, and was obliged, for lack of training space, to turn away qualified applicants. At Des Moines 70 women slept in poorly ventilated stable-barracks intended to hold 50; at Daytona Beach, trainees were housed five to a tent and eight to a double hotel room. Desperate calls and letters from training authorities indicated that "Training Centers cannot stand such overloading."[4]

It was realized that to turn away applicants was probably to lose them. In order to insure next month's quotas, Army recruiting stations therefore often swore in surplus applicants and placed them on inactive duty until training space was available.

By February this trick had backfired, placing the Corps under additional public and Congressional pressure. Enrollees who had resigned from jobs, given up apartments, and given away civilian clothing were vociferously indignant at months of delay and frequently wrote their congressmen. Negro recruits on the list alleged that they were not being called up because of their race. The number of enrollees on inactive duty, awaiting orders to report, was by this time almost one fourth of Corps strength. Some authorities attributed the later difficulties of WAAC recruiting to the fact that the presence of thousands of recruits awaiting training in these early days convinced other prospects and the public that the Army actually had no need for Waacs.[5]

As a result, conferees decided that the sensible course was to make available to the WAAC enough additional training space to scoop up at once all inactive members and current applicants—a course that appeared doubly wise, since Army jobs were already waiting and applicants would probably accept other war work unless taken at once. It would then be appropriate to decide, on the basis of the national picture, how much farther it would be possible to go and whether further legislation should be sought.

Accordingly, the goal finally set was that which General White of G–1 Division had earlier recommended—150,000 by the end of June 1943, a mere one tenth of G–3's first total. Minutes of the meeting noted that "present training facilities could . . . provide for a total enrollment on June 28 of 122,234 . . . and an additional training capacity of approximately 10,000 . . . will permit a total enrollment by June 28 of 150,234." The matter of later expansion was "discussed, accepted in principle, and left for future detailed consideration, with the idea that a

---

[4] (1) Min cited n. 3(2). (2) Weekly Rpt, WAAC Hq to CofAdm Serv, 14–20 Mar 43. SPWA 319.12.

[5] Contemporary Rpts, 1 Mar 43: Active—35,662 (21,925 in tng, 13,737 in fld); Inactive—8,022.

training capacity adequate for 150,000 by June 30 would be adequate for a greater number at the proper time." [6]

The greatest obstacle to the training of such a number was seen as the matter of supply, since, in both the previous recruiting step-ups of June and September, the Services of Supply had not been able to meet its commitments. However, there was placed in the record a schedule furnished to Colonel Catron by Requirements Division, Services of Supply, which indicated that in the new program all essential items for the numbers contemplated could be provided. [7]

The conference therefore directed, in language which in retrospect was to appear curious, that "a controlled recruiting of approximately 5,800 a week will be put into effect." Although this goal possibly appeared small by comparison with G–3's earlier ideas, actually the Corps was called upon to triple its size in four months. Corps strength in March would approach 50,000, of which only 14,000 would be trained or in the field, the rest being still in training or awaiting call to active duty. The new requirement meant that by 1 July there must be about 104,000 in the field and 46,000 in training. This was a voluntary recruiting effort unlike anything ever previously achieved by the U.S. Army in any comparable circumstances in its history. [8]

Within hours of the General Staff decision, the Corps was irrevocably committed to large-scale expansion. Recruiting quotas were at once doubled, with future tripling a necessity. Some 6,126 recruits had been admitted in December and 10,421 in January. With a fourth and fifth training center in prospect, the quota was now lifted to 18,000 for February and 27,000 for March. Thereafter it was expected to hold steady at around 33,000 monthly through June. [9]

The Services of Supply was already negotiating for a site for the Fourth WAAC Training Center. After conferences with the Chief of Engineers, it had recommended a part of Fort Devens, Massachusetts, which was excellently located to accommodate recruits from New York and New England. This site was shortly approved but, like the site for the Third, only after the General Staff overrode the nonconcurrence of the using command. It was directed that this center's staff of more than 1,000 be ordered in and be ready to open the training center in March. [10]

The site offered for the Fifth WAAC Training Center was less desirable; it consisted of three prisoner-of-war inclosures at Camps Polk and Ruston, in Louisiana, and Camp Monticello, Arkansas. This minimum-standards housing was available only because the Army had, at this date, taken few prisoners. Its use for Waacs was therefore proposed by G–3 Division, according to conference minutes:

General Edwards stated that the housing situation had been carefully surveyed and that neither the Ground Forces, the Services

---

[6] Min, Mtg in Office of G–3, 6 Feb 43. Only copy found in file of Dir Mil Tng SOS, SPTR 337, DRB AGO.

[7] Ibid.

[8] All figures are from M/R, WAAC Overall Picture, 1 Mar 43. SPWA 314.7 (1–7–43)(1) sec 1. No two sets of estimates in the files ever quite agree; all are unimportant in that even the lowest estimate was never reached. WAAC Daily Journal, Vol. I, 6 Feb 43, indicated that these goals were known to the WAAC by that date.

[9] For recruiting data, see Ch. X, and Table 2, Appendix A, below.

[10] (1) Memo, Tasker for Exec WAAC, 1 Feb 43. SPWA 600.914 (2–1–43). (2) WD Cir 63, 1 Mar 43. (3) Memo, G–3 for SOS and AGF, 3 Feb 43, and Inds. Tab, Fort Devens, WA 600.1 (7–2–42)(1) sec 2, 1943 WAAC Housing files.

FIRST OFFICER ELIZABETH H. STRAYHORN, *of the Fifth WAAC Training Center, with Governor Sam Jones of Louisiana, a visitor on the post.*

of Supply, nor the Air Forces could make any further housing available without deferring the activation of military units. He stated, however, that there was a possibility that Prisoner of War housing, much of which is now completed and unoccupied, might be temporarily made available. . . . The total housing program for prisoners of war was in the neighborhood of 196,000 spaces, of which we had commitments with the British for only 150,000 spaces, while actual prisoners of war therein total only 6,600.[11]

The Provost Marshal General concurred in allowing Waacs to train there, provided they did not modify the group toilets and showers and other masculine-type plumb-

ing facilities, and provided they would move out on thirty days' notice if German and Italian prisoners should need the place.[12]

The decision as to whether to accept this location was, according to Director Hobby, a difficult one. Its unattractive features were obvious, especially when compared to the WAVES and SPARS training schools at fashionable colleges. One recruiter asked, unnecessarily,

---

[11] Min cited n. 6.
[12] Memo, CofAdm Serv for TAG, 1 Mar 43. SPWA 314.7 (10–7–43)(1) sec 1.

whether the WAAC with its prisoner-of-war camps was not "suffering by contrast with the WAVES with Smith College, Holyoke, and Hunter?" [13] The Director therefore appealed to the Services of Supply for any other location, even city hotels, but was offered nothing else except a desert camp below sea level at Tulare, California. The WAAC therefore was obliged to accept the prison camps in order to comply with the directed expansion program.[14]

The three scattered branches of this training center, some one hundred miles apart, made administration difficult. The buildings were bare and rough inside and out, located in desolate sandy stockades. Colonel Hoag, who was ordered from Des Moines to be commandant, said: "It was necessary to place the moving-picture theaters of Ruston 'off-limits' until they were cleared of rats and other vermin. . . ." [15] General Marshall himself was concerned about the situation and, in a personal conference with Colonel Hoag, told him to push Special Services operations at this training center. However, the Eighth Service Command later turned down Colonel Hoag's request for these services on the grounds that it had had no instructions from the Army Service Forces.[16] Director Hobby, upon a later visit to the Fifth WAAC Training Center, said, "I know of no finer example of patriotism by Waacs anywhere than that which was shown by the women who worked and trained successfully at these camps." [17]

Expansion of WAAC Training

In accordance with General Staff directives, Brig. Gen. Don C. Faith's WAAC Training Command during the spring months underwent an expansion which overshadowed previous efforts. On 1 March the Fourth WAAC Training Center was activated at Fort Devens; on 15 March the Fifth WAAC Training Center was activated in the three prisoner-of-war camps, with recruits arriving a bare two weeks later. With these additions the five basic training centers had a capacity of 46,388. This meant that some 7,000 trained women—about 50 companies— could now be sent to the field weekly. There were 53 WAAC companies in the field at the end of February; by July, it was intended that there should be at least 375.[18]

In addition to the five basic training centers, several specialist schools were set up to relieve the training command of some of the load of specialist training. Most important of these were seven administrative specialist schools set up at women's colleges in the South and Southwest. These were under the jurisdiction of The Adjutant General, not General Faith, and were commanded by Army officers, with WAAC officers as instructors and company officers. Each had a capacity of about 600, and offered a six-week course designed to turn out trained administrative specialists.[19] Students of The Adjutant General's schools, like men, were given the rank of private first class, although graduates of identical courses at

[13] Miss B. Eugenia Lies, The Overall WAAC Picture (first draft), 28 Mar 43. SPWA 291.9, in Folder, Planning Serv Notes, WAAC Planning files.

[14] (1) Weekly Rpt, WAAC Hq to CofAdm Serv, 7–13 Feb 43. SPWA 319.12 (1942). (2) WAAC Daily Journal, Vol. I, 5 and 8 Feb 43.

[15] Ltr to Col Catron, 27 Apr 43. SPWA 291.1.

[16] (1) Statement by Comdt, Col Hoag, at mtg cited. (2) Ltrs, Col Hoag to Col Catron, 14 Apr 43, Tab, Ruston, and 3 May 43. SPWA 291.1.

[17] Lecture notes, Lt Col Jess Rice. WAC files, OCMH.

[18] M/R, 1 Mar 43, cited n. 8.

[19] WDBPR Press Release, 3 Mar 43.

WAAC training centers could not be so promoted, a circumstance that caused some discontent at the latter.

The new schools were shortly successful in removing a considerable load from the WAAC Training Command; on the other hand, inspectors soon noted a natural decrease in uniformity of operation, with some schools making no reports of personnel actions. There was also reported at some Army schools a growing need for a senior woman officer to correct a certain laxity of supervision of living conditions which was causing public comment unfavorable to recruiting.[20]

In addition, three Army schools to train WAAC radio operators and mechanics were set up at civilian schools in Missouri, New Jersey, and Pennsylvania. These had a capacity of about 300 each, and were under the jurisdiction of the Signal Corps.[21] In February, the Army Air Forces admitted 50 Waacs to the twelve-week photographic laboratory technician course at Lowry Field, Colorado, and others to later classes.[22]

From this time forward it became increasingly common to send Waacs to Army schools when their numbers did not justify separate schools for women. No particular difficulties were noted, and an ASF training inspector stated a few months later: "WAAC training, strangely enough, presents few problems. WAAC students at schools are eager to learn, and maintain discipline with less corrective action than men students in the same class."[23]

Delegation of Command Authority

Before the increased numbers of trainees could reach the field, hasty administrative changes were necessary.

While the training system was in process of expansion, WAAC Headquarters therefore hurried to complete the delegation of its command authority to the field. It was realized that such decentralization was perhaps too early for full justice to individuals, since the scanty field experience to this date had not provided a basis upon which all types of Auxiliary regulations might be carefully formulated, and Army Regulations could not yet apply; nevertheless, the approaching expansion made the step necessary. Ready or not, it was obvious that in a Corps of 150,000 women WAAC Headquarters would no longer be able to process the thousands of individual transfers, discharges, and promotions. Already the length of time required to process discharge cases was such that, the field reported, "Many of these members are rapidly becoming mental cases due to the length of confinement awaiting authority for discharge."[24]

It was desired to realign the WAAC organization in a way that would, as nearly as possible, parallel the command system for men and leave the Corps prepared for conversion to Army status, although, as the Director noted, planners were limited to doing "only those things which can be done legally" under existing legislation.[25]

Delegation of command authority to the service command level had been under way for some time. Before the end of 1942

[20] Memo, CG WAAC Tng Comd for Dir WAAC, 24 May 43. SPWA 319.1.

[21] WDBPR Press Release, 14 Apr 43.

[22] WDBPR Press Release, 5 Feb 43.

[23] Min, Conf of CGs of SvCs, Chicago, Ill., 22–24 Jul 43.

[24] (1) Ltr, 1st Tng Cen to Dir WAAC, 28 Jan 43; (2) Ltr, WAAC Stf Dir 4th SvC to Dir WAAC, 18 Feb 43; (3) Ltr, TAG to Tng Cen Dirs, 27 Feb 43, SPX 291.9 WAAC PR–W. All in SPWA 300.3 (1–7–43) sec 1.

[25] Min, Stf Mtgs, WAAC Daily Journal, Vol. I.

service commands had been given power to send Waacs on temporary duty and detached service away from their stations, provided that enrolled women were sent only to stations where they could be housed with a WAAC company. Army stations were also given power to grant WAAC leaves and furloughs, with no restrictions except those that applied to men.

At the end of December that much-disputed power—assignment and transfer—was delegated to the WAAC service command directors with no reservations, since these officers now thoroughly understood War Department ideas on safe and appropriate locations. The wording of the circular shortly had to be changed. It at first read: "Orders authorizing assignment . . . will be issued by the commanding general of the Service Command upon the request of the WAAC Service Command Director." This was pronounced offensive to commanding generals, since it appeared to place them under the command of a WAAC officer. Accordingly the wording was changed to: "The WAAC Service Command Director will request the commanding general to issue orders. . . ."

In February authority to promote enrolled women was delegated to WAAC service command directors and company commanders, likewise the authority to demote, with certain safeguards to protect the individual's rights. In March, after some delay to get the approval of the War Department, detailed instructions were published to guide in the selection of women for attendance at officer candidate school; Army commands would receive quotas, appoint selection boards, and issue orders sending the selected applicants to the school.

Finally, an even more important power was delegated, that of discharge, which would now be ordered by the commanding general upon the recommendation of his WAAC director, unless he was in doubt, in which case he could send it to WAAC Headquarters. This delegation had required months of study to set up exact and just grounds for each of the WAAC's three types of discharge—honorable discharge, discharge without specification as to character, and summary discharge—which did not correspond exactly to the Army's three types because they could not legally include a dishonorable discharge.[26]

At the conclusion of this series of delegations of authority, in early April, WAAC Headquarters retained within itself no more power over operating functions than that which The Adjutant General retained over male personnel—initial assignment of newly trained units, promotion of officers, and appeal on doubtful cases. Of these it could not dispose until Army status allowed The Adjutant General's Office to assume them.

Inclusion in the Troop Basis

At the same time, the General Staff decisions concerning Corps expansion and status had committed the Army to a course implicit in the program: the more complete integration of womanpower into every area and command. On 8 February, two days after the expansion program was launched, General McNarney informed the General Staff of a further decision which represented a new era in War Department thinking on the employment of womanpower: the WAAC strength was to

---

[26] WAAC Cirs 14 (4 Nov 42), 17 (29 Dec 42), 5 (13 Mar 43), with note, in SPWA 300.3 (1–7–43) sec 1; WAAC Cir 5 (10 Feb 43), 8 (17 Mar 43), 10 (9 Apr 43).

count against the Army's Troop Basis. G–3 Division, in recommending this action, stated:

Since the legislation was passed, conceptions as to the most profitable methods of employing members of the WAAC have undergone changes. . . . It is necessary to employ both soldiers and members of the WAAC only on those tasks which cannot otherwise be performed.[27]

General McNarney stated that the Army would voluntarily agree to draft one less man for every WAAC recruited, and that

From now on the strength of the WAAC will be included as a part of the authorized troop basis and will form a part of the 7½ million Army.

On 22 February the General Council noted:

General McNarney emphasized and re-iterated again that the purpose of Waacs is to replace soldiers. When Waacs are assigned to a post, a corresponding reduction of enlisted men must be made immediately. G–1 will check on this.[28]

Accordingly, the War Department directed that Waacs be removed from all employment that did not result in the replacement of soldiers. The decision particularly affected the plans, which some agencies still had not abandoned, to employ Waacs in laundries, post exchanges, officers' clubs, and similar duties which had no allotment of soldiers. It was directed that WAAC Headquarters refuse all such requisitions.

More important, the General Staff decision required the removal of approximately thirty WAAC units currently assigned to the Aircraft Warning Service.[29]

The demise of the Aircraft Warning Service WAAC units caused no grief in WAAC Headquarters. Nothing but diffi-culty had resulted from the use of Waacs mixed with civilians in city stations, with the Waacs inevitably getting less desirable assignments and becoming convinced that they had replaced not a soldier but a debutante. Already the possibility of an air attack on the United States appeared remote. The Aircraft Warning Service, on the other hand, declared Waacs essential and refused to give up about half of the women; instead, it allotted military vacancies for small clerical detachments at various operations and filter centers. The rest of the women were reorganized into the newly created post headquarters companies, AAF, similar to service command companies, for shipment to various air bases to perform real military duties.[30]

The Services of Supply now suddenly became concerned with the fact, which had not previously troubled it, that all WAAC units were assigned to the Services of Supply and only attached to the using service. It was immediately clear that Waacs would have to be assigned to the using commands in order to count against their troop allotment and not against the Services of Supply's. This coincided admirably with the desires of the Air Forces, which had endured the service commands' administration of the city-stationed Aircraft Warning Service units but could not view with equanimity a Services of Supply invasion of actual air bases.

Of the approved requests now on file, some 57 percent were from the Army Air

---

[27] Memo, G–3 for CofS, 7 Jan 43. WDGCT 291.2 WAAC, in OCofS 291.9.

[28] Min, Gen Council, for dates cited.

[29] Transcript of Mtg, 15 Feb 43 (Col Catron, Gen Grunert, Gen Madison Pearson). Dir Adm Serv ASF Sp Coll DRB AGO.

[30] (1) See Memo and Ltr cited n. 1. (2) Weekly Rpt, WAAC Hq to CofAdm Serv, 17–30 Jan 43. SPWA 319.12 (1942). (3) AAF WAC Hist, p. 14. See Ch. XVI, below, on AAF.

Forces and the remaining 43 percent from the Services of Supply and the Ground Forces combined. Accordingly, a tentative division of the first 150,000 was planned on this basis, with the Air Forces receiving the largest slice for field duty, although the training center allotment continued to belong to the Services of Supply:

Command	Strength	Percent
Total	150,000	—
Trainees, SOS	20,000	—
Field duty	130,000	100
AAF	70,000	54
SOS	55,000	42
AGF	5,000	4

Although this division had neglected to take into consideration the future needs of overseas theaters and the War Department and was soon to require revision, it roughly determined the proportion in which shipments were to be made for the next few months.[31]

On 17 February it was directed that all Waacs would in the near future be assigned, not attached, to the using agency, which might be the Army Air Forces, Army Ground Forces, Services of Supply (shortly renamed Army Service Forces), or an overseas theater. The formal transfer from attachment to assignment was set for 1 May.[32]

Staff Directors Assigned to New Commands

If there had been risk involved in early delegation of discharge and other powers to the service commands, where were located experienced regional directors, it was recognized that real danger lay in the necessity for scattering Waacs through all other Army commands and overseas theaters, which had neither WAAC advisers nor experience in Auxiliary administration. Therefore, it was decided that, before the formal assignment of enlisted women

on 1 May, a WAAC officer corresponding to the service command director must be assigned to each major command involved. These included an eventual fifteen Air Forces commands in the United States, two Ground Forces commands, and many of the Army Service Forces' administrative and technical services, as well as ports of embarkation, overseas theaters, and other miscellaneous commands. To designate all such WAAC advisers, the title WAAC Staff Director was devised, and the titles Service Command Director and Regional Director were dropped. All powers which had been previously delegated to a service command director were simultaneously made applicable to all WAAC staff directors.[33]

Immediate difficulty was experienced in finding qualified WAAC officers in sufficient numbers to fill these new and responsible positions. The best possibilities appeared to be those women with some experience as assistant service command directors, as senior recruiting officers, or in WAAC Headquarters. These officers, except for a few in headquarters, frequently proceeded hastily from the old assignment to the new without any such indoctrination as it had been possible to give the original nine service command directors.

Another problem in sending out these officers was posed by an unexpectedly

---

[31] (1) Transcript cited n. 29. (2) Memo, Dir WAAC for CofAdm Serv, 26 Jan 43. SPWA 320.2 (1–26–43)PS, in WAAC Planning files.

[32] (1) WAAC Daily Journal, Vol. I, 17 Feb 43. (2) WAAC Cir 11, 10 Mar 43. Since December, when there first appeared the possibility of unprecedented expansion into commands other than the service commands, WAAC third officers had been attached to the AAF, the Signal Corps, and The Adjutant General's Office, to assist those agencies in the necessary planning. WAAC SO 43, 5 Dec 42. SPWA 300.4 (8–18–42).

[33] Ibid.

quick transition from Auxiliary to Army rules of promotion. The system of requiring all officers to graduate from officer candidate school, with initial commissions only as second lieutenants, had, in Mrs. Hobby's opinion, proved sound and democratic in avoiding the choice of officers on political or personal grounds and in preventing the award of higher ranks to individuals who failed on the job. Nevertheless, as the WAAC Pre-Planners had recognized, the system was tenable only if women who had proved capable were advanced to ranks that would provide a normal spread of grades for Corps administration. In line with this policy, WAAC Headquarters had in December promoted service command directors and battalion commanders to the rank of first officer, or captain. It was planned to repeat the process in April to give equal rank to the new staff directors being sent out, to make experienced key officers majors, and company commanders captains.

However, when the Director proposed this move, she was informed by the Army Service Forces that the Army time-in-grade now applied to the WAAC, in anticipation of Army status later in the year. The Director protested that such abrupt application of the Army promotion system was impossible since the Corps had not initially followed the Army system of direct commissions:

The Army of the United States, faced with a similar necessity for providing officers for a rapidly expanding army, has commissioned many men directly from civilian life, determining their grades both by the nature of the job they have been asked to undertake and by the nature of their civilian experience and training.

If the WAAC had done the same, she noted that in February the WAAC with its current strength of over 30,000 members would have had, at least, on the Army ratio, 183 lieutenant colonels, 329 majors, and 848 captains; actually it had no lieutenant colonels, no majors, and only 82 captains. While no one desired these maximum numbers in a new organization, the Director suggested that staff directors and unit commanders be advanced to the rank to which their age, civilian experience, and military duties would have entitled them under the Army system of direct commissions. Otherwise, she noted, "The responsibilities devolving upon unit commanders and staff directors will not be adequately recognized, and they will be at a disadvantage in dealing with other officers of like responsibility but higher rank." Even under Army promotion policy, she noted that in similar emergencies West Point graduates and Air Corps men had been granted exceptions to the required time-in-grade.

However, the Army Service Forces' final decision was that the Army time-in-grade must thenceforth be observed; even women occupying Air Corps positions must observe the longer time-in-grade of the Army instead of the shorter time of men in Air Corps jobs. General Grunert noted: "Notwithstanding the contemplated expansion of the WAAC, there appears to be little justification for such rapid promotion." One concession was made, in which some promotions to captaincies were permitted in April, but none to field grade. As a result, the new staff directors went out as captains or lieutenants; by the end of the war, very few had reached the originally allotted rank of lieutenant colonel, and many company commanders were not yet captains. For promotions to the grade of major, only two exceptions were made during the remainder of the WAAC's existence, the first of these being for the officer sent to fill, in the Army Air Forces, a position comparable to Director Hobby's in the Service Forces.[34]

Major Commands Receive Waacs

Army Air Forces

At this point it was evident that the Air Forces' share of the WAAC field units would be almost double that of all other commands combined. It was currently scheduled to receive 253 field companies as against the Service Forces' 120 and the Ground Forces' 7. The receptive Air Forces attitude toward the employment of women was due largely to the announced policy of Gen. Henry H. Arnold, Commanding General, AAF, who repeatedly wrote field commanders that efficiency required the employment of Waacs to the widest extent possible, to make up manpower deficiencies.[35]

The Air Forces Waacs began arriving in March, accompanied by staff directors for the various subordinate air commands. The first unit, fifty-seven WAAC enrolled women and two officers, arrived at Jefferson Barracks, Missouri, on 3 March 1943 to work for the AAF's Map Chart Division. On 22 March the AAF's first two WAAC post headquarters companies arrived at Chanute and Scott Fields. Twenty-three more WAAC units arrived at air bases in April; by the end of the summer there were 171 air bases which had WAAC personnel as part of the permanent party.[36]

The choice of a woman to head this organization and to serve on General Arnold's staff was not announced until May. Although the importance of the position was second only to Director Hobby's,

and in fact equal in echelon as long as the Director remained assigned to the Army Service Forces, the top rank which could be allotted was that of lieutenant colonel, in view of the legislative restrictions which limited the Corps to one colonel. The position was given the title of Air WAAC Officer, and was set up as parallel to that of the Air Quartermaster, the Air Engineer, and other such staff officers.

The woman chosen for this position was the Director's former aide and current acting deputy, First Officer Betty Bandel, who upon assuming this duty was promoted to be the Corps' first field director, or major; she was to remain the WAC's second-ranking officer throughout Director Hobby's tenure of office. The new Air WAAC Officer was at this time thirty years old; as the Director's aide she had accompanied Mrs. Hobby to Europe and on most field trips and thus had a firsthand knowledge of the WAAC situation. As Acting Deputy Director since February, she had written many of the Corps' more important staff papers and had played an active part in co-ordinating the decentralization plans with ranking officers of other agencies.[37]

Army Ground Forces

Since the Army Ground Forces ordinarily trained on ASF-serviced posts and needed overhead only at a few schools, it had been allotted only about 5,000 Waacs of the first 150,000 expected to be re-

---

[34] Memo, WAAC Hq for CofS through CofAdm Serv, 18 Feb 43, and atchd corresp. SPWA 314.7 (6–2–41)(1) sec 3 (1941).

[35] See Ch. XVI, below, for details.

[36] AAF WAC Hist, p. 17.

[37] WDBPR Press Release, 4 May 43.

MAJ. BETTY BANDEL *receives her leaves from Colonel Hobby.*

cruited.[38] Comment within its headquarters was unfavorable to integration of even this number, and AGF Plans Section stated:

> In view of the educational, occupational, and physical training of the average American woman, it is anticipated that it would be extremely difficult to adapt them to military duties. . . . With the exception of a very limited number of assignments . . . there is no reasonable field for utilization of women in the military structure.[39]

Other comments added: "WAAC activities should not be expanded if it can be avoided . . . definitely opposed to coed

organization."[40] Accordingly, Lt. Gen. Lesley J. McNair, Commanding General, AGF, wrote the War Department that "for the present, the WAAC should be continued only in limited size," and should not be placed in the Army: "It seems premature to anticipate manpower shortages

---

[38] Ltr, TAG to CG AGF, 1 Apr 43. AG 320.2 WAC (3–12–43) PR–W–WDGAP.

[39] The WAC in Army Ground Forces in World War II (hereafter cited as AGF WAC Hist), Vol. I, p. 4. This study was prepared by the AGF WAC Officer, Lt. Col. Emily E. Davis. (See Biblographical Note.) Folder, WAC, AGF Sp Coll DRB AGO.

[40] *Ibid.*, comment of G–1 AGF.

so critical as to demand the extraordinary measures here contemplated." [41]

General McNair objected also to the allotment of 5,000, which had been based by the General Staff on proportionate overhead strength of male personnel, without his comment or consent; he asked that the allotment be set back to 3,600. This was done by the War Department, and the remaining 1,400 reallotted to overseas theaters.[42]

Under the impression that Waacs would always be administered by the Service Forces, the Ground Forces had already consented to receive some 1,700 Waacs at six different stations. The pioneer unit went to the Second Army at Memphis on 26 March 1943, and in April the others followed in rapid succession to Camp Hood and Forts Benning, Sill, Riley, and Knox. These installations followed their own inclinations, some allowing service commands to administer the Waacs, and some prematurely employing AGF channels to WAAC Headquarters. Within AGF headquarters, all WAAC matters were referred to G–3 Section rather than to G–1, under the impression that WAAC problems chiefly concerned units rather than personnel. The Ground Forces declined to accept the assignment of a WAAC staff director or any WAAC officer in its headquarters.[43]

Army Service Forces

Within the third of the major domestic commands, the Army Service Forces, the number of the service command staff directors was increased by the addition of other staff directors for the ASF technical services. This action was highly pleasing to most such services, which had long resented the interference of service command directors and had repeatedly asked

that their own command channels be used. For example, Aberdeen Proving Ground objected to sending officer candidate applications and discharges through the Third Service Command, since Aberdeen was under the Chief of Ordnance. Inasmuch as many of the technical services were engaged in highly secret research and other activities, most felt that inspection by a member of another command was inadvisable. The appointment of WAAC staff directors for Ordnance and other services ordinarily ended such objections, and made command channels the same as those for men.[44]

Employment of Waacs among these technical services now promised to become rather extensive. The Transportation Corps placed a senior WAAC staff director in its Washington headquarters, and others in the various ports where Waacs were to be stationed in numbers—New York, Hampton Roads, New Orleans, San Francisco, and Seattle. Since most ports were in labor-short areas, they were already hard-hit by the loss of general service men.

The Chemical Warfare Service likewise foresaw a future lack of military personnel for permanent domestic installations, and desired to obtain Waacs whose research, once begun, would not be interrupted by withdrawal for combat duty. A WAAC staff director was therefore requested by the Chemical Warfare Service in March of 1943, and its first Waac company arrived in April.

---

[41] Memo, CG AGF for CofS, Attn: G–3, 1 Jan 43. GNDCG 320.2 WAAC (12–7–42). Full text in appendix to *Ibid.*

[42] 1st Ind to AG Memo, sub: Utilization of WAAC Pers in AGF. GNGCT 320.2/5 WAAC (4–1–43). Copy in App. VI of AGF WAC Hist.

[43] AGF WAC Hist, pp. 12–13.

[44] (1) Memo, WAAC Hq for TAG, 5 Jun 43; (2) Ltr, Aberdeen Proving Ground to WAAC Hq, 7 Jul 43, and reply. SPWA 300.3 (1–7–43) sec 2.

The Corps of Engineers now also requisitioned Waacs for an important project at Oak Ridge, Tennessee, so secret that its character could not be revealed.

The Signal Corps secured adoption of a plan to place in the WAAC some 8,000 civilian women, known as WIRES (Women in Radio and Electrical Service), whom it was training in radio, telephone, and other communications work; a staff director had already been accepted.

Medical Department requests also came in for the first time on 13 March, and totaled 20,869 or from 30 to 50 percent of enlisted personnel in hospitals of 500 beds or more. The requests were for women trained in various medical skills and also for clerks, drivers, and mechanics, plus 4,000 orderlies and others for low-grade work around hospitals. No staff director was accepted.[45]

Overseas Theaters

The decentralization of authority applied even to overseas theaters, since approaching legislation would give the Waacs the military status that would make further shipment morally justifiable. Requests from the North African and European theaters were by now so extensive that a War Department decision on priority was necessary. Director Hobby favored priority to the zone of the interior, but theaters argued that skilled Waacs had proved able to replace from two to three men apiece in North Africa, and that, in view of the difficulty of maintaining personnel overseas, theaters should get the most competent. Both General Somervell and General Marshall inclined to this view, and finally informed the Director that overseas theaters' requests would have priority.[46]

The staff director for the European

theater, Capt. Anna W. Wilson, arrived in England on 13 April 1943 to plan for later shipments. No firm shipment priorities had yet arrived, and the several requisitions for Waacs were by this time so confused and overlapping that it was impossible to tell whether they concerned the same or separate units. Captain Wilson found that the theater had so little information about the Corps' mission and capabilities that specific requests were difficult; when this was supplied, the Eighth Air Force in the theater requested a WAAC battalion, and supplied a firm shipping priority. The first unit for England therefore began to be organized, and was to reach the theater in the summer shortly after the Corps obtained military status. Other earlier shipments to the North African theater were also authorized.[47]

Readiness for Increase in Numbers

By late spring of 1943 the WAAC organization was thus fully decentralized and well prepared, as far as mere skeletal organization was concerned, for Army status and for expansion to any number. Its staff advisers were in almost every important Army command, learning its needs and peculiarities; its command powers were so delegated that shift to Army status would scarcely be noticed; its training system was fully staffed and capable of accommodating large numbers of recruits. The administrative network was ready. Had no other factor been involved, expansion to a million or more upon this frame appeared easily possible.

---

[45] See section on each service in Ch. XVIII, below.
[46] Office Memo, WAAC Hq Opns Br for Exec WAAC, 29 May 43. SPWA 320.2 sec 4a.
[47] See Chs. XIX and XX, below.

CHAPTER VIII

Stresses of Rapid Build-up: Personnel and Training

In spite of its excellent framework, the expansion program was hardly launched before it became evident what stresses such a rapid build up would carry with it. In some respects these had been anticipated, since they were comparable to those which the Army as a whole had recently encountered; but there remained one major point of difference: the women's services were dependent upon voluntary recruiting. As the spring of 1943 wore on, it became clear that stresses easily supportable in themselves might nevertheless have an exaggerated effect upon public opinion and the supply of recruits. It was gradually recognized that any attempt at quick expansion by voluntary recruiting carried within itself the seeds of self-defeat.

Training Center Confusion

From the viewpoint of the WAAC training centers, the first six months of 1943 had all the aspects of chaos. As successive new centers were staffed, commandants and key officers seldom stayed more than a few months in any location; experienced instructors, cadre, supply officers, classification officers, all moved to open new centers before projects could be completed or reports made. As new field companies had to be formed, some basic companies were reported to have lost their cadre several times in the four-week basic training. A recruit who trained at Camp Polk wrote:

> We changed officers so often that no one knew who was looking after us. We seldom had the same instructor or classroom two days in a row, and some instructors must have just taken over classes because they knew nothing about them. We didn't learn a thing. We never even had a retreat parade the whole time, and I made a fool of myself during one when I got to Fort Riley later. In our last class the workmen walked in and took out the furniture and just left us standing there.[1]

Field complaints indicated that training authorities sometimes shipped units without advance notice to the station; service records and classification cards at times did not accompany unit movement but arrived as much as two weeks late, incomplete and incorrect, after assignments had been made without benefit of records. Stations protested when Waacs arrived after cross-country trips in dirty coaches without lights or sanitary facilities and with no one responsible in charge.[2] At one station

---

[1] Interv with Miss Dorothy Pat Costello, former WAC sergeant, 4 Aug 48.

[2] (1) Ltr, 2d SvC to Dir WAAC, 9 Mar 43, sub: 42d WAAC Post Hq Co. SPWA 319.1. (2) Ltr, Col Howard Clark, Chief, Opns Serv WAAC Hq to 2d Tng Cen, 20 Mar 43. SPWA 319.1–os. (3) Ltr, 2d SvC to Dir WAAC, 1 Dec 42, and Inds. WA 513 (11–26–42) Transportation.

the unit was in the field ten days before an officer arrived. The staff director reported, "Undoubtedly the timing went wrong somewhere, but it created an unfortunate impression of WAAC organization." [3]

There were also more lasting inconveniences to stations receiving units. Enrolled women of low ability or questionable character, who once had been weeded out at training centers, now were undetectable in the general confusion and were the subject of complaint when they arrived at field stations. Company officers and cadre for outgoing units were lumped together from whatever was available at the moment, without much consideration of such factors as relative age and civilian experience, although these were often the margin between success and failure in groups of women destined to spend the rest of the war together in one installation. Untried cadre were promoted by training centers to the grades specified in the Table of Organization, often leaving units in the field saddled with incompetents who had too much rank to be reassigned. Officers were sent out as company commanders who had little or no experience or aptitude for the work; Maj. Betty Bandel noted, concerning the Air Forces, "Our greatest problem is our company commanders. I make a special plea that at least one experienced officer go out with any new unit to the field." [4]

Field stations frequently complained that neither WAAC officers nor enrollees arriving from training centers knew anything about WAAC rules and regulations, and did not have copies of them. Some company commanders considerably embarrassed their staff directors by informing station commanders that the Army had no jurisdiction whatever over WAAC units. Others had little idea of real Army life in the field, and attempted to inculcate

a state of discipline and daily routine suitable only for a brief and strenuous basic course, but impossible to sustain in a working unit. [5]

Commissioning of Unqualified Officers

Among early casualties of the expansion program were the original perfectionist plans for avoiding British mistakes in officer selection. As soon as the expansion program was directed, it was evident that the original carefully selected 1,300 officers would be insufficient to staff the new units. Since officer candidate training was weeks longer than basic training, it became necessary to begin large officer candidate classes before the women to be commanded were even recruited. Unavoidably, almost all came from the training centers, since most companies in the field were still in transit or had not had time to set up boards and select officer candidates, although it was well known that many of the best-qualified women had been placed in early field companies, while those in the training centers had not yet had opportunity to demonstrate leadership under actual field conditions.

As available personnel in training centers was combed over again and again for successive classes, quality fell rapidly. Daytona Beach complained that it had to furnish four large groups of officer candi-

---

[3] Ltr, WAAC Stf Dir WFTC to Exec WAAC, 3 Jun 43. SPWA 319.1.

[4] Comment of Air WAAC Off, Min, Stf Dirs Conf, Chicago, 15–17 Jun 43. SPWA 337 (6–1–43). Also see: (1) other comments in Min; (2) Memo, Consultant (Miss Lies) for Dir WAAC, 6 May 43. Plng Proj 6, WAAC Planning files, 1943.

[5] (1) Rpt of 2d SvC, Min cited n. 4. (2) Interv with Lt Col Katherine R. Goodwin, former Stf Dir 1st SvC, 31 May 46. (3) Statement by Lt Col Jessie P. Rice, former Stf Dir 3d SvC, in speech at Purdue Univ., Apr 45. (4) Min, Stf Dirs Conf, New York, 1–3 Dec 43. SPWA 337 (11–10–43).

dates from its cadre alone, before trainees arrived, and that while the first group was good, the last three were extremely doubtful. Board members at Des Moines reported, horrified, that they had given the lowest possible scores to certain applicants who were judged impossible material because of poor appearance, manners, education, and possibly morals, yet to make up the required quota they were directed by the WAAC Training Command to go to the bottom of the list and accept every applicant on it.

General Faith, in directing this action, noted that the WAAC had no choice if it was to meet the expansion plans. He therefore ordered boards to be realistic and admit some candidates who would make good second lieutenants although they would never be able to advance higher: "The ability to advance to high rank, which was very important in the original selection of officer candidates, has become of less importance as the total number of officers already commissioned has increased." [6] He directed boards under his Training Command not to reject anyone finally, since the ones rejected one week might be better than those available the next. General Faith suggested to the Director that she order officer candidate boards in the field to follow this system, but she did not concur, and instead published a field directive which established a selection system much like the Army's. [7]

Even if good candidates were sent by posts or training centers, they did not invariably receive commissions. During the hectic months of expansion the WAAC Officer Candidate School came to share with men's schools a problem of which Army inspectors noted:

In many [Army officer candidate] schools, performance on the drill field was used as a means of separating those with 'leadership' qualities from those lacking such characteristics . . . a loud voice and a general air of confidence indicated that 'leadership' was probably satisfactory. [8]

Numerous field complaints were received on this score; for example, the Fifth Service Command protested the "washing out" of three of its candidates who, in spite of leadership ability demonstrated in the field, had been rejected for "no voice and command," "could not drill," and "no pep and enthusiasm." [9] Similarly, the Transportation Corps protested concerning thirteen women who had all "washed out for voice and command, nothing else." [10] After frequent complaints, Director Hobby sent to the Training Command for transcripts of "murder board" hearings, which convinced her that too much emphasis was placed on youth and physical contour, and too little upon character and past accomplishments. At a time when field stations were pleading for mature officers, boards had informed applicants that an age as advanced as 35 years, if apparent, was disqualifying. [11]

---

[6] Ltr, CG WAAC Tng Comd to Dir WAAC, 3 Feb 43, and pencil notes thereon with Dir's nonconcurrence. SPWA 291.9 (2-3-43).

[7] (1) Ltr, Dir Tng, 2d WAAC Tng Cen to Dir WAAC, 8 Mar 43. SPWA 319.1. (2) Rpt, 2d O Ann Danovsky, *et al*, to 2d O M. E. Treadwell, Des Moines Office Dir Tng. Confirmed by intervs with Maj Helen Hanson, head of OCS and Dir Tng, 3d Tng Cen. (3) WAAC Cir 8, 17 Mar 43, Sec VIII. Circular had been requested a month earlier, Memo for CofAdm Serv, 19 Feb 43. SPWA 300.2 (1-7-43) sec 1. (4) Speech by Dir Hobby, 9 Jun 43, Min, Conf of Offs to Supervise OC Bds. SPWA 334.9 (6-10-43).

[8] ASF Hist of Military Training: Officer Candidate Training, 1941-45. (Hereafter cited as ASF Hist of OCT.) OCMH.

[9] Ltr, 5th SvC to Dir WAAC, 27 Jul 43. SPKEB 341, in SPWA 341 R (1942).

[10] Min cited n. 4, especially rpts by San Francisco POE and by Dir Hobby.

[11] *Ibid.;* also interv with Maj Patricia Lee Chance, Exec WAC, 1945.

Her discovery of the collapse of standards at training centers came too late. In the few brief months before the end of the summer, half of all WAAC officers were women without previous experience in jobs more responsible than those of clerks, typists, stenographers, and secretaries—including sixteen actresses, fourteen chorus girls, fourteen waitresses, and varying numbers of beauticians, charwomen, laborers, chauffeurs, and housekeepers, as well as one undertaker. Education had also declined from earlier standards. About 31 percent of WAAC officers now had only high school education or less—about 5 percent had less—while another 28 percent had not completed college; only 41 percent were college graduates. Still worse, 30 percent of officers were less than twenty-five years old.

Upon learning these facts, WAAC Headquarters took action to set up another campaign to get more officer candidates from civilian life, but before this could well come into operation, the Corps had reached almost the top officer strength it was to be permitted. The WAAC by the end of its first year had over 5,800 officers, who were, with the later failure of the expansion plan, to be enough for the rest of the war. Only a few hundred more were to be commissioned in the remaining years, so that many of the unsuitable officers so hastily commissioned did not remain second lieutenants, as General Faith had expected, but were pushed up gradually as the Corps expanded. Embarrassing as this deficiency was to everyone concerned, the WAAC had experienced no more problem in this respect than the Army; remarkably enough, even this lapse had not brought the average of WAAC officer education below that of Army officers. However, even a minority of unsuitable or rank-happy officers were always to be extremely conspicuous in a women's service.[12]

Unsuitable Mentors

The expansion program also made it impossible to carry out Director Hobby's recent order that male officers in training centers be replaced by Waacs, the most unsuitable to be the first weeded out. The "man-woman factor," unprecedented in Army schools, afforded opportunities for maladministration which all too frequently were found to have been realized. General Faith later estimated that male offenders under his command totaled not more than 5 percent, and that these were immediately relieved from duty if discovered in misconduct. Nevertheless, scattered reports continued to be received from all training centers of cases in which women's advancement was allegedly based on matters other than merit.

The gravest situation in this respect was that at Daytona Beach, which was investigated at Director Hobby's request by operatives from the Military Intelligence Service in Washington as well as by the Fourth Service Command's inspector general. These inspectors' reports noted that certain of the Army officers in highly responsible positions were drinking and misconducting themselves with Waacs and were promoting to positions of leadership only those who offered them favors in return. Members of the Army staff, when written statements were taken, officially accused each other of "running around"

---

[12] (1) Memo, Capt Ruby E. Herman, WAAC Hq, for Dir WAAC, 12 Nov 43, with incl statistics, 12 Nov 43, made as of 15 Sep 43. Unnumbered folder, 1943 WAAC files. (2) ASF Hist of OCT, 1941–45, pp. 15–16, 74. OCMH.

and "carrying on" with Waacs, and of using force on enlisted women while drunk.[13] A Waac visitor described a resulting situation of "sycophancy" by senior WAAC officers and of "obsequious flattery" among junior ones. When a WAAC inspector arrived, she learned that women were in many cases not assigned in accordance with real skills and abilities.[14]

In view of the fact that many of the officers assigned to WAAC training centers had been pronounced "culls" by the commandant when first assigned, it was perhaps remarkable that more serious situations did not develop in all of the various training schools. Concerning the common practice of assigning second-rate officers to staff women's schools, the Bureau of Naval Personnel observed that in the WAVES' program "it was a penny-wise-pound-foolish policy not to detail the handful of first-rate men it would have taken to have established the whole program on the best possible basis."[15]

Observers noted that these unsuitable mentors often had an unfortunate effect upon newly commissioned, inexperienced, and eager-to-please female officers. Through a process of what Army psychiatrists called "mimesis," or unconscious imitation, as well as through a conscious desire to secure advancement, women copied supervisors who were not in themselves models of Army leadership. Imitation was noted not only in standards of morals and public behavior, but in language and attitude toward trainees. The senior WAAC officer at Des Moines, beset by critics at a staff directors' meeting, admitted, "I have been told that some of our officers are very rough in their language. I think it is due to some of our Army officers at the fort."[16] It was some time later that Director Hobby formulated the difficulty and told a group of women officers:

It seems to me lately that I have seen too many women officers who are hard. The last thing we want to accomplish is to masculinize a great group of women. . . . I think that [harshness] often comes from the officer's own insecurity. When she is at a loss how to handle a problem, she relies on what she thinks would be the Army attitude. Actually it is not an Army attitude among leaders. Only insecure persons revert to harshness.[17]

The "Nightmare" of Basic Training

In these months many recruits used the word *nightmare* to describe basic training, although at earlier and later periods the same course was pronounced "inspiring." One recruit, an Army wife, noted that this definition was literal: "For months after I left there, I used to wake at night crying, dreaming I was back at Des Moines."[18]

The difficulty, insofar as it could be diagnosed, appeared to lie chiefly in an overabrupt and deliberately harsh introduction to Army life. The early high state of training had been produced when recruits' ideas of membership in a military team had been more nearly met, with plentiful ceremonies and instruction in Army tradition which produced a lasting pride in military status regardless of what hardships followed. This system continued to be followed, by deliberate intent, at the

---

[13] (1) Memo, Dir WAAC for TIG, 13 Mar 43, sub: Request for Investigation, and atchd corresp. SPWA 330.14, Folder, Daytona Beach, Dir Adm Serv ASF Sp Coll DRB AGO. (2) Memo, IG 4th SvC for CG 4th SvC, 9 May 43, atchd as Exhibit B to Rpt, CIC to MIS, 19 Jul 43, sub: Origin of Rumors Concerning WAAC, G–2 files MID 322.12 WAAC. (3) Also see Ch. XI, below.

[14] Memo, 1st O Anna W. Wilson for Chief, WAAC Plng Serv, 11 Mar 43. SPWA 319.1 (3–11–43).

[15] WAVES Hist.

[16] Min cited n. 4.

[17] Speech at Stf Dirs Conf, New York, 1–3 Dec 43. Min cited n. 5(4).

[18] Diary of an Auxiliary, winter 1942–43, made available to the author in a personal interview, 31 January 1946.

WAVES' training centers, with the first weeks devoted to inculcating a knowledge of Navy tradition and ceremony, and with only fully trained women graduates instead of recruits being used for the more menial tasks about the school.

Gradual adjustment seemed even more necessary for female recruits than for male draftees, since the women were apt to be more uncertain about their ability to "take it," and had been subjected to the sales talks of recruiters who accented the glamorous side of Army life. At a later period these facts were to be recognized by WAAC training authorities, but during the winter and spring of 1943 there was reported, at most training centers, an initial emphasis on military "hazing" which, as one authority later noted, "tried to belittle a recruit's ideals, laugh at her patriotism, and make her a soldier in the first five minutes." [19]

Thus, one recruit's diary noted what other accounts confirmed as a typical experience at Fort Des Moines: "I was sent out to scrub one of the offices on my first day, before I got my uniform." Emphasis on fatigue duties continued to take precedence over military indoctrination:

We seldom got to attend classes regularly, as we were pulled off for all kinds of duties: we did KP at our own mess, the officers' mess, and the consolidated mess; we scrubbed classroom floors and the theater daily; we cleaned offices, orderly rooms, dayrooms, storerooms, cleaned the outside of buildings and washed the windows and the white pillars, though in zero weather. We hated to miss those classes as there was so much to learn in only four weeks. [20]

The absence of a uniform during much of the training period was also keenly felt, though to a less extent than the fact that "the men who drilled us and marched us through the snow had complete warm outfits." The fact that almost all recruits at one time or another during training contracted colds and coughs, sometimes influenza or bronchitis, did little to increase their endurance. Even more lamented was the lack of drill and ceremony, which was prevented at some centers by the winter weather and lack of warm clothing, and at others by lack of space, by scattered housing, or by the necessity for pulling out half-trained women to meet the shipment schedule.

Under these conditions, some women suffered breakdowns and had to be discharged before receiving a field assignment, in such numbers as later to cause investigation by The Surgeon General. For the majority, it was evident that surprisingly little permanent damage was done. The time of basic training was brief, the hoped-for military ceremonies were eventually encountered on Army stations, and in looking back from the vantage point of years, trainees were if anything inclined to boast about how they "took it." Morale was reported in even the most confused months of the expansion program as "unbelievably good," and "the women were excited about their work, determined to succeed, and felt that the worst would be over if they could only get to the field and to work." [21]

The women's generally good-humored reaction was fairly well expressed in their favorite songs, which grew up during these months: [22]

WAAC Days, WAAC Days,
Dear old break-your-back days. . . .

[19] Speech by Lt Col Jess Rice, "Development of the WAC," at Sch of WAAC Pers Adm, Apr 45, notes in WAC files, OCMH. Also see bulky studies in SPWA 331.1 (3–1–43), now in file of Dir Pers ASF.
[20] Diary cited n. 18.
[21] Ibid.
[22] Pamphlet, WAAC Parodies. The only song not from the pamphlet is "AR 35–1440," most of which is unprintable.

KP DUTY, *Daytona Beach, Florida. Note seersucker exercise dress.*

When you come to the end of a perfect day,
And you sit alone with your gigs. . . .

K-K-K-Ka-P, beautiful KP,
You're the only Army job that I abhor.
When the moon shines over the mess hall,
I'll be mopping up the K-K-K-Kitchen floor.

Troublesome rules and regulations were memorized to the tune of ditties such as:

AR 35–1440,
Deals with matters very naughty.

Running a close second to the earlier favorite, "The WAAC Is In Back of You," was a new original at Des Moines, entitled the "G. I. Song": [23]

Once her Mommie made her bed,
Cleaned her clothes and buttered her bread,
And her favorite dress was red—
Oh me, Oh my, that ain't G.I.

Hats and shoes and skirts don't fit,
Your girdle bunches when you sit,
Come on, rookie, you can't quit—
Just heave a sigh, and be G.I. . . .

In the Mess Hall she now stands
Buried 'neath the pots and pans
Getting pretty dishpan hands,
Oh me, Oh my, gotta be G.I.

Then she came to camp one day,
Quickly learned the WAACKIE way,
Underwear cafe au lait—
Oh me, Oh my, strictly G.I.

Winter, summer, spring or fall
Should you try to end it all
You can't die until sick call
You see, if you die, you gotta die—G.I.

However, even among such lighthearted versions of school days, the final song was:

We're in the Staging Area
And we soon will go away
We've finished all our basic
Glory be and happy day

Glory Glory we are staging
Glory Glory we are staging
Glory Glory we are staging
Before we travel on.

The more damaging aspect of the dislocations to basic training during the months of expansion appeared to have been the effect upon recruiting. In the letters written to friends and relatives during the first week or weeks, there was noted, at worst, a frightened disillusionment or frantic desire to escape from what at first glance seemed a trap and, at best, a tendency to boast about the unspeakable hardships the writer had survived. The Army as a whole was not unfamiliar with such a phenomenon, which had little effect upon draft boards. British women's services had noted a less favorable public reaction, and that "The large majority adapt themselves in time . . . but a certain number, when writing home, may easily exaggerate. . . ." [24]

Just how great a part the brief "nightmare" of basic training had played in the later failure of the recruiting program was never to be easy to determine. General Ulio, The Adjutant General, ascribed some importance, in a staff study made during these months, to "people writing home about . . . conditions." [25] Recruiters attributed damage especially to publicity on the prisoner-of-war camps, in which no male soldiers had been reported as required to train. Later Gallup surveys also showed that many acceptable recruits were allegedly deterred from enlistment by the belief that they lacked the necessary strength to survive the reputed rigors and hazings of basic training. [26]

It came to be the general belief within WAAC Headquarters that the echelon of the Training Command had been in itself

---

[23] Words and music by Lt. June Morhman.
[24] *Conditions in the Three Women's Services.*
[25] See Ulio rpt, Ch. X, below.
[26] See Gallup rpt, Ch. XIII, below.

one of the less happy results of the expansion program. The Acting Deputy Director noted:

We were completely cut off from the training centers and could not even communicate with them; instead, we should have had direct telephonic communication all winter in order to find out their difficulties and expedite corrective action in supply, officer selection and training, and other matters.[27]

In March, Director Hobby petitioned the Services of Supply to abolish the echelon of the Training Command and restore its functions to her office, as well as General Faith in person, for its better assistance and information:

The Training Plans Division [of WAAC Headquarters] has no authority and receives problems for decision which it is unable to give. In addition, it is uninformed on training activities and programs. . . . Since the functions now being performed by the WAAC Training Command are properly headquarters functions, it is recommended that . . . the functions of the Training Command be absorbed as rapidly as possible in the appropriate organizational units of WAAC Headquarters.[28]

This request was disapproved by the Services of Supply, but some increase in effective liaison was achieved by moving the Training Command headquarters from Daytona Beach to Martinsburg, West Virginia—a location as near to Washington as possible, and one removed from the scene of the scandal concerning maladministration at the Daytona Beach training center. At the same time, General Faith was given additional duty as head of a new Training and Field Inspection Division in the Director's office, where he now spent part of his time. It was hoped that the field inspection function would provide training centers with assistance and some guide to field needs.[29]

Personnel Problems in Headquarters

Its loss of control over the training program was only one of the difficulties that expansion had brought to WAAC Headquarters. The office still suffered from chronic understaffing and overwork; since January it had been reported that "the pressing common problem throughout Headquarters is a shortage of competent dependable civilian help. Officers are doing clerical work."[30]

The Director, while supplying thousands of Waacs to the Army, was in the position of being unable to get a requested allotment of eleven for herself, because of the Services of Supply's rule against bringing enlisted Waacs to Washington. Finally, a few enlisted women were brought in on temporary duty, which prevented their promotion, and were soon also suffering from overwork, while the headquarters feared to let them go lest shipment orders remain untyped and "a tremendous backlog accumulate at Training Centers."

Letters concerning individual Waacs were referred unanswered to their posts, and letters of inquiry from Army stations were answered without being seen by the Director or top authorities—a system that provoked much unfavorable comment from the public and the field, and resulted in vague or inaccurate routine replies from junior officers to inquiries which were really matters of policy. The volume of mail was clocked at an average of 406

---

[27] Interv with Lt Col Betty Bandel, 5 Oct 45.

[28] Memo, CofS ASF for Dirs of Stf Divs and Chiefs, Sup and Adm Svs, 1 Mar 43; Dir WAAC's reply, 19 Mar 43. SPWA 331.1. (3–1–43), located and read in Office Dir Pers ASF.

[29] TWX, Faith to Dir WAAC, 29 Jun 43. SPWA 314.7 (1–7–43)(1) sec 1.

[30] Memo, 1st O Anne Alinder for Contl Div WAAC, 6 Jan 43. WAAC files.

pieces daily. The stenographic pool in April had a ten-day backlog and was obliged to reject all but urgent work, while some 1,200 papers remained unfiled. In April, the headquarters petitioned the Service Forces for an increase of civilian personnel from 56 to 77, stating: "Necessary work is being delayed or left undone with the result that the WAAC program is being seriously impaired." [31]

The problems of an expanding organization did not receive too much sympathy from the Army Service Forces, which had passed its own critical period and was at the moment engaged in a drive to reduce personnel. On 1 March WAAC Headquarters, in common with all ASF offices, was required to report on steps taken to abolish nonessential functions and personnel. The Director protested that reductions could not safely be made at present, but that in a few months, if legislation passed, "it will be possible for WAAC Headquarters to avail itself of existing Army machinery for handling certain functions, which will permit dropping activities which parallel functions done elsewhere in the War Department." In this, she was overruled by General Styer, who indorsed the papers back with a demand for immediate reduction of the office force, stating: "You will submit a further report . . . [which] will list . . . the number of military and civilian personnel released." [32]

The Director took the occasion to point out that the January 1943 reorganization of her office by General Somervell's Control Division, like that of October 1942, was unworkable. She indicated that there were friction and confusion among her Army section chiefs, with different section chiefs claiming the same projects. She therefore asked that authority be given

her to redefine duties and regroup the sections concerned according to her own ideas of office organization. There was also some discontent among the WAAC officers who made up the junior working personnel, in that male officers still retained key jobs and policy-making powers and did not allow WAAC officers to say anything in staff meetings that had not been written out and approved in advance, or otherwise to give the Director "stories of what is going wrong." [33]

In late April, Control Division, ASF, partially acceded to the Director's request and again revised the WAAC Headquarters organization—the third revision in seven months—changing the wording of the ASF Manual accordingly. A personnel increase was also briefly granted, but nullified three weeks later, and a further cut ordered.

The headquarters situation, during the entire time when the expansion program ran its course, therefore remained generally critical. The only prospect of relief and improved efficiency was Army status, which did not come until the hope of recruiting success was ended. [34]

---

[31] (1) Memo, Dir WAAC for IPD ASF, 2 Apr 43, sub: Civ Pers, and atchd. SPWA 230.14 (4–2–43). (2) Memo, Dir Adm Div for Chief, Opng Serv WAAC, 31 Mar 43; Memo, Dir Adm Div for Dir of Opng Serv, 22 Jan 43. SPWA 311.1.

[32] Three studies: (1) Ltr, ASF to all Divs, SvCs, etc., 1 Mar 43; Dir WAAC reply, 20 Mar 43; 1st Ind, CofS ASF, 10 Apr 43. (2) Memo cited n. 28, and 1st Ind, CofS ASF, 14 Apr 43. (3) Memo, CofS ASF for CofServs and SvCs, 1 Mar 43; Dir WAAC reply, 30 Mar 43; 1st Ind, CofS ASF, 19 Apr 43; 2d Ind, Dir WAAC, 28 Apr 43. All in SPWA 333.1 (3–1–43), now in Dir Pers ASF Sp Coll DRB AGO.

[33] (1) WAAC SO 78, 22 Apr 43. SPWA 300.4 (8–18–42), 1942. (2) Interv with Maj Elizabeth C. Smith and Maj Irene Galloway, 11 Oct 45. (3) Interv cited n. 27.

[34] ASF Cir 30, 15 May 43; also SOS Manual M301, Jul 43, par 202.03.

Shipment of T/O Units

In the field, possibly the most serious publicly known personnel problem caused by the expansion program was in the matter of job assignments. Again, the difficulty was not the expansion itself, but the fact that it was required before the end of the Auxiliary system.

The separate WAAC Table of Organization—which could not yet legally be merged with military job allotments—had proved in itself a disaster for the Corps. Although large Army Tables of Organization had vacancies for almost any variety of skill, the small 150-woman T/O had positions for only a few general skills—chiefly office workers and chauffeurs. As recruiting restrictions were eased, recruits were accepted who had other and more varied skills. However, when a WAAC was recruited with some rare and badly needed skill, such as teacher of Braille, she could not be assigned as such because the WAAC allotment did not call for it. The WAAC T/O could not be amended to add the job without requiring every WAAC unit in the world to have a teacher of Braille.

Under this system, the temptation for training centers to misclassify women was great. The teacher of Braille sat waiting assignment which could never be given her; a WAAC company could not be shipped until a mail clerk was found to complete its T/O; the teacher of Braille overnight became a mail clerk. Still worse, a Table of Organization could not be amended by a post commander; when the WAAC unit reached a station, the station was helpless to remedy the misclassification and was obliged to assign the Braille expert as a mail clerk, even though its hospital was badly in need of her skill and had a military vacancy for it. "Many of our stations faced this problem," reported Staff Director Jess Rice of the Third Service Command.

The WAAC Table of Organization called for six housekeepers, so they fired the maids in the guest houses and put the Waacs to scrubbing floors, even though they might be doctors of philosophy, teachers, or technicians, who had been classified as housekeepers just to get them out of the Training Center.[35]

If training center classification teams rebelled at the dishonesty of falsifying such a woman's records and classified her properly, she could not be assigned at all. Training centers with such scruples gradually accumulated a number of women with more or less odd skills—dental hygienists, X-ray technicians, translators, key-punch operators, opticians, dietitians, and many others. These, although badly needed to fill military vacancies, could not be assigned in the WAAC T/O unless classified as unskilled. Training centers reported that these women were in a state of very low morale: many advised civilian friends that the Army could not use their skills; and some nervous individuals actually became psychopathic cases, after months of delay and malassignment, and had to be discharged.[36]

Malassignment of skilled workers was, of course, well known to Army men in times of rapid expansion. The effect of malassignment on a woman, however, was often greater, because she could not receive a combat assignment which might in her own eyes justify the waste of a special skill. The only reported cases in which malassignment caused no morale damage to Waacs were those instances in which a

---

[35] Speech, "Hist of WAC," at WAC Pers Adm Sch, Purdue Univ. OCMH.

[36] (1) Memo, Classif and Asgmt Sec WAAC Hq for Sp Consultant to Dir, 7 Jun 43. SPWA 201.6 (6–7–43). (2) Rpt of WAAC Stf Dirs, 2d, 3d, and 4th Tng Cens. Min cited n. 4.

clerical or sedentary skill was ignored in favor of a field-type job, which most women were found to prefer.

The whole WAAC training system was soon distorted to meet the rigid requirements of the separate WAAC T/O. Exact calculations were made as to how many cooks, clerks, and chauffeurs would be needed in a certain number of companies, and the WAAC specialist schools were geared to turn out this number. Once the school quota was set, it became an inexorable demand which had to be met weekly regardless of the qualifications of the new recruits who presented themselves that week. Thus, if in one week there were large numbers of typists, badly needed in the field, they must be divided into three parts, one for cooks and bakers school, one for motor transport school, and one for administrative school. If, a week later, the recruits were all skilled mechanics, they must nevertheless also be divided among the three schools.

General Faith admitted later, "We arbitrarily tried to maintain a balance. Women who hated to cook were sent to Cooks School and women who couldn't spell were sent to Administrative School." [37] One Air Forces representative noted:

We don't mean to complain of the classification at the Training Centers, but we received a unit of 76 from one of the centers and all 76 were supply clerks. When we interviewed . . . we found we had college graduates who had years of experience in hospitals or other jobs, and they had been sent to administrative schools to become supply clerks.[38]

Expert stenographers had been trained as cooks, while former cotton pickers were graduates of Administrative Specialists School. Women had been sent to radio school who had not only hated radio work but also had medical or clerical skills.[39] Airfields that requisitioned weather observers got former waitresses classified as "potential weather observers." [40]

The War Department had for some time realized that the T/O system, while appropriate for rifle companies and other identical combat units, was a poor means of supplying either men or women to zone of the interior stations, no two of which had exactly the same needs. The Bulk Allotment system, prepared during these same months, promised relief from the distortion of both WAAC and Army skills to fit an inflexible Table of Organization.

Both WAAC and Army allotments were eventually to specify only the numbers and grades of individuals sent to most noncombat commands, leaving their duties to be determined and requisitioned according to the needs of each station. Although WAAC Headquarters worked all spring to hasten the application of this system to the WAAC, such did not become possible until May. In late March Army commands were warned to prepare for the new system. For units already shipped, they were expected to prepare Tables of Allotment representing the women's real skills; for units yet to come, any desired assortment of skills could be requested. On 1 May WAAC T/O units were formally inactivated, and Army commands were on their own in determining WAAC jobs within the limits of the total Bulk Allotments.[41]

---

[37] Speech. Min cited n. 4.
[38] Speech of WAAC Stf Dir AAF Tng Comd. Min cited n. 4.
[39] Rpt of 2d SvC. Min cited n. 4.
[40] Rpt of Insp, Great Falls AAB, Montana, 20 Aug 43. SPWA 333.1.
[41] (1) WD Memo W635–3–43, 31 Mar 43. (2) Ltr, TAG to CG ASF (AGF, AAF), 1 Apr 43. AG 320.2 WAAC (3–12–43) PR–W–WDGAP.

Replacement of Soldiers

Even the Bulk Allotment system did not solve another problem that resulted from Auxiliary status, whether under a Table of Organization or a more flexible Table of Allotment: under either system it proved difficult to determine whether a Waac had really replaced a man. The General Staff sent out repeated injunctions that Waacs must count against the Troop Basis and replace men one-for-one; a series of increasingly stringent War Department directives required a full report by skill and rank of men shipped, to be tallied against the number of Waacs received. Only thirty days—fifteen in the Army Service Forces—were allowed for the replacement, a shorter time than customary with male replacements, on the theory that a Waac could learn a job faster.

Nevertheless, it became increasingly evident that few men were actually being sent away, and might not be until the WAAC became part of the Army and its allotments could be merged with the military. Through a technicality of paper work, minor but basic, it was found that most Army posts were able to retain both Waacs and men. Each station had an allotment of military personnel and an allotment of civilian personnel; when Waacs arrived it had a third type, since each company came complete with its own Table of Organization or Allotment under which its members could be promoted and paid. Whether Waacs filled military or civilian jobs, all three allotments remained intact. All efforts, therefore, to get many posts to send a soldier away failed except on paper. A Waac might actually be given a man's desk and see the man depart, only later to find him at a new desk a few doors down the hall, in work for which the installation often had a perfectly legitimate allotment. If the man actually departed, the station had a vacancy in its military allotment, and promptly requisitioned another man. So long as Waacs were not legally recognized as military personnel, and could not fill vacancies in military allotments, the General Staff directives concerning the Troop Basis remained administratively impossible to enforce.[42]

The apparently simple solution of reducing a station's military allotment for each WAAC allotment, although directed by the General Staff, was also administratively unworkable. A station's allotments, whether in the form of Tables of Organization or the later Bulk Allotments, were complicated affairs which could not be altered at station level. To reduce the allotment, it would be necessary to republish it each time a new WAAC unit arrived, or each time a Waac was promoted from one grade to another. The time lag in this process was such that, reports indicated, most stations would not apply to higher echelons for republication of their military allotments, but clung to both WAAC and Army personnel. Only approaching military status could entirely solve this problem, by making one military allotment apply to both men and women.

---

[42] (1) WD Memo W635–2–43, 10 Feb 43. (2) WD Memo W635–3–43, 31 Mar 43. (3) WD Memo W635–4–43, 31 Mar 43. (4) WD Memo W635–5–43, 26 Apr 43. (5) ASF Cir 39, 11 Jun 43.

CHAPTER IX

Stresses of Rapid Build-up: Supply and the WAAC Uniform

As was to be expected from past Army experiences, the difficulties of expansion were also felt immediately in the matter of supply. For the WAAC, supply problems had been more or less chronic since the Corps' establishment, with crises following each new expansion plan, none more than temporarily remedied.

Shortages of Clothing

Of these supply problems, the one most apparent to the public was the Corps' inability to issue even one set of military outer garments to recruits—a situation that rarely pertained to male draftees. As the Corps neared the end of its first winter, fully half of the women in some training centers still went through their entire training without uniforms, while at others only summer clothing was available. Fort Dix, New Jersey, for example, was surprised to see descending from a train—in the midst of a March snowstorm—the entire 42d WAAC Post Headquarters Company from Daytona Beach, dressed in summer cottons. The women were promptly restricted to barracks and put to bed to keep warm, while Fort Dix for-

warded comments derogatory to the intelligence of WAAC authorities in training centers.[1] One west coast airfield, expecting a company, received a single untidy-looking Waac whose only clothing was the begrimed civilian outfit she had worn from her home to the training center and throughout basic training. After acid comment by telephone to Washington, one uniform was obtained. Other Waacs arrived with one or two shirts at desert airfields where the daily temperature averaged 110 degrees. At other times stations complained that women had been given their complete clothing issue by a process of issuing them grotesquely ill-fitting garments and, still worse, wrong-sized shoes, with the assurance that "you can change them when you get to your permanent station," even though the stations obviously had as yet no maintenance supplies of WAAC clothing.[2]

---

[1] (1) TWX, Comdt 1st WAAC Tng Cen to Dir WAAC, 24 Dec 42. WA 421 (11–20–42) Status. (2) Ltr, 2d SvC to Dir WAAC, 9 Mar 43, sub: 42d WAAC Post Hq Co. SPWA 319.1.

[2] (1) AAF WAC Hist, p. 39. (2) Memo, Dir WAC for QMG, 30 Aug 43. SPWA 400.34 (3–21–42)(1) sec 4 (1942). (3) Ltrs, WAAC Hq to field, 24 Feb 43, and replies; Memo, Lt Ryan for Plng Serv, 3 Apr 43. Same file, sec 3a.

Such failures were generally attributed by the public, and by WAAC trainees, to the numbers involved in the expansion program, or to the difficulty of procuring women's garments in an organization accustomed to dealing only with men's. The latter view was at times held by WAAC Headquarters itself, which noted in one criticism of The Quartermaster General's action: "Two manufacturers of women's wear said . . . any one of fifty stores in the country supplied many more women with many more items." [3] However, upon later analysis, shortages—as distinguished from defects in style—were seldom found to be due to Quartermaster inexperience or inability to let contracts for the relatively small numbers of women in the Army, but rather to simple failure to let WAAC contracts to manufacturers in time. This in turn was caused by the repeated refusal of Requirements Division, Services of Supply, to approve The Quartermaster General's proposals without lengthy delay and debate over possible discrimination in favor of women. At other times failures resulted, in The Quartermaster General's opinion, from the Services of Supply's action in approving G–3's expansion plans without the concurrence of supply agencies.

Difficulties in this respect could be traced back to the moment, a few days after the passage of WAAC legislation, when WAAC Headquarters and The Quartermaster General completed and sent to Requirements Division for approval the Table of Basic Allowances for winter clothing. Its approval was believed routine, since General Marshall had personally viewed and approved every listed item at the time of the WAAC's establishment. Nevertheless, approval was not forthcoming, and upon inquiry it was found that Requirements Division took issue with the fact that women's military clothing, like their civilian clothing, was scheduled to cost more than men's. A Waac's outfit would cost $177.45 as against $102.33 for a man's. In its efforts to equalize the total costs, Requirements Division noted that, whereas men received only one overcoat, women were scheduled to get two—the heavy winter coat like the men's and the light waterproof utility coat instead of the men's field jacket. Requirements Division at once determined to save $15.00 per woman by deleting the utility coat.

Director Hobby, when informed, pointed out that Requirements Division's action had been taken in ignorance of the previous months of planning on the WAAC uniform, in which the whole outfit had been keyed to the two coats. Thus, women's winter uniforms and underwear were of a lighter weight than men's, and women were not given either wool shirts or field jackets. The heavy overcoat was too warm for wear in spring and fall, and she felt that sickness would result if women faced those seasons with only cotton shirts and light covert cloth uniforms. The Quartermaster General sided with the Director, pointing out that no saving would result from the deletion, since one utility coat and one overcoat would wear as long as two of the more expensive overcoats, while a utility coat would protect the overcoat from rough wear in rain, mud, and motor convoys. The Chief of Administrative Services, General Grunert, likewise backed the Director in her arguments. [4] Requirements Division nevertheless re-

---

[3] MS Draft, The WAAC—Its Mission, 6 Apr 43. Folder, Plng Serv Notes, WAAC Planning files.

[4] Memo, CofAdm Serv for Reqmts Div SOS, 25 Jun 42. Same file.

fused to restore the item: "Statement as to possible increase in sickness may be questioned. On a cold winter day, it is a common sight to see women dressed in light weight clothing, including silk stockings and light shoes, while men are clothed in heavy wool garments." [5]

For five weeks the matter remained deadlocked. The Philadelphia Depot telephoned to state, "The girls will freeze this winter," [6] and wrote, "The time has passed when they may elect the fabric they desire and must take that which is available." [7] Director Hobby twice more protested the refusal to approve her requests.

At the end of July, with Waacs already at Des Moines, The Quartermaster General's Office (OQMG) had still received no procurement authority for either coat, and in desperation telephoned Director Hobby to ask that she put "a lot of pressure" on Requirements Division. This feat she believed to be militarily impossible since Requirements Division was on a higher SOS echelon than her office and was headed by a major general. The Director stated, "It's going to be a tragedy," to which the OQMG representative added: "And we don't want to be responsible for it. I know damn well that we will be blamed for it if the things aren't available. And these people that sit up there and can't make up their minds are going to crucify us, and I don't like it. . . . God Almighty, they are grown people!" [8]

What happened next was not recorded, but two days later Requirements Division, SOS, agreed to permit the procurement of both coats. There was some indication that the matter had not previously reached a high echelon in the Requirements Division.[9] At all events, it was admitted that the delay in letting contracts

was already irreparable; [10] there shortly ensued the September and October supply debacle at Des Moines, with its accompanying high sick rates and adverse publicity.

Nevertheless, when increased expansion plans were adopted in September of 1942, the same situation arose again. In explaining his inability to supply uniforms to either Des Moines or Daytona Beach in November and December, as promised, The Quartermaster General stated that Requirements Division had again delayed letting of uniform contracts for six weeks, for unexplained reasons. In addition, it proved impossible for The Quartermaster General to get from the Services of Supply authority to procure emergency cold-weather items to make up the deficit. The climate at Des Moines by this time had proved such that, even had full winter uniforms been available, additional arctic-type clothing would have been needed for outdoor workers and for all who had to march or walk across the extensive post. Temperatures of from zero to 20 degrees below were not uncommon, and a foot or more of snow often covered the parade ground.

On 3 November 1942, the newly appointed commandant, Colonel Hoag, wired: DUE TO SEVERE CLIMATIC CONDI-

---

[5] (1) Memo, Dir WAAC for Reqmts Div SOS, 25 Jun 42; (2) Memo, Reqmts Div SOS for Dir WAAC, 2 Jul 42. SPWA 400.34 (3–21–42)(1) sec 1.

[6] Memo, OQMG for Dir WAAC, 20 Sep 42. SPQRP 421–C. Copy in SPWA 421 (9–30–42).

[7] Risch, *Wardrobe for Women of the Army*, p. 67.

[8] Tp Conv, Col Hugh B. Hester, OQMG, and Dir WAAC, 20 Jul 42. SPWA 400.34 (3–21–42)(1) sec 1.

[9] Memo, Reqmts Div SOS for Dir WAAC, 2 Aug 42. SPWA 400.34 (1943). The memorandum says only that the Director, Requirements Division, SOS directed its Allowance Branch, the contending party, to change its stand.

[10] Risch, *Wardrobe for Women of the Army*, pp. 70, 82–85.

TIONS, FOLLOWING ITEMS WAAC CLOTHING URGENTLY NEEDED TO PROPERLY PROTECT AND SAFEGUARD HEALTH OF THIS COMMAND. He asked for over 15,000 each of four-buckle arctic overshoes, nurses' lambskin-lined mittens, and wool-lined trousers, and concluded: IT IS IMPERATIVE THAT THE SUPPLY OF THESE BE EXPEDITED.[11] A few days later Colonel Hoag appealed again by letter, asking for wool socks, caps, shirts, and trousers, also mittens, wool underwear, and overshoes; for drivers, he asked for flannel-lined coveralls to replace the cotton ones.[12]

In Director Hobby's absence in England during this month, Colonel Catron immediately appealed to Distribution Division, Services of Supply, for orders to ship emergency cold-weather items. Some debate then took place between Distribution Division and Requirements Division. Distribution Division felt that action on the radio request should not be delayed but that the whole problem must be approached more deliberately:

With reference to the broad problem posed by basic radio, this division has noted numerous requests initiated, piecemeal, by the Women's Army Auxiliary Corps for the adoption of additional items of clothing. . . . It is recommended that caution be observed in authorizing any special procurement to assure the adequacy of items hurriedly requested to fill the requirement for which intended. This division has no information as to the adequacy of the trousers desired, nor as to the suitability of the Arctic overshoes requested for wear with shoes issued to the WAAC.[13]

As a result, no decisive action was taken except to schedule a conference for 25 November, some two weeks away.

The Quartermaster General also was unable to take action, and in fact was in a state of rebellion against the repeated expansion directives his office had been re-

ceiving. It was his opinion that the War Department supply agencies that agreed to G–3's expansion program—particularly Requirements Division—had not co-ordinated the matter fully enough with their operating agencies.

OQMG, which had requested twelve months' notice of expansion plans, now was lucky to get twelve minutes, so rapidly did the WAAC estimates go up. The Quartermaster history of women's clothing stated: "Army Service Forces did its planning at much too short range, without admitting the necessity for stock-piling cloth. . . ." Admittedly OQMG was kept fully informed, often by telephone, of the latest developments, but no sooner did it complete plans and let contracts than the figures were again raised. The figures furnished The Quartermaster General had increased within a few months from a March 1942 estimate of 12,000 in a year to later estimates of 53,000 for 1943; then 113,000; then 150,000; then half a million, although the last figure was not used for procurement purposes. As a Quartermaster historian later remarked, "The consternation this created can be imagined."[14]

Accordingly, an OQMG council was held in November of 1942, at which it was stated that no increased supply of winter uniforms could be procured and no cold-weather or arctic equipment, unless the office was given twelve months from date of notice if cloth must be bought, or six months if the items could be procured ready-made. This was the time customarily allowed for the procurement of men's

---

[11] TWX, Comdt 1st WAAC Tng Cen to Dir WAAC, 3 Nov 42. SPWA 420.
[12] Ltr, Col Hoag to Dir WAAC, 9 Nov 42. SPQ 420, in SPWA 400.34 (3–21–42)(1) sec 1.
[13] Covering Memo and Inds to TWX cited n. 11.
[14] Risch, *Wardrobe for Women of the Army*, pp. 5, 6.

clothing and equipment. This recommendation was approved by the Services of Supply's Chief of Staff, General Styer, in ignorance of the fact that the women were already at Des Moines.[15]

Upon Director Hobby's return from England in mid-November and her threatened resignation, General Styer shortly reversed this policy and directed The Quartermaster General to get 2,000 winter uniforms to Des Moines at once and 1,000 a week thereafter, regardless of his twelve months' notice. General Styer's immediate subordinate, the assistant chief of staff for operations—Maj. Gen. LeRoy Lutes—then directed The Quartermaster General to procure at once 2,500 wool-lined trousers, 2,500 wool shirts, and 2,000 pairs of gloves for WAAC motor transport personnel. General Lutes' immediate subordinate, the director of Requirements Division—Brig. Gen. Walter A. Wood, Jr.— also directed the Quartermaster Corps to procure 17,700 wool caps and wool gloves and 2,574 more overshoes, and to take action to standardize necessary articles for winter wear.[16]

To achieve this increase without diverting standard material from men's uniforms, the Philadelphia Depot was obliged to gather up various odd lots of different colored woolen materials which were then in the depot, and to have them redyed to the enlisted shade. These inevitably came out in a wide range of nonstandard colors. One branch of OQMG directed that some skirts, some jackets, and some caps be made in each shade, so that a woman might receive a complete matching outfit even if she did not match her neighbors. Since this would have caused administrative difficulty for the depot, another branch of OQMG canceled this order without the knowledge of the branch that

had issued it. As a result, skirts and jackets were of different shades and it was impossible to match them. Observed a Quartermaster historian: "The most grotesque combination was that of the chocolate-brown barathea and the mustard shade olive-drab."[17] From the viewpoint of the Recruiting Service, these uniforms were worse than the shortages, but they were at least warm.

To avoid such hasty procurement in the future, The Quartermaster General again recommended that his office be given twelve months' notice on any further increases, saying:

Experience indicates that it has required approximately twelve months from the initiation of procurement of cloth required for WAAC uniforms until the finished article is ready for issue.

WAAC Headquarters again professed its helplessness to give such notice:

Since the passage of the bill creating the WAAC, four (4) distinct expansion plans have been ordered by higher authority. In each instance the plan was ordered into operation immediately, and The Quartermaster General was given the proposed figures without delay.

Accordingly, the Services of Supply was forced in December of 1942 to give The Quartermaster General procurement authorization in advance of the General Staff decision on the Corps' future size, stating that the clothing could be used for main-

---

[15] Memo, CofS SOS for CofAdm Serv, 19 Nov 42. SPEX, SPWA 421 (11–19–42).

[16] (1) Interv with Lt Col Helen Woods, 9 Oct 48. (2) Weekly Rpt, WAAC Hq to CofAdm Serv, 15–21 Nov 42. SPWA 319.12 (11–9–42) sec 1. (3) Memo, ACofS Opns SOS for QMG, 27 Nov 42. SPDDQ 420 Clothing, in SPWA 421 (11–27–42). (4) 1st Ind, Reqmts Div SOS (Gen Wood) to QMG, 3 Dec 42. SPRMD 421 (11–26–42), in WA 400.34.

[17] Risch, *Wardrobe for Women of the Army*, p. 51, ns. 95, 97.

tenance stocks if the expected draft of women did not occur. The enormous amounts of 400,000 by the end of 1943 and 750,000 by June of 1944 were authorized, in the expectation that the plan for a draft law to obtain those numbers would be approved. In the light of future events, it was perhaps fortunate that the paper was recalled, and that it was decided to await the General Staff decision on draft plans.[18]

In spite of General Styer's intervention in November, there could be no immediate improvement in the supply of uniforms since the procurement process had been long delayed. On Christmas Eve Colonel Hoag again telegraphed from Des Moines, reporting many items exhausted, all stocks low. At Daytona Beach, which opened in December, only summer uniforms were available for most of the winter. Trainees were necessarily shipped out in summer khaki, regardless of destination. The Third WAAC Training Center, at Fort Oglethorpe, opening in January, reported that many women went through their entire training without uniforms; at the same time, the rate of respiratory disorders soared to twice that of men in the area. Graduates were at first held idle in staging areas. The previous shipment of women in civilian clothes to the Aircraft Warning Service had had such an adverse effect upon recruiting that Director Hobby had issued a ban on further shipments not properly uniformed. Overcrowded conditions in the staging companies soon forced repeal of this order, and a report from Fort Oglethorpe noted that "Fifty percent of personnel departing this station during the week of March 21–28 will not be uniformed." [19]

In early March WAAC Headquarters was informed that it was impossible for The Quartermaster General to meet the supply schedule furnished by Requirements Division at the time of G–3's February decisions on Corps' size. As a result, the Fourth WAAC Training Center was scheduled to open in the still-wintry Massachusetts weather without any clothing supplies whatever.

At this, the Director sent her chief of operations, Colonel Clark, to the training centers to determine the actual situation. Upon his return Colonel Clark directed sharp criticism toward the Army Service Forces' supply agencies. There had been minor administrative faults at the training centers, Colonel Clark reported, such as occasional failure to establish close cooperation with depots or to utilize stock fully. Thus, the Atlanta Quartermaster Depot had shipped items to Daytona Beach that were needed at Fort Oglethorpe, and vice versa, and Quartermaster had refused to exchange them:

He objected strenuously on the grounds that such action would confuse his records. My reaction to that is that records can always be straightened out but a death from pneumonia due to improper clothing can hardly be laughed off.

In spite of such occasional administrative faults, Colonel Clark concluded emphatically that fully 80 percent of the difficulties could be traced to insufficiency of production rather than of administration. He recommended that proper authority assure that individual contractors were on time, that surplus men's material "known to be available in abundance" be used,

---

[18] Memo, Dir Reqmts Div SOS for CofAdm Serv, 26 Nov 42, and Inds dated 5, 21, 27 Dec 42 and 12 Jan 43. SPRMP 291.9 WAAC, in Dir Adm Serv ASF Sp Coll DRB AGO.

[19] (1) Weekly Rpt, WAAC Hq to CofAdm Serv, 14–24 Mar 43. SPWA 319.12. (2) Ltr, 3d Tng Cen to Dir WAAC, 20 Mar 43. WA 421 (1942).

"that a determined inquiry be made at once to ascertain why certain articles are, and have been, habitually lacking over a period of months, and that steps be taken to remedy this deficiency." [20]

In reply to Colonel Clark's report, The Quartermaster General stated that WAAC supply had been "expedited in every manner"; "contractors are well ahead"; "this office, in supervising and directing the procurement of WAAC clothing through the procuring depot, has taken every action possible to eliminate delinquencies on current contracts." [21] This view was supported by General Madison Pearson, Deputy Chief of Administrative Services, SOS, who wrote, "The report of action taken by The Quartermaster General indicates that everything possible is being done to expedite the manufacture and shipment of clothing." [22]

Finally, representatives of WAAC Headquarters, in a meeting at OQMG, secured promise of makeshift action to supply the Fourth Training Center. A sufficient quantity of Civilian Conservation Corps spruce-green mackinaws were made available; trainees were issued Army officers' serge shirts in lieu of winter jackets; and 20,000 more off-shade skirts were procured, also shoes and raincoats. The Fifth Training Center, at Camps Ruston and Polk in Louisiana and Monticello in Arkansas, could fortunately get along with summer khaki. The Quartermaster General, said a WAAC representative, was "most sympathetic and cooperative."

The Quartermaster General now decided that the matter of supplying the WAAC warranted the full-time specialized attention of one officer, and a WAAC officer was assigned to his office to work on the problem. Such an assignment had not been possible previously because of General Somervell's order that no WAAC officers would be assigned to any office within his headquarters other than that of the Director WAAC. [23]

If the supply of uniforms to training centers was insufficient, that to field stations was virtually nonexistent. Army supply officers at these stations often were uncertain what the WAAC supply channel was or what depots stocked WAAC clothing, and they had no copies of the WAAC T/BA, T/E, and T/O, which were apparently not available at training centers or in the field. Even if requisitions were properly submitted, it took over a month to get them filled from the two depots—Kansas City and Atlanta—that stocked WAAC uniforms. Sometimes the requisitions were never filled, and the wait for shoes was often two or three months. As late as 15 March a service command which had administered WAAC units for seven months was told that there was still no schedule set up for maintenance allowances for Waacs at posts, camps, and stations, and that none could be set up until sufficient quantities of clothing were available for new recruits. [24]

Appearance of the Uniform

In addition to exaggerating shortages, the expansion program had permanently

---

[20] Memo, Chief, Opns Serv WAAC, for Exec WAAC, 6 Mar 43. SPWA 421 (11–20–42) 1942.

[21] Memo, QMG for WAAC Hq, 10 Mar 43. SPWA 421 (1942).

[22] Memo, DCofAdm Serv for Dir WAAC, 13 Mar 43. Same file.

[23] Memo, Chief, Opns Serv WAAC for Dir WAAC, 23 Mar 43. WA 421 (1942). For Somervell order, see pp. 94–95, above.

[24] (1) Ltr, OQMG to field, 23 Sep 42. SPQX 420. (2) Ltr, 8 Dec 42, sub: same. SPWA 421 (5–16–42) sec 1. (3) Memo, 1st Tng Cen for WAAC Hq, 29 Oct 42. SPWA 421. (4) Ltr, 1st SvC to Dir WAAC, 15 Mar 43. SPWA 400.34 (3–21–42)(1) sec 3.

affected the appearance of the WAAC uniform, by making correction of early mistakes impossible before mass production was required. For every amateur theorist who supposed that any other cause had damaged WAAC recruiting, there were ten who put the blame on the appearance of the uniform. Some nine out of ten of the unsolicited letters of advice received by the WAAC went so far as to place sole responsibility upon this one factor.

Actually, OQMG had been well aware from the moment uniforms were issued that many items of clothing needed modification, and plans for such modification were being made when the need for immediate mass production intervened. The Quartermaster General, soon after the opening of the First WAAC Training Center, sent to Des Moines an expert committee which included a representative of the Philadelphia Depot and a civilian consultant, Miss Dorothy Shaver, vice-president of Lord & Taylor. These catalogued various complaints, and Colonel Faith reported others. All garments were cut with wide collars and narrow hips, as for men; skirts, shirts, and jackets were for this reason generally ill fitting, uncomfortable, and unbecoming to the average woman. Hats were out of shape before they were issued; raincoats leaked at every seam in even a light shower; seams of hems were sewed down so that they could not be easily raised or lowered, and some garments had no hems at all. The suspenders on girdles were too short and pulled runs in stockings, as the War Production Board had allotted insufficient elastic.[25]

The attempt to discover the reason for the poor appearance of what had been a basically sound uniform design revealed that the Philadelphia Depot had never made a graded designers' model of the uniform, but had somehow got hold of a rough pattern cut by a manufacturer to estimate the cloth needed. This the depot had henceforth called "the master pattern," and from it each manufacturer had developed a set of sized patterns of his own. Those manufacturers who received contracts were all in the men's-wear industry, since, The Quartermaster General reported, "The manufacturers of women's clothing were not able to handle the production of WAAC uniforms at the prices which the Philadelphia Depot was willing to pay." Moreover, winter uniforms had already been made upon the defective patterns used for the summer ones.

For the poor results obtained, the Philadelphia Depot blamed The Quartermaster General for failing to consult it earlier, thus giving it insufficient time for development of patterns. Further developmental work was therefore relinquished to the depot so that it might not be hampered. A new jacket was developed, with a better-fitting collar. It had no belt, as the women had shown a tendency to pull the belt too tight. Unfortunately, the depot, in omitting the belt, respaced the jacket buttons so that the bottom one fell quite low; it was now impossible for a Waac to sit down without unbuttoning the lowest jacket button or suffering what Director Hobby described as an "unsightly gap." Since large quantities had been acquired, The Quartermaster General refused to correct the spacing. The new jacket, as turned out by the men's garment contractors, was also too flat across the bust and still too stiff and awkward.

[25] (1) Rpt, 20 Oct 42. SPWA 421. (2) Ltr, Faith to Dir WAAC, 12 Aug 42. SPWA 421 (8–22–42). (3) Risch, *Wardrobe for Women of the Army*, Ch. IV. The following paragraphs, unless otherwise stated, are based on Risch, especially pages 40–47 and 61–63.

WAAC BAND, *Fort Des Moines.*

The skirt pattern also was modified to round the hipline somewhat and to prevent wrinkling and rolling. The summer material was too stiff to permit insertion of a pleat, even if War Production Board rules would have allowed it. The 8.2-ounce cotton twill used in men's uniforms had admittedly proved totally unsatisfactory for women's; OQMG now tried to devise some other suitable summer material which would withstand laundering in Quartermaster laundries, but various cotton-rayon combinations all proved doubtful. Seersucker was dropped from consideration because it would have required a new uniform design and because of a shortage of production facilities, although the WAVES, SPARS, and women Marines all found an adequate supply for summer uniforms. Finally, it was decided that the khaki uniforms must be retained.

Until the spring of 1943, both the Director WAAC and The Quartermaster

General found themselves in the position of helpless bystanders, able only to make suggestions, which were accepted by the Philadelphia Depot but never seemed to appear in the finished garments. In May, OQMG discovered the cause—the depot was frequently ignoring its recommendations, and for six months had not made all the requested corrections, nor had it ever placed the pattern in the hands of a good tailor of women's clothing, which it had been directed to do.

The Quartermaster General now took back some control over developmental work and, at the request of WAAC Headquarters, called in representatives of four leading clothing firms and expert designers of women's patterns.[26] These immediately discarded the Army sizes, which had been set up in long, regular, and short, as

[26] M/R, 19 May 43, Min of Mtg, and atchd Memo, ASF for OQMG, sub: Summer Uniforms, WAAC. SPWA 421 (1942).

for men. Now at last patterns in the usual women's sizes were developed—half sizes, misses', women's, and long sizes. These proved better, but the Quartermaster's Storage and Distribution Division insisted that the old size designations and stock numbers be used on the new patterns, to avoid complicating its storage and issue system, which was geared to handle only short, regular, and long.

Even with improved patterns, the jackets still remained stiff and unbecoming, and it was not until some months later that OQMG detected the trouble: the Philadelphia Depot was still writing specifications, which manufacturers were required to follow, that called for the use of the same heavy construction with canvasses and interlinings of the weights used in men's uniforms.

In late 1943 and 1944 a satisfactory uniform pattern was to be gradually developed, but its production by this time was, as The Quartermaster General said, now merely a matter of academic interest, as large stocks of the earlier patterns had been ordered in an effort to meet the scheduled expansion program, and no new procurement could be authorized until these were worn out.

At first sight of the original ill-fitting uniforms, Director Hobby in July 1942 had recommended to Requirements Division, SOS, that Waacs going to the field or on leave be allowed to purchase individually tailored white dress uniforms, at their own expense, as were male Army officers, Army nurses, and, later, the Navy women's services. It was believed that such a measure would eliminate the worst of the general criticism encountered earlier, since the dress uniform could be worn for public ceremonies and appearances.

Requirements Division disapproved this request: "No useful purpose can be served in connection with efforts toward a successful prosecution of the war."[27] Three subsequent requests by the Director to General Marshall were stopped by the Services of Supply from reaching him, and the WAAC was not authorized a dress uniform until later entry into the Army automatically gave it to women officers.

The appearance of the WAAC cap was also much criticized. It was worked over by experts—the visor was made twice as thick and heavy, to prevent buckling; the side and top stiffening was increased; a new type of lining was devised. Still the cap remained almost impossible to clean and block. Director Hobby in January 1943 finally gave up the idea of a distinctive cap and requested a garrison (overseas) cap for all but dress wear. The Director pointed out that winter and summer garrison caps at a cost of 71 cents and 39 cents respectively would eliminate the need for issue of extra visored caps at $2.32 and $1.99 apiece. This request was refused by the Services of Supply on the grounds that it would increase the number of issued items. Although men got both dress and service caps, it was at the time believed that the War Department was shortly to cease issuing the garrison cap to men.[28]

The WAAC shirtwaist was also the subject of dispute, and more than one Army man reported, quite accurately, "I never yet saw a WAAC whose shirt collar fit her." Commercial producers of women's shirts had always sized them by bust sizes rather than by collar size, since civilian

---

[27] (1) Memo, OQMG for G–1, 18 Jul 42, with Inds and covering Memos; (2) Memo, Dir WAAC for CofAdm Serv, 24 Aug 42, and Inds. SPQRE 421, in SPWA 421 (7–16–42).

[28] Memo, WAAC Hq for CofAdm Serv, 20 Jan 43, and Inds. SPWA 421.

women's blouses seldom had a standing collar and tie and therefore did not require exact collar measurements. Men's shirts, on the other hand, were sized by neck and sleeve measurements.

The Quartermaster General now perceived that women's military shirts should have been sized like men's, but the shirt contracts had been let to manufacturers of women's garments, who were unable to produce men's-type shirts with a standing collarband and graded neck and sleeves. To cancel their contracts and let new ones would have caused a serious delay; it was therefore decided to retain the convertible collar and the original sizing system. Several sleeve lengths for each size were recommended, but the Quartermaster Storage and Distribution Division would not concur, because of the "extra work this would entail" in storing and shipping several types of shirts.

One difficulty was solved, however: The Quartermaster General discovered that the Philadelphia Depot had again been guilty of furnishing manufacturers a basic pattern cut by makers of men's shirts. A new pattern was devised with a collar that was smaller than the previous one and a bust that was larger, and this proved fairly satisfactory. Again, large purchases of the defective pattern had been made and had to be issued throughout 1943 and 1944, and complaints about the shirt never ceased to come in.

The problem of providing satisfactory government-issue shoes for women had from the beginning been difficult to solve so as to please everyone. The Director's Office made surveys of the women's opinions as to various types of shoes and found that there was a dissatisfied minority for any type. Medical opinion also was divided. One school of thought recommended a flat-heeled shoe like the men's for all purposes, pointing out that most orthopedic patients in WAAC training center hospitals suffered from sprains and fractures caused by marching or doing heavy work in the medium-heeled oxfords. Other experts said that, on the contrary, a sudden change to flat heels for constant wear would cause even greater foot trouble and fallen arches for the majority of American women. The dispute was resolved by the adoption of the nurses' high-laced flat-heeled field boot for outdoor work and marching and the service oxford for office and dress. Even for this limited use, the field boot had to be broken in by an elaborate routine involving heavy wool anklets and ten-minute daily wearings. The Director therefore recommended that the women get one pair of these field shoes in addition to the two pairs of ordinary shoes.

This request was refused by the Army Service Forces: men got only two pairs, both of course flat-heeled, so women could have only two—one of oxfords and one of field shoes. The Director appealed again, pointing out that in such case a woman could not let her service oxfords be sent away for repair, since repair of women's shoes proved to be always slower than that of men's and ordinarily took from two weeks to a month, a prohibitive length of time to be without shoes for office wear. Finally, after the Director wrote a memorandum on the subject to General Somervell, the ASF agreed to issue Waacs three pairs of shoes—two of oxfords and one of field shoes for office workers, one of oxfords and two of field shoes for outdoor workers.[29]

---

[29] (1) Request, Dir WAAC to OQMG, for field shoes, 4 Sep 42; (2) Rpt on test of 500 WAAC oxfords, 14 Nov 42; (3) Ltr, Surg, Ft Oglethorpe, to Dir

YOU'LL JUST HAVE TO GET USED TO LOW-HEELED SHOES!

The WAAC utility bag had likewise proved unsatisfactory. The cheap imitation leather adopted by the economy-minded Quartermaster General almost at once cracked and peeled. The Director then presented him with a leather bag designed by Richard Koret, and requested its adoption. Mourned a Quartermaster historian: "It was apparently immaterial that the bag was expensive and that it used calfskin leather, a critical material." [30] This sample was delivered to the Philadelphia Depot, which immediately let the contract to such low-priced manufacturers that the resulting bag was unrecognizable and quickly wore out. Finally, OQMG announced with pleasure that it had located a quantity of seal leather, tanned goatskin, and genuine water buffalo. These were durable and noncritical materials, and an excellent utility bag resulted.

The Navy avoided most clothing difficulties by giving its Waves a clothing allowance with which to purchase uniforms. Various commercial firms produced the uniforms, apparently without any of the Philadelphia Depot's misfortunes, and sold them through department stores which gave expert fitting. Shoes and other personal items could thus be chosen from standard models whose fit suited the individual. The Army was unable to adopt this system, since to provide a money allowance in lieu of clothing would have required Congressional action to amend existing Army legislation. Army women eventually benefited in that they received maintenance of the uniform by free re-

placement of worn-out items, whereas the Waves' monetary maintenance allowance of $12.50 every three months was reputedly scarcely enough to keep them in stockings, much less in new uniforms, shoes, and underwear.[31]

The Need for New Types of Work Clothing

As Waacs began, under the expansion program, to do various kinds of Army jobs which had not been anticipated by the WAAC Pre-Planners, a need arose for new types of work clothing. Of the four types of jobs which had been originally authorized—clerks, drivers, cooks, and telephone operators—the first and last could be performed in the A uniform. Accordingly, the only work uniforms authorized for Waacs were white dresses for cooks and coveralls for drivers to put on over their uniforms while making motor repairs. These work uniforms were issued only to the few specialists concerned. The majority of Waacs when shipped to the field had only the A uniform plus two of the seersucker exercise dresses, which were worn to protect the service uniform during physical training, kitchen police, and barracks fatigue duties.

With the expansion of the Corps, Waacs soon were working in hospital wards and laboratories, driving light trucks as well as staff cars, and being assigned as full-time mechanics, welders, pier checkers, messengers, and gas pump attendants. In the Air Forces many worked "on the line" in aircraft maintenance and in other jobs that required them to climb in and out of aircraft and up and down control towers. Neither the A uniform nor the fatigue

WAAC, 23 Feb 43, and Inds; (4) Ltr, WAAC Hq to Des Moines, 3 Apr 43; (5) Ltr, WAAC Hq to Reqmts Div ASF, 10 Jun 43, with Inds; (6) Memo, Col Hobby for Gen Somervell, 9 Jul 43; (7) Change to T/E 21, Sep 43; (8) Ltrs, Field Stas to Dir WAAC, various dates, atchd to above. All in SPWA 421.3 Shoes (9–4–42) 1943.

[30] Risch, *Wardrobe for Women of the Army*, p. 73.
[31] Memo, Asst Exec WAC for Dir WAC, 14 Mar 44, sub: Uniform Issue of Marines, WAVES, and SPARS. WDWAC 421.

dress was appropriate. The A uniform was easily ruined by grease or medicines, and its tight skirt made tower-climbing either impossible or immodest; the exercise dress was even skimpier, being well above the knee and unsuitable for appearance outside the WAAC area.

One of the most important reported work needs was for some form of trousers or culottes, requests for which poured in from the field. The Military District of Washington, after a study of the needs of Waacs in its motor pool, requested a culotte skirt for drivers. The regular skirt had proven

slightly embarrassing at times to the wearer, particularly in climbing over tail-gates into trucks, or standing on a rack about 3½ feet high and leaning over washing the tops of passenger cars. . . . The coverall currently provided has been found unsuitable and unsightly for wear when driving staff cars and the regulation skirt too short and tight.

WAAC Headquarters concurred in this request and asked the development of a divided skirt for drivers.

However, Requirements Division, Army Service Forces, refused the request on the grounds that the Director herself had rejected culottes at the time the uniform was decided upon. The Director thereupon acknowledged her mistake but renewed the request, saying, "In March 1942 there were no Waacs on duty in the field and therefore no recommendations or decision could be based on actual experience." This question went as far as the Acting Chief of Staff, Army Service Forces, who supported Requirements Division's view and refused the request.[32]

The demand for a work garment continued too strong to stem, and later in the spring of 1943 Director Hobby again appealed to the Army Service Forces: "It has become increasingly evident as larger numbers of WAAC units are assigned to the field . . . that a trousered garment for exercise, fatigue, and other heavy work is vitally necessary."[33] Since Requirements Division would not concur in the design and procurement of slacks or culottes for Waacs, Director Hobby requested, as the only other alternative, that the herringbone twill coveralls be issued to all Waacs, instead of only to drivers.

This action was agreeable to Requirements Division, but, since men had only one type of fatigue clothes, the seersucker exercise dress was deleted from the authorized issue except for use in the training center. Instead of two exercise dresses, each Waac assigned to the field was now issued one coverall. WAAC Headquarters requested two coveralls, but Requirements Division decided that one would be adequate and that Waacs in active work could later get two by turning in one skirt and one shirt. The Des Moines Motor Transport School attempted to get three or four coveralls for student drivers, so that coveralls could be sent to the ten-day Quartermaster laundries. The Quartermaster General's Office concurred in this, but Requirements Division disapproved it "in view of the requirements of the using arms and services and the production facilities of industry."[34] The later training centers for a time had difficulty in getting even the allotted number, and drivers at Daytona Beach wore men's Class B blue denim.[35]

---

[32] Ltr, MDW Motor Cen to CG MDW, 30 Jun 43, with Inds. SPWA 400.34 (3–21–43)(1) sec 4 (1942).

[33] Memo, WAAC Hq for Reqmts Div ASF, 21 May 43, sub: Trousers, HBT. Same file. Also Ltr, Camp Campbell, Ky., to 5th SvC, 20 Mar 43, and 16 Inds. Same file, sec 3.

[34] Ltr, Ft Des Moines MT Sch to CO 1st WAAC Tng Cen, 22 Sep 42. Same file, sec 1.

[35] Ltr, 2d WAAC Tng Cen to Dir WAAC, 18 Jun 43. Same file, sec 4.

PHYSICAL TRAINING *at an Army Air Forces Training Command base in 1943.*

The adoption of the coveralls did not solve the need for cold-weather work garments, for which requests continued to come in from both Army and Air Forces stations. Whereas a man might comfortably wear cotton coveralls over his long winter underwear and wool trousers, a Waac had nothing underneath but her winter panties, only one fourth as heavy as men's winter underwear. In March, what OQMG believed to be women's wool shirts and trousers were issued to drivers only, but these proved greatly oversized and unsuitable.

In late April of 1943, after the Waacs had somehow survived the first winter, The Quartermaster General sent a committee to investigate the situation at Fort Des Moines and make recommendations on winter clothing. The committee recommended that all Waacs in cold climates, regardless of job, get warmer panties and vests (50 percent wool instead of the current 25 percent) and also wool shirts and knee-length wool stockings. All outdoor workers should also get long wool drawers and long-sleeved undershirts, trousers with an inner wool liner and outer windproof cover, field jackets with liners and covers, leggings, and wool caps. Director Hobby concurred, pointing out that much training time had been lost at Fort Des Moines and Fort Devens for lack of warm clothing. However, Requirements Division did not favorably consider the field jacket, leggings, and 50 percent wool underwear for women, or the wool waist, trousers, and liner for any except drivers.[36]

Warm-weather clothing was equally deficient, according to reports from hospitals and stations in semitropical climates. These, finding the heavy A uniform totally unsuited to a hot climate or to hospital ward work, had fallen into the admittedly undesirable practice of allowing Waacs to wear the short seersucker exercise dress for many types of jobs, even desk jobs in headquarters where they were fully visible to employees and visitors. The dress was also worn for kitchen police and barracks duties where the long-sleeved coverall was too hot. Just as the decision was rendered to substitute coveralls for exercise dresses, many southern stations were writing to plead for four or more of the exercise dresses instead of two.

The Army Air Forces' large Training Command, which at one time utilized almost one sixth of the entire WAAC personnel, was particularly hard-hit, since the majority of its airfields were along the southern border in Florida, Louisiana, Texas, and the southwestern desert. A study prepared by this command pointed out that at many fields the temperature never went below 90° or 100° for months at a time and often rose as high as 135° F. Enlisted women were obliged to wear two shirts a day and wash them at night, since there were no laundries on the fields. The Air Forces study concluded that Waacs must be immediately issued at least five short-sleeved shirts in addition to their regular ones, three exercise suits instead of the two then issued, and four pairs of cotton anklets instead of the three wool ones then issued. In reply, the AAF received what it considered an inexplicable decision that no additional clothing would be issued and that even the two exercise suits would be taken away and replaced by a heavy coverall.[37]

In May of 1943, three months before the refusal of the Air Forces' request, the Director had made a similar recommendation: that the Quartermaster Corps redesign the exercise dress into a seersucker summer uniform like that of the WAVES and Women Marines. The Quartermaster General concurred and visualized the development of one standard short-sleeved work dress, longer and better fitted than the exercise dress, which could be worn by cooks, hospital workers, women in tropical climates, and any others who needed such a dress. The Quartermaster Corps began to study this problem in 1943 but no summer dress for universal on-duty wear was produced during World War II.

The lack of such a dress was felt most strongly by hospitals, where WAAC workers had no uniform comparable to the nurses' white or seersucker uniforms. Some Waacs wore seersucker fatigue dresses if they had received any before issue was discontinued. This practice was pronounced unsanitary, since the same dress was worn for physical training, recreation, kitchen police, and barracks fatigue duties, and with only two dresses a Waac could not

---

[36] Ltr, Comdt to OQMG, 22 Apr 43. Same file, sec 3a.

[37] Ltr, AAF CFTC, Randolph Field, Tex., with Ind, Hq AAF Tng Comd, Ft Worth, Tex., to Dir WAC, 20 Aug 43. Same file, sec 4.

use the hospital laundry but either wore her dress a week unwashed or washed one herself every night. Even so, the two exercise dresses were more suitable than the one coverall that replaced them.[38]

The Quartermaster Corps, on being informed of the problem, was agreeable to issuing hospital Waacs the WAAC cook-baker dress, a neat cool wrap-around white garment which could be dyed any desired pastel shade to distinguish Waacs from nurses. However, The Surgeon General's Office objected: "Fatigue clothes are worn by enlisted men of the medical department and there should be no exception for members of the WAAC stationed at hospitals." Waacs, this office said, could wear either their coveralls or surgical gowns. Requirements Division, ASF, concurred with The Surgeon General's Office and overruled the Quartermaster Corps. They held firm in this ruling all summer even after stations in the field pointed out that enlisted men on duty in clinics and laboratories often did get four pairs of cook's white trousers and six white coats. The surgical gown shortly proved most unsatisfactory for women working in men's wards: it was too long, frequently dragging on the floor. Worse, it was open all the way down the back and a uniform was not customarily worn underneath in warm weather.[39]

With hundreds of similar field requests on file, the Army Service Forces held unswervingly to its policy that no additions or changes would be made to the originally authorized uniform either in type or amount. Fort Bragg, North Carolina, asked increased issue of dresses and aprons for cooks and bakers because of the intense summer heat, the coal ranges used, and the ten-day laundry service. This was

refused by The Quartermaster General's Office on the grounds that the material was needed instead for grain bags and civilian clothing. Recruiting offices in Virginia asked that all stockings issued them be rayon instead of half the issue in cotton, which produced a bad public reaction. The Director approved this request and asked that all Waacs assigned outside Army posts be issued rayon stockings only, but was refused by The Quartermaster General on the grounds that rayon did not wear as long as cotton stockings.

Director Hobby asked that, if Waacs could not have a garrison cap, they be issued two summer hats, since the current issue of one made cleaning and blocking impossible. No immediate action was taken on this request; OQMG had on hand only 262,000 extra summer caps and feared that a sudden influx of recruits might cause a shortage. In only one minor case did the Army Service Forces grant a request for change: late in August of 1943 it authorized WAAC recruiters to receive an extra summer jacket, skirt, and cap, after it was demonstrated by a year in the field that recruiters had to wear the full uniform daily and could not wear fatigue clothing while their one jacket and cap were being cleaned.[40]

The trend of Requirements Division's policy was in fact in the opposite direction—the systematic deletion of all items of the original authorization that men did

[38] Ltr, CO Hosp Unit, Ft Oglethorpe to Dir WAAC, 10 Apr 43. Same file, sec 3.

[39] (1) Memo, SGO for QMG, 6 May 43, with Inds; (2) Ltr, Randolph Field, Tex., to Dir WAC, 20 Aug 43. Same file, sec 4.

[40] (1) Ltr, Ft Bragg to 4th SvC, 28 May 43; (2) Ltr, Richmond R&I Dist to Dist R&I Off, 23 Aug 43, and Inds; (3) Memo, ASF for Reqmts Div ASF, 30 Aug 43; (4) Memo, Reqmts Div ASF for OQMG. Same file, sec 4.

not wear. These included summer and winter pajamas, galoshes, handkerchiefs, dress shields, athletic shoes, and summer and winter bathrobes.[41]

Next, a Quartermaster committee "made personal investigations at Fort Des Moines" and found that only 25 percent of the women were wearing the issue girdles, others preferring to wear none or to purchase a favorite brand commercially.[42] The Quartermaster Corps felt that Waacs should be given, in lieu of the issue, money to purchase the brassières and girdles of their choice, and WAAC Headquarters concurred. However, this plan would have required amendatory legislation and, after various unsuccessful attempts to draw up the legislation in general terms, the Army's Legislative and Liaison Division retreated in disorder. One colonel in this division recommended that the proper physical appearance of Waacs be attained by exercise and good posture, and not by the use of "surgical contraptions." If the government was to issue brassières and girdles to women, he wrote, then "such devices could well be considered for the officers and enlisted men."[43] The issue of girdles and brassières was therefore stopped. Several months later, when such items became very scarce on the commercial market, the Director requested that the issue be resumed, but this request was refused by The Quartermaster General.

Public Reaction to Unsuitable Uniforms

By this time it was unfortunately impossible to conceal from the American public the fact that the WAAC uniform and supply program had become a tragicomedy of errors. Gallup polls showed that eligible prospects for enlistment rated the WAAC uniform last in attractiveness, after the Marines', Waves', and Spars' uniforms. The citizenry at large was inspired with a desire to be helpful, and letters poured in from housewives, designers, Congressmen, soldiers, and other interested bystanders. All writers were firmly convinced that adoption of their ideas would immediately end the WAAC's recruiting difficulties.[44]

Many ideas, particularly those from Army stations and Waacs in the field, were practical and sound, but required major revisions, which could not have been made during the expansion period without greatly delaying contracts, and which could not be made afterward in view of the necessity of wearing out huge stocks of already-procured items. The same public that condemned the Waacs' appearance was not ready to support expensive measures such as discarding thousands of dollars worth of unsightly and ill-fitting garments. When recruiting advertisements pointed out that Waacs received certain fine-quality items worth a total of $250 (although actually costing the government half that) irate readers wrote to ask why the taxpayers' money was spent in this fashion. Later, Congressional committees were to investigate the alleged expenses.[45]

[41] (1) Memo, Distrib Div SOS for Reqmts Div SOS, and Ind. SPDDQ 421 Shoes, in same file, sec 1. (2) Memo, WAAC Hq for CofAdm Serv, 23 Nov 42. SPWA 400.34.

[42] Rpt cited n. 25(1).

[43] (1) Memo, Col E. J. Walsh, L&LD, for G-1, 28 Oct 42. SPWA 422.2 (9–16–42) Foundation Garments. (2) Memo, QMG for USW, 16 Sep 42, sub: Proposed Amendment to PL 554. Folder, WAC Recruiting, ASF Sp Coll DRB AGO.

[44] See entire SPWA 400 files, as well as: (1) Memo, Dir WAC for OQMG, 20 Aug 43. SPWA 400.34 (3–21–42). (2) Ltr, Miss Erma Reece, Kansas City, Mo., to Mrs. Hobby, 10 Jul 43. SPWA 421. (3) Ltr, Mr. A. J. Drugan to the President of the U.S., 9 Oct 42. SPWA 421. (4) Comments in Min, Rctg Conf, Chicago, 7–8 May 43, SPWA 337. (5) For Gallup polls, see Ch. XV, below.

[45] *Ibid.*

The final solution of the WAAC uniform problems was impossible at this time. It waited upon the day when the Director's Office was removed from the Army Service Forces and when The Quartermaster General had organized a specialist group for the development of Wacs' and nurses' clothing. Meanwhile, the extent to which the state of the uniform had damaged recruiting in the intervening months was always to remain a matter for speculation. WAAC authorities actually attributed less importance to this factor than did the general public. Although many women informed recruiters that this was their reason for not enlisting, and although many men used this argument to discourage women from enlisting, later events were to indicate that this excuse was nothing more than a red herring offered by individuals who would have disapproved of enlistment in any case.

Director Hobby offered scant sympathy to those who wrote her that their patriotic desire to enlist was impeded only by the uniform. To one such person she personally dictated and signed a reply: "Since the uniform is of so much importance to you in making your decision to join one of the women's services, I suggest that you select the service which, in your opinion, has the most attractive uniform." [46] Significantly, the complainers did not do so. The WAVES, with their smart Mainbocher-designed uniforms, never recruited the numbers of women that the WAAC and WAC did, and the weekly intake of the WAVES, SPARS, and Women Marines fluctuated constantly in close proportion to that of the WAAC.[47] The cause of recruiting difficulty, for any women's service, was to be proved more complex than any mere reaction to the appearance of a uniform.

---

[46] Ltr, Miss Elizabeth Williams to Mrs. Hobby, 4 May 44, and atchd reply. WDWAC 095.

[47] See following chapters.

CHAPTER X

Stresses of Rapid Build-up: Recruiting

The Army Recruiting Service, to which had been delegated the recruitment of women, inherited a discouraging tradition: from Revolutionary days onward the Army had never been able to recruit the number of men needed to fill its ranks in a major war. The Continental Congress had been unable to persuade each colony to contribute its fair share of men, and General George Washington had lamented, "We should not have found ourselves this spring so weak as to be insulted by 5,000 men . . .; we should not have been for the greatest part of the war inferior to the enemy . . . for want of force which the country was completely able to afford." [1] In the War of 1812 and during the Indian wars, even the meager forces authorized by Congress could not be obtained by recruiting. Both the North and the South, during the Civil War, had to resort to conscription before the war ended.

With the first World War, it became an established tradition that the nation would draft soldiers if they were needed. Both the public and the Army accepted the fact that a volunteer system would never persuade the needed number of men to enlist in a national emergency. In the interval of peace between the two World Wars, Congress whittled the enlisted strength of the Regular Army down to

118,750 men—less than the total number of women who were eventually to be recruited for the WAC.[2] The Army Recruiting Service therefore was geared to bring in only a modest number of men, and this during the depression years when surplus manpower was abundant. Even before the nation entered World War II Congress again provided for conscription, so that the Army had never been obliged to perfect a high-grade sales organization. After enactment of Selective Service legislation, only limited personnel and facilities remained available to the Recruiting Service, which was devoted chiefly to Aviation Cadet recruiting and other special projects.

It was thus a severely handicapped organization that undertook WAAC recruiting upon the Corps' formation. In the opinion of the Army officers later assigned to salvage the program, the Army Recruiting Service was placed at a great disadvantage in being forced to attempt a feat entirely outside its experience: to bring in larger numbers of women than it had ever

---

[1] *Military Policy of the United States* (U. S. Military Academy, West Point, 1944), with foreword by Col. Herman Beukema, Prof., USMA, p. 8.

[2] *Ibid.* The top WAC strength at any one time was just below 100,000; total number recruited was 143,-435. See Tables 1 and 2, Appendix A. See also Ch. XXXIV, below.

obtained of men, and this in a nation that indorsed the idea that "women's place is in the home." The 1943 chief of the WAAC Recruiting Section, Captain Edlund, said, "The Army had never had a real recruiting setup. . . . It was never a sales office in any sense of the word, for in peacetime they were always able to get the quota they were after, without actually recruiting them." [3]

The Navy, in recruiting Waves, recognized the difficulty by giving direct commissions in high ranks to well-known advertising experts and authorities on sales methods. The enlistment of Waves was taken entirely out of the hands of the agencies that enlisted men and given to the Office of Naval Officer Procurement, in consideration of the fact that the recruitment of women was more selective than the drafting of men. In the Army, the Army Service Forces chose to use the personnel already assigned to its Recruiting Service, and The Adjutant General, General Ulio, stated that no intensive recruiting effort for women was deemed "necessary or advisable." [4]

The Army Recruiting Service responded well enough as long as no strain was put upon it. WAAC Headquarters furnished it with assorted instructions and pamphlets, and the numbers of applicants at first so far exceeded training space that the selection of well-qualified women offered no great problem. It was directed that recruits be thoroughly screened by mental and physical tests and by inquiries to their references and to police courts and schools. Women were also required to prove their occupational claims, and to be interviewed finally by a WAAC officer who had the power of administrative rejection. Even so, recruiting efficiency was far from 100 percent, for early reports showed that recruiters were losing sales in more than two thirds of all cases in which women were interested enough to approach them.

Staff directors also noted that recruiters frequently gave out untrue information, or took other action not in the best interests of the Corps. [5] About mid-November of 1942 Colonel Catron reported to General Grunert that there were some signs of what was called "careless enrollment." [6] Each applicant was at this time the subject of a Provost Marshal General check, although her enlistment could be completed pending its receipt, and an increasing number of derogatory reports began to be received which necessitated the discharge of women after enrollment. Particularly embarrassing was one case in which a recruit's unsuitability had not been detected in time, and, although discharged, she was thereafter able to bill herself as "The Original WAAC Strip-Teaser." A study was initiated to check such cases, and the office also took up with The Surgeon General the number of physically unfit individuals being accepted. Colonel Catron urged The Adjutant General's Office, which conducted WAAC recruiting, to increase its efforts both in numbers and quality.

---

[3] Memo, Conf of Offs to Supervise OC Bds, 9–10 Jun 43. SPWA 334.8 Conf 1943.

[4] Memo, TAG for CG ASF, 5 Apr 43. AG 341 (4–5–43) PR–I, in SPWA 341.

[5] (1) Ltr, TAG to all Corps Areas, 4 Jul 42; Additions: TWXs, TAG to all Corps Areas, 24 Jul and 12 Aug 42; also Ltr, WAAC Hq to Corps Areas, 16 Jul 42. SPX 291.9, in SPWA 341. (2) Weekly Rpt, WAAC Hq to CofAdm Serv, 7–12 Dec 42. SPWA 319.12. (3) Ltr, Stf Dir 2d SvC to Betty Bandel. Folder, WAAC Stf Mtg, SPWA 319.2 (12–2–42), WAAC Planning files. Also Rpts in Folder, Stf Dirs Conf, Chicago, 15–17 Jun 43, SPWA 337 (6–1–43).

[6] Weekly Rpt, WAAC Hq to CofAdm Serv, 8–16 Nov and 28 Nov 42. SPWA 319.12 (11–9–42) sec 1.

RECRUITING OFFICERS OF SIXTH SERVICE COMMAND *at a meeting to help promote enrollment in the WAAC, December 1942.*

Danger Signals

When the expansion program required a tenfold increase in quotas, The Adjutant General's Office began to put more pressure on its Recruiting Service. A booklet was circulated entitled *A Plan for Increasing the Rate of Enrollment in the WAAC.* In order not to disturb Army command prerogatives, the actual conduct of recruiting was left to the service commands, of which Captain Edlund observed, "In the Service Commands we had nine separate recruiting campaigns." [7] In January of 1943 all service commands received a visit from a liaison party consisting of representatives of The Adjutant General and WAAC Headquarters, accompanied by advertising experts from N. W. Ayer & Son, the advertising agency that held the

contract for WAAC recruiting. Advertising matter was placed in seven magazines and in many newspapers; several WAAC posters were printed and distributed by The Adjutant General's Recruiting Publicity Bureau in New York City; information pamphlets of several types were also provided. Through the Office of War Information, a radio campaign was obtained. [8]

In spite of these efforts, certain danger signals began to be apparent. One was the adverse attitude of the men of the armed forces. In early January of 1943 the unfavorable nature of soldier opinion had become so unmistakable that Director Hobby

---

[7] Memo cited n. 3.

[8] (1) Memo cited n. 4. (2) Memo, Col Charles A. Easterbrook for Dir WAAC, 1 Feb 43. SPWA 334.8 Rctg (12–28–42) 1942.

requested the Services of Supply to make a formal survey.[9] This was done at once by Special Services Division, and the results, available in March, were more unfavorable than even the worst expectations. When asked, "If you had a sister 21 years old or older, would you like to see her join the WAAC or not?" the reply was:

No........................... 40 percent
Yes........................... 25 percent
Undecided..................... 35 percent

The percentages were almost identical when men were asked whether they would advise a girl friend to join—only one fourth would. Those who said *no* gave as their reasons: "Women are more help in industry, defense work, farm"; "better off at home"; "Army no place for a woman"; "too close contact with soldiers"; "too hard a life"; "don't like Army life and wouldn't want her to be in anything similar."

When asked, "How do you think a young woman without family responsibilities can serve her country best?" over half designated war industry; others preferred farm or "government work." Only from 10 to 20 percent of different groups named the WAAC; only from 1 to 2 percent the WAVES. These opinions were offered although most had never seen a Waac. Almost none had any idea what the Waacs were to do; about 25 percent said "work for the government," and as much as 13 percent in some groups said "combat duty."

General Somervell expressed considerable alarm at the report and wrote, "This not only creates a severe drag on WAAC recruiting, but also creates an unnecessarily lengthy adjustment period when WAAC personnel reports for duty in the field." He directed that a high-priority film be made for the purpose of influencing soldier opinion, also a handbook to provide soldier information, and that any other media available to the Army concentrate on the problem. General Somervell also, upon the request of General Ulio, sent a letter to the commanding generals of service commands, stating, "Intimations have come to me that our men in the Army have not been too sympathetic to the idea of a women's auxiliary . . . ," and urging them to take steps to change the minds of their subordinates.

By early spring, however, the unfavorable attitude was still growing. General Madison Pearson commented on "the wave of letters coming from service men urging their wives, sisters, or girl friends not to join the WAAC." Director Hobby added that the WAAC had received fairly good publicity from press and radio, and only adverse comments on enlistment from men of the armed forces; she added, "WAAC Headquarters had been aware for some time of the attitude of the Army to the WAAC."[10]

Also ominous was the attitude of the newly created War Manpower Commission, which in December of 1942 had been given jurisdiction over the Selective Service system. Since one of the Commission's primary missions was to secure 4,000,000 women for civilian industry, its policies toward the womanpower needs of the armed forces from the beginning caused them some concern. The War Manpower Commission had immediately ended Army-Navy recruiting for men within draft age,

[9] Weekly Rpt, WAAC Hq to CofAdm Serv, 4–9 Jan 43. SPWA 319.12.

[10] (1) Memo, CG SOS for Dir Sp Serv Div SOS, 19 Mar 43. SPAP 320.2 WAAC. (2) Memo, TAG for CG ASF, 25 Mar 43. Vol. I, Gen Policy, WAAC Hist files. (3) Memo, DCofAdm Serv for CofS ASF, 5 Apr 43. SPWA 341 (4–5–43). (4) Memo, Dir WAAC for CG ASF, 7 Apr 43. SPWA 341.

limiting the armed forces to such man-power supply as could be obtained through authorized draft quotas. It was the Army's opinion that the Commission did not pos-sess powers so to limit female recruiting, since in this case the armed forces' needs were not supplied by a draft. Neverthe-less, in preliminary negotiations with the Commission over the extent of its influence, the suggestion was made that the WAAC restrict its recruiting to Group IV areas— the most limited and unpromising part of the nation's manpower area. It was also hinted that the WAAC should not recruit in occupational fields in short supply in in-dustry—namely, the clerical, steno-graphic, and other fields most needed by the Army. This action followed the stand-ard world-wide pattern: in almost every nation in which womanpower had become important, there had existed a stage in which military needs were considered sec-ondary to those of industry. In at least one country the pressure of industry upon the national control group had been such that an army had been ordered to release to factories the women it had already re-cruited and trained.[11]

For its first months the WAAC had had no restrictions upon the sources from which it might accept recruits, although almost every civilian concern expressed the opinion that its womanpower needs were more important than those of the Army. A typical protest was one for-warded to a United States senator by a state manufacturers association, which said:

A great deal of training is needed to pro-duce a cotton mill operator. . . . Don't you think these women are more needed in the cotton mills than in the WAACs? Can you advise us of any steps this mill can take to prevent these girls from leaving their posi-tions to join the WAAC?[12]

Early objections also came from govern-ment agencies, such as the General Ac-counting Office and the Federal Bureau of Investigation, which asked that the WAAC refuse to accept their female em-ployees.

At this time Director Hobby still clung to what she felt to be the "only tenable position":

So long as enrollment in this Corps is vol-untary, and [women] citizens of this country are free to choose whether or not they shall make a war effort and if so in what manner, the Corps cannot refuse to enroll those who desire to join its ranks if they are otherwise eligible.[13]

On 6 February 1943, when the General Staff conference met to decide the WAAC's future recruiting quotas, the im-minence of the Army's defeat in this en-counter was perhaps not fully realized. However, within three months tremen-dous pressure from government and indus-try was to compel the armed forces to agree to sweeping limitations on women's enlistment: no women federal employees to be accepted without a release from their agencies; no women from "war industries" to be accepted without a written release from their employers or a statement of compelling reasons; no agricultural workers to be accepted at all.[14]

The Director informed the General Staff that recruiting prospects, excellent in 1942, had by this date deteriorated badly. For its first six months the Army had en-

[11] New Zealand. Memos, Alice R. Randolph (Ci-vilian Consultant) to Dir WAAC, 1 Jan 43, and 4 Jan 43. WAAC Planning files.

[12] Ltr, 5 Jan 43, and atchd corresp. SPWA 201.6.

[13] Ltr, Atty Gen to SW, 15 Sep 42, and atchd re-plies. WA 044.2 FBI. Also Ltr, GAO to 1st Lt Henry Lee Munson, 5 Oct 42. SPWA 324.72 (1943).

[14] Ltr, TAG to all SvCs, 26 Feb 43. AG 341 WAAC (2-25-43) PR-I-A, in SPAP 341 WAAC (2-26-43).

countered little competition from the other armed services. However, in 1943 the WAVES, SPARS, and Women Marines began to offer numerous advantages to the better-qualified women: military status, direct commissions for college women, smart uniforms individually purchased, schools in attractive locations, and, in the case of the WAVES, technical assignments and a policy of permitting social association with officers. Also set up about this time was the government-financed U.S. Cadet Nurse Corps for civilian trainees, which gave attractive uniforms, free professional training, and a student's salary greater than that of a Waac private.

Disputes Over Lowering Standards

To overcome these obstacles, The Adjutant General took a step which, for the remainder of the Corps' existence, was to remain a most controversial issue. He lowered acceptance standards and simplified recruiting procedure in order to meet the increased quotas. Recruiters were permitted to enroll applicants before results of the serological test were obtained and to discharge them from the Reserve if the test proved positive. Presentation of a preliminary health certificate from a civilian doctor was no longer required, since this put the applicant to some expense and was supposedly duplicated by the Army examination. Letters of recommendation were no longer required, except in doubtful cases, and the WAAC questionnaire was eliminated, as well as the statements on occupational training. An aptitude test score of only 50 was made acceptable, and no educational requirement was included. Instead of the previous Provost Marshal General investigation there was substi-

tuted a check by the local office of the Retail Credit Company, Inc., optional with the recruiter.[15]

The place of WAAC Headquarters in this recruiting picture was not clear. Captain Edlund said later:

Back in November we had a recruiting section here in Headquarters which consisted of two people. We were called into The Adjutant General's Office and the only thing we had to say about it was not in regard to the way the job should be done. . . . As early as January we were convinced that the recruiting campaign would not be successful . . . we fought for all the things we felt were missing. The quality slipped badly.[16]

On the other hand, General Ulio said, "Close liaison has been maintained at all times with WAAC Headquarters"; and also, "All important changes in recruiting activities affecting the WAAC receive the comment or concurrence of WAAC Headquarters before issue."[17]

In spite of these drastic measures, the recruiting campaign gradually began to disappoint its sponsors. In January of 1943 the picture was still rosy—the higher quota of 10,000 was actually exceeded. In February the quota was raised to 18,000; most of those on the waiting list were called to active duty and all others who presented themselves were accepted immediately. Nevertheless, at the end of the month it was discovered that the quota had not been met in spite of the lowered standards:

---

[15] (1) Ltr, TAG to all SvCs, 14 Jan 43. SPX 341 WAAC (1–14–43) PR–I, in SPWA 341 (7–4–42) 1942. (2) Ltr, TAG to all SvCs, 26 Feb 43, AG 341 WAAC (2–25–43) PR–I–A, in SPAP 341 WAAC (2–26–43). (3) Historical Monograph, The Loyalty Investigations Programs, prepared by the Office of the Provost Marshal General, p. 17 and Tab 38A. OCMH.
[16] Memo cited n. 3.
[17] Memo, TAG for CG ASF, 25 Mar 43. Vol. Gen Policy, WAAC Hist files, 1943.

only 12,270 had been enlisted. This figure, had recruiters only known it, was to be tops for all time. The bubble had burst. The quota was raised to 27,000 for March— the number needed to fill the new training centers—and recruiters were urged to make new efforts. This quota was not met and the take for March fell below that of February—11,464.[18]

There was mounting evidence that the campaign was not recruiting from wider and more promising areas, but instead was merely scooping up the undesirables who had been previously rejected. One veteran WAAC recruiter described the situation:

In 1942 we had crowds of applicants and could pick and choose. By early 1943 these were well picked over, but the quota went up while the applications went down. Many of those whom we now called to duty were those who were acceptable but not quite the best. By March these were almost gone, and we were faced with a choice of accepting women we had previously rejected or of leaving our quotas unfilled.[19]

AGCT Standards

Within a few weeks, the results of lowering standards were so serious as to cause Director Hobby to appeal to General Somervell to overrule The Adjutant General. In the matter of AGCT standards, records preserved at Fort Des Moines illustrated the situation. In September and October of 1942 Army General Classification Tests given recruits at this training center showed that less than 10 percent fell into the lowest two grades, IV and V, 30 percent in Grade III, or average, while 60 percent were in Grades I and II, the two highest grades, in which Army officer candidates were required to score.[20] Even in December, only 12 percent were in the two lowest groups, as against the Army ex-

pectancy of 32 percent. However, during the first months of 1943 standards plummeted, and over 40 percent of all recruits received at Des Moines were in Grades IV and V. Similar records from other training centers were not preserved, but it was the opinion of authorities at Daytona Beach and Fort Oglethorpe, which drew from the Fourth and Eighth Service Commands, that they had an even higher percentage of Grades IV and V recruits. Almost half of all WAAC recruits were now falling in a group so low that their usefulness for any sort of skilled noncombat task seemed doubtful.[21]

Records at Fort Des Moines also showed a similar drop in the degree of education attained—in April a large number of recruits were found to have had only grade school education or less. Likewise, the degree of skill attained in civilian experience declined; of a typical group of women at Des Moines, about 70 percent were classified as semiskilled, unskilled, domestic service, or laborer. Not all of these records were available to Director Hobby when she began to make protests in March, but the trend was unmistakable.[22]

By the end of March about 1,000 of these women, about half of whom were white and half Negro, were waiting idly in the training centers, where they constituted a problem of morale and sometimes of discipline. It became clear now, if it had

---

[18] See Table 2, Appendix A.

[19] Intervs with Maj Jean Melin, then of New Jersey Rctg Dist.

[20] Grade I . . . . 130 or above
Grade II 110–129
Grade III . . . . 90–109 average; 100 median
Grade IV 70–89
Grade V . . . . 69 or below

[21] ASF Hist of WAC Tng, Ch. II, Table III and footnote. OCMH.

[22] Ibid., Tables IV, V.

not been before, that the Army literally had no military assignment for unskilled and unintelligent women. These could not be assigned to replace enlisted men of like category because such men were ordinarily assigned to heavy work which women could not perform. They could not be trained for more than a few types of military duties.

Colonel Branch, head of the WAAC Planning Service, suggested that they be formed into motor transport, mess, and laundry companies, but the idea proved unsuccessful. Laundry training was not attempted because no military jobs could have been filled. Cooks and Bakers School received many and failed to graduate most, pointing out that such women almost never made good cooks and could pass neither the cooks nor the bakers course; they were not even cleanly and reliable in lesser duties. The Motor Transport School was directed to take large numbers. When the women could not pass the driver aptitude test, they were assigned to the course without it; when they could not pass the course, the course was changed to eliminate all technical subjects. Even with these concessions the school was able to convert few into qualified drivers.

Next, attempts were made to train the women as ward orderlies in hospitals but were abandoned when it was found that the women could not replace men of like category because of the heavy lifting involved. The women obviously were useless for all except the most simple and repetitious duties in factories or the home. To enlist them was not only to deprive industry of needed factory workers but also to burden the Army's military manpower allotments with women who could not carry their share of the work.

Later, opportunity schools and special training units were to be attempted, but inasmuch as the women's deficiency was ordinarily mental and not educational, training authorities pronounced the time spent on them to be more than their subsequent usefulness warranted. Medical authorities also discovered that the rate of disability discharge among these women was about four times as high as among skilled workers. Psychiatrists noted that the continued failure to succeed on Army jobs provoked neurotic conditions and disciplinary infractions among the subjects.[23]

In addition to the low-grade personnel retained at training centers, thousands of others were placed in companies on various pretexts and shipped to the field. Their impact on field stations was unfortunate and threatened to destroy the Corps' early reputation of one-for-one replacement of men. An alarmed staff director reported that, at a certain Arizona airfield, 152 women had arrived, of which 53 were in Grades IV and V; 86 had scores below 99. At a neighboring field in California, 34 of 154 were in Grades IV and V, and 78 were below 99 in score. While such percentages were still within the Army average, they were not good enough for a headquarters company such as the WAAC provided. The staff director commented:

It would seem that no company going into the field should be burdened with such a large number of auxiliaries in the two lowest brackets. It makes an unfortunate impression of the Corps when the station contains so many women of low-grade mentality, which so often means low-grade behavior.[24]

She reported that all had been assigned to "grease monkey" work where it appeared

---

[23] For full discussion see Chs. XXXI and XXXII, below.

[24] Ltr, 1st O Helen Woods, WAAC Stf Dir AAF WFTC, to Col Catron, 3 Jun 43. SPWA 319.1.

doubtful that they could ever replace men, one for one. The Second WAAC Training Center was called upon for an explanation, since it had shipped the offending companies. Daytona Beach replied: "The only thing significant about the fact that these companies came from Daytona is that we have had the misfortune of having these people sent to us to train. There have been sent to us 3,576 Grade IV and V people." [25]

At Director Hobby's direction, training centers compiled detailed reports of all women in Grade V, giving the station of their enlistment. These she forwarded to General Ulio with the request that stations be reprimanded and individual recruiters penalized for all such women accepted, since they obviously could not have passed the WAAC intelligence tests which stations were supposedly giving. Since, in one week, three fourths of the number came from two stations in the Eighth Service Command, such corrective action appeared warranted. However, The Adjutant General did not reprimand the stations, but instead asked them to forward the test scores of the individuals concerned; these, somewhat naturally, were reported as passable, and no further action was taken. [26]

Medical Standards

As soon as the requirement for a civilian doctor's examination was dropped it quickly became clear that physical and psychiatric standards were falling alarmingly. Director Hobby gathered from training centers a list of the worst cases, including 30 women who were pregnant when accepted, 52 cases of psychoneurosis, 39 of menopausal syndrome, and miscellaneous other disorders such as fibroid uterus, rheumatic heart disease, chronic cystitis, duodenal ulcer, severe bronchial asthma, hyperthyroidism, arthritis, epilepsy, atrophy of left leg and thigh, and dementia praecox. Also, two babies had been born to new enrollees before they could be discharged—one only six weeks after the date of the mother's enrollment examination. [27]

Director Hobby forwarded these lists to The Surgeon General with names of the stations from which each had been recruited, with a request for corrective action in the case of the medical examiners concerned. The Surgeon General, however, refused to take any such action on the grounds that an Army medical examiner could not have been expected to detect any of these cases, except that of the advanced pregnancy, under the induction examination used. This examination included serological tests, chest X rays, urinalysis, palpation of abdomen, and tests of blood pressure, vision, and hearing. A pelvic examination had not been required and neither had a complete social history, since these were not required for men's induction examinations. Without them, The Surgeon General pointed out, many illnesses could not always be diagnosed. [28]

Fort Oglethorpe authorities complained that Army medical examiners seemed to think that the training center was an induction center like the Army's and that a thorough physical examination would be given there. WAAC Headquarters welcomed this, saying, "This confirms the

---

[25] *Ibid.*, 3d Ind.
[26] Memo, WAAC Hq for TAG, 16 Mar 43. SPWA 210.11 (2–17–43).
[27] Memo, WAAC Hq for CofAdm Serv, 11 May 43. SPWA 702.
[28] *Ibid.*, 2d Ind. SPMCS 322.5–1, SGO.

Division's contention that publication of a circular is necessary to clarify standards." [29]

Returns from the field indicated that the chief difficulty was not willful negligence, but either the absence of an adequate authorized induction examination for women or medical examiners' ignorance of proper standards of such an examination. Thus, early in 1943, rejection rates for mental diseases ranged from a low of 0.6 per thousand in the First Service Command to a high of 30.6 per thousand in the Sixth Service Command; either far more women in Chicago were deranged than in Boston, or the medical standards differed widely in the two service commands. [30] Evidence indicated that more stations were too lax than too strict: of all disability discharges granted until June, 1943, one half of the women discharged had been in service less than four months and three fourths less than five and a half months, which strongly suggested that the disabilities had existed before enlistment. Furthermore, analysis showed that 73.7 percent of all disability discharges were for two reasons only—gynecological and neuropsychiatric. This appeared to some to be rather strong evidence that medical examiners were more or less efficiently screening out the disabilities common to men and women, but were baffled by those peculiar to women. [31]

There were a few WAAC staff directors who felt that some examining psychiatrists, in the absence of guidance from The Surgeon General, were methodically screening out the more stable applicants. In one extreme case, a director noted that the local psychiatrist "maintained that the only way to determine a woman's stability was to require her to walk into his office naked, and to sit down and answer his questions in this condition." He then, in order to test her emotional balance, asked her, "How often during the past month have you had intercourse with a soldier or sailor?" The staff director added, "We lost a number of nice young prospects who never came back after he interviewed them. I could just imagine what they told their parents about the purpose of the Women's Army Corps." [32] There also continued to be a disconcerting number of unwise acceptances, such as the woman who reported to Fort Oglethorpe and nine days later informed authorities: "I am the Duchess of Windsor." [33]

A company officer at Daytona Beach found that the parents of one of her recruits had removed her from an insane asylum to enlist her; when the officer called the girl and her parents to the orderly room and presented them with her discharge, the parents wept, while the girl, it was related, "leaped over and bit her mother." [34]

To remedy such matters, Director Hobby urged The Surgeon General's Office to set up a specialist group to determine and publish detailed guides to the medical examinations required for women

[29] (1) Extracts from a large file of Tng Cen Rpts on WDAGO Form 40 (C.D.D.). SPWA 220.8 (9–30–43), 1943. (2) Ltr, 3d Tng Cen to Dir WAAC, 14 Apr 43; also atchd Memo, WAAC Pers Div to Dir WAAC. SPWA 314.7 (1–7–43)(1) sec 1.

[30] (1) Quarterly Rpt, Exam of Candidates for WAAC, Nov 42–Jan 43, SGO, Jan 43. WDWAC 702. (2) Memo cited n. 27. (3) Memo, SG for Dir WAC, 15 Sep 43. WDWAC 370.01.

[31] Memo, Med Stat Div SGO for Dir WAAC, 18 Jun 43. SPWA 220.8 (6–18–43).

[32] Interv with Lt Col Katherine Goodwin, ASF WAC Off (then Stf Dir 1st SvC), 8 Oct 45.

[33] Rpt of 3d WAC Tng Cen, Min, Stf Dirs Conf, New York, 1–3 Dec 43. SPWA 337 (11–10–43).

[34] Interv with Lt Col Mary Weems Fullbright (former CO of Tng Co.), Apr 51.

and to their later medical care. In May, she brought the matter to the personal attention of Generals Marshall and Somervell. In return she received from both the assurance that they would "personally OK procedure and it [would] soon straighten out."

The action of these authorities was unrecorded, but The Surgeon General shortly went on record that "there are problems of health peculiar to women." He therefore yielded in the matter of specialization and, a year after the WAAC's establishment, appointed the office's first Consultant for Women's Health and Welfare—Maj. Margaret D. Craighill, formerly dean of the Women's Medical College of Pennsylvania. Major Craighill became responsible for recommendations concerning the health of 60,000 Waacs and 30,000 nurses, and for visits to them at stations both in the United States and overseas. Director Hobby stated, "This is our first ray of hope. Now we have real co-operation from The Surgeon General. Major Craighill has been given the whole problem." Major Craighill at once set herself to secure published standards for proper gynecological and psychiatric screening of applicants and for other medical problems.[35]

Moral Standards

Even more distressing was the lowering of moral standards, although the relative number of women concerned was not great. Some lowering of behavior standards was inherent in the acceptance of women of low ability or of neurotics and other unstable persons. In addition, women were now accepted whose character and past record were questionable.

Early in November 1942 the Office of the Director had pointed out to The Adjutant General the dangers of attempting to apply to women the moral standards used for men. The Director's Office protested that the check on male inductees was handled so as to admit all but vicious criminals, chronic offenders, and habitual drunkards. The Director believed higher standards necessary for a volunteer non-combat corps of women and, in all cases referred to her, refused to accept women who had been convicted of any criminal offense.[36]

Until January, when references and other time-consuming checks were discontinued except for doubtful cases, a woman might possibly be screened out by reports received in this way, unless she applied in a state where she had no record, but after January this safeguard was absent. Recruiters were further handicapped in smaller towns by the fact that a traveling recruiting team, spending only a day or two in the town, might unknowingly accept a presentable-looking woman whose unsavory record was known to everyone in town except the recruiters. For men, such incidents were prevented by the fact that Selective Service boards gathered case histories, but the Director of Selective Service refused to extend this work to WAAC recruits.

One WAAC officer enlisted a woman, about whom she was a little doubtful, only after the local police chief assured her that the woman had no police record. The

[35] (1) Memo, Exec SGO for Dir WAC, 15 Aug 44. SPMC/DD 322.5, in WDWAC 720. Appointment of women doctors in the Medical Corps had been authorized by PL 38, April 1943; those already in the WAAC were transferred to the Medical Department. (2) Speech by Dir WAAC. Min, Stf Dirs Conf, Chicago, 15–17 Jun 43, SPWA 337 (6–1–43).

[36] Memo, WAAC Hq for Apmt & Ind Br AGO, 11 Nov 42. AG 000.51 WAAC PR–W, in SPWA 000.

woman was subsequently discovered to be a well-known prostitute and drunkard with a long police record. When the police chief was asked for an explanation, he replied frankly, "Well, I thought it would get her off our hands and probably do her good too." [37]

To prevent such occurrences, the Director and The Adjutant General joined in a petition to General Grunert that no woman be accepted without investigation and clearance by the Provost Marshal General's local investigators. The Director stated, "In the present stage of development, with the quality of material under close [public] scrutiny, . . . this office is of the strong opinion that all recruits should be checked . . . for the next 60 days." However, the Chief of Administrative Services and the Provost Marshal General opposed the idea, since such a check was not made for men. Instead, General Grunert informed the Director that, as a concession to the publicity problem, a spot check would be made of one in every ten recruits. [38]

Inexpert Sales Methods

The appearance of recruiting stations and the manners of recruiters also, in the Director's opinion, frightened off some applicants. To check on this suspicion, she secured authorization for a civilian agency to make an impartial survey. [39] This agency sent women employees to recruiting stations in all parts of the United States. Some sat for as much as forty minutes without attention; others were told that they were not needed and were given no informational pamphlets. [40] Still others were unable to find the Army recruiting stations, which were usually in inaccessible locations, although in searching for the station one agent found a Navy station where she was most politely treated and showered with literature and enthusiastic accounts of life in the WAVES. One who did find an Army station reported, "We had to go through about 100 selectees, whistling and making friendly remarks." [41] Another gave an account of her experience as follows:

Q: As you entered the recruiting station, what was the general reaction you got?
A: Rather unfavorable, unattractively furnished, and clouded with cigar smoke. Man in uniform looking out the window.

Q: What sort of reception did this person give you?
A: Turned around, gave a brief look at me, hollered "Sergeant!," and started looking out the window again.

Q: Was the recruiter a man or a woman?
A: A man . . . I felt that he thought the campaign was of little importance. Here is a verbatim report of our conversation.

Applicant: I just want to ask some questions about the WAAC.
Sergeant: Are you over 21 and have a birth certificate some place at home?
Applicant: Yes.
Sergeant: OK. There isn't anything you could ask me that isn't in there. (Hands over a pamphlet.) Take it home and when you make up your mind, come back. [42]

It was the agency's verdict that any business concern selling products to women would shortly go bankrupt if it hid its shops in places where women would not or did not go, or if it employed untrained salespeople who had no knowledge of the

[37] Co Comdrs Forum on Discipline. Files of Sch of WAC Pers Adm, OCMH.
[38] Weekly Rpt, WAAC Hq to CofAdm Serv, 14–21 Feb 43. SPWA 319.12 (11–9–42) sec 1 (1942).
[39] Young & Rubicam.
[40] Statement by Maj Rice, Min cited n. 33.
[41] Rpt, Young & Rubicam. Min, 6th SvC Rctg Conf, Chicago, 7–8 May 43, SPWA 337.
[42] *Ibid.*

product or any desire to sell it. It was discovered that, as a result of these sales methods, only one out of every ten women interested enough to find their own way to a recruiting station ever filed an application.[43]

The Director pointed out that surroundings which were acceptable to male draftees were not always acceptable to women volunteers. For example, male inductees who must spend the night near a station were ordinarily housed in the cheapest hotel available. Some WAAC applicants reported that they had to spend the night in questionable establishments. This point was not one on which The Adjutant General cared to make a stand for identical treatment, and a directive went out:

In contracting for lodgings for WAAC applicants for enrollment, the regulation . . . which requires the lowest available rate per man per day will be interpreted to mean the lowest obtainable rate per woman per day consistent with the proper standards of cleanliness and decency and the personal safeguards to which women are entitled.[44]

Although WAAC officers and enlisted women had at this time been assigned to the Army Recruiting Service for several months, protests had come in from almost every service command, saying that they had little voice in the selection of applicants. Not every station was criticized in this respect, but the condition was reportedly widespread. The Second Service Command's report on this matter was the most complete. It asserted that WAAC officers had been coldly received by the recruiting stations; they received orders from enlisted men; civilian women were used to interview applicants while Waacs sat idle. Army officers determined the disposition of WAAC mail without consulting the Waacs; they determined rejections;

they made requests for waivers after the Waacs had declared the applicant not qualified. The Staff Director, Second Service Command, noted: "It is felt that the special knowledge, skill, and training of WAAC officers assigned to recruiting in the Second Service Command are not being fully utilized." She recommended that their position be defined or that they be transferred from the Recruiting Service to other jobs.[45]

Reports from other service commands corroborated this report. In the opinion of the WAAC Staff Director, First Service Command, the difficulty was due to lack of orientation of the Army Recruiting Service in the field. "They had no idea what a WAAC Recruiter was supposed to do," she said. "When the first two officers arrived at a certain station, the officer in charge asked, 'Can you type?' and when they said no, he instructed them to attend night school and learn so that they could be assigned as office typists. Apparently it had never occurred to these officers that women could be expected to plan and conduct a recruiting campaign or to determine the merits of enlistees."[46] The first WAAC recruiters in the Fifth Service Command noted, "All the station commanders forced us to take in women with scores of 40; they just changed the score."[47] On the other hand, some WAAC recruiters alleged that they never permitted the enrollment of unsuitable applicants, al-

[43] Memo, Dir WAAC for CG ASF, 5 Apr 43. SPWA 341 (4–5–43)C.

[44] Ltr, TAG to all SvCs, 22 Jan 43. SPX WAAC (12–17–42) PR–I, in WA 513 (11–26–42), 1942.

[45] Rpt, WAAC Stf Dir to Dir Pers 2d SvC; copy in Ltr, 1st O Cora Webb Bass to Col Catron, 11 Feb 43. SPWA 319.1.

[46] Interv cited n. 32.

[47] Interv with Maj Marion Lichty, National Sel Serv Hq (former Rctg Off), 5th SvC, 4 Mar 46.

though they had to defy senior officers when quotas were not met.[48]

Transfer of Responsibility to WAAC Headquarters

By the end of March, less than two months after the expansion program was put into effect and before the worst of the results were felt, Director Hobby became convinced that the Army Recruiting Service's methods and failure to uphold standards were wrecking the Corps' mission. At a staff meeting on 25 March she directed her Planning Service to "present factual and irrefutable evidence to higher authority that will accomplish the immediate transfer of responsibility for the WAAC Recruiting Program from the Office of The Adjutant General to Headquarters WAAC."[49] On 5 April the Director submitted to General Somervell a detailed WAAC recruiting plan to raise standards and a request for control of acceptances.[50]

The Adjutant General countered by offering a radical concession. He stated that a separate specialist group was needed to recruit women and proposed entirely to separate the Army Recruiting Service and the WAAC Recruiting Service, having a "Service Command WAAC Recruiting Officer" directly responsible to the commanding general, and WAAC recruiters responsible only to her and with full control of the acceptance of Waacs.[51] He listed what he considered the chief causes of the difficulties, as concurred in by the Director:

1. The uncertainty of the proposed legislation. [The public had apparently, until the WAAC Bill received publicity, never before realized that the WAAC, unlike other women's services, had not been admitted to full military rights and benefits.]

2. The unsatisfactory setup at some of our service command headquarters and subordinate recruiting installations.

3. The disappointment and dissatisfaction of enrollees writing home and describing conditions.

4. The lack of proper outfitting at the time of enrollment.

5. Inadequate housing facilities to take care of more enrollees.

6. Lack of appreciation of the importance of the WAAC objective to the Army.

7. Competition with industry.

8. The fact that the recruiting service has been staffed largely with men who are not suited for and do not understand the psychology of recruiting women.[52]

To remedy these conditions, General Ulio proposed extensive reforms: better locations for recruiting stations; only Waacs allowed to process applicants; solicitation of help from women's clubs; follow-up inspection by his office. He planned to increase recruiting personnel, make a Hollywood film, conduct a Special Services campaign to change Army men's opinions, and call on all Army chaplains to assist. He proposed also to relocate some recruiting stations, increase the advertising campaign, and ask all Waacs to urge at least two friends to join.

More important, he proposed to lower the age limit to 19, lower the physical standards, and eliminate the aptitude test for high school graduates.[53]

---

[48] Maj Jean Melin, WAAC Stf Dir, AGF Repl and Sch Comd, formerly Rctg Off in New Jersey.

[49] Cited as authority in Memo, CofPlng Serv for Dir WAAC, 5 Apr 43, Tab A to Progress Rpt, 16 Mar–15 Apr 43. SPWA 600.14 (4–15–43).

[50] Memo cited n. 43 Also, for Director's list of deterrents, see Memo, Dir WAAC for CG ASF through CofAdm Serv, 31 Mar 43. SPWA 291.9 PS, under Planning Serv Notes, 1943 WAAC files.

[51] Rough Draft by buck slip, Col Vance L. Sailor, R&I Sec AGO, to Capt Edlund, WAAC Hq, 13 Mar 43. SPWA 341.

[52] Memo, TAG to CG SOS, 25 Mar 43. Vol. Gen Policy, WAAC Hist files.

[53] Memo cited n. 4.

General Ulio's plan was endorsed for the Chief of Administrative Services by his deputy, General Madison Pearson. General Pearson suggested that the age limit be lowered to 18, the physical standards be made less rigid, and an additional mental test or two be made available for those who failed the present one.[54]

The Adjutant General's proposals reached General Somervell on the same day that Director Hobby sent her request for transfer of control, 5 April 1943.[55] Called upon to comment, the Director gave the opinion that further lowering of standards would be a dangerous matter. She noted that what she had proposed was a major matter of policy concerning higher standards, whereas The Adjutant General's program of administrative detail would be highly appropriate for whatever policy was adopted.[56]

There was no reasonable compromise between the two points of view, since British experience had already strongly indicated that a women's corps dependent upon recruiting could not contain both types of workers: if low-grade personnel constituted the majority, office workers of good character and acceptable skill would not volunteer. Only selective service for women had eventually made it possible for the British forces to obtain adequate numbers of both types of workers in the same corps. The choice posed was thus whether the WAAC should continue its original mission of supplying the Army with those skills that were scarce among men—chiefly clerical and communications—or should relinquish this to invade the fields of heavy physical labor in which women were inefficient replacements for men, requiring possibly two-for-one replacement, but in which large numbers of low-grade women could easily be recruited.

General Grunert, after a flying trip to Daytona Beach, changed his office's previous stand and supported the Director's view, stating: "Enlistment of too many low grade factory, store, and restaurant workers . . . is a problem. WAAC clerical assignments predominate and this calls for class. We had better slow down and get quality than . . . speed up for quantity."[57] He therefore withdrew previous objections to better screening methods, and advocated that Provost Marshal checks be restored for all recruits.[58]

On the other hand, there was a considerable body of opinion within the Army Service Forces which held that the Chief of Staff's original policy should be reversed and low-grade women sought. This view was stated a little later in the summer by one of General Somervell's consultants in recommending that steps be taken to replace Director Hobby:

The techniques appropriate to the original conception of the WAAC as a small highly-qualified group of women enrolled for more or less morale and propaganda purposes are completely inappropriate for a Corps of 385,000 to take over all of the dirty work in the Zone of the Interior. . . .

This means drastic revision of the present policy insisting on the high standard of intel-

[54] Memo, DCofAdm Serv for CofS ASF, 5 Apr 43. SPWA 341 (4–5–43).
[55] The Director had discussed her plan on 3 April with both The Adjutant General's Office and the Chief of Administrative Services; she had held it for two days for their comments and incorporated in it the only suggestion, a minor one, received from them. The Adjutant General had not co-ordinated his paper with hers; neither had the Chief of Administrative Services. Memo, Gen Somervell for Dir WAAC, 6 Apr 43. SPEX, in SPWA 341 (4–5–43).
[56] Memo, Dir WAAC for CG ASF, 7 Apr 43. SPWA 341 (4–5–43).
[57] Folder, Daytona Beach, Dir Adm Serv ASF Sp Coll DRB AGO.
[58] Instead, a Retail Credit Company check was extended to all recruits, for which $2.25 per name was paid. For later types of checks, see Monograph cited n. 15(3).

ligence, dignity, and educational and social background. . . . Public Relations and Recruiting policies of WAAC Headquarters . . . [place] an overemphasis on high standards and dignity, which . . . are principally and directly responsible for decreasing WAAC enrollments.

The root of the whole matter is that Mrs. Hobby feels that deterioration of standards would result from any mass recruiting technique, yet, whether she admits it or not, she has to have 385,000 Waacs by 1 July 44. . . . Consideration [should] be given to the appointment of a new WAAC Director capable of mass organization. . . .[59]

One day after its receipt the Director's request for control of recruiting was approved. Some explanation of the decision was made in a note by the WAAC Planning Service: "We understand that the Director secured the concurrence of General Marshall to raise the enlistment requirements to insure better quality."[60] Thus, as in the crisis of the previous September when he had intervened to provide for more cautious administration, the Chief of Staff's personal decision now for a second time determined the Corps' future path and mission. For the next months the goal was to be quality, if necessary at the price of quantity—recruits with clerical, communications, and technical skills or the ability to learn them, rather than unskilled laborers.

The Adjutant General was directed to give the WAAC full co-operation and every practical assistance in its new responsibility. He shortly published a memorandum asking that all communications on recruiting be sent to the Director, and withdrew from any further part in operating details. The Chief of Administrative Services, as directed by General Somervell, notified the field of the new plan, inclosing copies of Captain Edlund's somewhat frank interoffice memorandum on the deficiencies of the Recruiting Service.

This rendered Captain Edlund *persona non grata* with so many Army recruiters that within a few months he was replaced by a WAAC officer. At the moment he continued as Chief, Recruiting Section, and guided the campaign which was to follow.[61]

The Restoration of Standards

Director Hobby's first act upon taking control of recruiting was, on 7 April, to restore the enrollment standards. A minimum of two years in high school and a score of 60 on the aptitude test were now required. While high, these standards were still below those of the WAVES, which required high school graduation. At once the number of recruits fell from 11,464 in March to 6,472 in April, and in May, when the new standards were in force all month, to only 4,064. In June the requirements were raised again, to a score of 70 plus two years of high school, or 80 without high school; in this month only 3,304 recruits were enlisted. By July classification officers at headquarters and training centers were able to report that "problems in making assignments have disappeared due to the present higher enrollment requirements." Records from Fort Des Moines showed that the number of recruits in Grades IV and V fell at once from 40 percent in April to 12 percent in July and 6 percent in October. In November 1943,

---

[59] Memo, "K. J." for Gen Somervell and Brig Gen Clinton F. Robinson, 12 Jul 43. Folder, WAAC Rctg, ASF Sp Coll DRB AGO.

[60] Memo cited n. 49.

[61] (1) 1st Ind, ACofS ASF to Dir WAAC, 8 Apr 43, to Memo cited n. 54. (2) ASF Memo S635-4-43, 14 May 43, signed by Gen Ulio. (3) Buck slip, Capt Edlund to Col Catron, May 43. SPWA 341 (4-5-43). (4) Ltr, CofAdm Serv to all SvCs, 10 Apr 43. SPAAS 341, incl Memo, 31 Mar 43, cited n. 50, in SPAP 341 WAAC (2-26-43).

after the WAAC was placed in the Army and The Adjutant General resumed operation, the figure jumped from 6 percent to 20 percent, which was to remain its average for the rest of the WAC's existence. The number of women with less than high school education fell from 36 percent in April to 20 percent in July.[62]

The expansion program had not so much collapsed as never begun. Numbers obtained monthly were now approximately the same as before the campaign began. The influx of the unqualified had lasted only a brief two months and had been checked before it lowered the Corps' average standards too far, but it was clear that the expansion program could not continue unless a real recruiting campaign could be devised that would increase numbers without lowering standards.[63]

The Advertising Contract

General Ulio was also overruled in the matter of the advertising contract, for which he favored the current contractor, N. W. Ayer & Son. This agency had adopted the campaign slogan, "Release A Man For Combat," and had given it wide publicity. The slogan had proved unfortunate in several ways. In view of the prevalence of punsters in the population, it was discovered that it would be wiser to use the expression "Replace A Man" instead of "Release" or "Relieve." Worse, as the "phony war" vanished and combat became more real to the American public, the slogan appealed to no one: Army men in clerical jobs did not particularly appreciate being replaced for combat; mothers did not wish a daughter to enlist if this would send a son to his death; and a woman whose husband or sweetheart was killed overseas did not like to think that

but for her or some other woman he would have been safe in a desk job.

Also, the advertising agency, in handling the WAAC account as part of the Army account, had not given particular consideration to women's psychology in the matter of advertising appeal, location of recruiting stations, training of recruiters, or other matters.

General Somervell's Control Division, after investigation, therefore recommended that the account be canceled because of a decision to revise the entire campaign and not for any particular fault. Accordingly, eleven of the nation's leading advertising agencies were invited to a meeting and asked to suggest campaign plans. On the basis of results, Control Division, ASF, and Control Division, Adjutant General's Office, awarded the contract to Young & Rubicam, called "the largest advertising agency in the country," and one which handled campaigns for many women's products and also had an unusually large number of women writers on its staff.[64] Young & Rubicam immediately began to make surveys, for which they employed Dr. George Gallup and a staff of female investigators, to determine the correct psychological approach. Every effort was made to suppress the theme of "Release A Man For Combat," but it was found that the slogan had sunk deep into the public mind and was by this time so widespread that for months every new re-

[62] (1) Memo, Capt Edlund for TAG, 7 Apr 43; (2) Memo, Dir Hobby for DCofS for SvCs, 6 Jun 43; (3) Memo, Lies, Special Consultant, for Dir WAC, 8 Jul 43. SPWA 341. (4) Tables III, IV, V, ASF Hist of WAC Tng, Des Moines figures only. (5) See Table 2, Appendix A.

[63] For a description of the average Waac, see Ch. XI, pp. 192–93, below.

[64] Rpt, Lt Col Paul V. Betters and Maj McGovern, Contl Div ASF; see Weekly Rpt, WAAC Hq to CofAdm Serv, 7–13 Mar 43 SPWA 319.12.

RECRUITING POSTER *used to induce women to enroll in the Corps. This recruiting theme was later discarded.*

cruiter, unless forewarned, enthusiastically launched forth with it.[65]

The Revised Campaign

Under the leadership of Maj. Harold A. Edlund, WAAC Headquarters with the assistance of Young & Rubicam at once launched a recruiting campaign which for desperate thoroughness had not been surpassed in Army history. The success of the expansion plan and the Corps' whole future hung upon the question of whether well-qualified American women could be induced to volunteer in the numbers scheduled.

Major Edlund, in civilian life a sales expert, believed that they could, but he did not underestimate the problem, which, he said, was believed by sales experts to be "one of the toughest selling jobs in the country today." He stated that recruiters who approached the problem casually had no idea of "the difficulties of persuading women of the sort we need in the WAAC to give up their homes and security and to voluntarily take on a way of life completely foreign to them." The WAAC recruiters, he said, were intuitively aware of the factors involved, but lacked sales training and the necessary authority. Nevertheless, Major Edlund's confidence in the infallibility of scientific sales technique was such that he predicted that 100,000 women could be recruited in the three months remaining before 1 July 1943, to bring the Corps' strength to the required 150,000 by that date.[66]

The first step of the giant campaign was the collection of accurate data, and a quick Gallup poll was made of a scientifically selected nationwide cross section of eligibles and the parents of eligibles. The results were admittedly shocking even to

those closest to the WAAC program. Until this time it had been believed that if the women of the nation knew the Army's need for their services they would respond at once. Publicity had therefore been centered around statements by President Roosevelt, General Marshall, and others of the nation's leaders, pointing out the Army's need for personnel. Now it was discovered that the public was perfectly well aware of the Army's need; an overwhelming majority (86 percent) replied "Yes, we know the need; we know the Army is calling for more." But women did not respond, according to the Gallup survey, for five reasons:

1. *Apathy:* "Sure, it's important, but let someone else do it."
2. *Fear of Army life:* Many women feared they would not be equal to the reputed rigors of training and regimentation.
3. *Misunderstanding as to the jobs Waacs did:* The majority were most familiar with the least attractive types of work—cooking, laundry, scrubbing. Thirty-one percent said the Waacs' main job was kitchen police.
4. *Attitude of relatives and friends:* Those considering joining were almost unanimously discouraged by parents and male advisers.
5. *Army attitude:* Almost all eligible women had heard, or had been told by soldier friends, that the Army was opposed to the WAAC.[67]

Other interesting facts were uncovered. It was found that more eligibles feared overseas service than desired it. Some would join only if they could be near home; others, only if they could travel.

---

[65] (1) Ltr, SW to Pres., N. W. Ayer & Son, Inc., 7 May 43. WDGAP 095. (2) Speech of Maj Edlund at the mtg. (3) TAG's opinion in Memos cited ns. 4, 17. (4) Memo, WAC Hq to RPB, New York, 16 Oct 43. SPWA 000.7. (1943). (5) Ltr, Dir WAC to CSigO, 2 Jul 43. SPWA 411.36 (4–10–43).

[66] Incl to Memo cited n. 43.

[67] Ltr, Young & Rubicam, Inc., to Maj Jess Rice, WAC Hq, 1 Oct 43. SPWA 000.7. (2) See also statement cited n. 40.

Half the women believed that a Waac could not marry an Army man; many others believed that a Waac was not allowed to marry at all, or to have dates, or to use cosmetics.

The new campaign was shaped by these discoveries. If apathy was the trouble, the war must be made real to women. If women feared a strange new life, every detail of the life must be publicized so that it was familiar and not frightening. If they had mistaken ideas about the Corps, these must be corrected: they must be told that Waacs did interesting work as well as menial, that Waacs dated, married, and used cosmetics. If families and Army men disapproved, some approach must be found to change their attitude. The keynote of the campaign, in short, would be to make familiar to everyone the life and work of a Waac, and especially the good side of that life.

Accordingly, Young & Rubicam hastily prepared advertisements that pictured the interesting jobs Waacs did; they devised quizzes with many small pictures and questions; and, believing that women were inveterate coupon clippers, they inserted small coupons that could be mailed to recruiting stations for free literature. At the same time there was assembled an array of supporting talent that dwarfed previous efforts. Among others, the Writers' War Board pledged co-operation—Rex Stout, Clifton Fadiman, Paul Gallico, Margaret Lee Runbeck, Sarah Elizabeth Rodgers, Katherine Brush, Laura Z. Hobson— each to write articles to reach a different type of national magazine and audience. Ten writers of this board were flown to Fort Oglethorpe and other stations to gather material.

Famous photographers were asked to take pictures for picture magazines. In addition to stories, many magazines agreed to use a WAAC cover girl—the July *American,* the August *Cosmopolitan* and others. The May *Reader's Digest* had a story; *Life* used pictures sent from North Africa; the August *Harper's Bazaar* showed WAAC physical training in its least terrifying aspects; a June *Saturday Evening Post* began a five-part serial. Through the co-operation of the Office of War Information, radio time was obtained, including plugs on shows by Bob Hope, Kate Smith, and others. Daily papers got news stories and pictures, and Sunday papers carried paid advertisements. Motion pictures also were contributed, by both Hollywood and the Signal Corps. All of these various media were co-ordinated through WAAC Headquarters in order to maintain the same theme throughout.[68]

To co-ordinate recruiters' efforts with the advertising campaign, there set out from Washington a flying task force which, traveling by plane, train, and subway, achieved the apparently impossible feat of a two-day conference with each of the nine Service Commands in sixteen days.[69] These included representatives of Young & Rubicam to describe the campaign, of General Motors to initiate expert sales training methods, and of The Adjutant General's Recruiting Publicity Bureau to display their newest wares of posters and booklets.

The conferences were generally well received, although, said Major Edlund, "The Army Personnel connected with recruiting didn't quite understand what this was all about and perhaps resented it a little

[68] (1) Ltr, Hq 2d SvC to Dir WAAC, 15 May 43. SPWA 334 with Min of mtg. Also, Min cited n. 41.
[69] The First, Second, and Third Service Commands met together in New York. Exhibit A to Memo, WAAC Hq for CofAdm Serv, 24 Apr 43. SPWA 341 (4-5-43).

bit. We had to make sure that they realized we were perfectly friendly and honest about the whole thing and that the main purpose was to help them do the job they had been asked to do with insufficient help." [70] Instead of scolding about unfilled quotas, Edlund congratulated them on the 60,000 women already recruited. "In Canada they have been going much longer and have less. In England they had to come to conscription." Even the Waves, he said, were having difficulty in getting the relatively small number they were then aiming for.

Major Edlund had made the decision not to separate the Army Recruiting Service and the WAAC Recruiting Section, although events were to prove that it would have been wiser to adopt at once General Ulio's plan of removing all authority from the regular Recruiting Service, since such action eventually proved necessary.

Major Edlund's keynote, later deplored by veteran WAC recruiters, was, "Let's turn the bright side of the apple toward the general public." He proposed that pictures and releases all feature the most interesting jobs and the best-looking Waacs, and that Waacs not be pictured driving heavy vehicles, or in fatigue uniforms, or doing strenuous calisthenics, or even marching, since this frightened away many desirable prospects. This approach was supplemented by Young & Rubicam's advertisements with captions such as,

"We're the luckiest girls in the world and we know it."

"I joined to serve my country and am having the time of my life."

"I felt pretty important when that tailor fitted that swank new uniform to me."

Such advertisements, while calculated to counteract previous misunderstandings, were also sufficient to bring on howls of derision from veteran Waacs, and to call forth complaints from later recruits who enlisted while under their spell.

The Cleveland Plan

Time was now working against the salesmen. The various surveys, the preparation of advertisements, and the flying tour had been accomplished in the unprecedented space of little over a month. Nevertheless, only six weeks remained to get the scheduled 100,000 women by 1 July. Major Edlund therefore determined upon a saturation technique of salesmanship that would literally hunt out and carry off potential recruits in a house-by-house canvass in major cities. He immediately began a demonstration campaign in a typical city. Cleveland, Ohio, was selected for the trial, and WAAC recruiters from every service command gathered to assist and observe. [71] The basic idea was that WAAC sales could be achieved only by personal interview, and not by rallies, bonfires, and previous tactics, of which Edlund said, "Everything that we could see being done [before] was a big rally or parade—a lot of talk mostly along patriotic lines and 80 percent of the people listening were not eligible to join." [72]

The Fifth Service Command ran the Cleveland Campaign, although Major Edlund had desired to do it. Theoretically such a campaign should have been preceded by a softening-up barrage of newspaper and radio publicity, but Cleveland's

---

[70] Speech by Maj. Edlund. Min cited n. 35(2).

[71] Cleveland was chosen because it was a representative large city, 52 percent of homes had telephones, and the Cleveland Advertising Club offered to help.

[72] Speech cited n. 70.

publicity media were busy "trying to buy a ship or something," and WAAC recruiters were obliged to land without protection. Since there were not enough WAAC recruiters in the nation to conduct a door-to-door survey in a city of this size, the Cleveland Plan called for the use of any civilian agency that had many women members in a city-wide organization. The American Red Cross was deemed the oldest and best organized, but when asked to assist, its officials replied that the Red Cross was "interested only in essential war work"; later they added that their charter did not permit help. The Office of Civilian Defense (OCD) therefore volunteered to assist, although its Block Plan was newly organized and its leaders inexperienced.[73]

The WAAC recruiters held meetings with the OCD sector leaders and supplied them with literature and questionnaires, which were passed on to block leaders. These leaders were not to attempt to enroll women, but only to locate eligibles. The final report stated that "block workers were most co-operative. Reports were that many women at home seemed to be waiting for someone to ask them to do something in the war effort. . . . The majority attitude represented complacency." These block leaders were soon able to furnish recruiters with the name and location of each eligible woman in the district.

WAAC enlisted women next went to work at a battery of telephones, trying to persuade each eligible to grant an interview to recruiting officers. These Waacs were especially trained by the Ohio Bell Telephone Company. They were instructed not to try to recruit, but merely to get an interview; when and if an interview was obtained, WAAC recruiters called on the prospect. The Realsilk Hosiery Company donated expert training in the technique of polite interviewing. All who still appeared eligible were urged to enlist, and those who seemed undecided were placed on a follow-up list.

The Cleveland Plan, supported by the nationwide publicity campaign, seemed the most intensive recruiting effort that it was possible for any organization to make. When the drive was finished and the score counted, it stood revealed as a miserable—almost an incredible—failure. The score was: [74]

Families contacted	73,589
Questionnaires completed	36,151
Considered eligible from questionnaire	12,886
Found eligible on contact	8,253
Signed applications	427
Enrolled	168

To achieve even the mere 100,000 female recruits that the Army needed immediately, recruiters would, if this rate held true, have to contact 43,800,000 families, although the nation was estimated to have only about 37,000,000 families. Interviews and sales talks would have to be held with almost 8,000,000 eligibles before 100,000 could be recruited. There were probably not that many qualified women in the United States.[75]

The Cleveland method, refined and improved by experience, was caught up and used all over the nation. Improvement in recruiting machinery continued. All summer the great radio and press campaign played upon the public. More and better-trained recruiters were thrown into

---

[73] This and the following are from a mimeographed booklet, WAAC Recruiting Plan, Cleveland, Ohio, June 1–10, 1943. SPWA 341.

[74] Memo, Asst Chief, WAC Rctg Serv, for Exec WAC, sub: Résumé of Rpt from 5th SvC, 4 Aug 43. SPWA 341 (1942).

[75] The Bureau of the Census in a Statistical Abstract estimated 37,100,000 families in 1944, in a civilian population of 126,606,000.

the battle. And still, amazingly, the number of qualified applicants fell. Finally, in August, the exhausted recruiters suspended their efforts to await completion of the conversion to Army status—the final hope. In this month only 839 recruits were enrolled—not enough to make up for normal attrition.

At last the full extent of public opposition stood revealed to the WAAC recruiters—an impenetrable wall against which the methods of supersalesmanship and expert recruiting techniques broke and fell ineffectually. It was not as yet fully understood why this wall had sprung up and solidified after the initial favorable public reaction, but it was all too clear that it had now done so.

CHAPTER XI

The "Slander Campaign"

British experience in two world wars had indicated that any women's service soon after organization would become the target of slanderous charges, which would lower morale, alarm parents, and make it impossible to secure a large corps except by drafting women. However, the WAAC had appeared to be relatively free of such charges during its first few months. It was therefore prematurely hoped that the American public had, since the early attacks on the Army Nurse Corps, outgrown the use of moral charges as a means of opposition to women in public life.

Record of the WAAC's First Year

This hope was sustained by the fact that the Corps' record, as it reached the milestone of its first birthday in May of 1943, remained good beyond even the highest expectations. Recruiting, training, and supply difficulties had had little if any effect upon the efficiency of WAAC units in the field. The War Department, which had supported military status in advance of proof of WAAC efficiency, now found its action justified by all field reports. From North Africa, Gen. Dwight D. Eisenhower's headquarters expressed enthusiasm for the performance of the first WAAC company and forwarded requests for hundreds more enlisted women, without whom, it was declared, it was "literally impossible to conduct effective administra-tion." The theater requested that these units "be given earliest priority . . . and shipped at expense of ground force replacements." [1] Equally important for public opinion, both health and discipline in North Africa had been good, and there had been only one pregnancy, that of a married woman.

From the secret antiaircraft artillery experiment, which was concluded about this time, came an official report that Waacs could fill more than half of the jobs in AAA units, and were "superior to men" in many operations requiring dexterity. [2] War Department files abounded in reports of sudden conversion, such as that of the post commander who informed Col. Frank U. McCoskrie that Waacs would be sent to his post only "over my dead body," but who, a few months after their arrival, was discovered to be not only alive but writing to Des Moines for two more companies. [3] From other station commanders came similar indorsement. [4] The commanding general of a port of embarkation wrote, "I am greatly impressed with their discipline, intelligence, efficiency, and devotion to

---

[1] (1) ETO WAC Hist, p. 7. (2) Cbl W3105, 20 Jun 43. WAAC 320.2 sec 5.

[2] Memo, G–3 for CofS, 7 Jul 43. WDGCT 291.9 in CofS file and in MDW.

[3] Related by Col. McCoskrie of a post commander in the Sixth Service Command.

[4] (1) Project 24, WAAC Planning files (1943). (2) Army Fact Sheet, Women in Uniform, 10 May 43, WDBPR. WAAC Hist files. (3) Dorothy D. Bromley, *New York Herald Tribune*, July 11, 1943.

duty. They have raised the standard of discipline of the command." Similar comment was received from the Signal Corps, Air Forces, Adjutant General's Department, and service commands, respectively: "Proved its value in hundreds of departments"; "Their work is splendid"; "looking forward to receiving more Waacs"; "highest type of intelligence and aptitude"; and so on.[5]

An Army Service Forces inspector in May of 1943 reported, after a visit to Waacs in the field:

My impression in general of WAAC personnel is:
1. They are doing a fine job in the training center. . . .
2. They are performing the jobs to which assigned . . . in an excellent manner.
3. The officers and enlisted personnel with whom the Waacs work are more than satisfied with the efficiency and manner in which the women perform their tasks, as well as their attention to military courtesy.
4. The WAAC personnel is happy and doing a fine job.
5. The conduct of the WAAC personnel both on the job and after working hours is satisfactory. . . . The using people heartily endorse the use of Waacs and want to know when they are going to get more.[6]

Remarks of service commanders at a conference in July of 1943 likewise indicated that they were unanimously satisfied with their WAAC personnel and had experienced no noteworthy difficulties except in recruiting.[7]

A newspaper commented in July, near the first anniversary of the Des Moines school:

The life history of the Waacs reads like the proverbial American success story. At their inception they were offered a chance to make good at only a handful of noncombatant jobs then considered suitable for women. Within little more than a year they had proved so effective that the Army now urgently asks that their ranks be increased to 600,000.[8]

In the summer of 1942 only four jobs had been authorized for Waacs; in the summer of 1943 Waacs were already filling 155 different Army jobs, and the number was increasing daily. In 1942 it had not been supposed that the WAAC's range of usefulness would require assignment other than to the Army Service Forces; in mid-1943 Waacs were already assigned to every major Army command in the United States and to two active overseas theaters; they were stationed in forty-four of the forty-eight states. In 1942 the admission of women even to auxiliary status appeared risky; in 1943 the War Department entertained no further doubts about the wisdom of full integration of women into the Army.[9]

General Somervell noted, in commending General Faith, "The excellent discipline, military courtesy, and appearance of the Women's Army Corps . . . are equalled by few and surpassed by no other group in the Armed Services."[10]

Statistical records in May of 1943 showed that, in spite of the brief lapse in recruiting standards, Waacs still surpassed in qualifications both the civilian average and that of Army men. The "average" Waac at this time was a mature woman, 25 to 27 years old, healthy, single, and without dependents. She was a high school graduate with some clerical experience. According to information derived from

---

[5] Quotations in Ltr, Dir WAAC to Edith Nourse Rogers, 26 May 43. SPWA 000.7.

[6] Rpt, Lt Col Hal P. Crane, GSC, to MPD ASF, 12 May 43. SPWA 319.1.

[7] Min of Conf, CGs of SvCs, Chicago, 22–24 Jul 43.

[8] *Washington Post,* July 10, 1943.

[9] Mimeo Sheets, 10 Jul 43, 142 Spec Jobs and 406 Suitable Jobs, and 9 Jul 43, 155 WAAC Jobs and Over 400 Others Suitable.

[10] Memo, Somervell to WD Decorations Bd, 15 Jan 44, sub: Award of DSM to Brig Gen Don C. Faith. Personnel Abstracts, WAC files, OCMH.

psychiatrists' interviews, she was inspired to enter the WAAC chiefly by a desire to do war work of a more active and responsible nature than was generally possible to a woman in civilian life. Of the small number of her eligible American sisters who were similarly inspired to the extent of getting an application blank, she was the one in three who completed it, after which she had survived tests and interviews that eliminated half of her fellow applicants. Before shipment to her job in the field, she had cost the Army only four weeks of basic training but no specialist training, which had not, for the average woman, proved necessary to successful assignment. On the men's AGCT test, she made an average score of 109. At her field station, she accepted assignment to routine clerical work although she would have liked to drive a truck. She had not yet been promoted, and her rank remained that of auxiliary (private), at $50 a month.[11] She constituted a permanent and reliable type of employee, not being subject to transfer to combat duty, nor to the usual causes of turnover in civilian personnel.

From the public viewpoint the Corps' moral record was even more important than its job efficiency. Statistical records indicated that, even with the brief lapse in standards during February and March, enlisted women's morality exceeded the civilian average. The WAAC rate of venereal disease was almost zero; many WAAC units had not experienced a single case, while training centers generally encountered only cases that had been undetected by faulty enlistment examinations. Even including cases existing before enlistment, the incidence in the WAAC was far below that of either the Army or of women in civilian life. As for pregnancy among unmarried women, the rate in the WAAC was about one fifth that among women in civilian life. This record was even better than that reported in 1942 by the British women's services, which was itself better than that of British civilian women.[12]

However, by May of 1943 it was already known within the War Department that the American corps, in spite of its actual record, was not to escape the traditional fate of slanderous attack, which became familiarly known to the Department's investigators as the "Slander Campaign," sometimes also called the "Whispering Campaign" or "Rumor Campaign." The slander campaign was, as its name implied, an onslaught of gossip, jokes, slander, and obscenity about the WAAC, which swept along the Eastern seaboard in the spring of 1943, penetrated to many other sections of the country, and finally broke into the open and was recognized in June, after which the WAAC and the Army engaged it in a battle that lasted all summer and well into the next year before it was even partially subdued.

Publicity Machinery

It was WAAC Headquarters' belief at the time that full and early publicity on the record of the WAAC's first year might have prevented what followed. However, during the period when the slander campaign took shape and gained momentum, it was the policy of the War Department

---

[11] Unless otherwise stated, all statistics in this and the following section are from two manila-bound typed booklets: (1) Info on WAAC, the Director's personal book of statistics, in the 1943 WAAC files, and (2) WAAC Pers Statistics, 6 Sep 43, 1943 WAAC files. See Table 3, Appendix A, for a breakdown of WAAC statistics.

[12] *Conditions in the Three Women's Services*, pp. 49–52.

Bureau of Public Relations to permit no specialized attention to the WAAC. There was no central agency charged with securing and releasing the true record and statistics of the Corps' first year; news stories on WAAC life were generally limited to those which news media secured and presented for clearance. The Bureau's Radio, Press, Pictorial, and Publications Branches all handled WAAC news releases separately and without co-ordination of policy.

General Marshall and others evidently supposed that there existed some central publicity group for the support of recruiting; as late as January of 1944 General Marshall addressed a memorandum to the "WAC Recruiting Section, Bureau of Public Relations,"although there was actually no such agency.[13]

To make up for the lack of a publicity campaign from the Bureau of Public Relations, the Director attempted to bring enough WAAC public relations personnel into her own office to supply good material to news media and guide them toward desired policies. For this purpose, she was allowed a small Office of Technical Information (OTI), such as other administrative services had, chiefly designed to check releases for technical inaccuracies but not to promote publicity. In the WAAC's first months the Director requested a larger allotment for this office, on the grounds that the WAAC must recruit personnel and was the object of more "extraordinary public interest" than other administrative services. The Services of Supply refused this request on the grounds that men's organizations, such as the Chemical Warfare Service, did not have a larger allotment.

Even had more personnel been allotted it, the WAAC OTI was not allowed by the

Bureau of Public Relations to handle publicity. In April of 1943, the OTI appealed to the bureau for permission to contact editors directly to get more accurate and positive articles in magazines and journals, since the "personnel shortage" in the bureau had apparently made it impossible for that agency to achieve the desired results. In reply, the Bureau of Public Relations published a directive that all inquiries concerning the WAAC received by WAAC Headquarters would be referred to the Bureau of Public Relations, and that inquiries received by the bureau would be handled by it without reference to the WAAC except by telephone.

The extent to which the WAAC OTI was allowed to influence the bureau's decisions was limited; in June, General Surles reminded the Director by personal letter that when his Review Branch asked any OTI for comment, it desired only views on security and accuracy, and not opinions on method of presentation or tone.[14] Projects originated by the WAAC were frowned upon; thus, when the Director desired to use the WAAC Band on a radio program, the bureau vetoed the idea on the grounds that "publicity is moving along very well and the orderly procedure of it should not be disturbed too often by special appearances." [15]

Under this system, press comment on the WAAC varied. Many newspapers faithfully and favorably reported all that was furnished them, although this was not plentiful enough to build public knowl-

---

[13] Memo, CofS for WAC Rctg Sec WDBPR, 26 Jan 44. CofS 324.5 WAC.

[14] (1) Memo, Dir Pers SOS for CofAdm Serv, 20 Nov 42. SPGAO 322.5 WAAC, in SPWA 020. (2) Memo, WAAC OTI for WDBPR, 21 Apr 43. Vol. Policy, WAAC Hist file, SPWA 314.7.

[15] Memo, "TS" for Dir WAAC, 15 Aug 42. SPWA 311.23.

edge and acceptance to a degree that would insulate the WAAC against the later rumors. Certain anti-Administration newspapers from the beginning made the WAAC the subject of caustic comment, evidently regarding the Corps as a New Deal creation. Even in the most favorable press, there was a natural tendency for "news" to consist of those items amusing or spectacular enough to reach reporters directly, such as stories headlined, STORK PAYS VISIT TO WAAC NINE DAYS AFTER ENLISTMENT,[16] or, ARE WOMEN PERSONS? DEBATED BY HOUSE VETERANS COMMITTEE.[17] There was also a tendency for headlines to include the word WAAC in reporting all accidents, murders, suicides, and family troubles involving a member of the Corps; a headline that might more properly have read ARMY OFFICER TRIED FOR BIGAMY became, instead, WAC BRIDAL BRINGS TRIAL.[18] Even when friendly newspapers arranged for visits of their own reporters and photographers or foreign correspondents, the results frequently tended toward the coy or frivolous rather than a serious emphasis on actual WAAC jobs.[19]

Also, from the first, cartoonists had found the WAAC amusing and had contributed caricatures which ranged from light humor to emphasis on anatomical detail. Of these, a training center commandant protested to WAAC Headquarters: "There seems to be no restraint on funny papers and cartoons with the WAAC as subject matter." He was informed that "legally there is nothing that can be done to restrain cartoonists from caricaturing the WAAC."[20]

The more extreme actually were seldom commercial cartoons, but were more often soldier products from camp newspapers, which held with rather monotonous lack of originality to the idea that the best way

of ridiculing a woman was to exaggerate those portions of her figure that differed from the masculine version. Although peculiarly masculine garments were not considered funny, the mere depiction of a brassière, empty or otherwise, was alone enough to seem comic to cartoonists.[21]

Certain clergymen had also published their protest against the Corps as an improper place for young Christian women. Of these, the Catholic chaplain at Fort Des Moines wrote:

It is unfortunate that the few clergymen who have sounded off against the Corps get so much publicity, while the thousands I know who are in favor of it get little or no publicity. . . . I have had to have three masses every Sunday—about 1,400 Waacs each Sunday.[22]

Attacks by Private Letter and Gossip

These relatively minor cases of poor published and broadcast publicity or ill-chosen humor bore little resemblance in degree of virulence to the slander campaign which followed, and which had an entirely different character. The first manifestations of a deeper change in public opinion came early in 1943, when there began to be evidences of more vicious attacks on the Corps spread by word-of-mouth gossip and by private letter. Some of these were merely the "nut" letters that any organization might expect; quite often these included miscellaneous charges of

[16] Washington *Times-Herald*, May 1, 1943.
[17] Washington *Evening Star*, February 3, 1943.
[18] Philadelphia *Evening Bulletin*, August 8, 1945.
[19] For WAAC clippings, see Vol. IV, WAAC Hist file, SPWA 314.7 (1942–43).
[20] Ltr, Comdt 5th WAAC Tng Cen to Dir WAAC, 3 May 43, with atchd comment. SPWA 319.1.
[21] Malvina Lindsay, in *Washington Post*, July 17, 1948.
[22] Ltr, Chaplain Urban J. Baer, Ft Des Moines, to Dir WAAC, 9 Dec 42. SPWA 319.12.

WHAT MAKES YOU THINK THE WAAC IS COMING TO THIS CAMP?

vice in the armed forces, or attacks on "the people in the White House" for permitting card playing and drinking by soldiers.[23]

Some letters were more dangerous than their character warranted. A typical example was a letter from an Army nurse to an Arkansas radio evangelist, which began, "I am a Christian and a member of the . . . Church and hate sin as bad as anyone." She then alleged that Waacs at training centers were lined up naked for men medical officers to inspect, that no sheets were used on examining tables, and that medical officers showed Waacs pictures of naked men and of men sitting on toilets. She concluded, "Christ loves these girls and I know he does not like for them to have to line up naked and it is embarrassing for our girls every month. Please send me your book *The Truth About the Mark of the Beast,* also *Satan's Children.*"

The radio evangelist naturally became indignant and wrote his senator, saying that he intended to warn Arkansas parents and, "I am not going to permit Arkansas to become a Socialist State under the New Deal." He also sent copies of the letter to the governor, the Secretary of War, and three editors.[24] Upon the senator's request, an Army inspector general flew to Arkansas, launched a full-scale investigation, and discovered that none of the allegations was true and that the nurse in question was currently hospitalized with a diagnosis of mild psychoneurosis; she had also written similar letters about the Army Nurse Corps.

This, of course, was merely one of hundreds of such letters; the WAAC seemed to be a favorite target of mentally unbalanced persons. Unfortunately, although disproof for such allegations was readily available, it did not always reach all who had heard the charges.

Other scattered reports indicated that the WAAC was also encountering gossip and animosity from more responsible elements of the population. This was particularly true around all training centers, where numbers of Waacs were so great as seriously to inconvenience civilian users of streetcars, shops, and beauty parlors. An Army Service Forces inspector noted that, while Des Moines merchants and civic leaders had offered much co-operation, certain citizens were displeased, and added:

It seems that any dislike of WAAC personnel is not caused by disorderly or promiscuous conduct, but rather by the fact that the WAAC personnel, in the strength superimposed upon a city the size of Des Moines, makes it appear that they take over the town at such times as they are free, particularly Saturday and Sunday, which causes some amount of inconvenience. . . .[25]

Investigation at Des Moines by the Army's Military Intelligence Service was unable to discover any basis for such dislike except "resentment on the part of local citizens . . . to the presence of strangers who they feel are usurping the old settlers in restaurants, stores, theaters, and hotels."[26] The Director of Intelligence, Seventh Service Command, after investigating Fort Des Moines, said "It was conclusively determined during the course of the investigation that the morals of the members of the Corps are exceptionally and surprisingly good."[27] He

---

[23] Photostat of anonymous Ltr to SW, 9 Jun 43. MID 322.12 WAAC (6–9–43) (6–11–43)

[24] (1) Ltr, Lt S., ANC, to Rev. James MacKrell, Little Rock, Ark., 18 Jan 44, and atchd. Hobby files. (2) Memo, CG ASF for TIG, 2 Feb 44, with 3d Ind SGO to TIG, 9 Mar 44. SGO Hist Div Cl file 322.5–1.

[25] Rpt cited n. 6.

[26] Memo, Chief CIC, MIS, for Maj Gen George V. Strong (G–2), 19 Jul 43. G–2 MID 322.12 WAAC.

[27] *Ibid.,* Des Moines Sec.

pointed out, however, that one example of WAAC misconduct in a bar would create much more gossip than identical conduct by scores of local civilian women.

As WAAC companies spread to the field, similar local animosity was sometimes noted near these units. For example, USO facilities and Stage Door Canteens at times discouraged or prohibited attendance by Waacs, defending this action by saying that Waacs broke rules by going outdoors with men between dances, which hostesses could not do. Waacs felt that they were not welcomed simply because USO hostesses were not interested in raising the morale of military personnel except of the marriageable variety.[28]

The Civilian Uniforms

Another variety of gossip began to plague the WAAC perhaps more than any other in the spring of 1943. It arose from the fact that the public began to attribute to the WAAC certain misconduct which, upon investigation, proved to be that of civilian women in near-military uniforms. For example, an Army recruiting officer in Louisiana reported that Waacs, probably on leave from the Fifth Training Center, were drinking heavily in Shreveport bars and taking men to their hotel rooms. Investigation by the provost marshal revealed that the women in question were indeed conducting themselves as stated; they were not Waacs but "a group of women ordnance workers wearing a uniform identical with that of the WAAC except for insignia." [29] The Women Ordnance Workers, better known as WOWS, were civilian employees of Army Ordnance; although the majority of such employees did not wear uniforms or misconduct themselves publicly, a certain number

caused rumors in all parts of the country. For instance, Ninth Service Command and AAF authorities in California both protested to the Director that some of the Wows were drinking to excess and engaging in barroom brawls, and being mistaken for Waacs. Investigation disclosed that the Wows at Stockton Ordnance Depot were wearing khaki shirts and skirts, garrison caps, and enlisted men's or officers' insignia.

The ordnance depot, after the investigation, ordered removal of Army insignia, but allowed retention of the uniform, which was optional with such workers all over the nation. Their winter uniform was of olive-drab elastique, like a WAAC officer's except for patch pockets and garrison caps; they also wore depot sleeve patches and miniature shields and ordnance insignia. Being civilian workers, they were under no restrictions as to conduct, hours, or neatness.

The same ordnance depot, like hundreds of other Army installations, also employed civilian women drivers who were allowed to wear khaki shirts, slacks, and garrison caps, with sleeve patch and shield insignia. The same region in California also had a civilian volunteer group, the Women's Ambulance and Defense Corps of America, which had a khaki uniform with Army insignia of rank and the letters WADC on a sleeve patch; these women, however, were forbidden by their bylaws to drink in uniform.

[28] (1) Rpt, Stf Dir 4th AF, 2d SvC, and others, Min, Stf Dirs Conf, Chicago, 15–17 Jun 43. SPWA 337 (6–1–43). (2) Ltr, Dir WAC to all Stf Dirs, 13 Mar 43, incl Ltr from Mrs. Eliot Cross. SPWA 250.1 (3–12–43).

[29] Ltr, 8th SvC to Dir WAAC, 3 Apr 43, incl comment of Maj Warner Bishop, Ft Humbug, Shreveport, La. SPWA 250.1. WAAC Headquarters, suspicious of this address, investigated and found Fort Humbug a legitimate Army district.

The Ninth Service Command investigators, after study of uniforms of the WOWS, women drivers, and WADC, concluded that the public was undoubtedly taking all of them for Waacs, unless they investigated insignia and button design closely.[30]

This was only the beginning of what seemed to be an attempt by every woman in America to get herself into a military uniform without the inconvenience of subjecting herself to WAAC discipline. Civilian clerical workers in many Army offices bought officers' "pink" skirts and olive-drab jackets with gold buttons. The Civil Air Patrol women were authorized by the AAF, without clearance from WAAC Headquarters, to wear WAAC uniforms with red braid and silver buttons. Even the WAAC "Hobby Hat" was not sacred; secretaries at Valley Forge Military Academy wore a close copy, with a uniform almost indistinguishable from a WAAC officer's. When WAAC authorities protested this to the academy, they were informed by the professor of military science and tactics that the uniform was not at all similar since the skirt had a pleat and the buttons had the academy crest and not the WAAC eagle. At Fort Devens a soldier's wife was found wearing a WAAC uniform with gold U.S. Army buttons and her husband's insignia; she said the uniform was one that "they sold in Philadelphia" to girls whose husbands were in the service.[31]

Eastern stores advertised a "junior WAAC uniform" in sizes up through 14, guaranteed to be "an exact copy of the real WAAC uniform." The Quartermaster General informed the Director that its sale was not illegal, although its wearing by an adult might be, depending on circumstances.[32] A New York manufacturer supplied dress shops all over the country with a uniform quite similar to the Waacs', advising them:

STAKE YOUR CLAIM. There is a vast new field open for you in selling to the army of Women Volunteer Workers—Air Raid Wardens—Minute Men—Canteen Workers—USO and scores of others. ALL DOING THEIR PART AND ALL WANTING TO DRESS THE PART.[33]

It was doubly annoying to WAAC Headquarters that these concerns were able to get olive-drab and khaki cloth in the early months when The Quartermaster General was still unable to get it for WAAC uniforms.

These department store uniforms were bought and worn not only by volunteer workers but by scores of organized prostitutes in Eastern cities. Staff Director Jess Rice of the Third Service Command, working with the provost marshal, gathered and forwarded to WAAC Headquarters irrefutable evidence of this practice. The streetwalkers, known as Victory Girls, were discovered in Harrisburg, Newport News, Baltimore, and other cities, wearing uniforms of material and cut very similar to the WAAC's. One was apprehended by military police while trying to buy a furlough-rate railroad ticket. Another was discovered when authorities checked a report that a WAAC officer was drunk in a disreputable Harrisburg hotel. The proprietress of a Baltimore clothing

[30] Ltr, Dir WAAC to 9th SvC, 4 Jun 43, sub: Unauthorized Wearing of Uniform, and Ind. SPWA 250.1.
[31] (1) Ltr, TAG to CG AAF, 10 Aug 43, sub: Authorization of WAAC Uniform for CAP Pers. SPWA 421. (2) Ltr, 4th SvC to 3d SvC, 26 May 43, sub: Valley Forge Mil Academy, Wayne, Pa., and Ind. SPWA 250.1 (4–3–43). (3) 1st Ind, WAAC Stf Dir to Dir WAAC, 11 Aug 43, to Memo, Chief of PM Br 3d SvC for Capt Rice, 11 Aug 43. SPWA 250.1 (4–3–43).
[32] Ltr, WAAC Hq to Legal Div OQMG, 14 May 43, and Ind. SPWA 421.
[33] Photo adv, Evelyn Alden Fashions, 134 W. 37th St., New York, incl with Ind cited n. 31(3).

253164 O—54——15

store claimed that she was doing a good business in sale of these uniforms and "desired to know if she was doing wrong in selling them." [34]

At the Hampton Roads Port of Embarkation, the camp followers, dressed in khaki skirts and shirts, were so bold as to wait outside the gate, claiming that they were Waacs and picking up soldiers as they left the port. Here, the commanding general ordered the enrolled women to pin their insignia on the collars of their cotton shirts, at that time contrary to uniform regulations, so that they could be distinguished from prostitutes in khaki shirts and skirts. [35]

Gathering together all these examples, Director Hobby requested the Army Service Forces to amend Army regulations so as to forbid the civilian use of WAAC uniforms and insignia, or that of any insignia, buttons, and clothing which very closely resembled the WAAC items. She also asked that the Quartermaster Corps and Army Exchange Service co-operate in discouraging manufacturers of these uniforms. Since the Army controlled the manufacture and sale of all material used in commercial manufacture of Army officers' uniforms, it could, by withholding material, force most manufacturers to cease wasting it in the production of nonmilitary uniforms.

However, the Army Service Forces rejected the Director's idea, saying that it would be too difficult to enforce and that the Quartermaster Corps and the Exchange Service already co-operated with manufacturers of male officers' uniforms, so that no new instructions to them were necessary. The ASF added "Due to the fact that the WAAC is a comparatively new corps, the casual and uninformed observer is apt to believe that every woman

in o. d. uniform is a Waac. It is believed that this situation will be overcome in due course." [36]

The Quartermaster General soon afterward authorized the lend-leasing of 5,000 WAAC winter uniforms, left surplus by the collapse of recruiting, to the French "WAAC" in North Africa—at that time a part-native corps without military organization. The Director shortly received a flood of derogatory letters from soldiers, in parts of North Africa where there were no Waacs, who nevertheless alleged that Waacs were disreputable in both appearance and conduct, wore earrings and bobby sox with uniforms, also long hair down their backs, and obeyed no military commands. [37]

The Organized Rumors

By late spring, even before the Cleveland Plan was launched, rumors were more widespread, more consistent, more vicious, and the tempo of their occurrence had quickened. Director Hobby and War Department officials now began to suspect that Axis agents had taken over the sporadic stories and were systematically spreading certain definite rumors in an attempt to discredit and wreck the WAAC and thus impede the Army's mobilization. This theory was supported by the fact that the onset of the more vicious rumors followed immediately after the Congressional hearings in March of 1943, in which Army

---

[34] Memo cited n. 31(3).

[35] Rpt, Stf Dir HRPOE. Min, Stf Dirs Conf, Chicago, 15–17 Jun 43. SPWA 337 (6–1–43).

[36] (1) 2d Ind, 19 Aug 43, to Memo cited n. 31(3). (2) D/F, MPD ASF for Dir WAAC, 1 Sep 43, atchd to same.

[37] 2d Ind, OQMG for Reqmts Div ASF, to Memo, Dir WAAC for Reqmts Div ASF, 16 Nov 43, sub: Redesigning of WAC Cap. SPWA 421.

leaders had asked Army status for the WAAC and had emphasized that thousands more women were sought to allow more men to be sent to strengthen the fighting front. The Waacs already obtained, it was said, would release for combat a number of men equal to that which had just defeated the Germans in North Africa.

As early as 18 May 1943, Director Hobby wrote to General Grunert that "there have been many indications of an organized whispering campaign directed against the WAAC" and asked investigation. The Army Service Forces sent the request for an investigation to G–2 Division, General Staff, which in turn sent it to the Federal Bureau of Investigation, claiming that it was out of the Army's jurisdiction.[38]

By early June, the situation was so far out of control that G–2 Division reversed its stand and requested the FBI to allow it to act. In a letter to the FBI, G–2 Division said:

Consequent to the formation of such a women's auxiliary to any of the military services, a certain amount of indecent humor was to be expected. However, the inevitable so-called humor first has been supplemented and subsequently has been replaced by a circulation of plainly vicious rumors . . . what appears to be a concerted campaign has assumed such proportions as seriously to affect morale and recruiting.[39]

Supporting evidence for this view was plentiful. An identical rumor appeared almost simultaneously in New York, Washington, Kansas City, Minneapolis, and other cities, to the effect that large numbers of pregnant Waacs were being returned from overseas. Camp Lee, Virginia, was swept suddenly by the report that any soldier seen dating a Waac would be seized by Army authorities and given medical treatment. A widely repeated rumor circulated at Hampton Roads to the effect that 90 percent of Waacs had been found to be prostitutes, 40 percent of them pregnant. In the Sixth Service Command an apparently organized rumor appeared in many localities to the effect that Army physicians examining WAAC applicants rejected all virgins. In Philadelphia a "War Department Circular" with obscene anatomical "specifications" was reproduced and widely circulated, finally being found even in the foxholes of New Guinea. From Florida there came numerous identical stories that Waacs openly solicited men and engaged in sex acts in public places.[40]

One favorite theme for these organized rumors was that Waacs were issued prophylactics or were required to take such items with them when they left the barracks, so that they could fulfill the "morale purposes" for which the Army had really recruited them. It was this story that finally brought the whole slander campaign into the open. Until this time, Army and WAAC authorities had felt it wiser to ignore all rumors, since to deny any publicly would merely have given them greater circulation. However, on 8 June 1943, the charge that Waacs were issued prophylactics was made in a nationally syndicated column, "Capitol Stuff," in the McCormick chain of newspapers, by a columnist

---

[38] (1) Memo, Dir WAAC for Dir of Adm ASF, 18 May 43, with incl evidence; (2) 1st Ind, ASF for G–2, 22 May 43; (3) 3d Ind, G–2 for ASF. G–2 MID 322.12 WAC (5–18–43).

[39] Ltr, G–2 to FBI, 9 Jun 43. G–2 MID 322.12 WAAC (6–11–43).

[40] (1) Weekly Intelligence Bull, MID, 11 Jun 43. G–2 MID 322.12 WAAC. (2) Memo, AAF Hq for Dir WAC, 5 Apr 45. WDWAC 330.14. (3) Exhibit D, Rpt, CIC to MIS, 19 Jul 43, sub: Origin of Rumors Concerning WAAC. G–2 MID 322.12 WAAC (6–11–43).

THE PRESIDENT AND MRS. FRANKLIN D. ROOSEVELT *visit the Waacs in the spring of 1943. Above, Mr. Roosevelt reviews the troops at Fort Oglethorpe, Georgia. Below, Mrs. Roosevelt with Director Hobby and Col. John A. Hoag, commandant of First WAAC Training Center at Fort Des Moines.*

who had continuously opposed Administration measures. It was noted that in the weeks preceding the appearance of the column Mrs. Roosevelt had visited the Waacs at Des Moines and the President himself had reviewed those at Fort Oglethorpe, after which he had informed the press that "those of us who have seen the work they are doing . . . have only admiration and respect for the spirit, the dignity, and the courage they have shown." [41]

On 8 June the column stated:

Contraceptives and prophylactic equipment will be furnished to members of the WAAC, according to a supersecret agreement reached by high-ranking officers of the War Department and the WAAC Chieftain, Mrs. William Pettus Hobby. . . . It was a victory for the New Deal ladies. . . . Mrs. Roosevelt wants all the young ladies to have the same overseas rights as their brothers and fathers. [42]

There was actually no truth in the statement. The Army did provide free prophylactic equipment for men, and it appeared theoretically possible that some station in the field might have attempted to apply the same rule to women. However, the most thorough investigation by Army operatives from G–2 Division failed to produce any such evidence. These operatives reported:

There is apparently no factual basis for the . . . charge that contraceptives and prophylactics are issued to WAAC personnel. It is indicated that these articles are not even generally purchased in Post Exchanges and drug stores by individuals in the WAAC; in all cases of recorded sales the purchasers have been married women. [43]

It was G–2's opinion that the "supersecret" document referred to was a War Department printed pamphlet for the WAAC, *Sex Hygiene,* which prescribed six

lectures to be given WAAC officers and officer candidates, to equip them to give their women a suitably modest version of the Army's required hygiene course for men. [44] This was, however, an unsensational document, part of the routine training course, which prescribed standard subjects no more radical than those given in high schools and colleges—feminine anatomy and physiology, the nature and dangers of venereal disease, and the facts about menstruation and menopause—and which said nothing whatever about the issue of contraceptives. Its wording had in fact been carefully reviewed by the Director, and its presentation limited to trained WAAC officers, because of the British experience:

Exaggerated rumors appear to have gathered about hygiene lectures in the forces. . . . The mental reaction of a girl unaccustomed to attributing precise meanings to words, and bewildered by the impact of new and unfamiliar terms, must be kept in mind. [45]

G–2 described the pamphlet as "an excellent, frank, and wholesome manual . . . [which] counsels continence." [46] It definitely did not authorize any issue of contraceptives, and did not even tell the women what they were or how to use

[41] (1) *Des Moines Register,* February 15, 1943, and AP release, February 17, 1943. (2) Press Release, 15 May 43, signed Stephen Early. Envelope, Roosevelt, F. D., Statements by, WDBPR file of WAC Gp. (3) Text on new application form for enlistment, 31 May 43. SPWA 062.1.

[42] Washington *Times-Herald,* June 8, 1943.

[43] Memo, G–2 for Dir WAAC, 21 Aug 43, sub: Origin of Rumors Concerning Waacs. G–2 MID 322.12 WAAC (6–11–43).

[44] WD Pamphlet 35–1, 27 May 43, *Sex Hygiene Course, Officers and Officer Candidates, WAAC.*

[45] *Conditions in the Three Women's Services.*

[46] Memo, Chief CIC for Gen Strong (G–2), 23 Jun 43, sub: Prelim Rpt on WAAC. MID 322.12 WAAC (6–11–43).

them. This, just published on 27 May 1943, could have been the "agreement" mentioned in the 8 June column, although it was not "supersecret" or even secret or confidential but merely restricted to military personnel. Save for this, G–2 found that no directives on the subject had ever been issued by WAAC Headquarters except one letter in May, in answer to an inquiry, which said definitely that Waacs would not be given even so much as instruction in the use of prophylactics, much less the prophylactics themselves.[47]

War Department Denial

The War Department thus was in an excellent position to force the columnist to retract his statement. The question was whether it would be wise to lend the affair the dignity of a formal War Department denial. Many of the Director's advisers counseled against it, pointing out that persons would read the denial who had never read the attack, and that the present distress, anger, and humiliation experienced by the Director and all other Waacs would in time be forgotten. On the other hand, the shock which the column had caused the Waacs and their families was so great that an immediate denial seemed necessary to preserve the faith and self-respect of the Corps. An Army officer described a typical reaction in the WAAC company on his post:

It raised hell with that company. Long distance calls from parents began to come in, telling the girls to come home. The younger girls all came in crying, asking if this disgrace was what they had been asked to join the Army for. The older ones were just bitter that such lies could be printed. It took all the pride and enthusiasm for the Army right out of them.[48]

An enlisted woman described the same reaction; she said:

I went home on leave to tell my family it wasn't true. When I went through the streets, I held up my head because I imagined everybody was talking about me, but when I was at last safe inside our front door, I couldn't say a word to them, I was so humiliated—I just burst out crying, and my people ran and put their arms around me and cried with me. I couldn't understand how my eagerness to serve our country could have brought such shame on us all.[49]

Director Hobby herself, when she gathered her staff to tell them what had happened, broke down and was unable to continue speaking. The severity of the reaction of all Waacs, in whatever ranks, could be explained only by the fact that all, at this date, were the early pioneers whose enlistment had been motivated by a perhaps impractical idealism, intense enough to sustain them through the supply and training problems of the first winter, but too intense to receive such a gross attack with the indifference its inaccuracy merited.

Director Hobby therefore made the decision to reassure the women and their parents by public denials, whatever the effect on newspaper readers. Such denials were thereupon immediately made by the President and Mrs. Roosevelt, by Secretary of War Henry L. Stimson, by General Somervell of the Army Service Forces, by members of Congress, and by Director Hobby and other WAAC officers. The President told his press conference that it was a "deliberate newspaper job" and that the reporter had merely taken orders

[47] *Ibid.*, with incl Ltr, WAAC Hq to CG 2d SvC, 14 May 43. SPWA 726 (5–6–43).
[48] Interv with Joseph A. Bourdow, 9 Aug 48, then of Ft Washington AGO Sch.
[49] Sgt Amelia Madrak, Hist Div SSUSA, secy of author, 1947.

"from the top." [50] Mrs. Roosevelt in her press conference on 8 June stated that rumors about misconduct among Waacs in North Africa were Nazi propaganda, and that "Americans fall for Axis-inspired propaganda like children." [51] Naturally, she said, the Germans were interested in discrediting an organization that released so many men for the fighting front. [52]

Secretary Stimson's denial was the most publicized, and did in fact reach many people, especially on the west coast, who had never heard of the columnist or the rumors:

Sinister rumors aimed at destroying the reputation of the Waacs are absolutely and completely false. Anything which would interfere with their recruiting or destroy the reputation of the Corps, and by so doing interfere with increase in the combat strength of our Army, would be of value to the enemy. The repetition of any unfounded rumor . . . is actually an aid to the enemy.

He pointed out that reflection on the WAAC was reflection on the whole of American womanhood, and that to malign the nation's women could easily destroy the morale of men at the front. [53]

In addition, General Somervell told a Congressional committee that the rumors were spread by a person sympathetic to the Axis and that the Waacs were "your and my daughters and sisters" and entitled to respect. [54] Representative Edith Rogers told Congress that "nothing would please Hitler more" than to discredit Waacs and American women. Representative Mary Norton said, "Loose talk concerning our women in the Armed Services cannot be less than Nazi-inspired." [55] Director Hobby told reporters that there was "absolutely no foundation of truth in the statement."

Under the barrage, the columnist was forced to retract his statement, which he did, although protesting that his information came from an "intelligent and trustworthy" official who swore that "his eyes had passed over" the alleged secret paper. [56] Nevertheless, three years later, religious publications were still to be found reprinting the story, and actually attributing the columnist's lines to Director Hobby. Director Hobby's picture was labeled "Astounding Degeneracy," and one article continued, "Mrs. William Pettus Hobby, chieftain of the WAC, says, 'Contraceptives and prophylactics will be furnished to members of the WAC according to a super-secret agreement reached by high-ranking officers of the War Department. . . .'" [57]

Investigation by Intelligence Service

In June, a full-scale investigation of possible Axis influence in the rumors was launched by the Army's Military Intelli-

---

[50] *Washington Post*, June 30, 1943.

[51] *Washington Daily News*, June 9, 1943.

[52] *PM* (New York), June 10, 1943.

[53] *Washington Post*, June 11, 1943.

[54] *Ibid.*, June 16, 1943.

[55] Both in the Washington *Evening Star*, June 10, 1943.

[56] "Capitol Stuff," June 10, 1943. The columnist later insisted he was vindicated when, in 1945, *Time* alleged the Army had declared surplus the remains of a stock of contraceptive jelly. He did not check far enough to discover that such jelly, if it existed, would have been sold in any Army PX, where Waacs formed an almost microscopic fraction of female customers, who included soldiers' wives and other authorized purchasers. In fact, upon investigation, Army officers were unable to locate any such stock of contraceptive jelly as reported by *Time*. Transcript of Tp Conv, Maj Chance and Mr. Marples, WDBPR. WDWAC 331.1 (1945–46).

[57] (1) *The Evangelical Beacon*, Vol. XIV, No. 22, February 27, 1945, incl to Ltr, AAF PDC to Air WAC Div, 20 Sep 45. WDWAC 330.14. (2) Ltr, Mrs. F. D. Roosevelt to Dir WAC, 25 Oct 44, incl Ltr from voter re religious magazine of alleged 1,500,000 weekly circulation, *The Missionary Worker*. WDWAC 330.4.

gence Service. The Federal Bureau of Investigation gave the Army full permission, in this one instance, to investigate persons who might otherwise fall under the investigative jurisdiction of the FBI.[58]

A more exhaustive investigation could scarcely have been made than that which Military Intelligence now undertook. First, Army agents covered sections of the nation near large WAAC installations, such as training centers. At Des Moines, for example, more than 250 interviews were held with a cross section of the local citizens, in an effort to expose the source of the rumors. Next, specific stories all over the nation were tracked down to their beginnings, each involving a large file of notes and records.[59]

The report reached a conclusion far less pleasant than the theory of Nazi activity:

There is no positive evidence that rumors concerning the morality of WAAC personnel are Axis-inspired. There is some evidence that the Axis-controlled radio has followed a line of rumors already widely circulated by . . . *Army personnel, Navy personnel, Coast Guard personnel, business men, women, factory workers and others.* Most . . . have completely American backgrounds.[60]

Evidence indicated that in most cases the obscene stories had been originated by men of the armed forces at about the time of the change from the "phony war" to real combat in North Africa, and of Congressional publicity on the thousands of women sought to release men for combat. From Army and Navy men, the stories had spread rapidly, first to their wives and women friends, and thence to the whole population. Eventually the rumor spreaders included, according to G–2 secret files:

(1) *Army personnel:* "Army officers and men who resent members of the WAAC . . . who have obtained equal or higher rank than themselves." "Men who fear they will be replaced by Waacs." "Male military personnel who are sometimes inclined to resent usurpation of their long-established monopoly." "Soldiers who had never dated Waacs . . . [or] had trouble getting dates."

(2) *Soldiers' Wives:* "Officers' wives over bridge tables." "Women whose husbands are shipped overseas."

(3) *Jealous Civilian Women:* "Local girls and women who resent having the Waacs around." "Younger to middle-aged women who deplore the extra competition." "Women who ordinarily participate in community enterprise and who are losing publicity as a result of women in uniform."

(4) *Gossips:* "Thoughtless gossiping men and women." "Men [who] like to tell off-color stories."

(5) *Fanatics:* "Those who cannot get used to women being any place except the home." "Those whose rabid political convictions cause them erroneously to see in the WAAC another New Deal creation."

(6) *Waacs:* "Disgruntled and discharged Waacs."[61]

A typical example of an unfounded rumor that spread in the standard pattern was the case involving a Midwestern city and the surrounding area. In this city, agents reported, enlisted men and officers in bars had begun the rumors with statements of which the more printable included, "Waacs are a bunch of tramps"; "All Waacs have round heels"; and "Waacs are nothing but prostitutes." In small towns nearby, officers' wives soon

---

[58] Memo cited n. 43. Also, Ltr, J. Edgar Hoover to Col Leslie R. Forney, MIS, 30 Jun 43. G–2 MID 322.12 WAAC (6–11–43).

[59] Specific references will be given in each case in following paragraphs. The entire file of the summer's investigation is found in G–2 files, MID 322.12 WAAC.

[60] Memo cited n. 43. Author's italics.

[61] (1) Memo, Chief CIC, MIS, for Gen Strong, 13 Aug 43, sub: Closing Rpt on Investigation of Rumors Concerning WAAC. MID 322.12 WAAC. (2) Memo cited n. 26. (3) Memo cited n. 46.

afterward stated to friends that Waacs were really taken into the service to take care of the sex problems of soldiers. An Army chaplain then advised Waacs not to re-enlist in the WAC. The rumors spread to Protestant and Catholic ministers in the vicinity, who then urged Waacs to get out of the service. These were investigated by the FBI for sedition in urging desertion.

Agents were not able to verify even one case of pregnancy of an unmarried Waac in that area, or any other notorious misconduct.[62]

In New England, especially in the Fort Devens area, agents found that a number of stories about mass pregnancy, venereal disease, and immorality had originated with military personnel. The G–2 report added:

Military personnel, commissioned and enlisted, were found to be a prolific fountainhead of WAAC rumors. Soldiers who had never dated Waacs, and consequently didn't know whether the stories were true, accepted the tales as gospel. Army nurses are allegedly jealous of the Waacs because the latter are promoted more rapidly, receive more publicity, and encroach on the nurses' dating territory. The wives of men replaced by Waacs are said to be angry because their husbands are sent overseas as a result of the Waacs supplanting them. No subversive intent is apparent in either case.

Soldiers in the Fort Devens area were credited by investigators with originating the rumor that "fantastic" numbers of pregnant Waacs had been sent back to Lovell General Hospital from North Africa. Agents descended on that hospital's records "without prearrangement" and reported, "No record of a pregnant Waac was found." In fact, no Waacs pregnant or otherwise had ever been returned from North Africa to Lovell General Hospital. Another Fort Devens' rumor among military personnel was that the WAAC venereal disease rate was skyrocketing. When 6,000 women were examined, only 11 cases were discovered, 8 of them having existed before enlistment and having been undetected by entrance examinations. This, agents said, was a rate which was "less than *any* civilian community." A third rumor in New England was that Waacs were officially advised to utilize contraceptives. Agents interviewed hundreds of Waacs and were unable to find even one who had ever been so advised; the Catholic chaplain also asserted that no Waacs in the area had ever to his knowledge been given such advice.[63]

In the Fort Des Moines area, where Waacs had been longest, rumors were not so vicious; the attitude of male military personnel, originally quite hostile, had reportedly upon closer acquaintance taken a marked change for the better. The Director of Intelligence, Seventh Service Command, concluded, "It is obvious that the Corps members, by force of their own composite opinion, do much to enforce proper conduct and freedom from even the appearance of evil on the part of other members."[64]

Agents at Fort Des Moines reported that no soldier could be found who had ever had sexual intercourse with a Waac; in fact, most had trouble getting a date. Sales of contraceptives at local drug stores had not gone up. Waacs drank less in public than civilian women, and it was found that "merchants agree Waacs are more courteous and patient, meet obligations more readily." All interviewed who knew Waacs placed the sexual morality of the

---

[62] Memo cited n. 61(1).
[63] *Ibid.*, Ft Devens area sec.
[64] Memo cited n. 26, Ft Devens area sec.

average member as higher than that of the average civilian girl. Nevertheless, a relatively few instances of drunkenness and misconduct had made a proportionately greater impression on local citizens. Since Waacs originally did not have to wear uniforms off duty, local citizens also showed a tendency to consider any drunken woman a disguised Waac, until training center authorities forbade wearing of civilian dress in the Des Moines area.[65]

Near the Fifth Training Center, a Capt. Charles S. wrote a Waac friend that he had heard there were 165 "pregnated" Waacs in one month at Camp Polk, and that before members went out on passes they were required to show that they had contraceptives with them. When asked for proof by Military Intelligence, Captain S. was, agents said, "much chagrined and embarrassed."[66]

In the area around Fort Oglethorpe, Georgia, agents reported evidence that rumors had been spread by men who resented WAAC rank or who thought they would be shipped overseas as soon as enough Waacs could be recruited to replace them. Local girls and women had picked up the rumors; one admitted to agents that she had spread stories which were not true but that, "I just get tired of seeing them around." A rumor about 100 pregnancies was traced to the local WCTU. Again, statistics failed to support the charges. Of 14,000 women trained or processed since the training center opened, three had been hospitalized for drunkenness, and eight had venereal disease, which agents described as a "negligible" percentage of cases compared to civilian rates. Hotel owners and the director of the Chamber of Commerce said Waacs conducted themselves better than civilian girls.[67]

Investigation at Daytona Beach

The most extensive training center investigation was conducted at Daytona Beach, where the Second WAAC Training Center and General Faith's headquarters had operated in the midst of a resort city. In January Director Hobby had renewed her attempts to get the women out of the city area, and in March the Services of Supply approved construction of classrooms and one theater but again refused to approve construction of recreational buildings.[68]

As a result, large numbers of recreation-seeking Waacs descended on the city nightly, provoking much civilian resentment and some of the most serious allegations encountered by investigators. At first these objections concerned only the crowding and food consumption by Waacs: one winter resident, who described himself as "a lover of the locality and its facilities as an adorable resort," wrote his senator to denounce WAAC service as "a grand vacation at Government expense . . . the Army group monopolizes our few sizeable restaurants to the detriment of civilians." Investigators found that most such complaints came from about 15 percent of the local residents described as "well-to-do property owners . . . the

---

[65] Memo cited n. 26. Also (1) M/R, 10 Jul 43, Summary of Investigation, sub: Origin of Rumors Concerning WAAC. G-2 MID 322.12 (6-11-43). (2) Ltr, Col Hoag to Dir WAAC, 11 Jan 43, sub: Wearing of Uniform. SPWA 300.3 (12-7-43) sec 1 (Cont). (3) WAAC Cir 2, 28 Jan 43. (4) Ltr, WAAC Hq to Tng Cens, 24 Feb 43, sub: Wearing of Uniform. SPWA 300.3.

[66] Memo cited n. 61(1), 8th SvC sec.

[67] (1) Memo cited n. 26, Ft Oglethorpe Sec. (2) Ltr, MID 4th SvC to MID (Washington, D. C.), 5 Jul 43, sub: Origin of Rumors Concerning WAAC. G-2 MID 322.12 WAAC (6-11-43).

[68] Ltr, 2d Tng Cen to Dir WAAC, 8 Jan 43, and Inds. WA 600.1 (7-2-42)(1) sec 2 (1942).

elderly conservative type." [69] Another civilian criticism alleged that WAAC messes wasted food so that their garbage cans were filled to overflowing while Florida civilians went hungry under the administration's food rationing system. Instead, investigators found that the disposable garbage rate in WAAC messes was only half that of the Army rate; the local garbage collector, when interviewed, stated that what he found in WAAC garbage cans was far less than that from "civilian sources." [70]

Rumors nevertheless grew more vicious. It was said that WAAC trainees drank too much; that they picked up men in streets and bars; that they were registered with men in every hotel and auto court, or had sexual relations under trees and bushes in public parks; that there was a nearby military hospital filled to overflowing with maternity and venereal disease cases. Finally, it was seriously stated that Waacs were touring in groups seizing and raping sailors and Coast Guardsmen. [71]

No evidence to support such statements could be found by military intelligence operatives, or by independent investigations by the Fourth Service Command, or by Colonel Clark of WAAC Headquarters. [72] The alleged government maternity home was nonexistent; only 18 pregnancies had been discovered, 16 of them among married women; inspectors could get locally only hearsay and gossip but "no single piece of correspondence which would indicate any tangible item." [73] Although the center had almost 10,000 trainees, the military police report for a typical Saturday night revealed a total of only 11 delinquencies:

2 kissing and embracing in public
1 no hat on
2 injured in auto accident
1 without identification card
1 walking with officer on street
2 found intoxicated
1 AWOL returned
1 "retrieved from Halifax River in an intoxicated condition"

---

11 Total

This was accounted a remarkable record in view of the fact that, among the thousands of women at the Second Training Center in this first week of May, 1943, many were the mental, moral, physical, and psychological problems that had been accepted in such large numbers before the restoration of recruiting standards. However, it was admitted that rumors would naturally spread through the local civilians if even one Waac out of 10,000 had to be retrieved from the Halifax River every Saturday night. [74]

The inspectors and the local authorities

[69] (1) Ltr, Mr. Fred Huntress to Senator Claude Pepper, 3 Mar 43; (2) Memo, Gen Grunert for Dir WAAC, 23 Mar 43. Folder, Daytona Beach, Dir Adm Serv ASF Sp Coll DRB AGO.

[70] For civilian complaints: (1) Memos cited n. 61. (2) File of Dir Adm Serv, with investigations, cited n. 72.

[71] Memos cited n. 61.

[72] (1) For MID investigation, see Memos cited n. 61. (2) For Col Clark's, see Memo, Col Clark, Chief Opns Div WAAC Hq, for Dir WAAC, 27 May 43. SPWA 319.1. For others, see (3) Ltr, Mr. Harry Hopkins to Brig Gen Frederick H. Osborn, 1 Mar 43; (4) Memo, Dir WAAC for TIG, 13 Mar 43, incl Ltrs from Senator Pepper and Gen White, SPWA 330.14 (3–8–43)E; (5) Memo, Exec 2d WAAC Tng Cen for Comdt, 13 Mar 43; (6) Memo, Gen Faith for Dir WAAC, 18 Mar 43, SPWA 250.1; (7) TWX, Gen Grunert to DCofAdm Serv ASF, 19 Mar 43, WA–212–119–Govt Z; (8) Memo, DCofAdm Serv for Dir Reqmts Div ASF, 20 Mar 43, with approval by Reqmts Div, 23 Mar 43, SPAAS 353.8; (9) Memo, CofAdm Serv ASF for Dir WAAC, 23 Mar 43; (10) Various Ltrs from White House, Congress, citizens, et al., atchd to above. Folder, Daytona Beach, Dir Adm Serv ASF Sp Coll DRB AGO.

[73] Rpt, CIC 4th SvC to MIS, 19 Jul 43, sub: Origin of Rumors. G–2 MID 322.12 WAAC.

[74] Ibid.

unanimously blamed the location and the lack of recreational facilities. The area was described as the week-end mecca of soldiers and sailors from surrounding military and naval stations. An Army investigator observed, "From Saturday noon until midnight Sunday, Daytona Beach takes on an atmosphere of a large coeducational institution at which the home team has just won an important football game." [75] One officer reported, "It was a crazy idea to try to set up a Military Training Center in a place like this where the girls live in hotels and are surrounded by a carnival atmosphere." [76]

The Fourth Service Command inspector general recommended more recreation facilities so that trainees would not need to roam the city at night. The military intelligence operative agreed: "It is the opinion of this officer that recreational facilities are inadequate." [77] Ninety percent of the women had, he said, stayed in their quarters and suffered low morale, while only about 10 percent were seen in the city, but this 10 percent totaled a thousand women. General Grunert, who investigated in person, immediately telegraphed his office:

RECREATION FACILITIES AVAILABLE TO WAAC TRAINING CENTER HERE AT DAYTONA BEACH ARE SO GROSSLY INADEQUATE AS TO MAKE IT NECESSARY TO RECONSIDER THE QUESTION OF PROVIDING TWO SERVICE CLUBS. . . . PRESENT USE OF INADEQUATE CIVILIAN FACILITIES HAS RESULTED AND WILL CONTINUE TO RESULT IN COMPLAINTS AND RUMORS AS TO DRINKING AND IMMORALITY AND DEPLETION OF CIVILIAN FOOD SUPPLY. . . . TAKE UP THIS MATTER WITH COMMANDING GENERAL ARMY SERVICE FORCES AT ONCE FOR EARLY ACTION. [78]

Now, belatedly, Requirements Division, ASF, reversed its earlier disapprovals and approved Director Hobby's four-month-old recommendation for two service clubs,

but the time required to bring them into operation was considerable, and in any event the damage was irretrievable. [79]

In addition, inspectors blamed some rumors at Daytona Beach on the conduct of female dischargees who remained about town "conducting a campaign against the WAAC." [80] General Faith noted that, in the weeks before recruiting standards were restored, about one half of 1 percent of the women sent him had previous records which warranted their immediate discharge, and that in addition another 4 percent were guilty of "unseemly conduct . . . specifically, drinking, boisterousness, and petting in public parks and on benches." The remaining 95 percent he believed to be of exemplary conduct and discipline, a good statistical average for any civilian community. General Faith stated, "I am convinced that faulty recruiting is the primary cause of the conditions described." [81]

No matter how promptly such women were discharged, civilian gossip had opportunity to multiply their numbers and to confuse the conduct of dischargees with that of trainees. WAAC military police attempted to take uniforms from dischargees who were wearing them for a purpose other than the official one of return to the place of enlistment, but in one such case a woman discharged for neurosis promptly ran screaming into the street disrobed, causing even worse public comment.

---

[75] Memo, Asst IG 4th SvC for CG 4th SvC, 9 May 43, atchd as Exhibit B to Rpt cited n. 73.

[76] Post Engr, in Rpt cited n. 73.

[77] Rpt cited n. 73.

[78] TWX cited n. 72(7).

[79] Memos cited n. 72(8) and 72(9).

[80] WAAC Cir 11, 1 Oct 42, and correspondence in SPWA 420 (8-25-42), 1942. Army Regulations shortly superseded this circular.

[81] Memo cited n. 72(6).

Colonel Clark, who investigated for WAAC Headquarters, said:

Being considerably alarmed by rumors . . . I took the trouble to ascertain from the hospital records the true facts with regard to pregnancies and venereal diseases. These figures are statistical and incontrovertible. . . . It will be seen at a glance that the experience of this center in this respect has been unusually fortunate. . . . It is extremely unfortunate that we have no recourse against these scurrilous and slanderous charges.[82]

The Army did have one recourse, and that was to abandon all city property—a move also dictated by the shrinking enrollment. At this, a local newspaper columnist cried:

It may be that the present scare that the War Department would forego Daytona Beach . . . will close the traps of some of the scandal mongers. . . . Had it not been for the coming of the Waacs, Daytona Beach would by now have been a ghost town.[83]

In July, the Waacs gave up the leased city buildings and withdrew within the cantonment area, and the local radio station broadcast, "Cool Daytona Beach can once again accommodate thousands of summer visitors."[84]

Other Investigations

It was from overseas, where most soldiers had not as yet seen a Waac, that the worst opposition came. The Office of Censorship ran a sample tabulation and reported that, of intercepts of soldier mail which mentioned the WAAC, 84 percent expressed disfavor and most advised a woman not to join; some threatened to jilt or divorce her, as the case might be, if she did join.[85]

The only Waacs then overseas were some 200 in North Africa and about 600 bound for England, but, according to the soldiers' reports, each must have been shipped home pregnant several times. A counterintelligence operative, sitting in a restaurant next to an Army major, heard him say loudly that the Army had sent "a whole boat-load" home and that it was "difficult to keep Waacs at any station over there for any length of time without fully two-thirds of them becoming pregnant."[86] A civilian just returned from North Africa cautioned his women friends against joining the WAAC because of the low moral character of nurses and Waacs, but when pressed for facts was unable to furnish the names of any specific persons or places, and admitted he had no direct knowledge of the matter.[87]

One favorite rumor was that General Eisenhower had said that he didn't want Waacs "dumped on his command area." Foreign correspondents interviewed General Eisenhower and found that he had not only requested Waacs but said he would get British servicewomen if American ones were not sent. One reporter discovered that Waacs in North Africa lived in a convent under strict discipline, rose early to catch a 6:00 A.M. military bus to town, worked hard all day, securing enthusiastic recommendations from supervisors, and retired to the convent for an 8:00 P.M. curfew. He therefore failed to see how their night life could be very exciting.[88]

---

[82] Memo cited n. 72(2).

[83] *Daytona Beach Observer*, May 22, 1943.

[84] July broadcast over Daytona Beach stations. Exhibit N, Rpt cited n. 73.

[85] Memo cited n. 46.

[86] Memo, CID agent for Chief CIC, 16 Jul 43, sub: Dissemination of Rumors. MID 322.12 WAAC (6–11–43).

[87] Memo cited n. 61(1).

[88] John Lardner's syndicated column, June 10, 1943.

Among all the comments reported in later samplings by the censors, who of course had no power to delete them, there were many praising the Corps and its work, but not one reported instance in which a man advised a woman to enlist.[89] Typical soldier comments, from many units and from widely separated parts of the world, were:

Wife of one of the men in my company joined the Wacs. She simply wrote and told him that, tired of living off the fat of the land, she had enlisted. With no further ado, the man wrote his father's attorney to institute divorce action . . . and is at present engaged in cutting off her allotments, changing insurance beneficiaries. . . .

You join the WAVES or WAC and you are automatically a prostitute in my opinion.

I think they are great organizations, but I don't want any wife, or future wife, of mine joining them.

Are you going in the Wacs, Mother? If you did or do, I will disown you.

Velva, please don't join the Wacs. I have good reasons for not wanting you to. I persuaded my sister not to. Some day I'll tell you why.

You ask me to tell you what I think of the Wacs and Waves with the idea of you joining in mind. Darling, that sort of puts me on the spot. If the idea of you joining were not involved, I would say that they have proven a proud, worthwhile part of our armed forces. . . . But from the standpoint of you joining is something else again . . . very emphatically I do not want you to join.

I think it is best that he and Edith are separating, because after she gets out of the service she won't be worth a dime. . . . I would not have a girl or wife if she was in the service even if she was made of gold.

Any service woman—Wac, Wave, Spar, Nurse, Red Cross—isn't respected.

I told my Sis if she ever joined I would put her out of the house and I really meant it. So if you ever join I will be finished with you too and I mean it.

I think it is enough to say that I am not raising my daughters up to be Wacs.

It's no damn good, Sis, and I for one would be very unhappy if you joined them. . . . Why can't these Gals just stay home and be their own sweet little self, instead of being patriotic?

I just spoke to a couple of officers one of whose wife was so smart she joined and then told him. To give you an idea of what officers think . . . he told his wife to get a divorce. The other officer had to really tell off his daughter before she got such ideas out of her head.

Darling for my sake don't join them. I can't write my reasons because the censors won't let it through.

Honey don't ever worry your poor head about joining the Wacs for we went over all that once before, Ha! (Remember, over my dead body. Ha! Ha!) You are going to stay at home.

I would rather we never seen each other for 20 years than to have you join the Wacs. For gosh sakes stay a good girl (civilian) and I'm not just kidding either.

Ruth asked about the Wacs. The idea is noble but the widespread attitude of the public is narrow and bad. So I definitely don't recommend it.

I don't want you to have a thing to do with them. Because they are the biggest hours (I hope this gets through the censor.) Lousey, boy, they are lousey, and maybe you think my blood don't boil and bubble. . . . God, I'd disown anybody who would join.

The practice of women in the Army, still in my mind, is a glorified form of cheap bolshevism.

Lets not say no more about the auxiliaries for the idea makes me mad in the first place

---

[89] Exception: one comment was found in which, toward the end of the war, a man stated that it would provide a woman friend with GI benefits for a few weeks' service before the Corps was demobilized. All soldier comments are from (1) NATO AG file 319.1 Morale, Vols. II–V; (2) Morale Evaluation Survey in Women's Services, GHQ AFPAC, 16 Jun 45, in possession of former Staff Director, AFPAC.

and I don't want you galavanting around over the country for another thing. You will be better off chopping cotton. . . .

Your letter shocked me so and it was not appreciated by no means. If you join the Wacs, you and I are through for good, and I'll stop all allotments and everything.

I remember distinctly telling you before that your joining the WAC was one thing I would not tolerate. I told you distinctly that I didn't want to discuss it. Why do you persist? . . .

The service is no place for a woman. A woman's place is in the home.

About joining the Wacs the answer is still NO. If they really need service women let them draft some of the pigs that are running around loose in every town.

When you asked me the first time whether you could join the Wacs I refused and I meant that for all time. I want to come home to the girl I remember.

I cannot put this on paper how I feel and I am ashamed to tell my fellow officers. She cannot even consider herself as my wife from now on. I am stopping all allotments to her and am breaking off all contacts with her. Why she did such a thing to me I cannot understand. My heart is broken.

Get that damn divorce. I don't want no damn WAC for a wife.

In the last year of the war a censor summarized the situation:

Comments on the WAC continue to reflect much credit on their ability. Their military bearing and adaptability to military life bring praise . . . [but] there is no indication of a lessening of U.S. troops' opposition to friends and relatives joining. WAC individuals indicate their disillusionment.[90]

In the spreading of rumors, the Waacs themselves were far from guiltless. Letters written home by disgruntled individuals frequently contained remarks about food, living conditions, and forced association

with low and unsympathetic characters. For example, a young woman just arrived at a new station wrote her father:

Dear Pop:
Please don't show this letter to Mom. This place is like a concentration camp and the C. O. and the First Sergeant have driven one girl to suicide and three to going AWOL. The girl who went AWOL last night was a fine, clean girl, and when she refused to submit to her Boss he threatened to court-martial her on a trumped-up charge. A boy in Co. W. killed himself last night, I saw the note he left with my own eyes. Two Chaplains have gone AWOL this week and can't be found. Please don't worry. I'll stick it out as best I can, but it is leaving its mark.

Somewhat naturally, her father sent this letter hastily to his congressman, who sent it to the Secretary of War, saying, "I have known her all of her life and have always found her to be honest, reliable, and trustworthy." A formal investigation was immediately held, at which it was discovered that none of the allegations was true: "Complainant stated that she addressed the letter to her father while in a mood of depression following her arrival at Camp D——. She acknowledged that the statements in her letter were based upon hearsay."[91]

The faulty recruiting techniques of the past months also resulted in receipt by civilians of long, incoherent letters from mentally disturbed individuals concerning persecution by officers, general misconduct among all officers and noncoms, or at least those who got promotions, and unwarranted punishments for the writer. Most alleged that they were sending copies to newspapers and friends. Investigation

---

[90] File cited n. 89(1).
[91] Ltr, Adm Asst to SW to Hon Michael Kirwan, 25 Sep 45; Ltr, Hon Michael Kirwan to SW, 6 Jul 45; Ltr, [WAC, Camp Davis], 6 Jul 45. CofS 324.5 WAC.

of such cases ordinarily disclosed only that the writer "had great difficulty in adjusting to the military service," [92] or had just been discharged.

With the approach of the conversion to the Women's Army Corps, many women deemed undesirable members of the company were refused re-enlistment by their commanding officers; these included neurotics, behavior problems, and other troublemakers. Recruiters came to dread the return of one of these rejects to her community, knowing that she would probably spread ridicule and falsehoods about the Corps. [93]

The Question of Axis Influence

Army intelligence agents at this point began to concentrate upon tracking down individual stories with, originally, the hope that Axis agents would be found at the source. In only one case was there any such Axis connection: this was the rumor about the return of thousands of pregnant Waacs from North Africa. When this was painfully traced to its beginning, it was found to be based on an actual incident in which the first three Waacs were shipped home, two sick, one pregnant, the latter having been for some years the lawful wife of an Army officer who had spent a leave with her a few months before.

The Axis radio station DEBUNK then broadcast in English to North Africa the modest amplification that 20 Waacs had been returned for pregnancy. This broadcast, however, was less effective than that of a Coast Guard lieutenant who told friends at the Capitol in Washington that he was a member of an armed guard which was required on a ship bringing back 150 pregnant Waacs "to keep some of the women from jumping overboard." On

a train from Washington to New York, a Navy commander gave the number as 300. By the time the figure was given in Minneapolis by a Navy enlisted man, it had reached 250,000. When questioned by the Office of Naval Intelligence, the Coast Guard lieutenant said, "It was spoken in jest." He was, the Navy said, then "admonished." The Navy commander had the misfortune to relate his story on the train to a man whose daughter was a Waac; this man took his name and wrote the Secretary of War. The Secretary of War asked the Secretary of the Navy for action. The commander then wrote the Waac's father, "The private conversation in which we engaged informally seems to have been seized on by you as the basis of some far-extending investigation, in which I do not intend to become involved." The War Department was not informed whether any action had been taken against the commander. [94]

No other cases showed even a trace of Axis influence. A typical case was that of an insurance salesman in Philadelphia who wrote an Army officer that WAAC conduct was deplorable. When military agents appeared in his office and pressed for details, he alleged that Waacs had at various times accosted him and his friends, entered his hotel room, and showed him contraceptives in their purses. He refused to give names of the men friends who he

---

[92] Ltr, Pvt Ruth F. Bolger to Dir WAC, 23 Jun 44, incl, with investigation, in Memo, Air WAC Off for Dep Dir WAC, 18 Oct 44. WDWAC 330.14.

[93] Office Memo, 1st O Virginia Martin, Rctg Sec WAAC Hq, for Exec WAAC, 24 Jul 43. SPWA 319.1.

[94] (1) Memo, G–2 for Dir WAAC [WAC], 12 Aug 43, sub: Origin of Rumors Concerning WAAC. G–2 MID 322.12 WAAC. (2) Memo cited n. 61(1), sec re Lt Dix W. P., Coast Guard, and Comdr Neil B. W., USN. Also, same file, Ltr, John W., Jersey City, N. J., to SW, 30 Jul 43, with atchd Ltr, Comdr W. to Mr. W. (3) Ltr, SW to SN, 28 Jul 43. CofS files.

said were present when the alleged offenses occurred. His neighbors were asked for opinions as to his reliability and described him as "not reliable," "know-it-all," "a blowhard." He was not an Axis agent.[95]

Miss Helen A., a businesswoman in New York City, wrote Army authorities concerning the disgraceful situation at the ——— Hospital of Jersey City, where, she alleged, there were 50 pregnant Waacs. When questioned by intelligence officers, she admitted that she had heard that story from a friend, Miss W. Miss W. said she had the information from another friend who was having a baby at the hospital and heard two nurses in conversation outside her door. However, Miss W. finally admitted that the real source was a conversation she had overheard between two unidentified women sitting at the next table in a restaurant. The hospital submitted four affidavits to show that no Waac, pregnant or otherwise, had ever been there. Confronted with this evidence, Miss A. reportedly said that she "regretted writing the letter." None of the individuals concerned were Axis agents.[96]

In South Dakota, a civilian woman who had been assisting recruiters told them that she could no longer help recruit women unless they took steps to see that no more Waacs were sent overseas "to be tempted." She had heard that 5,000 had just been sent home from England for pregnancy. Recruiters told her that she must be wrong, since there were not that many Waacs in England, but she replied that she had the facts from her son, Capt. Harvey H., a medical officer in England. Recruiters reported this to the Director, who promptly wrote to the European theater requesting that they call to Captain H.'s attention "the implications of such statements on American woman-

hood." Scarcely was Captain H. threatened with court-martial in England than his father telephoned from South Dakota to tell the Director that the whole thing had been a misunderstanding. None of the family were Axis agents.[97]

One of the lengthiest investigations concerned a suspected Nazi in New Jersey, Hugo S., recipient of the Iron Cross and former Bund member. This individual, working at his bench in a war plant, observed to fellow employees that 500 pregnant Waacs had just arrived in New York from overseas. A fellow worker, whose daughter was a Waac stationed overseas, promptly knocked him down and reported him. Intelligence agents made every effort to prove that Mr. S. was acting as a Nazi agent in repeating this rumor, but were unable to do so. Several weeks before, Representative Daniel S. had risen in the Massachusetts legislature to make the same charge. He alleged that the story was told him by an Army medical officer whom he refused to name, and the representative was not a Nazi agent.[98]

Even when a rumor could be traced to its originator, there was no legal means of punishing loyal American citizens for gossip. An Axis agent, if proven such, could have been jailed had he spread identical stories with intent to hinder mobilization. Members of the armed forces could be punished only if it could be proved that they used their position to

---

[95] Memo, MIS for Dir MI, 3d SvC, 16 Jun 43. MID 322.12 WAAC (6–16–43) (6–11–43).

[96] Ltr, 2d SvC Hq to G–2, 22 Jul 43, sub: Origin of Rumors Concerning WAAC. MID 322.12 WAAC (6–11–43). Sec re Miss Helen A. and Miss W., New York.

[97] (1) Memo, Dir WAC for CG AAF, 6 Dec 44, sub: Rumors. WDWAC 330.11. (2) Ltr, ETO Hq to ETO, 17 Mar 45, sub: Rpt of Investigation. AG 333.5 MPMGA, in WDWAC 330.14.

[98] Memo cited n. 61(1).

spread false official information detrimental to the war effort. Director Hobby reluctantly recommended such action to Waacs who reported, for example, that an instructor in an Army school had told his class that Waacs were "a prostitute Army," that an officer's wife had told everyone in a beauty shop that large numbers of Waacs were pregnant, and other such cases. Observing, "It is a bitter thing that this had to happen in the Army family," Director Hobby advised that in every such case the offender's name be obtained and a report made for investigation of the charges.[99]

The conclusion that Axis agents were not primarily involved was supported, after the end of the war, by captured German intelligence files. These indicated that German agents had collected newspaper clippings and other public announcements, and were well aware of the Corps' strength and the plans to recruit more womanpower, as well as of the plans to place the WAAC in the Army. However, there was no indication that the Germans had placed secret agents on this project, as they had on others; apparently they were content with information gleaned from news and radio sources. If any orders had been given to spread rumors, they were not recorded.[100]

Ineffectiveness of Denials

It proved all but impossible for a Waac to defend herself or the Corps against the various rumors. For example, a young recruiter, in her speeches to civic groups, attempted to spike the rumors by telling the absolute truth: not that all Waacs were angels, but that only one Waac in the area had ever been picked up by military police; only one out of many drank

heavily; the local police chief reported "very little trouble"; only nineteen women of thousands trained had ever been discharged for pregnancy and she "understood" that all nineteen were married. Spectators reported that "it appeared to give them more to talk about."[101]

At least one constructive countermeasure was put into effect by WAAC Headquarters. A planeload of the most prominent leaders of the Catholic, Jewish, and Protestant faiths had been carried to Fort Oglethorpe and Fort Des Moines for a visit shortly before the newspaper columnist's attack. They were given opportunity to inspect chapels, hospitals, clubs, and barracks, to talk to the staff and trainees, and to hold religious services. As a result, immediately after the attack, these clergymen issued a signed statement to the newspapers, saying, "We feel that parents concerned about the moral and spiritual welfare of their daughters can be reassured. A hopeful harbinger of the new world is evidenced by the sacrificial contribution which American women are making through the WAAC. [It] will strengthen their character." Monsignor Michael J. Ready told the Waacs, "We're proud of you." Dr. Carroll C. Roberts wrote the Director, "We were all deeply conscious of the earnestness of the young women and the quiet dignity with which they carried out their work."[102] These statements were reinforced by articles and

---

[99] Min cited n. 28(1).

[100] Sec F 22 d, "Frauen," Pol. 5, 2. Bd., Frankreich, FRA; file of German Intelligence, Army High Command, G-2 Sec, Foreign Armies West, H 2/2.

[101] Memo, 2d O D. L. Meyer for PRO, 3d WAAC Tng Cen, 7 Jun 43, sub: Rpt of Speech on Rumors by Rctg Off. SPWA 319.1.

[102] (1) Office of the Chief of Chaplains, Military History of the Second World War: The Corps of Chaplains, p. 95, on ministrations to WAC. OCMH.

CLERGYMEN VISITING FORT DES MOINES. *They are accompanied by (left)*
Maj. Margaret D. Craighill, Col. Frank U. McCoskrie, and the Director of the WAAC.

pictures in religious magazines by a group of religious writers and editors who received a similar plane trip.[103]

There was also some evidence that the newspaper blasts concerning Axis sympathizers, even though mistaken in where they placed their blame, had some effect in convincing rumormongers that they might be aiding the enemy.

Congressional committees were so alarmed by the rumors that, two days after the 8 June "Capitol Stuff" column appeared, they summoned Director Hobby to appear and bring statistics on the actual cases of pregnancy and venereal disease. After seeing these, they expressed a desire to be of assistance, and suggested that the Director publish the figures and some of the actual cases of rumor spreading, to prove to the public that WAAC morality was superior to that of civilian women.[104] One Congressional committee stated:

---

(2) Releases in numerous papers; for example, *Washington Post*, June 11, 1943. The group included Dr. Barnett R. Bricker, National Jewish Welfare Board; Bishop W. W. Peels, Council of Bishops of the Methodist Episcopal Church; Rt. Rev. Msgr. Michael J. Ready, National Catholic Welfare Conference; Dr. Almon R. Pepper, National Council of the Protestant Episcopal Church; Dr. S. Arthur Devan, General Commission of Army-Navy Chaplains; Dr. Joseph C. Hazen, Northern Baptist Conference; Dr. J. Quinter Miller, Federal Council of Churches of Christ; Dr William Barrow Pugh, Presbyterian Church; Dr. Carroll C. Roberts, International Convention of Disciples of Christ.

---

[103] M/R, 29 Apr 43, sub: Religion. SPWA 000.3.
[104] WAAC Daily Journal, Vol. I, 10 Jun 43.

The committee wishes to express its unqualified endorsement of this organization . . . [and] feels constrained to voice its condemnation in no uncertain terms of those who malign this splendid group of patriotic women. Certainly no self-respecting patriotic American would indulge in such a cowardly, contemptible, despicable course.[105]

Army commanders at many stations also immediately made their stand known to the troops; one stated to the men:

We have gained aid and help from the women of America. If we do anything to make their lot uncomfortable or unhappy, if we fail to give them a maximum amount of respect, if we fail to behave always as gentlemen, we have not only lost a contribution towards winning this war, but we have also lost some of the finer qualities of manhood.[106]

Others in Congress and elsewhere took the attitude that the stories were merely good clean fun and that the Waacs were spoilsports to object to them. According to a member from Alabama, WAAC stories were "like traveling salesman jokes" and he looked upon them as "the way this country keeps its sense of humor."[107] General Marshall was later to suggest that responsible Army officers might be able to distinguish between clean fun and a dirty joke by asking themselves if the stories would appear equally funny if circulated about Army wives and daughters instead of about Waacs. To Director Hobby for the WAAC, General Marshall wrote:

To me, one of the most stimulating aspects of our war effort has been the amazing development of the WAAC organization in quality, discipline, capacity for performing a wide variety of jobs, and the fine attitude of the women themselves. Commanders to whom the Waacs have been assigned have spoken in the highest terms of their efficiency and value. The best evidence in the matter are the demands now being made on the War Department for increased allotments of WAAC organizations. . . .

I wish you would reassure your subordinates of the confidence and high respect in which they are held by the Army.[108]

WAC leaders were later to conclude that the whole slander campaign had been to some degree unavoidable. In this, the British precedent of identical slander in two world wars lent strong support. One WAC leader commented, "Men have for centuries used slander against morals as a weapon to keep women out of public life." Mrs. Hobby, after a lapse of some five years, remarked, "I believe now that it was inevitable; in the history of civilization, no new agency requiring social change has escaped a similar baptism. I feel now that nothing we might have done could have avoided it."[109]

---

[105] HR Rpt 566, 78th Cong, 1st sess, Rpt of Com on Appropriations to Accompany HR 2996, Mil Establishment Appropriation Bill FY 1944. Hobby files, 18 Jun 43.

[106] Ltr, Base Surg to Mil Pers of Base Hosp, Tinker Field, Okla.; reprinted in Ltr, Base Comdr to All Mil Orgns . . . at Tinker Field, 23 Jun 43; copy in Folder, Slander Campaign, OCMH.

[107] *Washington Post*, June 16, 1943.

[108] Personal ltr, CofS to Oveta Culp Hobby, 15 Jan 43. Gen Marshall's personal files; read by author by courtesy of his secretary, December 1945. The Chief of Staff was in Africa at the time of the columnist's charges, and had just learned of the attack.

[109] Comments to author. British published reports reached the same conclusion. See Appendix B.

CHAPTER XII

July–September 1943: The Conversion to Army Status

By the middle of June 1943, after delay caused by the slander campaign, the WAC bill was at last nearing approval by Congress.[1] The Auxiliary Corps faced its final and most severe test, for every member must choose honorable discharge or immediate enlistment in the new Women's Army Corps, Army of the United States. Neither the modern Army nor any other women's service had ever faced such a trial, and no precedent existed as to how many of the enlisted personnel would depart when given such an opportunity.[2]

It had been known for some time that certain clauses in the pending WAC legislation would probably give every member of the WAAC the right to elect immediate honorable discharge rather than to enlist in the new WAC when it should be established. The Army's Judge Advocate General ruled that it did not lie within the Army's power to transfer women from the WAAC to the WAC without their consent, since only a selective service law could place a citizen under court-martial jurisdiction without his consent.[3] At first, few departures had been anticipated, but in June, following the newspaper attack, Colonel Catron was obliged to inform the War Department: "It looks as though more members of the old WAAC than we

had anticipated have it in mind not to join the WAC."[4]

Reporters and editors, sensing a spectacular story in the offing—possibly the end of the Corps itself—demanded confirmation of the fact that "the Army is very much worried about the WAAC situation." When estimates of probable losses were refused them, some intimated that they would publish estimates of their own.[5]

Director Hobby stated, just before the bill passed, "My feeling is that we don't want them if they don't want to stay in. I would hate to lose a great many but I would rather have a smaller Corps of women who are dedicated to this service. This is something that a woman must want to do if she stays in."[6] She therefore refused to take steps to persuade women

---

[1] Min, Gen Council, 31 May 43.

[2] The Army Nurse Corps a year later secured similar legislation placing it in the Army of the United States, but it was not necessary to discharge those members who refused AUS status, since there was an authorized peacetime component of the ANC which continued to exist and in which members could be required to continue service.

[3] M/R, 8 May 43. SPWA 300.3 sec 1.

[4] Memo, Exec WAAC for G–1, 20 Jul 43. SPWA 314.7 sec 3.

[5] File of Tp Convs, esp Jul–Aug 43.

[6] Min, Stf Dirs Conf, Chicago, 15–17 Jun 43. SPWA 337 (6–1–43).

to stay by emotional appeals or any other means.

The WAC bill itself, as it neared passage, offered women the mixed blessing of Army status, but few other inducements. Little was left of the simple version proposed by the War Department, which would have placed few limitations on the Secretary of War's power to decide administrative matters. The Congressional situation had continued unfavorable all spring. In April the War Department became so alarmed at the rejection of the Navy bill to send Waves to foreign countries that it withdrew the WAC bill entirely and submitted it again in May.[7]

Even so, a number of amendments had to be accepted: the Corps was to last only for the duration plus six months; it was limited to women aged 20–50 years; its commanding officer could never be promoted above the rank of colonel and its other officers above the rank of lieutenant colonel; its officers could never command any men unless specifically ordered to do so by Army superiors; physicians and nurses could not be accepted because of the Medical Department's insistence on autonomy.[8] Many even more hampering amendments had been narrowly averted—the Senate's proviso that the Corps expire on 1 January 1945, and the House's attempts to limit the Corps to 150,000, to set the top age at 45, to forbid WAC officers to be assigned to Army jobs, and to deny all dependency benefits to women—but all these were eventually eliminated in conference. Director Hobby stated that she was willing to accept any amendments if only the bill might pass.[9]

Just as they had been a year previously, the efforts of the Army's highest authorities were required to secure Congressional approval. General Marshall urged passage of the bill in a letter to Chairman Andrew J. May of the House Military Affairs Committee, and also intervened to secure the new age limit of 20–50, which would admit more recruits than the previous 21–45 limit. General Somervell was also summoned to testify when the Military Affairs Committee seemed about to disapprove the bill because of the erroneous idea that Wacs would be used to displace Civil Service workers in Washington. This had actually been done on a large scale by the WAVES without Congressional disfavor, but never by the Army. "They've got the Waacs and the Waves confused," noted the Office of the Secretary of War.[10]

The First Wac

The bill to establish a Women's Army Corps *in* the Army of the United States was passed by the Senate on 28 June and

---

[7] Min, Gen Council, 28 Apr 43.

[8] Whether to commission women doctors in the WAC or in the Medical Department was for a time a controversial problem. The WAAC had consented to commission women doctors recommended by The Surgeon General, and did commission several—the only exception to its rule that all WAAC officers must attend OCS. (WD Cir 23, Sec II, 18 Jan 43.) The Secretary of War had personally directed Director Hobby to include a clause in the WAC bill permitting commissioning of women doctors in the WAC. (WAAC Daily Journal, Vol. I, Feb 43.) However, Congress refused this and passed a separate law permitting direct commissions in the Medical Corps.

[9] (1) HR Rpt 595, 78th Cong, 1st sess, 24 Jun 43, sub: Establishing a WAC for Serv in Army of U.S., Conf Rpt to accompany S 495. SPWA 314.7 (1–7–43)(1) sec 1. (2) Speech, Min, Tng Cen Comdts Conf, Washington, 31 Mar 43, SPWA 334.8 (3–20–43).

[10] (1) Ltr, CofS to Hon A. J. May, 1 Mar 43. CofS 291.9. (2) Memo, Dir WAAC for Leg&LnDiv, WDSS, 24 Apr 43. CofS 291.9; also in SPWA 341 (4–7–43). with note re Gen Marshall's desire for this plan. (3) Quotation from M/R, Tp Conv, Mr. Mitchell and Dir Hobby, 11 Jun 43. SPWA 314.7 (1–7–43)(1) sec 1. See also pp. 557–59, below.

signed by the President on 1 July 1943.[11] On 5 July, in the presence of General Marshall and other dignitaries, Director Hobby took the oath of office as a colonel, Army of the United States, thus becoming the first woman to be admitted to the new component of the Army.[12]

The passage of the bill was the cause of general pride and pleasure to Waacs throughout the world. The commanding general of the Hampton Roads Port of Embarkation wrote to Colonel Hobby:

You would have been amused and, I think, pleased at the reaction of our personnel here to the news that the legislation had gone through. The Port Band at mess time, accompanied by a large part of our Headquarters Detachment of enlisted men, proceeded to the WAC barracks and serenaded the girls with "You're in the Army Now," and "This is the Army, Mr. Jones," and a general jollification ensued.[13]

Actually, "You're in the Army Now" was somewhat premature, for the WAAC did not automatically become the WAC. The law gave the Army ninety days to arrange for the dissolution of the Women's Army Auxiliary Corps. By the thirtieth day of September, all Waacs must be enlisted or commissioned in the WAC, or discharged, for the WAAC would cease to exist.

The Conversion

The following ninety days of the summer of 1943, informally called The Conversion, were perhaps the busiest in the history of the Corps. WAAC Headquarters' fourteen-hour day now approached a twenty-four-hour one as WAAC officers worked throughout the night to type, sort, and fold informational material and stuff envelopes. Director Hobby canceled all travel plans for July and August, and the headquarters braced itself for three

months of the most intense activity the Corps had yet experienced.[14]

WAAC Headquarters was immediately hit by "a flood of requests for information regarding the changeover."[15] Stations in the field had had no instructions or advice as to the nature of the conversion, and knew only what they read in the newspapers. Some stations immediately began to let women go home if they wished, without proper authority;[16] others began to swear them into the Army, also without authority—in fact, some enlisted women were sworn in by WAAC officers and served for months without ever knowing that they were not in the Army.[17]

Director Hobby had foreseen this confusion and had asked the War Department to permit her to send the complete conversion plan to the field far in advance of the event. This conversion plan had actually been carefully prepared over the past six months by WAAC Headquarters and The Adjutant General's Office, and included a detailed timetable based on T Day or Transfer Day. Women who desired to transfer to the WAC must complete a

[11] PL 110. Approved by WD in Ltr, SW to Bur of Budget, 1 Jul 43. SPGAL 291.9 Gen (6–30–43)–5, in WDCSA 291.9.

[12] (1) WDBPR Press Release, 5 Jul 43. (2) GO 1, Hq WAC, sub: Assumption of Comd. SPWA 300.4 (7–5–43)E (1943). She was not the first woman admitted to the AUS; this honor went to Major Craighill, the first woman doctor to be admitted under Medical Corps legislation of the previous month.

[13] Ltr, Brig Gen John R. Kilpatrick, CG HRPOE, to Col Hobby, 3 Jul 43. SPWA 314.7 (6–29–43).

[14] (1) Memo Routing Slip, Dir's secy to OTI, 25 Jun 43. Vol. I Gen Policy, WAAC Hist File, 1943. (2) Intraoffice Memo to Asst Exec WAAC, 28 Jul 43. SPWA 314.7 (1–7–43)(1) sec 3.

[15] WAAC Daily Journal, Vol. I, 1 Jul 43.

[16] Rectified by Change 2, 14 Jul 43, to AGO Memo W635–10–43, 7 Jul 43.

[17] Rectified by AG Ltr, 21 Aug 43. AG 320.2 WAAC PR–W, in SPWA 314.7 sec 4. Women later demanded release but were refused on grounds that they had been "constructively enlisted."

certain application form, must pass a stricter Army medical examination, and must also be recommended by their commanders. It was intended that this processing be completed by 1 September 1943, on which date Waacs all over the world would be sworn in with mass ceremonies.[18]

G–1 Division of the General Staff had refused the request to communicate this plan to the field in advance of the passage of legislation, stating that such action might be illegal or might adversely influence Congress, and had told the Director, "There will be plenty of time."[19] The Director persisted and finally, only a week before the passage of the bill, succeeded in getting a confidential letter sent to all commands, giving an enlistment plan that could be put into effect under any probable wording of the legislation.[20]

On 1 July 1943, a few moments after the bill was signed, Director Hobby telegraphed all Army commands telling them to begin the processes of this letter, and to abide by WAAC Regulations until new ones could be published. Unfortunately, the letter itself had not yet had time to filter down to most Army stations, since it had to be relayed through several command echelons, and those women who wished to leave, and their parents, became immediately frantic for reassurance. When the Director saw how little information had reached the field, she chose six of the Corps' best officers and sent them on tour to carry correct procedures to every WAAC company; she herself visited as many as possible.[21]

Even after stations received instruction, the apparently simple process soon proved unbelievably complicated: all of the administrative problems of the Auxiliary here converged and demanded a final

definitive solution as to the exact status of its members in all legal matters before WAAC records could be closed out. Some of these questions, but not many, could be answered by WAAC Headquarters. A number of red-bordered immediate-action letters were published by The Adjutant General, at WAAC Headquarters' request, to get answers to the field before 1 September, while others were answered by telephone and telegraph.[22]

In addition, there were about twenty major issues which neither the Army nor WAAC Headquarters had the power to decide; these were submitted to the Comptroller General, but decision was not received on some cases until the following October and November. Most stations desired especially to know whether WAAC service might be counted as Army service for purposes of longevity pay. Most Waacs and Army stations felt strongly that it should, since in actual conditions of daily living there was virtually no difference in WAAC and WAC life, which continued without a break in its routine. The Army Service Forces blamed the Director's

---

[18] (1) M/R, sub: Chronology, Conversion of WAAC to WAC. SPWA 314.7 (1–7–43)(1) sec 3. (2) Memo, Capt Bandel for Maj George G. Wolfe, AGO, 26 Apr 43. SPWA 300.3 (1–7–43) sec 1. (3) Memo, Dir WAC for Dir Pers ASF, 30 Jun 43. SPWA 291.9. (4) AGO Memo cited n. 16. (5) WD Cir 146, 26 Jun 43, sec III, Physical Standards.

[19] Memo, WAAC Hq for TAG, and Ind, 12 Jun 43. SPWA 314.7 sec 1.

[20] AGO Ltr, 24 Jun 43. AG 210.1 WAAC (6–23–43), in SPWA 314.7 sec 1.

[21] A week later, more specific instructions were published by TAG. The Director also telegraphed all WAAC training centers to issue simultaneous press releases. (1) TWX, Dir to all SvCs, Tng Cens, Ports, and Def Comds, 1 Jul 43, and Ltrs to AAF, AGF, and MDW; (2) TWX to all Tng Cens, 1 Jul 43. SPWA 314.7 sec 3. (3) Speech, Dir. WAC, Min, Stf Dirs Conf, New York, 1–3 Dec 43. SPWA 337 (11–10–43).

[22] W635 series, copies in Vol. AGO Memoranda, WAAC Hist File. Also Change 1, 13 Jul 43, and Change 2, 14 Jul 43, to AGO Memo cited n. 16.

Office for the delay in answering such questions, and one of General Somervell's consultants pronounced its organization "inadequate," saying, "Simple questions such as 'Does my service in the WAAC count so far as longevity benefits are concerned?' are unanswered. It is possible that five minutes would be required to settle a question of this type; the only possible answer is yes." [23] As a matter of fact, the only possible legal answer was *no*, and after some years of controversy and attempted corrective legislation, the answer was still *no*. [24]

Some Comptroller General decisions decided such issues as the fact that Waacs were not entitled to re-employment rights even if they enlisted in the WAC, since they had not gone directly from their civilian jobs to the Army; this issue was not finally settled until 1946 when corrective legislation was secured. It was also found that Waacs who enlisted in the WAC forfeited their eventual travel pay home upon discharge, and were entitled only to pay to the place where they joined the Army, their present station; correction of this matter luckily did not require legislation and was made by the Comptroller General in time to prevent wholesale failure to enlist. [25]

Still worse field confusion resulted when the physical requirements were changed in mid-August. For two months before passage of the bill, Director Hobby had argued with The Surgeon General over the physical standards, which she wished to adjust so as to admit every Waac who had been qualified upon her enrollment and who had since given satisfactory service, even though her physical condition might have declined since her enrollment. She felt strongly that these women should be admitted to the WAC and given reme-

dial treatment if necessary. This The Surgeon General refused, stating that routine granting of administrative waivers would negate the desired screening by virtually blanketing the WAAC into the WAC. Director Hobby especially objected to the high visual standards, seldom needed by enlisted women, and directed that her office "go to bat with the Surgeon General." Toward the end of June, G–1 Division decided in favor of The Surgeon General, and directives for physical examinations were published accordingly.

By August the numbers of Waacs rejected for physical reasons became so excessive that the decision was reversed, Colonel Hobby's plan accepted, and all discharges for physical reasons were stopped until the requirements were corrected. This action could not authorize recall of women who had already been discharged under the old standards, and considerable inequality of treatment to individuals resulted. [26]

---

[23] Memo, "WCM" for Dir Pers ASF, 10 Aug 43. SPAP 341 WAAC (2–26–43), ASF files.

[24] Comptr Gen to SW, Decision B–35441, 4 Aug 43. SPWA 242.2 (6–10–43). Service did count for Yeomanettes, Marinettes, Army field clerks, WAVES, SPARS, Women Marines. Army or Navy Nurse Corps service could be counted by enlisted women but not officers.

[25] (1) Memo, JAG for WAAC Hq, 19 Aug 43, sub: Eligibility for Re-employment Benefits, etc. SPJGA 1943/11282 in WAAC file. (2) Comptr Gen to SW, Decision B–36362, 26 Aug 43. SPWA 245.6 (7–1–43). (3) For a summary of controversy on legal status of WAAC, see Appendix C.

[26] All except (2) and (7) in SPWA 314.7 (1–7–43), secs 1 and 4 (1943): (1) Memo, Dir Pers ASF, 3 Jun 43. (2) Memo, Dir Hobby for SG, 26 Apr 43. SPWA 300.3 (1–7–43) sec 1. Director Hobby felt that nurses' standards on weight and eyesight were too high for enlisted Wacs, since Wacs often did more sedentary jobs. (3) Office Memo, WAAC Contl Div for Exec WAAC, 14 Jun 43; (4) M/R, 23 Jun 43; (5) WD Cir 146, sec III, 26 Jun 43; (6) Memo, CofS ASF for Dir WAAC, 21 Aug 43, and Ind, with AG Ltr 220.8 WAAC PR–W, 23 Aug 43. (7) Memo, Gen Styer for TAG, 23 Aug 43. SPEX.

First Companies in the WAC

Meanwhile, station commanders were alarmed to note that, during the two-month period of indecision and confusion, many women who had at first intended to enlist were changing their minds. The delay between passage of the bill on 1 July and the scheduled date for mass swearing-in on 1 September gave parents, friends, and former employers time to urge a return home. Moreover, Army supervisors were found to be offering certain women high civilian salaries to leave the Corps and continue in the same jobs as civilians—the advantage being, from the officers' viewpoint, that the women could then date officers and live where their quarters and hours were not supervised. This practice became so widespread that Colonel Hobby was able to collect evidence of it sufficient to secure an Army Service Forces directive forbidding such offers. Meanwhile, at stations where such transfers had already occurred, remaining Waacs were found less disposed to continue under military restrictions and enlisted wages.[27]

In late July, as the evidence of suasion by relatives and employers mounted, it was directed that each station swear in its company as soon as it was ready, instead of waiting for the scheduled 1 September date for mass enlistment. Only WAAC officers were required to wait until 1 September. Where 95 percent or more of a company intended to enlist, it was suggested that a mass ceremony be held with appropriate publicity.[28]

This move proved successful and field companies raced to be the first to enlist. One Army Service Forces and two Army Air Forces companies tied for first place, each with 100 percent enlistment.[29]

Others had only a few losses, chiefly for physical disability, and throughout August these were sworn in as fast as possible.

As the WAC waited to discover what the total loss would be, it became evident that there was considerable variation from station to station—some losing none, some losing 5 or 10 percent, many about 20 percent, and others as much as 50 percent. When the loss figures from their several stations were compared, higher commanders were presented with what amounted to a chart of relative efficiency in personnel management. Air and service command headquarters at once sent inspectors and WAAC staff directors to the stations showing high losses, in the hope that conditions might be corrected while there was still time for the women to change their minds before discharge. Commanding generals of major commands became generally aware of the matter; some actually went in person to speak to the women.[30]

Why Some Went Home

The combined discoveries of these inspectors gave WAAC Headquarters a reasonably clear picture of the reasons for which women were leaving. The most revealing discovery was that the majority was not quitting because of the hardships of Army life. On the contrary, at many

---

[27] (1) Memo, Dir WAC for Dir Pers ASF, 23 Aug 43, and Memo, Dir Pers ASF for TAG, 27 Aug 43. SPWA 314.7 sec 4. (2) WAAC Daily Journal, Vol. I. 28 Jul 43. Also M/R, 13 Aug 43. SPWA 230.14 (7–22–43).

[28] AGO Memo W635–14–43, 30 Jul 43.

[29] On 2 August 1943: Moody Field, Valdosta, Ga.; Mitchel Field, N. Y.; Edgewood Arsenal, Md. WDBPR Press Release, 3 Aug 43.

[30] Folder, Congratulatory Letters, SPWA 314.7 (6–29–43) 1943.

MASS ENLISTMENT CEREMONIES. *Camp Atterbury, Indiana, 10 August 1943, above, and Fort Oglethorpe, 11 August 1943, below.*

isolated and uncomfortable stations in deserts and swamps fewer left than at large comfortable installations. In one case, Waacs were stationed at two airfields near the same Texas city—one the handsome permanent headquarters of a commanding general, the other a hastily expanded training field; yet thirty-seven women left the first, none the second. Inspectors noted that the more isolated or less comfortable stations could not get civilians and therefore needed and appreciated the Waacs.[31]

One staff director reported, "The happiest girls are the ones doing the hardest work."[32] Inspectors' conclusions could be summarized in one statement: *Waacs remained at stations where they were wanted and needed in their jobs.* Even before the conversion started, Director Hobby had informed commands employing Waacs that only two things would be needed to make a woman wish to remain: "These are, first, that her job shall keep her busy and utilize her abilities to the best advantage, and second, that she shall feel that she is making a real contribution and that the Army is interested in her work."[33]

A frequently identifiable cause of loss was hostility toward Waacs on the part of a post commander, which set the tone for the entire post and was usually associated with poor job assignments for women. When Las Vegas Army Air Base lost 54 of its 151 members, inspectors reported:

The Unit Commander stated that she had met the post commander only on two occasions. Neither the Inspecting Officers nor the Staff Director was able to see him. . . . Women were assigned in the Officers' Mess and the Post Exchange. The Unit Commander has been allowed little part in the assignment of WAAC personnel.[34]

At Camp Lee, Virginia, 40 of 146 were leaving. Inspectors reported:

All records were satisfactory . . . [but] morale and company spirit were found to be very low. . . . Women stated that they did not have the proper respect of the enlisted men. They said they had discussed this with the post c.o., but he told inspectors he was unaware of it.[35]

At many other stations the fault did not lie with the post commander, except in failing to recommend removal of the WAAC commander, for inspection reports clearly placed the blame on unsuitable WAAC company commanders. At Richmond, Virginia, inspectors found records, buildings, mess, supply, recreation, and church facilities all adequate, but through the fault of the company commander many Waacs were malassigned, and "punishments have been given that are out of proportion for offenses committed."[36] At Fort Monmouth, New Jersey, inspectors noted: "The c.o. does not appear to have a sympathetic understanding of her troops as individuals, and many complaints were received that the EW could not readily contact her for confer-

---

[31] WAAC Daily Journal, Vol. I, 28 Jul 43, re Randolph Field and Brooks Field, San Antonio, Texas.
[32] Min cited n. 6.
[33] Personal ltr, Oveta Culp Hobby to each CG, by name, Air Comds, SvCs, AGF Comds, Def Comds, Ports, Chiefs of Servs, and Comdts of Schs, 29 Jun 43. SPWA 314.7 sec 1.
[34] Rpt of Insp, Las Vegas AAB, 31 Aug 43. SPWA 333.1 (8–20–43).
[35] Memo, 1st O Dora F. Petmecky and 2d O Lucia T. Hudgens for Dir Fld Insp Div, WAAC, 28 Jul 43, sub: Insp of Hq Co (WAAC) formerly designated as the 96th. SPWA 314.7 sec 3.
[36] Memo, Petmecky and Hudgens for Dir Fld Insp Serv, WAAC, 28 Jul 43, sub: Insp of 709th Post Hq Co. SPWA 314.7 sec 3.

ences."[37] Another station lost 35 percent of its women because the women believed their WAAC commander to be misconducting herself with the station commander, although inspectors could find no proof of this.[38] On the other hand, it was found that when companies had good WAAC commanders many enlisted in a body, even though every other outward circumstance was unfavorable.[39]

Many unsuitable WAC commanders were now relieved and replaced with women of understanding and integrity. Later, unsuitable WAC commanders could not be removed because the new Office of the Director WAC no longer had command power.[40]

When questioned, women gave various reasons for departure. Some of the more frequent excuses tabulated were:

Changed family and home conditions: "Husband now stationed in U.S. and I wish to be with him." "Mother is ill." "Enrolled expecting husband to be drafted, but he was rejected." Almost half of the excuses given fell into this category. Some women sought leave to try to pacify relatives and men friends before giving up all hope of enlisting.

Dissatisfaction with job assignment: "Feel I can do more good in war industry." "I can do more good teaching." "My qualifications are not of as much value to the Army as they are in civilian life." "Do not feel I am doing what I came in to do." "Resent working under civilians."

Emotional or physical difficulties: "Feel physically unfit." "Cannot accustom myself to military life." "Unable to concentrate since my husband reported missing." "My two sons killed in action. It has made me very restless."[41]

Impatience with Army errors: Two women,

removed from motor transport school and sent to cooks and bakers school, said, "We expected the Army to be a well-regulated organization that didn't make mistakes." Others took basic training several times, were put in the wrong specialist school, sat six weeks in staging area, and said, "We see by the papers that requests are on file for 600,000 Wacs and here we sit. What's the payoff?"[42]

Other miscellaneous undesirable conditions: These were analyzed by Colonel Catron as

Overstatements and unfulfillable promises by recruiting officers; inadequate physical examinations and consequent inclusion of too many physically and psycho-neurotically unfit; faulty classification and assignment; . . . some instances of assigning Waacs to jobs of less importance or dignity while civilians are used in the better positions; some cases of delay in having Waacs replace and take over the duties of soldiers and of appointing them to the grades presumably vacated by the men; . . . the public attitude that the war is all but won; the trait of women which, once they have decided to join a cause, demands that they be kept busy and that their abilities be used to the fullest; . . . recent unfavorable publicity and the indica-

---

[37] Memo, 1st O Frances M. Holbrook and 2d O Kathryn D. Neely for Dir Fld Insp Serv, 15 Jul 43, sub: Insp of WAAC Det, ESCTC, Ft Monmouth, N. J. SPWA 314.7 sec 3.

[38] Memo, Capt Frances M. Holbrook for Dir Fld Surv Br, 23 Oct 43, sub: Rpt of Investigation at Bergstrom Field, Tex. SPWA 331.1.

[39] See Ch. XXXIII, below.

[40] WAAC Daily Journal, Vol. I, 28 Jul 43.

[41] Reasons in three categories above are from tabulation at Fort Des Moines, copy in Folder, Classification Officers, 1943 WAAC Planning file. See also Memo, Exec WAAC for G–1, 20 Jul 43. SPWA 314.7, (1–7–43)(1) sec 3.

[42] Examples from Daytona Beach and Fort Des Moines, "Survey on Problems Most Frequently brought to Chaplains and Resident Counsellors," 9 Sep 43. SPWA 231.28.

tions that officers, enlisted men, and their families have not accepted the Waacs wholeheartedly, to say the least.[43]

Relatively fewer WAAC officers applied for discharge, although some were eliminated by a final screening board, called the AUS-WAAC Board, set up in Washington.[44] The board was unable to eliminate many of the unsuitable young officers just commissioned, since they were still in the officers' pool and could hardly be rejected until they had been given a chance at one assignment. The board was also hampered by the inconsistent recommendations of some field commands, which asked that certain WAAC officers not be admitted to the WAC, but at the same time gave them excellent and superior ratings.

Why the Majority Stayed

By this time the full extent of losses was fairly well tabulated. WAAC leaders had never ceased to predict that the majority of Waacs would not quit in spite of ample provocation. This prediction was now upheld to a surprising degree. Field stations' records of discharges were so uneven that it was not possible to determine how many of the losses were due to failure to pass the physical examination, how many represented women whose commanders had not recommended them, and how many had actually not applied; nevertheless, the total of all such losses combined was less than 25 percent. More than 75 percent of the WAAC had chosen to enlist and had been found physically and morally acceptable.[45]

Among the three major commands, the lowest average loss—about 20 percent—was found in the Army Air Forces. General Arnold, during the conversion period, directed all air inspectors to make WAC job assignment a special subject, in order that "the job assigned each individual will keep her busy and employ her abilities to best advantage and that she is given an opportunity to make a real contribution." General Arnold also took personal action by appearing in a camp newsreel sequence in which he delivered a message to Air Forces Wacs, emphasizing the AAF's need of them; this was shown to all Waacs at air bases before the final dissolution of the WAAC.[46]

The highest losses among the three major commands—about 34 percent—were suffered by the Army Ground Forces. Here, General McNair had refused to accept an AGF WAAC officer or any staff directors or WAAC specialists; he had repeatedly made known his opposition to employment of Waacs by the AGF and to the admittance of the WAAC to the Army. AGF assignment techniques had also been notably poor. In July, as manpower shortages became more serious, the AGF reconsidered its refusal to accept a WAAC staff director, and on 1 July Maj. Emily E. Davis, one of the first WAAC graduates of the Army's Command and General Staff School, reported to fill the position of AGF WAAC Officer, comparable to

---

[43] See tabulation and memo cited n. 41; also, Office Memo, Maj Gordon C. Jones for Exec WAC, 4 Aug 43, with Col Catron's comment in pencil note. SPWA 342 (7-30-43).

[44] Memo, Dir WAC for Dir Pers ASF, 7 Jul 43; also Memo, MPD ASF for TAG, 20 Jul 43. SPWA 314.7 sec 2.

[45] Losses totaled 343 officers and 14,607 auxiliaries. There is no available indication of the portion lost for medical reasons, rejection by commanding officer, or at own request. WDBPR Press Release, 1 Oct 43.

[46] (1) AAF Memo 121–1, 3 Aug 43. (2) AAF WAC Hist., p. 47; see Ch. XVI, below.

that of Major Bandel in the AAF. Major Davis at once made a hurried series of staff visits to AGF WAAC units.

The worst situation was at Fort Knox, where she found women of the Armored Replacement Training Center, declared unassignable for lack of typing skill some three months before, still sitting in the barracks without employment. She immediately secured their reassignment to other stations to duties commensurate with their Specification Serial Numbers. Major Davis made efforts to correct varied undesirable conditions in other WAAC units, but she had come too late to prevent extensive departures. Major Davis later noted:

The negative attitude of the command toward the utilization of women in the Army, which could not help but be transmitted to the field commanders, and through them to their staffs and to the enlisted women, had a part in this loss of personnel.[47]

WAAC observers had no difficulty in identifying the motivating force that had kept 80 percent of Waacs in the Army in the most friendly commands, and 66 percent even where employers were hostile. Most women felt that to leave would be moral desertion under the fire of the slanderers, and a betrayal of the ideals that had caused them to enlist. Enlistment was, like the original enrollment, ordinarily a matter of idealism rather than of logic. Observers at a training center reported that women who had asked discharge for good cause suddenly dropped their packed suitcases and ran weeping across a drill field to join their old platoons and take the oath of enlistment. Some who left soon asked to return.[48] Others who did not enlist later regretted it; one wrote two years later: "If I could only have that chance again. I haven't felt fine every time I think of it."[49]

Director Hobby said:

We lost a great many fine women because they could not pass the Army physical, but we also lost a great many women who would never have been soldiers. It makes me very happy to know that those who stayed, stayed because they know what true obligation is, and I for one feel that what we now have is a firmer core to build around.[50]

As bulwark against its inherited problems, the new Women's Army Corps had but one asset, but that an invaluable one—some 50,000 loyal members who now, in spite of full knowledge of its problems, followed the Corps into the Army of the United States.

The End of the WAAC

On the first of September, 1943, eligible WAAC officers were sworn into the WAC, in grades equivalent to their WAAC grade and with date of rank the same as in the WAAC. On the same date all WAAC units were officially redesignated as WAC. By this time enlistment of enrolled women was almost complete. Instructions were issued in September for the disposition of remaining WAAC members. Throughout the month, there was considerable scurrying both in headquarters and the field as stray Waacs were rounded up.[51]

On 30 September, the Women's Army

---

[47] AGF WAC Hist, particularly Vol. I, pp. 12–13 and 22.

[48] TWX, Hobby to 7th SvC, 10 Sep 43. SPWA 314.7 sec 4. AGO Memo W635–23–43, 28 Sep 43.

[49] Ltr, "Ex-WAAC" to CofS, 11 Oct 45. WDWAC 220.8.

[50] WAAC Daily Journal, Vol. I, 12 Jul 43.

[51] By WDGO 42, sec 1, 26 Jul 43, effective 1 Sep 43. AG Ltr 320.2 WAC PR–W, 2 Sep 43. SPWA 314.7 sec 4.

Auxiliary Corps ceased to exist. For the women who chose to remain with the Women's Army Corps, Colonel Hobby suggested, and got, a green and gold service ribbon to show their WAAC service. She said:

It is probable that this period will prove to have been the most difficult in the life of the Corps and the one which, because of its pioneering aspect with all that this implies, will be the source of the greatest pride to, and the reason of the strongest ties among, the members of the WAC.[52]

[52] Memo, Dir WAAC for G–1, 25 Jun 43. SPWA 200.6. Director Hobby intended the ribbon only for those whose service was continuous, but by an error in wording it also could be awarded to those who left the Corps and later returned. She was not able to get the wording changed to prevent this, as some such awards had already been made, and G–1 Division held it illegal to withdraw them. See Memo, Dir WAC for G–1, 19 Feb 44. SPWA 200.6 (1943).

CHAPTER XIII

Attempts To Revive Recruiting

The new Women's Army Corps began in spirit early in the summer, when groups of worried recruiting experts gathered in the Director's office to plan the first campaign. The whole future of the Corps quite evidently hung on the success of this effort. WAAC recruiting closed on 8 August 1943, and WAC recruiting opened without delay on the following day, yet in the entire month only 839 recruits were reported.[1]

At the same time, the Army's need for personnel had never been more urgent. The Adjutant General estimated that 2,000,000 more men must be drafted within the next year, of which 446,000 would be fathers of families. The Adjutant General stated that more than 600,000 of the jobs could more efficiently be done by Wacs, thus preventing the necessity of drafting any fathers whatever. General Marshall, after the ceremonies in which Colonel Hobby was sworn into the WAC, asked her if she could get the Army the 600,000 women it needed. The Director avoided a public reply.[2]

In fact, the real question was whether the WAC could survive at all, after the twin blows of the slander campaign and the conversion. In its first year, the Corps had recruited almost 65,000 members, but at the July recruiting rate it would take almost three years to get another 65,000; at the August rate, five years. At this point normal attrition overtook recruiting.

As the Corps waited for War Department solution to the recruiting problem, excess training centers were closed, surplus instructors were assigned to officers' pools, and recruiters were told to suspend their efforts pending new instructions.

The Search for a Recruiting Theme

In view of the gravity of the situation, both General White of G–1 Division and Brig. Gen. Joseph N. Dalton of ASF's Military Personnel Division personally participated in recruiting conferences during the summer. The ASF donated the full-time services of Maj. Robert S. Brown, rated as one of its best publicity experts, who was to give the problem concentrated attention until his death the following year. The advertising agency of Young & Rubicam sent numerous experts, including its adviser, Dr. George Gallup.

These planners fell into anxious debate over the theme of the next campaign,

---

[1] Figures as available to the War Department at the time. Table 2, Appendix A, gives accessions figures as revised by The Adjutant General's Office, 1 February 1948. (1) Memo, Dir WAC for TAG, 26 Jul 43; (2) ASF Memo S635–6–43, 30 Jul 43; (3) TWX, TAG to SvCs, 5 Aug 43, AG 341 WAAC PR–I; (4) Ltr, 6th SvC to Dir WAC, 13 Aug 43, sub: WD Memo S635–6–43. SPKOG 341–1 WAAC; (5) AGO Form 721, 1 Jul 43, Enlmt Rec, WAC, AUS. All in SPWA 341 (1943).

[2] (1) Min, Conf with Chief, Classif and Repl Br AGO. SPWA 337.2, incl Tables A, B. (2) WDBPR Press Release, 5 Jul 43.

which if not successful might well be the last. Dr. Gallup advocated an appeal to a woman's self-interest, with emphasis on the advantages of military status, the value of WAC training, and free clothes, food, and medical care. Colonel Hobby disliked such an approach, and held out for the straight patriotic appeal. Her favorite advertisement was a "shocker" which showed a wounded soldier dying on the battlefield while women played bridge, with the caption, MEN ARE DYING ON THE BATTLELINE—CAN YOU LIVE WITH YOURSELF ON THE SIDELINE?

This approach was vetoed by Generals White and Dalton, who were obliged to inform Colonel Hobby that the censors forbade showing dead American soldiers to the American public. Colonel Hobby next produced an advertisement showing soldiers' graves, with the caption, THEY CAN'T DO ANY MORE—BUT YOU CAN. She argued, "Something like this is needed to drive home a sense of shame to women not doing anything." Results would be better, she said, "the more difficult this job was painted to a woman, the more of a challenge it was to her . . . telling how hard, how drab, how routine it is. . . . Has she the courage to do the commonplace as against the courage of the spectacular?" Dr. Gallup disagreed with her, saying:

When you take into account all groups, I am afraid that would not be as good as some other appeal. There is too much competition from other things; there are too many ways by which people can rationalize their own situation. Almost every person has, in his own mind, become important, even though only growing a couple of cabbage heads.

Representatives of Young & Rubicam pointed out also that "what appeals to the manufacturer seldom appeals to the consumer," and finally decided to run only one advertisement of the shocker type to see if it "made the women mad." Colonel Hobby replied that, as far as she was concerned, they could be made as mad as hatters if it only drove them to the recruiting station.[3]

As a matter of record, when the soldiers'-graves advertisement was used in October, it was banned in Boston newspapers because it was "too gruesome" and might have caused "sad week ends" to sensitive citizens. Most later advertisements therefore emphasized the WAC's attractive jobs and its material advantages.

It was decided that advertising emphasis would be put on, first, the hundreds of types of Army work now open to Wacs, and second, WAC benefits, which now offered the greater advantage of full military status. It was noteworthy that the same decision concerning "glamorization" was also deemed essential, at different times, by both British and WAVES recruiters, in both cases over the objections of women directors.[4]

The Manpower Theme

Colonel Hobby took the occasion of her oath of office to launch another theme more congenial to the American public than the ill-fated "Release a Man" slogan; this was the WAC as the preserver of the American home. Pointing out that every

---

[3] All comments from min of conf, WAAC Daily Journal, Vol. I, 13 Jul 43.

[4] (1) Ltr, C. W. Rogers, Advt Dir, Boston *Post,* to Mr. Jim Mullins, Kelly-Smith Co., New York, 29 Oct 43. SPWA 000.7. (2) Draft, 2 Jul 43, sub: Notes for Publicity re WAAC Becoming Part of Army. Folder, WAAC to WAC, WAAC Planning files. (3) WAVES Hist; also *Conditions in the Three Women's Services.*

woman in uniform enabled a father to stay with his family, Colonel Hobby informed the press, "Women as a group have always been the exponents of family life. They may now preserve and protect this family life, the core of American civilization and culture."[5] Newspaper writers readily took up this idea, stating, "In the absence of a draft, it is just possible that the WAC will be filled by young women who would rather join the Army than see their married brothers taken from their children." War Manpower Commissioner Paul V. McNutt tentatively indorsed the theme, saying, "The number of Wacs and Waves has been increased. As a consequence the month when it would be necessary to take fathers has been pushed back. We do not yet know what the yield will be."[6]

This potentially powerful approach could not be pushed as far as was desired because of the refusal of the nation's highest manpower agencies to lend it any practical support. Attempts were made to get the national Selective Service system to credit WAC enlistments against local draft quotas instead of against national totals, so that women might see the results of their enlistment in their own towns, but this was repeatedly refused by Maj. Gen. Lewis B. Hershey because of the extra effort and the administrative changes involved.

The War Manpower Commission also, in spite of Mr. McNutt's public statement, continued to act on the assumption that WAC recruiting was a threat to the industrial war effort.[7] During these summer months, recruiters in the field forwarded surprising information concerning WMC's part in the recent failure of the Cleveland Plan. Colonel Hobby telegraphed all service commands for confirmation, and discovered that, during the Cleveland Campaign, the War Manpower Commission had effectively stopped all WAAC recruiting publicity in areas including about one half of the population of the United States.

The news appeared the more inexplicable in that the Cleveland Campaign had been cleared with national WMC headquarters before ever being launched. To obtain clearance, considerable concessions had been made by the armed forces in a joint Army-Navy agreement in April, in which they had renounced the right to recruit women engaged in aircraft production, shipbuilding, ordnance or signal work, war research and technical teaching, and wire or radio communication. Nevertheless, service commands indicated that, as soon as the Cleveland Campaign had been launched, the War Manpower Commission had directed its regional agencies not to allow the services to recruit any women, employed or unemployed, in labor-short areas.

While the WMC could not prevent recruiters from setting up offices in a city, it could, through its control of the Office of War Information, prevent them from making their presence known by way of radio, newspapers, or other news media. The OWI disclosed that it had received orders from the War Manpower Commission not to give any publicity to armed forces recruitment of women, and stated, "The War Manpower Commission is the ultimate authority on recruitment. The recruitment of women is limited to such areas as are agreed upon with the Re-

---

[5] *The New York Times,* July 5, 1943.
[6] Both from *The New York Herald Tribune,* July 11, 1943.
[7] For discussion of Selective Service's role, see Chs. XV and XXXIV, below.

gional War Manpower Commission Office."[8]

These areas were extensive, containing perhaps one half the population of the United States. It was also discovered that almost all large cities had been included: San Francisco, Los Angeles, Atlanta, Indianapolis, Baltimore, and many others— a matter that was serious to understaffed recruiting offices, since cities were the most easily accessible areas. For example, in New York state the OWI directed, "Recruitment of women WAVES, WACS, SPARS, and Marines is not considered advisable in Albany, Buffalo, Rochester, Schenectady, Syracuse, Troy, Utica, and [other cities.]" The stoppage was the more inexplicable in that, while affected areas were chiefly those labeled Class I or II— "labor-tight" areas—others were in Class III or IV, where there was supposedly no labor shortage.[9]

The Army at once took issue with this action, informing the War Manpower Commission that it was highly questionable whether the WMC Enabling Act gave the Commission the authority to limit recruitment of women by the armed forces. The executive order that gave WMC control of the Selective Service system directed only that "no male person," 18–38, should be inducted except through Selective Service. The WAC was not mentioned except that its training programs, with all others of the armed forces, should, if using nonfederal educational institutions, be co-ordinated to ensure full use. It did not appear to the Army that female soldiers could be considered "workers" in the passage which required "the hiring, rehiring, solicitation, and recruitment of workers . . . in any plant, facility, occupation, or area" to be done through the United States Employment Service.

In reply to the Army, the WMC retorted that WAC enlistments "shall be subject to the conditions of employment stabilization plans of the War Manpower Commission." It claimed authority not only over publicity media, but also to direct the Army not to send WAC recruiting teams to any area, or to use drill teams, bands, or local advertising, or to set quotas or take any other means of encouraging women to join the WAC. It also added thirty-five more exempted fields from which the WAC could not accept recruits, some of which were described in such broad terms as "industries" and "education services, public and private."[10]

The Army and Navy joined in protesting this action. They pointed out that it was extremely shortsighted to draft skilled male factory workers and teach them to type, thus forcing industry to replace them with women who had to learn the factory trade; both armed forces and industry would benefit by allowing a woman typist to enlist so that a skilled factory worker need not be drafted. Since competitive recruiting was admittedly to be deplored, the armed forces suggested instead a giant combined campaign, with resources of all agencies directed toward drawing women

---

[8] (1) Memo, Pers Div ASF for Enl Sec, 29 May 43, with incl copy of Memo, WMC for OWI, picked up by Army officer when a New York radio station refused to broadcast the WAAC news release. SPWA 000.77 (1943). (2) Almost identical Ltr from Georgia, SPWA 311.23. (3) Ltr, R&I Serv, 2d SvC to WAAC Hq, 30 Jun 43, saying that the WMC in Newark asked radio stations to hold off all WAAC publicity "owing to the womanpower drive of the WMC." SPWA 000.77 (1943).

[9] *Ibid.* Also Memo, WAAC Hq for WDBPR, 7 Jul 43, sub: WAAC Rctg, Class I and II Cities [incl telgs and lists of cities]. SPWA 000.77 (1943).

[10] (1) Exec Order 9279. (2) Draft of Ltr, SW to the President USA and to WMC. SPWA 000.77 (1943). (3) Ltr, Dep Chmn WMC to USW, 9 Jul 43. SPWA 341 (1943).

MAJ. JESSIE P. RICE

WMC.[12] It was only with this reassurance that the Army approved funds for the advertisements already selected, and for a new recruiting campaign to be co-ordinated with them. The campaign, unlike the advertisements, was shaped about the patriotic motif that the Director preferred.

The All-States Plan

Both the idea and the energy for the new campaign were supplied by a newcomer to WAC Headquarters, Capt. Jessie P. Rice of the Third Service Command, who was reassigned to the Director's Office in the summer. Captain Rice—a major in late August—was a woman of 42, described by reporters as "cheery, no-nonsense," and by all who knew her as "dynamic." She brought to the problem what proved an appropriate background—that of an industrial sales manager, history teacher, sports reporter, and native of a small Georgia town; she had also had a year's field experience as Staff Director, Third Service Command. For the next twenty months, first as head of WAC Recruiting and then as Deputy Director, she was to be, next to Colonel Hobby, the chief author of WAC policy. She was later credited by Director Hobby with, quite literally, saving the WAC from public defeat on two different occasions, of which the first was the present critical period. In her approach to the current problem, as to all later ones, staff members noted a rare combination of commonsense practicality with unabashed idealism

into war work, with the choice of job left to the individual. Otherwise, the Army pointed out, many unemployed women in labor-short areas would never be reached, since they would not take factory jobs and could not be offered Army jobs.[11]

As the War Manpower Commission refused action, the armed forces in August appealed the issue to the nation's highest manpower authority—Justice James F. Byrnes, the Director of War Mobilization. On 12 August 1943, the Director of War Mobilization informed the contenders that the WMC was forbidden to interfere in national recruiting campaigns even in labor-short areas. Its list of thirty-five essential industries was rejected in favor of the Army's shorter one of eight. The Army was in turn directed not to conduct any "intensive local campaigns" in Class I and II areas without clearance with the

---

[11] Memo, JND for Gen Somervell, 12 Jul 43. SPAP, in SPWA 341 (1943).

[12] (1) Memo, USW to Dir OWM, 21 Jul 43. WDGAP 320.2, in SPWA 341 (1943). (2) Memo, SW for CG ASF, 3 Aug 43. Same file. (3) Ltr, Dir OWM to SW, SN, WMC, OWI, 12 Aug 43. SPWA 000.77 (6–4–43), 1943.

for the nation's goals and the Corps' contributions to them.[13]

Major Rice strongly believed that the WAC would achieve lasting success and overcome the slander campaign only through the support of the American community, which was merely alienated by dazzling supersalesmanship and could be won only through giving community members a personal stake in the outcome. They must not be worked upon by outsiders but must do the work themselves, and its outcome must be made a competitive matter of local pride.

She therefore christened her plan the "All-States Plan" and credited the idea to a local success achieved by Baltimore recruiters. It called, quite simply, for each state to recruit a state company, which would carry its flag and wear its armband in training. The trick was in the mechanics, which involved participation of the states' most reputable citizens: General Marshall was to ask state governors to appoint local committees consisting of mayors and other prominent citizens in each town, who would be responsible for aiding recruiters to meet the quota. Major Rice said:

You will find in this plan nothing new—it is based on the oldest and most fundamental appeal any nation has ever used, and the device it uses is the oldest recruiting device in America, stemming from Colonial days. The appeal is the straight patriotic appeal. . . . By making this appeal by States we hope to reinforce it by the appeal of State pride. We have a big country with many state and sectional traditions . . . and they can be made to play their part only if the operations are conducted by people who know the States and the people in them.[14]

Another appeal was added by Colonel Hobby concerning the setting of the quota; each town would list the number of

its sons who had become battle casualties and would recruit a woman to replace each.[15]

The All-States Plan, Major Rice predicted, would not bring in astronomical numbers of recruits, but it could if properly handled pull the WAC out of its recruiting slump, ensure its continued existence, and help to squelch the slander campaign.

The Recruiters

The WAC recruiting machinery could scarcely have been in worse condition for a new effort. Recruiters had borne the brunt of a year of public hostility, and were so fatigued and discouraged that their relief would have been essential had any trained replacements been available. A typical example was one very junior North Carolina recruiter, who reported bitterly that she had made recruiting trips to all the main towns in nine different counties, secured seventy-three free articles and advertisements, got free radio time, secured lists of prospects in every town and sent them all letters, developed a trailer film and display boards, sponsored a state-wide high school poster contest, and distributed 10,000 copies of the winning poster. In return, she succeeded in giving out only ninety application blanks, received thirteen applications, and enrolled two women. Meanwhile, her four enlisted assistants became discouraged

---

[13] (1) WDBPR Press Release, 28 Oct 42. (2) "The Nine Old Women," *Time,* 1944. (3) Intervs with Mrs. Hobby, 29 Jun 48, and numerous others.

[14] Entire discussion from Min, WAC Rctg Conf, 7 Sep 43. WAC Daily Journal, Vol. II, SPWA 337 (9–1–43).

[15] Approved by D/F, G–1 to ASF through CofS, 2 Sep 43. WDGAP 341 WAC, in WDCSA 291.9 WAAC.

and applied for discharge from the WAAC to get defense jobs in California. For these tribulations, her only reward was a letter of reprimand from WAAC headquarters concerning the winning poster, which had been in such poor taste as to come to national attention.[16]

The burst of energy demanded by a new recruiting drive therefore presented a particular problem. Colonel Hobby wrote to the discouraged recruiters:

I know the difficulties, the loneliness, the heartbreaking apathy you have faced. I know how hard it is, after weeks and months of discouragement, to dip deep into inner resources and start again with fresh enthusiasm. But I know, too, that you have such inner resources. . . . If you can give fully of your own strength, your own conviction, your own faith and heartfelt patriotism, we will not fail now.[17]

For the success of the campaign, the WAC leaders depended frankly, as always in the Corps' history, upon these "inner resources," and upon motives which were matters of ideals and spirit. Major Rice took charge of the hundreds of conferences and interviews required by the All-States Campaign, quoting freely from Tom Paine concerning "summer soldiers and sunshine patriots," and using a modern quotation also favored by Colonel Hobby as typifying the Corps' present slim chances of success:

God of the hidden purpose
Let our embarking be
The prayer of proud men asking
Not to be safe, but free.[18]

As the Corps poised upon the threshold of this crucial effort to restore itself, Major Rice informed a conference of service command recruiters:

We know that there are millions of women who will join us now, if we can touch that spring of inner compulsion that causes people to forget self and fear of the unknown and strike out along the path that leads to their ideals.[19]

Sources of Assistance

The campaign's organization was nevertheless highly practical, and was to stand as a model for all future efforts. To avoid misunderstandings, Army recruiting and induction officers from each service command and their WAC assistants were thoroughly briefed in a Washington conference on the entire plan. At the same time, the Army's Recruiting Publicity Bureau, in New York City, set its presses rolling to produce, in an unprecedentedly short time, portfolios of instructions for recruiters, with brightly colored and attractive posters, window cards, stickers, manuals, envelope stuffers, clip sheets, mats, and advertisements of all sizes.[20]

Also, the War Advertising Council was approached and agreed to arrange free sponsored national advertising for the WAC as it was doing for other agencies. Recruiters were also instructed in how to get free advertising on a local level; many firms were found to be willing to aid the war effort by contributing advertising space, or by including a Wac in their usual advertisements. Many posters and other aids were also sponsored by various business groups. For example, the Stand-

[16] Ltr, WAC Hq to Rctg Off, Ft Bragg, N. C., 2 Aug 43, incl rpt of Lt Mary J. Norton, 22 Jun–20 Jul 43. SPWA 415.

[17] Ltr, Col Hobby to all WAC recruiters, 20 Sep 43. SPWA 341 (8–6–43) sec 1*b*.

[18] Henry Morton Robinson, "Litany for a New AEF," reprinted in *WAC Newsletter*, Vol. I, No. 8, 15 Jan 44.

[19] Speech. Min cited n. 14.

[20] Office Memo, "F" for "R" [Capt Ruth F. Fowler for Maj Rice, both of WAC Rctg Sec], 21 Sep 43. SPWA 341 (8–6–43) sec 1*b*.

ard Oil Company of Indiana sent its dealers 19,000 posters, "The Girl With the Star-Spangled Heart," to replace the previous "Drain Old Oil Now." [21]

National civic and business organizations by the dozen were approached by Colonel Hobby's staff, and agreed to mention the WAC in their trade publications and bulletins: the American Retail Association, the National Dry Goods Association, the National Association of Theater Owners, five press associations, most magazine publishing firms, several film companies, the Mayor's Conference, the National Association of Broadcasters, the U.S. Chamber of Commerce, and others as varied. [22]

Organized clubwomen of thirty-six national organizations announced their support after visits of their representatives to Des Moines.

The Executive Committee of the Governors' Conference also gave a preliminary indorsement which assured the Army that state governors would respond when officially called upon. [23]

Paid advertising was also authorized to supplement all the free publicity that the above agencies could contribute. Colonel Hobby asked that the Army allot $10.00 per needed recruit for this purpose, chiefly for systematic coverage of Sunday newspapers. General Dalton disapproved this on the grounds that "no business which is forced to operate at a profit would consider such an appropriation," but he was overruled by General Somervell, who considered that the situation merited the expenditure. As a matter of fact, the sum was somewhat less than that later used in postwar Army advertising to get comparable numbers of male recruits. [24]

As an added precaution Director Hobby in two different meetings with high

War Manpower Commission officials cleared the All-States Plan. She was informed that, from 27 September to 7 December, recruiting was authorized even in Class I and II areas, provided that no woman was taken from essential industry. A representative of WMC likewise stated this fact in a speech to the recruiters conference, and the Army published it to recruiters. In return the Army agreed to urge rejected WAC applicants to accept factory work. [25]

The Air-WAC Plan

Because the WAC's continued existence was virtually staked on this one campaign, the War Department decided to accept assistance from a source that it had previously rejected—the Army Air Forces. The AAF had for months begged to be allowed to send out its own personnel to assist regular recruiters, the only proviso being that recruits so obtained could be promised assignment to the Air Forces. Such special-promise recruiting was not unknown to the Army; the Air Forces' recruiting teams, in a recent campaign to get 57,000 male aviation specialists, had

[21] (1) Memo, Dir WAC for Dir Pers ASF, 28 Aug 43. SPWA 000.7 E, in ASF SPAP 341 WAAC (2–26–43). (2) Ltr, WAC Rctg Off, Chicago, to Dir WAC, 27 Oct 43. SPWA 415.

[22] Memo, Capt Fowler for Maj Rice, 21 Sep 43. SPWA 341 (8–6–43) sec 1b.

[23] (1) WDBPR Press Release, 20 Sep 43. (2) Min cited n. 14.

[24] (1) Memo, WAC Hq for CG ASF, 2 Aug 43; (2) Memo, Dir WAC for Gen Dalton, 25 Aug 43. SPWA 000.7 (8–25–43). (3) History: Office of the Director of Personnel, Army Service Forces 20 Jul 42–1 Sep 45. OCMH. Hereafter cited as ASF Pers Hist. (4) For army postwar advertising contract, see *Washington Post,* February 18, 1949.

[25] (1) Memos, Dir WAC for G–1, 16 Oct 43, 24 Aug 43, and 30 Sep 43. SPWA 000.77 (1–4–43). (2) Speech of Mr. Stephen W. Wood, WMC. Min cited n. 14. (3) Ltr, TAG to all SvCs, 12 Sep 43. AG 341 PR–I–E.

recruited 128,000 almost before the campaign could be shut off. Nevertheless, Colonel Hobby had consistently rejected these offers, pointing out that special promises to recruits—their choice of branch or station—were undesirable and that difficulty and hard feeling would later result, particularly since earlier recruits had no such choice.[26]

Army Service Forces recruiting experts now informed Colonel Hobby that the WAC would have to abandon its stand against special promises, saying, "The persistent decline in WAAC recruiting results, along with the increasing need for women in the Armed Forces, make it essential to open the door immediately for special WAC recruiting plans."[27] It was therefore decided to adopt the Air-WAC Plan to supplement the All-States Plan; the Air Forces would not compete, but would bring in women who would be part of the state companies until trained. Branch recruiting thus became an accepted fact, although the other two Army branches—AGF and ASF—did not at this time decide to give any personnel to the project. The AAF at once prepared to throw hundreds of additional recruiters into the struggle.[28]

The Quota

On the eve of the campaign, Major Rice estimated that the take would be 10,000 in the approximately two months between 27 September, when the campaign opened, and 7 December, when it closed. Colonel Hobby optimistically hoped for 35,000, and asked that Fort Sheridan be made available in case the three remaining WAC centers were inadequate. The Adjutant General insisted that the higher goal of 70,000 be set, since

70,000 casualties had been sustained to date. Colonel Hobby deplored this move, saying, "It is negative psychology to have an impossible quota"; she recommended a quota of approximately 17,000 for the entire period, which was disapproved by the Army Service Forces. Major Rice attempted to use merely the number of those killed in action instead of all casualties, but the number 70,000 was chosen by the Secretary of War and used in all publicity releases. Actually, G–3 Division of the War Department had hopefully included 200,000 Wacs in the Troop Basis for 1943, but with the provision that more men could be drafted if women failed to volunteer. The most impossible figure of all came from The Adjutant General's Office, which calculated that 631,000 Wacs were needed at once to prevent the drafting of fathers. The figure of 600,000 was used by General Marshall in his public speeches, to emphasize the extent of the Army's need, but was never considered a real quota.[29]

The Campaign

On the last day of August 1943, the All-States Campaign went into action with the precision and co-ordinated effort of a

[26] Memo, AAF for G–1, 29 Jun 43. Published 4 Sep 43, AGO Memo W635–21–43, Participation of AAF in WAC Rctmt. SPWA 341 (8–6–43) sec 1b.

[27] Memo, Lt Col C. C. Curtis for Dir WAC, 11 Aug 43. SPWA 341 (8–6–43) sec 1b.

[28] Ltr, TAG to SvCs, 12 Oct 43. AG 341 WAC PR–I, in SPWA 341 (8–6–43) sec 1a.

[29] (1) Rice estimate made to author and co-workers. (2) Hobby estimates in 1st Ind to Dir Pers ASF, to Memo cited n. 27. (3) Hobby quote from Min cited n. 3. Also Memo, Dir WAC for Dir Pers ASF, 19 Aug 43. SPWA 341 (8–10–43) R, in SPAP 341 WAAC (2–26–43). (4) Ltr, SW to Bur of Budget, 15 Jul 43. WDGAP 320.2 WAAC, in CofS 291.9 WAAC. (5) ByExec Order 9364, top limit to strength of WAC was set at 200,000, as published in WD Bulletin 17, 4 Aug 43.

ALL-STATES RECRUITING CAMPAIGN. *Governor Leverett Saltonstall of Massachusetts cuts the ribbon opening a WAC recruiting booth. Standing next to the Governor is Mayor Maurice J. Tobin of Boston.*

military invasion. Exactly twenty-seven days were allotted to softening up the public before the recruiters landed. General Somervell opened the barrage on 31 August with a personal telegram to the commanding generals of all service commands stating, DIRECTOR HOBBY WILL CONTACT YOU ON WAC RECRUITING PLAN WHICH HAS MY APPROVAL. URGE FULL SUPPORT. On the same day and the next, Colonel Hobby made personal long-distance telephone calls to these commanding generals, explaining the plan. In the following week, full details were placed in the hands of recruiters assembled in Washington.[30]

On 10 September, General Marshall sent a personal letter to each state governor, saying, "I am appealing to you for assistance. . . ."[31] This was followed by immediate visits to the governors by service command representatives. In the

[30] (1) TWX, CG ASF to SvCs, 31 Aug 43. SPWA 341 (8–6–43) sec 1*b*. (2) Min cited n. 14.
[31] The following discussion is based on: (1) Ltrs, CofS to the 48 governors, 10 Sep 43. SPWA 341 (8–6–43) sec 1*a*; also in CofS 291.9 with replies. (2) Ltrs, WAC Stf Dir 7th SvC, 11 and 30 Sep 43. SPWA 341 sec 1*b*. (3) Ltrs, Maj Gen Kenyon A. Joyce, 9th SvC, and others. SPWA 341 sec 1*a* (1943). (4) Proclamation, 18 Sep 43, with other proclamations. SPWA 341 (8–6–43) sec 1*a*. (5) Copy in Ltr, Young & Rubicam to Maj Jess Rice, 19 Oct 43. SPWA 000.7.

ALL-STATES RECRUITING CAMPAIGN. *Texas state flag is held by a WAC officer during a ceremony for recruits in front of the State Capitol, Austin, Texas.*

Seventh Service Command, Maj. Gen. Frederick E. Uhl took a plane and personally visited each state. The governors' responses were in most cases immediate; they appeared eager to be called upon for a further part in the war effort. Many issued proclamations such as

Whereas the successful prosecution of the war requires the enrollment of adequate manpower and [five other whereas's]. . . . Now therefore I, John W. Bricker, Governor of the State of Ohio, do hereby call for volunteers for service in the WAC. . . . I do further call upon mayors and other governmental authorities . . . upon all citizens, newspapers, and radio stations . . . to the end that the State of Ohio may fully achieve her goal in this great national objective.

The governors appointed committees in every community, consisting ordinarily of local officials and prominent citizens, whose efforts were co-ordinated by WAC recruiters. Many governors and mayors allowed the use of their names in local advertisements, for example:

WOMEN OF FITCHBURG

A Message from your Governor:

Throughout the history of America, men and women of the Commonwealth have never failed to answer the call of service to their country. . . . I am confident that once again the daughters as well as the sons of Massachusetts will have proved their right to our great heritage.

[Signed] Leverett P. Saltonstall

At the same time, the weight of General Marshall's personal prestige was thrown into the campaign in a national press release which, on 15 September, described the plan to the public. This was supported by paid advertisements on a co-ordinated theme placed in Sunday papers by Young & Rubicam.[32]

On 27 September, the doors were formally opened to All-States recruits. An unprecedented concentration of recruiting activity resulted: it appeared doubtful that any inhabitant of the United States failed to hear of the WAC if he could read, listen to the radio, or be reached by a citizen's committee. The Office of War Information for the next three weeks devoted to the WAC most of the free facilities offered it by radio stations, ordinarily used for such projects as bond sales and food conservation; 17,000 messages were broadcast over 891 radio stations, plus 150 plugs on network programs and special, national, and spot programs. The Army Air Forces on 18 October threw teams totaling 358 officers and 1,136 enlisted personnel into the campaign. The WAC Band toured; governors continued to issue statements, which Young & Rubicam caught up and published; governors whose states led were congratulated, others were chagrined, and some even went on personal speaking tours. In general, recruiters seasoned by earlier campaigns seldom fumbled, and publicity was uniformly good.[33]

State companies were shipped to training centers as fast as enough for a company were recruited. The women were ordinarily assembled at the state capitol building or some other historic spot, where they were sworn in with much ceremony, martial music, parades, crowds, and publicity, and presented by the governor with a state flag to carry at the training center. Some states thus recruited several companies in succession. No one WAC training center had sufficient capacity to hold forty-eight companies, but the spirit of the idea was preserved, and each training center parade had a display of from fifteen to twenty state flags. Competition among state companies was keen, and most recruits were kept in a state of high morale by the favorable attention given them by home-town newspapers and by their introduction to the governor and to other prominent citizens.[34]

Altogether, WAC and Army authorities were highly pleased with the prospects. Colonel Hobby called the plan "the best recruiting device we have ever had." The campaign seemed well on the way to achieving some of the more optimistic predictions. Well-nigh faultless in its organization, and highly effective in achieving the desired effect upon the public, it appeared that it could have been stopped only by one thing—an order from authority higher than the Army. And this was, in effect, what stopped it in many areas.

Opposition of the War Manpower Commission

No sooner was the All-States Campaign well launched than the Army discovered

[32] (1) WDBPR Press Release, 15 Sep 43. (2) Speech, Mr. Lenz, Young & Rubicam. Min cited n. 14.

[33] (1) Speech. Mr. Ferbanks, OWI. Min cited n. 14. (2) AAF WAC Hist, p. 57; also AG Ltr cited n. 28. (3) TWX, Comdt 1st WAC Tng Cen to Dir WAC, 4 Oct 43. SPWA 341 sec 1*b*. (4) Ltrs of thanks, Dir WAC to CGs of SvCs, 11 Sep 43. SPWA 341, sec 1*b*; and Ltrs, Governors to Gen Marshall, Nov–Dec 43. CofS 291.9. (5) Memo, Dir WAC for Secy GS, 12 Nov 43. SPWA 341 (8–6–43) sec 1*a*. (6) Speech, Maj Rice. Min, WAC Stf Dirs Conf. New York, 1–3 Dec 43, SPWA 337 (11–10–43).

[34] Ltr, Atty Gen of Ohio to Dir WAC, 5 Oct 43, and reply. SPWA 341 sec 1*b*.

that the War Manpower Commission was again ignoring not only its two agreements with the Army but the August directive from its superior, Director of War Mobilization Byrnes. In spite of WMC clearance of the All-States Plan, regional WMC offices in five of the nine service commands not only suppressed local WAC recruiting publicity, but, speaking as "The United States," released headlines such as one in Connecticut: U.S. FORBIDS WAC DRIVE IN CITY AS THREAT TO WAR EFFORT. In Macon, Georgia, bewildered recruiters were confronted with an ultimatum from the WMC area director saying, "I have decided it would not be feasible to continue with this [recruiting] program. This is a result of Macon being an extreme labor shortage area, and every woman who would be acceptable to the WAC could be used to advantage in war industries." The Office of War Information withdrew radio support in such localities as directed by local WMC officials saying that it had no other choice.[35]

The most charitable interpretation that could be put upon this action was that the War Manpower Commission had been slow in informing its regional offices of the Byrnes decision and of its own official clearance of the All-States Plan. When questioned by telephone, WMC officials at first gave this explanation, saying, "Frankly, they should have gone out quite some time ago." However, a few days later an executive staff meeting was held, of which Major Rice was informed, "Fact is, it was a complete nullification both in the chairman's office and the executive staff of the things we had discussed as exploratory." Major Rice at once pointed out that the WMC's commitments had not been exploratory, that WMC representatives had stated them at official meetings, that

the Army had spent a million dollars and staked the Chief of Staff's prestige upon them, and that "we are in a pretty desperate condition, with time running out on us."[36]

Director Hobby called to the War Department's attention "the fact that we had begun the All-States Campaign believing that we had clearance . . . the fact that with the best recruiting device we have ever had, we have been barred by the WMC area directors from making any effort to reach many thousands of women in areas of essential industry who are not themselves engaged in essential industry."[37]

High-level negotiations with the War Manpower Commission began again. The WMC now refused to inform its area directors of its previous clearance of the All-States Campaign unless the Army agreed to use the WMC list of thirty-five essential industries. which Director Byrnes had already disapproved, instead of the shorter Army list which he had approved. Mr. McNutt's office also demanded that its area directors be given power to add industries to the list at their discretion, to veto any objectionable activity, and to supervise all WAC advertising copy.[38]

Rather than thus renounce the advantages that the Byrnes decision had decreed for it, the Army chose to fight the matter

[35] (1) Sources cited n. 25. (2) Memo, Dir WAC for G–1, 4 Oct 43. SPWA 000.77 (1943). (3) Ltr, Ralph E. Haines, Area Dir WMC, Macon, Ga., to CO Cochran Field, 8 Oct 43. SPWA 341 sec 1b. (4) Memo, Maj Rice for Dir Hobby, with rpt of 5 Oct conf with TAG, G–1, and OWI; (5) Bridgeport (Conn.) *Post*, in Ltr, Maj Gen Sherman Miles, 1st SvC, to WAC. SPWA 000.77 (1943).

[36] (1) Tp Convs, Maj Rice and Mr. Broughton, 5 Oct 43, and another, no date. G–1 WAC 312.9, Drawer 6, DRB AGO.

[37] Memo cited n. 25(1).

[38] Tp Conv, Col Hobby and Mr. Broughton, 15 Oct 43. G–1 WAC 312.9, Drawer 6, DRB AGO.

through. The negotiations dragged on for some time and were not to reach a workable conclusion until the following year. Meanwhile, the brief All-States Campaign, which had depended for effect on its impetus and concentration, was somewhat blunted in many areas, and reached its final deadline on 7 December without feeling any benefit from the negotiations.

There was no way of computing the exact loss which had been occasioned by the War Manpower Commission's action. Major Rice believed that it was perhaps not as serious as the initial setbacks had indicated. In any case, it was clear that while the Army had at last made plain to the public its united support of the WAC, the government as a whole had not done so. Instead, the nation had approached a grave emergency without any clear definition of the role of womanpower and its apportionment among competing agencies.

Public Apathy

The lack of support by civilian manpower control groups of the United States Government explained to some degree the public conviction that the matter was not important, and the resulting apathy, which recruiters encountered as the All-States Campaign drew to a close in early December of 1943. One annoyed general reported that in his service command there appeared to be three types of women: (1) patriotic, who had already taken essential civilian work or enlisted in the WAC; (2) patriotic but mercenary, who were interested only in the highest-paying war jobs; and (3) "The leisure class, who like to go down to the USO, dance with the boys on Saturday night, and think they are making their contribution to the war effort that way. They make all these talks, ap-

pear in theaters, put up placards, appear before women's clubs, talk to everybody in the world, but when it comes to getting them to sign up, they say no soap." [39]

The Army's highest-ranking officers now became personally aware of the factors affecting WAC recruiting as never before in the Corps' career, since the All-States Campaign put the responsibility upon them as well as upon community leaders. General Dalton personally telephoned the commanding generals of service commands to read them a long list of ideas to get recruits. He told each pointedly, "I wonder if you've gotten word down to all ranks that General Marshall and the rest of the top people have an intense interest in this WAC recruiting." [40]

The difficulty in getting a woman recruit at first amazed, then exasperated, then spurred to action the commanding generals concerned. Even the service commander who led the field was dissatisfied and observed to General Dalton: "I don't know what is wrong. It just doesn't seem to take. . . . Well, we will put all we got in it, Joe." Another visited WAC recruiters at work and reported that "these people are up against a hard proposition" and needed all the co-operation that the Army could give. Still another noted how high-paying industry had stripped the area of qualified women, and stated, "If they're not just children, overaged, or a little moronic or something, they've quit, they've gone away." The interest and indignation of these officers worked to the WAC's advantage in that, recruiters reported, they were now able to get from their headquarters better transportation,

[39] Tp Calls, Dir Pers ASF to CGs of SvCs, 1 Dec 43, Reply of 2d SvC. ASF, SPAP 341 WAAC (2–26–43).
[40] *Ibid.*

personnel, and station locations than had previously been made available.[41]

The Army Air Forces recruiters received a similar shock. Employing tactics that had recruited 128,000 male mechanics in a short time, they were able to get, in the entire month of November, only about 1,500 Wacs. One AAF officer reported:

I never saw anything as tough. When our team hit one Florida city, we closed the place—actually got the mayor to close schools and stores so everyone would come to our parade and rally. We got important speakers, generals, war heroes. Better than 50 planes flew overhead forming the letters *WAC*. That night we had a big dance for prospects, with good-looking pilots as dates. Results? We didn't get one Wac in that town. Some of the local girls put in applications to please their escorts, but withdrew them the next day.[42]

It soon was apparent to the Air Forces that there was one important difference in the mechanics' campaign and the WAC campaign—the men had been faced by eventual draft and so had been happy to have a choice of branch, job, and station near home, whereas the women were not faced by any such compulsion. Nevertheless, the Air Forces persisted, and by December were getting more than half of the total intake.[43]

The Success of the All-States Campaign

In spite of the opposition of the War Manpower Commission and the public apathy, the All-States Campaign proved the most successful the Corps was ever to undertake. The intake of 4,425 in its final month was better than anything that had ever been achieved with comparably high enlistment requirements.[44] The final tally showed that the drive had netted 10,619 recruits, slightly over the 10,000

that Major Rice had predicted. No later campaign, even the highly successful General Hospital Campaign in 1945, was ever to achieve equal numbers in so short a time.

Even better than its immediate results, in Colonel Hobby's opinion, was its continuing effect in overcoming the slander campaign. Major Rice praised the "wonderful civilian cooperation, that will reap results for months to come."[45] A new Gallup survey in the closing months of the year showed that, the Director stated, "Public attitude is now definitely favorable to the WAC—more so than at any time since its organization."[46] Surveys showed that, among eligibles, 83 percent now knew that the WAC was part of the Army, and 85 percent knew that the WAC needed more women. When asked, "Which service needs women the most?" eligibles replied: WAC—58 percent; WAVES—14 percent; Marines—14 percent; SPARS—4 percent; Don't know—5 percent. If drafted, women stated that in making a choice they would give the WAC a slight edge on other enlisted women's service.[47]

General Dalton, while objecting to the cost per recruit, stated that the campaign had led to a better organized and successful recruiting service. Recruiting proved to be permanently restored, even though

[41] *Ibid.*, replies of CGs, 2d, 5th, and 9th SvCs.
[42] Related to author by Capt Dewey Couri, EFTC, at WAC Rctg Conf, Chicago, Feb 44.
[43] Memo, Maj. Rice for G–1, 28 Dec 43. SPWA 341 (1–1–43) sec 2.
[44] Higher totals had been achieved only in the winter of 1942–43 when enlistment requirements were drastically cut and unassignables admitted.
[45] Min cited n. 33(6).
[46] Memo, Dir WAC for CG ASF, 27 Nov 43, sub: Plan for WAC Rctmt, 7 Dec 43–15 Apr 43. SPWA 341 (11–27–43)B, in ASF, SPAP 341 WAAC (2–26–43). Also Min cited n. 33(6).
[47] Min cited n. 33(6).

to a modest level, and was to average more than 3,000 a month until the last days of the war. The campaign had thus answered the question of whether the WAC could survive: it could. On the other hand, the days of expansive planning in terms of millions were obviously ended, although it was always difficult for planners completely to relinquish visions, which had been held since the first World War, of the effortless and inexpensive acquisition of thousands of female volunteers.[48]

Revival of Plans to Draft Women

The ruinous expense of recruiting competition was now so clear that the Army, even before the end of the campaign, revived the question of drafting women, which had been rejected by the General Staff less than a year before as impossible. The Chief of Staff in early autumn personally directed Colonel Hobby to prepare a memorandum on the "selection of women for military duty."[49] This she did, noting, "A year's experience indicates the improbability of attaining, through voluntary enlistments, an adequate supply of womanpower to perform essential military services."[50] The Director was now thoroughly convinced that the American public looked on the draft as the proper means of meeting military needs. To a military conference, she stated, "I believe that it is as fair to ask volunteers for service as to ask for volunteers to pay taxes. . . . When people are asked, 'Why aren't you in the Service?', they remark, 'Oh, come now, if the Government really needs us they will draft us.' "[51]

The plans now made were far more extensive than those that the Army had attempted in its similar legislative study during the manpower crisis of the year before. It was noted that by this time the British Government already had registered women in the 19–40 age group and had power to direct some 17,000,000 of them into the armed services or industry. The British had found it advisable to give local industrial jobs to women with domestic responsibilities, and to emphasize mobility for the armed forces; younger mobile women were withdrawn from retail trades, the clothing industry, and even the government, and replaced by the nonmobile. By this means thousands of women were being successfully called up each week. Some 91 percent of single women and 80 percent of married women of ages 18–40 were already reported to be working directly in the war effort in Britain.[52]

The prospects in the United States looked even more favorable. Statistics from the Bureau of the Census showed that there were an estimated 18,000,000 American women in the 18–49 age group without children under 18, of which over 5,000,000 could probably meet the WAC's high requirements and pass all tests and investigations. Of these, the Adjutant General estimated that the Army would need to draft only 631,000.[53]

---

[48] ASF Pers Hist.

[49] (1) Memo, Miss B. E. Lies for Dir WAC 9 Sep 43. Folder, Plng Proj 27, WAAC Plng files. (2) Memo, Dir WAC for TAG, 11 Sep 43. SPWA 327.07.

[50] Memo, Dir WAC for CofS, 15 Sep 43. SPWA 327.02E.

[51] Remarks, Stf Dirs Conf, Chicago, 15–17 Jun 43. SPWA 337 (6–1–43).

[52] M/R, Summary of Certain Aspects of British Womanpower Policy, 19 Aug 43. SPWA 327.02 Great Britain (1–19–43).

[53] (1) Memo cited n. 49(1) contains varying figures from Bur of Census, Bur Labor Statistics, 1940 Census, and WMC. Some estimates, with deletions for lack of education, etc., still left over 3,000,000 qualified. (2) Memo, TAG for Dir WAC, 15 Sep 43. SPWA 337.02.

The submitted version of legislation was therefore extremely liberal, and would have exempted all married women living with their husbands, all women with children or other dependents, women in essential industry or agriculture, nurses, physicians, public officials, and others in like category. The proposed law stated, "An obligation rests upon women as well as men . . . to render such personal service in aid of the war effort as they may be deemed best fitted to perform." [54]

The Director's recommendation was that selection be scientific—by Army requirements, not numerical—since 80 percent of the jobs required skill and experience, and the other 20 percent required the ability to acquire skill with short training. Unskilled and low-grade womanpower was not wanted.

The American public seemed to be solidly behind the idea of drafting women. Gallup polls showed that 73 percent in October of 1943 and 78 percent in December believed that single women should be drafted before any more fathers were taken. Single women of draft age themselves endorsed their draft by a 75 percent majority, although stating that they would not voluntarily enlist so long as the Government did not believe the matter important enough to warrant a draft. Every section of the nation had large majorities favoring the drafting of women. [55]

Nevertheless, even its advocates soon realized that the plan would never be adopted unless serious military reverses occurred. Director Hobby stated in conference, " I think that what happens on the question of Selective Service depends on how long the war lasts. I do not think there is any thought of it in Congress at this time." [56]

Her prediction proved correct. The

General Staff's G–1 Division, after some consideration, decided that the only possible strategy was to wait until national service legislation was sponsored elsewhere and then to request that the Army be included. Some sponsorship was immediately forthcoming in the Austin-Wadsworth bill. [57]

The Austin-Wadsworth Bill

Scarcely three weeks after the close of the All-States Campaign, there ensued a national manpower crisis which caused an actual "universal service" bill to be considered. In the winter of 1943–44, the Army's major training effort ended and its all-out offensive began. Overseas, the invasions of Normandy and of New Guinea were in the making. In January, the War Department announced that by the end of the year some 6,000,000 men still on training stations must be shipped overseas; station overhead was to be combed for physically fit, well-trained troops. [58]

The nation's manpower economy was in poor condition to support the offensive, being at the moment in possibly the most critical condition of the war. Secret and pessimistic debates in the General Council showed that Selective Service calls were not being met and that there was small prospect that more than 80 percent of future calls would be met; planners con-

---

[54] Memo cited n. 50.

[55] Gallup Poll results in *Washington Post*, April 2, 1944.

[56] Remarks cited n. 51.

[57] (1) Memo, G–1 for CofS, 23 Sep 43. WDGAP 327 WAC. Handwritten note: "I agree. GCM." (2) HR 1742 and S 666, 78th Cong, 1st sess, 8 Feb 43. *Congressional Record*, Vol. 89, No. 21, A494.

[58] (1) *WAC Newsletter*, Vol. I, No. 8, 15 Jan 44. (2) Washington *Evening Star*, January 27, 1944, "Army Shakeup to Double Forces Abroad."

sidered calling up 400,000 men previously deferred as farmers.[59] The preliminary successes in Italy in the early fall had raised civilian hopes of immediate victory to such an extent that a stampede from war industries began. War Manpower Commission Chairman McNutt denounced the workers who "seek out a safe berth in nonwar work of a permanent character." Ship deliveries declined by 40 percent; war industry noted a severe slump in production goals; and the recruiting of workers by the armed forces and defense industry redoubled in difficulty.

Secretary of War Henry L. Stimson told the Senate Military Affairs Committee that "the home front is on the point of going sour," and that the morale of fighting men would be seriously affected if civilians were left free to snap up the best postwar jobs. Therefore, Secretary of the Navy Frank Knox recommended that workers be frozen in their jobs in order to prevent disastrous absenteeism and turnover of personnel. The Chief of Staff publicly warned the nation that it still failed to grasp the magnitude of the effort needed for victory.[60]

Heeding these pleas, Congress in January turned to active consideration of the pending Austin-Wadsworth bill for "civilian selective service." [61] The heads of the armed forces threw their support behind the measure as a means of equalizing the sacrifices of military and civilian personnel, warning that the war's great effort lay ahead of the nation and not behind it. From the viewpoint of the women's services, the measure appeared a sure means of ending recruiting costs and ensuring thousands of members. While the bill did not provide for the induction of women into the armed forces, it exempted enlistees from being drafted into farms and factories. British reports alleged that, under a similar act, some 40 percent of women had attempted to choose military service.[62]

Unhappily for such hopes, the Austin-Wadsworth bill was opposed by the American Federation of Labor—whose President, William Green, called a labor draft "servitude" and "unconstitutional"—and by the Congress of Industrial Organizations. Finally, when the Senate's Truman Committee announced its opposition, the bill was dropped. Wide-open competition for womanpower continued, under circumstances which made the manpower shortages of 1942 and 1943 appear mere preliminaries.[63]

No accurate estimate was ever possible as to the cost to the nation of the absence of some such law to direct women into industry or the armed forces. The Army's best estimate of the recruiting cost per Wac was $125, including advertising, recruiters' salaries, transportation, station rent, and all other expenses. This sum did not appear prohibitive when compared with the cost to the Army—$107—of recruiting a female civilian worker who might resign at any time. While no average figure was announced by civilian industry for its recruiting, the amount spent on rallies, bands, scouts, and other recruiting activities by the aircraft industry and others was undoubtedly comparable. The

---

[59] Min, Gen Council, 24 Jan 44.
[60] *Washington Post,* January 10, February 2 and 4, and March 3, 1944.
[61] HR 3944, 78th Cong, 2d sess, 11 Jan 44.
[62] National Service Act of 1941 (no. 2). Memo, MPD SOS for G–1, 4 Nov 42. SPGAM 320.2 WAAC (9–15–42).
[63] *Washington Post,* February 17 and 26, and March 5, 1944.

Army, in return for its expenditure, had at least the assurance that its Wacs must stick to their jobs, whereas Mr. McNutt reported that in industry eight women were quitting for every ten who were recruited.[64]

Army Manpower Crisis

As a result of the manpower situation, an Army directive advised all stations that they could not expect any additional military strength to replace, through the draft, the men shipped overseas. Commanders were told to replace their January losses and keep posts going as best they could by the use, in order of preference, of: (1) civilians, (2) Wacs, (3) men disqualified for overseas service, returned from overseas, over 35 years of age, or with less than twelve months of service.[65]

Misunderstandings at once arose over this order of listing, with Wacs and limited service men complaining that civilians were taunting them with being the less-desired type of personnel. The War Department hastened to explain that the situation was just the opposite: it had been intended that the few remaining men be saved for the jobs which only men could do, the Wacs for other completely military work, and civilians used for all else. When asked by a staff officer, "Why did the War Department, in their list of replacements, list civilians first and Wacs second?" General Dalton replied, "For the simple reason that Wacs are included in the military strength and we need the military for other purposes. We are trying to use as many civilians as possible to release the military, male and female."[66] The War Department's G–1, General White, added, "We never use military personnel on a job

that can be done by civilian employees if civilians can be obtained. . . . There is a serious shortage of WAC personnel. Military personnel must be used on assignments where we cannot use civilians."[67]

Sudden WAC Popularity

With unexpected suddenness WAC stock soared to new heights at Army commands and stations. Greatly increased requisitions for Wacs came from sources new and old. The Medical Department, which two years before had refused to employ Waacs, now stated, "With the expansion of hospitals and the withdrawal of enlisted men, there will be an urgent need for at least 50,000 additional Wacs to work in medical installations." The Chief Signal Officer asked that Wacs be increased from 9 percent to 16 percent of the military personnel under his jurisdiction, complained of the "special appeals" with which Air Forces was securing recruits, and called for "aggressive action" to get more for the Signal Corps.

Other administrative and technical services were in a similar predicament. Director Hobby returned from a brief trip to Europe in January of 1944 with further requests from the European and Mediterranean theaters for more Wacs. At the same time a request for 10,000 Wacs was received from the Pacific theater, which had refused to employ them up to this

---

[64] Memo, TAG for G–1, 28 Feb 44, sub: Estimated Per Capita Cost of WAC Rctg. PR–E, WAAC classif files, under "budget."

[65] WD Cir 293, 11 Nov 43; also ASF Cir 21, Sec II, 24 Jan 44.

[66] Min of Rctg Conf, Feb 44. SPWA 337.

[67] Ltr, G–1 to Hon Francis Case, 9 Mar 44. WDGAP 322 WAC, WDWAC 330.14.

time. The War Department, which had previously banned the use of Wacs in the Washington area, shortly reversed the decision and gave itself first priority on the most highly skilled recruits, to the considerable annoyance of field agencies. The agency habitually the most cautious about employing Wacs, the Army Ground Forces, had only a few months earlier asked that its Wac quota be cut from 5 percent to 3 percent of the intake; in a quick reversal it now asked for a "more equitable distribution" and that its quota be raised from 3 percent to 8 percent.[68]

The situation prompting this sudden popularity was graphically stated to the Air Forces by General Arnold:

If there is a man left in your organization who does not recognize that the bulk of the men he now has working for him are going to be shipped abroad, and that if he does not train and use the available Wacs, civilians, and soldiers physically unfit for combat, he will have no one to do his job—if there is such a man, he is a definite danger to your organization.[69]

In the Army Service Forces, General Somervell warned his service commanders that "You must . . . give your personal attention to the eventual taking over by the Wacs of many of the jobs in your command."[70]

The Chief of Staff himself went so far as to authorize release to the general public of the precedent-shattering statement that, for American women, "aside from urgent family obligations, *enlistment in the military takes precedence over any other responsibility.*" He added, "It is important that the general public understand the Army's urgent need for women to enable the military effort to go forward according to the schedule of operations in prospect."[71]

The Job-and-Station Promise

In response to the Chief of Staff's plea, the WAC was forced into its final compromise for recruiting success: the adoption of the plan labeled SJA or Station-Job Assignment. At an earlier date, the Army Air Forces had proposed that its recruiters be allowed to promise recruits not only assignment to the Air Forces, but assignment to a particular station for a specified type of work—a system quite comparable to the hiring of civilian employees. Such a plan was generally admitted to be the best possible means of securing parental approval to a woman's enlistment, or of recruiting women with responsibilities that made them unwilling to leave the area of residence. The system also had the advantage of making it possible to fit the stations' needs exactly, and to recruit no skills useless to the Army; it had in fact been developed originally in the days of expansion planning as a means of preventing overrecruiting in any one skill. The job promise was also expected to attract the

[68] (1) Memo, SGO for Dir Pers ASF, 11 Feb 44, with Inds, etc. SPAP 341 WAAC (2–26–43). (2) Memo, SigC for CG ASF, 7 Jun 44. SPSMP 320.2 WAC. SigC 322 WAC 1944–45, DRB AGO. (3) Ltr, SigC to CG ESCTC, Ft Monmouth, 15 Jun 44. SPSMP 320.2 WAC. (4) Min, Gen Council, 7 Feb 44. (5) D/F, G–1 for TAG through CofS, 31 May 44; Incl and M/R. CSA 324.5 WAC. (6) Memo, ASF for TAG, 11 Jul 44. SPGAC 341 Gen (7–11–44)–69, in SPAP 341 WAAC.

[69] Ltr, CG AAF to Air Forces and Comds, 22 Feb 44 (Tab D to Memo, Dir WAC for CofS, 16 Mar 44). WDWAC 341.

[70] (1) Min, ASF Conf of CGs of SvCs, Chicago, 22–24 Jul 43, p. 3. (2) ASF Ltr to all SvCs, 22 Sep 43. SPGAP 201.6 Gen (9–18–43). Folder, Plng Proj 26, WAC Plng files.

[71] Memo, Secy WDGS for WDBPR, 21 Mar 44, CofS Personal file, made available to author, December 1945, by courtesy of General Marshall's secretary. Author's italics.

skilled woman who had previously feared assignment to kitchen duties. A civilian survey revealed that 52 percent of the women questioned, although not planning to join the WAC, said that they might if they could be assured the job of their choice. Of this 52 percent, 50 percent wanted medical, radio, weather, clerical and other technical or mechanical work; only 2 percent wanted to be cooks or orderlies.[72]

At the time, the proposal had been rejected by Director Hobby, on the grounds that such promises were exceedingly difficult to fulfill; the promised job and even the station itself might have vanished before the recruit reported for duty. Also, such promises would plainly cause ill will among previous recruits who desired to choose another job or station.

A reversal of this decision was shortly proposed by the Army Service Forces. By the end of the All-States Campaign it was apparent that the Army Air Forces was, by means of the branch-assignment promise, getting about two thirds of the monthly take as AAF branch recruits. In addition to these branch recruits, the AAF under the War Department ruling got its original 40 percent of the general service recruits who elected no branch. A somewhat insignificant remainder was left to be divided on the customary basis of 57 percent to the ASF and 3 percent to the AGF.[73]

General Dalton, speaking for the ASF and AGF, demanded of Colonel Hobby why the AAF was getting more publicity. He was reminded that neither the ASF or the AGF had chosen to participate in branch recruiting when the choice was offered them the previous October, while the AAF now had some 1,500 of its personnel in the struggle. If anything, the War Department had hindered rather than helped the AAF in its publicity making, for it had forbidden the practice of saying, "Join the Air-WAC," which had occasionally caused the public to believe that a new and superior corps had been set up. The AAF was thenceforth obliged to say, "Join the WAC and Serve with the AAF," although the name Air-Wac was to stick as a title for the recruit herself.[74]

General Dalton therefore secured War Department approval for the publication of a circular giving the AGF and the ASF—but not the AAF—the authority to make the job-and-station promise to WAC recruits. An applicant's choice was limited to stations within the service command in which she applied, since before making the promise it was necessary to determine that housing and a job of the desired type existed at the chosen station. This bit of strategy gave the ASF and the AGF only a momentary advantage, since the AAF within a month secured G–1 Division's authority to make the same promise for air stations within designated air command areas.[75]

Station commanders now had a new and personal incentive to aid in WAC recruiting, since it was largely through their own efforts in the territory around their stations that their personnel needs might be filled. Many stations organized

---

[72] (1) Office Memo, "R. S." for Exec WAAC, 18 May 43. Proj 4, WAAC Plng files. (2) Folders 4, 19, 21, 23, 1943 WAAC/WAC Plng files.

[73] Weekly Rpt 22, O Dir WAC for ASF, 2–8 Feb 44.

[74] (1) Memo, Maj Rice for Dir Pers ASF, 15 Nov 43. SPWA 341 sec 1b, in SPAP 341 WAAC (2–26–43). (2) Memo, Col Catron for TAG, 27 Sep 43. SPWA 341 sec 1a.

[75] (1) WD Cirs 286, 296, 298, and 340 (1943). (2) AG Ltr 320.3 (12–28–43) PR–I, 28 Jan 44. SPWA 341 (8–6–43) sec 1a (1943).

part-time teams of station personnel to comb the surrounding area for recruits. General Arnold informed air bases, "The sole opportunity for station commanders to fill vacancies created by overseas shipments is to undertake active participation in Air-WAC recruiting." [76]

Considerable commotion and some confusion resulted as competing teams took the field. Airfield teams were especially numerous, but ports, hospitals, Signal Corps stations, and many others also participated in station-job recruiting. Posters for Air-Wacs, Port Wacs, and other varieties of Wacs offered a choice of advantages.

As expected, the administrative failure to fulfill these promises was higher than in the All-States Campaign: papers became lost; women insisted that they had been promised assignments which did not appear on their papers; Colonel Hobby's office was besieged by letters from Congressmen and parents, and was obliged to instigate endless investigations as to whether certain claims had any foundation. Some failures to comply with promises were inevitable, as the changing military situation caused certain jobs or even the stations themselves to be closed out before recruits finished training and reported for duty, or as women proved unqualified for the jobs which they had been promised.

Another disadvantage was the schism created in the previously close ranks of the Corps. Women who were approaching eighteen months' service, and especially those who were vainly applying for transfer to a different type of work, station, or climate, or to be nearer home, were likely to look with less than sisterly affection upon recruits who had not enlisted until the job-and-station promise was made.

The newcomers themselves were often ignorant of recruiting history and thus bewildered at their chilly reception by their barracksmates. Deputy Director Rice wrote all staff directors to appeal to the women's soldierliness: "I have the faith in the Corps that makes me believe that the vast majority of its personnel have learned that there is more to being a good soldier than just putting on a uniform and learning to drill and salute." [77] The veteran Wacs were to have need of this soldierliness often during the remaining months of the war, as more and more attractive promises came to be offered to meet the competition for womanpower.

Because of the women's reaction, Colonel Hobby consistently refused repeated recommendations that the WAC make an even more alluring promise: that of overseas assignment. Since it remained impossible to give overseas assignments to many Wacs who had continuously sought them during months of service, she believed it unwarranted to grant these scarce plums to attract latecomers.

Results of the Job-and-Station Plan varied with the energy and the natural advantages of the station. Some Air Forces stations, particularly the more glamorous ones of the Air Transport Command, doubled and tripled their WAC population, to the limits of their available housing. Others were not so fortunate. The commanding officer of the Infantry Replacement Training Center at Camp Roberts sent a letter to each soldier saying, "If each man at this center would assist in recruiting just one woman for the WAC, there would be a sufficient number for a

---

[76] Ltr, AAF Hq to Air Comds, 15 Feb 44. SPWA 341 sec 1*a* (1943).

[77] Personal ltr, Maj Rice to all SvC Stf Dirs, 10 Jan 44. SPWA 341 sec 1*b* (1943).

STATION-JOB RECRUITING DEMONSTRATIONS *used in Macon, Georgia, to enlist women for duty at Cochran Field, Georgia.*

complete Division." However, in the following months only two recruits were obtained and the proposed unit had to be closed out. Still other stations recruited well but not wisely; the Ground Forces replacement depot at Fort Meade found that it had selected women to do clerical work who were unskilled and untrainable for anything except car-washing. Furthermore, some stations found themselves with a group of women who needed frequent leave and holidays to manage outside responsibilities, or whose anxious parents attempted to take over company administration by telephone or in person.[78]

On a national scale, the returns were in direct proportion to the effort expended and to the attractiveness to the public of the various services. The Air Forces, which employed 1,500 recruiters on regular assignments plus uncounted others on part-time teams, got 5,000 of the first 5,270 branch and station-job recruits; the Service Forces 250, and the Ground Forces only 20. However, the Ground Forces had assigned only one officer, a first lieutenant, to recruiting duty, and had refused his request that returned combat heroes be added to his team; such, said the AGF, would be wasteful of personnel. The Air Forces never regretted the expenditure of recruiting personnel, and stated at the end of the war that the process "secured for the AAF over 27,000 workers, many of them highly skilled and many in the prized clerical field; and it tapped a manpower reservoir that could not otherwise have been tapped, so long as women were not directed into national service by some such system as selective service." [79]

Final judgments of the usefulness of the station-job system as a recruiting tool varied: on the one hand, it resulted in disappointments and administrative annoy-

ances; and on the other, it continued to secure recruits, in the face of increasingly desperate competition, who could have been obtained in no other manner. For this reason, in spite of its obvious drawbacks, the system was to continue up to the closing days of recruiting, and was to be picked up in postwar Army recruiting with even more sweeping promises to male recruits, such as choice of overseas stations.

Women-in-War Campaign

In early January of 1944, the long negotiations with the War Manpower Commission yielded the united recruiting drive that the Army had long been proposing. Labeled "Women in War," its aim was to urge women to accept some kind of full-time war work, whether in industry or in one of the military services. The OWI estimated that there were still five and one-half million idle women eligible for such work. However, questionnaires showed that the basic restraining factor was no longer a lack of knowledge of the need but a lack of interest.

The OWI leveled all of its very considerable forces against this apathy. Newspapers, motion pictures, magazines, radio, and all other civilian news media were fully at its command, and for several weeks all devoted their plugs to the theme of Women in War—urging women impartially to join one of the armed services or to take a job in industry. Fifty national radio shows a week and countless local shows used the OWI's Fact Sheet. Stars and producers of the motion picture industry co-operated by making two-and-

---

[78] See basic AAF, AGF, ASF refs in Chs. XVI, XVII, and XVIII.

[79] AAF WAC Hist, p. 72.

a-half-minute bulletins to be attached to newsreels, and 16-millimeter films for showing in churches, schools, and war plants.

In the magazine field, 548 editors simultaneously used the womanpower theme. Through its news bureau, the OWI placed free stories with every type of newspaper: news items were given to the wire services, human-interest stories to the syndicates, and special articles to the rural press, business press, labor, Negro. women's. and foreign-language press. Cartoonists and editorial artists at OWI's call featured an attractive Wac, Wave, nurse, or factory worker. As for posters, the nation's best artists contributed designs, while the OWI's Boy Scout Distribution Service handed out 750,000 posters bi-monthly, as well as 50,000 car cards a month. The Outdoor Advertisement Association contributed twenty-four different billboard spreads.[80]

All of this united activity had little perceptible effect on public apathy or on the armed forces recruitment of women: the WAC returns merely held steady at slightly below the level set by the All-States Campaign. Recruiters were inclined to believe that, had armed forces and industry earlier achieved a united front in harmonious publicity, greater results would have been obtained.

Campaign Conclusions

The All-States Campaign, the Station-Job Plan, and the Women-in-War drive had to some extent counteracted the slander campaign and restored recruiting to a level that permitted the Corps' continued operation. Neither they, nor any plan ever used by the naval women's services, could do more. The final lesson for the armed forces, after all the furor of effort and speculation had died, appeared to be merely the same that it had already learned in previous wars: the American public would not, without conscription, furnish the required number of volunteers for military success. In retrospect it became hard to understand why—in a nation that had been obliged to conscript men since the Civil War and in which women's service had never been popularly accepted—it had ever been imagined that women would make a better response to recruiting appeals than had men.

[80] Memo, Asst Dir Rice for Dir WAC, 12 Jan 44. ASF SPAP 341 WAAC (2–26–43).

CHAPTER XIV

Integration Into the Army

The business of changing the WAAC to the WAC had been virtually suspended while the All-States Plan was rushed into the line to make sure that there would be a WAC to continue. In October and November of 1943, as some measure of recruiting success seemed assured, planners turned back to the business of converting the obsolete WAAC organization, with its own operating headquarters, into the new WAC.

Upon the moment of conversion, an unidentified enthusiast in The Adjutant General's Office issued to the field the blanket directive that all Army Regulations would apply to the WAC until new WAC Regulations could be published. This superseded Director Hobby's plan to use WAAC Regulations in the interval. Outcry from the field soon made embarrassingly clear that the matter was more complex than expected. The Adjutant General hastily rescinded the directive and replaced it with one reinstating WAAC Regulations on clothing, housing, training, medical care, and all other matters with the exception of enlistment, discharge, and military justice, where Army rules would apply. The embarrassment continued: even this limited application of unqualified Army Regulations proved impracticable. In the matter of enlistment, there was a different legally established age and citizenship requirement and several practical differences concerning dependency and disqualifying defects; in the matter of discharge, there were differences in at least eight matters, including minority. As for pregnancy discharge, admission of infants to Army status was narrowly averted by resourceful field stations which gave discharges for disability to expectant mothers.[1]

Having thus perceived that some amendments to men's rules would be necessary, various Army agencies began to fight out the necessary differences. Disputes over the uniform regulations became so heated that it was necessary to detach them from the remainder of the regulations for later publication in the new year. Other matters were gradually agreed upon during the last months of 1943.[2]

Abolition of Separate Grades

In the months before complete agreement could be reached, a makeshift circular in late September took the first step toward integration by abolishing separate WAC grades, a step that appeared more startling to Army personnel officers than its nature merited. Civilian personnel allotments were of course not divided to specify which positions must be filled by

---

[1] (1) AGO Memo W635–14–43; changes 1 (31 Aug 43) and 2 (17 Sep 43). (2) Ltr, 2d SvC to O Dir WAC, 22 Sep 43, and reply. SPWA 314.7 (1–7–43)(1) sec 4.

[2] Memo, G–1 for G–1 Enl Br, 31 Oct 43. SPWA 300.3 (1–7–43) sec 2.

males and which by females, but for military personnel the merger of allotments aroused alarming visions of a merger of unit command and housing.

The Air Forces took the lead in pointing out that this need not necessarily follow: that women might well be assigned to the organizations for which they worked, while residing in their own barracks with a WAC commander possessed of full command powers. Major Bandel, Air WAC Officer, stated:

It had become apparent that the [accounting] troubles which arose came from thinking of WAC personnel as a special type of personnel which had to be assigned, counted, and administered apart from all other types of military personnel. Insofar as their housekeeping went, Wacs obviously had to be administered separately; insofar as their jobs went, if they were to be utilized with maximum efficiency they had to be administered as a part of the unit performing the job in question. Abolition of WAC grades would result in careful utilization, since Wacs would clearly count against a command's overall allotment of grades and personnel; maximum freedom of assignment, since Wacs could be assigned without delay to any job for which a military grade vacancy had been established; and elimination of duplication in manning tables and reports.[3]

Major Bandel therefore proposed to the AAF that each station, instead of having two types of Tables of Allotment, male and female, have only one, and that either a man or a woman be placed in any authorized job at the station's discretion, according to the qualifications and availability of personnel.

Major Bandel was obliged to do considerable sales-work before her headquarters assimilated the plan, but the idea appealed to the Air Forces once it was understood and was proposed to the War Department in August. A few months later the Air Forces also adopted a system for its men under which grades were not broken up among living units, but were retained at station level and distributed among various offices, while the squadron commanders retained all command and disciplinary powers. Major Bandel later received the Legion of Merit for her numerous contributions to the Air Forces' program, with particular reference to originating this idea for Wacs.

In late September the War Department approved the AAF proposal for both the AAF and itself. Thereafter, all War Department grade allotments to the major commands were without reference to the sex of personnel. Any command might place a Wac in any suitable job for which it had an authorized military vacancy, without further formality or bookkeeping. The only limitation was upon the number of Wacs that could be furnished any command; gradeless numerical WAC allotments continued to be made to Air, Ground, and Service Forces based on their usual shares.[4]

The Air Forces system of bookkeeping now became so simple that scarcely any extra load was incurred by the presence of women. Also ended was the whole cumbersome system of WAC requisitions, which had so frequently been outdated before Wacs could be recruited, trained, and shipped. Instead, each station merely reported its current personnel shortages, by specialty number, and its housing capacity, by sex, and was likely to receive either a man or a woman, according to availability. In filling such shortages, Air

[3] AAF WAC Hist, p. 33ff.

[4] (1) WD Cir 226, 22 Sep 43. Directed by D/F, G-1 to TAG through CofS, 13 Sep 43. WDGAP 220.3, in CofS 291.9 WAAC. Rescinds AG Memo W635-3-43, 31 Mar 43. (2) Memo, MPD ASF for TAG, 14 Oct 43. SPWA 320.2 sec 6.

Forces headquarters was no longer obliged to compute WAC requirements and place a requisition. Instead, The Adjutant General merely reported each week the numbers and skills of WAC graduates to which the AAF's percentage entitled it, and these were ordered at once to the station having the most immediate need and the necessary housing. There was almost no WAC skill so unusual that the woman could not be utilized somewhere among the thousands of military jobs thus opened to Wacs. There was also no longer any tendency for a station to think of Wacs as an additional allotment, since it clearly had only one military quota.

One major discrepancy in this integration system was the failure to allot grades for WAC overhead. While the size of a men's unit might be somewhat reduced by the arrival of Wacs, it still required a first sergeant, a supply sergeant, a company clerk, and other key cadre members. Part of the WAC cadre thus did not replace men and constituted an extra administrative load on the station.

Major Bandel's plan had included a provision for increasing each station's allotment by an allotment of WAC grades for cadre only; instead, the War Department went further and abolished all WAC grades. Stations were thus forced to make up an allotment for the cadre of the new unit by somehow withdrawing grades from other allotted activities. This was usually possible in the lower grades, but there was seldom a spare first sergeant's rating or a captaincy at any station, while other cadre members were more or less at the mercy of chance for their grades. Such a system not only lowered morale, but made it impossible to keep competent women in cadre jobs or as company officers.

Major Bandel repeatedly tried to secure the recognition of WAC administration as a duty that required an allotment, but without success. The Air Forces was able to solve a part of the difficulty by authorizing the promotion of WAC first sergeants to the grade warranted by their job regardless of station strength allotments, and their retention thereafter as authorized overstrength. No such solution for company officers was ever achieved.[5]

There was only one other flaw in this system: the fact that men's unit commanders were accustomed to command all assigned personnel, and frequently attempted to usurp the normal powers of the WAC company commander in such matters as discipline, uniform regulations, and hours of bed check. Such usurpation, where it occurred, invariably reduced unit discipline to a farce, divided the WAC company into quarreling factions under different rules and regulations, and resulted in insubordination to the WAC commander. The AAF solved this problem without difficulty by spelling out in its regulations the fact that all normal command powers were reserved to the gradeless WAC unit. Actions in which both office chief and company commander were interested could be originated by either and co-ordinated with the other. Discipline was reserved to the WAC commander, either on her own initiative or upon receipt of a report from the section chief.

One other difficulty, a psychological one, at times prevented full application of the system. The intention of the directive was that military personnel, like civilian, receive the grade allotted to the job each

---

[5] AAF WAC Hist. Also D/F, G–1 for Dir WAC, 31 Aug 43. WDGAP 320.2 WAC, in SPWA 320.2 (7–23–43).

was filling. Actually, at almost all Army stations, there appeared to exist a deep-rooted idea that there should be a "women's share," which should be equal to the "men's share"; that women should in fairness have the same percent of each grade that men held. In practice this caused widespread inequities, since all women sent to a station might be so unskilled that they merited no ratings, or they might all be so skilled that all merited ratings.

In checking on the application of the directive, the Air Forces found male office helpers promoted above the Wac who ran the office, and WAC cooks refused the rating that male cooks received, all on the grounds that the "women's share" was held by stenographers in headquarters. Another Air Forces directive promptly made it clear that the grade went with the job, regardless of the sex of the occupant. Elsewhere the idea of a share appeared too well fixed to suppress; even such a WAC authority as General White, on a visit to North Africa, directed that the theater provide "the same ratio of grades for WAC personnel as is provided for male." [6]

The Army Service Forces and the Army Ground Forces, for this reason, never chose to follow the Air Forces' system, but divided military grades into male and female, and maintained separate allotments for the WAC unit. The motive was frankly stated as a fear that women, if not limited, would eventually collect more than their "share" of grades, since they usually filled skilled jobs and were more permanent employees. As a matter of fact, in application the result was exactly the opposite: Wacs were fairly latecomers in the Army, and many commands were already so overstrength on rated men that promotions were frozen; thus the Air Forces Wacs

fared no better than male latecomers, while the Service and Ground Forces Wacs had a reserved quota and were promoted even though men inducted at the same time could not be. The well-integrated Air Wacs were shortly outstripped in ratings by the segregated ASF and AGF Wacs, and complained frequently at the loss of "our grades." [7]

The Office of the Director WAC

Second of the integration problems to be resolved was that of the reduction of WAAC Headquarters to form the new and smaller Office of the Director WAC, which had advisory duties but no operating functions. Only about 25 officers and 20 civilians were allotted the new Office of the Director; the remaining 75 officers and 46 civilians were scattered among the various Army Service Forces offices which now handled all operations. [8] With them went the files of their sections. All individual 201 files were sent to The Adjutant General, who was thereafter responsible for cases concerning individuals: initial assignment, transfers, promotions, filling of requisitions, classification, discipline, and discharge, as well as for answering inquiries from the public concerning the status of individuals. With this responsibility The Adjutant General received Capt. Clara G. Han and her assistants, who had been managing classification and assignment in the WAAC.

As for policy decisions concerning any

---

[6] D/F, G–1 for TAG, 18 Oct 43. WDGAP 320.2 WAC (9–10–43), in WDCSA 291.9.

[7] See details in chapters on services concerned.

[8] M/R, 15 Feb 44, Justification for Civilian Positions for FY 1945. WAC files.

of these personnel actions, the responsibility went to General Dalton's office, Military Personnel Division, ASF, with Maj. Florence Jepson to assist. Full authority over training policy as well as operation went to Military Training Division, Army Service Forces, accompanied by Maj. Elizabeth Smith. General Faith's Training Command was disbanded, and training centers were given to the service commands for administration, becoming Class I installations.[9] Similarly, recruiting, housing, supply, overseas selection, and other functions were all transferred.[10]

Such removal of operating functions was in general enthusiastically received by the WAC staff, since it was the same action that they had recommended a year before and that had then been impossible in an auxiliary status. In the first burst of enthusiasm for decentralization, the staff ruthlessly swept out of the office every discernible operating duty, and forwarded public inquiries and field requests unanswered to other offices.

In only two cases did the Director attempt to retain some supervision. She first asked that training centers be made Class IV installations, not under the service command for training doctrine and assignments, but this was refused by the Army Service Forces.[11] She also asked that she retain the power of final approval over the moral character of women officers selected by Army commanders for overseas shipment; this was also objectionable to the Director of Personnel, ASF, and was rejected by the War Department.[12]

The vague relationship of the Office of the Director WAC to the operating agencies was a source of confusion which Director Hobby in November requested the Army Service Forces to remove by publishing a circular defining responsibility. While she was permitted to recommend policy on all WAC matters, the other offices had always been finally responsible for policy, and there was no requirement that any co-ordination take place. The Director therefore asked that ASF divisions be charged with the responsibility of keeping her office fully informed of WAC matters and of WAC policy originated by them. This request was rejected by Brig. Gen. Clinton F. Robinson of the Army Service Forces' Control Division, on the

---

[9] (1) Routing Slip, Asst Exec WAAC to Chief, Operating Div, 26 Jul 43. SPWA 311.23 (1943). (2) Speech, Maj Jepson, Stf Dirs Conf, New York, 1–3 Dec 43. SPWA 337 (11–10–43). (3) AGO Ltr 320.2 WAC (10–7–43) PR–W–SPMOU, 31 Oct 43, incl WAC Tng Comd, effective 31 Oct 43. (4) Memo, O Dir WAC for MTD ASF, 19 Nov 43, SPWA 210.63 (11–19–43). (5) ASF Cir 110, 4 Nov 43.

[10] WAAC Supply, Housing, and Mobilization Sections to Mobilization Division, ASF; Control Division, Historical Section to Control Division, ASF; WAAC Office of Technical Information to Office of Technical Information ASF (later WD Bureau of Public Relations); WAAC Special Services to Special Services Division, ASF; WAAC Training Division to Military Training Division, ASF; Policy Functions of WAAC Personal Branch to Military Training Division, ASF; Classification, Assignment, Testing, Reassignment to AGO Classification and Assignment Branch; Recruiting to AGO Appointment and Induction Branch; Discharge, etc., of enlisted women to AGO Enlisted Branch; Discharge, etc., of officers to AGO Officers Branch. (1) ASF Adm Memo S–64, 14 Oct 43; (2) Drafts of same, Aug 43; (3) Memo, TAG for Dir Pers ASF, 5 Nov 43. SPWA 314.7 (1–7–43)(1) sec 4.

[11] (1) Memo, WAAC Hq for DCofS ASF, 17 May 43. SPWA 353 E; (2) Memo, Dir Tng ASF for DCofS for SvCs ASF, 21 May 43, 1st Ind, 22 May, DCofS ASF, 2d Ind, 27 May, MPD, 3d Ind, 1 Jun, Dir WAAC. WAAC Training Centers were made Class II installations by ASF Memo S210–14–43, 10 Jun 43, under the control of CG ASF and the technical supervision of the Director WAAC. ASF file, SPAP WAC (5–17–43).

[12] (1) AGO Memo W635–11–43, 8 Jul 43; (2) Memo, WAC Hq for G–1, 17 Sep 43; (3) Memo, TAG for Dir Pers ASF, 7 Sep 43. SPWA 320.2 (7–5–43) sec 1.

grounds that ASF divisions would ordinarily give the Director information about WAC matters of special importance without being directed to do so.[13]

The success of the several shifts in responsibility was therefore variable depending upon the degree of voluntary co-ordination between the offices concerned. The Adjutant General's Office was highly successful in removing a tremendous load of routine operations from the Director's Office, such as the receiving of availability reports and the issuing of assignment orders.

On the other hand, Military Training Division habitually took unilateral action in training matters, publishing training courses and circulars that had never been seen by the Director. Training center commandants complained of a perpetual conflict between training directives and other portions of the WAC program, such as recruiting. In a few cases the transfer resulted in total obliteration of a phase of the WAC program; work on the WAC history was stopped by General Robinson of ASF Control Division, who relegated the previous excellent WAAC collection to the files, disapproved collection of further material, and asigned the former WAAC Historian, Lt. Virginia Smithson, to a clerk's job.[14]

Several divisions, although assuming responsibility for part of the WAC program, did not accept assignment of a WAC officer or other specialist to help perform it. The Morale Services Division, for example, took the all-important responsibility for orienting soldier opinion, and its director, Maj. Gen. Frederick H. Osborn, after personal conference with Colonel Hobby, agreed to accept assignment of a WAC officer; but in spite of efforts of

Colonel Hobby's staff to remind him, no such assignment was made during the six months in which the WAC remained in the ASF. Similarly Brig. Gen. Joseph W. Byron of Special Services Division informed the Director that he intended to accept assignment of a WAC officer, but no assignment was accepted during this period.

Such reluctance appeared generally to be due to doubts concerning the propriety of employing a specialist for such a small group as the WAC, and to the belief that the regular staff could care for the additional responsibilities. However, within a few months it was apparent that little action was being taken on WAC problems in offices that did not have a WAC specialist. Her staff informed the Director, "There are certain operating divisions, ASF, which seem not to be fully aware that responsibility has fallen to them for matters concerning WAC personnel."[15]

The Director attempted to overcome such omissions by including, in her new office, a WAC liaison officer for each major ASF division. This system also did not work very well. Liaison officers noted that, even when a division was extremely co-operative in taking any action suggested by the Director's Office, it was inappropriate for their responsibilities to en-

[13] Memo, Dir WAC for CG ASF, 5 Nov 43, sub: ASF Cir, and 1st Ind, 13 Nov 43. SPWA 314.7 (1–7–43)(1) sec 4.

[14] (1) Speech, Maj George Martin, Chief, Contl Div WAAC. Min, Stf Dirs Conf, Chicago, 15–17 Jun 43, SPWA 337 (6–1–43). (2) Memo, Maj Anne Alinder for Exec WAC, 10 Sep 43. SPWA 314.7 (1–7–43)(1) sec 4. (3) Interv with Capt Virginia Smithson, Hist Div, AAF Hq, Dec 45. (See Bibliographical Note.)

[15] Memo, Well-Being Officer for Dir WAC, 20 Dec 43, with atchd drafts and buck slips. SPWA–W.

listed women to be constantly called to the divisions' attention by the Office of the Director, and also inefficient in view of the "complexity of the organization. . . . and the impracticability of one liaison officer from this office being aware of all the functions or activities of the many branches and sections of each division." The WAC liaison officer noted that, in order to get Wacs included in these divisions' activities, she was forced to undertake "action more in the nature of operations than advisory." [16]

In addition, such outside interference was not always popular. The Navy noted, concerning an identical situation, that so long as the WAVES liaison officer's assignment, or even her desk, was in the Director's office, other divisions tended to regard her as "a sort of polite espionage service," and that the only workable system was the location of a specialist in the division office itself.[17]

Especial deterioration was noted in the handling of public relations, never well co-ordinated. WAAC Headquarters' small Office of Technical Information was transferred to the ASF Office of Technical Information, and subsequently to the War Department Bureau of Public Relations, where material concerning Wacs was handled, with even less co-ordination than had prevailed before, by the respective assistant directors of the bureau for ASF, AGF, and AAF. In the Army Service Forces' opinion, the "overall WAC public relations job" would now have to be performed by the service commands.[18] Although General Somervell took steps to call this problem to their attention, there resulted during this six months a series of unfortunate releases which did little to assist the current recruiting drive.[19]

Even at best, considerable confusion

prevailed during the period of transfer of operating functions, and there were unavoidable lapses in continuity of operation. Files of the various transferred offices were shipped off bodily to offices in which they could not later be located, and other documents were destroyed for lack of space to house them. Continual office moves, an old Pentagon custom, added to the commotion. After two moves and one consolidation in the preceding twelve months, the office moved again in November of 1943 from the second floor of the Pentagon to the third; two months after this it was moved back to the second floor.[20]

General Impression of Director's Status

There was general failure on the part of Army and WAC personnel in the field to understand the Director's new status, and total failure on the part of the public. Few could grasp the fact that she no longer had any command power over individual women; fewer still realized that she was no longer consulted about every WAC directive nor informed of the policy in every matter. As a result, the Office of the Director constantly received many inappropriate requests, inquiries, and demands for corrective action. Service commands still telephoned the Director's Office with complaints, such as the failure of Army depots to distribute WAC Regulations on time. Others wrote her about matters under their own command, such as at what hour Wacs should go to bed and whether dating

[16] *Ibid.*
[17] WAVES Hist.
[18] Memo, CG ASF for DCofS for SvCs ASF, 18 Dec 43. SPWA 014.13 E.
[19] See Ch. XXXIV, below.
[20] (1) Hq Memo, 23 Nov 43; (2) Memo, MDW to CG ASF, 14 Jan 44. SPWA 310.2 (10–5–42).

should be permitted in the women's unit dayrooms.[21]

Following the conversion to Army status, the Army Service Forces refused to let the Director's Office have any further reports on WAC clothing status, training, station lists, or rank; it approved reports only on WAC strength and recruiting returns. The Director's Office continued negotiations in an attempt to get more.[22]

After this time, the Director had no means of discovering the problems of field units except by such visits as her staff was able to make, or by Congressional or other complaints; hence her later knowledge of field conditions tended to be based on a sampling rather than on a complete compilation. She succeeded in having written into the forthcoming regulations a provision, resembling that of certain British services, that any WAC commander might write directly to the Director on matters of women's well-being, provided that she routed her letter through the post commander. This provision proved virtually inoperative; the Director's Office noted at the end of the war that it had almost never been used, since a company commander obviously jeopardized her own local advancement by using the privilege, and therefore ordinarily did so only in the gravest emergencies.[23]

First WAC Regulations

Among all integration problems, the hottest debate concerned the matter of the special Army Regulations, if any, to be issued for the WAC. For almost a year, since the introduction of the WAC legislation, General Somervell's office and Director Hobby's office had been at odds on this matter.

The basic issue was the matter of mini-mum safeguards for women. Director Hobby maintained that this would require a directive stating that Army enlisted women would be assigned only to units commanded by a woman officer. The ASF disagreed, pronouncing any special regulations favoritism for women. Maj. Gen. Lorenzo D. Gasser, of the War Department Manpower Board, added that Army personnel officers would be hampered in exercising their prerogatives of transfer and assignment if they could assign enlisted women only to stations where a WAC officer was located.[24]

An ASF committee, appointed before the conversion to consider the matter, informed the Director that no changes in Army Regulations would be made, since "Experience has dictated that the effect of a regulation is often resented, especially if it seems to curtail power."[25] General Dalton, ASF's Chief of Military Personnel, also informed the Director: "It is highly undesirable that policies and regulations governing the control of WAAC personnel be more restrictive than those governing officers and enlisted men."[26] Upon reconsideration, the Army Service Forces decided that one basic Army Regulation for

---

[21] (1) Speech, Maj Mary-Agnes Brown, Min, Stf Dirs Conf, New York, 1–3 Dec 43. SPWA 337 (11–10–43). (2) Ltr, 9th SvC to WAC Hq, 17 Nov 43. SPWA 353.8.

[22] (1) Memo, Dir WAC for Col Conrad G. Follansbee, MPD ASF, 26 Nov 43; 1st Ind, MPD to AGO, 29 Nov 43. SPWA 201.7. (2) Memo, Miss Lies to Exec WAC, 15 Dec 43. Copy given author by Dr. Jessie P. Rice.

[23] Remarks, Dir WAC, Conf of Overseas Theater G–1's, 15 Oct 46. WDWAC 337 A–S.

[24] Memo, CofS ASF for Chiefs of Servs, 1 Mar 43, and 3 Inds. SPWA 333.1, now in Dir Pers ASF files.

[25] Memo, 2d O Mary Vann Racey for Dir WAAC, 1 Mar 43. SPWA 300.3 (1–7–43) sec 1.

[26] Memo, MPD ASF for Dir WAAC, 26 Apr 43. SPGAE 322.5 WAAC (4–26–43) G–1, in SPWA 300.3 (1–7–43) sec 1.

the WAC would be required: that under no circumstances would women command men.[27]

Director Hobby replied that, if less than a company with its own WAC commander was used at any station, it was not economical to provide women's clothing stocks, hospital equipment, post exchange items, recreational programs, and other needs that differed from those of men. Where these were not provided, the women did not receive care equal to that normally provided by the Army for its men. The Director also asked for a written definition of her own new noncommand duties in the WAC, which should, she stated, be those of advising on women's well-being, "defined to mean conditions of employment suitable for women, which shall remain the primary concern of the Director WAC."[28]

The Director's view was several times upheld by the Chief of Staff, General Marshall. In the spring of 1943, over ASF nonconcurrence, he authorized publication of the revised WAAC Regulations (1943), which contained the desired safeguards.[29] These governed the WAAC and WAC until late October 1943, when the General Staff was able to reconcile conflicting viewpoints and produce a final version of the WAC Regulations. The circular as published was drafted by G–1 Division, over the Army Service Forces' objection, personally discussed with Colonel Hobby by General White, and revised to incorporate her suggestions. On 9 November 1943 it was published as War Department Circular 289, the WAC's first important publication, which was to last, with amendments, for over a year, and to serve as a model for all later regulations.

Covering only six pages, it pointed out which Army Regulations were applicable

unchanged, and authorized certain exceptions and special provisions. The required differences were:[30]

1. WAC units would contain only women and be commanded by WAC officers, exactly as men's units were composed of and commanded by men.

2. Wacs would not be confined in the same building with men, except a hospital.

3. WAC messes would not be combined with men's messes except with War Department approval. [General Dalton almost immediately repealed this restriction without informing the Director.]

4. Wacs would not be used in "restaurants or cafeterias in service clubs, guest houses, officers' clubs or messes." [Such assignments were ordinarily not authorized for any military personnel.]

5. WAC officers would not be promoted to the grade of colonel. [By act of Congress.]

6. Wacs would not command men unless specifically ordered to do so. [By act of Congress.]

7. Wacs would not be employed as physicians or nurses. [By act of Congress, to avoid infringing on existing organizations.]

8. WAC officers would be appointed only from officer candidate school graduates, and officer candidates would be selected only from women already in the Corps.

9. Enlistment standards would differ from men's in the age and citizenship requirements set by Congress, and in a different physical examination; venereal disease was also disqualifying, and women with dependent children were ineligible.

10. Discharge was mandatory for minors [by act of Congress]; authority was included for discharge for pregnancy.

---

[27] Memo and Inds cited n. 24.

[28] Min cited n. 14(1).

[29] *Ibid.*, incl ltrs, SvCs to Dir WAAC, May–Jun 43.

[30] (1) Contl Div Rpt. Min cited n. 14(1). (2) Memo, Dir WAAC for Sp Serv Div, Chief of Chaplains, SG, CofFin, JAG, and Contl Div ASF, 11 May 43, SPWA 300.3 (1–7–43) sec 1. (3) Memo, "MGW" (Maj Gen Miller G. White, G–1) for G–1 Enl Br, 31 Oct 43. SPWA 300.3 (1–7–43) sec II. (4) Memo, G–1 for TAG, 3 Nov 43. WDGAP 300.3 WAC, in CofS 291.9. (Rescinds Cir 226.)

In addition, Director Hobby succeeded in getting spelled out certain other requirements which were identical with requirements for men, but which were still frequently violated because of the Corps' early ambiguous status: Wacs were to fill only military jobs, could not replace civilians, would not be assigned as permanent kitchen police, and were eligible for membership on courts and boards. It was required that courts and boards hearing WAC enlisted women include at least one WAC officer, in line with the general practice of including members of an enlisted man's arm or service. It was also required that commanders using WAC troops employ WAC staff directors, part of whose duties was "continuous inspection."

Rights and Benefits of the WAC

None of the circulars published made clear the differences between the rights and benefits of enlisted women and those of enlisted men. The Comptroller General decisions, requested in July, began to arrive in late September and defined some of these. On the question "May Wacs get allowances for dependents?" the Comptroller General ruled that it was clearly the intent of Congress to grant such allowances, since an amendment to forbid dependency allowances had been defeated. This, however, resulted in "material discrimination" against Waves and nurses, for whom the Comptroller had rendered an opposite opinion. The Comptroller decided that Wacs could not get allowances for husbands but could for parents and children in certain cases.[31]

The Comptroller General also reversed a decision of the Veterans' Administration that husbands were not eligible to receive the death gratuity, and made other re-

lated decisions. In addition, other decisions were made by the Army's Judge Advocate General and the General Staff. Many of these concerned the benefits toward which WAAC service might be counted, which were in constant question by every Army station. Wherever possible the General Staff attempted to give credit for WAAC service: it was decided to count it for time-in-grade for promotion purposes, for relative rank within grades, toward accrued leave, and toward overseas theater ribbons. As for the Good Conduct Medal, The Adjutant General first ruled that WAAC service did not count toward the time required to earn it, but was overruled by the General Staff. For other questions the answer had legally to be negative, since WAAC service had not been actually military service, and could not be counted for longevity pay or other such financial benefits.[32]

Colonel Hobby requested that these decisions be compiled in a new circular entitled Rights and Benefits of the WAC, for ready reference by puzzled field stations. The War Department decided against publishing such a compilation on the grounds that this would be a special publication for women and that it would be better to insert each reference in appropriate Army Regulations as they were revised from time to time. The Army Air Forces nevertheless obtained a copy of the rejected circular, mimeographed it, and

---

[31] Memo, Gen Styer (CofS, ASF) to Dir Fiscal Div, 21 Sep 43; Decision B–36497, Comptr Gen to SW, 24 Sep 43, SPEX, in SPWA 314.7 (1–7–43)(1) sec 2.

[32] See Ch. XII. Also (1) Decision B–35441, Comptr Gen to SW, 4 Aug 43. SPWA 242.2 (6–10–43). (2) Memo, JAG for Dir WAC, 3 Jan 44. SPJGA 1943/ 19509. Published in WD Cir 24, 1944. SPWA 314.7 (1–7–43)(1) sec 2. (3) Ltr, 3589th SU, Richmond, Ky., to TAG, 4 Oct 43, and 1st Ind from TAG, SPWA 200.6. (4) Memo, Col Hobby for G–1, 29 Dec 43; atchd to WD Cir 36, 28 Jan 44. SPWA 200.6.

sent it informally to AAF staff directors for their assistance in locating answers quickly. Many of these decisions never reached other field authorities; as late as 1946 War Department separation centers were discovered refusing to credit WAAC service for various benefits toward which it was creditable.[33]

Army Advisers Depart

The job of advising on Corps well-being under its new regulations now fell to an Office of the Director consisting of twenty officers, all women. The preliminary reduction, in November, had left the office with twenty-five officers, including Colonel Catron as executive and General Faith as head of the Field Survey Branch, but in December Colonel Hobby recommended that the office be still further reduced.[34] For service with the WAAC, General Somervell secured for General Faith the award of the Distinguished Service Medal, saying "To him, in large measure, belonged the responsibility of success in the whole program of women's participation in service with the Armed Forces."[35] To replace the departing officers Colonel Hobby gave key office positions to women brought in from staff directorships in the field. Major Rice left the recruiting office to become deputy director; Maj. Mary-Agnes Brown, formerly of the Eighth Service Command, was made executive officer. In civil life Major Brown had been an attorney for the Veterans' Administration and past president of the Women's Bar Association of the District of Columbia. Maj. Katherine R. Goodwin of the First Service Command became the personnel officer. Major Goodwin's civilian experience had been as head

of business administration in the Hartford, Connecticut, public schools.

Field Needs After Integration

Army commanders simultaneously took over the task of operating the Corps under Army Regulations. One WAC authority noted:

Generals, lieutenants, and sergeants who had long been privately certain that this business of utilizing women as soldiers would be perfectly simple, if the War Department would just let them handle it, now had a chance to prove their point. They went into action with all shades and degrees of concepts, from that which held that all women, in or out of uniform, were ladies who should be shielded from the rough ways of the world, to that which held that all soldiers were soldiers and should be treated alike, whether or not they were women. . . . Even for the many men who did not go to either of these extremes . . . women as soldiers were something new and different and required considerable getting used to.[36]

In spite of the inestimable advantages of Army status, field commanders faced certain disadvantages in attempting to begin operations under men's regulations, which were still largely unmodified. At Camp Gordon, Georgia, inspectors found that a WAC unit was getting all of men's T/BA equipment, including fifteen water tanks, spare gas tanks, a litter for carrying the wounded from the battlefield, and other property which it was unable to store in the space provided. Elsewhere just

---

[33] Memo, Dir WAC for TAG, 7 Oct 43; Memo, G–1 for CGASF, 4 Dec 43, WDGAP 243; SPWA 314.7 (1–7–43(1) sec 2. The informal AAF publication is in Policy Book, property of author.

[34] Memo, Dir WAC for CG ASF, 29 Dec 43. SPWA 320.2 E.

[35] Memo, Gen Somervell for WD Decorations Bd, 15 Jan 44. Personnel Abstracts, WAC files, OCMH.

[36] AAF WAC Hist, pp. 17–20.

the opposite idea prevailed, and because WAC units were gradeless, stations refused to issue them guidons, unit vehicles, or other standard equipment.

Army records and reports were now used for women and had to be modified in many cases. Officer candidates already processed and at the head of the waiting list had to be reprocessed under Army Regulations and take the test used for men, as well as appear before Army boards which sometimes differed considerably in judgment from the previous all-Waac boards. Commands were embarrassed when they tried women by court-martial and sentenced them to confinement without first providing a place of confinement. Stations and training centers that had previously weeded out prostitutes and other undesirables found that Army Regulations gave them no authority to discharge military personnel for prostitution.[37]

A major, if temporary, complaint was that no uniformity of personnel action was thenceforth possible for the "Corps"—now a corps in name only. Promotion was in the Army channel, and therefore could not be consistent from one command to another; junior officers were promoted before senior, women in less important jobs before those in more responsible, according to varying command and station policies and opportunities. Discipline was also a command matter, and major offenders went unpunished in some commands while minor matters in others were dealt with severely. Policies on dress, leaves, restrictions, and such matters varied. Training of various sorts, including physical training, was required by some stations and not by others.

Similarly, Corps-wide personnel programs were made impossible, including

rotation of training center officers to the field, relief of recruiters, or systematic advancement of company officers. The difficulty was intensified in that, while most Army commands had thousands of male personnel and could effect normal rotation among them, the average command had only a handful of WAC units and perhaps one staff job of field grade.

Another new difficulty was the lack of information. At Fort Moultrie inspectors noted, "Complaint was made that few notices of any nature were reaching the detachment from Headquarters Fourth Service Command"; at Camp Gordon, "The WAC Commanding Officer felt a need for more information about her job." It would obviously hereafter be more difficult to get WAC matters down to company level through the more complicated Army echelons than through the shorter WAAC channels.

To solve such new problems, there was noted a general tendency for the field to request directives from Washington to solve field problems and set Corps-wide policies. At a staff directors' meeting in December 1943, representatives asked the Director for a standard operating procedure to secure uniform punishments for women in various commands, adequate physical training, proper officers' quarters, and other items. Violations of uniform regulations by female personnel were in particular looked upon as a matter that some WAC authority should correct. Many asked to be allowed to assign worthless personnel to some sort of central WAC

---

[37] (1) Memo, WAC Hq for MPD ASF, 15 Sep 43, with atchd file. SPWA 315 (1943,) (2) WD Cir 240, 4 Oct 43, sec IV. (3) Memo, Dir WAC for G–1, 1 Jan 44. SPWA 424.2, 1942. (4) Folder Rpts of Stf Visits, esp rpts 24–29 Nov 1943. WAC Plng Serv files. (5) Ltr, WAC Stf Dir AAF WFTC to Exec WAC, 20 Nov 43. SPWA 320.2. (6) Min cited n. 21(1).

pool for disposition, as it proved extremely difficult to get male personnel to discipline and reclassify women. The difficulty of lack of uniformity was especially acute at places like Fort Riley, which had three sets of regulations for the three WAC units assigned respectively to the cavalry school, the replacement training center, and the post headquarters.[38]

Such difficulties, while very real, presented a peculiar problem in view of Colonel Hobby's determination to integrate the WAC in the Army. She repeatedly rejected any proposal which, she said, "tends to give the impression that the WAC is something apart from the Army."[39] Thus, while she marked for correction certain legitimate needs for new policies or amplified regulations, in general she replied to such requests that they were matters of command. The lack of uniformity of action among Army commands, although especially conspicuous among the WAC minority, was not a WAC problem but an Army one, concerning men as well as women, and inherent in the system of command responsibility.

Close of 1943

At the end of 1943, Wacs at a staff directors' conference pointed with pride to the WAC's progress since the previous December. Then, ten staff directors had attended the meeting; in 1943, fifty-three were present. Then the WAAC had boasted only two post headquarters companies plus the Aircraft Warning Service in the field; now

it had more than 260 companies. More Wacs were presently in each of two foreign theaters than had a year before been in the whole field. Then the headquarters and training centers had been run chiefly by men; now, they were run chiefly by women. Then, the training center had been the WAC world; now, it had receded to relative insignificance. Then, only service commands had employed Wacs; now all commands did. Wacs had been taken into the Army and had generally done away with separate grades, T/O's, and channels.[40]

The first of January 1944 found the WAC with a reported membership of 62,859 as against 20,943 a year before. Losses of the conversion period had almost been regained, several months before this had been believed possible. "We are very much encouraged," Colonel Hobby said. The Director added:

It is quite a consolation and encouragement to compare the difference in the questions and problems that arose at this Staff Conference with the ones that arose about a year ago and the ones that arose six months ago—partially a tribute to your indoctrination and understanding, and partially a tribute to the Army for the very fine and splendid assistance it has given the WAC, now one of its components.[41]

[38] Min cited n. 21(1).
[39] Memo, Dir WAC for CG ASF, 27 Oct 44, sub: Dr. Durfee's Tng MS on Leadership. WDWAC 353.
[40] Opening speech by Air WAC Off, Maj Bandel. Min cited n. 21(1).
[41] (1) WDBPR Press Release, 6 Jan 44. WAC Planning files. Strength reported at time. (2) Rpt, Machine Recs Div, AGO, 4 Mar 44. WDWAC 320.2 sec 4b. For adjusted total of 61,355 for WAC strength in January 1944, see Table 1, Appendix A.

CHAPTER XV

Removal of Director's Office to G-1 Division

There remained one step to be taken in the evolution of the WAC organization. This was the removal of the Office of the Director from the Army Service Forces to the General Staff level. During January and February of 1944, a number of contributing causes led directly to this move, the last in the series by which the Corps was fully integrated into the normal command channels of the Army.

There had for some time been general agreement within the War Department that the past two years' method of handling Corps' problems was unsatisfactory, and that some sort of remedial action was called for, with more high-level attention to its problems than the Corps had yet received. A prominent civilian special assistant, who was called upon by the Army Service Forces to diagnose the situation during the conversion crisis, bluntly informed it that its headquarters had in fact killed the WAAC with its left hand while publicly sponsoring it with its right. He wrote:

The situation with respect to the WAC is such that I believe immediate action is necessary, and that such action must be of rather far-reaching nature. Does the Army really want the WAC to succeed? I am not at all convinced that the answer to this question is "yes." . . . I have seen no real evidence of such a desire. . . . Are civilians really convinced that the WAC is an important organization? Civilians will be convinced of this only when the Army is convinced of it. . . . It should not be necessary to review arguments why the WAC must succeed. The Army started this program, and it is obviously a good idea to be associated with successful programs.[1]

A similar view had been voiced by Colonel Catron, after ten months of assignment to WAAC Headquarters. Later, "acting on my own initiative, but with the knowledge of Director Hobby," he had bypassed his former associates in the Army Service Forces to inform the General Staff directly, "In my opinion, the situation calls for . . . the military authorities to recognize an obligation to the WAAC, to the Army, and to the women of the country, to help make the WAC a go."[2]

G-3 Recommendation

At the time of the conversion, the Deputy Chief of Staff, General McNarney, therefore directed the General Staff to recommend a new location for the Director's Office. After analysis, G-3 Division

[1] Memo, "W.C.M." (Wilbur C. Munnecke, Vice Pres. of Univ. of Chicago, and wartime sp asst, ASF) for Gen Dalton, Dir Mil Pers ASF, 10 Aug 43. SPAP 341 WAAC (2-26-43).
[2] Memo, Exec WAAC for G-1, 20 Jul 43. SPWA 314.7 sec 3.

reported that the location in the Army Service Forces was not suitable. Although the Director WAC was a special adviser to the Chief of Staff, and was responsible for advice concerning Air, Ground, and Service Forces, she was currently obliged to submit all papers to or through the Army Service Forces. The G–3 planners noted: "This form of organization is not entirely satisfactory, as the scope of WAC matters is Army-wide and determination of all basic policies should properly be made at the War Department level."[3]

G–3 Division therefore recommended that the office be placed under G–1 Division of the General Staff, comparable in place to the Military Intelligence Division under G–2, or else, and preferably, be made an independent Special Staff division, like Civil Affairs Division. The Special Staff location, although it was never to be adopted, was always the one recommended by organizational experts. G–3 Division pointed out that the Director's responsibilities were not limited to G–1 matters and that the Special Staff location "will expedite direct consultation with appropriate divisions of the General Staff."[4]

Director Hobby concurred in either move, but General Somervell nonconcurred and presented a counterplan that would keep the Office of the Director under his jurisdiction. He proposed that it be attached to his own office, and not be placed under any subordinate office such as that of General Grunert or of General Dalton. He agreed also that the Director would be allowed to consult directly with Air and Ground Forces on matters that did not concern the Service Forces.[5]

General Somervell's plan prevailed; at the time of the conversion, General McNarney verbally advised Colonel Hobby

to try the plan for several months and see if it would work. As a matter of fact, it was to be exactly six months before all concerned were convinced that the plan would not work.

Handicaps on ASF Level

During the early weeks of 1944, General Marshall called to his office General White and other officers to express his dissatisfaction with the situation, particularly as it affected recruiting.

Among issues leading toward a move from the ASF level, the major one was that of supply. In the midst of debate over the Austin-Wadsworth bill, members of Congress began publicly to criticize the WAC uniform. Criticism from Army stations, particularly air bases, was equally severe. Very little honest defense against the criticisms was possible. In spite of the easing of the supply problem, which had presumably resulted from the collapse of expansion plans eight months before, the situation remained approximately where it had been at that time.

Severe shortages still existed on field stations; recruits in training centers still did not receive complete clothing issue, and still suffered high sick rates; and the appearance of the uniform had not been improved in any respect. Since the Army Service Forces had now been responsible for the WAC uniform for almost two years, it did not appear that either inexperience or rapid build-up could any longer be offered in explanation. However, eight separate proposals for improving the situation—made by the Army Air Forces, by

---

[3] Memo, G–3 for DCofS, 17 Aug 43. WDGCT 322 WAC (8–17–43), in CofS 291.9.

[4] *Ibid.*

[5] See pencil notation, *Ibid.*

The Quartermaster General, and by the Director—were all disapproved by Requirements Division, ASF, by the end of February of 1944, without any workable counterproposals. The last two proposals were addressed to the General Staff by authority of Circular 289, as a matter of the well-being of women in all major commands, but were disapproved by the Army Service Forces and turned back without reaching the General Staff.[6]

In the matter of public relations, a rapid deterioration had been noted after the Army Service Forces took over operating duties at the conversion. None of the Director's suggestions made at the time of the slander campaign were accepted, and in the first weeks of 1944, a series of publicity releases were so poor as to come to the attention of the Chief of Staff himself. General Marshall in January sent a stiff note to the Bureau of Public Relations: "It seems to me that very poor use is made of the best publicity possibilities in the WAC organization. . . . Who is handling this business?"[7]

As for soldier opinion, the Director had been unable, as late as February 1944, to secure the assignment of specialists to either ASF Morale Services or Special Services Divisions, to work on the improvement of soldier opinion or WAC morale.

Similarly, in November of 1943 General Marshall had directed that, in order to improve the supply and health situation at Fort Oglethorpe, a ranking WAC officer be made commandant. Although the Director twice reminded General Somervell's office of this directive, no action had been taken by late February.[8]

Also in November, General Marshall directed that some WAC officers now be made lieutenant colonels, to fill position vacancies that had existed for eighteen months. However, Air Forces proposals to this effect were subsequently refused by the Army Service Forces upon General Somervell's personal written advice. In a seperate study, General Somervell instead recommended giving direct commissions in this rank to socially prominent civilian women. It was this action that led the Assistant Chief of Air Staff to appear personally in the War Department seeking the removal of the Director's Office from General Somervell's jurisdiction.[9]

A particular cause of interservice friction was the handling of papers on WAC matters, which received Army Service Forces comment in cases that, had they involved men, would not have been handled by the ASF at all. For a time it had been hoped that the objections of the Air and Ground Forces, and of overseas theaters, could be met by the new status of the Director's Office as a part of General Somervell's own office, with authorization for direct communication with the Air and Ground Forces and the General Staff on matters that did not concern the Service Forces. Unfortunately, it soon developed that in actual operating practice there was little difference in the office's former position, since it became General Somervell's custom to route all outgoing WAC papers through the office's former superior, Gen-

[6] See Ch. XXVI, for details.

[7] Memo, "G.C.M." for WAC Recruiting Section, WDBPR (nonexistent section), 26 Jan 44. OCS 324.5 WAC.

[8] Memo, Dir WAC for DCofS ASF for SvCs, 26 Feb 44, with pencil notations. SPWA 210.31 (2–2–44).

[9] Entire discussion from: (1) Memo, Dir WAC for G–1, 27 Nov 43. SPWA 210.2, in SPAP 210.2 WAC. (2) Memo cited n. 8. (3) Entire file on controversy is also in CofS 324.5 WAC, and in SPWA 210.2 WAC Promotions, 1943. (4) Ltr, TAG to AAF, 18 Nov 43. 210.2 WAC (11–16–43) PR–W–WDGAP, in SPWA 210.2.

eral Dalton, as well as through other ASF divisions. Disapprovals of policy recommendations by General Dalton or by Requirements Division, ASF, excited increasingly unfavorable comment from other commands in matters which concerned them solely, or would not normally have received Army Service Forces' comment.[10]

Move to General Staff Authorized

In February of 1944, as a result of these complaints, Director Hobby went personally to General Somervell to ask clarification of her office's status. He asked her to present the problem in writing, which she did, attaching as corpus delicti some three defunct policy papers which she had addressed, supposedly directly, to the General Staff, all of which had been disapproved upon General Dalton's recommendation. All three concerned policies that were Army-wide, and one was solely an Air Forces proposal.[11]

Upon receipt of the Director's protest, General Somervell immediately recommended in writing to General Marshall that the Office of the Director be moved from his jurisdiction to that of the General Staff. General Somervell stated, "The office of the Director WAC is concerned primarily with matters affecting policy for the WAC which are applicable on an Army-wide basis in three major commands."[12] When later acquainted with his action, Colonel Hobby stated that, if allowed to comment, she would have expressed ready concurrence.[13]

As a result, General Marshall called Director Hobby in for a conference and directed that the Office of the Director be moved to G–1 Division, War Department General Staff, effective 1 March 1944.[14] Because of the small size of G–1 Division,

the Director's Office again had to be reduced in size, this time to the Director and four—later only two—other officers, including Major Rice as Deputy.

The Meek Report

The move was still in process, with office furniture not yet installed, when General Somervell's office received a lengthy written report, which it forwarded to General Marshall. The report was in the nature of a sweeping criticism of the conduct of the WAC program to date, alleging that Director Hobby and her advertising advisers had overlooked many obvious means of improving recruitment, had failed to improve the WAC uniform, and had allowed the WAC to fall far below the WAVES in public esteem. This study came to be called the Meek Report after its author, Mr. Samuel W. Meek, a member of the advertising agency of J. Walter Thompson, a competitor of the firm that handled official WAC advertising, Young & Rubicam.[15]

The Meek Report alleged, among other things, that the public was not aware of the urgency of the Army's need for Wacs;

---

[10] Specific examples in following text.

[11] Memo, Dir WAC for CG ASF, 5 Feb 44, sub: Functions of Dir WAC, with atchd papers. SPWA 314.7, Hobby files.

[12] (1) Memo, CG ASF for CofS, 9 Feb 44. Styer Files, Drawer 2197, DRB AGO. (2) Incl to Memo, Dir WAC for CofS, 21 Mar 44, sub: Comment on Public Opinion Concerning WAC, Tabs A to J atchd. WDGAP 341 (1944). (3) Min, Gen Council, 21 and 28 Feb 44.

[13] According to statement of Deputy Director to author.

[14] Memo, G–1 for CofS, 14 Feb 44. Approved by CofS, 19 Feb 44. WDGAP 320 WAC, in CofS 324.5.

[15] Manila Folder with 45 pages of surveys and statistics with atchd note, "HJK" to Gen Somervell, 21 Mar 44, and pencil notation: "Not to be use [sic] without my personal OK. BS." Somervell Files, Hq ASF, A46–257, DRB AGO.

that the WAC did not have the public standing of the WAVES; that three out of four women said they would choose the WAVES in preference to the WAC; that the public thought Waves got better treatment, more suitable jobs, more attractive uniforms; and that the WAVES had commissioned more outstanding women educators, whereas the WAC had not offered direct commissions to prominent women. Mr. Meek recommended that publicity tie-ins with high-ranking officers be used, that more prominent women be directly commissioned, and that society news pages then publicize the backgrounds of these new WAC leaders.

General Marshall called Director Hobby to his office on 15 March 1944 and, over Mr. Meek's objections, handed her the surveys and directed her to study these charges and prepare recommendations. This she did, first in a preliminary report and then in a confidential staff study which, because of its outcome, was to rank as perhaps the most important WAC policy paper of the Corps' career.[16]

The charges in the Meek Report proved, in themselves, unfounded and easy to counter. The only new survey of "public" opinion for which it contained documented statistics proved to consist chiefly of interviews with 111 college girls, 94 of them from Vassar, and with several prominent women, including women's magazine editors.[17] By contrast, the Young & Rubicam campaign had been based on a confidential Gallup survey of a scientifically chosen national sample of 1431 eligible women and 1415 parents of eligibles.

The two surveys often differed. Meek stated that the public was unaware of the urgency of the Army's need for Wacs; Gallup found that a record 85 percent said they were aware of it, and when

asked "Which women's service is in the greatest need of more women?" 58 percent said the WAC, only 14 percent the WAVES. The WAC advertising under Young & Rubicam thus appeared to have been more effective than was alleged. Meek stated that the public liked the WAVES better than the WAC, and that 66 percent of eligible women said they would choose the WAVES as against 20 percent the WAC; Gallup's non-Vassar eligibles answered: War work—51 percent, WAC—12 percent, WAVES—10 percent. The only statement which no one disputed was that about the uniform, for Gallup had always reported that only a few women preferred the WAC uniform.

Director Hobby was also able to prove that the WAC had, some months before, taken every action recommended by Mr. Meek except direct commissions and short-term enlistments: it had used publicity from every prominent person named, offered station assignment, used society pages, publicized overseas assignment as far as surveys showed desirable, obtained two Gallup and two scientific Army opinion surveys, mailed literature to parents, and so on. None of these steps had ended the Corps' problems or come near its basic difficulties.

---

[16] (1) Preliminary Rpt, Dir WAC for CofS, 16 Mar 44, sub: WAC Rctg. WDWAC 341, in CofS 324.5 WAC. (2) Memo cited n. 12(2).

[17] Following sources were listed in Meek Report: (1) 20 interviews with prominent persons, including ranking officers in the WAVES and Women Marines. (2) Unidentified surveys made by American Institute of Public Opinion and *Fortune* Magazine, Feb–Oct 43; statistics, dates, and scope not given. (3) Some 1,208 persons (473 young women, 377 young men, 358 parents) "interviewed in a national survey" in November 1943; surveying agency or method of selection not given. (4) Questionnaire to 240 staff members of *McCalls, Time,* and *Reader's Digest* and "advertising personnel." (5) "College Survey" of 94 students of Vassar and 17 from Sarah Lawrence.

In countering the various charges, it proved easily possible to discuss those of the Director's previous recommendations that the Army Service Forces had disapproved. The Director, perceiving this opening, at once drove straight through with two memoranda and ten appendixes.[18] These consisted of important parts of her own program, previously suppressed by the Army Service Forces, for improving the WAC's situation. This was the first opportunity to bring most of these proposals to the attention of the Chief of Staff.

When the Chief of Staff's final verdict was rendered, more of the Director's proposals concerning major issues had been approved in two weeks than had previously been done in the past two years in the Army Service Forces. The proposals were concerned chiefly with soldier attitude, public relations, and the uniform.

Corrective Action by the Chief of Staff

The first two issues, soldier opinion and public attitude, Colonel Hobby unhesitatingly named as the basic difficulty of the WAC program. Dismissing all lesser theories, which attributed recruiting difficulties to ignorance, WAVES prestige, the uniform, the failure to grant direct commissions, poor jobs, the desire for shorter enlistments, and other petty causes, she said flatly, "The two greatest deterrents to WAC recruiting are the attitude of soldiers toward women in the military service and the apathy of unmarried non-working women."[19]

General Marshall saw for the first time some of the slander campaign material, including literature which soldiers had mimeographed and circulated to almost every Army installation at home and abroad.[20] He saw a sample of the many letters, with which the WAC files were now bulging, from Wacs and eligible women.[21] He also saw cartoons from soldier publications all over the nation.[22] The most unexpected exhibits were certain anti-WAC statements made by high-ranking Army officers, all except one of whom were combat officers without experience in WAC employment. These Colonel Hobby revealed by name only after being twice expressly commanded to do so.[23] One general remarked, in a national magazine, "Fortunately I've no experience with that particular species [Wacs] and what's more I don't want any of them around here."[24] The Director commented, "The attitude of the officers and enlisted men in the field will never change to the degree desired as long as key personnel, whose expressions can be assumed to reflect the War Department attitude, make statements such as these."[25]

To remedy the Army attitude, Colonel Hobby proposed a campaign of re-education similar to that which General Bowley had proposed twenty years before. She asked that the Army attempt to change the soldiers' attitude by including material on the Corps' usefulness in the Army orientation course, by which other soldier attitudes were successfully influenced. She asked that available films on the WAC be shown in this course, and a new film

---

[18] Memo cited n. 12(2). Each Tab was a separate signed memorandum so that recommendations could be acted upon separately.

[19] Rpt cited n. 16(1).

[20] Memo cited n. 12(2), Exhibit I: "Characteristics, functioning, care, and preservation of the WAC, M-1 (model 1942-43)."

[21] *Ibid.*, Tab D.

[22] *Ibid.*

[23] *Ibid.*, Tab C.

[24] Maj. Gen. Lewis H. Brereton in *Liberty*, October 9, 1943.

[25] *Ibid.*

made, specifically designed to reach the soldier. She asked that a Wac officer be assigned to Morale Services, ASF, to direct the distribution and clearance of WAC news and cartoons to camp newspapers; also, that an enlisted woman be assigned to the staff of *Yank* magazine, previously unfavorable editorially. She asked that courses on the organization of the Army mention the WAC. And particularly, she asked that general officers clear with the Bureau of Public Relations before making public statements concerning the WAC.

General Marshall very soon approved much of this program. General Somervell now concurred in the orientation course material, and in the assignment to Morale Services and Special Services Divisions of a WAC officer and an enlisted woman. He protested that to require general officers to clear their remarks on the WAC was too drastic. He suggested instead that General Marshall write a letter to general officers discussing the problem, similar to the Marine Corps Commandant's letter sent out some seven months earlier concerning the treatment of Women Marines.[26] This alternative was acceptable to General Marshall, who immediately wrote not only to all generals but to all Army commanding officers, pointing out that the Army was about to launch another drive for Wacs to meet "imperative" needs, and that he expected to have the drive supported. He added:

The Women's Army Corps is now an integral part of the Army and a highly essential part of our war effort. . . . However, reports indicate that there are local commanders who have failed to provide the necessary leadership and have in fact in some instance made evident their disapproval of the Women's Army Corps. The attitude of the men has quickly reflected the leadership of

their commanders, as always.

All commanders in the military establishment are charged with the duty of seeing that the dignity and importance of the work which women are performing are recognized and that the policy of the War Department is supported by strong affirmative action.[27]

In the matter of the uniform, Colonel Hobby presented General Marshall with a list of her previous recommendations to the Army Service Forces, from August of 1942 to date. It appeared that General Somervell had not been aware until after the Meek Report was forwarded to General Marshall that the condition of the WAC uniform resulted from disapproval of the Director's proposals by various echelons of his own command. Colonel Hobby informed General Marshall that the Service Forces had already begun restudying some of her requests by direction of its commanding general.[28] General Marshall within a few weeks approved eight separate policy recommendations made by the Director and The Quartermaster General, all previously rejected by the Army Service Forces. These were shortly to work a considerable change in

---

[26] (1) Memo, CG ASF for CofS. SPAP 324.5 (3–29–44) ASF. (2) Ltr, Comdt USMC to all COs of posts and stations, 14 Aug 43, sub: Responsibility for Behavior of Men Toward Women of MCWR. "Information reaching this Headquarters indicates that in some posts and stations officers and men of the Marine Corps treat members of the Women's Reserve with disrespect. . . . In some cases, coarse or even obscene remarks are being made without restraint by male Marines in post exchanges, moving picture houses, and other places in the hearing of members of the Women's Reserve. . . . This conduct . . . indicates a laxity in discipline which will not be tolerated. Commanding officers will be held responsible to this Headquarters. . . ." [Signed] T. Holcomb.

[27] Printed Memo, CofS to all Hq divisions, overseas commanders, AGF down to tactical units, AAF, ASF, and Defense Commands down to posts, camps, and stations, 6 Apr 44. WDCSA 324.5 WAC.

[28] Memo cited n. 12(2), Tab I.

the appearance of the uniform, although many were unfortunately too late to reach the field in the one remaining year before the end of the war in Europe.

In the matter of public relations, the Director asked General Marshall to direct the formation of a co-ordinating board, which would not only initiate and direct an Army-wide constructive informational campaign, but would comment on the possible public relations effect of decisions concerning the WAC before the decisions were released. General Somervell stated, when asked to comment, that such a board was not necessary.[29] Colonel Hobby replied that General Somervell's attitude was "not in accord with fact or experience," and that "The present situation has been unfortunate and it can reasonably be expected that a continuation of uncontrolled and uncoordinated activity on the part of literally hundreds of issuing agencies will continue to be unsatisfactory. . . ."[30]

General Marshall, who had supposed that such a board already existed, overrode objections and directed General Surles of the Bureau of Public Relations to set up the co-ordinating group, saying, "I have personally taken every opportunity to support the WAC. . . . It is necessary that a central agency of the War Department be charged with the problem of keeping the public informed of matters concerning the WAC and of controlling the issuance of such information."[31]

Colonel Hobby also took this opportunity to secure the Chief of Staff's approval of several lesser projects which had previously been rejected at lower levels. One concerned equal provision for the WAC in the Army's demobilization plans, which were already being drawn up, and in which planners had made no provision for women. General Marshall approved the greater part of what she asked, which was to be of considerable importance at a later period.[32] Another proposal was for the centralization of recruiting control in the hands of specialists in The Adjutant General's Office, similar to that just approved in Public Relations. These and other recommended reforms in the Recruiting Service were all approved by General Marshall, with far-reaching later effects.[33]

The Director also concurred in one of the suggestions made in the Meek Report, the establishment of a civilian advisory committee composed of prominent women in each service command, modeled on the group that she had established in the Women's Interests Section of the Bureau of Public Relations, when she had organized that office in prewar days. This recommendation, providing for both local and national committees, was also approved. General Somervell concurred, provided that he be allowed to choose the prominent woman to head the national committee.[34]

Within a few weeks, by General Marshall's action, there were six WAC lieutenant colonels. In April, a WAC officer was also assigned as commandant of the Third WAC Training Center.[35]

In a final comment on the Meek Report, General Somervell sent the Chief of Staff another study recommending that key WAC officers be replaced by promi-

[29] Memo cited n. 26(1).

[30] Memo, Dir WAC for CofS, 4 Apr 44. WDGAP 341 (4–4–44), and in WAC Gp, WDBPR, under "Organization of the WAC Group."

[31] Memo, CofS for Gen Surles, 11 Apr 44. WAC Gp, WDBPR, and in CofS 324.5 WAC.

[32] Memo cited n. 12(2), Tab J.

[33] Memo, Dir WAC to CofS, 10 Apr 44, with CofS approval, 11 Apr 44. CofS 324.5 WAC.

[34] (1) Memo cited n. 12(2), Tab H. (2) Memo cited n. 26(1). (3) Memo, CofS for CG ASF, 11 Apr 44. CofS 324.5 WAC.

[35] Memo, ASF for TAG, 13 Mar 44. SPGAG 210.3 WAC (3–13–44)–129.

nent women to be selected by him and directly commissioned. He also stated that WAC leaders had too much control of WAC affairs, and that Colonel Hobby's current powers should be reduced by eliminating those of direct dealing with the major commands, of handling staff co-ordination on WAC matters, of taking any action, and of maintaining separate records.[36]

None of these recommendations was adopted. The Army's new policy toward the WAC, as forcibly inaugurated here by General Marshall, was keynoted by the introduction of specialist groups or specialist officers in almost every major office that handled WAC matters. The new location also ensured that Army-wide recommendations from the Office of the Director would not be rejected without consideration by the General Staff. From this time throughout General Marshall's tenure of office, specialist attention to women's welfare was to be the rule rather than the exception—with, however, the specialists concerned being fully integrated into their respective Army sections.

With the completion of the move to G-1 Division, and the accomplishment of the changes as approved by General Marshall, the Women's Army Corps completed its stage of organization and development, and entered a new phase of its career. Freed of the burden now assumed by the specialist groups, the small Office of the Director was to devote most of its time toward planning for the solution of the more intangible social and welfare problems which, although pushed into the background until now, had from the beginning attended the integration of women into military service.

The two years just ended had seen the discovery of the Corps' problems in public relations, clothing supply, administration,

and many others. The next sixteen months in G-1 Division, before the end of the war and Director Hobby's resignation, were to see workable solutions devised for all but five of the problems now on the Director's calendar.

The Corps was, by its second anniversary in May 1944, already world-wide in distribution and approaching peak strength in numbers. Corps strength in June was almost 77,000, with the peak of 100,000 not too far distant. In the United States, Wacs were present at 193 Air Forces installations, and 176 Ground Forces and Service Forces stations. Almost 10,000 women were already overseas in every major theater of operations—North Africa, Italy, England, Australia, New Guinea, India—as well as in Hawaii, Alaska, and other smaller bases.[37]

In May of 1944, the authorized strength was reallotted among the major commands:[38]

Army Service Forces	[a] 60,000
Army Air Forces	60,000
Army Ground Forces	7,500
War Department	1,050
Overseas theaters	21,450
	———
	150,000

[a] Including training centers

In these widely scattered Army commands, with their varying needs and policies, lay the further history of WAC employment, and success or failure on Army jobs.

---

[36] Memo, CG ASF, for CofS. SPAP 324.5 (3–29–44) in Dir Pers ASF files.

[37] (1) Memo, Dep Dir WAC for CofS, 21 Jul 44. WDCSA 324.5 WAC. (2) WDBPR Press Release, 17 Jun 44.

[38] D/F, G-1 for ASF, 8 May 44, WDGAP 320.2 Misc, WAC Cl files, based on Memo, Dir WAC for G-1, 17 Apr 44. For previous quotas, see: Ltr, TAG to CG ASF, 22 Oct 43. AG 320.2 WAC (11–19–43) PR–W–SPGAS.

PART TWO

WORLD-WIDE EMPLOYMENT

CHAPTER XVI

The Army Air Forces

Among the various Army commands, the Army Air Forces had been the first to employ Waacs and was now the first in field strength of WAC units. The history of the Air Forces Wacs was the story of almost one half of the Women's Army Corps—some 40,000 of the eventual 100,000 women.[1]

In spite of its enthusiasm for the use of womanpower, the Air Forces faced greater initial handicaps in employing Wacs than did other domestic commands. Subordinate air commands did not cover definite geographical areas as did service commands, but were strictly functional in nature, each having control of air bases scattered throughout the United States. Staff directors thus found the problem of supervision and supply more complex, and were obliged to take to the air to cover the distances between units assigned to their commands. The AAF's great Training Command had flying schools and technical schools from Florida to California; its Troop Carrier Command stations were less numerous but as widely separated; Air Service Command depots were scattered from coast to coast. The First, Second, Third, and Fourth Air Forces together covered the United States in their mission of forming men into combat groups for the numbered Air Forces overseas. The AAF's Materiel Command had one large WAC unit at Wright Field;

the School of Applied Tactics had an even larger unit at Orlando, Florida; and the Proving Ground Command had one isolated group at Eglin Field, Florida.

Although air bases were generally prepared to receive the women, they were caught without advance warning when the War Department ended the T/O system for the WAC some months before the Air Forces did the same for its men—a move that suited the Service Forces but left the AAF without means of accounting for the women. The new Air WAC Officer, Major Bandel, upon her arrival in 1943, found headquarters agencies shuttling the War Department directive back and forth from A–4 to A–1 and again to A–4. She noted later:

---

[1] (1) First Wacs to the field were in AWS units. While AAF WAC strength was greater in the field, ASF was greater if training centers were included. (2) The chief source of reference for this chapter is the AAF WAC Hist, by Lt. Col. Betty Bandel. (See Bibliographical Note). On the basis of 1945 reports, Colonel Bandel estimates 42,000 women as the AAF WAC top, including those in pipeline from training centers or to overseas theaters. Later AAF statistics set the actual top at about 40,000. Statistics used here do not always agree with later TAG re-evaluation of reports, but were those available to the AAF in its wartime planning. See Table 9: "WAC Asgd to AAF," and Table 13 (for 1946), in AAF Statistical Digest, World War II, prepared by Office of Statistical Control, AAF Hq. Hereafter cited as AAF Stat Digest. On file at U.S. Air Forces Historical Division, Air University, Maxwell Air Force Base, Alabama. Hereafter referred to as USAF Hist Div. See also Table 4, Appendix A.

To a headquarters wrestling with the problem of throwing thousands of fighting men and aircraft around the world, the entire WAAC program must have seemed at that moment a troublesome gnat buzzing around the head of a giant.

Promptly snaring the gnat on its return trip through A–4, the Air WAC Officer worked out a series of directives and accounting procedures which allowed the program to continue without interruption and which eventually led to full integration.

Acceptance of Wacs on Airfields

Wacs arriving on air bases ordinarily reported an enthusiastic reception. One company commander noted:

The friendly atmosphere and co-operative spirit prevalent throughout this post have made the Wacs feel that they are a definite part of the military life here. Everything is being done to further the comfort of the group.[2]

By mid-1944, Wacs became even more popular when, the supply of infantry replacements having proved insufficient, the War Department required the transfer of thousands of combat-fit men from the Air Forces to the Ground Forces. Airfields thus lost many of the specialized medical and technical personnel upon whom they had depended for normal operations, and Wacs became increasingly sought after as replacements.

Receptivity was also greatly increased by the official action of General Arnold and his staff, whose policy from the beginning was to neglect no measure that might impress upon the public the AAF's real need for Wacs and its cordiality toward them. When the Air-WAC recruiting campaign was launched in October of

1943, General Arnold issued a public statement that "members of the WAC have made an enviable record through their work at Air Force installations."[3] In November the Deputy Chief of Air Staff, Brig. Gen. William E. Hall, journeyed to Philadelphia to see the first all-Air-WAC company sworn in. In December Maj. Gen. Barney McK. Giles, the Deputy Chief of Air Staff, wrote to all Air Wacs that "it is the record you have made which has convinced the AAF of the great value of Wacs."[4] In the same month the AAF declared a national "Air WAC Week" in which airfields everywhere honored their Wacs at retreat parades and other ceremonies. Upon receipt of evidence that military personnel were involved in the slander campaign, General Arnold denounced such undercutting of his policy in an angry letter to the field.[5] With such constant and public declaration of policy, the Army Air Forces came to have the reputation in the eyes of the public and of the Wacs themselves of being friendly toward the employment of Wacs, and appreciative of their services.

The Air WAC Division

This attitude showed itself in AAF headquarters by a willingness to consider favorably the recommendations of the Air WAC Officer. A working WAC staff organization was set up which, in Lt. Col. Betty Bandel's opinion, was near-perfect under existing conditions. The Air WAC Division was granted a strength of six officers plus clerical help, and was eventually placed in the office of the Assistant

[2] WAC CO, Mather Field, Calif. AAF WAC Hist, p. 20.

[3] WDBPR Press Release, 20 Oct 43.

[4] AAF WAC Hist, pp. 62–64.

[5] Ltr, CG AAF to all Air Forces and Comds, 22 Feb 44. WDWAC 341 (3–16–44).

Chief of Air Staff for Personnel (A–1). Although in Colonel Bandel's opinion a location in the Special Staff would have insured easier co-ordination with other offices, in actual practice the policies and personal assistance of Maj. Gen. James M. Bevans and his staff in A–1 made for almost equal freedom and efficiency of operation.[6]

The generally co-operative spirit emboldened the Air WAC Division to divest itself at once of all operating powers, confining its activities to study of field conditions, formulation of policy recommendations, and co-ordination of the WAC program. It was able to take this action chiefly because each major operating division of AAF headquarters early accepted the assignment of a WAC specialist to perform the operating duties, either full-time or in addition to other duties. These offices included AAF's Military Personnel Division, both Officer Branch and Enlisted Branch; the Assistant Chief of Air Staff for Training; headquarters and regional offices of the Air Inspector; the Air Surgeon; and the Air Provost Marshal.

Together, representatives in these offices formed a good example of what was known to Wacs as the Tel-a-Wac system, reputedly faster than telephone or telegraph. The Air WAC Division was seldom left in ignorance of developments in the larger AAF program, and in return the various division chiefs, to whom the other WAC officers concerned owed primary allegiance, were seldom caught short by higher authorities concerning knowledge of WAC matters for which they were responsible. Policy papers were originated either by the Air WAC Division or by the division that discovered the need for them, and were mutually co-ordinated before publication. A headquarters regulation required all publications mentioning the WAC to be co-ordinated with the Air WAC Division. Offices were also reminded in writing that, in drafting all publications, they should remember that AAF Regulations were equally applicable to Wacs, unless specifically excepted, and that if any explanatory passages were needed they should be added.[7]

AAF "Firsts"

Under this system, a notable series of AAF "firsts" resulted, to which that organization was not backward about calling attention. The Air Forces was first in full integration and abolition of WAC grades; first to attempt branch recruiting; first to require WAC inspectors at all command levels employing Wacs. It was the first to make a woman a lieutenant colonel, and was stopped from going further only by Congressional limitations; first to request the employment of WAC officers in non-WAC or "operational" jobs; first and only domestic command to propose extensive improvements in the WAC uniform, and its recommendations in this field were the ammunition with which Colonel Hobby finally won many arguments. It was the first major command to allow its own insignia to be worn by Wacs and to recommend that they be detailed in the Air Corps or the appropriate arm or service, a move that did much to make the women feel an accepted part of the Air Forces.

The AAF was the first to admit enlisted women to all men's noncombat schools, including some previously deemed unusual for women; first to propose, even if unsuccessfully, that women officers be

---

[6] Before its assignment to A–1, the Air WAC Division had been briefly in A–4 (ACofAS for Matériel, Maintenance, and Distribution).

[7] AAF Hq Office Instruction 5–13, 29 Nov 44.

allowed to go to men's noncombat officer candidate schools if they were not intended as WAC administrators; the first major command to support a school for the advanced training of WAC troop officers. It unsuccessfully recommended that Wacs be sent to the Army's School of Military Government as a preparation for duty in occupied areas. It was the first to bring to the War Department's attention the need for interpretation of certain discharge regulations, and for establishment of a system of maternity care for discharged women. It was the first major command to supervise the overseas placement of its own women by studying the needs of its components overseas and guaranteeing to fill them at its own expense. As a result, the Eighth and Ninth Air Forces in England, and to a lesser degree the air forces in Italy, the Pacific, and India, received well-selected, Air Forces-trained Wacs in numbers greater than the War Department had proposed to supply them.[8]

The AAF did not share other commands' distaste for specialized explanatory publications in any matter in which Colonel Bandel reported widespread misunderstanding in the field. The Air Forces was first to publish a circular defining the WAC company commander's job, and thus to end the friction and misunderstanding prevalent over that point in other commands where section chiefs claimed the commander's normal powers.[9] Another directive cautioned local commanders against placing enlisted women on commutation of quarters and rations or ordering them to stations where no housing existed. In six separate publications the Air Forces discussed all phases of successful selection of women for overseas shipment.

After a series of poor selections of WAC officer candidates, AAF headquarters amplified the War Department regulation and spelled out a precise procedure, including the often-neglected provision that selection boards would contain one WAC officer—the AAF made it two—and that rating lists based on merit alone would be maintained at Air Command level, not lower. Likewise, the AAF published a WAC inspection manual, listing standards which should be expected in such matters as women's medical care, uniform and appearance, leadership, and the commander's handling of marital and social problems. Similarly, the AAF included in its personnel officers' handbook a chapter on WAC administration.[10]

AAF headquarters also permitted the

---

[8] In order: (1) Speech, Maj Bandel, Min, Stf Dirs Conf, New York, 1–3 Dec 43. SPWA 337 (11–10–43). (2) AAF WAC Hist, pp. 12, 49, n. 1, 67, 84; also AAF Ltr 35–83, 29 Apr 44, and 21 Aug 44, pp. 65, 85, 86–87. (3) Memo, Exec WAC for CG AAF, 22 Feb 44, returned, 9 Mar 44, by CG AAF for further study. (4) See overseas chapters below, particularly Ch. XXI.

[9] AAF Reg 35–44, 10 Nov 43, revised and amended 14 Sep 44, 18 Oct 44, and 19 Jan 45: "WAC squadrons will be commanded by WAC Officers, who will have administrative authority and duties analogous and equivalent to those of a company commander. . . . The WAC squadron commander is charged with housing, messing, supply, discipline, training, recreation, morale, well-being, maintaining WAC squadron records, and rendering necessary reports. . . . Recommendations for changes of status, including promotion, reduction, transfer, discharge, etc., may originate with the Officer in whose section or unit the Wac is working, or with the WAC squadron commander. In all such cases the recommendations must bear the indorsements both of the Officer in whose section or unit the Wac is working, and of the WAC squadron commander."

[10] (1) AAF Reg 35–49, 13 Jan 44. (2) AAF Ltrs: 35–119, 3 Aug 44; 35–152, 6 Nov 44; 35–175, 27 Dec 44 and 14 Feb 45; 35–175a, 6 Mar 45; 35–47, 6 Apr 45; 35–65, 12 Sep 44; 35–89, 9 Apr and 28 May 45. (3) AAF Manual 120–2, WAC Insp Manual, Hq AAF, 10 Apr 44. (4) AAF WAC Hist, pp. 45, 46, 67, and 84; AAF Reg 120–12, 25 Dec 43.

Air WAC Division to send an informal monthly mimeographed letter to its staff directors, explaining the reasons behind current actions by headquarters. The recipients of these letters were responsible for passing on this information to their WAC company commanders. This service was so popular with Wacs in the field that non-Air Forces staff directors overseas asked to be included on the mailing list, stating that they otherwise did not see even War Department regulations for months, if ever; and non-AAF company commanders set up regular correspondence with AAF WAC squadron commanders to learn what they could, stating that War Department circulars were seldom otherwise available to company commanders.

Flying Jobs for Women

In the field, the Air Forces' progressive attitude was demonstrated chiefly by an equal lack of inhibitions in the assignment of women to new and unconventional jobs. No AAF schools were barred to women except combat schools, and no AAF jobs for which they could qualify, however unusual for women. It was not even the Air Forces' intention to exclude women from the most extreme masculine province: its flying schools and assignment as pilot.

Women quite early had been hired as ferry pilots, on a Civil Service status. Air Forces headquarters had planned that this group, first called the WAAF and later the WASP (Women Air Service Pilots), would be placed in the Army as part of the WAC as soon as Congress had made the WAAC a part of the Army. Such an addition was agreeable to WAC authorities, in-

cluding both Colonel Hobby and the Air WAC Officer, since the number of women pilots was relatively tiny—some 800 as against Colonel Bandel's 40,000 Air Wacs—and could have been administered without additional expense. However, the proposed merger was blocked by the Director WASP, Mrs. Jacqueline Cochran Odlum, who recommended that women pilots not be grouped with other Air Corps officers, but given a separate military corps on equal status with the WAC, with a director equal in rank to Colonel Hobby. Legislation to this effect was attempted, but failed, and Congressional sentiment against the use of women as pilots was so strongly stirred up that the Air Forces was forced to disband the WASP without ever giving its members military status and benefits. Some WAC officers and enlisted women were also found to be qualified pilots, but it was deemed unwise ever to assign them as such in view of the emphatic nature of the Congressional decision.[11]

Enlisted flying jobs for Wacs, other than that of pilot, were never forbidden, although no such jobs had been considered by early planners because of the greater need for women elsewhere. As soon as assignment was turned over to local authorities, it proved impossible to keep a few women out of certain flying duties for which they had peculiar qualifications. Within two months Mitchel Field reported that it possessed the first two "flying Wacs," radio operators who were participating in B–17 training flights. This

---

[11] (1) Memo, CofAS for G–1, with Ind, WAAC Hq, 17 Apr 43. SPWA 314.7 (1–7–43) sec 1. (2) Memo, Arnold for Marshall [Jun 43], with reply from G–1, 20 Jun 43. SPWA 324.5 CAP (3–25–43). (3) Hist Recs Rpt 319, History of ATC: Women Pilots in ATC. USAF Hist Div. (4) For further discussion, see Summary of WASP Controversy, Appendix D.

precipitated scores of requests from other Wacs for flying duty. A few more WAC radio operators, mechanics, and photographers were soon assigned to regular runs. Several such Wacs actually received Air Medals, including one in India for her work in mapping the Hump, and one posthumously after the crash of an aerial broadcasting plane.

Both the women and the airfields concerned were ordinarily so pleased with themselves for accomplishing flying duty assignments that Air Forces headquarters, when it discovered them, published a directive authorizing such duty provided that the flights concerned were not for purposes of combat training, and that Wacs did not replace any man who might be receiving combat training on these flights.

The Air WAC Officer, while not discouraging such duty for women well suited for it, did not encourage any extension of it, or widespread training of women for it. Her opposition was due partly to the difficulty of housing a female crew member when nonscheduled landings were necessary, and partly to the danger of public outcry if any Wac was assigned to a position that even remotely involved combat training. Later in the war the Air Transport Command repeatedly proposed to use Wacs to replace male flight clerks on scheduled passenger runs. This was at first discouraged because of the irregular housing arrangements involved, but was eventually approved on a small scale and proved successful in flights such as those from Paris to London.[12]

Even including these flight clerks, the number of Wacs on flying duty, wearing wings and drawing flying pay, was never great. Only twenty Wacs held the Specification Serial Number of Air Crew Member, and flying radio operators and other technicians were equally scarce.

This comparative absence of a relatively exciting and popular type of Air Forces duty was one factor with which commanders of female troops had to reckon in maintaining morale. Many air-base commanders, recognizing the difficulty, directed that Wacs be allowed to go on local flights as passengers where space permitted, or for at least one orientation flight upon arrival at a station. Nevertheless, most AAF Wacs seldom saw the inside of a plane, and many were in the unfortunate position of Air Transport Command Wacs in Scotland and Wales, who were shipped overseas by boat and complained that they knew there was an outside world only by remarks dropped by transient men. Because of the value of occasional flights to women's morale, the Air WAC Officer secured a directive making clear that women were to have the same privileges as other military personnel in "hopping rides" or flying on military orders.[13]

Specialist Training

AAF headquarters from the beginning showed enthusiasm for training Waacs in other technical and mechanical jobs which were not ordinarily considered a woman's field. An elaborate training system was originally planned, with 8,000 women a month to be fed into AAF schools for training as everything from

---

[12] (1) AAF WAC Hist, pp. 19 and 41. (2) AAF Reg 35–45, 12 Nov 43. (3) WDBPR Press Release, 14 May 46. (4) Memo, AAF for Dir WAC, 30 Aug 45. WDWAC 319.1 AAF.

[13] (1) For list of Specification Serial Numbers see AAF Stat Contl Rpt SC–PS–123, sub: Strength of AAF Pers in WAC Within Continental U.S. by Comd, SSN, and Race. (2) Hist Recs Rpt 315c, Wacs in European Division, ATC, June 1944–August 1945, by European Division, ATC. USAF Hist Div.

TRAINING AT LOWRY FIELD, COLORADO, *in February 1943. Waacs learning camera operation, above, and making photographic mosaics, below.*

armorers to weather forecasters, in addition to 5,000 a month to be received already trained in WAAC schools as clerks. This plan was very similar to the system actually used on a smaller scale by the Naval Air Service, which determined in advance to employ set numbers of Waves as Link trainer instructors, control tower operators, and other specialists, and trained them accordingly. The Army Air Forces carried the plan so far as to set up Wac classes at the AAF Photolaboratory School at Lowry Field, which trained several all-WAC photolaboratory companies. The AAF also earlier encouraged the WAAC to set up its radio training school at Kansas City, and contracted to employ all graduates.[14]

However, as women began to arrive, the AAF was surprised to discover that the majority of women, unlike the 17- and 18-year-old boys who were being inducted, had a usable job skill before they entered the Army. To employ the average Wac successfully, it proved necessary only to place her, fresh from basic training, on almost any airfield, where, if not immediately snatched into too many pieces by competing section chiefs, she ordinarily soon found useful employment. The number of recruits arriving was never great enough to make placement a problem.

The Air Forces therefore soon dropped all but a few of its formal technical training plans for women, and adopted a system which was believed to be the most natural, speedy, and economical under the circumstances. Most AAF Wacs finishing basic training were shipped immediately to air bases having need of personnel in their civilian skills and were assigned to immediate duty or to on-the-job training, which was believed less wasteful of time than the average technical

course. If a station needed a specialist it was unable to train, or if a Wac showed such aptitude that higher specialized training was clearly indicated, the station was authorized to send her to any noncombat AAF school that could arrange to house her. In such cases the station ordinarily had to take the trainee back upon graduation and employ her in the new skill; training was thus seldom employed merely to gratify individual desires for unnecessary training or to get rid of troublesome individuals.

Unfortunately for the compilation of statistics, the attendance of Wacs at AAF technical schools was so well integrated and came to excite so little comment that it was later impossible to determine exactly how many women had attended each course and how their record compared with that of male students. It was known only that approximately 2,000 women successfully completed courses in AAF technical schools, including weather observers, weather forecasters, electrical specialists of several kinds, sheet metal workers, Link trainer instructors, cryptographers, teletype operators, radio mechanics, control tower specialists, parachute riggers, bombsight maintenance specialists, clerks, airplane mechanics, photolaboratory technicians and photointerpreters, chaplains' assistants, and physical and military training specialists. Lt. Gen. Barton K. Yount, commanding general of the AAF Training Command, wrote, "Their record of accomplishment reflects great credit upon the Women's Army Corps and the Army. . . . Their contribution to the Training Command's mission has been invaluable."[15]

---

[14] AAF WAC Hist, pp. 41–42.
[15] Ltr, Gen Yount to Dir WAC, 5 May 45. WDWAC 201.22.

Conventional Clerical Jobs

At the peak of enrollment, in January of 1945, it was estimated that about 50 percent of AAF Wacs in the United States held administrative or office jobs, being assigned as typists, stenographers, and various sorts of clerks.[16] This was a percentage of women in conventional jobs considerably smaller than that in most other commands or overseas theaters, where the numbers in "feminine" work ranged as high as 90 percent in commands such as the Eighth Air Force in England. The work of such Air Wacs did not ordinarily differ from clerical work in other commands, except that it required a knowledge of Air Forces nomenclature, organization, and administrative procedures.

The different air commands differed slightly from each other in certain uses for these clerical workers. The largest, the AAF Training Command, with its hundreds of flying training schools and technical training schools, found Wacs particularly useful in keeping the complicated records of trainees, training courses, and flight hours. The domestic air forces—First, Second, Third, and Fourth—likewise used Wacs to keep their personnel and flight records, and also to staff the assembly lines by which crews and equipment were processed for overseas shipment. The Air Technical Service Command used WAC clerks at its large depots to keep stock records of the thousands of items of Air Forces technical equipment. The Air Transport Command, running the Army equivalent of a commercial airline system, used numbers of Wacs at its information desks, in its dispatching offices, and to process passengers and supplies through aerial ports of embarkation. Toward the end of the war, the new AAF Personnel Distribution Command used Wacs to process personnel in replacement depots, redistribution centers, and convalescent centers.

Army Air Forces headquarters itself lagged behind its commands only because of the War Department ban on bringing Wacs into Washington. After repeated efforts to circumvent this policy, an opening was found in December of 1943 by the authorization to bring in twenty WAC messengers to handle secret and confidential mail, which had been repeatedly going astray under civilian operation. These were soon followed by weather observers, statistical machine operators, and others to a total of several hundred, housed at Bolling Field and working in the Pentagon.[17]

Technical Assignments

Technical jobs tended to increase in number toward the end of the war, as it became increasingly difficult for the AAF to get enlisted men in the top AGCT brackets necessary for some of the work. An especial competition for women of high ability developed between Air Forces agencies, which were frequently hard put to find men of suitable qualifications for technical work who were not immediately lost to officer candidate school or needed for overseas stations.

Weather Observers

AAF's Weather Wing, which sought Wacs long before it ever saw one, finally obtained a quota of 500. A few were sent

---

[16] Rpt cited n. 13(1). Administrative jobs totaled 46 percent, plus undoubtedly some of the group marked "Duty."

[17] AAF WAC Hist, p. 66.

to the regular Weather School, but most were trained on the job, five or six Wacs taking over the weather station at air bases where they could be housed with a WAC company. The majority of such Wacs were weather observers; only a few were ever trained for the more complicated job of weather forecaster, for which there was no shortage of men. The quota of 500 was never entirely filled in spite of all efforts.[18]

Radio and Cryptographic Work

The Army Airways Communications System (AACS), which had a quota of 1,450 and which competed for high-type personnel, chiefly sought radio operators. At the height of a shortage of this personnel, AACS discovered that several hundred WAAC radio operators and mechanics had been shipped under the old T/O system to airfields that did not need them. An individual search by name was instituted to unearth them. Some women were found suitably assigned to air-base radio stations, or as code instructors in schools such as the AAF Navigation School at Hondo, Texas, but others who were doing clerical work were carried off by AACS. These were assigned in groups of six or eight to operate AACS radio stations at airfields where a WAC unit was located. Most female radio operators recruited by the AAF were also given to AACS; when its needs still remained unfilled, AACS was also assigned Wacs without radio skills but of high intelligence and promising background. At a special AACS screening center, these women were tested and those with any radio abilities were sent to intensive training courses. Those with college or research backgrounds were

trained as cryptographers, for which women proved especially suitable because of the exacting and monotonous nature of the work.[19]

Control Tower Operators

Those with good diction and good nerves, such as former teachers and telephone operators, were trained by AACS as control tower operators, after a brief dispute concerning whether females should be given a position of such responsibility. Even the advanced British services did not at this time use women in this work.[20] Some objectors feared that a woman's voice would not be audible, that women would become hysterical in emergencies and be unable to give the necessary landing directions, or that women's training as control tower operators would interfere with men's training. One AACS region, in fact, put out a directive that "under no circumstances will WAAC personnel be permitted to operate the microphone in an airways station or airdrome control tower, or to operate on the net in an airways station." AACS headquarters quickly overruled the regional headquarters, stating that its need for personnel would require all qualified women as well as men.

From the end of 1943 onward, Wacs served successfully in these positions. Pilots seemed to experience no difficulty in following women's voices, and while no major emergencies occurred to test WAC operators' self-control, in several minor

[18] *Ibid.,* pp. 12, 42, 66–67. Appendix shows 242 WAC weather specialists.
[19] *Ibid.,* pp. 13, 31–32, 66.
[20] Memo, Sgt Goodwin for Col Hobby, 17 Apr 44, re inquiry from Air Chief Marshal Frederick W. Bowhill. WDWAC 211 Control.

crashes they rerouted aircraft and directed rescue apparatus in a manner that received praise. Colonel Bandel later reported, "Wacs love the work and have been highly commended. There seems to be no difference between men and women in adaptability to this work." [21]

The only difficulty experienced by AACS and Weather Wing in any of these technical assignments was a purely administrative one: they considered their Wacs, like their men, to be high-grade specialists who should perform no kitchen police or other duties for the unit with which they lived, whereas the WAC units, being smaller than men's units, seldom appreciated such exalted boarders, and demanded that these women share company rules and company duties. When differences threatened to result in eviction, both AACS and Weather Wing acquired WAC staff directors, whose chief duties were to travel continuously, persuading AACS supervisors that specialists could without damage be housekeepers, and convincing WAC commanders that some shift workers on exacting technical work might properly be given a few concessions. [22]

Business Machine Operators

In 1944 another shortage developed, that of skilled operators of business machines for AAF's statistical control units throughout the United States. Available trained men were required for mobile overseas units, and the need eventually became such that priority of assignment was given for 1,000 Wacs for statistical control work. Since few women skilled in this work could be recruited, women with suitable intelligence and aptitude were chosen and sent to a six-week intensive training course at the AAF School at Orlando, Florida. Women proved especially apt at the work, although many complaints were received concerning its monotony and the refusal of statistical control units to vary the duties or permit transfer or rotation between stations. [23]

Link Trainer Instructors

Another popular technical job for Wacs was that of Link trainer instructor. As early as November of 1942, AAF headquarters had proposed the use of Waacs in this work, since "Men suitable to act as such instructors are rapidly disappearing into officer candidate schools." Men qualified to do the work often were pilots or potential pilots themselves, and were not content to remain as enlisted instructors, once trained. A number of Wacs selected by local authorities were therefore trained in the men's training school for Link trainer instructors, and others learned the work on the job; the duties proved both successful and satisfying to the women. [24]

Mechanics

Had hundreds of thousands of Wacs been available, the AAF had planned to train many women as mechanics, but since all recruits obtainable were needed for other jobs, and since the work was less suitable because of women's lesser physical strength, no particular attempt was made to train large numbers of them. Nevertheless, several hundred women

---

[21] Memo, Air WAC Off for Asst Chief WAC Br G-1, 19 Apr 44. WDWAC 211 Control.

[22] Ltr, forwarded to Hq AAF by 1st Ind, Hq AACS, 4 Apr 45. AACS 220/1.

[23] AAF WAC Hist, p. 67.

[24] *Ibid.*, p. 13.

with civilian skills, requiring no further training, were assigned to the work. One station, by way of experiment, successfully set up an entire flight line staffed by some sixty WAC mechanics.

Some WAC staff directors were extremely doubtful about such work because of what they termed the coarsening effect on women of the average conversation encountered from men on most flight lines. However, the assignment was the only economical one for skilled women from civilian employment in the aircraft industry, and such women usually displayed a keen interest in assignment in their specialty and in the advanced mechanical training open to them, regardless of its effect on their vocabulary.

Medics

Some 6 percent of Air Wacs were medical specialists. Medical companies for larger AAF hospitals were requested as early as April and May of 1943, eighteen months before the ASF adopted WAC general hospital companies, but these had to be refused at the time for lack of trained WAAC personnel. As a result, no formally organized WAC hospital companies were ever employed by the AAF, which instead used whatever workers were available—clerks, receptionists, orderlies and medical technicians—as part of regular squadrons. These women were trained on the job instead of receiving special courses—a system that proved inferior to school instruction only in that it was necessary for inspectors constantly to prod hospital authorities to continue upgrading Wacs instead of leaving them as untrained orderlies. Nevertheless, twelve different medical Specification Serial Numbers came to be held by AAF Wacs.[25]

Aircraft Warning Service

Another group of specialists, veterans in length of service, were the approximately 1,000 women, remnants of the Aircraft Warning Service, who continued to perform duties with Fighter Command stations along the eastern seaboard. Theoretically these duties were clerical; actually, until near the end of hostilities the Wacs also continued to help in operations and filter centers when civilian volunteers defaulted. At the AAF School of Applied Tactics at Orlando, Florida, 500 more AWS veterans assisted in the aircraft warning portion of the school's training function. Women proved particularly suitable for this work, which was both monotonous and exacting, but as the danger of aerial invasion became more and more remote, women began to complain of fatigue after two or more years at this work, and to request transfer to other duties, which was seldom forthcoming.

Miscellaneous

In addition, some 5 percent of Air Wacs were drivers; 4 percent, supply experts; 3 percent, photographic technicians; 2 percent, telephone and teletype operators. Lesser numbers were radar operators, armament specialists, carpenters, dietitians, and interpreters. College women and others with responsible civilian experience were frequently assigned as librarians, classification specialists, instructors, personnel clerks, vocational advisers, occupational therapists, reporters and editors, and historians. The AAF's flexible system of assigning Wacs made it possible to fill special needs or to place un-

---

[25] *Ibid.*, pp. 13, 36.

usual skills found in only a handful of women: these included topographers, cartographers, sanitary inspectors, geodetic computers, chemists, and many others even more unusual.[26] A former watch repairwoman was trained in secret bombsight maintenance; six photographic airbrush artists illustrated technical manuals at Patterson Field; Russian interpreters found employment at ATC's Montana terminal. In California, the WAC's only dog trainer found that the AAF could also provide dogs to train.[27]

Officers

WAC officers assigned to the Army Air Forces were admitted to more than sixty different types of jobs in addition to that of company officer.[28] These were all full-fledged officer jobs; as soon as WAC officers arrived in AAF headquarters, a written directive made it clear that they were to replace commissioned officers only, and specifically not warrant officers or civilians.[29]

The majority were given administrative jobs in the fields of personnel, office management, mess, supply, and finance. Numbers were also found useful in jobs that involved dealing with people—special services, information and education, and public relations. A few WAC officers by the end of the war had worked up to positions of some responsibility; there was one air-base judge advocate, one inspector general, one base executive, and thirteen who held the coveted Specification Serial Number 2260, personnel staff officer.

Grades and Ratings

The wide scope of Air Forces jobs open to Wacs, both officer and enlisted, could be attributed chiefly to the AAF policy of full integration and the resulting abolition of all separate WAC grades, allotments, and Tables of Organization. An AAF Regulation stated, "Practices which tend to apportion grades and promotions by sex rather than by actual duty assignment are undesirable, as they serve to impair efficiency and morale."[30] Actually, when the total was reckoned, men were found to be far more highly rated than women, for most AAF Wacs had come on the scene in 1943 and 1944 when most high grades had already been distributed. Air Forces men in the United States still had four times the percentage of master sergeants' ratings that women did; twenty times the percentage of technical sergeants; ten times that of staff sergeants, and twice that of sergeants. Among officers, men had five times as great a percentage of field grade officers as did women.[31]

It was Colonel Bandel's opinion that there was no reason why late-arriving Wacs should have had higher ratings than the men who arrived in the same years, and that Air Forces procedure "resulted in greater freedom in utilizing Wacs and men doing similar jobs," even though in fewer guaranteed ratings for women.[32]

Toward the end of the war, officers of AAF's Military Personnel Division became concerned about the fact that WAC

---

[26] Memo, Chief, Classif and Repl Br AGO, for Dir WAC, 24 Apr 44. SPX 220.3 WAC (11–30–43) OC–H, in WDWAC 201.6.

[27] See Table 5, Appendix A, for division by occupational groups of total enlisted AAF Wacs in zone of the interior, 31 January 1945. The complete breakdown for both enlisted women and officers by SSN, race, and air command is given in the report cited n. 13(1).

[28] For a condensed summary of jobs held by AAF WAC officers in the United States, 31 January 45, see Table 6, Appendix A.

[29] AAF Hq Office Instr 35–25, 25 Sep 43.

[30] AAF Ltr 121–48, 29 Mar 45.

[31] AAF Stat Digest, Tables 9, 10, and 15.

[32] AAF WAC Hist, p. 34, n. 1.

officer grades included more first lieutenants and fewer second lieutenants than the men, and wished to forbid promotion of any more female second lieutenants. Air WAC Division killed this idea by pointing out that about 1,700 of the AAF's worldwide total of 1,900 WAC officers had come to it in 1943. After this, the WAC officer candidate school was virtually stopped, and while the supply of newly commissioned male second lieutenants continued, few more female second lieutenants were received. The WAC officers had received no more promotions than men who came to the AAF in 1943. Air WAC Division again pointed out that "separate" grades for women would have led to injustice.

Overseas Assignment

In 1944 several air commands received the hitherto unprecedented authority to move Wacs to overseas stations without reference either to the War Department or to AAF headquarters.[33] The AAF's Air Transport Command was the first to win permission to move its Wacs overseas as it moved its men, without reference to usual staging methods.[34] Air Transport Command had soon picked up Wacs from domestic stations, staged them, and set them down in Hawaii, Alaska, Bermuda, Labrador, England, Scotland, Wales, France, Africa, and India. Army Airways Communications System and AAF Weather Wing followed suit, attaching their Wacs to any convenient ATC unit. The several thousand women in these units, which remained under the command of the Army Air Forces, were in addition to some seven thousand Wacs furnished higher headquarters of combat air forces overseas.[35]

Such freedom of movement did not of course apply to combat units; AAF headquarters was kept busy refusing the requests of fighter and bomber groups trained in the United States who desired to ship out complete with two or three borrowed Wacs to whom they had become accustomed. After the defeat of Germany the U.S. Strategic Air Force was given permission to ship out its Wacs as it pleased, in its program to swing the bulk of its air power to the Pacific. This was the only combat organization to receive such authority and only a few women were ever shipped out in this manner.

Conclusion of Program

The high point of the AAF WAC program was reached in January of 1945, with a peak strength of almost 40,000 women. In Colonel Bandel's opinion there were few remaining difficulties in the employment of womanpower which the AAF had not solved.

Her final report listed only four remaining problems. One of these was the housing situation. As a matter of economy, initial mistakes in design could never be corrected once barracks were built, although both AAF inspectors and surgeons repeatedly objected. It was found that permanent employees like the Wacs suffered greatly in health and efficiency from being housed for two or three years in crowded

---

[33] Granted 10 Jun 44. AAF WAC Hist, pp. 74–81.

[34] Granted November 1943, ahead of blanket authority cited in preceding note. First ATC unit overseas was one to Hawaii, March 1944.

[35] WAC Pers with Air Forces Overseas, Jan 45, Table 28, AAF Stat Digest, 1946:

European Theater	2,835
Mediterranean	457
Pacific Ocean Areas	2
Far East Air Force	694
China–Burma–India	287
Air Transport Comd	2,755
Other (AACS, Etc)	285
Total	7,315

and flimsy temporary barracks with their hand-fired coal stoves, designed primarily for transient combat trainees. Another unsolved problem was that of the selection of WAC officers. The AAF felt that the War Department system of sending all candidates to a school for WAC troop officers was outdated, and that women should have been selected and trained as men were, in men's schools, except for those who would actually administer Wacs. Other unsolved problems were that of friction with civilian women workers, and that of disputes over fraternization of officers and enlisted personnel of opposite sexes; these could not be resolved within the limits of Army organization in World War II.[36]

None of these remaining problems was, in Colonel Bandel's opinion, a serious threat to the efficiency of the AAF WAC program. She concluded:

There can be little doubt that women did contribute many critically needed administrative and clerical skills—not generally possessed by men—to the AAF at a time when there was a very great need for such skills. . . . The WAC program in the Air Forces during World War II was a part of the natural evolution toward the full employment of a nation's manpower during a modern war.[37]

[36] See Chs. XXV and XXVII, below.
[37] AAF WAC Hist, pp. 94, 96, 97.

CHAPTER XVII

The Army Ground Forces

Although equal in echelon to the Army Air Forces, the Army Ground Forces offered a less favorable field for the employment of womanpower.[1] Ground Forces units were chiefly tactical in nature, depending upon the Army Service Forces for supply and other services. Except for its schools and replacement depots, the AGF had few permanent installations under its jurisdiction in the United States. There was some early debate within AGF headquarters as to whether Waacs could not be used to staff the rear echelons of separate corps, thus giving "a continuity of administration in the event a Corps is ordered overseas," but this idea was not approved. In general the WAAC was regarded as part of the Services of Supply, even when a few units were attached for duty at AGF installations.

It therefore came as an unexpected problem when, on 1 May 1943, the War Department formally assigned to AGF and other commands the units previously on loan from the ASF. The standard ASF Table of Organization units were not particularly suitable for the needs of the AGF, since most routine services were performed for it by the ASF, and only highly skilled typists and stenographers were wanted.

Upon her assignment as AGF WAC Officer during the period of conversion to Army status, Maj. Emily E. Davis visited all AGF WAC units and found that the only one with good morale was that at Fort Riley, which had been sent out after the end of the T/O system and thus fitted the needs of the station. Others suffered from malassignment and underutilization, and also had not received full uniform issue or been able to get salvage or repair of clothing. Some units were found to lack adequate housing and dayroom space, and had no recreational or special services program. Two units were under the command of WAC officers whom Major Davis pronounced "very weak" and immediately replaced; in three months these commanders had not made the most elementary arrangements for the welfare of the units.

For the remainder of the war the employment of Wacs in the AGF increased slowly. Replacements for the 34 percent losses of the conversion period were not forthcoming until early 1944, and additional requisitions were at first few. AGF headquarters voluntarily limited the number of Wacs by refusing all requests from the District of Columbia or installations "which are near large cities where they can procure civilian personnel." Requests from installations such as the Desert Training Center were also disapproved as unsuitable. Negro Wacs were rejected, since it was believed that they could not

---

[1] This chapter draws heavily upon the AGF WAC Hist, by the AGF WAC Officer, Colonel Davis. All direct quotations in this chapter, unless otherwise indicated, are from this history.

FIRST OFFICER EMILY E. DAVIS, *right foreground, with Colonel Hobby and Colonel McCoskrie on a tour of Fort Des Moines in June 1943.*

be employed in sufficient numbers to justify a detachment unless the War Department reconsidered their use to replace civilians in the operation of kitchens, dining halls, and cafeterias. For these reasons, the total number of AGF Wacs was never to be very great, at its peak strength amounting to less than 2,000, one twentieth of that employed by the Air Forces or the Service Forces.[2]

Lt. Col. Emily E. Davis remained the sole WAC representative in Headquarters, AGF. Although her responsibility was parallel to that of the Air WAC Officer,

smaller numbers of women were assigned to AGF, which never approved her request for an assistant in its own headquarters. At a later date a WAC staff director was assigned to the AGF's largest field command, the Replacement and School Command, and another to the Antiaircraft Command.

---

[2] (1) Ltr, Hq AGF to CofS, 1 Apr 43. GNGCT 320.2 WAAC. (2) For complete statistics on receipt of personnel by station by month, see AGF WAC Hist, Vol. II, App. XX. Peak strength in this chart appears as 1,950 women. See also Table 4, Appendix A.

WOMEN ASSIGNED TO THE ARMY GROUND FORCES *work alongside soldiers at Camp Davis, North Carolina, above; WAAC ex-school teachers outline courses for the enlisted personnel elementary school at Fort Sill, Oklahoma, below.*

AGF WAC Jobs

Wacs with the Army Ground Forces worked gradually into positions more diversified than the original assignments had promised. AGF requisitions continued to ask for women with a high degree of skill in some administrative or technical field, with the result that only 14 percent of its total enlisted women were in the two lowest AGCT classifications; the other 86 percent were in the top three groups, with 47 percent of enlisted women having the scores required of officers. These considerably surpassed the scores of Wacs in any other domestic command. A special arrangement was made whereby, if the AGF was accidentally assigned a Wac lacking in skill or aptitude, she was immediately reassigned to another command.

These women gravitated naturally toward a station's more responsible positions, especially since they were relatively more permanent employees than the enlisted men, not being subject to withdrawal for combat service. Wacs were finally assigned to every major training installation of the Army Ground Forces, both schools and replacement training centers: infantry, cavalry, field artillery, coast artillery, antiaircraft, tank destroyer, airborne, and armored force. They were also assigned to two overseas-replacement depots. Over 70 percent of the Wacs' jobs in these installations were clerical and administrative; others were technical, professional, mess, supply, or automotive.[3]

Type of Duty	Percent
Total	100.0
Administrative and Clerical	72.0
Automotive	8.9
Technical and Professional	8.2
Mess	5.4
Supply	4.8
Radio and Communications	0.7

Replacement Depot

One of the largest AGF WAC units was at the Ground Forces Replacement Depot, Fort Meade, Maryland, where over 400 women were assigned. To handle the tremendous volume of overseas replacements, a "belt line" process was established, by which each man's records were passed down a line where each checker took care of a single item. This process resulted in extreme accuracy but extreme monotony; it was performed on a twenty-four-hour basis, in shifts of from eight to twelve hours, depending on the load. It was reported that "WAC personnel became proficient in this type of operation, and as general-service men were released for overseas duty, they became the section heads of many of these processing departments."

In addition, many Wacs were used in training regiments in clerical capacities. WAC tabulating machine operators were in great demand by the Machine Records Unit, so much so that some showing aptitude were especially trained in the work, but the total number desired was never obtainable. Instead, many of the women recruited under the station-and-job plan with a promise of assignment to Fort Meade were so lacking in clerical aptitude as to be untrainable for the processing of papers, and 115 of them were used in the motor pool as dispatchers, drivers, mechanics, and attendants.

Antiaircraft Artillery School

In the Antiaircraft Command Wacs performed a variety of duties on the firing ranges where trainees were taught the

---

[3] Complete list of installations is given in AGF WAC Hist, Vol. I, pp. 47–48.

principles of antiaircraft defense. At some antiaircraft firing points the entire training operation, with the exception of technical supervision by male officers, was handled by enlisted women: WAC control tower operators kept the tow-target plane on the course, while other Wacs gave the fire signal over the field telephone, and WAC mathematicians computed the correct angle of fire and the accuracy of fire.

Other AGF Schools

At the Field Artillery School, a few Wacs were used as control tower operators to guide liaison planes. At the Armored, Field Artillery, and Cavalry Schools, Wacs were employed as radio mechanics, taking care of records and requisitions involving radio equipment, and repairing and installing radios in tanks, bantams, and other vehicles, both in camps and in bivouac areas. Other Wacs were radio operators and instructors in the Cavalry and Armored Schools, and in the communications school of the Field Artillery School, training men in code sending and receiving.

At the Parachute School, Fort Benning, Georgia, over one hundred women were utilized in the parachute rigging and maintenance sections. Women originally recruited for this work, under the station-and-job plan, were former textile mill workers and did not prove very apt, some 40 percent being unable to complete the training, with the average female rigger being able to rig only six chutes daily, as compared to ten rigged by the average man. Women were not allowed to jump with the chutes they had packed, as men were required to do, on the grounds that this was not an essential part of the job for a woman, but were allowed to fly with paratrooper trainees and watch them jump with chutes the women had packed. After station-assignment recruiting was discontinued and the requirements raised, women developed greater proficiency in this work and ultimately were considered "equally qualified with male personnel in rigging and better qualified in maintenance."

Women served also at various stations in such varied jobs as proofreaders on technical manuals, as photographic technicians, as sewing machine operators in a book stitching shop, as translators for the preparation of language courses, and as motion picture projectionists in training classes. One woman, as chief clerk of a department, was responsible for keeping track of its officer and enlisted personnel and 300 trainees, for checking the contents of all incoming and outgoing papers, for the computation of rations needed, and for maintaining records of completion of qualification courses. Another, a classification clerk, assigned all male cadre returned from overseas. One was personal secretary to two generals and a colonel. Another secretary prepared reports and took all testimony concerning cases brought before a board of officers.

Staff directors on field visits made a point of checking such job assignments against actual skills. While typists were usually well assigned, stenographers were frequently found to be dissatisfied, and staff directors reported, "The failure of staff officers to use stenographic ability persisted through the entire period of the war." Many complained of not being busy, saying, "I feel that the Wacs could handle much more work than is given them," or, "It is said there are five persons to each Army job and that statement seems believable." With these and a few other exceptions, the classification of enlisted women was, by 1945, pronounced "excellent" by the staff director.

Experiment With Mixed Tactical Units

The only official experiment with mixed tactical units in the United States was the early one made with antiaircraft artillery units under the actual command of the Military District of Washington. This experiment was made in spite of the objection of the Judge Advocate General that it would involve "assignment to combat units" and was thus probably illegal. However, the British experience in such mixed units had proved satisfactory, and the Antiaircraft Artillery (AAA) desired the action.[4] Civilian volunteers would otherwise have been required, and this involved difficulties of administration, discipline, control, and efficiency. Also, as the Army Service Forces noted, "it takes about ten volunteers to take the place of one soldier."[5]

No publicity was permitted on this project, partly because the unit was itself highly secret in nature, equipped with radar, height finders, fire directors, and other such apparatus, and partly lest WAAC recruiting should be harmed by mistaken notions that women were to fire guns or sleep in the men's barracks. The experiment actually offered little grounds for alarm, for the "tactical" unit in question appeared firmly rooted in the vicinity of Washington, D.C., and was "mixed" only during the working day, the Waacs enjoying their customary separate housekeeping at night.

In accordance with General Marshall's verbal instructions, two WAAC companies, totaling 10 officers and over 200 enrolled women, reported to the area in December 1942. With these, the AAA was directed to organize two composite batteries using women in at least 55 percent of the jobs, and to work out Tables of Organization showing exactly which jobs in AAA batteries, battalions, and regiments could be held by women, and whether the whole idea was workable.

The women concerned were carefully selected for their high AGCT test scores, although actually the AAA discovered that women of less ability could have performed certain routine jobs as well and felt less bored. They were never assigned a tactical mission, but did participate in the Eastern Defense Command's tactical problem. The women were not assigned to fire guns, nor were they given small-arms training. They were not assigned to outlying searchlight positions because of the isolation and the fact that the public would have observed the experiment. They were assigned to operate various instruments and machines, as well as to perform clerical duties, and the entire range section was completely manned by Waacs. The AAA reported, "WAAC personnel exhibited an outstanding devotion to duty, willingness and ability to absorb and grasp technical information concerning the problems of maintenance and tactical disposition of all types of equipment." Little administrative difficulty was reported, although separate housing was of course required, and there were separate dayrooms for men and women plus one for mixed groups.

---

[4] Cable 1101, 12 Aug 42, Eisenhower for Marshall, replies to Cable 2890, Marshall for Eisenhower, and gives data on use of ATS in AAA mixed batteries. Handwritten Ind, CofS, directs information be sent to G–1, G–3, Mrs. Hobby, Brig Gen Thomas H. Green, Maj Gen John T. Lewis, CG MDW. CofS 291.9.
[5] Memo, DCofAdm Serv for CG SOS, 18 Nov 42. SPAAS 320, Sp Coll DRB AGO.

At the conclusion of the experiment some months later, a full report was rendered to the War Department as to the possibilities of using women in such duties. The report concluded:

WAAC personnel can be used in performing many of the tasks of the Antiaircraft Artillery. They are superior to men in all functions involving delicacy of manual dexterity, such as operation at the director, height finder, radar, and searchlight control systems. They perform routine repetitive tasks in a manner superior to men. . . . The morale of women used in the AAA was generally high due to the fact that they felt that they were making a direct contribution to the successful prosecution of the war.[6]

As a result, the AAA requested that it be allowed to retain WAAC personnel and be given ten times more, to the extent of 103 officers and 2,315 enrolled women.

Since the need for antiaircraft protection in the area had subsided, G–3 Division decided instead that the most profitable immediate use for Waacs was in overhead installations to replace combat-fit men. With Colonel Hobby's concurrence, G–3 therefore directed that the AAA units be dissolved, their personnel reassigned, and records preserved to permit reactivation of such units should future need arise. This action was taken, over the protest of the AAA. Records were filed for future use, and G–3 Division concluded that "The experiment which has been conducted of employing WAAC personnel in antiaircraft artillery units has demonstrated conclusively the practicability of using members of the Corps in that role."[7]

Problems of Full Integration

Except in the one tactical unit, considerably more difficulty was encountered in achieving full integration of women into the Army Ground Forces than was the case in the AAF. From the enlisted women's viewpoint, the most visible distinction was the matter of insignia, in which it was the Ground Forces policy for women to wear WAC insignia instead of that which would have been worn by a man in the same assignment.

A more important handicap to integration, in the AGF staff director's opinion, was her inability to secure a merger of personnel allotments. Although allotments from the War Department no longer were divided into male and female, AGF headquarters continued to divide them, setting aside for each WAC detachment the exact number of grades the old WAAC Table of Organization had specified. These were designed for an ordinary ASF unit with many unskilled workers, and were somewhat modest for the average highly skilled AGF unit, allowing only 5 or 6 in each unit of 150 to hold one of the first three grades, and requiring about 80 to remain privates. These grades, however modest, were the sole property of the Wacs and were not interchangeable. Stations soon protested this lack of flexibility. The Armored Replacement Training Center wrote:

When we first received this company it was felt that our women were not qualified for the ratings in competition with the men, and our staff officers desired to give the ratings to men, which of course, we could not do. Now, with our expansion, the reverse is true . . . there are 41 privates in the WAC detachment, and we feel that most of these would be T/5's if all our ratings were pooled and they were in direct competition with the

---

[6] MDW Narrative Rpt, 10 Jul 43. 324.5 (151st WAAC Tech Co). Cited in mimeographed history, The Military District of Washington in the War Years (1942–1945), by William H. Cartwright, Jr. Copy in OCMH.

[7] Memo, G–3 for CofS, 7 Jul 43. WDGCT 291.9 WAC.

men. . . . Eventually our most competent administrative personnel will undoubtedly be women; some thought should be given to this and the War Department should initiate some policy.

The AGF WAC Officer therefore recommended that no separate grades be allotted for women, except cadre, but that grades be open to men and women alike. AGF's G–3 did not concur, and its system was continued throughout the war, with the modification that a revision of the WAC allotment could be obtained by any station upon formal request to Headquarters, AGF. Concerning this, AGF's Replacement and School Command protested that "such a recommendation requires extra paper work and loss of time. Normally, changes will be made only when a number of desired changes have accumulated, and individuals deserving of higher grades suffer from the lapse of time." AGF Replacement Depot 1 sent a similar protest. These protests from the field convinced AGF's G–1 Division, but not G–3, which maintained:

Since WAC personnel are in a more permanent status . . . and since they are used in large proportions in administrative job assignments where higher ratings tend to be concentrated, the proposed directive will tend to filter WAC personnel toward the higher grades and will exclude opportunity for male personnel returning from combat who may be qualified for such jobs. Although opportunity should be given all WAC personnel to qualify for promotion, it is believed that the present system should be continued as a means of control.

The separate allotments were therefore continued. This matter of ratings was a common cause of complaint among women. One wrote:

Many Wacs have taken over positions vacated by enlisted men and are performing the duties well, but due to current directives cannot be promoted to the grade they are occupying. . . . I believe that a Wac should be given the grade which belongs to the job.

The actual result of this policy was the opposite of that expected. As large numbers of highly rated men were returned from overseas, all male grade allotments were soon exceeded and male promotions were frozen, whereas Wacs, with a separate allotment and few WAC returnees, still received promotions. AGF Wacs soon came to have higher ratings than those in any other domestic command. Even so, the AGF WAC Officer continued to recommend that allotments be merged, saying that to promote AGF Wacs when men working with them in identical jobs could not be promoted "obviously had unfair implications from a practical point of view in the field."

Well after the end of the war, in October of 1945, Colonel Davis finally obtained publication of her 1943 recommendations: "Grades for enlisted men and enlisted women, other than detachment overhead, will be interchangeable without reference to this headquarters."

In the opinion of AGF staff directors, the failure to integrate womanpower, either in insignia or in grades, caused some loss of *esprit* among AGF Wacs. One enlisted woman wrote, "If the Army Ground Forces wants us to like it, why not give us an incentive?" Another said, "I am sorry to say that the girls in the other branches of the Service appear to have more to do, more responsible work, and are given more credit for the jobs they do." Like men serving under the same conditions, many objected to the more severe AGF discipline. One wrote, "I believe the Wacs in the AGF are disciplined far more than the Air Wacs and Service Force Wacs," and another added, "I cannot understand why we have less privileges and more severe discipline than the Air and Service Force Wacs. Restrictions concerning bedcheck, uniforms, dating officers, are more rigidly enforced, bordering in some cases on downright pettiness and hair-splitting."

One of the Ground Forces' characteristics that women found peculiarly objectionable was its policy of permitting very little transfer or rotation for women, and almost no overseas assignment. When the War Department directed the release of women for shipment overseas, the newest arrivals on a station were usually sent, partly because their low ratings fitted the requisitions, and partly because they were not as yet highly trained and indispensable.

One woman wrote, "Wacs do not rotate every year as the enlisted men do; the coveted overseas assignments go to the lower-ranking women, so here we sit year in and year out, same post, same job, which might account for our sinking morale." Dozens of women supported this view; one added, "as a matter of fact, this detachment has begun to be known as the Lost Battalion." Many who had no desire to go overseas believed that rotation of some sort was desirable. One enlisted woman summarized the general lack of *esprit* by concluding that "the lack of imagination on the part of some of the Regular Army men and their failure to understand that morale is based, among other things, on recognition of ability and the proper reward for such ability, has undoubtedly played a big part in the failure of the AGF WAC recruiting drive."

Effect of Manpower Shortages

Toward the end of the war, there began to be evident in the AGF a noticeable improvement in the integration of female military personnel. In part this change originated with the commanders of AGF installations in the United States at the time of severe personnel shortages. The manpower shortages of late 1943 and 1944 found the Ground Forces in the worst personnel situation of any major command, eventually requiring the emergency transfer of thousands of men from the Air Forces and Service Forces. At this time, and especially when the War Department required the shipment overseas of all general service men, many AGF stations began to show increased interest in obtaining WAC units. There was by this date little prospect of obtaining them, because of recruiting difficulties and increased competition from other commands.

The War Department's decision was that incoming WAC recruits would be divided among the three major commands according to the number of requisitions on file from each; the AGF's requisitions being less than 3 percent of the total, only 3 of every 100 women recruited were sent to AGF. This trickle was reduced still further when the War Department authorized branch recruiting, since the Army Ground Forces did not at first elect to recruit. In the first four months of 1944, the Ground Forces got only 20 branch recruits, as against the Air Forces 5,000; in addition, some 3,000 women enlisted without promise of a branch, and of these the AGF got only 3 percent, or about 90 women.

The AGF considered the assignment of recruiters as wasteful, and turned to efforts to get more Wacs without expenditure. First, the War Department was persuaded to give the AGF some 100 Wacs left surplus when the Eastern Defense Command was inactivated. Next, in April of 1944, the AGF requested the War Department to give it 8 percent instead of 3 percent of all recruits. This the War Department refused to do, since the increase would have meant a reduction in the shipments to other commands which had earlier demonstrated faith in Wacs and had made their housing plans accordingly.[8]

In July, the Army Ground Forces appealed again to the General Staff for a "more equitable distribution," asking that it be given almost all of the general assignment recruits, which were then being divided among the three major commands. This was opposed by other commands and by The Adjutant General, who pointed out that it would penalize the AAF and ASF, which had sent out recruiting teams when the AGF had not. However, it was agreed to grant the AGF a special favor, in recognition of its manpower shortages; it might recruit for job and branch in all service commands, whether it had a station there or not.[9] AGF now at last assigned small numbers of its own personnel to obtain recruits, and sent out station teams under the station-and-job recruiting system. The teams did not prove particularly adept at selection, and the desired type of recruit was not always obtained until after the station-assignment plan was ended.

As AGF personnel shortages continued, the War Department was finally obliged to increase its quota from 3,690 to 7,500, thus giving it a larger share of incoming recruits.[10] In early 1945 it was necessary to give AGF a further concession: that of dropping the previous system of apportionment of recruits, and acceding to the Ground Forces' request not only for top priority on WAC recruits but for the first choice on the scarce clerical skills. By this means, stenographers, typists, and clerks were diverted from other commands and sent to fill the AGF quota.

At the time of the Ground Forces' greatest crisis, the Battle of the Bulge, AGF WAC units were ordered withdrawn from its less active stations, such as those of the Antiaircraft Command, and rushed to stations where a heavy load was expected, particularly to combat infantry replacement training installations.[11]

Wacs also were relied upon in the great overseas replacement depot at Fort Meade, where it was stated that the women now "formed the backbone of the administrative organization of the installation, particularly since enlisted men in the headquarters were comparatively new because of the enforced rotation policies for men established by the War Department." Immediately after V-E Day, the women at Fort Meade were hastily transferred across the country to Replacement Depot 4 at Camp Adair, Oregon, to meet the expected heavy shipments to the Pacific. When V-J Day halted the expected rush of replacements westward and the west coast depot was inactivated, the Wacs were promptly shipped back to Replacement Depot 1, now at Camp Pickett, upon the insistence of the commanding officer of that installation.

At about this time the last major headquarters refusing to use Wacs—Army Ground Forces headquarters in Wash-

---

[8] D/F, G–1 for TAG through CofS, 31 May 44. See Incl and M/R. CofS 324.5 WAC.

[9] Memo, ASF for TAG, 11 Jul 44. SPGAC 341 Gen (7-11-44)-69. History of proposal summarized here, and disapproved by SW, in SPAP 341 WAAC (2-26-43).

[10] AGF WAC Hist, Vol. I, pp. 42–46, gives history of allotments.

[11] By May of 1945, 42 percent of AGF Wacs were in Infantry installations, 21 percent at Overseas Replacement Depots, and 30 percent divided among Armored, Field Artillery, Cavalry, and Tank Destroyer Training installations.

ington, D. C.—also yielded to the problem of the shortage of expert clerical help, and brought enlisted women into Washington. These women quickly became an integral part of a number of offices, so that the headquarters decided to retain them permanently and move them with it to Fort Monroe.

The close of the war was to see a complete reversal of original policy, with the Army Ground Forces taking the lead in urging a postwar WAC component, and spearheading the demand for a Regular Army WAC. "The services of these women proved of direct assistance in winning the war," observed one staff study, "A far greater number could have been effectively employed." Another study alleged: "Economical, efficient, and spirited results are achieved in military installations where both male and female personnel are on duty."

CHAPTER XVIII

The Army Service Forces

The Army's third major command, the Army Service Forces, had by mid-1944 been assigned some 40 percent of the WAC's enlisted women, including training center cadre. Upon the departure of Colonel Hobby's office for the General Staff level, the position of ASF WAC Officer was established, parallel to that of Colonel Bandel in the Army Air Forces and Colonel Davis in the Army Ground Forces. The first and only incumbent was Lt. Col. Katherine R. Goodwin, formerly staff director of the First Service Command and personnel officer in the Office of the Director WAC. Her office was located in that of the ASF Director of Personnel, General Dalton, but she had advisory powers direct to General Somervell on nonpersonnel matters. Because of its late beginning and because the ASF did not desire separate statistical studies for women, Colonel Goodwin's office had only one assistant.[1]

In the field, each of the nine service commands and the Military District of Washington continued to have its own WAC staff director. For a time the staff director's office was under the service command's director of personnel, until later raised by an ASF circular to the immediate office of the commanding general of the service command. In those commands which Colonel Goodwin considered the most successful in recruiting and public relations, notably the Third and Seventh,

the staff director also conducted periodic conferences of WAC company officers and recruiters in the area in order to improve efficiency and spread the latest information on personnel practices.[2]

The numbers of Wacs assigned to each service command varied greatly, from scarcely more than 1,000 in the First to 2,000 in the Eighth and more than 4,000 in the Fourth, which operated a training center. In general these were organized in regular post headquarters companies which, although no longer required to be identical, contained similar clerical and administrative personnel to help staff the post.[3]

Service Command	Officers	Enlisted Women
First	110	1,150
Second	120	1,371
Third	180	1,287
Fourth	600	a 4,600
Fifth	65	1,500
Sixth	170	1,140
Seventh	480	a 2,800
Eighth	240	2,190
Ninth	300	1,500
Military District of Washington	50	1,050

a Including training center.

[1] Distribution, Versatility, and Excellence of Wacs Serving with ASF, a 10-page summary prepared by Colonel Goodwin a year before the end of the war. Atchd to Memo, Dir WAC for CG ASF, 23 Sep 44, WDWAC 341, in SPAP 341 WAC (11–6–43). Unless otherwise stated, references are to this, by brief title, ASF WAC Summary. See Table 4, Appendix A.

[2] Interv with Lt Col Katherine Goodwin, 2 May 51.

[3] ASF WAC Summary.

LT. COL. KATHERINE R. GOODWIN (*center*) *visits the Signal Corps photographic laboratory at Camp Hood, Texas, August 1944.*

Other Wacs were allotted directly to the various ASF technical services such as the Signal Corps, for duty on Class II installations under the jurisdiction of the technical service, although located within the service command. Each of these services ordinarily had a WAC staff director, and sometimes several, as in the case of the Transportation Corps and its various ports. The ASF administrative services, such as The Adjutant General's Department, seldom had staff directors or assigned WAC personnel, since they had few if any Class II installations; personnel in their specialty was ordinarily assigned as part of post headquarters companies.

In this far-flung organization, existing records gave little clue to the exact jobs filled by Wacs and the exact numbers of Wacs in each job. Wacs on Class II installations, such as those of the Signal Corps, might accurately be assumed to be working for that service, but not all were necessarily in communications duties. Similarly, Wacs in post headquarters companies might be working for the post headquarters, but they might also be in suboffices of the administrative services, such as the post judge advocate, or in Quartermaster Corps, Signal Corps, Medical Corps, or other technical work not under the technical services allotment.

Even though exact statistics thus were never gathered, it was known that the Army Service Forces, as its name implied, offered large numbers of noncombat jobs intrinsically suitable for women, and that Wacs at the height of the war had worked their way into a wide variety of them. Especially from the individual administrative and technical services, some conclusions could be obtained as to the relative success and suitability of the duties.

The Signal Corps

The first of the Army Service Forces' agencies to request Wacs was, according to its own undisputed claims, the Signal Corps.[4] Even in World War I the Chief Signal Officer reported:

Our experience in Paris with the untrained and undisciplined English-speaking French women operators and experience elsewhere with the willing but untrained men operators was almost disastrous. The remarkable change in the character of the service at General Headquarters and other points when the American women operators took over was one of the features of the Signal Corps work of the times.[5]

In spite of this early enthusiasm, the Signal Corps experienced numerous delays and difficulties in launching a successful program to employ Waacs in World War II. In part this early delay resulted from a strong distrust of the Auxiliary status. In the earliest conferences the chief exponent of this view was Col. Henry L. P. King, Military Personnel Branch, Office of the Chief Signal Officer, who feared loss of trained personnel if the WAAC Director had command powers. In addition to seeking assignment and transfer control, the Signal Corps asked that the women wear Signal Corps insignia, that their units be designated Signal Corps and not

WAAC, and that communications training be given by the Signal Corps and not by WAAC training centers.

Such proposals for integration were deemed by the War Department illegal under the Auxiliary status, with the exception of the matter of technical training. WAAC Headquarters proved agreeable to abandoning its plans for a communications specialists school at WAAC training centers in order that the Signal Corps might send qualified personnel to whatever Signal Corps schools were indicated. The Director also gave reassurance that— as was later to be demonstrated—she would never move any such unit, once assigned. At this, the Chief Signal Officer expressed in writing his appreciation of the concession and added:

It is felt that as a result of the co-operation given . . . by the Women's Army Auxiliary Corps, the way has been opened for the release of needed enlisted men to field units and for a more extensive use of WAAC personnel.[6]

---

[4] Unless otherwise specified, statements through 1943 are from (1) Narrative OCSigO, Activities in Connection with WAAC or WAC Pers for Signal Corps Duty, October 1943, DRB AGO. Hereafter cited as SigC WAC Narrative. (See Bibliographical Note.) (2) Bound folder, WAAC Pers on Signal Corps Duty, Tab 1, Policy of CSigO Regarding WAAC Pers; loaned historian by Capt Jane Reeves, SigC WAC Stf Dir, 3 May 46, present location unknown. Hereafter cited as SigC Stf Dir file. (3) Interviews with: Maj Walter F. McDonald, SigC, OCSigO; Col Donald H. Nelson, OCSigO, Maj James L. Clark, OCSigO; Mr. Bruce W. Quisenberry, PRO, OCSigO; Lt Norma J. Fisher, OCSigO; Maj Charlotte E. Rhodes, former CO 334 1st Sig Serv Co, Germany, and 17th Sig Co, Ft Myer, Va.; all on 19 Sep 49; Capt Barbara Rodes, WAC Stf Dir, G–2, 22 Mar 46.
[5] Rpt, CSigO to SW, 1919, extract in Memo, Chief MPD SigC for Adm Div SigC, 29 Sep 42. SigC 320.2 WAC.
[6] Memo, Brig Gen Charles M. Milliken, OCSigO, for Dir WAAC, 26 Oct 42. SPWA 320.2 (10–26–42), unnumbered folder, Signal Corps, G–1 WD WAC files.

Proceeding with enthusiasm, the Signal Corps not only requisitioned Waacs for its Class II installations, but requested that all service commands be directed to requisition Waacs in every one of certain listed communications duties under their jurisdiction. Additional sweeping estimates were submitted to the Army Service Forces, as they had been periodically since the WAAC was organized, proposing to use women in literally every Signal Corps activity, from mixed tactical units to pigeon companies.[7]

The most important immediate proposal was that the WAAC aid in what came to be called the WIRES plan (Women in Radio and Electrical Service). Currently enrolled in Signal Corps schools were some 30,000 civilians, receiving free training and allowances during three- to six-month courses in radio and switchboard operation and related skills. Men in such courses were in the enlisted reserve and could be called to active duty upon successful graduation, but women graduates were necessarily hired as civilians, with the possibility that once trained they would seek better-paid jobs elsewhere. Use of the WAAC inactive reserve thus appeared a logical solution, and was generally agreeable to the women; a group at one school organized themselves as the first WIRES and appealed to Director Hobby to admit them. Upon the request of the Signal Corps, WAAC officers were dispatched to make necessary arrangements.[8]

Unsuitable Organizations and Locations

These extensive plans were shortly checked by the discovery that, while most Signal Corps jobs were perfectly suitable in themselves, they could not be given to Waacs without violation of numerous War Department policies on assignments for women. Since most Signal Corps jobs on Army posts were performed by civilians, the Signal Corps informed the Director that it would be necessary to rescind the ruling that Waacs would not replace civilians. There were also about 1,500 Signal Corp enlisted men who might have been replaced, but these were in small scattered detachments, the majority at stations where no WAAC unit existed. Therefore, the Signal Corps also asked the War Department to rescind the ruling that enlisted women would not be sent to any station without a WAAC barracks and commander for their adequate housing, supply, and protection.[9]

Both of these efforts were unsuccessful, since neither of these policies was ever to be relaxed by the War Department. Another point of dispute was the fact that Waacs, as civilians, could be assigned only to a WAAC unit and not to the Signal Corps; thus, the assignment of Signal-trained Waacs was a prerogative of the post commander and not the Signal Corps, and the WAAC Director could not guarantee their correct assignment.

On the other hand, the Signal Corps insisted that the WAAC must "guarantee them assignment on a communications basis and none other," and Colonel King wrote, "Tell the WAAC that since Signal

[7] (1) Stf Study, Maj J. K. Cunningham for G–1, 4 Nov 42. SPGAM 320.2 WAAC (9–15–42), in WD G–1 321 WAC. (2) Memo, CG ASF for CofS USA, 17 Jun 42. WD G–1 320.2 WAC (6–12–42), Tab A.

[8] (1) WDBPR Press Release, 9 Jan 43. (2) Ltr, Miss Stella Gunning, Pres WIRES, Trinidad Junior College, Colo., to Dir WAAC, 20 Nov 42, with Ind, Dir WAC to SigC. SigC 320.2 WAAC.

[9] (1) Memo, Maj. W. K. St. Clair, MPD OCSigO, for Chief MPB, 14 Oct 44. SPSMP 320.2 WAAC, in unnumbered folder, Signal Corps, WAC files. (2) Memo, Chief MPB OCSigO for Actg CSigO, 19 Oct 42, SigC 320.2 WAAC. (3) R&W Slip, Action 1, SigC Aux Br for MPD SigC, 9 Jul 42. SigC 320.2 WAAC.

Corps money is being used to train Wires we mean to keep same either as civil service employees or Wacks." [10]

Colonel King therefore returned to efforts to secure transfer of command from the Director to the Signal Corps, in the belief that the Signal Corps could then assign Waacs to replace civilians and to stations without WAAC companies. He wrote memoranda and made personal visits to most of the other technical and administrative services, urging their concerted action against the War Department policies involved. Securing the agreement of some, and noncommittal replies from others, he then attempted to call an ASF conference to force the issue. [11]

The Army Service Forces did not comply with the request, since it was at the time awaiting General Staff decisions as to the Corps' future status and size, and was unable to give the Signal Corps much more satisfaction than had WAAC Headquarters. At this time the Signal Corps noted, "The situation became so complicated that it was not known how requisitions were to be submitted, or how to procure Waacs for any type of installation under the Chief Signal Officer." [12]

Such squabbles over maximum replacement proved doubly futile, in that the numbers of WAAC recruits were never to be such as to warrant extension of employment to questionable locations or to replace civilians. The immediate result was that the Signal Corps delayed in opening its schools to Waacs, the WIRES plan lagged for some six months without action, and the Signal Corps established only the schools already agreed upon—three radio schools at civilian institutions, to provide radio operators for the AAF.

Thus, the first WAAC communications specialists to reach the field went in post

headquarters units and—other than radio operators—without Army training in Signal skills, relying wholly upon their civilian background. Recruiters continued to accept volunteers in Signal skills, and training centers to send them out, without much knowledge of actual needs. [13]

Signal Duties in the Field

Among the first communications specialists to reach the field were the bilingual telephone operators in the first overseas unit, which reached North Africa in January of 1943. Two WAAC officers also went to the Eighth Air Force in England, even before arrival of the European theater staff director, to plan for Signal Corps Waacs in that command. A considerable percentage of the first WAAC unit to reach England consisted of telephone operators and other communications personnel, sent with the approval of the Chief Signal Officer but without Army technical training.

At about this time, the first units began to reach the Signal Corps' own installations in the United States. First to arrive,

---

[10] (1) Comments to R&W Sheet, MPD OCSigO to Chief, 17 Nov 42; (2) R&W Sheet, Entry 1, Capt Kenneth E. BeLieu to Col King, 8 Dec 42. SigC 320.2 WAAC.

[11] Ltrs, Chief MPB OCSigO to Chiefs of Mil Br, CE, Ord Dept, 10 Nov 42, with incl; replies by 1st Inds. SigC 320.2 WAAC.

[12] SigC WAC Narrative; also R&W Slip, Capt BeLieu, MPB OCSigO for Chief, 9 Dec 42. SigC 320.2 WAAC.

[13] (1) Story of further WIRES planning: Stf Study, Capt BeLieu, MPB OCSigO, 15 Dec 42, with covering memos. SigC 322 WAC 1943. Memo, 2d O M. McCull for Dir WAAC, 5 Jan 43. Unnumbered folder, Signal Corps, WAC files. R&W Slip, Entry 1, Maj John W. Ramsey, SigC, for Exec OCSigO, 6 Jan 43. SigC 322 WAC 1943. Memo, 2d Os Brainerd and McCull for Dir WAAC, 11 Feb 43, with Incl and Inds. Unnumbered folder, Signal Corps, WAC files. (2) Two WDBPR Press Releases, 10 Dec 42, and 14 Apr 43.

in March of 1943, were units assigned to
Camp Crowder, Missouri, which by the
end of the WAAC totaled some 489 enrolled women and 100 officers. Another
unit under Signal Corps control went to
Fort Monmouth, New Jersey, in June, and
still others were on requisition. However,
most women in these units were not technical specialists, but clerical and overhead
workers to aid in running the schools.[14]

From the first there was no doubt of
these units' success in the assigned duties.
In Allied Headquarters in North Africa,
the assistant chief signal officer stated:

The manner in which they picked up the
work was outstanding. . . . Had we had
enough of them, we could have used them to
operate all our fixed communications installations—telephones and telegraph—throughout the rear areas. Every one . . . released
some man for Signal Corps duty up in the
combat zone.

The former chief signal officer of the AAF
in North Africa added:

Don't tell me a woman can't keep a secret.
Why, their own company commander
doesn't even know where the board is located—we've tested the girls again and
again.[15]

The Chief Signal Officer, Maj. Gen.
Dawson Olmstead, on a visit to the area,
was informed by the theater commander
that approximately 1,300 more Signal
Corps Waacs in ten different specialties
would be required if obtainable. The same
good reports were received from the European theater, where, after a one-week indoctrination course, 100 WAAC telephone
operators were assigned to operate multiple switchboards at five command headquarters. The officer in charge reported,
"Very soon I received praise of the improved service, as the good results were
noticed almost immediately."[16]

Another early success was the participation of twenty-nine WAC telephone operators in the Quebec Conference in
August of 1943. Rushed from train to
switchboard, the women were on continuous duty for eighteen hours and doubled
as secretaries and stenographers when a
shortage of these occurred. After seventeen days of secret duty, each member
received an individual commendation.
Wacs also served successfully on the
switchboards at the Cairo Conference and
the Potsdam Conference.[17]

Requests from Signal officers in the
United States continued to indicate an
urgent need for more Waacs, since current
directives required release of their general
service men. Civilian replacements were
scarce, and available limited service men
often were unsuitable.[18] In general such
requests also indicated a desire for Signal
Corps technical training for the women. In
England the using agencies, desiring teletypists, had been obliged to train WAAC
typists in the theater, which they protested
was a task more properly assumed by the
Signal Corps in the United States. Studies
showed that women could, with training,
fill seventy-eight different Signal Corps
jobs. Therefore, in May of 1943, Brig. Gen.
Henry L. P. King's successor, Col. Duncan
Hodges, put the long-delayed WIRES plan
into effect. The women were to be trained
first in Signal Corps duties in an inactive
WAAC status, and then sent to basic
training. Objectives were set at some 2,000

---

[14] SigC Stf Dir file.
[15] The WAC in the SigC, Speech by Col Oveta
Culp Hobby. SigC file, OCMH. See Ch. XX, below,
for North African Theater of Operations details.
[16] Appendix to SigC WAC Narrative.
[17] (1) *Ibid.* (2) Speech cited n. 15. (3) Interv with
Capt Jane Reeves, SigC WAC Stf Dir, 3 May 46.
[18] Ltr, Post SigO, Ft Bliss, Texas, to Chief MPB
OCSigO. SigC 322 WAC 1943.

QUEBEC CONFERENCE, AUGUST 1943

women, the first of whom reported in late May to a training course at the State Teachers' College at Livingston, Alabama, with eleven other schools scheduled for later opening.[19]

Effect of Army Status

The Signal Corps was highly pleased by the WAC's new Army status and the system of assignment, instead of attachment, to the using command. Signal Corps Wacs could now be assigned to the signal service company and not to the post, while the simultaneous multiplication of WAC units in the field made it possible to attach these women to existing companies in adequate numbers without violating War Department housing policy. On the other hand, Army status wrecked plans for WIRES training, since the new WAC legislation provided for no inactive reserve component. A mere 276 women were already in schools; these were given a choice of discharge or enlistment, and all enlisted.

The Signal Corps immediately began to seek some other system of earmarking acceptable recruits in order to retain Signal Corps control of qualified women during their basic training. For this purpose, the newly devised plan for branch recruiting appeared made to order, and it was with some disappointment that the Signal Corps received the Army Service Forces' decision not to join the AAF in branch recruiting at this time. The disappointment was alleviated within a few months by the authorization for station-and-job recruiting, which achieved virtually the same result. Under this plan, women received basic training first and then reported to the Signal Corps for either immediate assignment or specialist training.[20]

Some difficulty in obtaining recruits, even with the station-and-job promise, was caused by the high requirements of the Signal Corps. Women for attendance at the three radio operators schools were required to have near-officer qualifications: AGCT scores of 100 for radio operators and 110 for repairmen, as well as good scores on the radio operator's aptitude or mechanical aptitude tests.

By September of 1943 some 1,750 women had been trained, chiefly for the Air Forces, and the schools were discontinued. Thereafter the Signal Corps generally accepted only women with high AGCT scores as well as civilian skill "sufficient to qualify them for assignment with only nominal on-the-job indoctrination in Army procedure." Thus, women to be trained as tabulating machine operators were required to have clerical skill and an AGCT score in Grade III or better; women to be key punch operators required the same plus average typing speed; cryptographic clerks needed officer qualifications—an AGCT score in Grade I or II plus good education and mathematics or language background. Full civilian training in their fields was required of radio operators, radio and electrical repairmen, telephone operators, teletypewriter operators, draftsmen, and various photographic experts.

Such highly qualified personnel was not only hard to find, but the subject of competition from other agencies, particularly the WAVES, which offered officer status

---

[19] (1) Appendix cited n. 16. (2) Stf study cited n. 13(1). (3) Memo, Col James S. Willis, SigC for Brig Gen Frank C. Meade, OCSigO, 17 May 43. SigC 322 WAC. (4) WDBPR Press Releases, 11 and 21 May 43.

[20] (1) Ltr, Hq AAF to AACS, 31 Jul 44, and incls. WD G–1 220.3 WAC (8–7–44). (2) SigC WAC Narrative. (3) Memo, Dir MPD ASF for Dir Pers ASF, 26 Oct 43. SPAP 341 WAAC (2–26–43).

to cryptographers and other specialists. By June of 1944 the Office of the Chief Signal Officer was still highly discontented with the returns from station-and-job recruiting, which had produced Wacs only to the extent of some 1,100, or about 9 percent of the strength of the Signal Corps instead of the 16 percent that it had been authorized.[21]

Signal Corps Training

With a few exceptions, the Signal Corps did not find it necessary to give specialist training to the women who reported to it. It was stated that "substantial" Signal Corps classes, chiefly for overseas shipment, were conducted at Fort Monmouth and at Camp Crowder, but these were chiefly refresher courses in Army procedure for already-qualified women. For skills scarce or nonexistent in civilian life, such as cryptographer, classes were eventually held at Fort Monmouth. In general it was reported that women could master Signal training without alteration in course content, and presented no problems except in the matter of housing.[22]

Only one training difficulty was reported, that concerning the first cryptographic school. In the early months of this course, the officer in charge reported:

The WAC personnel we have received so far are almost without exception woefully uninformed about the personalities, the geography, and the matériel of the war. It is also evident that their intelligence, on the average, is decidedly inferior to the men they are replacing.

He asked that personnel be better selected according to prescribed standards: officer AGCT score (110 or better), wide vocabularies, technical skill, and knowledge of world events, and that they be chosen from among teachers in higher grades, librar-ians, editors, authors, and similar occupations. "They are not likely to be found among sales clerks, packers, restaurant employees, machine tool operators, beauty operators, and music teachers." [23]

With higher WAC enrollment standards, higher-grade personnel became more readily available. With the virtual cessation of the WAC Officer Candidate School at a time when the Signal Corps Officer Candidate School still received large quotas, it became still easier to get women of officer qualifications but enlisted status. Final reports indicated good results in training female cryptographers, and the instructor at Fort Monmouth reported that the women "far exceeded expectations" and could "hold their own with the best students." [24] Some WAC supervisors were of the opinion that cryptography would prove the most important future use for Signal Corps Wacs in occupied areas, since women did not fraternize with enemy nationals to the extent that men did, and were therefore less apt to betray secrets inadvertently.

Signal Corps Jobs

One of the first and most important assignments of Signal Corps Wacs was that in the War Department Signal Center in Washington, called "the world's most im-

---

[21] (1) Speech cited n. 15. (2) Quotation from Ltr, TAG for six SvCs, 25 Mar 44. SPX 341 WAC (3–22–44) PR–I. (3) WD Cir 340, 29 Dec 43. (4) Memo, Chief Pers and Tng Serv, OCSigO, for CG ASF, 7 Jun 44. SPMSP 320.2 WAC, in SigC 322 WAC.

[22] (1) WDBPR Press Release, Enlistment. (2) R&W Slip, Maj John W. Ramsey, SigC, for Exec OCSigO, 6 Jan 43. SigC 322 WAC.

[23] Memo, Lt Col Matthew G. Jones, SigC, OIC Code Cen, for Capt Louis F. Fuchs, 20 Jan 44. Unnumbered files of Career Management Br, OCSigO.

[24] The SigC Message, Ft Monmouth, N. J., July 21, 1944, p. 2.

portant communications center," [25] and hub of the Army's entire wire, radio, and cable system. With its outlying transmitting, receiving, and operating installations in the vicinity, it made up station WAR, in immediate contact by radio with all theaters and by land-line circuits with every major installation in the United States. Wacs for this service met the highest of intelligence and aptitude tests, and their loyalty records were minutely investigated. With the first assignment of a few Wacs to this work, the Chief Signal Officer, Maj. Gen. Harry C. Ingles, reported "an immediate improvement. . . . The loyalty and application to duty of these Waacs created an example which resulted in a noticeable increase in production." [26] By the end of 1944, some 235 Wacs were employed, chiefly in teletype operation, including radioteletype, and transmission and relay of messages translated into perforated tape on highspeed perforators. The chief of the Army Communications Service, Maj. Gen. Frank Stoner, stated, "We have found the Wacs conscientious, efficient, and dependable . . . thoroughly capable of filling many positions which formerly required trained men." [27]

The 2d Signal Service Battalion, which was under G–2 Division of the War Department for operations, employed some 1,000 Wacs at its stations at Arlington Hall, Vint Hill, and Two Rock Ranch. In general the secret work was routine, noisy, but of a nature requiring perfection in detail. The WAC staff director reported:

It was proven over and over again that women were far better equipped than men for routine but detailed work. They were not qualified for highly technical jobs in most cases, but were qualified for routine research and for specialists' jobs such as teletype and radio operator.

About fifty women were also assigned to the battalion's Miami detachment, which distinguished itself chiefly by attempting to operate with a male commander for the WAC unit, in violation of War Department regulations, to be found out only when improper administration resulted and was investigated. [28]

Other Signal Corps stations also employed appreciable numbers of Wacs. The Eastern Signal Corps Training Center at Fort Monmouth employed an eventual total of about 300, chiefly clerical and administrative personnel to run the center. [29] The Holabird Signal Depot near Baltimore employed some 100 women for similar duties, and a quota of 75 was allotted to the Army Pictorial Service and Signal Corps Photographic Center on Long Island, for work in film libraries and laboratories. [30]

The average Army post in service or air commands also employed a few Signal Corps Wacs, although in lesser numbers than enlisted men and civilians. For example, the staff of the Signal Corps office at Fort McClellan, Alabama, included 3 officers, 8 enlisted men, 5 enlisted women, and 55 civilians. All positions appeared to

[25] WDBPR Press Release, Wacs in the Signal Center; in *Washington Post*, November 12, 1944, and *Army Times,* December 16, 1944.

[26] Ltr, Gen Ingles to Col Hobby, 12 July 43. WAAC file and SigC 322 WAC.

[27] Release cited n. 25.

[28] (1) Interv with Capt Barbara Rodes, WAC Stf Dir G–2 WD, 22 Mar 46. (2) WDBPR Press Release, Enlistment. (3) Memo, Dir Pers ASF for CSigO, 6 Dec 44. SPAP 320.2 WAC.

[29] M/R, sub: Fld Trip to Ft Monmouth; also R&W Slip, MPB OCSigO for Pers and Tng Serv, 15 Jul 43. Folder, WAC Surveys, unnumbered files of SigC Career Management Br.

[30] WDBPR Press Release, Enlistment. (2) Interv with Capt Jane Reeves, SigC WAC Stf Dir, 3 May 46. (3) Memo, MPB OCSigO for CG SigC Photographic Cen, Long Island, 26 July 43. SigC 320.2 WAAC.

be essentially civilian in nature. The experience of WAC training centers, where Wacs necessarily composed most of the staff of the post signal office, indicated that Wacs could if necessary perform most of the Signal duties on an Army post. The question as to whether all or any of such jobs required military status was a technical one for higher authorities, but from the WAC viewpoint either all-WAC or all-civilian offices were preferable to mixed ones, which spotlighted differences in pay and privileges.[31]

Officer Employment

Employment of officers was in general seldom as efficient as that of enlisted women. Both in the United States and overseas the Signal Corps showed a propensity for assigning women officers to secretarial and similar duties scarcely requiring an officer's training. Eventually three WAC officers were allowed to attend the G–2 school, with the promise that if all graduated in the top 10 percent more Wacs would be accepted; all did. Several WAC officers also attended the three-month Advanced Radio Communications School at Arlington Hall and the Signal Corps Supply School at Camp Holabird.[32]

Signal Corps Jobs Overseas

Extensive employment of Signal Corps Wacs, both officer and enlisted, was made in all overseas theaters, although not to the extent that the Signal Corps desired, Brig. Gen. Jerry V. Matejka, the new head of Signal Corps personnel, complained:

Substantial requirements for Wacs on Signal Corps duty have existed in the various theaters, yet the furnishing of WAC personnel has been either retarded or abandoned because of apparent lack of the same co-ordination of interested agencies in the War Department as is applied to furnishing enlisted men as fillers and replacements.[33]

Some measure of the difficulty appeared due to the Signal Corps' own reluctance to part with Wacs on its stations in the United States. Thus, when requests from the European theater for a WAC signal service battalion of approximately 550 Wacs were approved by Operations Division, War Department General Staff, the Army Service Forces protested that male personnel should be sent in order to avoid disrupting the work of field stations using trained Wacs on key jobs. On Operations Division's insistence the unit was authorized for activation in the theater, but with the requirement that 200 of the Wacs be supplied by the theater.[34] Even when trained radio operators were found malassigned as clerks on Signal Corps installations in the United States, the Chief Signal Officer refused to release them for radio work overseas.[35] General Matejka further remarked that "use in overhead installations has been disrupted by the withdrawal of WAC personnel for overseas."[36]

In spite of the alleged difficulty of getting Signal-trained women for overseas duty, most overseas theaters by the end of the war had acquired relatively large

---

[31] (1) *The McClellan Cycle*, April 13, 1945, "SigC Job Big One on Post." (2) Press Release, 2d WAC Tng Cen, 1 Jul 43.

[32] (1) See overseas chapters. (2) Intervs cited n. 4. (3) Memo, Chief Pers and Tng Serv OCSigO for CSigO, 23 Sep 44. SPMSP 320.2 WAC, in SigC 322 WAC.

[33] Memo cited n. 21(4).

[34] Memo, Exec, G–1 Div for G–1, 12 Oct 44; Memo, "H.E.K." for Maj Gen Stephen C. Henry, G–1, 18 Oct 44. WD G–1 322 WAC.

[35] Memo, CofT for CG ASF, 30 Sep 44, SPTPM 220.3 WAC; with 2d Ind from CSigO and 3d from MPD ASF, SPGAC 210.3 WAC.

[36] Memo cited n. 21(4).

numbers, many trained in the theater. Some one third of all Wacs in the Mediterranean theater, or about 700 women, were estimated to be employed on communications duties—a percentage notably higher than that achieved in the United States.[37] In Europe, the 3341st Signal Service Battalion eventually reached a peak strength of about 28 officers and 738 enlisted women, and in Paris its women were employed in every department of what claimed to be "the largest message center in the world . . . with the exception of Washington, D. C."[38] Other units also contained some Signal Corps personnel, which brought the number in Europe to an estimated one fourth of the theater's WAC strength, or some 1,700 women. The Pacific theater reported that only about 3 percent of its Wacs, or 150 women, were in communications work, including secret duties with the Signal Intelligence Section. Lesser numbers were also used in smaller theaters.[39]

Peak of Employment

In September of 1944, some months before the WAC reached its peak strength, the Chief Signal Officer estimated that there were about 1,500 enlisted women at six installations under his own jurisdiction, or some 16 percent of the total enlisted strength. This, he believed, exceeded all other technical services in percentage of replacement with the possible exception of the Chemical Warfare Service. In addition, there were 236 enlisted women in the War Department Signal Center, and more than 700 performing Signal Corps duties in the service commands. To this could be added at least 1,700 in Europe, 700 in Italy, and 150 in the Pacific. It thus appeared likely that Wacs on Signal Corps

duties totaled at least 5,000, some 5 percent of the WAC strength.[40]

The general job groupings for Wacs, at least in the United States, were estimated by the Chief Signal Officer to include:

	Percent
Signal Corps Technical Specialists	63
Administrative and Clerical	25
Mess and Motor Pool Personnel	9
Miscellaneous	3

Special Problems of Signal Corps Wacs

In spite of such wide employment and consistent success on Signal Corps duties, it was evident by the end of the war that in employing women the Signal Corps faced several problems. The women described most Signal Corps technical jobs as "nerve-wracking"; after a few months they tended to become a nightmare of beeping earphones, clicking keys, or clattering machinery. A WAC inspector reported:

Severe nervous strain was imposed by the necessity for constant attention . . . no thought was required for much of it, yet the worker did not dare to let the work become automatic, as one slip wrecked everything, and the fear of costing men's lives was always with them.[41]

---

[37] For details, see Ch. XX, below.

[38] (1) Press Release, Hq ComZ ETO, Receipt No. 92782, 10 Jul 45. (2) Interv with Capt Jane Reeves, SigC WAC Stf Dir, 3 May 46. (3) M/R, 9 Oct 44, sub: Summary of Radiograms on WAC Sig Serv Bn for ETO. MTD OCSigO 322 WAC Sig Serv Bn. (4) Ltr, CSigO to Dir WAC, 5 May 49. PRO file, OCSigO.

[39] See Chs. XXI, XXII, below.

[40] (1) Memo cited n. 21(4). (2) Memo cited n. 32(3).

[41] Discussions of WAC staff officers' opinions are based on: (1) Interv with Capt Barbara Rodes, WAC Stf Dir G–2 WD, 22 Mar 46. (2) Intervs with Lt. Col Dorothea A. Coleman, WAC Stf Dir, NATO and MTO, 21 Jan and 8 Feb 46. (3) SigC refs in Chs. XX–XXIII, below. (4) Intervs cited n. 4(3).

Added to this was the ever-present strain of keeping security, and sometimes the knowledge that the operator, alone with a few of the Army's top authorities, shared secrets in which a slip of the tongue in public could cost the lives of hundreds of soldiers.

Most Signal duties also involved shift-work, which constantly rotated so that regular sleeping and eating habits were impossible. British inspectors had pointed out long before the WAC was formed:

A policy is present in the service of working watches or shifts with irregular hours of duty . . . it should have been known by now that the irregular rhythm of working hours is injurious to health.[42]

WAC inspectors repeatedly recommended that shift changes be less frequent than the customary two weeks, but this was nowhere possible under established Signal Corps policies. On ordinary posts the handful of Signal Corps Wacs was obliged to try to sleep at odd hours while barracks-mates engaged in normal activities. On all-Signal Corps stations, company commanders attempted to reserve one building for each shift, a move which seldom proved practicable since women worked in different offices on different schedules. At only one station, Arlington Hall, was some measure of relief achieved by the use of cubicle housing, four women to a cubicle. One WAC adviser noted:

One of our biggest problems was that of shift workers . . . we had to watch their health carefully. There was always the danger of emotional upsets caused by difficult sleeping arrangements.

The company commander's usual efforts to provide feminine-type sports, recreation, orientation, or even hot food and sympathetic counsel were often thwarted by the women's peculiar working hours and by the impossibility of keeping cadre on 24-hour duty.

In addition, at most stations the shortage of Signal Corps personnel was such that no leaves, furloughs, or passes were possible for months. WAC advisers recommended, without effect, that "it is most important that officers and enlisted personnel, both men and women, be required to take regular leaves twice a year."[43] There was on many stations also a certain reluctance to release women for any cause, even for officer candidate school, and Wacs were not eligible for the direct commissions that men of equal qualifications received in certain duties, or for admission to Signal Corps Officer Candidate School. Even appropriate enlisted grades were chronically scarce; remarkably consistent complaints were received from stations all over the world that enlisted Wacs had replaced men in top enlisted grades, or even officers and warrant officers, without receiving any ratings at all.

On restricted installations, particularly the several detachments of the 2d Signal Service Battalion, the situation was especially difficult. Here a woman, once assigned, was a virtual prisoner for the duration; men might look for enforced rotation to overseas service, but even this was not permitted for a woman until after the end of the war. If a woman failed in or was unequal to technical duties, she was retained on the station in menial or service duties on the grounds that she "knew too much" to permit her to be released for proper assignment elsewhere.

WAC inspectors reported that women for such installations should have been originally selected from volunteers who had been clearly informed of their pros-

---

[42] *Conditions in The Three Women's Services.*
[43] Sources cited n. 41.

pects, a method that was successful in other technical services. Instead, Signal Corps personnel went to Forts Des Moines and Oglethorpe and selected women who afterwards alleged that they had received promises of grades, overseas service, officer training, or "the glamor of working for intelligence." Women recruited directly for the station were not informed of its restricted nature. Neither had some of the company officers been well chosen, in the opinion of WAC inspectors. One observer recommended that in the future all company officers be chosen from among operational officers who had themselves worked shifts and were "aware of aching feet and backs and being unable to sleep in the daytime." [44]

Even if capable, the company officers on secret installations were often not "cleared" to visit the men or women on the job, and thus understood neither the working conditions nor the measures needed to provide outside rest and quiet. Inspection privileges were likewise denied to Army classification survey teams, staff visitors, and medical officers. Because of the highly secret nature of the installations, neither the Signal Corps nor G–2 Division believed it possible to permit interference by medical officers or inspectors on the grounds of health and well-being for either men or women. The Signal Corps employed a rapid succession of WAC advisers and staff directors—among them Capt. Susanna Turner and Capt. Zelma Hanson—but did not clear these individuals to visit secret work. [45]

Eventually the health and morale situation of the 2d Signal Service Battalion became so bad that G–2 Division, in the closing months of the war, was obliged to accept a WAC staff director and to clear her for visits to secret units for which the

Signal Corps staff director was not cleared. This officer, Capt. Barbara Rodes, expressed her belief that many of the problems had been preventable, and that "If they had had a WAC Staff Director in the beginning to pick personnel after a study of G–2's needs, they would never have had low morale in the WAC unit." Captain Rodes succeeded in getting a few women released for overseas duty and officer candidate school, and in getting ratings for others. She also gave considerable effort to helping women "to visualize the importance of a job and to get the whole war picture so that they could keep their perspective."

Independent reports from virtually every overseas theater showed an almost identical pattern of difficulty in Signal Corps work, mitigated only to some extent by the more stimulating nature of life overseas. In the Mediterranean theater, by the end of the war, some 8 percent of Signal Wacs, or an estimated fifty women, had suffered mental breakdowns, and others were believed to be on the verge of physical or psychiatric illness. In the Southeast Asia Command, the majority of all illnesses occurred in the minority of women who were assigned to Signal Corps work.

Since the end of the war intervened before women in most theaters and domestic stations had been on Signal jobs for more than eighteen months, there was no exact knowledge as to how long their efficiency could have been sustained under existing conditions. There were some grounds for belief that, under unchanged Signal Corps personnel and housing policies, two or two and a half years might be the maximum serviceability of the

[44] *Ibid.*

[45] Memo cited n. 21(4).

average Wac, after which disability discharge would be required and attrition might outweigh efficiency. Civilian experience indicated that the duties themselves were not at fault, since civilian women made careers of such work, with the aid of vacations, normal recreation, and private housing. One WAC commander reported, "When demobilization came, my women swore they would never come back to the War Department or to shift work, but about 25 percent eventually did—as civilians." [46]

Evaluation of Success in Signal Jobs

Apart from the question of how long it could be sustained, there was no doubt that WAC performance on Signal Corps jobs had been successful. A board convened in late 1948 at Fort Monmouth to consider the employment of the WAC in communications activities stated that it was "an accepted conclusion" that women were "more adaptable and dexterous than men in the performance of certain technical specialties." [47] A survey made of Signal officers in Army areas and overseas commands produced the opinion that women could fill approximately 50 percent of all operations, communications, and photographic positions within a communications zone. The consensus was that many maintenance functions could also be performed by women, with the exception of those involving heavy physical labor, and that "Wacs should be used as far forward as Army Headquarters."

It was concluded that women should be used in as many such activities as possible, with immediate emphasis on training in Army schools as teletype and telephone operator, message center clerk, radio and radio telephone operator, cryptographic technician, and facsimile operator. Similar studies within the office of the Chief Signal Officer indicated likewise that Wacs could be used in communications centers, on switchboards, in photographic detachments, in film libraries, and—provided that a WAC detachment was already at the installation—in Signal Corps administrative offices at Army posts, camps, and stations. The proper division of employment between civilian and military women was left for future resolution. [48]

Chemical Warfare Service

Second among the Army Service Forces agencies to obtain a WAAC staff director and the promise of WAAC personnel was the Chemical Warfare Service (CWS). [49] While the numbers involved were relatively small, never exceeding about 700 Wacs, the percentage of replacement achieved was higher than that in most larger agencies, eventually reaching, at different times, from 13 to 22 percent of the Chemical Warfare Service's domestic

[46] Intervs cited n. 4(3).

[47] SigC Bd Study 17, Employment of WAC in Communications Activities. FMSCB 324.5, 5 Oct 48, Hq Ft Monmouth, in SigC 200.3 WAC No 1, 1948.

[48] D/F, SigC Career Management Br to Maj. James L. Clark, 23 Mar 49, sub: WAC Problem, SIGMP–4 Comment 1, with reply, Maj Clark to Col Nelson, 24 Mar 49. Corresp folder, Career Management Br files, OCSigO.

[49] Unless otherwise specified, all references are from the following sources: (1) ASF WAC Summary, Sec With Chemical Warfare Serv. (2) Memo, WAC Stf Dir CWS for Asst ASF WAC Off, 10 Aug 44, copy furnished author by Stf Dir. (3) Interv with Maj Helen E. Hart, CWS WAC Stf Dir, 26 Mar 46. (4) CW Bull, Mar–May 45, Vol. 31, No. 2, "Here Are the WAC," pp. 4–11. (5) Comments, undated, by Lt Mary B. Warner, OTI CWS, on first draft of this section submitted to her for CWS comment. WAC files OCMH.

INSTRUCTION IN RADIO THEORY *for women attending the Midland Radio and Television Schools, Inc., Kansas City, Missouri.*

enlisted strength.[50] In early April 1943 the first CWS WAAC unit reached Pine Bluff Arsenal in Arkansas. A second WAAC unit reported in late April to Dugway Proving Ground, Utah, and a third and fourth in June to Camp Detrick, Maryland, and to the Chemical Warfare Center, Edgewood Arsenal, Maryland.[51]

Commanding officers of field installations did not entirely share the enthusiasm of the chief of the Chemical Warfare Service for requisitioning Waacs, and admitted later that "men busy on research projects where the slightest error might ruin months of experiments at first took a dismal view of female assistants in laboratories and proving grounds." [52] However, tentative inquiries a few weeks after the units' arrival brought the reply that "the Waacs at these installations are rendering excellent service." An early thousand-hour experiment with a detail of sixty at

[50] (1) Strength of the Army, STM 30, 5 Jul 45, p. 19. (2) Memo, Chief MPB OCSigO for Chief Pers and Tng Serv OCSigO, 16 Jun 44. sub: WAC Enl Str of Various Tech Servs. SigC Career Management Br files, OCSigO.

[51] Memo, Col Harold E. Brooks, CWS, for Maj Gen William N. Porter, 2 Jun 43. CWS 324.5 WAC (Apr–Jun 43).

[52] Bull cited n. 49(4).

WOMEN DECONTAMINATION EXPERTS *in the Chemical Warfare Service at Gowen Field, Idaho.*

Edgewood Arsenal, to determine to what extent Waacs might be used in the work of impregnating protective clothing with chemicals, met with "such surprisingly good results that we are about to recommend that some all-WAAC chemical impregnating companies be organized."[53] The WAAC staff director, Lt. Helen E. Hart, later stated that her chief contribution to the CWS program at this time was her success, after much pleading, in persuading her commanding general to change the name of this unit, which was finally given the name of WAAC Processing Company, instead of that which the

general had first directed—WAAC Impregnation Company.[54]

Very shortly, CWS inspectors were surprised to find the entire WAAC detachment at Pine Bluff Arsenal plunged into a serious state of low morale by what appeared to male inspectors to be a minor circumstance—the fact that Waacs had not replaced soldiers. As a matter of fact, the shortage of civilian personnel had made it possible to secure a bona fide military allotment for the installation, which

---

[53] Ltr, Col Brooks, CWS, to CO, Huntsville Arsenal, Ala. CWS 324.5 WAC (Apr–Jun 43).

[54] Interv cited n. 49(3).

eventually would have required enlisted men, but to the Waacs nothing was apparent except that they had filled former civilian vacancies. CWS inspectors noted in some surprise that the "insidious idea" that a woman should replace a soldier appeared to be "prevalent among all WAAC companies in the field." The situation was somewhat alleviated upon conversion to Army status, when "malcontents" departed Pine Bluff Arsenal en masse. Thereafter, the fact of Army status reassured the women that military jobs were being filled.[55]

While the diminishing supply of recruits made it impossible to fill all further CWS requisitions, three more detachments later reported respectively to Rocky Mountain Arsenal, Huntsville Arsenal, and the Office of the Chief of Chemical Warfare Service.[56] The Chief of the CWS, Maj. Gen. William N. Porter, noted that as the Corps ended its second year, the quality and efficiency of WAC personnel was holding up well and that there was "a high degree of enthusiasm in their respective tasks."[57]

CWS Jobs

The majority of these CWS Wacs were employed in routine post headquarters duties which differed from those of other commands only in subject and terminology. For example, at Pine Bluff Arsenal Wacs drove, serviced, and cleaned the large Army buses that connected the widely separated munitions buildings, transporting civilian shift workers twenty-four hours a day. Other Wacs ran the arsenal's military personnel section, handling records of both officers and enlisted men. Wacs in the quartermaster branch handled stock records, requisitions, inventories, shipping tickets, and reports. One

WAC sergeant ran the sales commissary; a corporal computed field rations for the post; others sorted the post's mail; the publications section was composed entirely of Wacs. One WAC officer was in charge of the motor pool; another was arsenal librarian; another the assistant to the chief of the payroll section. Two WAC officers inspected the seven post cafeterias and ran the officers' mess. Another WAC lieutenant was chief of the chemical production control section, co-ordinating manufacture and shipment schedules.

A minority of WAC jobs were the technical ones which concerned the real chemical warfare mission. "We got most of the scientifically trained Wacs there were," claimed the CWS staff director. For reasons which could not then be publicized, the CWS wanted not merely chemists but also pharmacologists, neurologists, and toxicologists. Other technical services frequently surrendered to the CWS any WAC scientist whose qualifications were too high to be utilized appropriately elsewhere.

Before admittance to the installations, a four-way loyalty check was required for each woman, which often caused a wait in staging areas of two months or more. Upon reaching CWS installations, women were surprised to find assembled many prominent scientists engaged in closely guarded research projects of great interest and variety. "Many of the women already had master's degrees," the staff director stated, "and I would estimate that they got about the same opportunities that a Ph.D.

---

[55] (1) Memo, Chief MPB CWS for CO WAAC Det, Pine Bluff, Ark, 17 Aug 43; (2) Ltr, Gen Porter, Chief CWS, to Dir WAC, 5 Jul 43. CWS 324.5 WAC (Jul–Sep 43).

[56] Memo, WAC Stf Dir CWS for CG ASF, Att: MTD, 29 Mar 44. CWS 324.5 WAC (Jan–Mar 44).

[57] Ltr, Chief CWS to Dir WAC, 6 May 44. CWS 324.5 WAC (Apr–Jul 44).

doing research would get." Many quickly became devoted to their projects; one woman, in rejecting a bid to officer candidate school, explained that she had previously shared the instructions of a certain famous scientist with a college class of seventy, but now had his exclusive supervision.

A few such enlisted women were eventually given work of real responsibility. A WAC pfc, with twelve years in public health work and an M.A. in bacteriology, sought new therapeutical methods of handling infections of gas wounds. Another WAC pfc, the former director of the Neuropathology Laboratory at Yale Medical School, investigated the effect of war gases upon the blood. At Johns Hopkins University, Wacs were directed by the staff in research concerning the use of penicillin spray in control of pneumonia which might be caused by chemical burns. At Dugway Proving Ground, a WAC T/4's research in heat radiation received a commendation from the U.S. Weather Bureau. Some of the Wacs were lured away by the Sanitary Corps, which was able to offer direct commissions, but others refused to leave their projects even for officer status. The extent to which such WAC scientists were employed was limited only by the fact that recruiters were unable to furnish them in the numbers desired by CWS.

Where college-trained scientists were not available, CWS requested and made good use of Wacs with lesser professional skills. WAC laboratory technicians were numerous at most installations, and WAC draftsmen were employed to design protective equipment. Dugway Proving Ground boasted the only WAC glass blower extant, who devised special sampling apparatus for experiments. Edgewood Arsenal used WAC photographers to photograph material for technical publications, and a former designer of fur coats to design and make canvas cases and protective coverings.

Women without skills could also be used by CWS with only on-the-job training. "It would be a mistake, in the future, to assume that CWS can use only scientists or technical experts," said the WAC staff director later. "For certain work all that is needed is a liking for outdoor work and for messing around with chemicals, smoke pots, and field instruments. We found that former factory girls were quite good at this, and interested in it." Perhaps the most colorful CWS job at Edgewood Arsenal was that of a WAC pfc who prepared colored-smoke grenades for signaling purposes and detonated them to test for brilliancy and duration of color; when the wind proved capricious this individual was habitually either green, yellow, or red from the—fortunately soluble—smoke clouds. At Dugway Proving Ground, Wacs were trained to participate in field observation during the mortar or rocket shoots, noting wind direction, air temperature, air pressure and humidity, and mastering the principle of the balloon run. They set up and oriented an artillery aiming circle and noted ballistic characteristics during rocket or artillery tests. Most women enjoyed outdoor work of any sort, and when shortage of personnel and periods of twenty-four-hour duty brought WAC office workers near the breaking point, it was found possible to revive them by brief rotation to field tests.

Problems Common Among CWS Wacs

The chief difficulties in CWS assignments for women were quite similar to those noted on secret installations of the Signal Corps. Because of the restrictions surrounding the more technical work, inspectors, staff directors, and company commanders were forbidden to check on any job assignments, even routine. As a result, some installations took advantage of this immunity from supervision to assign women to unsuitable duties contrary to War Department regulations. At various stations the requirement for WAC company officers was ignored. At another, enlisted women were assigned to a post commander's home to cook and act as personal servants to his wife. In several cases, civilian jobs in post exchanges and commissaries were staffed with Wacs. If detected, none of these violations could be reported, since it was alleged that security would have been endangered. The ASF WAC Officer, upon repeatedly receiving complaints from irate relatives, several times attempted to visit such installations, but was always informed that they were officially exempt from ASF inspection. Even the CWS WAC staff director was not cleared for such inspection.

Another factor which, in the staff director's opinion, caused lowered morale was the fact that women could not go into combat-supporting CWS units and that the CWS refused to release women for any other overseas assignments, on the grounds that such action would violate security and deprive installations of irreplaceable personnel. CWS was therefore exempted by the War Department from the WAC shipment quotas allotted to most other commands. The staff director estimated that only about 20 percent of the Wacs were employed on work that was too secret to permit them to go overseas or even on leave. She said, "The women could never understand it. I fought to get just two of them over, to give the others hope of reward for good service, but I failed."

Another problem faced by CWS units was that of obtaining good company officers. "We had a very high type of women on the average," the staff director stated later. "We found that WAC commanders had to treat them like intelligent adults. It was fatal to give unnecessary restrictions or to be too energetic in enforcing petty regulations." In general such restricted units, like those of other technical services, were found to require special attention to suitable recreation, rest, and living conditions.

In spite of various problems, as the war drew to a close ranking officers of the Chemical Warfare Service indicated satisfaction with the women's contribution. Army commanders in the field noted, "The men often consider themselves frustrated combat officers and thus lose interest in research and production work, but the Wacs eagerly plunge into their jobs with all their energy." General Porter, chief of the CWS, stated that Wacs had exhibited "all of the soldierly qualities of obedience, initiative, and devotion to duty. . . . The WAC has permeated our entire organization, and we owe them a great debt." [58]

The Corps of Engineers

The fact that Wacs had been assigned to the Corps of Engineers since early 1943 was almost as unknown, until August of 1945, as was the project on which they were employed, the atomic bomb. Not until then was it revealed that 422 Wacs, approximately eight and a half percent of the enlisted personnel under the command of the Chief of Engineers, had been employed on the project. Maj. Gen. Leslie R. Groves, commander of the project, wrote to these women:

---

[58] Bull cited n. 49(4).

Little is known of the significance of the contribution to the Manhattan Project by hundreds of members of the Women's Army Corps. . . . Since you received no headline acclaim, no one outside the project will ever know how much depended upon you.[59]

Manhattan District

The term *Manhattan District* was deliberately deceptive, for Engineer offices employing Wacs were located not only in New York, Washington, and Chicago, but also at Oak Ridge, Tennessee; Los Alamos, New Mexico; and Pasco, Washington. Here, the volume of classified material had recently become such that maintenance of security was a problem, and it was held essential that certain key secretaries and file clerks be under military control. A first cautious request was made for only 74 Waacs, who reported in June of 1943; others followed shortly.

The WAC staff director, who commanded the Oak Ridge company for most of its history, reported that she was sent to WAC training centers to select many members personally. The women interviewed were told frankly that, while the work was secret and vital, they would do a hard job, would never be allowed to go overseas or to officer candidate school, could never receive any publicity, and would live at isolated stations with few recreational facilities. A surprising number of highly qualified women responded. Women were rejected if they did not actively desire the work, or did not appear to possess "experience, judgment, earnestness, and sincerity of purpose." The staff director highly recommended this system of selection, to which she attributed her detachment's good fortune in avoiding many of the problems experienced by Wacs in secret installations of other technical services. As a matter of fact, it later proved possible to send a few women to OCS and overseas without violation of security.

There was likewise no pretense that women would do glamorous scientific jobs; the Corps of Engineers did not desire to use Wacs as engineers or technicians, but rather in general administration and paper work. Those assigned were therefore chiefly skilled stenographers, typists, telephone operators, clerks, and teletype and cryptographic technicians.

Exact job descriptions were never recorded, for reasons of security, but it could be stated that the women handled detailed records and technical reports. These included the classified files, communications, the production section, and all offices that handled scientific reports. The District Engineer, Brig. Gen. Kenneth D. Nichols, stated: "Members of the WAC were charged with a major portion of the responsibility for preserving project security."[60]

A minority of the women were assigned as chemists and other scientific technicians. A few, by the end of the war, had worked into various technical duties for which they proved apt and in which they received on-the-job training. WAC metallurgy technicians became qualified through work in ceramics, plastics, and powdered metals. Electronics technicians worked chiefly on the construction of needed electronics equipment. WAC photographers became specialists in photo-

---

[59] All references, unless otherwise stated, are to the following sources: (1) Ltr, Asst to Dist Engr, U.S. Engr Office, Manhattan Dist, Oak Ridge, Tenn, to Hist Div WDSS, 19 Apr 46. EIDMP-44, now in WAC files, OCMH. (2) Unit History, WAC Det, 9812th TSU–CE, Manhattan Dist. Copy in WAC files, OCMH. (3) Interv with WAC Stf Dir CE, Capt Arlene G. Scheidenhelm, 14 Feb 46. (4) STM 30, Strength of the Army, 5 Jul 45; WAC strength is from ASF WAC Summary.

[60] Commendations cited n. 59(1).

graphing metals and metallurgical processes. Spectroscopic technicians were eventually qualified for advanced work with the spectroscope.

Most of the Wacs' positions carried considerable responsibility, and as the project had a liberal allotment of grades, many of the women had received good ratings by the end of the war. Both the responsibility and the ratings were a definite factor in aiding morale, according to the WAC commander, but even greater was the fact that the work was hard and most women were always kept busy.

Problems of Engineer Corps Wacs

Only one major problem was encountered by Wacs serving with the Corps of Engineers, quite similar to that already reported independently by other technical services. This was the fact that the secrecy surrounding all installations prevented inspectors and WAC staff officers from checking on the accuracy of job assignment or the compliance of post commanders with War Department directives.

Serious morale situations soon developed in the Pasco and Los Alamos units, where Wacs were habitually used as babysitters, servants for civilians, and other nonmilitary jobs. In one, a number of highly qualified communications experts were assigned as barmaids to serve beer to civilian laborers. The women stated that they were subjected to rough language and insulted by the civilians, until one fled to Washington to appeal to the Air Forces to obtain their transfer to bona fide communications work.[61] The case was reported to the Chief of Engineers, who refused to transfer the women to the Air Forces; the ASF WAC Officer and the Ninth Service Command WAC staff director were both denied permission to visit the installation. At the second WAC detachment, an even more widespread morale problem developed when a young WAC officer without troop experience, sent to the station to do an office job, suddenly found herself in command of a newly acquired WAC company in addition to doing full-time office work, and without the assistant required by War Department regulations.

The problems presented at both of these stations eventually became so serious that, late in the war, the Corps of Engineers was obliged to appoint a WAC staff director. To avoid bringing in an outsider, Capt. Arlene G. Scheidenhelm was named staff director and was cleared to visit the other stations. At one station the detachment was reorganized; at the other, the staff director stated:

I merely told the post commander that he shouldn't use Wacs as barmaids or we should all get in trouble; he asked which women to reassign, I named them, and he reassigned them at once. All that was needed was a WAC Staff Director who was a part of the Corps of Engineers.

Commendations

The day when the A-bomb news could be released was dubbed by the Wacs "our day," and they were, according to the staff director, "the proudest Wacs in the Army," feeling that they had done more than most other Wacs to shorten the war and save the lives of American soldiers. At this time, the WAC units were awarded the Meritorious Unit Service Award; twenty women were presented with the Army Commendation Ribbon; and one received the Legion of Merit. Congratulatory messages were also received from the Secretary of War, from General Groves,

[61] Specifically, to the Exec, Air WAC Div, Maj Treadwell.

from the District Engineer, and from the WAC Director. General Groves wrote:

As one who observed your performances month after month, I wish to express my personal appreciation. . . . You can well be proud of your service with the Manhattan District and the part you played in saving countless American lives.

To this the District Engineer added:

No WAC assignment anywhere exceeded in importance their mission with the Atomic Bomb project.[62]

Ordnance Department

Some 700 enlisted women—over 5 percent of the enlisted strength—and 80 WAC officers were eventually employed in ten Ordnance installations in the United States, including five depots, two arsenals, two Ordnance districts, and the Office of the Chief of Ordnance. Other requisitions met with less success in that they sought Wacs to replace civilian employees, who "require fixed and steady hours of work" and would not accept undesirable shifts.[63]

The first official reference to Corps jobs at these installations concerned a controversy over the size of trucks which women might properly drive. WAAC Headquarters wished to set this limit at one and a half tons, but, upon the objection of the Army Service Forces and the reassurance of The Surgeon General, the limit was raised to two and a half tons. This provoked further objections from Aberdeen Proving Ground, which stated that the odd types of vehicles being driven and tested by its Waacs could not best be judged by tonnage. The Chief of Ordnance therefore asked an exception for this installation, which was concurred in by WAAC Headquarters.[64]

In the ballistics testing laboratories where ordnance equipment was examined,

Wacs were employed in computing the velocity of bullets, measuring the weight of bomb fragments to determine the degree of fragmentation of bombs, mixing gunpowder, and loading shells. They also worked as draftsmen, mechanics, and electricians, and received practical training in ordnance engineering. A good percentage of the women were employed in ordinary clerical duties. Reports from overseas theaters revealed that Ordnance Wacs were found especially valuable in handling the complicated stock records of ordnance equipment, its procurement, storage, and shipment.[65]

Ordnance Department also expressed itself eager to employ WAC officers in highly technical skills—engineers, mathematicians, analysts, designers, artists, statisticians, lawyers, and physicists. Unfortunately, the WAC Officer Candidate School was designed for troop officers and turned out very few such specialists, most of them considerably below the desired qualifications.[66]

The Quartermaster Corps

Contrary to the general impression, those units and installations under the

[62] Commendations cited n. 59(1).

[63] (1) ASF WAC Summary. (2) Memo, CG Erie Proving Ground for CofOrd, 30 Jun 44. Ord 322/731. (3) Places of employment: Ordnance Depots: Atlanta, Frankfort, Mt. Ranier, Red River, and Savannah, Ordnance Districts: Philadelphia, St. Louis. Arsenals: Raritan, San Antonio.

[64] (1) Ltr, 151st WAAC Tech Co to Dir WAAC, 10 Feb 43; (2) Memo, WAAC Hq for TAG, 19 May 43; (3) Memo, WAAC Hq for SGO, 2 Jun 43; (4) AGO Memo W635-3-43; (5) Ltr, Aberdeen Proving Ground to CofOrd, 27 Aug 43. WA 451 (7-25-42) 1942, Vehicles for WAAC.

[65] (1) ASF WAC Summary. (2) Account by Col Merle H. Davis, Ch. XXII, below.

[66] (1) Memo, Tech Div OCofOrd for MPB Ord, 16 Nov 43. Ord 322.436. (2) Memo, Dir Pers ASF for CofOrd, 5 Jun 44. SPAP 210.3 (8-30-43).

control of The Quartermaster General did not offer particularly suitable conditions for the employment of Wacs.[67] An early survey by the Office of The Quartermaster General pointed out that it was not advisable to use Waacs in graves registration companies; they could not replace men in salvage collecting companies because personnel had to be armed and had to perform heavy work in battlefield clean-up; they could not be employed in laundry battalions, companies, or platoons because these were mobile units operating in combat areas. It was suggested that Waacs could be employed in fixed laundries in the continental United States, which normally employed 89 percent women, but these were civilian job vacancies. As for bakery units, it was decided that bread-baking was definitely a man's assignment because of the strength required. It was not felt that Waacs should take over operation of light motor vehicles, which were used to train men for combat areas.[68]

Furthermore, as in the Signal Corps, employment was restricted by the requirement that enlisted women be assigned only in units. Most quartermaster depots employed only a small detachment of enlisted men, and in many depots only civilians were employed. The Office of The Quartermaster General stated that, if civilian replacement and use of small numbers were authorized, Waacs might be used in places where civilians were scarce, or to take night shifts and other work that civilians would not accept. The Quartermaster General did not particularly recommend such assignment, pointing out that provision of suitable housing and messing would be a problem for small numbers, and that it would be undesirable to mix Waacs and civilians because of the difference in pay and privileges.[69]

Therefore, by the time of the conversion to Army status, the Quartermaster Corps employed only one WAAC unit, located at Camp Lee, Virginia, where the women worked in the Quartermaster School and the ASF Training Center. Although The Quartermaster General assured Director Hobby at this time that "On the whole the girls are pleased with their assignments and are performing them in a satisfactory manner," the unit at Camp Lee suffered more than usual losses at the conversion. One possible explanation was The Quartermaster General's admission that some 20 percent of the women had at that time not yet replaced men. The women at Camp Lee eventually came to be employed also by the Quartermaster Board and the Quartermaster Replacement Training Center at that installation. Only one additional unit was recorded—that of the Fort Robinson Quartermaster Depot.[70]

The employment of WAC officers, who could be scattered about in small numbers, was more suitable to the Quartermaster Corps than that of enlisted women. In early 1944 the Office of The Quartermaster General stated that "within the next few weeks a shortage of QMC officers will develop. A number of units are scheduled for activation and demands for over-

---

[67] Text is based on (1) Seven documents found in OQMG files. (2) ASF WAC Summary.

[68] (1) Memo, Serv Installations Div OQMG for Mil Plans Div, 26 Jan 43, and 4 Incls. QM 321 WAC 1943. (2) Memo, by Brig Gen Henry D. F. Munnikhuysen, OQMG. QM 320.2 WAC 1942. (3) 1st Ind, "K.H." to SigC, 16 Nov 42, to Bsc Ltr, Chief MPD CSigO to OQMG, 10 Nov 42. QM 320.2 WAC.

[69] Ibid.

[70] (1) Ltr, Maj Gen Edmund B. Gregory to Dir WAC, 16 Jul 43, QM 321 WAC. (2) Memo, Capt Laura Asbury, WAC Asst, for MTD ASF, 29 Mar 44. QM 320.2 WAC.

seas requisitions are heavy." [71] Accordingly, it was suggested to depot commanders that they requisition Wacs, and a combined requisition for 340 WAC officers was placed with the Army Service Forces, which by mid-1944 had netted some 100 WAC officers. These officers ordinarily required no training other than a brief orientation course, although some were admitted to the depot course at the Quartermaster School and at the Columbus ASF Depot. A WAC staff director, Maj. Laura Asbury, was eventually employed.

The only available strength figures indicated that the Quartermaster Corps eventually employed at least 250 enlisted women and 125 WAC officers on its own installations. An unknown number, probably much larger, was also employed on posts, camps, and stations by local quartermasters in offices, warehouses, and sales commissaries—these being under the jurisdiction of an air or service command or overseas theater, and not counted apart from the rest of the overhead. In 1944, The Quartermaster General stated:

Personnel of the Women's Army Corps have become an integral part of this [QM] organization, and we now have unfilled requisitions from QM installations requesting more WAC personnel. [72]

The Transportation Corps

Early pessimists feared that ports of embarkation were no place for Wacs, who would undoubtedly be invalided by the rough physical work or seduced by the transient combat troops. Actually, the Transportation Corps proved second only to the Medical Department among Army Service Forces agencies in the number of Wacs employed, and first in the number

employed on its own Class II installations. With a peak strength of over 5,000 women, some 6 percent of its total enlisted strength, the Transportation Corps was able to maintain large WAC detachments in the eight major ports of embarkation— New York, Boston, Hampton Roads, Charleston, Los Angeles, San Francisco, Seattle, and New Orleans. Each port had one or more WAC detachments and its own WAC staff director, whose work was co-ordinated by a senior staff director, Lt. Col. Mera Galloway, located in the Office of the Chief of Transportation. [73]

These 5,000 women were obtained by the Transportation Corps by means of enthusiastic pursuit along every possible avenue of recruiting. Since most ports were in labor-short areas, they were hard hit by the ASF's directives that general service men be replaced by Wacs and civilians. Civilians were scarce, and Wacs were at once requisitioned for every manner of duty. Some of these uses were approved, while some, involving shipboard service, were at the time considered too unusual. [74]

The number thus acquired proving insufficient, other women were obtained by transfer from commands which found

[71] (1) Ltr, Gen Munnikhuysen, OQMG, to CG Boston Depot, 12 Feb 44. QM 210.31 WAC. (2) Ltr, OQMG to 20 QM depots, etc, 21 Mar 44. QM 210.31 WAC. (3) Memo, OQMG for TAG, 2 Mar 44. QM 210.31 WAC.

[72] ASF WAC Summary.

[73] Unless otherwise documented, this section is based upon: (1) History of Hampton Roads POE, *The Road to Victory*, Vol. II, pp. 174 ff. Copies in OCMH. (2) Intervs with Capt Jane Engleman, WAC Stf Dir TC, 1945–46; Capt Fay Foushee, WAC Pers Off TC, 1946–Oct 1947; Lt Key, WAC Pers Off TC, Oct 1947–48. (3) ASF WAC Summary. (4) STM 30, Strength of the Army, 5 Jul 45.

[74] Ltr, TC to Dir WAC, 16 Dec 43; also 1st Ind and Ltr, Dir WAC to CofT, 28 Feb 44. SPTPM 220.3 WAC, in SPWA 320.2 (8–18–42)(1) sec 6.

them unassignable because of low aptitude or lack of skill; the Transportation Corps was confident that it could assign and use any sort of Wac. Puerto Rican Wacs, whose possible language difficulties were feared by some commands, were requested and successfully employed. When WAC training centers were forced to relinquish their bands in the interests of personnel economy, the Transportation Corps acquired the musicians. When at last station-and-job recruiting was authorized, the Transportation Corps used its own recruiters to conduct such a lively campaign for Port Wacs that it, like the Air Forces, had to be restrained from implying that a new corps had been set up.

Transportation Corps Job Assignments

The women assembled by these means were assigned to a variety of duties. Some 700 of them, in New York and San Francisco, were assigned to postal battalions where all V-mail letters were processed. Wacs opened the letters, checked for correct form and for rips and tears, and sent them to the commercial company that photographed them; incoming letters were likewise processed, with Wacs operating the machines that put each letter in an envelope. This work proved extremely monotonous, calling for 24-hour duty on several shifts, and was successfully performed for over two years.

Large numbers of Wacs, both enlisted and officer, also worked on the piers at every port, assisting in the staging of troops for overseas and the reception of returning troops. This type of assignment began in a small way when Wacs were tentatively assigned to assist in staging female personnel—civilians, nurses, and Wacs. More than a hundred Red Cross women thus staged wrote to the commanding general:

It is our unanimous opinion that we have never been in an area where everything functioned more smoothly. There has been none of the confusion or discomfort which we had come to consider a normal part of the embarkation process.[75]

The use of Wacs in staging was soon expanded to include all types of personnel embarking or landing. WAC checkers on piers and ships processed not only outgoing personnel, but an estimated 800,000 items of supply for overseas forces. For example, in the San Francisco Unit Supply Office, Wacs not only kept records of the types of guns, the proper ammunition for each, and the type to be issued to each man according to his destination, but they also actually handed the gun to the man. One Wac said, "The soldiers come in unarmed and go out with a gun, and it gives me a pretty good feeling." As the men began to return from overseas, all-WAC bands in New York and San Francisco went out on small craft to meet the ships. As men came down the gangplanks, all-WAC teams met them for roll call and routine checking, after which other Wacs led them onto the proper train. Incoming officers also reported to a Wac's desk to receive any changes in orders. In this reception process, male military personnel were ordinarily employed only to check heavy baggage. The women generally reported no particular difficulty from the troops. One port noted, "Directions given [by Wacs] to troops debarking were cheerfully obeyed for the men 'just wanted to hear them talk.'"

In addition to postal and pier work, Wacs were employed in many other duties

---

[75] Ltr, Ruth Frederick, Gp Leader, American Red Cross, to CG NYPOE, 12 Nov 46. WAC Stf Dir TC file.

which differed little from those of other commands. At a typical large port, the Hampton Roads Port of Embarkation, it was reported:

> Though pier duty had priority over all other WAC assignments . . . [there were] dozens of other jobs in water, rail, motor vehicle, and mechanical maintenance, machine records, salvage, communications, photo-laboratory, mess, and supply. . . . The Wacs key-punched tons of manifests, cargo loading reports, convoy recaps, and what not . . . proofread passenger lists one inch thick, which were checked and rechecked. . . . There were 45 MOS numbers: butcher, sales clerk, auto-parts clerk, multigraph operator, quartermaster supply technician, tailor, photographer, movie projectionist. . . .[76]

At some ports, WAC medical companies were also assigned to administer shots, assist in processing, and keep records. During debarkations from hospital ships, these women were withdrawn from regular duties to act as guides, type admittance cards, and help in the Finance Department. On their own time, the women were discovered to be running errands and shopping for their patients, and carrying home the men's newly issued uniforms to iron. Most ports were deliberately striving to make wounded men feel that their country gave them a grateful and personal reception, and it was found that Wacs excelled in this effort. The effect on the women's morale was likewise good, as they felt less disposed to make known their own gripes when observing the greater discomforts of the wounded.

The chief difficulty encountered in the administration of Transportation Corps women concerned the fact that they often worked long hours and on night shifts as well as on monotonous duties, and were thus extremely susceptible to fatigue, nervousness, improper sleeping and eating habits, and impaired health. To combat this situation effectively, it was necessary for the cadre to maintain long and irregular hours. One commander of a postal battalion stated that for months she habitually slept for only two or three hours at a time, since the only time to discover the women's needs was when they were relaxing, talking, and eating after completion of their work shifts. As a result, where health and morale were maintained it was at the expense of the company officers, who wore out quickly.[77]

Later Experimental Assignments

As the Transportation Corps gained in experience in WAC administration, it began to show propensities, comparable only to those of the Air Forces, for experimentation with new and unusual duties. Soon after the invasion of Normandy in 1944, the all-WAC 29th Traffic Control Group was hand-picked from experienced Port Wacs and sent overseas. This group omitted the usual WAC overseas training at Fort Oglethorpe, and was entirely trained and equipped at the port, with such success that the European theater WAC staff director pronounced it the best-trained WAC group ever sent to Europe.[78]

Shortly afterward, to cope with the huge backlog of supplies for Europe which developed after the invasion of France, the Transportation Corps in September of 1944 organized a flying squad of approximately 100 Wacs, who were rushed to help clear out the jam at the Elmira Holding

---

[76] History cited n. 73(1), Ch. 14, written by Sgt Freda Zegman, HRPOE.

[77] Interv with Capt Theresa Davis, wartime CO WAC Det NYPOE.

[78] Sec Ch. XXI, below.

and Reconsignment Point. Here the Wacs found warehouses and a large open storage area crowded with an apparently hopeless assortment of boxcars, tanks, and other equipment. Much top-secret paper work was found to be involved in sorting manufacturers' lists and routing supplies to proper destinations. WAC clerks, checkers, and drivers worked outdoors for most of the winter, in three around-the-clock shifts, even operating the heavy lifts which moved and sorted supplies, and sleeping in the gymnasium of a local college. WAC officers later were of the opinion that the work involved had been too heavy for women, but no men were available to the Transportation Corps for the assignment and women performed it successfully.

With the end of the war and the resulting load of returning shipping, the Transportation Corps took a step not shared by any other zone of the interior agency, and set up rest camps similar to those used in combat areas. WAC camps were established shortly after men's camps were set up, one located near Camp Stoneman, California, and one at Vassar College. The idea proved extremely successful in combating fatigue, particularly for postal battalions and others in tedious and confining work.

Toward the end of the war, the Transportation Corps also achieved its previously thwarted objective of employing Wacs on shipboard. Earlier WAC objections to placing five or six enlisted women and a WAC officer on shipboard were based on fears that the women would either require expensive special provisions or would have none, since they could not use the men's recreational and living areas. Late in 1944 the Transportation Corps again requested Wacs for such duty, stating that "an urgent need exists for radio technicians for troop and hospital ships." [79]

WAC radio operators were by this time as scarce as male ones, and could not be provided by the Signal Corps, but the nature of the idea appealed to the Air Forces, which voluntarily furnished Wacs who merited reward for long and superior service in radio instruction in AAF schools. Three or four enlisted women and one WAC officer were assigned to each of several hospital ships, where they proved successful; one reported later, "It has been weeks since we have been referred to as experiments." [80] With the success of the WAC radio operators, other Wacs came to be employed on shipboard as clerical workers and as medical technicians to assist the nurses.

Quarters for such women did not prove a major problem, since they were usually housed in a cabin with its own toilet facilities, or with the nurses. As feared, the life proved confining and lacking in provisions for recreation for women. Enlisted women were not permitted to fraternize with passengers of either sex or with crew members of the opposite sex. On hospital ships, women not on duty were allowed to visit with patients, which proved of some morale value to both. One Wac reported: "Most of them are anxious for a game of bridge or just talking . . . it makes us feel that our job is worth while if we have a small part in helping to bring them home safely."

Nevertheless, "hospital ship fatigue" often developed; commanding officers believed that two months' unbroken duty without shore leave should be the maximum, although some individuals were able to continue for a year or more with-

[79] Memo, CofT for CG ASF, 30 Sep 44. SPRPM 220.3 WAC.
[80] Ltr, Sgts Brown and Niles and Cpl Kunmick, undated. Folder, Hospital Ships, WAC Stf Dir TC file.

out loss of efficiency. On other ships, where members were at sea only about ten days on each trip, with stopovers in foreign ports, the restrictions of shipboard life proved less important. The only reported casualties were two WAC officers who had to be reassigned for habitual seasickness.

The employment of WAC officers, originally requested only to secure approval of requisitions for enlisted women, soon proved so successful that WAC officers were assigned to other ships. Many such officers were graduates of the Army's School for Personnel Services, and were assigned as reconditioning officer, special services officer, and related duties. They were responsible for conducting discussions in the wards concerning veterans' benefits, hospital policy, and discharge procedure, for preparing a daily news sheet, for conducting the orchestra, and for arranging variety shows in the wards.

War Bride Ships and Dependents' Ships

With the end of the war, the employment of Wacs on shipboard expanded into a new and sometimes controversial duty: that on "War Bride Ships" and "Dependents' Ships." On Army ships bearing Italian, French, German, English, and Australian brides to the United States, one WAC officer was ordinarily assigned as assistant transport commander. This officer was responsible for stocking the ship's exchange with supplies needed by women; for the women's welfare in such matters as housing and feeding; for supervision of the nursery and diet kitchen. She was appointed liaison between the transport commander and the women, to explain his policies; she maintained regular office hours when passengers could present their personal problems, which were usually numerous; she organized discussions on

the monetary system, dress and customs, prices, products, and geography. Transport commanders confronted with voluble and excitable groups of passengers soon stated that WAC assistant transport commanders were invaluable, and eventually delegated to them the additional duties of post exchange officer and billeting officer. While Red Cross women, stewardesses, and Army nurses were also on board, the essential need was for a liaison officer in the chain of command and familiar with Transportation Corps policies.[81]

Good results were also obtained from the employment of enlisted women on the same ships, although there were ordinarily only a handful on any one ship. These were chiefly clerks, or medical technicians employed in the formula room under the direction of Army nurses, with little contact with passengers.

A different and somewhat greater problem concerned enlisted women passengers on the same ships. Such women, like enlisted men, were already resentful of the War Department policy which caused them to be allotted worse accommodations than the foreign civilian women who had married American soldiers. Their indignation frequently overflowed when, in addition to their ordinary work details such as kitchen police and latrine duty, transport commanders repeatedly assigned them to details involving day-and-night care of babies whose mothers were seasick, unsanitary in methods of infant care, or enjoying shipboard entertainment. The problem was not alleviated when war brides were supplanted by soldiers' wives and children en route to join men stationed overseas. These families, by Army Regulation, received better accommoda-

---

[81] For general discussion of War Bride Ships: Ltr, WAC Stf Dir NYPOE to CofT, 19 Jan 46, with incl. SPTAA 324.5 WAC, copy in WAC Pers Off, TC.

tions than male and female replacements on the same ships, and at the same time showed a certain tendency to regard the enlisted personnel as servants rather than as fellow passengers. Again, the Wacs' special objections concerned baby-sitting and other unmilitary work details often deemed especially suitable for enlisted women. In both cases, there appeared to be no solution as long as the Transportation Corps was required to carry civilian dependents while troops were still being transported, and to give civilian women better accommodations than those authorized for military women and men.

Evaluation

In discussions of a permanent women's corps, the Transportation Corps requested that from two to three and a half percent of its Regular Army strength be made up of Wacs in a variety of skills, principally clerks, postal workers, stenographers, typists, and communications experts.[82] Maj. Gen. Charles P. Gross, Chief of Transportation, stated:

> The Wacs have demonstrated thoroughly their value to the Transportation Corps. They have become an integral part of our ports, not only because of the quality of their work, but also because of the enthusiasm they have displayed and their loyalty to the Transportation Corps.[83]

However, with the placing of ocean transport for all services under the jurisdiction of the Navy, the Wacs on shipboard were scheduled for peacetime replacement by Waves, who had not previously been permitted to serve on ships.

The Adjutant General's Department

Although duties of The Adjutant General's Department were almost without exception suitable for women, that Department—like the other administrative services—did not have a number of Class II installations under its command as did the technical services, but merely provided personnel for station overhead. The AGD was co-operative in the matter of training, first admitting officers and then enlisted women to its schools at the request of the WAC. Such training was sometimes desired to qualify women for positions in WAC administration, and at other times to enable them successfully to replace male AGD personnel in various commands. WAC officers attended both the administrative and the classification courses at the AGD school and later the personnel consultants' course.[84]

Possibly the largest single group of AGD WAC employees was that assigned to the Classified Reproduction Section in the Pentagon, with the particular assignment of reproducing the weekly minutes of the General Council as well as other material for the office of the Deputy Chief of Staff—ordinarily top secret in nature. Of this work, the Deputy Chief of Staff, General McNarney, stated in 1944:

> WAC personnel were assigned to the Classified Reproduction Section in order to solve a most difficult problem. I feel that their performance has been a fine tribute to the Women's Army Corps, and I am extremely grateful for their fine work and loyal service.[85]

[82] Memo, CofT for TAG, 14 Jan 47, (Rpts Contl Symbol WDGPA–(OT)–78) file TCPER–MPB–320; in reply to Ltr, TAG for CofT, 26 Dec 46, A6AM–PM–320 (11–27–46).

[83] ASF WAC Summary, TC sec.

[84] (1) Memo, Dir WAAC for TAG, 17 May 43; (2) Memo, Exec WAAC for TAG, 4 Jun 43. SPWA 210.63, in AG file. (3) Memo, AGO Tng Br for Dir WAAC, 25 May 43. AG 210.63 (AG Sch) OT–S. (4) Memo, Exec WAAC for TAG, 23 Jul 43. SPAP 352 (5–19–43).

[85] ASF WAC Summary.

Finance Department

No statistics were preserved as to the numbers, if any, of Wacs on duty with the Finance Department in the service and air commands. Upon request, the Finance Department obligingly set up a quota of six for the WAC for its officers' course at Duke University, beginning in July of 1943. A little later, enlisted women were admitted to eight successive classes of the two-month enlisted finance course, to an eventual total of 305 women, of whom 266—about 87 percent—were graduated.

The only possibly unsuitable Finance duties for women were those in which it was necessary for the paying officer to wear or keep available a revolver or other weapon. Neither the Finance Department nor WAC Headquarters was able to see any reason why an otherwise qualified woman should not be allowed this privilege, inasmuch as the paying officer seldom was required to shoot anyone. However, the War Department refused to make an exception in this case to the general rule about "combat" assignments.[86]

Corps of Chaplains

When the WAAC was established, the Corps of Chaplains noted that there were two possible modes of utilization: that women ministers be used as chaplains for WAAC training centers, and that enlisted women be used as chaplains' assistants.[87] The first of these was never seriously considered. The Corps of Chaplains reported that, when the First WAAC Training Center was established:

Quick to take advantage of the new situation were the organizations of women preachers, and a considerable amount of agitation followed. . . . The statutes omitted any reference to the sex of chaplains, and at that time War Department directives did not make any specific statement on the subject. However, by tradition, as well as by general Army policy, chaplains were assumed to be of the male sex.

All applications from women ministers for commissions in the Corps of Chaplains were therefore refused. Ministering to the spiritual needs of the Wacs did not prove a problem to male chaplains, who stated, "Actually, the presence of Army women seemed to make very little difference in the work of most chaplains."

The use of enlisted women as chaplains' assistants was likewise originally disapproved by the Chief of Chaplains, who felt that it might prove compromising for a chaplain to be shut up alone in his office with a female assistant, and that even if it did not, the enlisted men who ordinarily revealed intimate problems to a chaplain would not do so if a woman was present. The assignment was not forbidden, but was left to the discretion of stations in the field. Within a few months, such assignments began to take place on the initiative of local chaplains and personnel officers.

Some of the women assigned were clerk-typists and general office workers, while others were musicians, such as organists and choir directors, or organizers of church activities. The Corps of Chaplains, after some experience with such employ-

---

[86] (1) Historical monograph, Personnel, General. Job A46–156, Drawer 4, ASF files of OCofFin, Jul 1940–Nov 1945. (2) Memo, Fiscal Dir for TAG, 21 Jun 43. AG 210.63 Army Fin Schs (2–9–43)(1). (3) Historical Monograph, Mil Tng, OCofFin, Tab G, Basic WAC Enl Fin Course. Job A46–156, Drawer 4, OCofFin.

[87] This section, including quotations, is based on: (1) Military History of the Second World War: Corps of Chaplains, Part III, pp. 95 ff. OCMH. (2) Memo, Lois Hill, Secy, for Dir WAAC, 10 Mar 43. SPWA 230.3.

ment, reported, "It was soon found that they could be used as Chaplains' Assistants to the same degree as men in the Army."

It was observed that women in the Army played much the same part in a post's religious life that civilian women did in the average community: they attended services more readily, formed more than a proportionate share of the choir, and in general were willing to lend more support to church activities. Under the circumstances, the employment of women as full-time chaplains' assistants ceased to excite comment. Estimates indicated that Wacs formally assigned to work with the Corps of Chaplains did not number more than a few hundred.

Only the Army Air Forces formalized the employment program to the extent of sending women to a school. Women already assigned to this duty were permitted to attend the AAF Chaplains' Assistants School for training in choir work, maintenance of records, and other necessary activities. These women represented all of the three major religious groups in the United States and both the white and the Negro races.

The Provost Marshal's Department

There was no official indication that Wacs were ever employed, in World War II, to replace male military police except at WAC training centers, where such employment was more or less necessary to avoid embarrassing male police. Early in the WAAC's existence, G–3 Division of the War Department had suggested that it was undesirable to assign men in the younger age groups "to units or activities not to be used for combat service" and that the necessary high caliber of military police be secured from older age groups, limited service men, and Waacs—the Waacs to be employed "to the fullest extent where appropriate." [88] Such assignment was never considered by WAAC Headquarters to be especially appropriate except in clerical positions in Provost Marshal offices or to assume custody of women.

Even this latter use was not realized to the extent deemed permissible by WAAC Headquarters. A request was made by Director Hobby in the summer of 1943 for WAC MP detachments at large centers of population where female absentees were often apprehended, but this was refused by the Army Service Forces because male MP's would not have been replaced. [89]

Throughout the war there were frequent rumors and reports that Wacs in scattered stations and overseas were being employed as military police; at times publicity photographs showed women wearing the armbands of MP's or parking guides. Upon investigation these were usually found to be office workers in a posed photograph. No employment involving the carrying of weapons was officially authorized for Wacs.

---

[88] Memo, G–3 for CG SOS, 26 Sep 42. WDGCT 322.999 MP (9–16–42), in SPAP 320.2 General.

[89] Memo, MPD ASF for Dir Pers ASF, 10 Aug 43. SPAP 320.2 WAAC (5–17–43).

CHAPTER XIX

The Medical Department (ASF)

Slowest of all ASF services to employ Wacs, the Medical Department by the end of the war had become the greatest user, employing some 20,000 Wacs, one fifth of the entire Corps, almost one half of Army Service Forces WAC personnel. These were to be found in general, regional, and station hospitals, ports, air bases, and convalescent centers, as well as in the few installations directly under The Surgeon General's command, such as the Army Medical Center in Washington.

The slow start resulted from the fact that well-trained civilian personnel and enlisted men were plentiful when the WAAC was organized. "It is the opinion of this office," stated The Surgeon General at that time, "that it is not desirable to utilize the WAAC in Army hospitals." [1] WAAC Preplanners had not pressed the issue, since requisitions from other agencies were already more than could be filled. [2]

In 1943, when the Service Forces surveyed the possibilities of expanding the Corps to a million members, The Surgeon General appointed a board of medical officers to reconsider the employment of Waacs. Hospital commanders, queried by the board, requested Waacs to a total of some 10,000 women for the ASF and almost as many for the AAF, to replace from 30 to 50 percent of their enlisted men. Nothing came of the study; Director Hobby informed the board that she was "in accord with the idea that members of the WAAC could be utilized in such a capacity," but the difficulties of recruiting prevented her from supplying the personnel. [3]

During the summer of the conversion, the WAAC was able to make available to The Surgeon General less than two hundred individuals a month, for technical training at the Army-Navy General Hospital. [4] Reports indicated that hospitals in the field were also obtaining certain numbers of women from post headquarters companies, although the women had been neither trained nor equipped for the work.

---

[1] 1st Ind, SGO to CG SOS, 14 Apr 42. SPMCP, SGO 322.5–1, in SPMCM 322.5–1 WAC, SGO Hist Div.
[2] Later comments from medical officers indicated a universal idea that the Director had attempted to force Waacs on Army hospitals. Actually, only two routine inquiries had ever been made, as a part of surveys—the first before Director Hobby's arrival in 1942, and the second by the ASF in 1943. No follow-up was made for agencies replying in the negative. See Chs. II and V.
[3] (1) Rpt of Proceedings of Bd of Offs, 11 Mar 43, appointed by Office Order 41, SGO, 26 Jan 43; (2) Ltr, SGO to all SvCs, AAF and CofT, 29 Jan 43. SPMCT, SPMCM 322.5–1 WAC, SGO Hist Div.
[4] Memo, SGO for CG ASF, 2 Jun 43. SPMCM 322.5–1 WAC, SGO Hist Div.

In early 1944, the nationwide personnel shortage caused the Medical Department an unprecedented loss: the forced transfer to the Infantry of some 5,000 combat-fit men, trained technicians upon whom hospitals had depended for normal operation. This loss brought about really urgent requisitions for Wacs. "The Medical Department is critically short," The Surgeon General's Office protested. "Efforts to hire civilians in sufficient numbers have as a whole failed. . . . With the withdrawal of enlisted men, there will be an urgent need for at least 50,000 additional Wacs to work in medical installations." The Surgeon General therefore asked an "extensive recruiting program" to recruit Wacs specifically for the Medical Department.[5]

The request for 50,000 Wacs was impossible of fulfillment, nor could the Medical Department be given first priority on even the actual intake without causing withdrawal of Air Forces, port, and other recruiting teams. Instead, Director Hobby was able to offer the Medical Department merely the privilege of recruiting for hospitals under the station-and-job plan, which was a simple matter of adding them to the existing list of participating installations. In the spring of 1944, the Corps' recruiting and publicity media therefore lent their support to what was called the Female Medical Technicians Campaign.

Female Medical Technicians Campaign

The Medical Department's demands were unusually difficult to meet, in that only highly qualified workers were acceptable.[6] Particularly sought were women with college training who could serve as bacteriologists, instructors in lip reading and Braille, pharmacists, optometrists, psychiatric social workers, orthopedic mechanics, and numerous other technicians.

Specifications were set for education, training, and experience which were so exceptionally high that the ordinary recruiting station was deemed unable to evaluate them accurately. The Medical Department therefore followed the WAVES' example and secured the assistance of the Officer Procurement Service, which assisted regular recruiters by filling out a qualification certificate guaranteeing assignment to, and suitability for, a technical job.

For example, a WAC psychiatric social worker (Specification Serial Number 263) was required to have "at least two years of supervised experience in social case-work . . . or a graduate degree in social work," and it was stated that those accepted "will be assigned directly upon completion of basic training and are eligible on the basis of such assignment to attain the grade of staff sergeant, dependent on individual ability and the existence of vacancies." A WAC laboratory technician was required

[5] (1) Memo, Brig Gen Raymond W. Bliss, Chief, Opns Serv SGO, for Dir Pers ASF, 11 Feb 44, SPMCP 322.5–1; Ind, Dir WAC to Dir Pers ASF, 12 Feb 44, SPWA 341. (2) Memo, Col Arthur B. Welsh for Col John R. Wood, re Off Procurement Serv. (3) Memo, MPD ASF for TAG, 11 Apr 44. SPGAP 341 Gen–69. (4) Memo, Chief, Pers Serv SGO, for Dir MPD ASF, 2 Jun 44. SPMCM 322.5–1 WAC, SGO Hist Div.

[6] This section is based on the following: (1) Memo, Lt Col Edward R. Whitehurst, Chief, Enlmt Br SGO, to Chief of Pers SGO, 13 Mar 44; (2) SGO Ltr, Chief, Pers Servs SGO to each SvC Surg, 15 Mar 44; (3) Memo, Chief, Enlmt Br SGO, for Dir Officer Procurement Service, 13 Apr 44; (4) Ltr, ASF Procurement Div for CGs of all SvCs, 24 Mar 44, FR–198; with incl Ltr, SGO to all SvCs, 15 Mar 44; superseded by Ltr, 15 Jun 44, FR–202. SPMCM 322.5–1 WAC, SGO Hist Div. (5) WD Cir 340, 29 Dec 43. (6) Interv with SGO WAC Stf Dir, Capt Maribeth Turnbull, 13 Feb 46. (7) SGO Tng Div, Rpt on Schooling of Enl Pers, MD, 1 Jul 39–30 Jun 44. OCMH. (8) Memo, G–1 for Asst DCofS, 11 Jan 45. CofS 324.5 WAC. June–December 1944 intake: 4.099.

to have a B.S. degree or three years' experience, and was similarly promised eligibility for a staff sergeant's rating. Other specialties were comparable. The Surgeon General agreed in return to accept the Officer Procurement Service's recommendation without change and to provide the guaranteed assignment.

In addition, regular recruiters were authorized to accept other women for three months' training as medical and surgical technicians, provided that the women had AGCT scores of 100 or better and had graduated from high school. Thus, only women in the upper half of the intelligence range of the population, and of near-officer caliber, were channeled to the Medical Department.

In spite of the high requirements, the Female Medical Technicians Campaign proved reasonably successful, the Medical Department's glamor obviously being second only to the Air Forces'. Women were recruited so surprisingly fast that the entire Medical Technicians' School reserved for WAC training proved inadequate. Within a few months some 4,000 well-qualified women had been recruited for Army hospitals—a number which, though short of 50,000, proved to be all that was required at the time.

Success of Training

It was quickly demonstrated that Medical Department training courses offered women no unusual difficulties. In early months, Medical Department schools were already carrying a peak load, and housing and sanitary facilities for women were so inadequate as for a time to cause a serious welfare problem. This condition was remedied gradually as male enlisted personnel for training became scarcer, un-

til by the end of the war over half of the students at the enlisted technicians schools were Wacs. No alteration was required in the usual training courses for men, except for omission of training in catheterization, which was considered unsuitable. Women in most cases qualified in two months for specialties that ordinarily required three months' training, and in three months for other specialties normally requiring four. Morale and discipline were generally high.[7]

Relative Success in Medical Jobs

The actual success of women in various types of hospital work varied with the duties. The most successful women were generally those who performed the more technical duties, especially ones related to patient care and reconditioning. Hospital authorities at first had felt that only male combat returnees should help rehabilitate the wounded, "due to personality changes of combat-wounded patients," which would presumably make them allergic to noncombat soldiers, especially female ones. When the first women began to be assigned to hospital work, authorities discovered, instead, that "the psychological reaction to feminine association has been most beneficial in combating certain prevalent attitudes of overseas returnees." Even untrained Wacs, according to commanders, showed natural ability for the work and obtained satisfaction from it. Authorities concluded that, "due to the personal services rendered and to the enthusiasm and understanding exhibited by

[7] (1) SGO Hist Div, Med Dept Tng Activities, 1 Jul 45–2 Sept 45, A Supplement. OCMH. During this period: *Enrolled:* 1,838 EM, 1,506 EW. *Graduated:* 588 EM, 1,329 EW. (2) Supplement to Rpt cited n. 6(7). (3) SGO Hist Div, Hist of Tng of MD Female Pers. OCMH.

such personnel, there has been a marked increase in the morale of the patients which is definitely considered to be an important part of the therapeutic regimen." In hospitals that pioneered in using Wacs in such work, complete satisfaction was expressed by all concerned.[8]

Psychiatric Social Worker and Psychiatric Assistant

Although earlier surveys had pronounced women unsuitable for any sort of psychological work with men, the Medical Department successfully employed more than 300 women as psychiatric social workers and psychiatric assistants. Women performed case work, interviewed patients and wrote case histories, carried out psychiatrists' mental hygiene prescriptions, and maintained necessary files and records on mental patients.[9]

Educational and Physical Reconditioning Personnel

More than 150 women with college degrees and teaching experience were enlisted and given one month's training in the educational reconditioning course at the Army's Special Services school. They were then employed to teach various school subjects to patients during convalescent periods in Army hospitals. Women were pronounced by medical authorities to be particularly successful in such teaching, since "men are conditioned to female instructors . . . and there is a psychological advantage to their employment."

The same school's course in physical reconditioning was barred to Wacs as inappropriate. One Wac accidentally attended, graduated, and was successfully

assigned; others did the work without such training and were pronounced "capable of fully participating in physical reconditioning, without specific limitations." When Wacs conducted games, recreational athletics, and exercises for male patients, there was noted "a marked increase of patient participation and enthusiasm." [10]

Therapy Assistants

Although the Medical Department had no authority to commission the highly trained civilian occupational therapists, as did the Navy, it succeeded in securing several on an enlisted status. In addition, more than two hundred women, experts in some handicraft, were recruited and assigned to convalescent hospitals to lighten the load on civilian occupational therapists by teaching leatherwork, weaving, and other crafts to the mentally or physically handicapped.

To assist commissioned physical therapists, the Medical Department gave a short course which successfully trained some 500 Wacs as physiotherapy aides, for duty in general and convalescent hospitals.[11]

[8] Memo, Fld Dir, Reconditioning Consultants Div SGO, for SG, 16 Feb 45. WDWAC 341.

[9] This and following subsections based on: (1) Rpts cited ns. 6(7), 7(1), 7(2). (2) Interv cited n. 6(6). (3) Final Rpt for 29 Jun–4 Aug 45, Lt Col E. R. Whitehurst, WAC in Procurement of Female Med Technicians, SGO Tng Div, 1945. It is not apparent whether this list includes both the Officer Procurement Service recruits in the 1944 Female Medical Technicians Campaign, *and* the General Hospital Campaign recruits of 1945, or only one of the two. In any case it has been used as a safe minimum.

[10] (1) Memo cited n. 8. (2) Rpt cited n. 7(2). (3) Interv cited n. 6(6).

[11] (1) Rpts cited ns. 6(7), 7(1), 7(2), and Interv cited n. 6(6). (2) Memo, Exec SGO for Dir WAC, 14 Aug 44. SPMC/DD–DW 322.5, in WDWAC 720. (3) Ltr, SGO to TAG, 2 Apr 45. SPMCM, in SGO Hist Div 220.1 WAC.

Laboratory Technicians

More than 700 women were recruited and assigned as laboratory technicians. Those with a B.S. degree or three years' experience were assigned immediately, while others were acceptable for the Army school if they had graduated from high school in the upper half of the class and had some laboratory experience. Women seemed entirely suitable for such duties, which consisted chiefly of analyzing specimens, making bloodcounts, preparing reagents, performing basal metabolism tests, and typing blood.

Similarly, some 500 women were recruited for X-ray work—those with experience for immediate assignment, and those with high school education, including physics and photography, for three months' training in Army schools. Technicians not only operated X-ray equipment, but prepared patients for treatment, managed protective measures, and developed film.

Medical Stenographers and Clerks

Recruiters had considerable success in locating recruits with both a knowledge of medical terms and the necessary clerical or stenographic skills. Such women were used in hospital offices to type records, prepare reports, take dictation at conferences, and construct technical charts.

Miscellaneous Technicians

With promises of a master sergeant's rating, recruiters succeeded in enlisting approximately a dozen dental hygienists, able to scale and polish teeth and perform other oral prophylactic work. Larger numbers of women with high school edu-

cation, and of the proper size and weight to fit into a dental cubicle, were also enlisted for three months' Army training as dental technicians and assistants.

The Officer Procurement Service also secured small numbers of recruits for various other technical duties: some forty pharmacists and pharmacists' aides, a half dozen lip reading technicians, and lesser numbers of Braille teachers, optometrists, hearing aids technicians, and others in rare specialties.

Only one flaw marred the assignment of such specialists during most of 1944. This was a certain lapse in liaison between procurement and employment authorities on the matter of salaries. Thus, the Officer Procurement Service's advertisements in professional journals had headlined the Medical Department's statement that Army specialist pay compared favorably with civilian technician pay, and that promotion to the specified rank for each duty depended upon "the proficiencies of the individual and existing vacancies." It had not been made clear that there were no existing vacancies and would not be for the current war; most hospitals' grade allotments were already exceeded by assigned men and by the daily return of highly rated men from overseas. Women recruited under the Female Medical Technicians Campaign therefore could rarely be promoted at all, and almost never to the specified rank. Hospital commanders naturally refused the requests for discharge of specialists who had enlisted under the wrong impression, and tended to blame the Officer Procurement Service for overglamorization of opportunities. On the other hand, that agency was able to show that it had merely operated on the written specifications furnished it by The Surgeon General's Office, and was not clairvoyant as to the internal conditions in Army hospitals.[12]

Commissioned Duties

Somewhat more fortunate were those few skilled technicians who were recruited on a commissioned instead of enlisted status.[13] Since The Surgeon General lacked Congressional authority to commission females in the Sanitary Corps, a special arrangement was made whereby WAC bacteriologists, serologists, and biochemists were commissioned in the WAC and detailed in the Sanitary Corps. Similarly, a number of WAC officers holding administrative jobs in hospitals were detailed in the Medical Administrative Corps to replace combat-fit male officers.

The Surgeon General had for some time had Congressional approval of commissioning women physiotherapists in the Medical Corps, without reference to the WAC. For a time the training course leading to a commission was open only to civilian women. Finally, at Colonel Hobby's insistence and because of difficulties in recruiting students, qualified enlisted women were offered the same opportunity, and several hundred were commissioned. Eventually the Medical Department's interests in this work were found better safeguarded by WAC recruitment of college graduates for training on an enlisted status and subsequent commissioning, and the greater part of the procurement of commissioned physical therapists was thereafter managed through the WAC.

Medical and Surgical Technicians

Greater in numbers than all of the skilled specialists obtained through the Officer

Procurement Service or by commissions were those women obtained direct through recruiting stations—the medical and surgical technicians.[14] These were to number from 6,000 to 10,000 by the end of the war. Such women ordinarily had no medical experience, but upon proof of the required education and AGCT score were promised training in the Army's enlisted technicians schools and subsequent assignment as medical or surgical technicians.

The duties of such ward personnel proved in general only slightly less suitable for women than those of the Officer Procurement Service technicians. Medical technicians made beds, gave baths, took temperature, pulse, and respiration; prepared patients for meals, carried trays, and fed patients if necessary; gave enemas and bedpans; filled icebags and hot water bottles; kept ward records, prepared dressings, and kept linen closets neat. Surgical technicians performed much the same duties, as well as sterilizing gowns and equipment and giving pre- and postoperative care. In general both were intended to assist nurses by relieving them of simple details of patient care.

Wacs ordinarily proved highly adept at such simple nursing duties, and approached the work with an enthusiasm and a sense of dedication not always found among male technicians. On the other hand, it was an accepted principle from the beginning that women could not replace all or even half of the male tech-

---

[12] Ltr, Dir Tng, MD Enl Techns Sch, Camp Atterbury, Ind., to Dir WAC, 28 Aug 44, and reply. WDWAC 210.3 (1945).

[13] Sources for this section cited ns. 9, 11.

[14] WD Cir 121, 19 Apr 45, defining duties of all SSN's. Ltr, Dir Pers ASF to Maj Gen Russell B. Reynolds, 15 Feb 45, with incl. SPAP 220.3 WAC (7–28–43). Statistics from Rpt cited n. 9(3).

nicians in any installation, since certain duties required great physical strength and others involved services for male patients that were considered inappropriate for women to perform. The accepted ratio was about 40 percent enlisted women to 60 percent men. Where these ratios were preserved, the jobs of medical and surgical technicians appeared extremely well suited for women.

The WAC medical and surgical technicians nevertheless suffered from a particularly obvious comparison with civilian women employed as paid nurses' aides. Trained by the Red Cross, these were almost identical in qualifications and training with the WAC medical technician, and were intended for similar duties. Civilian nurses' aides had figured in Medical Department history since World War I, and were frequently women with home responsibilities who had accepted the work for patriotic reasons. Nevertheless, it was a rare enlisted woman who did not remark the fact that civilian nurses' aides could quit if not given desirable duties, got three times the Wac's salary for half the hours per week, and in addition had officers' privileges on the post, all of which the Wac herself might have had but for the wiles of an Army recruiter.

Possibly no more unhappy example had yet occurred of the unwisdom of recruiting both military and civilian personnel for identical duties and of using them on the same installation. The final indignity to many enlisted women came when all hospital civilian employees were allowed to wear the Wacs' uniform, the surplus blue cotton dress formerly worn by nurses, thus depriving enlisted women of the only visible glory of military status.

The Hospital Orderly

The only hospital job on which women were admittedly unsuccessful was the least skilled: that of hospital orderly, or corpsman. Women had never been recruited for this purpose, but in 1943, when certain low-grade workers accumulated at training centers, the WAC requested the Medical Department to train them as ward orderlies.[15] The Medical Department accordingly set up an experimental training course, but within a few months was obliged to abandon it, pronouncing women unsuitable for hospital orderlies because of "the limited tasks to which this type of personnel might be assigned, and the impossibility of using them to replace enlisted men as ward orderlies."[16] These women, unlike enlisted men of the same category, could not successfully work long hours lifting heavy objects, pushing loaded food and linen carts, and scrubbing wards and corridors.

Two more attempts to train Wacs as orderlies, at Mayo and Nichols General Hospitals, likewise failed, and The Surgeon General informed the Director that such personnel required so much supervision that the nurses' load was increased instead of lightened. In any case women orderlies could not replace men on a one-for-one basis because of lesser physical strength. Therefore, the position of orderly was not represented in the Female Medical Technicians Campaign, and the standards set for recruits were far above that appropriate for such personnel.[17]

---

[15] Draft of Memo, WAAC Hq for SvCs, 11 Aug 43. SPWA 220.3.

[16] Rpt cited n. 6(7).

[17] Memo, SGO for ASF, 21 Oct 44. SPAP 319.1 WAC (10–9–43).

Under the circumstances, the War Department was at first unable to account for a growing trend that began to make employment of WAC orderlies the rule rather than the exception. Widespread reports indicated that in many hospitals ward orderlies were beginning to outnumber technicians among WAC personnel. Hospital commanders, for reasons not at once apparent, showed an increasing tendency to assign Wacs of high intelligence and technical training to duties that were exclusively those of charwomen and kitchen police, even when such women had in their possession written Recruiting Service guarantees of assignment as medical technicians, which by specification included no work heavier than "keeps bedside tables neat."

Repeated investigations shortly made clear that, although the Medical Department had acted on the assumption that technicians were needed, hospitals were if anything overstaffed on personnel for patient care and short chiefly in low-grade positions that civilians would no longer accept. A civilian observer reported, "Cadet Nurses, civilian nurses' aides, civilian nurses, Army nurses, and enlisted men are all above them [Wacs] in the hospital caste system and do all the actual medical care of the patients." [18] It was clear—at too late a date—that the Medical Department should instead have asked a campaign to recruit women in the lowest aptitude and educational group and without commitment as to duties.

All reports confirmed the situation. The commanding officer of Gardiner General Hospital told inspectors that he "had no use for Wacs except as ward orderlies whom he might use on cleaning and scrubbing duties." [19] At Fort Jackson,

South Carolina, the commanding officer published a memo stating, "All [WAC] personnel . . . will be used entirely for cleaning of wards." [20] From Halloran General Hospital, a Wac wrote:

If I had only known before I joined what I know now they could have shot me before I would have ever joined. Your people at the recruiting office show a beautiful film that shows the girls at work really doing things for the boys. . . . We scrub walls, floors, make beds, dust, sweep, and such only. . . . They should stop this farce of recruiting 'medical technicians' and ask for 'mop commandos.' [21]

Even an indignant civilian worker wrote, "Most of them [Wacs] had medical technician training [but] cleaning is all they do officially." [22] Civilian visitors to hospitals—including Mrs. Robert P. Patterson, wife of the Under Secretary of War—likewise protested to the War Department concerning conditions they saw. Mrs. Patterson commented on the WAC orderlies' makeshift uniforms, bedraggled appearance, overstrenuous duties in kitchens, long hours, and lack of the privileges and training given enlisted men. Military visitors carried the same report. Conditions discovered on one visit by the ASF WAC Officer, Colonel Goodwin, were so alarming that they were personally communicated to The Surgeon General's Office by General Dalton, with the advice that he would follow up on action taken. This he directed to include better attention to the women's appearance, better

---

[18] Ltr cited n. 14.

[19] Memo, Capt Chance, GSC, for Maj Gen Stephen G. Henry, G-1, 13 Mar 45. WDWAC 331.1.

[20] Memo, Asst CO for all Ward Offs, Ft Jackson Regional Hosp, 18 Feb 44, atchd to Ltr, Dir Pers ASF to CG 4th SvC, 26 Mar 45. SPAP 220.3 WAC (7–28–43).

[21] Atchd to Ltr, Dir Pers ASF to Dir Pers 2d SvC, 16 Feb 45. SPAP 220.3 WAC (7–28–43).

[22] Incl to Ltr cited n. 14.

salvage and supply, provision of one day off a week for kitchen police and orderlies, and an investigation of the chances of upgrading orderlies.[23]

By the summer of 1944, even before the end of the Female Medical Technicians Campaign, the problem had become one of the Corps' most serious. For the few women who had come into the Medical Department before the campaign, the question was merely one of malassignment to a duty possibly above their strength. For those who had been promised assignment as medical and surgical technicians, the matter was the more urgent one of the Army's good faith. A more unfortunate situation, or one more provocative of resentment on all sides, had never before occurred in the Corps' history. To the hard-pressed hospital commander, charged with maintaining patient care, the insistence upon fulfillment of the written recruiting promises seemed an unwarranted infringement upon his command prerogatives in assigning duties to keep the hospital functioning. For the WAC Recruiting Service, it was pure disaster. No other Army command, however much it deplored the necessity of recruiting promises, had ever deliberately violated them, and the Recruiting Service saw the source of supply of Wacs for the entire Army threatened by the personnel practices of one agency.

Request for Survey

By early summer of 1944, with the Female Medical Technicians Campaign still continuing, the number of complaints reaching the Director's Office "from civilian and Congressional sources" was so great that Deputy Director Rice asked the major commands for an investigation to determine the actual situation:

The few investigations conducted in response to some of these criticisms have substantiated the fact that conditions in these assignments are in many instances contrary to the well-being of women. Realizing the load on the hospitals . . . the Director WAC does not wish to recommend to the War Department that women not be utilized in this capacity, but because of conditions now alleged to exist in both time-length of daily scheduled duties (without commensurate time off) and in actual scrubbing work and other menial tasks, she feels that her responsibility for the well-being of women calls for study of such utilization.[24]

A simultaneous move came from The Inspector General, who informed the Chief of Staff, ASF, that "possibly there is misassignment of WAC personnel," and asked a survey.[25]

Reports of surveys, when received some months later, disclosed that the situation was in some respects worse than expected. In the Army Service Forces alone, over 1,200 enlisted women—about 5 percent of its total WAC strength—were found assigned as orderlies. Almost every station or general hospital was guilty in an appreciable number of cases. At one, ten technicians were used as orderlies, at another seven, at another six—in every case a percentage of the company large enough to cause comment. It was found that nonmedical specialists were also being mal-

---

[23] (1) Memo, "JND" for Gen Somervell, 13 Jul 44. SPAP 341 WAAC (2-26-43). (2) Routing Slip, Dep Dir Pers ASF to Gen Somervell, 13 Jul 44. Folder, WAC Rctg, ASF Sp Coll DRB AGO.
[24] Memo, Lt Col Rice for CG AAF, AGF, and ASF, 29 Jun 44. WDWAC 720.
[25] Memo, Gen Styer, CofS ASF, for Dir Pers ASF, 6 Jul 44, with Memo, ASF WAC Off for Dir MPD ASF, 31 Jul 44. SPEX, in SPAP 220.3 WAC (7-28-43).

assigned as orderlies, one station alone having converted thirty graduates of the motor transport school to this use.[26]

Hours of Work

Surveys also confirmed another fact which began to suggest that hospital work on an enlisted status was possibly not proper for women. This was the difference in hours of work for military and for civilian personnel. The customary hours in Army hospitals were 40 hours a week for civilian employees or 48 hours with overtime pay, and 8 hours a day for Army nurses. Enlisted men were believed to have more endurance, and traditionally worked a 12-hour day in Army hospitals.

The difficulty for Wacs was that they were both female and enlisted. As females, a 12-hour day was no more appropriate for Wacs than for nurses, and even less appropriate when Wacs were used for strenuous physical labor. As one female medical officer observed, "Wacs are replacing enlisted men but you are not turning women into men by an Act of Congress. . . . Wacs are enlisted women but they are still women."[27] On the other hand, Wacs were enlisted personnel, and if they worked only an 8-hour day the damage to the morale of enlisted men on the same wards was reported to be considerable because of the discrimination involved, and one-for-one replacement was made even more difficult.

The surveys revealed that enlisted women were almost without exception required by hospital commanders to work 12 hours a day and often more. Also, many were working 7 days a week and were not allowed compensatory time off during the work day or any leaves or passes. In addition to the regular 12-hour day, all were obliged to take night calls in emergencies, since civilian nurses' aides were not quartered on the post. Wacs also had to manage on their own time the four-hour-weekly continuation training courses required by the ASF, and other duties such as company fatigue, inspections, personal grooming, and sometimes laundry. As a result, enlisted women in Army hospitals were found to be working a minimum of 72 hours weekly and a maximum of at least 100, in addition to company duties. For example, Camp Wheeler, Georgia, employed trained WAC medical technicians as ward orderlies on a 12-hour, 7-day week, a total of 84 hours a week exclusive of emergency duty, training, and inspection. Camp Croft used a 13½-hour day, 6-day week, or 81 hours a week plus extras. Other variants at different hospitals produced the same general totals.[28]

These discoveries posed one of the most difficult questions to be encountered by the Army in its employment of womanpower: to what extent the Army could be bound by labor laws and civilian rules in the hours of work for women. Eighteen of the states had laws to the effect that 48 hours per week, or 8 hours per day for 6 days, were the maximum for women workers. In England, the Factory Act of 1937 placed the maximum for women at from 48 to 54 hours, and even in the darkest days after Dunkerque, the Ministry of Labour recommended that these hours not be exceeded. The U.S. Army Industrial Hygiene Laboratory, after a study of women in industry, reported:

[26] Memo, MPD ASF for G–1, 12 Sep 44. SPGAM 322.5 WAC (9–6–44)–97, in SPAP 220.3 WAC (7–28–43).

[27] Min, Med Tng Conf, Ft Oglethorpe, 1–3 May 45, pp. 29–30, comments of Maj Margaret Janeway. WAC folder, SGO Tng Div.

[28] Memo cited n. 26.

One of the lessons learned in World War I and again after the collapse of France in 1940 was that excessively long hours of work do not ultimately pay, even when considered solely on the basis of output and apart from the effect on health. . . . All of the available evidence from England and this country indicates that working hours in operations involving a fair amount of physical effort should not exceed 60–65 per week for men, and 55–60 per week for women.

A committee representing the Army, Navy, Public Health Service, War Manpower Commission, Labor Department and other agencies had agreed in 1942 concerning either male or female civilians that "one scheduled day of rest for the individual approximately every 7 days should be a universal and invariable rule." [29]

The Army Medical Department was therefore obviously exceeding all accepted safety limits in requiring a routine 72 hours a week and frequently 84 or 100 hours, and a 7-day week. On the other hand, the Army was in a somewhat different position from civilian agencies. Since it was entitled to ask a man's life in combat, it appeared equally entitled to ask that a woman sacrifice her health if required. There was a strong feeling in the Medical Department that any special regulations or labor laws concerning hours or type of work for women constituted discrimination; also, many Army doctors did not believe that any real damage to health would result. A representative of The Surgeon General stated, in refusing to accept the assignment of a WAC staff director for the Medical Department:

Some think that there has been entirely too much said on the subject of the physical capabilities of males vs. females and I can only say that I don't think any of them work as hard as they will when they become housewives and mothers.[30]

Director Hobby's recommendation, after she had considered the survey, was that any sacrifice was justified, either of health or life, if a true emergency required it; but that, since commanders did not deliberately kill men unnecessarily, the WAC should not unnecessarily sacrifice women's health. As a means of determining whether a true emergency existed, she proposed that the hours worked by Army nurses be considered the criterion. If nurses were not busy enough to require extended hours, and if the situation continued over months and years, there obviously was no emergency but rather a failure of hospital commanders to take aggressive action to improve personnel management. She therefore proposed that WAC and Nurse Corps hours be identical. This theory met with the general disapproval of hospital commanders, and was not to be acceptable for many months.

There was thus by the end of the summer of 1944 considerable doubt in WAC authorities' minds as to whether women should properly be employed at all in hospitals on an enlisted status, but should not instead be hired as civilians on a 48-hour week and with the privilege of quitting if overtaxed, a move that would also avoid the one-for-one replacement problem. To this was added the ethical question of whether recruiters were any longer justified in making commitments as to technical assignments which quite possibly would not be fulfilled.

Cessation of Medical Department Recruiting

Any such decision was postponed when, in late September of 1944, WAC recruiters

---

[29] (1) Baetjer, *Women in Industry*. (2) Helen Baker, *Women in War Industries* (Princeton University Press, 1942).

[30] Memo, Col Durward G. Hall, SGO, for Col Whitehurst, 15 Nov 44. SGO Hist Div 220.1 WAC.

received a request from The Surgeon General to discontinue the Female Medical Technicians Campaign. At this time, some months before the Battle of the Bulge, war news seemed good, and on the basis of low casualty estimates from overseas The Surgeon General believed that adequate hospital personnel had been obtained. Recruiting of paid nurses' aides was also scheduled for suspension; recruiting of nurses lacked only a few hundred of meeting the original ceiling. On the basis of similar reports from other agencies concerning the approaching end of the war, the entire WAC Recruiting Service made plans to go on a maintenance basis at the end of the year.[31]

It was thus prematurely hoped that a clash between procurement and medical authorities had been avoided for the duration. Surveyors, reporting finally in October, believed that they had corrected half of the cases of broken recruiting promises, and others were scheduled for correction if and when discovered. The ASF was not willing to take further action at the moment, since this "would harass commanders . . . corrective action is not now advisable"; it was hoped that time and the end of the war would bring the necessary readjustment.[32]

Resumption of the offensive in Europe brought greatly increased casualties, plus heavy hospitalization from combat fatigue, exposure, and trench foot. In one month the Army received more casualties from overseas than it had in all other months since Pearl Harbor, and soon the sick and wounded were being returned at the rate of 20,000 monthly. Almost overnight the situation regarding future medical care changed from comfortable to desperate.

A re-evaluation of the Nurse Corps ceiling indicated that installations in the United States would be short more than 8,000 nurses; only 41,839 nurses were in the Army, 75 percent overseas, of the 50,000 now believed needed at once. Also, although the Cadet Nurse Corps had absorbed some 177,000 young women and $192,285,518 in appropriations, it was chiefly designed to meet civilian nursing needs and had at this time furnished the Army only a few hundred cadets. In a final blow, more than 5,000 general service enlisted men were again ordered transferred from the Medical Department to make up Army Ground Forces casualties. This was the situation when, on 16 December 1944, the Battle of the Bulge began.[33]

At about this time a number of drastic measures were taken simultaneously by the Medical Department, any one of which would have been adequate to meet the situation that actually developed. In spite of certain objections from the General Staff, the Nurse Corps ceiling was raised to the total of 60,000 recommended by The Surgeon General. The Surgeon General on 19 November assured the Secretary of War that the nursing situation was "nearly hopeless." In an effort to arouse both the public and the General

---

[31] (1) M/R, Conf of Representatives of Dir WAC and TAG, 19 Oct 44. SPWA 341. (2) Memo, G–1 for ASF, 26 Oct 44, with Inds and M/R through 8 Dec 44. SPAP 341 WAC (11–6–44).

[32] (1) Memo cited n. 26 and Min cited n. 27. (2) Memo, MPD ASF for Dir Pers ASF, 7 Aug 44, SPGAA 210.3 WAC (7–6–44)–157; (3) Memo, Dir Pers ASF for MPD, 9 Aug 44; (4) Memo, MPD for Dir Pers ASF, 3 Oct 44, SPGAC 210.3 WAC (10–3–44)–157. All in SPAP 220.3 WAC (7–28–43).

[33] (1) Organized Nursing and the Army in Three Wars: A Political and Administrative History of the Army Nurse Corps, by Mary W. Standlee, Walter Reed Gen Hosp, in collaboration with Col Florence A. Blanchfield, R.N., ANC, pp. 461, 479, 606. MS copy furnished author for review and comment. Hereafter cited as ANC Hist. (2) Rpt cited n. 6(7).

Staff to his needs, he went so far as to by-pass the Bureau of Public Relations to give alarming statistics, based on the new Nurse Corps ceiling, to a well-known columnist. Great national concern resulted. Near the beginning of the new year, a proposal to draft nurses went from the Secretary of War to the President, and from him to Congress. Meanwhile, to fill the immediate gap, plans were made for the Red Cross to recruit 5,000 more nurses' aides. And even earlier, on 15 November, The Surgeon General's Office discussed plans to reverse the decision on WAC recruiting and to request some 8,000 more Wacs.[34]

Exact plans for these 8,000 WAC recruits developed slowly during the last six weeks of 1944. At first The Surgeon General, Maj. Gen. Norman T. Kirk, after receiving the pledge of higher authorities to do everything possible "to strengthen Kirk's hand,"[35] asked for 8,500 enlisted medical and surgical technicians, either men or women. It was stated that each could fill a nurse vacancy by assuming enough routine nursing duties to permit one nurse to handle the professional duties of two. For each of these men or women, The Surgeon General asked a rating of T/4, or sergeant, as befitted the skills involved. After discussion, both The Surgeon General and the Army Service Forces recommended that all of the technicians be Wacs, since the limited service men available for retraining seemed chiefly interested in getting out of the Army, and it was felt that women would have more enthusiasm for caring for the wounded in the long hospitalization and rehabilitation period ahead. Again the Medical Department asked for women in the upper AGCT and educational brackets.[36]

The Service Forces immediately authorized their hospitals to carry one WAC medical technician overstrength for each unfilled vacancy for a nurse. No announcement was made to the field as to how these extra technicians would be obtained, or whether they would get the T/4 rating previously recommended by The Surgeon General.[37]

Over this point, the General Staff disputed during the last days of 1944. Directives to curtail all WAC recruiting went to the field on 20 December, and an immediate decision was necessary if they were to be recalled. Resumption of the Female Medical Technicians Campaign would have been simple, but Director Hobby was not willing to sponsor a drive to induce highly qualified women to enlist unless some better assurance could be made that recruiting promises would be fulfilled. She sent The Surgeon General a list of questions concerning the means of providing the guaranteed job and grade, and in reply was assured only that the hospital training would be very valuable and would give the women an excellent chance, after the war, of being hired by the Veterans' Administration.[38]

The temper of the moment was one that made refusal to recruit for the purpose unthinkable. Director Hobby's telephone

[34] (1) ANC Hist, pp. 526 ff. Also Memo, SW for President of U.S., 30 Dec 44, Mr. Goldthwaite H. Dorr's file, Office of Records and Co-ordination, Office of SW. (2) Memo, Col Whitehurst, SGO, for Maj Gen George F. Lull, Deputy SG, 15 Nov 44. SGO Hist Div 220.1 WAC.

[35] Pencil note on Memo, SG for G–1 through MPD ASF, 23 Nov 44. SPMCM, in SPAP 220.3 WAC (7–28–43).

[36] (1) Memo Routing Slip, Exec SGO for Dir WAC, 22 Nov 44. WDWAC 341. (2) Memo cited n. 35.

[37] Ltr, Dir Pers ASF to SG and all SvCs, 9 Dec 44. SPGAS 320.2 Med (12–9–44)–285, SGO Hist Div 220.1 WAC.

[38] (1) Ltr, TAG to all SvCs, 20 Dec 44. SPXPR–I WAC (12–20–44), in SPAP 341 WAC, sec II. (2) Memo Routing Slip cited n. 36(1).

conversations revealed that she shared the general belief that "those boys are being wounded without people there to do things for them." Nevertheless, she cast about for any alternative to sending more women on enlisted status to Army hospitals. She went so far as to suggest in high places that nursing standards were too high, and that rather than use Wacs with a few weeks' training, the Nurse Corps should employ, as warrant officers or on a similar status, the practical nurses and graduates of smaller nursing schools who were not acceptable for commissions. This, she was informed, was impossible because of the pressure of civilian nursing groups against recognition of such women. Plans to recruit more Wacs therefore continued.[39]

Director Hobby's concern over the situation was such that she went in person to General Marshall to record her protests. General Marshall shortly thereafter interjected into the War Department conferences an opinion that sufficient women of the high caliber desired could not be recruited by the WAC for these jobs unless the Army could back up its guarantee of work involving patient care and a rating. Unless these could be assured the recruits, General Marshall refused to sanction any further recruiting of women as medical or surgical technicians.

Since such assurance was impossible under the current system, he proposed that the new Wacs be sent to hospitals in Table of Organization companies. The rigid T/O unit came equipped with its own extra allotment of grades, and with specifications as to the exact job of each member; neither the job nor the grade could be changed by field commanders. Such units for women had long ago proved impracticable for general duty Waacs, since few stations could use identical inflexible units, but general hospitals were a different matter, since all had almost identical missions and organization, and all used technicians.[40]

Wacs vs. Nurses' Aides

Before such units could be authorized, Director Hobby became aware of another fact which again caused her to consult General Marshall: The Surgeon General was asking the Red Cross for 5,000 civilian nurses' aides to be recruited at the same time that the WAC would be recruiting its 8,000 enlisted technicians. WAC recruiters feared that no WAC campaign, even if it guaranteed a good job and a rating, could succeed in competition with Red Cross offers of higher pay and officer privileges for identical jobs in identical hospitals on a civilian status. Instead, recruiting funds would be wasted and the government placed in an indefensible position.

On 5 January 1945, General Marshall wrote to his deputy, Lt. Gen. Thomas T. Handy:

I have just talked to the Director of the WAC and she tells me the ASF is going after 5,000 nurses aides.

My guess would be that this will ruin what I want to do in creating General Hospital companies in the WAC organization, because of the pay status and general competition with the Red Cross. . . .

Please look into this business and see that we are not working against ourselves in this enterprise. I want action.[41]

The decision between Wacs and nurses' aides at once involved the War Depart-

---

[39] Tp Convs, Col Hobby. Drawer 6, G–1 WAC files 312–312.9, DRB AGO.

[40] Memo, "JPR" for Dir WAC, 29 Dec 44. WDWAC 341. Describes 27 Dec 44 conf.

[41] Memo, CofS for Handy, 5 Jan 45; copy is Tab A to reply, G–1 for CofS, 5 Jan 45. WDWAC 341 WAC Hosp Units (4–22–45); also in CofS 324.5 WAC.

ment in much bitterness and misunderstanding. In training, the two positions were virtually identical, although graduates of the Red Cross course were considered by The Surgeon General to be "not as well trained" as WAC graduates of the Army's six-week course, and often needed retraining.[42] In relative cost, also, the WAC appeared to have a slight edge. A study made by the Chief of Staff's office indicated that a Wac cost from $1,032 to $1,368 yearly, including pay, housing, food, and clothing, while a civilian nurses' aide received $1,752 to $2,190 for a 48-hour week.[43]

However, civilian advocates of nurses' aides noted that there were always many hidden costs to military personnel and that the Red Cross bore the cost of recruiting and training aides. Army Nurse Corps leaders preferred civilian aides, stating that nurses would be needed to train Wacs, that Wacs were subject to redeployment, that WAC officers had been given Army rank a year before nurses, and that women under WAC command would be subject to call for drill without regard to patient care.[44]

In making its decision the War Department considered all of these arguments of less consequence than the decisive one: Wacs could not quit when the shooting ended. G–1 Division stated:

Since the personnel necessary for the care of the sick and wounded in Army hospitals must be available not only during the next . . . months but throughout the period when the Army hospitals must care for and rehabilitate all men wounded during the war, it is considered essential that a sufficient complement of military personnel, enlisted for the duration plus six months, be available.[45]

Breaking off with the Red Cross aide program proved a delicate business; the Red Cross for many years had been accustomed to recruit Army nurses as well as aides, and to set the standards of acceptance. Since Red Cross officials objected on the ground that commitments had been made to women already in training, it was agreed to hire all of these before discontinuing the program.[46]

Red Cross leaders co-operated in agreements by which their graduates might be guaranteed a medical technician rating without further training if they enlisted in the WAC. Resentment within some of the Medical Department offices was longer-lived. After the end of the war, Training Division, Surgeon General's Office, stated in its history that the Medical Department had never requested the 8,000 Wacs at all, or planned to use them, until Director Hobby had exerted influence upon General Marshall to cancel civilian nurses' aide recruiting, thereby forcing the Medical Department to take Wacs "to meet the shortage thus created."[47]

T/O Units for General Hospitals

Upon receipt of General Marshall's demand on 5 January, G–1 Division called from their evening meals WAC Deputy

[42] (1) Memo, Pers Div SGO for Tng Div SGO, 10 Feb 45. Tng Div SGO WAC file. (2) Memo, Lt Col Westray Battle Boyce for Col Charles F. Collier (G–1 Div) and Col Hobby, 24 May 45. WDWAC 220.3.

[43] Memo, G–1 for Col Frank McCarthy, Secy GS, 13 Jan 45. CofS 324.5 WAC.

[44] (1) ANC Hist, p. 492 ff. (2) Memo, Maj Edna B. Groppe, O Dir ANC, for Col James R. Hudnall, SGO, 10 Oct 44. File 23, Nurses' Aides, SGO Mail and Recs Br.

[45] Memo cited n. 6(8).

[46] (1) Memo, G–1 for CofS, 5 Jan 45. WDWAC 341 WAC Hosp Units (4–22–45). (2) Ltr, SW to Mr. Basil O'Connor, American Red Cross, 16 Jan 45. CofS 324.5 WAC. (3) Tp Conv, Col Rice and Mrs. Walter Lippmann, 1 Feb 45. Drawer 6, G–1 WAC 312–312.9.

[47] Rpt cited n. 6(7).

Director Rice and representatives of The Surgeon General, in various stages of off-duty attire, and the group worked all night to deliver to General Marshall the completed plan for WAC hospital companies.[48]

The Table of Organization, details to be prepared later by The Surgeon General's Office, was set at 100 women, in an assortment of technical and clerical jobs believed to be adaptable to any general hospital. Since no member was to be less than a skilled technician or clerk, no rating less than T/5 or corporal was included—a slight decrease from The Surgeon General's estimate that a T/4 or sergeant would be required for each, and one which gave the new units no higher spread of grades than that of men already in Army hospitals. Any hospital desiring one or more of such companies was to report the fact, and the women would then be recruited with complete assurance of assignment to that hospital and to a technical job, which would if successful automatically carry a T/5 rating.[49]

G–1 representatives pronounced the T/O an excellent idea, which would not only permit recruiters to make foolproof guarantees, but would also prevent hospitals from frittering away, in luxurious station overhead, personnel given them to care for the sick. The chief of G–1's Personnel Policy Branch stated later:

These units were developed to furnish medical and surgical technicians and other specialists in the hospitals, to assist the nurses. They were not developed for the overhead personnel of the hospital. Their purpose was to assist and care for the wounded and sick.[50]

To prevent injustice to women recruited earlier, the plan required that every Wac already working at such a hospital be incorporated into the T/O unit, or be transferred from the hospital if she was deemed incapable of performing a technician's duties. Pursuant to this scheme, The Surgeon General's Office was required on the night of 5 January to report the number of Wacs already at each hospital, which was subtracted from the number to be recruited to fill the unit. It was therefore confidently anticipated by planners that the establishment of the T/O units would remedy two ills at once: it would remove women from work as hospital orderly, which was officially considered beyond women's strength, and it would redeem all recruiting promises, past or future. The question of hours of work was also resolved by War Department approval of a circular requiring the same hours for all military women, commissioned or enlisted. Last, but far from least in the minds of enlisted women, the Director eventually secured authorization for a hospital uniform, a becoming rose-beige chambray, which could not be worn by civilians.[51]

General Hospital Campaign

Because the women had to reach the hospitals simultaneously with the peak of returning casualties, the General Hospital Campaign was launched almost at once. Women were required to have a score in the three upper AGCT brackets. White House co-operation was extended when Mrs. Eleanor Roosevelt invited Colonel Goodwin to share a press conference in

---

[48] (1) Completed plan: Memo cited n. 46(1). (2) Description of planning session by Col Collier, G–1 Div, p. 8, Min cited n. 27.

[49] Tab B of Memo cited n. 46(1). The T/O provided 67 T/5's and 33 higher grades.

[50] Remarks by Col Collier, n. 48(2).

[51] (1) Tab C of Memo cited n. 46(1). (2) Remarks of Col Whitehurst, SGO, pp. 26, 29. Min cited n. 27. (3) WD Cir 121, 19 Apr 45.

MEDICAL RECRUITING DISPLAY

January, and General Marshall again wrote to all state governors, seeking their aid.[52]

The appeal of nursing jobs to women was reported as "terrific," even in what the public now knew were the last days of the war. The General Hospital Campaign was soundly backed by public relations authorities, with numbers of local stories such as "WOUNDED APPRECIATE HELP," and effective local stunts. For example, Fitzsimons General Hospital received a giant bell, which toured Denver, tolling every eighty seconds to mark the return of one more American battle casualty who needed care.[53] A quota of about 6,000 by 1 May was set; in mid-career it was raised to 7,000; yet recruiters met and passed the number by the end of March, a month ahead of schedule.[54]

Training also went off well. The Third WAC Training Center at Fort Oglethorpe was turned over to medical recruits, and a shortened basic course was followed by a six-week medical course on the same post,

[52] (1) Memo cited n. 46(1). (2) Ltr, TAG to all SvCs, 13 Jan 45. AG PR–I 341 WAC (1–13–43). (3) Ltr, AGO to all SvCs, 23 Jan 45. SPXPR–I–341 WAC, copy in WDWAC 341 (1945). (4) D/F, G–1 for CofS, 5 Feb 45. WDWAC 000.7 (1945–46). (5) Ltrs, CofS to all State Governors, 7 Jan 45. WDCSA 324.5 WAC.
[53] *Omaha World Herald,* February 19, 1945; *Denver Post,* February 22, 1945.
[54] Memo, Dir WAC for CofS, 5 Apr 45. WDWAC 341.

staffed by Army doctors, nurses, and enlisted technicians from nearby hospitals. Both students and training authorities had only praise for the excellent and practical course and for the instructors.[55]

The recruits themselves were a promising group, extremely enthusiastic. Many were motivated by the fact that relatives had been casualties; they wished to give to some wounded soldier the care they had not been able to give personally to their own wounded. The majority were young single women of good character and intelligence; they successfully completed the three-month course in six weeks, with few failures even in cases where women with lower-than-qualifying AGCT scores had been erroneously recruited. About 5,000 were graduated as medical and surgical technicians, and 1,300 as medical clerks.[56]

However, the difficulties inherent in the whole General Hospital Campaign became obvious even before the women reported for duty. The Surgeon General's representative stated:

Utter confusion and conflicting policies and directives re ideas as to the utilization of this personnel have been flagrant since the original idea of WAC Table of Organization companies was conceived.[57]

Because of the confusion, repeated conferences were held with Director Hobby and with medical officers from every service command, without much success. Although the hospital T/O had been drawn up by The Surgeon General's Office itself, that office believed that changed conditions merited abrogation of recruiting commitments.

Even before the new recruits reached the hospitals, the Battle of the Bulge was won and January's fright concerning medical care was in the past. Just as V-E Day was in prospect, all of the drastic attempts

to get medical personnel were embarrassingly successful and bore fruit simultaneously. The nursing profession, under threat of the draft, had responded with a rush; in the three weeks between 8 and 29 January 1945, over 10,000 applications for commissions were filed. Draft rumors also stimulated 60 percent of senior cadets to choose the Army instead of civilian employment. Hospitals proved resourceful in hiring civilian nurses. In May, the director of the Army Nurse Corps, Col. Florence A. Blanchfield, returned from Europe to find that there were actually too many nurses. She recommended that 2,000 civilian nurses be released, and secured a recall of the proposed draft legislation. As a result, hospital commanders everywhere objected to the WAC T/O units, and pointed out that they no longer needed Wacs to care for the sick, but were in urgent need of more orderlies, kitchen police, and charwomen.[58]

The matter of grades was also a disappointment. It had been guaranteed by G–1 that these would be an extra allotment, but when the ASF appealed to Lt. Col. Westray Battle Boyce, the G–1 WAC officer handling the grades, it was in-

<hr />

[55] (1) Memo, SGO Tng Div for SGO Resources Analysis Div, 26 Jan 46; (2) Memo, ASF Plans and Opns Div for SG, 5 Feb 45, SPMOC 532; (3) Memo, Capt Turnbull for Dir Tng Div SGO, 23 Feb 45; (4) Min cited n. 27. WAC file, SGO Tng Div.

[56] (1) Rpt cited n. 7(2). (2) Remarks by Lt Col Elizabeth H. Strayhorn, Comdt, 3d WAC Tng Cen. Min cited n. 27.

[57] Memo, Col Hall, Actg Chief, Pers Serv SGO, for Surg Gen, 14 Mar 45. WAC file, SGO Tng Div.

[58] (1) M/R, Extract from SGO Diary, 28 Feb 45, initialed ERW, (2) Min, Mtg in O Dir WAC, 9 Mar 45; (3) Memo, Col Whitehurst to Col Hall. WAC file, SGO Tng Div. (4) Min cited n. 27. (5) Memo, SGO Pers Servs for CG ASF, 9 Jan 45. SGO Hist Div 322.5–1 WAC. (6) Memo, G–3 for CG ASF, 10 Feb 45. WDGCT 320.3 (1–5–45), in WDWAC 341. (7) D/F, G–3 to CofS, 30 Jan 45. CofS 324.5 WAC. (8) ANC Hist, pp. 553, and 584–5.

formed that "you must find them," and, after further appeals, it was six months before these were forthcoming from G–1 Division.[59]

Meanwhile, men and women already in hospitals felt that the new recruits were receiving their grades. They also failed to realize that the T/O grades were no higher than those already allotted hospitals, the only difference being that in the new units every member received a low rating at the expense of fewer high ratings than men in hospitals possessed. In any case the new arrivals could be promoted at once under the T/O while older hands had to wait for a vacancy in the existing overstrength.

The Air Forces solved the problem by getting War Department approval to the promotion of every Air Forces medical technician, man or woman, to the merited grade of T/5 regardless of other overstrength, but The Surgeon General asked instead that the situation be equalized by not promoting the new recruits. The Surgeon General's representatives privately admitted that they had concurred in setting up the T/O with rated technicians, and that "some of the things that you and I object to most strenuously were recommended by The Surgeon General's own office." Nevertheless, SGO Training Division now proposed that hospitals be freed to utilize the new recruits in any duties in which they were most needed, and to promote them on the same basis as other personnel. It was also proposed that some 1,800 recruits still in basic training not be given the technical training they had been promised, but be sent at once to unskilled work.[60]

Director Hobby opposed this plan on the grounds that recruiting promises made to women and affirmed by their state governors at the request of General Marshall could not be broken. The Surgeon General's representative objected:

Colonel Hobby has the idea that every company should be exactly as the Table of Distribution prescribes. . . . This is an unrealistic and impossible point of view. . . . In one breath, the theme of G–1 and the Director WAC appears to be to give the Surgeon General what he wants and needs and the next is to say that the Surgeon General will take what they give.[61]

Nevertheless, on this point the War Department's final decision was that recruiting pledges could not be broken.[62]

Even greater opposition from The Surgeon General's Office was offered toward the plan to assign all hospital Wacs to these companies. The directive produced after the all-night planning session of 5 January had stated specifically, "The WAC personnel now on duty at General Hospitals will be absorbed into the companies within the T/O strength." The Army Service Forces reported to the General Council as late as 13 March that the personnel on duty at general hospitals would be included in these units and be given at least 90 days to qualify for grades. On the next day it developed that the Office of The Surgeon General had not been aware of this clause; representatives also denied seeing The Adjutant General's

---

[59] (1) Comment 2, MPD ASF to G–1, 18 Oct 45, to basic D/F, WD Manpower Bd to G–1, SG, ASF. WDSMB 323.3 (Hospital), in WAC file, SGO Tng Div. (2) Interv with Col Goodwin, 2 May 51.

[60] (1) Memo cited n. 57. (2) AAF Reg 35–54 A (Amendment), 28 Jun 45, with notes. WDWAC 220.01. (3) Draft of proposed Ltr, SGO Tng Div to CG ASF, Jul 45. WAC file, SGO Tng Div. (4) Quotation from Comments from Pers Servs, 18 Jul 45. SGO Tng Div. (5) Memo, SG for MPD ASF, 23 Jun 45. SPMOM, WAC file, SGO Tng Div.

[61] Memo cited n. 57.

[62] AG Ltr to SvCs, 1 Jun 45. AG 322 (5–29–45) OB–I–SPMOU–M.

letters to the field that set up the companies on this basis. The Surgeon General had even issued contrary directives saying that WAC orderlies would be retained. On this point, since there had been no public commitment, Director Hobby was overruled and the directive rescinded.[63]

The general hospital T/O units lasted less than a year. Shortly after the defeat of Japan The Surgeon General obtained their dissolution on the grounds that they were too large for the decreasing size of hospitals, and would hinder demobilization. Wacs in these companies remained at hospitals as part of the regular bulk allotment, but the General Staff required, before permitting inactivation of units, that every woman receive the rating promised her. Thus the general hospital recruits could finally be used on any duties, as desired by The Surgeon General, but at least they had corporal's stripes.[64]

Conclusions

Final reports from inspectors in the last months of the Corps did little to dispel doubts concerning the suitability of hospital employment for women on an enlisted status. There was no doubt of its suitability for women on some status. The care of patients held an attraction for them, and even when Wacs were allowed officially to do nothing but scrubbing and cleaning, they devoted off-duty hours to the patients, writing letters, reading, shopping for them, and running various errands. Hospital commanders with few exceptions praised the work of Wacs to inspectors even while objecting to restrictions imposed by recruiting commitments. One said, "I'd rather have one Wac than three civilians." [65]

Final developments gave little indication that Medical Department policy could change to the extent necessary to protect the health of women in an enlisted status. In spite of the War Department circular requiring the same working hours for enlisted women as for nurses, the 12-hour day continued. When inspectors found women at Walter Reed Hospital working an 80-hour week long after the end of hostilities, the commanding general stated frankly that he had "circumvented the provisions of the circular by putting a small number of Army nurses on 12 hours duty."

The prominent women of the WAC's National Civilian Advisory Committee visited general hospital companies at work, after the Chief of Staff had overruled objections to the visit from both ASF and The Surgeon General; they reported themselves shocked at conditions. Barracks were frequently crowded, ill ventilated, and sprinkled with coal dust; workers on all shifts used the same bar-

[63] (1) Min, Gen Council, 13 Mar 45. (2) Min cited n. 58(2). (3) Ltr, AGO to SvCs, 12 Mar 45. AG 322 (3–8–45) OB–I–SPMOU–M. (4) Ltr, SGO to all SvCs, 15 Jan 45. SPMCM, SGO Hist Div 322.5–1 WAC. (5) Memo, Col Boyce for Cols Peter Schmick and Hobby, 21 Mar 45. (6) ASF Ltr SPGAC–210.3 WAC, 26 Apr 45. SPAP 220.3 WAC. (7) AG Ltr cited n. 62, and amendment, 13 Jul 43.

[64] (1) D/F, WD Manpower Bd to G–1 WD, SGO, ASF, 10 Oct 45. WDSMB 323.3 (Hospital), WAC file, SGO Tng Div. (2) Ltrs, AGO to all Comdrs, 3 Dec 45, and later dates. AG 322 (11–28–45) OB–I–SPMOU–M. (3) D/F, G–1 to CofS, 8 Oct 45. WDGAP 320.2 WAC in 320.2 (1945). Incl in Ltr, CofS to State Governors, 17 Oct 45. CofS 324.5 WAC.

[65] (1) Transmittal Sheet, MTD ASF to SGO, 7 Jun 45. Wac file, SGO Tng Div. (2) Memo cited n. 19. (3) Memo, Capt Margaret Stone for Dir WAC, 7 Jul 45. WDWAC 333.1, in WDWAC 319.1 Hosps. (4) Memo, Lt Col Mary-Agnes Brown for Dir WAC, 27 Jul 45. WDWAC 333.1. (5) D/F, G–1 to SG, 3 Oct 45. WDGAP 333 WAC, in WDWAC 333.1. (6) D/F, G–1 for CofS, 4 May 45, and D/F's, G–1 to ASF, 22 May, 29 May, 9 Jun 45. WDGAP 341 WAC.

racks, disturbing those trying to sleep either day or night; and hours had not greatly improved, with women still required to train and frequently to launder their clothing on their own time. There was also no evidence that the practice of malassigning technicians had abated. General Dalton eventually lost patience with repeated violations, and Colonel Goodwin ascribed to him personally most of the credit for redeeming such broken commitments as were redeemable.[66]

By some coincidence, the Navy reported the same experience, and the director of the Bureau of Naval Personnel stated later:

Experience indicated that in some jobs too much was asked of the women's physical strength. Oddly enough, the outstanding offender was BuMed. . . . As evidence mounted of women breaking under the strain of long hours, the office of the Women's Reserve put increasing pressure on BuMed to remedy the situation.

A 51-hour work week was regarded by WAVES authorities as "the desirable maximum," but the Bureau of Naval Personnel reported, "Efforts to have this cast in the form of a directive failed to overcome the opposition of Naval tradition against 'union hours'."[67]

Final recommendations by the Army Medical Department confirmed the fact that continued utilization of servicewomen was contemplated by Army hospitals. For commissioned positions, The Surgeon General asked and obtained legislation to allow women to be commissioned directly in a women's medical specialists corps,

headed by its own colonel, which would include dietitions, physical therapists, and occupational therapists.

The Surgeon General also advocated that enlisted women who worked in hospitals be enlisted in the Medical Department alone and not in the WAC. This move would have obviated the requirement for a WAC company commander and for compliance with War Department restrictions as to the hours and types of duty for members of the WAC. The War Department did not look with approval upon any such proposal for the setting up of independent women's corps in the different administrative and technical services, which tended toward compartmentalization as opposed to integration; it also did not agree to abdicate its Army-wide responsibility for safeguarding the well-being of women. Medical Department utilization therefore continued upon the wartime terms and without much greater clarification of the situation than had hitherto prevailed.[68]

---

[66] (1) *Ibid;* also series of ltrs, SPAP 220.3 WAC (7–28–43) beginning 1 Feb 45. (2) Interv with Col Goodwin, 2 May 51.

[67] WAVES Hist.

[68] (1) HR 1943, 80th Cong. (2) HR 3054, 80th Cong. (3) Final strength report: Memo, Dir WAC for Gen Henry, 18 Aug 45. WDWAC 319.1 Hosp.

ASF:	General Hospitals	12,087
	Convalescent Hospitals	423
	Regional Hospitals	2,203
	Station Hospitals	1,379
	Port of Embarkation	890
		16,982
AAF:	(as of 30 Jun 45)	3,055
		20,037

CHAPTER XX

The North African and Mediterranean Theaters

The North African Theater of Operations was the pioneer in employment of Waacs overseas.[1] The experiment owed its impetus to the first theater commander, Lt. Gen. Dwight D. Eisenhower, who had been impressed with the efficiency of British servicewomen, and to his deputy, Maj. Gen. Everett S. Hughes, who fifteen years before had prepared the General Staff study, Participation of Women in War. On most lower echelons there was a less favorable general attitude, ranging from mild skepticism in headquarters offices to bitter opposition in the great majority of soldiers' letters.[2]

The theater received its first five WAAC officers on 22 December 1942, some six weeks after the invasion of North Africa. The women, qualified as secretaries, were assigned by the War Department to England, but upon General Eisenhower's request were immediately placed by the London headquarters on a ship bound for North Africa. A day out of port, the ship was torpedoed, and the women came into port aboard a British destroyer, which had taken two from the burning ship and three from a lifeboat. The day in the lifeboat was remembered by the Waac participants as a hectic interval in which they lost all their equipment, the only crewman aboard became violently seasick, and the

women fished five or six men, one badly injured, from the water. When the Waacs arrived in port, dirty and bedraggled, they were greeted by anxious dignitaries who contributed oranges, toothbrushes, and other emergency items. General Matejka offered half a jar of hand cream, while Maj. Gen. Walter Bedell Smith procured small-sized men's trousers, which the women found they could not get into. General Smith immediately chose as his assistant one particularly filthy member who had lost hairpins and hat and been vomited on; he confided to her later that he "picked the worst-looking so her feelings wouldn't be hurt." The greatest con-

---

[1] No official WAC history was discovered in theater files. This chapter draws upon: (1) The sections concerning NATO in SPWA 320.2, WAAC classified files, DRB AGO. (2) WAC policy file, in possession of Lt Col Dorothea A. Coleman. Hereafter cited as Coleman file. (3) Intervs with, and written comments from, Lt Col Dorothea A. Coleman, 21 Jan and 8 Feb 46; Lt Col Cora M. Foster, 8 Mar 50; Maj Hortense M. Boutell, 8 Mar 50 and 6 Mar 51; Maj Ruth M. Briggs, 6 Mar 51; Maj Aline Drezmal, 6 Mar 51. (4) Memo, WAC PRO, Hq MTOUSA, for WAC Gp, WDBPR, 12 Sep 45, sub: WAC Redeployment. WDWAC 000.7. Hereafter cited as Redeployment Summary. (5) Clippings and publicity material, cited by name and envelope. DRB AGO. (6) Interv and written comments from Dr. Sidney T. Mathews. OCMH. (7) Review of this chapter by Col Westray Battle Boyce Leslie.

[2] For all excerpts from mail, see NATO AG files 319.1 Morale, Vols. II–V.

tribution came from General Marshall, who met the women at the Casablanca Conference and took home a list of lost equipment. Finding that there was no legal means of free replacement, he personally paid for and forwarded new clothing, refusing to accept repayment.[3]

Arrival of First Unit

The first enlisted women arrived in the theater a month later. The 149th WAAC Post Headquarters Company, called by newspapers "the first American women's expeditionary force in history," was one of the most highly qualified WAAC groups ever to reach the field. Hand-picked and all-volunteer, almost all members were linguists as well as qualified specialists, and almost all eligible for officer candidate school. The company was shipped from the United States on a regular military transport, which encountered no enemy action. The only difficulty was the loss of unit equipment, which never arrived in Algiers. The unit's vehicles were later found to have been issued to a male unit at the port, while cooking equipment, medical supplies, folding cots, recreational equipment, typewriters, and clothing maintenance supplies vanished, a serious loss in view of shipping conditions and the absence of women's supplies in theater warehouses. Such occurrences in later shipments were to be prevented by the prior appointment of a theater WAAC staff director to make advance preparations.[4]

The unit reported on 27 January 1943 to General Eisenhower's headquarters in Algiers, a location now considered safe, except for air attack, from the conflict still raging to the east. The women were housed in the dormitory of a convent school some distance from the headquarters. The unfamiliar climate and the unheated quarters caused almost every member to succumb immediately to colds and other respiratory disorders—a tendency noted also in newly arrived men. Waacs washed in an outdoor trough, carried water in helmets, and worried in their usual manner concerning the impossibility of careful laundry or neat appearance. Working hours were long; women were carried in trucks to the headquarters at an early hour, and home again for an early curfew. The nightly bombings, with brilliant displays of antiaircraft fire, made sleep difficult for the first weeks.

Nevertheless, most women managed a satisfactory adjustment, and most of the sick required no hospitalization.[5] Morale was high, and women called themselves the luckiest in the Corps, commenting variously, "Life has been one thrill after another"; "All my life I wanted to travel and see strange sights and now I am doing just that"; and, of the ack-ack fire and burning barrage balloons, "No Fourth of July celebration could be more spectacular."[6] Ecclesiastical authorities protested when Wacs were housed in church quarters, but soon admitted that they had "never imagined that a unit of American women could be so well-disciplined and so considerate as well."[7]

---

[3] Intervs cited n. 1(3); also two WDBPR Press Releases. (1) "Torpedoed," in Env, Africa—Interesting Backgrounds. (2) 27 Jan 43, in Env, Stories—1943.

[4] (1) Memo, CO 149th WAAC Post Hq Co, APO 514, for Dir WAAC, 8 Feb 43. WDBPR file of NATO correspondence, DRB AGO. (2) For theater strength figures, see Table 7, Appendix A.

[5] Ibid.; also Memo, CO 149th WAAC Post Hq Co for Dir WAAC, 23 Feb 43. Same file.

[6] WDBPR Env, Africa—Ltrs Written by Waacs.

[7] Ltr, Col Donald B. Adams to Dir WAC, 23 Mar 44. WDWAC 000.7.

As there were not enough Waacs in this first unit to supply every office's needs, the theater adjutant general reported an "inevitable scramble by chiefs of general and special staffs to obtain additional WAAC personnel." [8] The largest part of the company went to the Signal Corps and to the newly organized Central Postal Directory. Others were assigned, by twos and threes, to various headquarters offices: three to the Office of Psychological Warfare; three to the adjutant general's office; one as General Eisenhower's secretary and one as his driver; more than a half dozen to drive other officers. Ten more were assigned as cooks and bakers to keep food ready for workers on three shifts. [9]

Reports on initial job success were consistently good. Among the first to receive commendation were telephone operators and other communications workers in theater headquarters. The Voice of Freedom—the entire telephone switchboard system of theater headquarters, large enough to service a good-sized city—was eventually manned entirely by WAAC supervisors and operators. Many telephone operators had from ten to fifteen years of civilian experience as operators and supervisors, and some were bilingual. A record for calls handled was set, and the theater chief signal officer, Brig. Gen. Terence J. Tully, stated, "It is highly desirable that the use of Wacs be extended," particularly to message center and cryptographic duties. [10]

The first postal directory workers were likewise successful. Officers in charge reported that "since the Waacs have taken over with an entirely different attitude toward the job than the men who had previously handled it, the percentage of errors has decreased materially." [11] Although the job was considered by some to be a deadly routine, Waacs were somewhat romantically apt to visualize the pleasure of a soldier in getting long-delayed mail, or the anguish of a mother erroneously returned her letters, stamped "missing in action." The postal directory's Army supervisor stated:

The office was piled ceiling high. These girls came in and took over and worked from 8 a.m. until 9:30 p.m. seven days a week until it was cleaned up. . . . They never thought of asking for time off and I had to order them home nights. [12]

Administrative Difficulties

This early and continued job success was deemed remarkable in view of the administrative difficulties that the unit encountered during its first six months. Theater authorities attributed the confusion that developed to the absence of a WAAC adviser on the staff level, for the women had been sent without a WAAC staff director for the theater—the first and last time that such a mistake was made. [13] In the meantime, certain policy questions had arisen which even General Hughes, with his long study of the problem, felt unable to answer. He sought Director Hobby's advice by mail, but she felt it undesirable to attempt long-distance pronouncements in ignorance of local conditions. [14]

[8] Ltr, Brig Gen Thomas J. Davis, AG AFHQ, to Col Hobby, 29 Sep 43. SPWA 320.2 sec 7.
[9] Inez Robb dispatch, WDBPR Env, Africa—Opinion, Gen Offs.
[10] Memo, Gen Tully for CG NATOUSA, 27 Sep 44. Coleman file.
[11] Ltr, Gen Hughes, Dep Theater Comdr, to Dir WAAC, 29 Apr 43. SPWA 320.2 sec 5.
[12] AFHQ Press Release, "Postal," WDBPR, Env, Africa—Interesting Jobs.
[13] Cbl 3093, 20 Jun 43. SPWA 320.2 sec 5.
[14] Ltrs, Gen Hughes to Col Hobby, 17 Apr 43, and to Col Catron, 13 May 43, and reply 3 Jun 43. SPWA 320.2 sec 5.

MAJ. WESTRAY BATTLE BOYCE, *WAAC Staff Director, North African Theater,* *reads orders replacing enlisted men of the adjutant general's office with enlisted women, Algiers,* *North Africa.*

Finally, responsible commanders in the theater were stirred to action by the report that a large number of Waacs did not intend to enlist in the WAC. At this, General Eisenhower cabled a request for "a highly competent senior WAAC officer to be sent to this theater without delay." [15] Director Hobby promptly complied with the request and sent a theater WAAC staff director, Maj. Westray Boyce, previously staff director of the Fourth Service Command. Major Boyce, according to General Hughes' account, "arrived to find the girls in a state of mind which required immediate and drastic action. This she took." [16] The previous company officers and key cadre were returned to the United States in a body, since it appeared impossible to place individual responsibility or to restore the women's lost confidence; all later proved successful in a variety of duties in the United States. A request was cabled for "competent, experienced" company officers to fly to the theater.[17]

[15] Cbl cited n. 13.
[16] Ltr, Gen Hughes to Col Hobby, 1 Jan 44. SPWA 320.2 sec 9.
[17] Cbls W7186, 12 Aug 43, and W8669, 30 Aug 43. SPWA 320.2 sec 5.

Meanwhile, the company had been successfully pulled together by one of the five officer secretaries, Capt. Martha Rogers, who had not been previously considered for company duty for lack of "voice and command" presence. Major Boyce secured some reassignment of women who were unsuitably assigned or not kept busy. She also succeeded in slowing up the promotion of Waacs, which she felt that a few section chiefs had been making too indiscriminately. After the reorganization, morale soon improved, and the number of Waacs lost at the conversion to Army status was less than had been anticipated. Gen. Dwight D. Eisenhower personally addressed the women in mid-August and informed them that they were necessary to the fighting ahead, and that "if a single one of you goes home, it's too many." [18]

Because of the general alarm at the results of lack of staff supervision, General Eisenhower and General Hughes personally drafted and put into effect a system that gave Major Boyce greater power than any ever held at any other place or time by any other WAC staff director. Under the title of Theater WAC Executive Officer, she was given virtually complete command jurisdiction over Wacs in the theater, bypassing normal military channels in all matters except supply and routine post administration. She was supreme on all matters of promotion, job suitability, discipline, discharge, and well-being. In fact, the system was a complete reversion to the old WAAC regulations, although few WAAC officers in the United States had ever exercised all of these powers as fully as Major Boyce now did. [19]

These powers did not last long, for a new commander, Lt. Gen. Jacob L. Devers, replaced General Eisenhower a few months later, and soon restored the command prerogative of Army officers. He also placed the WAC staff director's office in G–1 Division; as a result, she could no longer consult directly with the deputy chief of staff. However, in the interim, the theater staff had become accustomed to consulting the WAC staff director on policy matters, and the habit persisted even after WAC command powers were revoked and after Lt. Col. Westray Boyce was succeeded, in less than a year, by Lt. Col. Dorothea A. Coleman. The headquarters eventually directed in writing that the WAC staff director be allowed to comment on all matters affecting Wacs before action was taken by any headquarters division. [20] With this precaution, it appeared to be a matter of little moment what command system was used, and the early administrative problems seldom if ever recurred in later units.

Further WAC Shipments

From the time of arrival of the first unit, theater requisitions for more Waacs had been repeatedly forwarded to the War Department, with the highest shipment priorities. As soon as approaching military status warranted, these began to be shipped, in accordance with General Marshall's policy of priority to combat theaters. The second shipment arrived in May, some four months after the first, and contained chiefly workers for the Central Postal Directory, although fewer than the chief of that agency had tried to obtain. In August of 1943, a platoon of about

---

[18] (1) Cir 205, Hq NATO, 23 Oct 43. Coleman file. (2) Ltr cited n. 16. (3) Quotations from AFHQ Press Release, 17 Aug 43. WDBPR Env, Africa—Opinion, Gen Offs.

[19] Cir cited n. 18(1).

[20] MTO Ltr, 7 Feb 45, sub: Responsibilities of WAC Stf Dirs. AG 322.01/234 A–O.

sixty members arrived in Casablanca and proceeded to Mostaganem for service with the Fifth Army. In September the 60th WAC Headquarters Company arrived to augment the 149th, and the 61st for SOS headquarters at Oran.[21]

The need to release more men to staff Signal Corps installations in Italy brought about the activation of a complete WAC Signal company, which arrived in Algiers in November. The women were welcomed by the Deputy Chief Signal Officer, Allied Forces Headquarters, who promised them long hours of work under "far from ideal conditions."[22] Members were assigned as route clerks, high speed radio operators, teletypists, cryptographic code clerks, and to cutting tape in radio rooms. On the same ship with the Signal company was the first WAC contingent for duty with the Air Forces in the theater, the Twelfth Air Force Service Command at Algiers. This unit was picked up at the port of debarkation by transport planes and flown direct to its parent organization. According to its chief of staff, "We have a lot of work for them to do right now; we can't afford to have them sitting around a port for several days."[23] Enlisted members, like those in preceding shipments, were again highly qualified, ranging from a former dean of women to a translator of African dialects. Most were assigned as telephone operators, file clerks, typists and stenographers, and to aid in the air service command's work of forwarding ammunition, engines, and other supplies to the front.

In January of 1944, the theater announced the arrival of another contingent for service with the Air Forces—some 372 enlisted women and eight officers, bringing the theater total to over 1,500. These were divided into four units for assignment to four different stations in North Africa.

Other shipments continued during 1944, eventually bringing the theater total to approximately 2,000. The theater thus assumed third place in the number of Wacs employed overseas, being eventually surpassed only by the European and Pacific theaters.[24]

These Wacs were processed in and out of the theater by a WAC replacement depot, operated in conjunction with the men's depot, but with its own experts in WAC clothing, equipment, records, and other processing. Here new arrivals were given orientation talks by the WAC staff director, with hints as to how best to profit from the past experiences of Wacs in the theater. New arrivals were interviewed and assigned by a WAC specialist in G-1 Division, who was aware of the probable training, capacities, and limitations of WAC personnel.[25]

Even before the full 2,000 had arrived, Wacs had begun to move out into Italy, beginning with the Fifth Army platoon in November of 1943. At the height of the Italian campaign there were fourteen WAC units with the various commands in Italy, including the Fifth Army, the Peninsular Base Section, and the Air Forces. By the end of the Italian campaign all of the theater's Wacs were in Italy.

---

[21] (1) ETO WAC Hist, p. 7. (2) Cbl W3105, 20 Jun 43. SPWA 320.2 sec 5. (3) Press Release cited n. 12. (4) Hist, 6669th WAC Hq Plat (Overhead), APO 464, Fifth Army. In possession of Lt Col Cora M. Foster. (5) Intervs cited n. 1(3).

[22] Press Release, 11 Nov 43, sub: WAC Sig Co Arrives; and Press Release 125237 AFHQ. WDBPR Env, Africa—SigC Co.

[23] Two Press Releases, subs: WAC, and WAC Air Corps Co Arrives. WDBPR Env, Africa—AAF Wacs.

[24] (1) Stars and Stripes, Algiers, January 20, 1944. (2) Peak strength: 1929, Jun 45 (96 offs, 1833 EW). Lowest: 206, Jan 43. Coleman file.

[25] Intervs with Col Coleman cited n. 1(3). (2) Ltr, Hq MTO to CO Hq Comd AF (Overhead), 2 Apr 45. AG 2220.3 298-P.

WACS ARRIVING AT CASERTA, ITALY, *17 November 1943.*

Fifth Army Wacs

The theater's most unusual experiment in WAC employment was that of the Fifth Army Wacs, who claimed the honor of being the first Wacs to set foot in Italy, and in fact on the continent of Europe. Although never more than sixty women were involved, the experiment was considered to be potentially more important than its size would indicate, since it might determine the degree to which women could in future emergencies make up part of tactical units.[26]

When the Fifth Army jumped off for Italy, the Wacs were not too far behind it, arriving in Caserta, via Naples, on 17 No-

vember 1943 under the command of 1st Lt. Cora M. Foster. The T/O called for 10 telephone operators, 7 clerks, 16 typists, 10 stenographers, 1 administrative clerk, and cooks and other cadre. In late January the unit split into forward and rear echelons, and the forward echelon, including all telephone operators and some stenographers, moved into the bivouac area near Presenzano. Here the women lived in pyramidal tents and worked chiefly in the Fifth Army's mobile switchboard trailer. By March the rear echelon was also in tents near Sparanise. Unit records noted

[26] All statements concerning Fifth Army Wacs are from: (1) Hist cited n. 21(4). (2) Intervs cited n. 1(3). (3) Redeployment Summary.

that the women "thrived on it; the sick call rate dropped way down."

For the rest of the Italian campaign, the units followed the Fifth Army up the peninsula, usually being located from twelve to thirty-five miles behind the front lines. From June to September the forward echelon's longest stay in any one place was five weeks, the average being two. The women lived in whatever billets were available—schools, factories, apartments, and chiefly tents. The forward section spent most of the winter of 1944–45 living in tents in the mountains above Florence. The women usually wore enlisted men's wool shirts, trousers, and combat boots, and carried only the few necessities that could be moved forward with them.

The unit proved unusually successful. It received Lt. Gen. Mark W. Clark's praise as well as being one of the few to receive both the Fifth Army Plaque with clasp, in 1944, and the Meritorious Service Unit Plaque in 1945. There were twenty-seven awards of the Bronze Star. The forward echelon included some of the most skilled telephone operators on the Continent, able in a matter of minutes to get through the complicated communications networks to the commanding officer of any unit sought by General Clark. The unit's morale and *esprit de corps* were perhaps highest in the theater's WAC units. Its members wore the Fifth Army's green scarf. "They were," said Colonel Coleman, "Fifth Army first and Wacs second—perhaps the best-integrated unit in the theater."

The dangers of a combat area did not present any great problem in this case. During the last days in Anzio, air raids offered the nuisance of noise and falling shell fragments, but fortunately the area had just been vacated by a combat unit that had left adequate foxholes and dugouts. The Wacs were lucky in having no injuries, in spite of some close calls. During the advance up the peninsula, they were frequently within sound of long-range artillery, and almost always in an area of complete blackout, but required no guard except the usual one that patrolled the entire camp. Italian service troops ordinarily set up the WAC and Nurse Corps tents, and the Wacs took them down themselves, with the aid of two Italian laborers to load them on trucks.

In spite of the fatigue that developed from repeated moves, officers noted that the women "griped and complained less than soldiers in rear areas." Signal Corps units in rear areas were surprised, upon offering Wacs rotation to less exhausting conditions, to find that not one telephone operator would agree to quit the Fifth Army unit.

WAC commanders credited much of the sustaining sense of integration to the personal policies of General Clark, who saw to it that a stirring ceremony was made of any occasion, such as the swearing-in of Waacs to the Army, or the presentation of medals and awards. When visiting dignitaries came to the area, Wacs stood honor guard with men of the 34th Division. Women were left in no doubt that they were considered useful and valuable members of the group. Such measures inspired a loyalty among the women that long hours, fatigue, and discomfort could not shake.

It was undoubtedly significant that Wacs under such circumstances seemed exempt from the pattern of administrative needs that was invariable in sedentary units. The almost total absence of grades and ratings did not noticeably affect morale, although an expert switchboard operator of two years' service was lucky to get a pfc. rating. The longer hours, the lack of privacy, the necessity for wearing clothing designed for men, all seemed to have little effect. Telephone operators seemed to be immune from the illness and tension experienced by women on identical shift work in more permanent companies a few score miles to the rear. Rude remarks from occasional unfriendly males, which caused a morale problem among Wacs elsewhere, were more or less brushed aside by women too busy to notice them and too assured of their own usefulness to doubt it. Under the circumstances, the staff director considered it a pity that all Wacs could not be employed in such units.

WAC advisers recommended that any such groups, for best success, be carefully selected. The best-suited type of woman was believed to be one whose physical stamina was average or better, who liked outdoor life, and who was well balanced mentally and emotionally. In a small isolated group, it was found fatal to include those with irritating habits and mannerisms—overtalkative, grouchy, or erratic. The ambitious or the highly qualified woman was also not a good choice, since top supervisory jobs in a tactical headquarters did not go to women, nor did they receive the high grades that those in rear areas did, many still being privates after two years. Emotional self-control was also vital, since the women were constantly surrounded by men, especially by combat troops coming back for a rest. Besides fending off advances, said the staff director, "The Wacs had to listen to the men and let them blow off steam, and this put an additional strain on the women's nerves." A mature woman was found preferable, especially one whose only interest was not the opposite sex. The lone company officer who accompanied each sec-

tion had to be especially self-reliant and self-sufficient; her conduct necessarily had to be above reproach.

It was Colonel Coleman's final judgment that WAC units similar to this Fifth Army unit might easily be used, if necessary, in army and corps headquarters, or wherever nurses could be used, provided that the women were as well qualified. The only limitation, she believed, was that too many women should not be used in any one headquarters, since the headquarters force was also the security force, and lost a combatant for every woman specialist present.

Headquarters Duties

With the exception of the small Fifth Army experiment, the remainder of the theater's Wacs were employed in ordinary headquarters duties not strikingly different from those in comparable agencies in the United States. Woman in Allied Forces headquarters and Services of Supply headquarters were employed by almost every staff section—ordnance, judge advocate, adjutant general, and others, and as secretaries to ranking officers. In addition, the headquarters of the Mediterranean Allied Air Forces and the Twelfth and Fifteenth Air Forces employed Wacs, in units stationed at various times at Caserta, Bari, Foggia, and Florence.

In organization, the most distinctive feature in the Mediterranean Theater's employment of Wacs was that all women, with the exception of Air Forces and Fifth Army Wacs, were eventually organized into a single battalion under WAC command. This unit was the 2629th WAC Battalion, stationed in Caserta, under the command of Maj. Hortense M. Boutell. The battalion included a postal company, a message center company, a WIRES company, two headquarters companies, a replacement depot detachment, and a small Signal group on detached service, first in Constantine and then in Rome. Eventual enlisted strength totaled approximately 900, about half of theater WAC strength, plus 52 WAC officers, and some 400 British ATS attached to the battalion and housed with it. With such a large concentration of female personnel under WAC command, matters of supply, administration, and discipline were considerably simplified.[27]

In all units—Air, Ground, or Service Forces—the most striking difference from employment in the zone of the interior was the higher degree of skill and ability involved. All but a negligible number of enlisted women were qualified for skilled jobs; there were only two WAC "laborers" in the theater—one basic, one repairman. The statistically average Wac in this theater was a trim, healthy young woman, unmarried, older than the average soldier, with better education than the zone of the interior Wac.[28] Thus, the theater never experienced the problems of the zone of the interior in assigning personnel of low aptitude or little training. The higher average ability was reflected in the final tally of WAC assignments in the various headquarters.[29]

Type of Duty	Percent
Total	100.0
Clerical	31.9
Communications	29.2
Stenographic	16.3
Miscellaneous	12.7
Headquarters Cadre	9.9

Such high percentages of skilled personnel not only made assignment easier, but minimized problems of maladjustment, mental health, discipline, and improper or too-heavy work. In most units women did not even have to perform

kitchen police and fatigue duties, since local labor was available and it was considered uneconomical to waste a skilled Wac's time in such heavy tasks. The large WAC battalion alone eventually had about 250 civilian servants.

The advantages that the theater enjoyed in such high-type personnel were made clear by its reaction when, in later shipments from the United States, the quality declined somewhat, especially for officers, concerning whom an observer protested, "If we cannot give them officers who are outstanding leaders, we should at least give them officers who are ladies and whose conduct is such that the enlisted women can respect them."[30] A corresponding decline in the care of selection of enlisted women more than doubled the number who promptly had to be returned to the United States because of physical breakdowns.

The only major problem in WAC employment encountered by the theater was that of the Signal Corps Wacs.[31] By midsummer of 1944, women in this work began to suffer from fatigue and depression; their sick rate was twice as high as other Wacs', and morale was low. The theater chief signal officer diagnosed the fatigue as "resulting from working long hours over a period of several months

[27] Interv with Maj Boutell, 8 Mar 50; interv and written statement, 6 Mar 51.

[28] Redeployment Summary.

[29] Ibid. Statistics in Coleman file are even higher for the period Jun 43–Jun 45.

[30] (1) Memo, Col Boyce for Dir WAC, 28 Oct 44. WDWAC 320.2. (2) Cbl W1960, 5 Feb 44. SPWA 320.2 sec 9.

[31] Discussion from: (1) Memo, WAC CO 6715th WAC Com Co, APO 512, for CO 2629th WAC Bn Hq 29 May 45. Coleman file. (2) Rpt, Bn CO 2629th WAC Bn to Dep CSigO NATOUSA, 11 Sep 44. Coleman file. (3) Memo cited n. 10, Tab A, 2 Sep 44. (4) Memo, Traf Off 3141st Sig Serv Gp for CO 2629th WAC Bn, 22 Sep 44; Tab B is D/F, Theater WAC Stf Dir, 10 Sep 44; Tab C is Rpt of Surv Com, 11 Sep 44.

under pressure caused by the necessity for speed and security in handling messages, and the realization of the operational importance of every duty they perform." WAC and Medical Corps officers felt that the difficulty was due, not to the work itself, but to the lack of leaves or furloughs, the rotating shifts so short that sleeping habits never became adjusted, and the long hours of off-duty training in other Signal Corps work. Most important was the shift work; Major Boutell later surmised that this alone was the chief problem, coupled with the lack of privacy or quiet in living quarters, which made sleep difficult for night workers.

By mid-1944 about 8 percent of the women who had been in Signal Corps work for a year or more were found already unfit for further overseas service, and others were, in the opinion of their commanders, building up a nervous tension that in time would permanently end their usefulness unless transfers or leaves could be arranged. The theater chief signal officer was unable to suggest any remedy except to try to enlist large numbers of Wacs for Signal Corps work with the promise that they would be discharged after two years in the Army. He also felt that, if a 2 percent overstrength of personnel could have been provided the Signal Corps by the War Department, the Signal Corps could have permitted rotation and leaves for all personnel. Major Boutell was of the opinion that there was no real solution for the Wacs unless one could be achieved by the Signal Corps as a whole.

With this exception, there could be no doubt that most of the women were happy in their overseas assignments; they commented variously: "I love my work and enjoy being overseas"; "I wouldn't miss being here for anything"; "I like being close to the war"; "I wouldn't change

places with any girl back home." One said:

Many wonderful things happen to us. We've sailed the seas as other troops have, served on foreign soil, marched in Allied Nations parades, have seen and met some of the world's most famous men.

Another wrote:

Mother, I have never before had the complete satisfaction of worth-while accomplishment that I get from my present work. And I greatly doubt that I shall ever be inspired to put such wholehearted energy and effort into anything which my life after the war will demand of me.[32]

There was considerable debate, as in most such theaters, whether special housing and security measures required for women outweighed their usefulness on the job. It was the opinion of the staff director that there was little truth to the allegation that women required extra guards. She added:

There was an M.P. at each barracks in the cities, but there was also one at the officers' club, the noncoms' club, and all enlisted men's barracks, to keep out the civilians. Even where women lived in tents, they needed only the usual patrol.

The only objection, in her opinion, was that Wacs, on moving to new quarters, usually needed help in setting up bunks, latrines, and showers.

Degree of Adjustment Required

At no time was there any serious question of the ability of enlisted women to adjust to conditions of life in a theater such as this one. Possibly the greatest physical hardship was the usual absence of heat and hot water in the quarters,

---

[32] (1) Press Release 117715, Wacs in Ord, Env, Africa—Ord Wacs. (2) Ltrs, WDBPR Env, Africa—Ltrs.

whether tents or mansions. Except for this, the usual billet was comfortable—frequently an apartment house, school, or hotel, considerably more pretentious than barracks in the United States. Theater authorities closely co-ordinated housing assignment with WAC advisers, leaving to them the matter of determination of suitability. The theater consistently maintained the requirement that Wacs be assigned only in groups of fifty or more, in spite of attempts by numerous agencies to scatter them about in small numbers; this requirement, in the opinion of WAC advisers, greatly facilitated control of housing as well as of discipline.[33]

Wacs in North Africa or Italy were seldom long without items of clothing necessary to health, if not to comfort and good appearance. Because of the relative difficulty of maintaining a stock of women's clothing, men's clothing frequently had to be issued in emergencies. Women's supplies were hard to come by. Women went months without their full issue of clothing; large and small sizes were scarce, shoe repair slow, the stocking situation often critical. Post exchanges did not always have items needed by women. Hairdressing facilities were often inadequate, since the men's barbershops were of course of little use to women. Supplies forwarded to units near the front were often lost, particularly in the case of small units like the Fifth Army Wacs, whose usual supplies filled only a small easily misplaced box. "Some of the stuff was never found; I suppose it's still over there," commented Colonel Coleman.

It was discovered that women in all kinds of work did not have enough warm clothing. For many work-type clothing needs, neither regulation WAC coveralls nor seersucker work dresses were suitable. For lack of a warm soft work jacket, over-sized wool shirts were cut off and made into battle jackets. In meeting these various emergencies, theater headquarters permitted close staff supervision by WAC specialists. The theater was always quick to requisition available new items of clothing, and protested whenever such items appeared in the United States before theater Wacs had them.[34]

Health, Discipline, and Morale

Theater Wacs were never in danger of capture, although they were frequently in air raid areas. The WAC billet in Naples was hit in one bombing, but, as members commented, "it only knocked down the ceiling and one wing." Maj. Margaret D. Craighill, inspecting for the War Department later in 1944, noted no serious tension among enlisted women as a whole. She stated, "The medical service given to the WAC is excellent," consisting of two women medical officers on full-time duty, which included a monthly trip to all units for the required monthly physical inspection. The only defect in care noted by Major Craighill was the fact that "sick in quarters" was not permitted, resulting in many subterfuges by women with temporary menstrual disorders who did not wish to be hospitalized. Major Craighill reported:

Dysmenorrhea seems to be more frequent among both nurses and Wacs in this theater. Some who were never before subject to difficulty during menstruation now complain of severe pain. Reasons for this are not apparent; fatigue and constipation may be contributing factors.[35]

[33] NATO Ltr, 9 Jul 44. AG 324.5–O. Coleman file.
[34] (1) Cbl W–464/6920, 19 Sep 43. SPWA 320.2 sec 7. (2) Ltr, Gen White, G–1, MTO, to Dir Hobby, 16 Sep 44. WDWAC 320.2. (3) Cbl W6706, 2 Dec 43. SPWA 320.2 sec 7.
[35] Memo, Maj Craighill for SG through SG MTOUSA, 20 Sep 44. SGO Hist Div 319.1 MTOUSA, Women In.

Administrative arrangements for WAC medical care, with minor exceptions, were pronounced satisfactory, with adequate unit dispensaries and beds in general hospitals. As a result, evacuation rates were not excessive, being somewhat less for Wacs than for nurses. As for time lost from work, the theater enjoyed the distinction of being one in which the annual noneffective rate for Wacs was less than the comparable nonbattle noneffective rate for men—about 2.7 per 100 strength for Wacs, and 3.6 for all personnel exclusive of battle injuries.[36]

The rate of venereal disease was so low as to be negligible, although for men in the area rates were frequently alarming and the disease endemic. Among Wacs, cases were pronounced by Major Craighill to be "very infrequent"—less than one per month, with only fourteen cases having been reported by the end of 1944. The rate of pregnancy was less than that in comparable civilian age groups in the United States, and quite similar to that of nurses in the theater. Although no records were kept as to marital status, it was known that more than half of such women were married, with the number of pregnancies increasing toward the end of the war as the theater began to provide hotel quarters for married couples.[37]

The number of courts-martial during the entire two and a half years, through June of 1945, was extremely small, records showing no general courts, only six special courts—chiefly for censorship violations—and thirty-two summary courts for almost 2,000 women. WAC officers felt that "the worst disciplinary problems have been created by a few women who obviously should not have come overseas because of lack of adaptability or emotional instability." Some cases of misconduct were attributed to unhappiness about job malassignment.[38]

There was every indication that WAC morale was good in most cases. Company commanders considered morale to be almost entirely dependent upon full utilization of time and skills; one observed, "They wanted not only to be useful but to be inwardly sure of their usefulness." In cases where low morale did occur, such as in certain Signal Corps units, investigators were unable to find any bad effect from rough living conditions or lack of recreational facilities or the desire to return home; the only factor that had a definite effect on health, morale, and efficiency was that of job satisfaction.[39]

For the maintenance of morale, off-duty classes of interest to women were sponsored by the theater early in 1944, even before Director Hobby was able to get the U.S. Armed Forces Institute and other agencies to provide special courses for women. When rest camps and recreation centers began to be established to permit brief passes and furloughs for male troops, Wacs were included and were provided with living quarters, messing facilities, and quotas for such locations as Algiers, Capri, Rome, and later the Riviera, Venice, Switzerland, and Jerusalem. Although the average stay was only from three to five days, the rest was found to be a great relief from barracks life for women, and served in lieu of a convalescent hospital, which was not provided for women. For a restful evening off, WAC authorities, working with British women's services, were able to obtain adequate separate facilities for women's clubs, where women could enjoy an evening of

[36] (1) *Ibid.* (2) Statistical Data. Coleman file.
[37] *Ibid.*
[38] (1) Statistical Data. Coleman file. (2) Rpts, WAC COs, 6715th WAC Com Co and 6667th WAC Hq Co, 29 May 45 and 7 Jun 45, respectively. Coleman file.
[39] Documents cited n. 31.

bridge, cooking, and feminine companionship. The theater also permitted the WAC staff director to call meetings of WAC company officers and to send them monthly news bulletins, in an effort to improve leadership and administration.[40]

In the matter of decorations and citations WAC units and individuals were also included. The WAC sergeant who had supervised theater telephone communications received the Legion of Merit from General McNarney himself in a retreat ceremony. General Eisenhower awarded the Soldier's Medal to a WAC private who saved a soldier from a pool of flaming gasoline, at the expense of severe burns. Other decorations and battle stars were not unusual. Grades and ratings were likewise generally good, except among Fifth Army and Signal Corps personnel, and by the end of the war in Europe only a few hundred women who had been long overseas were still unrated.[41]

Soldier opposition had possibly a worse effect on morale than it did in the United States, since not only the Corps' existence but its presence overseas was questioned. Even before the women's arrival, letters streamed homeward advising against enlistment, and afterwards came the mass-pregnancy rumors which helped to inaugurate the slander campaign. Almost 100 percent of soldier comment was unfavorable or obscene. An Army supervisor noted:

That sort of thing has a direct effect on the morale of the girls over here because their families write to them and want to know if they are true. . . . It bothers me because I can see the effect on the morale, spirit, and pride of the kids working for me.

Early arrivals also had to face insults in the streets. One Wac, advising her sister on enlistment, noted, "How many times I've heard some GI call us dirty filthy names, names that I would never allow anyone to call me if I were a civilian." WAC officers excited even more resentment than enlisted women, chiefly when they outstripped men in rank or promotions.

From those soldiers who worked in offices with Wacs, or were stationed in the same vicinity, the comments tended to become more favorable. The women's military bearing likewise was praised. Soldier comment noted:

As the girls came down the boulevard, they really drew the applause. You have to hand it to them, they look good on parade. I doubt if West Pointers could appear better.

Unfortunately, only a minority of soldiers ever worked in offices with Wacs, or had any opportunity for becoming acquainted with them. Even where soldiers and Wacs were stationed in the same cities, there were not enough Wacs to permit much firsthand acquaintance between the two. Women shortly became so surfeited with requests for dates that it was necessary to provide separate recreation rooms and snack bars where they might relax and enjoy feminine companionship. The conduct of combat men, particularly young Air Forces officers, was a problem, for, said the staff director, "They would just sweep into the dayrooms and take over the place, and nothing could be done with them." There was no doubt that a Wac date, where available, meant much to many American men. One wrote:

---

[40] (1) Intervs with Col Coleman cited n. 1(3). (2) MTO Ltr, 29 Apr 45, sub: Educational Interests of WAC Pers. AG 353.8/264 TWSD-O. (3) Memo, G-1 NATOUSA for Sp Servs, 29 Dec 44; Conf Notes; Monthly Ltrs. Coleman file.

[41] (1) Statistical Data, 1943–45. Coleman file. (2) M/R, 10 Jan 44, SPWA 200.6. (3) At end of War: about 34 Pvts, 207 pfc's, according to Coleman intervs.

Some of the boys and I have been dating some Wacs and having a grand time. They have a day room all of their own with ping-pong table, darts, and cards. They have a small library too. About eleven o'clock in the evening they get some sandwiches for us at the mess hall and we polish them off with a couple of cokes. They are a heck of a nice bunch of girls and full of pep and fun. It's nice to be able to talk to some feminine company that speaks your own language.

On the other hand, a Red Cross worker noted:

Too many GI's get out of hand and then wonder why the Wacs won't go out with them. There are about 10 percent of the GI's that spoil things for the other 90 percent.

From the viewpoint of the War Department, the most alarming thing about soldier opinion in the North African theater was its effect on recruiting. The theater, like others not surrounded by the American public, never displayed a highly developed sense of those public relations measures that might have counteracted the soldier comment and reassured the women's families. Thus, in the early days it failed to take any positive countermeasures, although as early as February and March of 1943 some American foreign correspondents attempted to do so, notably John Lardner, Inez Robb, and Ernie Pyle.[42]

Although the first overseas Waacs were the Corps' greatest potential recruiting publicity asset, few stories or pictures came back. Recognizing that such attention could not be afforded by a combat theater for a tiny minority, Director Hobby attempted to stem the flood of bad publicity by sending a Waac photographer and a writer on temporary duty to get favorable stories. These could be given little assistance in the way of Signal supplies, laboratory facilities, or transportation, since the problem of winning the campaign was immediate and that of recruiting Waacs was remote. The two officers nevertheless managed to secure much favorable comment in various news sources, and to send back pictures of Waacs with General Eisenhower, Maj. Gen. James H. Doolittle, Lt. Gen. Carl Spaatz, and Gen. Henri H. Giraud, and with Spahis in a colorful review.[43]

Social Association

Possibly the only other theater problem in WAC employment stemmed from the lack of a firm policy on officer-enlisted relationships. General Eisenhower and General Hughes, in setting the first policy, were of the opinion that no restrictions should be placed on social engagements. Any other policy appeared difficult to enforce because of the presence at Allied Forces headquarters of large numbers of Allied officers and American naval officers, whose services permitted off-duty social association of officers and enlisted personnel. After her arrival, Major Boyce concurred, provided that officers did not date enlisted women who worked for them, thus avoiding the danger of favoritism in promotion. When General Devers took command, he reversed this policy and, over the objection of Major Boyce, directed that both Wacs and nurses observe military customs in selecting their off-duty escorts. Exceptions were made only for relatives and fiancés, who had to carry a letter to prove their status.[44]

[42] WDBPR Env, Africa—Opinion, Favorable.

[43] Rpt, Capt Ann McIlhenney and Lt Charlotte McGraw to Dir WAC, sub: Rpt on NATO Pub Relations. SPWA 320.2 sec 5.

[44] (1) Hughes Ltr to Col Hobby cited n. 14. (2) NATO Cir 23, 26 Feb 44; Med Base Sec Cir 20, 3 Mar 44. Coleman file.

GEN. HENRI H. GIRAUD REVIEWING WAACS *in a colorful ceremony in North Africa.*

Neither system worked perfectly. Mixed dating in itself caused no difficulty, so long as women did not date their supervisors, except in a few instances in which officers brought enlisted women to their clubs against the wishes of other officers who did not wish to associate with them. Enlisted men were bitterly jealous when officers monopolized the Wacs, but when the Devers ruling restricted enlisted women to dating enlisted men, the unfavorable comments continued and worse problems arose. Major Boyce asked that British and Navy officers be made subject to the rul-ing, but this proved impossible, and unfortunate public disturbances resulted when military police arrested enlisted Wacs escorted by British or Navy officers.

WAC commanding officers also reported difficulty with Army officers who ignored the rule and then attempted to prevent punishment of enlisted women whom they had dated. WAC commanders were loath to enforce the ruling when officer escorts were not likewise punished, but were allowed no choice under the regulation. Violations were flagrant, and commanders feared that respect for all discipline was being damaged. It was attempted to allow some latitude by issuing letters of authorization for engaged couples, but when informed that notices of engagement would be mailed to home-town papers, all but two such couples withdrew their requests for authorization.

Inasmuch as over half of the enlisted women in the theater were eligible for officer candidate school, it was impossible to hope that "natural social level" would cause them to prefer enlisted men. Only the Fifth Army experienced little difficulty, because it was possible to maintain one policy in this command.

No solution was ever found to the problem, which enlisted women frequently cited as the reason for their desire to leave the Army as soon as eligible for discharge. Upon losing an excellent secretary, General White discovered that her departure was due entirely to one incident in the theater, in which she had been arrested for dining in public with her husband, an officer.[45]

Marriage was not forbidden, and in addition to the Wacs who married officers there were a number of the theater's 4,000 nurses who had married enlisted men. Theater authorities were shortly obliged to be realistic about the situation. Finally, hotels were set aside to which officers and enlisted men might take their wives, and a wife was authorized to take the status of her husband when accompanied by him to hotels, messes, and clubs. However, WAC weddings were not frequent; only about 135 had occurred by the end of the war.[46]

Other Women's Groups

Wacs in North Africa and Italy considered themselves particularly blessed in the relative scarcity of American civilian employees, who in many other theaters occupied the best jobs. In the few cases where civilian women were employed in this area, the WAC staff director succeeded in pulling Wacs out of the offices concerned, so that conflicts were avoided, and, said Colonel Coleman, "We also successfully ran the OSS civilian women out of the WAC off-duty dress." It was not until the virtual end of hostilities that good enlisted jobs began to be taken over by that phenomenon which always annoyed Wacs irrationally: numbers of civilian women, complete with officers' privileges, fur coats, and duly authorized WAC uniforms.

In addition to the few civilian women employees of the Army, there were other women's groups in abundance—civilian groups such as the USO and the Red Cross, and military groups such as the British ATS and the French "WAC." Of these, the British ATS were the most numerous. Some months after the arrival of the first Waacs, and especially when the theater's Supreme Allied Commander was British, British women in small numbers began to arrive. In general they were housed and fed with the Wacs and worked with the British sections of the various headquarters. The British women proved most generous in sharing their recreational facilities with the Wacs, and all services mingled companionably for tea and other occasions.

In the Fifth Army two groups of ATS women lived and ate with the Wacs. The British women were pleased with the American mess and, said Captain Foster, "it was a pleasure to have them." As much

---

[45] Intervs and excerpts from mail cited n. 1(3) and n. 2.

[46] MTO Cir 52 sec II, 3 Apr 45. Coleman file.

could not be said for certain USO women sometimes billeted with the Fifth Army Wacs, since they habitually managed to be absent at moving time, leaving their tents for the Wacs to take down. Also living with the Fifth Army Wacs were the chief nurse, Red Cross women, and several French women officers. In general Wacs had only praise for the French women's corps, which, after a confused start on ambiguous status, achieved military standing and discipline and whose ambulance drivers were often sent farther forward than the women of any other service.

As for the American Red Cross, personal relations usually depended on the individual; as a group, it appeared to WAC commanders that "there was no place in their program for us." The older British services, on the other hand, had by this time made provision for women in their recreational services. When the American Red Cross failed to provide for the Wacs, the British YWCA set up a series of rest camps in Italy, and General Sir Harold R. L. G. Alexander backed an Allied Women's Club in Caserta. All of these served as many Wacs as ATS, and made it possible for the Wacs to have recreation and three-day passes comparable to those which American services provided for men only. In general, WAC authorities noted that "American agencies were not too well set up to do anything as far as women were concerned, and more often the Wacs had to take care of them."[47]

For a time it was feared that the Wacs would have to take over supervision of some 500 members of the German women's forces captured in the area. The uncertain status of these women, which might or might not have been that of civilians, roused some doubts in the minds of WAC authorities as to the result if the situation had been reversed. Had German captors been forced to decide WAC status, there appeared some likelihood that Wacs would have been considered civilians through confusion with the numerous civilian women in the OSS, USO, and other groups, all of whom wore the WAC uniform.

Demobilization

As the end of the war approached, WAC advisers became increasingly concerned that in wartime there was no limit to the overseas tour of duty of administrative troops. WAC company commanders noted that there were a few women in every company who became physically or emotionally unfitted for efficient overseas service but who could not be returned, for lack of any authority, until totally disabled.

Colonel Coleman felt that for certain types of work, particularly in the Signal Corps, personnel should be able to look forward to relief at a definite time, and that it would in the final analysis be cheaper to return a good worker while he or she was still capable of rehabilitation and continued service in the United States. She advised theater commanders, "Good service should not be permitted to end in hospitalization if it is possible to avoid it."

It was also Colonel Coleman's opinion that women, if left overseas past the proper time for return, were affected spiritually, not by war and death so much as by long residence in war-disrupted countries where the standards of native life were low and heartbreaking destruction was widespread. Under such circumstances, WAC commanders noted that

---

[47] Intervs and statements cited n. 1(3).

"women gradually hit a place where they have to live on the surface," and a certain temperamental change, of which they were often unaware, appeared to have made them less vulnerable to the sight of others' suffering. For this reason, even when women's health and efficiency were untouched, Colonel Coleman concluded that it would be better, if replacements and shipping were available, to limit an overseas tour to eighteen months.[48]

When rotation to the United States was finally authorized by the War Department, it was clear that Wacs would not be eligible in competition with men who had much longer service, and in fact most women felt that return would be improper under the circumstances.

At Director Hobby's request, the War Department late in 1944 added a microscopic quota for Wacs and nurses, enough to assure return of emergency cases. Even when Wacs became eligible under regular rules, there was no immediate relief. The theater decided that directives on rotation did not oblige it to return Wacs until a "suitable replacement" was available, and that men even in the same skill were not suitable replacements for women. The theater's new G-1, General White, commented:

> I contend emphatically that you cannot cut us off from WAC replacements on the grounds that the theater is overstrength. That is like saying you won't give us any more shoes because we have too many caps.

Eventually the theater was obliged to permit a few Wacs to be returned without replacements, since the War Department decided that these were more badly needed in more active theaters.[49]

When actual demobilization began, some 80 percent of the women were found to be eligible for discharge under the point

system. In spite of some attempts to persuade them to sign up for longer service, some four fifths of eligibles indicated that they wished to be discharged. Many were retained as long as the "military necessity" clause permitted, until after the defeat of Japan, when the War Department directed return of remaining overseas Wacs. By the end of 1945, all enlisted Wacs were out of the Mediterranean theater.[50]

The Wacs' eagerness to depart indicated, by all evidence, merely a desire for discharge and no condemnation of theater employment as compared to that in the United States. When rotation first began, women who had returned to the United States wrote back comparisons highly favorable to the theater. Accustomed to being treated as essential employees, they found civilians in the best jobs in the zone of the interior, and the civilian population scarcely as respectful as that of occupied areas. Army barracks, even with heating and laundry facilities, were not as comfortable as the apartments and hotels that the Mediterranean theater had provided; neither were there civilians or prisoners to relieve the troops of kitchen police and fatigue duty. Upon receipt of such reports, an overwhelming majority of 95 percent of the remaining women in the theater stated that they preferred to stay overseas until eligible for discharge, rather than return

---

[48] (1) Memo cited n. 31(1). (2) Quotations from M/R, Stf Dir's Opinion, Rotation. Coleman file.

[49] (1) Memo, Col Hobby for Gen Henry, 21 Aug 44. WDWAC 320.2. Quota asked was 0.5 percent per month. (2) Memo cited n. 30(1). (3) Quotation from Ltr, Gen White to Col Hobby, 3 Jan 45. WDWAC 320.2. (4) Only 120 women were ever returned (1944–45), according to Col. Coleman. About 136 received a furlough in the United States.

[50] (1) Statistical Data, Jun 43–Jun 47; (2) MTO Ltr to all subordinate comds, 23 May 45, sub: Readjustment of WAC Pers. AG 370.01/746–A–O, Coleman file.

to face the hardships of life in the United States. When, upon the cessation of hostilities, a sizable number of individuals on temporary duty were obliged to remain for permanent duty in the United States, their protests were audible in Italy.[51]

Final comments of both Army and WAC authorities indicated that the theater's WAC experiment had been a successful one. The first theater commander, General Eisenhower, stated of the women:

The WAC in Africa has proved that women can render definite contributions to the winning of the war, and that their capabilities in this regard extend to an actual theater of operations. . . . In some cases one Wac has been able—because of her expert training—to perform tasks that previously required the assignment of two men. The smartness, neatness, and esprit constantly exhibited has been exemplary . . . their general health and well-being have certainly been equal to that of our best enlisted units.[52]

The Air Commander in Chief of the Mediterranean Allied Air Forces, Lt. Gen. Ira C. Eaker, added:

As a result of my observation of the WAC personnel to date, I am thoroughly convinced that it should be retained in the after-the-war peacetime Army. I believe it is an indispensable service to our Army in the present emergency. There are innumerable tasks which I have observed WAC personnel performing in the Air Forces with remarkable efficiency. . . . They have a capacity for many specialized duties essential to the Air Forces to a greater extent perhaps than any other Air Force soldier.[53]

General Clark of the Fifth Army called to tell the Director that he wanted to take his headquarters platoon into Austria with him: "They've plenty of points but I have to have them." [54] Col. Westray Battle Boyce, visiting the areas as second Director WAC, after the end of the war, noted that morale was good and the women well adjusted, with adequate provision by the theater for their welfare.[55]

---

[51] (1) Memo cited n. 30(1). (2) Coleman Interv.

[52] Statement by Gen Eisenhower, AFHQ, 9 Jun 43, Hist Background of WAAC–WAC, App. E. WDBPR file, DRB AGO.

[53] Ltr, Air CinC MAAF to Dir WAC, 27 Jan 44, in History of Mediterranean Allied Air Forces, Dec 43–1 Sep 44, by Hq MAAF, Vol. II.

[54] Memo, Exec WAC for Dir WAC, 16 Jun 45. 1945–46 WAC files.

[55] M/R, Rpt of Visit by Dir WAC, Tab B, Mediterranean. WDWAC 333.1 (1945–46).

CHAPTER XXI

The European Theater of Operations

The European Theater of Operations, the first to requisition Waacs, was the second to receive them. By the end of the war it employed 8,316 women, the largest number in any overseas theater.[1]

The first requisitions, made by the theater Services of Supply in the summer of the Corps' formation, were not pressed after Lt. Gen. Dwight D. Eisenhower's departure for North Africa. After some six months of waiting for shipping priorities, the first two units earmarked for the theater were disbanded and their members were sent either to North Africa or to stations in the United States. In the spring of 1943, the Services of Supply again sent a requisition, but again furnished no shipping priority and shortly thereafter canceled the request.[2] Impetus in the program passed to the theater's Air Forces, of which General Eaker noted later:

Shortly after I arrived in England the problem was presented to me. . . . The commanding officer counseled me against bringing Waacs over . . . he said that I would be held responsible.[3]

Accepting the responsibility, the Eighth Air Force requested an entire WAAC battalion and set a shipping priority for the summer.[4]

In mid-April of 1943 the theater WAAC staff director, Capt. Anna W. Wilson, arrived in London to make preparations for the unit. Small advance parties from the Signal Corps and other groups were also present. Captain Wilson made plans for reception, housing, and assignment of the women, and for such feminine needs as laundry rooms, sanitary facilities, special post exchange items, and clothing main-

---

[1] Unless otherwise indicated, all references and quotations are from the Report of the General Board, U.S. Forces, European Theater, Study of the Women's Army Corps in the European Theater of Operations. OCMH. (See Bibliographical Note.) Hereafter cited as ETO Bd Rpt. Other major references: (1) ETO WAC Hist. (2) WAAC classified files, SPWA (later WDWAC) 320.2 secs 1, 2, 4a, 4b, 6, and 8a, DRB AGO. (3) History of USSTAF, 516.01, Vol. III, Ch. II, pp. 150–58. USAF Hist Div. Cited as USSTAF Hist. (4) Historical Records Rpt 315c, Wacs in European Division, Air Transport Command. USAF Hist Div. Cited as ETO ATC WAC Hist. (See Bibliographical Note.) (5) Interv with Col Mary A. Hallaren, Dir WAC, and written comments, 14 Mar 50, (6) Comments on draft of MS by Dr. Hugh M. Cole, author of *The Lorraine Campaign*, UNITED STATES ARMY IN WORLD WAR II (Washington, 1950).

[2] (1) Ltr, ETO WAAC Stf Dir to Dir WAAC, 16 Jun 43. AG 322.3, SPWA 320.2 sec 4a. (2) Rad 8786, USFOR London to WAR, 15 Apr 43. (3) Ltr, WAC Hq to CG ETO, 20 Feb 43; Rad 7329, London to WAR, 17 Feb 43. SPWA 320.2 secs 2 and 4b. (4) Memo, WAAC Hq for CG ASF, 17 Mar 43. SPWA 320.2 sec 4a. (5) D/F, OPD WDGS for CG ASF, 22 Mar 43; 1st Ind to unidentified basic Ltr, Opns Div ASF to Dir WAAC, 12 Apr 43. SPOPU 320.3 (4–6–43).

[3] Address to WAC OCS 60th Graduation Class, 17 Nov 45. WDWAC 352.

[4] Rad 9130, London to WAR, 27 Apr 43. SPWA 320.2 sec 2.

tenance supplies. The WAAC's way was smoothed by the long-accepted presence of the many British women's services, as well as of the Voluntaires Françaises, the Norwegian ATS, the Polish ATS, the Canadian WAC, and other such groups.[5]

The arrival of the American WAAC was nevertheless of considerable public interest. Captain Wilson reported:

We were interviewed by the press and on short-wave radio, and were a little surprised to find ourselves near-celebrities. We are now settled in a very comfortable flat overlooking Hyde Park . . . two bedrooms, two baths, kitchenette, and a living room.[6]

Captain Wilson noted that a disproportionate amount of her time was consumed by the social and public relations activities required of her. As in other overseas theaters, there always existed a certain tendency for the WAC staff director to be considered dedicated to official teas, press conferences, and ceremonies instead of to her military responsibilities.[7]

First WAAC Separate Battalion

Upon receipt of the Air Forces' shipping priority, WAAC Headquarters rounded up as many members of the original units as could be found, with replacements for those who had gone to North Africa. These were rapidly organized at Fort Devens to form the 1st WAAC Separate Battalion, under the command of Capt. Mary A. Hallaren. Women were equipped with full winter uniforms, as authorized for England, plus gas masks, canteens, first-aid packets, utility packs, helmets, and pistol belts without pistols. Their training included judo, hikes with full packs, and an obstacle course which, although not required for noncombatants, every woman elected to go through. The

555 enlisted women and 19 officers were so eager for the long-awaited assignment that no case of AWOL occurred prior to sailing. On 16 July 1943, almost a year after the initial request, the battalion reached England.[8]

Upon arrival the women were divided into companies and assigned to various Air Forces stations. Housing consisted of "everything from castles to huts,"[9] generally being identical with the type used for male troops at the stations. Theater historians later noted, "It was anticipated that special housing and physical facilities would be required for the Wacs, but the problem of housing Wacs provided no particular difficulties."[10]

It was immediately apparent that WAC employment in England offered little more difficulty than employment in the United States, and had the advantages of new sights and experiences and the stimulus of closeness to combat. The regulation WAC uniform was obviously inadequate for work in unheated buildings during the approaching winter and for the projected movement to the Continent, but time permitted remedial action. The supply lanes to the United States were by this time open and were relatively short, and many items could be procured from British stocks. The dangers of the area were no more

---

[5] (1) ETO WAC Hist, pp. 7–13; also ETO Bd Rpt. (2) Ltr, Lt Gen Frank M. Andrews, Hq ETO to Dir WAC, 1 May 43. SPWA 320.2.

[6] Ltr, WAAC Stf Dir ETO to Dir WAAC, 30 Apr 43. SPWA 320.2 sec 4a.

[7] ETO Bd Rpt, incl App. 112.

[8] (1) Rpt of Tng and Staging, PRD, Camp Shanks, N. Y., undated. SPWA 320.2 sec 2. (2) Interv cited n. 1(5). (3) Series of documents, SPWA 320.2 secs 1 and 2. WAAC sources say 557 enlisted women.

[9] Statement by Col Hallaren, Nov 51. WAC files, OCMH.

[10] ETO WAC Hist, pp. 10–11; also ETO Bd Rpt.

DOCKING IN SCOTLAND. *Advance party of WAAC officers and enlisted women are greeted by a bagpipe band upon their arrival, 11 May 1943.*

than those confronting the civilian population, and appeared to have little effect on morale; General Eaker later noted, "One of the factors in their success was courageousness. I saw this demonstrated when German planes came over . . . they keep more calm than men in emergencies."[11]

The first arrivals were an immediate success to a degree which, in the opinion of Air Forces commanders, motivated the extensive requisitions that followed. General Eaker stated, "It was not long before they were the best we had . . . other forces followed our lead."[12] An Eighth Air Force supervisor stated:

Their work has improved the efficiency of my office tremendously. Their attitude, discipline, and efficiency are of such value that not only enlisted men but some officers have been released to perform other duties.[13]

In a typical Air Forces flight control room, Wacs were shortly assigned as teleprinters, typists, and switchboard operators.[14] General Eaker noted his surprise in finding that "military secrets were going to have to be kept by women," and added:

One of their most important duties was to keep secret and confidential files. They were intelligent and learned quicker. They were the best photo interpreters . . . keener, and more intelligent than men in this line of work.[15]

Build-up of Units Before D Day

Further requisitions followed from both the Air Forces and theater headquarters. Personnel for the next shipment was at first organized as the 2d WAC Separate Battalion, but at the request of the theater the battalion was inactivated and its members shipped as casuals without grade allotments. The move was made possible

by the Corps' recent military status, and was pronounced by the theater to be more suitable to its needs, since the women could be integrated into existing units. These Wacs arrived in the theater in September and November of 1943, and were assigned to both Air Forces and theater headquarters, bringing the total of theater WAC enlisted strength to 1,126. In October of 1943, as a result of continuing requisitions, the War Department raised the theater WAC quota to 2,775.[16]

Before this quota could be shipped, the War Department at the end of the year informed the theater that no more Wacs could be sent for several months. Losses of the conversion period had left existing units in need of replacements, while the manpower shortage of early 1944 was already being felt. Theater protests followed, citing the approaching invasion of the Continent. General Spaatz and General Eaker appealed personally to General Arnold in Washington, asking that he prod the War Department.[17]

The theater also asked permission to make up some of the deficit by recruiting and training American civilian women living in the British Isles, believing that considerable numbers might thus be obtained. This authority was not granted for some time, and even when later put into effect proved an insignificant source of recruits, as did a similar provision for transferring to the WAC the few American citizens in

---

[11] Address cited n. 3.
[12] Ibid.
[13] ETO Press Release 1601, 14 Aug 43. ETO PR file, Adm 365 WAC, DRB AGO.
[14] ETO Press Release 1832, 6 Dec 43. Same file.
[15] Address cited n. 3.
[16] (1) See Table 7, Appendix A. (2) ETO WAC Hist, pp. 8–9; also ETO Bd Rpt. WAC sources say September and October for arrival.
[17] Rad W8189, USFOR London for USAWW–WAR, 6 Dec 43. SPWA 320.2 sec 6.

the British women's services. It became clear that the European theater must depend upon recruiters in the United States for its supply of Wacs.[18]

There followed what was, over the next months, to be a continuing skirmish over the numbers and skills of Wacs who could be sent overseas. The War Department noted that, to meet the theater's heavy demands for skilled typists and stenographers, not only would the entire recruiting intake be required, but it would be necessary for stations in the United States to resort to the embarrassing expedient of using male typists to replace Wacs "for combat" instead of vice versa. The theater in reply urged that they be so embarrassed. In its opinion, overseas areas, being obliged to support and supply troops under difficulties, required the best workers for each type of duty; the argument was that one Wac typist could replace two men while eating only half as much.[19]

At the moment part of the dispute was resolved in the theater's favor by General Arnold of the Army Air Forces, who secured permission to cut loose the Air Forces quota from the rest of the theater's, and to supply all the Wacs that General Spaatz requested, provided that only AAF stations were called upon to supply them. In February of 1944 the War Department therefore approved a new quota for the theater, 4,448 Wacs for the Air Forces and 1,727 for all other commands, a total of 6,215 for the theater.[20]

Requests from the Services of Supply in Europe were slower to come in. It was not until just before D Day that the SOS requested several large groups, so hastily that some, especially telephone operators, had to be provided with air priority.[21]

Under the new quota, WAC shipments were at once resumed and, during the first half of 1944, arrived in the theater almost

faster than they could be accommodated at reception facilities. Just before D Day, theater WAC strength had reached 3,687. At this time the War Department was again forced to shut off the supply, pleading heavy shipments to the Pacific. In spite of theater protests, no further quota increase was to be granted for some months.[22]

By D Day, Wacs were assigned to Headquarters, Supreme Allied Expeditionary Force; Headquarters, ETO; to the Allied Expeditionary Force; and to other theater organizations. Within the Air Forces, they were in Headquarters, U.S. Strategic Air Forces; Headquarters, Eighth Air Force; Headquarters, Ninth Air Force; Headquarters, Allied Expeditionary Air Forces; Headquarters, VIII Fighter Command; Headquarters, IX Bomber Command; I, II, III Bomber Divisions; and the 2d, 14th, 20th, and 96th Combat Wings. There were also numerous independent organizations that used almost a thousand Wacs in Europe, including the Air Transport Command and the Office of Strategic Services.[23]

Before D Day, initial job assignment in some of these organizations suffered from the fact that only the Air Forces in Eng-

[18] (1) ETO WAC Hist, p. 9. (2) ETO Bd Rpt, Vol. I, p. 27. (3) Ltr WAC Stf Dir to Dir WAC, 7 Aug 44. WDWAC 352 British Stf College.

[19] (1) Cbl E–31714, Eisenhower to WD; (2) Cbl WAR 49888, 13 Jun 44; (3) Ltr, WAC Stf Dir ETO to Dir WAC, 24 Jun 44. WDWAC 320.2 ETO.

[20] ETO Bd Rpt; differs slightly from Ltr, TAG to CG ETO, 10 Mar 43, sub: Quota of WAC Pers for ETO. AG 320.2 WAC (2–18–44) PO–M–A, in SPWA 320.2 (1944).

[21] Sources cited n. 2.

[22] Sources cited n. 19. These say strength was almost 6,000; later TAG figures give 3,687. See Table 7, Appendix A.

[23] Later mentioned: U.S. Gp Contl Council, 12th Army Gp, First AB Army, and MIS. ETO Bd Rpt; also ETO WAC Hist, p. 19. Independent orgns: ACT, OSS, O of Mil Attaché, Governments in Exile, Br O of JAG MIRS, AACS, U.S. Strategic Bomb Surv.

land were as yet engaged in combat. Other headquarters still had plenty of enlisted men, and were still located in areas where competent civilian help was obtainable. Therefore, while Wacs would be needed in the future, and were welcomed by higher commanders who had requisitioned them for this reason, their welcome from subordinate commanders and enlisted men was less enthusiastic. In Lt. Col. Anna W. Wilson's opinion:

Male soldiers who were firmly established in their administrative, clerical, and communications jobs and were not trained for combat naturally were fearful of the arrival of WAC personnel. Their comments on and reception of WAC personnel were derogatory and cold. The Wacs felt that they were unwelcome, which in fact they were. Months passed before this feeling of ill-will disappeared.[24]

Censorship of letters showed that there was much bitterness in the accounts written home by enlisted men and Wacs alike, which upon investigation had "no reasonable basis" but which authorities feared would damage WAC recruiting.[25]

Until D Day, as a result of the abundance of personnel, Wacs therefore at times did not replace men, or were assigned to only part-time work, or were fitted into existing organizations in duties less responsible than those of enlisted men and British civilians and less useful than the positions the women had occupied in the United States. The staff director listed incorrect assignment as first among causes of low morale. The WAC personnel officer noted, "The greatest gripe from Wacs has constantly been, 'not enough work to do.' "[26] Luckily, the serious morale problems that usually accompanied such a situation in the United States did not develop, chiefly because of the women's sense of nearness to combat and the prospect of more useful days ahead.

Office supervisors discovered no loss of efficiency during the buzz-bomb raids, and in fact, as D Day approached, there were grounds for believing that the reverse was true. One unit, which arrived in London simultaneously with the V–1, reported:

At first the Wacs were up most of every night, spending much of their time in the improvised basement shelter. Since this area was not properly equipped, there was great loss of sleep, and the nervous tension which resulted was almost as bad as the bombs.[27]

However, the women soon became accustomed to the alarms and slept all night without going to the shelter, and they worked without interruption even when bombs fell close to their offices. Several Wacs were awarded the Purple Heart for injuries received in bombings; they were more fortunate than British servicewomen in that none died of these injuries.[28]

The Move to the Continent

Less than a year after the first group's arrival, the invasion of Normandy began and Wacs moved out into France and later into Germany. A lively dispute had raged all spring over the propriety of taking women along. The more gloomy objectors stressed the fact that the women would probably be killed or captured and, if captured, might not, under the rules of land warfare, be recognized as "protected personnel" and would not, like nurses, be entitled to officer prisoners' privileges. Some

---

[24] ETO Bd Rpt, Vol. I, pp. 10 and 12.

[25] (1) ETO Bd Rpt. (2) Morale Rpt, 1–15 May 43, to Chief Info and Censorship Sec ETO. ETO Opns Rpts, Adm 365 WAC, DRB AGO.

[26] ETO Bd Rpt, p. 55; also Vol. II, App. 17.

[27] ETO ATC WAC Hist.

[28] Six deaths of Wacs were reported as of December 1944: 2 accidental poisonings, 2 auto accidents, 1 peritonitis, 1 meningitis. ETO Bd Rpt, Vol. III, App. 114.

LANDING IN NORMANDY, *14 July 1944, above. Photographs, below, were taken in the WAC camping area on 1 August 1944.*

feared that fighting men would worry so much over the Wacs' safety that their efficiency would be impaired. Others questioned whether women could live in tents under field conditions. Officers on the other side of the argument declared that their offices required their Wacs and that conditions on the Continent would be no worse than those in London under the buzz bombs, which had not disrupted office work. The WAC staff director was of the opinion that Wacs should move with their headquarters, in view of the reported success of the Fifth Army's experiment in Italy. The Wacs themselves were, as always, inordinately eager to go.[29]

The theater's decision was that the Wacs would go along, and that 50 percent of the personnel of Forward Echelon, Communications Zone, would be WAC. Necessary plans were made for clothing and maintenance, tentage, and well-trained cadre. An initial attempt was made to select personnel carefully on the basis of ability, physical stamina, and emotional stability; the group selected to follow invasion troops onto the beaches was also given a strenuous training program, plus field clothing and equipment. Unfortunately, it was soon clear that the whole WAC population of England would shortly be on the move, and that other units coming directly from the United States would have to go to France without special screening or acclimatization.

As the time approached for movement to the Continent, certain bookkeeping difficulties had to be solved. When the WAC's own Table of Organization units had been dissolved, the War Department had specified that overseas Wacs would be asigned only to large headquarters operating under bulk allotments. Assignment to vacancies in men's T/O units was prohib-

ited because of the notion that every T/O unit would sooner or later move out to do battle.

Actually, Air Forces and Signal Corps headquarters, although under T/O's, were able to operate from bases farther behind the lines than were some of the bulk-allotment Communications Zone headquarters. To avoid violating the T/O ban, the Air Forces for the first months employed Wacs on an impractical and confusing lend-lease basis from theater headquarters. Bookkeeping difficulties almost wrecked this program and shortly forced the War Department to relax its ban and permit Wacs to be assigned to men's T/O units, to "suitable noncombatant positions in fixed headquarters or installations."[30] With this, the stage was set for easy movement of Air Forces and Signal Corps Wacs to the Continent. As a matter of fact, the term "fixed installation" was shortly to be interpreted by the theater to mean a tent moved forward not more than once a day.

The first Wac to arrive on the Continent was a stenographer who, on 22 June, flew in and out of one of the beachheads to record a conference. The first regular WAC unit landed in Normandy on 14 July 1944, almost a year to the day after the first group had arrived in England, and thirty-eight days after D Day. These Wacs, assigned to Forward Echelon, Communications Zone, arrived on the Normandy beaches in LST's, and camped out in an apple orchard. They slept under shelter halves or in pyramidal tents on Army cots, received the usual field rations, and washed in cold water carried in hel-

---

[29] The entire account of the movement into France and Germany, unless otherwise stated, is from ETO Bd Rpt and ETO WAC Hist.

[30] Ltr, TAG to CG ETO, 10 Mar 44. AG 320.2 WAC (2–18–44) PO–M–A, in SPWA 320.2. Change was later written into WAC Regulations.

mets. They immediately went to work as telephone operators, typists, and clerks, working in tents, cellars, prefabricated huts, and mobile switchboard trailers. Because of the cold and mud, they wore leggings, trousers, and combat jackets; even long underwear was now popular.[31]

It was not noted that the men's anxiety over WAC safety impaired their efficiency, as had been feared; in fact, historians recorded that men were glad to have American women to talk and sing with, and "just to look at." However, since living and working conditions were equal, the normal amount of masculine griping was found to be definitely hampered.

More Wacs arrived at once, by plane and boat, some in units and some with their sections—Normandy Base Section (Supreme Headquarters, Allied Expeditionary Force), and Air Forces units, also Quartermaster, Transportation, Engineers, Ordnance, and others. Large groups of Signal Corps telephone operators arrived, many having been hastily flown in from the United States on a high-priority requisition. The most forward and mobile WAC detachment was reported to be the unit with the 12th Army Group, which advanced with its headquarters close behind the fighting lines.

On 31 August, five days after the fall of Paris to the Allied forces, a WAC advance party arrived, and on 1 September Wacs began pouring into the city from Normandy and England, by plane and by truck convoy. WAC telephone operators at once took over French switchboards just abandoned by the German army; office workers operated with captured German office supplies; cooks and mess sergeants assumed supervision of French cooks and waitresses in the various messes; and the Wacs themselves moved into and gradually filled a number of hotels in the city.

By October, 3,000 Wacs were in France; by the end of 1944 over half the ETO WAC units were there.

The Transportation Corps shortly sent picked personnel from the United States to form a traffic regulating group entirely composed of Wacs; many of the map tracings for routing combat supplies were made by this group. The Signal Corps organized an all-Wac battalion, composed of switchboard teams, message center teams, and teletype teams. This could not be called a WAC battalion because its tables called for combat equipment, and Wacs were noncombatants; Signal Corps authorities therefore called it the % 3341st Signal Service Battalion, with the % mark indicating, to the initiate, Wacs. Another all-Wac battalion, composed of Negro personnel, came in a unit toward the end of 1944 and took over half of the Postal Directory for the theater. Besides these all-WAC units there were Wacs in almost every command echelon down to the Army group level.[32]

In the eight months before V-E Day, Wacs followed closely behind the fighting forces. Food, quarters, and supplies were the same as those available to the men. The only reported difficulty concerning quarters was the absence of heat and hot water; doctors estimated that 25 percent of the women in one unit had chilblains. Conditions were extremely unsettled, medical and hospital care uncertain; there was cold, rain, snow, and mud; it was seldom any longer possible to have advance inspection of housing. Nevertheless, the strenuousness of this period had no perceptible effect; authorities were in fact

---

[31] See also Synopsis Hist of WAC, atchd to Memo WAC Gp WDBPR for Dir WAC, 31 Jul 45, sub: Proposed ETO WAC film. WDWAC 062.

[32] After V-E Day, Wacs were also assigned to the Third, Seventh, and Fifteenth Armies, and to the 40th Bombardment Wing.

LT. COL. ANNA W. WILSON, *WAC Staff Director, European theater, lunches in the field in France, 1 August 1944.*

surprised to discover that the WAC sick rate was the lowest of the year. During the initial six weeks when Wacs were landing on Normandy beaches, only one woman had to be sent back to England because of illness. Wacs noted that after the V-bombs in England, the sound of distant artillery fire in Normandy was a relief. Morale remained high in direct proportion to the women's sense of playing an immediate and essential part in the winning of the war. With civilians temporarily left behind, and men for office work scarce, Wacs were at last the valued employees they had been in some units in North Africa. This period, in spite of its lack of physical comforts, was reportedly the one in which

ETO Wacs were happiest. In December of 1944, during the dark days of the Battle of the Bulge, offices depended greatly on their women, and WAC morale and efficiency were at a peak.

At the time of the Battle of the Bulge, theater representatives went to Washington and personally sought and obtained resumption of Wac shipments. These, by V-E Day, had raised the ETO WAC strength to more than 8,000—the largest number of Wacs utilized by any foreign theater. The number was only half of the 16,000 that had been requisitioned, and much less than the 25,000 to 50,000 that the WAC staff director felt would have been requisitioned had there been any hope of receiving so many. As the Air Forces mission shrank after V-E Day, greater proportions of the total came to be employed by field and service forces.[33]

When, in the spring of 1945, the First Tactical Air Force and the 12th Army Group headquarters opened in Heidelberg and Wiesbaden, no one debated whether or not to take Wacs to Germany; they moved with their headquarters as a matter of course. After V-E Day, only a handful of Wacs were left in England; the majority came to be concentrated in Germany at Berlin, Frankfurt, Wiesbaden, Heidelberg, and other headquarters. Here and in Paris, living conditions became luxurious in comparison to wartime billets and to the average accommodations of troops in the United States.

In Paris, Wacs lived in hotels with maids, dining rooms, no work details, and good recreation and sight-seeing facilities. In Frankfurt, they were housed in a well-heated apartment building, ordinarily with only two women to a room, and ate at an excellent mess boasting small tables and tablecloths, with civilians to do all but supervisory work. There were available a complete and quick civilian laundry service and good recreational facilities. In Wiesbaden, women lived in cold but comfortable apartments and a handsome private home. In Heidelberg, a comfortable hospital building was used for housing. Visiting War Department inspectors late in 1945 reported that "with few exceptions, these Wacs were living under better conditions and with more comforts than it was possible to have during the war." [34]

WAC Job Assignments

During the entire period of employment, the most notable difference from the pattern of job assignment in the United States was that a higher type of personnel was available to the theater. As in the North African theater, the women who made up these shipments constituted, on a statistical average, the cream of the Corps. Records showed that 99 percent of ETO Wacs were skilled, and that more than 50 percent of enlisted women had the AGCT scores required of officers. Such women were not only easier to assign but, as later studies showed, were less liable to become disciplinary problems, suffer low morale, or require medical discharge. No "holding depot" to accommodate unassigned personnel was ever needed for women, since all were readily assignable.[35]

Another notable difference in the employment pattern resulted from the theater's decision to limit women's jobs to a rather narrow range. Like most overseas theaters, the European theater considered women's job superiority proven only in routine clerical, stenographic, and communications duties, and was loath to risk shipment of other skills in which a man might not be efficiently replaced. Final records of WAC assignment indicated that about 35 percent of the theater's enlisted women were employed as stenographers and typists; another 26 percent were clerks; 22 percent were in communications work. These percentages of scarce skills were considerably higher than those available to the Corps as a whole. In the United States, as in Britain, personnel shortages had admitted servicewomen to a wide variety of work and had made it necessary to accept recruits in any skill. In the European theater, only 8 percent of American servicewomen were employed

---

[33] ETO Bd Rpt, Vol. I, pp. 26 and 27; Vol. II, App. 10, pp. 4–5, and p. 14.

[34] Rpt, Maj Frances Clements, G–3, and Capt Velma P. Griffith, PRO. WDWAC 333.1 (1945).

[35] ETO Bd Rpt statistics.

POSTAL DIRECTORIES IN THE EUROPEAN THEATER

in the more unusual skills: medical technicians, mechanics, draftsmen, interpreters, weather observers, and photographic specialists.

The maintenance of this policy at times was carried so far as to result in the malassignment of women with "unfeminine" skills. Thus, some one hundred WAC mechanics in the Air Service Command, although pronounced "highly satisfactory" in this work, were ordered reassigned to unskilled desk jobs on the grounds that it was not appropriate for Wacs to wear coveralls. Other WAC mechanics remained unassigned at ports, and were eventually transferred to the Air Transport Command.[36]

The policy also made it increasingly difficult for the War Department to approve theater requisitions, and for shipping agencies to fill them satisfactorily. Many requisitions, while numerically reasonable in view of the total strength of the Corps, would have required skimming almost all stenographers and many typists from stations in the United States—a sacrifice which the War Department deemed unjustified in view of frequent reports that there was already widespread theater use of WAC stenographers as typists and of typists as clerks. Stations in the United States experienced difficulty in providing even the numbers approved. The theater reported receiving typists labeled stenographers and clerks called "potential typists." Also, as volunteer stenographers and typists were all shipped, it became necessary for stations to send nonvolunteers who were known to be more liable to psychiatric breakdowns. Plenty of volunteers for overseas service remained in the Corps, but not in the requested skills. Eventually the War Department was obliged to inform the theater that its requisitions could no longer be approved if they asked percentages of scarce skills higher than could reasonably be supplied. The theater's requisitions thereupon dropped a notch in skill, but continued to concentrate upon clerical fields, in spite of the staff director's attempts to interest offices in using Wacs in medical, mechanical, and other work.

An additional complication in shipment was the matter of grades. Since arriving casuals were assigned to existing units, the theater asked that they arrive with low grades in order not to outrank men and women already in those units. Expert stenographers were sought in the grade of private, and experienced company officers in the grade of second lieutenant. The Army Service Forces filled several shipments with Wacs who voluntarily relinquished their ratings for a chance at overseas service. However, when later nonvolunteer shipments arrived with ratings, a morale problem arose and the War Department ordered the ratings restored to earlier arrivals, not wishing to establish a policy of reducing to the grade of private all men and women sent overseas. Eventually the War Department was forced to apply a percentage ruling to WAC shipments, requiring the theater to absorb a percent of higher grades equal to the over-all distribution.[37]

Rather than ship women who did not meet the exacting specifications in theater requisitions, incomplete shipments were sometimes made, a practice that also met with objections from the theater, since short shipments upset assignment plans almost as seriously as did unqualified ones. At other times, shipments were delayed until after the theater's need had changed

---

[36] ETO Bd Rpt statistics, Vol. II, App. 12 of App. 1, and Vol. III, Apps. 95–96.

[37] (1) ETO WAC Hist, p. 26, 34. Also ETO Bd Rpt. (2) D/F, G–1 to MPD ASF, 10 Mar 45. WDGAP 320.2 WAC, in WDWAC 320.2 ETO.

or had been filled from other sources. Colonel Wilson later commented:

The fluctuating supply of WAC personnel, engendered by the voluntary recruitment policy, prohibited firm planning . . . and resulted in an immeasurable expenditure of money, time, and effort, all of which would have been avoided by the application of selective service to women.[38]

Officer Assignments

As was generally true overseas, ETO WAC officers were frequently less fortunate than enlisted women in the variety of their assignments and the degree of responsibility delegated to them. Several WAC officers attended the British Staff College in a class with British women officers, but an assignment adequate to justify this high-level training could not be found. Wacs who had graduated from the Army's own Command and General Staff School were assigned to jobs such as photointerpreter. A generous portion of 32 percent of the WAC officer strength was made available for WAC administration. A high percentage of the others was used in routine jobs which were similar to those of enlisted personnel except that an officer was required for security reasons—code and cipher officers, watch officers, signal officers, photointerpreters, censors, and military secretaries.[39] In spite of a War Department letter prohibiting the employment of WAC officers as stenographers, aides, and chauffeurs,[40] by the end of the war, no less than forty-five WAC officers—14 percent of the total—were serving as personal assistants to ranking officers in the European theater.

Such employment of WAC officers caused other ranking officers in the theater to ask that their enlisted WAC secretaries be directly commissioned and continue on the same job. Director Hobby steadily opposed all of these proposals, maintaining that if the women were more worthy of commissions than other Wacs in the theater, they should be selected by an officer candidate board, and that to open the door to such a policy would mean yielding to the political pressure of hundreds of other prominent sponsors who still sought WAC commissions for friends and constituents. The War Department therefore never wholly sanctioned the European theater's request, but a concession was made which permitted deserving cases to be forwarded for review in Washington. Under this authority several direct commissions were eventually granted— none to secretaries, but several to technicians such as the WAC sergeant who, as an expert on bridge demolition, was already filling the job of a major in the Corps of Engineers.

Because of a peculiar loophole in the WAC legislation, there was no legal barrier to the direct commissioning of British civilian women in the WAC; however, in the European theater only one civilian, General Eisenhower's chauffeur-secretary, was commissioned in this way, over Director Hobby's protest.[41]

---

[38] ETO Bd Rpt, Vol. I, p. 27.

[39] ETO Bd Rpt statistics as of 1 Nov 44.

[40] Ltr, DCofS USA to AAF, ASF, AGF, and overseas theaters, 11 Aug 44. CofS 324.5 WAC.

[41] For details see Chs. XXII and, below. Colonel Hobby had repeatedly discouraged ETO inquiries in this matter, and General White had written General Eisenhower a long personal letter citing obstacles, but after three Allied citizens were commissioned in Australia without her consent, the Director received a note from Colonel McCarthy, Secretary to the General Staff: "After a talk with Gen Eisenhower, Gen Marshall decided that Miss Summersby should be commissioned directly. I understand that the WAC will have objections but I believe that the decision is final." Memo, Secy WDGS for Dir WAC, 31 Oct 44. WDWAC 320.2 ETO.

WAC Staff Director's Office

Some initial difficulty was reported by Colonel Wilson in establishing her own office and her relative responsibilities. In her opinion, theater authorities, while welcoming the enlisted women, were not initially receptive to an active role by WAC staff officers, particularly in the first months before General Eisenhower's return in 1944. The title of Director was objectionable to the headquarters because "by definition and practice in the civilian world [it] implies a certain amount of the command function." [42] As a result, Colonel Wilson and her subordinate staff directors in air and service forces headquarters found that

. . . until the WAC Staff Directors became personally known in the commands, they met many difficulties in the performance of their mission, especially with respect to making staff visits and collecting information necessary for making long-range plans and policies.

Equally objectionable to theater authorities was the word *inspection* in the War Department's provision that "a principal function of staff directors will be continuous inspection . . . for the purpose of gaining information upon which to base recommendations on . . . plans and policies." In spite of the War Department directive, the theater refused to authorize staff advisers to visit WAC units, on the grounds that this usurped the inspector general's duties or those of male commanders. Theater authorities also were reluctant to allow WAC staff officers to receive statistical reports on WAC strength, losses, disciplinary action, and other problems.

Until the end of 1943 the theater did not define the position of the WAC staff

director's office, which was unofficially that of a section of G–1 Division. As a result, other sections of the headquarters co-ordinated matters with the staff director only when the existence of the section was known to them.

Colonel Wilson noted that staff actions and directives which supposedly applied to both men and women frequently omitted any provision for women, with resulting confusion in the field, but that "failure to provide adequately for female personnel was never the result of intentional neglect, but of oversight resulting from the magnitude of the overall European Theater planning job."

Soon after General Eisenhower's return from North Africa at the end of 1943, a formal announcement was made of the establishment of the WAC Section, G–1 Division, and it was required that "all matters pertaining exclusively to the Women's Army Corps and necessitating the formulation or interpretation of policy will be referred directly to the WAC Section."

WAC officers also became part of the offices of the quartermaster, the provost marshal general, Special Services, Information and Education, the adjutant general, and the inspector general. This generally proved a great advantage from the Wacs' viewpoint. Not until a WAC officer was assigned to Special Services in April, 1944, was a complete recreational program designed to fit the needs and interests of women. The assignments also generally proved acceptable to the office concerned; the theater's chief quartermaster later noted that numerous early mis-

---

[42] This and following, including quotations, all from ETO Bd Rpt, Vol. I, pp. 16–17, 17, 19, 20, 21, 43, 80–82, and Vol. II, App. 2 of App. 1, and Apps. 7 and 10, p. 11.

takes would not have occurred except "for lack of a female advisor in OTCQM prior to the arrival of the first women troops." [43]

In the next few months, subordinate headquarters employing numbers of Wacs acquired their own WAC staff directors. A directive was published officially authorizing field "visits" by the staff director. The informal collection of a monthly statistical report through "technical channels" was also sanctioned, although only the Air Forces in the theater ever agreed to require this officially.

In spite of these great improvements, the position in G–1 Division did not prove entirely satisfactory to Colonel Wilson, who found that her office's nonconcurrences were often lost in the final G–1 decision and were not apparent to either higher echelons or other staff sections. With the establishment of Supreme Headquarters, Allied Expeditionary Force, at some distance from the rest of the headquarters, the WAC staff director was not again officially able to see the general whom she was responsible for advising; at this time there were nine intermediaries between them.

On the other hand, the staff director, who had left the United States in WAAC days, retained many operating functions that in the United States were willingly dropped as soon as military status permitted. The staff director's office had powers of assignment and reassignment of Wacs; it approved or disapproved all promotions of WAC officers, even those employed on duties unrelated to the Corps; it requested and suballotted quotas, requisitioned personnel, and took action on requests for the discharge or return to the United States of individuals in the WAC. In general, it performed for G–1 Division all personnel functions relating to women.

Here, as elsewhere in WAC administration, it proved to be difficult to relinquish operating powers until some voice was obtained in the shaping of policy.

It was not to be until after the end of the war, and after Colonel Wilson was replaced as staff director by Lt. Col Mary A. Hallaren, that earlier efforts bore fruit in a directive stating:

Although her office is an adjunct of G–1 Division, the position of the WAC Staff Director is on the same level as the assistant chiefs of staff with respect to all matters pertaining to the WAC. On such matters she is advisor to the Chief of Staff and the chiefs of the general and special staff divisions. . . . Channels of communication between . . . divisions and the WAC Staff Director are direct.

This circular also repeated War Department directives insuring "continuous inspection." [44] Colonel Hallaren later stated, "From the day this went out, we had no problem; it was a joy to be in the Headquarters." [45]

Housing, Supply, and Clothing

From the first it was clear that administrative arrangements for Wacs in a theater of this type would present no insuperable problem even in the absence of a strong staff planning section. In general, Wacs received exactly the same type of housing that was provided for male administrative troops, which was usually much superior to that provided for troops in the United States. The majority lived in hotels and houses, although a few others had barracks, Nissen huts and, temporarily, tents.

[43] Memo, Actg Theater Chief QM to Theater Gen Bd, USFET, 5 Dec 45. ETO Bd Rpt, Vol. III, App. 75.

[44] Ltr, Hq USFET to all CGs, 8 Aug 45. AG 322.01 GAP–AGO.

[45] Interv, 14 Mar 50.

While the women remained in England the theater required that all proposed WAC housing be inspected by a representative of the staff director before a unit moved in. On the Continent such inspection was not always possible.[46]

The locating of most WAC housing in civilian communities made extra protection for women's quarters unnecessary, and also eliminated the need for excessive restrictions upon the women's freedom except those required of the entire population. The theater found that Wacs resented even minor restrictions such as "march outs" to work during morning and evening dark hours, preferring to get about independently. Because of the uncertain nature of transportation facilities, enlisted women were not sent from station to station without a WAC officer escort, unless a woman's commanding officer certified that the travel concerned did not require an escort. Other than these, there were no restrictions for Wacs which did not apply to men.

Organizational supplies were also generally superior. Because of the precedent of the British women's services, the Wacs obtained bed linens and mattresses, plus a limited number of electric irons and some hairdressing equipment, although this last was never rated entirely adequate. Post exchanges were ordinarily as good as those in the United States. Mess equipment was also generally adequate. In spite of the absence of milk, fresh fruits, and other items, the WAC messes were well rated, with cooks showing ingenuity in preparing dehydrated foods and other standard Army rations, which were superior to those of the British. Wacs usually had a separate mess only if civilian employees could be obtained for all heavy labor; kitchen police and similar fatigue

duty became almost as unknown as it had been in Italy.[47]

The only immediate problem presented by the area was that of suitable clothing. The standard winter uniforms that Wacs had brought from the United States were considered inadequate, especially in the Air Forces, where many women were assigned to night shifts in unheated buildings and underground operations centers. The situation was declared an emergency, and the issue of enlisted men's long-sleeved undershirts and long drawers was authorized. Since Wacs were found to be catching colds because of a certain reluctance to wear these ill-fitting garments, the theater immediately requested many extra items above the regular issue: wool underwear designed for women, wool shirts, a field jacket and wool liner, with matching trousers and trouser liner, combat boots, and long wool hose. Most of these were obtained from the United States after much delay. Because of the limited cleaning and repair facilities, all Wacs in the theater also received extra exercise dresses, wool skirts, and field shoes.

The Quartermaster-designed trousers and jacket, when finally received from the United States, were found to be bulky and unbecoming, could not be tailored to fit the figure, and shrank and faded when laundered in the field. A smart three-piece wool uniform was therefore designed by the European theater—slacks, skirt, and battle jacket—which was found to be durable, warm, lightweight, and becoming for wear either under field conditions or in the city. A request for this was for-

---

[46] ETO WAC Hist, pp. 10–11; also ETO Bd Rpt.

[47] (1) ETO Bd Rpt, incl Vol. III, App. 75. (2) Ltr, Asst Theater WAAC Stf Dir to Dir WAC, 5 Jun 43. SPWA 320.2 sec 4a.

warded to the War Department, which refused to authorize it on the grounds that all available material was being used to produce the new ETO battle jacket uniform for men. At this, the European theater found means of procuring in England enough of these uniforms to furnish each woman at least one. With the benefit of these additions, Colonel Wilson noted that ETO Wacs were better dressed than those in the United States, where cold-weather garments and other extra items were not issued except to a few outdoor workers.[48]

Maintenance supply of uniforms was also good in comparison to that of other overseas locations. The theater engaged in a continual struggle to keep up adequate stocks of women's clothes, and had chronic shortages, particularly in small sizes, but this was no more than could be said of most stations in the United States. The theater experienced an additional difficulty in that purchase of rationed clothing in civilian shops was forbidden to American troops in England. Wacs needed many items that were no longer issued, such as warm bathrobes, bedroom slippers, brassières, and handkerchiefs. As items brought from the United States began to wear out, the theater cabled to The Quartermaster General to point out that, while in the United States it might be practicable to call these items nonessential and to require a woman to buy her own, such procedure was inappropriate in an overseas area where the items required ration cards that the Wacs did not possess. Fully 60 percent of the women, the theater estimated, were in need of girdles. The Quartermaster General refused to resume issue of these items, but eventually arranged for their purchase and resale through post exchanges to women overseas.[49]

Health, Morals, and Discipline

During the entire period of employment, there was little to indicate that service in the European theater was more detrimental to women's health or behavior than service in the United States, or produced any problems that would have rendered the employment of Wacs uneconomical. For most of the war months, the WAC attrition rate remained the same as that of noncombat men—one half of one percent.[50] This was in spite of startling statistics computed in the early days, when it was reported that ETO Wacs, unlike those in the United States, appeared to be losing twice as many days from work as men. This rate seemed due chiefly to the high incidence of respiratory disorders. Upon investigation it was found that most of the Wacs at this time were newly arrived in England, and that the rate of respiratory disorders among newly arrived male troops was also twice as high as that of the theater as a whole. In addition, Wacs were chiefly office workers, and the rate of respiratory disorders among male headquarters troops was also twice that of the field forces.

An odd additional factor was the unsatisfactory model of military shoes for women, and the shortage of proper sizes, which, according to a medical report, .

. . . loomed large in the noneffective rate for Wacs during the period when they were being admitted to the hospital for adjustment of

---

[48] (1) Rpt, by ETO WAC Stf Dir, 12 Jul 44. WDWAC 421. (2) ETO Bd Rpt. (3) ETO WAC Hist, p. 14.

[49] (1) Cbl W8720, USFOR London to AGWAR, 16 Nov 43, SPWA 320.2 sec 6. WAAC Cl file. (2) ETO Bd Rpt, Vol. III, App. 121.

[50] This and following from ETO Bd Rpt, Vol. I, pp. 48, 58–60, 123; Vol. II, Apps. 1 and 13; Vol. III, Apps. 114, 117.

shoes. . . . The proper fitting of shoes is still an unsolved problem. Metatarsal bursitis and fallen arches are common disorders.[51]

The WAC illness rate was further increased by the fact that pregnant women, although not ill, were hospitalized and returned as patients, for their better protection. As Wacs became acclimated, and as improved administration caused less delay in processing of female patients, the final rate of time lost in hospital was found to be only 2.2 percent for Wacs as against 2.5 percent for all troops, nonbattle cases only.[52]

Women were found to develop psychological disorders somewhat less frequently than men, and records kept for the first year and a half showed that only a dozen requests for return home had been initiated. "Female complaints" caused almost one-fourth of WAC hospitalizations, and were serious enough to cause the Air Forces surgeon to recommend that "women with menstrual disorders should be eliminated prior to their dispatch to a Theater of Operations."[53]

However, this rate of time lost because of female complaints was exactly compensated for by the higher rate of venereal disease among men. The WAC venereal disease rate was variously computed at from one sixth to one ninth that of the men, and considerably less than that of civilian women in the United States. In the first year, with over 6,000 women, there were only about 10 cases, including both married and unmarried.[54] Most of the latter were from a small minority of women who, in the theater's opinion, should not have been enlisted and should certainly not have been sent overseas. After inspecting the theater Wacs for the Medical Department late in 1944, Major Craighill stated, "We have found that the

medical problems as respects morals are much better controlled in WAC than in civilian units."[55] Army historians later noted, "venereal disease among the Wacs was conspicuous by its almost total absence."[56]

The WAC pregnancy rate was likewise negligible.[57] For unmarried women it was estimated as about one a month, out of 6,000 women then in the theater, while about two married women a month were returned for pregnancy, the total rate being less than one sixth of the rate among civilian women in comparable age groups in the United States. The number of Wacs returned because of pregnancy did not raise the total WAC attrition rate above that of the men. The infrequency of discharge for this cause was such that no entirely satisfactory system of processing pregnant returnees was ever worked out, with some hospitalized women awaiting return for as much as two months, and at least three babies being born in the theater.

Both the WAC pregnancy rate and the venereal disease rate compared favorably with statistics available on Wacs in the United States. Fearing that overseas conditions placed a greater strain upon accepted standards of conduct, Colonel Wilson and the ETO medical consultant

[51] Memo, Maj Craighill for SG, through Chief Surg, ETOUSA, 30 Nov 44. SGO Hist Div 319.1 ETO, Women In.

[52] Bull, U.S. Army Med Dept, Vol. VI, No. 3, Sep 46, p. 285.

[53] ETO Bd Rpt, Vol. II, App. 1

[54] (1) ETO WAC Hist, p. 32. (2) ETO Bd Rpt, Vol. II, App. 13, p. 9.

[55] Min, Senior Offs Mtg, Celtic Hotel, 6 Nov 44. ETO folder Adm 534, Mss — Wacs in ETO, Opns Rpts, DRB AGO.

[56] USSTAF Hist.

[57] This and the following paragraphs are based on and quote: ETO Bd Rpt, Vol. I, p. 59, Vol. II, App. 13, p. 6, Vol. III, Apps. 114, 115, 121. Also see Ch. XXXI, below, for details.

decided that Colonel Hobby's moralizing approach to the facts of life, as incorporated in hygiene manuals, was too Victorian and that it "had been a mistake" not to include very frank sex advice. Several "fairly vigorous lectures" were therefore presented to the enlisted women, but because of "reverberations" from the WAC unit, medical authorities were obliged to desist. The British women's services likewise discovered that their women preferred advice that was moral rather than chemical or mechanical in nature.

Medical care provided for women appeared to be quite similar to that available in the United States. Like the War Department, the European theater appointed a woman doctor to be medical consultant for women, suffered setbacks in its attempts to provide service for scattered WAC minorities, and did not until the end of the war get around to appointing gynecologists on the staffs of general hospitals that treated Wacs and nurses. The War Department's medical consultant for women's welfare, Major Craighill, reported:

> The medical care of Wacs in England and France is excellent . . . dispensaries, station and general hospitals having special medical facilities for women. Very few hospitals are equipped for gynecological or obstetrical cases. . . . The health of the WAC is good . . . there is no evidence of undue fatigue. Tension is apparent only among those groups having insufficient work to occupy them fully.[58]

There was no indication that ETO Wacs were appreciably less healthy than those in the United States. Some reports showed that ETO Wacs lost less time in the hospital than Wacs in the zone of the interior, but ETO authorities believed their WAC noneffective rate to be slightly higher.[59]

WAC disciplinary records were also good. Statistics compiled by the Air Provost Marshal showed that men committed various offenses from ten to a hundred and fifty times as often as women.[60] On a percentage basis, men were AWOL 89 times as often as women, drunk 85 times as often, and violated miscellaneous Articles of War 150 times as often.[61]

Commands reported that "Wacs classed among the most smartly and neatly dressed troops on the stations." Serious misconduct was lacking, and the advance plans for a group of female military police were never carried out. Court-martial cases were few; there were only two general courts reported among Wacs in the history of the theater. Historians, questioning whether this rate resulted from good behavior or from undue leniency of WAC company commanders, examined company punishment records closely and determined that there had been "no tendency to coddle or minimize punishment for misdemeanors. . . . Supervision at the detachment level was more thorough and constant than among males."[62]

Of aid in maintaining this record was the fact that the theater acted to make clear the disciplinary powers of WAC commanders by reaffirming the War Department's two safeguards: that enlisted women would be assigned only in groups, and only under the command of a WAC officer.

---

[58] Memo cited n. 51.
[59] Weekly Health Rpt, Vol. V, No. 9, ASF, SGO; ETO Bd Rpt, Vol. I, p. 123; Vol. III, Apps. 114, 119, 121. Hospitalization rate:
  35 per 1,000 for U.S. Wacs
  34 per 1,000 for Army, less evacuees
  27.18 per 1,000 for Wacs in ETO
[60] ETO Bd Rpt, Vol. I, p. 40.
[61] ETO Bd Rpt, pp. 37–42.
[62] USSTAF Hist.

Civilian Competition

Final theater reports indicated only one important handicap to WAC employment in an area such as this one: the competition with civilian employees. This problem, although appearing minor at first consideration, became more prominent in the period following the slackening of hostilities and was eventually rated the European theater Wacs' number one difficulty by both WAC staff directors, as well as by returning enlisted women.

It had been originally contemplated by the Chief of Staff that no civilian women would be employed overseas, but by the time of the WAAC's formation it was already clear that such employment could not be prevented in certain areas. As early as 1942, Director Hobby had therefore proposed that difficulties between the two groups be minimized by directing that "no organization or group of women employed by the American forces . . . wear a uniform or parts of a uniform which are of a color or a pattern which would cause them to be confused with members of the WAAC." [63]

She pointed out that existing regulations provided a satisfactory uniform for American civilian employees—the blue hostess-librarian uniform—which was ordered through Special Services from commercial firms that were ready to supply them. However, the Army Service Forces refused to send this proposal to the War Department, and it was not considered. Instead, at a meeting at which the Director was not represented, it was decided to sell the WAAC officer uniform to any civilian women going overseas. [64]

The problem had small immediate importance, since until after the cessation of buzz-bomb danger very few American civilians went to the area, and British employees lived at home and seldom wore uniforms. To Colonel Hobby's inquiry, Colonel Wilson replied, "This is a situation about which we are not unduly concerned." In the early and dangerous days of the invasion, Wacs were the only female employees in most cases. Later, the theater decided to take female civilians to the Continent as soon as conditions became safe and stable, and it was necessary to provide them with quarters and identifying uniforms. Colonel Wilson concurred in a recommendation that civilians get separate messes and distinctive uniforms, but instead the theater authorized officer accommodations for them and allowed each command to prescribe its own uniform. At this, a considerable morale problem resulted among equally qualified enlisted women, mitigated somewhat in cases where British civilians were veteran employees who had shared the bombings and rationings. [65]

Early in 1945, a morale crisis was precipitated by news of plans to send overseas large numbers of American civilian women as soon as hostilities ended. At this time Director Hobby's staff learned that "a meeting was held in the Secretary of War's office, at which representatives of the Quartermaster and G–1 were present, but no representative of this office . . . those present agreed that the WAC uniform should be provided for civilians overseas." In a series of confidential memoranda, the

[63] Memo, Dir WAAC for CofS, 10 Oct 42, sub: Ltr of Instr to CG ETO. SPWA 320.2 sec 1.

[64] D/F, Dir Mil Pers ASF to Dir WAAC, 16 Oct 42. SPGA M/322.5 WAAC (10–10–42), in SPWA 320.2 sec 1.

[65] (1) ETO Bd Rpt, Vol. I, pp. 71, 21; Vol. III, App. 135; Vol. III, App. 10, p. 7. (2) Quotation from Memo, WAC Stf Dir ETOUSA, for Col Howard E. Kessinger, Exec, G–1 WDGS (on tour of ETO), 28 Aug 44. WDWAC 421.

Director protested that WAC enlisted women were as well qualified as the civilians who would wear the officer uniform; that civilians should not receive officer privileges without accompanying military responsibilties and discipline; that the social association problem would be hopelessly complicated if civilians wore the WAC uniform; and that the practice "would react to the serious detriment of the morale of the enlisted women who have served the Army well and faithfully under the rigorous conditions of overseas life without [such] pay or privileges. . . ." [66]

The Director shortly succeeded in getting a directive to the European theater that civilians would get only the enlisted uniform, and this with the addition of conspicuous colored shoulder straps, sleeve braid, and cap crown, plus a blue hostess-librarian overcoat. The theater cabled back for a reconsideration of continued issue of the unchanged WAC uniform, which would considerably simplify its supply and storage problems. This was not granted, but hundreds of unmodified uniforms were already in the hands of civilians, and War Department attempts to get the directive enforced in the theater were never wholly successful. Colonel Wilson was not asked to comment; she noted, "The problem was of such a controversial nature that it was impossible for the WAC Staff Director to initiate a paper as a branch of G–1." [67]

With the posthostilities arrival of American civilian women, the Wacs' *esprit* vanished, as well as pride in Army status and uniform. The women talked of little else; the gist of their more printable comment was that they had been hooked as sentimental suckers by a government that penalized enlisted service and handsomely rewarded those who stifled their patriotic fervor until the danger was over. The theater noted numerous "natural jealousies" that arose between the two groups. The Wacs' chief complaint was not the pay or officers' mess and quarters, but the uniform, and the fear that the Corps' hard-won reputation for neatness and good conduct was rapidly vanishing in the eyes of the occupied nations and the American soldiers alike as a result of the way in which their uniform was worn by civilian women untrained in military customs and unsupervised as to appearance or living habits.

In addition to the civilian employees in WAC uniform, there were women movie stars, newspaperwomen, Congresswomen, society women, and the entire casts of traveling shows such as *Panama Hattie*. Further indignation was provoked when these women, as well as USO workers and nurses, got priority on the scanty WAC maintenance stocks, resulting in shortages to enlisted women. Also, civilians could date officers and attend officers' social functions. They had different housing standards, less restrictions, no inspections, and no company punishment. Though holding jobs similar to enlisted women's, their top salary was $745 a month as against the WAC maximum of $138. [68]

---

[66] (1) Memo, Exec for Dir WAC, 24 Feb 44; (2) WD Cir 118, 22 Mar 44; (3) Memo, "KKJ" for Dir WAC, 26 Feb 45, WDWAC 319.1 Johnson (1945–46); (4) Memo, Dir WAC for Col Guenther, 1 Mar 45; (5) Memo, Dir WAC for G–1, 27 Mar 45; (6) Cbls CM–OUT 57510, WD to ETO, and CM–IN 26948, ETO to WD, 25 Mar 45. All in WDWAC 421.

[67] *Ibid.* Quotation from ETO Bd Rpt, Vol. II, App. 7: Memo, WAC Stf Dir for G–1 SHAEF, 4 May 45.

[68] Min cited n. 55. ETO Bd Rpt, Vol. III, Apps. 71, 132, 134. Monthly salaries:

	Minimum	Maximum
U.S. civilian in ETO	$220.00	$745.00
Continental civilian	110.00	372.00
WAC	50.00	138.00

The theater also admitted that "occasionally there was a tendency to cater to the civilians in order to keep them happy and on the job, and on the other hand to delegate to WAC personnel in the same office the more difficult and less pleasant jobs and overtime work because they were military personnel and subject to orders." [69] When questioned by WAC officers concerning the necessity for this practice, ETO's Chief of Military Personnel replied: "The matter is a command function based on the overall view which probably the individual does not understand." [70]

The civilian women themselves were equally resentful. They felt that their quarters were often worse than the WAC officers' quarters, sometimes lacking in heat when WAC quarters were heated. Civilian personnel also lacked the many military benefits and provisions for morale-building recreation and entertainment that enlisted Wacs had. No system of hearing civilian women's complaints was set up until 1947, and no action was taken on them. [71]

It was in vain that WAC officers attempted to point out to the enlisted women that the fault lay in Congress' failure to draft women as well as men, thus forcing the Army to employ civilians to make up the deficit, and to grant extra privileges to attract them. The women's hostility remained unabated through the final days of the war, and was reflected in postwar refusal of former Wacs to accept civilian employment with the Army. As Wacs became eligible for discharge, the theater, with the War Department's approval, worked out a system that would permit former Wacs to transfer to civilian status and good civilian jobs in the Army of Occupation, but of more than 8,000

Wacs, only 126 chose to accept the offer. Neither did the majority desire to serve the Army any longer on military status. [72]

Social Association

A second policy problem, which became more noticeable in 1945 as a complication of the civilian importation, was that of the social association of officers and enlisted personnel of opposite sexes. [73] Until American civilians arrived and began dating their section chiefs, Wacs had lived without too much objection under General Devers' written directive that the customs of the service would apply except to relatives and fiances carrying letters of authorization. This prohibition, during the war months, was fairly well observed in the subordinate commands and in the rural areas, but was generally ignored in cities and higher headquarters because of the anonymity which couples could easily find in large cities such as London and Paris. Enlisted men made sporadic objections when Wacs dated officers, although believing that they themselves should be allowed to date nurses, but the relative abundance of dateable women in England prevented any real hard feeling.

It was only with the move to Germany and the end of the war that feelings on the subject became more intense. For the eighteen months after his return to Europe, General Eisenhower was not informed of his theater's policy in this

---

[69] ETO Bd Rpt, Vol. I, p. 132.
[70] Min cited n. 55.
[71] Intervs with civilians returned from Europe.
[72] ETO Bd Rpt, Vol. III, Apps. 131, 133, 134; Vol. I, p. 133.
[73] Unless otherwise stated, discussion is from ETO Bd Rpt, Vol. I, pp. 6, 25, 135–39; Vol. III, Apps. 137–49.

regard. After V-E Day he discovered it from "gripe letters" from Army nurses to *Stars and Stripes,* complaining that it would be less evil to go out with "good respectable privates" than with officers who were always married men. General Eisenhower asked what the "alleged regulation" was that prevented a nurse from going out with an enlisted man, and added, "What is all this?" Upon learning that the theater had a written restriction against social mixing, he wrote:

I want *good sense* to govern such things. Social contact between sexes on a basis that does *not* interfere with other officers or enlisted persons should have the rule of decency and deportment—not artificial barriers.[74]

Colonel Wilson had not brought the matter to General Eisenhower's attention because she believed that distinction was advisable and had a basis in civilian life, where, "for example, no railway company exists in which section hands or brakemen expect or want social intimacy with the president of the company."[75] In answer to General Eisenhower's query, Colonel Wilson recommended, with the concurrence of all subordinate Army commanders, that the current situation be allowed to continue. She informed General Eisenhower that Colonel Hobby favored such a policy, although actually the opposite was true.

Colonel Hallaren, upon assuming office as ETO WAC staff director, advocated a reversal of the policy. She felt that she spoke for the enlisted women, who still resented social discrimination, and that while Wacs probably would not take undue advantage of a relaxed policy, "they get claustrophobia with the door closed."[76]

In the commotion of demobilization, the theater commander failed to approve either proposal. Without rescinding the written ruling, he authorized establishment of an all-ranks restaurant in Paris where "mixed" couples could get food. Later, after civilian restaurants were opened, there was no particular problem for violators of the rule.

Policy on Marriage

Closely connected with the social association problem was that of marriage of military personnel. The theater's written orders were, "When two members of this command marry, thereafter either they will be stationed at widely separated posts, camps, or stations, or, when appropriate, one of the parties will be removed from the theater."[77] The orders applied only to nurses and Wacs, and not to American and Allied civilians and women of liberated countries. They directly contradicted the War Department circular, which stated that Wacs would not be transferred solely because of marriage to persons serving in the same station.[78]

The theater chaplain protested to General Eisenhower that, since engaged couples did not wish to be separated because of marriage, "a condition of concubinage" was resulting, and the WAC staff director put it more explicitly that "military couples lived together without the marriage ceremony for fear of being separated." General Eisenhower, upon reading these statements, personally reaffirmed his policy that "Persons in the military service will not be permitted to establish homes and families in this active theater."

---

[74] ETO Bd Rpt, Vol. III, Apps. 136, 146, (11–23 May 45)

[75] ETO Bd Rpt, Vol. I, pp. 136–39.

[76] ETO Bd Rpt, Vol. III, App. 147.

[77] Hq ETOUSA Cir 41, par 5*a*, 17 Apr 44.

[78] WAAC Regs, 1 Jun 43; WD Cir 462, 1944, par 12*b*.

Although medical reports indicated that "arbitrary separation of husbands and wives within the theater does not tend to reduce the incidence of pregnancy," [79] it was not until after the end of the war in Europe that the transfer requirement was relaxed. The WAC marriage rate at once quadrupled. Even so, a station was forbidden to allow married couples, military or civilian, to be domiciled together—a provision that later resulted in publication by an interested newspaper of a reprimand to an Army captain beginning, "It has come to the attention of this headquarters that you are living with your wife. This must cease at once." [80]

There were only 323 WAC marriages in the theater, of which all but eight were to Americans. Historians noted, "It has always been a rare sight in London to see a Wac with a member of any foreign service or with a civilian from any country other than her own." Women noted that "almost any man from the States seemed to think it was a crime for any Wac to cast more than a pleasant glance at a foreigner, when there were so many Americans in Europe who preferred American women. . . ." Likewise, the Wacs mixed less with the British civilian population. Reports noted:

Though a large majority of the Wacs were entertained in British homes, few of them visited these homes more than once or twice. Wacs were in a rather different position from that of the American men in the Army. . . . [81]

Public Relations

A last management problem, which was intensified with the close of hostilities, was that of WAC public relations. [82] Wacs in the European theater, like those in other overseas areas, never had a public rela-

tions problem in the sense that Wacs at home did, where they were constantly observed by critical American civilians. ETO Wacs generally encountered only respectful Continental audiences. However, war correspondents did their best to substitute for the home folks in this respect, from the day that the 1st WAC Separate Battalion landed and was met by thirty-eight correspondents and publicized in 600 newspapers. Press relations were so time-consuming that a WAC staff officer was installed in the ETO Public Relations Office, to cope with news requests. Here her work resolved itself chiefly into a struggle to produce favorable news releases faster than enterprising reporters could produce unfavorable ones.

On the credit side, the European theater quickly reached a volume of WAC news stories equaled by few others, in spite of disagreements with Washington as to a reasonable compromise between the capacity of cable facilities and the needs of recruiters in the United States. Because of the news value of overseas items, Director Hobby sent a WAC writer and a photographer to stimulate output, and later devoted much of her own 1944 visit to England to this purpose. The theater obligingly produced many general-interest stories on the WAC, plus home-town releases on almost every Wac in the theater. The WAC Public Relations Officer, Maj. Henriette Horak, also publized events that would put the WAC in a good light:

---

[79] Memo cited n. 51.

[80] (1) Hq ETOUSA Cir, 9 Jun 45, par V. (2) Above passage based on ETO Bd Rpt, Vol. I, pp. 55–58, and Vol. II, Apps. 39–47. General Eisenhower's policy: App. 39. Chaplain's protest: App. 42. Newspaper quote: *Washington Post*, March 2, 1947.

[81] ETO ATC WAC Hist.

[82] All statements on public relations, unless otherwise indicated are from ETO Bd Rpt, Vol. I, pp. 115–18, and Vol. III, App. 112.

the "adoption" of British war orphans; visits of Wacs to Paris cathedrals; the story of the responsible work done by Wacs at the Postdam Conference and the Nuernberg trials. Stories were placed in *Yank, Life, Vogue,* and many others; newsreel coverage was obtained; Wacs were pictured with Generals Eisenhower, Smith, Doolittle, Eaker, Lt. Gen. John C. H. Lee, and others.[83] To promote GI-WAC friendship, much was made of the naming of a bomber the "Pallas Athene-GI Jane" and a locomotive the "WAC Blazer." By the machinations of the WAC Public Relations Officer, Wacs were slipped into Berlin ahead of other women to achieve a noteworthy "first."[84]

The size of the theater nevertheless made it necessary for the WAC Public Relations Officer to decentralize control of releases to various lower echelons not having Wacs on their public relations staffs. The unfavorable stories that slipped by male public relations officers were all of one type: derogatory comments about Wacs by the soldiers, which reporters seemed to take especial pains to evoke. The WAC Public Relations Officer admitted that one of her "chief headaches" was "the antagonism between the Army male and the Army female." As a result, there were frequent releases such as one from Eighth Air Force headquarters, which consistently refused to accept a Wac public relations officer, "Soldiers Prefer English Girls to Wacs."[85]

The worst releases of this type came toward the end of hostilities, when Field Marshal Sir Bernard L. Montgomery's headquarters released a statement that numbers of the WAC and ATS would be sent into Germany to prevent soldiers from fraternizing with German women. The women's duties, said the story, were to act as dance partners, to chat, and to drink tea.[86] This appeared in *Stars and Stripes,* in the *London Daily Mail,* and in the *New York Times.* The story was widely reprinted in the United States; some writers and one radio religious hour stated that Wacs were being transferred to camps where men visited German brothels too often, and that the brothels were now being filled by Wacs.[87]

In the United States, the National Federation of Press Women asked that the War Department take a definite stand against this type of overseas "propaganda," but the head of the War Department Bureau of Public Relations took no action because, as he informed Director Hobby, "I think the statement [from Montgomery's headquarters] was well meant, even if poorly advised . . . I smell the needling by correspondents."[88] This type of release continued, fostered somewhat by soldier letters in the European theater *Stars and Stripes,* which in August of 1945 printed what United Press reporters called "a blizzard of bitter letters" from soldiers; this was also picked up in the United States.[89]

---

[83] Ltr, PRO ETO Hq to Dir WAC, 30 May 44. WDWAC 320.2.

[84] ETO Press Releases 8296, 29 Jan 44, and 9747, 16 Nov 44. ETO Adm 365 WAC, DRB AGO.

[85] Eighth AF Hq Release, *Des Moines Register,* January 20, 1944. Also: (1) Memo, Dir WAC for CG AAF, 2 Feb 44, and reply, 21 Feb 44, from CofAS, Gen Giles, citing cbls. SPWA 001.–N. (2) *Chicago World Herald,* August 21, 1945, UP release, "Soldiers Lambaste Wacs."

[86] *New York Times,* December 5, 1944, by *Times* correspondent with British Second Army.

[87] (1) Ltr, Dr. K. Frances Scott to Dir WAC, 14 Jan 45, and atchd file. WDWAC 330.14. (2) *New York Journal-American,* December 8, 1944.

[88] Ltr, Natl Fed of Press Women to Dir Hobby, 16 Dec 44, and Inds. WDWAC 080.

[89] *Chicago World Herald,* August 21, 1945, UP release.

WAC recruiters in the United States lived in constant apprehension of these periodic outbursts, which got wide publicity because of public interest in overseas news. This particular problem never found a solution; even in the Army of Occupation damaging releases continued to be permitted and even originated by Army public relations officers.[90] From the European theater viewpoint the problem had no great effect on WAC efficiency, although it did tend to hamper recruiting in the United States.

Posthostilities Period

While the WAC's problems of public relations, civilian competition, and social discrimination were considered worthy of record by students of personnel management, they were not conspicuous in the general morale let-down that followed the end of hostilities in Europe, nor as serious as the social and moral problems of men in the occupation forces.

In this period, the efforts of the theater as a whole were turned toward the maintenance of morale and good conduct for both men and women. Women received furloughs and passes under the same rules as for men, were included in Information and Education plans, and were provided with facilities at selected leave areas. Wacs were generally less able to avail themselves of those facilities than were men, since most Wacs were employed in critical categories and could not be released by section chiefs to participate in programs designed mainly for idle troops. Wacs were permitted to take courses such as those at Shrivenham and Biarritz, but few were able to attend.

American Red Cross authorities had from the beginning endeavored to provide identical services for Wacs and enlisted men, but reported themselves handicapped by the attitude of their women field workers: "Many of the women approached [to run a WAC rest area] said they had come over to serve the men and not the women." [91] Clubs for enlisted women and WAC officers were eventually set up in London. After some delay, a WAC rest home was established near Oxford soon after the invasion, and moved to Nice after V-E Day; it proved extremely useful, since the Wacs had no convalescent hospitals.[92] The men's program of return to the United States—Rehabilitation, Recuperation, and Recovery—was never applied to Wacs, because of their shorter length of service, although Colonel Wilson felt that if a small quota had been included in the program it would have aided morale.[93]

In this period various devices were employed by WAC commanders to help in sustaining morale: unit clubs; a relaxation of regimentation; athletic tournaments; the salvage of toys, food, and clothing for homeless children; and the hospital visitation program.

Demobilization

Colonel Wilson was not included in planning conferences for the Army of Occupation, but the theater planners determined independently to employ even

---

[90] Memo, Actg Chief, WAC Gp WDBPR for Dep Dir WDBPR, 29 Jan 45. WDBPR WAC Gp file Organization of WAC Group.

[91] Ltr, Miss Eleanor C. Vincent, Asst National Dir, Mil and Naval Welfare Serv, Red Cross, to Miss Helen Walmsley, 7 Sep 44. WDWAC 080 Red Cross (1945).

[92] This was administered by the Army with recreation furnished by the Red Cross. ETO WAC Hist, pp. 30–32; ETO Bd Rpt, Vol. II, App. 10, p. 10.

[93] ETO Bd Rpt, pp. 52–55 and 69–70.

more Wacs than had been used in wartime. It was decided that 50,000 Wacs could be used in the Army of Occupation, but that in view of the size of the Corps, only 10,000 would be asked, these to be in addition to the thousands used by the Air Forces in Europe.

Further disagreement with the War Department followed as to the relative needs of the zone of the interior and the Army of Occupation. Theater representatives asked, in conference, "Why is it difficult to get personnel now? What are the Wacs doing over there that they can't be spared to come here as replacements?" To this, War Department spokesmen replied that the administrative load of demobilization would fall on the United States, not the theater, and that "Wacs [in Europe] gripe that there isn't enough work to do—that they would go in the Army of Occupation only for fraternization—they resent it." [94]

The War Department therefore at first refused the request for more WAC personnel, stating:

The average limited service man in the United States has a much lesser degree of intelligence and effectiveness than the average Wac, and it would thus be most difficult to have limited service soldiers take over the jobs which Wacs are now performing. [95]

The General Staff also objected that ex-combat returnees could not be traded for Wacs in the United States because the men had too high grades, were lacking in skills, or were temperamentally unsuited for the work.

Director Hobby did not take sides in the matter, other than to recommend that all or no requests be approved, in order that Wacs not be used in the Army of Occupation except in sufficient numbers to give them a "recognized status" and to make provisions for their health and supply economically justifiable. [96] Finally, a compromise was reached: the War Department refused to exclude the AAF's quota from the requested quota of 10,000, but agreed to raise the theater quota, including Air Forces, from 8,000 to 10,000—thus in effect permitting shipment of 2,000 more women. [97]

Shipments to supply the additional women had already begun when the onset of demobilization intervened. At this time the European theater used its unfilled WAC quota of 10,000 as an excuse for refusing to release women eligible for discharge, saying, "This personnel will necessarily be considered essential if the theater quota has not been reached, and will not be eligible to return to the Zone of the Interior." [98]

As in the Mediterranean theater, male replacements in the same skill and MOS were not considered acceptable. The War Department therefore took a step that would have forced return; it cut the theater quota from 10,000 to 6,000 on the basis of "other needs" elsewhere. [99] The theater refused to comply; while returning a few women in unwanted skills, it informed the War Department that it had "frozen" the return of WAC stenographers and typists until WAC, and not male, replacements in these skills were received.

This proved a fruitless move, for after the defeat of Japan and the end of WAC

---

[94] Min cited n. 55. Also ETO Bd Rpt, Vol. II, App. 7.

[95] Memo, Secy WDGS for Dir WAC, 12 May 44. WDCSA 424.5 WAC, in CofS 324.5 WAC.

[96] (1) D/F, G–1 for CofS, 2 Feb 45. WDGAP 320.2 WAC, in CSA 324.5 WAC. (2) Memo, Exec WAC for Dir WAC, 21 Feb 45. WDWAC 201.6.

[97] ETO Bd Rpt, Vol. I; also D/F, G–1 WD to MPD ASF, 10 Mar 45. WDGAP 320.2 WAC in WDWAC 320.2 ETO. Quota was 200 offs and 10,400 EW.

[98] Memo, ETO for TAG, 6 May 45. AG 387 RCGA, in WDWAC 320.2 ETO.

[99] D/F, G–1 Div WDGS to TAG, 7 Jul 45. WDGAP 320.2 WAC (2–2–45), in WDWAC 320.2.

recruiting, the European theater, like all others, was informed that no more Wacs would go overseas. Soon after, the War Department forbade any theater to retain discharge eligibles, men or women, on the grounds of "military necessity." Thereafter, demobilization of nonvolunteer Wacs proceeded rapidly. The theater reported that the War Department's action "was a serious blow to the European theater, which considered Wacs its primary source of critically needed clerical and communications personnel, and [it] required the revision of plans for their utilization in the Army of Occupation." [100]

Appraisal

The statements of both theater commanders and the women themselves indicated that WAC service in the European theater was considered suitable and successful. General Eisenhower informed the War Department:

During the time I have had Wacs under my command they have met every test and task assigned them. I have seen them at work in . . . England, France, and at Army installations throughout the European Theater. Their contributions in efficiency, skill, spirit, and determination are immeasurable.

General Lee added, "The work of the organization has been superior." The Chief Signal Officer, Maj. Gen. William S. Rumbough, called their work with the Signal Corps "superior." Maj. Gen. Willard S. Paul, G–1 of ETO, reported, "I have received nothing but the highest praise for the results you have achieved." [101]

The Air Forces in the theater added similar praise. General Spaatz of USSTAF stated:

The WAC has been of inestimable value. . . . Its members have worked devotedly,

often at arduous tasks requiring exceptional performance. [102]

General Eaker later added:

Women made, in my opinion, the best soldiers in the war. I feel that Wacs should be retained as part of the postwar military plans. [103]

The Air Forces in the theater summarized their conclusions concerning WAC employment favorably:

Wacs proved much less of a problem than had been envisaged. . . . It was found that Wacs could live under conditions substantially the same as those of male personnel. . . . Perhaps the greatest achievement of the Wacs was their triumph over the prejudices of the male military mind. The half-amused, half-scornful attitude of some officers in responsible positions was not justified by the performance of the Wacs. A balanced judgment would find that the Wacs have been deserving of any extra time and effort which might have had to be expended on them because of their sex. [104]

The verdict of the Wacs themselves was also favorable. The life of a Wac in the European theater was obviously superior with regard to housing, recreation, sightseeing, and the absence of kitchen police and other work details. ETO Wacs were more smartly and warmly dressed than Wacs elsewhere. They had experienced the morale lift of constant forward movement to new and exciting areas, as opposed to the tedium of years at one station in the United States; the element of shared dangers had added to Corps *esprit*. Also, in spite of the poor start in obtaining appropriate ratings, ETO Wacs by the end of the war had more than twice as high a percentage of the first three grades

---

[100] ETO Bd Rpt, Vol. I, p. 114.
[101] All from ETO Bd Rpt, Vol. I, p. 11.
[102] *Ibid.*
[103] Address cited n. 3.
[104] USSTAF Hist.

as did Wacs in the United States, even though they still had only half as many high ratings as ETO air force men.[105] WAC officers also had twice as high a percentage in the grades of major and captain as did those in the United States.[106]

Awards and decorations were plentiful. Besides three presidential citations, there were about two hundred Bronze Stars and a few other decorations, and the percentage of women receiving the Legion of Merit was considerably higher than that in the United States.[107] As a result of all these advantages, ETO Wacs were distinctly proud of their period of service, and upon discharge frequently protested turning in their battle jackets, the only means of distinguishing themselves from the 92 percent of the Women's Army Corps that had not been sent to Europe.[108]

On the other hand, only a fraction so small that it was not recorded volunteered to stay in Europe, either as Wacs or civilians, beyond the date of discharge eligibility. Only 30 percent said they would later be interested in joining an inactive WAC reserve if one should be created.[109] Theater surveys by ETO Special Services Division, attempting to find out how many women would stay, started much unrest and eventually caused Congressional investigation of charges of undue influence in forcing women to volunteer.[110] One such allegation stated, "Their officers want to keep the Wacs overseas but the girls themselves do not want to stay." [111] However, while asking discharge, some 63 percent of enlisted women and 85 percent of WAC officers preferred to stay in the theater until eligible for discharge, instead of again serving in the United States.

The approval of both ETO Wacs and the theater commanders of the conditions of WAC service, as they had known it in England and Europe, was to have an effect upon the future of the Corps far beyond that which might have been expected from their small numbers. From Colonel Wilson and theater commanders there came repeated and enthusiastic recommendations that Congress be asked to provide for "the inclusion of women as an integral part of . . . the Regular Army and Reserve Corps." These recommendations were later to be revived when the postwar War Department and the Director's Office were taken over by new staffs from the European theater. At that stage, WAC demobilization plans were to be reversed, and the Army of Occupation was to receive its Wacs. At that time also Generals Eisenhower, Devers, Spaatz, and Eaker were to spearhead the successful drive to ask Congress to continue the Women's Army Corps in the peacetime Regular Army.[112]

---

[105] The exact comparative figures are not given on the graph (ETO Bd Rpt, p. 45; also Vol. II, App. 1) from which the comparison is taken, but seem to correspond to those from Strength of the Army, STM-30, June 1945.

[106] ETO Bd Rpt, Vol. I, pp. 14, 71: ETO approximate grades as of 31 Aug 45; WAC officers, worldwide, are from Strength of the Army, June 1945.

[107] ETO Bd Rpt, p. 48 and App. 26: 4 Meritorious Unit Plaques, 3 Presidential Citations, 15 Purple Heart, 9 Legion of Merit (7 to officers), 229 Bronze Star, 2 OBE, 1 Legion of Honor, 6 Croix de Guerre, 113 Certificates of Merit, 7 MBE, 2 Luxembourg Couronne de Chene. For final TAG figures on decorations and awards, see Table 8, Appendix A.

[108] (1) Cbl WAR–65259 to CG ETO, 17 Sep 45; (2) D/F, G–1 to ASF, 25 Sep 43. WDGAP 421 WAC, in WDWAC 421.

[109] ETO Bd Rpt, Vol. I, pp. 7 and 133.

[110] (1) Rpt, Nov 44, sub: Postwar Plans of EW in WAC; (2) Rpt, Nov 44, sub: Attitude of 175 WAC Offs Toward Remaining in WAC Overseas. WDWAC 320.2.

[111] Ltr, Dir WAC to Clare Boothe Luce, 15 Jun 45, in reply to correspondence, 7 Jun 45. WDWAC 095 Forsht. Also similar letters in this file.

[112] See Ch. XXXVI, below.

CHAPTER XXII

The Southwest Pacific Area

The last of the major overseas commands to employ considerable numbers of WAC personnel was the Southwest Pacific Area (SWPA). Here, although the first shipment did not arrive until the middle of 1944, some 5,500 women eventually served—the second largest number to be employed by any overseas area.[1]

The delay in employing Wacs was readily explained: there was no shortage of female clerical workers in Australia, where some 20,000 civilians were employed by the American forces. Therefore, when Army-wide surveys were made at the time of the Auxiliary's formation, and again at the time of its contemplated expansion, the theater rejected the idea of using Waacs, stating that all available shipping was needed to bring combat personnel to its authorized level.[2]

Until late in 1943, several of the headquarters in Australia had entertained the hope that civilian employees would be permitted to move with them when the northward attack was launched through New Guinea and the Philippines. At this time, a personnel crisis was precipitated by the immediacy of the offensive combined with the final refusal of the Australian government to let its women move from the continent, in view of existing labor shortages. The theater therefore began a series of requests to Operations Division of the War Department General Staff, seeking to raise its Troop Basis to permit the shipment of general service men to replace the civilians. Limited service men were not wanted, in view of the unpromising nature of available material.[3]

These requests met with consistent refusal from the War Department. The theater was already authorized to have 3.2 percent of its military strength in overhead, as against only 1.5 percent for the

---

[1] No official WAC history was prepared by SWPA. (For a description of the sources used in this chapter, see Bibliographical Note.) All references, unless otherwise indicated, are to: (1) 30 folders of SWPA material, now at Kansas City Records Center, cited by folder and drawer number. (2) Historical material, WAC Assigned to SWPA, typed, undated, and unsigned, although Capt Velma P. Griffith (WAC PRO, SWPA—an eyewitness to many events and with access to theater WAC data) acknowledges authorship. Cited hereafter as Griffith Account. (3) Rpt, GHQ USAFPAC to TAG, 1 Nov 45, sub: Rpt on WAC Pers in SWPA Prepared in Accordance with AG Ltr 333.5 (9-27-45) OB-S-A, 1 Nov 45. Official copy in G-1 WD 321-333 WAC, 18 May 45, AGOF-C-333 WAC, DRB AGO. Cited as AFPAC Reply. (4) Draft of the above, prepared by WAC Staff Director, AFPAC, and approved by WAC Staff Directors, AFWESPAC and FEAF. Now in WAC Classified file. Cited as WAC Draft AFPAC Reply. (5) Official Rpt, Col Westray Boyce, Dir WAC, to CofS USA, 22 Mar 46, sub: Rpt of Visit to WAC Pers in Overseas Theaters. Also earlier draft of same. WDWAC 333.1. Cited as Boyce Rpt. (6) For list of interviews, statements, and comments, see Bibliographical Note.

[2] Rads: 1122 (CM-OUT 7466), 22 Aug 42, and reply by C-484 (CM-IN 5492), 13 Sep 42; 1631 (CM-OUT 508), 2 Mar 43, and reply by C-724 (CM-IN 2934), 6 Mar 43.

[3] Unless otherwise cited, all references to OPD action are to OPD 320.2 Australia, Sec IX, Cases 265-303, Dec-Apr 44, DRB AGO. Cited as OPD file.

European theater, and stations in the United States were by this time almost stripped of general service personnel. Instead, it was suggested that the theater render its headquarters mobile by screening the half-million troops it already had, among whom there were believed to be numbers of clerically skilled men.

This move was considered impracticable by the theater. Instead, there was some discussion within the several headquarters of the possibility of employing Wacs, under the misapprehension that they could be requisitioned to fill civilian job vacancies. The move was generally favored by Headquarters, Fifth Air Force, and by the Services of Supply, but rejected by the higher echelon, U.S. Army Forces in the Far East (USAFFE).[4]

In the early days of 1944, Operations Division of the War Department received a personal visit from Lt. Gen. George C. Kenney, Commanding General, Allied Air Forces and Fifth Air Force, who expressed a desire to get WAC personnel for his command. However, a call to ASF Military Personnel Division revealed that, of the Wacs who were expected to be available for overseas shipment during the entire year, only about 800 enlisted women and 200 officers remained unallotted. OPD at once acted to freeze this number until the Pacific's needs could be considered. Director Hobby was then overseas, but a call to her office revealed that, at the current rate of recruiting, a "reasonable number" of this 800 women could probably be obtained within a few months. At this, OPD radioed the theater asking whether General Kenney's request represented theater opinion. If so, it was promised that the theater's Troop Basis would be increased by 1,000 in order to accommodate the shipment.[5]

SWPA protested by radio:

Proposed allotment totally inadequate for minimum theater requirements. . . . Can use 10,000 or more Wacs. . . . Theater Chief of Staff who should reach Washington today has data on theater overhead requirements and on positions which Wacs may advantageously fill.[6]

Director Hobby first learned of the new development on 11 February 1944, soon after her return from Europe, when Lt. Gen. Richard K. Sutherland, General MacArthur's chief of staff, came to her office and informed her that at least 10,000 Wacs would be immediately required by the theater. "He appeared," she stated later, "to be under the impression that Wacs were still Auxiliaries and would not count against the Troop Basis."[7]

The Director informed General Sutherland that in her opinion the shipment could not be made for two reasons: first, Wacs were military personnel and would require a military allotment just as men would; and second, the WAC had not yet recovered from its conversion losses and from heavy shipments to Europe, and could not provide women in any such numbers in the clerical skills requested.

---

[4] No supporting documents were found. The WAC Staff Director, USAFFE, recalled seeing in the files a USASOS request disapproved by Maj. Gen. Charles P. Stivers (USAFFE) without stated reason. Brig. Gen. Harry H. Baird (USAFFE) stated in 1948 that earlier staff studies questioned supply, housing, protection, etc.; these were not found, nor any evidence of why such doubts were not communicated to the War Department by Lt. Gen. Richard K. Sutherland in his 1944 request for Wacs. Ltr, Mary-Agnes Brown to OCMH, 23 Apr 51; Memo, Col Harry H. Baird for HD SSUSA, 29 Jul 48. OCMH.

[5] (1) M/R, 1 Feb 44, sub: WAC Pers in SWPA, with copy of rad atchd. OPD file. (2) For final theater strength figures, see Table 7, Appendix A.

[6] Rad C–1319 (CM–IN 4025), GHQ SWPA to WAR, 6 Feb 44.

[7] WAC Daily Journal, 11 Feb 44; quotation from tp conv, Mrs. Hobby and author, Oct 50.

General Sutherland refused to accept this rejection as final. A few days later the Director learned that, in a conference with General Somervell, a plan had been devised whereby 4,000 of the theater's civilian allotment would be given to the ASF in the United States in exchange for 4,000 of the ASF's military allotment. General Somervell also agreed to supply 4,000 Wacs from those under his control, to fill the allotment. This arrangement was approved by the War Department, and the theater was advised by radio that its Troop Basis had been increased by 4,000.[8]

This transaction naturally differed from those concerning initial shipments to Africa and England, in that plans were no longer made by the Director WAC, in accordance with the system adopted at the end of Auxiliary status. Thus, matters concerning the Troop Basis and overseas shipment were now properly planned by OPD and were carried out by the various ASF operating agencies.[9] The staff studies and directives concerning the 4,000 allotment bore only the concurrence of agencies that normally concurred in such matters for men: G–1, G–3, Military Personnel Division of the Army Service Forces, and the War Manpower Commission.

At a later date the question was to be raised as to whether the General Staff should have requested the Director WAC to make a study of the area from the standpoint of the well-being of women. However, her new small staff no longer contained inspectors, and in any case the original destination, Australia, appeared considerably more safe and stable than had North Africa at the time of initial shipments. As of this date, small groups of Wacs were also successfully serving in India, Egypt, and New Caledonia. To assist the theater in planning for any contemplated forward movement of Wacs, comparable to those into Italy and Normandy, it was determined that a WAC staff director would be sent in advance of the enlisted women, and the Director was allowed to nominate this officer. As OPD began to order shipments to the port, the Director was generally furnished with an information copy of their composition.

In three matters the Director attempted to secure retention of Auxiliary procedures different from those for shipment of men. In December of 1943, and again in the following March, the Office of the Director asked ASF's Mobilization Division to provide any Wacs going to the Pacific with the same tropical clothing and equipment already authorized for the China–Burma–India theater, since no maintenance stocks for women yet existed in Australia.[10] This was not done; Wacs being ordered to the port were authorized only winter clothing, in line with the custom for the shipment of men to Australia in its winter season. The Office of the Director also requested that WAC company commanders continue to have a voice in the approval of the stability and character of Wacs sent overseas. This request was disapproved upon the recommendation of ASF's Director of Personnel. Finally, Director Hobby requested The Surgeon General to continue giving Wacs a com-

---

[8] D/F, OPD for DCofS, 2 Mar 44, sub: Increase of Overseas Establishment in SWPA, with approval "OLN" for DCofS. OPD file.

[9] For a discussion of the relations between OPD and ASF operating agencies, see: (1) Ray S. Cline, *Washington Command Post: The Operations Division*, UNITED STATES ARMY IN WORLD WAR II (Washington, 1951). (2) Chester Wardlow, *The Transportation Corps: Responsibilities, Organization, and Operations*, UNITED STATES ARMY IN WORLD WAR II (Washington, 1951).

[10] Memo, Asst Exec WAC for ASF Mobilization Div, 11 Dec 43; and Memo, Actg Dir WAC for same, 21 Feb 44. SWPA 320.2 (8–18–42)(1) sec 6.

plete overseas physical examination, as had been previously done in Auxiliary days to detect gynecological disorders or pregnancy, but this was also refused as too time-consuming, since men going overseas had no such examination, only a briefer physical inspection.[11]

The assembly of shipments proceeded with unusual speed, because of the immediacy of the move from Australia. On the basis of informal lists of needed personnel furnished by General Sutherland, orders for the first shipment of 1,000 women were issued by OPD on 15 February even before the request for 4,000 was formally approved. A formal requisition for 270 WAC officers and 4,730 enlisted women was forwarded from the theater on 11 March 1944. The majority of the requests were for clerical and stenographic skills such as had already been requested by other theaters. This requisition was approved by the General Staff, plus other later requests from the Far East Air Forces in the theater, to a total of 7,500—a quota that was never to be entirely filled.[12]

Direct Commissions

The first three Wacs in the theater were appointed by local action before any shipments were made from the United States. General Kenney during his visit had requested WAC status for his Australian secretary; General Sutherland during his stay sought the same for his receptionist and for the secretary of Maj. Gen. Richard J. Marshall, Deputy Chief of Staff, SWPA. It was stated that key officers would suffer a serious lapse in efficiency if obliged to part with their experienced Australian and British personnel. Although the act of Congress limited WAC enlistments to American citizens, appointment to officer status was not mentioned; since all WAC officers were derived from the ranks, the possibility of appointing noncitizens had never been considered. Previous requests from the European theater had, up to this time, been withdrawn when the WAC policy was explained to General Eisenhower. However, General Sutherland refused to withdraw his requests, and, over Director Hobby's nonconcurrence, direct commissions were immediately given to the three Australian and British employees. Although all WAC officers to date had been initially commissioned second lieutenants, two of the women were commissioned as first lieutenants and one in the grade of captain.

This action was taken over the adverse recommendation of General White, G–1 of the War Department General Staff, who felt so strongly on the matter that, after being unable to dissuade theater representatives, he personally walked with them to the Chief of Staff's office to register his protest. General White was finally overridden when General McNarney, Deputy Chief of Staff, was informed [13] that the commissions were personally desired by General MacArthur as essential to headquarters operation.

When Director Hobby also called to register her protest, she was informed that it was the Chief of Staff's policy never to refuse any urgent personal request of a theater commander if it was possible to grant it.[14] She nevertheless placed in writing her request that the three commissions be revoked, stating:

---

[11] See Ch. XXIX, below.
[12] AFPAC Reply. FEAF requisition, 15 Jul 44: 84 offs, 2,916 EW.
[13] By Gen Sutherland, according to Gen White's diary, entry of 3 Jan 44.
[14] *Ibid.*, and intervs with Gen White, 5 Jan 51, and with Lt Col Mary-Agnes Brown, Jun 45 and 5 Jun 47.

I believe that the policy of appointment cited above will cause the personnel of the WAC to feel that the War Department has broken faith with them, and that the continuance of such a policy will be a great blow to the morale of the entire Corps. . . . The policy of selecting officers only from graduates of officer candidate school, and of selecting officer candidates only from the ranks, has been presented to the American public throughout the history of the Corps as a soundly democratic one.[15]

This apparently minor event received widespread and generally unfavorable publicity in Australia, which had it own women's services for qualified women, as well as British women's services. An even worse reaction came from Army men, particularly young combat officers who had not yet been promoted to equal ranks. Soldier mail, in the month before the first American Wacs arrived, showed that 90 percent of the comments about all Wacs were unfavorable, many obscene, alleging that all Wacs would be used only for "morale purposes" for officers.[16] This situation was to cause a serious morale problem among arriving Wacs.

In the United States, General White's office was at once swamped with renewed demand from Congressional and military sources for direct commissions for American civilian women with prominent sponsors.[17] The War Department held that the three commissions were irrevocable, but public reaction continued to be so adverse that G–1 Division succeeded in blocking any further appointments, except the one in Europe which was requested again in view of the exceptions made for SWPA. However, the Director secured a ruling against further such action in the future.[18]

In the theater, commanders noted continuing bad effects for months after the event, especially upon the morale of highly qualified enlisted men and women. Some

commanders were obliged to forbid the women to talk or write of the subject, on threat of disciplinary action. The women's reaction was generally surprising to those not informed of the Corps' previous history and basic problems.[19]

Arrival of WAC Staff

Director Hobby released for assignment as staff director an experienced officer from her own staff, Lt. Col. Mary-Agnes Brown. Since the Southwest Pacific Area was known to be headed by ranking Regular Army officers with World War I experience, Colonel Brown was believed especially qualified by virtue of twenty-five years' acquaintance with Army channels. She had been employed in Army finance in World War I, had ten years' experience as executive secretary to ranking Army medical officers, and was thereafter an attorney for the Veterans' Administration, holding the degrees of A.B., LL.B., and S.J.D. In the Army she had been the first staff director for the Eighth Service Command and later executive officer in the Office of the Director WAC. With four officer assistants, Colonel Brown flew to the theater, arriving on 15 March 1944, to

[15] D/F, Dir WAC for G–1, 25 Feb 44. SPWA 320.2 (2–25–44)B, in SPWA 314.7 (1–7–43) sec 5.

[16] (1) See Chart, p. 000. (2) MI Rpt 107, 31 Aug 44. SFPOE, in MID files. (3) Personal ltr, Catholic priest to Col Hobby. WDWAC 330.14 (1945).

[17] Numerous ltrs, especially to and from Senator Charles O. Andrews, 10 Apr 44. WDWAC 095 and SPWA 095.

[18] D/F, G–1 for TAG, 21 Apr 44, WDGAP 210.1 WAC (4–17–44), approves attached Memo, Dir WAC for CofS, 14 Apr 44. Approved by CofS, 18 Apr 44. WDWAC 210.1.

[19] (1) Seminar comments. (2) Griffith Account, "Awards and Decorations." (3) Intervs with Col Brown, Col A. Robert Ginsburgh, and Miss Dorothy Pat Costello, former sergeant in GHQ detachment. (See Bibliographical Note).

help prepare for the arrival of the enlisted women two months later.

Upon her arrival, the staff director was assigned to the senior American administrative headquarters, USAFFE. No WAC personnel was assigned to General Headquarters, an operational Allied headquarters, except for two of the directly commissioned officers. The staff director was not delegated the customary responsibility [20] for the WAC program. This was instead placed upon G–1 Division, USAFFE, headed by Col. Harry H. Baird. Subsequently, G–1 Division noted:

The G–1 Section originally was charged with the handling of WAC personnel due to: (a) Their newness in the theater; (b) The fact that they were covered by a special allotment of overhead grades and ratings by the War Department; (c) The fact that it was necessary to keep in complete touch with the strength of the WAC Corps and the utilization of members during the period of arrival in the theater.[21]

Most of the duties assumed by G–1 were merely the normal staff duties now commonly performed by similar commands in the United States; however, it also held responsibility for policy matters. It believed that, so far as possible, enlisted men's policies should be applicable to the WAC. Colonel Baird recalled later that, "As far as the theater was concerned, there was no 'WAC program' except for an evident required publicity program." [22] There existed some belief that WAC advisers' experience and training were not always adequate to cope with the conditions that existed in the area. Colonel Baird later noted:

Almost every one in top positions in GHQ, USAFFE, and SOS had served a generation in the Regular Army, as well as having seen service in World War I. For them to have formed very definite ideas on staff procedure, command, and military custom—which was

the situation—was natural and logical. The Wacs lacked the background of military custom and they had little understanding of the possible far-reaching and serious effects of an action or decision.

The staff director's office was set up as the WAC Section of the Special Staff and, in the months before the Wacs' arrival, was called on chiefly to attend conferences and for public and social duties. In the matter of public relations, Colonel Brown was given a free hand and was encouraged by USAFFE to take all necessary steps to establish good will prior to WAC arrival. In the following weeks the staff director received calls from heads of the Australian Women's Auxiliary Service, YWCA, and Red Cross, and other officials. She attended theatrical performances, the Australian Arts and Crafts exhibit, a memorial mass, a WAAF ceremony. She went to receptions, gave luncheons, made formal calls at Admiralty House, Government House, and the American consulate. She broadcast radio programs, met visiting celebrities, and was photographed with koala bears. As a result, before the arrival of the first shipment in May, public attitude was believed to be definitely more favorable.[23]

---

[20] All WAAC and WAC Regulations without exception required every commanding general employing WAC personnel to employ also, on his staff, a WAC staff director who would be responsible for continuous inspection and for advising him on the welfare of the women. WD Cir 462 (1944) was latest wartime statement.

[21] Check sheet, G–1 USAFFE for CofS USAFFE through WAC Sec, 11 Apr 45, Tab 6 to WAC Draft AFPAC Reply.

[22] All of Col Baird's statements from Memo, Col Baird for HD SSUSA, 29 Jul 48.

[23] Monthly Historical Reports, WAC Staff Section, USAFFE, for Jun, Jul, Aug, Sep 44, Incl in Ltr, WAC Stf Dir USAFFE to Dir WAC. WDWAC 319.1 SWPA (1944); also in Folder, Monthly Historical Rpts, WAC Sec USAFFE, at Kansas City Records Center. These reports hereafter cited as WAC Sec USAFFE Hist Rpt, by month.

The only serious deficiency in planning at this date appeared to be in the matter of clothing. During a visit to the United States in March, Colonel Baird urgently recommended that two skilled WAC supply officers be sent by air to the theater. Queried for confirmation of this request, the theater authorized air shipment of one supply officer and one public relations officer. The supply officer, Capt. Lavern Bartholomew, was first ordered to OPD for indoctrination on supply needs of the area, and arrived in the theater in mid-April. Since at the same moment the first large group of enlisted women was boarding ship on the U.S. west coast, and the second was under orders, her supply planning was limited to later shipments. Planning was further delayed by the fact that Captain Bartholomew was not at once assigned to the office of the theater chief quartermaster, although Colonel Brown recommended this action on the grounds that supply planning was not a function either of the WAC Section or of G–1, which lacked the necessary data and authority.[24]

On 4 May 1944, a week before the landing of the first ship bringing Wacs, Colonel Brown and her assistant, Capt. Charlee L. Kelly, were sent to New Guinea to inspect the first advanced location, Port Moresby, to which some of the women would be sent two weeks after arrival. No unusual difficulties were expected in the area, since Port Moresby had long been regarded as a rear echelon, at which American nurses and Red Cross women had been stationed for about two years.

At the camp site, it was discovered that the quarters were entirely adequate but not prepared for troop occupancy; the staff director secured from the local quartermaster an agreement to prepare the quarters as soon as possible. Colonel Brown also discovered a fact not previously considered by supply officers—that malarial control regulations required all women in New Guinea to wear trousers both at work and off duty. The regular issue for men assigned to headquarters duty was six pairs of summer khaki. As officers, nurses had been able to purchase the trousers through commercial civilian channels in Australia, and were now required to have six mosquitoproof khaki shirts and six pairs of slacks apiece, which the chief surgeon described as "the minimum number which would take care of requirements." [25]

Returning immediately to Australia, Colonel Brown informed Brig. Gen. William F. Campbell, Chief Quartermaster, U.S. Army Services of Supply, Southwest Pacific Area (USASOS), that there was no such item as slacks in the WAC wardrobe, and that the nearest approach was the heavy herringbone twill coverall, of which arriving Wacs would have only one pair apiece. On the same day, the WAC supply officer was assigned to General Campbell's office, and a radiogram was sent to Washington requesting that the issue of two-piece coveralls to Wacs not already en route be increased to five pairs per individual, pending study of the problem.[26]

On the following day, Colonel Brown and her staff were received by General MacArthur, who, according to historical reports,

[24] WAC Sec USAFFE Hist Rpts, Apr, May 44; also in OPD file.

[25] Annual Rpt, 1944, Chief Surgeon USASOS SWPA, pp. 36–37.

[26] Rpts cited n. 24; also interv with Col William F. Campbell, 31 Jul 47.

ARRIVING IN SYDNEY, AUSTRALIA, *on 12 May 1944, above. Two days later members of the first contingent board buses for their new camp at Yeronga Park.*

... welcomed the WAC; spoke of the magnificent contribution of Australia to the war effort; praised the nurses and Red Cross women; spoke of how horrible war is; the two enemies our men have to fight—Japs and nature; and the morale factor of the presence of the WAC besides their contribution to their jobs ... that he had asked the War Department for 10,000 Wacs and that he was getting less than half that number.[27]

This was the last official conference with General MacArthur until just before the Wacs departed at the end of the war.

First WAC Contingent in Australia

A few days later, after all preparations had been made for the reception of the first Wacs at Brisbane, it was discovered that the ship was about to put in at Sydney. Colonel Brown and other welcoming officers flew to Sydney, where it was found that USASOS personnel, long desirous of obtaining Wacs, had planned a cordial reception. On the morning of 12 May, an impressive number of general officers, heads of Australian services, and curious soldiers and sailors were on the pier to watch the first 640 Wacs disembark from the transport *West Point.*[28] The Wacs made a good military appearance in their winter uniforms, according to a public relations officer:

With every eye trained on them, the Wacs marched off in their best military formation to pile into trucks. They were dressed in Class A uniform plus utility coat, field shoes, helmet, full field pack strapped on the back, and they carried in their hands everything from Red Cross ditty-bags to pillows, candy, radios, typewriters, and other cherished treasures. One Wac even carried a guitar. "Gee, they're real American girls," remarked one GI unbelievingly.[29]

The Wacs proceeded at once to Brisbane, which was only a two-week stopover for the first group destined for New

Guinea, but where others were to stay for several months while civilian employees were replaced and the various headquarters rendered mobile. The 526 enlisted women and 114 officers were divided between USAFFE and USASOS. Most of the officers, and one company of the enlisted women, were assigned to operate the Central Postal Directory at Port Moresby, New Guinea. USAFFE's remaining 198 enlisted women were assigned to various headquarters offices, including 55 to the adjutant general, and from one to ten each to G–1, G–2, G–3, G–4, the chaplain, inspector general, headquarters commandant, judge advocate, provost marshal, special services, information and education, and finance. USASOS assignments were not recorded, but were presumably similar.[30]

Army officers responsible for the women's placement reported strong initial resistance on the part of many section chiefs, who were not enthusiastic about releasing civilian employees, but such objections were usually short-lived in view of the prospective departure from Australia.[31] An additional difficulty in replacement was presented by the fact that the first to arrive were in many cases not clerical workers, the higher clerical skills in the United States having been already well combed over by the European thea-

---

[27] WAC Sec USAFFE Hist Rpt, May 44.

[28] Paragraphs on landing and stay in Australia, unless otherwise specified, are from: (1) Griffith Account, "Australia." (2) AFPAC Reply, both draft and approved versions.

[29] Griffith Account. Numbers are from AFPAC Reply, although Colonel Brown later believed that nearer 1,000 had landed.

[30] Folder 203.1, 1st Contingent, Theater WAC Stf Dir files.

[31] Col. A. Robert Ginsburgh, "The Good Staff Officer in the Field," *Infantry Journal*, August 1946, pp. 10–11.

ter. Also, theater requisitions had included drivers, mechanics, radio operators, and other specialists who, it was now decided, could not safely be used in New Guinea. As a result, a headquarters in the urgent days of preparing for movement was faced with the necessity for retraining chauffeurs and other workers as clerks and typists—a problem which occasionally left the impression that untrained Wacs had been shipped.[32] In August the theater requested deletion from future shipments of fifty-four drivers, as well as some draftsmen, cashiers, bookkeepers, and other specialists, but the War Department reply was, "Impossible to delete . . . as personnel already en route to theater or under shipment orders."[33]

Under the circumstances, it was surprising to staff officers that the replacement was none the less accomplished speedily and successfully. General Campbell noted later:

I was assigned 39 Wacs to replace 78 Australian girls. The Wacs didn't know one Quartermaster report from another but they quickly caught on: even those who had been drivers showed aptitude for it, and did more and better work than civilians. I never saw a bunch more willing to do a job.[34]

In one other respect, that of selection, several of the Wacs were inferior to the initial shipments to other theaters. A few days after the arrival of the first group, one member went AWOL and was finally apprehended only after conspicuous misconduct in the city of Brisbane, which came to the attention of the American consul and of some of the citizenry. Inspection of her records showed that she had been shipped overseas after a series of disciplinary offenses and courts-martial. Further investigation uncovered several more records of the same character. The women were promptly shipped back to the United States, accompanied by a report pointing out that Wacs should not be selected on the same basis as combat troops, and that as the first ambassadors and representatives of American womanhood in a foreign country, such women left something to be desired.

Using this evidence, Colonel Hobby finally secured re-establishment of the requirement—a considerable deviation from men's rules—that WAC company commanders must certify the suitability of any enlisted woman sent overseas, and that WAC staff directors must certify any officer.[35] Later selection was reported as much improved. Theater medical authorities felt that many physical and mental breakdowns could have been avoided had women with known records of instability not been sent. A subsequent report commented:

It appears that the selection of WAC personnel sent to this theater was not made carefully enough, especially in the case of commissioned personnel. The "unloading" of less than "excellent" type personnel on an overseas requisition was a practice which flourished to the detriment of the WAC in this theater. WD Circular 362, 6 Dec 44, put a check on this practice, but a great deal of damage had already been done. Conditions of this theater put the greatest demands on women commanding other women as regards stability and judgment, and the calibre of many company officers sent here leaves much to be desired.[36]

As expected, the Australian stopover presented no important difficulties in housing or supply. Wacs were housed at

---

[32] Tech Int Rpt T/PFI–2472, Strategic Int Det, Hq 4th SvC, 7 Jul 45, to CG ASF. MID files.
[33] Folder 203.6, 6th Contingent.
[34] Interv, 31 Jul 47.
[35] (1) Ltr, Col Brown to Dir WAC, 7 Aug 44. WDWAC 320.2. (2) WD Cir 291, 11 Jul 44, Sec IV, succeeded by WD Cir 362.
[36] WAC Draft AFPAC Reply.

Yeronga Park, generally riding to work on city trams; USASOS Wacs later transferred to Victoria Park. The lack of heat in some offices and part of the quarters, customary as it was to Australians, caused a high incidence of minor pulmonary disorders, seldom disabling in character. Barracks were somewhat more primitive than those in the United States, with bucket latrines, outside showers, and limited laundry facilities, but were in general superior to those of male troops in the area. Wacs enjoyed city recreational facilities, and stated that they had plenty of Australian fruit and green vegetables and more than plenty of Australian mutton.

Arrival in New Guinea

Beginning on 28 May, only two weeks after the landing in Australia, 100 WAC censorship officers and 88 enlisted women left by air for Port Moresby.[37] As perspiring Wacs stepped from the first plane, clad in coveralls and wool-lined field coats, and carrying full field pack, they were met by an advance party with cameras and flashbulbs, intent on preserving the moment for recruiting purposes. Driving along the 14-mile road from Port Moresby to their camp site at John's Gulley, they found much of the way lined with fuzzy-haired natives, and with soldiers who shouted, waved, whistled, and called out such questions as "What State are you from?" or "How's San Francisco?"

The WAC quarters, inside a hot and dusty barbed-wired enclosure, were among the best enlisted housing in New Guinea—long wooden barracks with iron roofs, cement floors, and screened walls, with outside showers and toilets, but boasting a water-borne sewage system.

The barracks were not yet fully prepared for troop occupancy, and the women, fresh from the United States, were at first baffled by the lack of furniture except Army cots, which thwarted their attempts to unpack clothing or set up the orderly room typewriter. They were also worried about prospects of doing their laundry without laundry facilities or hot water, or of eating, since the WAC mess was choked with debris and there was no drinking water.

However, a friendly men's unit nearby loaned the women a Lyster bag for drinking water, and fed them bread and jam, after which they borrowed trucks and set out to scavenge supply dumps for boxes, crates, tin cans, nails, and broken furniture. "The Quartermaster salvage dump proved a fascinating place," wrote one woman. They also borrowed a tool kit from the men, and improvised shelves and hangers for clothing and stands for the orderly room typewriter and files. By nightfall they considered themselves theater veterans. An enlisted woman wrote, "Now that we have our boxes, we are different people. We have found our sense of humor, and a sort of objectivity."

The work at Port Moresby proved heavy but routine, the operation of the Central Postal Directory in general offering nothing unfamiliar. The enlisted women sorted, checked, readdressed and forwarded soldier mail in what inspectors pronounced a highly competent manner. The WAC officers were employed as censors to replace male officers, and were also

---

[37] All descriptions of Port Moresby, unless otherwise specified, are from: (1) Monthly Hist Rpts, 5203d WAC Det, May–Aug 44, incl in Ltr, WAC Stf Dir USAFFE to Dir WAC. WDWAC 319.1 SWPA. (2) Griffith Account, "Port Moresby." (3) AFPAC Reply, both WAC Draft and final versions.

complimented by their supervisor, who observed:

I don't know what there is about women that makes them so sharp-eyed in reading letters, but the ones I have here possess an uncanny knack for picking up hidden security breaches, such as tricky codes a soldier may devise to tell his wife where he is. . . . They are turning out more and better work than the male officers they released to the combat area.[38]

The only immediate difficulty in the area was that of the uniform. The skirted winter uniforms had necessarily been left behind for storage in Australia, leaving each woman, for her entire supply of outer garments, only the one pair of herring-bone twill coveralls that had been issued for shipboard wear. Since there were no WAC maintenance stocks in the theater, each woman was provided with two more pairs of coveralls by the expedient of withdrawing them from other Wacs still in Australia. The heavy coveralls proved too hot for the climate and irritating to women's skin, as well as being so unsightly that nurses and other female personnel in the area were not permitted to wear them. Heat and skin diseases soon made it necessary for the headquarters to authorize the wearing of the WAC cotton shirt with the trousers of the two-piece coveralls, a practice that eventually became theater-wide, although officially forbidden by the theater surgeon, since the WAC shirt was lighter than the men's khaki, and below the weight believed safely mosquitoproof. The unit historian noted also that a few lucky women "had adopted suntan pants." Gifts of flowers and candy were scorned, and the successful applicant for a date was one who came carrying, as well as wearing, khaki trousers.

An additional problem that soon became evident was the unexpectedly re-stricted life of the enlisted women. WAC advisers, having been informed of the safe and civilized nature of the Port Moresby area, had believed that, as in Italy and Normandy, the ordinary camp security system would afford women sufficient protection, since there was little danger at this date from either the enemy or the natives. Instead, the headquarters directed that, in view of the large number of male troops in the area, some of whom allegedly had not seen a nurse or other white woman in eighteen months, Wacs would be locked within their barbed-wire compound at all times except when escorted by armed guards to work or to approved group recreation. No leaves or passes, or one-couple dates, were allowed at any time. The women's reaction was unfavorable; inspectors reported that they believed that higher commanders thought them "children or criminals," and therefore confined them in "a concentration camp." On the other hand, those restrictions that also applied to men were accepted by the women without comment.[39]

Within a few months the WAC area had been rendered more comfortable than most of those that were later to be found at more advanced bases. For labor beyond their strength, the women gave the natives cigarettes, candy, and even the otherwise useless WAC hats. Visitors reported considerable shock at beholding the natives dressed in WAC hats and very little else.

There were soon shelves, a graveled walk through the mud, a dayroom set up by the Red Cross, and even improvised dressing tables. The women learned from the men to wash their clothing in cold

---

[38] Griffith Account. Copy of commendation also in Folder, 5203d WAC Det, Drawer X–28040.

[39] AFPAC Reply, both versions. Also interviews. (See Bibliographical Note.)

water and to press it by sleeping on it or by hanging it up very wet. WAC cooks eventually cleared the debris from the WAC mess hall, overhauled the stoves, and soon had a mess which, their historian reported, "had a steady stream of daily business calls from officers who usually arrived just before dinner."

The women later obtained two washing machines, electric lights, and electric irons. In a few more months the Wacs had such luxuries as a recreation hall, a softball team, and a jukebox. They also persuaded the nurses to move their hairdressing shop so that Wacs could share it, since they could not use the men's barbershop. A Wac was put into the post exchange to order items women needed.

In spite of initial adjustments, only one woman in the detachment showed complete "inability to adjust to a tropical environment," and had to be returned to Australia. The unit grew in size, and was soon bypassed by Wacs moving north.

Headquarters Rendered Mobile

Meanwhile, with the aid of two more large shipments of WAC personnel, the various headquarters in Australia had succeeded in making themselves mobile. On 26 June 1944, the second WAC contingent landed in Brisbane—357 enlisted women and 28 officers—which was again divided, with USAFFE headquarters receiving about 99, the Port Moresby detachment 68, and the remainder going to Headquarters, USASOS. Included among the various skills were 75 clerks, 65 stenographers, and 52 typists. On 10 July a third contingent landed at Brisbane—8 officers and 371 enlisted women—again in chiefly clerical skills, and again divided among USAFFE in Australia, USAFFE

in Port Moresby, and USASOS in Australia. In addition, 84 women of this last group were given to the newly formed Headquarters, Far East Air Forces (FEAF), which had not filed its own formal requisitions until July and thus had not received any on the scheduled date for movement in August.[40]

A matter which unit organization did not reveal was that not only USAFFE, USASOS, and FEAF, but also GHQ, were employing Wacs. By August of 1944, shortly before the jump-off from Australia, GHQ had borrowed 74 Wacs from USAFFE and 31 from USASOS—a total of 105, with 150 more on requisition. Colonel Brown recommended that these women be organized into their own detachment when numbers warranted, and assigned to GHQ, as were enlisted men, and Dutch, Australian, and British women. This request was refused, since it was the Supreme Allied Commander's desire that American women not be assigned to GHQ, but attached for duty from some lower administrative echelon. Of these 105 women, 56 worked in GHQ's Signal Intelligence Division, 28 as telephone operators, 10 with the Chief Regulating Officer, and lesser numbers in other offices.[41]

Scarcely any one policy, supply situation, or personnel practice was common to all of these groups—GHQ, USAFFE, USASOS, and FEAF—even when they shared one camp. Because of the poor communications and local differences in climate and facilities, it was USAFFE's practice to promulgate only broad instructions and to leave the subordinate com-

---

[40] (1) Folders 203.2, 2d Contingent, and 203.3, 3d Contingent. (2) List of shipments, AFPAC Reply.
[41] Correspondence folder, 5205th WAC Det, Drawer X–29853.

mands free to meet the changing situation. For this reason, Colonel Baird noted that "the theater was most reluctant to publish a fixed policy or general rule to establish uniformity in WAC control and administration. This was true for the men also." Exceptions could therefore be found to almost any general statement which could later be made concerning theater Wacs as a group. A theater housing policy for Wacs was almost the only published over-all policy, and even this was found impracticable outside of Australia.[42]

A source of some later comment was the fact that Wacs were assigned to the advanced echelons of all of these headquarters. For nurses, the theater had formerly adopted a contrary policy of "using them only in rear areas," causing them to be replaced by male corpsmen in evacuation hospitals and in field hospitals during active phases of service—a practice which, inspectors reported, had caused low morale and psychiatric casualties among the women.[43]

Theater historians later expressed some doubt as to the necessity for the opposite policy concerning Wacs, since Australia was, to the end, a great supply base at which some noncombat men remained, and certain other headquarters, such as Air Transport Command, winnowed the necessary male clerical personnel for more advanced bases from among ordinary troops.

Maj. Gen. William O. Ryan of the ATC, upon inspecting the New Guinea bases, declared the area unsuitable for women and canceled the orders of ATC Wacs about to fly in from Hawaii. Nevertheless, responsible Army officers were unanimous that the theater could not have taken similar action. Col. A. Robert Ginsburgh, who was both G–1 and G–3 of USASOS, stated later:

USASOS could not possibly have moved from Australia without the Wacs. . . . Except for the Wacs, I had only the few clerically skilled men which higher headquarters let trickle through to USASOS, plus a few malarials and other men sent back from combat, naturally not very useful at exacting office work.[44]

Colonel Baird of USAFFE likewise indicated that the decision was a military necessity. General MacArthur himself, when later questioned as to the advisability of this course, replied:

I moved my Wacs forward early after occupation of recaptured territory because they were needed and they were soldiers in the same manner that my men were soldiers. Furthermore, if I had not moved my Wacs when I did, I would have had mutiny . . . as they were so eager to carry on where needed.[45]

The Wacs themselves were eager to get forward, and the staff director later expressed "complete accord" with the decision.[46]

Oro Bay

Wacs began to move out of Australia early in August of 1944; by October only

[42] AFPAC Reply, both versions; also Memo cited n. 22.

[43] (1) Memo, Maj Craighill, MC, Consultant for Women's Health and Welfare, SGO, for TAG through CG USAFFE, 8 Jun 45, sub: Med and Social Conditions of Women in Mil Serv in SWPA. WDWAC 333 Pacific, and in SGO Hist Div 319.1–2 Women, SWPA. Hereafter cited as Craighill SWPA Rpt. Attached is a list of interviews with more than 200 individuals in SWPA, including chief nurses, WAC detachment commanders, hospital commanders, Army commanders, inspectors, etc.; also Table of Comparative Rates of Medical Evacuation for Wacs and Nurses, 1 Jul 44 to 1 Apr 45. (2) Data in possession of Col Brown.

[44] Seminar Comments. (See Bibliographical Note.)

[45] Statement to Col Boyce in Tokyo, 14 Oct 45, quoted by her in Boyce Rpt.

[46] Ltr, Miss Mary-Agnes Brown to OCMH, 23 Apr 51. OCMH.

COMMANDING OFFICER OF THIRD CONTINGENT OF WACS *to arrive in Australia is greeted at the pier on 10 July 1944. In the group greeting Capt. Ida M. Ross from left to right are Brig. Gen. Homer C. Brown, Lt. Col. Mary-Agnes Brown, Capt. Charlee L. Kelly and Lt. Vera Mankinen.*

a negligible number remained on the continent.[47] First to move was USASOS, which on 9 August 1944 sent an advance unit to Oro Bay for service with its Intermediate Section (Intersec). These were shortly reinforced by the arrival at Oro Bay on 6 September, direct from the United States, of the largest WAC shipment yet received—47 officers and 1,253 enlisted women. These were divided between Intersec headquarters at Cape Sudest and USASOS Base B at Oro Bay proper. On 30 October another large shipment of 21 officers and 571 enlisted women for USASOS also landed at Oro

Bay, followed later by a final smaller one in January of 1945. A WAC staff director for USASOS was designated, the position being held successively in the next twelve months by Capt. Natalie Reebel, Maj. Ellen Bailey, and Maj. Annie V. Gardiner.[48]

The supply situation of the Oro Bay Wacs was not improved, for the first few months, by the fact that the entire September shipment arrived completely equipped with arctic clothing, including ski pants and ear muffs. No explanation

---

[47] Oro Bay discussion, unless otherwise stated, is from Griffith Account and AFPAC Reply.

[48] Sources cited n. 40.

or comment on this phenomenon was ever advanced by supply agencies in the theater or in the United States; no arctic shipment of Wacs had ever been directed by the War Department during World War II.[49]

The Oro Bay area proved generally suitable for women, with WAC camps, carved from the jungle, lying along the seashore, with beaches for front yards and palm trees for shade. Swimming was permissible under certain conditions. Barracks were made of wood and screens, with a large recreation hall and mess hall already built nearby. The staff director, Colonel Brown, accompanied by Captain Reebel, had visited and slept in these barracks before the arrival of the women, and had checked with the Base B staff on other necessary preparations.

Since Oro Bay was principally a major supply base, much of the Wacs' duties concerned the stock record reports and other paper work necessary to get matériel forwarded to combat troops. The Distribution Office was almost entirely staffed by Wacs, who kept track of the ships and supplies in New Guinea, whether mobile or at bases or consigned to the area from Australia or San Francisco. Army service command units to enter Leyte with the next wave of combat troops included men pulled out of offices at Oro Bay and replaced by Wacs.[50]

As at Port Moresby, the only unexpected difficulty in the employment of women in the area was that of restrictions not applied to men at the same base. Colonel Brown noted that before her departure the base commander, Brig. Gen. Clarence L. Sturdevant, had agreed to treat the women like other troops. General Sturdevant, one of the few members of the Pacific staff who had observed WAC administration in the United States prior to his assignment to the Pacific, believed that "overly protective measures such as barbed wire fences and armed guards were unnecessary and undesirable."[51] However, before the troops' arrival this decision was reversed. Thereafter, all USASOS bases used a system of protective custody for women. Barbed wire was put up around the Oro Bay WAC area, and the women were forbidden to leave "any area at any time" without armed guards, even being marched to approved movies in formation under guard. A list of further restrictions was published in order to prevent "regrettable incidents and unwholesome impressions of any nature."[52]

Off-duty activities were limited to approved unit parties and other mass entertainment to which women could be taken under guard, and even for these a woman's date had to be named twenty-four hours in advance, subject to disapproval by the senior WAC officer. Outside the WAC area, vehicles carrying women could not stop en route to the approved destination, or any woman leave the vehicle, or the vehicle leave the main road. Women were forbidden to board boats, ships, or craft of any sort, or to ride in aircraft. "Informal social gatherings of males

---

[49] Description of arctic shipment was deleted by theater from WAC draft report, but is well substantiated by interviews with participants. The only arctic shipments were those made to Alaska and Labrador by the ATC, which staged, equipped, and shipped its own Wacs.

[50] (1) Interv with Col Ginsburgh, 25 Jul 45. (2) M. Hamlin Cannon, Leyte: Return to the Philippines, a forthcoming volume in this series.

[51] (1) Marginal note on draft of this chapter. For fuller documentation see: (2) WAC Draft AFPAC Reply. (3) Memo 90, Hq Base B USASOS, 21 Nov 44. (4) Reg 10–55, Hq USASOS, 19 Dec 44. (5) Reg 10–100, Hq AFWESPAC, 2 Sep 45. (6) Ltr cited n. 46.

[52] Memo 66, Hq Base B USASOS, 22 Aug 44. This replaces an earlier Memo 15, 8 Apr 44, with C–1, 5 Jun, and C–2, 25 Jul.

and females" were forbidden unless the commanding officer designated the spot for them. All women were required to be in quarters by 2300 unless authorized to stay out until midnight, which was the absolute deadline.

Because of the growing effect of these provisions upon discipline and mental health, Colonel Brown later appealed again to USASOS headquarters to revert to the system first approved by the base commander. Although Maj. Gen. James L. Frink later agreed to authorize his base commanders to grant Wacs "the greatest possible freedom consistent with their personal safety," very few actual modifications ever resulted.[53]

Hollandia

On 31 August 1944, three weeks after the first Oro Bay shipment, a group of Far East Air Forces Wacs took off from Brisbane for the next stop, Hollandia, some eight hundred miles beyond Oro Bay. Here the environment was far less favorable and, while combat troops had landed four months before, the last Japanese raiding parties had still not been driven from the hills. The prudent FEAF Wacs, having heard that wild country lay ahead, climbed from their air transport laden with sixty baby chicks and twenty-five laying hens—which, incidentally, never laid thereafter. USAFFE and USASOS Wacs followed, until there were shortly more than a thousand in the Hollandia area.[54]

Climate and living conditions in Hollandia, except for GHQ's elevated camp site, were in general the least favorable yet encountered by the advancing headquarters. Rain was continual in some seasons, clothing was generally wet from perspiration, and heat prevented more than a few hours sleep at night. The red New Guinea clay apparently had the ability simultaneously to blow into the hair as dust and stick to the clothing as mud. During the first weeks there were no laundry facilities for men or women, and the slow-drying coveralls proved difficult to keep clean. For some time women had no hairdressing facilities, of which a medical officer noted, "They have as much need of them as men do of barbershops."[55]

Also, everyone shortly turned yellow from the required atabrine. One officer reported, "Frankly, women who had looked very well in Australia looked like hell in Hollandia." Men and women alike began to get skin diseases; some had to be sent back, including one competent WAC commander whose loss, USASOS authorities stated, "we could very ill afford." Weather conditions often prevented active recreation, while attempts at approved social entertainments bogged down under the weight of heavy coveralls and field shoes in 100-degree temperatures.

These conditions were particularly felt by USASOS personnel, both men and women, in their hot and humid camp site on low ground near the harbor. Here Wacs shared, with assorted insects, wooden-floored tents and a converted warehouse. The FEAF camp site was scarcely more healthful, with tents pitched on ground subject to flash floods of mud

---

[53] (1) Memo, Gen Frink, CG USASOS, for CG Intersec, 23 Oct 44, with incl Stf Dir Recommendations re WAC Pers at Intersec and Base B. GSCG 324.5. (2) Ltr, Stf Dir SWPA to all WAC Dets, 27 Oct 44, with incl Ltr. Folder, 5200th WAC Det, Drawer X–29443.

[54] Hollandia account, except as cited, from: (1) Griffith Account. (2) AFPAC Reply, both versions. (3) Interv cited n. 50(1).

[55] Major Craighill. See Table of Comparative Rates of Medical Evacuation for Wacs and Nurses, atchd to Craighill SWPA Rpt.

and water, and at the foot of a hill a strenuous hike from the offices on top. For a time the FEAF unit also housed the USAFFE Wacs, most of whom worked for GHQ, but within a few weeks this arrangement became so unsatisfactory to FEAF that, without warning, it bodily ejected the GHQ Wacs and their belongings, without a company officer.

Emergency housing was hastily worked out, and the GHQ Wacs eventually benefited by a move to tents in the GHQ area on a cool mountain top. To prevent such misunderstandings in the future, the staff director recommended in September and again in January that the unit be formally organized and assigned to GHQ as were enlisted men, but she was again informed by USAFFE that "The Commander-in-Chief did not want Wacs assigned to GHQ and under the circumstances no attempt would be made to do so." [56] Because of its ambiguous status, the GHQ unit suffered chronic supply difficulties, and eventually departed from Hollandia without ever receiving its organizational equipment.[57]

The GHQ unit, upon Colonel Brown's recommendation, attempted the experiment of housing Wacs, nurses, and Red Cross women in one camp without barbed wire, and with a minimum of restrictions. No particular difficulties were experienced, and there were only two instances of prowlers, of whom it was reported, "The Wacs took care of them." [58] The success of this experiment did not, as the staff director had hoped, persuade other commands to try it. USASOS units at all stations, employing some 60 percent of all Wacs, continued to use varieties of the unpopular "concentration camp" system. Air Forces units ordinarily relaxed the system to abolish locked compounds, requiring only armed escorts and traveling in minimum groups of four. The FEAF

staff director noted that "No serious incidents were reported as a result of the wider degree of freedom exercised by Air Force units." [59]

A fourth WAC unit was eventually organized in Hollandia by the Far East Air Service Command (FEASC). Although handicapped when the departing FEAF transferred to it more than sixty WAC drivers and other unassignables needing retraining, the FEASC detachment requisitioned more Wacs and reached an eventual strength of approximately seven hundred.[60]

At this time premature optimism was general when, toward the end of 1944, the WAC medical evacuation rate for the first six months in the theater was computed and proved to be not too much higher than the men's, the loss rate being 62 per 1,000 per year for men (nonbattle causes only) and 98 per 1,000 for Wacs. This rate appeared especially good in view of the current rate of 202 per 1,000 for Army nurses, a rate that had generally prevailed since their arrival. Theater reports stated that the WAC rate compared "very favorably" with the men's, and that the difference was due to gynecological disorders, other disabilities incurred by the Wacs being generally of the same nature and degree of severity as those incurred by men.[61]

---

[56] (1) WAC Hist Rpt (shows Stf Dir check sheets on 23 Aug and 7 Sep). (2) Folder, 5205th WAC Det, Drawer X–29853. Also minutes of seminar.

[57] From 16 different items of correspondence in Folder, 5205th WAC Det, Drawer X–29853.

[58] Statements by Colonel Brown at seminar and on margin of draft of chapter.

[59] Ltr, Lt Col Mary L. Kersey, WAF, to OCMH, 21 Apr 51.

[60] Hist Rpts, Jan, Feb 45. Folder, FEASC WAC Det II.

[61] WAC Draft AFPAC Reply, cited in D/F, G–1 WD to CofS USA, 13 Sep 45. WDGAP 330.11 WAC (5–26–45).

HOLLANDIA, NETHERLANDS NEW GUINEA. *Wooden-floored tents occupied by the women.*

Other evidence tended to support even more optimistic conclusions. For one period, during which the average length of nonbattle hospitalization was computed separately, the average stay for Wacs was only 10.5 days as compared to 18 days for men. There was a slight suspicion among the Wacs themselves that they could withstand the hot weather better than the men. On the other hand, while many Wacs had gained weight in Australia, they, like many men, now began to lose; some suffered a "gradual and continuous" loss from the time of their arrival. Authorities blamed this on "loss of appetite after long periods of diet composed principally of canned and dehydrated foods." [62]

The Philippines

Wacs arrived in the Philippines on 26 November 1944, some thirty-six days behind the first wave of combat troops. The Wacs' presence was again required by USASOS' personnel plan, a repetition of its previous maneuver. To man the immediate northward push from Leyte, it was again necessary to pull men out of the organizations that had landed on Leyte and to send them forward in the island-hopping toward Manila. The mechanics of this exchange was handled by a WAC enlisted woman, later a warrant officer, Margaret Sterling, who received high commendation from USASOS authorities

[62] AFPAC Reply, both versions.

HOLLANDIA, NETHERLANDS NEW GUINEA. *Women at work in the finance office.*

for her management of the selection and training of WAC replacements in this and previous moves. GHQ and FEAF also made the decision to move their women to Leyte.[63]

Colonel Brown attempted to move the staff director's office forward from Hollandia ahead of the enlisted women, and succeeded in getting orders for a permanent change of station to Leyte. However, these orders were shortly revoked by G–1 Division, over her protest, and no representative of the WAC Section was permitted to visit the Leyte area until some weeks after the enlisted women's arrival.[64]

The first enlisted women, the GHQ unit, took off for Leyte accompanied by "Tokyo Rose's" prediction, "Of course

they won't get there." As promised, trouble was encountered when the first planes were obliged to circle for some time before they could land, and were immediately strafed when they started to unload. Arriving Wacs, accustomed to being a sensation, were nevertheless surprised to see hundreds of men fleeing the airstrip and plunging into brush and foxholes. The women soon grasped the maneuver, and hit the foxholes as promptly as did the combat veterans on the same planes; from this vantage point they cheered as two

[63] (1) Interv cited n. 50(1). (2) Griffith Account, "Citations."

[64] Colonel Brown's notes on draft of chapter. WAC file, OCMH. USAFFE orders: WAC Sec USAFFE Hist Rpts.

Japanese planes were shot down in flames.[65]

Conditions during the rainy season nevertheless proved so unexpectedly bad as to raise the issue of whether or not the Wacs should be sent back, even over their objections. Proceeding through hub-deep mud to Tacloban, the GHQ Wacs were housed in a deserted mission school where Japanese soldiers had been recently garrisoned. Fortunately, the yards were already honeycombed with Japanese foxholes; the entire day and night were described as "a series of enemy air-raids and ducking for shelter." [66] USASOS men and women, arriving soon after, shared an area in a sea of mud, in which frameless tents were pitched so closely that they had to be tied together. FEAF Wacs were slightly better off. On the day after their arrival General Kenney himself inspected the area, and in the next month drainage ditching was performed by "shovel-equipped Colonels, Majors, Lieutenants, and non-coms from the A–2 Section." [67] However, the chief WAC problem on Leyte was not housing, which was the same for men and women, but rather the lack of suitable equipment. There were no overshoes for women, and only four of the GHQ Wacs had more than one pair of field shoes, which never dried out but had, the commander reported, to be "cleaned and put back on while still wet." The supply of coveralls was still so poor that, she noted, "there is no way of keeping in dry clothes." [68] A search was made for men's overshoes or field shoes in small sizes, but even after calling upon the Navy it was impossible to find enough to equip the women.

Nevertheless, the women were averse to leaving Leyte, and no move was made to return them. The History of USAFFE reported:

They kept communications open at Leyte between alerts that sent them into foxholes, only to return to take more messages all through the night.[69]

The deputy chief ordnance officer noted:

The Advance Section, USASOS, which went into Leyte, worked long night hours in the lantern-lighted tents when we were getting ready for an operation. We were interrupted frequently by air-raids, but they didn't panic.[70]

After a rough three months on Leyte, conditions improved as they had at previous stations; food and supply were better, laundry and hairdressing facilities were obtained, and emergency housing was improved. Troops of both sexes had more time for swimming, sight-seeing, and shopping at the local market. The chief interest was the battle for Manila; as usual, the Wacs again wished to move forward. As released prisoners, wounded, and sick began to be evacuated, some Wacs took up clothing collections among their own scarce stores for the women and children from internment camps, and volunteered off-duty help in hospitals.

Other Bases

Meanwhile, during and after the move to Leyte, Wacs had been sent to other bases.[71] The decision was made by USASOS headquarters that Wacs must go out to all of Intersec's lettered bases

[65] (1) Folder, 5205th WAC Det, Drawer X–29853. (2) Griffith Account.

[66] Descriptions of Philippines experiences not otherwise documented are from: (1) Griffith Account. (2) AFPAC Reply, both versions.

[67] Folder II, WAC Det FEAF, Drawer X–25096.

[68] Folder, 5205th WAC Det, Drawer X–29853.

[69] History of the United States Army Forces in the Far East 1943–1945, by Hist Sec, G–2 Far East Command. OCMH. Cited as USAFFE Hist.

[70] Interv with Col Merle H. Davis, 24 Jul 47.

[71] This section based on Griffith Account, AFPAC Reply, and Interv cited n. 50(1).

WAC AREA, TACLOBAN, LEYTE ISLAND, *27 December 1944. Note regulation dress shoes worn by woman.*

except those already to the rear, even where somewhat primitive conditions existed. As a result, USASOS Wacs were moved from Oro Bay not only to Hollandia but, on 24 November, to Base E at Lae and, on 6 December 1944, to Base F at Finschhafen. The USASOS staff director visited these bases in advance of troops, to help select WAC areas, and no particular difficulty was reported. Wacs at Lae lived in a hospital area, and those at Finschhafen in quarters of native construction, which were considered superior to tents. Both groups were later to be the last to leave as other bases moved forward. Jobs remained the familiar USASOS routine of cargo tonnage, troops movements, vessel routing reports, and other service paper work.

On 13 February 1945, the USAFFE mail and censorship unit likewise moved forward from Port Moresby to the coral island of Biak. Although the location presented problems of heat and glare, it eventually offered many conveniences. Except for an air raid in which no WAC casualties were suffered, the Biak Wacs' closest approach to war came with their visits to hospital ships and general hospitals.

Manila

On 7 March 1945, four days after organized resistance ended in Manila, the GHQ Wacs left Leyte and reached the area by air, across a bay still clogged with sunken ships. A WAC officer described their arrival:

The plane landed on a black-top highway[72] that served as an air-strip. Wacs climbed out and sat cross-legged on the ground taking in the scene. Down this modern roadway passed an array of assorted vehicles . . . people and their belongings coming back to the city. . . . Heavy artillery fire could be heard in the distance routing the Japs out of the hills only a few miles away. The route into the city led past . . . a once thriving business section, now a pile of crushed buildings, twisted iron gratings, debris. . . . Dead Japs still lay along the streets awaiting burial. GHQ and USAFFE Wacs were housed in De La Salle College . . . called "atrocity college" because of the atrocities committed there by the Japanese. Bodies had been removed a day previously and floors and walls creosoted and fumigated.[73]

Fighting was still going on in the outskirts of the city, snipers were being routed out, and guards were heavy. One Japanese prowler was later caught in the WAC mess hall, and two others were shot down and died at WAC onlookers' feet, but there was, an observer reported, "no hysterics" among the women.

The disturbed conditions continued for some weeks. Water was scarce and had to be hauled. The GHQ Wacs bathed in helmets, lived by candlelight at night. Latrines were erected in the courtyard, with half a dozen shower heads. Men's mess halls lacked space to serve the women, and Wacs lived on K rations until they could get their own mess hall into operation. Dehydrated food was the chief sustenance for all troops; some women lost their appetites, preferred to sleep at mealtimes, and often ate only one meal a day. Until blood and filth could be removed, flies were so numerous that a severe epidemic of dysentery afflicted the GHQ Wacs. Their commander's greatest fear was that some of the violently ill women, groping their way in the blackout to the outdoor latrines, would fall and detonate the remaining Japanese booby traps believed to be on either side

---

[72] A later description refers to the highway as a city street and gives a route somewhat different from that in the present account.

[73] Griffith Account for entire Manila discussion unless otherwise cited.

of the board walks. Nevertheless, there was soon set up what was described as "an orderly efficiently operating headquarters in the midst of chaos, confusion, and destruction." In buildings full of bullet and shell holes, GHQ Wacs for the first weeks propped up broken desks and chairs, used crates for file cases, chunks of twisted metal for paperweights, and fragments of exploded shells for ash trays.

The USASOS Wacs delayed their arrival until, in the opinion of their battalion commander and later staff director, Major Gardiner, the worst of the dirt with the resulting dysentery was eliminated. They were housed in the Far Eastern University and in overflow tents on adjacent areas. Buildings were in relatively good condition, and the headquarters was quickly established.

As various New Guinea stations were closed, Wacs were moved into the Manila area until eventually most of the entire five thousand were concentrated there. Army Forces, Western Pacific (AFWESPAC), the successor to USASOS, used over a thousand women who were housed in frame-and-burlap barracks on Ascarraga Street. A small general depot group at Quezon City lived in floored tents in an area which the Wacs soon neatly landscaped. At the demolished Fort McKinley, FEAF Wacs lived in an attractive breezy camp with partitioned buildings, neat dayrooms, and their own club for dancing. At Nichols Field, FEASC Wacs had hot and dusty tin barracks. The Philippine Base Section WAC detachment drew comfortable but crowded nurses' quarters, where they lived six and eight to a two-woman compartment, and enjoyed that novelty, clothes closets. Wacs at Santa Ana Racetrack, working for the Allied Translator and Intelligence Service, lived

for a time in muddy unfloored tents, later moving to thatch-roofed huts of 20-Wac capacity. Wacs with the signal intelligence section were housed at San Miguel Plantation in frame and tin barracks, and lived a very quiet country life.[74]

For some time restrictions in Manila were even tighter than elsewhere, since the city's remaining recreation facilities were generally off-limits, and a seven o'clock curfew was imposed for security. Also, the move to Manila did little to improve the supply situation. One company commander was obliged to ask that Wacs not be arrested by military police for not being dressed in the khaki uniform now required of all men and nurses, since "WAC personnel are not out of uniform when wearing coverall trousers with cotton shirts, because of the necessity for such wear as Class A uniform due to lack of supplies. Some members have only one pair of [men's] khaki slacks."[75] Just after the first Wacs' move to Manila, the WAC Section sent a memorandum to G–1 of USAFFE pointing out that while the supply difficulties for male troops in the area were great, those for Wacs had been even greater: "No supply has been available for Wacs where I have been stationed since our departure from Australia."[76]

Job Assignments

In Manila, and in the outlying bases, final records of WAC job assignment were scanty. The theater estimated that, as of the spring of 1945, 70 percent of the Wacs were engaged in administrative and office

[74] For WAC detachments at end of war see Griffith Account.

[75] Correspondence Folder, 5200th WAC Det, Drawer X–29443.

[76] Memo, Capt Juanita Stryker, WAC Sec USAFFE, for Gen Baird, 12 Mar 45. Tab 12, WAC Draft AFPAC Reply.

work. The most common WAC jobs were, in order: clerk-typist, clerk (general), stenographer, typist, message center clerk, chauffeur, cook, and file clerk.[77] The estimated percentages in each type of job were, toward the end of the war:[78]

Duties	Percent
Technical and Professional	2.52
Radio and Electrical	.08
Communications	2.04
Mechanical and Trade	.81
Administrative and Office	69.33
Motor Transport	6.45
Food	4.52
Supply and Stock	8.77
Miscellaneous	5.48

By comparison with world-wide employment, the Pacific had used notably fewer women in communications, and more in routine office and supply jobs.

The approximate peak distribution of WAC troops among the several commands was estimated as: [79]

Command	Percent
USAFFE (including GHQ)	23
USASOS	60
Air Forces: FEAF	6
FEASC	11

Concerning the work done by the 23 percent assigned to USAFFE and GHQ, the History of USAFFE noted:

The WAC were typists, switchboard operators, administrative officers in signal centers and message centers, chief clerks, mess sergeants, translators, historians, Personnel and Transportation Officers, Top Secret Officers, Executive Officers, and Assistants to Adjutants General. They drove heavy vehicles; handled stock reports, censored the mail of the whole theater.[80]

In addition to such duties, Wacs were by 1945 also assigned to the Joint Supply and Survey Board, the Radio and Radar Unit, the Psychological Warfare Board, the USAFFE Board, the fiscal director, the Civil and Military Censorship detach-

ments, the A-D Board, and Section 22 of GHQ.[81]

Within USASOS, its 60 percent of Wacs were assigned not only to the headquarters but to ten base depot companies including quartermaster, ordnance, signal, engineer, chemical warfare, and medical.[82] For example, the ordnance office of USASOS employed several hundred Wacs, of whom its chief noted:

Ordnance had more than 100,000 line items on which it maintained stock control in the theater, first by cards and later by IBM. Most men do not like this type of work, and even so the women are more painstaking. Each enlisted Wac would handle one small group of items, and each WAC officer would supervise several such groups. Our tendency was to leave them on the group they had learned, but they did not show signs of weariness. Many of the women were outstanding in morale.[83]

Percentages of Wacs in the various USASOS offices were not recorded, with two exceptions: the finance office at Intersec, serving approximately 2,800 personnel, was staffed entirely by Wacs; the editorial section of USASOS headquarters was composed of one WAC officer, eight enlisted women, and two enlisted men, who reviewed all publications.[84]

The 17 percent of Air Forces Wacs did, in general, the same type of work as that in the Service Forces. No record of FEAF jobs was preserved, but as of June 1945, FEASC employed 574 Wacs.[85] Of them,

---

[77] "Suggested Materials for a WAC Newsmap . . ." Material in possession of Mary-Agnes Brown.
[78] AFPAC Reply.
[79] Ibid.
[80] USAFFE Hist.
[81] List in possession of Mary-Agnes Brown.
[82] Ibid.
[83] Interv cited n. 70.
[84] Newsmap material cited n. 77.
[85] Folder I, WAC Det FEAF, Drawer X–25096.

Maj. Gen. Clements McMullen of the Far East Air Service Command stated:

> The FEASC WAC Detachment rendered superior service to this command. Our Wacs typed letters, ran mimeo machines, almost entirely manned an International Business Machine Statistical Unit, filed papers, drove automobiles, worked in dispensaries, and maintained their own homes, in a wonderful manner. . . .[86]

Signal Corps duties were common to GHQ, USAFFE, USASOS, and the Air Forces. In the Intersec Signal Center, Wacs at teletype machines handled an average of 100,000 coded groups a day. During the Leyte campaign, 130,000 words a day were handled, including coding and decoding. One four-position telephone switchboard averaged 6,500 calls daily. GHQ's Signal Operations Group commended the Wacs handling the Bataan exchange, saying:

> Many favorable comments have been received by this office recently on the operation of the Bataan Switchboard. The speed, efficiency, and courtesy with which calls are now being handled have been highly commended by representatives of the Chief Signal Office, GHQ.[87]

FEASC reported that during the move of its advanced headquarters to Manila, six WAC telephone operators "without assistance, for two consecutive weeks ran the FEASC switchboard at its new headquarters on a 24-hour 7-day week." [88]

Several hundred women were employed on skilled work of a classified nature. The Allied Translator and Intelligence Service had 150 Wacs, including nisei, who did what was described as "important secret work" as interrogators and translators. This unit maintained a high morale, and was regarded as outstanding. Equally secret although more monotonous was the work of the 120 Wacs with the Signal Intelligence Service. The women were described as "highly skilled technicians," but it was admitted that "the secret nature of their work, regardless of how interesting and stimulating it was, in time became tiring due to the fact that it was confining and restricted the individual." [89]

The work of the censorship unit and the Central Postal Directory, successively at Port Moresby and Biak, continued almost unchanged. Approximately a million wrongly addressed pieces of mail were processed monthly by the Wacs, who received reports of all changes of status or location of theater personnel and worked seven days a week checking cards in huge locator files. The censorship group received the Meritorious Service Unit Plaque for having censored not only ordinary mail but "practically all the foreign-language mail written in the theater, involving a knowledge of 31 languages." [90]

Nevertheless, inspectors found that censorship work, which at first had appeared highly suitable for women, offered a definite mental hazard. One reported:

> Much of what the men wrote was so obscene that the women became demoralized from having to read it all day. . . . The WAC censors became nervous, temperamental, and complaining; first they thought they would lose their eyesight, then their minds. All came to complaint hour. By the end of the war . . . many of them had become definitely neurotic if not actually psychotic.[91]

An inspector general report in April 1945

---

[86] Ltr, CG FEASC to Dir WAC, 3 Jan 46. sub: Commendation. WDWAC 201.22 and 330.13. (1945–46).

[87] Correspondence folder, 5205th WAC Det, Drawer X–29853.

[88] Hist Rpt, Jul 45, Folder II, WAC Det FEASC.

[89] Boyce Rpt.

[90] GO 157, GHQ USAFPAC, sub: Meritorious Serv Unit Plaque Award (5203d WAC Det). Tab 14 to WAC Draft AFPAC Reply.

[91] Interv with Capt Jeanne K. Letallier, WAC IG SWPA, 9 Jan 46. Similar rpt in Craighill SWPA Rpt.

stated that an extremely low state of morale existed and that the health record
was poor: 20 percent were on sick call
daily, 50 percent suffered from eye strain,
and approximately 8 percent had already
been evacuated due to tropical. diseases
and psychoneurosis.[92] After the unit was
returned to the United States, the postwar
theater staff director wrote, "In any future
planning, I definitely oppose the use of
women in censoring male correspondence."[93]

A few other defects marred the WAC
job-assignment program, of a type which
in less active theaters had caused more
serious difficulty than was reported in the
Pacific. In some units, women, especially
stenographers, were not always kept busy
enough to suit them. Inspectors reported
of the FEASC detachment that "the largest percentage of complaints from this
group involved job utilization . . . complaints were registered in regard to the
limited amount of work actually being
performed."[94]

Nevertheless, women were apparently
more fortunate than men in this respect,
for a FEASC management control survey
reported the job utilization of enlisted
women to be better than that of enlisted
men in the same offices.[95] On the other
hand, highly skilled women technicians
were more subject to malassignment than
men, for the environment greatly limited
the extent to which women could be scattered about, and WAC radio operators,
photographic technicians, drivers and
mechanics usually had to be retrained to
other skills.

In almost all commands, job promotion
was slow and skilled workers did not receive the ratings that the War Department, in allotting Wacs to the theater, had
provided. This spread of grades and rat-

ings would have been generally appropriate for the MOS numbers held by the
women, but after a few months these were
not reserved for the Wacs but made available to the men, according to the system
of integration favored by WAC advisers in
the United States. Any other course, according to Colonel Ginsburgh, "would
have caused much ill-feeling among the
men."[96] Grades received by Wacs were
below the theater average for men in
skilled jobs; they were also somewhat
lower than those received by Wacs in
Europe and Italy. On the other hand, they
were higher than those of male labor battalions and unskilled service troops in the
theater, and even a single stripe on a
woman's sleeve provoked so much caustic
comment from unrated men that Colonel
Ginsburgh recommended that, in the
future, women in the Army be given no
grades. WAC officers' promotions were
likewise slower than in other theaters,
about half never being promoted in the
theater.[97]

Because theater policies differed, awards
and decorations were given less frequently
than in other theaters. Although Pacific
Wacs had moved more rapidly and lived
longer under field conditions than those in
Europe, they received only about one
fourth as many Bronze Stars. In some
cases there existed some feeling that

[92] Material atchd to Ltr, WAC Stf Dir AFPAC to
Dep Dir WAC, 8 Nov 45. Hobby files.
[93] Personal ltr, Lt Col Mera Galloway, WAC Stf
Dir AFPAC, to Dir WAC, 28 Dec 45. WDWAC 320.
[94] Memo, WAC Stf Dir FEAF for CG FEAF.
WDWAC 319.1 Pacific.
[95] Hist Rpt, May 45. Folder II, WAC Det FEASC.
[96] WAC Draft AFPAC Reply. Confirmed by Interv
cited n. 50(1).
[97] (1) AFPAC Reply, both versions. (2) STM-30,
Strength of the Army, Jul 45, p. 41. (3) Morale Evalu-
·ation Rpt on Women's Servs, AFPAC, Jul 45, incl in
Ltr, Actg Stf Dir AFPAC to Dir WAC, 11 Aug 45.
WAC Cl files.

Bronze Stars and similar awards were inappropriate for women. One WAC sergeant noted that identical recommendations were forwarded by her section chief for herself and for the men under her supervision, but that only the men's were approved.[98] There was only one award of the Meritorious Service Unit Plaque, elsewhere quite common among WAC units.[99]

The Question of Expense

There existed from the beginning the question of whether the expense of maintaining women in such an area was not so prohibitive as to nullify any possible gain from even the most superlative efficiency. Theater authorities discounted this view almost completely, and were unable to understand how it had become so widely circulated. To some extent its spread seemed due to hundreds of statements in soldier mail, such as "As far as replacing men, that is purely a myth; it takes more poor GI's to work for them, and more to guard them, than they come anywhere near replacing"; or, from an officer, "The lady GI's haven't freed any men for the fighting fronts. They require special quarters, special handling, and so damned many MP's to guard them that it more than eats up the manpower relieved." Some thought that it took "three or four GI's" for every Wac, or even, "For every Wac that is sent overseas it required approximately eight soldiers to take care of her."[100]

Actual employers of Wacs could find little basis for such charges. "Wacs needed some extra care and help in setting up their housing," the USASOS G-1 stated, "but a headquarters has to have administrative troops, and where will you find male stenographers?"[101] A section chief noted, "When we moved, we had to provide areas for women, but we would have had to set them up for the nurses anyway; it was only a few days' work, and didn't have to be done again for months."[102] The general view was that it was not an uneconomical procedure to employ service troops to set up facilities for key office workers, regardless of sex, although the service battalions concerned could not be expected to concur in the opinion.

Some guards had also undoubtedly been required, much against the women's wishes, but in daylight hours only one or two were employed to march the whole unit to work, which took a very few minutes. At night, for attendance at unit parties, the duty was a purely voluntary one. As for gate guards, the comment of Colonel Boyce, the second WAC Director, after a visit late in 1945, was:

It was noted that guards were considered necessary and were therefore assigned to all the other groups in the forward area, i.e., nursing personnel, medical groups, and general headquarters areas. It was established that no more guards were required for WAC personnel than for other types of noncombat personnel assigned to duty in these forward areas.[103]

Apart from the labor involved, there remained the question of whether WAC housing, messing, and other accommodations had not been prohibitively expensive, or cost much more than the men's. There was little evidence that they had, although

---

[98] Interv with Miss Dorothy Pat Costello, 4 Aug 48.

[99] AFPAC Reply, both versions: 1 Meritorious Service Unit Plaque; 4 Legion of Merit; 3 Soldier's Medal; 50 Bronze Stars.

[100] All except second from GHQ AFPAC Summary, Comments on Women's Servs, 16 Jun 45, in possession of former WAC Stf Dir; second from WDBPR file.

[101] Interv with Col Ginsburgh, 24 Jul 44.

[102] Interv with Col Merle H. Davis, Chief OO WESPAC, 24 Jul 47.

[103] Boyce Rpt.

Wacs were often allotted the best of the enlisted accommodations already available to a headquarters.[104]

The choice of camp site went according to the priority rating of each organization. Thus, USASOS usually rated housing, on a priority basis, after GHQ, USAFFE, FEAF, and the Sixth and Eighth Armies. The housing of USASOS Wacs was therefore ordinarily less desirable than that of the men of those groups, although possibly superior to that of USASOS men. The History of USAFFE noted briefly, "The WAC were not accorded special quarters and special transportation or special supplies. In New Guinea, their quarters, mess, and recreation were comparable to those of male troops." [105]

The general impression that Wacs had more expensive quarters seemed due largely to the fact that visitors and historians arriving several months after the advanced echelons found some comforts present. Reliable sources ascribed these only to the persistent scavenging of the women themselves, abetted by the ever-willing labor of the endless supply of GI suitors. In a typical camp on Leyte, Wacs were assigned the usual dirt-floored tents, but the women's dates brought them floors for the tents, a piece at a time. Wacs also traded with the natives for heavy labor and useful or decorative items.

A far more useful source than either Army men or natives was the Navy, particularly the Seabees, who were no less willing to assist and far better supplied with the wherewithal. A settled WAC unit with reasonable access to land, sea, and air forces was therefore likely to have a landscaped camp site, graveled paths, floors in the tents, dressing tables, and, overhead, forming a heat-resisting space below the iron or canvas roof, the billowing nylon of a discarded parachute. Rec-

reation halls were likewise decorated with native thatch, palms, trophies, and bright-colored supply parachutes.[106]

WAC messes, equipment, and rations were identical with those of male units. The Southwest Pacific Area was the only overseas theater that could not ordinarily relieve skilled office workers of kitchen police duty, since civilian labor in New Guinea was limited, although some was available in Manila. Wacs staffed their own messes or, if eating at the consolidated mess, generally furnished their proportionate share of kitchen police, as they did in the United States. Two men were usually assigned to large WAC messes to service the field ranges and do heavy lifting.[107] Again, it appeared that any appearance of superiority was due only to improvised decorations or well-prepared food, which often ranked a WAC mess with higher headquarters messes. The Biak historical report stated, "The WAC Mess Hall soon became the envy of the post . . . the rumor flew that Wacs had better rations, but the Wacs refuted this." [108]

As for the matter of clothing, there would have been no question of unusual expense even had the Wacs received any. WAC staff members estimated that, even if the Army's usual policy of issuing all needed items had been followed, the cost of a Wac's clothing in malarious areas would have been only $124, in nonmalarious areas $143, as against $233 for comparable items for Wacs in the United States.[109]

---

[104] D/F cited n. 61.
[105] USAFFE Hist.
[106] (1) Boyce Rpt. (2) Griffith Account.
[107] AFPAC Reply, both versions.
[108] Folder, 5225th WAC Det, Drawer X–28368.
[109] *Ibid.* Also (1) Memo, Capt Stryker for Gen Baird, 12 Mar 45. (2) Check Sheet, Capt Stryker to CofS, USAFFE, 2 Apr 44. Tab 12, WAC Draft AFPAC Reply. (3) Personal ltr, Maj Gen R. J. Mar-

Medical Evacuation Rate

The greatest question concerning the efficiency of WAC employment in the theater did not concern expense of maintenance. It began to come to light only after the move to Manila: this was the increasing rate of loss for medical reasons. The earlier favorable rate had continued through the first months of 1945, even during the emergency period in Leyte. The change in health was at first not startling; in April the GHQ detachment noted a high percentage on sick call, but no serious diseases, and concluded, "Apparently many are in a somewhat run-down condition." In May the trend continued, again without serious disorders but with "the usual complaint [of] boils and other skin ailments, colds, or other manifestations of fatigue." [110]

When the evacuation rate was computed theater-wide, it was obvious that in these few months it had suddenly jumped from 98 per thousand per year to 267 per thousand. The chief surgeon's office informed Colonel Brown in February of 1945 that "At this rate, almost 20 percent of the command will be lost per year by evacuation." [111] By April, it was clear that the figure was more like 25 or 30 percent, and as much as 60 percent per year in some units, such as FEASC. The significant fact in this connection was that the 6 percent rate for men had not increased to any comparable degree. The rate was even more startling when compared to that of the Wacs in Europe and to those in India and China, whose losses were the same as the men's in those areas. The Pacific WAC rate was now virtually the same as that which Army nurses had experienced since their arrival, and four or five times that of the men. [112]

The onset of this loss rate had come too late to damage the efficiency record of the WAC's first year, but at this time commanders believed that this efficiency would have to be sustained for still another year of war in the Pacific. It therefore appeared urgent to discover, and if possible remove, the cause of the increased loss rate before it began to affect WAC strength more seriously. Brig. Gen. Guy B. Denit, Chief Surgeon, USASOS, stated emphatically that the increase had no medical or geographic cause: "Under the sanitary system we had by that time, a white woman could live in the area for any length of time as easily as a white man." [113]

Neither did the chief surgeon agree with some medical officers who believed that the Pacific theater, unlike the European, had no facilities for treating disorders peculiar to women, which thus required evacuation, whereas a man could be treated and returned to duty. One doctor alleged that he and other medical officers were

. . . unable to do anything for Wacs reporting to the hospital with such diseases, as there are no instruments or medications furnished to Army hospitals overseas for their treatment. It seemed a waste of space and manpower to send Wacs overseas and then not have medical instruments and medications available to treat them. [114]

[110] Hist Rpts, Apr, May 45. Folder, 5200th WAC Det, Drawer X–29443.

[111] Memo, Asst Chief Surg for WAC Dir USAFFE, 16 Feb 45. REMD 704.11. In possession of Mary-Agnes Brown.

[112] All rates and other health statistics cited, unless otherwise specified, are from Craighill SWPA Rpt or AFPAC Reply.

[113] Interv, 24 Jul 47.

[114] Tech Int Rpt T/PFI–2614, SID, Hq 4th SvC, to CG ASF, 23 Jul 45. G–2 MID files.

shall, CofS AFPAC, to Gen Stivers, OPD, 14 May 45, (4) Ltr, Asst AG USAFPAC to CG USAFWESPAC, 31 Jul 45. AG 420 (7–31–45) WA. Tab 12, WAC Draft AFPAC Reply.

No women medical officers were employed in the Pacific as they had been by the European and Mediterranean theaters.

This explanation of the loss rate was contradicted by General Denit, who stated that he had available every supply and facility, could get any needed gynecological instrument by air, and had deep X-ray machines, radium, and other equipment. General Denit's view was for the most part supported by the statistics, which showed that less than one fifth of the total loss was due to disorders peculiar to women. The War Department's medical consultant, Major Craighill, after a visit, noted, "Gynecological conditions are usually mild in character and transitory in occurrence." [115]

Neither could the high rate be attributed to undue medical lenience in the return of women to the United States. Major Craighill indicated that "an even more lenient policy in regard to return . . . would seem indicated for the good of the group and to salvage individuals for continued service in the States."

The only notable medical deficiency which was cited by theater authorities was that of poor initial medical screening in the United States. Major Craighill reported:

Medical officers in all overseas theaters commented on the inadequacy of screening of women for overseas duty. It was thought to be the primary cause of medical evacuation rates for women, especially in the Southwest Pacific, where they were far higher than for other personnel.[116]

A survey in the FEASC WAC detachment indicated that as many as 50 percent of the medical returns were attributed to poor medical screening in the United States, with a few evacuees having been in the theater less than a month.[117] On the other hand, the screening of women for service in the Pacific had been as good as that of men, with identical selection procedures. Also, four fifths of the European theater's Wacs, and most of those for India and other areas, had been selected, like the Pacific's, after the end of the Auxiliary requirements for physical examinations.

With no medical deficiency thus entirely sufficing to explain more than a part of the loss, General Denit stated instead that in his opinion the primary cause of the higher loss rate was to be sought among theater policies other than medical. Independently, WAC inspectors also arrived at the conclusion that the cause of the higher WAC rate of loss did not lie in the environment but in theater policies toward women that did not apply to men. Colonel Boyce, the second WAC Director, stated after an inspection visit, "It is believed that the experiences of Wacs in the Pacific which adversely affected their effective utilization were not inherent in the geographical location." [118] The same view was expressed by Major Craighill after an inspection trip in 1945. Major Craighill felt that there was nothing necessarily dangerous about the area for women, and made recommendations for improvement that were all in the fields of supply and administration.

Deficiencies in Uniform and Supply

Among nonmedical deficiencies which had possibly contributed to the medical loss rate, the most conspicuous was that of

---

[115] Unless otherwise cited, all of Major Craighill's comments are from Craighill SWPA Rpt.
[116] Hist of Women's Med Unit, draft by Lt Col Margaret D. Craighill, 23 Jul 46. SGO Hist Div.
[117] WAC Sec USAFFE Hist Rpt, Mar, Apr 45. Folder II, WAC Det FEASC.
[118] Boyce Rpt.

the clothing supply.[119] Women had in fact faced a difficult and dangerous environment less well equipped than the men in the same headquarters. It was noted particularly that dermatitis, sometimes popularly called "jungle rot," led all other causes for evacuation of women, even though medical officers had originally believed that women would prove less susceptible because of higher standards of personal cleanliness and more frequent laundering of garments. There appeared to be some obvious connection with the fact that the WAC service uniform had been the heavy herringbone twill, well known to cause skin irritation to women even in the United States. In fact, in the India–Burma theater the chief surgeon had refused to let Wacs wear this garment at any time, pronouncing it a major health hazard in a tropical climate. On the other hand, some medical officers noted that even had the Wacs possessed summer khaki like the men's, women might possibly still have had a higher dermatitis rate because of their more sensitive skins.

In addition, it appeared possible that the rate of loss for malaria had increased wherever Wacs substituted their cotton shirts for the coverall top, since the shirts were lighter in weight than the men's and not believed mosquitoproof by The Quartermaster General. On the other hand, as both General Denit and Colonel Brown pointed out, experimentation had never conclusively indicated what weight of shirt was really mosquitoproof, and Navy nurses in the area wore skirts instead of slacks, so that the Wacs' uniforms might possibly have offered as good protection as any other type of garment.

Other minor possibilities were also noted. It appeared that the rate of respiratory disorders might have been increased by lack of protective footwear. The shortage of all garments had apparently increased illness during rainy seasons when not enough dry coveralls were available to permit a change. There was also some evidence that the regular WAC wool socks, heavy rayon underwear, low oxfords, and other issue items were not particularly suitable to the area.

Up to this time, all attempts at remedial action had merely demonstrated that, if women were launched into a campaign improperly equipped, no "business as usual" would produce the requisite supplies. Theater action to secure mosquitoproof slacks for women, and all other needed items, was begun in 1944 in the month of the Wacs' arrival in Australia.[120] The months of May and June were consumed in Quartermaster staff studies as to the proper amendments that should be recommended in theater Tables of Equipment. The matter was not as simple as it appeared to nonexperts in supply matters, since there were many items of WAC uniform, undergarments, and footgear to be considered, as well as the opinions of medical and technical specialists on the proper weight and design of slacks and shirts. On 6 July 1944, a large-scale conference on WAC supply was held by representatives of USAFFE and USASOS with visitors from Operations Division of the War Department General Staff. This produced no immediate results, and later in July the assistant staff director appealed by personal letter to Colonel Hobby to expedite matters by securing immediate War Department authorization for ordinary khaki slacks. In reply she was informed that The

---

[119] Interv with Capt Letallier, 9 Jan 46. Entire following discussion is based on interviews and statistics already cited.

[120] Except as otherwise documented, the supply discussion is from the monthly WAC Sec USAFFE Hist Rpts.

Quartermaster General was already developing specifications for a slacks suit, but could not expend funds to procure or ship any item without requisitions and shipping priorities from the theater. It was not until after the movement of most of the Wacs from Australia had begun in August that the theater requisition for slacks went forward.[121]

Among women moving out to Hollandia and other bases, only the 6 percent working for FEAF were reported as equipped as well as men, since General Kenney had refused to let them board planes until they had been issued men's khaki trousers from the ample stocks of men's clothing in Australia.[122] Issue of men's clothing was considered by some other commanders, but generally rejected because the garments were ill-fitting and required "unsightly" alterations; it was decided to await arrival of women's slacks from the United States.

However, following the theater's requisition in August, there ensued another two months' delay for queries and replies concerning specifications. On 14 October 1944, the War Department gave its final approval to specifications for women's slacks, and informed the theater that the slacks would be available in only ninety days—one fourth the usual procurement time for men's clothing. This schedule was very nearly met, and in only four more months the first shipment of slacks and proper-weight shirts was on the pier in California. Not only was this still a considerable distance from New Guinea, but it was by this time February of 1945, and the Wacs were moving on to Manila.

It was confidently expected that the slacks would reach the women in Manila; some 75,000 pairs were promptly shipped from the United States, 5,000 of them by air. However, upon reaching the theater,

they were off-loaded at way stations and never reached the Wacs. When queried by the War Department, the theater explained that it lacked transportation to lift the newly received slacks from various depots, so that assembly in the Manila area was never accomplished.[123]

A similar difficulty accounted for the lack of normal maintenance stocks of standard items such as field shoes, coveralls, and undergarments. Maintenance stocks had been routinely authorized for shipment even before the first Wacs left the United States for Australia, and numerous shipments had been made, few of which reached the Wacs.[124] The difficulty was the same as that already discovered by the Fifth Army in Italy—that the supplies for a tiny group became lost or misplaced when handled in the routine supply channels for men's clothing. In this case the difficulty was a hundred times intensified by the distances and shipping problems in the New Guinea area, which had no highways or railroads and few good docks.

The problem was illustrated by six WAC clothing shipments that were eventually traced.[125] Two of these shipments reached the areas before the Wacs, were put on sale in officers' stores, and were "badly depleted" by unidentified custom-

---

[121] (1) Personal ltr, Capt Juanita Stryker, Asst WAC Stf Dir SWPA, to Dir Hobby, 12 Jul 44, and reply from Capt Patricia Lee Chance, Exec WAC, 16 Aug 44. WDWAC 320.2 SWPA. (2) WAC Draft AFPAC Reply, Tab 12 (omitted from theater-approved version).

[122] According to his memoirs, *General Kenney Reports* (New York, 1949).

[123] AFPAC Reply.

[124] Ltr, TAG to COMINCH SWPA, CG SFPOE, and CofT, 21 Apr 44. AG 400 (4–18–44) OB–S–E–SPMOT; Tab 8 of WAC Draft AFPAC Reply.

[125] Discussion from theater-approved version, AFPAC Reply. Six examples are in WAC Draft, deleted by theater.

ers before the Wacs arrived. Two others went to a base where Wacs were never stationed, and remained there. General Campbell noted, "You don't run a Liberty ship up and down the coast to pick up a few WAC shoes." [126] One went to a station where about one half the theater's Wacs were then located, and was well utilized. The remaining one also reached a WAC detachment, although months after its arrival. General Campbell added, "Supply for a million men spread over 4,000 miles was difficult, but for 5,000 Wacs in small scattered groups it was desperate." [127]

Even if supplies were received by the women, it was difficult to keep them, in view of the usual system of movement of Wacs by air. This explained part of the situation of the GHQ detachment on Leyte. As early as September of 1944, Colonel Baird had unsuccessfully recommended to USAFFE's deputy chief of staff that, when a WAC unit moved by air, its equipment accompany it, since "Experience has shown that otherwise it is a long time before such items become available." [128] This was not considered practicable, but upon departure from Hollandia the WAC supply officer had personally watched the crating and loading on a ship of whatever clothing and equipment could not be carried by air. When this did not arrive in Leyte, investigation disclosed that the vessel was at another base, towing two barges, and could not be turned around for a few crates of WAC clothing.

Similarly, when the censorship unit moved by air from Port Moresby to Biak, some forty-eight tons of equipment and personal baggage had to be left for shipment by water. Two months later, when this still had not arrived, the detachment commander protested that it was "critically needed . . . especially clothing of personnel," but the regulating officer in-

formed her that there was no prospect of any ship calling at Port Moresby to pick it up. [129]

As for nonissue items such as girdles, brassières, and pajamas, purchase of these was not possible in Australia because of rationing restrictions. Wacs got 25 clothing coupons a year, but the purchase of a girdle required 10 coupons, pajamas 12, and a brassière 5. In New Guinea and the Philippines these were unprocurable. Colonel Brown recommended to USASOS that brassières be added to allowances:

These items are absolutely necessary and are peculiar to the needs of women. Enlisted men are furnished all necessary items; therefore enlisted women should not be expected to buy items which are necessary for wear. Women are continually requesting families and friends to mail these articles, but with the uncertainty of arrival by mail, they are often without these necessary articles.

The theater therefore four times submitted a request for the issue of such items, but was four times refused; it never achieved the solution, found successful in other overseas theaters, of procuring the items for sale in post exchanges. In fact, post exchange supplies of any sort for women were extremely scarce. Several large groups had never to this date been able to purchase any sanitary napkins—these also being considered "nonessential" items which were not issued to women, but in other theaters usually purchased at post exchanges. [130]

In the final analysis, most observers concluded that the factor of supply had been a major one in the WAC loss rate,

---

[126] Interv, 31 Jul 47.

[127] Unless otherwise documented, entire discussion above is from: (1) Monthly WAC Sec USAFFE Hist Rpts. (2) Tp Conv, 2 Feb 51.

[128] Check Sheet, 30 Sep 44. Folder, 5205th WAC Det, Drawer X–29853.

[129] Folder, 5203d WAC Det, Drawer X–28040.

[130] AFPAC Check Sheet, WAC Sec to G–3, 19 Apr 45. In possession of Mary-Agnes Brown.

particularly in the rate of loss for dermatitis, malaria, and respiratory disorders. Had it been possible to retain the women in Australia until they were fully equipped for field conditions, as had been possible in England, the educated guess was that the rate in excess of men's losses might have been lowered.

Morale

There was every indication that the women's morale had held up excellently at most stations. All observers agreed that, as in Italy, the one factor which had done most to sustain morale was the nearness to actual combat. Units in the most forward areas were consistently found to have the highest morale. The race to get forward had become a matter of competition, and WAC officers reported that the panacea for supply shortages and primitive living conditions consisted in "excitement and pride in being the first Wacs." [131] A typical group upon disbandment wrote sentimentally of the Leyte experiences—tents, candles, no supply, mud, foxholes, air alerts, rain—and added, with no apparent sense of incongruity, "We'll never have a detachment so ideal and so perfect again." [132]

Even when Wacs were not actually near the combat area, the constant presence of combat-wounded and released prisoners gave a sense of immediacy to their efforts. Wherever possible—as for example at the 51st General Hospital—women were allowed to visit hospital wards. They saved their beer and cigarette rations, cookies from home, and flowers grown around their tents to share with the patients, with resulting good effect not only on the wounded, but on the women themselves. [133]

Units everywhere had adopted mon-

keys, dogs, chickens; smuggled a duck on shipboard; cherished unidentifiable native animals. Songs were invented for all subjects ("If you meet a looie with big blue eyes, you can look but you can't fraternize".) [134] The women took pride in improvising: a Christmas tree was made of native thatch tied to a bamboo trunk, decorated with scrap metal from enemy planes. When most Christmas packages failed to get through, inspectors noted that "they opened the few that came and shared them like sisters," while one supply sergeant filled their shoes with "gifts" of pistol belts and towels. Desiring a green-and-gold WAC guidon for the funeral of a member of the FEASC WAC detachment, the women improvised one from parachute lining, dyed with atabrine and green ink. [135]

By comparison with problems of morale among noncombat men, the Wacs' good morale appeared even more striking, for women seldom complained about, or were depressed by, factors that were high on the men's list—mail service, rotation, officers' superior privileges, and the lack of good movies and other entertainment. The only common complaint factor was that of food. Particularly noteworthy was the mildness of WAC complaints about their company officers' deficiencies as compared to the complaints by noncombat men about their officers. [136]

[131] AFPAC Reply, both versions. See also Hist Rpts. Folder, 5225th WAC Det, Drawer X–28368.

[132] Correspondence folder, 5205th WAC Det, Drawer X–29853.

[133] Hist Rpts, Jan, Feb 45. Folder II, WAC Det FEASC.

[134] Interv with Lt Mary B. Warner, 3 Oct 47.

[135] (1) Folder I, WAC Det FEAF, Drawer X–25096. (2) Hist Rpts, Jan, Feb 45. Folder II, WAC Det FEASC. (3) Quotation in Folder, 5225th WAC Det, Drawer X–28368.

[136] For typical noncombat male complaints, see History of South Pacific Base Command by Hist Sec, G–2, Hq SOPACBACOM. OCMH.

However, there appeared to be a possibility that the generally high morale had accounted for the moderate loss rate of the first year. Company commanders voiced the opinion that there was a general "end of the line" feeling in Manila, at which time women who had actually been ailing for months suddenly gave up to their illness. Medical officers noted that, with women, illness was more likely to mark the breaking point in tension, rather than the spree of some sort in which men might seek escape from prolonged strain.

In addition, there was some evidence that the factor of social pressure, which had helped to sustain morale, had simultaneously damaged health. At all stations not under actual attack, there continued to be more unit dances and approved group parties than the women had energy to attend. The enlisted Wacs were the chief source of American dates for the enlisted men, who vied for invitations to the WAC recreation halls and in providing unit entertainments approved for WAC attendance, with bands, decorations, refreshments, and other inducements. WAC bulletin boards in Manila were filled with bright-colored posters carrying mass invitations. Some listed the menu, promising ice cream or some other rare delicacy, for the Wacs soon became blasé about masculine company and refused to stir without the guarantee of food.

On one occasion fraternal bloodshed was narrowly averted when one unit's trucks appeared, flying false colors, and carried off the Wacs destined for another unit's dance. No Wac was so old or unattractive as to be neglected, although commanders feared that this would some day cause a painful readjustment to the facts of life in the United States. While such attention was of great assistance to morale, the constant social pressure increased the ever-present problem of fatigue. Group or mass entertainment had always proved tiring to WAC units, but in most Pacific bases there was often no alternative recreation. Colonel Brown early recommended that, at well-established camps, service clubs for joint use be provided, but this was seldom considered practicable.[137]

Length of Working Day

In accordance with tropical custom, working hours generally began at seven or eight in the morning and ended at nine or ten at night, in order to permit time off in the heat of the day for leisurely meals. Thus, at Intersec headquarters the working day covered fifteen hours, from seven in the morning to ten at night, with three-hour breaks for meals.

While the relative merits of the system on a six-day week were not primarily of WAC concern, since all personnel was affected, inspectors noted adverse results in certain organizations staffed almost completely by Wacs and which, because of the pressure of work, were obliged to work these hours for seven days a week. The all-Wac Central Mail Directory was reported as working such hours for seven days a week, with no day off for five months; the same was true of the all-Wac Casualty Section and the Machine Records Unit.[138] In some cases it appeared that women did not avail themselves of the full time off for meals when work was heavy or an operation being launched. An FEASC management control survey noted, "In general the enlisted women were working longer

[137] Memo and Ltr cited n. 53.

[138] (1) Interv cited n. 119. (2) AFPAC Reply, both versions, except that official version omits names of specific offices having no time off.

hours than enlisted men performing similar skilled duties." [139] Also, women's time-consuming chores such as laundry were usually not done during the mealtime breaks but after hours, by their own preference. [140]

Inspectors were unable to determine whether adverse effects were due to lesser endurance than men in the same offices, or to the women's tendency to put in overtime. In any case, even without overtime, the hours of work were longer than those used successfully with civilian women in either the United States or Britain.

Among reported instances, the greatest damage to health occurred among the Hollandia Wacs in General McMullen's Far East Air Service Command. These stood reveille every morning at 0530, walked back and forth some distance to work three times a day in all weather, worked an official minimum of ten hours a day, until ten o'clock at night, seven days a week, with only Sunday afternoons off, these being reportedly spent standing in line to get to laundry facilities. After less than a year of this schedule, the medical loss rate in the FEASC WAC detachment jumped alarmingly, from 3 per month in January of 1945 to 30 per month in June.

The Air Surgeon reported that "an increasing number of cases are on record for nervousness and exhaustion," and recommended that personnel be given one full day off per week to relieve "nervous tension." The June rate, if continued, would total more than 62 percent medical evacuation per year, an unprecedented loss even for combat troops. The staff director for FEAF supported the Air Surgeon's recommendation, noting that offices were not really busy; it was believed that the day off could profitably be applied to all personnel to avoid discrimination in favor of women. However, General McMullen rejected the request for Sunday mornings off, and informed the surgeon, "Medical records do not indicate any situation . . . to cause me serious concern." [141]

Discipline and Morals

In the minds of some observers a question arose as to whether the medical loss rate could have been affected by the type of moral disintegration popularly supposed to afflict men and women in the tropics. However, if such disintegration took place, it was more subtle than could be measured statistically, and did not consist of the gross sexual immorality about which most rumors centered. On the contrary, the pregnancy rate for the Wacs' chief period of service in the Pacific was, like that of other overseas theaters, less than one half the world-wide WAC rate, which was itself low by civilian standards. During the period after the arrival in Manila, with the relaxation of previous restrictions on marriage, the WAC pregnancy rate rose considerably, but was still less than the world-wide rate, and about the same as that for nurses in the Pacific. Of the theater's 5,500 Wacs, only 111 were reported returned home pregnant, with an estimated half of these being married women. However, in spite of the frequent restriction to compounds, the Pacific Wacs' rate was considerably higher than that of the European theater, which placed no special restrictions on women. [142]

---

[139] Hist Rpt, May 45. Folder II, WAC Det FEASC.

[140] Interv with Maj Charlee L. Kelly, 28 Jul 47.

[141] Memo, WAC Stf Dir FEAF for CG FEAF through CG FEASC, 19 Jun 45, with Rpt of Surg and Ind, CG FEASC to CG FEAF, 22 Jul 45. AG 333.1. Correspondence folder, WAC Det FEAF, Drawer X–25096. See also Ltr cited n. 86.

[142] For world-wide rates, see Ch. XXXI, below. For SWPA rates, see Craighill SWPA Rpt.

Venereal disease rates were likewise so low as to be negligible. One commander of a unit of over 700 women stated that she did not, in the entire time, have any new cases.[143]

Further evidence that no gross moral breakdown occurred was offered by the fact that the Wacs were gradually able to convince the enlisted men that their mission in the area was a military one. Statistics on the trend of enlisted men's comments showed that a remarkable decline in the number of derogatory comments took place as soon as the men actually met the Wacs. From a high of 90 percent unfavorable comments in the month before the Wacs arrived, the number fell slowly until, in the month in which demobilization began, only 28 percent of comments were still unfavorable, many of these being from units that had never seen Wacs.[144]

WAC detachment commanders frequently expressed an uneasy belief that the discipline or perhaps merely the *esprit* of their detachments was not as high as that which they had known outside the theater. Some felt that the women's habitual evasion of petty restrictions had undermined respect for more important rules and for those in authority. Others noted a lessened sense of conventionality, decorum, or discreet behavior; the WAC inspector general added, "Dress them like tramps and they may act like tramps."[145] However, detachment disciplinary records seldom revealed other than exceedingly minor offenses attributed chiefly to tension, exhaustion, or loss of respect for authority. One detachment's worst case was a woman who was AWOL from midnight until three in the morning. Another detachment's worst was a woman who, after fifteen months on a particularly exhausting job, was "on the verge of a complete physical and mental breakdown,"

went AWOL, and "spent her entire absence in a native hut sleeping."[146]

A number of minor offenses concerned violation of the ban on officer-enlisted dating, although the theater experienced fewer problems in this respect than the European, since most Wacs were already restricted to approved group entertainment. Restrictions on officer-enlisted association were frequently severe; at some USASOS bases in New Guinea, even husbands and blood relatives were for a time not permitted to see Wacs of a different status. WAC staff officers stated, "It is believed that this has resulted in resentment of persons concerned and in flagrant violations."[147]

The prohibition was originally adopted only over the nonconcurrence of the staff director, in line with a previous ruling that nurses would not be allowed to date corpsmen. WAC company officers noted that they were obliged to punish their enlisted women while officer dates were not punished; officers sometimes removed their insignia to attend unit dances, and at other times flagrantly violated the rule. Combat units in the area merely tore up such notices; while in one case the officer concerned was the head of the local military police who were charged with enforcement. Air Forces and USAFFE headquarters ordinarily enforced nonassociation rules less strictly than USASOS, thus fur-

---

[143] Craighill SWPA Rpt.

[144] (1) Tab 13, WAC Draft AFPAC Reply. Also Surv, Comments on Women's Servs, 16 Jun 45, GHQ USAFPAC, copy in possession of former WAC Stf Dir. (2) Morale Evaluation Rpt, Attitude Towards Women's Servs, Jul 45, Hq AFPAC, incl in Ltr, Actg Stf Dir AFPAC, to Dir WAC, 11 Aug 45. WAC C1 file SWPA.

[145] Interv cited n. 119.

[146] Folders, 5200th, 5203d, 5205th, and 5215th WAC Dets. Quotation from 5215th WAC Det, 21 Aug–20 Sep 45.

[147] WAC Draft AFPAC Reply.

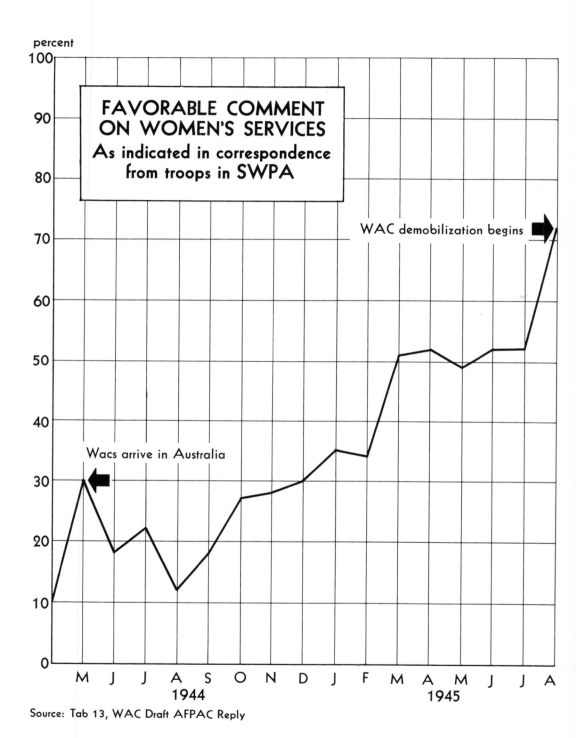

percent

FAVORABLE COMMENT ON WOMEN'S SERVICES
As indicated in correspondence from troops in SWPA

WAC demobilization begins

Wacs arrive in Australia

1944

1945

Source: Tab 13, WAC Draft AFPAC Reply

ther complicating the problem of unequal punishment.

After Wacs reached Manila, the problem began to assume added importance, and the WAC staff director again requested permission for the social association of "relatives and friends of long standing" carrying passes from their WAC commanding officers. The theater again refused to set an over-all policy. WAC company officers, when asked to make suggestions for the improvement of discipline, included "a definite policy for officer-enlisted relationships"; "fewer rules and more rigid enforcement of same." [148]

An additional restriction, more severe than any in the European or Mediterranean theaters, was FEASC's customary prohibition against marriage of its members; as applied to women, it allowed them to marry only if they became pregnant. In this command, women engaged to men about to leave for combat often quite frankly consulted the WAC staff director and the chaplain to ask why they should not take that course. To prevent this, the staff director repeatedly attempted to secure more lenient terms for both men and women of American citizenship; this was eventually granted by General McMullen only after the headquarters reached Manila. [149] Only 121 of the theater's 5,500 Wacs married in the theater during the war. [150]

Restrictions on Daily Life

In the opinion of many observers, one of the most serious handicaps to the health of women in the area had been the restriction to locked compounds in the majority of stations in New Guinea, a factor which did not affect male troops. It was noted that, among medical causes of evacuation for women, psychoses and neuropsychi-

atric disorders were second only to dermatitis. It was always to remain a matter for debate whether the unusual restrictions placed upon women were necessary and inherent in the dangers of the Pacific area, or were an unnecessary creation of arbitrary theater policies. Colonel Brown continued throughout the stay in New Guinea to recommend the abolition of the system, but few modifications were ever reported with the exception of the GHQ unit in Hollandia, the smaller Air Forces group, and minor adjustments elsewhere. [151]

Three resulting unfavorable factors were noted. The most obvious was the noise, crowding, and lack of privacy which, in the opinion of medical officers, fostered mental disorders. Even if the area was not noisy, women experienced a "sense of confinement" which made them unable to relax after strenuous office hours or tiring mass entertainment. Major Craighill reported that women appeared to value privacy more than men, and that even among nurses, who as officers were less crowded in tents than enlisted women, the rate of loss for psychiatric reasons was increased by lack of privacy.

More important, in medical officers' opinions, were the physical disorders fostered by simple lack of physical exercise, recreation, and rest. Major Craighill wrote, "Facilities for exercise are lacking in most places. . . . In the tropics, more

---

[148] (1) Marginal note by Colonel Brown on draft of this chapter. OCMH. (2) Fraternization in FEAF was forbidden by Stf Memo 15, 30 Jul 44. Folder, WAC Det FEAF I. (3) Interv with former CO of a USASOS WAC Det, 22 Jul 47. (4) Check Sheet, Hq USAFFE, WAC Stf Dir, to DCofS, 23 Jul 45, Tab 15 to WAC Draft AFPAC Reply. (5) Quotation from Correspondence folder, 5200th WAC Det, Drawer X–29443.

[149] Memo cited n. 141.

[150] Griffith Account, "Statistics May 44–Sep 45."

[151] Sources cited n. 51.

than elsewhere, proper exercise is important." According to one WAC adviser,

> The greatest deficiency in recreational facilities since the Wacs left Australia has been that at no time has there been a place to which they could go for a three-day pass and get away from the mental strain of group living.[152]

The Pacific area obviously offered few advantages in this respect. Leave areas for men existed in Australia, operated by the Red Cross, but in spite of Colonel Brown's repeated recommendations, the handful of Wacs remaining in Australia were refused permission to use them until near the end of the war, when the Red Cross replaced one of its workers who had blocked admission of women.[153] The Air Transport Command also operated a regular "leave shuttle" to Australia, carrying men from New Guinea on 3-day passes. Although this shuttle was organized in Hollandia by the date of the Wacs' arrival, and although ATC historians noted that it often operated half empty, it appeared to be seldom employed by most headquarters, and in any case Wacs were not given a quota.[154]

Army nurses were originally allowed leaves from forward areas every six months, and were transported by special planes to leave areas,[155] but as the headquarters advanced, this privilege was also considerably restricted, and it never applied to Wacs. During the entire stay in New Guinea, no leaves or passes were reported as given to enlisted women at most installations, because of the absence of any approved place to spend them. Major Craighill noted that, for both Wacs and nurses:

> Recent restrictions against nurses' leave to Australia completely deprive personnel of all rest areas. None are provided in the islands for women for even short periods. Such facilities are especially needed because of the unusual restrictions on women's activities and the lack of outside places for recreation.

In those areas where men also had no rest areas or were not allowed to use the leave shuttle, the situation appeared unavoidable, although some WAC advisers questioned whether a local commander's action in restricting women to compounds did not obligate him to find some means of equalizing the resulting mental tension and physical sluggishness.

Also increased, in company officers' opinion, was the women's resentment, disobedience, and immature conduct. As the women were well aware, "restriction to quarters" was ordinarily employed by the Army only for punishment. When restriction to quarters was imposed by court-martial, Army Regulations contained the caution that it "will not be imposed in excess of three months."[156] Even though the Wacs' custody was protective and not punitive, it was difficult to find a previous occasion in Army history in which a soldier had been kept in protective custody for a year or eighteen months. If the system was indeed required, as theater authorities insisted, to prevent rape of Wacs by Negro troops in New Guinea, the War Department was not in a position to protest command policies. However, to WAC leaders in the United States, viewing the problem from a distance, it appeared that, if an area was so dangerous as to require the long-term confinement of soldiers of one sex, such soldiers should not be considered for employment in that area.

---

[152] AFPAC Reply, both versions.

[153] Ltr cited n. 46.

[154] (1) Interv with Dr. Samuel Milner, author of Victory in Papua, a forthcoming volume in this series. (2) The ATC in the Pacific, 7 Dec 41–1 Aug 44, p. 148. USAF Hist Div.

[155] Annual Rpt, 1944, Chief Surg, USASOS, p. 35. SGO R–3232 (1–7–47).

[156] A Manual for Courts-Martial, U.S. Army, pp. 94, 104.

In her final report to the War Department, Major Craighill stated that in her opinion the rate of WAC loss was definitely increased by the lack of healthful recreation, the undue restriction in compounds, and the failure to treat women as responsible adults. This opinion coincided closely with that reached by The Surgeon General's Office in Washington concerning the rate of loss for men in the area:

The health of troops is directly affected by command policies and procedures governing rotation, discipline, recreation, and the provision of incentive and motivation. It seems probable that these are influential factors.[157]

Inferior WAC Commanders

Inspectors' reports indicated that in certain detachments the sick rate had possibly been aggravated by inferior WAC command practices. It was known that some company officers with low efficiency ratings had been unloaded on early shipments by commands in the United States. However, these were not unduly numerous, and a number of excellent company officers were also in the theater. Unfortunately, by a combination of circumstances, quite often the inferior officers were placed initially in company work from which staff directors were later unable to get them removed, while trained company officers were assigned to office work.

Thus, the first shipment of Wacs had contained a number of trained company officers, intended to staff future companies. Instead, since USAFFE headquarters desired to set up its censorship detachment immediately, these officers were included, with the promise of reassignment to company work when more enlisted women arrived. However, in spite of the efforts of the staff director, their later release was

never concurred in by the central directory.[158]

In several cases, officers were assigned to company work who had already failed at it in the United States. Possibly the worst example cited in inspection reports was that of the FEAF WAC detachment. Soon after its establishment, the USAFFE inspector general discovered improper assignments, low morale, irregularities in detachment records, undue delay of mail, partiality and lack of interest in enlisted women's needs, and profane language on the part of the WAC commander, as well as threats to enlisted women in detachment meetings.[159] Unsatisfactory conditions were attributed by the inspector general chiefly to the WAC unit commander, who had been sent overseas by the Fourth Service Command after being relieved of two different WAC commands in the United States, one with an efficiency rating of Unsatisfactory. The situation also reflected the initial lack of a staff director. Because of the unit's unexpectedly sudden beginnings with borrowed personnel, the FEAF WAC staff director, Maj. Mary L. Kersey, did not arrive from the United States until the unit was already in Hollandia, and was then unable to correct the already-established situation.

At this time Brig. Gen. Harry H. Baird informed the USAFFE chief of staff:

A recent inspection of the FEAF WAC Detachment by the Inspector General of this headquarters makes it clearly evident that adequate supervision of the WAC Company Commander and administration of the WAC Detachment has not been exercised. . . . It

[157] Memo, Dir Contl Div SGO for Gen Kirk, 12 Jul 45, with Tab A from Chief Consultant in Medicine, Tab B from Chief Consultant in Surgery, and Tab C from Dir Neuropsychiatry Consultants Div. SGO Classif MEDC–701.
[158] Boyce Rpt.
[159] WAC Draft AFPAC Reply only; certified copy of USAFFE Inspection Rpt atchd.

is apparent that full use had not been made either of Major Kersey's abilities or her prescribed duties as WAC Staff Director. It is the opinion of G–1 that Headquarters FEAF should either be required to conform to War Department and Theater policy or that the Women's Army Corps should be withdrawn from that command.[160]

As a result, in January of 1945 FEAF headquarters belatedly required its various sections to co-ordinate with the staff director when setting WAC policy. Although the inspector general also recommended removal of the WAC detachment commander, General Kenney refused to effect a replacement, since he had personally selected the officer. Instead, she remained with the detachment until its inactivation, was promoted to the rank of major, and received the Bronze Star.[161]

In another case, the WAC commander of a USASOS detachment had been removed from a "large" command of 500 in the United States in the belief that she would be "all right in a small command overseas." Instead, she was assigned to command almost 1,000 women at one of the most difficult stations. As in the previous case, difficulties developed and the inspector general recommended her removal, but she was retained and promoted.[162] In one instance, in which a commander was sent direct from a WAC training center, she was found to know little of field life, and inspectors discovered her women to be near collapse from keeping the floors polished, barracks shining, shoes and clothing in basic-training spotlessness, while working long hours in hot weather.[163] In still another case, an officer without previous company experience was assigned as commander of a large detachment, over Colonel Brown's protests. Inspectors noted, "Many problems, which would have been routine for an experienced company commander, arose and

had an adverse effect upon the detachment." [164]

Not all WAC units were so afflicted; in many cases WAC commanders were outstanding. Colonel Boyce, on a visit to the area, particularly cited the commanders of the FEASC detachment, which, after the end of the war, she found still suffering from illness and a long working day. Colonel Boyce found the unit living in tin barracks in an area without shade or trees, very muddy or very dusty by turns, with the women drenched by torrential rains as they attempted to get to mess or to the outside latrines. Dead Japanese were buried so close to the surface that women had to scatter lime around the mess hall daily to control the stench. Nevertheless, since the unit's establishment it had had WAC commanders who were sincerely interested in the women's welfare, and Colonel Boyce reported the unit's state of morale and discipline at that time far better than that of more healthfully situated units.[165]

However, even where good company officers were assigned, they were frequently found under a strain caused by overwork and shortage of assistants. The FEASC WAC detachment had 714 en-

---

[160] Check Sheet, G–1 USAFFE to CofS USAFFE through WAC Dir, 29 Dec 44. Folder, WAC Det FEAF.

[161] (1) FEAF Stf Memo 4, 15 Jan 45. (2) WAC Draft AFPAC Reply only. Records of FEAF Detachment are incomplete; files noted destroyed by authority of company officers included: WAC Disciplinary Problems, Questionnaire Rpt to Maj Kersey, Leyte to Manila Move, Check Sheet re AAF Policy, Conditions of Latrine, Unauthorized Departure, Policy of Beach and Facilities, etc. Remaining are only Commendations, PRO file, vehicular reports, etc. (Envs 1 and 2, Folder, Correspondence, General, Drawer X–25096. (3) Interv with Lt Col Mary L. Kersey, 23 Jul 47.

[162] Insp Rpt, atchd to WAC Draft AFPAC Reply; Boyce Rpt.

[163] Interv cited n. 119.

[164] Boyce Rpt; Rpt cited n. 162.

[165] Boyce Rpt.

listed women and only three officers, the number commonly assigned to a unit one fourth that size in the United States. Inspectors recommended more, since work was heavy, but more were not assigned, although ten other WAC officers at the same base were assigned operational duties. The GHQ detachment for a time had only one officer for 386 women; eventually one more was added. The huge AFWESPAC battalion of some 3,000 women never had more than seven officers, even when it was scattered over three widely separated stations with the commanding officer alone in Manila attempting to prepare for reception of the women. In all, only 15 percent of the WAC officers in the Pacific were assigned to WAC administration, as against 32 percent in the European theater. There was only one troop or staff officer for approximately 100 women, as against the one per 20 believed suitable in the United States.[166]

Command of Enlisted Women by Male Officers

In several detachments, although WAC officers of proven ability were in charge, they were considered to have no powers other than those of providing food and housing, command and discipline being the prerogative of male commanders to whose units or offices the women were assigned. The situation was parallel to that of enlisted men assigned to one command and merely attached for quarters and rations to another. Even the ordinary Army unit, formally activated and with its own grades, encountered some friction between commander and section chief over such matters as promotions. Most WAC units in the area, with a few exceptions such as those in the Air Forces, were even more vulnerable, being gradeless and without "assigned" personnel other than cadre.

Noting that the command of enlisted women by male officers was in her opinion contrary to War Department regulations, Colonel Brown soon after her arrival recommended publication of a clarification such as that used in the European theater and in the Army Air Forces in the United States, to the effect that the WAC commander had full disciplinary powers even though her unit was gradeless or not activated. When this was refused, she attempted to send a letter through channels to the War Department, asking clarification of its ruling under the circumstances, and stating that she considered the current system "dangerous" in view of certain factors involved in the command of enlisted women by male officers. This letter was stopped by USAFFE on the grounds "that it did not pertain to the health, well-being, or morale of women," and Colonel Brown was informed by Maj. Gen. Charles P. Stivers, "Matters of assignment of Wacs, determination of this headquarters."[167]

Discipline in the GHQ USAFFE WAC detachment eventually reached a crisis. The WAC commanding officer, although responsible for almost 400 enlisted women, had no "assigned" personnel except one assistant, and had in the detachment not only Wacs working for GHQ but personnel assigned to nine other separate detachments as well as to Air Evaluation Board and Philippine Base Section.[168] After women guilty of disciplinary offenses in

---

[166] (1) Memo, WAC Stf Dir FEAF for CG FEAF, sub: Inspection of WAC Det FEASC, 4–6 Feb 45. WDWAC 319.1 Pacific. (2) Folder, 5200th WAC Bn, cx–447. (3) AFPAC Reply. Griffith Account gives 5 percent of officers on WAC administration, 95 percent elsewhere.

[167] (1) WAC Sec USAFFE Hist Rpts, particularly Dec 44 and Jan 45. (2) Check Sheets in same folder, particularly Check Note to CofS USAFFE, 2 Feb 45, re Stivers decision. (3) Colonel Brown's marginal note on draft of chapter. OCMH.

[168] Folder, 5200th WAC Bn, cx–447.

the detachment were promoted by their male commanders, one only a few days after conviction by court-martial, General Baird informed General Stivers:

It has come to our attention that there have been a number of instances where enlisted women have taken up matters concerning WAC detachment internal administration with section chiefs. In several cases, staff officers have suggested that enlisted women follow a course of action directly in opposition to the orders of their company commander. It is obvious that a complete breakdown of internal company command will result if the above situation is allowed to continue within this headquarters.[169]

USAFFE headquarters therefore published a memorandum, for its own detachment only, stating:

Enlisted women seeking advice or decision as to internal detachment administration will be referred to the Commanding Officer, WAC Detachment, by the section chiefs concerned.[170]

This directive, published without co-ordination with the staff director, still was not effective, and squabbles ensued, such as one in which the USAFFE board informed a WAC commander:

You, as commander of the detachment serving this, as well as other units, in an administrative capacity, have no discretion in the matter [of WAC discipline in an off-duty offense.] [171]

In any case, the ruling was applicable to the USAFFE unit only, and did not solve the problem elsewhere. WAC company commanders, asked to comment on the causes of delinquency, noted, "Most of our troubles arose from a divided command which created and fostered a disregard for authority," and "Many Army Section Chiefs tend to encourage infraction of rules and try to protect the enlisted women working for them." [172]

Major Kersey, the FEAF staff director, noted later:

The Air Force WAC Detachments, FEAF, and FEASC, had all personnel assigned to the WAC Squadrons, and consequently the WAC commanders did not encounter the same problem of disciplinary control.[173]

Some WAC commanders of proven ability eventually asked to be removed from company work because of their ambiguous status. One capable officer quit after eight months because, "I could not do anything about the things that were being done and I could not stay there and see what was happening to [the women]." Another WAC commander developed a mental condition that required a disability discharge. Still another, of previously irreproachable character, had to be relieved of command after she formed the habit of drinking too much and spending the evenings on the beaches in a state of blissful unconsciousness.[174]

It eventually came to be Colonel Brown's opinion that no mere publication concerning disciplinary authority would correct the situation, and that the enlisted women should be formally assigned to WAC units, the device adopted in the Mediterranean theater and in the Army Ground Forces. In spite of the cumbersome bookkeeping involved, such a command system was considered more nearly foolproof.

---

[169] D/F, G-1 USAFFE to DCofS, 26 Mar 45, atchd to WAC Draft AFPAC Reply.

[170] Stf Memo 31, Hq USAFFE, sec III. Atchd to WAC Draft AFPAC Reply.

[171] Memo, Det Comdr, USAFFE Bd, to CO 5200th WAC Det, 1 May 45, sub: Restriction of WAC Pers, with 4 inds. Atchd to WAC Draft AFPAC Reply.

[172] Folders, 5200th WAC Det, Drawer X-29443, and 5205th WAC Det, Drawer X-29853.

[173] Statement on draft of chapter, incl to Ltr, Col Kersey, WAF Stf Dir, Hq Strat Air Comd, to Chief, Mil Hist, 21 Apr 51. OCMH.

[174] Interviews listed in Bibliographical Note.

Transfer of Responsibility to WAC Section

In attempting to solve the various WAC problems, Colonel Brown's office came to the opinion that "in all headquarters, full advantage was not taken of the experience and knowledge of WAC staff officers."[175] Her own office was, in her opinion, handicapped not only by lack of formal responsibility but also by its inability to secure transfer to the advanced echelon where were located higher commanders and many of the enlisted women. Shortly before the move to Manila Colonel Brown informed a critic:

Until it is possible for me to talk to General Richard Marshall [Deputy Chief of Staff] personally, we shall have to do the best we can. I have every confidence that the General will make it possible for me to carry out the functions of a Staff Director as listed in the War Department Circular 462.[176]

In the spring of 1945, the WAC Section finally overtook the advanced echelon in Manila, and Colonel Brown was able to confer with General Richard Marshall. She noted later, "General Marshall was more than willing to seek and act upon the Staff Director's recommendations."[177] However, no written directive from General Marshall proved necessary, for shortly thereafter G–1 Division of USAFFE recommended of its own accord that "all policy and supervision of the WAC corps in this theater be immediately taken over by the WAC Section." It was stated that G–1 Division had felt it necessary to retain control during the experimental stages of the WAC program, which now, being safely established, could be turned over to WAC officers.[178]

This transfer was only a part of the general reorganization going forward at the time, during which GHQ and USAFFE were consolidated to form the new Headquarters, Army Forces in the Pacific (AFPAC). At this time the USAFFE WAC Detachment working for GHQ at last found itself working for the headquarters of assignment, AFPAC.

The powers transferred to the staff director in no case included command. G–1 Division and the adjutant general's office retained all normal operating functions such as promotion and assignment. Even in policy matters it developed that not too many of the WAC Section's recommendations were accepted.[179] Nevertheless, it was Colonel Brown's opinion that her office was now in a position to take action against the several probable causes of the medical evacuation rate.[180]

One immediate action was the publication of a directive concerning the disciplinary power of company commanders:

Where enlisted women are assigned to a unit or organization other than a WAC detachment, the commanding officer of the WAC detachment to which they are attached for rations, quarters, and administration will exercise disciplinary control.[181]

This directive applied only to the USAFFE GHQ detachment, its promulgation to other units being prevented by the command policy of noninterference. Colonel Brown was never entirely satisfied

---

[175] WAC Draft AFPAC Reply only.

[176] Personal ltr, CO 5205th WAC Det to Col Brown, 11 Mar 45, and reply, 14 Mar 45. Folder, 5205th WAC Det, Drawer X–29853.

[177] Written comments on draft of chapter; also comments in seminar.

[178] Check Sheet, Hq USAFFE, G–1 for CofS through WAC Sec, 11 Apr 45, signed H.H.B. Approved by Comment 2, CofS to G–1, 12 Apr 45. Tab 6 to WAC Draft AFPAC Reply.

[179] USAFFE Check Sheet, WAC Sec to G–1 Div, 27 May 45, sub: Critical Score, Deployment Plan, and comment 2 from G–1. FEWAC.

[180] List of "Subjects for Discussion with the Dir WAC." Copy in possession of Mary-Agnes Brown.

[181] Atchd to WAC Draft AFPAC Reply: (1) D/F, WAC Stf Dir USAFFE for G–1 Div USAFFE, 8 May 45, sub: Restriction of WAC Pers. (2) Stf Memo 52, Hq USAFFE, 18 May 45.

with the resulting situation, and in her final recommendations proposed that, regardless of accounting difficulties, all women be clearly assigned to WAC companies. Otherwise, War Department regulations were ignored and "the placing of enlisted women under the immediate command of male officers . . . had an adverse effect upon their well-being." [182]

A second issue immediately forced by the WAC Section was that of supply. A memorandum to General Richard Marshall asked that the theater take decisive action to get proper clothing, and that a representative be sent to the United States to trace supplies. Much activity resulted in the spring and summer of 1945, when General Richard Marshall personally wrote friends in the War Department to try to expedite shipment. The matter eventually came to be considered important enough to merit air priority, which had to date proved the only means by which minority supplies had any chance of reaching their goal. In May of 1945, Colonel Brown was ordered to return to the United States and personally check the status of each requisition. By these means, Manila Wacs obtained some supplies before the end of the war with Japan. With the end of hostilities, it was believed that a reasonably satisfactory supply system would have been perfected had any Wacs remained in the theater. [183]

War Department Investigation

A few days after transfer of responsibility to the WAC Section, the theater was the object of a War Department "Investigation Concerning the Morale, Health, and Living Conditions of WAC Personnel in the Southwest Pacific Area." [184] Disquieting reports on the women's health and well-being had been reaching the

War Department since the beginning of the move to New Guinea. While many were obviously exaggerations—particularly those from parents alleging that all Wacs were being eaten up by "jungle rot"—yet the area in any case was believed to merit a visit from Director Hobby such as the two that she had already made to Europe and Africa.

From May of 1944, when the first Wacs went to New Guinea, Director Hobby therefore planned to visit the area, but was prevented by repeated hospitalization. In October of 1944, she placed Deputy Director Rice on orders to go in her place. Again at the last moment the Director's illness intervened to cancel the trip, since during these months the Director had only a deputy and one assistant for her entire staff.

At this time, the Director secured permission for an inspection trip by Major Craighill of The Surgeon General's Office. This visit proved of little immediate assistance to the women, as it became part of a tour of all theaters.

It was not until after the end of the war that the second WAC Director, Colonel Boyce, reached the area. Colonel Hobby's resignation at this time was in fact hastened by the need for the Director to visit the Pacific and her own inability to do so.

Meanwhile, the War Department's concern was spurred by the condition of Wacs who began to trickle back from the Pacific, of whom it was reported, "Not only do these women arrive without adequate clothing and equipment, but their state of

---

[182] AFPAC Check Sheet, WAC Sec to CofS through G-1, 28 May 45. FEWAC.

[183] Sources cited n. 109.

[184] (1) Ltr, TAG to CINC SWPA, 9 Jun 45, sub: Request for Investigation Concerning Morale, Health, and Living Conditions of Members of WAC in Pacific Areas. AGOB-C 333 WAC (5-18-45). (2) See also n. 1(3).

mind is very low and their health below par." [185] Immediate action was precipitated when similar reports reached Congress and resulted in Congressional demands for an explanation. At this, General George Marshall requested of General MacArthur a full confidential report of the condition of Wacs in his command.[186]

The reply to this inquiry proved unsatisfactory to the War Department; it consisted chiefly of a copy of a press release made by Colonel Brown, who was then in the United States checking supplies, plus the 1944 statistics on evacuation, which indicated that Wacs were in good health. The War Department immediately demanded a second report, stating sharply, "A release for publicity purposes made here in the War Department is not considered adequate as a confidential report to the War Department. . . ," and adding that other statements were "very general in content and the code indicates that it was prepared by G-1 and not by the WAC Staff Director's office or the Inspector General." [187]

A more detailed reply was then prepared in the WAC Section of AFPAC, but was considerably censored by G-1 Division, so that the version which reached the War Department was rather short. The staff director noted:

G-1 here decided to scrap my report. . . . They had some Major who has not long been in the theater do the principal amount of work on the one that was sent. So far, I have not been able to get a copy of their finished product.[188]

The theater-approved version gave only two adverse items: (1) the failure of Christmas presents to arrive on time, and (2) the death of eight of the Wacs in a plane crash.[189]

As a result, before illness finally forced

Colonel Hobby's resignation in the summer of 1945, several decisions were reached by the Army's highest authorities, with her concurrence. One was a general decision to return all Wacs from all overseas theaters as soon after the end of hostilities as they became eligible for discharge, and not to send replacements. This measure would have been required in any event to permit demobilization of the Corps as required by the current legislation. To cover the period before demobilization, a second plan was prepared, which would have permitted voluntary rotation of Wacs after 12 months in the Southwest Pacific, and mandatory rotation after 18 months. These decisions effectively prevented WAC employment in the Army of Occupation in Japan. It was the theater's verdict that it would not be worthwhile to prepare housing and move the units to Japan in view of the few remaining weeks. A computation of point scores for discharge eligibility showed that by the end of 1945 all but 500 of the Pacific's Wacs would be eligible for return under the Army's Adjusted Service Rating System, and that even these 500 would be eligible in a few more months.[190]

The War Department also refused to allow the Pacific theater to keep dis-

---

[185] Memo, Lt Col Helen H. Woods, Deputy Dir WAC, for G-1, 10 Oct 45. WDWAC 330.11. She refers to returning Wacs of previous months.

[186] Ltr cited n. 184(1). Inclosure 1 is Congressional request.

[187] D/F cited n. 61. Incls show: Congressional Inquiry, 18 May 45; first request to Pacific, 26 May 45; interim Ltr to Congress from CofS, 8 Aug 45; first SWPA Rpt, 21 Aug 45, rejected for reasons given above.

[188] Ltr, WAC Stf Dir AFPAC to Col Boyce, 28 Dec 45. WDWAC 320.

[189] Rpt cited n. 1(3). All supporting documents were omitted in theater version.

[190] (1) See Ch. XXXVI, below. (2) Memo, KKJ (Maj Katherine Johnson, Exec WAC) for Dir WAC, 11 Jun 45, sub: Rpt of Action 6–11 Jun 45. WDWAC 319.1. (3) Boyce Rpt, draft version.

charge-eligibles who volunteered to remain. These were not many. Surveys before the defeat of Japan showed that 57 percent of WAC eligibles—80 percent of the AFWESPAC (formerly USASOS) group, 82 percent of FEAF—wanted to go home; by comparison, only 5 percent in Italy and 38 percent in England had expressed a desire to go home before the fighting ended.[191]

Extensions and exceptions were later to be given to the European and China theaters, so that their volunteer Wacs were not forced to return; no such extension was allowed the Pacific theater. Colonel Brown, herself a victim of amoebic dysentery that had already required hospitalization, believed an extension should have been granted, but was not called on to comment in the matter and did not return to the Pacific after demobilization began. She was awarded the Legion of Merit and a high efficiency rating personally signed by General MacArthur.

Lt. Col. Mera Galloway, formerly WAC Staff Director, Transportation Corps, was sent to the theater with the assigned mission "to close WAC History in the Southwest Pacific in an efficient and successful manner."[192] Colonel Boyce also arrived in the area as the closing-out began; until her report was received there remained the possibility that an extension of the return date of WAC volunteers would be granted.

Colonel Boyce was accompanied on her visits by the new staff director, by a War Department representative of G–3 Division, and by Dr. Marion Kenworthy, a prominent psychologist and member of the National Civilian Advisory Committee. The team talked individually with hundreds of enlisted women, and visited remaining WAC units on Hollandia, Biak, and Luzon.[193]

Their impression was not favorable. From Manila, Colonel Boyce cabled to the War Department: "I recommend all enlisted women in this theater be enroute USA for discharge or reassignment not later than 1 January 1946."[194] The medical loss rate had declined only slightly and Colonel Boyce, although a veteran of the North African crisis, was disturbed by the apparent poor health of members still on duty. Most were underweight, and all were highly fatigued. When the headquarters attempted to hold a parade formation in her honor, and delay resulted in an hour's wait, eight women fainted. Many were still working seven days a week with additional evening duty. Food was still poor, some quarters still unhealthful with beds standing in an inch of water, while few women yet had adequate clothing and footgear for protection against the daily rainstorms.

Colonel Boyce advised theater commanders that the women's condition required immediate action: less overtime office work, granting of quotas for rest areas, and more suitable clothing, such as that provided enlisted men for protection from the rain. Her advice was not accepted, although a service club and a rest camp were eventually opened to women a few weeks before they left. Colonel Boyce, after her encounter with theater authorities, wrote to Colonel Brown: "I want you to know that my observations in the theater simply confirmed the faith I have always had in your ability to perform

[191] "Readjustment Rating Scale Figures, Manila Area." In possession of Mary-Agnes Brown.

[192] Boyce Rpt, draft version.

[193] Ltr, Lt Col Mera Galloway Ferrin to OCMH, 22 May 51.

[194] Cbl, CinC AFPAC Comd, Manila, Boyce for WD, 27 Oct 45. C–19184, WDWAC 320.01.

difficult assignments in a superior manner."[195]

Many section chiefs, as well as Colonel Brown, felt that the refusal to permit WAC volunteers to be retained was unwarranted and deprived them of needed office help. The Commanding General, AFWESPAC, Maj. Gen. Wilhelm D. Styer, requested that the War Department at least allow a short extension; he proposed to make all Wacs warrant officers if this would allow them to remain. Colonel Boyce replied from Washington that the War Department was extremely sorry not to grant the request but that the January deadline could not be extended. Women were extended the same privilege offered in the European theater, that of remaining as civilian employees if they desired, but only about 200 elected to remain.[196]

Demobilization

A final problem was presented: the shipment of the women to the United States. Colonel Boyce while still in the theater found the first large group already boarding the ship *Evangeline* for return. The ship appeared unsuitable—vermin-ridden, ill ventilated, with men obliged to walk to mess through the WAC sleeping quarters. The women's physical condition left much to be desired. They had no woolen clothing, such as was issued to men for a comparable voyage, the original clothing in which they arrived having long since deteriorated in distant warehouses. Colonel Boyce, however, was unwilling to stop the shipment in view of the crowded state of port housing, the scarcity of ships of any sort, and the women's eagerness to get home. She radioed her office that she was "extremely disturbed" at the condition of the women, and feared that they "will make a very poor impres-

sion upon their communities unless their general condition can be improved upon their arrival." Accordingly, the War Department directed that the AAF WAC Officer and the ASF WAC Officer, Colonels Bandel and Goodwin, hurry to a west coast port to meet the shipment. This was accomplished, but obviously little could be done in the few days before the women were discharged, and the precautions did not prevent unfavorable publicity and headlines, such as VERMIN-RIDDEN TROOPSHIP, in both the Associated and the United Presses. WAC authorities feared the Corps' whole hard-won public relations victory might be jeopardized if the entire 5,500 women returned to their forty-eight states in a physical or mental condition alarming to the public.[197]

The second WAC group was being loaded on another ship, previously used to transport Chinese laborers, when the commanding general of the Hollandia Base saw it and refused to allow his Wacs to join those already on it. Colonel Boyce hurried to the scene and, without authority, ordered the remaining Wacs off, and port commanders thereupon turned the ship back to its owners as unfit for military use.

Before she left the theater in November, Colonel Boyce conferred with the chief of the transportation section and secured the assignment of a WAC officer to the office of the port director, to co-ordinate future shipping arrangements for Wacs and nurses. The WAC staff director or her assistant thereafter personally inspected shipping space assigned to women before

---

[195] Ltr, Dir WAC to Mary-Agnes Brown, 12 Dec 45. Personnel Abstracts, WAC file, OCMH.

[196] (1) Ltr, Dir WAC to WAC Stf Dir, AFPAC, 11 Dec 45. WDWAC 320. (2) Ltr cited n. 193.

[197] (1) Memo cited n. 185. (2) UP Release, 23 Oct 45, with headlines such as that in the Denver, Colo., *Rocky Mountain News*.

the date of loading. No further difficulties were noted.[198] On 10 January 1946, the last major shipment of returning enlisted women was loaded onto the *West Point,* the ship that had brought the first group to Australia, and from which the last now waved farewell to Manila.

Conclusion

The Director WAC, when later asked whether she would recommend that women ever again be stationed in such areas, was exceedingly doubtful as to the correct reply. Some of her advisers felt that the greater sacrifices of combat troops in the area made it impertinent even to question whether women should be sent to any area in which men were required to fight. Others commented:

Men had to be there; nurses had to be there so long as the Army had no male nurses; but Wacs didn't have to be there; and it seems important to discover whether a decision to use enlisted women in such an area is wise and economical or not.[199]

Theater authorities with one exception agreed that the WAC experiment was an unqualified success. General MacArthur stated to WAC leaders that he was satisfied with the results of WAC employment. When Colonel Boyce consulted him in Tokyo, he praised Wacs highly, calling them "my best soldiers," and alleging that they worked harder than men, complained less, and were better disciplined. He informed Colonel Boyce that he would take any number of the Wacs the War Department would give him in any future command he might ever have.[200]

General Styer, commanding general of the Army Forces in the western Pacific, called the Wacs' service "a matter of everlasting credit to the Women's Army Corps," and said that the Wacs were

"courageous soldiers," who from Australia to Manila "more than carried their share of the burden."[201]

General Kenney, commander of the Far East Air Forces, stated that his Wacs' work "has been of the highest caliber. Each has better than replaced a soldier."[202] General McMullen of FEASC said, "The detachment in every way upheld the fine traditions of American womanhood and their departure is a distinct loss to the command."[203]

Colonel Ginsburgh of USASOS added, "The Wacs did a job. We never had the sense of frustration which a discussion of their problems gives you; we only had a sense of achievement."[204]

On the other hand, General Baird, G–1 of USAFFE, later wrote:

I cannot truthfully say that their contribution, great as it was, outweighed the difficulties. On the other hand, nothing I could say would quite do justice to the loyal and efficient effort they put forth under all conditions and circumstances; to their courage and fortitude. . . . I do not believe that Wacs should be sent outside the limits of the United States until every general service man has been replaced by a Wac, and until every other available limited service man has been replaced. . . . The hardships, isolation and privation of jungle theaters are jobs for men. Women should be employed there only as a last resort.[205]

[198] Ltr, WAC Stf Dir AFPAC to WAC Stf Dir SFPOE, 8 Nov 45.

[199] Interv with Lt Col Mera Galloway, second AFPAC Stf Dir. (See Bibliographical Note.)

[200] (1) In interv with Col Boyce, 14 Oct 45, quoted in Rpt to Gen Marshall. Also see his statement in booklet "The 5205th WAC Det, GHQ," published in theater. WDWAC 000.7. Incl in Ltr, CO, 5205th WAC Det to Dir WAC. (2) Statement by Colonel Boyce to author and others, 19 November 1946, upon her return from SWPA.

[201] Griffith Account, "Commendations."

[202] *Ibid.*

[203] Ltr, CG FEASC to Dir WAC, 3 Jan 46, sub: Commendation. WDWAC 201.22 and 330.13.

[204] Interv, 13 Aug 47.

[205] Memo, Col Harry H. Baird for Hist Div SSUSA, 29 Jul 48. OCMH.

An opposite view was offered by the first WAC staff director, Colonel Brown, who wrote later:

The fact that the mission was successfully performed is much more important than a hind-sight consideration of whether it was wise to use Wacs in SWPA. . . . In my opinion the service of WAC members was essential to the success of Army operations in New Guinea and the Philippines. I deplore the failure of those immediately over the Staff Director . . . to accept my recommendations on procedures to assure the well-being of WAC personnel, but the WAC mission was accomplished in spite of these and other obstacles and at not too great a sacrifice.

Colonel Brown joined with the staff director of the European theater in advocating a permanent WAC in the Regular Army, and pointed out:

Colonel Hobby's recommendation to General Marshall that Wacs be withdrawn from SWPA was made without consulting the Staff Director. . . . When General Marshall decided to send Colonel Boyce to the theater to "put the lid on," the recommendations or opinions of the Staff Director . . . were not sought.

Colonel Brown also was of the opinion that the heavy loss rate would have slackened eventually with improved supply and other provisions.[206]

From the War Department's Army-wide viewpoint, the verdict was less positive. Even in the few brief months between the incidence of the loss rate and the recall of the women, heavy casualties had been suffered, while the future usefulness of many of the other women was questionable.[207] The War Department inspection team noted, of the entire group:

It was evident that in their forced adaption they had no realization of their physical and mental sacrifices. It is possible that not until they return to the Zone of the Interior will they acknowledge the changes which have taken place within them.[208]

These were, to the War Department, expensive losses. A skilled Wac was valuable Army property, representing a considerable investment in recruiting and training, and was needed for assignment in four or five jobs for every one that could be filled. Had the same 5,500 women been assigned to any of the other numerous overseas or domestic commands that had unfilled requisitions, few of these losses would have occurred under prevailing loss rates.

It therefore appeared to have been poor economy to employ women in circumstances where the loss among an equal number of men would have been only one fourth as great. If men in the proper skills were unavailable, the loss was obviously required in winning the war. The question of whether the entire Army of 7,700,000 men was not at this stage able to afford 5,500 men in clerical skills was one to be answered by students of the world-wide replacement system, and was a matter beyond the scope of either WAC or theater knowledge. Operations Division's decision to send Wacs had been made in the belief that, in the moment of manpower shortage, there existed no such 5,500 men. Thus, the original decision to send Wacs needed no justification; any future decision concerning the use of women in such an area would require consideration of the existing manpower shortage versus the probable loss rate.

It came to be the final opinion of most WAC leaders that women not only should be sent to such an area under equally desperate circumstances, but that they could

[206] Memo, Lt Col Brown for OCMH, 23 Apr 51, and comments at seminar, 1948.

[207] All from AFPAC Reply, both versions, except nonmedical evacuations, which are from WAC Stf Dir's file.

[208] Boyce Rpt.

probably be employed without any comparable loss rate by application of the principles of WAC employment used elsewhere. These included, particularly, advance planning, a definition of the place of WAC advisers, command of women by female company officers, specialist attention to tracing the supplies of the relatively small group of women, and consideration of women's psychological need for treatment as responsible adults. In her final report to General George Marshall, Colonel Boyce summarized the WAC impression:

> Women in the Army should be required and permitted to serve wherever the Army serves when their services are needed. However, in . . . New Guinea, Biak, and the Philippines, it is apparent that essential safeguards to the effective utilization of WAC personnel were not applied.[209]

A clue to an explanation of this lack of safeguards could be found in world-wide WAC experience, which indicated that the fault lay in the time factor as much as in any human element. In both other major theaters, a considerable shakedown period was required after WAC arrival in order to set up a satisfactory administrative system and specialist attention to supply and other needs. The Fifth Army experiment had not been attempted until eleven months after the first Wacs' arrival; the Normandy move, until twelve months after arrival. In the Pacific, the world-wide norm of a WAC administrative system had also been worked out at the end of a year. It was the theater's misfortune that, because of the lateness of its requisitions for Wacs, the achievement of this system had coincided with the end, and not with the beginning, of a risky experiment.

---

[209] *Ibid.*

CHAPTER XXIII

Other Overseas Theaters

In addition to being employed in the three major overseas theaters, Wacs were stationed in every other active theater of war. In each case the employment was relatively minor, never exceeding a few hundred women. Nevertheless, remaining records of the various experiments often provided clear-cut indications of the practicability of employment of womanpower in differing climates and administrative situations.

Southeast Asia Command

Pioneer in the employment of American Wacs in India was Vice-Adm. Lord Louis Mountbatten's Southeast Asia Command. The headquarters already employed nurses, British servicewomen, members of the Indian WAC, and local civilians, so that no great venture was undertaken when a small unit of sixty-two enlisted Wacs and four officers was added to the staff in October of 1943. After six months in New Delhi, the unit was transferred in April of 1944 to Southeast Asia Command headquarters in Ceylon, where it remained for the duration.[1]

Fourteen of the enlisted women were assigned to Signal Corps duties, and the remainder to routine clerical work in offices of the headquarters, both British and American. Officers, in addition to company duty, were assigned operational jobs in the same offices.

No great difficulties were encountered by the unit in the performance of its jobs. The two stations of assignment, while by no means pleasure resorts, were not the most trying in India. New Delhi, the capital, was one of India's cleaner and more healthful cities in spite of temperatures ranging up to 110° F. The Wacs nevertheless soon discovered the ailment theater veterans designated as "Delhi belly." The climate of Ceylon was tropical, without extremes of heat but with excessive humidity during the rainy seasons. Enlisted women were housed in barracks in the WRNS area, which inspectors pronounced excellent in spite of the customary bucket latrines and absence of hot water. Both men and women ate at a joint mess, which lacked cold-storage facilities and thus had only small amounts of meat and few fresh vegetables. Drinking water was boiled and stored in Lyster bags. The working day generally followed the nonstrenuous British schedule, with an 8-hour day and one day off per week.

Major Craighill, who visited the unit after Wacs had been in India for some

---

[1] No records of this group were found, with the exception of Memo, Maj Craighill for The SG through SEAC and IBT, 6 Apr 45, sub: Med and Social Conditions of Women in Mil Serv in Ceylon. SGO Hist Div 319 Special, Ceylon, Women In. In addition, comments on drafts of the present chapter were given by Charles F. Romanus and Riley Sunderland, authors of *Stilwell's Mission to China*, UNITED STATES ARMY IN WORLD WAR II (Washington, 1953).

eighteen months, stated that "the general health of the detachment is excellent." Except for dengue fever, mild gastrointestinal conditions, and skin infections, there had been no notable illnesses, and especially no amoebic or bacillary dysentery, or malaria. One serious exception was the Signal Corps women, who were on around-the-clock shifts, rotating every four days. Major Craighill noted:

A high incidence of sickness among the group working on irregular hours with the Signal Corps is significant. Of the 58 admissions for all causes, 20 were from this group of 14 women. This includes the hospitalization of ten of the fourteen: the other four have all been on sick call. These conditions are attributable to the irregularity of meals and the loss of sleep due to constantly shifting hours of work.

In spite of Major Craighill's recommendations, the headquarters did not modify the shift changes, since they were "in accordance with the present British system." [2]

No final recommendation was on record from the headquarters concerning the success of employment of Wacs. There appeared to be no very valid reason why women could not successfully fill many of the jobs in any such high administrative headquarters. On the other hand, there was no proof that local employees could not have done the work adequately without the importation of American women.

The China–Burma–India Theater

The intrinsic suitability of the China–Burma–India (CBI) theater for WAC employment was by no means identical with that of the Southeast Asia Command. [3] Principal supply installations were in Calcutta, a city noted for oppressive heat, disease, and filth, and generally considered even more unhealthful for unacclimated

white women than the more sparsely populated New Guinea islands. However, there were certain advantages not possessed by the Southwest Pacific Area, notably the fact that in Calcutta, a city approximately the size of Chicago, there were available civilian shops and tailoring facilities, as well as some approved recreational facilities. Nevertheless, the experience of nurses and Red Cross women already in the area was not encouraging; nurses had previously suffered from clothing shortages, emotional strain, tension, and a medical evacuation rate four times that of the men. [4] "Wacs in India were definitely on trial," a later report stated, "as many Army officials believed that women would not be able to stand for long the climate and diseases found in Asiatic countries." [5]

It was therefore not until July of 1944, two years after the Corps' establishment, that the Air Forces headquarters in Calcutta received its first Wacs. Earlier attempts to bring in Wacs had been blocked by the theater commander, Lt. Gen. Joseph W. Stilwell, who eventually yielded to the Air Forces' requests only after receiving the express pledge of the Air

---

[2] 1st Ind to Memo cited n. 1.

[3] (1) CBI WAC files, by folder number and specific document therein. (See Bibliographical Note.) Other important sources are: (2) Rpt, AAF, IBT to TAG, 5 Jul 45, sub: Surv of WAC Health and Living Conditions in India–Burma Theater. AG 321 WAC, Hobby files, also in CBI WAC files. Hereafter cited as IBT WAC Survey. (3) Rpt, Maj Craighill to The SG through CG IBT, 30 Mar 45, sub: Med and Social Conditions of Women in Mil Serv in IBT. SGO Hist Div 319.1-2, Women, India–Burma; hereafter cited as Craighill IBT Rpt. (4) Comments on draft of present chapter by Maj. Beryl Simpson, wartime WAC Staff Director, China Theater, and Maj. Betty Clague, wartime WAC Staff Director, CBI Theater.

[4] Incl 3 to Craighill IBT Rpt.

[5] Rpt, WAC Stf Dir AAF CT, 25 Oct 45, sub: Narrative Account of WAC Activities in Chungking, China, 15 Jul–13 Oct 45. WDWAC 319.1; also in Folder, Chungking, CBI WAC Sec files.

Forces commander, Maj. Gen. George E. Stratemeyer, that any Wacs brought in by the AAF would never under any circumstances be assigned to other than Air Forces headquarters.[6]

Scrupulously careful advance preparation was the keynote of the entire Air Forces project. Wacs for shipment to India were selected by the Army Air Forces from among women proved capable and emotionally stable by service at airfields in the United States. The result was so good that General Stratemeyer, upon later checking their job performance, congratulated Director Hobby, who congratulated General Arnold, who congratulated air commands in the United States, who passed the commendation on to selecting officers at airfields—the whole project ending in a glow of mutual admiration.[7]

This success was the more remarkable in that the theater, with typical overseas optimism, asked percentages of scarce skills never remotely approached in the United States—one fourth stenographers, one fourth typists, and the rest all highly skilled in other fields.[8] It was possible to supply these satisfactorily only because the total original request was not large, less than 300. Selection was marred only by seven cases in which the routine physical inspections failed to detect serious physical disqualifications that caused the women to be returned to the United States. Much to the theater's chagrin, the first report of its WAC experiment was given to the press by one of these women, who had never set foot in India except to enter the comfortable port hospital but who was described by reporters as the heroine of a bout with jungle, heat, and disease-bearing insects, as she personally battled her way through Burma side by side with General Stilwell.[9]

The actual reception of the Wacs was considerably less alarming. "Never has any WAC contingent received a more cordial welcome than this group," wrote the WAC staff director, Maj. Betty Clague.

> Everyone from the Commanding General on down has apparently had a personal interest in our welfare and happiness. . . . Everyone is impressed with the fact that they must not let down these men who have expressed such a satisfaction in having us as an integral part of their headquarters.[10]

Accommodations were unique, consisting of a section of a huge eight-acre jute mill, which also sheltered headquarters' offices and many of the officers' and enlisted men's quarters. Space allotment per individual was somewhat greater than that of the zone of the interior, and Wacs had not only single-decked beds with sheets and pillows, but dressers, chests of drawers, overhead fans, and mosquito nets. Latrines had toilets, showers, tubs, and mirrored washbasins. For the less than 400 enlisted women[11] who eventually lived in these quarters, there were 23 Indian sweepers and about 50 ayahs, who

[6] Ltr, CG AAF IBT to Dir WAC, 15 Nov 44, sub: WAC Utilization, (Incl 1 to IBT WAC Survey).

[7] *Ibid.* Also Ltrs, Dir WAC to CG AAF and CG AAF IBT, 18 Dec 44. WDWAC 320.2.

[8] IBT WAC Survey, p. 6. The 257 enlisted women on duty at that date: 67 stenographers, 61 clerk-typists, 69 clerks, and the rest qualified in such jobs as key punch operator, draftsman, radar specialist, intelligence specialist, photolaboratory technicians, classification specialist, telephone operator, medical technician, cadre, and the like.

[9] *Ibid.,* p. 9. See also (1) Memo, CO WAC Det for WAC Stf Dir, 14 Feb 45; (2) Ltr, WAC Stf Dir to Air WAC Off, 22 Feb 45. Folder IBT, CBI WAC files.

[10] Ltr, WAC Stf Dir AAF CBI to Air WAC Off, Hq AAF, 21 Aug 44. WDWAC 320.2 CBI.

[11] IBT WAC Survey shows 257 EW as of that date. In her comment on a draft of this chapter, Major Simpson shows 397 as the highest number ever on Morning Report. For final theater strength figures, see Table 7, Appendix A.

TAJ MAHAL *is seen by four women of the Southeast Asia Command on a sightseeing tour.*

made beds, shined shoes, washed underwear, and policed the area. There was also provided a hairdressing shop, a dispensary in the WAC area, and a dayroom with piano and radio. The only obvious objection to the arrangement was, according to medical inspectors, the noise in the big building, which made it difficult for night workers to get any sleep. In the future, living accommodations for not exceeding 75 in a group were recommended. With this exception, quarters were possibly more comfortable than the average barracks in the United States, although members expressed a mild initial surprise at observing large rats frisking through the machinery overhead, and birds roosting on the beds.[12]

Other advance preparations had been carefully made. The post exchange stocked needed women's items—cosmetics, stockings, brassières, girdles, and garter belts. Wacs were admitted to the Red Cross club and to the enlisted men's club, where tea was served daily. There was a free movie theater, and free hourly bus service to Calcutta, with its Army-approved swimming pools and dining and dancing places. Provision was made for Wacs to share in the theater authorization for yearly 15-day rest leaves in mountain resorts, with breakfast in bed and sports such as golf, riding, and tennis.[13]

Wacs ate at the men's large consolidated mess, where supervision was taken over by an experienced WAC mess officer, Capt. Roslyn Katz, a WAC mess sergeant, and other Wacs who supervised Indian cooks and kitchen laborers. Some 8,000 meals a day were served at this mess, which was later rated as "well above the average in this theater." Food was generally considered to be as attractive and appetizing as was possible in the absence of salads, milk, fresh butter, and other uncooked items. Besides regular meals, a midnight snack of hot coffee and sandwiches was available.[14]

Air Forces authorities believed that they had been equally careful in making advance provision for suitable uniforms, but immediately discovered that in fact they had shown scarcely better foresight than had the Southwest Pacific Area. At the written request of the theater, each woman had been issued six off-duty dresses for office wear, since this, although not the ideal dress that could have been designed for the area, seemed the coolest garment already stocked by quartermaster depots. It was soon discovered that the dresses were "washable" only by methods seldom known to local ayahs, and "couldn't stand beating on a rock for two or three changes a day"; even when later reserved for dress, they did not prove durable. Furthermore, although malaria control restrictions required wearing of slacks after 1800, the need for them had not been foreseen and again the only available items were herringbone twill coveralls. These, however, were pronounced totally impossible by theater authorities, since the weather was too hot to make them endurable and they "would have increased alarmingly the incidence of skin infections."[15]

The theater was saved from consequences similar to those in the Southwest Pacific Area by the fact that local shops could provide the necessary items if the Wacs had the money to purchase them. The theater could find no Army funds for the issue of men's slacks, but medical offi-

---

[12] (1) Craighill IBT Rpt. (2) IBT WAC Survey, pp. 1–2. (3) Intervs with CBI Wacs.

[13] IBT WAC Survey, pp. 2–5, 10 and Incl 3.

[14] *Ibid.*

[15] Comments of theater staff director on draft copy of chapter, and in interview.

cers refused to let the women leave the barracks for their evening meal until so equipped. Therefore, most enlisted women bought slacks tailored of an Indian mesh cotton. Mosquito boots were also purchased, as well as cotton anklets, sandals, and sometimes bush jackets. Also, Air Forces headquarters proved prompt in remedying deficiencies, and some months later succeeded in getting shipment for each woman of five cotton skirts and seven short-sleeved shirts for office wear, as well as three pairs of women's khaki slacks for wear after 1800. For the two or three colder months, wool clothing was provided. Eventually, CBI Wacs, by their own and theater efforts, had about double the amount provided for Wacs in semitropical climates in the United States, although no more than medical authorities deemed necessary in view of the frequent changes of perspiration-soaked garments that were required to prevent illness.[16]

All of the provisions of Air Forces headquarters for its men and women, although frequently exceeding the average for military facilities elsewhere, paid off in respect to the health rate. At the time of Major Craighill's inspection in March of 1945, no Wacs had been evacuated to the United States for medical reasons, except the original seven, who had disqualifying defects upon arrival. If these were counted, the loss rate was still only about 2 percent per year as compared with 2.1 percent for the theater.[17]

Major Craighill reported, "The medical care and condition of women is in general, good. They seem to stand the strain of overseas service as well as do men."[18] Both WAC and theater authorities attributed the low loss rate to the fact that Wacs were not only encouraged but ordered to report to the sick bay in their barracks at the slightest sign of any disorder, or even

for advice. As a result, as many as 10 percent of the women in winter months, and 20 percent in summer, reported each month to the sick bay for cases not requiring hospitalization, as against 5 and 9 percent, respectively, for men. Theater authorities urged women to patronize medical facilities even more frequently if necessary, and provided not only a nurse for the well-equipped dispensary, but a gynecologist in the local hospital.

There was every indication that, without such constant care, the health hazards of the area would have been comparable to those of the Southwest Pacific Area, for illnesses included both amoebic and bacillary dysentery, impetigo, hepatitis, various fevers, and respiratory disorders. Major Craighill recommended that two years' service in the area be the limit, since "Among nurses who have been overseas two years or more, there is an obvious increase in tension, manifested by irritability, depression, insomnia, and loss of effective energy."[19]

An additional health problem was what Major Craighill called the "great emotional strain" from the social demands of "a group of isolated and lonesome men." While Wacs were by no means the only white women in the theater, they were nevertheless overwhelmed upon arrival with such numerous offers of social engagements that not all could be accepted. In the interests of health and working efficiency, WAC commanders from time to time prescribed dateless nights, quiet

---

[16] *Ibid.* Also (1) IBT WAC Survey, pp. 9–10. (2) Ltr, WAC Stf Dir to Air WAC Off, 7 Oct 44. Folder CBI, CBI WAC files.

[17] From Stat Div SGO: total over-all loss by medical evacuation in 1944 was 2.1 percent; in 1945, 2.7 percent.

[18] Craighill IBT Rpt.

[19] (1) *Ibid.* (2) IBT WAC Survey, pp. 10–13: Comparative statistics for men and women.

hours, and other expedients. After the first months, most Wacs were fatigued by the constant masculine attention, and found organized parties and mass invitations especially tiring.[20]

Coupled with the theater's precautions concerning health were, in the early days, numerous protective restrictions which, although not comparable to those in the Southwest Pacific Area, the Wacs found annoying. Wacs could not participate in airplane flights, had bed check even though men did not, could not accept overnight invitations from local families, could not spend the night away from their quarters even in approved service centers, could not date officers, and could not marry.[21] These restrictions caused a certain number of Wacs to inform the chaplain that they were being "treated as children."[22]

Most of these restrictions were therefore quickly abolished as initial misgivings concerning the employment of Wacs subsided. Although bed check was retained as a health safeguard, hours were usually lenient, and Wacs were eventually allowed to stay overnight at the women's service center. Wacs were also soon allowed in aircraft, and at least one technician was placed on regular flying duty for which she received the Legion of Merit and the Air Medal.[23] The restriction on dating officers was not removed until Wacs reached Shanghai, and some difficulty was caused by the fact that Air Forces Wacs were liable to punishment while officers of theater headquarters, which had no such rule, were immune.[24]

The restriction on marriage, a theater ruling, was the most objectionable to the women. The rule had been designed to prevent the marriage of soldiers to noncitizens, and had been modified just before the Wacs' arrival to permit marriage only

if a soldier was leaving the theater within thirty days. Cases involving pregnancy were considered individually on their merits. At the time of Major Craighill's visit, Wacs still had a pregnancy rate of zero, but WAC commanders considered the system, for obvious reasons, incredibly shortsighted. In April of 1945, after receipt of Major Craighill's recommendations, and after the first Wac achieved marriage by the only theater-approved method, Lt. Gen. Daniel I. Sultan liberalized the policy to permit marriages between two United States citizens after a three-month waiting period. With this one case, the WAC pregnancy rate was only one fourth of one percent, or considerably less than the average. No cases of venereal disease were discovered among any WAC personnel.[25]

As always, factors of physical surroundings proved less important to the women than that of job satisfaction. Initial job assignment was far from perfect, a condition that General Stratemeyer attributed chiefly to "a failure on the part of officers

[20] (1) Rpt cited n. 5. (2) Memo, WAC Stf Dir for all offs, 26 Mar 45. Folder IBT, CBI WAC files.

[21] Memo, WAC Stf Dir for CO WAC Det, 16 Sep 44, sub: Policies Applicable to WAC Pers. Folder IBT, CBI WAC files.

[22] Memo, Stf Chaplain for CG AAF IBT, 10 Jul 45, sub: Morale of Wacs; also Memo, WAC Stf Dir for CG, 15 Jul 45. Folder IBT, CBI WAC files.

[23] WAC citations, 7 Dec 45, Folder Shanghai II, CBI WAC files.

[24] Entire lengthy dispute: (1) Ltr, Hq SEAC, 5322 D/U.S. Army Sec, 14 Jul 44. WDWAC 421. (2) Draft of Statement, 23 May 45. Folder IBT; (3) Routing Slip, Comment I, WAC Stf Dir AAF CT to AC, 28 Aug 45, Folder Chungking I; (4) Memo, WAC Stf Dir Hq USFCT for CofS, 25 Jan 46, Folder Theater WAC III; (5) Cir 7, Hq USAF China, 9 May 46, sec 1, Folder Shanghai V. All in CBI WAC files. (6) Interv with Maj Simpson, 23 Jun 47. (7) Boyce Rpt, Tabs: India–Burma, and China. WDWAC 333.1 (1945–46).

[25] (1) Memo, Capt Chance, Exec WAC, for Col Hobby, 3 May 45, sub: Marriage Policy. WDWAC 291.1. (2) MS History of India–Burma Theater, 25 Oct 44–23 Jun 45. OCMH.

to appreciate capabilities, and overstaffing during the period of orientation prior to the transfer of enlisted men replaced by Wacs."[26] General Stratemeyer took immediate and vigorous action to correct the situation.[27] As a result, the expected 30-day on-the-job training was reduced to 15 days.

A few months later General Stratemeyer directed his WAC staff director to make a survey of job utilization. It was found that, "with a very few exceptions, the qualifications of Wacs were being fully employed in jobs commensurate with their training and experience," and the exceptions were at once corrected. Some problems still remained. The offices were not exceptionally busy, at least not enough to satisfy the Wacs. Also, civilian competition was present from female citizens of Calcutta. The staff director remarked:

I believe that the biggest hindrance toward the proper utilization of WAC personnel in this Headquarters is the usage of inefficient civilian help. Because of their employment in the majority of stenographic positions, the Wac is compelled to watch someone else do a job which would ordinarily take her one-half of the time to complete.

Because of the constant attention to the matter of correct assignment, however, lack of work never became a morale problem. An Army observer confirmed this assertion about Wacs' high morale and its cause, stating that:

The women look well, work efficiently, are universally cheerful and seem almost without exception to feel that they are doing an important war job. . . . The WAC personnel are universally admired and respected by male officers and enlisted men here. They have made a definite contribution to the morale of the base and the efficiency of the headquarters here, and I believe that their excellent attitude reflects their pride in this fact.[28]

General Stratemeyer, at the time of the separation of the China theater from the India–Burma, reported to Generals Stilwell and Arnold:

Experience of the past several months has proved any doubts concerning the propriety of the experiment to be false. It is with enthusiasm that this Headquarters reports the substantial overall improvement in efficiency as a result of the placement of Wacs. . . . Officers and enlisted women alike have quickly adjusted themselves to the climate, food, and the somewhat rugged living conditions. . . . Deportment is superior. Not one untoward incident has occurred as a result of their presence in this Headquarters. . . . This Headquarters recommends without hesitation to other Headquarters overseas the excellent benefits to be obtained through the placement of Wacs in theaters of operations.[29]

The newly organized Services of Supply headquarters in Kunming, China, immediately petitioned the commander of the U.S. forces in the China theater, Lt. Gen. Albert C. Wedemeyer, for permission to bring in a WAC company almost identical with the Air Forces' company, saying:

It is virtually impossible to obtain competent civilian clerical employees in this theater. . . . Male enlisted personnel trained in typing and stenographic duties are not available in sufficient numbers. . . . Where the civilian employee is not a citizen of the United States, as is almost invariably the case in this theater, effective security is largely unknown.[30]

---

[26] Ltr cited n. 6.

[27] D/F, Gen Stratemeyer to Col David Barret, 21 Sep 44. Folder IBT, CBI WAC files.

[28] (1) D/F, WAC Stf Dir to Orgn and Plng, 8 Nov 44, Comment I. Folder IBT, CBI WAC files. (2) Statement by Maj Philip Boyer, Jr., Actg PRO. Incl 2 to IBT WAC Survey.

[29] Ltr cited n. 6.

[30] Ltr, Hq SOS, USFCT, APO 627, to CG USFCT, APO 879, 26 Nov 44, sub: Establishment of WAC Co at SOS Hq, 13525–322. Folder 5, Hq SOS USFCT file, AG 322.

However, theater headquarters refused this: "The decision of the Theater Commander is that no Wacs will be brought into the China Theater for the present." Six months later, the SOS asked again and was again refused on the grounds that "we cannot quarter these people . . . including mess, toilet, and living space."[31]

There was also some objection to the Air Forces' proposal to take Wacs to China when its headquarters moved to Chungking in July of 1945, but because of General Stratemeyer's insistence, the objection was overcome. It was known that living conditions would be far less favorable than in India, but two hundred of the Wacs volunteered to go and about a hundred were chosen, this being all that the reduced headquarters could employ. Again, preparation was careful. Maj. Beryl Simpson, who had replaced Major Clague as staff director, visited the new site to check on all accommodations before the order was given to send the enlisted women. The first WAC contingent flew the Hump on 3 August 1945, closely followed by others.[32]

The China Theater

As expected, living conditions in Chungking were less settled than in India.[33] With much work and close sanitary supervision of native help, an attractive mess hall was maintained, and within three days the Wacs had set up their own laundry and trained local help to give good personal service. The hundred women eventually employed some sixty Chinese servants for mess, laundry, and yard work. Housed in dormitories similar to the civilian women's, Wacs eventually obtained a few fans, an improved water supply, and better electric lights. In spite of predic-

tions, the headquarters reported that a "low rate of sickness" prevailed among Wacs, and that "the sweltering heat failed to impair efficiency." As in India, Wacs were urged to seek medical advice frequently. Records showed that in six weeks over half of the women had been on sick call, although much of the rate resulted from the fact that almost all members were getting daily treatments for prickly heat, an annoying but nonfatal malady, which caused little loss of work time.[34]

In accordance with General Wedemeyer's policies, the headquarters was careful to allow no appearance of favoritism to women, who were trucked to work as were men, issued supplies in the same manner, and generally treated as other troops. In this respect, the move to China accomplished several goals that the WAC staff director had never been able to attain in India. The extreme friendliness of the Air Forces headquarters in India had always been such that WAC staff directors and unit officers were occasionally hard put to maintain strict discipline and military appearance. Before the Wacs arrived, nurses had been allowed to wear civilian evening dress in spite of Army Regulations and rules on malarial control, and it did not prove easy to convince the headquarters that the WAC was best treated as a fully military organization.[35]

[31] *Ibid.*, 1st Ind, 7 Dec 44; 2d Ind, 2 Apr 45; 3d Ind, 25 Apr 45.

[32] (1) Memo, WAC Stf Dir for Col J. S. Clark, 9 May 45, sub: China Survey—WAC. CBI WAC files. (2) Rpt cited n. 5.

[33] Account of China tour of duty is, unless otherwise specified, from: (1) Rpt cited n. 5. (2) All CBI references. (3) Memo, Maj Craighill for The SG, through CG CT, 11 Mar 45, sub: Conditions Affecting Women Pers in China. SGO Hist Div 319.1 China. No Wacs were in the area at the time of this report.

[34] *Ibid;* also interv with Maj Simpson, 23 Jun 47.

[35] Craighill IBT Rpt.

Late in 1944 the staff director discovered a move by junior WAC officers to override the regulations on conduct and uniform by securing from senior Army officers contradictory statements, which were "usually made in a spirit of conversation at mixed parties." [36] These attempted violations the staff director was able to quash, but there remained the problem that Army officers were often "accessible and sympathetic to personal requests." [37]

Some months later the staff director reported that "a good many enlisted women are relaxing their efforts with regard to their personal appearance and individual conduct." She also called the women's attention to the fact that some Wacs were not "promptly and properly rendering the salute." Detachment regulations thereupon required that hair must be neater, T shirts invisible, shirt sleeves up or down but not halfway; no flowers or "other articles of non-military nature" could be worn in the hair; short or tight skirts must be let down or out. "It is essential," the staff director informed the women, "that the reputation thus far enjoyed by all members be maintained, that no relaxation be permitted that might adversely affect the generally accepted idea that American women soldiers are well-dressed, personable, and conduct themselves as ladies." [38]

A few weeks after the stricter detachment regulations had been published, they were partially canceled by General Stratemeyer, who, on a visit to the Southwest Pacific Area, had noted that General MacArthur's Wacs and General Kenney's Wacs "were wearing decorations such as flowers and ribbons in their hair during working hours." Being ignorant of the fact that General MacArthur's Wacs by this date had nothing resembling a military uniform, General Stratemeyer was favorably impressed. Over the staff director's protests, new official uniform regulations contained the provision—probably unique in the history of the Army—that "Flowers or ribbons are authorized and encouraged for wear in the hair." [39] The staff director conceded defeat, with the notation:

There is absolutely nothing General Stratemeyer would not do for his Wacs to make them happier . . . we will therefore accede to his wishes, though they are contrary to the military indoctrination we received. . . . [40]

The move to China, combined with the location of the Air Forces headquarters in the same compound with General Wedemeyer's headquarters, caused considerable change in policies in this regard. Corrective action was first undertaken informally by a memorandum:

General Stratemeyer this morning expressed a personal hope that all his Wacs would be so prompt and snappy in their saluting that General Wedemeyer would voluntarily say to him, "Boy! Are those Wacs good!" He pointed out that sometimes we get so interested in the conversation that we fail to notice an officer, and often that very officer is just the type to report the failure to General Wedemeyer. [41]

This document having had all the effect that might have been expected, a month

[36] D/F, Chief of Air Stf to WAC Stf Dir, 29 Dec 44, sub: Comd Channels. Folder IBT, CBI WAC files.
[37] Ltr, WAC Stf Dir AAC CBI to Air WAC Off, 6 Aug 45. CBI WAC files.
[38] Memo, WAC Stf Dir for CO WAC Det, 17 Mar 45, Folder IBT, CBI WAC files.
[39] (1) Memo, Exec for CO WAC Det, 23 Jun 45. (2) Mimeographed Memo, Chief of Air Stf to all Wacs, 8 Aug 43. Folder IBT, CBI WAC files. (3) Ltr cited n. 37.
[40] Ltr cited n. 37.
[41] Memo, WAC Stf Dir AAF CT for all EW of Det, 10 Aug 45. Folder Chungking I, CBI WAC files.

later General Stratemeyer noted, "Saluting by enlisted women was still extremely lax." He therefore issued more unmistakable orders that "the situation be corrected at once." At this the staff director, expressing considerable pleasure, showed great alacrity in informing the women that they would be court-martialed in a most military manner if that was the only way to get them to salute and to wear hats on the street.[42]

Happily for all concerned, the women reverted to their military training without noticeable loss of efficiency or morale, and impressed General Wedemeyer sufficiently to cause him to request General Stratemeyer to contribute Wacs to theater headquarters. At the close of the stay in Chungking, General Stratemeyer informed the women:

You have . . . established an enviable record of efficiency which has immeasurably facilitated the accomplishment of the mission of my command. . . . Your performance stands as a worthy goal for any military unit in the Armed Forces of the United States.[43]

With the defeat of Japan, the headquarters moved to Shanghai, taking the Wacs with it. With the approaching inactivation of the Air Forces headquarters, General Wedemeyer's headquarters took over all of the women, including the staff director. He later requisitioned and obtained double their number direct from the United States.

Even in the postwar wave of demobilization fever, less than half of the Wacs eligible for discharge desired it, and the headquarters strongly urged them to stay.[44] In Shanghai, the Wacs were visited by the new WAC Director, Colonel Boyce, who had intended to direct their return to the United States, as had been necessary in the Pacific. Upon seeing the women,

Colonel Boyce changed her mind, pronouncing them a carefully picked, seasoned group, all volunteers, who felt that their services were needed by the headquarters, and whose morale was correspondingly high. Most had by this time worked their way into key positions, and many were section chiefs, so that the headquarters was reluctant to part with them. The women themselves stated that they were willing to remain either as Wacs or as civilian workers. As a result, Colonel Boyce agreed to leave them indefinitely and to support General Wedemeyer's requisition for more.[45]

The China theater Wacs later moved from Shanghai to Nanking and Peiping; the group in Peiping staffed General Marshall's mission to China until its return. In both cities, the staff director noted that "their living arrangements and job assignments were as carefully prepared in advance as was their original entry into China." As the American forces quit China, some women moved to Japan and others returned to the United States.[46]

The employment of Wacs in India and China, although on a small scale, had done much to counteract the impression that women could not be successfully em-

---

[42] Memo, WAC Stf Dir AAF CT for CO WAC Det, 17 Sep 45, sub: Mil Customs and Courtesies of EW. Folder Chungking I, CBI WAC files.

[43] Ltr, CG AAF CT to WAC Stf Dir, 14 Sep 45, sub: Commendation. AAF 201.22, in WDWAC 319.1.

[44] Of 77 enlisted women, 50 were eligible for discharge, but only 23 desired it. Routing slip, Exec for Adm Serv AAF CT, Comment 1, 31 Aug 45. Folder Chungking I, CBI WAC files.

[45] Boyce Rpt, Tab China. WDWAC 333.1 (1945–46).

[46] (1) Interv with Maj Simpson, 19 Jun 43. (2) Ltr, WAC Stf Dir CT to Dir WAC, 18 Mar 46. WDGAP 320. (3) Memo, Exec, O Dir WAC for Maj Gen William E. Bergin, G–1, 25 Apr 46. WDWAC 320. (4) Quotation from comment by Maj Simpson on draft of chapter.

ployed in a tropical or disease-ridden area. The low medical evacuation rate, and the willingness of the women to remain for indefinite periods, both indicated that they were adaptable to such employment. However, all WAC advisers noted, in conclusion, that such success was likely to occur only in headquarters that made careful advance preparation and maintained a constant friendly alertness to detect developing problems.

The Middle East Theater

An example of the use of Wacs in an inactive theater was furnished, on a small scale, in the Middle East theater.[47] Here were assigned two WAC companies, totaling slightly less than three hundred members—one located in the city of Cairo, the other several miles outside it at Camp Russell B. Huckstep.

The first request for Wacs in Cairo was received in the fall of 1943 from Maj. Gen. Ralph Royce. General Royce at this time asked only for twelve WAC secretaries "to prevent the constant and sometimes serious leaks in information."[48]

The request was approved, and in December of 1943 ten enlisted women and two WAC officers were flown to the area. Capt. Josephine Dyer headed the group and later served as staff director. Other requests followed: one for 240 women for theater headquarters, which was approved; one for 600 women for Tehran, which was disapproved on the grounds of nonavailability of WAC personnel; and two others, of 150 more Wacs for theater headquarters and 104 for the 19th Weather Squadron, which were disapproved by Operations Division of the War Department on the grounds that no military vacancies existed in the command. Before making these requisitions, the thea-

ter had entertained some hopes of on-the-spot enlistment of American women living in Cairo, but it was found that 49 out of 50 eligible civilian women refused to enlist, and the idea of local recruiting was abandoned as it had been in Europe.[49]

The shipment of 240 women for the Cairo area was accordingly organized in the United States in February of 1944. It reached the theater only after an exhausting four-month struggle to get shipping space, during which the unit spent a month at Fort Oglethorpe, a month in one area at Camp Shanks, three weeks in another area, a week at Camp Patrick Henry, three weeks on shipboard, and ten days in Naples. The delay proved trying for the women, who were so eager to get overseas that 118 of them, 13 in the first three grades, voluntarily relinquished their ratings in order to comply with the theater's requisition for unrated personnel. The women were described as "dejected and disillusioned" during the months of waiting, but their morale rose rapidly as soon as they were in transit.[50]

Arriving in Cairo on 16 June 1944, the women were sent to Camp Huckstep,

---

[47] (1) Historical Data, WAC Det, Middle East SvC, Camp Huckstep, 11 Sep 44, by Lt. Jane A. Riebesell, WAC Hist Off, with appendixes for Jul, Aug, Sep, and Oct 44. Hereafter cited as Unit Hist Camp Huckstep, by month. (2) Hist Review, WAC Det Cairo Mil Dist, 28 Aug 45; last 13 pages pertain to Huckstep unit, Sep 44–Apr 45. Hereafter cited as Unit Hist Cairo Det. (3) Summary: WAC–AMET, prepared by Sgt Birdie Weisbrod, Jun 45, based on file of G–2 Hist Sec AMET. Hereafter cited as WAC AMET Summary.

[48] Memo, MPD ASF for TAG, 10 Nov 45, sub: WAC Pers for Gen Royce per Msg JM 1814, 27 Oct (CM–IN 16628). SPGAR 220.3 WAC, Dir Pers ASF, DRB AGO.

[49] (1) Cbl CM–IN 3072, 4 Feb 44; Cbl 2442, 9 Feb 44. (2) Memo, Stf for Dir WAC, 31 Jan 44. WDGAP 320.2 sec 8a. (3) WAC AMET Summary.

[50] Unit Hist Cairo Det; WAC AMET Summary; and esp Unit Hist Camp Huckstep, p. 4.

where living conditions were pronounced by detachment officers to be "far superior to any experienced by the unit since its inception." The brick-and-wood barracks were clean, modern, and airy, and latrines were in the same building. There was plenty of hot water, and a laundry with ironing boards and washing machines. In this the women's barracks were superior to those of some of the men's units, which did not all at this time have hot water. Barracks had single-decked beds, pillows, bedding, and shelves and hangers for clothing; there was also a well-furnished dayroom with recreation equipment. On the whole, the accommodations were described as being "in striking and overwhelming contrast to the haphazard facilities encountered in the United States." The only difficulty was a temporary one when, on the first morning, it was announced that Maj. Gen. Benjamin L. Giles was to review the Wacs immediately, and 240 travel-wrinkled women descended simultaneously on ten electric irons.[51]

Within a week, 126 of the women moved to Cairo for duty with Headquarters, Africa–Middle East Theater; the remaining 114 at Camp Huckstep were assigned to the Middle East Service Command. The unit in Cairo was billeted in the New Hotel, two to five women to a room. At the end of the year, after winter rains had flooded parts of the building, and after the arrival of more Wacs left it overcrowded, the Wacs moved to new quarters in a modern building with a bedroom for every three women and a complete post exchange and hairdressing shop.[52]

As the women were interviewed and assigned to duty, a fundamental problem emerged: the theater was already at full authorized strength and not in desperate need of personnel. If Wacs replaced enlisted men, the men were idle, and if Wacs were merely added as supernumeraries, there was only part-time work for all concerned. The majority of the women were stenographers, clerks, and typists; others were messengers, bookkeepers, telephone operators, and teletypists. Many were assigned as secretaries to ranking officers, and others were placed in almost every staff section of the two headquarters, with the largest numbers in the adjutant general's office, the Signal Corps, and the Censorship Section.[53]

While most women were well satisfied with the type of work assigned them, the fact that it was not full-time caused a continuing morale problem among both men and women. At Camp Huckstep, the WAC historian reported:

Morale was affected by the existent morale at Camp Huckstep, which was poor and contagious. The majority of the men, and consequently of the women, felt that they were not actually needed and that what they were doing was not important to the war effort. Wacs were resented by some of the men.[54]

Promotions could not be given to any of the Wacs, even to a few who had replaced master sergeants, so long as the command remained overstrength. The Cairo report added:

Comfortable living quarters and opportunities for enjoyment seem to be secondary in building morale . . . the important factor is the feeling that they are needed and that individual assignments keep them busy.[55]

[51] *Ibid.* All quotations from Unit Hist Camp Huckstep.
[52] Unit Hist Cairo Det, p. 3.
[53] Asgmts at Hq not listed; July asgmts at Camp Huckstep given in Unit Hist.
[54] Unit Hist Camp Huckstep, p. 20.
[55] Unit Hist Cairo Det, Aug–Sep 44.

During the first summer, only 56 of the 240 Wacs replaced enlisted men. Toward the end of this time, the theater appealed to the War Department for authority to return the surplus men to the United States. By October, enough men had been removed from the theater so that 157 promotions were made among the Wacs, chiefly to the grades of private first class and corporal. These were followed by others at intervals. By the following spring the Cairo detachment reported:

The morale for the past period has improved . . . due partly to the fact that most of the women are now fairly busy, and also to the fact that they have a feeling of being generally accepted as a part of Headquarters.[56]

The theater consistently directed its efforts toward devices to maintain troop morale, and in these the Wacs were allowed to share fully. At Camp Huckstep, women were admitted to the excellent recreational facilities—a theater, a service club with cafeteria, game room, and library, and sports equipment. In Cairo, women were allowed to join a club with swimming, tennis, and golf facilities. At both stations, Wacs shared athletic programs in league baseball, volleyball, hockey, basketball, and even touch football, although such programs appealed only to the younger women. Women were also admitted to off-duty classes offered by the Armed Forces Institute in such subjects as French, Arabic, shorthand, and photography. Social activities were also encouraged, with organized parties and holiday celebrations, but the Wacs reported that such activities soon became burdensome and most women declined unit invitations.[57]

Wacs likewise were given the same amount of leaves and passes as the men, and were provided with equal transportation and accommodations to visit various points of interest for sightseeing or recreation. There were frequent conducted tours of the environs of Cairo, and visits by some of the women to Bengasi, Alexandria, Cyprus, Palestine, and other areas.

Restrictions were seldom sufficient to cause complaint. Marriages were permitted, suitable married quarters were provided, and women were allowed and even encouraged to spend furloughs with husbands stationed elsewhere. Nevertheless, WAC marriages in the theater were not frequent.[58]

Considering the climate and the sanitary hazards of the surrounding cities, the women's health remained good. A sanitary mess was maintained, and the nature of the area caused only minor discomforts. During the winter a water shortage was suffered, and cold weather made the unheated buildings chilly, but kerosene stoves were soon obtained and men's pile jackets were issued to the women. Heavy winter rains found a small Nile coursing through the WAC barracks; the boiler broke down; a high wind blew down the reed blind fence around the WAC area and the improved view was enjoyed by both women and men until the fence was put back up. None of these minor environmental difficulties had any appreciable effect on morale or health.

Major Craighill, who visited the area late in December of 1944, found the women's health good and illnesses "relatively less than in other units in the area."

[56] (1) WAC AMET Summary. (2) Ltr, ME to TAG, 15 Aug 44. AG 320.2, Hobby files. (3) Quotation from Unit Hist Cairo Det, p. 7.

[57] Unit Hist Camp Huckstep, Jul and Oct 44 appendixes.

[58] WAC AMET Summary gives 10; Unit Hist Cairo Det gives 17.

In the Cairo unit, women suffered the usual respiratory and gastrointestinal conditions, but in less degree than the men, and there had been no cases of venereal disease, pregnancy, malaria, or the hepatitis that was prevalent in the area. Emotional maladjustments had been minor, only one case requiring return to the United States.

Camp Huckstep Wacs had likewise had no unusual medical conditions except an incidence of appendectomies to a total of almost 10 percent of the group. There had been no cases of venereal disease, and only one pregnancy, which had existed before arrival in the theater. However, Camp Huckstep Wacs had experienced a number of minor maladjustment problems and two serious psychiatric cases, one of which had to be sent back to the United States. These cases were not more numerous than similar cases among men and, according to Major Craighill, "were reflections of the enlisted men's attitude of frustration in an area removed from the combat zone." Improvement in this respect was noted when surplus personnel was shipped out. Gynecological conditions were minor and caused no loss of time from work or any evacuation of personnel from the area.[59]

The only policy problem noted by historians was a minor version of the Pacific and European theaters' major problem: the question of direct commissions for enlisted women who were secretaries to ranking general officers. As soon as the news of such commissions elsewhere reached the theater, General Royce repeatedly applied to the War Department for permission to commission his secretary. The request, with others like it, was refused upon the insistence of Director Hobby, who had secured a ruling against any further such

action as a result of the bad publicity accompanying earlier cases. The Director suggested instead that the woman, if qualified, be selected by regular board procedure and returned to officer candidate school with promise of return to the area upon graduation. General Royce instead preferred to appoint the secretary a warrant officer, which he did. No further comment resulted except sharp newspaper criticism of the commanding general's wisdom in using public funds to make his personal plane available to the secretary and her husband for an extended honeymoon tour of the Mediterranean.[60]

As the end of the war neared, restlessness increased, and both men and women were heard commenting that they wished they were in Italy, France, America, or almost any other place. Luckily the waiting period was not long, and soon after V-J Day shipment began, with the last Wacs returning home in October 1945. Colonel Boyce, who stopped in Cairo shortly afterward on her way home from India, interviewed the chief of staff and stated that "The Wacs were highly commended for their work and they were released only when there was no longer a job to be done."[61]

Although recommending a two-year limit on the tour of duty, Major Craighill stated that the theater's experience with the employment of Wacs and nurses had

---

[59] Passage on health, including quotations and statistics: (1) Memo Maj Margaret Craighill for The SG USA through Chief Surg USAFIME, 8 Jan 45, sub: Health Conditions of Nurses and Wacs in USAFIME. SGO Hist Div 319.1 Spec Rpt—Middle East. (2) Incl 3 to Craighill IBT Rpt.

[60] Memo, Dir WAC for CofS USA, 14 Apr 44. WDWAC 314.7. Approved by CofS, 18 Apr 44; forwarded to TAG, 21 Apr 44. WDWAC 210.1.

[61] Boyce Rpt of visit to WAC Pers in Overseas Theaters, 21 Sep–26 Nov 45, Tab F: AMET. Hobby files, also OCMH.

proved that "women can adjust satisfactorily to difficult environmental problems
under proper administrative control."
Other authorities concurred, with the additional comment that employment in an
inactive theater would possibly always
present problems of full-time employment
and therefore of morale.

Other Overseas Areas

At various times requisitions and inquiries were received from other overseas
areas, all of which were disapproved or
withdrawn. In general, refusals were due
to a desire to reserve the WAC's services
for more active theaters, or to the fact that
civilian help was plentiful in the areas
concerned.

Hawaiian Department

A tentative requisition from the Hawaiian Department was received in late 1942
for one or more WAAC companies, and
was favorably considered by WAAC
Headquarters.[62] However, further investigation revealed that Waacs were chiefly
wanted to replace civilian women in the
Aircraft Warning Service. With the decision to count Waacs against the Troop
Basis, such requisitions were automatically
eliminated. No Wacs served in Hawaii except those with the Air Transport Command, which employed them in military
duties.

Canada and Alaska

Requisitions were received in 1943 for
about 700 women for stations in Canada
and Alaska, including Edmonton, White-
horse, and Dawson Creek. These were refused, not by the WAC, but by OPD and

by ASF's Military Personnel Division. At
a later date, and after arctic clothing for
women was standardized, Air Transport
Command Wacs served in both areas
without reference to the War Department
for approval.[63]

New Caledonia

Inquiries were received from New Caledonia in 1943 concerning the possibilities
of getting some 40 WAC telephone operators and an unspecified number of other
workers. Both were disapproved by OPD,
for the stated reason of shortage of WAC
personnel. A few WAC officers were later
stationed in the area for varying periods.[64]

Puerto Rico

When the WAAC was organized, the
Antilles Department rejected the idea of
employing its members, as a large Puerto
Rican labor supply was already available,
and housing would present problems.
Therefore, for the rest of World War II,
Wacs were not requisitioned or employed.
In April of 1944, the Antilles Department
recommended that a WAC recruiting
party be sent to Puerto Rico, inasmuch as
the WAVES had already been there. The
War Department accordingly sent one
WAC officer and three enlisted women,
authorized to recruit not more than 200
women for service in the United States.
There was an enthusiastic response—some
1,500 immediate applications—but many
had to be rejected for failure to pass the
aptitude test, or because of parental ob-

[62] 1st Ind, TAG to CG Hawaiian Dept, 23 Dec 42.
AG 320.2 WAAC (11–19–42) PR–W, Folder, WAAC,
Contl Div ASF Sp Coll DRB AGO.
[63] Memo, Actg Dir WAC for CG ASF, 3 Nov 43.
SPWA 320.2 sec 6.
[64] Ibid.

jections. Also, later employment was handicapped by language difficulties.[65]

Independent Commands Overseas

In addition to overseas personnel under the command of the various theaters, there were several thousand overseas Wacs who were not assigned to any theater but to the numerous independent commands authorized to send part of their personnel overseas. Neither the allotment nor the command of such personnel was a prerogative of the theater, but remained with the parent organization. Such commands included various War Department boards and groups, the Office of Strategic Services, the AAF Weather Wing and Army Airways Communications System, and especially the Air Transport Command. Most such commands seldom employed more than five to ten women at any one station, and ordinarily attached them to the nearest WAC unit for housing.

Just as in the United States, unit problems and schisms frequently resulted from the presence of these privileged outsiders with different schedules, rules, ratings, and status in general. No particular solution was reported by the theaters, other than to suggest that full disciplinary control was essential to the unit commander. As a result, theaters did not encourage most independent commands to more widespread employment of women.[66]

Of the independent commands, the ATC was by far the largest, employing Wacs in such numbers as to make possible establishment of its own detachments to

a total of some 1,300 women overseas. By special War Department authorization, ATC was empowered to determine suitable overseas stations, and select, stage, and ship WAC personnel without reference to Air Forces headquarters or to the War Department. By the end of the war it had some 241 Wacs in Alaska, 236 at two stations in Africa, 460 at five stations in the European theater, 156 in Labrador, and 227 in the Pacific.[67]

On the whole, the results of assigning Wacs overseas in such independent and often unsupervised situations compared unfavorably with the experiences of those under theater jurisdiction. While efficiency seldom was affected, morale, conduct, and the full utilization of skills suffered. Theater experiences had, with one exception, indicated that Wacs overseas were uniformly successful and presented few problems, but the example of the independent commands, as well as of the North African theater before the arrival of its staff director, strongly suggested that such success was by no means as inevitable as its universality suggested, but instead depended to some extent on close and careful selection and supervision.[68]

[65] Antilles Dept Hist Studies, Sec VI: Puerto Rican Induction Program and Use of Puerto Rican Troops, Ch. IX, p. 70. OCMH.

[66] ETO Bd Rpt, Vol. I, p. 21.

[67] Directory of the AUS Outside Continental U.S., AG 461 (6–1–45) OB–I–M, gives ATC WAC strength.

[68] (1) ATC Hist Rec Rpt, West Coast Wing, 1 Jan 43–30 Jun 44, pp. 50–53. (2) ATC Hist Rec Rpt 308, Alaskan Div, Nov 44–Sep 45. (3) Hist of 1306th AAF Base Unit, ICD ATC, Jul–Aug 45, pp. 18–21. USAF Hist Div. (4) Memo cited n. 59(1). (5) ETO ATC WAC Hist.

CHAPTER XXIV

The Office of the Director WAC

At the top of the world-wide WAC organization was the Office of the Director WAC—a small advisory group of from three to five officers located in G–1 Division of the General Staff. For the eighteen months between its establishment and the end of the war, the office, although too small for field inspection or supervision, was the Corps' nerve center for policy and information. Director Hobby later noted, "The need for placing the Director's office on the General Staff level cannot be emphasized too highly. It is absolutely necessary." [1]

It was from the first obvious that the duties of the Office of the Director could not be crowded under the G–1 roof, in spite of the fact that G–1 proved a co-operative host. The part of the Director's responsibilities concerning "personnel as individuals" fitted neatly into G–1 Division—induction, transfer, discharge, morale, uniform design, and insignia. Left unhoused were all other responsibilities, which had to be co-ordinated not with G–1 but with G–2, G–3, G–4, and the Special Staff divisions. These proved a continuing puzzle not only to G–1 Division, but to other General and Special Staff offices, which were unaccustomed to co-ordinating their business with a branch of G–1.

A first attempt to solve the problem was made by splitting the Director's Office into two unequal parts, the larger one to handle G–1 matters only, the other for the rest of her responsibilities. The Director was given two titles and two sets of procedures: as Chief, WAC Branch, G–1, she sent papers to G–1 for approval and signature; as Director WAC she corresponded directly with all other staff divisions and the Air, Ground, and Service Forces on matters that did not concern G–1 Division. [2]

This peculiar organization lasted only three months, and never in reality functioned as two halves. Many of the Director's projects were an indissoluble mixture of G–1 and non-G–1 elements; her staff debated, consulted the G–1 staff, and was still unable to decide who should sign which paper. Also, the volume of work upon the Director WAC part of the office was so much greater than that upon the larger G–1 part that members of one had no desire to sit idly upon their organizational charts while members of the other worked overtime.

---

[1] Interv, 23 Aug 48.
[2] G–1 Office Memo, printed, 26 Feb 44. CofS 324.5 WAC.

In June of 1944 the G–1 part of the office was merged with other G–1 personnel branches, and its members moved to other offices, in a general G–1 consolidation.[3] Remaining in the Director's office were, for most of the following year, only Director Hobby, Deputy Director Rice, and Capt. Patricia Lee Chance, Executive Officer.

This—the number assigned to run an average WAC company—was the smallest number of officers with which the office was ever to attempt to operate. With the separation of the WAC Branch, G–1, the peculiar situation of the Office of the Director was that of having no real connection with G–1 Division, in which it was located. In the ensuing months, some confusion was inevitable. As G–3 Division had earlier pointed out, the Office of the Director was in nature, if not in size, actually a Special Staff division, and, while the position in G–1 proved more suitable than that in the Army Service Forces, it was never as appropriate to the military organization as that of a Special Staff division. The location nevertheless lent itself to relatively smooth operation during the remaining months in which the position of chief of G–1 Division was held by General White, an officer with wide knowledge and experience in WAC administration dating from the Corps' earliest days. After his departure, there was noted an increasing tendency toward activity by G–1 Division in projects more properly the concern of other staff divisions. No final solution to this dilemma was achieved at the War Department level, although some air commands began to place their WAC advisers on the special staff level, while the nine service commands moved them from G–1 to the immediate office of the commanding general.

MAJ. GEN. MILLER G. WHITE

Removal of Operating Duties

The assumption that the Office of the Director could function with so small a staff was based upon the belief that all operating duties could be removed and delegated to the new specialist groups in other divisions. To some extent this hope was justified when the WAC specialist groups in other offices, established at General Marshall's direction, came into full operation. For the last months of the war, a complete and harmoniously operating network of WAC specialists covered most of the headquarters offices, so that inquiries, investigations, calls, and necessary studies could be referred rapidly, and successfully, to recruiting experts, public relations experts, The Inspector General, and other

[3] G–1 Office Memo to Div Chiefs, 25 May 44, Incl 1. WDWAC 314.7.

staff divisions, or to the major command or overseas theater having responsibility in a given case.

The accord and unity of action existing among such offices were, in the opinion of WAC staff officers, among the most important achievements of the new organization. The invariable practice of the Air WAC Officer, the AGF WAC Officer, and the ASF WAC Officer was to act in closest co-ordination with one another and with the Director and her deputy. Not only were personal relations friendly, but advances and improvements in one command were communicated to others before being put into effect, rather than afterward. The Director never at any time during Colonel Hobby's tenure of that office approached individual cases or policy concerning Wacs in the United States except through the WAC advisers to the three major commands, thus maintaining not only military channels but the prestige of these officers within their own headquarters.[4]

Unfortunately for the high hopes of complete delegation, the next months were to demonstrate that—as was also discovered by the British and the WAVES—the efficient operation of such a network depended upon an efficient nerve center, and that there were certain operating duties that could never be removed from a director's office by any amount of effort. These duties seemed to be inherently inseparable from the head of a woman's service in the twentieth century. In General White's opinion the office's situation was comparable to that of his own G–1 Division, which also found itself performing many onerous operating duties required of it by the Deputy Chief of Staff that were not, until after the end of the war, reflected in its personnel allotments.

Few if any of these duties were military functions of any other office. Deputy Director Rice ruthlessly swept out every duty that could be delegated, and that any other agency could or would accept. Out also went routine indorsements, records, reports from the field, and other paper work not essential to planning, including much useful material that no one had time to read.

For example, reports from WAC training centers were discontinued, since the Director no longer had any jurisdiction over their activities in any case. Bulletins from field units, even if sent, could no longer be read. No more historical material could be collected, and the only agency that could be persuaded to continue the historical file was the Bureau of Public Relations, which added a few press releases from time to time. When a WAC officer wrote to ask whether material from the field was being collected for a WAC history, Colonel Rice replied:

The Director has now only myself and Captain Lee assigned to her immediate office. Naturally we cannot do anything about collecting such data: we can only hope it is finding its way into the proper files and is being kept by the commands.

The Director constantly received communications from Wacs in the field which indicated that they believed her to be responsible for supervising a much wider range of activities. One asked why she did not send out a touring group of artists from her office to sketch WAC life in the field; others thought she should visit every one of the approximately 500 WAC units every year; one requested a chart of her

---

[4] According to statement of three officers concerned.

"headquarters," only to be told, "There is no organizational chart . . . Colonel Hobby and her staff of two officers are located on the War Department General Staff, G–1, Personnel Division." [5]

However, in spite of strenuous efforts to simplify the office's duties, certain operating duties proved impossible either to discard or to delegate. One of these was the *WAC Newsletter,* a monthly 8-page pamphlet that went to all commands and units in the field, much like that later adopted by G–1 Division to keep field personnel officers abreast of War Department policy. The value of the *Newsletter* was attested by hundreds of letters from field units, which pronounced it invaluable in promoting discipline, morale, appearance, and understanding of the Corps' mission and work in the Army. The Director therefore asked the new WAC Group, Bureau of Public Relations, which had twelve officers, to take over this project, but the group refused on grounds of insufficient personnel. Captain Chance of the Director's Office was therefore obliged to continue writing the *Newsletter* in addition to her other duties. [6]

Another operating duty resulted from the fact that the Director's Office was required from time to time to compile, check, or certify special Army-wide summaries of information or policy, as requested by particular offices. [7] The second WAC Director later noted, "some uniformity in policies has been necessary; consequently, the Director WAC's office has been used as the co-ordinating office by the major commands and all staff divisions." [8]

However, the most troublesome of the "operating" duties of which the Director's Office was never able to rid itself did not

concern such responsibilities within the Army, but rather liaison with outside agencies and the public as a whole. This type of duty, although never recognized upon any organizational chart or in personnel allotments, in actual fact consumed more than half of the office's time.

Liaison With Other Women's Services

One frequent liaison duty outside the War Department was that of co-ordination with other women's services of the United States and Allied nations. Liaison with the WAVES, SPARS, and Women Marines was more time-consuming than the general public realized. The directors of the four services formed a special subcommittee of the Joint Army-Navy Personnel Board, and met regularly. A major disciplinary or personnel policy was seldom adopted for one service until the other three had opportunity to consider

[5] (1) Ltr, ASF to all SvCs, 12 Aug 44. SPXPO–A 210.31 WAC, in WDWAC 300.4. (2) Memo, Dir WAC for WDBPR, 5 May 44. WDWAC 000.7. (3) Ltr, Lt Harriet Barr to Lt Col Jess Rice, 8 Sep 44. WDWAC 007. (4) Chart quotation in Ltr, Lt Freddie Boyle to Dir WAC, 5 Sep 44. WDWAC 000.7. (5) Query on WAC hist from Ltr, Lt Virginia Smithson to Lt Col Jess Rice, 30 May 44, and reply. WDWAC 323.3.

[6] (1) Note, 1st O Louise Goeden to 1st O Gretchen Thorpe, re action of ASF Publications Review Bd, 22 Apr 43. (2) Memo, TAG for Dir WAAC, 26 Apr 43. SPWA 062.1. (3) Memo, Dir WAC for Dir, Bur of Budget, 20 Mar 44. WDWAC 000.76 *Newsletter*. (4) Memo cited n. 5(2). (5) Memo, Dir WAC for G–1, 12 May 44, with Tab B, Gen Surles' refusal. WDWAC 000.7. (6) Memo, Dir WAC for AGO Publications Div, 28 Jun 44. WDWAC 000.7. (7) Correspondence in WDWAC 000.76 *Newsletter*, 1945–46.

[7] (1) Memo, Dir WAC for I&E Div ASF, 2 May 45. WDWAC 201.22. (2) Memo, Exec WAC for CGs AAF, AGF, ASF, 14 Jun 44. WDWAC 000.7. (3) Other requests in SPWA 300.3 (1943).

[8] Draft (not used), 14 Nov 45, sub: WAC Hist, with Note, Dep Dir WAC, re intended use in speech. WDWAC 314.7.

it. Often identical policies were arrived at and announced jointly. The three other services, having been established later, were at times several months behind the WAC in administrative detail, and often copied almost verbatim the directives and circulars that had been used successfully by the WAC. Literature was regularly interchanged. The four directors were on the friendliest of terms and met often for lunch or informal conferences. The WAVES' assistant director later wrote to Colonel Hobby, "We have leaned heavily on the experience of the Wacs and we are extremely grateful for the assistance your staff members have given us." [9]

Liaison duties with Allied women's services were somewhat less frequent, although British and Canadian services had sizable units in Washington. Information of common interest was regularly exchanged and the Director WAC or her deputy was the expected representative at many ceremonial functions of these services, and was hostess to them in return. Arrangements were made for British and American women officers to be exchanged for attendance at their respective armies' highest staff courses. The Consulate General of the Republic of Poland arranged for a tour of Polish Wacs (called, unfortunately, *Pestkas*) to WAC installations. French authorities requested full information on WAC administration for use by their own women's corps, as well as a supply of WAC uniforms. The Netherlands Embassy requested and obtained permission to train Netherlands women at WAC training centers to form the nucleus of a Netherlands women's corps for service in the Pacific. All such negotiations with high-ranking Allied officials frequently required the personal presence of the highest-ranking WAC officer the Army was able to offer. [10]

Liaison With the National Civilian Advisory Committee

Equally official in nature, and required of the Director by War Department directive, was liaison with the WAC's National Civilian Advisory Committee. This organization had been established, upon General Somervell's recommendation, at the time of the Director's transfer to G–1 Division, in order to bring to bear the influence of prominent civilian women "to advise on WAC matters, assist in disseminating news about the Corps, and aid in recruiting." [11] This committee consisted of the chairman of each service command committee, plus twelve others selected by the Director, representative of various occupations, faiths, and races. These women maintained contact with the Office of the Chief of Staff through that of the Director WAC. It was necessary for the Director's staff to collect information and write the committee a monthly bulletin on events in the WAC, to receive and act on their recommendations, to call twice-yearly conventions, and in general to render appropriate recognition to the interest and helpfulness of these prominent women. [12]

Such a group, with its energies properly directed, proved invaluable in improving the community standing of the WAC and thus the number and type of recruits. On the other hand, to keep its members prop-

---

[9] (1) See Part Three, below, for instances of joint action. (2) Ltr, SPARS to WAC, 3 Nov 44, thanking WAC for info on Negro dets. WDWAC 080. (3) Ltr, Dep Dir Rice to Capt Mildred McAfee, 7 Jul 44. WDWAC 080. (4) Ltr, Asst Dir WAVES to Dir WAC, 14 May 45. WDWAC 370.01.

[10] ATS and Polish correspondents, WDWAC 080 (1944).

[11] ASF Summary, ASF Cir 101, 15 Apr 44.

[12] Ltr, Dir WAC to CG ASF, 9 Oct 44, sub: National Civilian Advisory Committee. WDWAC 334, in SPAP 319.1 WAC.

erly informed, to give proper individual attention to their suggestions, and to keep up the close relationship directed by the Chief of Staff, all could well have absorbed the entire time of one staff officer, had liaison with this organization been reflected in personnel allotments.

Liaison With the American Red Cross

The Director's Office held a similar responsibility in regard to liaison with the American Red Cross. This organization was committed to the principle of employing its funds and staff for the assistance of military personnel regardless of the race or sex of the persons assisted. Actually, in most overseas theaters, the organization had not proved sufficiently flexible to adapt to the needs of feminine newcomers to the armed forces, although not for lack of effort on the part of the national headquarters, which received high War Department praise for its efforts and cooperativeness. Frequent conferences were held by the Director's Office with national representatives, during which a maternity care plan was worked out and field recreational facilities for women discussed, as well as other needs of women on Army stations, which the local Red Cross field director might help to meet. The Red Cross likewise fulfilled for women certain functions in connection with dependency investigations which, for men, were handled by Selective Service boards. A Certificate of Appreciation was recommended by the Director WAC for Miss Helen Walmsley, assistant director of the Military and Naval Welfare Service, for her effective liaison with the WAC. Again, while certain discussions could be delegated to the Air, Ground, or Service Forces, on an Army-wide level there re-

mained no liaison agency able to coordinate final plans with the Red Cross except the Director's Office.[13]

Liaison With Other National and Local Organizations

A similarly unrecognized but frequent duty of the Director's Office was that of liaison with the many other national organizations—civic, professional, social, and patriotic—which desired to consult someone in the War Department in connection with WAC affairs.

The United Service Organizations' national headquarters, in an effort to overcome the somewhat chilly initial reception of Wacs in USO facilities, asked for lists of all WAC locations, and in repeated conferences made plans to assist each unit. The American Women's Voluntary Services offered assistance to Wacs, and asked for messages for the AWVS Bulletin. The American Association of University Women was always a strong supporter of the women's services, and AAUW representatives frequently consulted or wrote the Director's staff. The same was true of the National Federation of Business and Professional Women's Clubs, a consistent advocate of universal service laws for women. The Association of Junior Leagues of America arranged for all local Junior League presidents to assist in recruiting, saying, "The number of Junior League members who are able to enlist is not very large," but that members would be urged to join or to help recruit nonmembers. The WAC Mothers Association desired to contribute parties and dayroom furniture, and wrote for detailed information. The

---

[13] (1) See overseas and policy chapters for details of Red Cross activity. (2) Memo, Exec WAC for AGO, 3 Jan 44. SPWA 001. (3) Memo, Dir WAC for Civ Awards Bd, 16 Apr 46. WDWAC 201.

Theater Wing of the Stage Door Canteen requested WAC representatives and a WAC band for a bond rally. The National Press Club desired to arrange parties for enlisted women.[14]

An extremely brief sampling of the list of other organizations corresponding with the Director's Office during this period included the National Education Association, the National Editorial Association, the National Council of Jewish Women, the National Jewish Welfare Board, the National Association for the Advancement of Colored People, the American Legion and other veterans' groups, the American Association for Health, Physical Education, and Recreation, Zonta International, the Women's Overseas Service League, the American Social Hygiene Association, and the National Federation of Press Women.[15] The national representatives of organizations of this stature, when desiring an interview with the Director or Deputy Director, obviously could not be shunted by the Army to any other source of information even if one had existed, nor could their offers of assistance be rebuffed without at least a hearing or a reply to their correspondence.

Local civic and patriotic groups were in a different category from national representatives; nevertheless, the Director's Office was obliged to reply to their inquiries, even when their requests had to be refused. For example, the Saturday Afternoon Club of Vanderbilt, Pennsylvania, asked a statement on "What America Means to Me"; the W.I.V.E.S., a group of married women dedicated to urging people to donate money and blood, asked permission to name a chapter for Colonel Hobby; the Las Vegas Chamber of Commerce asked that a WAC hospital be located in its city.

Still more difficult to refuse gracefully were hundreds of requests for personal appearances—many of them in connection with recruiting, but the majority for non-WAC patriotic activities such as bond drives, plant security awards, ceremonies to recognize civilian women's volunteer work, and other similiar festivities. These were almost all refused "because of the press of military activities" or "because of previous engagements," but nevertheless required a prompt acknowledgment.[16]

Liaison With Congress

Liaison with Congress was another delicate and time-consuming duty. Supposedly all such work was done by the War Department offices that handled Congressional liaison for the Army, but it seemed difficult to educate Congress to this belief. Although the WAC was a part of the strength of the Army, the War Department required the Director personally to prepare material for yearly budget hearings, and to attend them at the call of Congressional committees to justify and explain WAC activities separately. It was also necessary for her to answer the daily Congressional letters and telephone calls that asked for a full explanation of WAC policies. These, even if properly addressed to the Legislative and Liaison Division or the Chief of Staff, were ordinarily routed to her for consideration as to possible

[14] (1) Ltr, Secy Joint Army-Navy Committee on Welfare and Recreation, to Lt Col Rice, 21 Apr 44; (2) Ltrs from AWVS; (3) Ltrs from AAUW, 18 Jul 44, and others; (4) Ltr, Exec Secy, Assn of Jr Leagues of America, to Dir WAC, 16 Feb 44. WDWAC 080.

[15] WDWAC 080 (1944). The 080 files (1942–46) are full of letters from such groups.

[16] 1944 files, WDWAC 080, 000.7, and 350.001. Also Ltr, Mrs. William Bacon, President, Veterans Guild of Association of Army and Navy Wives, to Col Hobby, 3 Aug 44. WDWAC 080.

policy changes or explanations of existing policy. The bulk of Congressional mail asked for special favors for constituents, which could not be routinely refused without a polite explanation of the policy concerned. Hundreds of these asked waivers of entrance requirements. Dozens of congressmen asked the Director to waive the act of Congress that barred 18-year-olds and aliens from the WAC. Hundreds of other letters concerned the desire of women constituents to receive direct commissions or to attend officer candidate school—a favorite request. Others asked promotion, transfer, investigation, award of contract, and so on.[17]

Liaison With Private Citizens

All such calls, correspondence, and liaison with Congress, civic groups, and women's services were insignificant when compared with those involving the general public. No Dorothy Dix was ever taken more thoroughly into the troubled confidence of the average American than was Director Hobby. Such attention was not unknown to the Army's highest-ranking leaders, who ordinarily had large staffs equipped to handle it; but it was almost unique in War Department history that an officer of the grade of colonel, and in a subordinate staff position, should be deluged with public correspondence which, for scope and variety of subject, seemed comparable only to that received by the Chief of Staff and others with Army-wide responsibility.

Parents, husbands, and other relatives of Wacs formed the largest group of these writers. Distraught parents accused the Director of every station commander's failure to protect, promote, or otherwise care for their daughters; others feared that

harm had come to daughters overseas who had not written recently. A heartbroken mother could not understand her daughter's reduction in grade, and asked that Colonel Hobby restore the rank; the father of a prospective recruit wrote to discuss with Colonel Hobby whether his daughter should join.

Husbands and would-be husbands were particular nuisances. A soldier overseas wrote that he would probably soon be sent into combat, and if so he would probably be wounded, and if so he would probably be transferred home to recuperate, and if so he would want his wife with him; therefore, would Colonel Hobby discharge her from the WAC immediately so that she could be ready to rush to his bedside as soon as all this occurred? An Army chaplain asked that a soldier's wife, who was about to get a divorce, be transferred within persuading distance of her husband. A husband wrote that his wife had joined the WAC after a fight with him, but that they had made up a few days later, and would the Army please discharge her at once before she had to report for training? Another husband said that he realized that his wife was in the Army when he married her, but that her job was "breaking up our marriage"; he asked that she be allowed to come home and care for him properly.[18]

Hundreds of letters also came from women who had been rejected by recruiters. One woman protested, in nine pages, that she was "thwarted by a psychiatrist"

---

[17] (1) Yearly Folders, Material for Budget Hearings, WAC C1 file. (2) Ltrs in 1942, 43, 44, and 45–46 files, under 080, 032.2, 095, 330.14, and others. (3) Ltr, Rep. Frances P. Bolton to Oveta Culp Hobby, 7 Jun 44. WDWAC 032.2.

[18] These and following personal letters unless otherwise indicated, are in 1944 files, SPWA and WDWAC 095 and 330.14. There are dozens like each case cited.

in getting into the Corps. Another, "a honorable discharge Waac," asked, "Why do a discharge Wac has to may a mental test over again?" Others wrote, "Dear President Rosevelt, I am a girl of 17 year old and would love to join the Wacc," or "I am 62 years old. Please don't let my age interfere." Many begged pitifully that physical defects, "nervousness," and past records not be held against them. One distracted eligible, in doubt as to whether to enlist, bared her entire financial, emotional, and physical condition in a long letter and asked Colonel Hobby to make up her mind for her.

Many of the letter writers sought personal advantages—promises of commissions, promotion, or special assignments. Most of these went on to say that, while they preferred to enlist as ordinary privates, their special qualifications were such that it would not be fair to the nation for them to come in unless they were made officers.

Some of the personal requests were more or less matters of business. *The Army-Navy Journal*, the *Britannica Book of the Year*, and others asked for personal statements or articles. Emily Post wrote to inquire how a wedding invitation should be worded if the bride's mother was a lieutenant and her father only a mister. Clothing manufacturers desired to know where to write for models and materials. A New York carnival owner asked for a WAC band, WAC exhibits, and WAC personnel, and, without waiting for a reply, advertised that they would be a carnival attraction. A gentleman asked that he be employed to go to Latin America and recruit "senioritas" for the WAC. Approximately a hundred persons sent WAC songs, such as the man who said, "A good popular WAC song to make the Wacs more popu-

lar would do the trick for you and step up recruiting"; then they asked her to get music publishers to accept their manuscripts.[19]

There were numbers of friendly citizens who either asked or contributed small gifts. A kindly housewife donated a good recipe for scrambled eggs for WAC messes. Others sent poems, scrapbooks, and pictures of their baby girls in miniature WAC uniforms. A grandmother sent a square of cloth to be autographed and returned to her for part of a quilt. The numbers who wanted autographs and autographed pictures were in the thousands, ranging from private citizens to a Boy Scout museum. Another began, "I am a Senior in High School and all Seniors must write 7,500 words on some subject we prefer," and asked for 7,500 words. Several museums asked for one of Colonel Hobby's uniforms for their collections.[20]

Many letters asked no favors but were merely generally abusive. Vague charges of immorality still were received. Many berated the uniform; others objected to the Army's class distinctions or other policies. Local and long-distance calls were received and had to be listened to; registered letters were received and signed for. Mentally deranged individuals were especially threatening. Vindictive women demanded harsh punishments for erring Wacs, especially after each case of newspaper publicity such as the one concerning a Wac who became engaged to a German prisoner. When one of the service commands was forced into the unpopular role of strikebreaker, it was its command-

---

[19] (1) Tp Conv, Chief, Plng Br for WAC Rctg and Exec WAC, 22 Jun 44. WDWAC 341. (2) 1944 files, WDWAC 000.7, 007, and 095. Song writer quoted, 4 Sep 44, WDWAC 000.7. The Director declined to express an opinion of any song.

[20] 1944 files, WDWAC 000.7, 007, 062, and 095.

ing general who put a Wac at the telephone switchboard of a strike-bound plant, but it was the Director WAC who received the complaints.

Somewhat lost among the requests, complaints, and abuse were a few lonely letters of thanks or praise, and descriptions from pleased parents of how their daughters had benefited by Army training.

Almost all letters betrayed a misunderstanding common to both civilian and military personnel: that Director Hobby was in immediate and supreme command of all Wacs. Correspondents regularly assumed that the Director was the final authority upon all of these matters, and could grant any favor she pleased. They assumed also that she had in her office large files of information on every Wac, and was personally responsible for all the events that occurred to Wacs world-wide, or was at least equipped to discover and explain what had befallen a daughter or wife.

Answering this public correspondence proved to be the greatest of the semimilitary operating duties that the Director was never able to get out of her office. Many solutions were tried and found wanting. A plausible one, for example, was to make no acknowledgment to correspondence before forwarding it to the responsible Army command. This proved highly unsuccessful in view of the time lapse involved in the command's investigation and reply, which required several weeks for cases on domestic stations and months for overseas theaters—by which time the average distressed parent had several times more written and telegraphed the Director's Office, his congressman, the President, and any other available dignitary, thus involving the office in more negotiation than would have been re-quired for a simple acknowledgment. Another and equally ineffective approach was to make a brief acknowledgment by form letter; this, particularly when a refusal was involved, also brought down upon the office the wrath of correspondents.

Furthermore, there were some letters that could not be forwarded to any other command. There appeared to be no other office that was responsible for placing the Director's signature upon a quilt square, resolving Emily Post's dilemmas, or writing repeatedly, "Upon behalf of the Corps, may we express our appreciation of your interest." Even had there been, the mere task of sorting and forwarding communications was a formidable one, since it appeared impossible to learn the nature of a letter or telegram without opening it, or of a telephone call without accepting it.

The final solution, perforce adopted by the Office of the Director, was highly unsuccessful from the standpoint of work load, but highly successful from the public viewpoint. Upon receipt of the daily accumulation of correspondence, it was sorted and certain routine items were sent directly to The Adjutant General or other responsible agencies, without acknowledgment from the Director. Items that could be handled in this fashion included thousands of requests from lawyers and friends for the addresses of Wacs or women believed to be Wacs, since no litigation could be taken against a missing woman who might be in the Armed Forces.

Requests for recruiting information went to the Planning Branch of The Adjutant General's Office, and requests for stories or articles were sent to the WAC Group of the Bureau of Public Relations. Gifts and other expressions of interest were acknowledged by Captain Chance with a note of thanks, and routed to the proper agency for storage or file. Inquiries from distressed relatives were referred to the Army command having jurisdiction over the Wac concerned, but with a letter of acknowledgment stating that this agency, and not the Director, had command of the Wac concerned, would investigate and make the required reply, and should receive any further inquiries.

There still remained, after such actions, a formidable daily pile of correspondence which required the drafting by Deputy Director Rice of a carefully worded individual reply, suitable for the signature of the Director, the Chief of Staff, the Secretary of War, or whatever office had received the request. These replies of necessity constituted formal Army policy and required a phrasing that might subsequently appear in print without causing embarrassment. Typical explanations required by Congress and private citizens concerned the reasons why more WAC officers could not be commissioned, why some enrollment requirements could not be waived, why the Army could not transfer or discharge all Wacs who requested it, what spiritual or medical facilities were available to protect ailing members, why British or Australian civilian women had been commissioned, and, particularly, what the current moral, venereal, and maternity situation was in the Corps.

The inevitable result of such voluminous correspondence was a load of work that was staggeringly heavy for the three staff members. In view of the apparent relation of the experiences of the year 1944 to the Director's hospitalization and later retirement, and to the Deputy Director's death a few years later,[21] it was essential to understand the motives that caused the War Department neither to increase the staff

nor to decrease the duties until shortly before the end of the war. In effect, the delay was chiefly caused by a hope that the load of operating duties was merely a temporary hangover from Auxiliary status, and would diminish as soon as the public and Congress realized that the Director was not the women's commander.

Thus, General Somervell wrote to General Marshall, at the time of the office's transfer, that the WAVES had no such "operating" problem, having never gone through an auxiliary status or been allowed much voice in their own management, and that "All that is necessary to do is to place Colonel Hobby in approximately the same position as Captain McAfee."[22] As a matter of fact, postwar studies revealed that the WAVES had an identical problem. The Bureau of Naval Personnel, in a final report, stated:

Public opinion would tend to watch jealously the health, safety, and morale of women serving with the Navy, and it would naturally tend to address its inquiries to the "Director." . . . This public position of responsibility had to be backed by some substance of authority in the Bureau, else the sham would sooner or later appear, and not just the Women's Reserve but the Navy as a whole would suffer from the resulting lack of confidence. Even if another war should bring Selective Service for women, with consequent elimination of a recruiting campaign, policy would probably again require that a woman represent women in the Navy to the public.[23]

An identical conclusion was reached by British investigators, who noted, "It may be that parents of girls . . . like to think that a woman is finally responsible for

[21] See Ch. XXXV, below, on resignation of Director Hobby. Deputy Director Rice died 11 September 1949 of cancer which was first detected and treated during the months under discussion.
[22] Memo, CG ASF to CofS USA. SPAP 324.5 (3–29–44).
[23] WAVES Hist.

their well-being and not a government department." [24]

The fact that certain duties could not be delegated to any other existing agency was also well known to experienced WAC staff officers. After months of effort to rid the office of the load, the second Director WAC likewise noted that it was impossible to do so. Not only was the Director's Office, a policy agency, unable to refer certain letters to operating agencies, but they continued to refer to her for reply many inquiries which had been addressed to them.[25] Colonel Boyce summarized the experience of years as:

All efforts to route these inquiries to other divisions or agencies for original handling result in return to the Office of the Director, WAC for a statement of policy, for information seemingly not available elsewhere, or in some cases in second letters condemning the Army for "buck passing." No amount of effort ever succeeded in eliminating this load of work from the Office of the Director, WAC.[26]

The actually intolerable nature of the situation was masked for a time by the concentrated activity of the Director's staff, which until well into 1945 worked 12-, 14-, and 16-hour days of 7-day weeks. At this time, upon Colonel Rice's departure to other duties, three officers were eventually necessary to replace her. In the interim, only the weight of collected carbon copies in the files made credible the fact that any one individual could dictate and sign in one day as many pieces of correspondence as did the Deputy Director. Her only apparent rebellion was a brief scribble on one particularly insulting letter of complaint, "I guess we shan't live long enough for this to stop." [27]

At the same time, the Director's major official duty—her policy responsibilities to the War Department—had not ceased to be fulfilled, even though staff studies were generally written by Colonel Rice in the late evening hours after visitors and conferees had been cleared from her office. These policy solutions, which came freely after the office's removal from the ASF, constituted in some respects the real history of the wartime Women's Army Corps, and its legacy to the future. Although any one of the major policy fields would require a separate chapter, if not a volume, for proper discussion, the problems arising within them did not occur separately, but were handled simultaneously with each other and with outside liaison duties during the last eighteen months of the war.

[24] *Conditions in the Three Women's Services.*

[25] For example: (1) D/F, TAG to Dir WAC, 8 Feb 44, sub: Request for Info re WAC. SPWA 095. (2) Ltr, Mrs. M. V. Moore to TAG, 1 Feb 44, asking for a copy of WAC regulations; TAG sent this to Dir WAC.

[26] Draft, WAC Hist, 14 Nov 45. WDWAC 314.7.

[27] Undated handwritten note to Executive WAC in Colonel Rice's easily identifiable handwriting. WDWAC 421.

PART THREE

WAR DEPARTMENT POLICY CONCERNING THE WOMEN'S ARMY CORPS

CHAPTER XXV

Legal, Social, and Moral Problems

For the Corps' first two years, its policy problems had been chiefly those of survival—the provision of clothes to wear, places to train, officers and cadre, a recruiting campaign to beat down public disfavor. For the last eighteen months, its leaders were able to turn to the more complex and less tangible problems of successful integration of womanpower into an Army. These problems, although existing from the beginning, became increasingly important as the exciting days of establishment gave way to the long haul of endurance.

A common error among both WAC and Army authorities was the optimistic assumption that the number of special rules and regulations for women had decreased toward the end of the war. Thus, ranking Wacs could be found stating, "As men have become more and more familiar with the WAC program, there has been less and less need for special directives." [1] As a matter of fact, this was an optical illusion. By the end of the war the number of amendments to Army rules had grown from zero to well over two hundred, ranging from Athletic Activities through Barber and Beauty Shops and Physical Profile down to Use of Weapons or Arms. [2] The apparent simplification of women's administration that prevailed at the end of

the war could be traced to the fact that differences had been catalogued so well that field agencies were no longer at a loss on how to deal with them, and therefore were scarcely conscious of them.

Discharge

From the conversion period to the end of the war, the enlistment standards for women remained relatively unchanged except for minor modifications and the polishing of the screening process. [3] On the other hand, standards for discharge were almost totally undeveloped. Women were placed under the discharge rules of the Army with only one hasty addition, apparently in the belief that the dischargeability of women would not differ from that of men except in the matter of pregnancy. This proved a considerable oversimplification, and in the following months

---

[1] AAF WAC Hist.

[2] A complete list of directives pertaining to the WAC was never published. A list compiled and mimeographed in 1945 by the School for WAC Personnel Administration included about 225, but was admittedly incomplete. Copy in possession of author.

[3] Only notable new requirements: (1) WD Cir 162, 1944, Re-enlistment after discharge; (2) WD Cir 156, 1945, Enlistment over age 38 prohibited (in accordance with new circular on discharge of men and women over 40).

a number of other changes in Army Regulations were requested by the Director.

Minority Discharge

A male minor who misrepresented his age in order to enter the Army was, according to Army Regulations, not discharged if discovered, provided that his parents did not request his discharge. Many stations thereupon decided that a woman discovered to be under age could also remain in the Army if her parents concurred. However, the WAC age limit of 20 had been set by act of Congress and not by the War Department; it was therefore necessary to publish a change making mandatory the discharge of a woman found to be under age.[4]

Fraudulent Enlistment

Army Regulations provided that men concealing any fact, except minority, that would have made them ineligible for enlistment would be given a discharge other than honorable (blue). Minority was excepted, since it was felt that the excess of patriotism that prompted this concealment should not be stigmatized as was concealment of previous conviction or other major offenses. Women, unlike men, were ineligible for enlistment if they had children in certain age groups. The Director argued, for a time unsuccessfully, that concealment of children was in the same category with concealment of minority, and did not merit the blue discharge given those who concealed criminal records. It was near the end of the war when she finally secured partial acceptance of this theory; authority was then written into Army Regulations for the discharging authority to give either a white or a blue

discharge for this offense, at his discretion. The Secretary of War's Discharge Review Board was then asked to review all previously issued blue discharges in this category.[5]

Discharge for National Health, Safety, and Interest

Discharges to accept essential employment were given to men who could bring proof of an offer of such employment plus certification from a Selective Service board that the holder of the job was exempt from draft. There was at first some difficulty in deciding how to get, for a woman, certification equivalent to that of a man's Selective Service board. Moreover, it was impossible to ensure that a woman would take or keep an essential job after discharge. A man who failed to do so was at once drafted again, but there was no way to get the woman back in the Army; women could accept such a discharge and then enjoy perfect idleness or a more lucrative nonessential job.

The War Department's first solution was to forbid any women at all to be discharged for this reason. This, however, was manifestly unfair to a few scientific technicians and farm managers who had enlisted from patriotic motives and now found themselves less useful to the nation in the Army. Finally, a new procedure was worked out, for both men and women, which eliminated reference to Selective

---

[4] (1) Memo, Actg Dir Rice for G–1, 25 Jan 44. SPWA 220.8 (9–20–43), in AG 320.2 WAC. (2) WD Cir 65, 12 Feb 44, sec VI; also Cir 96, 1944, and AR 615–362.

[5] (1) Memo, Dir WAC for G–1, 15 Dec 43. SPWA 220.8 (E), in SPWA 220.8 (9–30–43). (2) C–2, AR 615–366, 22 Aug 45. (3) Memo, G–1 for SW Discharge Review Bd, 23 Aug 45; (4) D/F, G–1 to TAG, 23 Aug 45. WDGAP 220.8, in WDWAC 220.8.

Service boards. Nothing could of course solve the problem of the absence of a selective service law for women; in any future legislation it appeared desirable to provide in some way for this contingency, possibly by reserve specifications if selective service was not applicable.[6]

Dependency Discharge

As soon as the first WAC applications began to ask discharge because of the dependency of relatives, it became apparent that there was one fundamental difference in the social responsibilities of men and women, which speedily caused difficulty in the application of the men's rules of discharge. This difference, as expressed briefly by Deputy Director Rice, was, "Dependency [of relatives] on a man is ordinarily financial; dependency on a woman is more often dependency for care."[7]

Thus, it was necessary for a man desiring discharge for dependency to submit documents showing that his presence was required for the "care or support" of a dependent, "to prevent or relieve destitution." Evidence from the field indicated that post judge advocates ordinarily interpreted "destitution" strictly to mean only financial destitution. Case after case quickly accumulated in which dependency discharge requests from enlisted women were disapproved because financial destitution was not a factor. Many of these concerned sick or aged parents. A parent might have a dozen sons and one daughter in the Army, yet when a lengthy illness set in it was the daughter and not the sons whose release from the Army was demanded. If the head of a family died, it was the daughter and not the sons who must come home to care for the younger

children. Community pressure generally enforced these duties on a daughter. From one small town the mayor, minister, and other prominent citizens wired Director Hobby asking release of a woman to care for her aged parents. In most of these cases, Army discharge authorities in the field refused to allow discharge of the women concerned, since the dependency was not financial. Many other such cases concerned children who, although of independent age or legally adopted by others, encountered changed conditions through the death or disability of a guardian or through other misfortunes.[8]

Even more trouble than the parents and children, as the war progressed, were husbands. One veteran wrote to the Director: "I am asking information concerning a discharge for her due to the seriousness of my condition. As you know, it is imperative that I remain on a special diet."[9] In such cases, whether the husband was still in an Army hospital or retired on a pension, he could not be said to be financially dependent on his wife.

Continued reports from the field indicated that, whether parent, child, or husband was concerned, there was little uniformity in the interpretation of "care or support" by Army discharge authorities. Some were endeavoring to interpret "care or support" according to the American

[6] D/F, G–1 to CG AAF, 2 Jul 45. WDGAP 220.8 WAC, in WDWAC 220.8.

[7] Memo, Col Rice for Col Richard R. Coursey, G–1 Div, 23 Aug 44. WDWAC 220.8.

[8] (1) Ibid. Also AR 615–360, sec V, later AR 615–365. (2) Entire files SPWA 220.8, esp Ltr, WAC Stf Dir, Eastern Flying Tng Comd, to Dir WAC, 31 Jan 44, in SPWA 220.8 (9–30–43). (3) Ltr, Mrs. T. W. Boman to Exec WAC, 11 Sep 45. WDWAC 095 Boman. (4) Discharge files for Air WAC Div, ACofAS Pers, AAF Hq, 1944–45, esp case from AAF Troop Carrier Comd.

[9] Ltr, Mr. Dave Ferguson to Dir WAC, 3 Feb 45. WDWAC 095 Ferguson.

social concept of a woman's duties to her husband, parents, or child, but others were applying the men's "care or support" rule concerning financial destitution.[10] The Office of the Director, after study of the problem, believed that the Army should not attempt to ignore the different social responsibilities of men and women in American civil life, but should accept and acknowledge the difference in an amendment to the Army Regulations. This proposed amendment would have allowed a woman to be discharged:

. . . when, by reason of death or disability of a member of her family, she becomes the person primarily responsible for the care of a child or disabled or ill adult who is a member of her family. . . . In such case the evidence required need not include evidence that discharge is necessary to prevent or relieve financial destitution, but . . . that [it is] necessary to provide that type of care which is normally the responsibility of a woman to provide.[11]

Such a rule would have been quite similar to that used for the WAVES, who—although making no changes in published regulations—required such cases to be routed to the Bureau of Naval Personnel, which treated them more liberally on the grounds that "it was felt that an ill parent would typically depend more on a daughter in the house than on a son." [12]

This concept was not acceptable to G–1 Division, except as it applied to the wives of "dependent" veterans. For all other types of dependency—parents, children, relatives—the rules on destitution remained unchanged. For discharged husbands the reaction was sympathetic, and the Army Regulation on dependency was amended to allow the wife of a disabled veteran, or of a soldier awaiting disability discharge, to be discharged to care for him, provided that medical authorities

certified that her presence would aid in his recovery. This provoked some dispute between husbands and medical authorities; shortly before the end of the war, an amendment provided that the wife of any veteran, disabled or not, could be discharged upon presenting proof of her husband's discharge from the armed forces or Merchant Marine. This policy was announced jointly by both military and naval women's services.[13]

Discharge for Misconduct

The delicate problem of prescribing WAC standards of conduct and morals had not fully taken shape until the end of the WAAC. In general the Auxiliary's discharge rules had been far more strict than comparable Army Regulations. The original WAAC Code of Conduct, in addition to the usual enjoinders against mutiny, riot, fray, desertion, and disrespect, also made it an offense to be found drunk in uniform or otherwise to bring discredit upon the Corps, either being grounds for various punishments including discharge.[14]

Director Hobby later directed that "drinking unwisely or without moderation" be considered such a violation,

---

[10] Draft of Memo, G–1 for TAG, 5 Jun 44, in WDWAC 220.8. Prepared by Office of Director for G–1 signature, but not approved by G–1. See M/R.

[11] Memo cited n. 7.

[12] WAVES Hist, pp. 52 ff.

[13] (1) RR 1–1, par 12d. (2) WD Cir 146, 17 May 45. (3) Joint Army-Navy Agreement on Policies for Separation from Service and Leave or Furlough Status for Women in Armed Forces Whose Husbands Are Discharged Veterans or Overseas Returnees, 24 May 45; (4) Women's Reserve Cir Ltr 4–45, Members of Women's Reserve Married to Servicemen Returning from Overseas, PERS–170–MEK. WDWAC 370.01. (5) Memo, Col Boyce, G–1 Div, for Dir WAC, 11 May 45. WDWAC 220.8.

[14] WAAC Regs 1942, sec V.

whether or not actual drunkenness could be proved.[15] It was in general considered undesirable to drink at all while in uniform, or to buy packaged liquor, or to be found all evening in bars even if sober.[16] Other "conduct bringing discredit upon the Corps" was not specified, but gave discharging authorities considerable latitude. Director Hobby noted:

Particularly, we want to emphasize what it means to be a gentlewoman and . . . interpret the Corps to the public. I want you to impress each one that she is not one person being judged by the public, but the Corps is being judged by the things she does.[17]

When the Corps came under Army status and discharge regulations, it quickly became apparent that many Army discharge boards did not consider it just to discharge a woman except for misconduct and "habits and traits" for which they would discharge a man. Some Army commanders favored the recognition of the "single standard." One judge advocate wrote to the Director:

For goodness' sakes treat these girls like the enlisted men of the Army and do not try to chaperon and shelter them in too exacting a fashion . . . their private lives should be more or less left to their own guiding.[18]

On the other hand, regardless of such abstract arguments, one concrete fact was soon clear—the majority of American citizens condemned misconduct in a woman, and the majority of Wacs also condemned it. Statistics showed that the WAC average still remained high as to character, ability, and morality, and it was found that women in the average WAC barracks could be brought almost to open rebellion when forced to share their "home" with even one woman who was a prostitute, or diseased, or given to frequent carousing and drunken nausea, cursing,

and fighting, although none of these private activities was usually considered grounds for discharge of an Army man, provided that the individual fulfilled military duties in a reasonably efficient manner.

It soon became plain from experience that the presence in a WAC unit of one such individual would inevitably wreck first the morale and then the efficiency of the majority of the women who, through the fact of enlisted status, were forced against their will not only to share barracks life with her, but also to face the jokes and innuendoes of other military and civilian personnel at the station, who assumed that all Wacs' morals must be the same. To keep one such woman was to inspire requests for transfer or discharge from the others. Whatever the merits of a theoretical single standard, the practical fact was that at the current moment in society, and in recruiting, the habits and traits that rendered a woman undesirable as an associate of enlisted women were somewhat different from those that made a man an undesirable associate of enlisted men.

It came to be Director Hobby's opinion, after study of reports from the field and on the basis of her legal training, that the clue to a solution lay in the Army's well-recognized duty to protect the rights of all individuals. The female moral offender, in strict justice, could not be punished more severely than a male soldier for

[15] Memo, Dir for all Stf Dirs, 9 Feb 43. SPWA 250.12.
[16] Ltr, 13th WAAC Filter Co, Richmond, Va., to 3d SvC, 2 Feb 43, and Ind. SPWA 250.12.
[17] Speech, Min, Stf Dirs Conf, 15–17 Jun 43. SPWA 337 (6–1–43). See also: (1) WAAC Regs 1943, par 63c; also WAAC Cir 9, 9 Apr 43. (2) Ltr, Dir WAAC to CG WAAC Tng Comd, 10 Mar 43. SPWA 250.12.
[18] Ltr, Chief, JA Br 8th SvC, to Dir WAC, 15 Jul 43. SPWA 250.

identical offenses. On the other hand, the 149 other members of a WAC unit also were entitled to protection from damage to physical or mental health or well-being, and the Corps, as a volunteer group, had the right to choose its members and give honorable discharges to the unfit. Whether or not the standards of conduct of twentieth-century American women were overstrict or illogical, the fact was that they existed and could not be converted to those of men by an Army Regulation. The Director therefore recommended that discharge boards be informed that it lay within their authority to define "habits and traits" in line with the right of unit members to decent surroundings as defined by American religious and social usage.

Unfortunately for its promulgation, this policy would have deviated from Army Regulations for men, and the Director was never able to secure its formulation in writing. She did succeed in including counsel to company officers, in their refresher training, that they present such cases to Army boards in terms of the effect upon the company as a whole and upon members' efficiency, rather than the relative seriousness of a moral offense for a man.[19]

Discharge for Inadaptability

For the type of discharge given men for "inadaptability," or hopeless ineptitude on Army jobs, there was a similar difficulty for women. A man was not considered eligible for discharge under this authority so long as he could perform the work of a laborer; a woman was actually useless to the Army if she could not do one of the more limited duties open to women—clerical, technical, food preparation, or other work within her physical capacity.

She could not be assigned to work such as ditch-digging, lifting boxes and cartons, battlefield salvage, or similar service duties. Nevertheless, reports from the field indicated that Army boards, in a commendable effort at strict justice, were applying to men and women the same standards of intelligence and training in this respect, and frequently refused to discharge any woman who, had she been a man, would have been able to dig a ditch.[20]

It was Director Hobby's opinion that, as in other cases, some modification of the Army Regulations was necessary for women, to assure discharge boards of their authority to apply the "inadaptability" provision to such women and to give them an honorable discharge. Such discharge appeared desirable both to free Army manpower allotments from the burden of unassignables, and to permit the individual to find happier employment in farm or factory. Again, the Director was not able to secure War Department approval of any published deviation from men's rules. She was able only to mention the problem in officer refresher training. Officers were counseled to present the case to Army boards in terms of the military duties within a woman's strength, and not in those of the woman's relative intelligence and training as compared to an inadaptable man's.[21]

Pregnancy Discharge

The Auxiliary Corps upon its establishment encountered a situation in which, for Army nurses, a sharp distinction had always been made between the types of

---

[19] (1) AR 615–360, sec VIII, which became AR 615–368 and AR 615–369. (2) See Ch. XXXV, pp. 716–17, below.

[20] *Ibid.*

[21] (1) *Ibid.* (2) Ltr, Dir WAC to all WAC Stf Dirs, 11 Sep 46, re WD Cir 241, 10 Aug 46, sec III.

discharge for married and unmarried pregnancy: unmarried nurses found to be pregnant were given a dishonorable discharge, elsewhere reserved for convicted criminals. The whole subject was in fact of such abhorrence to the Nurse Corps that no attrition rates were officially collected, and the word *pregnancy* itself was replaced by *cyesis*.[22] In conformity with this tradition, the earliest WAAC Regulations, written before Director Hobby's appointment, contained the provision that only married women would get an honorable discharge for pregnancy, others receiving the worst type within the Auxiliary's power to bestow, a summary discharge.[23]

It was immediately evident to the Director upon her appointment that the distinction was untenable, from a legal standpoint. A military discharge "other than honorable" was never decreed except for definite violations of military or civil law, and there generally was no legal charge that could be brought against a pregnant unmarried woman in either civilian or military courts if her public conduct was not disorderly. The Army's only legal grounds for discharging such a woman was that she was no longer physically capable of military service. Therefore, in December of 1942, Director Hobby secured a change in the regulation to permit an honorable discharge by reason of "unsuitability for the service."[24] Certain officers who still felt that only married women should get honorable discharges were forced into hasty retreat when the Director inquired if they were also going to require legal proof that the married woman's husband was the father of the child. Where a couple had not met for several years a wife's claim to a better type of discharge appeared slim, yet had the Army investigated every time lapse, it would manifestly have been placed in a somewhat ridiculous situation.

All subsequent WAC and Army Regulations therefore required an honorable discharge for all pregnant women, with the eventual entry on the discharge certificate being merely "By reason of Sec. III AR 615–361," or other appropriate regulation, without reference to marital status.[25] The Army Nurse Corps, after its later entry into full Army status, likewise authorized an honorable discharge.[26] In the Navy women's services, pregnant enlisted women were also discharged honorably, "For the Convenience of the Government."[27] The War Department's official policy on the matter was formally stated early in 1945 in a letter to Congress concerning the Army Nurse Corps, which applied equally to the WAC:

Pregnancy in the case of an unmarried woman is not cognizable by the criminal law. . . . Thus, the manner in which the Army disposes of such cases is consistent with the manner in which such cases are handled in civilian society. This office is aware of no justification for considering pregnancy of a militarized single woman as a crime, when civilian society does not thus consider it.[28]

In the United States, those cases in which a child was born before a woman could be discharged were ordinarily handled, for lack of any other authority,

---

[22] ANC Hist, p. 407. For WAC pregnancy discharges, see Table 9, Appendix A.

[23] WAAC Regs 1942 (Tentative) par 38a.

[24] WAAC Cir 17, 29 Dec 42.

[25] WAAC Cir 10, 9 Apr 43; WAAC Reg, May 43; WD Cir 289, 9 Nov 43, AR 615–361, 4 Nov 44, sec III, pars 16–24, EW only; WD Cir 404, 14 Oct 44, sec III, for offs.

[26] AR 40–20, C–5, 9 Jan 44; see also ANC Hist, p. 407.

[27] Bupers Directive PERS–66–THT–QR 8/P19, 23 May 43. WDWAC 702 (1945–46).

[28] Ltr, TAG to Rep Joseph C. Baldwin, 3 Feb 45. AGCH–P 321 Nurse Corps (15 Jan 45). WDWAC 702.

by dependency discharge. If this did not apply, either because the child died or the mother announced her intent to give it away, authority for discharge was, for the duration of the war, solved only by emergency requests to headquarters, which obligingly furnished authority to discharge the woman "by authority of the Secretary of War." It was not until 1947 that authority was published for "pregnancy" discharge if a child had already been delivered, living or stillborn.[29]

Delay in discharge was particularly conspicuous in overseas theaters. Director Hobby was eventually obliged to obtain a directive stating that, if discharge had been delayed until pregnancy was so advanced that the mother's or unborn child's life would be endangered by travel, the mother might be retained in service overseas until the infant was born, and both returned to the United States. Authority was provided for getting the baby past immigration officials and into Army hospitals as a "patient," and for discharging the mother when she was no longer pregnant. The Navy Department very shortly published an identical circular.[30]

A related problem was the type of discharge, if any, that should be given for abortion. The problem occurred very rarely, but in early 1944 there came to Director Hobby's attention four or five recent cases in which Army commands had given the offender a blue or "other than honorable" discharge. It was the Director's reaction that a woman guilty of deliberate abortion, married or unmarried, should be promptly discharged, both for the sake of the other women in the Corps and for the good of the individual herself, who would ordinarily be emotionally and physically unfitted for exacting military duty for some months. However, a check

by legal officers revealed that abortion was ordinarily not a civil or criminal offense for a woman, but only for the practitioner who performed it. Furthermore, legal and medical authorities agreed that it was ordinarily impossible, after the event, to certify to a court whether abortion or miscarriage had actually taken place and, if so, whether it was illegal or accidental.[31]

The Army courts that had given blue discharges to enlisted women for this action had therefore been guilty of applying legal penalties to women who had violated no law. In accordance with her previous policy concerning pregnancy, Director Hobby sought some means of honorable discharge, which would protect the individual's rights while preserving the right of the Corps to choose the type of members it desired. She found the WAVES in an identical dilemma. That organization could find no legal basis for discharge but had hesitated to publish this fact, fearing to appear to condone abortion, and so had done nothing, the decision being left to field commands. The SPARS had an ingenious system: a woman was required by regulation to report her possible pregnancy as soon as she suspected it, and was

[29] WD Cir 43, 15 Feb 47, sec IV.

[30] (1) ETO Bd Rpt, Vol. I, pp. 25, 124–25, and Vol. III, App. 114, p. 7. (2) Ltr, ETO to Dir WAC, 10 Oct 44. WDWAC 702. (3) Ltr, AGO to all Maj Comds, ATC, Ports, and Theaters, 20 Oct 44. AG 704.11 (9–22–44) OB–P–SPGAM–MP–M; in WDWAC 702 (1945). (4) Ltr, Asst Dir WAVES to Dir WAC, 14 May 45. PERS–170–MEK, in WDWAC 370.01.

[31] Folder, WAC Separation for Pregnancy, esp Ltr, 4th SvC to CO Ft Oglethorpe, 10 Feb 44, directing "Section VIII" discharge for EW, with Ind from JAG. WDWAC 702 (2–23–44). Comments on Colonel Hobby's deliberations on the matter are from the memory of Maj. Mattie E. Treadwell, Assistant Chief, WAC Branch, G–1, who shared the conferences on the subject.

then given an honorable discharge upon medical confirmation; but if she failed to report, and termination of pregnancy occurred, she was discharged for violation of the regulation that she report her pregnancy.[32]

Director Hobby seriously considered adopting the SPARS plan, but consultation with the Office of The Surgeon General brought forth many objections. Female medical officers maintained that, since spontaneous abortion often occurred even before a woman suspected pregnancy, an other-than-honorable dismissal would be an injustice to many. Also, medical officers believed that the threat of a blue discharge would not prevent abortion, since an estimated 700,000 were performed yearly on civilian women. Medical officers also feared that a system like that of the SPARS would lead to concealment from medical officers of after-abortion hemorrhage or infection, with possible death of the victim resulting.[33]

The Director was therefore forced to drop all attempts to make induced abortion a cause for discharge. The only published reference to the problem was a line in Army discharge regulations which provided that pregnancy "and the direct complications and sequelae thereof" would be considered as incurred "not in line of duty" but with no misconduct involved. However, if the medical officer was able to prove illegality, "illegal abortions complete or incomplete will be regarded as misconduct." [34]

Discipline

The conversion to Army status presented an equally serious policy problem to the Army commanders now charged with WAC discipline. Evidence from the field soon indicated that the punishments given Wacs by Army board procedures varied widely for identical offenses. At one extreme were found those commanders who dealt out a double standard of justice, with the result that female military personnel received heavier fines and penalties for identical moral offenses than did male personnel.

At the other extreme, there was evidence that more courts were too lenient with women than too strict; many found great difficulty in punishing a woman for anything. A woman might be a habitual troublemaker and insubordinate to her commander, but if she was at all attractive and articulate, or able to shed a tear, she could frequently convince a court that she was the injured party and her company commander an old sourpuss. A comparable situation could have been imagined only had it been necessary for Army company commanders to attempt to secure discipline of handsome young men before an all-female court.

It was Director Hobby's opinion that more uniformity might be obtained, without interference with command prerogative, by including WAC officers on boards or courts trying WAC offenders. A provision was therefore included in the first WAC Regulations to the effect that at least one member of every such group would be a Wac. Reports from the field soon indicated that the provision was not

---

[32] (1) Memo, WAC Legal Off for Exec, 10 Feb 44; (2) Memo, 23 Feb 44, SPWA 220.8. Folder, WAC Separation for Pregnancy, WDWAC 702 (2-23-44). (3) Memo, Maj Treadwell for Dir WAC, 25 Mar 44, sub: Tp Convs with WAVES and SPARS Hq. WDWAC 702 (2-23-44).

[33] Informal Memo, SGO for Col Hobby, marked "not for record," 6 Apr 44, WDWAC 702.

[34] (1) AR 615-361, par 22. For illegal abortions, AW 107 applied. (2) Women's Res Cir Ltr 3-45, 7 Jun 45. PERS-170-MEK-AR 8, in WDWAC 702.

uniformly effective. At times the one WAC member was a very junior officer. Frequently the requirement was entirely circumvented when the defendant's counsel used his right of peremptory challenge to remove the one woman board member, particularly if he planned to base his client's defense on emotional grounds. Such practices became so common that some Army commanders recommended all-WAC boards for women. The commandant of the Command and General Staff School pointed out in connection with a local case that such boards should not include any male officers "since men do not seem to be able to mete out punishment to women."

Director Hobby did not incline to such an extreme, believing that Army officers' greater length of service lent valuable knowledge, that they would in time achieve the necessary objectivity, and that one WAC member would suffice. She therefore requested publication of a letter or circular inviting the attention of field commanders, and of the Judge Advocate General's Department, to the requirement for a qualified WAC officer on every board, which would necessitate provision of alternates in the event one was challenged. However, such a publication met with the objection of the Judge Advocate General, and was never promulgated. The Army Air Forces nevertheless invited the attention of inspectors to the requirement, and also informed them that it was considered "sound administration" to appoint a WAC officer as the summary court to hear charges against Wacs.[35]

The Navy experienced an identical problem. The Bureau of Naval Personnel stated:

The administration of discipline was one respect in which it was definitely felt that the "woman's point of view" should be represented, though this worked out somewhat differently than the men had anticipated . . . The Women's Reserve representative who had been provided for to guard against injustice . . . more often than not provided the saving element of objectivity to hold the line. It was often the experience that commanding officers began by manifesting a paternal tolerance of minor infractions of discipline and then felt somewhat helpless when they discovered that women would take advantage of this as readily as men. The sex difference introduces a certain amount of misplaced chivalry to upset the objectivity with which one man would view the inadequacies of another. . . . The best that could be done was to introduce the detached appraisal of Women's Reserve representatives. . . .[36]

Since the same problem occurred in higher courts, the Director sent to the Judge Advocate General a list of forty-four Wacs who were lawyers, with the suggestion that he might wish them to attend his school at Ann Arbor so that some might be qualified to sit on the Army's highest Boards of Review. The Judge Advocate General refused the offer, stating:

The Boards of Review constituted by the Judge Advocate General, pursuant to AW 50½, are statutory boards composed of members of the Judge Advocate General's Department. . . . I do not deem it practicable or desirable to change the membership of such a board merely for the consideration of a particular class of cases . . . to appoint members of the Women's Army Corps to such boards is not now contemplated.

He also refused to send WAC lawyers to Ann Arbor, saying:

The legal fields in which a member of the

<hr />

[35] (1) WD Cir 289, 9 Nov 43. (2) Quotation from Memo, Maj Selma H. Herbert, Command and General Staff Sch, for Col Boyce, 29 Jul 46; incl is CG opinion. (3) Memo, Actg Dir WAC for Dir Pers ASF, 7 Jan 44; Memo, JAG for Dir MPD ASF, 31 Jan 44, SPJGO. SPWA 250.4 (1945–46). (4) AAF Manual 120–2, WAC Insp, Hq AAF, 10 Apr 44.

[36] WAVES Hist, pp. 116–23.

Women's Army Corps may be used are so limited . . . it appears to me to be neither practical nor, from the standpoint of training, advantageous.[37]

The problem of WAC representation on boards and courts was thus never completely solved, although the requirement for one WAC representative remained in effect where not locally circumvented. The Director advised staff directors to attempt, at every station, to make arrangements for providing WAC officers of sufficient number and experience to serve on courts and boards if the local commander saw fit.

Confinement

The question of WAC confinement was difficult to discuss without any number of puns, but insofar as it was defined as imprisonment, it presented an immediate problem which eventually required a published directive to the field. The problem of where to put delinquent women had first arisen in WAAC days, in connection with the detention of AWOL women who were found to congregate in large cities.

A typical field protest from Los Angeles revealed that the local provost marshal did not know where to house them. He put one in the city jail and newspapers got the story; he dumped others on a nearby WAC company which, after four in one week, objected vigorously. It was ordinarily necessary to house an AWOL several days or even weeks until return to her station could be arranged. The protesting local officers asked Director Hobby for some place of detention for women, saying:

Here is one of the particular cases where it seems to us the War Department must recognize that the fundamental difference in sex, so often referred to in regulations, demands that in big cities where Wacs will congregate there must be adequate arrangements set up to take care of them.[38]

Accordingly, Director Hobby asked for an experiment in one city of the Western Defense Command, which would require one WAC officer and two enlisted women as military police, plus some small quarters for detention. The Provost Marshal General concurred in the proposal. For a time it appeared that General Somervell would approve the plan. However, it was eventually disapproved after Military Personnel Division, ASF, pointed out that the plan would not permit reduction in the number of male military police, and that extra allotments to take care of the WAC were not justified since Wacs formed less than 2 percent of the Army.[39]

The matter of the housing of WAC AWOL's was thus left to local arrangements—a WAC detachment if it would take them, the city jail if it would not—until just before the end of the war, when Director Hobby, with the backing of the Air Forces, succeeded in getting a directive requiring local WAC companies to accept custody when requested to do so. This was never particularly acceptable to the companies concerned, since it had an undesirable effect upon their personnel as well as requiring expensive guards and separate facilities. Nevertheless, it seemed the best compromise in the absence of female military police stations.[40]

---

[37] JAG Memo cited n. 35(3).

[38] (1) Tp Conv, Stf Dir 9th SvC and Stf Dir WFTC with Dir WAC, 23 Jul 43. (2) Ltr, 1st O Helen Woods to Dir WAC, 24 Jul 43. SPWA 320.2 (7–23–43).

[39] (1) Memo, Actg Dir WAC for G–1, 2 Aug 43, with concurrence PMG; (2) Memo, Maj Gen Russell B. Reynolds, Dir MPD ASF, for Dir Pers ASF, 10 Aug 43, with Director's second appeal, 25 Aug, and G–1's final refusal, 31 Aug. SPWA 320.2 (7–23–43).

[40] D/F, G–1 to TAG, 23 Feb 45, sub: Custody of WAC Offenders. WDGAP 250.1 WAC, in WDWAC 250.

A still more serious problem after the integration in the Army was that of finding a place to confine Wacs who were sentenced to long terms by Army court-martial. Director Hobby had always advocated that, for minor offenses, some punishment more suitable than confinement or restriction to quarters be found, since, she said, "no military purpose is served by taking a woman off the job in wartime." [41]

Since serious offenses meriting such punishment were rare among WAC members, an entire service command covering several states ordinarily had only one or two women to be confined. One inspector found a station with its one WAC offender installed in a separate guardhouse with a necessarily private bath, with a detail of three able-bodied military police to guard the door night and day. From her window she received a stream of sympathetic military and civilian visitors, bearing gifts, so that her sufferings seemed to be slight. In another case the Eighth Service Command hopefully requested that a woman just sentenced to two years confinement be transferred to the "WAC Stockade, Fort Des Moines"—unfortunately, a nonexistent institution. [42]

A WAC disciplinary barracks at one of the training centers was actually under consideration at the time, since one such centralized institution would have been adequate to care for the few WAC prisoners from all over the nation. The Commandant, Fort Des Moines, advised Colonel Hobby in response to her inquiry:

I believe that one place under competent administration could restore many of the women as good Wacs. . . . With the increase in the size of the Corps we must recognize that a few undesirables will slip in, and make provisions for their welfare. [43]

Accordingly, the Director recommended that suitable training center facilities be provided for the confinement of women serving short-term sentences. For those with longer sentences, she suggested that arrangements be made to transfer them to the Federal Industrial Reformatory for Women at Alderson, West Virginia, which she believed to be a recognized institution with long experience in the scientific rehabilitation of female prisoners. This was in line with existing policy, which provided that federal facilities might be used for male military prisoners. [44]

The portion of her recommendation concerning transfer to Alderson was approved and put into effect. Cases accepted, however, were only those in which the individual had committed a felony or violated a civil law. Still undisposed of were sentences, like the two-year sentence in the Eighth Service Command, that were imposed for violation of military regulations only. The War Department never approved Colonel Hobby's recommendation for disciplinary barracks at WAC training centers for these women. High-level negotiations were involved. The Navy Department could never be persuaded to set up a similar institution for convicted WAVES and SPARS, whom it preferred to discharge, and the War Department felt that extremely unfavorable publicity and loss of recruits might result if it was known that the WAC was

---

[41] Min, Stf Dirs Conf, 15–17 Jun 43. SPWA 337 (6-1-43).

[42] Ltr, Hq 8th SvC, 20 Jan 44, A–902 359. SPWA 250.3 (11–22–43).

[43] Ltr, Col Frank U. McCoskrie, Comdt 1st WAC Tng Cen, to Dir WAC, 17 Jan 44. SPWA 250.3 (11–22–43).

[44] Memo, Dir WAC for Dir Pers ASF, 22 Nov 43, sub: Places of Confinement for Members WAC, re conf with Dir Pers, JAG, TAG, etc; two tng cens' concurrences atchd. SPWA 250.3 (11–22–43).

the only women's service maintaining such an institution.

As the only alternative, a confidential letter was sent to all commands stating that, while courts would adjudge sentences as usual, the reviewing authority would direct discharge instead of confinement for Wacs who could not be transferred to Alderson and who did not appear to be useful members of the Corps. Under this policy, the Corps operated for the duration. Although confidential, this policy came gradually to be known and occasioned some unfavorable comment from men who felt that "nothing could be done to Wacs who break rules." Such an impression was entirely erroneous, as all penalties remained identical with the sole exception of confinement over thirty days for offenses that did not violate civilian law. Director Hobby felt that the discrimination was in fact in the other direction— that male offenders had an opportunity for rehabilitation and return to service where they could earn an eventual honorable discharge. A paragraph was inserted in the directive admonishing reviewing authorities against the natural tendency to give a woman, in lieu of confinement, a more severe type of discharge than the case merited.[45]

All women's services in the United States adopted an identical policy in this respect. The officially approved explanation stated:

The laws creating the Women's Services set up voluntary organizations. . . . Women volunteering for these services are not subject to the draft law. It is presumed that if volunteers are no longer in a position to fill a military mission, they should be returned to civilian life. It is not believed that there was any intent to place them in confinement for such offenses as would not be punishable by civil law.[46]

It was also felt that there was little economic value to the armed forces in attempting to rehabilitate women offenders, since a man who spent most of his time in the guardhouse might eventually make a good combat soldier, but a female habitual offender would seldom settle down to be a good clerk.

Maternity Care

Another of Director Hobby's first projects after her arrival in G–1 Division was a hitherto unsuccessful plan to provide some form of maternity and postnatal care for Wacs discharged from the service for pregnancy. Soldiers' wives were entitled to maternity care in Army hospitals,[47] but a Wac was not eligible to receive it on the basis of her own service, since upon discharge she was not a soldier but a veteran. As for the chances of care in veterans' hospitals, the Veterans' Administration from the beginning had refused to provide care for women discharged for pregnancy, maintaining that it might legally provide only for "defect, disease, or disability cases," and that pregnancy was not a disability but a normal condition.[48]

The War Department's reluctance to take any action apparently stemmed from the fear that attention to the problem might lead the public to exaggerate the numbers involved, which actually continued to be less than comparable civilian rates. However, the infrequency of occurrence did not, in the Director's opinion,

[45] AG Ltr, 29 May 44. AG 250.04 OB–S–M.

[46] Memo, Exec WAC for Col Hobby, 25 Apr 45. WDWAC 250.3.

[47] WD Cir 305, 5 Oct 45, sec VII, replacing earlier Cirs.

[48] Memo, G–1 for Exec WAC, 27 Apr 44, sub: Maternity Care for Mil Pers (describes conf with VA representatives, 25 Apr 44). WDWAC 702.

warrant neglect of the individuals concerned.

A woman discharged for pregnancy, and without other means of support, was frequently obliged to wander from one social institution to another, seeking charity—a situation undesirable not only for humane reasons, but for the prestige of the Army and of the Women's Army Corps, particularly if she did her wandering in uniform. WAC company commanders or staff directors habitually attempted to help such women find care, but were usually unable to do so for lack of familiarity with social agencies in the city or state to which a woman was returning. The situation was admittedly so undesirable that the Chief of Chaplains himself protested that "inadequate provisions are available for the care and rehabilitation of the members of the Corps who become pregnant." [49]

The Director did not support the extreme view held by some authorities, that pregnant women should remain in the Corps. One command protested the discharge of such women:

The regulation does not give to the members of the WAAC the same consideration and care that is given the men in the Army who become physically disqualified for active duty. . . . In a majority of pregnancy cases the Waac so discharged will have no means of support, no opportunity for securing medical care, so will become an indigent. Discharge is not a proper solution to this problem either from the point of view of the Waac as an individual, the WAAC as a Corps, the Army, or Society.[50]

This command proposed care in a special confinement sanitarium, with discharge after the child was born unless it died or was adopted. Director Hobby objected to this idea, partly because it seemed to encourage a woman to give away her baby in order to remain in the Corps, and partly because it might appear to the public that the Army was running government-supported baby farms after the German model. She believed, however, that medical care after discharge, on a veteran's status, should be made available to both married and unmarried women discharged for pregnancy if they had inadequate private means.

After a series of fruitless attempts to convince the Veterans' Administration that childbirth required medical care, Director Hobby turned to the possibility of care of discharged Wacs in Army hospitals.[51] She secured a decision from the Judge Advocate General that it was legal to care for such veterans in Army facilities; she also obtained concurrence from The Surgeon General, and a plan whereby certain Army hospitals could accept maternity cases. She then reported to G–1:

Every way I know of providing for the care of this personnel has been explored during the past year. We have been able to develop no other way that is suitable and satisfactory. It is War Department policy to provide maternity care for wives of soldiers. I believe it is therefore in keeping with this policy to provide maternity care for female military personnel whether or not they are married to soldiers.[52]

This plan was approved by G–1 and sent to the Chief of Staff's office. Here it incubated for approximately nine months

---

[49] Ltr, Chief of Chaplains, to Dir WAC, 22 May 44. WDWAC 702 (1945–46).

[50] Ltr, AAF Tng Comd to Dir WAAC, 13 Apr 43, sub: Reconsideration of Par 38a WAAC Cir 17 re Discharge of Pregnancy Cases. SPWA 300.3 (1–7–43) sec I.

[51] Memo cited n. 48; also Memo, Maj Kathleen McClure for Col Hobby, 18 May 44. WDWAC 702 (1945–46).

[52] Memo, Dir WAC for Gen Henry (G–1), 16 Sep 44. WDWAC 702 (1945–46). Tab X has SGO plan. Tab Y has JAG opinion.

until finally, in late May of 1945, shortly before the end of the war, it came to light in the form of a War Department circular. Whereas the recommendations of Director Hobby and the Chief of Chaplains had not sufficed, the War Department was finally moved to action by the repeated urgings of the prominent civilian women of the National Civilian Advisory Committee. A month later the Navy Department issued an identically worded circular permitting Navy hospitals to extend the same type of care to Waves, SPARS, Women Marines, and the Navy Nurse Corps. This problem, which had existed since the establishment of the women's services, was thus solved only after three years and in the last days of the war.[53]

Meantime, Director Hobby, while waiting for this directive, had succeeded in getting a second and supplementary plan: the help of the American Red Cross in advising discharged pregnant Wacs. Red Cross representatives were already performing this service for the Army Nurse Corps,[54] and were agreeable to aiding enlisted women. Without applying any persuasion to follow a certain plan, the female Red Cross representative at a discharged Wac's station was instructed to talk to the woman, discover her wishes, and within two weeks arrange for a complete plan covering temporary employment, maternity care in the community of her choice, and later employment to enable the mother to keep her baby if she so desired. This was accomplished by direct communication with the Red Cross representative in the community concerned, who was ordinarily familiar with all the possibilities of help from available social agencies, could arrange financial assistance if necessary, and could keep the matter confidential while sparing the pregnant

woman the ordeal of applying in person from one agency to the other.

This plan was opposed by Personal Affairs Division, Army Service Forces, which felt that the Army's personal affairs officer at the station concerned should make the arrangements. However, the Director, Army Emergency Relief, as well as Director Hobby, felt that the Red Cross could reach more communities and more specialized service agencies; and the Red Cross plan was eventually adopted. To this was soon added the authorization to use Army hospitals if the woman concerned preferred.[55]

In general, the combined system worked admirably during the remaining months of demobilization, with the Red Cross planning all needed community services and Army hospitals furnishing care when necessary. To this was added a new decision by Veterans' Administration that pregnant women were entitled to regular unemployment compensation during confinement provided they registered with the United States Employment Service while still employable for light work for a few months.[56]

---

[53] (1) D/F, G–1 to DCofS, 22 Sep 44. WDGAP 702, in WDWAC 702 (1945–46). Concurrences: TSG, AAF, AGF, ASF, JAG. (2) WD Cir 141, 12 May 45, sec I. Amended by WD Cir 146, 17 May 45. WD Cir 292, 25 Sep 45, sec II, gives servicewomen priority over other maternity and infancy cases and dependents. (3) Memo, G–1 for CofS, 13 Oct 44. CofS 324.5 WAC. (4) Min, NCAC Conf, 16–18 Feb 45. WD Lib and Hobby files. (5) Comment 4 to Memo, Dir Pers ASF for G–1, 28 May 45. WDWAC 720. (6) Navy Dept Cir Ltr 45–612, 15 Jun 45. PERS–170–EAN–P3–2, in WDWAC 702.

[54] Ltr cited n. 53(6).

[55] Summary Sheet and incl discussion, Dir WAC to DCofS (co-ordination of G–1 Div), 10 Feb 45. WDWAC 702.

[56] (1) Memo, Capt Jeanne K. Letallier, O Dir WAC, for Col Woods, Dep Dir WAC, 10 Oct 45. WDWAC 702. (2) See Summary Sheet cited n. 55.

Marriage

Marriage, according to the Army Nurse Corps precedent, had always been classed in the same category as illegitimate pregnancy; married nurses were not allowed in the Corps, and those who married while on active duty were dishonorably discharged.[57] The WAAC chose to follow the Army example; marriage was considered neither disqualifying for enlistment nor grounds for discharge. Soon after the WAAC's establishment, the Army Nurse Corps also permitted its members to be married, but not to serve on the same station as their husbands.[58] The WAAC never sanctioned any such restriction. Quite early in Auxiliary days, it was discovered that some station commanders and WAAC company commanders were refusing to permit the marriage of WAAC personnel, or were breaking up the association of married couples by transferring either husband or wife if both were stationed at the same installation.

In answer to a query as to whether a Waac required her commanding officer's permission to marry, the reply was, "The Director WAAC will authorize no action to prevent marriages of WAAC officers or enrolled women, whether to officers, enlisted men, or civilians."[59] Director Hobby then secured the War Department's concurrence to a circular which provided:

The marriage of a WAAC officer or enrolled member to a member of the armed forces will not be allowed to effect an advantage or a disadvantage in her assignment of duty, nor will it be allowed to preclude the privileges normally allowed to such personnel. WAAC officers or enrolled members will not be transferred solely because of marriage to persons serving at the same station.[60]

A provision to this effect was included in all subsequent WAC Regulations, and was generally well enforced in the United States.

Only two other amendments to Army Regulations were required concerning marriage of Wacs. One of these provided authority for change of name, which was discovered to be lacking in the existing provisions by which an enlisted man might change his name. This action—for females only—was made mandatory, not optional.[61]

The other amendment concerned the burial of husbands. As members of the Army, Wacs were entitled to burial in national cemeteries with the customary Army honors if their relatives so desired. The question eventually arose as to whether or not a Wac's husband might be buried in a national cemetery with her, in accordance with the rule which permitted wives to be buried with Army husbands. The Quartermaster General proposed that such interment be refused to servicewomen's husbands unless they had been soldiers and were entitled to it in their own right. Director Hobby appealed the question to the Under Secretary of War on the grounds that WAC legislation provided for equal rights for servicewomen. The Under Secretary agreed and directed that permission be granted, but asked that no publicity be given to the matter, since it was feared that it would be harmful both to the WAC and to the Army if the public knew that husbands

---

[57] ANC Hist, p. 108.

[58] *Ibid.*, p. 317.

[59] Ltr, 2d SvC to Dir WAAC, 12 Jan 43, and Ind. SPWA 291.12.

[60] (1) WAAC Cir 4, 5 Feb 43, sec I. Cf. WD Cir 462, 6 Dec 44, sec II, par 12*b*. (2) Memo, Dir WAAC for CofAdm Serv ASF, 13 Jan 43, and approvals from ASF and G-1. SPWA 300.3 (1–7–43) sec 1.

[61] M/R, 11 Sep 43. SPWA 201.7.

were being given the rights of wives in this respect.[62]

The Social Caste System

The WAC never, in the opinion of its members, experienced any problem comparable to that of the Army concerning restrictions on the social association of officer and enlisted personnel of the same sex. Almost all WAC officers had risen from the ranks through officer candidate school, and for this reason WAC leaders noted that the distinction "did not affect the morale and well-being of female enlisted personnel to the extent reported for male personnel."[63]

On the other hand, where personnel of opposite sex was concerned, the problem was one of the Corps' most serious. The year of the Auxiliary's existence saw the evolution of Director Hobby's views from an original acceptance of the Army tradition in this matter to a final advocacy of a more liberal policy for personnel of opposite sexes. WAAC Regulations never mentioned the matter, which was in fact never mentioned in Army Regulations, but trainees were informed that the WAAC would abide by all Army traditions. This tradition proved understandably difficult to enforce, particularly as some male instructors proved of little assistance in inculcating in enrolled Waacs a respect for the Army custom. It was, in fact, necessary for a directive to be issued saying that enrolled Waacs in training centers were not bound to obey "orders of a social nature" issued by their male officers. Trainees at General Faith's headquarters at Daytona Beach were permitted to date officers if they desired.[64]

In addition to being hard to enforce, the caste system was bitterly resented by many women who suddenly found themselves unable to associate with former friends and, on leaves at home, obliged to decline dates and stay away from parties because of their supposed social inferiority. Therefore, toward the end of the WAAC period, Director Hobby placed herself on record as opposed to the Army tradition as between opposite sexes, at least in wartime. She said, "Most of the young people of this country are in uniform. I do not think you can change a social pattern in wartime."[65] She stated that she believed there should be no bar on off-duty social engagements between officers and enlisted personnel of opposite sexes, with the exception that an officer should not date enrolled personnel under his supervision, by analogy with the civilian custom by which a good supervisor ordinarily did not date one of his employees.

Nothing came of her objections at this time, nor was any reference to the matter placed in WAC Regulations; in reply to inquiries, it was stated that "orders or regulations of local authorities will govern policies."[66]

Letters and reports from the field soon after the conversion period indicated that the unpopularity of the caste system as applied to opposite sexes was steadily increasing. Of all the reasons that civilian

---

[62] Memo, Dir WAC for Under SW, 25 Oct 44, with 1st Ind, Under SW to QMG, 8 Nov 44. WDWAC 293.

[63] Memo, Dir WAC for Col Whalen, Welfare Br, G-1, 12 Apr 46. WDWAC 334 Caste System (4-12-46).

[64] (1) Ltr, 9th SvC to Dir WAAC, 13 Apr 43, and 1st Ind. SPWA 250.1 (4-13-43). (2) Tng Memo 2, 27 Jan 43, Hq WAAC Tng Comd, Daytona Beach. Vol. Gen Info, WAAC Hist files. (3) Ltr, Army Adm Sch to 2d WAC Tng Cen, 8 Sep 43, and Inds from Tng Cen to Dir WAC and Dir WAC to Tng Cen. SPWA 250 (8-21-42), 1942.

[65] Speech cited n. 17.

[66] Ltr cited n. 64(3).

women gave for refusing to enlist, this was one of the most frequent and most plausible; of all the objections that enlisted women felt toward military life, this was the most bitter. Enlisted women from a Florida airfield wrote to President Roosevelt:

In civilian life we associated with people of our own choice, and that is one of the many reasons why we are serving in the Army; to preserve our rights for equality. . . . Many of our fathers, brothers, husbands, and sweethearts are now officers in the armed forces; according to this regulation, it is necessary for us to have permission to be seen even with our nearest relatives. Don't you think this is absurd?[67]

Another enlisted woman wrote the Director:

Thousands of the girls in the Corps have friends that are officers, and should they meet on the street, they can't stop and talk without first securing a pass . . . you are sending the girls back to their home towns where all their friends will be returning on furloughs, and how do they feel when we turn them down for a dinner date? The girls in civilian life have officer friends and they do not want anything like this to happen to them, so it is much easier to stay out of the WAC.[68]

It was a new experience for American women to be told that they were socially inferior to anyone. Colonel Hobby added:

There exists no precedent for social distinction among the women of the nation beyond the normal relationships of employer and employee.[69]

To make the situation worse, there was no uniformity of practice in this respect among the Allied nations, the U.S. armed forces, and even within the Army itself. In most Allied forces, officers were not bound by such a custom and could not be punished for dating an enlisted Wac. The U.S. Navy also promptly announced, upon the formation of the WAVES and SPARS, that off-duty social association was permissible. As a result, the WAC suffered considerably by comparison, especially in recruiting publicity, and also was faced with the problem of punishing enlisted women for dating naval or Allied officers who were not punishable.

The Army itself had no Army-wide rule on the matter. The Army had always kept its social caste system unwritten, as one of the "customs of the service," and each local commander was therefore entitled to interpret the custom, or to ignore it, as he saw fit. In the United States most commanders enforced the "custom"; a few did not. For example, the Fourth Service Command and the Third Air Force, covering in part the same territory, had different rules, and an Air Forces enlisted woman was punished for being caught dating a service command officer, who was not punished. From every Army command, and especially from overseas theaters, there was continuous evidence that the rule was habitually violated and that the impossibility of enforcing it had merely caused loss of respect for all rules.

Ranking officers such as Maj. Gen. Charles H. Bonesteel at Fort Benning reported that it would be helpful to them for the War Department to announce a firm policy, but the War Department refused to do so, pointing out that the customs of the service were not written, and should not be. The War Department noted that it would be especially difficult to put in

---

[67] Ltr, 4 EW at Buckingham Field, Ft Myers, Fla., to President USA, Dec 43. SPWA 335.11 (12–25–43).

[68] Ltr, Sgt Gwendolyn Keeney, Ft Lawton, Wash., to Dir WAC, 12 Feb 44. SPWA 335.11 (12–24–43) 1943.

[69] Memo, Dir WAC for G–1, 6 Jan 44. SPWA 335.11 (12–24–43).

writing the prohibition of association, since the wives and daughters of many Army officers were enlisted women; such Army officers would thus be placed in the embarrassing position of violating a written regulation instead of merely a custom of the service.[70]

In January of 1944, just before her move to G–1, Director Hobby again petitioned the Army Service Forces to permit off-duty association, adding:

Since most of the youth of the country is in uniform . . . they are faced with the problem of dislocation by the very process of their service. Every indication tends toward the realization that there should be no more restrictions on those in uniform than are essential to their military mission. . . . As long as this is a war-time Army, every allowance should be made for a normal social life as far as it is compatible with any stated regulations and policies governing the efficient operations of all branches of the service. In this respect it must be recognized that this is a people's army rather than a regular peace-time army, and traditions temporarily waived accordingly.[71]

The Army Service Forces nonconcurred in these views and General Dalton made the suggestion "that WAC personnel at Training Centers be apprised that literal observance of pertinent Army custom is recognized as being impracticable under wartime conditions with respect to nonofficial or private social functions."[72] G–1 Division, War Department General Staff, concurred in General Dalton's suggestion.[73] Colonel Hobby refused to make any such suggestion to training center authorities, who had at a previous meeting already stated that WAC training centers would not teach enlisted women anything that they would discover to be untrue when they reached their stations in the field.[74] Instead, she indorsed the papers back, submitting as new evidence

the WAVES policy, which stated in writing:

The custom of the Service requires great circumspection in social relationships in order to avoid any compromising of their relative military positions. However, the commanding officer of the WAVES has ruled that officers and enlisted personnel of opposite sexes may attend social functions together so long as they conduct themselves in accordance with the general rules of conduct applicable to ladies and gentlemen in any social or nonmilitary situation.[75]

However, the Army Service Forces refused to let this new request reach G–1 Division, on the grounds that the War Department had already disapproved its substance.[76]

It was almost four months before Director Hobby returned to the project, this time from the vantage point of her new office in G–1 Division. To avoid the danger of loss of discipline if enlisted women dated officers on the same post—in which case they had shown some tendency to give orders to their WAC commander instead of vice versa—the Director proposed that permission for off-duty association be limited to personnel not assigned on the same installation. In the Army chain of command, almost any officer at a given station might be regarded as the supervisor of any enlisted woman, whether or not she worked in his office. The Director therefore proposed that the Army policy be worded:

Army officers and enlisted personnel assigned on the same post, camp, or station will

---

[70] Min, Gen Council, 7 Feb 44.
[71] Memo cited n. 69.
[72] *Ibid.*, 1st Ind, Dir Pers ASF to G–1, 15 Jan 44.
[73] *Ibid.*, D/F, G–1 to Dir WAC, 26 Jan 44.
[74] Min cited n. 17.
[75] (1) D/F, Dir WAC to G–1, 5 Feb 44; (2) Bupers Info Bull, Jan 43. SPWA 335.11 (12–24–43).
[76] *Ibid.* D/F, CG ASF to Dir WAC, 9 Feb 44.

observe all established customs of the service in their social relationship at all times. Army officers and enlisted personnel *of opposite sexes, not* assigned on the same post, camp, or station, when on leave, furlough, or off duty in the continental United States, may have social engagements and attend social functions together so long as they conduct themselves in accord with the accepted rules of conduct.[77]

General White, then Assistant Chief of Staff, G–1, postponed decision on her proposal for several months, during which Colonel Hobby drafted several alternate wordings, with the advice of the WAC staff directors of the Air, Ground, and Service Forces. General White eventually concurred and, after private discussion with General McNarney, Deputy Chief of Staff, was instructed to get a directive published. At this moment General White was replaced by Maj. Gen. Stephen G. Henry. Although General White person-

ally oriented General Henry on the situation, and although General Henry at first penciled "okay" on the proposed directive, within a week he had disapproved it, saying "I have personally taken this matter up with General Surles [Director of Bureau of Public Relations]. He will *not* clear for release. Must be handled orally as any other 'custom of the service.'"[78]

Before her resignation, Director Hobby was to propose her policy twice more. In all, she had proposed seven times that the Army's social caste system be modified for personnel of opposite sexes not assigned to the same station; she was seven times refused.[79]

---

[77] Memo, Dir WAC for Gen White (G–1,) 1 May 44. SPWA 335.11 (12–24–43), 1943. See Tab C.

[78] Memo, Dir WAC for G–1, 8 Jan 46. WDWAC 335.11 (1943). Tab A is summary of all action on the proposal to date.

[79] *Ibid.*

CHAPTER XXVI

Housing, Food, and Clothing

Housing

It was the Army's policy that "standards for housing of the WAC approximate the standards for housing of male personnel, varying only where the differences between men and women necessitate changes and adjustments."[1] The modifications deemed necessary to convert Army barracks for female use were in general of two types: those essential to safety and segregation from men, and those required to adapt the plumbing and similar facilities.

For proper segregation, it was required that WAC barracks be at least 150 feet from men's barracks, or with an intervening structure; in no case were women to be housed in barracks in the midst of enlisted men's barracks. Wacs were also to be allowed window shades, where necessary, for privacy. The WAC latrine was required to be inside, or attached to, the WAC barracks, for safety as well as for privacy. For the same reasons, and to permit walking to work, it was suggested that WAC housing be in the station-complement or headquarters area, never with field troops.[2]

Modifications in the plumbing included not only the elimination of certain fixtures, but the provision of others believed needed for feminine hygiene, such as two bathtubs per 150 women. British experience pointed to the advisability of partitions or curtains between showers and toilets. Sheets were authorized for the beds in the barracks, after The Surgeon General expressed the opinion that sanitation problems peculiar to women would make it easier to launder sheets than blankets.[3] For laundry one tub and ironing board were allowed for each twenty women, plus drying racks for garments. Enlisted women ordinarily provided their own irons.[4]

Experiences of the first year gradually dictated a few more modifications. It was found that women in the WAC service uniform, with its narrow skirts, had difficulty in jumping from windows to the standard fire escape ladders, and fire stairs were ordered substituted on two-story barracks. After several women received severe shocks from using electric irons while standing on wet concrete floors in laundry rooms, duckboards were authorized beneath ironing boards.

It was found that the Army-type mess hall tables with benches attached were unsuitable for individuals in skirts because of the difficulty in climbing over the

---

[1] AGO Memo W–100–9–43, 15 Apr 45; superseded by WD Cir 325, 14 Dec 43.

[2] (1) *Ibid.;* also Ltr, AAF to CofEngrs, 16 Sep 42; (2) Ltr, CofEngrs to WAAC Hq, 6 Jan 43, and 1st Ind. WA 600.1 (1942).

[3] Ltr, EDC to 2d SvC, 12 Apr 43. QM 430. 1st Ind, 2d SvC; 3d Ind, OQMG; 6th Ind, SGO, Reqmts Div. SPWA 400.34 (3–21–42)(1) sec 3 (1942).

[4] Memo cited n. 1.

bench; it was therefore directed that the benches in WAAC mess halls not be attached to the table, or that stools be substituted.

Also, since most women carried their personal belongings in ordinary luggage rather than in barracks bags when on leave or individual travel, two square feet of luggage storage space per enlisted woman was authorized, provided that no great cost was involved. Such space was usually available, since women's units required only 330 square feet for company supply as against 1,037 for men's supply and combat equipment.[5]

*Decline in Housing
Standards*

With the exception of these improvements, all later modifications in housing made during the first years were in the nature of successive compromises with expediency, involving gradual reduction of standards. Except at Fort Des Moines, no training center housing conformed to standard. Most schools were occupied hastily and for a short time only, and had outside latrines, uncurtained showers and toilets, and sometimes men's plumbing fixtures. Port and transit facilities were of course never modified for women. The earliest WAAC barracks on Army posts in general were constructed according to specification, but when Waacs began to count against the Troop Basis, new construction became the exception rather than the rule, being authorized only where it was impossible to convert the barracks of the men who had been replaced.[6]

At the same time, standards for Army construction were falling rapidly as the supply of materials became more critical.

Construction at Army camps had long since ceased to be of a permanent type. The "mobilization-type" construction, which was at first substituted, permitted a fairly substantial frame building, usually with central heating. WAAC Headquarters immediately agreed to the Chief of Engineers' plan for mobilization-type instead of permanent housing for Waacs, except for his proposal to eliminate the two bathtubs formerly installed in new construction. Supporting WAAC Headquarters' view, The Surgeon General again stated that tubs were necessary for feminine personal hygiene, but Requirements Division, Army Service Forces, refused to permit further installation of bathtubs, and later barracks had none.

WAAC Headquarters also agreed, in the interests of economy, to abandon the earlier plan for housing a company in three one-story barracks for fifty women each, in favor of a new plan for two two-story barracks of seventy-five each. This plan, while saving one building, required the women's beds to be double-decked and crowded closely together, with less space for wall and foot lockers. This type of construction was used for many of the Air Forces WAC barracks and for some in other commands.[7]

As the war continued, the mobiliza-

---

[5] (1) Memo, Reqmts Div ASF for CofEngrs, 14 Apr 43. SPPMC 600.12, in WA 600.1 (1942). (2) Memo, WAAC Hq for CofEngrs, 22 Jun 43. SPWA 438. (3) Memo cited n. 1. (4) Memo, Exec WAC for Dir Plans and Opns ASF, 4 Jan 44, with 1st Ind, ASF to CofEngrs, 15 Jan 44. SPWA 400.242.

[6] (1) Memo, WAAC Hq for CofAdm Serv, 28 Sep 42. SPWA 314.7 sec 3 Housing Sec. (2) Memo, Housing Br WAAC Hq for Opns Div WAAC Hq, 1 Jan 43. SPWA 020 Orgn of Opns Div. (3) Memo cited n. 1.

[7] (1) Memo, WAAC Hq for CofAdm Serv, 21 Nov 42, Inds from SGO and Reqmts Div. WA 600.1. (2) Memo cited n. 6(1). (3) New 75-woman type: Memo, WAC Hq for Reqmts Div SOS, 23 Oct 43. WA 600.1 (1942).

tion-type housing was succeeded on many stations by the highly temporary "theater-of-operations-type," warmed only by coal stoves and easily penetrated by heat or chill. Here a soldier's allotted home was frequently an upper bunk so near the ceiling that he could not sit up, plus a coat rack and shelf for personal possessions, in a barracks stiflingly hot in summer and drafty in winter, with coal dust sifting over the sleepers.

Colonel Tasker, at that time in charge of WAAC housing, protested to the Army Service Forces that theater-of-operations-type housing was intended only for temporary emergency use by transient trainees and that "permanent or semi-permanent housing facilities provided for units of the WAAC are not considered emergency [housing]." [8]

Nevertheless, Requirements Division directed the WAAC to use theater-of-operations-type housing, which cost only $8,720 per unit as against $13,300 for the sturdier mobilization type. A 74-man barracks was used for 81 women, or a 63-man building for 74 women, which gave each woman a space allowance of 50 square square feet as against the previous 60 for men. The Chief of Engineers soon informed the Director that the 50 square feet was a miscalculation, and that only 42.5 per woman could be allowed in converted buildings, or 45 in new ones. Although WAAC Headquarters entertained considerable doubts of the wisdom of the decision, Director Hobby felt unable to object, and informed staff directors, "We will have to compromise. We cannot use critical material for construction of new barracks." [9]

By the end of 1943, reports brought in by General Faith's Field Inspection Service and other agencies indicated that the current policy was a miscalculation of the actual need in two directions. Wherever the employment of WAC units paralleled the employment of Army units, almost no modification proved really essential. Most Army units were merely in training for a relatively brief time at various posts in the United States, preparatory to overseas shipment. Even in station-complement units an able-bodied man was virtually certain of overseas shipment within a year or eighteen months. Wherever women were similarly treated—brief periods at various training schools, staging areas, ports, and in overseas theaters—they proved able to sleep in crowded double-decked barracks, use communal showers and outside latrines, or live in tents, huts, hutments, trailers, or any other emergency form of housing, without special modification for women.

Unfortunately, since 85 percent of the WAC never got overseas, in the great majority of cases the experience of a WAC unit was not at all comparable to that of Army units. Women, after a brief training course, found themselves at the station at which they were to remain for several years. Under the circumstances, their needs for housing resembled those of the peacetime rather than the wartime Army. [10]

British inspectors had come to an identical conclusion:

[8] Memo, Col Tasker for Reqmts Div SOS, 21 Nov 42, and Inds. WA 600.1 sec 1.

[9] (1) Ibid. (2) M/R, 3 Feb 43. WA 600.1 sec 2 (1942). (3) Memo, CofEngrs to Reqmts Div SOS, 31 May 43. CE–320.2, in WA 600.1 sec 2 (1942). (4) Quotation from Min, Stf Dirs Conf, 15–17 Jun 43. SPWA 337 (6–1–43).

[10] (1) Memo, OCofEngrs for CG ASF, 16 Aug 43, and Inds, incl Memo, Dir WAC for CG ASF, 30 Aug 43. WA 600.1 (7–2–42) sec 3. (2) Memo, Maj Mary Durr for Maj M.-A. Brown, 4 Dec 43. WA 600.1.

WAC HOUSING. *Exterior, above, and interior, below, of two types of quarters furnished women at an air base in England.*

WAC HOUSING. *Brick barracks at Fort Des Moines, above; below, interior of mobilization-type construction with central heating.*

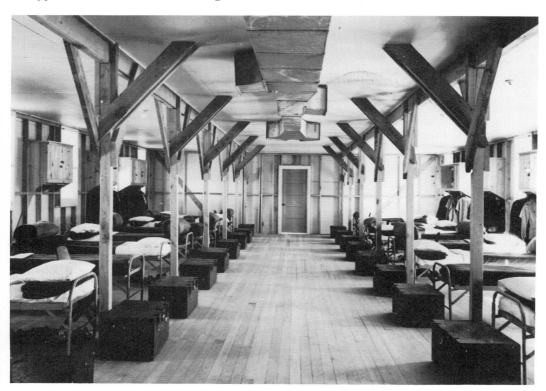

We do not find that hardships or rough conditions are resented on operational sites; on the contrary, they are willingly accepted by women who feel, when serving guns and balloons and radio-location, that they come near the actual war and that they are playing their part in the struggle. It is the boredom of non-operational units in old-fashioned barracks or uncomfortable quarters which is a more potent source of discontent than real hardship. . . . Grumbling does not arise over temporary conditions, however hard, which the girls instinctively feel are part and parcel of the war.[11]

The Navy, recognizing the permanent nature of WAVES employment, provided two- and four-woman rooms similar to the dormitories of civilian women workers. The Bureau of Naval Personnel stated:

Adequate housing was an especially urgent problem for the Women's Reserve in view of the relative permanence of the women's assignment to a station, compared to the men. . . . Housing for women called for certain features not provided in men's barracks: ironing boards, lounges, and the semi-privacy of a four-person cubicle (because women spend more time in quarters than men), more stowage space (the women's uniforms called for more space if they were to be kept in good appearance), more laundry facilities. These features were called for not as special factors or coddling but because they made the women more efficient members of the organization.[12]

For the WAC, it appeared that something resembling the peacetime Army barracks would be adequate for permanent units, although division into cubicles also appeared advantageous in a nonhomogeneous unit where members were on different shifts and schedules.

As early as the summer of 1943, the Director therefore held numerous conferences with representatives of The Surgeon General, Requirements Division, ASF, and the Chief of Engineers. For housing already built, it was too late to change the

standards, but addition of more space appeared possible. The Director noted that the low ceilings in theater-of-operations-type housing, which prevented occupants of upper bunks from sitting up to read or write letters, made an uncomfortable off-duty home for women in permanent units. She therefore asked that the 42 square feet per individual be increased to 60, which would remove the need for double-decked bunks and permit more space for clothing.[13]

The Army Service Forces concurred in this request, but virtually nullified it by stating that the provision would not be retroactive. Since housing for 98,000 women had already been built, there was to be little new construction to benefit by the improved standards. After another six months, the commanding generals of the Air Forces and Ground Forces and the Chief of Engineers supported the retroactivity clause, and eventually secured the concurrence of the Service Forces.[14]

This decision marked the limit of wartime changes in WAC quarters. Nothing could be done about the flimsy theater-of-operations-type housing for permanent units, concerning which poor reports continued to come in. Near the end of the war, WAC inspectors found that six out of six general hospital WAC detachments visited had this type of barracks, heated only by "space heaters." In no case, inspectors reported, was this the desire of the hospitals, which felt that the maintenance cost was higher than that of central heating, in spite of the lower initial cost. Wards also lost in efficiency when obliged to relieve women from their regular duties

---

[11] *Conditions in the Three Women's Services.*
[12] WAVES Hist, pp. 111–15.
[13] Memo cited n. 10(1).
[14] *Ibid.;* also Memo cited n. 10(2).

in order that they might stoke the coal stoves. In one hospital, use of poor-grade coal caused hospitalization of a large part of the detachment for carbon monoxide gas poisoning. An Army Air Forces study likewise concluded that theater-of-operations-type housing was uneconomical for permanent occupancy because of the greater number of days of hospitalization for respiratory disorders, and the long-term effects of inhalation of coal dust.[15]

All authorities also agreed that, if further construction had permitted, women's efficiency would have been promoted by some additional measures for privacy in permanent quarters. Major Craighill commented, concerning nurses' housing:

> The use in a few overseas areas of large open barracks for nurses was found unsatisfactory. It seems apparent that women value privacy more than do men, and living together under these circumstances tended to increase tension.[16]

The second WAC Director also noted:

> Lack of privacy in housing affects mental and physical health of women. It is essential that housing scales be established that will assure more privacy. The contrast between living conditions of WAC officers and WAC enlisted personnel would be more equalized if partitions are established in barracks to provide cubicles.[17]

These recommendations were generally in accord with those concerning permanent peacetime housing for men, in which cubicle-type quarters were also deemed superior where circumstances permitted.

Dayrooms

Women had particular difficulty in adapting Army dayrooms to the needs of a permanent unit. The Army-issued furniture was heavy and depressing and could seldom be made homelike by any feats of ingenuity. While many men apparently did not seem to mind the bleakness, WAC company officers pointed out that for a woman the dayroom was a substitute home—the family parlor in which the younger woman entertained her guests, and the fireside which the older women preferred to going out in the evenings. Attractively furnished dayrooms, said one authority, "go far toward offsetting the harmful effect of regimentation on women."[18] For women who did not date, there was literally no other place to spend most evenings except perhaps lying down in a double-decked bunk.

The problem of contriving cheerful dayrooms was increased by the fact that not one but two were needed. By social custom, women entertained their dates in their "home" instead of going to the men's home, yet a dayroom filled with dating couples dancing to a jukebox was scarcely a comfortable place in which older women and nondaters might lounge about in fatigue clothes and bathrobes. It was seldom found a wise solution to forbid daters the use of the dayroom, since, as Major Craighill noted:

> All women personnel need a dayroom in which they can lounge informally together, as well as a recreation or reception room in which they can entertain men. If adequate facilities are not available, the incidence of pregnancy and venereal disease is likely to increase.[19]

[15] (1) Memo, Exec WAC for Gen Henry, G-1, 13 Mar 45. WDWAC 331.1. (2) AAF WAC Hist.

[16] (1) T/S, Consultant Women's Health and Welfare SGO to Actg Dir WAC, 5 Nov 45. WDWAC 314.7. (2) Craighill SWPA Rpt.

[17] Memo, Dir WAC for Welfare Br G-1, 12 Apr 46, sub: Caste System as Affecting WAC Pers. WDWAC 334.

[18] Memo, WFTC for Air WAC Off, 30 May 45. WDWAC 353.1-369.

[19] Craighill SWPA Rpt.

The British had noted a similar need for two rooms:

> The gregarious are well cared for by wireless, games, concerts, and dances, but more quiet rooms are needed by women who wish to relax.[20]

Therefore, as the best possible solution under existing circumstances, most WAC units attempted to partition their dayroom space into two parts, or converted the noncommissioned officers' quarters in each barracks to tiny sitting rooms with facilities for writing or sewing. Furnishings were bought with private funds, sent from home, or begged, borrowed, or scrounged from local women's clubs, sorority sisters, churches, or charitable organizations. It was seldom that a WAC unit in the field any length of time did not somehow contrive a cheerful dayroom and a date room.

However, this practice was ended when the Army, early in 1945, forbade solicitation of basic dayroom furnishings from civilian organizations. Another circular prevented the use of company funds for the purchase of lamps and floor coverings.[21] For WAC units sent out after this date, any solution appeared difficult.

Hairdressing Facilities

During the first year of the Corps' existence, the provision for women of the equivalent of the men's barbershop was left to local initiative. Some stations already possessed a civilian-operated hairdressing shop for nurses and civilian employees; others did not and expressed some uncertainty as to what if any funds could be used to provide it. Such facilities often appeared even more needed by Wacs than by civilian women, because of the regulation that hair must not touch the coat collar. To meet this requirement,

many women needed permanent waves every two or three months. While the women could usually wash, set, and cut their own hair, the home permanent was not yet generally on the market.

Since the six-day work week left Wacs little time to patronize city facilities, Director Hobby recommended and the Chief of Engineers approved a directive which, at the end of the first year, authorized partitioning off part of the Wac dayrooms and the installation of water connections, if the unit could equip and operate the shop. There still remained considerable field confusion as to the financial authorization involved, and a year later a War Department directive defined the application by Army Regulations. Unit beauty shops and barbershops operated by enlisted personnel for their own use were permitted to be defined as "minor profit-making activities of a unit fund." Civilian-operated post barbershops and beauty shops were specified as functions of the Army exchange, with provision for purchasing from a unit any equipment that it had already bought.[22]

In another addition to regulations, permanent wave operators were required to have a state license, and authority was published for expenditure of unit funds for the required insurance. Director Hobby also requested and secured permission to include in overseas shipments some women who possessed licenses as hairdressers in addition to the military skill for which they were selected.[23]

---

[20] *Conditions in the Three Women's Services.*

[21] WD Cir 126, 26 Apr 45, and WD Cir 168, 1943.

[22] (1) Memo cited n. 1; also Memo, Dir WAAC for CofEngrs, 22 May 43. WA 600.1 sec 2 (1942). (2) WD Cir 321, 3 Aug 44, sec I, defining AR 210–50, 1 Jun 44.

[23] (1) Cirs 258 and 462, 1944. (2) Memo, Dir WAC for G–1, 18 Feb 44. WDGAP 320.2 sec 8a.

RECREATION ROOMS *for enlisted personnel at Brisbane, Australia, above, and North Africa, below.*

Company Officers' Quarters

For economy, WAAC Headquarters had been forced to consent to construction of company officers' bedrooms and latrine in a wing of the same building that housed the WAAC orderly room, supply room, and recreation room. By the end of 1943, reports from every command indicated that the economy had the unfortunate effect of lengthening the company commander's working day to 24 hours, since she was accessible at any hour to visits from company members, unless she arbitrarily denied herself. There was also a tendency to summon her in minor accidents, emergencies, and problems that might properly have been handled by the first sergeant.

As a result of an inspection trip, the Army Air Forces recommended that WAC officers, like male company commanders, be housed away from their units—not off the station, but in a location that would "remove them from the enlisted women so that they would not be on call 24 hours a day." Again, it was too late to correct housing plans after buildings had been constructed; no general relief was ever obtained, although stations sometimes, when other quarters were available, permitted company officers to live elsewhere. In some cases stations went to the other extreme and permitted company officers to live off the post where they were not accessible in any emergency. In the Air Forces this practice was checked by a circular requiring one duty officer to be quartered on the station, although not necessarily in the unit.[24]

Future Housing

Elaborate plans were drawn up by G–4 Division and the Chief of Engineers for the proposed peacetime WAC housing.[25] Privates, corporals, and sergeants in field units were to have hotel-type housing, only two to a room, with 120 square feet per enlisted woman (the wartime officer allowance). Each building was to have a kitchen, a dayroom, and a date room, and bountiful latrine facilities, including bathtubs. Enlisted women might also look forward to even greater privacy and comfort as they grew older and attained the first three grades; there were to be provided two-bedroom apartments for every four such women, each apartment with its own living room, kitchen, and bath. Even in training center barracks, recruits were to have 90 square feet per person, and window shades, hairdressing facilities, a dayroom, and a date room, a storage room, and adequate laundry and latrine facilities.

Junior officers were not quite so well off as top-grade enlisted women, since in accordance with the nurses' requests they were to be given only a bedroom and bath apiece, with a living room for each 12 to 18 officers, and a communal kitchenette. Only the chief nurse, assistant chief nurse, and senior WAC officer at each station would have private apartments.

Such accommodations, which met and surpassed most of the proven needs of women for privacy and home comforts, could actually, it was discovered, be provided at a lower average cost to the government than housing for Regular Army enlisted men and officers. This surprising

[24] (1) Memo cited n. 6(1). (2) Rpts of Serv and Air Comds. Min cited n. 9(4). (3) Direct quotation from Ltr, AAF to Dir WAC, 11 Dec 43. SPWA 620. (4) AAF Ltr 85–6, 3 Jul 44, superseded by AAF Ltr 35–245, 7 Jun 45.

[25] (1) Ltr, Chief of Plans and Opns OSG to CofEngrs, 13 Sep 46. MEDCH–CR, in WDWAC 622. (2) Memo, Dep Dir WAC for Col Calloway, 26 Sep 46. WDWAC 600.1.

saving resulted from the fact that most career Army men were married and drew dependents' quarters, to which women were not entitled. The provisions for women were designed to provide a semblance of home life for career women who would perforce be denied children or settled married life if they remained with the Army. Most of these plans remained on the drawing board, since the Army would not for years be in need of much new construction.

Unit Messes

In most respects the WAC unit mess was identical with similar Army messes, except for detached benches at the tables. Many messes also had any number of adjustments needed by women and contrived by the unit or by post carpenters. These included duckboards to limit the depth of sinks to a woman's reach, shelves and wheeled carriers to minimize lifting and bending, and similar mechanical contrivances to make it possible for women to manage heavy equipment designed for men. No catalog was ever made of such local inventions, although one had been begun by WAAC Headquarters before operating functions were transferred to the Army Service Forces, which discarded the material.[26]

Wherever local authorities permitted, WAC messes frequently took on an appearance quite different from that of the average men's mess, chiefly by the use of color, potted plants, and sometimes curtains, all either salvaged at no expense or acquired from unit or personal funds. One staff director recalled later, "I'll never see a sweet potato vine without thinking of the WAC."[27] At holiday seasons, decorations were generally put up, evergreens at

Christmas, autumn foliage for Thanksgiving, bunting on patriotic occasions. Quite often a piano or phonograph was borrowed from recreation buildings and installed in the mess hall to provide music with meals. The WAC unit mess invariably tended to take on something of the function of the kitchen in pioneer homes—a center for family life, visiting, and entertainment. Where there was no unit mess, and Wacs ate in consolidated messes or in city restaurants, a sense of unit solidarity was more difficult to maintain.

Consolidation of Messes

In spite of the vital role played by unit messes in morale and company unity, their maintenance presented certain difficulties. The provision of kitchen police details to staff these messes invariably caused complaint in headquarters offices, which lost a WAC working day once or twice a month. For this reason, Director Hobby for a time considered closing WAC unit messes, and allowing Wacs to eat with men at large consolidated messes where these existed.[28] Inquiry soon revealed that in the few cases where Wacs did not have separate mess, company commanders reported not only loss of *esprit,* but a serious nutritional problem. In a consolidated mess, the food was often too heavy and fattening for women. Also, women, after a hard day's work, were found to be going supperless to bed rather than change to clean uniforms, walk some distance to the consolidated mess, and brave the attention

---

[26] Memo, WAAC Hq to Fld, 24 Feb 43, and replies; Memo, Lt Ryan to Plng Serv, 3 Apr 43. SPWA 400.34 sec 3a (1942).

[27] Interv with Lt Col Helen H. Woods, USAF Res, 9 Jun 50.

[28] Draft of Memo, not sent, Dir WAC for G–1, 22 Jul 43. SPWA 220.6 (1943).

of hundreds of men. Women also often skipped breakfast for the same reason, substituting oversweet snacks or candy bars at the post exchange. On the other hand, both health and morale were improved when women could enjoy a leisurely meal at their own small quiet mess, where they did not have to dress or walk far, but could sit and talk, read mail, or listen to records.[29]

On discovering this, Colonel Hobby dropped the idea of consolidating messes, and instead requested that they not be consolidated without War Department consent to each exception. G–1 Division concurred, and a provision to this effect was placed in the first WAC Regulations in November of 1943. At once the Army Air Forces requested that authority to make exceptions be given to its headquarters, and Director Hobby agreed that such delegation might safely be made even further, to each general officer who had a WAC staff director on his staff. However, General Dalton instead decided that the authority should be given to "local commanders," which would permit station commanders to consolidate men's and women's messes without consulting higher authority. Over Director Hobby's nonconcurrence in this wording, he directed publication of a circular to this effect.[30]

Upon discovering this publication, Director Hobby renewed her recommendation to the General Staff, fearing damage to women's health if they did not eat regularly. Finally a compromise was obtained when the Army Service Forces agreed upon the wording "the Commanding General who is responsible for the operation of the post, camp, or station." While this did not necessarily bring the decision up to the level of a command having a WAC staff director, it prevented

most station commanders from acting without higher consideration of the factors involved. In view of the central role of the WAC mess in maintaining unit morale and efficiency, its abolition was ordinarily regarded by WAC advisers as a last resort where a unit had shrunk beyond any reasonable hope of maintaining its own mess.[31]

WAC Master Menu

It quickly became known to every mess officer that Wacs did not want, and could not eat, all of the items on the standard master menu for men, which were issued to each unit on a station. In general women wanted less potatoes, bread, flour, lard, syrup, pork, and other heavy or fattening foods, and more fresh vegetables and salads. Even of foods popular with both men and women, such as eggs, lean meat, and coffee, lesser quantities were consumed by women.

For the first years of the war, adjustment was attempted on a local level, with the WAC mess sergeant ordinarily adept at swapping mayonnaise for salad oil, potatoes for lettuce, and large quantities of pork for small steaks. By the end of 1944, research by the Office of The Quartermaster General, with control tests at selected installations, had established a WAC master menu that made swapping

[29] (1) Draft of Memo, Dir WAC for G–1, 23 Aug 43; (2) Memo, Dir WAC for Dir Pers ASF, 31 Aug 43. SPWA 220.6 Kitchen Police.

[30] (1) Memo, CG AAF for G–1, 2 Dec 43, with Ind, Dir Pers ASF for G–1 WD, 10 Dec 43; Ind, Dir WAC for G–1, 20 Dec 43, and Ind, Dir of Pers for G–1, 4 Jan 44. SPWA 331.4 (1943). (2) Memo, G–1 for Dir WAC, 11 Jan 44. WDGAP 331.4 WAC, in SPAP 220.3 WAC. (3) WD Cir 20, 17 Jan 44. (4) Memo, Dir WAC for G–1, 21 Jan 44. (5) Memo, ASF for G–1, 2 Feb 44. SPAP 220.3 WAC.

[31] *Ibid.*

unnecessary, and that authorized issue of the types and quantities of food proven by experience to be needed by the average WAC unit.[32]

Not only did such a master menu prove useful in improving appetite and controlling weight, but considerable saving to the Army resulted. During 1945, studies showed that the average cost per man per day was $0.58015, and per woman $0.52264. This, for the WAC strength of 100,000 as compared to an equal number of men, would result in a yearly saving to the Army of $2,099,115.00, provided that WAC unit messes were maintained.[33]

Clothing

Controversy over the main body of WAC Regulations was mild compared to that which accompanied the writing of the detailed uniform regulations after the Corps' entry into the Army, and which soon witnessed the Air Forces in mortal combat with the Ground Forces over lapel insignia, and the WAC in unsisterly dissension over the disposal of the necktie. Such commotion over articles of uniform was not unknown to the Army, where old-line officers could not recall any item changed without lengthy dissension. It was therefore not until the first days of 1944 that clothing regulations could be agreed upon,[34] and frequent amendments were necessary thereafter.

Director's Proposals

After the WAC's admission to the Army, possibly the most frequent cause of criticism was the continued use of the mismatched uniforms—nonmatching skirts and jackets of chocolate brown and mustard yellow shades—which women had

received during the early days of the expansion program. Many of these, turned in by the 15,000 women leaving at the conversion, had been repaired and re-issued to new recruits. In late December of 1943 Director Hobby submitted to the Army Service Forces a plan to eliminate them, noting that "These uniforms, which are obviously not of authorized shades, have had definite reflections on recruiting and on the morale of the troops." Since there was now a surplus of uniforms of the authorized shade, she asked a liberal salvage policy, whereby women need not wait until mismatched items were badly worn before turning them in. This request was approved by The Quartermaster General, but disapproved by Requirements Division, ASF, since it was standard Army policy that earlier procurement must be worn out, and reissued as long as repairable, before new stocks were used.[35]

The issue of secondhand clothing to new recruits was also a cause of criticism. The Director informed the ASF:

Innumerable reports to this office have indicated that the issue of used or substandard uniforms is disparaging to morale . . . and detrimental to enlistment in competition with other women's services.

Since other servicewomen got a clothing allowance with which to purchase new

[32] Memos, OQMG for Dir WAC, 29 Jan 44, and 27 May 44. WDWAC 430 (1944).

[33] Memo, Dir Subsistence Div OQMG for G-1 Welfare Br, 26 Apr 46. OCMH.

[34] AR 600-39, 5 Jan 44, Prescribed Service Uniform. For discussion of detailed policy, see discussion below. See also Erna Risch, *The Quartermaster Corps: Organization, Supply, and Services, Volume I,* UNITED STATES ARMY IN WORLD WAR II (Washington, 1953).

[35] (1) Memo, Dir WAC for CG ASF, 21 Dec 43, with Ind, OQMG, 3 Jan 44; (2) Memo, Maj Mary Durr for Dir WAC, 26 Jan 44. SPWA 421 (1943). (3) Memo, Reqmts Div ASF for Contl Div ASF, 11 Feb 44. SPRMA, in SPWA 421 sec 2 (1942).

clothing, she asked that no further Class B clothing be issued to new recruits, and that women already in the field be given one new skirt and jacket if their entire issue had been secondhand. This proposal was also rejected by Requirements Division, ASF, insofar as it concerned women already in the field, but it was agreed that new recruits should be issued one new skirt and one new jacket.[36]

A third proposal from the Director concerned an off-duty dress similar to those already authorized for the Army Nurse Corps and Army physical therapy aides. Before the conversion, Waacs had been able to discard ill-fitting or mismatched uniforms in favor of civilian clothing on off-duty occasions or when on leave, but this was no longer possible under Army status. Even had the tailored uniforms been adequate, there appeared, in the opinion of all women's services, to exist some universal psychological need of servicewomen for feminine-type attire for social occasions. The WAVES, SPARS, and Women Marines therefore authorized dress uniforms for both officers and enlisted women, while Army and Navy nurses had dress uniforms, plus summer and winter off-duty dresses in a simple shirtwaist style.

In consideration of the expense involved, the Director did not ask for the issue of such items for Wacs, but only that women be authorized to buy an approved model if they wished. She added, "It is considered by this office that a provision for an off-duty dress is necessary as a matter of well-being." However, Army Service Forces disapproved this request, stating that the WAC was not analogous to the Army Nurse Corps and that enlisted men were not allowed to buy off-duty dresses. Although Director Hobby addressed this

request to the General Staff by authority of Circular 289, as a matter of well-being, General Somervell's office returned it disapproved without allowing it to reach the War Department.[37]

As one alternative, the Director asked that The Quartermaster General consider a different fabric for the stiff and heavy summer uniform, one that would eliminate wrinkling and improve the fit. In January of 1944 the Quartermaster reported no solution and recommended that "the importance of the problem be considered insufficient to warrant a change in the fabric of the summer uniform." The retention of the men's-weight 8.2-ounce khaki was approved by the ASF and by G–4.

Likewise bypassed was the Director's attempt, concurred in by The Quartermaster General, to add more color to the uniform by the addition of an inexpensive yellow cotton scarf and gloves, similar in effect to the Women Marines' red scarf and the Navy women's blue or white shirts.

A sixth proposal, which also met defeat, was that of redesigning the WAC jacket, summer and winter, since nothing had yet been done to correct the inadvertent error of the Philadelphia Depot in respacing the jacket buttons. The Quartermaster General concurred, recommending that three buttons be used in future procurement instead of four. However, ASF's Director of Matériel refused to allow the Quartermaster to undertake developing a new design.

A seventh refusal was that of the Director's renewed request for a garrison cap

---

[36] Memo, Dir WAC for Contl Div ASF, 11 Feb 44, with atchd. SPWA 421 sec 2 (1942).

[37] (1) Memo, Dir WAC for G–1 through ASF, 16 Feb 44; (2) Memo, ACofS ASF for Dir WAC, 25 Feb 44. SPWA 421 (5–16–42) sec 2 (1942).

like the men's. She noted that men had both dress and garrison caps and that "The wearing of a garrison-type cap has been found necessary for many jobs to which WAC personnel are now assigned," the number of which "has been increased to 239 different jobs." Wacs, she said, had also been sent overseas where cleaning and blocking facilities for the dress cap were not available. Although the Director addressed her request to G–1 Division of the General Staff, as an Army-wide matter, it was disapproved by Requirements Division, ASF, on the grounds that there was a large supply of dress caps on hand.[38]

Although such surplus stocks of caps and uniforms were allegedly on hand in sufficient quantities to make changes impossible, in actual practice, the Director noted, there had been little improvement in supply. Stations reported not only that they were unable to obtain maintenance stocks and replacements for salvaged items, but that women continued to be shipped by training centers without complete clothing issue, and sent to cold climates without either caps or coats.[39]

Station commanders and inspectors in the field repeatedly protested to the Director the state to which the appearance of the WAC uniform had been reduced, in this second winter of the Corps' existence, by the failure to take action against existing defects. Inspector General reports noted that the clothing of Wacs in units inspected was of poor quality cloth, secondhand, and showing signs of much wear even when first issued, and that "Such clothing does not conform to AR 850–126 [for men] which states 'correctly fitted smart uniforms are a basic factor in the creation and maintenance of morale.'" The report of one service command caustically recommended that each Wac get

"at least one complete outfit of outer garments suitable for appearance in public."[40]

Early in 1944 members of Congress began publicly to criticize the WAC uniform. One senator informed the press in a widely quoted interview that the uniform was responsible for the lag in enlistments and that "a woman need not look like a man to make a good soldier."[41] There was no doubt that the public sided with the criticizing congressmen. A Gallup poll in January of 1944 asked, "Which uniform worn by women in the Armed Services do you like the best?" and received replies:[42]

	All replies	*Percent* Men only	Women only
Waves or Spars best	49	40	57
Marines best	26	28	24
WAC best	15	17	13
Undecided	10	15	6

Soon after the Director's move to G–1 Division, she was charged by the Meek Report with responsibility for failure to improve the uniform. In reply, the Director presented General Marshall with a list of her previous recommendations to the

---

[38] The preceding discussion is based on: (1) Memo, OQMG for G–4, 5 Jan 44. SPRMD 421.1, in SPWA 421 (5–16–42) sec 2 (1942). (2) Tab I of Memo, Dir WAC for CofS, 21 Mar 44. WDGAP 341, in WDWAC 341. (3) Memo, Dir WAC for Dir Mat ASF, 16 Nov 43, and Inds. SPWA 421. (4) Memo, Dir WAC for G–1 through CG ASF, 18 Feb 44, with comment, Dir Reqmts Div ASF for Dir MPD ASF, 1 Mar 44, and Ind, Dir Pers ASF to Dir WAC, 8 Mar 44. WDWAC 421.

[39] (1) AGO Memo W635–22–43, 10 Sep 43, changed by WD Cir 239, 30 Sep 43. (2) Memo, OQMG for Dir WAC, 6 Jan 44. SPQXK 420, in WDWAC 421. (3) Ltr, Hq Montana R&I Dist to CG 9th SvC, 22 Jan 44, with Inds. SPWA 400.34.

[40] Ltr, Asst SC IGD to CG 8th SvC, 8 Dec 43, sub: Action Ltr IGD . . . with Inds. SPLVI 333.1, in SPWA 421 (5–16–43) sec (1942).

[41] Sen. Edwin C. Johnson of Colorado, in newspapers 3–7 Jan 44, from Press Release, 2 Jan 44.

[42] As reported in newspapers, January 29, 1944.

ASF, from August 1942 to the current date, all disapproved.

The Chief of Staff's problem in determining needed action was not greatly clarified by Congressional attitude toward the matter. Unfavorable publicity originating in Congress continued throughout the spring of 1944. In one case a Representative from New York released to the press a letter to Colonel Hobby—which she had not yet received—headlined LACK-LUSTER WAC UNIFORMS HELD FACTOR IN RE-CRUITING LAG. The Congressman alleged that the uniform lacked "military pertness," and should be "piquant yet dignified, stern yet charming," and more "coruscant." He urged that New York stylists be allowed to redesign the entire uniform, which they had assured him they would, and as for the cost, he stated:

From a strictly military and economic point of view, it may be argued that there is a stock pile of half a million old WAAC uniforms. What of it? They should be used for junk. They are utterly valueless. . . . It is worth putting this stock pile on the scrap heap if you can appreciably recruit your full quota of Wacs.[43]

The language of such press releases contrasted considerably with that of a private letter, entitled "Senate Investigation of the WAC," which was shortly received from the Truman Committee, more properly known as the Special Committee Investigating the National Defense Program. This committee displayed particular interest in the stockpiles of unused material procured in the days of hoped-for expansion of the WAAC, and requested justification of the Army's action in the "reduction in WAC enlistment program," which had caused such surpluses. While the War Department was easily able to convince the committee that it had not deliberately cut down WAC enlistments, it was obvious that remedial action could not include any move to discard stockpiles of unsatisfactory uniforms.[44] Therefore, General Marshall's decisions were necessarily those which could be put into effect without much financial expenditure.

Chief of Staff's Approvals

Among the first of the Director's proposals approved by General Marshall was that of a chamois-colored cotton scarf and gloves, both actually less expensive than the leather gloves alone, but adding a becoming color to both summer and winter uniforms. The official "chamois" color was actually a pale yellow.

Possibly even more popular with the women was the new garrison cap, similar to the men's but designed to fit over women's longer haircuts. For this item, the ASF withdrew its disapproval before General Marshall directed adoption.[45] Although costing only about 39 cents in the summer version, the cap was so becoming, and so essential for many types of duties and for overseas stations, that the WAVES and women Marines shortly adopted a cap of almost identical cut. The combination of new and becoming cap, scarf, and gloves was found to add considerably to

[43] (1) *Washington Post*, April 22, 1944. (2) Ltr, Rep. Emanuel Celler (N.Y.) to Dir WAC, 21 Apr 44; this reached her after the news release; (3) Ltr, Dir WAC to Rep. Celler, 29 Apr 44. WDWAC 421.

[44] Army reply made clear that the estimated WAC strength used in procurement had never been more than 162,000. (1) Ltr, Chief Counsel, Senate Sp Com Investigating Natl Def Program, to Sp Asst to SW, 16 Jun 44, R-616-S; (2) Memo, Sp Asst to SW for CG ASF, 17 Jun 44; (3) Memo, Dep Dir Pers ASF for Dir WAC, 19 Jun 44. SPAP (6-17-44); (4) Memo, Dep Dir WAC for Dir Pers ASF, 21 Jun 44. WDWAC 319.1. (5) D/F, Dir Pers ASF for CofS, G-1, S/W, 11 Jul 44. SPWA 320.2, in SPAP 319.1 (7-11-44).

[45] Memo cited n. 38(4).

the smart appearance of the WAC uniform without the necessity for further and more expensive changes in the design of the uniform itself.[46]

Concerning the search for a nonwrinkling material for summer uniforms, it was found that a number of tropical worsted uniforms in the standard design were already on hand. These had been procured in the days when uniforms were issued to WAAC officers but had arrived too late, just as this practice was discontinued in favor of a monetary allowance for officers. With hasty procurement of a few more, it proved possible to give every WAC enlisted woman one such outfit during the summer of 1944.

The change wrought in the appearance of the WAC summer uniform by the difference in weight of materials was remarkable. Impartial observers now stated that a Wac in the summer, from being the most unbecomingly dressed of all servicewomen, now had become the smartest looking. So great was the difference from the stiff men's-weight cotton that the Chief of Staff later in the spring directed that not one but all cotton uniforms be replaced by tropical worsted. This was more than Colonel Hobby had asked, and drew protest from The Quartermaster General, who was obliged to postpone for two months delivery to sales stores of male officers' tropical worsted uniforms. Nevertheless, the Chief of Staff did not change his mind; the cotton uniforms were thereafter used only for training centers, the Pacific area, and certain other climates and duties.[47]

The last new item approved was the off-duty dress, somewhat similar in design to the approved off-duty dress of the Army Nurse Corps. General Marshall first directed that it be procured by the Quarter-master for resale to Wacs at cost. After learning that the dresses, although attractive and comfortable, would cost only about $10 each, he decided that each enlisted Wac should be issued one without cost. A jury of enlisted and officer Wacs shortly thereafter surprised Colonel Hobby by rejecting a smart model by a famous designer in favor of a more military basic dress with a collar for insignia. The dress was made up in a becoming beige shantung for summer, and in a gray wool shade close to the officer's "pink" for winter. The Quartermaster protested that immediate procurement was impossible, but at General Marshall's urging was nevertheless able to get the summer dresses out by summer.[48]

The off-duty dress proved well-fitting, being the first garment for which women's instead of men's sizes had been used in procurement. The Office of The Quartermaster General warned the field that "the patterns from which these dresses are made are basically different from the patterns used for jacket and skirt issue items of clothing; hence, the sizing will correspond to the civilian 'ready-to-wear' sizes."[49]

In general the dress proved most successful; requests for samples came from the Canadian joint staff and from other nations. Only in overseas areas were washing difficulties reported. In the United States there was much competition for issue of the dress: first priority was given to the Military District of Washington, where

---

[46] Risch, *Wardrobe for Women of the Army*, pp. 52–64.

[47] (1) *Ibid.* (2) Memo, G–1 for G–4, 20 Dec 44, with pencil notes, WDGAP 421 WAC, in WDWAC 421.

[48] Risch, *Wardrobe for Women of the Army*, pp. 53–58.

[49] Ltr, OQMG to all SvCs, Air Comds, all QM and ASF Depots, etc., 3 Jun 44. SPQXC 421 WAC Clo, in WDWAC 421. Each enlisted woman received issue of one beige chevron, if rated, one cap, and one dress; each officer could buy one cap at $1.93 and one dress at $9.97.

women were exposed to the view of the War Department; second, to recruiters, who were exposed to the public; third, to the Fourth and Eighth Service Command areas, which were exposed to the hottest summers; all others followed in order of receipt. The winter dress was issued, in the last winter of the war, to all commands.[50]

In addition to authorizing such new items, General Marshall also directed that the mismatched winter uniforms be replaced by those of authorized shade already in warehouses, and that Wacs be supplied new uniforms from the same source and no longer issued secondhand outer garments. The Quartermaster General welcomed this move, stating that the Army Service Forces policy of hoarding new uniforms had been "a shortsighted view . . . detrimental to the further recruitment of members."

The approval of the last of these changes in May of 1944 left the WAC uniform program in a state satisfactory to Director Hobby, except for specialized work garments that were to be added at a later date. The WAC now had a wardrobe comparable in neat appearance to those of the other women's services.

The WAC's service uniform remained, with a few modifications, where General Marshall had left it at this time. Even the many improvements did not make the public universally happy or silence all of the self-appointed critics. Enlisted women, who had seemed unanimously opposed to the stiff WAC cap, now in some cases perversely mourned its loss, saying, "I loved those peaked hats"; "They looked so much more military"; "Could you please reconsider your order?"[51]

After the appearance of the new items authorized by the Chief of Staff, Congress also was heard from with a "Complaint that Soldiers Receive Less Clothing than Wacs."[52] In reply, the War Department stated its final WAC clothing policy: "As a result of two and a half years experience with women personnel in the Armed Services, the Army has found that just as in civilian life women require more clothes than men."[53] The "more" was not, however, prohibitive in cost, amounting finally to only about five dollars a year per person, which would have been about $500,000 for peak WAC strength, less than one fourth the amount women saved the Army by eating less.[54]

In quantity of issue, G–1 Division noted that there were only two real differences, the chief being that Wacs got off-duty dresses, unlike men but like the nurses and all other women's services. The other difference was in the number of pairs of shoes in the initial issue, where men got two and women three, in order to provide different heel heights for service and field. In this case, G–1 noted that the Army actually had five types of men's shoes, which were issued as needed for special operations and climates, as against the WAC's two types, service and field, for all uses.

The Overcoat

The overcoat for enlisted women never offered any great problem after the issue of both overcoat and utility coat was restored. That of the officers was a different

---

[50] (1) Memo, OQMG for Dir WAC, 4 Sep 44. SPQRD 420, in WDWAC 421. (2) Ltr, Canadian Joint Stf to Exec WAC, 11 May 44. WDWAC 421.

[51] Ltrs, EW in fld to Dir WAC, esp 20 Jan 45 and 9 Feb 45. WDWAC 421.

[52] D/F, G–1 to Leg and Ln Div, 2 Oct 44. WDGAP 421, in WDWAC 421.

[53] *Ibid.*

[54] See Chart, p. 751, below.

matter, for their only authorized coat remained the rough field coat. The old WAAC "beaver" coat of light olive drab, comparable to the enlisted women's overcoat, was not restored because of shortages of its particular material, and in any case had never been authorized for nurses. As a result, women officers began wearing unauthorized overcoats of various designs and colors, especially "pink" coats modeled upon those of the men—likewise unauthorized, but worn by many officers. To stop this practice and standardize the coat, both Wacs and nurses agreed upon a coat cut exactly like the enlisted women's, but of dark olive drab to match the winter uniform. Its adoption came too late to standardize field practice to any great extent.[55]

Battle Jacket

The only other addition to the service uniform after 1944 was the battle jacket, resembling the civilian lumber jacket, first procured in England by the European theater. As European theater personnel, male and female, began to bring battle jackets to the United States, it proved impossible to stem the tide of their popularity, and it was necessary to authorize their wear by men in the zone of the interior. Many women officers also began to purchase them, and since the men's jacket could not be purchased by women, The Quartermaster General, after consultation with prominent New York stylists, produced a design for women. This lacked the pockets of the men's version, and had more of a bloused effect, since the men's bepocketed jacket had an unbecoming appearance when worn by short or plump women. Except for those individuals who had received them in Europe, the garment

was not issued, but purchased at the wearer's expense.[56]

Necktie and Handbag

The complexity of setting up rules for a new group in an army was well exemplified in a minor controversy over the necktie and the handbag. The shoulder strap of the handbag had originally been worn on the right shoulder, crossing the body diagonally, with the handbag resting on the left hip. This system was abandoned in WAAC days because the diagonal strap wrinkled the shirt and was awkward to put on and off; when worn by women of heavier build, it cut beneath the bust line to produce an undesirable profile. The rule was therefore changed to authorize wearing of the handbag on the left shoulder, hanging straight down. This method proved even worse; most women did not have large enough shoulder muscles to prevent it from slipping off, so that many handbags were lost and police reported an epidemic of handbag-snatching. Also, tailors reported that Wacs hunched the left shoulder to keep the strap on, and were rapidly becoming deformed; the marching gait was also uneven because the left arm swing was restricted. The original diagonal system was therefore restored, although later those who wished were allowed to remove the strap and

[55] D/F, G–1 for TAG through CofS, 6 Nov 44. WDGAP 421, copy in WDWAC 421.

[56] (1) Memo, Dir WAC for Col Kessinger, G–1 Div, 4 Sep 44. WDWAC 421. (2) Memo, Dir WAC for CG ASF, 4 Oct 44. WDWAC 421. (3) Memo, Dir Research and Development ASF to OQMG, 17 Oct 44. SPROG, in WDWAC 421. (4) Memo, Exec WAC for WAC Stf Dir ETO, 31 Oct 44. WDWAC 421. (5) D/F, G–1 for TAG, 4 Jan 45. WDGAP 421 WAC, in WDWAC 421. The design was approved by the Directors WAC and ANC, and by G–1, G–4, and the DCofS.

ON LEAVE IN PARIS, 1945. *Note off-duty dresses, above, and battle jackets (left), below, worn by the women.*

carry the purse in the hand when not in formation.[57]

Tucking the necktie into the shirt in the Army fashion was likewise forbidden because it added a certain undesirable bust fullness to individuals not in need of additional fullness in that respect. This provision had also shortly to be dropped in favor of the original system, for Wacs complained that the necktie hanging loose flapped in their eyes, became caught in machinery, was dipped in soup, or caused them to be arrested by military police who were not aware that the WAC had a different rule. The extra bust fullness was eventually deemed the lesser evil.

Work Clothing

The WAC uniform regulations from time to time added authorization for various types of work clothing that had been proved essential to replace the drivers' cotton coveralls, which from the first had proved an extremely poor substitute for either summer or winter work garments.

The herringbone twill cotton coveralls, as originally issued, had been designed only for tire-changing and emergency repairs. Both one- and two-piece models were used at different times, but all were ill-fitting and unbecoming garments. They were too hot for summer and for work in kitchens, too thin for protection in winter, too clumsy for use in laboratories, too unsightly for chauffeurs of staff cars, too unsanitary for hospital work. In warm climates they scratched the women's skin, causing rashes and infections, and some women proved allergic to the dye used in them. Their weight made them difficult for women to launder in the barracks, especially when the garments were grease-stained, and women who had only

one pair found that they would not dry overnight.

Even in Auxiliary days, various Army commands bombarded Director Hobby, whom they considered responsible, with requests for a substitute for the coveralls. The Army Air Forces requested a different type of work garment for Waacs engaged in aircraft maintenance, declaring that the drivers' coveralls lacked the necessary tool-holding devices for a mechanic's efficiency and were not designed for safety around moving machinery. The AAF's First Mapping Group also asked for medium-weight culottes for Waacs on duty in photo-laboratories and darkrooms: "The culotte uniform will improve the operating efficiency of personnel to such an extent as to warrant its procurement." [58] Such early requests were all disapproved by the Army Service Forces.

By mid-1944, complaints concerning the WAC herringbone twill coveralls had come in from every part of the world where Wacs were stationed, including the four major overseas theaters. In the United States, the most complete study of the deficiencies of the herringbone twill coveralls was made in the Air Forces' testing center at Wright Field. It found that the material was too thick to allow circulation of air during physical training, long sleeves and trousers limited free movement during formal exercises, the allowance of two per person was insufficient for duty assignments on flight lines or in warehouses, and the material was too hot for wear in warehouses. The uniform was supplied only in three sizes, and "The woman who needs a size 10 is a very

---

[57] Intraoffice Memo, Well-Being Div for Dir WAC, 6 Oct 43. SPWA 300.2 (1–7–43) sec 2.

[58] Ltr, 1st Mapping Gp AAF to Dir WAC, 24 Jun 44. SPWA 400.34 (3–21–42) sec 4 (1942).

pathetic figure in this garment." Its ill-fitting cut and limited size range made the garment an accident hazard; its poor fit "is humiliating to the enlisted woman and causes needless morale problems"; and the weight of the garment presented a laundering problem. This study was, however, rejected by G–4 of the General Staff on the grounds that the evidence of a single command was insufficient.[59]

Nevertheless, as a result of the cumulative requests, by the summer of 1944 the Office of The Quartermaster General was engaged in adapting the nurses' seersucker slacks design to wool and khaki for both Wacs and nurses. Unfortunately for speed of action, favorable consideration was not given to the simple request of most areas for a slacks suit of the same weight and general appearance as the men's. Instead, the Quartermaster attempted to employ the latest ideas of the Chemical Warfare Service regarding protective clothing in case the women should enter a gassed area, and the latest camouflage color.

As a result, at the end of the summer of 1944 there had been developed and approved a garment in poplin, not twill, in a muddy olive drab instead of the men's khaki, and with various flaps, drawstrings, and buttons for protection against gas. To this, the Pacific theater continued to object, stating that poplin was not mosquito-proof and that there was no reason why women's uniforms should be made unsightly with protective coloration and gas-proofing when those of men in the same area did not need these features. Eventually, a trim regulation khaki slacks suit, resembling the Army summer uniform, was approved, and the same design was applied to wool trousers. However, this action came too late in the war to be of anything but future interest. The experi-

ences of World War II had demonstrated beyond doubt that Wacs and nurses in overseas theaters, and those in active work in the United States, would inevitably require slacks resembling men's trousers in design and material.[60]

In the same months The Quartermaster General also developed various types of clothing for even rougher cold-weather wear. The "layering" principle currently employed for men's garments was also applied to women's, particularly in a field jacket and trousers with a windproof outer cover and wool innerliner. For arctic wear, pile-lined overcoats and hoods were also developed. Except in the coldest weather these garments were generally less favorably regarded by overseas theaters than ordinary slacks, partially because of their bulkiness and clumsiness.

Even after suitable work clothing was developed, stations in the United States were able to get it only for women whose occupational specialty number was on the approved list of "outdoor workers," or, in the case of winter clothing, if the station was located in the northern part of the United States. Many requests from field stations indicated that certain women not listed as outdoor workers, such as stock clerks, nevertheless often performed active work outdoors or in unheated buildings. In addition, stations in the southern zones of the United States complained that they were unable to get WAC drivers the necessary winter trousers and warm underwear, these sometimes being needed even more than in northern climates because there was no authorization for vehicle heaters in the south.

---

[59] Memo, Air WAC Off for Air QM, 9 Jun 44, incl ASC Study. AFPAW, WDWAC 421.

[60] Extensive descriptions are available in Risch, *Wardrobe for Women of the Army.*

In response to these requests, Director Hobby proposed that the commanding general of a service command be authorized to define "outdoor worker" and to determine when the climate required warm clothing. The Quartermaster General, fearing that this privilege might be abused, consented only to permit the commanding generals of service commands to declare women outdoor workers to no more than the extent of one fourth the company in Zone 3 and one third in Zone 2. This system was approved by Requirements Division in January of 1944, and put into effect.[61]

Hospital Uniform

With the move of the Director's Office from the Army Service Forces, the policy of providing no work uniform for hospital Wacs changed gradually. Soon after Major Craighill's appointment as Medical Department consultant, she discovered warehouse stocks of surplus blue cotton uniforms, now outmoded for Army nurses. Since no cost was involved, the Army Service Forces consented to their issue to Wacs working in hospital wards. However, the dresses were not available in all size ranges, and caused Wacs to be mistaken for the civilian employees who also wore them. Therefore, in September of 1944, G–4 Division authorized the wearing of the cooks' white uniforms in hospitals. This immediately proved unsatisfactory, since the cooks' uniforms had been designed to be worn over other clothing, and did not provide sufficient covering. Next, The Quartermaster General's Office experimented with the dyeing of nurses' white uniforms, but this also proved unworkable.

Finally, just before V-E Day, the Quartermaster General was authorized to provide green poplin dresses especially for hospital Wacs. Upon the advice of his civilian consultant, Miss Dorothy Shaver, vice-president of Lord & Taylor, the material was changed to rose-beige chambray. An extremely practical and becoming dress was evolved, and issue of nine dresses to each enlisted woman on hospital duty was authorized, a number that permitted Wacs to make use of hospital laundries as did other employees.[62]

Wacs not on duty in hospitals, but working after hours as volunteer nurses' aides, received published authorization to wear the usual blue and white cap and apron of the volunteer aide.

The Service Shoe

Another reform made by the last year of the war was in the fit of the WAC shoe. Throughout 1943, attempts to improve the shoe brought only complaints that new issues were worse than the previous one. In one "improved" type of shoe, salvage rose from 20 to 50 percent and wearers complained that it lacked arch support, did not fit the female foot, was too wide, too stiff, and with too low a heel for office wear. In 1944 the men's foot-measuring outfit proved unsatisfactory and was replaced by a new Foot-Measuring Outfit, Women's, one for each detachment, in order to eliminate the problem of

---

[61] (1) Change to T/E 21, 21 Oct 43; (2) Memo, Reqmts Div ASF for Dir WAC, with Ind from Dir WAC, 6 Jan 44, and 3d Ind OQMG to Reqmts Div. SPRMA 421 in SPWA 400 (1942).

[62] (1) Memo, G–1 for G–4, 21 Oct 44. WDGAP 421, copy in WDWAC 421. (2) Ltr, Miss Dorothy Shaver to Dir WAC, 4 Nov 44, and Memo, Dir WAC for ASF Mobile Div, 10 Nov 44. WDWAC 421. (3) Ltr, OQMG to all SvCs, 9 Apr 45. SPQXA 420, copy in WDWAC 421.

ordering wrong-sized shoes. With this improvement, and with The Quartermaster General's decision to issue only shoes made on government-owned lasts, most problems in the fit of the service shoe and the field shoe were eliminated.

The Quartermaster General concluded that earlier troubles had not arisen from poor shoes but from imperfect fit. Earlier shoes had been procured on as many as twelve different commercial lasts and, while each was of good design and construction, attempts by field companies to order by size were thwarted as the "result of stocking shoes made on different lasts under the same stock number." [63]

No similar solution was ever found to the need for an athletic shoe, since neither the high-laced field shoe nor the medium-heeled service shoe proved suitable for the required physical training. Quartermaster Corps investigators late in 1944 found that Wacs were wearing for this purpose and for kitchen duty what remained of the discontinued issue of tennis shoes, in "an advanced state of disrepair," as well as bedroom slippers, moccasins, and civilian sports shoes, presenting a "shabby and unsightly" appearance. The issue of tennis shoes could not be resumed, since all available materials were needed to produce canvas rubber footwear for combat men.

The Quartermaster General's Office was able to devise a substitute of non-critical materials, but the Army Service Forces and the General Staff refused to permit procurement of this item for women. Since WAC physical training was seldom done in public, the item was not, in the women's opinion, unduly important; most Wacs would have been glad to dispense with the physical training as well as with the shoes. [64]

Stockings

In tropical countries, and in semitropical areas of the United States, it proved virtually impossible to keep the Wacs in stockings. The five pairs of rayon stockings per quarter—one and two thirds pairs a month—which had by this time become the authorized issue, deteriorated badly in hot climates, forcing the women to buy their own or go stockingless. In any event, many women preferred to leave off stockings in the interests of comfort. Both the Air Forces and the Ground Forces recommended to the War Department that Wacs be authorized to omit stockings from the uniform between reveille and retreat, on the post only, at the discretion of the commanding officer. On the other hand, health authorities pointed out that at least clean socks or other foot coverings were required in the interests of health and shoe preservation.

The socks proposal was vetoed by The Quartermaster General's Office, which had not procured women's cotton socks except for use with the exercise or tennis shoe, long since discontinued. The stockingless state, particularly off the post, was frowned upon by both the first and second WAC Directors, since it became only those whose legs were shapely, well-tanned, and well-shaved—and there were, all too obviously, many Corps members not thus qualified. Finally, after V-J Day, a new authorization was published for eight pairs of stockings per quarter in tropical countries and Zone 3 of the United States—a provision that was supposed to

---

[63] (1) Ltr, WAC Stf Dir TC to QMG, 14 Dec 43. SPWA 421. (2) Memo, Research and Development Div ASF for OQMG, 4 Sep 44. WDWAC 421. (3) Quotation from Risch, *Wardrobe for Women of the Army*, pp. 76–78.
[64] *Ibid.*

end the need to go stockingless. However, nationwide reports from numerous interested observers indicated that such was not necessarily the result in all cases.[65]

Insignia

The WAAC lapel insignia of branch had always been the Pallas Athene, but under the WAC legislation the Corps was designated, not a basic branch, like Infantry or Cavalry, but a component of the Army. It thus became the only component to have its own insignia, which was ordinarily issued to women at training centers regardless of the branch that was their ultimate destination. After the conversion, the question at once arose from many field stations whether Wacs should continue to wear the Pallas Athene, or should change to the insignia that men would have worn if filling the same position vacancy— Quartermaster Corps, Signal Corps, Medical Corps, and the like.

One strong faction, composed of the Army Air Forces and certain of the Army Service Forces' administrative and technical services, insisted that women should wear the insignia that would have been worn by a man assigned to the same job. In fact, even in Auxiliary days WAAC Headquarters had noted with some amazement that The Inspector General had ordered WAAC officers in his office to violate War Department directives by putting on Inspector General insignia. Many air bases and some Signal Corps stations had unofficially been reported doing the same thing, and it came as no surprise that these agencies considered women entitled to wear their insignia as soon as Army status was achieved.[66]

The opposing faction consisted of the Army Ground Forces and certain headquarters agencies of the Army Service Forces. ASF's Military Personnel Division proposed that the women should continue to use up stocks of the old Auxiliary buttons, cap insignia, and lapel insignia, "thus maintaining the Corps as a separate unit" from the Army. General Dalton stated:

The WAC may be considered in effect as a separate corps or another service. As such it is appropriate that the WAC have distinctive lapel and collar [branch] insignia as prescribed for other arms and services. . . . The wearing of the lapel insignia of the arm or service to which WAC personnel may be detailed would be unsatisfactory as it would add unnecessary administrative complications concerning orders of assignment and relief, designation on rosters, strength returns, and signature legend.[67]

The Ground Forces also reported itself as horrified at the prospect of seeing crossed rifles, sabers, or cannon on women's uniforms, even though the woman was filling a job that would entitle a man to wear them. To the Air Forces' proposal, the Ground Forces sent a reply which the AAF interpreted as a deadly insult—that it was very well for women to wear Air Corps insignia, but not that of "a combat arm."[68]

The only compromise that could be reached in the first WAC uniform regula-

<hr>

[65] Memo, G-1 for CG ASF, 10 Oct 45. WDGAP 421 WAC (7-27-45), with atchd file, incl AAF proposal 5 Jul and AGF 27 Jul. WDWAC 421. Publication was WD Cir 287, 20 Sep 45.

[66] Intraoffice Memo, Onthank for Exec WAAC, 22 Mar 43. SPWA 421 (1942).

[67] Memo, OQMG for G-1, 11 Jul 43. Ind, G-1 to MPD ASF, 12 Jul, for remark; 20 Jul MPD draft of reply; Dir WAC's comment to MPD, 26 Jul; MPD reply to G-1, 4 Aug; G-1 concurrence, 9 Aug 43. SPQRD 421.4 WAAC, in SPWA 421.4 Insignia (1942).

[68] See Ch. XVI, above.

tions was a weak one: the insignia of another arm or service would be worn during the period that a WAC was "detailed in or assigned to" that arm or service. This phrase was virtually meaningless: *detailed in or assigned to* was technically used, for officers, to describe a change in branch which required War Department orders "by Direction of the President." [69] Since such orders were never used for enlisted personnel, there was extreme lack of uniformity in field practice. The Air Forces put its women in its own insignia, and, to insure against misunderstandings in this respect, secured a sweeping directive detailing all its WAC officers in the Air Corps by direction of the President, with provisions for change to the appropriate arm or service in the case of technicians.[70] The Ground Forces did not authorize a change in insignia, and various other services left the matter up to stations in the field, which were understandably confused about the whole matter.[71]

This confusion eventually made some further Army-wide clarification necessary. Instead of simplifying strength accounting, the retention of a separate designation by Wacs assigned to other arms and services actually forced statistical control units to add another column to reports, with apparent resulting discrepancies in reported personnel of Signal, Ordnance, Medical, and other troops, which were not really understrength but partially represented in the WAC column. The resulting confusion could have been heightened only if statisticians had been forced to carry all Negroes, or all Texans, or all left-handed men, or other minority groups, in a separate Corps instead of in the arm or service for which they were working.

Colonel Hobby's comments to this

effect were sent back by General Dalton while her office remained in ASF,[72] but upon the move to G–1 Division she was in a position to bring them to the attention of the General Staff. Meanwhile, one Army-wide clarification was achieved by the action of the Air Forces, which inquired whether Wacs might wear Army "distinctive insignia"—the metal devices for officers' shoulder straps and enlisted men's lower lapels, which marked certain regiments, commands, or other units. G–1 Division ruled that assigned women not only could but must wear these, since wearing of a unit's distinctive insignia was required of all members.[73]

On the more controversial issue of insignia of branch, for over a year the War Department was unable to devise any clarification of the 1944 regulations that would suit all factions. So bitter were the differences over this question that, in 1945, it was necessary to publish a final circular which permitted three different policies in the three major commands. In the Army Air Forces, all Wacs were permitted and required to wear Air Corps or ASWAAF (Arms and Services with the AAF) insignia. In the Army Service Forces, women also assumed the insignia that a man in the same assignment would have worn, but with exceptions made for the Judge

---

[69] AR 600–39, 5 Jan 44.

[70] AAF Ltr 35–83, 21 Aug 44, sub: Insignia and Detail of WAC Offs.

[71] Example: Ltr, Engr Sch, Ft Belvoir, to CG Ft Belvoir, 29 Jan 44. 1st Ind to MDW, 2d to TAG, D/F to Dir WAC and back to TAG, 3d Ind to MDW. SPWA 421.4 Insignia (1942).

[72] Memo, Dir WAC for Dir Pers ASF, 23 Aug 43, returned by MPD on 27 Aug. SPWA 421.4. Insignia (1942).

[73] (1) Memo, Maj Bandel for Dir WAC, 20 Oct 43, sub: Wearing of Distinctive Insignia for WAC (AR 600–40, par. 5); (2) WD Cir 216, 17 Sep 43; (3) Memo, Dir WAC for G–1, 4 Nov 43; approved by G–1, 5 Nov 43. SPWA 421.4 Insignia (1942).

Advocate General's Department, the Medical Department, and the Corps of Chaplains, none of which would concur in wearing of their insignia by females except when specifically detailed to their Corps by their own action in individual cases. In the Army Ground Forces, it was ruled that under no circumstances, no matter how assigned, or even if replacing men who had worn this insignia, would women ever wear the insignia of the Infantry, Cavalry, Field Artillery, Coast Artillery, Tank Destroyer, Armored Force, or any other Army Ground Forces command.[74]

Clothing Depots

The size of the Corps was never great enough to permit a system of stocking clothing and insignia comparable to that used for men. In the first months after the Corps' establishment, only WAAC training centers stocked women's clothing; later, two Army depots took over the task of supplying all field installations. This system proving unsatisfactory, in September of 1943 the Director's Office was informed by The Quartermaster General that, under an improved system, five depots would carry stocks of WAC clothing, and over 300 stations in the field would be authorized maintenance stocks. It was soon discovered that the list had neglected to provide for Air Forces Wacs and, after certain comment from that command, Air Forces stations were added.[75]

In spite of these improvements, field stations reported that their requisitions to authorized depots were still returned with the reply that no stocks were available.[76] It was also noted that filling of requisitions for women's uniforms generally required longer than those for men, while salvage and repair were likewise slower, presum-

ably because of the greater distances of shipment or unfamiliar nature of the items. In a later effort to improve the speed of supply, stations at which over 300 Wacs were stationed were authorized to keep maintenance stocks to supply the needs of smaller units in the vicinity. Obviously, however, no system as satisfactory as that for men's garments could be established for so small a group.

Allied Women's Services and the WAC Uniform

The whole progress of the WAC uniform and equipment program was of considerable interest to several of the Allied nations, which desired to equip their newly organized women's forces by lend-lease arrangements for American supplies. A number of WAC uniforms had already been shipped to the French forces in North Africa when, early in 1944, Director Hobby succeeded in getting a War Department directive that any further such shipments would be of a cut distinctive from the WAC uniform, or WAC uniforms dyed a distinctive color.

This rule did not meet with the general approval of foreign forces. The French Military Mission objected on the grounds of time: 100 Frenchwomen recruited in the United States were already awaiting shipment as soon as they could receive complete WAC uniforms, which were desired unchanged because the uniform of the French Feminine Volunteer Corps was "basically the same design and color as the WAC uniform." The Netherlands Purchasing Commission, for its women to serve in Australia, wanted merely different but-

---

[74] D/F, G–1 to MPD ASF, 19 Mar 45. WDGAP 421, in WDWAC 421.
[75] Memos cited n. 39.
[76] Ibid.

tons and sleeve patches, and objected to the orange lapel pieces, shoulder straps, and other distinguishing marks which Colonel Hobby suggested. International Division, Army Service Forces, sided with the governments concerned, since men's uniforms were lend-leased unchanged.

It was virtually impossible, in the interests of international tact, to point out to such nations that their female corps were seldom fully militarized or under military discipline, that some had no women officers and were unsupervised as to housing or conduct, that in others women officers were chiefly traveling secretaries of male commanders, and that at least one corps had practiced mass recruitment of native women, whose unsanitary appearance and conduct in WAC uniform had played a part in bringing on the rumors that had crippled recruiting. The Director's position was still further weakened when The Quartermaster General found that the large stocks of surplus winter uniforms, chiefly mismatched discards, could not be dyed successfully without wadding and shrinking. Reports from overseas areas indicated that in most cases unchanged uniforms had been acquired by local action. The problem appeared one not likely to be resolved until the application of selective service to women should have made public opinion of "WAC" conduct no longer a factor in recruiting costs.[77]

[77] (1) WD Cir 32, 25 Jan 44; (2) Ltr, Netherlands Purchasing Commission to International Div ASF, 11 Apr 44, with atchd rec of conf, 8 Apr 44; (3) Memo, OQMG for Dir WAC, 8 May 44, SPQRD 421; (4) WD Cir 217, sec VII, 1 Jun 44; (5) D/F, G–1 for G–2, 11 Aug 44, WDGAP 421. WDWAC 421.

CHAPTER XXVII

The Employment of Personnel: Enlisted Women

In all Army commands and overseas theaters, the experience of the war years produced very few Army-wide policies or restrictions on the job assignment of WAC personnel. The very considerable freedom that field commands had enjoyed in this respect seemed due in part to the small numbers of WAC personnel. Studies for the use of a million or more Wacs all indicated that hard and fast rules would have been required for this number, with explicit War Department directives to the field as to exactly what categories of jobs, or what entire organizations, would be staffed by Wacs.[1] In actual practice, with never more than 100,000 women to assign, a far more informal system remained possible, with women merely sent as casuals to field commands, and with little limitation on the types of jobs or organizations to which they might be assigned.

War Department regulations on the WAC allowed women to be assigned to "any suitable noncombatant overhead positions" or even to a combat unit organized under a Table of Organization, provided that the job itself was noncombatant and located in a "fixed administrative headquarters or installation." No limitation was placed upon a commander's discretion, except that men must be replaced one-for-one, that the duties must be within

the strength and endurance of "the average woman," and that the environment and working conditions must be suitable for women. Commanders were enjoined to remember that "procedures for the utilization of Women's Army Corps personnel both in their living and working conditions will vary from the procedure for utilization of male Army personnel," especially with respect to "hours of employment . . . number of women needed to perform heavy tasks . . . provision for safety and security . . . general standards of discipline . . . insurance of suitable recreation, education, and morale provisions." There was also, of course, never any wartime relaxation of the requirement that women be assigned in units of fifty or more, under the immediate command of a WAC officer.[2]

That such a lenient system was by no means inevitable was demonstrated by the Navy's dissimilar system. Here, the Bureau of Naval Personnel reported that it "kept full control of the detail of WAVES, enlisted as well as officer," primarily because it "did not have confidence that its

---

[1] Whole series of memos in WAAC and WAC Planning Serv files; for example, Memo, Sp Asst for Dir WAC, 13 Dec 43, sub: Pers Function of Dir WAC, draft 4.

[2] WD Cir 462, 1944; also earlier regulations.

directives on housing and placement policies would be observed by the District Commandants." Although the WAVES director and field agencies desired to assign women to any job for which they were qualified, the Bureau of Naval Personnel arbitrarily limited assignments to certain approved jobs, noting:

The Women's Reserve had originally fought to have all rates open to women, but the Bureau rejected this contention. . . . Field activities, with a commendable desire to give the enlisted women similar opportunities for advancement to those open to men, for a time permitted Waves to strike for a wide variety of rates which had not been officially opened to them; and it became necessary for the Bureau to issue firm instructions.

The Bureau also determined that certain jobs such as control tower operator would be largely taken over by women, and trained and shipped personnel accordingly.[3]

The Army's policy, on the other hand, began at the time of the conversion to Army status with almost no limitation upon the station commander's power to determine WAC jobs, and added restrictions only as they were proved essential by experience. By the end of the war, the limitations that had grown up could almost be numbered upon the fingers of one hand.

Restrictions on Nonmilitary Assignments

Of these restrictions, the most important grouped themselves about the always-uncertain distinction between military and civilian jobs, which for women appeared to present a special problem, particularly since assignment to civilian vacancies had been permitted in early Auxiliary days.

The issue did not, as it frequently did in the Navy, concern the replacement of Civil Service personnel, which in the Army was absolutely forbidden, and for which Congressional critics remained always alert even had the Army grown lax. Paradoxically, Congress did not object to the practice in the Navy. The Bureau of Naval Personnel noted that it secured a "gentleman's agreement" from the Naval Affairs Committees that it might use Waves when it could not get Civil Service personnel for jobs in the Washington area. As a result, as much as one third of the WAVES' entire corps was assigned to civilian work in Washington, the bureau protecting itself by certification "that civilians could not be found to fill any given jobs for which Waves were requested by a Washington office." Such assignment did not prove wholly satisfactory, the bureau noting later that "use of WAVES for essentially civilian work soon became a morale problem and a detriment to procurement. . . . Many of the women could see that they were not directly replacing men."[4]

For the Army, the question concerned only the non-Civil Service jobs on field stations.[5] It was ordinarily forbidden to use soldiers in civilian-operated laundries, as post exchange sales clerks, as waiters in officers' messes (except as extra paid employment), and in other more or less

---

[3] WAVES Hist.

[4] *Ibid.*

[5] For preconversion period: (1) Draft of Memo, Dir WAC for G–1, 4 Nov 43. SPWA 320.3. (2) Rpt of Insp, Colored Det, Ft. Knox, Ky., 6 Aug 43. SPWA 331.1. (8–20–43). (3) M/R, Faith, 8 Jul 43, sub: Rpt of Sp Insp. SPWA (11–16–43) Utilization. (4) Memo, Lies for Dir WAAC, 13 Jul 43, sub: Analysis of Insp Rpts. Proj 25, WAAC Plng Serv files. For postconversion period: (5) Memo, Dir WAC for Dir Pers ASF, 25 Aug 43. SPWA 222.6 KP, in Folder 22, WAAC Plng Serv files.

menial tasks not essential enough to merit military personnel. Before the conversion, however, inspectors discovered on field stations a common practice of assigning Waacs to a station's nonmilitary work, generally of menial character, to which soldiers could not be assigned and which civilian women could not be persuaded to accept. In part this practice appeared to result from the anomalous nature of the WAAC's status under its separate T/O, which seemed half-civilian, half-military, in character. In part it was ascribed to traditional ideas of the proper work for women.

Classification survey teams noted that while this practice was not universal, it was exceedingly widespread. At many stations Waacs were found assigned as personal orderlies by both Army and WAAC officers, and at several others they were used to fill low-grade civilian jobs in laundries. At Fort Knox, school teachers and college graduates were found assigned as dining room orderlies, food cart pushers, and garbage rack details. At Camp Breckinridge, Kentucky, five Negro Waacs, described as "well-educated," were assigned to sweep out warehouses, while fifteen others worked in the service club and thirty in a civilian-operated laundry. At Valley Forge General Hospital, four women were assigned as unskilled orderlies although, inspectors reported, "Two are really clerk-typists, one a graduate cook, and one a classification specialist with an AGCT of 137 and college degree."

Very few stations were entirely free from such practices. For example, in the Fourth Service Command alone, inspectors found Waacs waiting on officers in clubs and messes at Camp Forrest, Forts McClellan, Jackson, and Benning; Waacs were replacing civilians as post exchange clerks at Fort Jackson and at the Charleston Port of Embarkation; Waacs at Fort McClellan were performing "menial tasks far below their highest ability." The women so assigned included radio operators, cryptographers, dietitians, linguists, and others with useful skills.

Soon after the conversion to Army status, General Faith's Field Inspection Service brought in repeated evidence to the effect that female military personnel was still being considered especially suitable for assignments in post exchanges, laundries, canteens, service clubs, restaurants, and officers' clubs and messes. General Faith noted that all such assignments which did not result in filling a military job were "not very successful," and invariably caused resentment and low morale.[6]

As a result, in August of 1943 and again in October, Colonel Hobby recommended publication of a regulation specifically forbidding assignment of Wacs to jobs not authorized for soldiers. She added:

The sole source of personnel for the Women's Army Corps is by voluntary enlistment. Applicants are informed by recruiting officers that they will release soldiers for combat. The use of women, so recruited, as sales clerks in post exchanges and as laundresses leads not only to dissatisfaction but to reduced numbers of recruits. No objection is offered to the use of enlisted women in administrative [military] positions in Post Exchanges and laundries.

Over the Army Service Forces' objections, G–1 Division therefore placed a restriction in the first WAC Regulations against the use of Wacs in any civilian jobs, but with specific prohibition only of jobs in

---

[6] Min of Conf, WAC Classification Teams, Sep 43. WA 201.6.

restaurants or cafeterias in service clubs, guest houses, and officers' clubs or messes.

Shortly afterward, Director Hobby again appealed for a more specific prohibition on jobs in laundries and post exchanges. She also asked a written definition of the basis by which Wacs might be employed as orderlies, since "abuses in the field" had caused her to believe that Wacs should not be assigned as personal orderlies to male officers, even when, as rarely, a military allotment was provided, and that they should not even be permitted to accept off-duty paid employment as orderlies except with female officers. Again the Army Service Forces objected, concurring only in specific prohibition of nonmilitary assignment in laundries. This was published in late 1943. Nothing specific was ever published on the subject of employment in post exchanges or as orderlies, with the implication that such assignment was permissible if a military allotment could be contrived.[7]

Although inspection teams arriving before these publications found many women in unmilitary work and service commands most reluctant to remove them, teams arriving after publication found that many stations had just reassigned Wac waitresses and cooks from officers' clubs and messes. Other stations did not comply with the circulars until they heard that the teams were coming; still others agreed to make the corrections on the spot while teams were at the station.[8]

These prohibitions, however, did not actually constitute restrictions on the use of Wacs other than those already placed on the use of soldiers; the only difference was that the prohibitions were specifically restated for women as a result of numerous abuses.

Restrictions on Permanent Kitchen Police Duty

A similar problem concerned the assignment to kitchen police (KP) duty, which was authorized for military personnel, but not as a permanent job. It was considered unsuitable to use the duty for punishment or to assign any soldier to perform it continuously. WAC inspectors therefore expressed some surprise in discovering that this rule was more frequently ignored for women than for men, with a few Wacs at a number of stations being assigned the duty on a permanent basis. Upon investigation, the violation was readily understood: the number of men at any station was ordinarily so great that the duty could be handled on a roster basis without falling too frequently upon any one individual, while in a unit of 150 women the duty occurred once or twice a month. The difficulty was redoubled when Wacs began to receive ratings, since by Army custom noncommissioned officers and key office personnel were exempt from the KP roster. In the small WAC

---

[7] Entire discussion is based on Memo cited n. 5(5), and the following in AG 320.2 WAC (10–7–43) WAC Regs, AGO Gen Rec Sec; many also in ASF Dir Pers file SPAP 220.3 WAC (7–29–43): (1) Memo, Col Catron for TAG through ASF and G–1, 7 Oct 43. SPWA 320.2. (2) Memo, same, 7 Oct 43. SPWA 220.3. (3) T/S, Dir Pers ASF to G–1, 18 Oct 43. SPGAS 210.3 WAC–64. (4) T/S, same, 22 Oct 43. SPGAS 210.3 WAC–65. (5) D/F, G–1 for ASF, 25 Oct 43. WDGAP 220. (6) D/F, same, 25 Oct 43. WDGAP 220.3 WAC. (7) Cir 289, 9 Nov 43. (8) Memo, Dir WAC for G–1 through Dir Pers ASF, 4 Nov 43. SPWA 320.2. (9) T/S, Dir Pers ASF for G–1, 24 Nov 43. SPGAS 210.3 WAC. (10) D/F, G–1 for ASF. WDGAP 220.3 WAC. (11) Memo, MPD ASF for TAG, 13 Dec 43. SPGAS 210.3 WAC. (12) WD Cir 337, 28 Dec 43.

[8] For team reports see: (1) Prelim Rpt, Lt Alice Knight to Opns Div WAC Hq, 18 Oct 43. WA 201.6 (6–18–43). (2) Rpts of teams, Tabs to Memo, Lies for Dir WAC, 14 Apr 44. Folder, WAC Classif Surv, WAC Plng files. (3) Memo, Chief, AGO Classif and Repl Br for Dir WAC, 24 Apr 44. SPX–220.3 WAC (11–30–43) OC–H, in WDWAC 201.6 (1944).

company such exemption caused the duty to fall even more frequently to the remainder of the women, sometimes as often as every two or three days. The reaction of Army section chiefs was almost unanimous. As one staff director reported, "The Army officers said it was impossible to let them do KP. Offices had let men go and could not spare the girls even for a half-day."[9] The usual field solution was to assign a few members of the company on a permanent basis to do KP and other menial roster duty for the office workers.

This solution was not acceptable to Director Hobby, who noted:

With the new standards for recruiting, it would be unfair to have permanent kitchen police. . . . From now on we are not going to get the people who are suited for permanent KP's unless there is selective service for women.

Even if low-grade personnel was accidentally admitted, it was her opinion that American citizens who were induced to volunteer for military work should not find themselves forced to perform menial nonmilitary services for other volunteers. The Director stated:

We are in danger of building up a caste system in the WAC, whether we like it or not. . . . [It] is undemocratic and unfair to the women.

This view was supported by Deputy Director Rice:

We need to build in the company a spirit of respect for the job no matter what the job is. Everyone should take her turn at KP.[10]

The Navy reported an identical problem among the WAVES, and attempted to solve it by recruiting women as seamen (utility) expressly for this work, but this failed when "morale was chronically poor . . . too few would volunteer to enlist therein and those who did became dissatisfied when they discovered the nature of the work." Finally the seaman rating had to be dropped, and the work returned to a roster basis.[11]

As the only remaining solution, Director Hobby therefore asked publication of a circular requiring WAC noncommissioned officers, who were ordinarily exempt, to share KP with the other women in order that no woman would be too frequently absent on this duty. This recommendation was not favorably considered by Military Personnel Division, ASF, since "The privates cease to regard the noncoms with the respect which they are due if the noncoms are forced to work in the kitchen side by side with them."[12] General Dalton's opinion was not concurred in by the Director, who held the view that, except for the few command cadre positions, there was no reason why a truck driver should regard a stenographer with respect, or one member of the company be afforded more privileges than another on the grounds of superior education or skills. British services had entertained the same opinion, and had gone so far as to make a training film in which a rated office worker was reprimanded by

---

[9] Stf Dir MDW, at Jun 43 Conf. Min, Stf Dirs Conf, 15–17 Jun 43. SPWA 337 (6–1–43). Also opinions of all other reporting officers.

[10] All quotations from Min cited n. 9.

[11] (1) Memo, Gen Faith for Dir WAC, 14 Aug 43, also draft of Memo, 17 Aug 43; (2) Memo, Dir Pers ASF for G–1, 14 Sep 43. SPWA 220.6 KP. (3) WAVES Hist.

[12] (1) Memo, Col Catron for TAG through ASF and G–1, 7 Oct 43. SPWA 320.2. (2) T/S, Dir Pers ASF for G–1, 22 Oct 43. SPGAS 210.3 WAC–65. (3) D/F, G–1 for ASF, 25 Oct 43. WDGAP 220.3 WAC. (4) Memo, Dir WAC for G–1 through ASF, 4 Nov 43. SPWA 320.2. (5) WD Cir 289, 9 Nov 43. (6) T/S, ASF for G–1, 24 Nov 43. SPGAS 210.3. WAC. (7) D/F, G–1 for ASF, 29 Nov 43. WDGAP 220.3 WAC. All in AG 320.2 WAC (10–7–43) WAC Regs, and most are also in SPAP 220.3 WAC.

her company commander for a snobbish attitude toward a scrubwoman, and was informed that in winning the war the contribution of every member was equally important.

Director Hobby therefore made a third appeal for a written prohibition on permanent KP for Wacs, which would force station commanders to set up the work on a roster basis. Again General Dalton objected, stating that men were never used on permanent kitchen police and that there was no need to restate the prohibition for women. However, the General Staff supported the Director's request in view of reports of numerous violations of the rule, and the policy was published in the first and all later WAC Regulations.[13]

From the standpoint of the physical well-being of women, the solution to the KP problem achieved by many field stations, even on a roster basis, was doubtful. Desiring to cut absences from the office to a minimum, station authorities frequently elected to put women on one long detail, from before dawn until late at night, rather than to permit two shorter absences which disrupted work on two days instead of one.

In 1944 Director Hobby requested the major commands to check on this practice, since "letters to this office, some of them Congressional inquiries, have indicated that there has been an increasing tendency in WAC units to make schedules for KP duty so that individuals draw long hours and sometimes arduous continuous details."[14] Investigations revealed some cases of 14-hour details without rotation from heavier to lighter tasks. Many Wacs were found to prefer one long day of KP rather than several partial ones, although admitting that the resulting aches, pains, and strains caused additional loss of time

from the office. Inspectors at every opportunity questioned the practice, but it was difficult to alter.

Even selective service for women did not appear to offer a solution to the problem, since under this system the Army did not sanction permanent kitchen police for a soldier. In overseas theaters, a solution was achieved by the use of civilian labor, thus permitting key office personnel to work as steadily as section chiefs desired. Since funds did not permit this practice in the United States, some stations gave thought to the use of prisoners of war—a system which was informally discouraged after the first Wac was court-martialed and discharged for becoming engaged to one.[15] Under the circumstances, it could only be hoped that section chiefs would eventually cease to protest at allowing Wacs to fulfill their military roster duties as did other military personnel.

Restrictions on Food Service Assignments

While the WAC always ran its own messes, it never attempted to take over those of men's units. This system had not been the Corps' original intent. Women's civilian monopoly in the fields of cooking and home economics strongly suggested that the Army's entire food supply and service system, with the exception of combat units, might eventually benefit by acquiring a feminine staff. WAC advisers reported that many Army men felt that "there is nothing that the WAC might do

---

[13] *Ibid.* Also (1) British film, *We Serve*, 528–285, Verity Films Ltd., July 1942. (2) WD Cir 289, 9 Nov 43, and 486, 29 Dec 44.
[14] Memo, Exec WAC for CG AAF, ASF, AGF, 29 Jun 44. WDWAC 720.
[15] (1) Memo, ASF for Exec WAC, 23 May 45; (2) Memo, ACofAS Pers for Dir WAC, 26 May 45. WDWAC 220.4.

that would give it greater popularity with the Army or make itself more useful in the war effort."[16] This conjecture was supported by the precedent of the British women's services, which entirely staffed most officers' messes and many general messes.

For the American WAAC's first year, Director Hobby and her advisers therefore contemplated the eventual formation of mess companies, although deferring these in order to meet the shipment schedule for the standard Table of Organization companies. As late as June of 1943 WAAC Headquarters went on record as approving the establishment of WAC mess companies to operate men's messes. The action in fact appeared essential at this time, since the collapse of recruiting plans had left the WAC with a surplus of cooks, trained to staff WAC companies that had failed to materialize. However, before this personnel could be organized into mess companies, a requisition was received from the Army Air Forces to assign the cooks to its hospital diet kitchens to prepare food for patients. Since the need of the sick appeared worthy of priority, the women—some 700 in all—were assigned to the Air Forces and, under its flexible assignment system, added to existing WAC units at stations having hospitals large enough to require them.[17]

With the establishment of higher recruiting standards, no such surplus of cooks ever again accumulated. The number of recruits skilled as cooks and home economics specialists was never greater than could be employed in WAC units and hospital diet kitchens. At the same time, several developments convinced the War Department that no steps should be taken to stimulate the enlistment of WAC mess personnel. One important consider-

ation was the working environment, which appeared unsuitable except in the larger messes where an all-WAC mess company could be employed.[18]

Also, many duties in an Army mess proved to be beyond a woman's strength. Even in the small WAC unit messes, some assistance from men was often required in unloading hundred-pound cartons or in lifting garbage and grease containers. In the larger messes the kettles and other cooking utensils, when filled, were sometimes too heavy for women to lift, while few women could for many months sustain even such duties as large-scale meat-cutting and baking. Obviously even an all-WAC mess company would necessarily be confined to skilled cooks and mess sergeants, unless troop allotments could be expanded to allow two women for one man in heavier work. Under the circumstances, Colonel Catron informed the War Department at the time of the conversion that priority would be given to WAC messes and hospital messes, and consideration of running enlisted men's messes postponed until these needs were satisfied.[19]

This priority was never to be reversed. Not only were recruits too few to fill more urgent needs in offices, but the results of recruiting surveys indicated that any public awareness of the use of Wacs in cooking duties constituted a severe drag upon the recruiting of skilled and capable women. Even the limited use already undertaken had shown adverse effects, and after a receipt of one Gallup report to this effect,

[16] Ltr, Capt Ruth Woodworth, 6th SvC, to Dir WAC, 9 Oct 43. SPWA 331.4.

[17] (1) Min cited n. 9. (2) Memo, WAAC Hq for G–1, 23 Jun 43. SPWA 331.4. (3) AAF WAC Hist.

[18] Memo, G–1 for CofS, 16 Jun 43. CofS 219.9.

[19] Memo, Col Catron for Dir Opng Div WAC, 6 Jul 43. Plng Proj 22, WAAC Plng Serv file, 1943.

Director Hobby urged staff directors to "discourage as much as possible" pictures of women in the kitchen, particularly since these usually showed a background of oversized ladles, monumental cooking pots, and wholesale quantities of food.[20]

There was never to be any conclusive explanation of why the expectation of cooking duties should drive recruits away by the thousands, as it was well known to do. Classification experts were of the opinion that women with other skills feared, in spite of all job guarantees, that they would be forced into kitchens. Psychiatrists noted that many recruits wanted to do a man's job, and felt that kitchen duty was not particularly military. Possibly the best explanation came from civilian social analysts, who noted that domestic service had been steadily dropping in popularity, with "reluctance of workers, in the face of growing opportunities in factories and shops, to enter a field with low standards of work and wages and inferior social status." [21]

This hypothesis was confirmed by the example of the British women's services, which indicated not only that well-qualified women would not enlist for mess work, but that they would not enlist in, and wear the uniform of, a corps that earned a reputation for specializing in mess management.[22] In the WAC, it was noted that "those in charge of recruiting found that it was almost impossible to recruit office workers so long as the general public believed that women in the armed forces were used largely as cooks, waitresses, etc." [23] Only selective service had ever enabled any women's service to get numbers of skilled "white-collar" workers and mess personnel in the same corps.

For this reason, no recruiting campaign to organize WAC mess companies was ever sponsored. Early in 1945, Director Hobby obtained publication of a War Department circular forbidding the assignment of Wacs to men's messes, except in hospitals and except when Wacs ate in consolidated messes and furnished a proportionate share of personnel.[24]

Other Questions of Proper Employment

Thus, the only two major policies on WAC jobs ever to be adopted by the Army centered around the decision that Wacs would perform only military duties, and that the Corps would continue to specialize in office work rather than food service. Of all other questions concerning proper employment, most were satisfactorily settled at a field level; only a few ever received War Department attention.

In the field there seemed to be some impression that a list of other prohibited duties did exist, or should, and in its early days WAAC Headquarters constantly received queries concerning the maximum size of the trucks women might drive, the weights they might lift, and similar matters. Such inquiries continued to be so frequent that WAAC representatives worked long and painfully with Military Personnel Division, ASF, to compile a list of prohibited duties, which would have included some 150 occupations such as blacksmith, boilermaker, and bath attendant. The attempt seemed more amusing than useful, and was finally abandoned, as it appeared

---

[20] Min, WAC Stf Dirs Conf, New York, 1–3 Dec 43. SPWA 337 (11–10–43).

[21] U.S. Dept of Labor, *Women's Occupations Through Seven Decades*, Women's Bureau Bull 218. 1947, p. 141.

[22] Gen. Sir Frederick Pile, *Ack-Ack* (London: Geo. Harrap & Co., Ltd., 1949).

[23] AAF WAC Hist, pp. 2 n. 2, 36, 37.

[24] WD Cir 76, 9 Mar 45.

somewhat unlikely that anyone would assign women to such work in any case.[25]

Furnace Firing

One minor question, which arose at many stations lacking central heating in barracks, was whether the women could fire their own barracks furnace on roster duty as did most men's units. Since the answer varied according to the size and nature of both the furnace and the Wacs, the Director believed that the matter should be left to the discretion of Army stations.

For example, the Second Service Command reported to the Director an "acute problem" at Camp Upton, New York: the women's health was affected because they had to fire furnaces, while Waacs at nearby Fort Dix had such work done for them. The service command asked that the Director set a uniform policy. In reply, WAAC Headquarters refused to try to set a policy, stating that the matter was one of command, and that its only policy was that Waacs should not do work that overtaxed their strength. Colonel Clark write:

If the work of manning furnaces at Camp Upton is reasonably beyond the physical capacity of women, manifestly they should not be required to do it. It is believed to be purely a matter within the province of the Post Commander, who will undoubtedly take such action as is deemed necessary, upon the request of the WAAC Company Commander.[26]

In most instances local commanders solved the problem with considerable common sense. Where one post service detail did this job for men's barracks, the Waacs' could easily be included. If each barracks did its own, the WAC commander was usually able to arrange for the duty to be assumed by women of suitable strength, who often preferred it to kitchen police. If the unit contained no such strong women, or if section chiefs refused to release office workers for the task, civilians or male service troops were given the detail without causing any great comment.

This local-option view was not shared by the Chief of Engineers' office, which informed the field, without consulting the Director WAAC:

With proper training, the members of the WAAC can operate furnaces and water heaters in the same manner as enlisted men. No change is contemplated in the established policy that such equipment be operated by the personnel occupying the quarters in which it is installed.[27]

When it was discovered that the commandant at Fort Oglethorpe was using labor troops to fire furnaces and heaters for the whole post, rather than drawing details from Wacs for this purpose, ASF headquarters took these men from his allotment and stated, "War Department policy does not contemplate the use of station complement personnel to fire small heating units."[28] During the following winter, Fort Oglethorpe was subject to severe Congressional and public criticism for repeated cases in which recruits reported to cold barracks, and spent much of their so-called basic training period in firing furnaces, with a resulting high rate

---

[25] (1) Memo, Lt Ruth Spivak for Col Clark, 11 Jun 43; (2) Draft of Memo, 18 Jun 43. Folders 21 and 22, Plng Serv file.
[26] Ltr, 2d SvC to Dir WAAC, 8 Mar 43; 1st Ind, 19 Mar 43. SPWA 220.8.
[27] Ind, CofEngrs to CG 1st SvC, to Inquiry, 19 Mar 43, with notation. SPWA 320.2.
[28] Ltr, Post Comdt Ft Oglethorpe to 4th SvC, 22 Jul 43, with 3d Ind, MPD ASF to 4th SvC. SPWA 320.2.

of hospitalization and disability discharge.[29]

The WAC was not in a position to argue with Army-wide policies on furnace firing, but field inspectors found in some cases that any economy resulting from Wacs doing the work was indeed doubtful. WAC office and hospital workers suffering from sprained backs were frequently hospitalized and absent from their duties following furnace-firing detail. A large-scale study by the Army Air Forces showed that respiratory disorders were increased by the duty, with corresponding loss of time from work. Furthermore, at several stations the heating equipment suffered expensive damage from the unskilled ministrations of the Wacs. At one station steam instead of water emerged from certain fixtures in the WAC latrines, and geysers erupted on the post grounds. At one training center, women in the latrine were quite seriously scalded in a way that made desk work impossible for weeks.

The Army Air Forces achieved a partial solution to this problem by rescinding directives that required unit personnel to fire their own furnaces, thus leaving the post commander free to take any steps deemed necessary to prevent the absence of key office personnel, male or female. No similar Army-wide solution was ever promulgated.[30]

Use of Weapons

Another minor job-assignment question was that of the use of weapons. Although Wacs were clearly labeled noncombatants, and thus supposedly not concerned with the use of weapons, it soon developed that in their private lives a few were good marksmen, and that Army men took a friendly interest in instructing them and allowing them to qualify on firing ranges. The War Department judged the matter unimportant because of the few cases concerned. However, in this it reckoned without the newspapers, which shortly spread one or two pictured instances nationwide. There resulted what WAC advisers called "a serious public relations problem," with semihysterical accusations from many citizens (1) that the country was in such bad shape that women were about to be sent into combat, or (2) that Wacs were not needed and were obliged to while away their time in this manner, or (3) that Wacs were wasting the powder which munitions workers sat up nights to manufacture. Even a case in which Wacs were photographed drilling with wooden guns provoked condemnation when published in a blurred newspaper version.

Accordingly, Director Hobby requested and secured a stringent prohibition on the use of weapons, which stated sweepingly that "no weapon or arm, nor any replica or imitation thereof, will be used or carried by any member of the WAC, nor will any training in the use or firing of any weapon be afforded any member."

Almost immediately the regulation proved hampering to field commanders charged with assigning Wacs. Certain Air Forces women instructors had been accustomed to use gun-shaped training devices. Fiscal authorities protested that the ruling would require the removal of WAC officers from duty as disbursing officers. WAC officers attending the Army Finance School were unable to receive the same training as male students. Certain emi-

---

[29] See Ch. XXXII, below.
[30] AF Ltr 85–15, 26 Dec 44, Pers for Operating Heater and Boiler Plants.

nently suitable signal and communications duties were also jeopardized, since regulations required that a revolver be kept in the code room. In overseas areas there were also usually regulations which prevented taking out any vehicle without arms.

Director Hobby admitted that her original recommendation had been overstringent, and asked that the prohibition be reworded to permit women to carry such weapons as were required by their specific assignment, if the assignment was otherwise suitable and noncombatant, and if the women had suitable training. This request was refused by the Director of Personnel, Army Service Forces: "Not favorably considered in view of War Department policy that members of noncombatant branches will not be trained in the use of weapons."

Since the WAC was the only noncombatant branch assigned to duties in fiscal and other work requiring firearms, this restriction continued to prove most unpopular with the field, and Director Hobby, after her move to G–1 Division, continued to ask that it be rescinded. As a result, G–1 Division soon published what was believed to be a discreetly worded circular which allowed commanding generals to grant exceptions, for specifically named individuals only, provided that the duties were suitable and the women properly qualified.

Within six months, this authority was so extensively abused by field commands that G–1 Division rescinded it, stating that, with the circular as an excuse, "WAC personnel are being required to drill in the use of arms and at some localities there is wholesale participation by WAC personnel in familiarization courses in the use of weapons and arms." Since

Colonel Hobby did not wish to impose another absolute prohibition on such field assignments, G–1 merely rescinded the authorization, thus leaving neither approval or disapproval in the regulations, except for a passage which stated that "the wearing of badges representing qualification in arms by Women's Army Corps personnel is prohibited." This also did not prove too popular with Wacs, who felt it peculiar that they should be allowed to qualify but not to receive the badge. British precedent indicated an eventual solution of the problem only if future emergencies should make home defense as acceptable a female occupation as it had once been in pioneer days.[31]

Use in Public Theatricals

A more serious and frequent question was that which concerned the duty assignment of Wacs to theatrical performances designed for public entertainment. This question was entirely apart from that of participation in camp and company shows and skits, which had always been encouraged, although requests for Special Services material for this purpose were refused by the ASF for two years. Not until July of 1945 was there published a booklet of all-girl skits and other entertainment material suitable for WAC company parties. Such camp shows were done on the individual's

[31] Entire section based on: (1) AAF WAC Hist, pp. 18, 41, and n. 2. (2) WDAGO Memo W635–19–43. (3) Memo, Maj Rice for Dir WAC, 22 Dec 43. SPWA 620. (4) Memo, O Dir WAC for G–1, 13 Jan 44; Inds, 20 Jan 43, Dir of Pers ASF, and by G–1, 27 Jan. SPWA 620 (1943). (5) D/F, G–1 for TAG, 23 Apr 44. WDGAP 385.2 WAC, in AG 320.2 WAC (10–7–43) WAC Regs. (6) WD Cir 163, 26 Apr 44. (7) D/F, G–1 for TAG, 29 Aug 44. WDGAP 385.2 WAC. (8) WD Cir 354, 1 Sep 44.

own time and offered no question concerning duty assignment.[32]

On the other hand, many talented Wacs—writers, musicians, actresses, singers—had obviously hoped to use their talents on a full-time basis in the war effort, with Army sponsorship. The question of whether or not they would be allowed to do so first arose at Daytona Beach, where Waacs wrote and produced a show called *On the Double,* with dances directed by a former Broadway teacher and costumes by a former professional theatrical costumer. The production was such a success that firemen had to be called to turn away hundreds of curious civilians. Posts in the surrounding area requested that the show go on tour, and its WAAC sponsor wrote the Director, "We feel that this show would definitely be one of the greatest recruiting factors that the WAAC could have if it were possible for us to put it on in other places than Daytona Beach."[33]

After some consideration, Director Hobby disapproved the idea of a tour, and asked ASF to inform the service commands that it was improper to use Wacs for "singing and dancing in connection with any presentation put on for the public on behalf of recruiting."[34] There was considerable indication that the value of such expensive productions to recruiting was small, and at times actually negative. Thus, the successful Daytona production received newspaper "praise" calling it "the Amazon's answer" and stating, "Hold your hats, fellows—there's a strip-tease act so good the MP's have to break it up."[35] Even if such publicity was considered desirable, there remained the problem of expense. In one case in which the First Service Command tried such an experiment on its own authority, it was

soon obliged to report that recruits obtained by this means cost $1,200 more apiece than ordinary recruits.[36]

Therefore, although members of the press applied some pressure on behalf of talented WAC friends, informing the Director that she was making a "great mistake," she nevertheless proposed and secured publication of a War Department policy against the use of Wacs in theatricals for the civilian public. Wacs were allowed to appear only in those shows performed at home stations for soldiers and their families, which did not take them off their jobs and for which no admission was charged except to defray costs. This rule was published in July 1943, and with minor modifications remained the WAC's policy for the rest of its career.[37]

This prohibition often appeared unreasonable to stations in the field, since male military personnel were frequently used in traveling productions such as *This Is the Army.* There was every evidence that the regulation was frequently violated. Nevertheless, no change in ruling was ever made by the War Department. The distinction in such assignments for men and

[32] (1) Memo, WAC Hq to DCofS for SvCs ASF, 8 Oct 43, and refusal, 21 Oct 43, atchd. SPWA 353.8. (2) WD Pamphlet 38–13–A, Blackouts, Crossovers and Parodies for WAC Variety Nights. AG 461 (7–21–45). Copy in OCMH.

[33] Entire discussion in SPWA 353.8 (5–29–43) 1943, incl: (1) Ltr, Sp Serv Br 2d Tng Cen to Recreation Br WAAC Hq, 2 Jun 43. (2) Clippings from unnamed Daytona Beach newspapers, 12–13 Jun 43. (3) Ltr, PRO Ft Benning to WAAC Hq, 23 Jun 43. (4) Ltr, Henry Pringle to Capt Ruth F. Fowler, 26 Jun 43.

[34] Memo, WAAC Hq for DCofS for SvCs ASF, no date, sub: Directive to SvCs. SPAP 341 WAAC (2–26–43).

[35] Sources cited n. 33.

[36] Memo, Dir WAC for Chief, Plng Br for WAC Recreation, 1 Apr 44, sub: WAC Theatricals. SPWA 353.8 (1943).

[37] Memo, Dir WAC for G–1, 3 Jul 43. SPWA 353.8, in WD AGO Memo W635–15–43, 1 Aug 43.

for women was based partly upon the opinion that

. . . members of the public, not yet convinced of the advisability of having women in the military service, were prone to think, if they saw women in theatrical performances, that the Army had no real need for them.[38]

For men, especially where returned combat heroes were used, there seemed to be a more favorable public impression that singing and dancing assignments were only a brief interlude in combat. Eventually even this tolerance was at times overstrained, and the Director's staff noted that "the Bureau is having the same type of trouble with men participating in theatricals." [39] A great many such projects for men came to be refused, "because of the critical manpower situation and the present need for all available military personnel." [40]

For the WAC, the problem continued to be one not merely of economy but of public acceptance. Director Hobby stated, as one of the Corps' major principles:

It is contrary to policy to . . . sanction appearance in public where this might give the impression of frivolity or lack of serious purpose or occupation. . . . It is also contrary to policy to move WAC units over considerable distances except for necessary and official purposes.[41]

As the Army's practice of fostering home-talent post shows grew, the War Department, at the request of field stations, permitted Wacs to appear in such shows even when they journeyed to nearby stations, provided that their absence from home stations was not more than twelve hours and that they were accompanied by a WAC officer. Later, at the request of Miss Sarah Blanding of the Secretary of War's Recreational Committee, this ruling was extended so that commanding generals might authorize a longer period of absence from duty for performances before audiences composed entirely of patients in Army hospitals.[42]

There was no equally successful solution to the demand for WAC units to appear in civic parades and other celebrations. Military posts were accustomed to contributing a company to grace patriotic occasions in nearby communities, but could ordinarily divide the honor among a number of companies. Since the WAC ordinarily had only one company at a station, and was in great demand as a curiosity, its members were frequently forced to augment their military schedule with long marches in local parades, often with the loss of most of a working day. Colonel Hobby stated forcibly to WAC staff officers her opinion that "they must not be pulled off their jobs because somebody wants to see a parade." [43]

Post commanders ordinarily agreed heartily and did what they could to check the practice. Unfortunately, civilian patriotic groups were numerous and their requests not only incessant but difficult to refuse diplomatically. For example, in one brief period in one city, Masonic and Eastern Star groups asked for "from 60 to 100 Wacs to participate in a pageant"; the Confederate Memorial Committee asked

---

[38] AAF WAC Hist.

[39] Ltr, WAC Stf Dir AAF WFTC to Exec WAC, 23 Dec 43, and reply. SPWA 353.8.

[40] Ltr, Chief Ord Info, New York, Ord Dist, to Dir WAC, 29 Dec 43, and answer, 4 Jan 44. SPWA 353.8.

[41] 10th Ind, Dir WAC to Dir Contl Div ASF, 27 Oct 43, to Bsc Ltr, Air IG to CG AAF CTTC, sub: Alleged Discrimination Against Negro Soldiers at Sioux Falls, S. D., SPWA 291.2.

[42] (1) D/F, G–1 to TAG, 31 Jan 45, sub: Revision of WD Memo W635–15–43, 1 Aug 43. WDGAP 353.8, in WDWAC 353.8 (1945–46). (2) D/F, G–1 for TAG, 28 Jun 45. WDGAP 353.8 WAC, in WDWAC 353.8 (1945–46).

[43] Min cited n. 9.

for members to "display a banner in our procession"; and the American Legion asked for "such units as may be available" for their annual convention parade.[44]

Refusals of such requests were frequently appealed from a post commander to a service commander and even higher. Thus, Colonel Hobby on one occasion received a telephoned request—which she was of course unable to grant—that she "force" the Commanding General, Second Service Command, to ship his WAC band from New York to Philadelphia, at Army expense, for the bond parade sponsored by the Philadelphia War Finance Committee. In other cases, civilian groups, refused by the commanding general of a service command, appealed to Congressmen who forced the commanding general to yield. No reasonable compromise solution to the problem was ever discovered.[45]

Travel Orders

Only one restriction was necessitated concerning transportation orders for women. Conditions of shipment were the same for men and women—troop trains for whole units, and travel of individuals or smaller groups by coach for short trips and Pullman for overnight travel. In practice such standards were of course seldom met for either men or women. WAC training centers were finally authorized to use coaches regularly for trips up to 36 hours, with a WAC officer in charge of each WAC shipment.

As unit shipment declined and individual shipment as casuals increased, disturbing reports were received concerning the shipment of mixed groups of men and women—particularly in one case in which seven enlisted women were sent on an overnight trip in a coach with enlisted

men, with only a male corporal in charge. At this, the Director asked that shipments of men and women not be consolidated. The Army Service Forces did not approve or publish this request, but after the Director's move to G–1 Division a War Department circular was published which required that, if it was necessary to ship enlisted men and women in the same car, a ranking member of each group would be in charge.[46]

Legal Restrictions on WAC Jobs

In order not to conflict with the prerogatives of the Army Nurse Corps, the WAC was forbidden by act of Congress to perform nursing duties. Nurses who had joined the WAAC could transfer to the Army Nurse Corps if eligible, but as the top age limit was 45 for nurses and 50 for Wacs, a number were not eligible and chose to continue in the WAC. Many registered nurses in this age group apparently failed to understand that they could not employ their skills under these circumstances, and some complaints were received. There was, however, no authority for discharge of such enlisted women, who ordinarily were employed as orderlies or technicians under the supervision of younger Nurse Corps officers. The same

---

[44] File of D. C. area requests to Dir WAC, all forwarded to MDW as matter under its jurisdiction, WDWAC 370.7 (1945–46).

[45] (1) Tp Conv, Mrs. Gruber, Dir WAC, and Mr. Lee, War Finance Committee, 9 Jun 44. WDWAC 000.7. (2) Min cited n. 20.

[46] All in WA 513 (11–26–42) Trans of WAAC Units: (1) Ltr, 3d SvC to WAAC Hq, 26 Nov 42; reply by 1st Ind. (2) Ltr, 2d SvC to WAAC Hq, 1 Dec 42, and 3 Inds. (3) Memo, WAAC Hq for CofTrans, 21 Dec 42, and reply. (4) Ltr, 8th SvC to OCT, 16 Apr 43, 4th Ind, Dir WAC, 21 May 43. (5) TWX, 3d TC to Dir WAC, 8 Jul 43; reply 12 July. (6) Memo, Dir WAC for CG ASF, 7 Dec 43. (7) WD Cir 154, 18 Apr 43.

prohibition applied to doctors, but as none of these were reported as remaining in the WAC, the problem of their assignment as enlisted women did not arise.[47]

There was likewise no authority for transfer of members of the WAC to the U.S. Cadet Nurse Corps for training. The Cadet Nurse Corps was a civilian organization organized by the U.S. Public Health Service to give free nurses' training to "cadets" who received their keep, allowances, and attractive uniforms. It possessed considerable attraction for members of the WAC, especially those in hospitals who were performing the duties of orderlies and receiving little or no useful training for the future.

Unfortunately, an early bulletin of the Public Health Service gave the impression that qualified members of the WAC might be released by the Army to take cadet nurse training. This was soon corrected at the request of WAC authorities, but meanwhile a number of requests for transfer had been received, accompanied by Congressional backing. To these the WAC was obliged to reply that there was no existing authority to transfer members from military service to civilian groups, since this would in effect have required discharge of all soldiers who could do better for themselves in civilian life. Nevertheless, it was months before such inquiries ceased to come in from Wacs who felt that they were being penalized for their early enlistment before cadet training was offered by the government. In general, the problem remained merely one small facet of the larger question of national versus voluntary service for women.[48]

A similar refusal was received by WAC officers and enlisted women who were qualified as pilots or as pilot trainees and who desired to transfer to the WASP (Women Air Service Pilots). Since this organization was a civilian group, there existed no authority for release of military personnel to accept flying duties. While it would have been possible to accomplish the same result by placing the WASP in the WAC, a solution agreeable to WAC leaders, this step was rejected by the director of the WASP. Again, the problem appeared part of the larger need for a clearer line of distinction between military and civilian duties and status.[49]

Restrictions on Assignment to Washington, D. C.

One other restriction on WAC assignments, which soon proved so unpopular as to be unenforceable, was General Somervell's early order barring assignments in the District of Columbia. Although replacement of Civil Service workers in this or any other location was forbidden, there was a limited number of fully military jobs in Washington, in which enlisted men were employed. In the Corps' first month the Chief of Staff approved the use of the first group of enlisted Waacs in the Pentagon, to monitor telephone calls for G–2 Division, but any further use was strictly prohibited.[50]

In view of the stringency of these orders, the General Council was surprised at the end of the Corps' first year when General McNarney demanded an explanation of

[47] See overage nurses' ltrs in SPWA and WDWAC 330.14 (1944).

[48] (1) Ltr, U.S. Public Health Serv to Exec WAC, 3 Apr 44. WDWAC 080. (2) Ltr, Rep. Frances P. Bolton to Dir WAC, 15 Nov 44. WDWAC 032.2.

[49] For full discussion, see Ch. XVI. Also Hist Recs Rpt 319, History of Air Transport Command: Women Pilots in Air Transport Command, by Hist Br ATC. USAF Hist Div.

[50] Memo, Dir WAAC for CG ASF, 21 Sep 42, Folder, WAC Rctg, ASF Sp Coll DRB AGO.

why "a number of them have infiltrated into jobs here."[51] Upon investigating, General Dalton was startled to discover that the ASF had 259 Waacs in Washington. He requested explanation of how they got there, since, he said, "General S. still does not want Waacs assigned to ASF activities in Washington."[52] Actually, all proved to be properly authorized personnel who had been approved by the Chief of Staff from time to time, particularly in G–2, WAC Headquarters, and later as staff directors for the administrative and technical services.[53]

In spite of all resolutions, Wacs continued to filter into Washington. Almost immediately after his protest, the manpower shortage forced General McNarney to approve an exception for the classified message center of his own office, and for Operations Division of the General Staff. At the same time a request from Military Intelligence Service for Wacs to man its message center was disapproved. Military Intelligence Service persisted, and in September of 1943 the Chief of Staff finally authorized 77 Wacs for this work; a little later it was necessary to add 22 more.[54]

This concession marked the beginning of the end of the policy. In November of 1943, the ban on WAC officers in the ASF in the District was removed, with the precaution that a report of the total be sent to the Deputy Chief of Staff every two months. By May of 1944, a large percentage of the enlisted personnel being brought to Washington was female, for service at the secret Signal Corps installation at Arlington Hall, or with the Air Forces at Bolling Field and the Air Transport Command at Gravelly Point. By August of 1944 there were 2,045 enlisted women in the Military District of Washington alone, and the ceiling was raised to 3,202 to per-

mit more to enter. Just before the end of the war, the last opponent to Wacs in Washington—the Army Ground Forces—yielded to the manpower shortage and asked permission to bring in 55 women for military jobs in Headquarters, AGF.[55]

By this time the War Department's policy had been entirely reversed; not only did it permit Wacs to work in the General Staff in Washington, but it awarded itself top priority. It was directed that War Department needs would be filled from surplus personnel, if possible, but if not, it would receive Wacs regardless of the branch that had been promised them when recruited. If this was inadequate, the Air, Ground, and Service Forces would be called upon to supply Washington's demands from field stations.[56]

Since all General Staff requisitions called for highly qualified personnel, they remained unpopular with field commands, as well as with many of the enlisted women, who preferred the more military atmosphere of an Army post. On the other hand, since allotments often permitted top ratings, the requisitions were more easily

---

[51] Min, Gen Council, 3 May 43.

[52] Pencil note, "JND" for Col Wood. SPAP 320.2 WAAC (5–17–43).

[53] Memo, Dir MPD ASF for Gen Dalton, 19 Jul 43. SPAP 320.2 WAAC.

[54] (1) Memo, Secy GS for Gen McNarney, 2 Aug 43. WDCSA 291.9. (2) Memo, G–1 through CofS for G–2, 2 Aug 43. WDGAP 320.2 WAC, in WDCSA 291.9. (3) D/F, G–1 for CofS, 3 Sep 43, WDGAP 320.2 WAC; and later D/F, G–2 for DCofS, 1 Dec 43. MID 320.2, in CofS 291.9 WAC.

[55] (1) Memo, G–1 for ASF through DCofS, 16 Nov 43. WDGAP 320.2 WAC (10–15–43), in OCS 291.9. (2) Min, Gen Council, 15 May 44. (3) D/F, G–1 for MPD ASF, 14 Aug 44. WDGAP 320.22 WAC. (4) Memo, AGF for Dir WAC, 5 Aug 45. WDWAC 220.8.

[56] (1) Memo, MDW for DCofS, 14 Mar 44, SPWPM 341 WAC. (2) D/F, DCofS for TAG, 15 Mar 44. WDCSA 324.5 WAC.

filled than those of overseas theaters. Only military vacancies continued to be filled; as a result the total employment in the Washington area remained only about a fifth of that achieved by the Navy Department. Thus, the War Department priority never became the problem that was reported by the Navy, where, it was stated, "the over-riding priority given . . . cut across and upset all principles of equitable apportionment."[57]

Results of Enlisted Personnel Policies

With the removal of restrictions on assignment in Washington, there remained no type of fixed installation to which WAC assignment was forbidden. There was, likewise, with the possible exception of "entertainer," no noncombatant MOS to which field commanders were forbidden to assign enlisted women, although some, like food service, were restricted to WAC administration. The result of these lenient assignment policies was, as might have been expected, a rapid multiplication of the number of WAC enlisted jobs from the time of the conversion onward, limited only by the civilian skills that women were found to possess.

Records in the Corps' second year showed that already women had been recruited in more than 300 different civilian occupations, from gunsmith to electrical engineer, and from psychiatric social worker to horsebreaker. Almost every language skill was represented, including Chinese, Finnish, Lithuanian, and Swahili. While obviously not all of these skills could be used by the Army, by the summer of 1943 the number of military occupational specialities held by enlisted women was estimated at 155; by early 1944, at 239; by May of 1944, at 274. No final count was ever reported. It did not appear

likely that the estimated possible total of 408 suitable Army jobs had been reached, but it had undoubtedly been approached within all reasonable expectation under a voluntary recruitment system.[58]

Under the informal assignment system, about half of the assignments were to administrative and office work, in which women predominated in civilian life. Toward the end of the war a mild trend had set in away from such work in favor of increased technical and professional assignments—at least in the United States—but office work still took first place.[59]

	Percent	
Type of work	1943	30 Sep 44
Administrative and Office	53	45
Technical and Professional	13	18
Motor vehicle	10	9
Foods	8	9
Supply and Stock	7	8
Mechanical and Trade	5	4
Communications	2	5
Radio and Electrical	2	2

As might have been predicted from the higher WAC enlistment standards, the average enlisted woman was found to be somewhat ahead of the average enlisted man in aptitude as measured by the Army General Classification Test.[60]

	Percent	
AGCT	EW	EM
Group I	4.90	6.34
Group II	37.07	31.00
Group III	39.89	30.68
Group IV	17.87	25.12
Group V	0.27	6.86

[57] WAVES Hist.

[58] (1) D/F, TAG for Dir WAC, 27 Apr 44. Folder, Rpt of Unusual Qualifications, WAC Plng file. (2) List, copy in Plng Proj 4, WAAC Plng Serv files (1943). (3) Table, Utilization of EW in 274 ASF and AFF Jobs, 2 May 44. Folder, Statistics, WAC files, OCMH.

[59] Memo, G-1 Stat Br for Dir WAC, 26 Feb 45. WDWAC 201.6.

[60] William C. Menninger, Psychiatry in a Troubled World (New York: The Macmillan Company, 1948).

SUITABLE ARMY JOBS FOR WOMEN. *Above, Wac laboratory technician conducts an experiment at Fort Jackson Station Hospital, South Carolina. Below, two women work at a trailer repair unit, Fort McPherson, Georgia.*

SUITABLE ARMY JOBS FOR WOMEN. *Above, a Wac is at work in the Ordnance Section at Camp Campbell, Kentucky. Below, women pack a parachute, part of their duties as riggers, Fort Benning, Georgia.*

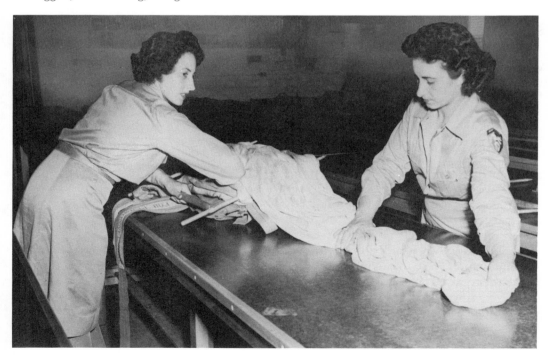

For the same reason, in educational level enlisted women appeared even more noticeably superior to the enlisted men of the Army, with 62 percent of enlisted women having a high school education or better as compared to 39 percent of enlisted men.[61]

Educational Level	Percent EW	Percent EM
Grammar school only	8.99	28.6
1, 2, 3 years high school	28.62	32.6
High school graduate	42.21	27.6
1, 2, 3 years college	13.76	8.2
College graduate	5.36	2.1
Postgraduate	1.06	.9

In ratings the enlisted women were nevertheless considerably behind the men of the Army. Obviously, under the decentralized system of control, women had not received the ratings that would have gone with their skills under a more formal system.[62]

Grade	Percent EW	Percent EM
Master and 1st Sgt	0.6	1.5
Technical Sgt	0.6	2.9
Staff Sgt and Tec/3	3.5	8.1
Sgt or Tec/4	11.8	14.1
Corporal or Tec/5	19.6	21.0
Pvt 1st Class	25.4	28.1
Private	38.5	24.3

The relative success of the decentralized and flexible system of enlisted assignments, as contrasted with the Navy's more formalized one, was difficult to determine. There were indications that the Navy suffered some wastage of civilian skills by arbitrary denial to women of certain categories of jobs, as well as what it called "misplacement and under-utilization of women, which were to have far-reaching consequences on morale and procurement."[63] However, in the Army also there was evidence that, while outright violations of regulations were few, the standard of utilization of skills was not high.

In late 1944 a War Department personnel auditing team surveyed a large sample of the Army's enlisted women and discovered that, of women who had specialized civilian skills urgently needed by the Army, 23 percent were not using them. If this sample ratio held true, almost one fourth of the Corps' skilled workers were being underutilized through poor personnel practices. It was also found that 22 percent of graduates of service schools were assigned to duties unrelated to their schooling, thus indicating that almost one fourth of the Army's specialized training of women was being wasted.[64]

Various inspection teams at different times also detected a notable trend toward underutilization of the higher skills. In the Air Forces, college women were pronounced "usually well-assigned," but in the Army Service Forces, only about 20 percent of enlisted college graduates were in jobs requiring their training, and 4 percent were actually in menial jobs. One team captain reported:

Women with degrees in home economics and one to fifteen years experience in food planning were working as Second and Third cooks. Women with years of photographic experience were working on one simple phase of that job. Expert linguists—German, Polish, Spanish, French, Chinese—some of whom could take dictation in the language— were not using their language skill.[65]

---

[61] Data as of 31 May 44 for EW and 30 Jun 44 for EM; Memo, G-1 Stat Br for HD SSUSA, 14 Mar 46, sub: Stat Mat for WAC Hist. WDGAP 314.7 WAC.

[62] As of March 1945. From George R. Powell, Chief, Statistical Advisory Sec, HD SSUSA.

[63] WAVES Hist, p. 58.

[64] Hist of Dir of Pers ASF. OCMH. Rpt of Team, 8 Nov 44, Southern Area. Sample: 28 WAC units of 3,742 EW.

[65] This and following discussion is based on team reports cited n. 8.

Skilled stenographers were especially liable to malassignment, as civilians often occupied an office's only stenographic job. Malassignments also were found among telephone operators, typists, clerks, chauffers, key-punch operators, dietitians, and other specialists.

Everywhere women were conscious of the lack of ratings. Surveyors noted that "in some instances, promotions have been given to enlisted men rather than Wacs when an opening occurs, even though the Wac may have filled the opening. . . . Enlisted men resent Wacs being given ratings rather than themselves."

Survey team captains reported that the Army Air Forces generally showed a more favorable attitude toward WAC classification. Various teams stated: "Wacs are very well received in the AAF, not only by section chiefs but also by enlisted men"; "The type of jobs open to Wacs was more varied in the AAF"; "AAF jobs were far more in agreement with WAC Regulations than ASF."

There was no indication that the wastage of skills of enlisted women was worse than that among enlisted men, with two exceptions: there was a general tendency to use women in nonmilitary work or lower-rated jobs, and there was also a tendency to accept as normal among women a percentage of malassignment which, for men, resulted from the necessity for combat assignments. All inspectors continued to note that failure to use their skills had a proportionately greater effect upon women than upon men, who expected eventual combat. One team captain noted, "Morale and classification

seem to be almost synonymous as far as Wacs are concerned."

There was every evidence that both the Army and the Navy had pursued the correct policy in limiting their women's corps to skilled personnel who could fill skilled jobs. Survey teams reported that women with less than two years of high school education had seldom progressed well in the Army, and those who had no essential skill, particularly in the older age group, had especial difficulty in adjusting to military life. Women's lesser physical strength effectively prevented success of such women on those Army jobs within their mental capacities.

In the last winter of the war, ASF's Military Personnel Division reported itself still unable to find suitable assignments for such women, after a series of futile attempts to train them as ward orderlies, shoemakers, and sewing machine operators. It therefore recommended that the women be discharged and no more recruited. This decision obviously represented a major reversal of the ideas of a decade before—or even a year before—concerning lowering of standards for women recruits. Both Army and Navy experience indicated that in future planning, and particularly if selective service was applied to women, the armed forces had good grounds for accepting only women of a skill and aptitude somewhat above that of drafted men and of the population as a whole.[66]

---

[66] (1) Hist cited n. 64. (2) Memo, MTD ASF for Dir Pers ASF, 16 Nov 44, sub: Tng for Grade IV and V WAC Pers, and 1st Ind, MPD to MTD, 25 Nov 44. SPTRP 353 WAC, in SPAP 353.

CHAPTER XXVIII

The Employment of Personnel: Officers

Few if any of Director Hobby's recommended policy changes concerned the well-being of WAC officers, whom she believed to be in a position to solve their own problems. She stated, "The WAC is an enlisted women's Army component. . . . The enlisted woman is the Corps. We, the officers, exist for the prime purpose of insuring her welfare. . . ." [1] For this reason, most of the provisions made for the employment of officers were concerned only with insuring adequate numbers for troop duty, proper selection, and suitable training. In other matters it was assumed that WAC officers—as had nurses for decades—had the pay and the freedom to provide for themselves without much special provision on the part of the Army.

Officer job assignments included not only Corps administration, which had existed since WAAC days, but also jobs in replacement of an Army officer, which were dubbed "operational." Some attempt was made, when WAC officers first became eligible for this latter duty, to analyze all Army officer jobs and list those suitable for women, as had already been done in the case of enlisted jobs. In this process, The Adjutant General's Office listed only those officer assignments that were noncombatant, suitable in environment, and within a woman's strength.

Automatically eliminated were all duties requiring unusual civilian experience or long training time, all usually held by senior officers, and all dealing exclusively with men. Such analyses, like those of enlisted jobs, proved fruitless under the actual assignment system, because various Army commands to which WAC officers were assigned determined their assignment without reference to The Adjutant General. [2]

Restrictions on Officer Assignment

Only two restrictions were ever placed upon this power of local commanders to determine WAC officer assignment, and neither was committed to a formal War Department publication. One of these, as in the case of enlisted women, concerned nonmilitary assignment. In late 1944 the director of ASF's Control Division noted:

The attention of this office has been called recently to instances in which it appears that WAC officers are not being assigned to jobs which are commensurate with their grades,

---

[1] *WAC Newsletter*, Vol. I, No. 6, 15 Nov 43.

[2] (1) Office Memo, Lies for Dir WAAC, 1 Jul 43. Proj 18, Plng Serv files. (2) Office Memo, Dolores Christy for Studdeford, 9 Jul 43. (3) Memo, Lies for Tng Off, 2 Feb 44. Papers of Dep Dir WAC, DRB AGO.

or which could not be performed by civilian clerks.[3]

The tendency to assign WAC officers to such work appeared related to misunderstandings as to status, dating from Auxiliary days. The Army Air Forces, as soon as it received WAC officers, therefore published instructions pointing out that they must fill bona fide officer allotments.[4] The Service Forces did not publish instructions on the subject, but attempted to correct individual cases wherever they were discovered by inspectors.

A second and somewhat related restriction concerned the assignment of WAC officers as aides, secretaries, and sometimes chauffeurs to general officers. Even if an officer grade was provided, the assigned duties seldom sounded like those of officers. One such Wac upon her return to the United States gave reporters a description of her duties which got national publicity:

I took all the dictation and did the typing. . . . I did the filing and answered the telephone. . . . I always saw to it that he had his eyeglasses and his wallet. . . . I kept a check on clean shirts. I laid out clean clothes and I would pack his bags for trips. I also sewed on ribbons and buttons. . . . I always had so much to do, with my office in my bedroom.[5]

She also, she added, served as hostess at parties. For these duties, she was promoted to the rank of major and received the Legion of Merit.

In spite of the danger of poor publicity on these assignments, they eventually became so prevalent that the War Department acted to forbid them. At Director Hobby's request, the Deputy Chief of Staff, General McNarney, wrote personal letters to the commanding generals of all major domestic commands and all overseas theaters, saying:

It has recently been brought to the attention of the Chief of Staff that commissioned officers of the Women's Army Corps have sometimes been assigned or utilized as aides to general officers, as chauffeurs, and for routine stenographic duty normally performed by enlisted or civilian personnel.

While such assignments of female officers are considered inappropriate and inadvisable, it is not desired to issue any formal War Department regulation on this subject, nor is it desired that your headquarters issue any formal instructions. On the other hand, if instances of such improper use . . . occur in any activity under your command, you should take appropriate corrective action.

It is particularly desired that there be no publicity on this subject.[6]

Commanders in the field frequently failed to comply with the provisions of this letter, especially overseas where such War Department opinion was at best deemed merely advisory. In the European theater, by the end of the war, no less than forty-five WAC officers—14 percent of the total—were serving as personal assistants to ranking officers. In almost every such case, unwarranted criticism was incurred by both employer and subordinate, and the impression sometimes created that officers of the Women's Army Corps received promotions and awards for duties that were not essentially those of an officer. Inasmuch as male officers were also at times employed in the same duties of aide and handy-man, the problem could not be considered entirely a WAC one, although newspaper innuendoes were pos-

---

[3] Memo, Dir Contl Div ASF for Dir Pers ASF, 5 Oct 44. SPAP 210.3 WAC. The above-cited survey resulted.

[4] AAF Hq Office Instructions 35–25, 25 Sep 43.

[5] "Missouri Girl Went Through War Overseas," *Kansas City Star*, September 23, 1945.

[6] Ltr, DCofS USA to CGs of AAF, AGF, ASF, EDC, WDC, ETO, NATO, POEs, USAFIME, SWPA, CBI, 11 Aug 44. WDGAP 210.31 WAC, in WDWAC 210.31.

sible that were usually not applied to male aides.

Limitations on Further WAC Commissions

Almost all other War Department directives on WAC officers concerned the numbers and skills needed properly to administer enlisted personnel.[7] Soon after the conversion, Director Hobby recommended to the War Department that the WAC ratio of officers to enlisted be the same as that of the Army, or about 1 to 11. The WAAC ratio had been somewhat lower, 1 to 14, in view of the fact that officers of the Auxiliary had not been eligible for other than troop duty. After discussion, General White of G–1 Division agreed to issue the necessary directives to set the ratio of 1 to 11.[8]

A nonconcurrence to the proposed action was offered by ASF's Military Personnel Division. In view of the current overstrength of male officers, Military Personnel Division proposed that the WAC officer-enlisted ratio be set at 1 to 20, stating:

It is believed that the ratio of 1 to 20 will provide adequate numbers of officers for all known needs. It will not provide officers for wholesale replacement of AUS [male] officers in installations in which either AUS or WAC officers could be utilized. Until the present overstrength of AUS officers is absorbed, it is not believed advantageous to commission, train, and utilize large numbers of WAC officers in positions which these AUS officers can fill.[9]

To bring the Corps down to this ratio, ASF proposed that the WAC officer candidate school be cut to the lowest possible amount that would permit its continued operation—100 every 3 months. These proposals were approved by the War De-partment, and the Director's Office was so advised.[10]

This move was not satisfactory to the Office of the Director, particularly since the output of male officer candidate schools for troop duty was not similarly curtailed in spite of the overstrength of male officers.[11] Also, WAVES recruiters still continued able to offer 250 monthly commissions to prospects, although the WAVES already had a higher proportion of officers than the WAC.[12]

A short time later, the War Department Manpower Board recommended that the WAC officer candidate school be entirely suspended. Director Hobby objected, pointing out, "Such action would be demoralizing to morale within the Corps and would be a serious deterrent to recruiting."[13] The Army Service Forces agreed that "the effect of such action on recruiting would not only result in a decrease in the number of women recruited but also in the caliber of women recruited."[14] At ASF's recommendation, the WAC officer candidate school was

---

[7] Minor exceptions: (1) Limited Service: Memo, Dir WAC for G–1, 11 Feb 44. SPWA 220.4. (2) Request by Name: Personal ltr, Dir WAC to Maj Gen Carter B. Magruder, G–4 USFET, 10 Jan 46. WDWAC 210.31. (3) Age Requirements: Memo, Dir WAC for CG ASF, 17 Sep 43, re AG Memo W605–35–43, 4 Sep 43. SPWA 210.31.

[8] Draft of Memo, Dir WAC for G–1, 6 Aug 43, with pencil note. SPWA 314.7 sec 4. See Table 10, Appendix A.

[9] Memo, Gen Reynolds, MPD ASF, for G–1, 1 Oct 43. SPGAS 320.2 WAC (9–29–43), in SPAP 320.2.

[10] Memo, MPD ASF for TAG, 20 Oct 43. SPGAP 320.2 WAC (9–29–43), in SPAP 320.2. See M/R. OCS was lengthened from 8 to 12 weeks.

[11] ASF Hist of OCT, Fig. 7. OCMH.

[12] Memo, Dir Pers ASF for G–1, 8 Apr 44. SPAP 352 WAC.

[13] Memo, Dir Contl Div ASF for Dir WAC, 9 Feb 44, Incl, Bd Rpt, 12 Jan 44. SPWA 319.1.

[14] Memo, MPD ASF for CofS ASF, 25 Feb 44. SPAP 210.3 WAC.

therefore not abolished, but its capacity was further reduced, this time to only 50 every three months, or 200 a year. This was a token enrollment that would not make up officer attrition, and that would allow each WAC company on the average to send only one candidate every two years.[15]

The Officers' Pool

Director Hobby's office was not at the moment in a position to offer strong objections to these decisions, in view of the current numbers of unassigned WAC officers. Although requisitions for enlisted women were plentiful, most Army commands had not, as of this date, shown any similar enthusiasm for WAC officers.

The officers' pool began its existence soon after the collapse of the short-lived WAAC expansion program. As training centers and specialists' schools closed, most of their officer cadre was assigned to an officers' pool. To this group was added each week the graduates of the large officer candidate classes which had been enrolled to administer the expected recruits. By the time of the conversion to Army status, the WAC officers' pool included over 1,000 officers, almost one fifth of the Corps' total officer strength.[16]

The seriousness of the situation was not immediately realized, since it was expected that, under the newly acquired Army status, jobs would be immediately forthcoming. In the Auxiliary Corps, women officers had been eligible for troop duty only, but Army membership opened to them the whole range of technical, professional, and administrative officer duties.

Immediately upon the effective date of the WAC legislation, the Army Air Forces requisitioned and successfully assigned 800

of these officers. However, with the closing of further training centers, the officers' pool quickly refilled itself. The Army Service Forces, which assumed control of the pool at the conversion, proved unable to assign any number of these women. In attempting to do so, ASF first informally directed its service commands to submit requisitions. The response was not enthusiastic, since too many noncombat men had been commissioned and were in some cases being relieved of active duty for lack of assignments. Eventually, ASF was forced to direct service commands to take 800 WAC officers on temporary duty, with the understanding that the women would be permanently assigned if they proved able to take over the duties of male officers gradually being sent overseas. This move was not a success either, as officers did not move overseas in sufficient numbers.[17]

By the end of the WAC's first six months in the Army, the situation was critical. The WAC officers' pool now contained about 1500 members, or about one fourth of all WAC officers, and was incurring

[15] (1) Memo, MPD ASF through G–1 WD for TAG, 16 Feb 44. SPAP 210.3 WAC. Approved 29 Mar 44 by G–1. Supported by Memo, Gen Styer, CofS ASF, for G–1 WD, 18 Feb 44. SPGAP 352 OCS (2–14–44) 245, in SPAP 352 WAC. (2) Attrition was later estimated at 360 per year. D/F, G–1 for TAG, 6 Mar 45, approved by DCofS, 7 Mar 45, with atchd stf study by Maj K. McClure, and Tabs A–F. Folder Statistics WDGAP 352 OCS.

[16] (1) M/R, 20 May 43. SPWA 300.6 (3–30–42) sec 2 (1942). (2) Memo, Col Catron for Dirs, Opns Div, Tng Div, Rctg Contl, 21 May 43. SPWA 341 (5–21–43)E, in SPAP 341 WAAC (2–26–43).

[17] (1) Memo, Lies for Dir WAC, 8 Feb 44. Folder 13, WAC Plng Serv files. (2) Memo, Dir Pers ASF for CofS ASF, 25 Feb 44. SPGAC 210.3 WAC (2–14–44). (3) AAF WAC Hist, p. 49. (4) Personal ltr, Chief, Strength Authorization Br ASF to Dir Pers in each SvC, 15 Jul 43. SPWA 314.7. (5) Memo, G–1, for Dir WDBPR, 18 Apr 44. WAC Cl file. (6) Memo, Dep Dir WAC for CofS, 21 Jul 44. CofS 324.5 WAC. (7) AGO Ltr, 12 Jan 44. AG 210.85 (12–30–43) PO–A–A.

severe public and Congressional censure and causing internal morale problems. Had the idle members been inanimate objects, no problem would have existed, since all would be needed within the next two years to staff new companies, but it was increasingly apparent that they could not be kept indefinitely, like so many cold-storage eggs, without spoilage.

The unhappy officers were formed in companies and commanded like enlisted women. As weeks passed in inactivity, there was afforded again an example of the reaction of women to idleness—or, as some psychiatrists termed it, the "volunteer" reaction. The unassigned officers' morale quickly vanished, and their attitudes plumbed the extremes of despair, anger, and disillusionment. Years later, no officer who had spent months in the officers' pool could be found who did not denounce the experience, and it appeared to many authorities that if WAC leadership had not already been ruined by poor selection, many potential leaders were now permanently warped beyond restoration. Officers in the pool, instead of aiding in WAC recruiting in order to secure themselves companies, were frequently found to have been advising friends that "it was a horrible mistake to join the WAC." [18]

When, six months after the ASF took it over, the officers' pool was not reduced, Maj. Katherine R. Goodwin, soon to be designated ASF WAC Officer, went personally to General Robinson of Control Division, ASF, to ask decisive action. [19] This also produced no discernible results.

Reclassification Proposals

To assist the ASF in fulfilling its assignment responsibilities for these officers, the Director proposed measures to reclassify and relieve from service all WAC officers, wherever located, whose performance had been unsatisfactory, thus leaving vacancies for more capable ones. A committee of the Director's staff, including General Faith before his reassignment, informed her that it was "common knowledge within the corps" that there were some WAC officers whose ability and behavior did not merit commissioned status and whose commanders repeatedly asked to transfer them to a training center or pool but, upon being told to reclassify them under Army Regulations, could not bring themselves to do so. [20]

Upon General Faith's advice, the Director proposed to the War Department that, to stimulate reclassification, commanders in all major commands be allowed to send such women for 90 days to a review board at Fort Des Moines, which, after medical examination and on-the-job observation in different duties, would return them with a recommendation for appropriate action by the command. The Director noted, "Commanders in the field are loath to apply the same standards of efficiency to WAC officers which they require of male officers." [21] However, this proposal for reducing the number of unassigned officers was refused by ASF on grounds that it might usurp the prerogatives of field commanders by preventing them from reclassifying an officer without first sending her to Des Moines. [22]

---

[18] Speech by Comdt, Sch of WAC Pers Adm, "Development of WAC." Notes in OCMH.

[19] Memo, KRG, then Pers Off, O Dir WAC, to Dir WAC, no date (about Feb 44). WDWAC 201.6.

[20] Memo, Faith for Dir WAC, 5 Nov 43. SPWA 201.6.

[21] Memo, Dir WAC for G–1, 15 Nov 43. SPWA 201.6 (11–5–43).

[22] Ibid., 1st Ind, MPD ASF for G–1, 12 Jan 44.

Until after the Director's move to G–1 Division, no solution to the problem could be found. However, within two weeks of the move, a dramatically sudden solution occurred, creditable to General Somervell. At a meeting of the commanding generals of service commands in March, General Somervell called for a vigorous drive to assign WAC officers to permanent jobs which would release male troop age officers needed for overseas shipments. So emphatic was his language that within a few weeks all but 250 of the 1,515 officers in the WAC officers' pool had been permanently assigned.[23]

Shortage of WAC Troop Officers

Within a few months a sudden reversal of the situation took place, and there was a shortage rather than a surplus of WAC officers. Had it been possible to hold the pool officers idle for another year or six months, troop assignments would have been eventually forthcoming. New recruits required officers; training centers needed to rotate fatigued senior officers to the field; field companies needed new junior officers to permit normal upward progress among troop officers; overseas theaters needed junior officers for the same purpose. In all of these jobs, WAC officers were essential, since men could not be substituted on WAC administration.

Director Hobby therefore, with the support of ASF's Director of Personnel, proposed that the WAC officer candidate school output be raised to meet minimum needs. It was pointed out that if even the 1-to-20 ratio, and not the Army ratio, was applied to the 4,000 new recruits entering monthly, the WAC would be entitled to 200 officer candidates a month instead of the current 200 a year.[24]

This request was refused by the General Staff "owing to the present officer strength of the Army." [25] Instead, it was suggested that some of the almost 2,000 WAC officers recently forced on service commands for non-WAC duties be retrieved and reassigned to troop duty. No great difficulty was anticipated, since the pool officers had been in fact a shotgun allotment. A survey was therefore launched, with each Army command required to state how many WAC officers it was not using on WAC administration, and how many of these could be released for assignment to duty with WAC troops.

Unfortunately for this project, it was found that the Wacs could no more be recovered than water from sand. Domestic Army commands admitted that, of their 5,038 Wac officers, only 1,626 were being used on troop work, and the remaining 3,412 were in staff jobs that could be filled by a male officer. Of these 3,412, commands alleged that all but 63 were now in work too essential to permit them to be released and replaced by a man, even though some had been unwillingly accepted only six months before. Only 63 unsatisfactory officers were offered for transfer to WAC troop duty.[26]

At this there began an undignified scramble for the acquisition of the 200-yearly output of officer candidate school, punctuated by frequent allegations of unsportsmanlike methods by contenders.

The ASF, which controlled the training centers, directed that all graduates be as-

[23] Memo, ASF for TAG, 13 Mar 44. SPGAC 210.3 WAC (3–13–44)–129.
[24] Memo, Dir Pers ASF for G–1, 8 Apr 44. SPAP 352 WAC (4–8–44).
[25] Memo, G–1 for ASF, 27 May 44. WDGAP 352 OCS.
[26] Memo, "KM" for Col C. F. Collier, Br Chief, G–1, 23 Aug 44. WDWAC 320.2.

signed to training centers to permit rotation of tired training officers to the field.[27] Training authorities felt that the efficiency of training centers was the primary consideration; that a new officer needed such assignment "to become used to her bars";[28] and that seasoned training center officers "are the best source of officers for field company duty."[29] The AAF nonconcurred when it discovered this action, since it contributed 42 percent of the officer candidates and expected 42 percent of the graduates, preferably the same individuals it had sent. Newly commissioned second lieutenants were badly needed to permit promotion in field companies; fatigued captains with training center experience were useless because of their rank and sometimes because they had acquired a training center concept of discipline and daily routine that proved unworkable in the field. Still a third viewpoint was offered by some of the technical services concerning new graduates who had signal, scientific, or other specialized skills desired by these services, which would be wasted in troop duty.

G–1 Division, from which Director Hobby was now operating, agreed with the Air Forces that the welfare of WAC detachments in the field took precedence, and ordered The Adjutant General to give first priority to company duty, with all graduates returned to the major commands with which they had served as enlisted women. The Adjutant General by August of 1944 was in the position of having 650 urgent requisitions for WAC troop officers and only 182 available from all sources to fill them.[30]

This competition, while gratifying to those who previously had found a WAC officer unassignable, resulted from an absence of normal officer candidate grad-

uation that proved unfortunate for the leadership for WAC troops. Of some 70,000 new recruits obtained after the virtual cessation of officer candidate training, very few ever had opportunity to be commissioned, although many of these women appeared far superior in leadership potentialities to those so hastily commissioned earlier.

Among those women already commissioned, troop duty, which was intended to be their primary interest, became a matter of abhorrence and was abandoned by many of the most capable officers. In the absence of a supply of second lieutenants, troop officers were frozen in their jobs and company duty became a dead-end street, with no chance of progress for junior officers or relief for tired commanders. On the other hand, WAC officers in Army staff jobs progressed normally and soon had too much rank to be rotated to junior company jobs even if the branches that had given them specialist training would have released them. Non-WAC staff jobs offered not only more progress but also less strenuous hours. The tired and unpromoted company commander, hurrying from dinner back to company conferences of an evening, was obliged to behold less capable but higher-ranking desk officers enjoying their afteroffice leisure at the officers' club.

Over a period of time, many of even the most devoted troop officers requested relief from troop duty; and the cause of WAC leadership, far from attracting the

[27] Memo, MPD ASF for TAG, 30 Jun 44. SPAP 210.3 WAC (8–30–43).
[28] ASF Hist of WAC Tng, p. 294.
[29] Memo, MPD ASF for G–1, 17 Jul 44. SPAP 210.3 WAC.
[30] *Ibid.;* cites 5 Jul G–1 directive to TAG and 13 Jul TAG report of contradiction. See also Memo cited n. 26.

best officers, gradually fell more and more to those unable to qualify for staff jobs or unable because of inferior ability to rise above the grade of lieutenant.[31]

The War Department was never willing to interfere in the command prerogative of Army commands by directing them to release WAC officers to company duty, and all efforts to get any number released by milder methods failed completely. In the case of officers who had not yet been trained as specialists and who were obviously malassigned, individual requests for release to troop duty were made.

For example, in one case in Army Service Force Headquarters, General Dalton's request noted:

The stenographic work performed by the incumbent does not warrant the services of an officer. . . . In view of the acute shortage of company officers and Lt. F's demonstrated ability as a company officer, it is recommended she be made available for transfer.

This was refused by the office of assignment, and almost without exception other offices refused to release such women for company work.[32]

Proposals for an A Corps

The solution proposed by Director Hobby was the same that certain British services had previously been forced to adopt: a formal division between administrators of female troops and those detailed to other corps. British women officers who were specialists in female administration proudly wore the "A" (for Administrative) lapel insignia to mark the distinction. Under Colonel Hobby's plan, an officer-enlisted ratio would be set for WAC administrators only, and might well be even less than 1 to 20. The WAC officer candidate school would be reserved for these

women; selection and training methods would be beamed toward production of a leader; separate allotments of grades and career management plans would insure rotation and progress; advanced leadership training would be given as WAC administrators were rotated to recruiting, training, staff, and company work, and progressed upwards from junior officers to commanders to staff directorships; and a special insignia would mark what would thus become the proudest instead of the most scorned branch of service for a woman officer.

The WAC would, in effect, become an arm or service like any other, training its own officer and enlisted specialists in its own limited field, the leadership of women, but not all women would belong to this service. All other officers and enlisted women, perhaps 90 percent of the Corps, would be cut loose from WAC designation and quotas, and become part of the arm or service in which they were detailed, attending its schools under its own quota.

Under this plan, the WAC would have exercised no more control over the selection of a female signal officer than a male. Since the Signal Corps at this time had a yearly quota of 2,600 officer candidates to meet its needs,[33] the new plan proposed that the enlisted woman specialist appear before the Signal Corps officer candidate board, not the WAC board. If she qualified in competition with male applicants, she would attend the Signal Corps officer candidate school or any desired combination of WAC and Signal Corps schools, be

---

[31] See Ch. XXXIII, below.
[32] Tab A, Memo, ASF WAC Off for Dir Pers ASF, 9 Dec 44. SPAP 210.3 WAC (10–5–44).
[33] Ibid., atchd Ltr to all offices from Gen Dalton, 21 Dec 44, and their replies.

commissioned in the Signal Corps under its quota and not in the WAC, and thereafter be entirely under Signal Corps control. She actually would not be a Wac, but a Signal Corps officer, and could not be arbitrarily removed by the WAC, or returned to the WAC if she failed in Signal Corps work. WAC staff officers believed that women could successfully attend the officer candidate school of any noncombat arm or service, with only minor modifications in physical training and similar courses, just as enlisted women were already successfully graduating from the corresponding Army enlisted specialist courses on a coed basis.

The general outlines of such a plan were arrived at simultaneously by so many agencies that it appeared an inevitable development. The Army Air Forces had repeatedly objected to the discrimination against its enlisted women. AAF enlisted men could be sent to the Air Forces administrative officer candidate school, while equally qualified women could not be commissioned except by attendance at the WAC school, for which the AAF got a quota of only 12 a month for 40,000 women. The Air Forces first attempted to raise this quota; it pointed out that it had 700 accepted WAC officer candidates, and an urgent need for 300 of them to fill officer vacancies, and asked for special large Air WAC classes to be scheduled at WAC officer candidate school.[34] This was refused by the War Department, with what the AAF believed to be consequent detriment to the leadership of its WAC squadrons. The Air WAC Officer later expressed a belief that the refusal resulted in a waste of training and loss of woman specialists, "who should have been used in their specialties rather than as company officers," and was not in accordance with

"everything that had been done in the WAC program during the previous three years [which] pointed to greater integration of WAC personnel into all commands and organizations of the Army. . . ."[35]

ASF training center authorities also independently arrived at this view:

Many officers have proven totally unsuited by reason of ability, personality, or past training and experience to serve as company officers. This has proved true to a point that it would seem desirable to commission as WAC officers only those individuals regarded as qualified to serve as company officers with WAC units. If it is necessary to commission female individuals for specialized assignments not connected with WAC administration, it would be best to . . . commission them in the branch in which they would be classified in such a manner as to avoid their subsequent assignment to WAC administration.[36]

This principle was never to be accepted during World War II, chiefly because arms and services such as the Signal Corps refused to share their officer candidate school quota with women, and, while still requisitioning qualified women officers, continued to insist that these come from the small WAC quota.

By the end of the war, with the continued refusal either to expand the WAC officer candidate school or to admit women to other schools, the WAC ratio of officers to enlisted had shrunk to approximately the intended 1 to 20, as against about 1 to 10 for the Army. Reports from various commands indicated that as high as 85 percent of these in some areas had been removed from WAC administration.

---

[34] Quota given as 7,710 for 1943, 2,640 for 1944. Fig. 1, of ASF Hist of Mil Tng: OCS Tng, by MTD ASF.

[35] AAF WAC Hist, pp. 85, 86, and 94.

[36] ASF Hist of WAC Tng, p. 112.

The precarious state to which the leadership of WAC companies had thus been reduced indicated that, had the war continued, some War Department decision would have been required, either to restore the WAC to the Army ratio of officers, or to give the Office of the Director power to withdraw women specialists from the arms and services over their nonconcurrence, to staff WAC companies.

Just before the end of the war, the General Staff authorized an emergency WAC officer candidate class of 200 for the month of May 1945, with increased classes intended thereafter. None of these officers reached the field in time to benefit the Corps before demobilization began, nor would these small numbers have offered any final solution to the basic dilemma had the war continued.[37]

Integration of Specialist Officers

Although other officer candidate schools were not yet open to them, the process of integrating women officer specialists into the arms and services had begun in a small way before the end of the war. When the Sanitary Corps requested that certain enlisted women with the necessary scientific training be commissioned and assigned to it, Director Hobby concurred, provided that the women did not count against the WAC officer candidate quota and would, if later found unsatisfactory as laboratory officers, be reclassified by the Sanitary Corps and not returned to the WAC for troop duty. When the Bureau of Public Relations requested that twenty enlisted women with civilian public relations experience be commissioned as public relations officers to fill existing shortages, a special WAC officer candidate class was set up which did not reduce the regular quota for troop officers. The Medical Department already had authority to commission women directly under its own quotas, and qualified enlisted women were commissioned as hospital dietitians, physiotherapists, or nurses without counting against WAC officer candidate quotas or even, in this case, against the WAC's 1-to-20 ratio.[38]

In time, Director Hobby departed from her rule against direct commissions insofar as to ask that enlisted women be given equal rights under any Army procurement objectives for commissioning of technical specialists. Thus, when direct commissions in The Adjutant General's Office were offered to enlisted men qualified as clinical psychologists, she asked and obtained an amendment to include equally qualified enlisted women. Finally, in 1945, G-1 Division authorized direct appointment of enlisted women under any suitable authorized procurement objectives for male officers. These, at this date, were very few, chiefly Japanese linguists, acoustic technicians, and similar specialties, for which it was known that only a handful of women would be eligible. All of these women, with the exception of some in the Medical Department, had to be commissioned in the WAC and detailed in The Adjutant General's Department or other service, since the WAC was still not designated an arm or service for female admin-

---

[37] Except as otherwise cited, above section is based on D/F cited n. 15(2).

[38] (1) Memo, Dep Dir WAC for Maj McClure, G–1, 26 Aug 44. WDWAC 210.14. (2) WDWAC 352 OCS and WDWAC 352 Special OCS Class, 1944. (3) Memo, Dir MPD ASF for TSG, 27 Jan 44. SPGAM 210 Taylor, Jan F, in WDWAC 210.1. (4) Bound file, SPWA 231.23 Med Dept Dietitians (8 Jan 44) 1944. (5) Memo, Dep Dir WAC for Col Coursey, G–1, 22 Sep 44. WDWAC 220.33. (6) Draft of Memo, SGO for CofS, 8 Apr 44. WDWAC 211.

istrators only, but remained a catch-all title for anything in skirts.[39]

The Question of Direct Commissions

In none of the foregoing cases were direct commissions offered to civilian women but only to qualified enlisted women. The decision to hold this line against direct commissions for civilian women was not easy, since the Director's office was still assaulted by undiminished numbers of would-be leaders. The number of letters on file from members of Congress and from prominent military and civilian figures, all seeking direct commissions for protégés, indicated that the character of WAC leadership would have been entirely altered had this bar fallen. Many wanted not only commissions but promises of choice assignments. For example, one senator asked Colonel Hobby's assistance in getting a direct commission for a young woman who, although without college education or responsible experience, was "much interested in obtaining a commission and especially desirous of being assigned to overseas duty." [40] In view of the fact that thousands of better qualified enlisted women were denied officer candidate training under current quotas, such applications received scant attention.

Only in four cases—one in Europe and three in the Southwest Pacific Area—did Colonel Hobby fail to maintain her policy on the direct commissioning of civilian women. Although unable to secure revocation of the four appointments, the Director did succeed in blocking the numerous other requests that immediately followed. At her request, and after much bad publicity, the War Department established the policy that women recom-

mended in this way could be commissioned only through the usual channel of competitive selection by officer candidate boards and attendance at officer candidate school. No exceptions to this policy were permitted during the remainder of Colonel Hobby's tenure.[41]

Promotion of Officers

Considerable interservice friction was habitually caused by the differing policies of the Air and Service Forces in officer promotion. No Wacs had, by the end of the Corps' first eighteen months, been made lieutenant colonels, although most staff directors had occupied position vacancies of this grade since their assignment. Recommendations had been received from the Second and Third Service Commands for promotion of their staff directors to this grade, but these had been refused by the Army Service Forces.

In November of 1943, a request was received from the Army Air Forces for the promotion of Major Bandel, with the notation that she had been in grade eight months, was responsible for recommendations pertaining to 25,000 Air Wacs, and, if an Army officer, would have been made at least a colonel under Air Corps promotion policies. This was refused by the

---

[39] (1) Memo, Dir WAC for G–1, 10 Jan 45. WDWAC 210.14. (2) D/F, G–1 for TAG, 6 Mar 45. WDGAP 210.1. See D/F cited n. 15(2), Tab B.

[40] See all WAC files, especially 1944, under SPWA and WDWAC 095.

[41] See Chs. XXI and XXII, above. Also: (1) Memo, Dir WAC for G–1, 25 Feb 44. SPWA 320.2, in SPWA 314.7 (1–7–43)(1) sec 5. (2) D/F, G–1 to Dir WAC, 21 Mar 44. WDGAP 210.1 WAC. (3) D/F, G–1 to TAG, 21 Apr 44, WDGAP 210.1 WAC (4–17–44), with atchd Memo, Dir WAC for CofS, 14 Apr 44, WDWAC 314.7, approved 18 Apr 44. WDWAC 210.1.

GENERAL MARSHALL *confers with Capt. Florence T. Newsome in his office at the Pentagon.*

Army Service Forces without being sent to the Chief of Staff.

In the following week, General Marshall, in a personal conversation with the Director, informed her that, in his opinion, it was time to bridge the gap between her own rank and that of key WAC officers. Accordingly, the Director recommended to G–1 Division the promotion of the two WAC majors in her office who had replaced General Faith and Colonel Catron. She also informed the commanding generals of the Air, Ground, and Service Forces of the Chief of Staff's decision in the event that they wished to submit—or, in the case of the Air Forces, resubmit—any promotion recommendations.[42]

---

[42] Entire discussion from: (1) Memo, Dir WAC for G–1, 27 Nov 43. SPWA 210.2, in SPAP 210.2 WAC. (2) Memo, Dir WAC for DCofS ASF for SvCs, 26 Feb 44. SPWA 210.31. (3) Entire file on this controversy is also in CofS 324.5 WAC, and in SPWA 210.2 WAC Promotions (1943). (4) Ltr, TAG to AAF, 18 Nov 43. AG 210.2 WAC (11–16–43) PR–W–WDGAP, in SPWA 210.2.

The Air Forces promptly resubmitted its recommendation concerning Major Bandel. With the Director and Major Bandel both overseas, the Army Service Forces again recommended rejection and the War Department Personnel Board again rejected the AAF request without reference to the Chief of Staff.

The Air Forces immediately demanded an explanation of Acting Director Rice, who informed the Personnel Board that the action it had refused had been directed by "The Chief of Staff, United States Army." Further delay resulted when the Personnel Board refused to credit the Chief of Staff's approval, and sought to reach him for confirmation. Meanwhile, General Somervell sent General Marshall a memo saying, "I do not concur . . . ," and stating that no exceptions for Wacs should be made to the time-in-grade requirements, which were waived only for men in Air Corps positions or in "meritorious cases." However, General Somervell called the Chief of Staff's office and withdrew his comment before it was shown to General Marshall. On the next day the Chief of Staff directed that until further notice the Personnel Board be lenient with time-in-grade requirements on promotions of certain cases submitted by the commanders concerned and approved by the Director WAC. Accordingly, Major Bandel was promoted at once, becoming the first WAC lieutenant colonel. On the following day General Marshall promoted to the same rank a Wac in his own office, Maj. Florence T. Newsome, who, as Assistant Secretary to the General Staff, filled a position vacancy calling for that grade,

On her return in late January, Director Hobby followed these with the promotions of Maj. Jessie P. Rice, Deputy Director, and Maj. Mary-Agnes Brown, Executive. She also secured the recommendation of the Commanding General, Fourth Service Command, to the promotion of Maj. Elizabeth H. Strayhorn, senior WAC officer at Fort Oglethorpe. A short time later the Commanding General, Army Ground Forces, reversed his original decision and promoted the AGF WAC Officer, Maj. Emily E. Davis. These six promotions were followed shortly by one more, that of Maj. Westray B. Boyce of the North African theater, at which time the exceptions to time-in-grade were ended. Future WAC promotions to the grade of lieutenant colonel were, with two exceptions, to wait for the regular time-in-grade. These exceptions were for Maj. Katherine R. Goodwin upon her assignment as ASF WAC Officer, and Maj. Anna W. Wilson in the European theater.[43]

Under the circumstances, although the grade of lieutenant colonel had been declared appropriate for staff directors since the establishment of the Corps, very few staff directors of subordinate field commands had attained it by the end of the war: two of the Army Service Forces' fourteen, three of the Air Forces' fifteen, neither of the Ground Forces' two, and three of the overseas theaters' six.[44] As a result, at the end of three years of existence, and at its peak strength in the spring of 1945, the WAC was far from approaching the percentages of field grade officers to which its strength would have entitled it under a policy of direct commissions or equal ratios.[45]

---

[43] Ibid.

[44] Approximate totals; numbers varied at different times.

[45] From Statistical Sec, OCMH.

	Actual Officer Strength May 1945	Entitled by Army Ratio
General officers.........	0	20
Colonels................	1	129
Lieutenant colonels.....	16	336
Majors	146	331
Captains	1,024	2,325
First lieutenants........	3,646	3,849
Second lieutenants......	975	2,483
	5,808	9,973

The absence of top grades was of course due to legislative restrictions; the deficiencies in company grades, and in the two lower field grades, had been of more actual significance in troop administration.

Officer Education

Final tallies on WAC officers showed "unusually high intellectual caliber." [46] The educational level of WAC officers slightly surpassed that of male officers. [47]

	Percent	
Educational Level	WAC Officers	Male Officers
Grammar school................	.26	1.5
1, 2, 3 years high school..........	4.01	12.0
High school graduate............	27.84	22.2
1, 2, 3 years college.............	26.98	26.2
College graduate................	26.23	21.7
Postgraduate	14.68	16.4

Army observers considered the high educational level of WAC officers to be "even more remarkable in that they were not chosen as specialists, [while] the male officers included all the professional workers who came into the Army as specialists, such as physicians, engineers, lawyers, teachers, and chaplains." [48]

Possibly even more surprising was the fact that, while the Army had a high percentage of success in finding officers who rose from the ranks to develop into accept-able WAC staff directors, the Navy reported less satisfaction with directly commissioned women serving in the comparable position of Women's Reserve Representative in naval districts. It noted the "unsatisfactory quality of the officers placed in these billets in some districts in the early haste of organization." [49]

Warrant Officers

For some time there existed a question as to whether or not Wacs might be appointed warrant officers if they held posts such as band leader, which, for a man, carried the grade. The WAC legislation did not mention the matter, but the Judge Advocate General ruled that appointment of women was illegal because the law did not specify that it was legal. Within a few months the question was brought to the War Department's attention by the North African, European and China–Burma–India theaters, which wished to appoint to that grade women who were filling warrant officer jobs. At this time the Judge Advocate General was overruled. G–1 Division held that such appointment was legal under the general authority to admit women to full Army status, and the Chief of Staff upheld this opinion. However, by the end of the war only 42 women had been reported in this grade. [50]

---

[46] Menninger, *Psychiatry in a Troubled World.* This and subsequent quotations used with the permission of The Macmillan Company, the publisher.

[47] D/F, P&A Contl Gp, WD, for HD WDSS, 14 Mar 46. WDGAP 314.7 WAC, in Folder, Statistics, WAC files, OCMH. Only available comparisons are of summer, 1944.

[48] *Ibid.*

[49] WAVES Hist, p. 132ff.

[50] Memo, G–1 for CofS, 26 Jan 44. OCS 324.5 WAC. Approved by DCofS, 29 Jan 44. Also ETO Bd Rpt, pp. 25, 46. See Table 2, Appendix A.

CHAPTER XXIX

The Employment of Personnel: Overseas Shipment

For both officers and enlisted women, a special group of personnel regulations centered around selection and assignment to overseas duty. The Auxiliary system of overseas assignment had not in many ways borne any resemblance to the Army's wartime system for men. Fearing that women overseas would be in an extremely conspicuous and demanding position, the Director's Office had issued orders:

. . . that WAAC officers selected for all overseas units be especially chosen for experience, strength of character, firmness of discipline; that auxiliaries be of a mature age and emotional stability and well-suited to perform the duties assigned.[1]

Candidates for shipment were habitually rejected for such causes as "fully qualified but emotionally unstable and too immature for overseas service"; "fully qualified but evinces very poor attitude."[2]

Since WAAC units for overseas shipment were made up at training centers from new recruits, and were completely trained and processed on the spot, it was easy to achieve a thorough screening, with physical and mental examinations as well as job classification tests. Final movement orders were arranged by WAAC Headquarters only after personal examination of the records of each officer and auxiliary chosen.[3]

This system proved deficient in only one respect: while the women thus selected were on the whole highly qualified, they were only a few weeks removed from civilian life and had only a theoretical knowledge of Army terminology and procedures. Valuable time had to be spent in active theaters in giving this experience. Also, field experience often revealed unsuspected physical or emotional difficulties. Company officers just out of officer candidate school were under an especial handicap in taking a company into field conditions. While WAC personnel possibly did not require the year or eighteen months ordinarily required for men before shipment, some on-the-job training was obviously needed.[4]

The problem of lack of experience was intensified when the system of shipping Waacs in Table of Organization units was abandoned in favor of shipment as casuals. Shipment as casuals meant that unit training was omitted and that women could be sent overseas after only four weeks of basic training, or even less if a shipment was waiting.

---

[1] Ltr, Exec WAAC to Comdt 5th WAAC Tng Cen, 2 Apr 43. SPWA 320.2 sec 4a.
[2] Ltr, WAAC Hq to Comdt, 1st WAAC Tng Cen, 7 Jun 43, and 1st Ind, 14 Jun 43. SPWA 320.2 sec 4a.
[3] Office Memo, Opn Div WAAC for Exec WAC, 14 Apr 43. SPWAO, in SPWA 320.2 sec 4a.
[4] AAF WAC Hist.

To solve this problem, WAAC Headquarters adopted a system by which all new recruits, after training, were assigned to Army stations in the United States to gain experience, and were sent overseas only after proven successful on Army jobs in the field. A requisition from an overseas theater was filled by calling upon each unit in the field to give up one or more of its most successful women; these women were assembled at a central point, processed, and shipped.

A further refinement to the system was soon added by drawing women from the appropriate major command. Women destined to serve with the Air Forces overseas were taken only from air stations in the United States; hence they were familiar with the necessary terminology, regulations, and clerical forms. Similarly, women for overseas service with Ground Forces, Service Forces, Transportation Corps, and other such organizations were, insofar as possible, drawn from those organizations in the United States. This system pleased the theaters; it was also enthusiastically received by Wacs in the United States. The hope of selection for overseas service was always to remain one of the greatest morale factors in sedentary WAC units.[5]

Before this system was well begun, the conversion to Army status abruptly ended all special rules of selection for women. The necessary operating procedures to select and ship women were transferred from WAAC Headquarters to the Army Service Forces, which now called upon Army commands and stations, not upon WAC company commanders, to select the women. The central assembly point at a WAC training center was retained for convenience in processing, but the training center itself was also now under ASF direction.[6]

Informal reports from many commands indicated that quite often the difference in systems was not very great, since most station commanders, while now allowing station personnel officers to choose women as they did men, also continued to allow WAC company commanders and staff directors to comment. Formal reports from overseas, on the other hand, soon indicated that not all stations did so, and that the previous problem was in many cases being reversed: instead of receiving personnel of excellent qualifications and no field experience, theaters were receiving women with plenty of experience and no qualifications.

Protests from overseas theaters soon testified to the receipt of women with records of previous court-martial offenses, those who were habitual troublemakers, sexual offenders, and neurotics, as well as some who were merely ill, unskilled, or morons. Such theaters claimed to be at a disadvantage in that they had no time, especially during rapid forward movement, to collect evidence for board action to discharge an individual. Only one theater, the India–Burma, solved this problem to its satisfaction by merely authorizing the staff director to ship improperly selected women home with the Army board recommendation "that they be returned to the continental limits of the U.S. for reassignment to duty without stigma and that they not be reassigned to the India–Burma theater."[7]

---

[5] (1) AG Memo W635–11–43, 8 Jul 43. (2) Memo, Dir WAC for Gen White, G–1, 3 Jun 44. WDWAC 320.2.

[6] D/F, MPD ASF for TAG, 18 Feb 44. SPAP 320.2 WAC (2–10–44). Rescinds AG Memo 210.31 (12–14–43) 23 Dec 43. See M/R.

[7] (1) Ltr, Asst AG USFOR CT, to CG AAF CT, 12 Aug 45, 322 WAC. (2) Ltr, WAC Stf Dir AAF CT to Air WAC Off, Hq AAF, 22 Feb 45. CBI WAC files.

In recommending corrective action, Director Hobby pointed out that in her opinion conditions of overseas service were not identical for men and women. For an able-bodied man, overseas duty was an almost inevitable requirement, whereas less than one out of five Wacs could expect to go overseas, and the assignment tended to become a prize. For a man, overseas shipment meant probable combat service, but for a woman, merely the excitement of proximity to action. Misbehavior in a male soldier overseas was not as conspicuous as in a female one, since a female could not be sent to the front lines. Male soldiers looked upon shipment as a duty which a man should not be allowed to escape through malingering or misconduct, whereas Wacs considered the assignment a reward of merit.

A few months after the transfer of her office to G–1 Division, the Director secured publication of the requirement that WAC company commanders must certify the character of any enlisted woman shipped overseas, and that staff directors must certify WAC officers. The circular was approved by the War Department only after being carefully worded to indicate that the choice of Wacs for overseas service would still be made by male commanders in accordance with their command prerogative; the station commander's choice was merely limited to those women whose conduct was good according to WAC standards. This certification was generally effective, and overseas theaters shortly reported a noticeable improvement in the qualifications of new arrivals.[8]

Medical Screening

The character-screening powers of WAC officers could not be stretched to veto the shipment of any woman whose behavior record was good, even if her physical stamina or stability appeared dubious. Army doctors and psychiatrists believed that there were many women physically and emotionally capable of service in the United States who would crack up overseas, and recommended careful physical examinations before shipment. In Auxiliary days, the European theater also requested that women get a complete physical examination before shipment, as the arrival of large numbers who had to be immediately returned for any cause, but especially for pregnancy which had existed before shipment, "would present an embarrassing situation."[9] The War Department accordingly directed that Waacs going overseas be given a complete physical examination that would detect pregnancy and any disease or defect.[10] This thorough WAAC examination was a departure from the Army system, since men going overseas merely got a superficial inspection.

Incorporation of the WAAC in the Army ended the authority for a physical examination for women, but, by some oversight, WAC training centers, in assembling shipments, continued to give complete overseas physical examinations under the old WAAC system for seven months after the ASF assumed control. In March of 1944, The Surgeon General's Office discovered that women were being given such an examination and ordered it

---

[8] (1) D/F cited n. 6. (2) WD Cir 291, 11 Jul 44. (3) See ASF WAC Officer's file of acceptances and rejections in SPAP 210.3 WAC; also WD Cir 362, 6 Dec 44.

[9] Rad 982, USFOR London to WAR, 17 May 43. SPWA 320.2 sec 4b.

[10] D/F, G–1 for CG ASF, 3 Jul 43. WDGAP 201.5 WAC, in SPWA 320.2 sec 4b.

stopped, saying that men received no such examination and that

. . . it is the opinion of this office that routine mental and physical examination of every individual prior to departure for overseas duty is not essential or practicable and that the amount of work involved would not be justified, particularly in view of the shortage of medical officers.[11]

Director Hobby had also requested, for WAC shipments already at a port, that The Surgeon General's Office authorize a pelvic examination immediately before departure, followed, if there was any indication of pregnancy or venereal disease, by the proper specialized tests. However, it was the opinion of representatives of The Surgeon General's Office that such a system would not detect early pregnancies and that

. . . even with any means we would adopt we would be bound to have some cases of pregnancy after they get overseas. Wouldn't it be better to accept that as one of the costs of war?[12]

Thereafter, the physical check given women before overseas shipment was the same in all respects as that given men, although most overseas theaters were under the later impression that it had not been equally satisfactory. Some women arrived with obvious disqualifications that necessitated immediate return, including advanced pregnancies, which resulted in headlines such as one from the Associated Press: WAC GIVES BIRTH TO BOY IN DUTCH NEW GUINEA.[13] Major Craighill, The Surgeon General's consultant on women's health, stated, "Medical Officers in all overseas theaters commented on the inadequacy of screening of women for overseas duty."[14] Major Craighill noted that she considered the overseas screening system unsatisfactory but that "repeated

efforts to change the policy were unsuccessful." The Director's Office therefore replied to all complaints that The Surgeon General believed the cost of returning the women to be less than the cost of physical examinations for all women sent overseas, especially since men in the Army did not receive overseas examinations.

Psychiatric Screening

Major Craighill likewise never succeeded in getting a psychiatric examination for women going overseas, although Army psychiatrists reported that female mental and moral crack-ups overseas could have been almost eliminated by such an examination.[15] No such examination was given for men, where the problem of screening would have been extremely complicated because of the combat factor. Although Wacs did not face the mental strain of entry into combat with the enemy, Major Craighill believed that they faced a type of combat which men did not, the defense of their character structure and their double standard of morality. She stated:

Women overseas were subjected to more tension than men by reason of their scarcity, which resulted in more emotional pressure, and because there was a more radical change in the pattern of their lives.[16]

---

[11] 1st Ind, SGO to Dir MPD, ASF, 30 Mar 44, SPMCB 322.5–1. Folder, Capt Berlien notes, SGO Hist Div.

[12] Tp Conv, Capt Strayhorn and Col Freer, 9 Jul 43. G–1 WAC 312–312.9, Drawer 6, DRB AGO.

[13] *Denver Post,* July 4, 1945.

[14] History of Women's Medical Unit (rough draft, only one ever filed) by Lt Col Margaret D. Craighill, MC, 23 Jul 46. SGO Hist Div 314.72.

[15] All references to opinions of psychiatrists, unless otherwise stated, are from History of Psychiatry in the Women's Army Corps, 1946, by Maj. Albert Preston, Jr., MC. SGO and Hobby files.

[16] Hist cited n. 14.

Women who showed marked emotional disorders on the eve of shipment were sometimes referred to the training center psychiatrist, and some were eliminated on his recommendation, but regulations did not permit him to interview every woman. Maj. Albert Preston, Jr., the Army psychiatrist at Fort Des Moines, felt that a reasonably accurate screening process would have been possible, but in the absence of a similar requirement for men, no such system was authorized.

For psychiatric screening, as for medical, the dilemma was identical. The WAC, because of its small size, could probably with existing facilities have achieved better screening than was possible for the Army as a whole. On the one hand, the efficiency of overseas theaters would have been improved and female crack-ups prevented, but on the other, the principle of "identical" treatment would have been jeopardized by giving women more complete examinations. It was the decision of The Surgeon General's Office in both cases that improvements in screening would not be made for women until they could be made for men.

Shipment of Nonvolunteers

One point on which psychiatrists disagreed with Director Hobby was as to whether women who did not volunteer to go overseas should be forced to go if needed. It was soon proven that such women were more apt to develop psychiatric disorders which eventually forced their return to the United States. Thus, a rough psychiatric screening would have been accomplished merely by elimination of all nonvolunteers.

During the first months of the Corps' existence, there were so many volunteers that the problem never arose. As overseas shipments increased, and as overseas theaters persisted in requesting women in scarce skills, a choice was more and more often necessary between sending nonvolunteers in the desired skill or not filling the shipment. In a typical case, one company commander protested to Colonel Hobby that the station had only four WAC stenographers, none of whom wanted to go overseas because of objections from their families, yet the unit had been directed to ship two. The commander added:

> The fact that we are soldiers cannot be offset in their minds by the fact that they were not drafted but came in voluntarily and on the basis that they would not be sent overseas against their wishes. Many families would never have consented had overseas duty been anything but optional.[17]

Congressional protests in this vein were also received, although as a matter of fact no authorized publicity and no regulation had ever promised WAC recruits that they would not go overseas if needed. Even the station-job recruiting campaign was careful to state that only initial assignment to a given station was promised, with transfer not precluded.

It was the belief of Army Service Forces' Military Personnel Division that women should not be required to follow the men's rules in this case:

> This distinction between male and female personnel of the Army can have no detrimental effect upon the efficiency of the WAC nor the morale of the male personnel.

However, Director Hobby recommended against any such differentiation and G–1

---

[17] Ltr, CO WAC Det 1, Camp Butner, N. C., through Camp Comdr to Dir WAC, 11 Aug 44, with Inds. WDWAC 220.3.

Division upheld her, pointing out that volunteers in scarce skills would become fewer as the war continued.[18] In writing and conferences, Colonel Hobby several times stated emphatically her position:

They're soldiers now, and we have never, as you know, given out any promises of any kind. . . . They're in the Army and they're soldiers and if they are needed they are going.[19]

However, the Director authorized a circular which stated that volunteers would be chosen "to the maximum extent possible." Her office also suggested that stations not having volunteers should so inform their command headquarters, so that attempts might be made to get volunteers from other stations. The Army Air Forces devised and published an authorization for a process of quick reference to other stations in order that no nonvolunteer might be sent if there were any volunteer Wacs in the Air Forces in the same skill. In June of 1945, The Adjutant General directed all commands to survey and report the number of eligible volunteers in various skills, but V-J Day intervened to nullify the usefulness of the results.[20]

Objections to Filling Requisitions

The system of selecting experienced personnel from field companies, while highly popular with the enlisted women themselves and with overseas theaters, met with increasing objections from commands in the United States as the war continued. A typical objection was that offered by General Gross of the Transportation Corps, in a telephone conversation with Colonel Hobby:

General Gross: I just want to tell you of my difficulties with women. . . . We have of course great enthusiasm for their use and we replaced enlisted men with them and released the enlisted men because we thought we had something stable. Now, we are forced to fill allotments for overseas. . . . I think your organization should have its own replacement center.
Colonel Hobby: . . . You think we should take them directly from the training center and send them overseas without proving them in any way at all?
General Gross: Well, at least not prove them in the Transportation Corps.
Colonel Hobby: Maybe everybody feels that way. The War Department—and I want you to get that clear when you say my office—the War Department has approved the requisitions for the personnel where they are fighting the battles. . . . We try to cause as little dislocation as possible but we can't pull them out of thin air.[21]

There seemed to be no very ready solution to the problem. It appeared to be as unwise to ship Wacs without field experience as it would have been to ship men after four weeks, yet to maintain a replacement training center for the sole purpose of giving Wacs six months or more of field experience also appeared prohibitively expensive. The Adjutant General's assignment authorities attempted insofar as possible to co-ordinate assignment of new recruits to the field with simultaneous

[18] Memo, MPD ASF for G–1, 24 Nov 43. SPGAP 322.5 WAC (11–24–43). Incl is WAC objection. Disapproved by G–1 on 13 Dec 43, appealed by MPD on 17 Dec, and refused again by G–1 on 1 Jan 44. All in SPAP 341 WAAC (2–26–43).
[19] (1) Tp Conv, Col Hobby and Maj Galloway, 22 Mar 44. Tp Transcripts, G–1 WAC 312–312.9, Drawer 6, DRB AGO. (2) Min of all WAC Stf Dir Confs. SPWA 337.
[20] Memo cited n. 18. In same file: (1) Ltr, Dir WAC to Rep. Edith Nourse Rogers, 25 Aug 44. (2) Ltr, Stf Dir WFTC AAF to Dep Dir Rice, 11 Aug 43; reply 26 Aug 43. (3) WD Cir 61, 10 Feb 44; Cir 462, 1944, Sec II, par 14d. (4) See also AAF Ltr 35–175a, 6 May 45; and Hist of O Dir Pers ASF. OCMH.
[21] Tp Conv, Gen Gross and Col Hobby, 24 Mar 44. Tp Transcripts, cited n. 19.

withdrawal of experienced personnel for shipment, but such action was seldom possible when overseas shipments were made in large increments while replacements arrived in an uncertain trickle, and often in skills less essential than those withdrawn for overseas theaters.

Furthermore, The Adjutant General's allotments of new recruits were made to the major command concerned and not to the station level, so that it had no means of forcing a command headquarters to send replacements to any given station, regardless of the indignation of the station commander, if some other station had a higher priority on personnel. In any case, since only some 15 percent of the total WAC personnel ever served overseas, it did not appear that the problem of their loss had been a major one. The War Department therefore made no change in the system of shipment.

Processing for Shipment

To process overseas shipments, the Army Service Forces set up a unit called the Extended Field Service (EFS) Training Battalion. This unit, commanded by Maj. Frances M. Lathrope, operated at Fort Oglethorpe until just before that training center closed, when the unit moved to Fort Des Moines. The battalion fulfilled the functions of an overseas replacement depot for women, and in addition furnished the women's clothing and supplies that local stations and ports did not stock. No exactly comparable organization existed for men, who could ordinarily be processed locally. The unit was responsible for receiving the women, checking on their classification, forming them into casual detachments, providing clothing and equipment as specified in overseas orders, completing immunization, and adminis-

tering necessary training. Women found unqualified during this time were removed and replaced from training center overhead or from a special overstrength allotted for this purpose.[22]

Whatever the merits of the idea, the battalion operated under such considerable handicaps as not to come into most efficient performance during the period of heaviest shipment. Enlisted women staged here wrote, "We have never, from Sidney to Port Moresby to the Philippines, found any quarters that remotely resembled them in discomfort."[23]

For most of its existence the area was classified as "temporary," which by Army Regulations meant that very little construction or repair work was permitted. Buildings had been unoccupied for some time and previously had been used by a men's reception center. They were not in the best of repair, one section being known as "Bedbug Row." In trying to eliminate this appellation, it was found that the post engineer acted upon the corpus delicti principle; even when the necessary evidence was finally caught it was discovered that fumigating materials were on the critical list and took some weeks to secure.

Before improvements could be effected, the battalion had been the subject of derogatory reports from escort officers of all of the first shipments to be processed. Transportation difficulties caused women to be retained until 2,500 were housed in space for 1,000. Through some failure of co-ordination in the first months, clothing supplies were inadequate; the Atlanta Depot refused requisitions on grounds that

[22] (1) ASF Hist of WAC Tng. (2) ASF Cir 35, sec VI, WAC Pers, 31 Jan 44. (3) Memo, MPD ASF for CofS ASF, 10 Feb 44, SPGAA 320.2 WAC, in SPAP.
[23] Extract, Mil Censorship WAC Det Bull, 4 Star Final, p. 19, Tab 1 to AFPAC Reply. See also Unit Hist Camp Huckstep.

it had never heard of the organization, and several shipments went to port before the situation was remedied. As a result, ports of embarkation rendered unsatisfactory reports on the first women who reached them, who were said to be poorly trained, untidy, furnished with improper equipment and ill-fitting clothing.[24]

Within several months, the situation was greatly improved by the efforts of inspectors from Washington, who put considerable pressure on Fourth Service Command agencies, as well as by those of the cadre, who at times worked as long as eight weeks without a day off. Removal to Fort Des Moines also made available better facilities for such small groups as remained to be processed in the final days of the war.[25]

Since the training center was not officially informed as to unit destination, except as the designated port gave some clue, it was not always able to prepare individuals specifically for the proper overseas area. Also, none of the cadre or instructors had ever been overseas, and attempts to get Wacs returned from overseas met with the reply that there were, at this date, none who had completed the prescribed tour.

The ASF training course, which the EFS Battalion had no power to alter, was patterned on men's combat courses, without much consideration of the ways in which women's overseas service differed from men's. Wacs were toughened, and incidentally given head colds, by long hikes in the rain in unsuitable clothing; they swarmed up and down cargo nets; they crept up on the enemy in the field, adjusting their gas masks as gas bombs exploded around them; and practiced dispersion and seeking cover. They studied first aid, map reading, defense against chemical attack and air attack, malaria

control; they got practical experience in using a compass, messing in the field, and extended kitchen police duty; they were, as one shipment said, "given endless lectures designed to confuse us about our destination."[26] Their training films included such unlikely items as *First Aid for Chemical Casualties, Rations in the Combat Zone, Combat Counterintelligence,* and *First Aid for Battle Injuries*—probably as good a selection as was possible in view of the fact that there were no films to prepare women for their specific overseas problems.[27]

In the opinion of the Army psychiatrist at Fort Des Moines, Major Preston, women should have been prepared, not for combat first aid or map reading, but for the peculiar social environment of a woman overseas; the certainty of an exaggerated popularity and the danger of an overemphasis on social life; the tendency of unfamiliar surroundings or homesickness to cause quick friendships, overdependency on other women, or liaisons with married men; the probable effect of lack of privacy, lack of customary conventions, and the opportunity for excessive drinking; and especially the psychological effect of danger and restrictions.

In the last year of the war, there arose some question of the economy of the system: women already stationed on the west coast and destined for the Pacific had to be shipped to Georgia or Iowa and back for two weeks' processing, and the same was true of women in the New York area

---

[24] (1) 1st Ind, WAC Stf Dir, TC, to Dir WAC, 4 Jul 44, with incls. SPTPM 220.3 WAC, in WDWAC 320.2. (2) ASF WAC Off to Dir Mil Tng ASF, 22 Jul 44, with 1st Ind. SPAP 210.3 WAC. (3) Buck slip, WAC Br G-1 to Dir WAC, atchd to rpt 25 Mar 44. WDWAC 330.14.

[25] EFS passage, except as otherwise stated, from written statement by Maj Lathrope, and interv with Maj Lathrope, 6 Apr 48.

[26] Sources cited n. 23.

[27] For subjects taught, see ASF Hist of WAC Tng.

OVERSEAS TRAINING. *Women practice going down a cargo net at Fort Des Moines.*

destined for Europe. After a training inspection, G–3 Division of the General Staff recommended that EFS be abolished and that two processing centers, under the control of the Chief of Transportation, be set up at ports on the east and west coasts. This recommendation was concurred in by the Air Forces and by Director Hobby. However, Military Training Division, ASF, objected to removal of the unit from its authority, saying that it would be costly to maintain stocks of WAC clothing and equipment at two places instead of one. As a result, and because of the imminent cessation of overseas shipment, no action was taken, although the subject remained open for consideration in the event of future resumption of heavier shipments from one or both coasts.[28]

Rotation

By the end of the war there had begun to be considerable evidence that female personnel could not sustain as long a period of overseas assignment as could noncombat men. As early as the summer of 1944 Director Hobby had given some consideration to formulation of a rotation policy, and informed Maj. Gen. Stephen G. Henry, the new G–1 of the War Department, that in her opinion it might be necessary to have a policy for Army women as a separate group, "provided it can be done without detriment to the morale of enlisted men."

She recommended that a small quota of one half of one percent a month be set for those with 18 months' service. This would affect very few individuals, yet might improve the morale both of those in need of return and of those still eager to go overseas. The Director added, "I do not want to make overseas service for women so long

that they will crack under it or come back abnormal in any way."[29]

Meanwhile, Major Craighill, after a tour of all theaters, informed The Surgeon General that in her opinion a 2-year tour should be the maximum for women. Major Craighill diagnosed the lesser endurance of women overseas as partly emotional:

Women overseas, because of their scarcity, are subject to great emotional strain. . . . There tends to be a change in standards and sense of values in both sexes. Their previous and future lives become vague and unreal so that only the present is of importance. . . . Men are apparently better able to partition off their lives adequately so that they do not as readily become deeply or permanently involved emotionally. They are, therefore, less liable to lasting psychic trauma from transient attachments.[30]

The recommendation of the second WAC Director, Col. Westray Battle Boyce, upon return from a postwar overseas tour, was that the maximum tour of duty for female personnel should be not more than 18 months, since "Statistics indicate that medical evacuations increase sharply for female personnel with longer service."[31]

While no such wartime policy was ever adopted, these opinions were reflected in the first postwar directives, which set a maximum tour for men of 30 months with a possible 6-month extension, and for Wacs, nurses, physiotherapists, and dietitians of 24 months with a possible 3-month extension. Colonel Boyce noted that this shorter tour for women was made possible

---

[28] (1) Memo, Dir WAC for CG ASF, 4 Jul 44; (2) Memo, MTD ASF for G–1, 1 Aug 44, SPTRP 353 WAC; (3) Memo, MTD ASF for G–3, 9 Sep 44, SPTRP 353 WAC (8–24–44). WDWAC 353.
[29] Memo, Dir WAC for Gen Henry, 21 Aug 44. WDWAC 320.2.(C).
[30] Craighill IBT Rpt.
[31] Rpt, undated, sub: Final Rpt of Dir WAC on Return from World Tour, Tab B: General Observations in All Theaters. WDWAC 333.1 (1945–46).

only by the high percentage of Wacs who had never been overseas and were eager to go, as against lesser percentages of men, and that "it was agreed that a two-year tour of duty for all was advisable, but present conditions would not permit it for men." [32]

Shipment in T/O Units

It was Colonel Boyce's opinion that the system of shipment of Wacs as casuals had been hard on morale and should be abandoned in favor of shipment as Table of Organization units. When shipped as casuals for assignment to vacancies in men's groups, Wacs found others already promoted to the grades to which their skills would have entitled them, and were often given the least desirable or responsible duties, or malassigned to work that did not use their highest skills. In a T/O unit organized in the United States, women would be assigned in accordance with real skills and would receive the grade their position was allotted. Also, in such units the WAC company commander was recognized as being in command, and thus avoided possible disciplinary complications.

Unfortunately, as its sponsors recognized, the T/O proposal had serious limitations. It would be effective only if a women's force existed in the earliest days of a mobilization period, before most of the T/O units had been organized and shipped and the need became merely that for casuals as replacements. Even if employed so early, the plan would limit women to units in which they could perform all duties, such as signal or postal. In view of the near-disastrous experience with T/O units in the United States, it would be inapplicable to large-scale use of Wacs in theater headquarters and over-

head, and would prevent the overseas employment of women with unusual skills not included in a standard T/O. On the other hand, if the overseas program of the WAC remained, as in World War II, a minor part of its whole program, it appeared that serious problems of assignment would not be caused by use of the T/O system for all WAC overseas units wherever practicable. [33]

Effectiveness of Shipment Program

While all evidence indicated that the program of overseas shipment of Wacs could have been more effective than it was, and while deficiencies were habitually distressing to WAC personnel, there was no indication that difficulties had been as serious as those encountered by the Army in selecting, training, and shipping male personnel, especially combat troops, whose problems were considerably multiplied. The chief peculiar difficulty remained that of sending overseas only women of highly selected moral character and stability, in which respect lapses were criticized by overseas theaters considerably more than similar lapses in shipment of men. In spite of occasional perfectionist complaints from overseas theaters, the final outcome of the WAC effort to put its best personnel overseas could only be evaluated as highly successful. On a statistical average, Wacs in all overseas theaters had been the best educated, the most intelligent, and the most highly skilled of the Corps. [34]

---

[32] Remarks of Dir WAC, Conf of Overseas Theater G-1's, 15 Oct 46. WDWAC 337 A-S.

[33] Rpt cited n. 31.

[34] All available reports indicate that at least 55 percent of all women shipped overseas were in AGCT Groups I and II. See Chs. XX-XXIII, above; also ETO Bd Rpt, p. 129. A list of the Overseas WAC Units as of June 1945 may be found in Directory of the AUS Outside Continental United States, AG 461 (6-1-45) OB-I-M pp. 269-270.

CHAPTER XXX

The Employment of Personnel: Minority Groups

The only sizable racial minority group in the WAC was that of the Negro, although a few women of Puerto Rican, Chinese, Japanese, and American Indian descent were also enlisted. Members of most of these groups, except the Negro, were very rarely recruited, and were not segregated, but scattered through ordinary WAC units according to skills.

One exception was the group of Puerto Rican Wacs, who were enlisted, trained, and assigned as a unit. It had been intended to integrate them into other WAC units, but language difficulties made this step impractical. The women presented no notable problems except that of language, which possibly prevented them from receiving assignments commensurate with their intelligence.[1]

Considerable numbers of nisei recruits had been expected when, in 1943, the Army began to admit Americans of Japanese descent. In this hope, the Director's staff went to some pains to publish the necessary waivers on height and to request small-sized uniforms. Some five hundred nisei recruits were wanted for employment as translators, but in spite of visits of WAC recruiters to relocation centers, only thirteen could be obtained in the first six months of enlistment, and negligible numbers thereafter. Parental opposition to

military service for women was believed to have been the chief deterrent, as well as the fact that the women were by this time permitted to leave the relocation centers for other employment.[2] Somewhat later, the Military Intelligence Language School was able to locate and enlist a few more women who agreed to enter specifically for service at the school. Four more such women, especially enlisted in Hawaii for the language school, were appropriated by the Office of Strategic Services in Washington. There was sometimes a tendency to expect that all nisei Wacs could be assigned as translators, although in actual fact some of them proved to know no more of the Japanese language than any other American.[3]

Negro Personnel

Even before the passage of the first WAAC legislation, the War Department

---

[1] See Chs. XVIII, p. 332, and XXIII, above.
[2] (1) Tp Conv, Mr. John J. McCloy and Col Hobby, 13 Jan 43; (2) D/F, G–1 to Dir WAC, 26 Feb 43, with atchd, WDGAP 291.2 WAAC; (3) Ltr, TAG to all SvCs, 20 Jul 43, AG 291.1 (7–23–43) PR–I; (4) Memo, Dir WAC for G–1, 17 Feb 44. All in Enrollment of Japanese-American Women, SPWA 291.2 (1–13–43).
[3] (1) Memo, MIS for TAG, 16 Jul 45; (2) Memo, Tng Br MIS for Pers Br, 15 May 45, MID 908. G–2 MID 324.5 WAC (3–8–43).

announced that the new Corps would follow Army policy by admitting Negroes to basic and officer candidate training, and that two of the first eight companies sent to the field would be composed of Negroes. Forty of the WAAC's first 440 officer candidate vacancies were allotted to Negro women.[4]

Equality of treatment was also required by the confidential official policy which was formulated and approved shortly afterward and which stated:

On posts where these companies are stationed it should be fundamental that their reception and treatment should be an exemplification of the rights and privileges accorded officers and soldiers of the United States Army. . . . There will be no discrimination in the type of duties to which Negro women in the WAAC may be assigned. . . . Every effort will be made through intensive recruiting to obtain the class of colored women desired, in order that there may be no lowering of the standard in order to meet ratio requirements.[5]

The WAC, like the Army, was directed to accept 10.6 percent of its strength in Negro recruits. In accordance with the policy for men, it was deemed most desirable for adjustment to assign units to posts where a number of Negro troops were stationed, or where there was a large Negro population in nearby cities. Assignment overseas was also approved, contingent upon the request of the overseas commander.[6]

Reports from the first Negro trainees indicated that these prohibitions against discrimination were being upheld to the satisfaction of national Negro organizations. At the request of Dr. Mary McLeod Bethune of the Federal Security Agency, a Negro lawyer in the city of Des Moines questioned the Negro officer candidates closely to see if they could not recall some

evidence of discrimination, and found none:

Question: Are Negro girls made to feel that a special concession is being made to them in permitting them to attend this school?
Answer: Yes. The white girls are made to feel the same.[7]

General Marshall himself watched closely for compliance with these directives, and reported with satisfaction to the War Council that a reporter from the *Pittsburgh Courier* had inspected the Negro candidates and after urging them to make complaints could find none. All Negro Waacs assured the investigators that no school subjects were denied them, or jokes or sly remarks made. Some discrimination was noted in the city of Des Moines, but none among the other women, particularly those from the South, of whom Secretary Walter White of the National Association for the Advancement of Colored People (NAACP) asked, "When is Des Moines in general going to become as democratic as the white Waacs from the South?"[8]

---

[4] (1) Min, Gen Council, 4, 12, and 19 May 42. (2) Senate Com on Mil Affairs, 77th Cong, 2d sess, *Hearings on HR 6293*, 1 and 4 May 42, p. 1. (3) Draft of Ltr, SW for President, U.S., 14 May 42. WDGAP 320 WAAC, in WDGAP 291.2. (4) Intervs with Maj Ulysses Lee, OCMH, author of The Employment of Negro Troops, a forthcoming volume in this series. (5) See Table 11, Appendix A.

[5] (1) Memo, Tasker for Hobby, 14 May 42. G-1 291.21 WAC. (2) D/F, G-1 for MPD SOS, 24 Aug 42. WDGAP 322.99 WAAC, in CofS 291.9. (3) Memo, MPD SOS for G-1, 12 Sep 42. SPGAM 322.5 WAAC, in G-1 291.21 WAC.

[6] *Ibid.* Also Memo, Opns Div SOS for G-1, 4 Sep 42. SPAOO WAAC (9-3-42), in SPWA 291.9.

[7] (1) Ltr, Dr. Mary M. Bethune to Civ Aide to SW, 2 Sep 42. SPWA 291.21. (2) Rpt, Charles Howard to Dr. Bethune, Aug 42. CofS 291.9 WAAC.

[8] (1) Min of War Council, 16 Sep 42, remarks of Gen Marshall. (2) *PM*, Daily Picture Mag, undated copy in Folder, Negroes—Morale, WDBPR, file, OCMH.

Segregation

While thus approving other provisions, Negro organizations and investigators without exception objected to the segregation of Negro personnel, in which the WAAC had been directed to follow the Army policy. During the Corps' first months, numbers of Negro and white investigators arrived at Des Moines to search for bad results of segregation. The NAACP, after a visit by its representatives, wrote both the Secretary of War and the Director to protest the restriction of Negroes to separate barracks, separate tables in mess halls, and different swimming pool hours. Secretary White of the NAACP also repeatedly called at WAAC Headquarters in person to protest the Corps' action in following the Army policy on segregation. The National Board of the YWCA also investigated and wrote the Director to protest segregation. The Boston Urban League did the same. The Julius Rosenwald Fund sent a committee to Des Moines and concluded that segregation in housing would cause a falling off in Negro applications for enlistment.[9]

This concentrated activity within the space of a few weeks caused considerable concern to the WAAC staff. However, it was finally concluded that any new agency would probably receive similar visits, and that Negro organizations, like almost everyone else, did not realize that the WAAC was not an independent command in policy matters. One adviser reported to the Director:

The War Department, WAAC included, is gradually being maneuvered into the position of being forced to make decisions relative to racial matters which the government and/or the citizens should have made long ago, by legislation and the establishment of a different policy. . . . The Director is going to be in a better position if she allows the Army to care for the things that they normally do. Housing is one of them and it is the camp commanders' problem.[10]

All requests to the WAAC for independent action were necessarily referred to the War Department for consideration, as part of the Army policy. In November of 1942, officers' housing and messing at Fort Des Moines were merged, and also service club facilities, and officer candidate companies became nonsegregated, there being precedent for these steps at some men's schools. On the average Army station, no change in the Army policy was deemed possible, since there was ordinarily only one WAAC unit on a station and its housing was of course segregated regardless of the race of its members.[11]

In attempting even a limited relaxation of segregation at Des Moines, a women's corps dependent upon voluntary recruiting proved to be in a less advantageous position than the rest of the Army. There was some evidence that WAC recruiting soon suffered by comparison with that of the Navy women's services, which did not at this time accept Negro women. One congressman objected to the situation at Des Moines, stating of a constituent, "This fine girl along with others is now forced to share the same living quarters, bathroom facilities, restrooms, and reception rooms with Negroes."[12] Some Louisiana radio stations refused to aid WAC recruiting be-

[9] (1) Ltrs, Walter White to SW and to Dir WAAC, 28 Oct 42, with M/R atchd; (2) Ltr, Natl Bd YWCA to Dir WAAC, 14 Oct 42; (3) Ltr, Julius Rosenwald Fund to Dir WAAC, 23 Sep 42. SPWA 291.2.

[10] Intraoffice Memo. SPWA 291.21 (1942).

[11] M/Rs, 4 and 19 Nov 42, of mtgs with Secy NAACP; also Rpt of Investigation by Lt West. SPWA 291.2.

[12] Ltr, Rep. George H. Mahon to Dir WAAC, 22 Apr 43. SPWA 291.21.

cause a local woman, while housed on a separate floor of the Chamberlain Hotel in Des Moines, had to eat and do kitchen police with Negro women on the next floors.[13] An Army officer reported:

I am hearing constant rumors as to a re-laxing of segregation of Negroes at Fort Des Moines. Such rumors are horrifying to people in this section and I know are interfering seriously with recruiting.[14]

In any attempts to change the Army pol-icy, a newly established volunteer corps, under orders to attempt an expansion pro-gram unsupported by selective service, ob-viously offered the least promising point for a beginning. Only Director Hobby's personal convictions prevented the wiping out of the steps already taken at Fort Des Moines.

Recruiting

Most Negro organizations alleged that the policy of segregation would deter the best-qualified Negro women from enlist-ment, and this possibility was recognized and provided for in the original War De-partment policy concerning Negro Waacs, which stated:

There is a definite reluctance on the part of the best qualified colored women to volun-teer in the WAAC. This is brought about by an impression on their part that they will not be well received or treated on posts where they may be stationed. This could be over-come by an intensive recruiting campaign with the idea in view of interesting the de-sired class of colored women in this project and arriving at a thorough understanding of their rights and privileges while in the serv-ice. . . . An eminently qualified person, preferably a Negro recruiter, will be sent out to colored colleges in order to secure the proper class of applicants.[15]

Definite instructions requiring the ac-

ceptance of Negro applicants were sent out to recruiting stations. Noncompliance was discovered in only five cities and was corrected by telegraph in the WAAC's first week of recruiting.[16] One of these cases, in Pittsburgh, caused the editor of the *Pitts-burgh Courier* to demand that a woman from his staff be assigned to the Director's Office, since "We wouldn't want the pub-lic to deceive itself with the notion that what happened in Pittsburgh was due to the fact that the Director of the WAAC is a white woman from Texas." [17] The de-mand for such an adviser became a nationwide campaign with as many as thirty-five mimeographed letters being re-ceived from one small Virginia city.[18] However, the work of checking on such complaints was instead given to one of the first Negro officer candidates, Lt. Harriet West of the Director's staff, a former as-sistant to Dr. Bethune. Later charges of recruiting discrimination were investi-gated by Lieutenant West. In most cases records revealed that identical recruiting standards had been used, although re-jected Negro applicants sometimes tended to blame discrimination rather than their own failure to pass aptitude or physical tests.[19]

[13] Ltr, Manager KWKH and KTBS, Shreveport, La., 17 Apr 43. SPWA 291.21.

[14] Ltr, Comdt 5th Tng Cen to Exec WAAC, 3 May 43. SPWA 319.1.

[15] Memos and D/F cited n. 5.

[16] Cities were Pittsburgh, Winston-Salem, Colum-bia, S. C., Dallas, and St. Paul. File of action is WA 291.21 (5–27–42), 1942. See large file in SPWA 201.2 (1942).

[17] Ltr, Percival L. Prattis, Exec Bd, *The Pittsburgh Courier*, to Dir WAAC, 28 May 42. WA 291.9.

[18] (1) Mimeo Ltrs, from Lynchburg, Va., 21 May 42. WA 291.21. (2) Memo, G–1 for Exec WAC, 7 Aug 43. WDWAC 291.2.

[19] (1) Ltr, Walter White, Secy NAACP, to Dir WAAC, 8 Jun 42, and reply. SPWA 291.2. (2) Ltr, Maj Harriet West to Frances L. Munson, 1 Sep 43. SPWA 291.2.

Although Negro WAAC recruiting officers were sent to the field as soon as the first class graduated, Negro recruits from the first months failed to come up to expectations in either quantity or quality. An early check made by the Recruiting Service indicated that there were plenty of Negro applicants but that in some localities as many as 85 percent failed the various tests. Also, skills were scarce, and the whole Second Service Command reported that in several months it had been able to secure only one qualified typist and one clerk against its quota.[20]

During the first months of 1943, when standards for all recruits were unwisely lowered to meet expansion quotas, Negro recruits quickly presented a special problem, in that most of those who met enlistment standards tended to meet only the minimum requirements. As soon as educational standards were restored, in April of 1943, this condition became less common, but meanwhile the assignment problem for Negro women had become acute. A Negro training company in this month contained 225 members of whom 192 had no usable military skill. In the same month, the pool of unassignable women contained 180 whites and 776 Negroes.[21] The only available comparison of test scores showed that, of a May 1943 sample, 66 percent of Negro recruits were in the two lowest AGCT groups, IV and V, as against only 15 percent of white recruits; only 6 percent of Negro Wacs were in the two upper brackets, I and II, as against 43 percent of white Wacs.[22] The WAAC Control Division commented that the problem was one of the Corps' most serious, and would become worse when the women reached the field.[23]

Attempts were made to discharge the most hopeless cases, and it was believed that the higher enrollment standards just adopted would prevent similar future difficulty. As for women who could not be discharged, Capt. Harriet West, after an inspection, recommended that they be formed into companies for unskilled work in hospitals, messes, and salvage depots. However, this could not be done because of the War Department policy that Negroes would be assigned to the same type of units as whites, and because most allotments for such jobs were civilian. To ease the situation at Des Moines, a number of the women were shipped to the Fourth Training Center at Fort Devens for general use about the post and for training in motor transport. After about three months, Fort Devens closed out and they were shipped back to Des Moines.[24]

The situation quickly became highly embarrassing to the War Department. Although white women with equal lack of qualifications were equally unassignable, it frequently appeared to Negro organizations that race rather than ability was the determining factor in Army job assignments for Negro women. Every possible solution appeared tinged with discrimination. The WAAC Table of Organization unit had only seventeen vacancies for unskilled women, so that to form such companies of the Negro women was impossible, yet to devise a different T/O for Negroes, entirely composed of menial workers, would have been actual instead of apparent discrimination. Attempts at

[20] Ltr, 2d SvC to TAG, 11 Sep 42. SPWA 291.21.

[21] Memo, Col Howard Clark, Chief, WAAC Operating Serv, for Dir, 21 Apr 43. SPWA 291.2 (1942).

[22] Plng Proj 5, May 43, Sample of 1400 of each race. WAAC Plng Serv files.

[23] Memo, Maj Martin, Dir Contl Div WAAC, for Dir WAAC, 24 May 43. SPWA 291.2 (1942).

[24] (1) Tab I, Memo, Col Branch, Chief WAAC Plng Serv, for Dir WAAC, 15 Apr 43. SPWA 600.914. (2) Memo, same, 31 Mar 43. SPWA 291.2 (1942).

specialist training were equally futile. For Negroes only, the requirements for motor transport school were waived, and technical subjects removed from the course, but even with this assistance very few qualified drivers could be produced.[25]

In April of 1943, the Secretary of War's civilian aide, Truman Gibson, sent the War Department a complaint that the failure to give Negro women radio and other specialist training represented manipulation of test scores rather than the women's inaptitude; this was formally denied by training authorities. In May, representatives of the NAACP called on Colonel McCoskrie at Des Moines with the same and other complaints, and were again informed that women's alleged qualifications for radio and other training did not show up on tests.

In September of 1943 the civilian aide to the Secretary of War again complained that Negroes were being sent only to cooks and bakers school instead of to higher technical schools, and that white women were being assigned to field jobs while Negro women were not. The Director replied that Negroes could and did go to every specialist school upon the same basis as other women, and in fact had received more educational attention than white women in an effort to make up their deficiencies and permit their assignment to military jobs. The Secretary of War's civilian aide also objected to the fact that Negro women in the pool of unassignables had been allowed to go home on furlough while assignments for them were being sought; this, he charged, was also discrimination, in that white women did not get such furloughs.[26]

Especial protests concerned the recruiting situation, in which it was felt that the Army was not making every effort to re-

cruit more Negro women. The basis for such complaints was the fact that, in July of 1943, Negro WAC officers were withdrawn from recruiting duty and returned to training centers, in what was announced as a move to provide instructors for unassigned Negro women in order to get them assigned to the field as quickly as possible. Under the circumstances, it appeared to the Negro press that the Negro recruiters were being blamed for the low-grade women admitted, or that the move was a prelude to refusal to admit Negro recruits. In spite of this protest, the Negro recruiters were not returned to duty, since a check revealed that their absence had caused no decline in the numbers of Negro recruits.[27] It was known that the presence of Negro recruiters had caused situations prejudicial to white recruiting; in Sacramento, California, intelligence operatives reported a serious situation caused by Negro WAC recruiters who "appeared in public places giving public speeches." [28]

With the end of the T/O system, it became possible to ship to the field a unit chiefly composed of unskilled personnel, and the pool of unassigned women gradually diminished. The difficulty was, however, merely shifted to Army posts. An Army inspector reported that station commanders were quite at a loss as to how to assign the women without putting them into civilian jobs in laundries and service clubs. For example, one Negro unit in the field complained to an inspector of wom-

[25] See Ch. XXXII, below.

[26] (1) Ltr, Comdt Ft Des Moines to Exec WAAC, 13 May 43. SPWA 319.1. (2) Ltr, Detroit NAACP to SW, 29 Sep 43, with Inds. SPWA 291.2.

[27] Ltr, Dallas Negro Chamber of Commerce to Dir WAC, 2 Jul 43, and atchd correspondence. SPWA 291.2.

[28] Ltr, MID to MIS, 30 Mar 43. MID 291.2/7490-WAAC, in SPWA 291.2.

en's assignments, but it was found that only three women of the 135 were above Grade III on AGCT score, while 108 were in Grades IV and V. Their average civilian salary was $13.16 per week, and in civilian life they had been maids, waitresses, laundresses, and housewives. Nevertheless, they said that recruiters had told them that they would be trained to do skilled jobs and promoted at once to the grade of sergeant. Three in the company were described as "agitators," who threatened the other women for refusing to strike against their jobs.[29]

All attempts to place such low-grade women in Army jobs met with opposition. In 1943 and again in 1944 The Surgeon General's Office refused to accept them even as ward orderlies, saying:

No suitable assignments exist for such personnel upon completion of training and further accumulation of surplus colored WAC enlisted women thus trained would constitute an increasing embarrassment to the service.[30]

At the same time The Surgeon General's Office also refused to accept Grades IV and V white women.

The unassignability of unskilled Negro recruits merely served to reinforce a discovery that hardly needed reinforcement: that the Army had few jobs for unskilled and untrainable women of any race, and that to recruit them was invariably illadvised. For skilled Negro recruits, the situation was considerably different. Negro women who met the intelligence requirements were successfully given specialist training including that of medical and surgical technicians, as well as laboratory, X-ray, and dental technicians; these women proved able to complete the regular course on the same terms as other Wacs.[31] Army posts and air bases where Negro

troops were stationed expressed a consistent eagerness to obtain Negro WAC units containing stenographers, typists, and other office workers.

Skilled Work Done by Negro Wacs

Scattered reports from Negro WAC units at Army stations showed successful performance by Negro Wacs of a wide variety of administrative and technical work. At Fort Jackson, a Wac sergeant was medical stenographer to the chief of general surgery. At Fort Bragg, a Wac T/5 taught arts and crafts to soldiers in the recreational therapy shop. At Fort McClellan, fifteen Wac clerks staffed the locator section of the post office, forwarding wrongly addressed mail and packages and keeping locator card files for the post. At Fort Riley, members served not only as ward orderlies but in the more skilled jobs of physical therapy aids, laboratory technicians, X-ray technicians, and dental technicians. At Fort Sheridan, Illinois, the women worked at graphotype machines, processing soldiers' records. At Camp Knight, California, 105 Negro Wacs performed clerical work in the overseas supply division.

In the Army Air Forces, whole units, such as that at the Walla Walla air base, were reported as succeeding in the same type of clerical and other duties performed by white Wacs. At the Sioux City Army air base, Negro Wacs worked in the tech-

[29] Rpt of Insp, WAC Det Ft Knox, Ky., 6 Aug 43. SPWA 333.1.

[30] (1) D/F, Opns Serv SGO for MTD ASF, 17 Aug 44. SPMCT, in SGO Hist Div SPMCM 322.5–1 WAC. (2) Draft of Memo, Dir WAC for SvCs, 11 Aug 43. SPWA 220.3.

[31] (1) Memo, Tng Div SGO for MTD ASF, 19 Oct 43, and 1st Ind; (2) Memo, Tng Div SGO for MTD ASF, 25 Apr 44. MDETS, SGO 353.1 Ft Huachuca.

nical inspector's office. At Douglas Army Airfield, the women were assigned to aircraft maintenance, the flight line, and laboratory work; one also served as photographer in the post public relations office. In the Air Service Command at Fresno, two women served in map and editing work in the war room.

Other duties noted at different stations were those of teletype operators, motion picture projectionists, parachute packers, drivers, cooks, chaplains' assistants, and librarians.[32] The commanding officer of Fort Huachuca wrote, "These young women are showing marked ability in taking over essential jobs. . . . The performance of the Wacs has been very satisfactory in every respect."[33] The commanding officer of Douglas Army Airfield stated, "I've found them cooperative at all times, and their enthusiasm, industry, attention to duty and conduct make them a real asset to this post." "In several cases," Colonel Bandel reported later, "their efficiency and spirit were highly praised by airbase commanders."[34]

Negro WAC officers served not only as troop officers and instructors but in operational jobs, a number also being graduates of the Army's Quartermaster School at Camp Lee.

With the higher enrollment standards, recruiters experienced increased success in obtaining qualified women. A survey of skills in 1944 showed that about one fourth of Negro recruits had clerical and professional skills, as against one half of white recruits. In addition, about 30 percent of the Negro recruits, as compared to 34 percent of the whites, had experience in skilled or unskilled trades.[35] Although thus not as good as the WAC average, the Negro Wacs appeared to be considerably superior in skills to the average for Negro

civilian women workers in the United States. Here, more than 64 percent of civilian women were reported to be in service occupations, as against only 35 percent of Negro Wacs with this background.[36]

In employing higher skill and aptitude standards, recruiters were never able to reach the desired goal of 10 percent of the Corps' strength.[37] The peak strength of Negro WAC troops was reached early in 1945 and totaled approximately 4,000 or about 4 percent of the Corps.[38] These women were assigned to some twenty stations in the Army Service Forces and ten stations in the Army Air Forces. The Army Ground Forces employed no Negro Wacs,

[32] (1) R&R, Air WAC Off to PRO, 26 Sep 43. AAF 291.2. (2) *Mason City, Globe-Gazette*, Iowa, January 16, 1945. (3) Atlanta, Ga., *Daily World*, February 15, 1945. (4) Story, "Locator Wacs," by Mary F. Green in undated, unmarked clipping. Folder, Negroes—Field Installations, WDBPR files. (5) *Kansas City Call*, January 26, 1945. (6) Study, Facts About Negro Women in the WAC. Folder, Negroes—Field Installations, WDBPR files. (7) Detroit *Chronicle*, November 25, 1944.

[33] (1) File, Ft Huachuca, SPWA 291.21. (2) Extract from Army Fact Sheet, Women in Uniform, 10 May 43, Radio Br BPR. Folder, Negroes—Facts, WDBPR files.

[34] (1) WFTC News Release, undated. Folder Negroes—AAF, WDBPR files. (2) WAC AAF Hist, pp. 14, 40.

[35] Study made by SGO (incidental to determining factors in health record) of 22,000 accepted applicants, Oct 43–Mar 44. SGO Med Stat Div.

[36] Janet M. Hooks, *Women's Occupations Through Seven Decades*, U.S. Dept of Labor, Women's Bureau Bull 218, pp. 143–44. The 64 percent applies to "nonwhite" women and does not include charwomen, and the like, who were apparently included in the WAC's 35 percent.

[37] See breakdowns of rejection rates by race, printed by Stat Analysis Br Med Stat Div SGO, Feb–Mar 43, and Med Rejections, Nov 42–Dec 44. Med Stat Div SGO.

[38] (1) As of 31 Mar 45. See also Memo, Dir WAC for G–1, 14 Mar 45. Folder, Material, 10 Apr 45, for Cong Appropriations Mtg for Year 1945–46, Tab 7. (2) Memo, Dir WAC for G–1, 14 Mar 45. Hobby files.

since most of its troops trained on stations administered by the Service Forces.[39]

Problems of Negro Units

There was little indication that, with a few exceptions, the problems experienced by these Negro WAC units in the field were greatly different in nature from those of other WAC units, but in some cases the normal difficulties of women in the Army were apparently intensified. Unskilled women of any race had been found harder to assign and harder to discipline. Thus, the Negro company officer frequently faced a more difficult command situation than did the average WAC company commander, in proportion as her unit contained more than the average of such women. The post commander at Fort Huachuca noted that the enlisted women were prone to develop "jealousies and cliques" and "bickerings which seem to date back to school days at Des Moines . . . with various kinds of personal gossip about each other."[40]

Unit members also showed a tendency to complain to inspectors about the education and ability of Negro company commanders, who were in fact as well educated and trained as the average WAC commander. To deal with such units frequently required a skill and a degree of leadership highly taxing to the company officer. Some Negro WAC company commanders were reported to have met the challenge with an ingenuity, energy, and sense of humor seldom equaled among other WAC commanders. On the other hand, some were found to share their women's deficiencies; an intelligence report from Fort Des Moines found that jealousy and rivalry had arisen among Negro WAC officers, resulting in a "heated argument" and "emotional display" in the presence of the commandant.

Negro WAC officers also had an especial problem of loneliness on many stations; the WAC policy was to have Negro company officers for Negro troops, but many male Negro units had white officers, so that the WAC officers were apt to be the only Negro officers on a station.[41]

While all WAC units had at first encountered some degree of skepticism concerning their mission in life, this difficulty was apparently intensified for Negro Wacs. The first requisition from the European theater, rejected by Colonel Hobby at the time of the Corps' formation, had been so plainly for "morale purposes" that the Secretary of War's civilian aide, William H. Hastie, protested that "the assignment of units of the WAAC to afford companionship for soldiers would discredit that organization" and was "contrary to its whole plan and purpose."[42]

The first units at Fort Huachuca encountered an exceptionally difficult situation in this respect during the early weeks.[43] While such impressions on stations of assignment could be remedied only by time and demonstrated military behavior, every effort was made to avoid exposing the women unnecessarily to situations that encouraged the misapprehension. Thus, when the inspector general at Sioux Falls suggested that large groups of Negro Wacs be brought by truck from Des Moines to make up for the recrea-

---

[39] *Ibid.*

[40] File, Fort Huachuca, SPWA 291.21.

[41] (1) TIA Rpt, 1 Sep 43, Ft Dix, N. J. (2) Statement to author by Stf Dir 5th SvC. (3) Memo, CI Br ASF for Chief, Opns Div WAC Hq, 15 Sep 43. SPWA 291.2. (4) Min, Stf Dirs Conf, Chicago, 15–17 Jun 43. SPWA 337 (6–1–43).

[42] Memo, SW's Civ Aide for USW, 17 Aug 42. AG 291.2 Race, Negroes.

[43] File cited n. 40.

tional deficiencies of Negro men at that air base, Colonel Hobby replied with some emphasis that one of the War Department's invariable policies was that Wacs, regardless of race, would not be removed from their jobs to be "social companions."[44]

Negro WAC units also experienced a special problem outside their control in that in some cases a serious race problem had already arisen in certain areas before their arrival, including what was described as "race riots," "unrest," "inflammatory gossip," and "rumor of a nature to incite the men."[45] Not only did such emotions prove contagious, but the sentiment in neighboring civilian communities was also sometimes anything but favorable toward the women's arrival. When it was planned to send a unit to Gardiner General Hospital in Chicago, where a strained situation already existed, protests were received by the Army from four suburban civic groups, to the effect that stationing the women in a restricted white residential area, near a white bathing beach, might cause "incidents" and race riots. Although the Army ignored these protests and successfully stationed the unit at Gardiner General Hospital, such a community reaction obviously presented an adjustment problem to unit members.[46]

The women's adjustment to the Army situation was also rendered more difficult by well-meaning civilian groups in their constant watchfulness for discrimination. It was not surprising that many of the experiences that had been encountered by white Wacs everywhere, and attributed to their sex, should be interpreted by Negro Wacs as racial discrimination: these included the early malassignments, clothing shortages, malicious gossip, and other common difficulties. Possibly the most

serious report investigated was one of "terrorization and mistreatment," which actually proved to be the common experience of many WAC units—a chilly initial reception, rude remarks by civilian employees, lack of enthusiasm about Wacs on the part of USO hostesses, and pranks by soldiers. The unit, except for three complaining members, was actually found to be in good morale, satisfied with its recreational facilities, and satisfactory in its duties.[47]

A similar situation arose when, in the last days of the war, both white and Negro units were recruited for general hospitals. Shortly afterward, Congressman Adam C. Powell informed the War Department that "Trouble is brewing at Fort Oglethorpe." Upon investigation it was found that Negro civilian employees were being given better hospital jobs than Negro Wacs; that Negro Wacs worked in hospitals 12 hours a day and civilians only 8; that Negro Wac orderlies had to take orders from civilian nurses.[48] These were exactly the problems currently reported from white hospital units.

An almost identical and widely publicized case of alleged discrimination concerned the court-martial of four Negro Wacs at Lovell General Hospital in Massachusetts. A summary of their grievances was endorsed by white medical technician recruits everywhere:

---

[44] Ltr, Air IG to CG AAF CTTC, with 10th Ind, Dir WAC to Contl Div ASF, 27 Oct 43. SPWA 291.2.

[45] Ltr, CofS to AAF, AGF, ASF, with 1st Ind, 13 Jul 43. SPWA 291.2.

[46] (1) Memo, Col John Nash for Dir Pers ASF, 6 Apr 45. SPDC, in SPAP 220. (2) Memo, Exec to CG ASF for TSG, 3 May 45. SPDC, in SGO 330.14 Gardiner GH.

[47] Ltr, Mrs. Eleanor Roosevelt to Dir WAC, 25 Oct 44, and reply, 16 Jan 45. WDWAC 330.14.

[48] D/F, G–1 for Leg and Ln Div, 3 May 45. WDWAC 291.2.

They don't want to scrub. . . . They want a future, i. e., training . . . they don't like the civilians because the civilians are late, lazy, and mean . . . they said they knew they weren't wanted in the beginning . . . they want promised ratings.

The conviction that racial discrimination was involved led a part of this Negro unit to refuse to report for duty even after personal pleas from the WAC staff director, two colonels, a judge advocate, an inspector general, and the commanding general of the service command, which finally caused all but four members to return to work. The court-martial of these four was declared proper even by the NAACP, which issued a statement that "We recognize that there is no right to strike in the Armed Services." Although the commanding general upheld the court-martial proceedings, the conviction was reversed by the Judge Advocate General, and the women restored to duty on the technicality that the court was improperly convened.[49]

Negro Wacs Overseas

The European theater was the only overseas theater to employ Negro Wacs. ETO policy vacillated. Negroes were requisitioned in 1942 with the declaration that "in time of war it is the privilege of all American citizens regardless of race or sex to serve in and with the Armed Forces." However, when Director Hobby refused to let the women be scattered in uncontrolled small field units near male Negro troops, the theater hastily canceled the requisition and stated that "colored Wacs will not be requisitioned until such time as the War Department announces that their shipment to theaters of operation is a necessity."[50]

Pressure of Negro groups finally forced the War Department to direct the European theater to accept Negro Wacs. As directed, the European theater submitted a requisition for approximately 800 Negro women to set up half of a central postal directory. Declaring that these women would not fill any existing military jobs, the theater asked and expected an additional allotment of grades, but none was received.

The unit, the 6888th Central Postal Battalion, was selected from both the Air Forces and the Service Forces in order to give all women a chance at overseas service, but sufficient volunteers to fill the unit could not be found. One Negro editor had alleged that "they are heartbroken because they cannot serve overseas like their white GI sisters,"[51] but this opinion apparently did not accurately reflect the sentiments of all of the women, one of whom suggested to an inspector that they ship the NAACP instead.[52]

The battalion arrived in Europe in February of 1945, under the command of Maj. Charity Adams, later promoted to lieutenant colonel. The unit contained 40 percent unskilled workers, as against 1 percent for white Wacs in this theater, and 40 percent in the two lowest AGCT grades, as against 10 percent for white Wacs.

As a separate T/O unit, the battalion

---

[49] (1) Ltr, CG 1st SvC to CG ASF, 13 Mar 45, with incls. SPBVG. (2) Memo Slip, Int Div ASF for Dir Pers ASF, 21 Mar 45, with atchd; and another, 3 Apr 45. (3) Clippings in same file. (4) Weekly Int Summary 164, Hq 1st SvC, 31 Mar 45. SPBIB 350.09, Racial Situation Annex.

[50] Following, unless indicated, based on ETO Bd Rpt, Vol. I, pp. 126–29 and Vol III, Apps. 85d and 125.

[51] Ltr, Malvina Thompson to Dir WAC, 1 Nov 44, incl Ltr from city editor of *AFRO-American*, 26 Oct 44, and reply, 4 Nov 44. WDWAC 330.14.

[52] Interv with Maj Marjorie Ludwigsen, Hq AAF, inspector of unit for AAF.

naturally had segregated housing and working quarters, but there was no segregation in the use of Red Cross clubs, leave areas, and schools. No particular difficulties were reported in discipline and administration. The unit was congratulated by the theater on its "exceptionally fine" Special Services program. Its observance of military courtesies was also pronounced exemplary, as were the grooming and appearance of members and the maintenance of quarters.

Unit efficiency was difficult to evaluate. Before the women's arrival, the central directory operated with enlisted men and civilians and reported itself "swamped by mail" and with an undelivered backlog of over three million pieces; it also faced the necessity of a move to France, where English-speaking civilians would be more difficult to find.[53] The Wacs' performance was not entirely satisfactory to inspectors, who stated that "production appeared to be low" and that "the girls relax on their jobs while mail accumulates." The women in turn believed that too much pressure was being brought to bear to increase mail output, and that they had not been awarded a well-deserved unit citation.

Some 11 percent of the detachment also had cause for considering themselves malassigned; about 10 percent were typists, and 1 percent were stenographers, and these were admittedly underutilized in a postal directory. Had not the segregation policy prevented, these could have been scattered through other WAC detachments where their skills could have been employed. The other 89 percent appeared to be properly assigned but, like most newly arrived personnel, had difficulty with respiratory disorders; they also reported considerable fatigue.

Some six months after the end of the war in Europe, with the departure of discharge-eligibles, the battalion had shrunk to about 300 members, and its morale and efficiency were pronounced so "exceptionally low" by a WAC inspector from the War Department that she recommended its immediate return to the United States.[54] The theater preferred not to return the unit under circumstances implying failure, which was believed unwarranted, but eventually, with the reduction in size of the theater, there was little work remaining for the women, and they were returned to the United States as a unit. The theater's conclusion was that the problems experienced by Negro Wacs in the European theater were similar to those experienced by other Negro troops and were not peculiar to women, and that the War Department's eventual solution should apply to both.

As soon as shipment was made to the European theater, Negro groups turned toward efforts to get Negro Wacs sent to the Southwest Pacific Area.[55] Such action was never directed by the War Department, since they were not requisitioned by the theater, and since the end of the war intervened. Also, the difficulties currently being encountered by white Wacs in the Pacific would have been difficult to explain to Negro organizations. In any case, the percentage of Negro Wacs overseas was, on the strength of the European battalion, as high as that of all Wacs, or about 20 percent.

---

[53] Rpt on Postal System in ETO 10 Jan 45–15 Feb 45 Rpt 30, Hq ETO Gen Inspectorate Sec. Copy in WDWAC 333.5.

[54] Rpt, Maj Frances Clements, G–3, Visit to 6888th Cen Post Bn. WDWAC 333.1 (1945–46).

[55] (1) Undated Q and A Series. SPWA 291.2 (1943). (2) Ltr, Editor, *Amsterdam News*, N. Y., to WD BPR, 23 Jul 45, and reply. WDWAC 000.7.

Conclusions

It proved difficult to evaluate the success of the program of employment of Negro Wacs. The second WAC Director, Colonel Boyce, when asked to comment, replied, "The Negro women in the Army are a part of the WAC. The record of achievement of the Corps cannot be attributed to any individual or to any group but to the whole Corps." [56] Training center authorities were inclined to wonder if the nuisance value of the constant civilian searching parties had not outweighed the military contribution by the women.[57] In the field, comments of post commanders applied to ability rather than race: every skilled Wac was assignable regardless of race, and unskilled ones were never wanted. When the WAVES, near the end of the war, were considering admitting Negroes, a WAC authority advised them,

To speak very frankly, the problems are fundamental ones—charges of segregation, discrimination, not giving them clerical jobs. . . . Success depends in the main on (1) the caliber of officers . . . (2) intelligent assignment and utilization.[58]

It appeared that in some respects the Navy policy had been more successful than that of the Army. The WAVES had not admitted any Negro women until 1945, by which time the Navy had announced an end of segregation for men. At this time the WAVES accepted only 70 Negro enlisted women and no company officers. By virtue of the small numbers, enlistment was highly selective, and only women of high aptitude and skill and good personal appearance were chosen. For this reason, the WAVES were able to abolish segregation from the beginning, and to incorporate the few skilled specialists into existing units. The approval with which the Navy policy was received by Negro organizations strongly suggested that, had the WAC never set a 10 percent quota, and instead limited Negro enlistment to a few women who met the highest standards, it might not only have avoided the burden of unassignable low-grade personnel, but also have successfully abolished segregation. However, the WAC could hardly have adopted this policy in the absence of a change in Army policy.[59]

There was some indication that, as compared to the relative problems of Negro men in all services, the WAC had experienced lesser problems and been more highly regarded by the Negro civilian population. When asked in a nationwide survey "What are your chances in the different services?" more Negro women answered "Good" concerning the WAC than did Negro men concerning any of the armed services.[60] It appeared that the armed forces' eventual decisions concerning male Negro troops would apply equally well to female troops, with the exception—which applied to women of all races—that higher-grade female personnel would continue to be required in view of the fact that women could not perform combat and heavy service duties.

[56] Series cited n. 55(1).
[57] Ltr, Comdt 1st Tng Cen to WAAC Ex, 19 Aug 43. SPWA 291.2.
[58] Ltr, ASF WAC Off to Dir WAVES, 4 Nov 44. SPAP 220.3 WAC.
[59] (1) Ltr, Headlines and Picture Editor to Dir WAC, 31 Jul 45. SPWA 291.2 (1943). (2) Navy Press Release. (3) WAVES Hist, pp. 78–79.
[60] Study, 8 Jul 43, sub: The Negroes' Role in the War, OWI Memo 59, pp. 9–10. SPWA 291.2.

CHAPTER XXXI

Health and Medical Care

Responsibility for providing medical care for the 160,000 Wacs and nurses of the Army was placed upon the Office of The Surgeon General, both in Auxiliary days and after the change to Army status. As directed by The Surgeon General, any inquiries received by Director Hobby concerning medical problems of members were sent to his office for reply.[1] The Surgeon General's responsibilities were threefold: setting medical standards for enlistment, providing suitable medical care after enlistment, and recommending hygiene courses and other preventive measures to maintain women's health.

For the year of the Auxiliary's existence, these responsibilities toward Waacs were handled as part-time duty by a Medical Corps officer. Shortly before the conversion, the responsibility was delegated to the first woman Medical Corps officer, Maj. Margaret D. Craighill, former dean of a woman's medical college in Pennsylvania.[2] Major Craighill gradually acquired an assistant and two secretaries, and undertook visits to training and field installations and overseas theaters.

Her unit was, she reported, handicapped from time to time not only by its small size but by lack of sufficient authority or delineation of responsibilities within The Surgeon General's Office.[3] There also existed a divided responsibility with Military Training Division, Army Service Forces, which sometimes issued directives on medical training for Wacs without coordination with either Major Craighill or Director Hobby.[4]

By the end of 1943, Major Craighill was nevertheless embarked on plans for a coordinated health program for women. If it had taken a year for The Surgeon General to recognize that "there are problems of health peculiar to women," [5] it was to take the rest of the war to solve most of them.

Medical Standards for Enlistment

One of Major Craighill's first actions after her appointment was a tour of Army induction stations to seek the cause of medical examiners' errors, which had seriously affected the early recruiting program. The cause, she discovered, was simple: most stations were not giving any

---

[1] Memo, Consultant for Women's Health and Welfare to Dir WAC, 4 Jul 44. SPMC DD–DW 322.5, in WDWAC 220.

[2] References to Craighill opinions, unless otherwise cited, are from: (1) History of Women's Medical Unit, rough draft narrative by Lt Col Margaret D. Craighill, MC, 23 Jul 46. SGO Hist Div 314.72. (2) Rpt, Maj Craighill to Hist Div SGO, 26 Sep 45, sub: Logistics of World War II. SPMDF–W, in WDWAC 314.7.

[3] For development of unit, see history cited n. 2(1).

[4] (1) Memo, WAC Well-Being Off for Dir WAC, 6 Jan 44. SPWA 211. (2) Memo, ASF Pub Contl Off for Maj Craighill, 4 May 44. WDWAC 300.6.

[5] (1) WAAC Regs 1942, par 21–25. (2) AR 40–100, Change 5, 27 Sep 43. (3) Rpt, Enlistment, Health, and Discharge of the WAC, by Med Stat Div SGO, in Army MD Bull, Vol. VI, No. 3, Sep 46. (4) Memo, SGO for Dir WAC, 14 Aug 44. SPMC/DD–DW 322.5.

MAJOR CRAIGHILL, *the first Consultant for Women's Health and Welfare in the Office of The Surgeon General (right). Dr. Elizabeth Garber (left), a member of the WAAC on the hospital staff at Fort Des Moines, later sworn into the Medical Corps of the U.S. Army.*

pelvic or gynecological examination at all; neither were many giving a psychiatric examination. Instead, the prescribed examination for men was being used, which made it understandable why the rejectable gynecologic defects were overlooked.[6]

Upon her return to headquarters, Major Craighill at once secured a directive that gynecological and psychiatric examinations would be given every WAC applicant. Instead of leaving exact gyne-

cologic standards to the medical examiner's imagination, as formerly, she secured appointment of a board of Army doctors to set standards of acceptability, and these were shortly published. Exact directions were given for administering a suitable pelvic examination, the list of disqualifying gynecologic defects was ex-

[6] See Ch. X. Also Rpt 3–W, WAAC Enrollment Data, SGO Med Stat Div Bull, 17 Aug 43.

panded, and it was required that the menstrual history be recorded.[7]

In spite of the publication of standards, the circumstances of WAC enlistment did not lend themselves to sudden improvement. Wacs were enlisted at many widely scattered stations, where the relatively small numbers of women processed made it necessary to use the medical staff that processed inducted men; it was impossible to provide every small station with a gynecologist. Also, medical examiners were generally uninformed about the work the WAC would do, and admitted a tendency to underrate the physical and mental strain of military life. In addition, examining officers pointed out that they were frequently urged by recruiters to overlook "minor" disqualifications, particularly in matters involving personal judgment, such as stamina and personality defects. Doctors were also hurried by recruiters who wished to swear in an applicant before she changed her mind, without waiting for a full check on her records of civilian hospitalization.

As a result, while the number of psychiatric and gynecological rejections increased, 1944—and the beginning of the Corps' third year—found the situation still unsatisfactory. Almost 75 percent of WAC disability discharges continued to be for psychiatric and gynecological reasons, most of them occurring within a few months of enlistment, and rates from different service commands still varied widely.[8] Training centers continued to send reports of causes for which new recruits had to be discharged at once: dementia praecox, schizophrenia, manicdepressive psychosis, epilepsy, fibroids of the uterus, tumor of the ovary, and advanced pregnancy, as well as other matters such as diabetes, arthritis, goiter, pep-

tic ulcer, tertiary syphilis, and tuberculosis.[9]

By February of 1944, all responsible officers were seriously concerned about the situation. The Surgeon General, Maj. Gen. Norman T. Kirk, informed General Somervell at this time that "the physical examination of Wacs at induction stations and other stations is not being conducted satisfactorily and is not sufficiently thorough."[10] The Director's staff noted that "the enlistment of unqualified women continues to create serious problems for recruiting, for the Corps, and for the individuals concerned."[11] Reports from service commands noted that among the "worst deterrents to recruiting" was faulty psychiatric screening. It appeared to be equally bad to accept an applicant known to her community to be "queer" or seriously delinquent, or to select one well thought of in the community who immediately broke down and had to be discharged.[12]

The Administrator of Veterans' Affairs, Brig. Gen. Charles Hines, wrote to the Secretary of War concerning cases in which women had been discharged for neuropsychiatric disorders immediately after enlistment, and thrown upon veter-

---

[7] Change 5, AR 40-100, 27 Sep 43. See also D/F, Dir WAC for SGO, 20 Dec 43, incl 1st Ind from SGO, SG 322.5 (1st SC) AA. SPWA 220.8 (9-30-43).

[8] Bull, SGO Med Stat Div, *WAC Enlistment Data,* 6 Mar 44, Rpt 5-W, Contl Symbol SPMCS-96.

[9] (1) Memo, Craighill for Gen Bliss, SGO, 28 Apr 44. SGO Hist Div folder. (2) Ltr, Post Surg to Comdt Ft Oglethorpe, 11 Nov 43, and Inds; (3) Ltr, Post Surg Ft Oglethorpe to SGO, 21 Jan 44. SGO Hist Div 322.5-1.

[10] Memo, The SG to CG ASF, 7 Feb 44. SPAP 341 WAC (11-6-43).

[11] M/R, O Dir WAC, 29 Feb 44. WDWAC 326 (1945-46).

[12] (1) Speech of Dir WAC, Recruiters Conf, Chicago, Feb 44. WDWAC 337. (2) Memo, Sp Asst Elizabeth DeSchweinitz for Dir WAC, 12 Feb 44. WAC files, OCMH.

ans' hospitals for what appeared to be indefinite future care.[13] Brig. Gen. William C. Menninger reported that the need for good psychiatric examinations was even greater for women than for men, because of the greater number of peculiarly motivated individuals who applied for a volunteer corps as contrasted to those called up in a nationwide draft, and also because of the higher age limits for acceptance of women.[14]

During these months every possible means of improving the situation was explored, with disappointing results. At The Surgeon General's request, the National Committee for Mental Hygiene made a study of neuropsychiatric induction procedures for both men and women. The committee recommended that women psychiatrists examine women—a suggestion that could not be adopted for lack of women psychiatrists at the hundreds of recruiting stations enlisting Wacs.[15] The committee also recommended an elaborate system of investigation of each applicant's medical and social history, which was found to be too time-consuming to be practical.

Director Hobby next proposed that Selective Service boards assist the WAC "in securing medical history on prospective WAC recruits." For men, such histories were compiled by Selective Service boards and their medical field agencies in the home locality. They included verification of identification, education, medical and social history, and other material of much assistance to induction examiners, who could not otherwise have detected certain traits in one interview. However, General Hershey refused to allow his local boards to extend this service to Wacs, stating:

The gathering of information in connection with WAC recruiting would not appear to be part of the duties for which they are appointed or compensated . . . it is not deemed advisable that the agencies assume the additional work.[16]

As an alternative, Director Hobby proposed a "New England Plan," used successfully by WAC recruiters in New England, with information derived from both local Selective Service boards and from social agencies. Typical of cases thus detected were that of a woman who had "a call from God" to enlist but many home anxieties; a well-educated and presentable woman found to be unable to hold a job because of fits of depression and hysterical blindness; a woman whose father wept and begged that she be taken away from association with his younger children. However, this plan was frowned upon by ASF's Military Personnel Division, which feared it might give outside agencies undue control of acceptances.[17]

The Surgeon General's Office next turned to an attempt to get WAC enlistments limited to the few large stations where qualified gynecologists and women psychiatrists could be stationed.[18] To this end, Major Craighill worked for some weeks with The Adjutant General's recruiting staff, preparing lists of stations and plans for detailed instruction. Unfortunately for this idea, it came at a time of manpower shortage, when the Army was

[13] Memo, Dir Pers ASF for G–1, CofS, and SW, 15 Jan 45. SPGAP 710 Gen, in CofS 324.5 WAC.

[14] Menninger, *Psychiatry in a Troubled World*, p. 112.

[15] (1) Memo, SG for Dir WAC, 4 Oct 43. WDWAC 702. (2) M/R, 3 Feb 44. SPWA 080 (9–9–43), copy in OCMH.

[16] Memo, Dir WAC to G–1 WD through CG ASF, 6 Jan 44, and atchd reply. WDWAC 341.

[17] (1) M/R, sub: Memo on WAC Screening in New York City. WDWAC 201.6 (1944). (2) Memo, MPD ASF for Dir Pers ASF, 2 Feb 44. SPGAP 342 Gen, in SPAP 320–340 WAC.

[18] Memo, The SG for CG ASF, 7 Feb 44. SPAP 341 WAC (11–6–43).

redoubling efforts to get WAC recruits, and when posts and air bases were contributing additional teams. Recruiters, from a study of the reactions of hesitant prospects, felt that it was difficult enough to secure an enlistment when the applicant could be rushed through processing in her own home town and sworn in before she repented her decision. It was deemed impossible to persuade most applicants to take leave from their jobs and travel several hundred miles for an examination which, if unsuccessful, would leave a woman in the embarrassing position of having publicly announced her intentions and then having been publicly rejected. Therefore, the whole plan of centralized screening was dropped, and the number of enlistment stations was actually increased instead of decreased.

Finally, in March of 1944, a conference of all interested agencies adopted a plan proposed by Director Hobby's representatives. This solution, similar to that which had proved successful in The Surgeon General's Office and in other agencies, called for centralizing responsibility in a WAC specialist. Accordingly, a highly qualified WAC officer was appointed in each service command to improve screening procedures as best she might. She was responsible for giving medical examiners the proper background material for an understanding of Corps jobs, and for obtaining for them such reports on doubtful candidates as would assist their judgment, such as case histories and hospitalization records. If qualified psychiatrists were unavailable locally, she was authorized to pay $2.50 per doubtful applicant to recognized social agencies for a full investigation—a small investment compared to mustering-out pay and veterans' benefits, and one that left the final decision in the hands of military personnel. It was also re-

quired that a qualified WAC officer be placed in each recruiting station where WAC enlistments were processed, to render much the same assistance and to assume responsibility for a final review of acceptances.[19]

The Surgeon General called the attention of service command surgeons to these measures and directed that they assist the WAC liaison officer in every possible way. A conference was also called in May of 1944, of one member from each service command, to clarify procedures. In August of 1944, a more forceful directive to recruiting stations reiterated the requirement that the neuropsychiatric examination must be made by a qualified neuropsychiatrist, and that the gynecological examination must not be omitted. It was stated that "experience has shown unequivocally" that there was an undue discharge rate of women accepted by stations where such examinations were "omitted or inferior." Finally, in the fall of 1944, a medical technical bulletin gave an extremely clear statement, in medical language, of the conditions of WAC life that medical officers must consider in approving an applicant.[20]

This last combined effort seemed to be moderately successful. The rejection rate rose markedly and the disability discharge rate dropped.[21] It appeared that the work of educating medical examiners to WAC

---

[19] M/R cited n. 11.

[20] (1) Ltrs, AGO to all SvCs, 1 Apr 44, AG 341 WAC PR–I; 19 May 44, SPX 341 WAC PR–I; 10 Jun 44, AG 341 WAC PR–I. (2) Ltr, SGO to all SvCs, 13 May 44. SGO Hist Div folder. (3) Memo, MPD ASF for Dir Pers ASF, 3 May 44. SPGAP 342 Gen–123, in SPAP 341 WAAC. (4) Memo, Actg Dir WAC to SGO, 3 Mar 44. SPWA 330.14 R. (5) Direct quotation from Memo, MPD ASF for TAG, 19 Aug 44. SPGAP 342 Gen–141, in SPAP 342 WAC.

[21] Rpt cited n. 2(2). Also Chart by Med Stat Div SGO, 12 Mar 45, sub: Trend of Med Rejections, WAC Candidates, Nov 42–Dec 44. Copy in WAC files, OCMH.

enlistment requirements had been done as well as possible under the voluntary enlistment system where recruits of any sort were at a premium. As Major Craighill pointed out, these results were not achieved until the main WAC recruiting effort was over, but the system remained on record for later use.

Rejection and Discharge Rates

Toward the end of the war, The Surgeon General's Medical Statistical Division completed a study of the factors affecting enlistment. It was now confirmed that applicants over 40 had only one chance in three of passing the entrance physical examination, while those under 25 had an even chance; also, that Wacs over 40 were three times as apt to get a disability discharge. Less easily explicable was the fact that married applicants also had less chance than single women of passing the physical examination, and married Wacs were almost three times as likely to get a disability discharge. Disability, in all these cases, did not include pregnancy rates, so that there was no easy explanation of the poorer health of married women.

Also unexpected was the factor of education. Women who had not completed high school got four times as many disability discharges as did those who had completed high school or better. There were three times as many psychiatric discharges and six times as many gynecological discharges among the less educated group. Grammar school graduates received seventeen times as many disability discharges as did college graduates.

There was a similarly unexpected relationship to previous employment. Wacs who had never held a paying job, including housewives, got three times as many

disability discharges as those who had held clerical or professional jobs. Domestic and service workers were almost as bad a risk as the unemployed and housewives. Those never gainfully employed had three times as many psychiatric discharges as self-supporting women, and four times as many gynecological discharges. These "unemployed and housewives" were not a large group, however: 95 percent of married Wacs and 96 percent of single ones had held paying jobs outside the home before enlistment.[22]

According to this analysis, the lowest possible disability discharge rates would be achieved by the WAC if it were possible to restrict its membership to young women who had never been married, whose schooling included at least high school graduation, and who were previously employed in paying jobs as other than service workers or housekeepers.

It was always emphasized by The Surgeon General's Office that medical rejection rates for WAC applicants should not be compared to the higher rejection rates among males, which might have given the impression that the nation's women were

---

[22] Study, Trend of Med Rejections in WAC, and A Sample Study of Med Defects . . ., 147 pages, 30 charts. SGO Med Stat Div. The Certificate of Disability Discharge rate per 1,000 for the year October 1943 to October 1944 was:

Age:
20–39	18
40–50	59

Marital Status:
Married	73
Divorced or widowed	68
Single	27

Education:
4–7 years	189
8 years	185
1–3 yrs high school	73
High school graduate	26
1–3 yrs college	24
College graduate	11
Post graduate	11

Skill:
Employed in skilled work	36
Unemployed	115

healthier than its men. The rates were not, in The Surgeon General's opinion, strictly comparable, since the WAC was a self-selected group, in which only those women applied who had reason to believe that they could meet the requirements, and who desired to do so.[23]

Monthly Physical Inspection

After passing the medical enlistment examination, a normally healthy Wac next encountered the Medical Department at the monthly physical "inspection" required for all Army personnel. By Army Regulations, this included, for men, inspection of the feet, mouth, and teeth; investigation for venereal disease and vermin infestation; and observation for chronic diseases.[24] When the Auxiliary was organized, no indication was given the field as to whether or not the requirement applied to women.

In October of 1942, the post surgeon at Fort Des Moines called this omission to the attention of The Surgeon General. He pointed out that venereal disease in women could not be detected by inspection, as in men, and suggested that the more complicated pelvic examination required to detect it be given only every six months, since it called for hospital facilities. In reply, The Surgeon General refused to set a policy, recommending that the training center determine for itself "such special examinations as may, in the opinion of the Surgeon, be required for the prevention and spread of communicable disease."[25]

This information was given only to training centers, and field stations shortly began to inquire about the same problem. At one, the post surgeon refused to fill out the necessary monthly venereal disease reports for the company unless he could give a complete pelvic examination to each woman each month. Such inquiries were answered to the effect that, pending publication of instructions, stations should hold the inspection but omit the venereal disease check. Since this information was given only to the stations that inquired, Director Hobby's office in December of 1942 requested The Surgeon General to amend the Army Regulation to make the matter clear to all, and to forbid routine pelvic examinations.[26]

By the time of establishment of the WAC, some seven months later, no such action had been taken, and reports from the field indicated that at some stations pelvic examinations were given monthly. Such practices invariably called forth protests from the women, since the examination was often a painful business which most women were willing to undergo once or twice in a lifetime, but scarcely every month. As the public pointed out to Mrs. Roosevelt, who pointed it out to Director Hobby, a woman might suffer pain for a week after a rough or inexpert examination.[27]

Therefore, one of Major Craighill's first acts after her appointment was to secure

---

[23] (1) Inquiry from U.S. Office of Education, and reply, with M/R, SPWA 353.8 (1943). (2) Chicago *World Herald,* June 30, 1945. (3) Memo, Stat Br G-1 for Dir WAC, 3 Mar 45. WDWAC 720, 1945–46.

[24] AR 615–250.

[25] Ltr, Post Surg 1st Tng Cen to TSG, 20 Oct 42, with Inds. SPWA 201.6.

[26] (1) Ltr, 6th WAAC Opns Co, Boston, to 1st SvC, 7 Nov 42, and Inds. SPWA 201.6. (2) Memo, Col Karl R. Lundeberg, MC, for The SG, 2 Dec 42. SPMCM 322.5–1 WAC, in SGO Hist Div. (3) Memo, WAAC Hq for SGO, 5 Dec 42. SPWA 201.6. A monthly physical inspection was directed by WAAC Circular 1, 23 January 1943, which, however, had no power to prescribe procedure, and did not.

[27] Ltr, Secy to Mrs. Roosevelt to Dir WAC, 30 Dec 44. WDWAC 330.14.

publication, in the summer of 1943, of a medical circular giving detailed directions as to the proper procedure for conduct of the monthly physical inspection for female troops. This definitely made it clear that a pelvic examination would not be given routinely; if it seemed indicated by other symptoms, it might be made in a dispensary or hospital. It was also specified that the pelvic examination would be made rectally "where indicated"; this provision met the objections of young unmarried women to enlistment. It was required that the monthly inspection be simple and private, preferably in the WAC barracks, with the subject suitably draped; inspections in the nude were forbidden.[28]

Even after this action, objections continued to come in. Company commanders pointed out that their women were of excellent moral character and found the monthly inspection embarrassing. Women also frequently questioned the necessity for any examination at all, since it could not detect venereal disease and was so brief— 15 seconds in one training center—that in their opinion it served no purpose but to waste time and require undressing and dressing. Major Craighill in reply urged WAC commanders to educate their women to the purposes of the examination, which was not intended to imply a suspicion that they had contracted venereal disease, but rather to detect any deterioration in physical condition before it became serious, and to promote a friendly doctor-patient acquaintance that would make medical care easier in the event of illness.[29]

To this end, another Surgeon General letter was sent out, advising doctors that more care should be taken to consider the modesty of the individual and to explain the purpose of the examination. It was added that a female company officer should be present at all times, that personnel would wear underwear in addition to being covered with a sheet or blanket, and that an inspection of the pubic hair would not be made routinely. This last requirement alone did much to end the near-rebellion with which many women had regarded the monthly inspection.[30]

Women's higher degree of modesty in physical matters obviously posed a continuing problem for examiners, and one which, in the opinion of medical authorities, was not likely to be changed in the current century. General Menninger noted, "Girls are raised in a manner entirely different from boys in relation to the emphasis on modesty and privacy in dressing, bathing, and toilet."[31] Equally important was the fact that examining physicians were of the opposite sex in all but the very few installations that employed women doctors. It appeared that male personnel likewise might have offered some objections to monthly nude examination by women doctors. Well toward the end of the war, The Surgeon General's Office continued to receive objections based on this factor, and to find evidence that some medical officers were still unfamiliar with the precautions prescribed in medical directives, particularly that concerning the presence of the female commanding officer.[32]

---

[28] SGO Cir Ltr 135, 27 Jul 43, in SPWA 314.7 sec 3.

[29] Memo, Craighill for Gen Bliss, 25 Mar 44, sub: Visit to Ft Des Moines and Chicago. Folder Capt Berlien, SGO Hist Div.

[30] (1) Ltr to 3d SvC, 4 Dec 43, with 1st Ind, SGO to Dir WAC, 25 Jan 44; (2) Ltr, SG to all SvCs, 9 Feb 44, incl Change to SGO Cir 1, 1 Jan 44; amends SGO Cir Ltr 135, 27 Jul 43. SPWA 702 (12–4–43), 1943.

[31] Menninger, *Psychiatry in a Troubled World*.

[32] (1) Memo, Asst Consultant on Women's Health for Col Freer, SGO, 27 Sep 44. SGO Cl 321 WAC. (2) D/F, G–1 to SGO, 29 Sep 45. WDGAP 201.5 WAC, in WDWAC 201.5.

Sick Call, Dispensary Care, and Hospitalization

In every type of medical facility, the necessary segregation of the WAC minority presented a problem to medical officers. The easiest solution was possible to the larger hospitals, that of merely designating one or more wards for female patients, including Wacs, nurses, and soldiers' dependents. Smaller hospitals could ordinarily designate several rooms for the same purpose. Even at best, Major Craighill noted that the small number of women involved made it inevitable that types of personnel and of cases were not always segregated in the manner customary for hospitals. Sick call and dispensary care presented the greatest problem. Separate dispensaries were provided only where large groups were handled; otherwise different hours were set for women. A practice generally objectionable to WAC commanders was that of having Wacs report to sick call in the orderly room of men's units, which frequently required a sick woman to walk for some distance, or made her unwilling to report at all.[33]

A particular problem for the WAC company commander, because of the non-activated nature of her unit, was sometimes that of securing reports, which were frequently sent instead to the commander of the men's unit or section to which the Wac was formally assigned. Some WAC commanders were able to make local arrangements by which they were allowed to keep the women's sick book entries, these being relayed by telephone from the various units of assignment; others had more difficulty in checking on the women's status.

In either case there was noted a certain difficulty in maintaining the confidential character of medical records. In fact, evidence from all overseas theaters indicated that, whether reasonably or not, women objected so strongly to having records on their gynecological disorders handled by male cadre and civilians that the efficiency of medical care was lowered by the women's failure to reveal difficulties. Objections especially centered around such practices as writing the diagnosis on the passenger list for Wacs returning from overseas, or on the card attached to the Wac's coat. Major Craighill noted:

> Privacy in regard to medical conditions is deplorably lacking in Army hospitals, as was pointed out in War Department Circular 310 . . . "Maintenance of Ethical Standards by non-Professional Personnel." The practice of passing the records through numerous hands . . . quickly makes a diagnosis common knowledge and a topic of conversation. This is particularly embarrassing to women . . . and leads to hesitation about seeking medical advice.[34]

Partial local solutions to this problem were sometimes achieved by using WAC medical technicians in dispensaries during hours of service to women, or by special precautions in handling records.[35]

WAC Morbidity Rate

A complicating factor in medical care for women was the higher WAC rate of morbidity, a term used to indicate the frequency of reporting to sick call. Industrial surveys had indicated that civilian women sought medical advice twice as frequently as did men, but that as a result the average duration of an illness was less for women. The British women's services had

---

[33] (1) Sources cited n. 2. (2) Memos, Civ Consultant for Dir WAAC, 6 and 17 May 43. Folders 6 and 15, Miss Lies' file, 1943 WAAC Plng Serv file.

[34] Craighill IBT Rpt.

[35] (1) Memo cited n. 1. (2) ETO Bd Rpt, App. 121, p. 5.

noted an identical effect. Industry found that the excess of medical visits by women was not due to female disorders but to the common cold and other minor respiratory disorders and digestive upsets. Men, when they finally sought advice, were more apt to have pneumonia, heart disease, or other more serious illnesses requiring longer absence from work.[36]

When the WAC began to note an identical phenomenon, Director Hobby was at first distressed and, in company with many medical officers on posts and stations, felt that the women were perhaps "goldbricking" or malingering. She therefore consulted The Surgeon General's Office as to whether steps should be taken to indoctrinate WAC company commanders to discourage women from reporting to sick call for minor ailments. Major Craighill and The Surgeon General's Office strongly advised her to take no such action, since the tendency was considered a desirable preventive medicine practice.

Army medical statistics soon confirmed this fact. While the WAC sick call rate was found to run about 36 percent above that of the rest of the Army, some 30 percent of WAC cases could be treated in quarters, as contrasted to 8 percent for men. As a result, the rate of admission to the hospital was about the same for women as for non-battle cases among men, and the length of stay was less. Wacs actually lost less time from work because of hospitalization than did men, a fact attributed by The Surgeon General to the less serious character of the illnesses common among women. Thus, while women reported about 70 percent more colds than did men, and twice the amount of dysentery, men had about twice the WAC rate of pneumonia, measles, mumps, scarlet fever, rheumatic fever, and other more serious diseases.[37]

These statistics seemed to confirm The Surgeon General's belief that a higher sick call rate was good preventive medicine. Therefore, in order to eliminate the resentment of medical officers against enlisted women appearing on sick call, The Surgeon General's Office published a summary of the findings in several of its progress reports, stating, "The higher morbidity of the WAC need occasion no concern. . . ."[38]

Gynecological Care

The WAC's smaller loss of time by hospitalization could not be attributed to especially efficient gynecological care, which in Major Craighill's opinion was largely nonexistent in Army hospitals. Such hospitals, naturally enough, were not originally set up with a view to caring for female patients. Even after the Army ceased to be exclusively male in composition, Major Craighill noted:

Gynecological and obstetrical conditions have not been given the recognition which the size of the problem warrants when it is considered that over 156,000 women were in the military service at one time, and that there were approximately 31,000 deliveries occurring in dependent civilian wives during 1944 in Army hospitals.

An exactly parallel situation had been found by inspectors of British women's services, who recommended the appointment of more gynecologists, preferably women.[39] In late 1943 The Surgeon Gen-

---

[36] (1) Baetjer, *Women in Industry*, pp. 39 ff. (2) *Conditions in the Three Women's Services.*

[37] (1) ASF Monthly Progress Rpts, Sec 7, "Health," for 31 Jul 44, 31 Oct 44, and 31 May 46. (2) Rpt cited n. 5(3). (3) WD Press Release, 18 Oct 46. (4) Annual Rpt of The SG for Fiscal Year 1945.

[38] Rpts cited n. 37(1).

[39] *Conditions in the Three Women's Services.*

eral's Office made surveys of the locations of Army doctors who had been civilian specialists in gynecology,[40] but Major Craighill noted that it was not until after the victory over Japan that a systematic effort was made to place such specialists in hospitals serving the largest numbers of women. She also reported:

Equipment and supplies for use in these conditions have not been readily available in many places because these items were not included in the early equipment and medical supply lists.

It did not appear that, while the WAC remained a tiny group in the Army, the Medical Department would find it possible to fulfill its responsibilities to women soldiers as well as it did to men on all of the scattered stations employing a few Wacs. Major Craighill was of the opinion that at least one consultant in gynecology and obstetrics could reasonably be appointed in the Office of The Surgeon General, but this was not done, these specialties instead being handled by the Surgical Service.

For this reason, very little information was collected on the extent of gynecological problems among Wacs and nurses. Only scattered reports were made on the causes and cures of the various disorders in menstruation and menopause, or the extent to which they were influenced by military service or were a handicap to it.

Menstrual Disorders

In 1943, a brief and sensible discussion of the anatomy and physiology of menstruation was included in WAC training courses. This was supplemented in 1945 by a general hygiene film, brief sequences of which mentioned menstruation by way of exploding popular superstitions and fal-

lacies on the subject and teaching women a sensible health regime.[41] No further attention was given the matter. However, it was ordinarily apparent to a woman, even before completion of basic training, that one of the most frequent effects of military service upon her physical condition was some change in menstruation. Some women noted considerable improvement, with less painful and more regular periods. A few experienced an increased and often debilitating loss of blood (menorrhagia), or the absence of one or more periods with consequent gain in weight and general sluggishness (amenorrhea), or increased pain and disability for a day or more each month (dysmenorrhea).

Incidental notes made on the subject by medical officers were frequently contradictory. Thus, British reports indicated that "the best menstrual health prevails among women doing strenuous and active work," and that the worst disorders were found among clerical, medical, and communications personnel and waitresses.[42] This view was supported by Major Preston of the Fort Des Moines consultation service, who noted a complete lack of serious menstrual difficulties among student drivers, as contrasted with higher rates among cooks and clerks.[43] On the other hand, a survey made near the end of the war noted that drivers and women who had been long in other strenuous outdoor work suffered from menorrhagia to an extent that was a distinct occupational hazard, although they experienced less

---

[40] Rpts by Paul Titus, MD, Consultant to SG, in Hist Div SGO 210.01; info from Mr. Clarence Smith, SGO Hist Div.
[41] WD Pamphlet 35–1, Sex Hygiene Course, 27 May 43, and later edition, May 45. WDWAC 720 (1945).
[42] *Conditions in the Three Women's Services.*
[43] Ch. XXXII, below.

pain than other workers.[44] In the absence of any more specific studies on the subject, the validity of these observations appeared difficult to determine.

The only agency to undertake any serious research on the problem was the Army Air Forces, which reported that numbers of women at certain stations in the Florida swamps were all but disabled by menorrhagia. Some study was made of the effect of climate upon menstruation, and of the relative effectiveness of different treatments, but with little conclusion except that the sufferer usually recovered if transferred to a climate or duty to which she was accustomed.[45]

Unfortunately for this solution, previous regulations of The Surgeon General provided that a soldier who was a noneffective at any station would not be transferred to another to secure his recovery, but would be discharged. This regulation had been designed for male patients with asthma and similar complaints, and was intended to prevent the Army from becoming immobilized by too many members who could work only in certain climates or situations. WAC authorities protested its application to menstrual disorders, since badly needed WAC typists and clerks who could have given good permanent service were discharged because of it. Nevertheless, no change was made in the ruling, since The Surgeon General considered it impractical to amend Army Regulations for one type of case.

Another amendment thought desirable by WAC advisers, but never granted by The Surgeon General, was one to allow post surgeons to authorize two hours or a half day in quarters for women with menstrual cramps. These ordinarily abated in the time required for aspirin to take effect, but meanwhile, under Army Regulations,

a medical officer was required to commit the woman to a hospital if she was unable immediately to return to work. Since several days were ordinarily required to secure release from a hospital, increased loss of work time resulted. Industrial advisers noted an identical problem:

> Industries can reduce the time lost due to dysmenorrhea by providing a place for the women to rest, hot drinks, local heat, and simple medication. . . . If such provisions are made, many women will be able to return to work after a short period, whereas otherwise they would leave the plant.[46]

The Surgeon General was never willing to authorize any such solution, although reports indicated that some stations had solved this and similar problems by maintaining dispensaries in which any patient might be allowed to rest for a brief period. Such dispensaries, if locally devised, had to be managed through unofficial reallotment of grades, since they were never authorized on any Tables of Organization.

Even without the recommended amendments, the efficiency of the Corps as a whole was not perceptibly affected by menstrual problems. This fact appeared the more remarkable in view of expressed opinions before the war that woman's menstrual function rendered her so "abnormal, unstable," and so on, as entirely to disqualify her for military service. Instead, while individual women had been disqualified for certain duties or for military service, there was no instance in which the sex as a whole had been disqualified for this reason from serving in any particular Army job or in any station,

---

[44] Memo, SGO for G–1, 19 Dec 45. SPMC/DF–W, in WDWAC 201.6.

[45] Health files (unnumbered) of Air WAC Div, ACofAS Pers, Hq AAF, 1943–45.

[46] Baetjer, *Women in Industry*.

climate, or area. Industrial surveys similarly concluded that "it would appear that the ability of women to perform mental or muscular tasks is not essentially altered by the menstrual cycle." [47]

A strictly parallel conclusion was indicated by the more complete records kept for civilian women pilots by the Army Air Forces. Here, the Ferrying Division had at first forbidden women to fly from one day before the beginning of the menstrual period until two days after it, since the Civil Aeronautics Board handbook stated that "many women pilots have fainted while flying during this period with fatal results." This statement, the Ferrying Division noted with interest, seemed to have no foundation; many women flew steadily without fatal results, and the rule could not be enforced because

> Actually, without the rather intimate cooperation of the women pilots concerned, it is difficult to understand just how the Group Commander could tell when a Waf was in a period. . . . There was little anyone could do if a Waf denied being in that condition.

Even among those women who observed the rule, it was noted that few were forced "to take to their beds," but instead used this time for the required paper work and ground school and therefore lost no more flying time than men. [48]

Menopause

Menstrual disorders tended to merge into menopausal difficulties in a few older women or in younger women suffering from surgical menopause. These disturbances were ordinarily more distressing than those of menstruation, and Director Hobby, soon after the formation of the first WAAC companies, called the problem to The Surgeon General's attention, asking whether medical examiners could not reject women who would be problems because of menopausal difficulties. The Surgeon General replied that there was no way in which the approach of menopausal difficulties could be foretold, and believed it unnecessary to take any specific action. [49] No provision was made for treatment or discharge of such cases. Upon her appointment, Major Craighill reported the policies regarding menopause to be in "a most confused state."

Throughout the next two years, WAC inspectors were informed by company commanders in the field that the problem was more important than the number of affected individuals would indicate. A company ordinarily had only one or two sufferers, yet the morale of an entire barracks could be affected by one such individual's constant complaints and chronic depression. Such women, although no asset to the Army, could not be discharged under any existing Army Regulations unless their difficulties became disabling or their conduct punishable, which was usually not the case.

Because of the number of such inspection reports, the Army Air Forces recommended to The Surgeon General that there be authorized a separate type of honorable menopause discharge for women "for the convenience of the government," similar to the special pregnancy discharge. However, this was refused by The Surgeon General on the grounds that menopause was a normal condition and not cause for discharge unless it became so

[47] *Ibid.*, p. 196.

[48] Hist Recs Rpt 319, History of the ATC: Women Pilots in the Air Transport Command, by Hist Br, Hq ATC (1946). USAF Hist Div.

[49] Memo, WAAC Hq for SGO, 23 Jan 43, and reply 26 Jan. SPWA 210.13 and SPMCM 322.5–1 WAC, SGO Hist Div.

disabling that a disability discharge was appropriate.[50]

The Surgeon General in return repeatedly proposed that the maximum age for enlistment in the WAC be lowered from 50 to 38, to avoid admitting women liable to menopausal difficulties. Statistics revealed that the disability discharge rate for women over 40 was almost three times the average rate. Director Hobby and The Adjutant General's Office refused this suggestion, pointing out that the WAC badly needed recruits. Even under the higher discharge rate, 9 out of every 10 older women remained, and many of the most valuable skills were in this group. It was therefore believed undesirable to bar many useful mature women in order to avoid finding some means of discharging the few who had difficulty.[51]

Medical supply catalogs, which originally authorized only those items needed for the treatment of men, were belatedly amended to add the drugs and hormones needed for women. However, many medical officers, according to inspectors, were unaware of this, and required enlisted women to buy necessary supplies if they wished treatment.[52]

Major Craighill therefore in 1944 proposed to The Surgeon General that some definitive policy concerning treatment and discharge be established by headquarters. She reported that discharge of menopause cases was often refused to genuine but not "disabled" sufferers, while elsewhere disability discharge was "being used loosely, especially to avoid the stigma of psychiatric conditions, or to get rid of people who had undesirable traits of character or could not adjust." About a year later, a policy was published in a technical bulletin; the type and length of treatment was specified, and discharge was authorized if

a patient showed no improvement after six months.[53] By this time, as Major Craighill noted, the advice was not greatly needed, since, with V-E Day past, the Army had already authorized the discharge of any man or woman over the age of 38.

Social Hygiene

By the guarded title of *Social Hygiene*, WAC authorities usually avoided potentially sensational terms such as sex hygiene and venereal disease control, believing that they would affect recruiting adversely if they appeared in the public press. The Surgeon General's Office, however, although silent on the innocent problems of menstruation and menopause, had a large and active program for combating venereal disease, headed by an officer with the title of Director of Venereal Disease. This office, where dormancy would have been welcomed by WAC recruiters, promptly sprang into activity at the prospect of setting up a thorough venereal disease control program for women. In its efforts to devise a program comparable to that for men, this office was always to feel itself hampered by the Director WAC, and Director, Army Nurse Corps, because of their belief in different moral standards for women.

Thus, in the initial and all wartime admission standards, venereal disease was made a cause for rejection of women, although The Surgeon General's specialists believed that from a public health stand-

[50] Memo, Exec WAC for Air WAC Off, 16 Jun 44. WDWAC 720.

[51] (1) Memo, SG for CG ASF, 7 Feb 44, SMPDA 322.5–1, with remarks of MPD ASF, 15 Feb, SPGAP 342 Gen, and Dir WAC, 3 Mar, WDWAC 341. All in SPWA 341 (1942). (2) Rpt cited n. 5(3), p. 285.

[52] Memo cited n. 32(1).

[53] T. B. Med 158, May 1945.

point it would be better to take such women off the community's hands and treat them, as was done with men.[54]

In August of 1942, there occurred a clash over what Director Hobby described as

. . . the calling of a meeting of civilians, at the request of the Surgeon General, to discuss the details and scope of the sex hygiene instruction to be given by the WAAC, without reference to the Director WAAC either as to the necessity for or the advisability of such a meeting . . . to the serious jeopardy of the military and civilian acceptance of the whole idea of the Corps.[55]

The civilians thus consulted were scientists of the National Research Council, who were accustomed to advise The Surgeon General on venereal disease control among men, and who emerged with a proposed venereal control program for women so thorough as to disconcert even The Surgeon General. The scientists proposed that Waacs, like men, be taught all of the facts of life concerning sex and how to prevent venereal disease and that, since unmarried women would be too modest to request issue of prophylactics as men did, these be dispensed from slot machines in WAAC latrines.

WAAC Headquarters, shocked but not speechless, denounced this idea, and The Surgeon General hastily rejected it. This apparently Victorian reaction was not so exaggerated as it appeared to disciples of pure science, since the decline of WAAC recruiting a year later was in fact closely connected with the unfounded public charges, possibly based on this incident, that the Army issued Waacs prophylactics which it expected them to put to good use for "morale purposes" among the soldiers.[56] Director Hobby stated that The Surgeon General, in calling such a meet-

ing without her approval, might have wrecked the whole WAAC program had news of the meeting reached the newspapers. To this The Surgeon General replied, "It has never been considered necessary to request the permission of the Chiefs of the various Arms and Services to discuss health problems." [57]

The problems of preventing and treating venereal disease in women were admittedly more complex than those for men, partly because of social taboos and the double standard of morality, and partly because the physical organs involved were less easily protected from infection and less accessible to treatment. Medical officers gave fleeting consideration to setting up prophylaxis stations for women such as those for men, and to providing women with suitable prophylactics comparable to those given to men. Chemical agents, however, were known to offer little protection to women. Mechanical means were not much more reliable, and had an associated contraceptive use that made their issuance even more dangerous from a recruiting standpoint. Also, it was realized that women, unlike men, would not spontaneously avail themselves of such a station's facilities.

In any case, the whole idea was never remotely considered by the directors of the women's services. Early medical meetings concluded that, because of the high type of woman expected in the Corps, no control measures would be needed except a good training course in physiology and hy-

[54] Sources cited n. 5.
[55] Memo, Dir WAAC for CofS, 4 Aug 42, sub: Status of WAAC Hq in WD Consideration of WAAC Matters. Copies in SGO Classif SPMC 322.5–1, and Adm Serv ASF, DRB AGO.
[56] See Ch. XI, above.
[57] 1st Ind, SGO for CofAdm Serv, 8 Aug 42, to Memo cited n. 55.

giene such as was given in some women's colleges. In December of 1942 Director Hobby requested that The Surgeon General's Office prepare such a course for WAAC officers to use in instructing women in health and hygiene.[58]

This pamphlet,[59] after a rewriting by Director Hobby's office, sounded more like a moral than a medical discourse. "We all desire the Corps to be the finest organization in the world," officer candidates were taught. "Every member must insist that the conduct of the Corps be irreproachable. . . . It is difficult for one person to realize the damage she can do the Corps by her conduct alone."

After further pages in this key, a certain amount of medical information was given: woman's physiology and the proper functioning of her reproductive organs in menstruation, childbearing, and menopause; the frightful effects of venereal disease upon herself and her children; the difficulty of protection and treatment. Prospective WAAC officers were taught that war traditionally placed many stresses upon standards of conduct, and that their women must be protected against these and should be encouraged to bring all such questions to the WAAC officer. Officers were cautioned to avoid letting their women be led into injudicious conduct because of boredom, poor recreational facilities, lack of appreciation and praise of their work, or ignorance of the facts regarding sex and of how to control their own desires.

All references were in moral terms: venereal disease was "a national menace"; illegitimate pregnancy "a personal tragedy as well as a loss in womanpower"; and as for abortion, "no woman should resort to this." There was absolutely no reference to prophylaxis except to say that, for

women, all means were "neither effective or practicable." There was no discussion of the various chemical and mechanical means of avoiding infection and pregnancy, nor were women told where to get these prophylactics, or how to use them. In the opinion of annoyed medical officers, a more Victorian approach to the facts of life could scarcely have been contrived.

Nevertheless, it was shortly after the restricted publication of this course of instruction that there ensued the newspaper attacks of the slander campaign, which charged that a "secret document" directed that contraceptives be issued to Wacs.

The training course was not withdrawn, although the Navy Department delayed from 1943 to 1944 in distributing the WAVES' sex hygiene pamphlets and films because of the "publication of erroneous and distorted information regarding a similar program of the WAC."

The Surgeon General's Office desired to follow the pamphlet with a letter to Army medical officers in the field, directing them to assume the same responsibility for venereal disease control that they had for men, but this was discouraged by WAAC Headquarters. Instead, selected WAAC instructors were sent to a meeting discreetly titled A Conference on Preventive Medicine, and thence to a tour of the field to lecture to those company officers who had not had the new course in basic training. This avoided the possibility that some field medical officer, uninstructed in the explosive possibilities of the subject, would say something in his lecture to Wacs that the American public could consider immoral.

The Surgeon General's Office also made repeated recommendations that training

---

[58] Memo, WAAC Hq for SG, 5 Dec 42, sub: AR 615–250. SPWA 201.6 R.
[59] Pamphlet cited n. 41.

material and films on disease control be sent to the field, as well as pamphlets and posters. These ideas were all rejected by the War Department for almost another year. Finally, in 1944, permission was granted to show certain Public Health Service and Canadian films especially designed to avoid shocking the public. A carefully rewritten pamphlet was also approved, and finally a second one for women overseas, although, as Major Craighill pointed out, this appeared just as most women were nearing the end of their overseas service. All of these training aids continued to have a moral tone and gave no instruction in prophylaxis.[60]

Director Hobby's chief fear during this period was that, in the hundreds of stations to which Wacs were now assigned, some medical officer would erroneously apply the regulations governing men, and thus supply enemies of the Corps with grounds for stating that Wacs were urged to use contraceptives. The danger was redoubled in that the Medical Department and Military Training Division, like almost all other headquarters agencies, occasionally forgot that all Army Regulations were applicable to the WAC unless otherwise specified, and published directives that made no exceptions for women.

Thus, in April of 1944 the circular on Training in Basic Medical Subjects was already cleared for publication by Military Training Division before Colonel Hobby discovered, from an information copy, that it prescribed instruction in "individual methods of preventing venereal disease" for "all military personnel." [61] To prevent such accidents in the future, Director Hobby secured publication of a War Department circular stating plainly:

It is contrary to War Department policy either to provide instruction in venereal dis-

ease prophylaxis for female personnel of the Army of the United States, or to issue venereal disease prophylaxis materials to such personnel. The provisions of Army Regulations and directives concerning these matters are intended for male personnel only and are not applicable to female personnel.[62]

The Director also secured publication of a circular stating that WAC unit commanders would give or arrange the periodic instruction in social hygiene that was required by Army Regulations.[63]

These precautions proved useful, for as late as 1945 an Army Regulation declared that "Commanding Officers will make readily available to all military personnel such venereal disease prophylactic items as are prescribed and furnished by the Surgeon General," and that instructions would include "routine use of prophylactic methods during and following possible exposure." [64] In such cases it could only be hoped that field authorities were aware of the earlier circular and would not interpret "all military personnel" as including women.

If any danger to women's health resulted from a disease control program based on recruiting considerations rather than medical ones, such danger was not apparent in the rates of infection. In fact, it quickly became clear that among Wacs venereal disease was so rare as to be a neg-

---

[60] (1) Pub Health Serv Films: *Fight Syphilis* and *The Magic Bullet;* Canadian film: *For Your Information;* American film: *Our Job to Know.* (2) Pamphlet: *You'd Better Know,* printed by V. D. Education Institute, Raleigh, N. C. (3) WD Pamphlet 35–4, 1945, *For Women Overseas.* AG 461 (3–13–45), in WDWAC 720.

[61] Memo Routing Slip, MTD ASF to Dep Dir WAC, 7 Apr 44, re Draft of Change to Cir 48, 3 Feb 44, with atchd note.

[62] WD Cir 172, 2 May 44, sec IV.

[63] WD Cir 6, 4 Jan 44, amended by WD Cir 163, 26 Apr 44.

[64] AR 40–210, 25 Apr 45.

ligible health problem. Although the rate for civilian women in the United States was only slightly lower than that for men—87 to 90 percent of the men's rate in 1945—the WAC rate was in all reports considerably below the men's rate, being estimated finally by Major Craighill as only about 18 percent of the men's rate. It was especially noted that, in overseas areas designated as "epidemic," where men's rates considerably exceeded the rates for the United States, the WAC rates showed no notable difference.[65]

The lower WAC ratio seemed partially due to the fact that the WAC excluded women infected at the time of application or with a history of venereal disease. While infections existing before enlistment were also not counted in the yearly incidence rates for men, the WAC system tended to prevent admission of "repeaters." Another factor was the smaller number of Negroes in the WAC, which had only 4 percent of Negro personnel as against 10 percent for the Army. Since rates for both men and women were higher in the Negro race, an additional 6 percent of Negroes might have raised the WAC rate somewhat. Also, the moralizing approach used by the WAC was later tried in several postwar groups of men, with some indication that, at least for younger men, it appeared to result in lower infection rates.[66]

These statistics were repeatedly made available to investigating groups, but were never fully credited by the general public. Thus, toward the end of the war, a congresswoman received a letter complaining, "The rate of venereal disease among the women in our forces is increasing at an alarming speed." Director Hobby again called at the Capitol in person with the statistics, and again secured written Congressional assurance that "the matter has

been answered wholly to my satisfaction. I think you should feel exceedingly proud of the Wacs."[67]

At only one early period was the Corps' ability to maintain this high standard in doubt. This occurred during the Auxiliary period just before control of recruiting was taken over by WAAC Headquarters, when lowered entrance requirements caused an influx of diseased women into training centers in such numbers as, in a few units, to equal or surpass the men's rates.[68] This trend was checked before it produced any notable fluctuation in the over-all rate, but gave evidence that a women's corps was by no means exempt from the Army problem, and that of civilian society, except by strict maintenance of enlistment standards. The Surgeon General ruled that women with venereal disease, although barred from enlistment, could not be discharged if admitted by faulty examinations.

The diagnosis and treatment of syphilis in women presented no particular problem for medical officers, since it was similar to that in men. The diagnosis of gonor-

---

[65] WAC rate is from Major Craighill's final report. Her sources were regular monthly reports from all service commands, received throughout the war. Civilian comparison is from: (1) Office Memo, U.S. Pub Health Serv VD Div for OCMH 13 Jul 50, sub: Morbidity Rates by Sex and Color. OCMH. (2) Telephone conversations with Dr. Johannes Stuart and J. Wallace Rion of that division. The Public Health Service stated that, due to differing methods of determining rates, no exactly comparable figure could be given for civilian women, but that the ratio of male to female rates should hold true under any method of collection of data, and that studies indicated that incidence for men was about the same whether in or out of Army.

[66] Notably at Universal Military Training test groups at Fort Knox, visited by the author.

[67] Ltr, Rep. Frances P. Bolton (Ohio) to Dir WAC, 5 Dec 44, incl Ltr from constituent, and another, 16 Dec 44. WDWAC 720.

[68] Ltr, Post Surg to Comdt 4th WAAC Tng Cen, 14 May 43; 3d Ind, SGO to Dir WAAC. SGO Hist Div 322.5–1.

rhea in women was more difficult, as smears were found unreliable and cultures required expert laboratory technique which was available in few places. The Medical Department expressed an interest in experimenting with the hitherto-unproved penicillin treatment for gonorrhea and salpingitis in women. A treatment center was established, but, said the disappointed authorities, "Unfortunately for study, very few cases were discovered for this treatment," and the test had to be completed by civilian agencies with civilian women. Effective standards for this and other treatments were eventually developed and published.

Pregnancy

The WAC pregnancy rate, like that of venereal disease, was never great enough to require any special studies or recommendations from the Office of The Surgeon General. The total rate varied from 0 to 7 per 1,000 per month at different times. Toward the end of the war a noticeable increase occurred, which was attributed to the return of husbands from overseas, their wives' desire to get out of the Army, or "a family was desired before becoming too old." Even so, the final average of 4 per 1,000 per month or 48 per 1,000 per year was considerably less than the rate of 117 per 1,000 per year for civilian women in comparable age groups.[69] Since the WAC rate was computed on the basis of pregnancies, and the civilian rate on actual births, the gap was obviously even greater.

Medical authorities were of the opinion that the lower WAC rate did not indicate that military service was damaging to the fertility of women. It was in fact reported that many married women who had never before been able to become pregnant now

did so, perhaps because of "a routine healthy life, plus the temporary separation from the husband . . . [or] high emotional states while on leave."[70]

As for the necessary medical considerations for treatment of pregnant servicewomen, the Office of The Surgeon General found that these differed from existing provisions for nurses and soldiers' wives only in that most Wacs were enlisted personnel with certain service records to be kept. Thus, soon after the Corps' organization, inquiries were frequent from station hospitals as to whether pregnancy should be entered in the individual's records as incurred "Not in line of duty," and if so, whether time lost should be required to be made good, as it was for certain other "NLD" cases, and also how these decisions would apply to the complications and sequelae of pregnancy, such as hemorrhages, toxemias, abortions, and miscarriages.[71]

In 1944, the Army Regulations were amended to make clear that, while pregnancy would be recorded as "not in line of duty," the individual would not be required to make good lost time, and neither AR 35–1440 nor AW 107 would apply. The same ruling was applied to the sequelae of pregnancy, except for illegal abortions.[72]

A particular problem for medical officers was that of quick and accurate certification of pregnancy in order to expedite discharge. Where delay occurred, protests were frequently received from husband or

---

[69] Med Stat Div SGO analysis. Also see Table 9, Appendix A. Civilian rate for 1944 is from U.S. Bureau of the Census, *Statistical Abstract of the United States: 1948*, Table 69, p. 67; rate for each age group of civilian women has been weighted according to the percent of Wacs who were in that age group.

[70] Menninger, *Psychiatry in a Troubled World*, p. 114.

[71] Ltr cited n. 68.

[72] AR 615–361, 4 Nov 44, sec 22.

parents that miscarriage had been caused by work assigned during that period. One, for example, charged that loss of a much-desired heir was "due entirely to the long hours and constant work, and the fact that as soon as her condition was known she was not discharged." [73] Legal action against the responsible medical or company officers was sometimes threatened. Also, delay was highly undesirable from the public relations viewpoint, since women whose condition had become obvious were seen by the public in near-outgrown uniforms and were invariably assumed to be unmarried. [74]

In Auxiliary days, WAAC Headquarters had requested The Surgeon General's Office to work out a means for applying a laboratory test to ensure very early diagnosis. However, the request was rejected by The Surgeon General as "not practical" because it required a large supply of nonpregnant rabbits and quarters for the same, both being difficult to find. [75] Late in 1944, an addition to Army discharge regulations required that "the diagnosis will be certified as early as possible in pregnancy. . . . This does not preclude observation for a reasonable period of time in which to make certain that the diagnosis is correct." [76] At this time, medical officers were also authorized to use any biological or other tests that they desired, without cost to the patient.

The only further step that Director Hobby was able to obtain to expedite discharge was an administrative one, which prevented transfer of a woman to another station or overseas before a medical officer had completed his observation: "No transfer will be effected if there is reason to suspect the existence of pregnancy until clearance has been obtained from the medical officer responsible for the care of such personnel." [77] Even with this safeguard, Major Craighill noted that in overseas theaters, "Cases of pregnancy which were reported as likely prior to overseas shipment have been sent overseas, even against the protest of the unit commander." [78]

While the incidence of unmarried pregnancy was not regarded as great enough to merit any special studies, Major Craighill and her staff on field visits made incidental notes of the factors that seemed to them to lead unmarried women into misconduct and resulting pregnancy. It was noted that the rate varied surprisingly in detachments within the same area—from only 1 pregnancy in 15 months in one detachment, to 7 times that many in a neighboring one. Several factors were isolated that appeared to have some relationship:

Detachments with a good company commander had low pregnancy rates.

Most pregnancies occurred, oddly enough, where women were subject to the most restrictions, bed check, etc.

Detachments with the least recreation facilities had the most pregnancies.

Length of service was a positive factor, and possibly length of assignment to one station, with resulting fatigue and boredom.

Women a long distance from home were more susceptible.

None of the cases occurred in women who were accustomed to drinking. [79]

[73] Ltr, Mrs. M. T. Kramer to Dir WAC, 2 Jun 44. WDWAC 330.14.

[74] D/F, Dir WAC for ASF Com on Awards, 12 Jun 44, sub: Amendment of AR 615–40. WDWAC 300.3 (6–8–44).

[75] Memo, SGO for Col Catron (Exec WAAC), 24 Mar 43, sub: Test for Pregnancy. WDWAC 702, Hobby file.

[76] AR 615–361, 4 Nov 44.

[77] Ltr, TAG to AAF, AGF, ASF, 7 Oct 44. AGPE-A–WDGAP 200.3 WAC (10–2–44), as printed for AAF fld stations by AAF Ltr 35–148, 20 Oct 44.

[78] Craighill SWPA Rpt.

[79] Memo, Maj Margaret Janeway, MC, Asst Consultant for Women's Health and Welfare, to Col Freer, SGO, 27 Sep 44. SGO Cl 321 WAC.

Psychiatric Problems

Major Craighill upon her appointment found that no action had yet been taken toward the study or analysis of women's psychiatric disorders. Upon visiting training center hospitals, she noted that they "were being filled with inadequate persons whose cases presented a major problem in disposition." At recruiting stations, she found that all types of psychiatric examinations, or none, were being given, with psychiatric rejection rates varying from 3 per 1,000 examined to 89 per 1,000. It was evident that the first figure was too low, since four out of five of all discharges for neuropsychiatric reasons followed quickly after enlistment.[80]

In an attempt to meet the problem, Colonel Hobby requested that psychiatric examiners be given better instructions and that mental hygiene units be set up in WAC training centers, to screen out the worst of the examiners' mistakes before they reached the field, and to salvage recruits with minor difficulties.[81] Little action was taken on the request until the spring of 1944, when Col. William C. Menninger was appointed to head The Surgeon General's Neuropsychiatric Division. Colonel Menninger's attitude toward the problem was expressed in a memorandum to his staff:

I raised quite a little hell about the fact that psychiatrists in the field who were supposed to examine Wacs didn't know about the WAC program in many instances. . . . What did you ever do about it? Let's get going.[82]

By the end of 1944 Colonel Menninger had secured explicit directions to medical examiners, and had also established a pioneer mental hygiene unit at Fort Des Moines under the direction of a Menninger-trained psychiatrist, Maj. Albert Preston, Jr. During the eighteen months of its existence the unit compiled, from 18,000 interviews, extensive statistics on the psychiatric problems of women in military service and the differences of such problems from those of men.[83]

Much of the success of the project was attributed by Major Preston and by the commandant of the training center to the fact that the unit, called the Consultation Service, was not attached to the hospital but worked closely with classification and assignment officers. According to these authorities, women would seldom voluntarily seek out a psychiatrist at a hospital, knowing that his duty was to use their disclosures against them in obtaining their discharge, but when a psychiatrist was available in a separate office, to give advice and counsel on job difficulties and adjustment, women would and did flock to see him.[84]

Such a unit was also found more suitable than the Auxiliary's earlier system of employing a civilian resident counselor, similar to the British system of traveling counselors called The Twelve Elder Sisters. Such counselors, while badly needed in the absence of any others, were found to be handicapped by the danger that their

---

[80] Memo cited n. 29.

[81] (1) Rpt cited n. 2(2). (2) Ltr, Dir WAC to CG 4th SvC, 12 Nov 43, and 3d Ind, SGO to Dir WAC, 8 Mar 44. WDWAC 211 (1944).

[82] (1) Memo, Col Menninger for Maj Berlien, 26 Jun 44. SPMDU, Capt Berlien folder, SGO Hist Div. (2) Memo, Col Menninger to Maj McClure, O Dir WAC, 10 Mar 44. WDWAC 000.7.

[83] All references to psychiatrists' opinions, unless otherwise specified, are from: (1) Preston, History of Psychiatry in the Women's Army Corps, 1946. Copy in SGO and O Dir WAC. (2) Menninger, *Psychiatry in a Troubled World.* Used with the permission of The Macmillan Company, publishers.

[84] Interv with Col Frank U. McCoskrie, Comdt 1st WAC Tng Cen.

advice might be regarded as civilian interference.[85]

The Consultation Service rendered "psychiatric first aid" to Wacs, advised commanding officers and classification officers, and gave mental hygiene lectures. It was discovered that women showed less resentment than men to psychiatric referrals, which Major Preston attributed to "the fact that in women the socially acknowledged and permitted emotionalism is accepted and not judged as a conflict, stigma, or weakness, as in men." About 25 percent of the women treated by the Consultation Service were discharged; the remainder were salvaged with some degree of success.

The success of the unit prompted the WAC's National Civilian Advisory Committee to recommend, at its meetings in October of 1944 and again in February of 1945, that more mental hygiene facilities of the same type be provided, with mobile units to reach those companies too small to merit permanent consultation service. This measure was believed impracticable for either men or women by The Surgeon General, who reported that "this office is unable to see clearly the need for mobile mental hygiene units." [86]

Material collected by the Des Moines unit convinced psychiatrists that "women faced definite psychological factors of significance" in attempting to adjust to military life, where they must "subordinate traditional feminine attitudes and functions." By the "adoption of a severely masculine and identical style of dress," women were believed to have lost one traditional feminine means of "individuality, competition, and gratification," a problem not experienced to a like degree by men, who were customarily more regimented in dress and expressed their individuality by other means. Because of their early training, women were also believed to require a greater effort at adjustment to the lack of privacy in bathing, dressing, and other living arrangements.

Most important, General Menninger believed, was the conflict with public opinion. Inconsistently enough, the approved feminine role was "a passive and dependent one . . . even in our own democracy," while at the same time "the modern girl child in America is not taught to be the passive, dependent individual our culture has conceived of as the normal of adult femininity." This conflict, although existing for all American women, was intensified for Wacs, even as contrasted with the Army Nurse Corps, whose military status might meet public disapproval but whose profession was at least "universally regarded and accepted as a feminine function." On the other hand, military service was believed to offer some psychological compensation through an opportunity for women to release many feminine frustrations and become active, independent individuals.

Psychiatrists also noted that the Corps as a whole faced one special problem because of its volunteer nature. Volunteers, as contrasted to draftees, included more "unsuitable individuals such as the maladjusted and those seeking glamour." They were also apt to feel "some inherent right to have some choice in their assignments, duties, and locations." If improperly assigned they were more likely to be

---

[85] Memo, Well-Being Off for Dir WAC, 3 Jan 44, and atchd file. Personal papers of Dep Dir WAC, in OCMH.

[86] (1) Memo, G–1 for CofS, 13 Oct 44. WDGAP 334, in CofS 324.5 WAC. (2) Min, Conf, 16–18 Feb 45. WD Lib and Hobby files. (3) Comment 4, to memo not found, Dir Per ASF to G–1, 28 May 45. WDWAC 720.

"wondering if they were contributing enough," or contrasting Army jobs with those for which they might more wisely have volunteered elsewhere.[87]

The control group of 18,000, which Colonel Menninger called "a cross-section of WAC's," contained 10,000 patients and only 8,000 normal women interviewed for other purposes. It was therefore not surprising that, as expressed in psychiatric language, almost all volunteers' motives appeared alarming to the layman: those who wished to play an active part in the war effort were displaying signs of "masculine identification"; those who wished to share war's sufferings with the men were termed "masochists," while those who thought the WAC would be enjoyable were "escapists"; and even those carried away by patriotic emotions were probably "hysterical."

Major Preston observed, "It was found that neither emotional, practical, or intellectual motivation was a guarantee for success in the WAC. . . . The greater the opportunity given for fulfillment of the motivation for enlistment, the greater were the gains both personal and military." Thus, a former file clerk who enlisted because of a desire to do outdoor work appeared to be more useful if allowed to work in that capacity than if forced into a sedentary or "feminine" field.

Among patients of the Consultation Service, as contrasted to Wacs generally, Major Preston found "selfishness predominant . . . the hoping to gain something from the Army. They are much more anxious to gain than to give." Many had also hoped that the Army would be more pleasant than their homes, would "make them well," or "make a woman of them." Others hoped that they would be treated harshly, desiring to punish themselves for

some reason. One candid individual observed that "her husband was such a good man and spent so much on her and her family, that she was so happy, that she felt she didn't have the right to be so happy, so she enlisted in the WAC." [88]

A composite picture of "the maladjusted WAC" was compiled by Major Preston as an example to recruiters of a type which could easily be detected and avoided:

She is 26 years of age; she is careless and untidy in her personal appearance. . . . She has completed the tenth grade at an advanced age, stopping school after several failures because she was embarrassed at being older, or was tired of it. After leaving school she usually stayed around home doing nothing, being dependent upon her family financially and emotionally, and then is apt to have had multiple periods of brief employment of an unsatisfactory type, clerking in 5 and 10 stores, being an elevator operator, waitress, grocery clerk, or some similar occupation.

She has had several abdominal operations, perhaps even a complete hysterectomy in her early twenties, or if she has not had such a history, the patient describes several episodes of what she terms as a "nervous breakdown." . . . Most frequently she comes from a broken home and had poor relationships with her step-parents . . . one or more of whom have been in some difficulty, legal or psychiatric. She married impulsively at 18 or 19 and chose a man whom she had known for only a brief period of time. Her first marriage usually ended in divorce and again she married impulsively. She has had a life of constant conflict between herself and her environment. . . . Finally and again impulsively she enlisted in the WAC as an escape from an intolerable home situation, often leaving a dependent child at home to be cared for by her parents. She states that when she was re-

---

[87] See also Dr. Marion Kenworthy, in Rpt of Dir WAC, sub: Gen in All Theaters. WDWAC 333.1 (1945–46).

[88] Min, Conf of NCAC and WAC Stf Dirs, Ft Des Moines, 16–18 Feb 45, pp. 11–18. OCMH.

cruited, she was promised a good job, early promotion, a furlough . . . that her lack of education did not matter and that she would not have to do physical training, drill, classwork. . . . When this utopia has finally exploded, she comes to us again seeking an escape from an environment which is too rigid for her quotient of adaptability.[89]

As compared to a well-adjusted group of women whom he approved for leadership school, Major Preston noted that the disturbed group had twice as many cases of broken homes as did the normal group, four times as many divorces, five times as many abdominal operations, seven times as many "nervous breakdowns." It also had at least twice as many married women.

If any material was collected by the Consultation Service concerning the technical manifestations of neurotic and psychotic traits in women, or the treatment of the same, this did not remain in War Department files.[90] The only exception was the subject of homosexuality, which was investigated briefly because of the apparent public impression that a women's corps was the ideal breeding ground for it. One accuser stated that Fort Oglethorpe was "full of homosexuals and sex maniacs."[91] Director Hobby upon receipt of this allegation at once requested the Army's Inspector General to determine the true situation. The Inspector General complied, but was able to find very little evidence of homosexual practices; the incidence seemed no greater and probably less than in the civilian population.[92]

The only explanation that could be found for such accusations appeared to be the vague and erroneous nature of popular ideas on the subject: any woman who was masculine in appearance or dress, or who did not enjoy men's company, was apt to be singled out for suspicion. Medical authorities pointed out that the true female homosexual was only occasionally of this type, and more often just the opposite. WAC company commanders were especially cautioned to avoid witch-hunting based on such amateur impressions.

The problem was complicated by the fact that emotional demonstrativeness was an accepted trait among women, who thought nothing of kissing or embracing female friends or walking arm-in-arm with them, while medical officers sometimes viewed these traits with the alarm that would have been attached to identical behavior among men. It was also true that the nation, where masculine comradeship was commonplace, had few traditions of friendship between women; a woman who was capable of liking other women was popularly regarded as slightly peculiar. In actual fact, many members of the women's services noted that there was possible a comradeship among women quite similar to that which men had traditionally enjoyed, and which for honesty, loyalty, and freedom from tension and selfish motives often surpassed the average man-woman relationship. Army psychologists encouraged this loyalty of woman to woman, as an aid to growth in maturity and leadership.[93]

Because the problem of homosexuality

<hr>

[89] *Ibid.*

[90] It is understood, from an interview with Major Preston, that he retained these records upon return to civilian employment in the Menninger clinic, and intended to write a book concerning psychiatric problems of women.

[91] Ltr to Dir WAC in WDWAC 330.14 (1944).

[92] Memo, Dir WAC for CG ASF, Att MTD, 26 Aug 44, sub: Course of Instruction on Homosexuality, with 2d Ind, SGO to Dir WAC; IG investigation is described. SGO Cl SPMC 330.14 Ft Oglethorpe.

[93] Pamphlet cited n. 41.

occurred so rarely in the WAC, The Surgeon General believed that no course of instruction in the problem was needed, but merely a reference to it in lectures by the psychiatrist. There were some indications that in a peacetime career service the problem might require more specific action, but that a wartime "citizen's Army" would present no more problem than did the rest of the nation.

Accidents and Injuries

All evidence indicated that the rates of accidents and nonbattle injuries were almost identical for enlisted men and women in the Army. The rates as recorded for a six-month period in 1944 showed 72 injured per 5,000 strength each year for women and 70 for men, while an eighteen-month survey near the end of the war corrected this figure to show a slightly lower rate for women—about 50 per 1,000 per year for women against about 55 for men. No studies were made by The Surgeon General's Office that would have indicated the nature and causes of the accident rate for women.[94]

The only detailed study in this respect was made by the Army Air Forces, which employed a WAC officer in its Ground Safety Division. There was found to be considerable difference in the type, place, and cause of injury for men and women, according to the Air Forces statistics in a limited survey. It appeared that women had less than half as many motor vehicle accidents as men, either on or off the post. When assigned to perform technical work, women also had less than half as many accidents on the job. In mess hall work and kitchen police, women might have more strained backs but had fewer other

injuries, so that total rates were much the same for men and women.

On the other hand, the advantage of women in driving and technical work was evened in the total rate by the fact that when a Wac was placed on some level or generally harmless area she would, a third again as often as men, fall down and acquire a sprain or strain. The Air Forces noted with curiosity that most of women's injuries had no relation to their jobs and that "one of the most common types is falls—falling on stairways and curbings, falls on ice, or stumbling while simply walking on the post. . . . About one half of all the injuries studied thus far are stumbling, tripping, and falling *on the same level.*"

Recurring frequently in reports were falls while entering and alighting from vehicles or jumping from the backs of trucks; falls due to running in barracks, especially on stairways; falls due to jumping off porches or down stairs; slips and falls on freshly mopped floors; back sprains due to improper lifting; slips while climbing on boxes and chairs to reach high places; and tripping, sliding, slipping, or colliding in games and sports. Surveyors were unable fully to account for this Wac propensity, noting only that "the question of why women have such accidents is complicated."

There appeared to be some relation to the fact that a wholly satisfactory women's military shoe had never reached some stations, and that in any case a woman's medium-heeled oxford was obviously less suitable for action than a man's shoe. Even if the proper footgear for sports had been issued, it appeared highly probable that the average woman was also less ac-

---

[94] Rpts cited n. 37(1). Figures are given in a chart that cannot be interpreted exactly.

customed to baseball, football, and other active sports and athletics for which an Army station had facilities.

While the total rates for both men and women appeared relatively tiny, the Air Forces made every effort to lower them, pointing out that the rate showed one injury per 28 women each year, with about 8,000 workdays lost. Women's injuries appeared to be slightly less serious than those for men; for each injury, women remained hospitalized a total of 15.59 days as against 18.19 for men.

Some commanders reported good results from warning signs or posters at spots in halls, stairways, and porches where members were particularly prone to run or jump. On the other hand, civilian studies indicated that such an approach might actually increase accidents by implanting unconscious ideas of a fall in such locations, and that the best preventive measures required psychological assistance to those "accident-prone" individuals who ordinarily accounted for a disproportionate share of accident rates. If any later emergency should require large-scale use of women in more active physical work, some further evaluation of preventive measures seemed useful.[95]

Weight and Diet

The WAC master menu, published by The Quartermaster General in 1944, came too late to prevent what appeared to observers to be a widespread condition of overweight among Wacs, who for two years had eaten Army menus while performing chiefly sedentary jobs. A somewhat inconclusive sample of Wacs in training indicated that 82 percent gained weight, to an average gain of 6 pounds,

during the six weeks of basic training, at the end of which period some 45 percent were overweight; some 42 percent had gained an inch in waist measurement and 59 percent of them in hip measurement.[96]

The Director, perceiving the trend, consulted The Surgeon General's Office in 1944 as to the best means of bringing to Wacs' attention the relationship of weight to health. The result was a War Department circular appearing late in 1944, entitled Weight Control in the WAC. Unfortunately, its chief result, insofar as could be determined, was to bring down on Wacs in the field an unmerciful ribbing from male personnel who found the circular enjoyable reading matter. Any more beneficial results, although possible, had not been reported by the end of the war.[97]

Fatigue and Health Impairment

As the war neared its end, one of the more important medical problems began to be the onset of fatigue, with corresponding adverse effects upon health and efficiency. As distinguished from combat fatigue in men, the problem for women appeared to be just the opposite, caused by unrelieved sedentary work that had long since lost any visible closeness to the war effort.

In order to define the problem, and counteract it if possible, Director Hobby

---

[95] Memo, AAF Ground Safety Div for Air WAC Div, 5 May 45, sub: Study of Injury Experience of AAF Military Women, AFPGS. The survey covered women in six different Air Commands for a 10-month period, May 1944 through February 1945.

[96] Memo, Capt Donna Niles for Dir Tng Div SGO, 12 Apr 44. Folder, Berlien—Reports on Weight, SGO Hist Div.

[97] (1) Memo, Exec WAC to SG, 13 Jun 44. WDWAC 702, 1944. (2) Memo, SGO for G–1, 23 Oct 44. SPMC/DF–W, in WDWAC 720.

in April of 1945 requested The Surgeon General to make a survey of the Factors of Fatigue Influencing the Effectiveness of WAC Personnel.[98] Little was known on the subject. Industrial surveys recognized that there existed "a decreased capacity to work as a result of previous work or activity," but were unable to state exactly what caused it, except that it did not appear to be related to strength, health, injuries, or blood cell count.[99]

Returns from The Surgeon General's survey indicated, as hoped, that the situation had not yet caused any noticeable diminution of WAC efficiency, in the opinion of Army commanders. When asked to what extent their Wacs' efficiency had declined since the beginning of the war, section chiefs replied overwhelmingly that it had not declined but increased. It was estimated by these section chiefs that they would have rated 74 percent of the women excellent or superior when they first began their jobs, and that by the end of the war 85 percent were considered excellent or superior.

On the other hand, the opinion of medical officers and of the women themselves was that fatigue and health impairment were rapidly mounting with each month of service. Almost one half of the women were found to be more nervous than before they enlisted, about one fourth suffered from increased mental depression, and one fourth had more colds. Only negligible numbers were found to be in better health, less nervous, or less depressed, and less than one percent had fewer colds. A startling 40 percent were diagnosed as suffering from "true fatigue," defined as decline in efficiency, loss of interest in outside activity, and listlessness, accompanied by "the weariness which does not respond to

the usual form and amount of relaxation." Medical surveyors did not count as "fatigue" the mere weariness that vanished after proper sleep or recreation.

It was found difficult to isolate the factors that had caused this fatigue. It appeared that some factors which had no perceptible effect in six months or a year began later to exert influence. Thus, it was found that 50- and 60-hour work weeks were the rule, and that many Wacs worked more than 60 hours a week, but these showed no more fatigue than those on an easier schedule. Similarly, the type of messing facilities seemed to make little difference, and the availability of recreation facilities made only slight difference. However, length of service was an important factor, with fatigue growing in direct proportion to months served, until in those with over two years' service, half were fatigued. This factor was puzzling, since the duties were not greatly different from those of which civilian women made lifetime careers without any such adverse results.

The type of housing proved to have a direct relationship to fatigue, with those who slept in rooms being considerably less fatigued than those who were in barracks. The Surgeon General's Office noted, "The rooms [for two to four women] were well-ventilated; the women had similar working hours and were able to choose their own room-mates. This led to similar sleeping habits and congeniality."

The effect of age was the opposite of that expected, as older women were less

---

[98] Following, unless otherwise indicated, is from Memo, Exec SGO for G–1, 19 Dec 45, in compliance with directive 30 Apr 45. SPMC/DF–W, in WDWAC 201.6.

[99] Baetjer, *Women in Industry*.

tired than the younger ones. Women with family responsibilities, particularly those worried about their parents, were slightly more tired. The number of months a woman had gone without a promotion also had some influence, but slight.

One single factor appeared to have more influence on fatigue than all the others combined, and this was occupation—the woman's job and her interest in it. The group of women not interested in their work showed almost twice as much fatigue as those with keen interest. Medical surveyors reported:

The women felt that they had entered the service to do a job; they expected many changes in their lives and many inconveniences, but if they had work they liked and felt was worthwhile, the unpleasant things paled to insignificance.

In every occupational group, this held true. Cooks, who were fatigued in spite of little actual damage to health, were revealed to have least interest in their jobs; drivers were very little fatigued, in spite of heavy work, because they thought their jobs interesting. Greatest fatigue was found among shift workers whose sleeping, eating, and recreational habits were necessarily irregular.

Medical surveyors also attempted to judge the impairment of health by military service, and the causes of damage. As in industry, it was found that poor health and fatigue had no necessary connection, since some women in perfect health were suffering from fatigue and decline in efficiency, whereas others whose service had actually damaged their health still enjoyed their work and felt no fatigue or loss of efficiency. About 20 percent of the Wacs appeared to have suffered some loss of health through military service, including

more days of illness, more visits to sick call, more respiratory and menstrual disorders, and more headaches and nervousness.

Again, a woman's job appeared to be the greatest factor influencing her health. Clerical workers showed the greatest health impairment, due largely to frequent respiratory infection, headaches and nervousness attributable to poor office ventilation, unbroken sedentary work, and eye-straining jobs. Drivers were second in health impairment. Surveyors noted, "The very factor of constant driving which gave drivers a variety of scenes and associates and was functional in decreasing their fatigue was resultant in their menstrual difficulties." Cooks were well below other groups in respiratory infections and sick call visits.

Although the survey came too near the end of the war to effect changes in current personnel, housing, or medical practices, it appeared significant that military service in the type of work of which civilian women made lifelong careers should, after a mere two or three years of military service, produce "true fatigue" in 40 percent and health impairment in 20 percent.

Reconditioning

There was no provision for women in the physical and occupational reconditioning programs provided for men. There were no accommodations for women at convalescent centers. In the last year of the war, the WAC's National Civilian Advisory Committee recommended to The Surgeon General that women be included in the Army's physical and mental reconditioning programs, but the recommendation was never favorably considered, for unspecified reasons presumably related to the expense of facilities for such a small group.[100]

Separation

When WAC demobilization began, the Office of The Surgeon General succeeded in getting the system of a few centralized stations for medical examinations of women, which it had never been possible to get in recruiting. Although men were demobilized through dozens and later hundreds of points, women were processed through only six, where women medical officers made certain that adequate gyne-cological examinations were given. Major Craighill felt that the process was "a most interesting and valuable medical proce-dure in indicating the health of large groups of women of varied social, eco-nomic, and age distribution"—a cross section more varied and therefore more valuable than a similar number of exami-nations of more homogeneous groups in industry and colleges. She recommended, "This mass of information should be more carefully studied by analysts for the future welfare of civilian women."

[100] See n. 2; also Memo, G–1 for CofS, 13 Oct 44, sub: NCAC. WDGAP 334, in CofS 324.5 WAC.

CHAPTER XXXII

Training

The fact that Wacs received military training at all was a departure from the precedent of the Army Nurse Corps, which at the time of the WAAC's establishment did not give any such orientation to new members.[1] In Director Hobby's opinion, the training needs of Wacs were simple: a brief basic military course to inculcate Army customs and discipline more quickly and efficiently than these could be acquired on the job, plus specialist training only for those few women who could not fill an Army job without it. The majority of Wacs, like nurses, possessed a civilian skill that required little modification to be of use to the Army.[2]

General Marshall's original decision to employ womanpower had been strongly influenced by this factor, since a woman with civilian clerical skill could be trained and placed on the job within a month, as against the six months or more required to train a man lacking this civilian skill. This departure from the Army's length of training was affirmed in the WAAC legislation, which stated the Corps' intent to make available to the Army the already-existing "knowledge, skills, and special training of the women of the nation."

From the time of the disbandment of General Faith's Training Command, shortly after the conversion period, responsibility for WAC training rested with the Director of Military Training, Army Service Forces. The WAC representative in this office was Maj. Elizabeth C. Smith, formerly a member of General Faith's staff. Military Training Division's responsibilities to the WAC extended to three major fields: the supervision of WAC training centers, the arrangements for coeducational specialist training at Army schools, and the training of units in the field.[3]

WAC Training Centers

Of these, the largest responsibility concerned the WAC training system. Even after the bestowal of Army status, recruits for Air, Ground, and Service Forces continued to be trained on ASF installations, although some division of this authority had been contemplated by the AAF had the number of trainees warranted. Instead, the failure of expansion plans made further reduction a necessity. At the peak of the expansion plans there were five training centers, six separate administrative schools, and two radio schools. These, with the failure of expansion plans, had four times as much cadre as trainees; the WAC at one time had 148 percent overhead as against the average of 30 percent in male replacement training centers.

---

[1] ANC Hist, p. 321.

[2] (1) Memo, Dir WAAC for CG ASF, 6 Apr 43. Folder, Planning Serv Notes, WAC Plng Serv file. (2) Memo, Dir WAC for Dir Mil Tng ASF, 21 Dec 43. SPWA 353.

[3] Unless otherwise stated, all references are to ASF Hist of WAC Tng.

Reluctantly, steps were taken to close out the additional training centers and specialist schools, which had just been so painfully established. One staff member reported, "At first we were frantic because we didn't have enough cadre to take care of the trainees, and now we didn't know what to do with the cadre." [4] For a time the schools were held intact, and instructors and cadre sat idle, while still-hopeful planners informed them, "If we send overhead personnel to the field, when recruiting picks up again we will have to start all over in the Training Centers." [5]

The first to go was the Fifth WAAC Training Center, with its three prisoner-of-war camps in Arkansas and Louisiana. By June of 1943 the Army in North Africa had taken sufficient prisoners to require the housing. When the Provost Marshal General requested the return of this establishment, the WAAC relinquished it without reluctance. The Fifth Training Center had lasted for three months. [6]

Next to close was the Fourth WAAC Training Center, at Fort Devens, Massachusetts, which had opened in March of 1943. After a hectic six months during which it had four different Army commandants, it was ordered to close in mid-August. [7]

Next, the various separate specialist schools—administrative, radio, and signal—faded from the scene. The three remaining training centers were able to train all specialists except for small numbers in radio and other highly technical training, who could be accommodated in Army schools on a coeducational basis.

When the last proposals for draft legislation were shelved, Director Hobby recommended to General Somervell that the remains of the Second WAC Training Center, at Daytona, be closed, that all remaining specialist schools be closed and their functions consolidated at training centers, and that all leased buildings at Des Moines be given up. This view was endorsed, with some emphasis, by General Gasser of the War Department Manpower Board. [8]

By March of 1944 only the First and Third WAC Training Centers survived, at Fort Des Moines and Fort Oglethorpe respectively. Until after the victory over Japan, the First WAC Training Center was commanded by Col. Frank U. McCoskrie. The Third had a succession of Army commandants, replaced in April of 1944 by Lt. Col. Elizabeth H. Strayhorn, the only woman officer to serve in the capacity of training center commandant.

As Class I installations of a service command, these centers were under the Seventh and Fourth Service Commands respectively. All matters of command, supply, and personnel were prerogatives of the service command and did not come to the attention of Washington agencies except upon inspection or investigation of complaints. Neither the training centers nor their service commands had any control over the content of the course of study, which was prescribed by Military Training Division of the Army Service Forces. Gen-

---

[4] Rpt of 4th WAAC Tng Cen, Ft Devens, in Min, Stf Dirs Conf, Chicago, 15–17 Jun 43. SPWA 337 (6–1–43).

[5] 1st O Florence Jepson, *Ibid.*

[6] Memo, WAAC Hq for Dir Pers ASF, 18 Jun 43, sub: Abandonment of 5th WAAC Tng Cen. SPWA 291.9 (6–18–43) O–O, in SPAP 353' WAC. Release was effective 30 Jun 43.

[7] Hist of 4th WAAC Tng Cen. Looseleaf vol, WAAC Hist files.

[8] Memo, Dir WAC for CG ASF, 16 Nov 43. SPWA 353. Also: (1) Memo, WD Manpower Bd for CofS, 9 Dec 43, WDMB 324.5 WAC; (2) Ltr, DCofS to CG ASF, 11 Dec 43, (incl to above); (3) Ltr, ASF to DCofS, 16 Dec 43, SPTRR 354.1 WAC (12–11–43). OCS 291.9 WAC.

PROCESSING AT TRAINING CENTERS. *Trainees receive a throat check at Fort Des Moines, above. Below, new recruits are given a clothing issue at the warehouse, Daytona Beach.*

eral policy supervision in training matters was exercised by G–3 Division of the General Staff, but since courses of study were considered routine operating matters, they did not often come to the attention of that level, or require the approval of either G–3 or the Director WAC.[9]

Basic Military Training Courses

WAC training centers had at various times from four to six weeks in which to accomplish their mission of transforming a civilian woman into "a physically fit, psychologically well-adjusted, well-disciplined soldier who was informed of the duties, responsibilities, and privileges of women in the Army."[10] This was of course a shorter time than that required to train a man, who had to be prepared also for combat.

The WAC recruit upon arrival at a WAC training center was met by Army trucks, to and from which she carried her own luggage like other recruits. Most commandants insisted upon personally meeting as many incoming shipments as possible, or later talked informally to each company. Recruits straggled in all week from recruiting stations all over the nation, and were grouped into basic classes that began weekly.

WAC training centers, unlike men's, faced the problem of processing these women, issuing clothing, accomplishing immunization, and providing orientation. For men, these functions were generally performed at reception centers, of which there were none for women because of the Corps' small size. After a few hectic classes in which the entire basic course was disrupted by such matters as uniform fittings, illness from shots, and visits to classification offices, the training centers solved the problem by activating reception and stag-

ing companies or battalions, which received the women and completed their processing in the first week, before turning them over to a basic company. Colonel McCoskrie, later noted, "Nearly every Personnel Board visiting this station demanded justification of this organization. Few realized that all of the normal Reception Center processing had to be done somewhere."[11]

For a time the women waiting in the reception battalion appeared to authorities to be ideal candidates for the omnipresent classroom-scrubbing and kitchen police duties, but it was eventually realized that such an abrupt greeting paid poor dividends in the individual's attitude toward the Army, and in the public's opinion. Thereafter such duties were instead given so far as possible to those who had completed training and were awaiting shipment. The weekly strain of receiving new, bewildered, and questioning recruits soon told upon most reception company cadre, and Colonel McCoskrie insisted that insofar as possible "only personnel genuinely interested in people, who have patience and sympathy, tempered with good judgment, should ever be used in connection with either Receiving or Staging."[12]

Although basic companies at times were housed in everything from hotels to tents, the average and the most effective housing proved to be the standard company unit with a central building for orderly room, supply, and dayroom, and a separate barracks for each of the three platoons. Most training authorities agreed that it was better for morale and scheduling to avoid

---

[9] Ltr, CO 3d WAC Tng Cen to Dir WAC, 15 Apr 44, with incl.
[10] ASF Hist of WAC Tng, pp. 62–63.
[11] Ibid., pp. 66–69.
[12] Ibid., pp. 68–70.

huge consolidated facilities and to have separate buildings assigned to each company, and a small separate mess to each one or two companies.[13]

Basic Course Content

There was never any division of opinion among WAC authorities as to the proper minimum course content in basic training, as all agreed that noncombat courses exactly like those used in the first weeks of men's training most quickly oriented women to the Army situation and gave them a common background of experience, even though having little connection with most WAC jobs. The first WAAC basic training program, as devised in Auxiliary days by Colonel Faith, followed quite closely the first four weeks of the men's basic course. The usual subjects were included: military courtesy, Articles of War, Army organization, drill, and so on. Waacs had a somewhat easier training day: for some 91 hours of combat courses there were substituted 20 hours of the necessary reception and processing, plus courses in current events, map reading, and property responsibility. After completion of the first four weeks, men went on to further basic training prescribed by the different chiefs of services, but women, unless they went to specialist school, were at once assigned to the field.[14]

In Auxiliary days, minor changes were continually made in the basic program. At Director Hobby's instigation, there began a major trend in the direction of the adaptation of the course to feminine needs. It was directed that Colonel Faith "keep and stress those subjects which make a definite contribution to the production of women soldiers [and] make all courses deal with

practical problems to the greatest possible extent."[15]

This trend continued for the next ten months, until the end of the WAAC. General Faith, while retaining all noncombat courses given to men, was able under a heavier work week to add a number of courses expected to be of interest to women: Army Administration, dealing with required reports and correspondence; Army Mess, dealing with mess supplies and reports; and Explanation of the Allied Cause. Also, the unfortunate drop in the AGCT level of WAAC recruits early in 1943 for a time required a longer initial indoctrination course to explain Army rules and procedures and the importance of personal hygiene. By August of 1943 these various additions forced extension of the course from four to five weeks.[16]

The trend toward addition of practical courses was abruptly arrested with the end of the WAAC, when control of the training program passed from General Faith to Military Training Division. At this time Director Hobby forwarded to the Director of Military Training a summary of General Faith's conclusions, notably that WAC basic training might be accomplished in four weeks for normal individuals if it consisted primarily of

. . . those developments essential to the performance of military duty which women may be called upon to perform, and those soldierly qualities that distinguish the trained from the untrained enlisted woman. . . . The true objectives of training are factors of growth

---

[13] *Ibid.*, pp. 106–07.
[14] *Ibid.*, p. 64. Also Memo, 28 Aug 42, SPTRU 353.01 (8–27–42), cited in Unit and Replacement Training, by MTD ASF, p. 16. OCMH. See Appendix E, Course Content, for the various courses discussed in this chapter.
[15] ASF Hist of WAC Tng, pp. 65, 71, 72.
[16] *Ibid.*, pp. 74–75, 87.

and development rather than bodies of subject matter to be mastered.[17]

Some six months later the basic course was revised by Military Training Division, and a copy sent to Colonel Hobby with the note that it was now "in conformity with basic training of male personnel."[18] To achieve this conformity, the WAC basic training period was extended to six weeks, or 288 hours, the exact equal of the men's course, in "an effort to insure that WAC personnel had training comparable to that given enlisted men."[19]

Since 153 of the men's 288 hours were devoted to combat subjects, retention of the WAC basics for an equal six weeks allowed a considerable increase in available time. To utilize this time, most courses were increased in length. Wacs now received about five times as much instruction as men in the organization of the Army, four times as much in military courtesy and the Articles of War, three times as much in safety measures, sanitation, social hygiene, first aid, and inspections. Women also got one third again as much drill and physical training as men.[20]

This additional two weeks' extension of the course was never generally agreeable to Army personnel officers. Inasmuch as the educational and aptitude level of enlisted women remained considerably above that of the Army as a whole, their need for more training in basic subjects than men received was questioned. Although the number of weeks involved appeared insignificant, it amounted to a perceptible number of workdays lost to Army stations in the field. Thus, for each WAC unit so detained, the loss caused by the new policy was 4,500 man-days of work; for the Wacs trained from this time onward, the loss was about 1,000,000 man-days.

However, training center medical officers expressed a belief that the extra two weeks would have been justified if the hours that men spent on combat subjects had been used for new courses of comparable value to women, particularly those concerned with mental health, conduct, character, and adjustment to military life. Major Preston of the Consultation Service noted, "The chief defect in the training of women was that . . . apparently no effort was made to adapt the training to their probable needs in the Army."[21] Finally, at the insistence of medical officers, two hours of mental hygiene were included "to assist women in their adjustment to Army life and to relieve tension caused by uncertainty in the beginning of the training period."[22] This two-hour course was the only one, among the 288 basic hours, ever added by Military Training Division to the usual subjects for men.

Although most other courses were, on paper, identical for men and women, it was the Army practice to give different practical application in the different branches of service. Surviving studies did not indicate to what extent, if any, such practical application was found possible for women. The only course that appeared to be materially altered was that on social hygiene, variously called personal hygiene, sex hygiene, and preventive hygiene. Here, the Army Service Forces approved continuation of the WAAC course, and like-

---

[17] Memo cited n. 2(2).

[18] Memo, MTD ASF for Dir WAC, 2 Jul 44. SPTRP 353 WAC, in WDWAC 353. Course was MTP 35–10, WD Mobilization Tng Program for WAC Enl Pers of ASF, 1 Jul 44.

[19] ASF Hist of WAC Tng, p. 77.

[20] *Men:* MTP 21–3, 1 May 44, cited in Unit and Replacement Training, MTD ASF, p. 38. OCMH.
WAC: ASF Hist of WAC Tng, pp. 77–78.

[21] Preston, Hist of Psychiatry in WAC, p 14. See also Memos cited n. 2.

[22] ASF Hist of WAC Tng, p. 99.

CHEMICAL WARFARE TRAINING. *Women remove their gas masks before leaving the chamber, as ordered, thus experiencing the effects of tear gas.*

wise sponsored one of the only two training films produced especially for Wacs— *Strictly Personal*—which was not issued until 1945.[23]

In the subject of military courtesy, Director Hobby recommended development of lectures on "manners for military women," which would give Wacs detailed instructions on how to make the best impression in many specific places where female conduct was the subject of particular comment—trains, hotels, clubs, and public dining places. However, Military Training Division, after a study, concluded that "differences [from men] were so slight that the establishment of new doctrine was unnecessary."[24] Colonel Hobby also requested that this course devote more time to explanation of officer-enlisted relationships, which were a source of particular annoyance to Army commands where they concerned personnel of opposite sexes. Military Training Division replied that such training was not needed and that the regular men's course, concerning the relationships between members of the same sex, "is considered to be sufficient."[25]

The course on care of clothing and equipment was of necessity different concerning some of the items to be arranged and cared for, but otherwise was the same except that "instruction in hair dressing and proper application of cosmetics was presented by demonstrations." The course on interior guard duty differed only in that Wacs were not armed and were required to perform tours of daylight guard duty only. Close order drill likewise differed only in that Wacs were not armed.[26]

For all other courses, basic instructors were without the advantage of being able to pretend that the courses had any practical future usefulness for women. Instruc-

tors in map reading could preface courses with "Now, if you were ever separated from your companions in an enemy-occupied area, and had a map and a compass . . . ," but it was well known that no Wacs during the entire war had ever found themselves in such a predicament. Similarly, it was ordinarily impossible to personalize the studies of chemical warfare, aircraft recognition, field messing, emergency first aid, or even drill, which most Wacs seldom used after leaving training centers.

Nevertheless, the more inappropriate a subject was for women, the more most women appeared to enjoy it. Wacs plunged delightedly through gas chambers, viewed with interest films on battlefield first aid, and hiked willingly about the countryside seeking a given point on a map. Drill was a favorite subject. Spectators noted that "Many spent off-duty time in small groups practicing," and those who missed this instruction during the severe winter months at Des Moines felt themselves defrauded. Training authorities also noted that weekly parades and ceremonies of any sort were very popular with trainees, since they "tended to enhance the feeling of belonging to the military team."[27]

Physical Training

Only one masculine-type course encountered serious objections on the grounds that it might be harmful to women. This was the course in physical education, in which it appeared impossible to please everybody. According to staff

---

[23] TF 8–2093. *Ibid.*, pp. 86–88.

[24] *Ibid.*, p. 79.

[25] Memo, Dir Troop Tng Div MTD ASF for Dir WAC, 6 Sep 44. WDWAC 353.

[26] ASF Hist of WAC Tng, pp. 84, 89.

[27] *Ibid.*, pp. 81–98.

members in Auxiliary days, more time and concern was given to this one course than to any other, with less satisfactory results. Although Wacs did not require hardening for combat, and would perform jobs similar to those they had done in civilian life, some moderate exercise or sports appeared desirable to offset sedentary work.

In determining the necessary measures, the WAC was handicapped by the fact that there apparently flourished in the United States at least two large and mutually hostile schools of physical education, as well as a considerable body of those who felt some antipathy toward any form of required exercise.[28]

For the first training classes, civilian experts were hired, who set up a course based on Swedish-Danish gymnastics. The student body reaction was generally critical. One school of thought asserted that the exercises were "positively harmful to women over the age of 18," [29] while another—that of a group of former physical education teachers—held that they were not strenuous enough, in that "strength-building exercises were not included." [30] The latter opinion prevailed when a group of newly commissioned women officers was assigned to revise the course. These officers immediately substituted a program designed to increase the strength of the women, who, they alleged, "are greatly in need of development. This puts a temporary strain on their physiques, but will pay dividends in the future." [31]

From this time to the end of the war, the WAC physical training program remained in the hands of WAC physical education experts of the strength-building school, whose chief, Capt. Donna Niles, informed a staff conference, "It is as much a part of our responsibility to keep physically fit as to uphold the Code of Conduct." [32] Ac-

cordingly, there was produced a WAC physical training manual, which prescribed a warm-up "cadence series" followed by muscle-building "strength progressions" designed to give women strong muscles in arms and shoulders, abdomen, upper back and neck, and legs. "Progressions" started with simple exercises for these areas and worked up to very difficult ones; they were virtually identical with push-ups and other exercises given men. The manual also contained a number of careful photographic illustrations, which for some cause proved extremely popular with male personnel.[33]

Opinion on the success of the course was as divided as was that of the civilian profession in the United States. Civilian physical educators of the strength-building school highly approved the program. One wrote:

Many of the most prominent women in the physical education profession feel that the WAC has the best physical training program for women of any of the branches of the Armed Forces.[34]

On the other hand, the nationally prominent women of the WAC's Civilian Advisory Committee recommended that more relaxing sports and recreation be

[28] (1) Interv with Lt Col Helen H. Woods, 9 Oct 48. (2) M/R, 26 Jun 43, sub: Program Relative to WAAC Physical Tng. SPWA 353 (9–22–42), 1942.
[29] Memo, 3d O Helen H. Woods for Dir WAAC, 11 Dec 42. SPWA 353 (9–22–42) Phys Tng.
[30] ASF Hist of WAC Tng, pp. 91–92.
[31] Memo, 2d O Donna Niles for 1st O Dorothea A. Coleman, Tng Plans Div WAAC Hq, 13 Jan 43. See also Ltr, Dir Tng, Ft Des Moines, to WAAC Hq, 22 Sep 42. Both in SPWA 353 (9–22–42), 1942.
[32] Min, WAC Stf Dirs Conf, Chicago, 15–17 Jun 43, SPWA 337 (6–1–43).
[33] WDFM 35–20, 15 Jul 43. The manual was reproduced and sold by The Infantry Journal.
[34] Ltr, Mabel Lee (Member, NCAC from University of Nebraska Department of Physical Education for Women) to Dir WAC, 13 Mar 45. WDWAC 720.

substituted for the calisthenics, which in their opinion had little practical value and were sometimes damaging to the health of women over 30.[35]

WAC company officers in the field alleged that exercises were "too strenuous," were less useful for female office workers than ordinary women's sports and recreation would have been, and were at times detrimental to health and job performance.[36] ASF investigations of the problem established only that there was no provable connection between muscular "physical fitness," as developed by these exercises, and the type of physical-mental fitness that kept a woman working efficiently at her desk.

The program was eventually discontinued by all Army stations as not worth the time it required, and replaced by group recreation. Military Training Division directed its continuance in WAC training centers, and the discontinuance of required group sports and recreation, which were sometimes considered a substitute. The second of the two WAC training films, *Figures Don't Lie,* completed in June of 1945, was sponsored to encourage the program. Training centers generally experienced less difficulty with the program than did field stations, since they were able to provide expert instruction to ensure that each woman followed the "progressions" to more difficult exercises only as fast as she could without overexertion.[37]

Basic Technical Courses

Considerable debate took place concerning the value of sending women for technical training immediately following their basic course. Male ASF units automatically continued in training centers

for seven more weeks in various technical specialties, of which cooks', clerks', and drivers' courses were standardized for all branches. The trend of Military Training Division's policy for men was to increase rather than decrease this training time. After complaints that male units with thirteen weeks' total training were still lacking in discipline, sanitary standards, and skills, the ASF lengthened the course to 17 weeks, and later added an additional 13 to 17 weeks of advanced unit training where possible.[38] Much of this training concerned the use of weapons, and other combat subjects.

Neither General Marshall nor Director Hobby favored such extended technical training for women if they could fill an Army job without it. General Marshall pronounced it "a waste of time which we didn't have." While the Auxiliary established short technical courses for clerks, cooks, and drivers, most Waacs who could qualify were assigned to field units without further training.[39]

When WAC training passed to the control of Military Training Division, this trend was reversed in accordance with that division's policy of lengthening training wherever possible. It therefore became the standard practice to route as many Wacs as possible through some specialist course immediately following

---

[35] Min, NCAC Mtg, 16–18 Feb 45, Ft Des Moines. WD Library, also Hobby file. Action refused by Comment 4, ASF to G–1, 28 May 45. WDWAC 720.

[36] See below. "Physical Training of Field Units."

[37] ASF Hist of WAC Tng, p. 95.

[38] Unit and Replacement Training, by MTD ASF, foreword and p. 21.

[39] (1) Except for the errors common in the first months, whereby skilled stenographers inveigled their way into Motor Transport School or were erroneously assigned to fill quotas in Cooks and Bakers School. (2) For the more complete statement of General Marshall's opinion, see Ch. I, p. 20, above.

basic training, thus requiring retention in the training center for another four to twelve weeks, with an average of eight.

However, the Army Air Forces refused to concur in retention of its recruits, preferring on-the-job training similar to that used for civilian women employees. The retention for an average of eight weeks of technical training cost an additional 9,000 man-days of work for each entire unit so detained. For this reason, the AAF forbade WAC training centers to retain more than 5 percent of its Air WAC recruits—often the majority of trainees—for further training after completion of basic.[40]

Although the ASF was thereby prevented from sending many AAF Wacs to its courses, more and more of the Service Forces Wacs came to be routed routinely through the basic technical courses at WAC training centers. Until 1945 The Adjutant General retained power to order assignment of trainees at the end of basic training if they were already qualified in skills urgently needed in the field, but at this time Military Training Division at last, after repeated recommendations, secured the power to determine sufficiency of training. Thereafter it refused to release most ASF recruits for assignment until they had received from four to twelve weeks of technical training. This was late in the war, so that actually only 42,000 of the 140,000 Wacs to go through training centers ever received such technical training, at an estimated cost of about 2,000,000 man-days.[41]

An identical difference of opinion between personnel and training officers existed in the Navy, where training authorities sent even higher percentages of their women to specialists' schools— from 70 to 80 percent—over the objec-

tions of the Bureau of Naval Personnel:

. . . from an economy viewpoint, the Navy got more use from the girls by sending them as rapidly as possible to the jobs where while learning they were contributing something to the going enterprise rather than just being sent to school.[42]

Clerks Course

Most important of these basic technical courses was the administrative or clerks course, which Military Training Division adapted from the regular Army one after discarding the shorter WAAC version. Here student clerks became familiar with Army correspondence and filing systems; with regulations, manuals, and other references; with company records and reports; and with the records used in disciplinary procedures, fiscal accounting, and personnel offices. These subjects were made as practical as possible, although this was difficult in view of the fact that few field commands used identical systems. Material was deliberately chosen that did not concern the WAC. Thus, Wacs practiced activating and managing an infantry company, and studied Army organization and chain of command with relation to groups, armies, divisions, regiments, and battalions. The Army Ground Forces systems were used in exercises in personnel accounting. Although the practical usefulness of this appeared doubtful to trainees, 97 percent of whom would not be assigned to the AGF, WAC instructors nevertheless succeeded in arousing interest by the use of many ingenious training aids and mock-up rooms, in which Wacs acted out

[40] See AAF WAC Hist, Ch. 18. Also AAF Ltr, 50–47, 31 Jul 44.
[41] ASF Hist of WAC Tng, pp. 343 and 348–49.
[42] WAVES Hist, p. 100.

the parts of cadre for combat infantry companies.[43]

No records were retained of the total number of Wacs who attended clerks courses, although records of individual classes indicated that this might have been around 300 monthly—possibly one tenth of the month's basic graduates. No comparative studies were made that would conclusively determine the relative success of the school-trained and the job-trained WAC clerks. The Consultation Service at Des Moines noted many referrals from this group, and observed:

There were numerous psychological handicaps to the training: The attitude that attendance was an unnecessary delay from a field assignment; many women enlisted to avoid the monotony of their civilian stenographic jobs . . . women already trained as stenographers were required to complete the same course as those inexperienced. This . . . could have been avoided by early and consistent motivation for Clerks training and . . . by separation of the training groups.[44]

Typing Course

Less difference of opinion existed concerning the four-week typing course, which was given independently to Air Forces recruits, and as part of the clerks course for others. This consisted chiefly of 80 hours of touch-typing, a subject which seemed universally useful to Wacs, but which could not be given prior to the summer of 1943 because of the inability of training centers to obtain typewriters. The subject proved more and more essential as skilled women became harder to recruit and as Army requisitions for WAC typists grew heavier; it was approved even by the AAF for those of its nontyping recruits who showed clerical aptitude. It was admittedly impossible in 80 hours to bring a

beginner to the expert typist speed of 45 words per minute, but the course succeeded in teaching beginners a speed sufficient for typing cards and other records—18 words per minute—as well as increasing by almost the same amount the typing speed of women who could already type to some extent.

WAC instructors who had formerly operated civilian typing schools considered the concentrated military course more successful than most civilian courses, even though it was handicapped by inadequate equipment, by the frequent absence of trainees for kitchen police, by assignment of inept beginners, and by the mixture in one class of women with typing speeds ranging from 0 to 76 words per minute. Nevertheless, instructors stated:

. . . training classes had distinct advantages over civilian teaching: there were no discipline problems; the instructor had the stimulation which comes from teaching mature women conscious of the urgency of the job and . . . the women applied themselves with a zeal rarely seen in civilian classes.[45]

Cooks Course

Training center authorities noted that "assignment to the Cooks' Course was not popular with the trainees except in isolated instances."[46] Women regarded the assignment as menial; many women who had previous cooking or dietary experience had enlisted to escape from their occupation. High sick call rates and minor psy-

---

[43] ASF Hist of WAC Tng, pp. 125–52.

[44] (1) Ibid., Table VI: 19 classes of about 150 per month at Des Moines alone. (2) Quotation from Preston, Hist of Psychiatry in WAC, p. 23.

[45] ASF Hist of WAC Tng, p. 31.

[46] Cooks Course is described in ASF Hist of WAC Tng, pp. 155–63. See also Preston, Hist of Psychiatry in WAC, p. 18.

chiatric casualties resulted. WAC instructors were of the opinion that many women actually liked to cook but resented the low social status and lack of advancement, and the fact that training center officers at times employed enlisted specialists for food service at officers' off-duty social affairs.[47]

Instructors were unable to discover any easy rule for selecting successful WAC cooks. Some civilian cooks made good Army cooks, and some did not, while many women with no previous experience proved very efficient. Former restaurant cooks were usually more of a problem than beginners, since they had to forget previous work habits and learn new ideas of orderliness and cleanliness. Women with college training in home economics were likewise found to have "very little knowledge of cooking," although assignable elsewhere as experts in some specialized dietary field.

School authorities also lamented the tendency of assignment officers to consider the cooks course a haven for women of low aptitude. These, although assigned in large numbers, could seldom be made into satisfactory cooks. In addition, their presence lent the course a certain stigma which made it unpopular with more capable women, as reflected in a favorite song:

> I am the girl with the low I.Q.
> I can prepare a good menu
> But you do not need brains to make a stew
> So I'll be at home on the range.[48]

As a matter of fact, women with low AGCT scores seldom could qualify as cook, baker, or mess sergeant, which in an Army mess demanded considerable alertness.

In 1944, the WAC cooks course was lengthened by Military Training Division from the six weeks used in Auxiliary days to the eight weeks needed for men. Most "instruction," as in men's schools, consisted in preparation of food for training center messes; this was supplemented, between meals, by lectures and demonstrations in the mess halls. Army films and film strips were found valuable, although not all were suitable for the smaller scale of operation of WAC unit messes.[49]

Motor Vehicle Operators Course

Most popular of the technical courses offered at WAC training centers was drivers' training, although, because of the relatively smaller demand for WAC drivers, only 3,000 women were ever trained at Fort Des Moines, and lesser numbers at other centers. The original six-week Auxiliary course was lengthened to the men's eight-week course by Military Training Division.

It was reported that "devices for driver-selection and methods of instruction were substantially the same as those used throughout the Army."[50] The course included not only vehicle operation, but first and second echelon maintenance, repair and lubrication, convoy operation, vehicle recovery, blackout driving, and motor pool administration. Maintenance above the second echelon was not given Wacs, although a third-echelon course had been prepared before recruiting difficulties ended possibilities of replacing many men in such work.

---

[47] Interv with Miss Margaret E. Tackley, former director of the school, Lt USA Res, OCMH, 4 Mar 49.

[48] *WAAC Parodies,* WAAC Publications Office, Ft. Des Moines, May 1943. Copy in OCMH.

[49] Course established by MTP 35–10, 1 Jul 44.

[50] Course discussed in ASF Hist of WAC Tng, pp. 164–84. Exact attendance not given. Course established by MTP 35–10, 1 Jul 44.

MEMBER OF THE COOKS COURSE *prepares cake batter in a training center mess hall, January 1943.*

Student drivers were supposed to score at least a Grade III (average) in general aptitude, and motor transport instructors reported:

... difficulty was experienced all through the history of Motor Transport in the effort to establish the fact that people with low AGCT scores would not make dependable drivers. Hardly any Army job calls for quicker thinking, more instantaneous adjustments, cooler nerves—yet the section was sent grade IV's and V's.[51]

From the beginning the course operated successfully in spite of this and other handicaps. Training aids could seldom be obtained, but many ingenious ones were constructed by the faculty. The Fort Des Moines school reported that, since engines for instruction were not issued it, several were "assembled in their entirety from miscellaneous parts retrieved from the dump, salvage, or other unidentified sources."

WAC instructors went to the Army school at Camp Holabird, and took over all teaching almost immediately. WAC trainees felt themselves handicapped by lack of a proper uniform for women. The WAC chief of the motor transport school went in person to Washington to plead with ASF for ordinary slacks and shirts in summer, and lined trousers and flannel shirts in winter, as well as a brimless cap that would not blow off. She received promises of such items, but reported later that "nothing was ever realized from such promises."[52] The appearance of women drivers in their clumsy and unbecoming coveralls led, in training authorities' opinions, to "the development of marked masculine traits and unwarranted criticism of the women drivers because of their masculine uniforms, appearance, and mannerisms."[53]

All of the men's motor transport courses appeared useful and practical to the Wacs with the exception of those on blackout driving and decontamination of gassed vehicles, which hours could, they felt, have been better spent on other subjects. Nevertheless, women were found to be not averse to driving the most inappropriate vehicles they could obtain, including Army tanks. They also enjoyed "bug hunting" in the engine laboratory, assembly of dismantled engines, convoy driving, and the recovery of mired vehicles; even Des Moines' icy winters were approved for providing the opportunity to rescue stalled trucks.

Contrary to pessimistic expectations, the Des Moines motor transport students drove 1,500,000 miles without a traffic accident, and were awarded a safety plaque by grateful Des Moines citizens. This course was called by the Consultation Service:

... one of the most satisfactory basic technical training schools, and the one which was most desired among trainees of all degrees of intelligence and all variety of occupations. ... The low sick call rate, the minimum psychiatric referrals, the lack of serious menstrual difficulties and of fatigue ... illustrates the advantage of assignments fulfilling motivation for enlistment.[54]

Medical Technicians Training

For a brief period in 1945 there existed at Fort Oglethorpe the fourth and last type of basic technical course to be given at WAC training centers: that for medical

---

[51] Maj Eleanor Garber, in ASF Hist of WAC Tng, p. 177.
[52] *Ibid.*
[53] Preston, Hist of Psychiatry in WAC, p. 28.
[54] *Ibid.*

MOTOR TRANSPORT TRAINING. *Students standing in formation alongside recon-naissance command cars, ½-ton pick-up trucks, and carryall trucks.*

and surgical technicians and medical clerks. Wacs had long received such training on a coeducational basis at Army medical schools, where they had completed men's courses successfully. The WAC course was merely a transplantation of these courses to Fort Oglethorpe in order to instruct centrally the thousands of recruits obtained by the General Hospital Campaign in the spring of 1945.

At the instigation of the War Department, and because of the immediate need for technicians, Military Training Division in this one instance reversed its usual policy and shortened rather than lengthened the training time. Basic training was reduced from six to four and a half weeks, and the men's twelve-week medical technicians course was given in six weeks.[55] Nevertheless, the training was pronounced highly successful by using agencies, and The Surgeon General informed training

authorities that the manner of performance of its graduates was "admirable."[56]

Miscellaneous Courses

In addition to the regular basic military training and basic technical courses, WAC training centers from time to time gave various minor courses to meet particular needs or emergencies. Of these, perhaps the most significant were the Opportunity School and its successor, the Special Training Unit. These illustrated again the fact that unskilled women of low aptitude were a particular problem to the Army, especially since they could not be trained for heavy labor as could men in like categories.

Opportunity School

Although recruiting standards recognized this difference and kept the Wac

---

[55] Course described in ASF Hist of WAC Tng, pp. 185–97. Subjects, (C–1 to MTP 35–10).

[56] SPMCT, 13 Sep 45, cited in ASF Hist of WAC Tng, p. 190.

average intelligence and skill above men's, small but embarrassing numbers of inept women continued to arrive at training centers. Training centers found that such women were literally unassignable to fill any Army requisitions for women. For the first year this misfortune was ignored and the women were shipped out to hapless stations in the field, which quickly protested. Since such women could not ordinarily be discharged under Army Regulations based on men's standards of ineptness, an opportunity school was eventually established at Fort Des Moines, to which field stations were permitted to ship back their unassignables. Some 552 women were shipped back under this authority, about half of whom were Negroes.[57]

These women spent half a day in formal training and the other half in on-the-job training. The formal instruction put great emphasis on military courtesy, drill, and a locally devised course called Manners for Military Women, of which this personnel seemed in visible need. In the apprenticeship period attempts were made to train women as hospital orderlies, messengers, supply clerks, assistant librarians, mimeograph machine operators and in many other jobs.

Under this intensive grooming, 70 percent of the students qualified in various skills, chiefly in hospital work, as mail clerks and orderlies, as machine operators, messengers, photographic technicians, and stock clerks and checkers. Some qualified in even higher specialties, such as radio operator. Under the apprenticeship system of actual training, many reported themselves "crazy about their work," and only some 64 women had to be discharged. Nevertheless, an additional and expensive three months beyond basic training, and the help of the most expert instructors and

cadre, were required to accomplish this result. The Consultation Service noted that "a number of the women who successfully completed the course required administrative separation at a later date," and concluded that "the results of the school did not justify its existence."[58]

Special Training Unit

Opportunity School was succeeded, as soon as Military Training Division took control, by the Special Training Unit, which did not attempt to give women usable skills, but merely to assist through basic training those with educational deficiencies.[59] The course was exactly like that of men's special training units, except that weapons training was omitted. It emphasized reading, writing, arithmetic and all military subjects, including even tent pitching and knots and lashings.

Since the WAC enlistment standards, unlike the Army's, now included an educational requirement, few Wacs had real educational deficiencies, and much difficulty was experienced when basic companies sent this unit disciplinary problems and maladjusted women who did not lack education. Some 426 women were eventually trained by this unit—a tiny fraction of the Corps, which testified to the average efficiency of recruiters. Of these, some 80 percent were able to return to basic training, but no records of their later assignability were maintained. The Consultation Service noted:

The greatest problem of the women with borderline intelligence is their utilization on

---

[57] Opportunity School discussed: ASF Hist of WAC Tng, pp. 200–18. Established: ASF Cir 88, 24 Sep 43.

[58] Preston, Hist of Psychiatry in WAC, p. 20.

[59] ASF Hist of WAC Tng, pp. 219–28. Established by ASF Cir 76, 15 Mar 44. Opportunity School was ended by ASF Cir 147, 19 Mar 44.

jobs. There were never a sufficient number of routine and simple tasks to which these women could be assigned. When assigned to a specialist school or jobs above their intellectual level of comprehension and performance, frequent psychosomatic complaints developed which rendered them unfit for efficient duty or created behavior problems and AWOLS. . . . In a volunteer organization such as the WAC, the problem of women with low intelligence should not exist.[60]

WAC Officer Candidate School

The WAC officer candidate school continued to specialize in the production of officers for WAC troop administration, since it would have been impossible to duplicate the training of officers in the dozen or more arms and services to which Wac officers might be assigned. The conduct and policy of the WAC officer candidate school were, from the time of the establishment of the WAC, of minor importance to the Corps, since in its entire two years of existence the WAC school was allowed to receive only 750 candidates, in contrast to the 5,675 that had been received in only one year by the WAAC school. Later improvements were therefore of little effect upon Corps leadership. It could be said of the WAC, as of other Army Service Forces officer candidate schools, "It was not until the OCS were considerably past the peak of their greatest usefulness that they reached their highest development as training agencies."[61]

Actually, in the case of the WAC, there were few noteworthy new developments. The greatest change was in length; as soon as the ASF took charge of the school in 1943, it extended the course from the previous eight weeks to three months, since men's officer candidate courses averaged about this length. Director Hobby's office

was not consulted about either the extension or the new curriculum, but was informed of its content.[62]

The extension to three months made a greatly increased number of hours available, since women could not be given subjects such as weapons training and combat orientation. Most of these extra hours were used on conventional subjects: twice as much time as the Auxiliary had given to map reading, defense against air attack, military courtesy, and physical training; four times as much in medical instruction; five times as much in organization of the army. Several new courses were added: some, like signal communications, because they were required for men, and others, such as duties of a staff officer, in consideration of the wider scope of officer employment in the WAC.

Wacs now received more hours of army organization than The Adjutant General's officer candidates, more mess management than The Quartermaster General's, and more physical training than the Medical Administrative Corps. In general, every noncombat course directed for men's schools was also added to the WAC course, with the sole and inexplicable omission of Defense Against Paratroops. The only courses in the 578 hours that had no parallel in men's courses were 6 hours devoted to public relations and 5 to recruiting, in

---

[60] Preston, Hist of Psychiatry in WAC, p. 25–27.

[61] All OCS references unless otherwise stated from: (1) ASF Hist of Mil Tng, Officer Candidate Training, MTD ASF. OCMH. Hereafter cited as ASF Hist of OCT. (2) ASF Hist of WAC Tng, pp. 254–98, and Tables XV and XVII, which do not agree exactly. Quotation from pp. 45–46. (3) Figures from Statistical Sec, OCMH.

[62] (1) Memo, Asst Dir MTD ASF for Dir WAC, 11 Nov 44. SPTRP 352.11 WAC, in WDWAC 352. (2) Memo, Dir Troop Tng Div MTD ASF for Dir WAC, 5 Dec 44. SPTRP 352.11 WAC, in WDWAC 352.

recognition of the fact that the WAC had to recruit instead of draft its personnel.

Courses that aimed at developing leadership and the ability to manage a group were in a minority. Only 79 of the 578 hours could even remotely be considered to fall in this category, and even of these, many were more concerned with teaching the correct paper work than with the psychology of leadership. WAC candidates had more hours in map reading than in duties of an officer; three times as many hours in courts and boards as in leadership; five times as many in drill as in morale.

Consultants at the school observed:

In Officer Candidate Schools, the emphasis on the transmission of information could have been changed to an emphasis on developing the characteristics and attitude of an officer, and thus many of the deficiencies of leadership might have been averted. . . .[63]

This deficiency was of course not peculiar to WAC schools, and Service Forces historians later noted of men's schools, "The courses most frequently omitted from curricula were those concerned with morale, management, and training of men."[64]

There was considerable effort by instructors to make all officer candidate courses practical, but this was seldom possible except in the small group of leadership courses, where lively student discussion of actual problems took place. Material of other subjects was less easy to adapt, typical difficult subjects being organization of the field army and other tactical groups, malaria control, map and compass exercises, radio and pigeon communication, gas identification, camouflage, and others. In some subjects, such as supply, it was found that practical experience was a handicap. In order not to confuse the standard lecture, it was necessary to suppress student discussion of the varying procedures actually used by commands in the field in which many officer candidates had worked as enlisted women.

Instructors' efforts to make courses practical were handicapped also by the fact that most instructors had never been out of the training center, a problem common to other ASF officer candidate schools, of which it was said:

Most of the instructors were recent OCS graduates often totally lacking in field experience. . . . Even those in charge were too often those who had a background of school experience and training instead of service in the field or on-the-job training. . . . Later, when rotation policies were put into effect, . . . policy-making personnel [were seldom replaced].[65]

Intermediate Officers' School (IOS)

Shortly before the conversion to Army status, Director Hobby attempted to put into effect a plan for improving the standards of WAAC leadership by establishing an advanced officer training school modeled on the British system, to which the most capable officers would be returned for preparation for higher jobs.[66] Unfortunately, the Intermediate Officers' School upon establishment coincided with the growth of the officers' pool, and was used to provide occupation for the unassigned pool officers. Attendance at IOS, instead of an honor, therefore came to be considered a blot upon an officer's record. General Faith tried to convince the inmates that instruction such as Advanced

[63] Preston, Hist of Psychiatry in WAC, pp. 13–14.

[64] ASF Hist of OCT, pp. 45–46.

[65] *Ibid.*, p. 93.

[66] Min, Stf Dirs Conf, Chicago, 15–17 Jun 43. SPWA 337 (6–1–43). Also Memo, WAAC Hq for CofAdm Serv, 7 May 43. SPWA 314.8 (1–7–43)(1) sec 1.

Mapreading was valuable, saying, "Some of our folks are going to far places and you wouldn't get far on the instruction you have previously received in Mapreading." [67] However, as months passed, and the IOS was succeeded by the Advanced IOS and other endless instruction, the training center abandoned all pretense of giving the women any useful training while they waited. Army Service Forces authorities admitted later that the various courses, which were devised to kill time, "produced no significant training result and met no training need," and also that the "inexperience of instructor personnel rendered the training practically valueless." [68]

Leadership Courses for Enlisted Women

The absence of a course for the training of enlisted leaders was a serious omission in the opinion of some training center authorities, who believed that the daily adjustments of a member's life were as often in the hands of the company cadre as of the officers. A school to train cadre had not been originally established in the erroneous belief that lower-rating WAAC officer candidates would be used as cadre until their deferred commissioning. When immediate commissions were granted all graduates, the various training centers began belated efforts to set up cadre schools, but these were scattered and un-co-ordinated. Finally, in June of 1944, ASF headquarters directed both men's and WAC training centers to set up such courses. [69]

By this time only limited progress was possible. Most companies in the field and in the training center already had their cadre, who had too much rank to be reassigned elsewhere. Station-and-job recruits,

who constituted the bulk of trainees, could not be withdrawn for these assignments, and the available general service recruits were few and often unqualified. The school therefore, in its fourteen months of existence, produced only 500 graduates, most of whom were used only in training centers.

Nevertheless, training authorities pronounced the course a notable success. Colonel McCoskrie stated that, of all the activities at Fort Des Moines, he was most proud of the development of noncommissioned leaders. Outstanding women to attend this course were selected toward the end of basic training and were referred to the Consultation Service, where they were interviewed by the psychiatrist to determine emotional stability and maturity, and were given personality inventory tests. Selected women were then assigned to training under officers who had demonstrated outstanding leadership. Sleeve and pocket patches marked "Leadership" were worn and proved to be an excellent morale factor in developing pride in the course.

Military Training Division left the curriculum to the training center, and the result was an eight-week course of more practical application than anything else at the center. Although only 12 of the 96 lecture hours concerned leadership, map reading was conspicuously absent, and other courses concerned the everyday cadre duties of administration, supply, drill, and instruction. Two weeks of theory were followed by six weeks of supervised work as acting cadre, with careful plans,

[67] *Ibid.*

[68] ASF Hist of WAC Tng, pp. 199, 251.

[69] (1) Preston, Hist of Psychiatry in WAC, p. 21–22. (2) Interv, Col McCoskrie, Comdt, Ft Des Moines, 29 Jan 46. (3) ASF Hist of WAC Tng, pp. 243–49. (4) See Cadre Training Course, Appendix E.

discussions, and critiques. The Consultation Service's psychiatric workers lectured on adjustment problems to be expected in companies, and discussed the individual cases that arose.

The success of the school and its graduates, in the opinion of training center authorities, more than justified its existence. Moreover, officers pointed to the trainees' "marked changes in qualities of leadership" as proof that leadership could actually be taught. Had such a course been perfected before all field units had been shipped out, instead of after, its value to the efficiency of stations in the field apparently would have been considerable.

Testing Procedures

Very few reliable statistics were ever compiled as to the performance of women on Army tests and the applicability of the tests to women. It was the preliminary opinion of The Adjutant General's testing experts that women probably did not score as well on the Army General Classification Test as did men of the same actual intelligence, since the test had been designed for and validated with men. They therefore recommended the use in training centers of the Women's Classification Test (WCT), then used in recruiting stations, which was especially designed for women and on which the scores were slightly higher.

However, the Office of the Director WAC was not able to see any significant injustice to women in the Army test—especially since Wacs were highly selected and most groups exceeded the men's average in spite of any handicap. Had women of all types been drafted as men were, the question might have assumed more importance. The ASF WAC Officer also noted that the AGCT had more significance and

was more readily understood by personnel officers on Army stations. The use of the men's AGCT was therefore continued in classification procedures at training centers.

Another test developed for early recruiting—the Mental Alertness Test (MAT)—did not correlate too highly with later success. The Clerical Aptitude Test seemed only of moderate value in predicting women's success on clerical jobs; the Radio Operators Aptitude Test was found by training centers to be very poor when applied to women; the Driver Aptitude Test, on the other hand, had high accuracy.[70]

Evaluation of Effectiveness of Training

Very few field comments of any sort were recorded as to the adequacy or inadequacy of WAC school training. The fact that a Wac had received several times the number of hours in many basic subjects that a man received had practically insured that she would be at least as well indoctrinated. Since a woman's survival in the field did not so visibly depend upon the adequacy of her training as did a combat soldier's, the matter was not in any case unduly conspicuous. Most field commendations concerned merely the women's neatness and military bearing; most complaints related only to administrative matters such as supply, records, and classification.

[70] In SPWA 201.6 Mental Alertness Test (10–11–43): (1) Memo, TAG for Dir WAC, 17 Aug 43. (2) Memo, TAG for Dir WAC, 16 Dec 43. (3) Memo, Dep Dir for Dir WAC, 13 Jan 44. The WCT and GCT seemed about equal in predicting success in basic, OCS, and specialist schools; the MAT not so good. The R–1, a short test, seemed as good as the WCT–2 (85 percent received same disposition), and was therefore adopted for recruiting stations as a timesaver. The WCT and MAT–2 were reserved for retests in cases where recruit failure seemed due to fright.

Concerning the academic courses themselves, the only notable field objection was that they had seldom reflected the experience gained by WAC units at Army stations in the field. As a result of lack of rotation, training center instructors and cadre were generally attempting to prepare recruits for a field service of which they themselves had no knowledge.

Problem of Rotation

The problem of rotation appeared to be even more difficult than that experienced by men's training centers, in that the numbers of WAC field units in the Fourth and Seventh Service Commands were insufficient to manage normal rotation of Wacs from field to training center. When training centers appealed to other commands for an exchange, they discovered with regret that the only ones offered were those who

. . . had not been successful at previous assignments . . . this condition was generally recognized by WAC officers, so that an assignment "back to the Training Center" carried a certain stigma and was dreaded by most officers.[71]

Training center authorities recommended:

A sound officer rotation policy should contemplate reassignment of old, experienced officers prior to the time that they go stale on the job; this period varies with the individual, generally between 12 and 30 months.[72]

When visiting instructors could be obtained who illustrated precepts with actual experiences, trainee interest was found to be much stimulated.

There was similarly noted a lack of information in training courses as to the latest War Department directives and policies concerning the WAC, particularly in matters of recruiting. The attenuated channel of communication for training centers led from service command to The Adjutant General to Military Training Division. Somewhere along the line blockage occurred; Colonel Strayhorn was of the opinion that it was "on the Washington level."[73] The WAC was not the only organization to note a lack of liaison between Military Training Division and the chief of an arm or service. For the Judge Advocate General and other services, the view was also expressed that training schools should have been Class II installations:

The final responsibility for the competence of the product lay not in the Service Command but at the door of the Chief of Service or Division Director. Direct control over the personnel engaged in this phase of training should have accompanied this responsibility.[74]

Medical Evaluation

A more serious criticism of the WAC training system was offered early in the spring of 1944 by The Surgeon General, who raised the question of whether the whole system of military training patterned on that for men was too strenuous for women. At this time, a few months before Colonel Strayhorn's appointment at Fort Oglethorpe, the incidence of colds and influenza among women at that installation was almost double that of the Fourth Service Command as a whole.

---

[71] (1) ASF Hist of WAC Tng, p. 353; also see p. 114. (2) Hist of Ft Des Moines, 1 Jan–30 Jun 45. WD Lib, 000.4 Historical.

[72] ASF Hist of WAC Tng, p. 113.

[73] Ibid., pp. 102–03.

[74] ASF Hist of OCT.

The Surgeon General reported that both training centers were "noting a high incidence of physical disability" and that 52 percent of all disability discharges that ever occurred in the WAC occurred in the first three months of a recruit's service. Training centers blamed this fact entirely on poor screening by recruiters, but The Surgeon General inclined to the view that some part of the responsibility belonged to the WAC basic training program. Psychiatric problems and questions of mental adjustment were reported by medical inspectors to be frequent at both training centers, and the injury rate was almost double that of men's training centers.

As a result, The Surgeon General undertook a survey called "Study of the WAC Basic Training Program in Relation to the Physical Fitness of Women." Since the WAC admitted women up to 50 years of age, enlisted chiefly for sedentary jobs, it appeared possible that the whole theory of giving women a training course was unsuitable and wasteful of personnel, especially since women did not require hardening for combat.[75] At the same time the Fourth Service Command's inspector general made a similar investigation, prompted by complaints from women's relatives and from Congress. As one irate relative put it, "It is the consensus of the civilian population that the basic training given a WAC should be only schooling for a particular job."[76]

Director Hobby, while favoring a basic training course, was also inclined to believe that no training should be given which was so strenuous as to cause a breakdown and discharge that the Army job itself would not have caused. In late 1943 she informed Military Training Division that one of the criteria of successful basic training of Wacs should be that "the indi-

vidual has not become physically unfit for military duty."[77]

In all of the resulting investigations, reports confirmed the fact that an excessive number of breakdowns had resulted from the training period. On the other hand, there was no evidence that these breakdowns had any provable connection with the noncombat basic training subjects, most of which were not strenuous. Instead, disability was almost invariably traced to administrative practices or conditions not at all intrinsic in the basic course.

Of these, mismanagement of fatigue duties appeared prominent. In some cases the women's "basic training" had apparently consisted less of the prescribed courses than of scrubbing and cleaning the various classrooms and offices of the headquarters, kitchen police in officers', consolidated, and unit messes, furnace firing, window washing, and most of the heavy labor about the training installation. Women had usually proved unsuccessful in permanent assignments to such heavy duties at field stations, and it appeared no reflection upon the academic training that women of 50 previously employed in desk jobs proved unable to complete classwork while carrying the additional load of training center upkeep.

The inspector general reported that no precautions had been taken to keep the length and nature of fatigue duties within a woman's strength. In a typical case a 25-hour detail of furnace firing was immediately followed, without time for sleep, by

---

[75] All in file of SGO Hist Div, unnumbered folders marked Capt Berlien: (1) Memos, Craighill for Bliss, 11 and 25 Mar 44. (2) M/R, SGO Med Stat Div, 6 Apr 44.

[76] Ltr, Fred C. Haase to Dir WAC, 25 Mar 44, with Ind, Dir WAC to CG ASF, 1 Apr 44, and Rpt, IG 4th SvC to CG 4th SvC atchd. WDWAC 330.14.

[77] Memo cited n. 2(2).

a 14-hour kitchen police detail during which heavy lifting and scrubbing had been continuous, resulting in hospitalization and discharge of a skilled recruit. As a result, the inspector general recommended that commandants take steps to see that continuous arduous duties were not assigned during the entire fourteen hours of kitchen police, and that the scheduling of fatigue details was done so as to insure rotation from heavier to lighter duties.[78]

In addition, some of the disability discharges seemed directly traceable to deficiencies in clothing and housing which also had no necessary relation to the basic course as such. At Fort Oglethorpe in January and February of 1944, the inspector general reported that new arrivals had been housed for several days in poorly heated barracks, and had walked through rain and mud to class, mess, and the outside latrines before receiving any issue of protective military clothing and footgear. Even at the end of basic training, the inspector general noted:

A check on one group of 30 recruits showed that no one member had received all the clothing allowed. . . . The supply situation had existed for several months with no apparent attempt by the Commandant to remedy it.[79]

By contrast, Fort Des Moines, which had steam-heated brick buildings, indoor latrines, and a better-established clothing supply, reported a rate of respiratory disorders only 60 percent of the service command rate, as against twice the service command rate at Fort Oglethorpe. This again offered proof that the military training itself had not caused the excessive illness.

As a result, neither The Inspector General nor The Surgeon General made any recommendation to abolish the basic course as such, but there appeared to be a definite need in administrative matters for more consideration of women's lesser physical strength, greater enlistment age, and previous sedentary occupations. The Inspector General also required the Atlanta Depot to increase the supply of clothing to Fort Oglethorpe. In April of 1944 the Army Service Forces also published detailed instructions for the fitting, alteration, and inspection of women's clothing.[80]

In the same month, from her new office in G–1 Division, Colonel Hobby secured the appointment of Colonel Strayhorn as commandant of Fort Oglethorpe. For the last year of the war, no further question was raised concerning the value of a military indoctrination course for women, although medical inspectors continued to point out recurring failures to recognize the limitations of women's physical capacity in fatigue details.

The Army Nurse Corps, soon after the WAAC's establishment, also accepted the value of such an indoctrination course before a Nurse Corps officer reported for professional duty, although prohibitive injury rates resulted when it was attempted to use men's obstacle courses unaltered. The Navy found that WAVES officers who were directly commissioned without a military indoctrination course were perceptibly embarrassed and handicapped. In all corps, the evident final solution was to continue military indoctrination while avoiding blind imitation of overstrenuous systems used by men.

---

[78] Investigations atchd to refs cited in ns. 75 and 76.
[79] Memos cited n. 75(1).
[80] (1) OQMG Ltr to all Tng Cens, 20 Sep 43, and all depots, 8 Apr 44. (2) ASF Cir 103, 14 Apr 44, Sec VII. (3) WD Cir 204, 23 May 44.

Recruiting Liaison

A particular set of problems revolved around the always-delicate relationship of the WAC recruiting and training organizations, which were frequently at cross-purposes. Even in the earliest and least complicated days of recruiting, both commandants agreed that the WAC training centers' greatest problem—not shared by most Army schools in wartime—was its dependence upon recruiters' success.

In view of the unpredictability of intake from one week to the next, few firm schedules could be drawn up. At times training companies were activated and staffed only to sit idle, with the cadre "suffering a marked lowering of morale and efficiency." At other times too few companies were ready, resulting in the "hasty activation of units and procurement of trainer personnel from whatever source possible." [81] There was believed to be no real solution short of selective service for women, although Colonel Strayhorn attributed part of the difficulty to the ASF's "failure to furnish training centers with recruiting figures," [82] which might have been obtained through better liaison by Military Training Division with The Adjutant General's Office at the Washington level. [83]

Problems redoubled with the advent of the various special recruiting schemes to which the War Department was forced to resort to obtain personnel. From the viewpoint of the training centers, the ideal training situation was one in which trainees arrived without strings attached, thus leaving the centers free to determine for what job a woman would be classified and trained. Maj. Elizabeth C. Smith, of ASF Military Training Division, pointed out:

Under this plan it is obvious that the Training Commandants could not exercise their normal prerogatives of classification and training. . . . The attitude of many a station-job-assignment recruit was that she could (and did) tell the Army *where* she was going to work and *what* she was going to do. [84]

In this respect, it was obvious that there could be no exact parallel with the classification practices of men's training centers until the latter in peacetime were also confronted with the problems of career promises to recruits. From the fall of 1943 onward, training centers were presented with a series of "named companies" such as the state companies of the All-States Campaign, the Wainwright Company, the Benito Juarez Company, and others recruited as units under various national or local projects. Some of these were of much less than company strength, and caused waste in overhead and housing in order to meet the commitment that they be trained as a group. Others were overstrength for a standard company, with consequent overcrowding of barracks and classrooms. There followed the branch recruits, who had been promised shipment to a particular branch of the service, and the station-job recruits, who had been promised assignment to a specified station and job.

Training center resentment against these systems was sharp. While most recruiters' classifications were found not to be grossly inaccurate, in some cases women had not elected a job in their most essential skill, or had been led to expect further training,

---

[81] ASF Hist of WAC Tng, pp. 102–03.
[82] *Ibid.*
[83] Congress had not authorized a WAC Reserve, in which recruits could have been held on inactive duty to stabilize inflow. See: (1) Hist cited n. 71(2). (2) ASF Hist of WAC Tng, pp. 344–45.
[84] ASF Hist of WAC Tng, pp. 56–58.

which could not be provided. Training center reports added:

Some recruits expected to be exempt from kitchen police duties; to be destined for superior assignments; to be entitled to more consideration than other Wacs. Naturally this attitude quickly aroused resentment among other trainees and training center personnel.[85]

Whatever the cause, the War Department soon began to receive numerous allegations that recruiting promises were being violated by training authorities. For the duration of most recruiting campaigns, inspectors were kept busy checking upon cases in which it was alleged that certificates of enlistment had been ignored or destroyed at training centers, recruits classified in unwanted duties or shipped to other than the promised station, or ridiculed for their branch or state armbands. Low morale among branch recruits was reported as so prevalent that a War Department representative was sent to investigate.[86]

Recruiters objected that they had received letters from their recruits to the effect that commitments were being violated and that

. . . it makes the job of recruiting an almost impossible one for those of us who are interested in the future and welfare of the women . . . especially when the responsibility lies on our shoulders for having encouraged them to join.[87]

Through the efforts of various inspectors, a number of cases of erroneous shipment were discovered and corrected. In some cases certificates were still in the possession of recruits, while in others papers had been lost and training centers had not sent for duplicates before disallowing claims. In most cases the numbers of such

shipments were no greater than might have been attributable to error, haste, or ignorance of the significance of certificates. In some cases, women who had not been promised branch assignment had merely taken advantage of the general confusion to assert that they had.[88]

Colonel Strayhorn was of the opinion that training authorities in the ASF had again not co-ordinated matters fully with recruiters on the Washington level, and that there was "failure to properly advise the training center prior to the actual arrival of troops recruited under such recruitment programs of the nature of the program and of the promises made." [89] Visiting War Department representatives agreed that "the Third WAC Training Center has not been informed of changes in organization and planning for WAC recruiting." [90]

Air Forces Evaluation

A particular problem was posed by the presence in one installation of Air Wacs, Port Wacs, Ground Wacs, and others who arrived complete with factional spirit. Because of its relatively small size, the WAC was forced to train in one installation recruits guaranteed assignment in different branches of the Army, a situation that sel-

---

[85] (1) *Ibid*, pp. 58–59. (2) Ltr, Comdt 1st WAC Tng Cen to Dir WAC, 9 Mar 44. SPWA 333.1.
[86] (1) Memo, Rctg Off for Dir WAC, 3 Mar 44. WDWAC 333.1. (2) Ltr, Gen White, G–1, to Rep. Francis Case, 9 Mar 44. WDWAC 330.14.
[87] Ltr, Lt Virginia Williams to Dir WAC, 8 Feb 44. SPWA 330.14.
[88] (1) Files of Air WAC Div, Hq AAF, ACofAS Pers, Recruiting. (2) AAF WAC Hist, p. 70 n. 1. (3) Intervs with AAF WAC Off, and Capt Corene Brooks, AAF Ln Off, during 1946.
[89] ASF Hist of WAC Tng, pp. 102–03.
[90] Memo cited n. 80(1).

dom if ever confronted men's basic training centers. Training center officers remarked:

Many recruits earmarked for AAF assignments were difficult to orient to basic military training. This was a result of a preconceived idea that training provided by the ASF was not applicable in the Air Forces.[91]

To deal with the problem, an approach was adopted by training centers which in turn drew objections from other commands: that of temporarily eradicating branch loyalty. Des Moines training authorities noted:

One of the primary objectives of basic training is, of course, the inculcation in the trainee of a feeling of unity and identity with the Corps. . . . The leadership of a strong Company Commander was necessary to overcome the . . . sense of separateness, of an already-developed pride in belonging to a special unit.[92]

This view was not concurred in by Director Hobby, who wrote to ask Military Training Division to stress "building of pride with the unit in which the soldier serves rather than building pride in the WAC." She asked, unsuccessfully, that passages in training courses be deleted which "give the impression that the WAC is something apart from the Army."[93]

By mid-1944, mounting Air Forces indignation at the number of lost recruits, plus dissatisfaction with training given in Air Forces organization and nomenclature, brought the AAF to the point of requesting its own basic training center in spite of the expense. This action was averted only by the Air WAC Officer's substitute proposal for a less expensive measure: the assignment of one experienced Air Forces officer to each of the two training centers, to act as liaison. This plan was fought by the

ASF upon Major Smith's recommendation, and was rejected by G–3 Division of the General Staff on the grounds that it was "wasteful of personnel."

Colonel Bandel resubmitted the papers in person, and eventually prevailed; the two officers were assigned in 1944, and were authorized to communicate directly by mail or telephone with Air Forces headquarters and its subcommands.[94] They proved most successful, in the AAF's opinion, in securing speedy solution to difficulties: new recruiting appeals were coordinated, Air Forces job classification systems installed, individual misunderstandings and claims given immediate attention, and training instructors provided with recent organizational charts.

There was, however, obviously no way of arriving at an exact parallel with the practices of men's training centers, until the peacetime realignment made it possible for each branch to train its own female recruits.

Other Evaluation

Most other aspects of WAC training center operation required no comment, being identical with those of all Army installations of a similar nature. Both Colonel Strayhorn and Colonel McCoskrie shared the belief that the quality of instruction at WAC installations, as distinguished from course content, was generally superior. Trained teachers were easily found among WAC officers. A survey in

[91] ASF Hist of WAC Tng, pp. 56–58.
[92] ASF Hist of WAC Tng, pp. 58–59.
[93] Memo, Dir WAC for CG ASF, 27 Oct 44. WDWAC 353.
[94] AAF Ltr 80–27, 25 Sep 44.

1944 showed that over 20 percent of WAC officers were former teachers, with 16 percent being principals or teachers in universities or secondary schools. These instructors were particularly successful in preparing training aids, instituting approved teaching methods, and inspiring trainee interest. An ASF inspector commented, of both officers and enlisted cadre, "I was impressed by the manner in which they conducted themselves, the prompt and courteous attention paid to superiors, and above all, the effort put forth to do a job." [95]

Training centers also maintained a superior record in respect to food and mess management. Meals were generally well planned and included plenty of the fruits and salads that women were found to prefer. In some months, reports showed a disposable garbage rate only half that of the Army average. Colonel McCoskrie's special pride was his establishment of a "birdseed table" of low-calorie diet, to which he directed women whose weight seemed to him to require it, regardless of their age or rank. The women, however, felt that certain Army men on the installation might profitably have received the same treatment. [96]

Great effort was also expended by WAC training centers in uniform issue and shoe fitting, which commandants believed got more attention than at most Army centers. Such efforts, however, were often fruitless in view of the shortages of clothing, the lack of proper sizes, and other problems connected with the relative difficulty of standardization and shipment of women's supplies. Whenever, as was not frequent, receiving companies were able to issue women complete and well-fitting uniforms, commandants noted that women were "more receptive to training." [97]

Closing of Training Centers

With the planned reduction of recruiting at the end of 1944, it was clear that one of the two remaining centers must close. Major Smith and Military Training Division favored retention of Fort Oglethorpe on the grounds of its warmer climate and greater capacity. Director Hobby preferred consolidation at Des Moines, in consideration of the needs of Negro recruits and of the superiority of the permanent brick buildings. The AAF supported this view and so, finally, did G–3 Division of the General Staff, which directed the choice of Des Moines. [98]

Closing of Fort Oglethorpe was delayed by the training of hospital technicians. When it eventually closed in September of 1945, Colonel Strayhorn was transferred to Fort Des Moines as training center commandant, while Colonel McCoskrie remained as post commandant. With the beginning of WAC demobilization and the cessation of WAC recruiting, Fort Des Moines likewise closed out its training activities in December of 1945. This marked the formal end of wartime WAC training, except for such scattered attendance at Army specialist schools as took place thereafter. [99]

---

[95] Rpt, Lt Col H. P. Crane, GSC, to MPD ASF, 12 May 43. SPWA 319.1. Also see Preston, Hist of Psychiatry in WAC, p. 14.

[96] (1) Rpt, Col Howard Clark, Chief, WAAC Opng Div, to Dir WAAC, 27 May 43, sub: Visit of Info to 2d and 3d WAAC Tng Cens. WPWA 319.1. (2) Ltr, Col McCoskrie to Dir WAC, 9 Mar 44. SPWA 333.1.

[97] ASF Hist of WAC Tng, p. 115.

[98] In WDWAC 353: (1) Memo, Dir WAC for G–3, 4 Jul 44. (2) Memo, MTD ASF for G–1, 1 Aug 44, SPTRP 353 WAC (7–4–44). (3) Memo, MTD ASF for G–3, 14 Sep 44, SPTRP 354.1 WAC. (4) Memo, G–3 for MTD ASF, 17 Nov 44, WDGCT 322 WAC (8–24–44).

[99] Ltr, Mrs. Elizabeth Strayhorn Walsh to OCMH, 14 Jun 50, with incl comments.

LAST BASIC TRAINING INSPECTION *by Colonel Strayhorn, commandant of the First WAC Training Center, and Colonel Rice, October 1945.*

Attendance at Army Specialist Schools

No bars were generally interposed to the attendance of Wacs at Army noncombat specialist schools on a coeducational basis, other than the limitations of available housing for women. The number of WAC students varied, from entire classes to a few individuals. In the latter case it was sometimes necessary to delay approval of a Wac's attendance until enough applications were on hand to justify use of a housing unit. Some students were sent direct from training centers to fill WAC quotas allotted by the school concerned, and others were sent by Army stations. The relatively small size of the Corps, and the fact that many women already possessed civilian skills or were given specialist training in WAC training centers, prevented coeducational specialist training from reaching any considerable proportions, although obviously the program would have ceased to be a minor one had it been necessary to fit a million women into the Army scheme, or to accept untrained younger women.

WAAC and WAC officers also attended the Army's Command and Staff School at Fort Leavenworth,[100] The Adjutant General's School, Ordnance School, Quartermaster School, Cooks and Bakers School, the Chemical Warfare School, and many others.[101] In most such cases, women proved able to take the full course successfully. Instructors at the Chemical Warfare School reported, "We pulled no punches," as Waacs went through the obstacle course, complete with tear gas, mustard gas, and exploding booby traps.[102] In addition, faculties noted with approval a certain increased industry among competitive-minded male students.

The only apparent defect in the informal and flexible assignment system was a lack of knowledge in the field as to how it operated. Recruiters, personnel officers, and individual women vainly wrote to training authorities for "a list of [specialist] schools, their mission, scope, prerequisites, and classification of successful graduates." [103] At the time of the conversion, WAAC Headquarters had begun preparation of a list, but the project was never completed. By the time that Military Training Division assumed authority, such a list would have been difficult to compile, in view of the wide decentralization of power to authorize attendance.

Not only were WAC quotas for specialist schools set up by Air, Ground, and Service Forces headquarters, but many Army stations made the proper arrangements with training commands at a lower level. Thus, it was frequently discovered that several Wacs were attending a class for aircraft mechanics, or other specialists, without any record of the fact in headquarters.

For this reason, and because the ASF disapproved of separate studies for women, no over-all report was ever made by Military Training Division as to which Army specialist schools Wacs had attended, in what numbers, and with what success.[104]

---

[100] In the first class, a Waac scored fourth in a class of about 400. The best reported Wac record was in a later class: fourth in the General Staff Course (AAF Tactical subdivision), in a class of over 1,000.

[101] WDBPR Release, 13 Oct 42.

[102] Chemical Warfare Bull, Vol. 31, No. 2, Mar–May 45.

[103] Ltr, Chief, R&I Br, 7th SvC, to TAG, 12 Feb 44. SPKPI 353 WAC, in SPWA 353.

[104] See Chs. XVI–XIX, above, for technical schools of the AAF, AGF, and ASF.

Army Specialized Training Program (ASTP)

There was, at different times, some consideration of allowing women to attend not only Army specialist schools but the civilian colleges that were concurrently training enlisted men under the Army Specialized Training Program. Soon after the Medical Department received authority to commission women doctors, The Surgeon General recommended that women be included in the ASTP, whereby young men were being sent to medical school at Army expense. He proposed that women medical students with two years of training be enlisted in the WAC for completion of a medical education of eighteen months, followed by a commission in the Medical Corps. This, he said, would assure a supply of women doctors for the Army, and would encourage women already doctors to serve with the Army, since "it will eliminate much of the prejudice . . . which is currently a large factor in their reluctance to enter the Army Medical Corps." [105] This proposal was rejected by Military Training Division, ASF, on the grounds that it would reduce the number of men who could be given medical training, and that women did not need the aid, as they could not be drafted and thus their medical studies could not be interrupted.

In the following year, when the ASTP for men was drastically cut during the manpower shortage of early 1944, bereft college authorities turned with some hope toward the WAC to fill the vacancies. At this time Military Training Division reversed its earlier stand, and proposed that 19-year-olds be enlisted in the WAC and given a year of college training at Army expense, which would include medical, communications, dietetic, statistical, or other work.

Many considerations caused the proposal to be unanimously rejected by the Director WAC, the Army Service Forces, and the War Department. Legislation would have been required to enlist women under 20, involving delay and possibly difficulties with Congress. Since there was no draft of women, it could not be said that the Army was drying up the source of college material and of future women scientists. Most girls of 19 would have been past college entrance age, yet to lower the entrance age to 17 or 18, with two or three years of training, would have been unjustifiably expensive and of little value in the current war. Furthermore, the WAC already had some 6,000 enlisted college graduates and some 10,000 more with partial college training, very few of whom were being used to fill assignments that required such training. For these reasons, no Wacs were ever sent to school under the ASTP. [106]

Continuation Training in the Field

The War Department had for some time accepted the principle that "continuous refresher training" was necessary for male troops not engaged in actual combat; such troops were excused from their duties for several hours of training each week so that a review of basic training was accom-

---

[105] (1) Memo, SG for CG ASF, 30 Oct 43, and 1st Ind from MTD, 30 Nov 43. SPWA 353. (2) Ltr, ASW to Senator George L. Radcliffe, 14 Oct 44. WD 095 Bentz, Frank L. (Mrs.), in CofS 291.9.

[106] (1) Memo, Sp Asst for Dir WAC, 8 Apr 44; (2) Memo, Lt Vera Mankinen for Mrs. Gruber, 28 Feb 44; (3) Memo, CG ASF for CofS, 7 Mar 44. WDWAC 353.

plished every six months.[107] In the early days of the WAAC, no decision was made about such "continuation training" for Waacs after they left the training center. Director Hobby proposed a directive placing responsibility for instruction on the WAAC company commanders, but General Faith decided that no special directives for women were necessary, upon "the assumption . . . that local commanders would discharge their command responsibility for the training of WAAC personnel." As a result, no directive was issued until just before the establishment of the WAC, when General Faith's inspectors discovered that "almost without exception no provision was being made for WAAC unit training," because of "confusion in the minds of station commanders" and "the inexperience of WAAC unit commanders."[108]

General Faith at once issued a directive on the subject, Mobilization Training Program 35–1. Since there was as yet very little knowledge of women's actual training needs in the field, it was merely provided that WAC units would spend not less than three hours a week, and not more than four, in a repetition of basic training, including drill, physical training, military courtesy, and hygiene. The directive also contained authority for station commanders, at their discretion, to substitute on-the-job training for part of these hours, or professional courses such as typing and shorthand.[109]

This directive was revised somewhat by Military Training Division when it took over WAC training, chiefly by adding map reading and by omitting the authority for station commanders to substitute on-the-job training, typing, or professional courses. The physical training period was also changed from 1¼ hours once a week to 15 minutes a day, since experts believed

daily exercise more beneficial. The Air and Ground Forces delegated to the Service Forces the right to prescribe this training for WAC units world-wide, believing at the time that unsisterly dissension would result if Wacs on neighboring stations or combined installations were required to take different types and amounts of training. The ASF's revised version at first occasioned little comment when published in a directive entitled Mobilization Training Program for WAC Detachments in the Field, familiarly known as MTP 35–2. This repetition of basic training every six months was, it was stated, expected to maintain "efficient job performance . . . military discipline, and physical fitness."[110]

Opposition of Personnel Officers

Within six months of the date of publication, this directive was under fire from Army section chiefs, station and company commanders, and personnel officers. The heart of the opposition was the question of whether, for permanent-type noncombat troops, the repetition of basic subjects every six months had enough value to compensate for time lost from other duties, or in fact had any value at all. Although the minimum requirement of 3 to 4 hours a week appeared small, it in fact added up to two working days a month, or 24 working days a year. From the section chief's viewpoint, such loss was the equivalent of giving all Wacs a furlough for one month of the twelve, or of shipping them all back

[107] FM 21–5, WD, esp. par 44 of 1943 edition.
[108] Whole discussion, unless otherwise specified, based on ASF Hist of WAC Tng, pp. 323–25.
[109] MTP 35–1, Unit Tng Program for WAC Units in Field, 21 Aug 43.
[110] MTP 35–2, WD, 15 Oct 44. Notification to Director in: Memo, Dir Troop Tng Div ASF for Dir WAC, 23 Sep 44. SPTRP 300.8, in WDWAC 353.

to the training center for another four weeks' basic course each year.

WAC staff directors believed that enlisted women felt the impact of this problem more keenly than the average men's unit, for several reasons. Of these, one obvious difficulty was that women were more permanent employees than men; 85 percent of Wacs never went overseas, and therefore heard the same course in defense against chemical attack given by the same company officers, not once or twice, but four, five, and six times during the course of the war. Such prolonged repetition in time provoked insufferable boredom among the victims. The ASF WAC Officer, Colonel Goodwin, reported later:

One of the deterrents to morale among enlisted women in the field has been a constant repetition of such basic military subjects as Defense Against Chemical Attack, and Map and Aerial Photograph Reading, which in no way contribute to the efficiency of women on the job.[111]

A more important factor was the nature of women's work, as distinguished from that of the average men's unit. All Army personnel were required to be excused from their duties for the weekly training "wherever practicable," but the majority of women, unlike the majority of men, were in clerical or other office work from which they could seldom be released. As the war situation grew worse and combat-fit men were transferred away from offices, Wacs came to hold many key office jobs which required constant attendance plus night and Sunday work.[112]

As a result of the opposition of section chiefs, almost no cases were reported in which a WAC company was allowed to conduct its training during duty hours. To long hours of office work were already added duties from which civilian women employees were exempt: barracks fatigue,

kitchen police, parades, and ceremonies. The addition of four hours of weekly training on off-duty time therefore posed a serious problem for enlisted women, since it occupied from two to four nights a week of supposed "recreation" time.

The Air WAC Officer, Colonel Bandel, noted

Commands had placed women on key clerical assignments, would not release them for training during the day, and yet expected them to take three or four hours of training weekly. The result was that women were working, training, or doing housekeeping from early morning until late at night.[113]

Even overseas, this difference was noted. In the European theater's great training programs prior to D Day, men and nurses took the training during duty hours, but Wacs, because of the pressure of office work, were obliged to take it in their off-duty time, a fact that some Army doctors blamed for the higher sick rate among Wacs at this time.[114]

The difficulty of scheduling required courses was further increased for women by the fact that most WAC units were not homogeneous, as men's often were, but contained workers of every type employed in different offices on different hours and shifts. Thus, company officers and cadre were obliged to repeat each course several nights a week to catch all members off duty.

An additional objection from station commanders was that the program made it difficult to find time for more urgently needed practical courses. Many stations

---

[111] Memo, Asst ASF WAC Off for MTD through MPD ASF, 29 Jun 45. SPAP 353 (5–17–43).

[112] Min, Med Tng Conf, Ft Oglethorpe, 1–3 May 45, p. 14, in SGO Tng Div, unnumbered.

[113] AAF WAC Hist, p. 42 and n. 1.

[114] ETO Bd Rpt, Vol. III, p. 5, App. 114, Rpt of SGO Consultant for 1944; and pp. 69–70.

and Army commands followed a consistent program of upgrading both military and civilian workers by providing free off-duty training in typing, communications, and medical skills, or whatever was needed in the local situation. The staff directors of every service command informed Colonel Goodwin that "Training Directors of Service Commands and Technical Services often superimpose additional training requirements over those of MTP 35–2." [115] The Air Forces noted the same problem, but the weekly four-hour program of map reading and other courses was already so heavy that it was necessary for Air Forces Headquarters to forbid more practical training. [116]

Physical Training for Field Units

The most unpopular of the required subjects was the course of muscle-building calisthenics, identical with that used in the training center. From the beginning, training inspectors had noted a certain laxity concerning this requirement. Units in double-decked barracks ordinarily had no indoor room for active exercise, since it was impossible for members to bend, fling arms and legs, or lie on the floor without hitting the beds, coal stoves, or each other. Outdoor training, even if weather permitted it, was hampered by the usual lack of nearby areas large enough and smooth enough for the prescribed exercises. Company commanders had sometimes solved the problem by securing permission to use some large post recreational hall or area, where the company was assembled once a week for an hour of miscellaneous games or exercises, but this system could not be used when the requirement was changed by Military Training Division to 15 minutes a day instead of 1¼ hours a week. Commanders soon protested that it was

impossible to secure a suitable area and assemble the company five time a week. The time consumed in donning proper clothing and marching back and forth to the area was often nearer to an hour a day than to 15 minutes. [117]

WAC staff directors of Air, Ground, and Service Forces, after a conference, therefore appealed to Military Training Division to remit the daily requirement because of "the administrative difficulty involved in scheduling and operation." [118] However, ASF's physical training experts refused, saying, "There was no evidence that the training as required was not expedient from the point of view of the purpose of physical training." [119] This, being translated, meant that 15 minutes of daily exercise was considered important enough to merit further efforts to overcome administrative difficulties. Unfortunately, the eventual solution arrived at by most WAC companies was, before dressing for reveille, to spend 15 minutes in such exercises as could be taken in double-decked bunks without awakening shift workers sleeping in neighboring beds. These, although duly entered on company records, were often invisible to the naked eye of the inspector.

Therefore, to enforce more active exercise, Military Training Division proposed a program not used by men: that WAC field units be required to administer a physical fitness rating test every three months, the rating to consist of scores made on four exercises requiring considerable strength, which were currently taught at training centers. These four were known,

---

[115] (1) Min, Stf Dirs Conf, Feb 45, Ft Des Moines. (2) Memo, ASF WAC Off for Dir Mil Tng ASF, 23 Feb 45. SPAP 353 WAC (5–17–43).
[116] AAF WAC Hist, p. 42 and n. 1.
[117] ASF Hist of WAC Tng, p. 330.
[118] Min cited n. 115(1).
[119] ASF Hist of WAC Tng, p. 339.

respectively, as the "dip," the "sit-up," the "wing-lift," and the "squat thrust." WAC advocates of these exercises pointed out that these four taken together would develop muscular strength in every part of the body, which random sports and recreation would never do. Skeptics, on the other hand, noted that the exercises were quite similar to exercises for men, and questioned whether women's efficiency in any capacity would be improved by giving them broad shoulders, narrow hips, and muscular arms and legs, which the exercises undeniably aimed for.

To make the required score of *Good,* a woman was expected to perform all four exercises in succession with a speed dependent on her age. For a woman of 50, from 3 to 8 full dips first had to be made without pause, with the body supported on hands and toes and lowered by bending the elbows until the chin touched the floor and then returned to position. Second, from 28 to 48 sit-ups had to be performed, also without pause, with the body brought from a lying to a sitting position without the use of the hands. Third was the wing-lift, in which the body was face down with the hands clasped behind the neck, and the upper part of the body then raised until the breast left the floor; a woman of 50 was required to do from 69 to 85 of these lifts in one minute. Last was the squat thrust, in which the subject squatted, thrust the legs out behind until the body was straight and rested on hands and toes, returned to a squat, and then to a straight-knee stand; a woman of 50 was required to do from 15 to 18 such thrusts in 30 seconds. For a younger woman, the required scores on all four tests were considerably higher.[120]

Colonel Hobby immediately objected to this test when it was proposed. She informed Military Training Division:

This office is not in agreement with the principles of the proposed Training Circular "WAC Physical Fitness Rating." This disagreement is not based on any expert knowledge of physical training, but on the opinion that, from the point of view of the welfare of the enlisted women, such a system is not appropriate or suitable for women in the field.

The basic mission of the Women's Army Corps is to accomplish given military jobs. Physical training in the field should be held to the minimum necessary for a woman to keep fit to perform her assigned duties, most of which are not strenuous.[121]

Colonel Hobby privately remarked to her staff, "Are they trying to make Amazons of our women?"[122]

In spite of this opposition, ASF training authorities refused to make the physical fitness rating less strenuous. Captain Niles of The Surgeon General's Office, the physical training expert who had devised the exercises, wrote, "It is essential that the organic vigor of WAC personnel in the field be improved." The medical consultant, Major Craighill, likewise favored the exercises as a means of offsetting sedentary work. Finally Major Smith secured Colonel Hobby's approval on the grounds that the test merely provided the field a convenient way of measuring exercises already taught in training centers and illustrated in the WAC Physical Training Manual, and would not be competitive.[123]

Upon publication, however, the directive stated that the test was not optional but "will be administered once every 3

[120] WD Tng Cir 62, 16 Jun 44 and 10 Oct 44.

[121] Memo, Dir WAC for Dir Mil Tng ASF, 13 Apr 44. WDWAC 353.

[122] According to Maj Mattie E. Treadwell, Asst Chief, WAC Br G-1.

[123] (1) Memo, SGO Tng Div for MTD ASF, 9 May 44. WDWAC 353. (2) Memo, SGO Consultant for Women's Health and Welfare for Dir WAC, 18 Apr 44. WDWAC 353. (3) Memos, Dep Dir WAC for Dir WAC, 20 May 44, and for MTD ASF, 22 May 44. WDWAC 353.

months," and that women of all ages would be excused only by authority of an orthopedic surgeon.[124] Protests at once arose in the field. Enlisted men had no such test, which appeared to Army commands to be an unnecessary burden for women. The AAF reported with alarm that their first woman to try the test, although herself a young physical training teacher, was hospitalized for a week with a strained back.[125] Most women alleged that, although always perfectly healthy, they could not perform the exercises at all.[126] Some alleged that only those women with the build of a man would ever be able to do them correctly, since most women's bone and muscle structure was unsuitable for successful performance, particularly in required shoulder width and narrowness of hips.

Captain Niles, on the other hand, believed that the unpopularity of the tests was due to lack of knowledge on the part of supervisory officers, and asked that traveling WAC teams be sent to major commands to demonstrate. This was done, but a year later the program still remained very unpopular. One Air Forces command, after carrying on what it called "a vigorous program," discovered no improvement in women's scores, with most still below "average," and concluded that the test did not measure real physical fitness for women.

WAC company commanders, when polled, were found to be 95 percent opposed to the whole physical training program. So-called physical fitness as measured by this means often, according to their observation, actually had a negative correlation with job efficiency. Instead, the almost unanimous demand of Wacs in the field was for permission to replace the muscle-building calisthenics with some re-

laxing form of group or individual sports suitable for women, such as bowling, hiking, or swimming.[127]

All such field protests were not effective; Military Training Division refused to alter the requirement. Major Smith replied to advocates of a recreation hour:

We have to recognize the difference between planned training and a morale-building program for recreation. . . . Play loses its value if forced. Therefore the point of substituting recreation for planned exercises is not valid.[128]

Personnel vs. Training Needs

The entire issue of continuation training was finally forced, just before V-E Day, by a concerted campaign of personnel advisers in all major Army commands. As early as April of 1944 Colonel Hobby informed Military Training Division, "The time of the enlisted women in the field is ordinarily so valuable that none should be devoted to unnecessary training activities." [129] In February of 1945, as hospitals and personnel centers braced themselves for record loads, a meeting of all Air, Ground, and Service Forces WAC staff directors re-

---

[124] Cir cited n. 120.

[125] Maj Gwendolyn Watson, AC, then WAC Stf Dir, AAF Mat Comd, Wright Field.

[126] Including the author, who, although not having lost a single day from work during five years in the Army, was unable to arise from the floor after one half of one full dip. The AGF WAC Officer, who performed the experiment at the same time, achieved an identical result.

[127] (1) Memo, Opns Serv SGO for MTD ASF, 3 Jul 44. SGO Hist Div 322.5-1. (2) Ltr, AAF ATSC, Wright Field, to Dir WAC through CG AAF, 21 Jul 45. WDWAC 720, 1945-46. (3) Memo, Asst ASF WAC Off to MTD ASF, 29 Jan 45. SPAP 353 WAC (5-17-43). (4) Poll of company officers. Files of Sch of WAC Pers Admin, WAC files, OCMH.

[128] Min cited n. 112, p. 17.

[129] Memo, Dir WAC for Dir Mil Tng ASF, 13 Apr 44. WDWAC 353.

ported the unanimous opinion of their commands: that authority must be decentralized to them to determine their own continuation training needs. ASF's report to this effect was prepared by Colonel Goodwin and forwarded by General Dalton of Military Personnel Division, who stated, "Because enlisted women are working longer hours and harder than at any time since the Corps was established, it is felt that consideration should be given to reducing the number of training hours required." [130] AAF's objections were even more strenuous, since that command had now abandoned any continuation training program for its men, and saw no reason for special requirements for women in a time of great manpower shortage. [131]

All such requests for modification were consistently refused by Military Training Division, with the statement that continuation training could not safely be decentralized to the station commander, since the resulting programs would not be uniform and thus would not produce an identical Army-wide state of training. In rejecting the recommendations, Military Training Division pointed out that the opinion of personnel officers could not be considered formal complaints until approved by directors of training in subordinate commands and submitted to headquarters through channels. [132]

General Dalton replied:

Admittedly not all the Staff Directors are training specialists, but . . . post commanders, section chiefs, and hospital commanders complain to them of the difficulties in carrying out the present training program. [133]

He suggested that Brig. Gen. Arthur G. Trudeau verify their comments by inviting the formal opinions of the service commands and technical services. This, the Director of Training, ASF, refused to do. [134]

In any case, the comments were inapplicable to the Army Air Forces. Colonel Bandel had opposed an earlier break with the ASF because she preferred to use the powerful lever of AAF opposition to force Army-wide reforms, rather than to rescue Air Wacs alone. After the failure of Colonel Goodwin's efforts in March, Colonel Bandel made a final attempt to prevent a division by requesting a conference of Air, Ground, and Service Forces officers with a representative of the War Department's G–3 Division. At this conference the AAF's argument was supported by the AGF and by the ASF WAC Officer "in view of pressing work demands on assigned personnel."

Military Training Division again refused to consider this recommendation on the grounds that:

This opinion was based on administrative and morale problems evolving from the field approach to the training requirement. It did not represent an evaluation of the ability of the training program to accomplish its stated purpose.

Therefore, Military Training Division still refused to modify the program in any command. [135]

At this, the Air Forces recommended that continuation training of AAF Wacs be made a responsibility solely of the AAF, in line with the system for men's training.

---

[130] Memo, ASF WAC Off for Dir Mil Tng ASF through Dir Pers ASF, 23 Feb 45. SPAP 353 WAC (5–17–43).

[131] AAF Ltr 50–18, 18 Jan 45.

[132] Memo, MTD ASF for Dir Pers ASF, 2 Mar 45. SPAP 353 WAC (5–17–43).

[133] *Ibid.* 1st Ind, Gen Dalton to MTD ASF, 13 Mar 45.

[134] *Ibid.* 2d Ind, MTD to Dir Pers ASF, 22 Mar 45. See also Speech by Maj Smith, pp. 10–11. Min cited n. 120.

[135] Above based on ASF Hist of WAC Tng, p. 339, except for Colonel Bandel's opinions, obtained by interview.

This recommendation received Colonel Hobby's concurrence and was approved by G–3 Division of the War Department for both the AAF and the AGF, becoming effective 15 July 1945, a few weeks before the end of the war. The requirement for a physical fitness rating test was also suspended about the same time by separate action.[136]

The Air Forces immediately published a simplified continuation training program for Air Wacs, in which only two hours weekly were required. One of these was the orientation hour directed by the War Department for all Army men and women. This offered no problem since it was not repetitive, was given during duty hours, and was ordinarily prepared by a specialist for presentation to both men and women of an entire station. The second hour was one of "exercise and sports," with time, place, and type to be determined by the station concerned. All other subjects were to be conducted only when believed necessary by local commanders, and in no case could exceed one additional hour weekly. One day later, the Army Ground Forces published an identically worded continuation training program for its Wacs.[137]

Military Training Division prepared for ASF Wacs a continuation training program that was virtually unmodified. Military Personnel Division at once objected to publication of this program, since the expanding mission of the Service Forces after V-E Day had placed even greater loads on ports, hospitals, and separation centers. Military Training Division again refused to consider this recommendation, and unsuccessfully attempted to revise the ASF WAC Officer's assigned duty of advising General Somervell on the WAC program to that of advising him on the WAC program except for WAC training. At this, General Dalton appealed to the Chief of Staff, Army Service Forces, to override its Training Division on the whole matter. Both Control Division, ASF, and the Chief of Staff, ASF, approved General Dalton's appeal, and directed Military Training Division to publish an easier program like that of the Army Air Forces and Army Ground Forces.[138]

The program was published as directed. Only three months later, Military Training Division's policies met an even greater setback when the pressure of work forced the ASF to remove all requirements for continuation training of all operating personnel, both male and female. Since the AAF and AGF already had no such requirement, the theory that routine continuation training was practicable in time of emergency was generally discarded. It was subsequently made clear by Major Smith that Military Training Division had not altered its opinion as to the ideal course content when time permitted. Since the objections of most Army station commanders had chiefly concerned the loss of work time and efficiency in an emergency, it appeared that there would be less active opposition to repetition of basic courses in peacetime when personnel became plentiful.[139]

[136] (1) Memo, ACofAS Tng for G–3, 11 May 45; Comment 1, 17 May 45, G–3 to Dir WAC; Comment 2, 26 May 45, Dir WAC to G–3. AVACT–4, in WDWAC 353. (2) WD Tng Cir 31, 2 Jul 45.

[137] (1) AAF Reg 50–34, 23 Jun 45 (effective 15 Jul 45). (2) AGF Ltr 461/150, (MTP) (24 Jun 45) GNGAP.

[138] (1) Memos, Asst ASF WAC Off for MTD ASF, 29 Jun 45, and no date. SPAP 353 WAC (5–17–43). (2) Memo, Gen Dalton to CofS ASF, 12 Jul 45. SPAP 353 WAC. This outlines briefly the entire history of negotiation discussed in this chapter.

[139] (1) ASF Cir 289, 30 Jul 45. (2) ASF Cir 359, 25 Sep 45. (3) ASF Hist of WAC Tng, p. 354, final critique by Maj Smith.

CHAPTER XXXIII

The Leadership of Women

If the development of leaders among men was one of the Army's major problems, the development of women leaders was equally urgent for the Women's Army Corps, and even more difficult, since the Corps began its career without a nucleus of experienced personnel. Soon after the conversion to Army status, field commands noted that one of the Corps' most pressing needs was for good WAC detachment commanders; those sent out were frequently found to be deficient in the training, the experience, and the temperament for leadership.[1]

There were those who held that the task was impossible, in that the terms *female* and *leader* were self-contradictory. This prevalent view was set forth, soon after the move of the Director's Office to G–1 Division, in a nationally syndicated newspaper column, which alleged:

The War Department has received thousands of letters from Wacs suggesting that officer personnel in their outfits consist of men instead of women. The revolt is so bitter and widespread that the recommendation may be accepted. . . . The gist of the general complaint seems to be that the gals would have more respect for a male boss than for a female commander. . . . Most of the communications charge that women are too "petty" to handle large groups of the same sex.[2]

This statement was, fortunately for the WAC, entirely inaccurate. No such avalanche of letters was received by the War Department; there was no hint of any such "revolt"; no recommendation that WAC commanders be replaced was ever received from any major commander.[3] There was much question of the way in which to discover the best female commanders and remove unsuitable ones, but there was never, after the first officer candidate classes, any question of the necessity for unit commanders of the same sex as the troops. Only the first seven WAAC training classes had male officers, who were replaced by female officers as rapidly as possible.

The question of "leadership" as here raised was distinct from the administrative and disciplinary aspects of command. In mere administration, women officers for female troops had a natural advantage: the WAC company routine of inspection, sick call, monthly physical examination and similar matters was, if not impossible, at least embarrassing for the male commander, and in all private interviews he was forced to remain constantly aware of possible charges that might be brought against him unless witnesses were present at all times. In disciplinary matters, reports on file from field commanders also attested that the average male officer was more

---

[1] Min, Stf Dirs Conf, New York, 1–3 Dec 43. SPWA 337 (11–10–43).

[2] The column "National Whirligig," 11 Apr 44. WDWAC 000.7.

[3] Only one such early document was discovered, and this was never forwarded to the War Department.

hampered by "misplaced chivalry" than a female officer, when required to adjudge disciplinary penalties against women.[4]

However, the real question concerned the more positive aspects of leadership—whether women officers were "too petty" to handle large groups of women, or were unable to inspire troop loyalty, devotion, high morale, and good conduct. This was the view commonly supported by popular surveys concerning women supervisors in business offices and by public opinion in general. If this was true, and if women would not follow the leadership of a woman, it would be necessary to train male leaders for women's units in spite of their natural handicaps along administrative and disciplinary lines.

The Army found no basis for any such belief. Women leaders were found to exist, both those with natural ability and those capable of being trained, and the conditions and qualities of female leadership seemed reasonably in accord with those already understood for men.[5] There was no reliable basis for estimating the relative numbers of leaders among women, although it appeared probable that they were scarcer than among men for lack of previous opportunities to develop. Nevertheless, leadership ability appeared to be latent in a number of women, and the woman leader, once found, was able to draw from her female troops a devotion, respect, loyalty, obedience, and self-sacrifice which resembled in every way that obtained from men by the best male commanders.[6]

In the opinion of Army psychologists, a woman was, on the company level, the only natural and possible leader of women in the truest sense of the word, since real leadership involved psychological processes of identification and mimesis which

for women properly required a superior woman as the object. Some of the undesirable mannishness of early projects of WAAC training centers appeared due to the fact that the first women trainees had imitated their male commanders in the matter of voice, dress, walk, manners, and other standards. Psychologists told the WAC officer:

The strongest and most direct motivation is identification with yourself. . . . People gain emotional security by modeling themselves on a leader in whom they have confidence . . . attitudes, mannerisms, gestures, even voice tones, are contagious.[7]

Capabilities of the Woman Leader

Testimony as to the existence of the successful woman leader was offered by every command. The Army Air Forces reported:

The WAC squadron commanders have been extremely important factors in the (WAC) program. . . . Women lean on their company commander for advice and guidance considerably more, evidently, than do men. . . . A good WAC Commander could and often did increase the actual job efficiency of an entire WAC unit.[8]

WAC training centers reported the same phenomenon:

The strength and ability of the commanding officer of a training unit has probably influenced the training result of a unit more

---

[4] See Ch. XXV, pp. 503–05, above.

[5] All references to established principles of leadership for men are based upon: (1) FM 22–5, WD, Feb 46, Leadership, Courtesy, and Drill. (2) Speech by Maj. Gen. Orlando Ward to Fort Jackson Rotary Club, 1945. (3) Interv with Mr. Charles McDonald, OCMH, author of *Company Commander* (Washington: The Infantry Journal Press, 1947).

[6] See quoted passages below.

[7] (1) Preston, Hist of Psychiatry in WAC. (2) Dr. Hildegarde Durfee, *The WAC Officer, A Guide to Successful Leadership*, WD Pamphlet 35–2, Feb 45.

[8] AAF WAC Hist, p. 96. See Ch. XVI, above.

than any other single factor. In many instances a superior commanding officer has been able to attain a good training result even where handicapped by inadequate junior officers or cadre, inadequate housing, and an inadequate flow of supplies. Her importance in the training picture cannot be overemphasized.[9]

In the field, a survey of several detachments brought forth the same comment:

The enlisted women attribute everything that happens to the company commander. The policies were made by the post [but] as far as the women are concerned, the company commander could change them if she would do so. . . . Her attitude and her moral tone set the tone for the entire company. If you study the attitude of the days or weeks when she is feeling low, the company follows the same trend.[10]

Various other surveys repeatedly confirmed not only the existence of the woman leader, but also her surprising ability to dominate all other factors in her unit's surroundings. The Transportation Corps studied two WAC companies stationed near the same port: the first company had a superior location, was more warmly received by its employers, had more convenient transportation and better recreation facilities, more passes, more promotions; nevertheless, the members of the second company were found to be happier, to like the food better, to be better pleased with recreation facilities, to consider themselves in better health. Investigators were unable to find any cause except the superior leadership ability of the commander of the second detachment.[11]

In another survey of forty-four WAC detachments, investigators found that no environmental factor had serious effect upon company morale in companies with good leadership. In such companies women took more pride in their unit, believed themselves better adjusted to the Army, liked their jobs better, thought that there were fewer discomforts in Army life, that their housing and sanitary facilities were superior, post recreational opportunities better, and medical attention more satisfactory. In an especially striking case, two WAC companies on the same post used the same medical facilities, yet women in one company thought they were getting better medical care than the other did, the only real difference being in the leadership ability of their WAC commander.[12]

This control that the WAC company commander exercised over apparently unrelated matters never ceased to astonish investigators. Concerning the cause of widely different unmarried pregnancy rates at five stations in the same area, inspectors reported, "In those detachments where there has been continuous good leadership, the pregnancy rate has been low."[13] At other stations, statistical studies showed that the number of entries in the sick book increased when the company commander was changed; when the company commander got married, the number of disciplinary offenses increased; when the officers went on leave, both offenses and sickness increased.[14]

The existence of the female leader, and

---

[9] ASF Hist of WAC Tng, pp. 111–12.

[10] Remarks of S/Sgt Doris Todd re Det Pers. Min, of TC WAC Stf Dirs Mtg, 1–4 May 45. WDWAC 337 Stf Dir Mtg.

[11] *Ibid.*

[12] Hq Rpt C–102, How Enlisted Wacs in the U.S. View Their WAC Officers. ASF/AG 461 (6–4–45), DRB AGO, and OCMH.

[13] Memo, Maj Margaret Janeway, MC, Asst Consultant, for Col Freer, SGO, 27 Sep 44, sub: Visit to WAC Dets at NYPOE and Sepn Ctr, Fort Dix, N.J. SGO 321 WAC.

[14] Min cited n. 10.

the tremendous power that she was capable of wielding, were therefore undeniable; it was also undeniable that not every woman officer was so qualified.

Efforts To Determine Qualities of Leadership

After two years of experiment it was clear that the successful leader could not be determined entirely by age, or previous occupation, or education or the lack of it, or intelligence, or any other circumstance. This was in accord with Army experience with men.[15] Later statistics revealed that some successful women leaders were married, some unmarried; many were college graduates; a few never went to high school; their ages ranged from 21 to 50. Many former teachers did well, but were almost equaled in number by former clerks and secretaries. Some former office managers succeeded, but so did former bookkeepers. Librarians were leaders as often as reporters, housewives as often as buyers, beauticians as often as lawyers.[16]

Neither did the ability to lead women automatically follow from instruction in voice and command, military manners, or Army Regulations. In fact, the only reliable method of discovery in the Corps' first years was that of trial and error, of sending commanders out with companies and advising Army stations to replace those who proved unsuccessful. This was costly, and involved the loss of real or potential leaders and damage to units.

The task of collecting and verifying available evidence on the nature of leadership was delegated to Dr. Hildegarde Durfee, a psychologist employed as civilian consultant by the Office of the Director and, after the conversion, by the Army Service Forces. It was Dr. Durfee's opinion that the general principles of leadership for men would apply equally to women, but that women would have certain special and additional problems. She added:

> They are newcomers in a male setting; hence tend to feel on trial and under special pressure to make good. . . . They have volunteered their services, are apt to be more eager and more individualistic. . . . Their problem is not the overcoming of fear in combat, but more often the endurance of routine and monotony. . . . Women as a whole have had less experience in group discipline and leadership. Theirs has been at once an over privileged and an under privileged status in our society. They have been given more attention and consideration, but the price of this has been less opportunity and recognition.[17]

It was therefore anticipated, and later proved true, that certain established leadership principles would receive peculiar emphasis for women, and that new principles might emerge.

Sensitivity to Discipline

The first and most obvious difference to confront researchers was one of degree rather than intrinsic quality: that of responsiveness to leadership. All observers agreed that women were more dependent upon their company commander than were most men. A poor commander had

---

[15] Lecture, Psychology of Leadership and Motivation, Lt. Col. T. Ernest Newland, USMA, 24 Mar 47, to seminar in advanced psychological principles of personnel administration, George Washington University, (D. C.), and on file there in mimeographed form.

[16] Statistics concern 818 WAC officers who attended the School for WAC Personnel Administration in 1945. Routing Form, G–1, 26 Oct 45, sub: Final Rpt of Sch for WAC Pers Admin. SPTRP 352 WAC. Incl, Rpt of Comdt to G–1, 19 Oct 45. WDWAC 352.

[17] References to Dr. Durfee's opinion are from her pamphlet, The WAC Officer.

an exaggerated effect upon women, who were unable to take her shortcomings lightly and were completely demoralized, while a capable commander found them unprecedentedly malleable, and was able to build an unusually high company discipline and spirit. Army men commented that women seemed noticeably more sensitive to discipline than were the average male troops whom they had commanded. "Women don't require the needling that men do," said Colonel McCoskrie of Fort Des Moines.

Women hate to fail. Words of encouragement go further with them than blame. It is fatal to assume the same attitude one would with men—you just scare them and then get nothing further from them.[18]

This difference appeared partly due to women's social training, which, according to Dr. Durfee, "makes them tend to want to please and not offend," and partly due to the fact that they were volunteers, above average in aptitude, and eager to demonstrate the abilities of their sex.

Because of this trait, the successful WAC commander was always obliged to have positive qualities of leadership instead of merely negative ones of authority. "You don't command women—you lead them," Colonel McCoskrie reported. Dr. Durfee noted that "there is a great difference between ordering your women around because you are their commanding officer and winning their cooperation because you are their leader."[19] Colonel Hobby urged selection boards to consider this factor, saying:

In the beginning we put too much stress on this business of command anyway. We never want to make the mistake of substituting force for real leadership. My experience is that leadership is mostly by example.[20]

The Maternalistic Commander

Women leaders, apparently more than men, also needed to guard against an overprotective attitude toward their companies. In spite of the Wacs' dependency upon their commander, they seldom enjoyed being the recipients of applied child psychology, in which too many WAC officers appeared to be experts. The leadership situation was definitely not that of parent and child, nor even that of teacher and child. Dr. Durfee noted:

The criticism most often heard of WAC officers is that they treat their troops too much like children and talk down to them too much. This tendency to fall into a housemother role is understandable, and is probably due, in part, to the natural maternalism of women, in part to the dependence of troops on their company commanders. It is well for WAC officers to remember that they are dealing with grown women, many of whom have managed their own affairs for years.

Of officers who failed on this score, enlisted women commented:

"She treated her command as she probably did her 4B grade class."

"She never seemed to realize we might be intelligent too."

"She regarded us as so many figures to be pushed around on a checkerboard."

Of those whom they considered real leaders, enlisted women said:

"She acted as though she thought highly of everyone of us and gave us fair adult treatment."

"She treated us with respect and automatically received in kind."

---

[18] Interv, 29 Jan 46.

[19] The WAC Officer, p. 11.

[20] M/R, A Statement of Policy on Selection of OCs, 12 Mar 43. SPWA 314.7 (1–7–43)(11) sec 1.

"She not only demanded respect, she gave it."

"She always expected the best of people—and got it." [21]

Overmaternalistic officers, in addition to irritating their women, were usually failures at developing leadership in subordinates. Case histories revealed that some officers could not qualify as leaders because, although intelligent, conscientious, and hard-working, they did not only their own job but that of the rest of the cadre, making all the decisions, and failing to give the proper training to junior officers. It was significant that failure of this type caused the first recorded removal of a woman commander in a WAAC training center, in which testimony stated:

The morale of this Battalion is at a low state. The basic difficulty is that Lt. ——— has tried to treat adult, intelligent women as high school freshmen, and it won't work. Lt. ——— uses her staff practically entirely as a source of information; in most cases she neither asks nor accepts the advice of members of her staff. . . . On numerous occasions I have heard Lt. ——— reprimand officers in the presence of other officers. Officers and auxiliaries are motivated by fear accompanied by a lack of respect. . . . Lt. ——— has completely stifled the initiative of members of her staff.

To this the commandant added:

I am of the opinion that . . . in her every act, Lt. ——— has honestly believed that she was carrying out instructions . . . that the present difficulty has arisen through her zeal, her lack of understanding of human nature, and her arbitrary manner. [22]

Leadership courses for men likewise emphasized the delegation of authority; for female leaders, its observance appeared especially important.

Even excellent leaders with no tendencies toward maternalism had to guard against the zealousness for work that had been previously remarked as a characteristic of most volunteers, and that in a company commander could easily result in nervous and physical exhaustion and loss of perspective. Colonel Hobby wrote, "It is absolutely necessary for a good leader to have a life of her own with interests other than the WAC in it." [23] Published leadership studies added:

The officer who thinks—talks—breathes of WAC affairs, out of a natural but mistaken enthusiasm and conscientiousness, narrows her mental and emotional horizon to the detriment of her own enrichment of living and her effectiveness as a leader. . . . Maintain your individuality so far as possible within the Army framework. Strive to keep up your interests in the outer world; read, play, cultivate social contacts. [24]

Psychological tests also indicated that the WAC leader should be a woman of energy and quick action rather than of abstract ideas; the responses of successful leaders to word associations suggested that "the leader is the doer, the one whose primary associations are with actions and not merely with activity in the abstract." [25]

Other Leadership Problems

Many other traits required of their leader by enlisted women seemed to differ from those of male leaders in degree of intensity if not in kind. It appeared that women's curiosity could scarcely have been

---

[21] All above from *The WAC Officer*, pp. 26–27.

[22] Memo, Comdt 2d Tng Cen for Dir WAAC, 27 Nov 42. SPWA 320.2 (8–18–42)(1) sec 1.

[23] Memo, Dir WAC for CG ASF, 22 Oct 44, sub: Dr. Durfee's Tng MS on Leadership. WDWAC 353.

[24] *The WAC Officer*, p. 13.

[25] Ltr, Exec WAC to Miss Florence L. Goodenough, Prof., University of Minnesota Institute of Child Welfare, 15 Mar 46. WDWAC 095 Goodenough.

exceeded, and leadership studies cautioned women officers: "Wherever possible, explain the reason for orders and regulations, especially disagreeable ones." Numerous cases came to light in which disappointment, resentment, and low morale followed a commander's repeated failure to give simple explanations—which would in no way have compromised security—in such matters as the cancellation of passes, the extra policing of grounds, or a delay in orders.

Colonel Hobby also noted a tendency for women, more than men, to value their individuality, possibly because of their lesser regimentation in civilian life in dress, schools, clubs, and employment. The Director urged training authorities to point out to WAC leaders that

. . . one of the main distinctions between successful leadership of women and similiar leadership of men is that women need to remain individuals to such an extent that group activity, outside of office hours, can very easily be overdone with them.[26]

Because of this natural individuality, prospective WAC leaders were cautioned to emphasize group loyalty. Dr. Durfee stated:

Women have not, as a rule, had much organizational experience in civilian life, and sometimes lack a concept of what loyalty to organization means. They tend to be personal and subjective in their attitudes, to feel free to criticize each other as if they were merely separate individuals. This attitude may lead to jealousy and backbiting which can disturb the unity of command and seriously affect the morale of troops.

The successful WAC leader therefore was obliged to set a perfect example of loyalty to the Army, to the station and its policies, to fellow officers, and to the members of her company. When inspired by such an example, the women's natural idealism was apt to produce group loyalty and *esprit* of an unexcelled intensity. When not so inspired, a WAC unit seemed particularly liable to degenerate into feuding cliques and factions. Wac leaders were warned to avoid building "a selfish personal following," but instead to promote loyalty to the Army.

A forceful example of the dangers of personal followings was given early in WAAC history, when the commandant of one training center secured to himself the loyalty of one segment of the WAAC staff to such an extent that, upon his removal, these officers telegraphed hundreds of personal protests to the War Department. Colonel Hobby in return severely reprimanded these women for unmilitary conduct and misplacement of their loyalties. No commander of women was ever to be counted successful who permitted any such cleavage within his command.[27]

The prospective WAC leader was told:

If once the impression is created that she plays favorites, is inconsistent in her discipline, or that her word is not to be trusted, she might as well walk East until her hat floats.

Enlisted women serving under poor leaders said:

"You can't beat the clique in this detachment. There's no team spirit since the new CO came. It's split the company right in two."

"Our CO caters to a little group of apple polishers . . . It makes us sick to see how hard she falls for their line."

"If you don't stand in with the first sergeant, you're out of luck."

"There's no use trying . . . what few grades there are all go to the CO's pets."[28]

---

[26] *The WAC Officer*, p. 13.
[27] Hobby files.
[28] *The WAC Officer*, p. 29.

In exact proportion as women appeared to be more sensitive than men to the approval of their leader, it became more essential that there be no clique, group, or individual to which that approval appeared to be especially given.

Problems Peculiar to WAC Leaders

In a few respects women leaders faced especial problems with little Army parallel. One of these concerned the feminine interpretation of the Army leader's responsibility "to teach and encourage high moral standards in troops." Since military regulations had been modeled on men's moral standards, but not on women's, leaders were cautioned:

Although some [women] may feel that they should be able to exercise a man's freedom in their conduct, they must bear in mind that they are in the Army to do a job, and not to settle an old social problem.[29]

To maintain the women's reputation and their social adjustment, the WAC leader was required far to exceed the male commander in the moral standards that she instilled and maintained. Release of personal tensions by means of alcohol, sex, or disturbing the peace ordinarily had far more serious social consequences for women than for men. Many women had been previously more sheltered than men, and were now given more unaccustomed freedom, which presented a situation more difficult for the commander to manage. In the leader's own life, whatever her previous habits or beliefs, she was also obliged to exemplify the strictest of feminine codes; nothing less was found to hold the respect of the average WAC company.

In many cases a female leader also needed leadership qualities in even greater degree than the average male leader, in order to hold her position without the combat incentive. Army manuals stated, "The necessity for discipline is never fully comprehended by the soldier until he has undergone the experience of battle,"[30] and this no WAC unit would ever know. To overcome the meaninglessness of noncombat routine, WAC commanders were urged to

. . . bring the realities of the war home to your women in every possible way. . . . Try to make each woman realize what it would mean to her, as a woman, to live in a Nazi-controlled world; what it would mean in the education of her children; what the Nazi state could and would do with her menfolk; what restrictions would be placed on her opportunities as a woman.[31]

This remote stimulus was the WAC leader's only substitute for combat discipline.

A WAC company commander was at times under an additional strain in introducing female troops into a location in which they had not previously served. While the needs of male troops on the average station were well documented and remedies prescribed, the WAC commander was sometimes obliged to meet peculiar and unforeseen needs, and to advise the station commander in a way not commonly expected of the average male captain or lieutenant. There was also at times a problem of public relations and of community and post acceptance, in which the WAC commander had to lead the way for the women, as well as minimizing any initial friction. Failure in this respect was not uncommon. One staff visitor noted:

---

[29] *The WAC Officer*, p. 50.
[30] FM 22–5, Feb 46, Leadership, Courtesy and Drill, p. 6.
[31] *The WAC Officer*, p. 4.

At one extreme is the C.O. who tries to run her detachment as an autonomous outfit; at the other, an officer who is merely a funnel through which post rules are transmitted. The former has not learned how to mesh gears with the command for the most effective development of its mission; the latter fails to realize that if she does not function in an advisory capacity, she is useless to the Army and the WAC.[32]

The One Essential Quality

Toward the end of the war, a survey was made by the ASF's Information and Education Division of the attitudes of more than 6,000 women in all types of units. As a telling commentary on the popular belief that women could never like a woman supervisor, it was found that as many as 90 percent of the women in some companies had only favorable attitudes toward their WAC commanders.[33]

The ASF study, as well as that by Dr. Durfee, came independently to the same surprising conclusion: the real qualities that made a woman a leader of women had little to do with those that had often been attributed to a female leader in civilian life, or with the concept of "command" and efficiency so laboriously inculcated at officer training schools. Both studies made it clear that the human values, and these values only, constituted the ability to lead women. Dropped to the lowest place in the scale were many commonly praised factors of efficient paper work, knowledge of regulations, supervisory thoroughness, commanding voice and appearance, and military bearing. Leading the list were personal and individual matters—fairness, friendliness, unselfishness, sincerity, courage, and a genuine concern for the women. If a woman possessed these traits, the women would follow her, but, the ASF

surveyors noted, *"If a C.O. is deficient in these traits, it is likely that no amount of efficiency or administrative skill will win for her the enthusiastic support of her enlisted women."*

Of their successful leaders, women said:

"She is fair and square with everyone and shows no partiality."

"She obeys the rules she makes for us."

"She is fair to Wacs, enlisted men, and civilians."

"Doesn't punish all for the misdeeds of a few."

Typical adjectives were *just, dependable, objective, impartial, unselfish,* and *honest.* Of the poor leader, women said:

"Very unfair to the majority. Makes too many exceptions for those she likes."

"She bucks dirty jobs to those under her but breaks any good news to us herself."

"She will say *yes* when *no* is the right answer, if it is unpleasant to say *No.*"

"Some get punishment for infringement of rules, some don't."

The quality of friendliness ranked high:

"She is a regular. I can talk to her better than anyone I know."

"Her ability to be one of us and yet hold the complete respect of all of us."

"She is cheerful and interested in individuals."

"She is available and willing to listen to our troubles."

"She is a good sport and really sympathetic."

"She has a ready smile."

---

[32] Memo, Dep Dir for Dir WAC, 16 Sep 46. WDWAC 333.1.

[33] Rpt cited n. 12. The survey points out that the women's opinion was not necessarily a true picture of their commander's efficiency, in that difficulties unknown to the women existed at certain posts, but as far as the qualities preferred or disliked were concerned, there was no room for mistake.

Of unfriendly commanders, it was said:

"C.O. is too impersonal. Doesn't try to get acquainted with her company except in that 'holier than thou' attitude."

"She means well, but lacks the democratic way of making me feel at ease in her presence."

"Much too G.I. She outshines the meanest male officer."

"Her manner is unfriendly, almost discourteous."

"She is too G.I. and rank conscious."

"She is not interested in individuals."

"She's as cold as a fish and gives the impression she's god and almighty and we're nothing."

The women were quite well aware that their correct assignment and general welfare often depended upon their commanding officer's willingness to "go to bat" for them, even when this might cost her own promotion, advancement, or popularity with higher authorities. Of real leaders, women said:

"She cares about the enlisted women—really cares."

"She is loyal to the company."

"She thinks and acts for the welfare of all the girls."

"She has improved our mail system . . . our medical treatment . . . housing conditions . . . recreational facilities . . . company policies, and morale."

Typical unfavorable comments were:

"She looks out for her own skin first, then will do something for us if it may help her."

"She is partial to anyone who can further her personal interests."

"She is more concerned with personal affairs than with the welfare of the women."

"She is indifferent to the welfare of the WAC."

"She'll never do anything for you—never pursue your problem."

"She shows a complete lack of interest towards our job."

"If she would be more interested in you and your job instead of the way you wear your hair, the Wacs would be more interested in being Wacs."

The factor of appearance—so much stressed in officer candidate school—did not impress the Wacs in proportion to the other qualities, and their views were sometimes unorthodox. Their approved leaders were described as "ladylike . . . lovely looking . . . dignified, courteous, poised . . . neat, clean." They disapproved of an oversevere or overglamorous appearance as much as they did a careless one, and said, "She is too hard and mannish . . . ," "I don't like her G.I. haircut . . . ," "She wears her skirts too short."

The quality of technical competence, so thoroughly stressed in schools, was likewise of secondary importance to the enlisted women. Surveyors reported that, while administrative ability might be more important to the general success of an officer than the women realized, it was not leadership: "It lacks the 'personal relationship' aspect which appears to be highly important." Since the women's lives did not depend, as did those of combat soldiers, upon an officer's technical competence, they were apt to lay less stress upon ability to memorize regulations and correct procedures. While even the best female leader obviously profited by knowledge of technical details, no amount of study of Army Regulations appeared sufficient to make a leader of a woman lacking in personal qualities.

Absolutely disqualifying to leadership was one trait seldom mentioned in officer candidate selection or training instructions: selfish ambition, or rank-consciousness. All evidence indicated that, quite simply, the WAC leader was a person whose primary and genuine concern was for her troops and not for herself. In the makeup of her character, there must be no primary interest or motivation which concerned the importance of her own rank, authority, promotion, or economic advancement, for if so, the women would inevitably discover it and would not respect her, whatever her other abilities.

Enlisted women gave no respect to any woman who was a bully, rank-conscious, or an "apple-polisher." Comments on this type included: "Gold bar crazy," "The Great I-Am," "Power hungry," "Grandstand Officer," "Her bars weigh heavy," "Her bars go to her head instead of her heart," "Uninterested in her job because there's no promotion in it." Even though an officer refrained from the more obvious tyrannical tactics or "throwing her rank around," enlisted women seemed to know her inner motivation. Trouble shooters sent out to inspect ailing companies reported "the lowest morale where company commanders are too interested in their social life or their personal advancement." [34]

Objective psychological tests confirmed their surmise; the typical WAC officer "profile" showed "a far higher social motivation and lower economic motivation than the population in general." The higher the rank of the officer tested, the greater was her emphasis on human values. [35]

Unfortunately, the selfish officer was difficult for superiors to detect, since she often presented a most attractive and capable appearance. Colonel Hobby admitted later:

I was often misled; for example, when I first met Captain S. at Des Moines, she talked of nothing but her enlisted women's welfare, until I was much impressed with her devotion; only after she had been given a better job and promoted did I discover that her only devotion was to herself. [36]

Director Hobby in her speeches and Dr. Durfee in her published studies constantly exposed the pretensions of the rank-conscious or selfishly ambitious individual, in the hope that the developing leader would not be misled. Director Hobby said:

I should consider it very unfortunate if any of us should ever forget that the only reason for our existence as officers is the Women's Army Corps—and that the Women's Army Corps is its enlisted personnel. [37]

One published study added:

Your rank gives you many privileges. . . . These are not just tributes to your natural superiority, nor do they in themselves make you superior. . . . Many an enlisted woman has as good educational background and civilian experience as her officers. . . . You are not their master but their servant. Your only reason for being, in fact, is the enlisted women of the Corps.

The discovery of this basic requirement for the leadership of women appeared to offer a key to the myth that women leaders did not exist, and to the fact that many women bosses and supervisors were heartily disliked in civilian life. The career woman, who by hard fighting rose to the top of a profession in a man's world, had sometimes, by the very intensity of the struggle, lost the concern for others that was essential to the leadership of women. Such civilian "leaders" often failed in the WAC as completely as did some women

---

[34] *The WAC Officer*, pp. 1 and 25.
[35] *The WAC Officer*, p. 22.
[36] Interv, 15 Jan 46.
[37] Min cited n. 1.

unaccustomed to authority. In civilian life a compulsive drive for self-advancement had propelled them to professional or business success, but it had simultaneously denied them the respect of their women subordinates, over whose figuratively dead bodies they sometimes rose.

The natural leader of women was, in the Army experience, distinct from the nervously ambitious office supervisor, the technically competent specialist, the aggressive professional woman, the busybody clubwoman, and the wealthy social leader, all of whom had previously usurped the title. In the WAC such women could succeed in other types of work, but not as leaders of women. The true leader's ambition had to be all for her troops, her Corps, and the Army—never, even secretly, for herself first. The possession of this honest selflessness lent a woman, in the eyes of the women who followed her, a certain dignity, strength, and even greatness.

Selection and Training of Leaders

These discoveries, if applied, might have effected considerable changes in the methods of selection and training of WAC officer candidates. Unfortunately, Dr. Durfee's studies were not published until February of 1945, and the ASF survey not until April, by which time all but about two hundred of the WAC's some seven thousand officers had been selected. Even had earlier results been obtained, it appeared unlikely that the WAC system would be modified until the Army selection and training system was also changed.

Some eighteen months previously, Director Hobby had proposed a changed officer candidate selection system based on very similar British conclusions. The British women's services, like the American, had discovered by experience that a woman leader could not be detected by any external factor, but only by the "personal" qualities that emerged upon contact with a group of women. British women officer candidates selected by field stations were therefore screened by a brief sojourn with a small group of women who included not only other candidates but testing experts, who administered a series of group tests—written, oral, and practical. These women, identically dressed without sign of rank, and living in an informal group, were placed in a number of real-life situations, and led to discuss company problems with the group, while experts made notes of their reactions. The testing officers were thus able to discover much the same personal qualities that would have been apparent to a company of enlisted women over a period of weeks.[38]

The American adaptation was fully worked out, with specific tests and procedures and with selection and training of team members. The team actually functioned in dry runs at the training center, during which groups of thirty officer candidates spent a two-day "live-in" period with team members, taking psychological and performance tests, before going on to regular officer candidate school. Director Hobby's proposal was, however, rejected by the War Department for numerous reasons. The Adjutant General's test construction experts rejected it because commercial psychological tests were used

---

[38] (1) Remarks of Dr. Durfee and Dir Hobby. *Ibid.* (2) Entire file new OCS procedure; submitted Dec 1943; disapproved Jan 1944; in SPWA 352 OCS, 1943. (3) *WAR*, Bull of Army Bur of Current Affairs (British), 17 Apr 43, Sec. 2, p. 7. OCMH.

which they had neither made nor validated, and the use of such tests was not in accordance with policy, while the construction and validation of such tests by the Army would have been more expensive than the small numbers of Wacs merited. Even could this obstacle be overcome, the Army Service Forces nonconcurred on grounds that the system would be a violation of command prerogative: the selection of officer candidates, male and female, was a function of field commands, and to reject their selected candidates after only two days would have been offensive to them. In England this problem had not arisen because of the short distances involved: an applicant could with little travel be sent where the team was located, and was not placed on a command's eligible list prior to a successful sojourn with the team.[39]

The only partial solution available to the WAC was therefore to use a modified testing team as an advisory committee to the officer candidate "murder board"; this was reported to be helpful, although its efficiency was "relative to the cooperation and understanding of the officers."[40] After the end of the war, the ASF arrived at the conclusion that such a system of pre-officer candidate school screening would have been valuable for male candidates, to avoid the "waste of man hours" and the "tremendous burden of eliminating misfits," which in its absence fell upon the schools themselves. There appeared to be a good chance that such a system would eventually be adopted for men as well as women. ASF inspectors also recommended at the end of the war "that the definition of leadership as the ability to command troops in close order drill be discarded and that leadership be defined as an element in every relationship."[41]

The Army Commander as a Leader of Women Troops

While educating the WAC officer to be a leader of women on the company level, the Army also had to consider the knowledge and training required by Army commanders above that level in the leadership of female troops. In the opinion of Army psychiatrists, above the company officer level it was not only safe but proper and natural for women troops, like the citizenry in general, to identify themselves with great military heroes, commanding generals, station commanders, or whatever other Army leaders were best known to them. Such identification promoted morale and pride in military status and a more uncomplaining acceptance of hardships shared by leader and follower alike.

There was considerable evidence that such motivation operated with Wacs, and that they followed meticulously and even blindly any example set. From the first days of the Auxiliary, the Chief of Staff's office took the attitude that Army officers, being senior to the Waacs, were responsible for setting them an example. In one case in which a commander subjected newly arrived WAAC officers to public criticism by inviting them to have drinks in his hotel room, the Chief of Staff's office directed a reprimand:

The War Department regrets that members of the WAAC have cause to be disappointed in a natural expectation that an officer of the Regular Army of thirteen years

---

[39] *Ibid.* Also: (1) Preston, Hist of Psychiatry in WAC, p. 12. (2) From Maj Treadwell, Asst Chief, WAC Br G-1, who discussed tests with TAG. (3) Memo, MPD ASF for Dir Pers ASF, 31 Dec 43. SPGAP 352 OCS (12-23-43) 232, in SPAP 352 WAAC (6-14-43).

[40] Preston, Hist of Psychiatry in WAC.

[41] ASF Hist of OCT 1941-45, p. 87.

service could be looked to as a mentor of what was customary and expected in their association with officers of the other arms and services.[42]

The chief difficulty for the Army officer in fulfilling such expectations lay in the necessity for separating his personal and lifelong attitudes toward women from his military behavior. It was quite simple to recite the only precept necessary for success in Army leadership of women: that women troops should be treated with the same justice, concern, and objectivity that a good commander applies to any troops. It was quite another matter to apply such a precept in the minutiae of daily personal encounters. From the officer whose Wac driver assisted him from a car, to the section chief requested to rescue a tearful secretary from kitchen police, each separate decision frequently required deliberation and good judgment to determine the wise and objective course. Neither was it always possible to follow exactly the same course that could have been followed with a male subordinate, since many situations—such as the case of hotel room drinking—obviously had different implications to society where different sexes were concerned.

Fortunately, the penalty for such failure of objectivity was severe in only one respect. No irreparable damage was usually done by the officer who allowed a personal misogyny to cause a military overseverity, or by the officer who translated a personal gallantry into a military overleniency. WAC units could and did survive both situations. Somewhat more dangerous was the commander whose age and fatherly attitude produced a paternalism that stifled the growth of responsible and mature conduct among women. However, even in this case the worst possible result was ordi-

narily his own disappointment in the unit's performance if responsibility was suddenly thrown upon it. In none of these cases, unless carried to pathological extremes, was the partial failure of a higher commander's objectivity and leadership sufficient totally to undermine unit spirit and efficiency.

One type of failure in leadership, and only one, invariably seemed to end a WAC unit's usefulness and damage its members personally: this was that of the commander who allowed his military decisions to be affected by "the man-woman factor." In civilian life, this officer had his counterpart in the boss who favored one secretary with his personal attention to the disadvantage of other employees. Such a practice habitually damaged civilian office morale even when not aggravated by the greater control superimposed by the military system. Although the relationship that caused the favoritism might be a completely innocent one, bad results were felt by the WAC unit in every case in which an officer attempted to secure special favors, exceptions from rules, or unwarranted advancement for a member. If the relationship was not innocent, it likewise incurred the disfavor of the WAC unit, a thousand times intensified if a unit officer was concerned. The worst possible situation was the combination of an immoral relationship with open and unconcealed favoritism in promotion and other advantages. From the point of view of leadership of women troops, such action by a higher commander constituted complete betrayal, and almost invariably ended the unit's morale, discipline, and efficiency in a way that no other known factor in the Army

---

[42] Memo, TIG for Dep CofS, 2 Jan 43, sub: Investigation Concerning Treatment of WAAC Offs in Norfolk Air Def Wing. IG 333.9 Wilmington, N.C., with incl. WDCSA 291.9.

environment had ever succeeded in doing.

The difficulty in the man-woman factor in the field was not that it occurred frequently, and not that it could not be easily detected by observers, but rather that in such cases as did occur, outside advisers often found themselves powerless to correct the situation. In one extreme case, which went as far as the War Department, both the Chief of Chaplains and the ASF WAC Officer asked transfer of a WAC company officer because her close association with the post commander "is occasioning much comment." However, the commanding officer of the subordinate command and the Chief Signal Officer himself refused to take action, pronouncing the request "idle gossip." As a result, the situation brought on low morale in the detachment, and the divorce of the officer concerned.[43]

Such situations were regarded by reasonably competent WAC staff officers as simple to detect and correct by transfer, had recommendations on the matter always been backed by superiors. With such backing, the man-woman factor was pronounced no serious threat to the integration of women in the Army. The only sure preventive, however, appeared to be the indoctrination of every Army officer in the full consequences of such situations, and his recognition of their relation to his responsibilities for troop leadership.

---

[43] (1) Memo, 9 Jun 44, ASF WAC Off for CSigO, incl request of Chief of Chaplains; (2) 1st Ind, CSigO to ASF, 13 Jun 44, SPSAC 200 WAC; sequel furnished author by ASF WAC Off. SPAP 333.1.

CHAPTER XXXIV

Recruiting and Publicity

Recruiting

The solution to the riddle of WAC recruiting developed, in the opinion of some observers, into a favorite indoor sport. To the end of the war, it never lost its appeal for amateur and professional alike. The letter-writing public, in particular, was fascinated by the problem, and WAC files were filled with helpful letters, such as, "I read with a great deal of interest . . . the recruiting difficulties of the WAC. An idea occurred to me which is so simple that I am surprised that no one has thought of it."[1]

Insofar as this riddle was ever solved in World War II, the solution was not simple, but a matter for constant and painful attention. Following Director Hobby's move to G–1 Division, the principle was fully accepted by the Chief of Staff that continued recruiting success would require not only specialization, but expert specialization, in the recruiting of women. One of the more significant developments of the last months of the war was the perfection within The Adjutant General's Office of a precision recruiting machinery, previously unknown in the Army.

For the last eighteen months of the war, the Recruiting Service faced a tremendously more complicated national problem, and a generally admitted "War-Is-Won" attitude, with those few applicants who still presented themselves including greater numbers of culls and previously rejected women.[2]

Under the circumstances, there existed some question as to whether a continuation of WAC recruiting was possible at all. Some staff offices, such as G–3 Division, recommended against making the effort. During the last year of the war the Army was already overstrength, and the draft was able to supply enough limited service men for replacements. Since there was no longer any numerical compulsion to recruit, the decision hinged upon the relative efficiency of Wacs and limited service men.

It was the General Staff's decision that WAC recruiting must be continued in spite of the greater effort and expense involved. It was noted that all available general service draftees were required as combat replacements. Therefore, men drafted to fill clerical jobs would be not only limited service but frequently lacking in clerical skills. It was also reasoned that, although the Army was overstrength, there were many able-bodied soldiers still in the zone of the interior who were needed overseas, and skilled Wacs could be trained and as-

---

[1] Ltr, Mrs. F. L. C. to Dir WAC, 15 Jan 44. SPWA 062.2.

[2] (1) D/F, ACofAS Pers for CofAS, 1 Jan 44. (2) M/R, 30 May 44, Conf (Mbrs: Gens White, Surles; Cols Hobby, Rice; Dr. Gallup and other Young & Rubicam representatives), sub: Formal Presentation of Nationwide Attitude Survey Made in April. WDWAC 341.

signed to replace them within six to ten weeks, while men could not be. The final decision was that the overstrength could best be taken care of, not by cutting off the supply of needed skills, but by discharging noneffectives, thus "improving efficiency and avoiding aggravation of the current overstrength." [3]

"Fighting Men and Wacs"

This decision was announced by Secretary of War Stimson in widely quoted interviews: "The need at the moment is for fighting men and capable Wacs." The Secretary specifically repudiated the decades-old view that male 4–F's and limited service personnel, whenever obtainable, should be used for noncombat Army jobs. One reporter noted, "Secretary Stimson added that the Army doesn't think very much of 4–F's and would prefer a good capable Wac any day." The Secretary added:

We can fit them into the Army with the minimum of training and use them on jobs where men are seldom as well-trained, as efficient, as well-suited by temperament, or as willing to work as women are.

In another press release a month later, Secretary Stimson again stated:

We need women because they have the skills we are looking for. . . . It is not economy to take men from their families and from jobs in essential industry to do the work in the Army which women who are mobile and without dependents could do with less training.[4]

Such a statement was at first shocking to press and public, which clung to the World War I view that limited service men, however sickly or unskilled, should be used by an Army in preference to women, however healthy or skilled. In response to an appeal from the Bureau of Public Relations, which was deluged by complaints, G–1 Division stated the War Department's position unequivocally in writing:

1. *If the Army is up to troop strength, why are more women needed?* Answer: From 75,000 to 100,000 men or women a month are needed to keep the Army up to strength.

2. *A million men have been discharged. Couldn't they have been retained to do the work Wacs do?* Answer: These men were discharged for physical reasons, for essential civilian jobs, for age, or because unskilled and unsuited for combat. Some could have been placed by the Army, but they have a high sick rate, and would have had to be trained for jobs for which they had no aptitude.

3. *Some 5,000,000 4–F's have not yet been called. Couldn't they be drafted to keep the Army up to strength, without using women?* Answer: Most such men would have to be trained, while women have previous civilian skills. Also, 3 medical persons are needed for every 4 hospital patients, so that the Army does not want 4–F's.

4. *About 10,000,000 men aged 26–38 are deferred. Why not use them instead of Wacs?* Answer: Most are in essential jobs; many are fathers. It is better to take women already skilled in clerical work than to take these men from industry and retrain them.[5]

This concept of the ideal composition of the Army became so well accepted that when, in late 1944, economy-minded congressmen again demanded reasons for not stopping WAC recruiting, the Army replied that in future its activity would be

---

[3] Entire discussion from Memo, G–1 for ASF, 4 Jul 44; incl G–3 noncurrence, 26 Jun 44; DCofS approval, 3 Jul 44. WDGAP 341 WAC, in SPAP 341 WAC.

[4] (1) Stimson statement and reporters' comments, 11 May 44. SPWA 000.77. (2) WDBPR Release, 17 Jul 44.

[5] Memo, G–1 for Dir WDBPR, 18 Apr 44. Hobby files.

. . . in line with the statement of the Chief of Staff to the effect that the personnel needs of the Army are now for *fighting men and Wacs*—men qualified for combat, and women qualified for those jobs requiring the technical and administrative training commonly found among women.

A letter from the Secretary of War to an inquiring congressman further stated:

As you know, selective service calls are now confined almost entirely to combat replacements, whereas the recruitment of Wacs is based upon the Army's need of those skills and training largely held by women.

The need for administrative skills in fact was found to be increasing rather than lessening in the last days of the emergency, because of the need for hospitalization of wounded and for paper work to redeploy or separate others.[6]

The General Staff decision constituted, in effect, a new Army personnel policy. Until this time, it had been customary to group female military personnel with other "limited service" personnel, without much distinction. The new policy recognized three types of military personnel: general service men who were available for combat, women who were "limited service" only with respect to combat, and finally, the genuine limited service category, men or women with physical and mental handicaps requiring additional medical attention or consideration on Army jobs. The Secretary's statement made it clear that in the future "fighting men" would be preferred for combat and "capable Wacs" for office work, with the real limited service category a distinctly last choice for either.

The General Staff thenceforth turned upon the WAC Recruiting Service a close and specialized attention that was to produce, by the end of the war, a streamlined and efficient recruiting and publicity machinery which compared favorably with civilian sales organizations, and which was later to serve as a model for the Army's own postwar Recruiting Service.

Improvement of Recruiting Machinery

In preparation for its resumption of recruiting responsibility at the end of the All-States Campaign, the Army Service Forces began a stock-taking of the state of The Adjutant General's Army Recruiting Service. Investigators, sent out to compile the working recruiters' needs, found an organization scarcely improved since the days of World War I, and recruiters fatigued and in need of attention. Offices were still unattractive and poorly located, transportation still inadequate, funds not properly distributed. Ratings were so poor that only low-rated and therefore often unqualified men and women could be assigned to recruiting duty, while those already assigned could not look forward to promotion no matter how capable their work. There was no training course by which recruiters might be helped toward a proper pride in their specialty, nor bulletins to encourage them. Not even a sufficient supply of uniforms for satisfactory public appearance was provided.[7]

The inadequacy of those in command of recruiting stations, as well as that of the enlisted personnel, was also frequently noted by these investigators, who reported:

Personnel assigned to recruiting is generally below standard and seems to be in

---

[6] T/S, G–1 for CofS and SW, 22 Sep 44, with incl ltr for signature of ASW to Joint Com on Reduction of Non-Essential Federal Expenditures. CofS Cl 324.5 WAC.

[7] Memo, Capt Joseph D. Neikirk, AGD, for Gen Dalton, 20 Jan 44. SPAP 341 WAAC (2–26–43). Incl 1: Memo, Lt Col Hall C. Park, Chief, Mobilization Br, 5th SvC, for Capt Neikirk. SPVPM.

direct relation to the results achieved. Particularly the Army officers in charge of districts seem unsuitable, by the admission of Service Command Headquarters. WAC officers for the most part seem average or better but need training. Enlisted women were below standard in many cases.

Those in charge of stations were found to include such persons as a professor of botany, a linguist, and a man who "is inefficient and drinks too much." Even in the far more important position of director of recruiting in service command headquarters, there were found to be no top-flight sales personnel, but a former farm manager, an accountant, a bookkeeper, an ordinary salesman, and others even less qualified. General Dalton suggested strongly to the service commands that they replace such directors of recruiting with Army officers with a civilian background of responsible sales experience—by definition, those whose salaries had been at least $7,500 yearly—but unfortunately no such officers could be found in most service commands.[8]

It was impossible at all stages to avoid frequent unfavorable comparisons with the Navy recruiting service. One Army investigator reported:

The WAVES have enjoyed a constant and aggressive recruiting policy, backed by highest Headquarters. Offices have been manned with personnel of civilian sales experience, both officer and enlisted. Sales managers have been commissioned. Sales education and training have been available for all levels. They have enjoyed abundant advertising material and transportation.

A comparison of one recruiting area revealed numerous differences:

	Army	Navy
Personnel on recruiting duty	205	375
Number of substations	53	63
Number of vehicles	19	63

Army recruiters had nevertheless, at the time of the survey, got 70,000 women as against the Navy's 48,000—the difference being chiefly due to the Army's six months' start—but the Army had been forced to spend a million dollars on paid advertising while the Navy experts had obtained almost an equal amount free, and had been able to limit acceptances to women with a high school education. The Navy's savings resulted, in Director Hobby's opinion, from the fact that, before WAVES recruiting began,

The leading male sales managers of leading industries were contacted and offered a commission in the grade of Lieutenant Commander to participate in the WAVES recruiting program at one of their approximately 500 Navy recruiting stations. . . . This highly trained sales organization promptly obtained so much free sponsored advertising that the paid advertising test was cancelled.

It was the Director's opinion that reform in the recruiting organization could eventually enable the Army to do the same.[9]

In remedying these ills, it became increasingly obvious that, as General Ulio had predicted a year before, the recruiting organization for men was inadequate to cope with the problems of recruiting women: specialization was the only means of lasting success. In January of 1944, this principle was first applied by the establishment, within The Adjutant General's Office, of the Planning Branch for WAC Recruiting. The Planning Branch's staff was chosen from Army officers of proven ability, most of whom had years of civilian experience in the field of life insurance

---

[8] Ltrs, Gen Dalton to CGs of SvCs, 31 Dec 43, and 12, 13, and 15 Jan 44; and replies. SPAP 341 WAAC (2-26-43).

[9] (1) Memo cited n. 7. (2) Memo, Dir WAC for CofS, 3 Apr 44. WDWAC 341.

sales management. Brig. Gen. Edward F. Witsell, of The Adjutant General's Office, noted:

This decision was based on the realization that the problem is not only one requiring expert sales technique, but the personalized technique best found in the life insurance field, where salesmen deal daily with the intimate personal relationships of all types of individuals.[10]

As chief of the branch, The Adjutant General appointed Lt. Col. John F. Johns, a former insurance sales executive who had for two years been Director of Officer Procurement, Fifth Service Command.

To advise the Planning Branch, there was set up at the War Department level a Planning Board for WAC Recruiting. The Planning Board had an impressive membership of the highest personnel advisers available to the Army—not only General White of G–1 Division, but the personnel chiefs of Air, Ground, and Service Forces, at that time General Bevans, Brig. Gen. Clyde L. Hyssong, and General Dalton, respectively—as well as The Adjutant General and the Director WAC. This board met occasionally as needed to settle major questions. With such a battery of talent turned upon the problem, there was little chance that earlier errors would be repeated.[11]

An auspicious factor for the success of further recruiting efforts was the close and friendly co-operation that existed from this time forward between The Adjutant General's Office and the Office of the Director. Colonel Johns' group met frequently with Deputy Director Rice, with Col. Vance L. Sailor of The Adjutant General's Appointment and Induction Branch, and with representatives of Young & Rubicam. With the establishment of the Planning Branch, the Director's Office routinely referred to it a considerable burden of recruiting inquiries—suggestions from the public, protests, and requests for changes in standards.[12]

At the time of its establishment, it appeared to the men of the Planning Branch that their powers to improve the Recruiting Service were limited. In her reply to the Meek Report, Colonel Hobby therefore asked that this group be given power to institute approved sales policies and methods, supervise and visit the field, and integrate advertising and publicity. These recommendations were all approved by General Marshall.[13]

Diagnosis of Resistance to Enlistment

As the first step in improving both the recruiting and the publicity machinery, a national conference of Army recruiters from every service command was held in Chicago; its keynote was the discovery of handicaps and the polishing of method.[14] Veteran recruiters at the 1944 conference no longer expressed any doubt as to the basic cause of women's resistance to enlistment. Recruiters stated the conviction that the cause of recruiting difficulty did not lie in any of the earlier diagnoses such as women's aversion to Army housing, uniforms, pay, jobs, or any other WAC deficiency. Instead, it appeared to them to be almost solely due to the poor public at-

[10] Opening Remarks, Min, WAC Recruiters Conf, Chicago, 21–23 Feb 44. WDWAC 337.

[11] Planning Board set up by AG Ltr 341 WAC (1–27–44), 29 Jan 44. SPAP 341 WAAC (2–26–43).

[12] See examples in WDWAC 341 (1944).

[13] Memo, Dir WAC for CofS, 10 Apr 44, with CofS approval, 11 Apr 44. CofS C1 324.5. WAC, also SPWA 341, in SPAP 341 WAC (2–26–43).

[14] (1) Memo, TAG for Dir Pers, 12 Jan 43. SPAP 341 WAAC (2–26–43). (2) Memo, Dir WAC for CG ASF, 27 Nov 43. SPWA 341 sec B, in SPAP 341 WAAC.

titude toward women in the armed forces, which in turn was largely traceable to the opposition of Army men.[15]

Brig. Gen. Henry S. Aurand of the Sixth Service Command voiced the service commanders' opinion to this effect:

We are all convinced that the attitude of the buck private is the reason for slow enlistment of Wacs. That is unanimous, and we all say you cannot do anything about it. You have to recruit in spite of it. Let's take this Command for example. Less than ten percent of the enlisted men are in combat organizations. Just tell those fellows to go out and get Wacs so they can be sent overseas, and you will see how far you get. You cannot do anything about that. You have to do it in spite of the attitude of the Army. You might just as well put that in your pipe and smoke it. You are not going to change the way these men think.[16]

This opinion was supported by thousands of letters and statements to recruiters from hesitant prospects. A typical letter from an eligible stated:

The trouble lies with U.S. men. The average serviceman absolutely forbids his wife, sweetheart, or sister to join a military organization, and nearly all U.S. women are in one of these categories.

When a girl sees an Army officer refuse to return a WAC salute and even leave a restaurant just because a group of Wacs walk in, is that any inducement for her to enlist? The catcalls, filthy remarks and dirty stories floating among soldiers and sailors about servicewomen make a decent American girl shudder. From Nebraska to California to Montana to Florida I have heard servicemen's opinions, all the same. . . . Ever since I can remember I have thrilled to military music, marching feet, and uniforms. When the WAC was formed I desired to go right in but the boy I was going with said it would be the end of our romance. Now . . . my husband is an Army officer overseas and my brother is overseas. This state is filled with servicemen's wives living at home. . . . There is nothing I would rather do than join . . . but if I do, I

would probably be disowned by my father, my brother would be ashamed to admit relation to me, and my husband would be heartbroken. . . . The WAC hat is atrocious and the whole uniform a definite drawback, but if men would give their OK, women would gladly wear them. Other objections raised are low salary, long hours, and adverse living conditions, but . . . the expenses I have each month leave about the same amount of money a Wac clears. . . . All those silly reasons are just excuses for pleasing a man.[17]

Even the most loyal Wacs themselves, and the parents of Wacs, dared not gloss over this factor in advising other women to enlist. A typical Wac letter to a prospective recruit stated:

You make up your own mind what you want to do about joining up with the WAC . . . I'm not homesick and I'm not sorry for myself, but I've had the biggest disappointment of my life. You know I loved basic training with all the hard work, discipline, and things I felt I was "taking" in order that I might become a good soldier. I still do not mind having to sleep in an upper bunk with few comforts that I had at home. . . . I have no complaints about the requirements and restraints . . . but the biggest disappointment is the utter lack of respect for the personnel of the WAC. At first I was indignant, but lately . . . instead of being a proud soldier, I am embarrassed that I am a Wac. The soldiers have absolutely no respect for us.[18]

There was little tendency among service commanders to make light of the American woman's subservience to masculine opinion in this respect; the emotional suffering of women and their parents under such social disapprobation was too intense

---

[15] See Ch. XI, above.

[16] Min cited n. 10.

[17] Ltr, Mrs. R. L. C. to Dir WAC, 3 Feb 44. SPWA 095.

[18] Incl to Ltr, CG AAF to all Air Comds, 22 Feb 44; Tab D to Memo, Dir WAC for CofS, 16 Mar 44. WDWAC 341.

to be discounted. One mother sent to the President a daughter's letter, adding:

> It is a terrible thing to have one's child write such a letter, when there is nothing a mother can do but pray. . . . Is it such a terrible thing that girls are in the Armed Forces? It seems they are very much resented.[19]

There existed considerable differences of opinion among conferees as to whether the Army man's thinking could be changed. The vice-president of Young & Rubicam, Mr. Jack Reeder, alleged:

> I would want to resign from Young and Rubicam tonight and go into some other kind of business if I agreed that you cannot change the attitude of the Army men in regard to the WAC. I have never seen any public attitude yet which could not be changed if gone about intelligently. Some of the things we have persuaded Americans they would want . . . makes me think that this is not a particularly tough job, especially when the Wacs themselves are doing such a wonderful job of changing the opinion of the men.[20]

Most service commanders, at a conference in Dallas, agreed that there was nothing wrong with the product for sale, and that men's attitude rapidly changed wherever they had actually worked with Wacs. Maj. Gen. David McCoach, Jr., of the Ninth Service Command, added: "There is no question of the popularity of the Wacs in those services which have them. Right in my own headquarters everybody is enthusiastic. . . ."[21] Nevertheless, only a small fraction of enlisted men were ever thus exposed, and even Young & Rubicam's experts admitted that when they started a survey of what men thought about Wacs, "Our first man was arrested and put in jail in Omaha and we were called off."

Commanding generals of service commands generally refused to abandon the project as completely hopeless. Maj. Gen. J. Lawton Collins stated, "The enthusiasm of the Army can be obtained by the 'center of influence' method." He recommended that senior officers demonstrate to their juniors by concrete action, not speeches, that they approved of the WAC. Maj. Gen. Richard Donovan of the Eighth Service Command called for the ASF to take the lead in "breaking down opposition on the part of the enlisted men" and selling them the idea that "each of them can and must recruit a Wac. . . . We have an Army of seven million men . . . if one out of twenty can induce some woman to apply, we would have 350,000 applications."[22]

In this respect, the most confident of the service commands was the Seventh, which had already developed and tried out an orientation program for male Army personnel, with very encouraging results. This program employed enlisted men and women with professional stage and radio experience in a lively dramatization of the WAC's jobs and mission. At every Army station where the show had been presented, a notable improvement in soldier understanding and friendliness had been reported. Although it was physically impossible for the actors to visit every station in the United States, the Seventh Service Command made available the script and instructions for use by other commands.[23]

Out of these conferences and simultaneous telegraphed instructions to the field,

---

[19] Incls to Ltr, Air WAC Off to Dir WAC, 6 May 44. WDWAC 330.14.

[20] Min cited n. 10.

[21] Min, Conf of CGs of SvCs, Dallas, Tex., 1944. WDWAC 337.

[22] Min cited ns. 10 and 21. Also Memo, Dir Pers ASF for CofS ASF, 14 May 44. SPAP 210.3.

[23] Memo, TAG for Dir WAC, 31 Mar 44, sub: WAC-Army Orientation Movie. AG 341 WAC (3–31–44) WR–E.

there came for the first time a clear and uniform understanding in all commands of the policies basic to successful recruiting. The first of these, not new, was a matter which a year's previous effort had not succeeded in informing all recruiters: "Request omission from announcements of reference to the fact that Wacs 'replace men.' Imply that men are destined to move overseas leaving work to be done here." Colonel Hobby added:

I think that the WAC is old enough to stop talking about 'replacing' a man . . . manpower has become so acute that we should not think in terms of womanpower replacing a man. The soldier does not like it. There is not always a good civilian reaction to it, and we mothers are jealous, perhaps, of our sons . . . we do not like to think that some girl has replaced our son. The WAC is now a total part of the man and woman power of this nation.[24]

Quite closely related to this principle was the Director's request—somewhat startling at first sight—that recruiters cease from public praise of the WAC. She noted:

I think that the day of speaking of the WAC as something new or novel should be over. We should stop saying what a good job the WAC does. I think it should be an accepted part of the war effort. We should simply appeal to the manpower and the womanpower of this nation.

Telegraphed suggestions to the field added:

Because it will antagonize male listeners, don't imply that women do a better job than men except on work in which men recognize women's superiority, such as stenography.

Recruiters were also warned that it was no longer enough to state that the Army needed personnel, because surveys showed that the public realized the need. Director Hobby said, "We know that a great many

women are rationalizing the job they do. If they work . . . two hours a week, they think they are doing a war job." As a "simple measuring stick," she suggested that recruiters ask such women whether their work could be justified as essential in countries that drafted women.

All present at the conference deplored the widespread misunderstandings about recruiting promises. Recruiters were told emphatically that they must make clear to the prospect the limitations on even the station-and-job promise, and Colonel Sailor of The Adjutant General's Office added, "The interested prospect is almost sure to overlook the phraseology, *unforeseen military exigencies*—I wish I could catch up with the guy who coined that. . . ." He advised avoidance of all promises where possible. Colonel Hobby especially insisted that additional and undignified inducements not be added at a local level, with particular emphasis on a rumor that nylon hose, unobtainable on the civilian market, were being offered.

Service command representatives also unanimously objected to impossible quotas, which had previously been based on the astronomical numbers of Wacs wanted by the Army, instead of upon what might reasonably be obtained. Director Hobby agreed, and stated that it was possible that quotas had been the basic reason for the defeatist attitude about the failure of WAC recruiting.

Another demand of service commanders was for the establishment of a recruiters' school. A few service commands, on their own initiative, had taken some earlier steps to train WAC recruiters. The Ninth Service Command's indoctrination pro-

---

[24] All, including following discussion, from: (1) Min cited n. 10. (2) TWX, Dir WAC to all WAC Ln Offs in SvCs, 19 Feb 44. SPWA 000.77.

gram had included a study of WAC Regulations, local news files, common errors, and what not to say for publication.[25] It was Colonel Johns' first opinion that all could do likewise. He informed service command conferees:

The nine Service Commands have men who are possessed of a sufficient knowledge of the problem to start the training procedure, so that you do not have to wait until we set up a school. May I suggest that you try to solve the problem in your own commands?

Service command representatives disagreed, stating variously: "We have done that, but have not been successful"; "If we could have them go to school outside the Service Command, it would be much better than the effort we can put forth"; "Recruiting is primarily AG work . . . you have the Fort Washington School." When Colonel Johns called for a vote, six of the nine favored a centralized school.

Remedial Action by The Adjutant General

During the first six months of 1944, Colonel Johns' Planning Branch took swift remedial action against all such defects in organization that might hamper or discourage the working recruiter. In January The Adjutant General's Office published the first issue of its *Recruiters' Review,* designed to inform recruiters in the field of the latest developments and to exchange workable ideas between commands, as well as to reveal the comparative record of each area's progress. The Air Forces already used a similar bulletin to spread knowledge of successful devices.

By the first day of February, The Adjutant General's Recruiting Publicity Bureau was ready to distribute more than 39,000,000 pieces of literature, including recruiter's kits, booklets, cards, posters, a more attractive application blank, a booklet for servicemen, a reassuring letter for mothers of recruits, and other aids.

In March, as a result of suggestions made at the conference, widespread use was made of ideas and devices that had proved successful in various commands. Small information booths were set up in department stores, theater lobbies, and other places where women were more likely to go than to the main Army recruiting station. Columns were written by enlisted women for home-town newspapers, letters of information were mailed home from training centers and new stations, home-town mayors proclaimed "WAC Day," and the Air Forces bombed whole communities with recruiting literature. A moving picture short subject was planned, to orient Army men to the useful work done by Wacs.

The Planning Branch sponsored a concerted drive on women's colleges, universities, and business and technical schools, with the object of getting skilled workers and at the same time "to improve the general opinion of the nation regarding the type of women which make up the WAC." Nationwide publicity was directed to particularly successful local results. For example, when General Somervell's daughter and six other highly eligible young women enlisted from Sweetbriar College, General Dalton was rushed to the spot to administer the oath, and widespread news stories resulted.

Also in March, for the first time in over a year, a recruiting quota was set that was humanly capable of being met. In April, for the first time in most recruiters' memory, this quota was exceeded—a

[25] Ltr, Hq 9th SvC to Dir WAC, 10 Mar 43. SPWA 201.6.

psychological triumph which, without any great increase in recruits, caused a more optimistic feeling to be reflected in press and public opinion.[26]

In late April, a WAC recruiters' school was established in conjunction with The Adjutant General's other schools, taking fifty women at a time for classes of two weeks' duration. To be eligible for the school, enlisted women were required to be high school graduates of good character, with at least two months' recruiting experience and previous experience in dealing with people.

To improve the type of personnel assigned to the WAC Recruiting Service, the Planning Branch proposed a special allotment of grades that would make it possible to assign and keep competent specialists, comparable to the Navy's ratings.

This effort was for a time blocked by General Dalton, who stated that he did not wish to restrict the service commands in how they utilized their bulk allotments. Colonel Hobby therefore included in her reply to the Meek Report a recommendation that appropriate grades and ratings be provided. This was approved by the Chief of Staff. General Marshall, at her request, also directed each service command to bring recruiting personnel up to authorized strength and assign a full-time supervisor of WAC recruiting.

In this month, members of the Planning Branch spent two thirds of their time in the field. Service command organizations were revised, supervisors appointed, and attempts made to keep up recruiters' enthusiasm. More uniforms were obtained for recruiters, and they were given a priority on the new tropical worsted summer uniforms.[27]

In May, after two months of furious activity, the Planning Branch published a selection procedure for WAC applicants. This was later, for convenience, incorporated in an ASF manual. It gave a detailed compilation, in one convenient publication, of the many rules, procedures, and policies that now applied to WAC recruiting. For new or untrained recruiters, such a book of reference was expected to be especially valuable.[28]

In all these efforts, good use was made of the National Civilian Advisory Committee, by which prominent women lent their assistance in many localities. One report from an especially active group in the Second Service Command, headed by Mrs. Oswald Lord, showed that it had approached numbers of eligible women for enlistment, obtained much free advertising, persuaded 300 theaters to show WAC recruiting films, put displays in various department store windows and in Pennsylvania Station, New York City, got spot announcements from seventy-five radio commentators, met with local groups and churches, arranged trips for reporters, and persuaded the Fifth Avenue Coach

---

[26] (1) *Recruiters' Review*, first issue. Copy in SPAP 341 WAAC (2–26–43). (2) Memo 5, Hq AAF Tng Comd, WAC Rctg Publicity Campaign, 11 Nov 43. SPWA 007. (3) Min, Mtg in O Dir WAC, 14 Dec 43. SPAP 341 WAAC. (4) Memo, Maj McClure for Dir WAC, 26 Jan 44. SPWA 000.7. (5) Memo, Plng Br for TAG, 3 May 44. SPAP 341 WAAC (2–26–43). (6) Memo, Capt P. Spofford for Lt Col Robert S. Brown, ASF, 18 Apr 44. ASF Folder, WAC Rctg, DRB AGO. (7) Rpt, Plng Br for WAC Rctg to Plng Bd, 26 Apr 44, and incls. WDWAC 341.

[27] (1) Rpt cited n. 26(7). Also Memo Routing Slip, AGO for Dir WAC, 19 May 44; incl, Revised Program of Instruction for WAC Recruiters. WDWAC 341. (2) Memo, Gen Dalton for TAG, 9 Feb 44. SPGAS 220.2 Gen (2–9–44)–49, in SPAP 220.4 WAC 319.1 WAC folder. (3) Memo cited n. 13.

[28] ASF Manual M208, 23 Jan 45, sec III. Earlier ltr, 19 May 44. See Comment 4, Dir Pers ASF for G–1, 28 May 45. WDWAC 720.

Company to repaint one of its buses with WAC advertising.[29]

At the same time, with the aid of Director Hobby's appeal to the Chief of Staff, funds for paid advertising for another four months were secured. The ASF opposed the further use of funds on the grounds that the Navy did not require it, but the Director noted that, in spite of planned improvements, the Army did not yet have the necessary trained and capable personnel, nor was there any one unified WAC recruiting service comparable to the Navy's. Without such central coordination, she stated, the use of free sponsored advertising was ineffective, since each sponsor followed a different theme. Paid advertising was thus as yet the Army's only means of maintaining centralized control of advertising policies and coordination of the sales approach of the field recruiters.[30]

The importance of the expense of the measure depended on the viewpoint; thus, although about $2,000,000 was spent on paid advertising in the fiscal year 1944, this was little more than half that appropriated to give soldiers free lapel buttons with certain medals.[31]

Establishment of a Separate WAC Recruiting Service

All of these improvements, while valuable, did not yet solve the problem of creating efficient recruiting machinery. In late May of 1944, the Planning Branch finally admitted the necessity of the one last step that had been foreseen by General Ulio more than a year before: the complete separation of the WAC Recruiting Service from the Army Recruiting Service in the service command organization. In spite of other improvements, final

control of acceptance or rejection still did not always lie with personnel trained to meet the problem or sympathetic to it. At a meeting of the Planning Board in late May, the inadequacy of this organization to meet continuing needs was noted, and it was decided that "definite steps must be taken immediately to gear the recruiting organization to the mission to be accomplished." [32]

The seriousness of The Adjutant General's proposals caused considerable General Staff debate. Complete specialization was recommended, with the WAC Recruiting Service entirely divorced from the Army Recruiting Service, and responsible only to the director of personnel of a service command and thence to The Adjutant General. Acceptance and rejection would be entirely in the hands of the service command's WAC recruiting officer and her assistants, and could not be overruled by the parallel Army recruiting office. The service would have its own appropriate allotment of grades, with assignment and promotion entirely in its own control. It was also proposed that order be brought out of the hodgepodge of personnel by permanently assigning to the WAC Recruiting Service those temporary-duty

[29] Rpt, 2d SvC CAC to ASF, 1 Sep–15 Dec 44. SPAP 319.1 WAC (10–9–44).

[30] On WAC advertising in this period, see: (1) Memo, Dir WAC for CG ASF, 27 Nov 43. SPWA 341, in SPAP 341 WAAC. (2) Memo, Dir WAC for Budget Off for WAC, 23 Dec 43. WAC C1 file, unnumbered. (3) Memo, TAG for G–1, 28 Feb 44. Same file. (4) Memo, Dir WAC for CofS, 3 Apr 44; (5) Memo, Plng Bd for WAC Rctg for TAG, 30 Jun 44; (6) Memo, Dep Dir WAC for Col Coursey, G–1 Div, 21 Oct 44; Rpt, Plng Br AGD to Plng Bd, 23 Oct 44; (7) Memo, WAC Gp WDBPR for Dir WDBPR, 27 Oct 44. WDWAC 341.

[31] G–4 Rpt, Min, Gen Council, 21 May 46.

[32] (1) Memo, TAG for G–1, 14 Jun 44. AGWR–E 341 WAC. (2) Memo, G–1 for CG ASF through CofS, 23 Jun 44; with DCofS approval, 3 Jul 44. WDGAP 341 WAC. All in CofS 324.5 WAC.

recruiters now on loan from Air or Ground Forces, currently only partially under Recruiting Service control, and unable to be rated until returned to other duty.

The drastic nature of the proposed action brought objection from several agencies, particularly G–3 Division, which in July of 1944 believed the war's end too close to warrant the effort and recommended that WAC recruiting cease. However, in view of the continuing need for the administrative skills found among women, it was the General Staff's decision that the reorganization was warranted, and the establishment of the WAC Recruiting Service was directed.

With the addition of former temporary duty personnel, a total of almost 4,000 persons—both men and women, officers and enlisted personnel—was assigned to the WAC Recruiting Service. The assignment of men was limited, since past experience showed a bad public reaction, partly because men were kept from combat to recruit women, and partly because

... many of the enlisted men who have been assigned to WAC recruiting have proved actually harmful because of their wisecracking and scornful attitude towards members of the WAC in the same office and because of blunt and often fresh remarks to prospective recruits.[33]

It was finally decided to allow only a minimum use of returned combat men, who could not be accused of avoiding active duty, and whose status as war heroes lent a certain prestige to the recruiting station, particularly if they could be kept busy making public speeches to civic groups. The Navy some time before admitted that, even though men in its recruiting stations had no authority over WAVES acceptances, they were not even satisfactory in a limited role as processing

agents because they "did not pay sufficiently careful attention to weeding out underage girls and some who proved to be marked disciplinary problems."[34]

With the completion of this reorganization, the WAC recruiting machinery reached the peak of its wartime efficiency. In July of 1944, Colonel Johns and Planning Branch members visited all service commands, and reported:

The program on an over-all national basis seems now to be well underway, and definite accomplishments should shortly begin to result, providing the public does not become too thoroughly convinced that the war is about over.[35]

At this inopportune moment, the brief honeymoon between the WAC and the nations' manpower agencies was ended when the Office of War Information, objecting to the WAC decision to spend its advertising money in newspapers instead of radio, stopped all radio co-operation. OWI's national headquarters wrote to all radio stations in the United States that, since the War Department had decided to spend its WAC advertising appropriation by buying newspaper space exclusively, the Office of War Information therefore "feels that the WAC Recruiting Campaign will be adequately handled in this media" and that free radio facilities should not be given to recruiters. Colonel Johns reported:

The withdrawal of OWI radio support has affected every Service Command ... this has proved inestimably detrimental to the Recruiting Program and ... even in the event radio support is soon reestablished, the posi-

[33] D/F, Plng Br AGO for Dir WAC, 29 Jan 44; 1st Ind, 2 Feb 44. SPWA 341.

[34] WAVES Hist, pp. 66–69.

[35] Memo, Col Johns for Plng Bd for WAC Rctg, through TAG, 9 Aug 44, sub: Rpt of Visit to All SvCs and MDW, 17 Jul 44. SPAP 341 WAAC (2–26–43).

tion we formerly held in relation to this medium can never be fully regained.[36]

The national situation had not improved, with even military authorities implying that the war was over. Colonel Johns reported:

Continued adverse publicity has had a very detrimental effect. . . . It is doubtful if we will exceed our quota . . . , because of headlines and statements such as ARMY IS ALREADY OVERSTRENGTH, or MORE THAN A MILLION MEN HAVE BEEN DISCHARGED, or MEN BEYOND 26 YEARS OF AGE ARE NOT NEEDED, and numerous other negative pronouncements by Army and Government officials.[37]

Achievements of the WAC Recruiting Service

In the face of these difficulties, the new and separate WAC Recruiting Service nevertheless accomplished what, in the first months of the year, had seemed unlikely: the maintenance of recruiting for the rest of the war at a level not too far below that set earlier by the All-States Campaign, with an actual rise in recruits in the summer of 1944 in spite of the optimism engendered by the Normandy invasion.

Even more remarkable was the WAC Recruiting Service's success in preventing enlistment of unqualified women. Records of training centers indicated that discharges for erroneous enlistment, minority, and dependency were wiped out by the new system; the Army thus saved thousands of dollars in terminal bonuses alone, as well as in clothing, transportation, and training costs. Discharges for undesirable traits and for fraudulent enlistments were almost eliminated. At the same time there was a reduction of 35 percent in the number of women who had to be sent to the Special Training Unit.[38]

Also, after six months of the new system, Director Hobby was able to recommend the abolition of paid advertising, since the Army now, like the Navy, had a specialist group with centralized control. The Planning Branch estimated that, in the last nine months of 1944, the value of free sponsored advertising obtained by the WAC exceeded $15,000,000. As a result, the WAC was able to turn back unspent some $200,000 of the earlier appropriation for paid advertising. Had the Planning Branch and a separate WAC recruiting service operated from the beginning of the war, it was estimated that the economy would have been even greater, to the sum of several million dollars.[39]

Last Days of WAC Recruiting

Cessation of recruiting began gradually in the fall of 1944 by the simplification of mechanics. It was at the time hoped that a need for lesser numbers would permit abandonment of the various special inducement systems such as branch or station-and-job recruiting. There were two major objections to these systems. The ASF and AGF objected to them on the grounds that the AAF continued, by means of them, to get the majority of recruits; the majority of women in the top AGCT brackets also chose the AAF.[40] The ASF also objected on the grounds that ASF training centers could not classify

---

[36] Ibid. Incl is OWI Ltr, Chief, Station Relations Br to all radio stations, 15 Jul 44.

[37] Rpt, Plng Br for WAC Rctg to Plng Bd for WAC Rctg, 26 Apr 44, and incls. WDWAC 341.

[38] (1) Memo, Maj Katherine K. Johnson for Dir WAC, 23 Feb 45. WDWAC 220.8. (2) Rpt, Plng Br to Plng Br, 23 Oct 44. WDWAC 341.

[39] (1) Ibid. (2) Memo, Dep Dir WAC to Col Coursey, G–1 Div, 20 Oct 44. WDWAC 341.

[40] D/F, Classif and Repl Br AGO for MPD AGO, 17 Jun 44. WDWAC 319.1.

and assign, as they saw fit, the women already promised a branch, job, or station.[41]

The AAF concurred in dropping the station-job system, always troublesome, but refused to allow the 1,500 members of its recruiting teams to continue unless branch recruiting also continued. In late August of 1944, letters therefore went out directing the end of station-and-job recruiting on 1 November.[42]

The next step was intended to be the reduction of recruiting to a maintenance basis immediately following the defeat of Germany—which, it was prematurely expected, would take place by the end of the year. Plans made in late October called for the strength of the Corps to be frozen at the end of 1944, recruiting thereafter to be limited to 500 or 700 women a month in essential skills to make up attrition. This reduction would, in The Adjutant General's opinion, make possible a simultaneous 65 percent reduction in facilities and 77 percent in personnel.[43]

In pursuance of this plan, letters went out to all service commands on 20 December 1944, virtually ending active WAC recruiting. Effective 1 January, each service command was directed to reduce its service to 20 officers and 41 enlisted personnel. Each command had a quota of only 68 each month, the women to get a choice only of the major branch of service, not job or station.[44]

Unhappily for this plan, and for the relief to which recruiters were looking forward, the Battle of the Bulge made this directive obsolete even before it was sent out. In the first days of the new year, the relief orders were rescinded and recruiters learned of the General Hospital Campaign with its system of recruitment for specific installations.[45]

In every way the General Hospital Campaign, which occupied the first four months of 1945, made the fullest use of the technical knowledge evolved by the Recruiting Service, and avoided the pitfalls revealed by past experience. The original directive plainly stated that, while women could be promised initial assignment to a unit, the recruiter must make clear the meaning "initial" and also that the members might be trained as either technicians or medical clerks, according to the needs of the service. To prevent misunderstandings and later disputes as to what had been promised, it was specified that a qualification certificate be completed in quadruplicate: the original to be placed in the service record, a duplicate to go to training center classification officers, the third copy to the woman herself, and the fourth to the service command file.[46]

So thorough did the WAC recruiting organization eventually become that, in the last days of its operation, it appeared doubtful whether any eligible prospect or avenue of approach in the entire nation was ignored. In fact, the Director received a congressman's complaint that recruiting literature had been sent to a former constituent, although the lady had died the previous year at the age of 95.[47]

After almost three years of continuous

[41] Memo, MPD ASF for Dir Pers ASF, 27 Apr 44. SPGAP 341 Gen (4–19–44)–69, in SPAP 341 WAAC (2–26–43).

[42] D/F, G–1 for TAG, 29 Aug 44. WDGAP 341 WAC, in WDWAC 341. Published in AG Ltr to SvCs, 31 Aug 44. SGPR–I–A 341 WAC (8–29–44).

[43] Memo, G–1 for ASF, 26 Oct 44, with inds and M/R through 8 Dec 44. SPAP 341 WAC (11–6–44).

[44] Ltr, TAG to all SvCs, 20 Dec 44. SPXPR–I WAC (12–20–44) in SPAP 341 WAAC.

[45] Ltr, TAG for All SvCs, 13 Jan 45. AGPR–I 341 WAC, in WDWAC 341.

[46] *Ibid;* also Ltr, TAG for all SvCs, 23 Jan 45. Same file.

[47] D/F, Dir WAC to TAG, 16 Jan 45, incl ltr to Rep. Paul W. Shafer. WDWAC 341.

campaigning, the unrelieved proximity to public opinion had been sufficient to reduce even the most normal and extroverted of recruiters to what most believed to be incipient paranoia with delusions of persecution. Relief had been promised upon successful completion of the General Hospital Campaign, since there was no legislative authorization for a peacetime women's Corps and demobilization was at hand. With the campaign completed and V-E Day at hand, G–1 Division of the General Staff hastened to restore the earlier orders to cease WAC recruiting except for attrition replacements.[48]

Effective 15 May 1945, the WAC Recruiting Service was abolished, its separate Table of Organization was rescinded, and it was again integrated into the Army Recruiting Service. Its personnel was cut from 3,600 to 300, the excess being returned to the major command that had contributed it. The Planning Branch for WAC Recruiting was also abolished as of 15 May 1945. The recruiting effort for women of all services appeared over. Even the War Manpower Commission declared an end to the joint statement of policy, and noted that, because of the lessened need in industry, "Army-Navy recruitment of women will no longer be subject to the restrictions and policies set forth in the joint statement." [49]

For a few weeks it appeared that this action had been premature. In the uncertain days of the early summer of 1945, both the Army and the Navy decided that it had been a mistake to cut recruiting of women to an attrition basis, since the demobilization process began to present unprecedented demands for clerical personnel. As a result, soon after Director Hobby's resignation, G–1 Division presented the service commands with a new quota of 10,000 in six months—fully half that which the highly organized WAC Recruiting Service had been able to get in its most intensive campaign. In addition, it was demanded that 75 percent of recruits be in the scarce clerical skills, and another 25 percent in other skilled specialist fields.

With something of the optimism of early WAAC days, the General Staff indicated that the Army Recruiting Service should be able to get these numbers without the expense of reactivating the WAC Recruiting Service. Some surprise was expressed that WAC recruiting had promptly slumped to insignificant numbers as soon as the WAC specialist groups were disbanded, and that low-grade recruits were again being erroneously admitted. Officers sent to the field to investigate reported that WAC recruiting "had been relegated to a position of minor importance."[50]

The renewed demand, therefore, caused some concern to former WAC recruiting authorities, who had always held the unanimous opinion that recruiting would never succeed without organization:

Chevrolet, or General Electric, or any big concern trying to sell a large quantity of goods could not do it without retail salesmen . . . to try to do this job without people . . . would be just about suicide.[51]

---

[48] Memo, G–1 for TAG, 27 Mar 45. SPAP 341 WAC.

[49] Ltr, WMC to all Regional Dirs, 20 Jun 45. WMPE, in WDWAC 341.

[50] Above and following based on: (1) M/R, Memo for Presentation at Mtg of Plng Bd for WAC Rctg, 26 Jul 45; (2) Memo, Dir WAC for Dir WDBPR, 27 Jul 45; (3) Memo, Dir WAC for Dir WDBPR, 27 Jul 45; (4) TWX, TAG to all SvCs, 29 Aug 45, AGSE–P 341 WAC, Priority, in WDWAC 341. (5) TWX, TAG to all SvCs, 13 Sep 45. AGPO–A–SPGAG, 210.31 WAC (9–1–45) in WDWAC 210.31.

[51] Remarks of Vice-Pres, Young & Rubicam, In Min, WAC Recruiters Conf, Chicago, 21–23 Feb 44. WDWAC 337.

At a meeting of the divisions concerned, it was pointed out that the Army Recruiting Service faced an impossible situation: the Navy had just launched a specialist-sparked campaign for 20,000 Waves; the skills asked were short nationally; the pay and advancement offered could not compare to industry's; and women were reluctant to enlist just as men were being redeployed from Europe.

Bombs dropped at Hiroshima and Nagasaki intervened to spare recruiters this ordeal. Soon after V-J Day, the wartime history of WAC recruiting was closed out by a telegram to all service commands:

DISCONTINUE WAC RECRUITING AND WAC ENLISTMENT. DO NOT REPEAT NOT COMPLETE ENLISTMENTS BEING PROCESSED. REPLACE WAC RECRUITING PERSONNEL WITH MALE PERSONNEL END.[52]

Public Relations Support

During the last eighteen months of the war, an identical course of development had been experienced in the parallel problem of providing public relations support for WAC recruiting. Although the policies for presenting the Corps in a dignified manner had been established since the day the WAAC was launched, the average public relations officer in the field did not have the advantage of familiarity with these policies. Recruiters in the field complained that, with a remarkable unanimity considering the lack of co-ordination, almost every post public relations officer had decided that it was funny or effective to pose a woman peeling mountains of potatoes or onions, or to smear her face with grease and show her peering from under a truck. One male recruiter noted:

Post Public Relations Officers, with the best intentions in the world . . . would send out pictures of somebody doing a tough job. Making your pictures of pretty girls panting and in awkward positions won't win friends and influence people.[53]

Local radio shows were even more difficult to control; a typical early protest went to the Fifth Service Command concerning a soldier broadcast which was "in poor taste, with kidding back and forth between the Waacs and soldiers of a sort that sounded cheap on the air."[54] Overseas theaters in early days were also habitually blind to the effect of their news releases on the home-town recruiters. Soon after Waacs arrived, the North African theater created a minor sensation by releasing pictures of veil-skirted Waacs in what appeared to be a harem, but which NATO public relations officers insisted was a "light, clean comedy put on under the supervision of staff officers. . . ." The public nevertheless persisted in writing to the Director for information on "the burlesque show being put on by Waacs in North Africa"; one told her: "I am about to prepare a study on causes of delinquency and would appreciate the details you have uncovered."[55]

The agencies releasing publicity material in this un-co-ordinated fashion included not only posts, camp, and stations, but overseas theaters, the various divisions of the Bureau of Public Relations itself, and all War Department personnel who

---

[52] TWX cited n. 50(4); also Ch. XXXVI.
[53] Min, Rctg Conf 6th SvC, 7–8 May 43. SPWA 337.
[54] Ltr, Actg Dep Dir WAAC to WAAC Stf Dir 5th SvC, 26 Apr 43, re broadcast from Camp Campbell.
[55] Ltr, Mansur B. Oakes to Lt Pat Lee Chance, 25 Mar 44, and reply, 3 Apr 44. WDWAC 330.14.

mentioned the WAC in public interviews.[56]

By the time of the move to G–1 Division, the WAC file of clippings labeled "Horrible Examples" included many unlikely releases originated by station public relations officers, such as FORMER CIRCUS FREAK NOW A WAC AT THIS POST. Wacs in leopard skin sarongs and Wacs in nude-colored bathing suits vied with overweight Wacs and stern-faced mannishly barbered Wacs for Army publicity pictures.

Negative public statements were also frequent, with typical headlines such as: RESULTS SO FAR POOR, GENERAL UHL REPORTS; WAAC DRIVE GOES SLOWLY; RESPONSE IN NEBRASKA UNSATISFACTORY; LAG IN WAAC ENLISTMENTS IS DISAPPOINTING TO THE ARMY. At the same time other services, with smaller actual enlistments, were releasing statements such as WOMEN MARINES' RECRUITERS SWAMPED WITH APPLICATIONS. Some public commendations were ill-chosen to soften soldier opinion, such as a statement from a post commander: "Their coming here has literally shamed the soldiers into a little more conscientiousness and neatness." Errors of fact were common; Wacs were pictured in jobs that they did not actually perform, or in unauthorized uniforms. Possibly most damaging were press stories to the effect that MALE RIDICULE RETARDS WAC ENLISTMENT, or WOMEN IN WAR OPPOSED.

Since all such efforts of local public relations officers had been guided by very little knowledge of national recruiting policy, it was possibly more surprising that some had achieved effective and positive publicity, such as MEDAL GIVEN HUSBAND RECEIVED BY AIR-WAC, or PLANE NAMED PALLAS ATHENE . . . AS TRIBUTE TO GIRLS AT THIS BASE.[57]

In January of 1944, the Chief of Staff became aware of the problem through one of the worst *gaffes* yet committed by the publicity organization. In this month public relations officers in the European theater released to a national pictorial magazine in the United States a series of pictures of grotesque mannish-looking "Wacs" in obscene poses and engaged in soliciting men. The captions did not make it clear that the subjects were men dressed in WAC uniforms. Once released, the pictures were beyond recall by the War Department. Director Hobby protested:

These pictures together with the captions, are a reflection on both the serious purpose and the morals of the WAC. . . . The WAC is a component of the Army, and War Department policy contemplates that there shall be no discredit to any member of the Army of the United States because of sex, as well as none because of color or creed.[58]

This incident for the first time brought the Chief of Staff into the problem of coordination of publicity with recruiting expenditures. In a personal note to the bureau he commented, "We do not appear to have made the best of the picture." General Marshall listed cases that he would have used to aid recruiting if he had been a public relations expert: General Arnold's WAC adviser, representative of 20,000 women; the five WAC officers in

[56] Memo, Dir WAC for CofS, 21 Mar 44, with Tabs A to J atchd. WDGAP 341.

[57] All from press scrapbook on loan to author; specifically (not in order): *Omaha World-Herald*, April 12 and 21, June 21, and December 16, 1943, February 19 and August 31, 1944; Pueblo (Colo.) *Star*, May 21, 1943, and January 31, 1944; Springfield [?] *Leader*, March 11, 1943; Denver, Colo., *Rocky Mountain News*, March 2, 1943; *Denver Post*, March 23, 1943; *Fargo Forum*, (N. D.), February 20, 1944; *St. Paul Dispatch*, January 19 and 20, 1944; *New York Times*, June 16, 1943 and February 14, 1944; *Des Moines Register*, June 27, 1943, and January 20, 1944.

[58] Memo, Dir WAC for CG AAF, 2 Feb 44. SPWA 001.–N.

Africa, present at Casablanca and entertained at dinner by President Roosevelt and Prime Minister Churchill; the fact that General Eisenhower's driver was a Wac and that "my driver in Africa was a Wac and a very efficient one." From his own office he contributed a case, saying:

There came to my office, shortly after the initiation of the WAAC, a Lt. F. T. Newsome. She was used to replace an officer in the outer office to meet people. Her work proved so valuable that she was gradually moved from job to job until she is now my personal secretary for all matters pertaining to the U.S. Chiefs of Staff and combined Chiefs of Staff, briefing the papers, making contact with the interested parties who include General Arnold, General Somervell, and General Handy, and apprising me of the pros and cons of the various issues. That is certainly an important job. Furthermore, during certain periods on off hours she performs the duty of Acting Secretary, General Staff.

I am sure that there are a number of somewhat similar cases, none of which I have seen featured. Who is handling this business?[59]

The answer, not rendered in exactly those terms, was that there was no section or individual in the Bureau of Public Relations charged with co-ordinating WAC publicity on an Army-wide basis. On 18 February, at his request, the Director submitted to General Surles of the bureau a twelve-page summary of problems and deterrents connected with WAC recruiting.[60] This received no immediate reply.

Establishment of the WAC Group

A month later, in her reply to the Meek Report, the Director recommended formation of a specialist group, under General Surles' jurisdiction, to co-ordinate publicity with recruiting policy. She stated:

Civilian experience has shown that in the information field there are two distinct and separate functions to be performed. The personnel required to perform these functions is different in temperament and training and never grouped together in civilian practice. One is the creative type which thinks of ideas which, when they occur, will create an impression on the public mind. The other is the type which tells what has happened: factual reporting. The personnel of the Bureau, in keeping with its mission, has been selected from this latter type. . . . A group must be established whose primary mission is to prepare plans and follow through. . . . This must be a professional job, competing in a well-organized field for the attention and interest of the civilian public against professional attempts to attract the same people in other directions.[61]

Over the objections of both General Somervell and General Surles, General Marshall directed formation of such a group. General Surles stated that he could spare no personnel for the project. Accordingly, G–1 Division augmented the Bureau of Public Relations by twelve officer grades to form a WAC Group.[62]

Six field grade male officers and six company grade women officers were assembled to form the WAC Group, headed by Col. J. Noel Macy, formerly the WAAC's first deputy and public relations officer. Specialists were included in the fields of radio, photography, newspapers, magazines, and other publicity media. The group was formally charged with developing a favorable public reaction to

---

[59] Memo, "G. C. M." for WAC Rctg Sec, WDBPR (nonexistent sec), 26 Jan 44. OCS 324.5 WAC.
[60] Memo, Dir WAC for Dir WDBPR, 18 Feb 44. SPWA 341 B, in WAC files, OCMH.
[61] Memo, Dir WAC for CofS, 4 Apr 44. WDGAP 341, WDBPR files—Orgn of WAC Gp.
[62] (1) Memo, Chief, News Div WDBPR for Dir WDBPR, 13 Apr 44. (2) WDBPR Office Memo 22, 25 Apr 44. Establishes WAC Gp, with 12 offs. Both in Folder, Orgn of WAC Gp, WDGAP 341 (4-4-41).

WAC recruiting, and its relations to The Adjutant General's Planning Branch were formally defined. It was directed to devise a proper approach, gather material, write releases, review copy for accuracy, and guide field public relations officers toward the original idea of the WAC as a serious and dignified organization, which General Marshall had attempted to inculcate at the WAAC's first press conference almost two years before. It was Director Hobby's opinion that such a group, operating from the beginning, might have saved the WAC from much of its recruiting difficulties and public misunderstanding.[63]

From this time onward, it was not always possible to tell which improvements in national opinion could be credited to Army recruiters and which to Army public relations officers, since they were no longer employing contradictory approaches. The WAC Group set itself to obtain from posts and stations a stream of information and pictures that would make good news stories, which soon began to flow out to the recruiters and to publicity media—radio, newspapers, and magazines. It was hoped that enough emphasis upon accurate publicity of this type would eventually counteract other stories shocking enough to reach reporters unassisted.[64]

By the summer of 1944, the WAC's first real public relations campaign was under way. For the first time a full-scale publicity campaign was designed to reinforce a recruiting campaign, and for the first time public relations officers in the field learned exactly what the Army wished of them in the way of presenting the Women's Army Corps to the public. The rules, as laid down in classified bulletins to field public relations officers, were quite similar to those which Colonel Hobby had adopted for her own office two years before, with some additions. The chief ideas to be keynoted by stories and pictures were:

1. Wacs are just as feminine as before they enlisted. They gain new poise and charm. They do feminine jobs much like those of civilian women. They have dates and are good friends with Army men.

2. The Women's Army Corps is no longer an experiment. It has public acceptance and prestige. "Present it as a success story." Parents are proud. Requirements are high. Only attractive pictures should appear.

3. Army jobs performed by Wacs are necessary to the war effort. Dramatize the job. Show Wacs working with men. Avoid pictures of kitchen police.

4. "Uncle Sam provides for the welfare of his Army nieces." Emphasize advantages of travel, new friends, medical care, recreation.

5. Adopt an affirmative approach. Don't be on the defensive. The WAC has a right to be proud of its record.

For the first time also the field public relations officers learned the "do's" and "don'ts" which had long been common practice in the Director's office: Say *women,* not *girls.* Show the proper uniform always except in sports pictures. Show attractive women but not cheesecake. Use the Corps' full name once—Women's Army Corps—and thereafter in an article it is permissible to say *the WAC* or *Wacs.* Avoid pictures of Wacs smoking or drinking. Do not put Wacs on radio programs in competition with male personnel, nor as stooges, nor as romantic interest. Avoid using Wacs in off-the-post theatricals.

---

[63] *Ibid.*

[64] *Ibid.* Also Draft of Memo for WAC Gp, undated. Same file.

Avoid "humor" in camp newspapers which creates the public impression that the Army does not have the proper regard for Wacs. "Would you object to your wife or daughter being identified as the subject of an article or cartoon?" Avoid showing Wacs doing jobs which Wacs do not really do. Do not guarantee assignments, commissions, or ratings.[65]

There were now many obstacles to the success of the campaign that had not existed two years before. The WAC Group found that the WAC was no longer "news" in itself, and that editors who previously had fought to get any sort of story about the Corps now refused to print anything that was not in itself noteworthy. It now required good writing, good photography, and good liaison to persuade news media to give recruiters the free publicity that formerly had been abundant. Also, public relations officers and civilian reporters were now well set in their previous attitudes, and could not be re-educated overnight.

In spite of the handicap of a late start, the new publicity campaign achieved substantial results. A random sampling of the press scrapbook of a Midwestern headquarters showed that the field had seized on the leads offered. Headlines read: MORE ENLISTING IN WAC—PLEASED AT RESULTS; or SECOND WAC GROUP FILLED—RESPONSE OF NEBRASKA YOUNG WOMEN GOOD. The European theater had in January released a story headlined PREFER ENGLISH GIRLS TO WACS, but in July it sent a wirephoto of the first Wacs on Normandy Beach, labeled YANKS WELCOME WACS. The "general's daughter" theme took hold at once, with such items as GENERAL'S DAUGHTER ARMY PRIVATE, COLONEL'S MOTHER JOINS WACS, WACS TO MAKE BETTER WIVES SAYS COLONEL, HUBBY'S FOOTSTEPS

FOLLOWED BY DEVOTED WIFE, and so on. The number of positive headlines swelled: WAC ENLISTS AND MAKES FAMILY 100 PERCENT IN WAR EFFORT, SOLDIER MEETS WAC SISTER IN AUSTRALIA, FOUR WOUNDED SOLDIER HEROES HELP RECRUIT WACS, MARCH QUOTA EXCEEDED IN WAC ENLISTMENTS, WAC SIGNS LEAVE PAPERS FOR HUSBAND, WAC CREDITED WITH SAVING LIVES OF PLANE CREW, and many others.[66]

The files of the WAC Group revealed that in one week alone at least two hundred free news stories and pictures could be attributed to material supplied to news media by the group. Press releases to national agencies were mimeographed and mailed to some three hundred recruiting offices as well as to public relations officers in the field, the Office of War Information, and the War Advertising Council. This caused the amount of news coverage to soar as local newspapers and radio stations picked up items that national services had not featured.[67]

Material about Wacs overseas was particularly easy to peddle to news agencies, but difficult to get. The North African theater had an early rule that all film must be used to record combat activities. The

[65] (1) WDBPR Bull, 24 Jun 44. WDWAC 014.13. (2) WDBPR Continental Ln Bull XXV, 30 Sep 44. WDWAC 062. (3) WDBPR Bull., "Public Relations Activities Pertaining to WAC," 1–30 Jun 44. WDWAC 000.7.

[66] In order: *Denver Post*, April 22, 1944, and *Omaha World Herald*, March 21, 1945, *Des Moines Register*, January 20, 1944, and *Minneapolis Star-Journal*, July 22, 1944; Denver, Colo., *Rocky Mountain News*, February 12, 1944; *Minneapolis Star-Journal*, July 13, 1944; *Omaha World Herald*, July 3, 1944; *Denver Post*, May 5, 1944 and November 6, 1944; *Pueblo* (Colo.) *Star-Journal*, June 18, 1944; same; *Minneapolis Star-Journal*, May 15, 1944; *Denver Post*, May 5, 1944; *Des Moines Register*, March 30, 1944; *Omaha World Herald*, November 14 and 16, 1944.

[67] Office Memo, Actg Chief, WAC Gp, for Dep Dir WDBPR, 18 Feb 45. Folder, Orgn of WAC Gp, WDGAP (4-4-41).

European theater permitted WAC pictures, but with so little forethought in public relations policy that releases were often more harmful than helpful. The Pacific theater's stricter control of reporters' activities prevented any great number of derogatory stories, but likewise did not produce any positive material. An appeal for better recruiting aids produced only five pictures of the staff director with koala bears and three of Wacs doing kitchen police.[68]

Again, the only solution was found to be specialization, with a WAC publicity expert and a photographer sent to tour overseas theaters and obtain newsworthy stories about actual jobs and interesting locations. The result was a considerable jump in sound publicity. In the Pacific theater alone a volume of about 1,000 stories monthly was attained by one permanently assigned specialist. In one month she arranged for 1,360 home-town stories, 6 general stories, and 235 pictures and captions. Overseas pictures and stories were featured to good effect: Wacs dancing with soldiers in New Delhi or studying Paris styles in liberated France, local stories like FOUR KANSAS WACS FLY TO AFRICA, or MINNESOTA WAC, AIDE TO GENERAL IKE, WEDS HIS ORDERLY.[69] These were willingly given space by most newspapers; almost every Wac overseas was good for a story and picture in her home-town paper.

Because of the greater apparent importance of overseas stories in the minds of newspaper editors, the Chief of Staff also cabled all theater commanders:

Because of the emphasis placed on all news coming from the theaters of operations, special care must be taken that news stories, radio scripts, or other publicity material about the WAC or in any way referring to the Wacs be in good taste and free from unfavorable innuendoes or coarse humor

injurious to the general reputation of the WAC.[70]

The WAC Group at the same time made efforts to establish friendly liaison with editors and reporters, in the hope that newspapers would gradually learn to consult the group before printing damaging stories. This type of diplomacy occupied a good part of the group's time; unfavorable stories that did reach print were isolated and prevented from spreading, and poor or ill-timed photographs were quickly replaced with better ones.[71]

National surveys soon gave grounds for hope that the tide of public opinion against the Women's Army Corps had been almost arrested, at least in its more frequent published manifestations; there was now some chance that a more favorable feeling would set in. The WAC Group reported:

The most recent study of public opinion toward the Wac indicates an increased favorable public attitude and that the public is receptive in general to the purposes and objectives to which the 1945 recruiting program is geared.[72]

---

[68] (1) Ltr, ETO to AAF, 3 Feb 44, with incl. WDWAC 000.7. (2) Cbl R9627 (CM–OUT 8528), Surles to Eisenhower, 19 Feb 44. WDWAC 000.7. (3) Memo, Dir WAC for WDBPR, 25 Feb 44. SPWA 062. (4) Ltr, Exec WAC to Capt Juanita Stryker, 16 Aug 44, with incl. WDWAC 320.2 SWPA. (5) Memo, Women's Interest Sec AFPAC for all WAC PROs in AFPAC, 2 Oct 45. WDWAC 319.1.

[69] Ibid. Also Denver (Colo.) Rocky Mountain News, February 3, 1944; Greeley (Colo.) Tribune, May 1, 1945; Topeka Daily Capital, November 4, 1944; Minneapolis Star-Journal, December 16, 1944.

[70] Cbl (CM–OUT 2890), WD to all overseas Comds (from CofS), revised by DCofS), 7 Feb 44. WDGAP 320.2 (8–18–42) (i) sec 8a.

[71] (1) Memo, Actg Chief, WAC Gp, for Chief, Press Br WDBPR, 23 Feb 45. (2) Memo, Lt Carroll for Dep Dir WDBPR, 29 Jan 45. Both in Folder, Orgn of WAC Gp, WDGAP 341 (4–4–41).

[72] Memo, Chief, WAC Gp for Dep Dir WDBPR, 20 Dec 44. Same file.

It was never to be known to what extent the tide could have been turned. The WAC Group had been founded by General Marshall only over the Bureau of Public Relations' objections. Four months after its establishment, the bureau began to consider reducing the size of the group after the defeat of Germany. Three months later, in December of 1944, although Germany was still undefeated, the bureau informed the group that it was to be discontinued, since the only purpose in improving public opinion had been "to support all-out recruiting." [73] At this moment the Battle of the Bulge and the resulting extension of WAC recruiting automatically postponed the disbandment of the WAC Group, but it shrank in size until only a few junior officers remained. These pleaded for retention until the Corps was demobilized, citing the volume of output of desirable stories,

. . . which by their very appearance and availability will serve to discourage and offset a return of the previous unfavorable publicity. . . . Should [this] be denied, the needs and accomplishments of the Corps will rapidly disappear from the classification of genuine news, and the unfavorable publicity will again become a fact.[74]

Nevertheless, at the end of February, 1945, the WAC Group had vanished. To support the General Hospital Recruiting Campaign, there were left three WAC officers in the Press Branch of the bureau. A month later, in an undocumented reversal, the group was suddenly re-established, with eight WAC officers assigned. In May of 1945, upon reduction of WAC recruiting, the group asked to be retained on the grounds that it must now carry alone the load of "prestige publicity" that had previously been shared by hundreds of WAC recruiters in the field. It was therefore left intact for the time being, but was not long to survive the departure of Colonel Hobby in the summer of 1945.[75]

Support by Films and Stage Shows

Possibly nine out of ten suggestions from amateur critics advocated an additional form of supporting publicity for recruiters: the use of films, stage shows, motion picture stars, and other theatrical means, which, it was confidently stated, would bring the American woman to enlist as would nothing else on earth. In spite of this opinion, no great use of this form of recruiting support ever proved possible, for a number of reasons.

From its earliest days the Corps offered an irresistible attraction to the theatrical-minded. The WAAC had not graduated its first members before a Hollywood company had asked permission to star them in a musical comedy. This and the other frequent requests to make films about the Corps were refused by the Bureau of Public Relations, which replied:

The WAAC is a new thing in the lives of the American people, and so being, is for the present on trial. Its success is dependent upon two effects: first, the achievement of its objective in an efficient, dignified, and military manner, and two, the approval by the American people and their acceptance of the organization as necessary in the war effort. While serious treatment of the organization

---

[73] *Ibid.* Also see Memo, Col Macy, Chief, WAC Gp, for Dir WDBPR, 15 Sep 44. Same file.

[74] Memos cited n. 71.

[75] (1) Memo, Actg Chief, WAC Sec Press Br, for Press Br WDBPR, 26 Feb 45. Folder, Orgn of WAC Gp, WDGAP 341 (4-4-41). (2) Ltr, Maj Louise Goeden to Maj Henriette Horak, PRO SHAEF, 25 Apr 45. (3) M/R, 28 May 45. Folder, Orgn of WAC Gp, WDGAP 341 (4-4-41)

in dignified, dramatic structure is one thing, its portrayal in musical comedy is another, and one which cannot receive official sanction.[76]

In spite of rebuffs, private producers remained interested. It was with something less than appreciation that public relations authorities received offers from unknown producing agencies, such as one which stated, "We are about to produce a legitimate stageplay . . . based on the Women's Army and entitled *They All Do It*." [77] The typical producer desired to "glorify" Wacs in a nonprofit show for the benefit of some Army cause; the producer would furnish the writer, and the Army would furnish the material, the talent, the equipment, probably the funds, and, usually, indorse the producers' songs as official. All such ideas for gaining producing fame at the expense of the government were politely refused by the Bureau of Public Relations, in consideration of the expenditure involved and the frequently dubious picture of the WAC that would have resulted.[78]

Even in the case of reputable film companies eager to contribute their services to the war effort, the results were discouraging. As soon as the WAAC was formed, an attempt was made to get a recruiting film from this source. Top-flight talent was contributed, with Warner Brothers sending its director, Frank Capra, to Des Moines to photograph the short subject, *Women at War*.

The result was pronounced "a very fine picture photographically"; the pictures of Des Moines were "superb," and the film had "great dramatic appeal." Unfortunately, the script as cleared by the Bureau of Public Relations, which at that date had no WAAC specialists, contained considerable untrue information, including a final battlefield scene, with Wacs rushing into combat to take over the work of frontline Signal Corps troops. By the time the film was seen by a WAAC adviser, changes would have been prohibitively expensive, and the studio refused to make them since the script had been cleared by the War Department. The film was therefore shelved for a time, and eventually released commercially with the substitution of dialogue stating that the "combat" was merely a maneuver in the United States—a statement equally erroneous as to WAC participation, but less alarming to the public. Its value except as a work of art remained dubious: at best it gave recruits an overglamorous idea of WAC activities, and at worst it perhaps alarmed timid prospects and parents.[79]

While this particular fiasco was solely the fault of poor co-ordination within the War Department, in general the scripts later submitted by both military and nonmilitary writers proved unmalleable, with errors so integral to the structure that it was impossible to correct them. The difficulty seemed to lie in a certain unbridgeable gap between the real facts of WAC

---

[76] Telg, Republic Pictures to Dir WAC, 23 Jul 43, with reply by Ltr, Chief, Pictorial Br WDBPR to Republic Pictures, Inc., 4 Aug 42. WA 413.56 (7–23–42)A.

[77] Ltr, Society of American Talents, Inc., to Red Cross Auxiliary, 15 Jun 44. WDWAC 080 Relief Fund.

[78] (1) Ltr, Lee M. Rousseau to Dir WAC, 26 Nov 43, sub: *Salute to the Wacs;* (2) File showing previous rejections by ASF OTI and AER as well as by Dir WAC; (3) Rejections from Gen Surles, WDBPR. All in SPWA 062 (1943).

[79] (1) Transcript, Long Distance Tp Conv, Dir Hobby and 1st Off Woods, 21 Aug 43. G–1 WAC 312–312.9, Drawer 6, DRB AGO. (2) Memo, Sp Serv Div for CG ASF, 12 Apr 44. SPRPS 413.56, in AG 341 9th SvC.

existence and the workings of the theatrical mind.

For this reason, requests to use WAC training centers and units as the background of commercial feature films were generally refused. Among the dramatic stereotypes suggested for such stories were the ancient rival-buddies theme, which in females looked like a mere cat fight; the bad girl reformed by the Army; the woman who discovers she must shed her Army uniform and don black lace to recover her husband's love. None of these appeared particularly helpful to recruiting, and it proved impossible to interest film makers in the real, although less conventional, drama of a Wac's actual life.

Nevertheless, many critics of WAC recruiting policies believed that the Corps was losing much valuable free publicity by rejecting such offers. Finally it was agreed to let a major company produce a WAC picture provided that the script was approved and a WAC adviser kept on the scene at all times. In spite of such precautions, the resulting effort was an embarrassment to Wacs everywhere. One of Hollywood's most glamorous stars was compressed, rather unsuccessfully, into a WAC uniform, and portrayed as receiving an officer's commission after a writer's idea of "feminine" behavior such as jealousy, tears, hysteria, and face-slapping on the drill field, which would have disqualified any real Wac officer candidate. Real Wacs in the audience fled in tears, accompanied by the jeers of soldier-spectators.[80] It was difficult to see what such productions added to public acceptance, other than the idea that all Wacs suffered from emotional instability but nevertheless were promptly made officers.

Thereafter, Army assistance was not given to further fictional films, and such recruiting short subjects as were necessary were made by the Signal Corps. Even with military producers, the proper straightforward and realistic tone was difficult to achieve. A few excellent and successful short subjects were nevertheless produced, particularly in support of the General Hospital Campaign.

Invariably rejected were the hundreds of suggestions that enlistment be stimulated by the use on recruiting duty of Hollywood stars then in the military establishment, particularly Clark Gable and James Stewart. This idea, in addition to its unpopularity with the individuals concerned, would have violated War Department policy on the assignment of prominent persons. As recruiting policy it was likewise frowned upon as being in the same category with offers of free nylons to potential recruits, and other misrepresentations of the advantages of life in the services.

Whether or not, in the future, this advertising medium could be more successfully exploited remained an unsolved problem. After the end of the war, the second Director WAC was of the opinion that the thousands of existing feet of film on WAC activities should be cut and consolidated for a historical record, and for the training of future Wacs, "since enlisted women were used in this war for the first time in the history of the United States Army." The proposal was rejected, however, by Maj. Gen. Russell L. Maxwell of the Army Pictorial Board, as not worth the expense of preparation.[81]

---

[80] Observed by author and others.

[81] (1) Memo, Dir WAC for G–4, 27 Nov 45, and inds; (2) Min, 20th Mtg, Army Pictorial Bd, 8 Jan 46. WDWAC 060–06.2 (1945–46).

Evaluation

From the parallel patterns of the Planning Branch and the WAC Group, two final conclusions were reported. One was the unvarying unpopularity of their efforts with other agencies, which opposed their establishment as long as possible and proposed their disbandment at the earliest opportunity. It was inevitably irritating to established services to see one Corps publicized, groomed, and pushed to the forefront of public attention—pictures of WAC recruits mailed to home-town papers when men's were not; prominent personages rushed into WAC ceremonies while those for men were ignored; publicity given to the WAC's first steps in paths anonymously trodden by men for years.

The other and equally unpleasant conclusion was also inescapable. There was every evidence that no corps or branch, whether of men or women, could recruit any number of individuals, in active competition with industry and the other services, without the expert, hard, and constant attention that had been given to the WAC Recruiting Service. Both the Army and the Navy had found, even after recruiting was seemingly well established, that when recruiters were cut and the machine disbanded, recruits vanished. The General Staff noted:

Experience has conclusively proved that recruits are only obtained by direct and repeated personal interviews and that the average good recruiter can at best actually enlist not more than 2 or 3 prospects out of every 20 interviewed.[82]

Any corps obliged to recruit in this manner while all others were supplied by the draft was obviously placed in a position to incur animosity. Among the many benefits that selective service would have brought to the WAC, not the least would have been freedom from the resentment of other services, as well as from the strain of keeping itself in the state of spotless saleability ordinarily required only of soap flakes and cigarettes.

It seemed important that future planners realize that an Army which wished to employ women in wartime must either summon its forces to back draft legislation, or pay the price of ungrudging specialization in women's publicity and recruitment. The early failure to commission the most highly qualified experts available, and to centralize control, was a luxury too expensive to be repeated, costing millions of dollars in advertising and thousands of potential recruits. In peacetime, when equal measures were required to recruit men, the problems of WAC recruiters and publicity experts would obviously be less conspicuous, and all branches would be more likely to receive equal publicity.

---

[82] Memo cited n. 3.

PART FOUR

LAST DAYS OF THE WARTIME WAC

CHAPTER XXXV

1945: The Closing Months of the War

The prospect of victory in Europe brought to the WAC, as to the Army as a whole, the last of its problems before demobilization: that of maintaining efficiency in a period of war weariness. Symptoms, as they appeared in the last winter of the war, were not in themselves any more alarming for the WAC than for the Army as a whole, except as trends which, if continued, would render the Corps ineffective at the moment the expected strain of redeployment to the Pacific would tax all administrative facilities. In January of 1945, the rate of medical discharge for Wacs was found to be more than double that of January of the preceding year. The rate of discharge other than honorable (blue) was many times greater than that of the year before.[1] WAC uniform violations became increasingly common, as well as mere untidiness. WAC officers, who should have set an example in this respect, instead were frequently the worst offenders. Director Hobby moved to secure publication of two separate admonitions, stating that "it is manifestly unfair to require and expect enlisted women to abide strictly by Uniform Regulations when the officers of their Corps are guilty of flagrant abuse thereof."[2]

Possibly more important was the intangible but unmistakable crumbling of that high morale and idealism upon which the Corps had always depended in surmounting pioneering obstacles and public disapproval. Among company officers, visitors reported a definite feeling that they and their women had been forgotten by those in authority. Most of the reforms in the uniform supply, job assignment, medical care, and other policy matters, which had been fought over for two years in the War Department, had reached the field so late as to make little impression, or had not arrived at all at some isolated stations.

Even at best, the earlier crusading spirit, with its rosy expectation of capturing the citadel of full acceptance, had long since been replaced by a more realistic evaluation of the situation. The familiar gibes and gossip had ceased to be a challenge and had become merely wearisome, and the average woman now realized that, so long as women did not share in combat, they would never be full-fledged military citizens. As one dispirited Wac put it in a letter to Director Hobby, "We don't want

---

[1] See Tables 12 and 13, Appendix A.

[2] (1) Ltr, Dir WAC to CGs AAF, AGF, and ASF, 18 Sep 44. WDWAC 421. (2) Memo, Dir WAC for WAC Offs on Duty in Washington, 20 May 45. WDWAC 421. (3) Ltr, Hq MDW to all Stations, 12 Sep 44, SPWBG 420 WAC, in WDWAC 421. (4) *St. Louis Post-Dispatch,* November 14, 1944. (5) Min, Stf Dirs Conf, 1–3 Dec 43. SPWA 337 (11–10–43).

appreciation; we only want to go home." [3]

The British Auxiliary Territorial Service had reported the same situation some months earlier, with particular reference to female troop officers stationed permanently in isolated spots. Having coped with all of the changes that naturally accompanied the growth of a new organization, they were described as needing "a shot in the arm." [4] In the American WAC, urgent cases of company officer fatigue had been reported as early as 1943, with officers vainly seeking transfer on grounds that they had "gone stale" and had nothing more to give to their units. [5]

Rotation Proposals

Inasmuch as medical surveys showed the job-interest factor to have more influence upon both fatigue and health than all other factors combined, first WAC proposals for combating a slump in efficiency hinged upon a transfer or rotation system that would approximate for female personnel the normal rotation in the armed forces. Women in both the Army and the Navy had generally lacked the job rotation customary for men. Except for the few released for officer candidate school or overseas service, most had remained at the station of initial assignment. The Navy Department was the first to note the problem in this system, reporting:

Since the familiar shore-sea duty rotation did not apply to the Women's Reserve, it was originally contemplated that their initial assignments to duty would probably be for the duration of the war. As the war lengthened, it became clear that this was not a sound policy. Morale in general was injured by a pervading policy which apparently froze all hands in whatever billets they had first chanced to find themselves. . . . Women assigned to out-of-the-way or otherwise less de-

sirable stations were considerably worse off than the men, who at least had a prospect of sea duty as a change. [6]

In November of 1944, the Navy Department therefore adopted a system whereby Waves who had given two years of good service, exclusive of training time, could request transfer to another location, approval to be contingent upon military necessity. Women whose original assignments remained responsible and absorbing to their interests did not request such rotation, but of others who did, it was noted that 90 percent wanted duty nearer home. Even if a new assignment held little more interest than the old, the change of scenery and renewal of family contacts appeared to improve efficiency. [7]

No comparable solution was arrived at by the Army. In a conference early in 1945, Army Service Forces staff directors recommended that the Army add a similar provision to its directives governing rotation, to apply only to individuals who had served at least two years either on "isolated stations" or "on duties the nature of which on a prolonged assignment is detrimental to the individuals concerned." Final approval of such a change in jobs would have remained a prerogative of command, dependent upon the situation.

This proposal met the opposition of Military Personnel Division, ASF, on the grounds that "the assignment and reas-

---

[3] (1) Extracts from Rpt of Asst ASF WAC Off, 18 Jul 44. SPGAS 319.1 WAC, in SPAP 319.1. (2) Quotation from D/F, G-1 WD to TAG, with incl Ltrs, 4 Sep 45. WDGAP 220.8 WAC, in WDWAC 220.8.

[4] Cbl and Ltr, Asst Mil Attaché, London, for Dir WAC, 8 Feb 45. WDWAC 320.2 WAC.

[5] (1) Min cited n. 2(5). (2) Memo, Miss Lies for Dir WAC, 19 Apr 44, with 9 atchd tabs. 1944 Plng Serv files.

[6] WAVES Hist, pp. 142 ff.

[7] Ibid.

signment of military personnel is a command function" and that rotation should therefore be left to a station commander to initiate if necessary. An eventual stalemate resulted from the fact that there was no reliable estimate of the number of men who would be affected by such a provision. Director Hobby believed it to be so small as to permit equal applicability of the provision to men and women, while General Dalton feared otherwise and that to apply it to women alone would appear discriminatory. For this reason, no such rotation was authorized until just before the end of the war, and WAC advisers instead sought other means of arresting a decline in efficiency.[8]

Refresher Training of Officers

British experience indicated that good results in combating fatigue among women troops could be obtained by combating it in their officers, by means of refresher training to impart new ideas and encouragement. The ATS had therefore established both junior and senior officers' schools, later merged, with reportedly excellent response.[9] As early as August of 1944, Director Hobby approached the Chief of Staff concerning the advisability of establishing a refresher course, because of the increasing fatigue of WAC troop officers and the unavailability of replacements.[10] She noted:

These officers . . . should be a very proud group, a group recognized throughout the Army. . . . Instead, there has been a growing tendency to regard the assignment to an operational job as a "plum." . . . A WAC detachment officer, if she does her job properly constantly has to listen to the problems of the women of her unit. Conditions in military service are more strange to women than to men, home situations often bear more

heavily, the very type of work they perform is more monotonous because the chances of transfer and change are less, outside diversions are fewer. The result is that at the present time many WAC commanders, many of the best ones, have been so drained of inner strength that they feel that they have nothing else to give and would like to be transferred to routine operational jobs. . . . I do not feel that the Corps can afford to transfer good detachment officers. . . . I do feel that something must be done to refresh the tired ones and constantly improve the work of all.[11]

In spite of General Marshall's immediate approval of this suggestion in August of 1944, ASF's opposition delayed the school's beginning until April of the next year.[12] Military Training Division took a firm stand against the school, on the grounds that there were no problems peculiar to females in the Army:

It is not apparent to this office what functions are peculiar to a WAC Staff Director that are not common to other officers performing staff assignments. Furthermore, it is not understood what functions are peculiar to WAC Detachment Commanders that are

---

[8] (1) Min, ASF WAC Stf Dirs, Mtg, Feb 45, with transmittal slip. SPAP 210.3 WAC. (2) Memo, G–1. WDWAC 220.3 (1945–46). (3) Memo, Dir MPD for Pers ASF, 6 Aug 45. SPAP 210.85 WAC. (4) For final action, see Ch. XXXVII, below.

[9] Cbl and Ltr cited n. 4.

[10] Summary of entire procedure for establishment of school in D/F, G–1 to Dep CofS, 9 Feb 45. WDGAP 353 WAC, in CofS 324.5 WAC. Approved by CofS, 14 Feb 45.

[11] Memo (draft for discussion), Dir WAC for Gen Henry, G–1, 21 Aug 44. WDWAC 352 WAC Pers Admin.

[12] For description of series of conferences see: (1) M/R by ASF WAC Off, 12 Oct 44, SPAP 352 WAC. (2) Memo, Chief Tng Gp G–3, for Dir WAC, 11 Nov 44, WDWAC 352 (1945). G–3 meetings: 3, 11, and 17 Oct. (3) Buck slip, Dir Pers ASF for Dir Mil Tng ASF, 13 Oct 44. SPAP 352 WAC. (4) Memo, Dir Pers ASF for CofS ASF, 20 Nov 44. SPAP 352 WAC (6–14–43). (5) Memo, MTD ASF for Dir Pers ASF, 21 Nov 44. SPTRD 352 WAC (10–12–44), in SPAP 352. (6) Memo, Dir Pers ASF for MTD ASF, 23 Nov 44. SPAP 352.

not common to all Detachment or Unit commanders.[13]

The Office of the Director disagreed with this opinion, believing that, while subjects such as hygiene, recreation, and discipline might be identical in title for both men and women, the practical application differed at least as much as the course content in Infantry School differed from that of the Field Artillery or Armored Force School. Colonel Rice added:

The only two new jobs added to the Army by the inclusion of the WAC have been those of WAC detachment officer and WAC Staff Director. While these carry the same MOS numbers as similar jobs for men, the actual duties, and therefore the elements in successful accomplishment, are somewhat different. . . . *The personnel administration of women is now an Army job* and I fail to see how an officers' school for that training is a different idea from an officers' school for any other specialized job such as QM School, Signal, CWS, Ordnance, or any technical and professional job.[14]

Nevertheless, Director Hobby decided to ask the opinion of the three major commands concerning the appropriateness of the school and of its proposed course of study. This was done, and two of the three commands proved receptive.[15] The Army Air Forces stated:

. . . it would be of particular value to secure by this means a digest of the best practices which have been developed in the administration of female military personnel over the past two and a half years, and thus to lay the foundation for a manual or guide to be used in the training of future WAC administrators.[16]

The Army Ground Forces likewise agreed, saying that the school "will be of real military advantage in the command and administration of members of the WAC." [17] AGF suggested that the course

include especial help in guiding women's recreation and physical training activities, education, and preparation for demobilization. On the other hand, in the ASF, Military Training Division alleged that there were plenty of Army schools already in existence. General Dalton added that the development of women leaders was no proper concern of the War Department: "After assignment, the efficient administration of a WAC company is one responsibility of command. . . ." [18]

Director Hobby offered the opinion that no Army school, even The Adjutant General's School, included courses on women's health, jobs, recreation, and physical, moral, and social problems. She also pointed out that she was not asking a women's school but an Army school, for the instruction of any Army officer whose business happened to be that new Army specialty, the personnel administration of women.[19] Male officers were therefore eligible to attend if interested in this specialty, or if assigned to WAC recruiting and similar fields.[20]

G–3 Division and the Chief of Staff both agreed with this statement, and establishment of the School for WAC Personnel

---

[13] Memo, MTD ASF for CofS ASF, 23 Oct 44. SPTRP 352 WAC (10–12–44), in SPAP 352.

[14] Memo, Dep Dir for Dir WAC, 20 Nov 44. WDWAC 352 WAC Pers Admin.

[15] Memo, Dir WAC for CGs AAF, AGF, 28 Dec 44. WDWAC 353, in WDWAC 352 (1945–46).

[16] Memo, ACofAS Pers, Hq AAF, for G–1, 4 Jan 45. WDWAC 352.

[17] Memo, Ground AG, Hq AGF, for CofS, Att: G–1, 3 Jan 45. 353 GNGAP–W, in WDWAC 352.

[18] (1) Memo, MTD ASF to Dir Pers ASF, 4 Jan 45. SPTRP 353, in SPAP 352 WAC. (2) Memo, Dir Pers ASF for G–1, 10 Jan 45. SPAP 352 WAC (1–4–44), in WDWAC 352.

[19] Memo, Dir WAC for G–3, 20 Jan 45. WDWAC 352.

[20] None did.

Administration was directed.[21] Thus, as the Corps neared completion of its third year, there was set a new major principle: that the leadership of women was a recognized specialty and branch of the science of personnel administration, and an Army responsibility. In an important restatement of the Corps' mission, the Director noted:

The WAC mission as a Corps is to procure, train, and supply personnel to the Army, and to administer that personnel. When trained personnel has been supplied to the commands, the mission of that personnel becomes the mission of the command to which it is assigned. . . . There is only one small group that performs a Corps mission. That group—consisting of officers assigned to detachments and WAC staff work—is charged with the administration of WAC troops because they are women. . . .

My concern with this matter is purely my concern with officers whose duty is the well-being and morale of women. All matters which can be handled by Army mechanics seem now to be well-understood and well-handled within the established framework of the Army.[22]

School for WAC Personnel Administration

By April of 1945, when the School for WAC Personnel Administration opened its doors, the plight of WAC leadership in the field appeared to be desperate almost beyond the point of remedying. The most capable WAC troop commanders were by their own admission exhausted and embittered. Critiques submitted by members of the first class of students revealed that they knew little of the attempts at progress and improvement in clothing supply, public opinion, and regulations that had been taking place in the War Department, and most stated frankly that they and their women desired nothing so much as

to get out of the military establishment.[23]

To counteract an attitude that seemed about to nullify the Corps' previous accomplishments, Director Hobby called upon the woman whose initiative had rallied the Corps once before in the days of recruiting failure, Colonel Rice, the deputy director. Although herself, in the opinion of doctors of the Army Medical Center, now so exhausted and ill that continuance of service was dangerous, Colonel Rice was given the final task of reviving, by exposure to her own leadership, the courage and idealism of troop officers and thus of the entire Corps. It was intended to assign Colonel Rice as commandant only long enough for her to establish the curriculum. It soon became evident, however, that, in the task of reviving exhausted leaders, the curriculum was less important than the commandant's personality, which a witness called

. . . the type of leadership based on personal integrity, selfless devotion to the cause she serves and the people she leads, and the vision to see and interpret for others a program in its broadest and most constructive aspect which inspires those who follow her.[24]

Colonel Rice therefore relinquished her post as deputy and remained with the school until its closing. In the Director's Office, she was replaced by Colonel Boyce

[21] (1) Memo, G–3 for G–1, 30 Jan 45, WDGCT 322 (1–20–43). (2) D/F, G–1 for DCofS, 9 Feb 45. WDGAP 353 WAC, in WDWAC 352. (3) Memo, G–1 for ASF, 8 Feb 45. WDGAP 353 WAC.

[22] Memo cited n. 11.

[23] Unless otherwise stated, entire section based on files of Sch for WAC Pers Admin: Critiques, etc., filed with Prof of Mil Science and Tactics, ROTC, Purdue; other student papers shipped to OCMH. Also, Preliminary Rpt, Sch for WAC Pers Admin to WDGS, Jun 45, with rosters. WDWAC 352 WAC Pers Admin.

[24] Memo, Hq AAF for Dir WAC, 23 Oct 45, sub: Expression of Appreciation. WDWAC 353.

as deputy, as well as by two other officers, a major and a captain.

The entire curriculum of the refresher course was designed by Colonel Rice. Both G–3 Division and Director Hobby had agreed that the War Department, not ASF, must control training doctrine, since students came from all three major commands and overseas theaters. ASF was given control of routine supply and administration.[25]

General Marshall himself vetoed Director Hobby's earlier plans to place the school on a military post, and insisted that its mission of restoring energy and perspective to troop administrators could best succeed in an informal atmosphere. Accordingly, the chosen site was Purdue University at Lafayette, Indiana, a school centrally located and one that already housed a Navy technical school and an Army ROTC. WAC administrative officers were ordered to this school at the rate of 90 every three weeks, for a two and a half weeks' course. In contrast to the custom at WAC training centers, a deliberately democratic and informal atmosphere was maintained; the commandant directed that the relative rank of students and faculty be ignored in the interests of maximum free discussion.

The school, as established at Purdue, set an example in personnel administration by proving the least expensive per student per month of all officers' schools conducted by the Army. Colonel Rice was assisted by a permanent staff of only four officers, with an additional rotating staff of four outstanding WAC administrators attending each class as temporary instructors.[26]

The most outstanding characteristic of the school was that no course was given that could not be given by a top authority in the field; thus, maxims and precepts were to a large extent replaced by a firsthand account of the Corps' experience. Colonel Hobby visited every class until her retirement, after which Colonel Boyce came often. The Air WAC Officer visited every class and addressed AAF students; the ASF and AGF WAC Officers came frequently, furnishing latest authoritative information on policies of those commands.

Lectures on mental health were given to each class by the WAC's psychiatric authority, Major Preston of Fort Des Moines. Medical problems of women were discussed by Colonel Craighill and Maj. Margaret Janeway of The Surgeon General's Office. Reliable information on demobilization and women's job opportunities was furnished each class by the WAC representative in Selective Service headquarters, Maj. Marion Lichty.

Purdue University, noted for its close working liaison with industry, furnished experts in personnel administration. Its psychology department likewise offered authoritative condensed lectures on the psychology of the adult female. Favorite subjects were the technique of the company interview, the psychology of punishment of women, and women's readjustment problems.

Lectures on War Department organization and policies, and on approximately two hundred War Department regulations peculiar to the WAC, were given chiefly by Colonel Rice, who had personally written most of the regulations under discussion. Prominent lecturers on the other women's services included Director Doro-

---

[25] (1) Memo, Chief, Tng Gp G–3, for Dir WAC, 11 Nov 44; (2) Memo, Dep Dir for Dir WAC, 20 Nov 44. WDWAC 352.

[26] WDBPR Release, 3 Apr 45.

thy C. Stratton of the SPARS, Director Ruth Streeter of the Marine Corps Women's Reserve, and representatives of the WAVES, ATS, and Canadian WAC.[27]

Also included, both for rehabilitation of students and for their use in teaching their units, was instruction by the college faculty in women's sports, as well as in a posture clinic, and in the organization of games, square dancing, and group singing.

The most important visiting experts, however, were believed by the commandant to be the students themselves, experienced troop officers. Therefore, group conferences and forums followed each lecture and emphasized the sharing of practical experiences.

In a conference on Morale, specific devices were discussed—crafts and homemaking classes, cheerful date rooms, women's sports tournaments, future wardrobe planning. In Public Relations, commanders related ways in which they had encouraged co-operation with local churches, newspapers, women's clubs, and civic groups so as to secure pleasant relations and recreational opportunities for the women. In Discipline, actual problem cases and most effective methods were discussed, as well as successful means of preparing courts-and-boards cases concerning women who injured company morale and reputation. The conference on helpful administrative devices discussed such matters as the best means of coping with the heterogeneity peculiar to WAC companies: how to arrange sleeping quarters for workers on different shifts, as well as barracks duties, training and meals. A dozen conferences of this nature left few original devices and discoveries unshared by the group.

Because officers from many different commands were included, the school offered no "approved solution" to any problem, but merely allowed women to observe the best solutions that fellow students had been able to achieve under varying command situations. Visiting psychiatrists pronounced the conferences "group therapy" as well as instruction. Commanders who, at isolated stations, had long borne in silence the responsibility for their women's lives and behavior now discovered dozens of individuals with identical experiences. Even after classwork, there was a torrent of extracurricular conversation, which filled every spare minute and lasted well into the night, and which Colonel Rice viewed with extreme approval as being more important than the course of study.

Many commanders were found to have labored under a weight of guilt and depression in the belief that certain problems were limited to their own companies, and were amazed and exhilarated to discover that identical problems had been met by every other commander and by Navy and British services. The only complaint was that this release and reassurance had come too late for many. One student wrote, "If only I could have talked about these things before my nerves were shot instead of after!" Others speculated bitterly on enlisted women whose lives or moral standards might have been saved had such shared information been available earlier to enable the commander to handle their cases more wisely.

Evaluation of Refresher Training

The effectiveness of the School for WAC Personnel Administration in combating troop fatigue was commended by most of

---

[27] For course of study, see files cited n. 23.

the commands that had sent WAC students. The AGF's adjutant general commented to General Marshall:

It has been apparent that all officers who attended the school received invaluable training in personnel procedures, designed to develop and maintain high morale among the enlisted women in this command. This has been indicated by the increasing number of units which have been awarded the Meritorious Service Unit Plaque and by the increased enthusiasm of the Commanding Officers themselves, which has in turn been reflected in the attitude and morale of the enlisted women under their immediate jurisdiction.[28]

As a result, AGF sent to the school every WAC company officer and staff director under its jurisdiction, except a few newcomers who were too late to participate.

The AAF noted:

Officers who attended the course returned to their bases not only with sound information . . . but also with a renewed zest for their own jobs, gained from the opportunity they had been given to assess the overall progress which had been made during the past three years in the program to utilize WAC personnel in the military service.[29]

The AAF likewise sent every WAC staff director, every WAC air inspector, all Wacs who handled WAC business in Air Forces headquarters, and almost all company officers, to the full extent of their quota for each class.

ASF sent none of its service command staff directors except those requested by name as temporary instructors, very few of its training center personnel, and only a scattering of company officers and recruiters.

The WAVES shortly secured authorization to set up an identical school for Wave troop officers and Women's Reserve representatives in each naval district. Only the

end of the war prevented this program. The SPARS, without waiting for the proposed Navy school, sent women to the WAC school. Although Spars met separately when specific Army Regulations were being discussed, it was found that almost every practical problem was identical for women in the Army and in the Coast Guard. After a visit to Purdue, Col. Ruth Streeter also requested permission to send members of the Marine Corps Women's Reserve. She said:

If the British ATS, the Canadian WAC, and the U.S. WAC have all had the same experience, it is only common sense for us to anticipate a similar situation." [30]

Colonel Streeter's request was disapproved by Marine Corps headquarters. The Canadian Wacs, however, sent representatives to obtain successful procedures for use in their own advanced school for leaders of female troops.[31]

With the defeat of Japan and beginning of rapid demobilization, Colonel Rice recommended that the school be closed. In spite of the officers' initial fatigue and disillusionment, Colonel Rice considered their reaction excellent, and wrote, "Based on what we have seen and heard here, I think we have a right to be very proud of the WAC officers, the jobs they are doing, and the attitude they have toward their jobs." [32] The course had come too late for

[28] Ltr, Hq AGF to CofS, 24 Oct 45. 362 (WAC) GNGAP–W, in WDWAC 353.

[29] Ltr, Dep ACofAS–1, Hq AAF, to Dir WAC, 23 Oct 45, sub: Expression of Appreciation. WDWAC 353.

[30] Ltr, Col Streeter to Col Hobby 25 May 45. WDWAC 352 (1–20–45).

[31] (1) Memo, Asst Exec WAC for Dir WAC, 6 Jun 45. WDWAC 319.1 Johnson. (2) Memo, Dep Dir WAC for Dir WAC, 19 Jun 45. WDWAC 352 (1–20–45)

[32] Ltr, Col Rice to Maj Johnson, 15 May 45. WDWAC 352.

its results to be reflected in more than a few months of administration; but not too late to aid in demobilization and readjustment, and to send women administrators and their troops home with some feeling of increased understanding and good will toward the Army.

Colonel Rice, at the instigation of the Air and Ground Forces,[33] was awarded the Legion of Merit for this and earlier assignments:

... As Chief of the Recruiting Division of her Corps ... she developed and supervised the All-States Recruitment Plan in a manner which swelled enlistments during a critical period ... she was successively Assistant Director, Executive Officer in the Office of the Director, and Deputy Director, Women's Army Corps, positions in which she applied her ingenuity, forcefulness, and rare ability to the solution of weighty problems affecting the military service of women. She initiated, developed, co-ordinated, supervised, and recommended many important changes which accomplished the thorough integration of the Women's Army Corps into the Army. Her suggestions brought about many plans for the welfare, health, and increased morale of the Corps. As Commandant of the Women's Army Corps School for Personnel Administration at Purdue University, she devised, co-ordinated, and executed a program for training officers in personnel management. In all these varied assignments, Colonel Rice, by her indefatigable energy, organizing ability, and steadfast devotion to duty helped to guide the Women's Army Corps through a difficult period of growth and contributed in a marked manner to the effective utilization of women in the Army of the United States.[34]

Director Hobby said later:

It is impossible to say too much about what the school accomplished. I really think it held the Corps together during the last hard days.[35]

Director Hobby's Resignation

Two months after launching the School for WAC Personnel Administration, a month after the victory in Europe, Director Hobby made a long-postponed decision to leave the Corps. For the past months the increasingly precarious state of her health had been common knowledge within a limited circle of the General Staff. In 1944 she had been hospitalized several times at Walter Reed General Hospital in Washington, for anemia, exhaustion, and a throat ailment which prevented speaking. Eventually Army doctors ordered her for six weeks to Brooke General Hospital in San Antonio and thence to an address known only to her family, with orders that not even policy matters could be communicated to her.

At this time she had attempted to resign in favor of her deputy, Colonel Rice, who carried the weight of Corps' policy during this time with the aid of the one remaining staff officer, Captain Chance, and the civilian adviser, Mrs. Gruber. Colonel Rice had dissuaded her from this step in view of the probable effect of such action on a Corps which was already becoming demobilization-conscious. The hope of a partial recovery proved justified, and in the fall of 1944 the Director was able to return to a limited amount of activity, although from time to time ordered back to the hospital for additional treatment. At this time she informed an inquirer, "I expect now to be able to 'finish out the war.' I hope that it will not be too long."[36]

During 1944 the entire staff was hospitalized for various causes; in particular

---

[33] See ns. 24 and 28.
[34] WDBPR Release, 30 Nov 45.
[35] Interv, 23 Aug 48.

[36] Ltr, Dir WAC to Gen White, 2 Oct 44, WDWAC 320.2. Also: (1) Intervs with participants. (2) Ltr, Maj Chance, Exec WAC, to Maj Gen Philip Hayes, CG 3d SvC, 10 Oct 44. WDWAC 335.2.

Colonel Rice, who spent a month in the hospital for a major operation but was obliged by the Director's equally poor health to return to work while still undergoing X-ray treatment. Her inability to visit the field during this year was a constant source of distress to the Director. Files were by now filled with urgent requests from various agencies: training centers asked her to attend graduation ceremonies, and the enlisted women themselves were pathetically eager for a glimpse of her. Not realizing that one day at each of the more than 500 WAC units would have taken more than a year, field commands hopefully invited her to visit all their detachments.[37] Companies that she did manage to see wrote, "Since your visit, the morale of our girls has been improved one hundred percent."[38]

In October of 1944, an attempt to send Colonel Rice to the Pacific had to be canceled, on the very eve of departure, because of the Director's renewed illness. In December of 1944, the Director requested the War Department Manpower Board to allot her another officer, and informed overseas staff directors that "if they approve the request, I have made a plan to spend a great deal of time at field installations and to send Colonel Rice out when I am in the field."[39] This hope proved vain; by the time another captain was allotted, her full-time work on demobilization planning was required, and the later allotment of a major came after Colonel Rice's reassignment, too late to make the plan practicable.

In connection with her retirement, there was also in the Director's mind a consideration that she admitted later: a comparison with the British women's experience, in which the head of one of the largest services had retired, as soon as its

problems were worked out, in favor of a successor who had been less active in early months. Her quite similar career had included successful crusades for equal status, full military rights, redesign of the uniform, elimination of the "snob element" and choice of officer candidates from the ranks, and other identical policy problems. "It was my feeling," Mrs. Hobby noted later, "that any woman who brought a Corps through its early difficulties had to fight so many battles and antagonize so many individuals that she must eventually destroy her usefulness to the Corps."[40]

Nevertheless, as late as the end of May 1945, two weeks after V-E Day, Colonel Hobby was still hopeful of being able to continue. At this time she told a reporter, "Until everybody can get out of the Army—I won't. . . . No matter what you've heard, I'm staying in until the Pacific war is over."[41]

In late June, the serious illness of the Director's husband required her immediate presence. Her own further hospitalization was imminent. At this time, General Marshall informed her that the situation in the Pacific area required a visit from the Director. All other Corps business appeared settled; even the demobilization policy was now approved. Colonel Hobby therefore reluctantly directed her office to draft a statement that would explain her action. The draft, intended for public release, made clear that she had meant, in 1941, to remain away from her husband and children only for a few months while

---

[37] Invitations cited, with many others, in WDWAC 335.2 (1944); also WDWAC 333.1 (1945–46).

[38] Ltr, CO WAC Sq, Chatham Field, Ga., to Dir WAC, 21 Jun 44. WDWAC 062.2.

[39] Ltr, Dir WAC to Overseas Stf Dirs, 1 Dec 44. WDWAC 320.2.

[40] Interv, 23 Aug 48.

[41] *St. Louis Post-Dispatch*, May 28, 1945.

organizing the Woman's Interest Section of the Bureau of Public Relations. This had taken longer than expected, and she was then "asked to stay a little longer and help organize the new Women's Army Corps. This organizing job lasted three years. Problems came up . . . at no time did she feel she could leave." [42] With this draft, the Director sent to General Marshall a note, with a barely legible signature, to the effect that "due to circumstances which have recently arisen it is necessary for the undersigned to be placed on terminal leave status." [43]

Recommendations for Promotion

During these last few days of the Director's tenure, there was again raised an issue that had recurred periodically: whether legislation should be requested to authorize her promotion to general officer rank. Among Congressional supporters of this measure one stated:

In no other branch of the service does an officer holding the rank of colonel command so many troops. Under the Tables of Organization of the Army, a brigadier general is supposed to command a triangle division consisting of 10,000 troops. In the Wacs, a colonel commands ten times this number. This is not fair to the head . . . it is not fair to its officers . . . Colonel Oveta Hobby is entitled to the rank of major general. [44]

There was also within the War Department some feeling that, even as staff adviser, the Director's rank should be more nearly comparable to that of the British women's equivalent, or major general. A staff study to this effect was therefore initiated at the last moment, proposing that the necessary legislation should be sought. This encountered delay in the Army Service Forces, and came up only

much later, after demobilization was well under way, at which time it was deemed inappropriate to promote her successor, the head of a small peacetime Corps, to a rank that had not been awarded to the full Corps in wartime. [45]

In any case, it was the general opinion that a Congressional majority for such legislation would not have been forthcoming. Some six months before, the Director had received the Army's highest noncombat award, the Distinguished Service Medal. On this occasion General White had noted, "Since our friends on the hill won't let us pin stars on you, this is the next best thing." [46] The award of the DSM was regarded as some measure of substitute recognition, as much to the Corps as to the Director. Its citation stated, in part:

Without the guidance of precedents in United States military history to assist her, Colonel Hobby established sound initial policies, planned and supervised the selection of officers and the preparation of regulations. The soundness of basic plans and policies promulgated is evidenced by the outstanding success of the Women's Army Corps, composed of nearly 100,000 women and comprising an essential and integral part of the Army. [47]

Choice of Successor

With her resignation, the Director submitted to the Chief of Staff, for consideration in choosing her successor, the names

---

[42] Draft, no date, sub: The Mission That Grew. WDWAC 314.7 (1945–46).

[43] D/F, Dir WAC for CofS, 26 Jun 45. WD G–1 WAC 210.31–.482.

[44] Congressional Record, 11 Jul 45, Mr. Overton Brooks of Louisiana, pp. 7416–17.

[45] Interv with Mrs. Hobby.

[46] Ltr, Gen White to Col Hobby, 3 Jan 45. "MTO," Hobby files.

[47] WDBPR Press Release, 12 Jul 45 (has copy of citation).

of five WAC lieutenant colonels listed in the order of her preference.[48] It was natural that members of the Corps staff should expect the new head to be the former deputy who for twenty months had been Colonel Hobby's chief assistant and at times Acting Director, Lt. Col. Jessie P. Rice. However, it may have appeared unwise to ask Colonel Rice, in view of her poor health, to leave her job as head of the School for WAC Personnel Administration and assume a new and more formidable post. Another consideration may have been the fact that Colonel Rice had not found herself in harmony with the views of the Assistant Chief of Staff, G–1, Maj. Gen. Stephen G. Henry, the Director's immediate superior. A particular disagreement, occurring some months before, had centered around language which Colonel Rice reported that General Henry applied to Negro Wacs in her presence. In protest, Colonel Rice had submitted her resignation and Colonel Hobby had supported her deputy by proffering her own resignation. Later, both resignations were withdrawn at the request of General Henry, who apologized for his language.[49]

In any event, Colonel Hobby's first listed choice for her successor was Deputy Director Lt. Col. Westray Battle Boyce. Earlier she had served as a staff officer in General Henry's Personnel Policy Branch, where she had handled numerous projects, including the allotment of grades for WAC general hospital companies. She had been the first staff director of the North African theater, and, before that, staff director of the Fourth Service Command. General Henry, in approving Colonel Hobby's nomination of Colonel Boyce as Director, stated that "she will make a better director in the eyes of the public, a better 'front' for the Corps," that she had shown her capacity to win the support of influential organizations of women, and also that she was "more the feminine type than any other candidate." General Marshall, about to leave for Potsdam, approved the choice, after obtaining the concurrence of Secretary Stimson, who was already on shipboard.[50]

Colonel Hobby elected immediate resignation instead of a medical discharge, since this enabled her successor to be promoted on the same day to the rank of colonel and the full status of Director, without waiting upon lengthy board proceedings. On 12 July 1945, the closely guarded secret was revealed, and in the presence of the Acting Secretary of War, Colonel Boyce took office as the second Director WAC. Acting Secretary of War Robert P. Patterson praised the first Director's work and informed a press conference, "She had to fight many obstacles in promoting a program that was unique in the history of the Army, but she did it with great distinction." Mrs. Hobby thanked the War Department for "The great assistance always at hand," and the press for their "constructive interpretation." She added:

I have been a member of the greatest democratic fraternity in the world. I shall always be grateful for my service in the Army

---

[48] Memo, Dir WAC for CofS, 26 Jun 45, sub: Recommendations. WD G–1 WAC 210.31–.482.

[49] The account of this incident is based on the author's recollections. The clash with General Henry was reported to a few WAC staff officers, including the author, as well as to Colonel Hobby. According to Colonel Rice, she had walked out in silence after General Henry's remarks, but had immediately returned to offer her uncensored opinion and resignation saying, "Sir, your staff officer just went out and a citizen of the United States walked in."

[50] (1) Memo, ACofS G–1 for CofS, 8 Jul 45, sub: New Director, WAC, with handwritten notes by CofS and SGS. WDGAP 210.31 WAC (6–21–45). (2) CM–IN–10024, Stimson to AGWAR (for Marshall), 11 Jul 45.

of the United States. . . . After three years, the Women's Army Corps has reached its authorized strength. These women are serving in more than two hundred and fifty Army jobs. They are performing their tasks in every theater in the world. The Women's Army Corps is no longer an experiment. Through the measure of its performance, it is accepted by the Army and by the public as an integral part of the team.

So, I feel that my mission of organizing the Corps has been completed. In resigning as Director of the WAC, I would like to say that I have had no comparable experience. . . .

Reporters were, as always, unwilling to let the subject drop so easily, and there followed a question-and-answer exchange not unlike that which had inaugurated the Director's term of service:

Press: What will be the most vivid impression you take away?

Mrs. Hobby: You cannot shed a four-year experience with people in the War Department, and with the great number of women that I have served with, without taking back the knowledge that you are a much richer woman.

Press: Would you like to see the WAC made a permanent part of the Army?

Mrs. Hobby: That is, as you know, a Congressional decision, and I wouldn't comment on it.

Press: Have you bought any new civilian hats?

Mrs. Hobby: Do you mind if I don't end this conference on a note of levity? [51]

The violence of the women's reaction to Mrs. Hobby's departure, although expected by the Office of the Director, was surprising to those who had not understood to what extent the small all-volunteer Women's Army Corps had been knit together and sustained in its pioneering by purely emotional motives—idealism, patriotism, and fierce loyalties to fellow members and to its leaders. Now the women's expected reaction was unfortu-

nately intensified by the manner of the press's relating of the event. The vital phrase in the prepared release, "that her mission *of organizing* the Corps had been completed," was omitted by the Associated Press, which reported, "Colonel Hobby said her mission was completed and that she is returning to her family." [52] The United Press retained the phrase "of organizing," but most newspapers did not print the long explanatory material.

As a result, many Wacs felt that if the Director's mission was ended, so was theirs. From as far away as New Guinea there came the disillusioned protest, "Fine thing—she helped us get into this mess, then she turns around and resigns and here we sit. Nice war, isn't it?" Others said, "If she can go, why can't we?" Because of the Director's desire not to reveal the personal matters that made her eligible for discharge on three different counts under Army Regulations, including the Adjusted Service Rating score, women said, erroneously but indignantly, "Men Army officers can't resign." As expected, parents also wrote to attack Colonel Hobby for resigning when their daughters were unable to do so. [53]

The total effect on the Corps soon became quite serious. Colonel Rice responded to a plea for help from the new Director's staff with a speech to troop commanders at the Purdue school in which, mincing few words, she defined a soldier's proper attitude in such crises, and defended the choice of Colonel Boyce, who was not well known to the Corps. The

---

[51] All from Transcript, Press Conf of Col Hobby with Actg SW Robert P. Patterson and Lt Col Westray B. Boyce, 12 Jul 45. WD G–1 WAC 210.31–482.

[52] AP; see *Chicago World Herald*, July 13, 1945.

[53] Ltrs in WDWAC 095 (1945–46) esp Ltr, Exec WAC to Mrs. D. F. Pattison, 22 Sep 45.

student response was good and Colonel
Rice predicted that the Corps' reaction,
though extreme, was a purely personal
one, and being such, would pass of itself
as soon as the shock wore off. In this she
proved correct, and within a few weeks the
normal routine of WAC life had been resumed. The women's reaction had, however, obliged Mrs. Hobby to make public
the state of her health, which she had desired not to mention, and to allow release
of the fact that she had been admitted immediately to Doctors' Hospital in New
York.[54]

Final Recommendations

The War Department soon discovered
that even in departure Colonel Hobby
had seized the opportunity for a post-
humous effort in favor of certain favorite
recommendations. In her final report, she
brought to the attention of the Chief of
Staff the only five major policy matters on
which she had been repeatedly defeated,
and which she considered important omissions from the perfection of the final WAC
program.[55] Although General Henry held
the paper for two months before presenting it to General Marshall, there appeared
to have been a good chance that the former Director would have scored final victory on all five counts had not the atomic
bomb brought the war to a close.

The most serious of these proposals was
that the War Department establish a
policy, comparable to the Navy's, to permit enlisted women to associate socially
with male officers. This proposal Colonel
Hobby had already presented seven times
in the past two years. General Henry
again disagreed, saying, "The traditional
relationship between officers and enlisted
personnel is a strongly entrenched custom

of the service, and any exception which is
made for Wacs will be a step in the direction of its complete elimination." This proposal now at last reached General Marshall himself, who noted, "I am inclined
to agree with Colonel Hobby. The situation between the sexes is very different
from that in the male Army."[56] However,
General Marshall's deputies urged him to
reconsider this decision, and finally, in
view of the unsettled postwar conditions,
and the prospective demobilization of the
Corps, General Marshall decided to make
no change in policy for the present.[57]

The other four proposals, made while
the war seemed of indefinite duration, returned to the problem of fatigue. The report noted that barracks which were
adequate for shorter occupancy by women
could produce excessive fatigue over a
period of years, and asked that "the housing regulation be amended to provide
some privacy" in the latter case. Although
the idea was approved in substance, with
the end of the war no new housing was authorized.

In a third proposal, the Director again
attempted to get a rotation policy after
two years of service. This also was approved to the extent of a nonmandatory
letter of advice to each major command,

---

[54] Announced by press (AP), 19 July 1945.
[55] Memo, Dir WAC for CofS through G–1, 11 Jul
45. WDWAC 319.1. Forwarded by Summary Sheet,
Gen Henry, G–1, for CofS, sub: Final Rpt on WAC
by Col Oveta Culp Hobby, Retiring Dir, 10 Sep 45.
WDGAP 319.1 WAC (7–11–45). Co-ordination of
G–3, 21 Sep 45, and G–4, 27 Sep 45. Approved by
Brig Gen Henry I. Hodes, Asst DCofS, 30 Sep 45.
[56] *Ibid.*, Atchd Note, CofS for Gen Hodes, 1 Oct 44.
[57] *Ibid.*, Atchd Notes. Brig Gen Robert W. Berry,
Dep G–1, prepared a memo for General Handy
(DCofS). General Handy did not sign this but talked
to the Chief of Staff, 15 October, according to an at-
tached note from General Hodes, (Asst DCofS), 15
October 1945. Copies of document were forwarded to
author by Deputy Director WAC. WAC files, OCMH.

although only the Air and Ground Forces accepted the advice, and the beginning of demobilization effectually prevented such rotation in any case.

A fourth proposal was also approved: that WAC officers in the older age bracket be eligible for discharge as men were, a provision that had been omitted from the directive on the discharge eligibility of officers.

The last proposal, that noncommissioned officers' schools be set up in the major commands, similar in purpose to the officers' school at Purdue, became unnecessary with quick demobilization at hand.

In addition to her formal report, Mrs. Hobby also wrote personally to General Marshall:

Serving under your leadership was one of the great experiences of my life. I shall ever be grateful to you for the opportunity and the never failing assistance.

Upon his return from Potsdam, General Marshall thanked the former Director for her service, and wrote:

Your firm leadership and unselfish purpose were a tremendous factor in the outstanding success of the organization. You made a great sacrifice in the effort which I hope will not prove costly to your future health.[58]

Upon her resignation in mid-July, 1945, Colonel Hobby had come nearer to seeing the wartime WAC to its end than she realized. She later remarked that, had she known how suddenly Japan would be defeated, she would have endeavored to remain for a short time thereafter. A few weeks after her departure, the first atomic bomb fell, and in the next month demobilization was on.

---

[58] Ltr, Oveta Culp Hobby for CofS, 10 Sep 45, and reply, 18 Sep 45, both in personal file of CofS. Made available to author, December 1945, by courtesy of his secretary.

CHAPTER XXXVI

Demobilization

Before her departure, Director Hobby had secured approval of a demobilization policy that would permit Wacs to be separated from the service in a fair and orderly sequence, a movement already begun in a small way with V-E Day. The process was, inevitably, to remain orderly for scarcely as long as was required for Japan to capitulate or the nation to succumb to a panic for quick demobilization.

Two years before, while the Auxiliary was still struggling to establish itself, it had been confronted by the War Department's Special Planning Division with the incongruous necessity of planning for demobilization. Three vital decisions were required: whether the WAC should get out faster, slower, or at the same rate as the men; which women should get out first; and the manner in which they could best be processed through separation facilities.[1]

Director Hobby's unvarying conviction, then and later, was that the WAC should be disbanded as soon as possible after the war was over. She replied to the Special Planning Division that the WAC was so small that even its complete and sudden postwar demise would upset neither Army demobilization nor the civilian economy; that Waacs legally had no re-employment rights even if they had joined the WAC; that without these rights, jobs for women would be scarce in peacetime and therefore an early start in searching for them

was advisable; and that the nation would wish its homes re-established as soon as possible. Unlike the Army, the WAC, under existing legislation, had no peacetime component toward which to build, nor even an inactive reserve. She therefore recommended a quick demobilization, in the order of length of service, with priority for former Waacs, veterans' wives, women with dependents, and women with guaranteed civilian jobs. The last to go, in her opinion, should be volunteers who elected to remain for a time.

These ideas were rejected in their entirety by Special Planning Division, which stated that "military necessity"— the essentiality of the job—could be the only governing factor, and that the length of a woman's service could not be considered. This view caused some concern to Director Hobby, since women were chiefly located in overhead jobs, where it might be deemed a military necessity to keep every Wac clerk until the last man was discharged. She asked also what community agency could be expected to assist WAC veterans as the Selective Service

---

[1] Entire planning project, except as cited in later notes, from: (1) WDWAC 370.01, containing: Memo, SPD WD for Dir WAC, 31 Jul 43; two Memos, Stf for Dir WAC, one 25 Aug 43, one undated; M/R, Miss Lies for Dir WAC, 28 Dec 43. (2) Folder, Plng Proj 26, WAAC Plng Serv files, including: M/R, 13 Jul 43; Memo, Miss Lies for Dir WAC, 24 Mar 44, with incl Memo, Dir WAC for SPD WD, 6 Sep 43, reply from SPD, 1 Oct 43, and from Dir WAC, 21 Jan 44.

boards would assist returning draftees. As a result, the Office of the Director formulated the policy to which it held while Director Hobby was in office: "It is not intended to suggest any preferred treatment for WAC personnel . . . however, it is believed that a percentage of discharge should be established for the WAC, and that this percentage should be the same as that which the total number of Army separations bears to the Army." [2]

Special Planning Division refused to take any action to authorize such a percentage. Accordingly, General Somervell, the Director's superior at the time, recommended that no plans be made for WAC demobilization until the War Department had decided whether to keep a Regular Army WAC—a decision that actually was not to be made until three years after the victory over Japan. In this he was eventually overruled by General Marshall, to whom the Director carried the issue at the time of her transfer to G–1. General Marshall directed that the WAC be immediately included in the Army's demobilization planning. General Somervell and the Director were in agreement on one point: that there should be quick postwar demobilization. General Somervell noted, "It is believed that all women who wish to leave the service after the defeat of Germany should be permitted to do so as fast as they can be replaced by men with the proper qualifications." [3]

In spite of the Chief of Staff's directive, as late as April of 1945 the War Department's readjustment plan still made no definite provision for female personnel, although the Adjusted Service Rating System had been developed for men, which gave particular weight to combat service and number of children. Director Hobby therefore submitted to G–1 Division a request that the WAC's strength, like the Army's, be reduced by one sixth after the victory in Europe. [4]

While most G–1 planners were favorable to equal percentages, a particular difficulty developed. G–1 Division noted that, since the WAC had virtually ceased recruiting while the Army was still drafting men, it would be more economical to discharge only men on point scores, and let normal attrition take care of reduction in the WAC. Director Hobby opposed this view, because she felt that it was not the enlisted women's fault that recruiting had ceased. On the matter of giving priority to women married to veterans, which the Special Planning Division favored, Director Hobby did not object, provided the purpose was to aid veterans' readjustment. She believed, however, that such priority should not affect the percentage of women to be discharged on their own merit. [5]

As a result of Colonel Hobby's request, a point score of 44 was set for the WAC, which permitted it, like the Army, to be reduced on merit after V–E Day. The discharge of married women did not prevent the departure of those with 44 points, nor did normal attrition. Director Hobby also received from G–3 Division the informal commitment that, while the remainder of the WAC, like the Army, must be kept until Japan surrendered, the Corps would then be quickly demobilized. [6]

---

[2] Memo, Jessie P. Rice, Dep Dir WAC, for SPD, 21 Jan 44. WDWAC 370.01.

[3] Memo, CG ASF for CofS, 29 Mar 44. SPAP 324.5 (3–29–44), ASF. For Gen Marshall's action, see Ch. XV, above.

[4] Memo, Dir WAC for G–1, 28 Apr 45. WDWAC 320.2.

[5] See n. 1; also Memo, Capt Margaret Stone, WAC, for Dir WAC, 12 Apr 45. WDWAC 370.01.

[6] Memo, Capt Stone for Dep Dir WAC, 12 Jun 45. WDWAC 370.01.

Before her departure, Director Hobby also secured the assignment of a WAC officer, Major Lichty, to the Veterans Placement Division, Office of the Director of Selective Service, to aid in applying the re-employment program to WAC veterans insofar as legally possible. A Wave and a woman Marine officer were also assigned.[7]

Only one provision of the final plan was not wholly satisfactory to Director Hobby. This was the requirement that the WAC use the Army system of computing point scores for discharge eligibility; G–1 Division considered it uneconomical and confusing to print and distribute separate cards and separate instructions for women. Of the four factors that determined a final score, only one really fit the WAC—"length of service." Of the others, "number of children" was manifestly inapplicable, since women with children had not been allowed to enlist after the first month of recruiting. Most "combat decorations" were also inapplicable, since women had not been admitted to combat, although they received Bronze Stars and lesser awards. "Overseas service" applied, but in the wrong way, since overseas service for Wacs had been generally considered a privilege, and those without it were often more in need of discharge than those with it.

No inequity was caused by the fact that men's scores computed under this system necessarily ran higher than women's, since the WAC was guaranteed an equal percentage of reduction. The inequity occurred among members of the WAC, where those with overseas service outscored those who had enlisted long before them. Nevertheless, this difficulty was not at the time deemed prohibitive, as less than one fifth of the Wacs had been overseas. In a quick demobilization, numbers of those at home would go out almost as fast as women abroad could be returned for separation.

With the understanding that Wacs would get equal discharge percentages on length of service, and after seeing some 2,500 women demobilized under the system, Colonel Hobby resigned.[8] Less than a month later, the sudden defeat of Japan disrupted both Army and WAC plans for demobilization; the armed forces found themselves powerless to stem the tide of public demand for more immediate and drastic action than had earlier been deemed wise.

Action Following V-J Day

In the ensuing scramble, the WAC was overlooked in War Department press releases. Public announcements were made about the future demobilization of Army men, and the Navy issued announcements about its men and about the WAVES, SPARS, and Women Marines, but nothing was said about the WAC's plans.[9] The WAC discharge score was left at 44, where it had been since May, a score that allowed no Wacs in the United States to be separated on length of service. Women who had no children and no overseas service could not have accumulated more than 36 points even had they enlisted on the day the WAAC began.

The new Director, Colonel Boyce, undertook a tour of training centers and service commands to check on the situation. She was immediately struck by the overwhelming sentiment of Wacs in the field in favor of quick demobilization,

---

[7] 1st Ind (to unidentified Ltr), TAG to Dir SS, 23 Nov 44. AG PO–M–A 320.21 (11–13–44), in WDWAC 353.

[8] M/R, 5 Jul 45, sub: WAC. WDWAC 220.8.

[9] Memo, Dir WAC for Gen Henry, 27 Aug 45. WDWAC 370.01.

especially of women with long monotonous service in the zone of the interior. She reported: "There is a growing feeling among WAC personnel with long Zone of the Interior service on isolated posts that they are being discriminated against" by discharge of overseas Wacs with shorter service. Colonel Boyce therefore recommended "an early press release in order that the questions in the minds of the Wacs, the public, and Congress may be answered." She expressed herself in favor of beginning WAC demobilization in the zone of the interior by dropping the point score from 44 to 30, thus allowing demobilization of women who had enlisted in the Auxiliary's first six months, even if they had had no overseas service.[10]

Colonel Boyce's recommendations were not favorably considered by the War Department. On the day following her request, General Henry spoke before the Military Affairs Committee of the House of Representatives, giving only the plan for demobilization of men.[11] Colonel Boyce at once protested:

. . . the inadvertent omission of any reference to the lowering of the point score [for women] is particularly unfortunate in view of . . . my memorandum. It is hoped that an immediate decision will be reached. When the necessary policy decisions are made, this office will prepare a separate War Department release on the future of the WAC, to try to offset the detrimental effect of past silence.[12]

A week later the War Department decided on a drop in the point score. It proved to be a disappointment, since the drop was from 44 to only 41 for enlisted Wacs, instead of to 30. WAC officers' scores were set at 44. This score still prevented the discharge of Wacs in the United States, some 85 percent of the Corps. Since overseas theaters, with most

of the discharge eligibles, were extremely slow about returning Wacs, the result was that almost no women moved toward separation centers.[13]

With this announcement, the Director's Office was all but submerged in a wave of bitter letters from Wacs in the field. Even before she received these protests, Colonel Boyce in September drafted a memorandum pointing out that, when the men's score dropped to 80 points, the WAC score should drop to 33, if the percentage of Wacs allowed to go home was to equal the percentage of men leaving. This memorandum was not sent. In the meantime the War Department had directed that on 1 October the men's score was to fall further, to 60 points, but the Wacs' only to 36, and that in November, when the enlisted men's score fell to 55, the Wacs' would fall only to 34.

Thus, six months after V-E Day, the principle of equal discharge percentages on point scores was abrogated, and no Wacs in the United States, except the handful of enlisted women who had enrolled during the Auxiliary's first two months, were yet eligible for discharge on the basis of points.[14]

Slowing of WAC Demobilization

What had actually been repudiated was the plan that the percentages of Wacs

---

[10] *Ibid.*

[11] Gen Henry's mimeographed statement, 28 Aug 45. WDWAC 370.01.

[12] Memo, Dir WAC for Gen Henry. WDWAC 370.01.

[13] (1) WDBPR Press Releases, 3, 6 Sep 45. (2) Cbl, G–1 overseas commands, 6 Sep 45, by WDGAP 220.8 to TAG. WDWAC 370.01.

[14] (1) Draft (not used) of Memo, Dir WAC for Gen Henry, (Sep 45). WDWAC 370.01. (2) WD Policies on Discharge, par II, 6. (3) WDBPR Press Release, 20 Sep 45.

to be discharged on length of service should not be affected by the numbers discharged because they were veterans' wives or for any other reason. Even before Colonel Hobby left, G–1 Division's Statistical Branch had objected to this system, saying:

In order that the relative importance and prestige of the WAC be maintained throughout the entire demobilization period, it seems necessary that the present WAC percentage of the total Army strength be maintained. . . . Although the WAC is under moral obligation to release women who have performed long and arduous service, yet . . . it seems necessary to sacrifice a few for the good of the many.[15]

Attrition losses were by this time considerable. First, several thousand veterans' wives had been discharged. Next, the Army let men and women over 38 years old leave if they wished, and some 7,000 more women were made eligible for discharge. No sooner were these gone than the outcry of nonveteran husbands forced the release of all married women. Their discharge was authorized regardless of length of service, at the same time that men with three or more children became eligible for discharge regardless of length of service. The WAC took this step reluctantly, and only at the insistence of G–1 Division, and after the Nurse Corps, WAVES, SPARS, and Marines had already taken it, since this made 13,000 more women eligible. In order to maintain Corps strength after recruiting had ceased, these women had been substituted on the monthly demobilization quota for those who would ordinarily have been made eligible by a lowering of point scores comparable to that of the men's scores.[16]

Even more significant for the future was the refusal of the General Staff to approve

public announcement of the final demobilization date of the WAC, still tentatively set as June 1946. At the same time, the Navy Department was also considering holding the WAVES beyond the originally scheduled June date, over the protest of the WAVES leaders.[17] This delay, in all the armed forces, was generally related to the discovery that the need for the skills common among female personnel had been underestimated, to an extent that raised doubts as to whether enlisted women could be allowed to leave at the same rate as enlisted men. Overseas theaters in particular had resolutely refused to face the fact that the WAC could never be entirely demobilized, as required by law, until male replacements were accepted for discharged Wacs. In justification for its action in retaining dischargeeligibles, the European theater pointed out that, when it had returned a few women for discharge, these had not been separated as men were, but had been pulled out by Army Service Forces' separation centers to process men for discharge, on the grounds of "military necessity."[18]

The Army Service Forces informed the War Department that, in order to main-

---

[15] Memo, Maj A. J. Bonis, G–1 Stat Br, for Dir WAC, 28 Apr 45. WDWAC 370.01.

[16] (1) Memo, Maj Bonis for Dir WAC, 5 Sep 45. WDWAC 370.01. (2) Memo, Dep Dir WAC for Col Boyce, 14 Nov 45. WDWAC 319.1. (3) Memo, Exec WAC for Col Boyce, 27 Nov 45. WDWAC 220.8. (4) Memo, Maj Bonis for Col Boyce, 10 Sep 45, atchd to Memo, G–1 for MPD ASF, 6 Sep 45. WDWAC 354.1.

[17] Memo, Dep Dir WAC for Dir WAC, 23 Jan 46, sub: Rpt of Mtg of Dirs of Women's Servs, 22 Jan 46. WDWAC 337.

[18] (1) Memo, "KKJ," WAC Exec, for Dir WAC, 13 May 45, sub: Rpt for Week 7–13 May 45. WDWAC 319.1. (2) Ltr, WAC Stf Dir ETO for Dir WAC, 6 Aug 45, and Reply, 13 Aug 45. WDWAC 320.2. (3) 1945 Budget Hearing material. Hobby files. See also Chs. XX and XXI, above.

tain separation centers, 5,000 Wacs should be transferred from the Air and Ground Forces. Both Air and Ground Forces offered objections. AGF was hard-pressed to find enough Wacs to replace high-point men in its commanding general's office in Washington and at the Army War College. It was in fact preparing to request the War Department to remove Wacs from other commands in order to fill its needs. For this reason, the War Department was able to allot ASF only 2,600 of the requested 5,000 and was obliged to direct the AAF to furnish all of them.[19]

Over the issue of demobilization, WAC leaders split into two opposing camps—those who believed that WAC demobilization should be effected in accordance with original commitments to former Director Hobby, and those who favored keeping as many women as possible as long as possible, in the hope that Congress would authorize some type of peacetime group. By what appeared more than coincidence, the majority of Wacs who supported a permanent Corps, or desired to remain in one, were those whose service had been chiefly overseas. The nonsupporters included the WAC advisers in almost all air, ground, and service commands in the United States, the most eager to depart being those whose service had been entirely in the War Department.

These officers' desire for a speedy demobilization was based on various factors. There was at the time no prospect of a Regular Army corps, and it seemed futile to keep a handful of women on an ambiguous status. In addition, a recent Information and Education Division survey showed that only 2 percent of the enlisted women were actively interested in remaining, and that these constituted the Corps' bottom 2 percent from the point of view of education, maturity, and ability.[20] Just before WAC recruiting ended, Colonel Boyce reported that, with the WAC Recruiting Service disbanded,

. . . the recruits received since V-E Day include an increasingly high number of Grade IV's and V's despite outstanding directives that only the equivalent to Grade III's or better are acceptable. . . . It is the opinion of recruiting officers that the number and quality of enlistments will decrease as time goes on.[21]

There were also reports from the field, such as one from a staff director who wrote:

We have noticed a definite change in the attitude of male officers and enlisted personnel toward the WAC since the cessation of hostilities. . . . Present pressure for demobilization will undoubtedly influence public opinion against the wearer of the uniform. . . . Today the majority of the people in America would give us a vote of confidence. I am fearful that four months from now the fickle public will be questioning the reason for women being in uniform. . . . I am leaving in any event.[22]

An additional objection, as voiced by Colonel Bandel, was the belief that peacetime Army life, as contrasted to emergency wartime service, presented an unnatural situation for a woman. A woman choosing the Army for a thirty-year career would,

---

[19] (1) Memo, Dir Pers ASF (Gen Dalton) for G–1, 13 Aug 45. SPGAC 210.3 WAC, in SPAP 220.3 WAC. (2) D/F, G–1 for DCofS, 15 Aug 45. WDGAP 220.3 WAC, in CSA 324.5 WAC. (3) Memo, Dir WAC for CG ASF, 18 Aug 45. WDWAC 220.3. (4) WDBPR Press Release, 5 Sep 45. (5) AGF Hist, Vol. I, p. 77, and Vol. II, App. XXVII.

[20] I&E Div Rpt B–166, 14 Sep 45, Postwar Job Plans of Enlisted WAC. WAC files OCMH.

[21] *Ibid.* Also, D/F, G–1 for CofS, 28 Aug 45. WDGAP 370.01 WAC, in WDWAC 370.01. Approved by DCofS, 29 Aug 45. See WDBPR Press Release, 30 Aug 45.

[22] Ltr, Maj J. S. Phillips, WAC Stf Dir EFTC, to Col Woods, 25 Sep 45. WDWAC 330.14.

she stated, have to face the fact that her husband could not be considered a dependent and thus could not live with her on a military post. If he was an Army man he could live on the post, if by chance the stations of husband and wife coincided, but questions would arise as to who took the social status and quarters of whom. In any case, if Wacs married, the loss from pregnancy would be high, or a woman bent on a career could not permit herself any children. Under the circumstances, while most Army career men lived normal lives with homes and families, it appeared that career women would be denied both.[23]

WAC Effort To Hasten Demobilization

In September, Colonel Boyce left for the Pacific without having secured a decision on the Corps' future. In November, Acting Director Helen Woods made a final effort to secure total demobilization. In a memorandum for the new Assistant Chief of Staff, G-1, General Paul, she recommended that the Corps' fourth birthday, 14 May 1946, be chosen for the closing date, and that the WAC go out proudly in a burst of ceremonies and with the public announcement that the War Department had requested Congress to bestow Reserve status on all women who had served honorably. By the Corps' fourth birthday, its strength would have been reduced to about 20,000 after which point, said Colonel Woods, it would be "unsound economically and administratively to keep the Corps in operation at a figure much below this." [24]

Colonel Woods was later reinforced in her position by written memoranda from the Army Service Forces WAC Officer and the Army Ground Forces WAC Officer. The ASF WAC Officer, Colonel Goodwin, concurred in the choice of the WAC fourth anniversary as closing day, for WAC officers as well as enlisted women, since officers would not be vitally needed with the women gone. The AGF WAC Officer, Colonel Davis, likewise urged speedy demobilization, but preferred the thirteenth of June as the final deadline.[25]

The Air WAC Officer, Colonel Bandel, had already taken a more practical step. Taking advantage of an obscure provision that gave the Air Forces the right to discharge its women as well as its men at its own rates, she persuaded her headquarters to release Air Forces Wacs as fast as it was releasing AAF men. This at once cut the critical score for Air Wacs from 34 to 18, and opened floodgates which by December had let out of the Army all but 10,000 of the AAF's 39,000 Wacs, and which threatened by the fourth anniversary to have settled the dispute, at least for the Air Forces, in a most effective manner.[26]

At this point, Colonel Boyce abandoned her overseas tour and hurried home, recording the fact that

. . . information received by the Director WAC in a teletype conference with her office on Saturday, 10 November, indicated that plans and policies affecting the future of the Corps were being discussed, and she felt it

---

[23] AAF WAC Hist; also intervs.

[24] Above and below from Memo, Dep Dir WAC for Gen Paul G-1, 8 Nov 45. WDWAC 370.01.

[25] Memo, ASF WAC Off for Dir WAC, 11 Dec 45, and Memo, AGF WAC Off for Dir WAC, 10 Dec 45. WDWAC 370.01.

[26] TAG Ltr to major comds, 24 Sep 45. AGPW-A-WDGAP 220.8 (9-22-45), in WDWAC 220.8. Also WDWAC 370.01, 1945-46, documents dated 13, 19, 20, and 26 Dec 45.

advisable for her to return to Washington rather than complete the tour.[27]

Colonel Boyce returned to a War Department that had been virtually taken over by the staff of the European theater. As a result of the high caliber and skills of WAC personnel employed in wartime by that theater, the idea of a permanent Corps was now favorably viewed by General Eisenhower as Chief of Staff, General Paul as G–1, General Devers as AGF commander, and Generals Spaatz and Eaker as AAF commanders.

Soon after Colonel Boyce's return, the Air Forces' independent discharge authority, insofar as it concerned women only, was withdrawn. Thereafter the WAC critical score fell slowly. By January of 1946 the score remained at 32 points or two and a half years' service.[28]

WAC officers' scores fell even more slowly; on 1 November the score of 37 was adopted, the first point at which any WAC officer who had not served overseas became eligible for discharge. At this score, 800 veteran officers from the first classes became eligible, including many of the key officers of the WAC. In January those officers with three years and three months of service were also released. It proved difficult to lower the WAC officers' score much more, since few had been commissioned since 1943, and all but one tenth had three years of service by the spring of 1946.[29]

Cessation of WAC Demobilization

In the first days of January 1946, the War Department was faced with the necessity of slowing all demobilization, an unpopular move that was to produce a crisis in Army public relations.[30] At this time the issue was finally forced as to whether the WAC should be retained after June of 1946. A memorandum in Colonel Boyce's file indicated that she or her staff prepared one last strong objection to retaining the WAC:

It is the considered opinion and urgent recommendation of the Director WAC that the enlisted personnel and administrative officers of the Corps be demobilized by the end of the fiscal year, 30 June 1946.[31]

Six different objections were advanced: *First,* as WAC units shrank, constant and expensive transfer and consolidation would be necessary. *Second,* "it is not efficient or economical to continue to utilize WAC personnel beyond a minimum strength level, since administration and supply become impractical at a certain point." *Third,* "it is becoming increasingly apparent that, with an indeterminate demobilization date for the Corps, utilizing agencies are finding it impossible to plan intelligently on the use of Wacs." *Fourth,* morale would become steadily worse as women waited for long-delayed information. *Fifth,* "the public relations aspects of having the Corps dwindle to small scattered groups of personnel remaining to an undecided date are highly undesirable." *Sixth,* embarrassing errors would be inevitable in view of the uncertainty as to

---

[27] Rpt of Dir WAC on overseas tour, undated, Tab B, sub: General Observations on All Theaters. WDWAC 333.1 (1945–46).

[28] Memo, Dep Dir Woods for Col Boyce, 7 Dec 45. WDWAC 370.01.

[29] D/F, G–1 for TAG, 10 Oct 45. WDWAC 370.01.

[30] (1) Memo, Maj Chance, Exec WAC, for Lt Col McClure, G–1, 23 Oct 45. WDWAC 370.01. (2) Memo, Dep Dir Woods for Col Boyce, 5 Dec 45. WDWAC 370.01. (3) Memo, WDBPR, 15 Jan 46. WDWAC 350.001. (4) For final WAC separation figures for both officer and enlisted personnel, see Tables 12 and 13, Appendix A.

[31] Memo, Dir WAC for G–1, 17 Jan 46. WDWAC 320.2.

whether the services would be merged, the Air Forces made independent, or the Army placed on a peacetime basis. As a result, the WAC recommendation concluded, "It is not practical to contemplate an Interim WAC."

This proposal was rejected by G–1 Division. Instead, General Paul recommended that the WAC be retained indefinitely, possibly as long as the Army retained any non-Regular Army men. He explained the action to a Senate committee, saying:

We fully expect to have a small permanent group of women in the Army. . . . For that reason the directive did not direct the abolishment of all of our women from the Army by June 30. . . . The women have done a very outstanding job in this war, and in line with getting more men out of the Army we should use every available replacement we can get.[32]

The stoppage of the critical score for women was approved by the Chief of Staff, General Eisenhower, in a directive that stated: "There is a potential shortage of skilled personnel for utilization in the Interim Army."[33] At the same time the Navy Department also decided to retain the WAVES beyond June 1946, although only on a volunteer status with offer of inducements to remain. This policy was adopted over the nonconcurrence of the WAVES director. The women Marines were likewise retained. Only the SPARS managed to secure demobilization by June 1946.[34]

Accordingly, the War Department announced that the release of Wacs with twenty-four months' service would be delayed from April to June, and that those with less than twenty-four months would not be released until some indefinite future date. The men's discharge rate was

also slowed, but their critical score, which had been twice as great as the Wacs' in the beginning, fell so rapidly that by June it was identical with the Wacs', and remained so thereafter.

With this decision to hold the Women's Army Corps involuntarily, there ended a sixth-month period in which Colonel Hobby's policies for demobilization had been gradually but completely reversed. As the WAC headed into the troublesome two-year interim period ahead, the face of the Corps was completely altered by the departure of those in key spots and their replacement by officers who approved of the new policy. First to go, in December of 1945, were Colonels Bandel and Rice; Colonel Bandel left the Air Forces only after having successfully demobilized three fourths of her women. Colonel Woods left in February; Colonel Goodwin stayed only for the inactivation of the Army Service Forces in June. Within a few months almost every wartime WAC leader had left the Corps: fifteen of the seventeen women who had been wartime service command staff directors, and almost all of their assistant staff directors,[35] twenty-three of the twenty-five wartime

---

[32] Statement to Senate Subcommittee on Mil Affairs, in Ltr, Asst Exec G–1 to Mr. James L. Conners, 28 Jan 46. WDGAP 095 Conners, in WDWAC 095. See also D/F, G–1 for CofS, 1 Feb 46. WDGAP 370.01 WAC (1–4–46), in WDWAC 370.01.

[33] *Ibid.*, Tab A to D/F.

[34] (1) Memo cited n. 17; (2) M/R, 22 Jan 46, by Maj Jere Knight; (3) Memo, Asst Exec WAC for Dir WAC, 23 Feb 46. WDWAC 337.

[35] *Remaining:* Boyce (4th SvC, later Dir WAC), Bell (7th SvC, later overseas).

Discharged: Goodwin, Stearns, Perry (1st SvC); Bass, VanBolt, McQuatters (2d SvC); Rice, Wilson, Kerens, (3d SvC); Wolcott (4th SvC); Miller, Hedekin, Werbach (5th SvC); Epperson (6th SvC); Welch (7th SvC); Brown, Stillwell (8th SvC); Milburn, Gardiner (9th SvC); Keplinger (MDW).

air command directors,[36] and all of the Army Ground Forces staff directors in field commands.[37] All wartime staff directors of overseas theaters also left, even including such strong advocates of a permanent Corps as Colonel Wilson, who left to be married, and Colonel Brown, who returned to the Veterans' Administration.[38] After Colonel Bandel, two more Air WAC Officers left in rapid succession;[39] and after Colonel Davis, two more AGF WAC Officers elected discharge.[40] The ASF WAC Officer's only assistant left with her when the Service Forces closed.[41] The only Wac to have been a training center commandant, Colonel Strayhorn, likewise departed. All former officers of Colonel Hobby's staff elected discharge.

Colonel Boyce's office—like most other General Staff sections—was now entirely staffed with officers from the European and Mediterranean theaters. For her new deputy she chose Lt. Col. Mary A. Hallaren, former staff director of the Air Forces in Europe, in civilian life a teacher and lecturer for women's groups, and a strong advocate of a peacetime WAC.

Separation Procedure

While some 20,000 members of the Women's Army Corps were held in service by the frozen discharge criteria, the other 80,000 were in the process of leaving it. A year before, the commitment had been secured that women would be separated at only five of the many separation centers for men, to permit the assignment of specialists in women's medical and vocational problems. With the beginning of demobilization, women began to be processed through these five centers— Fort Dix, Fort Bragg, Camp Beale, Fort

Sheridan, and Fort Sam Houston. Fort Des Moines was added at a later date.[42]

Although these centers had a year's advance warning, the idea of adequate facilities for women and of skilled processing teams never was brought to fruition at all of them. War Department inspectors early discovered that medical teams examining women lacked gynecological specialists; a woman doctor was shortly ordered to each of the five centers, to be responsible for detecting gynecological disorders requiring treatment.[43]

At Camp Beale, physical surroundings were found to be undesirable and only a few women a day could be processed, with others waiting indefinitely.[44] At Fort Dix, barracks were overcrowded and unsanitary. Some correction was undertaken, but a full year later hundreds of Wacs at Fort Dix still had to wait over a week for sepa-

---

[36] *Remaining:* Hague (CFTC), Kersey (2d AF).

Discharged: Freeman (TC and Air WAC), Woods (WFTC and Dep Dir), Phillips (EFTC), Stryker (TTC), Hardesty (WTTC and Air WAC), Johnson (CTTC), Lea (ETTC), May (ATC; recalled 1946); Gilbert (1st AF), Watson (2d AF), McCauley (3d AF– died); Clague (recalled 1948), Marshall (4th AF); Elrod (Mat C–recalled 1948), Kennedy (ASC), Kerr (TCC), Guild (PGC); recalled 1947), Sweet, McKay (AFTAC), Morris (PDC), Barth (AACS; recalled 1948), Pease (WW), Ludwigsen (Hq AAF).

[37] Melin, Riley.

[38] *Remaining:* none.

Leaving: ETO: Wilson. SWPA: Brown. MTO: Coleman (Colonel Boyce, first MTO Stf Dir, remained until May 1947). ME: Dyer. CBI: Clague (returned to RA, 1948).

[39] Lt Col Mary Freeman, Maj Elizabeth Hardesty.

[40] Maj Louise Neilson, Maj Geneva McQuatters.

[41] Maj Margaret Perry.

[42] (1) Min, Conf, 17 Jun 44. WDGAP 354.1 (1945– 46). (2) Memo, G–1 for MPD ASF, 6 Sep 45. WDWAC 354.1. (3) Memo, SGO for Dir WAC, 6 Jul 44. WDWAC 220.8.

[43] D/F, G–1 to CG ASF, 19 Jun 45. WDGAP 321.02, in WDWAC 720.

[44] Memo, Dir WAC for G–1, 14 Jul 45. WDWAC 220.8.

VOCATION COUNSELING *at the separation center, Fort Des Moines.*

ration, since only 35 could be processed daily.

Eventually a series of incidents of illness and improper housing caused a War Department survey team to be sent to visit all five centers. Only Fort Des Moines received unqualified praise from this team. Here were employed medical officers and vocational counselors experienced in women's needs, and a final impressive ceremony with a band sent women away in an apparent glow of good will. Fort Sheridan was also praised for its separation ceremonies, in which men and women participated together.[45] A later limited survey showed that only about 3 percent of women in some areas had received any of the prescribed counseling prior to discharge. Even in these cases, counselors had little or no information on job opportunities for women.[46]

The War Department overlooked female personnel in most of its directives on separation. It was discovered that all reference to women had been omitted from the official War Department pamphlet, *Going Back to Civilian Life,* which was given to each person leaving the service to inform him of his rights and responsibilities and of the assistance available to him. This pamphlet was often inapplicable to Wacs, who did not have to report to Selective Service boards, could not join the Reserve or National Guard, had different dependency rules, had special provisions concerning WAAC service, and experienced other unique problems of status. Accordingly, a

[45] Unfavorable rpts in 1945–46 WDWAC 333.1 and 354.1.
[46] Helen G. Brown (former 1st Lt WAC), "Adjustment of problems of College and Non-College WAC Veterans," M. A. thesis, Stanford Univ, 1947.

WAC supplement to the pamphlet was hastily published, but this did not reach the field until 1946, when more than half of the Corps had already been separated.[47]

At the same time, it was discovered that instructions to separation centers had neglected to provide for entry concerning Auxiliary service anywhere on the standard discharge records, and former members of the WAAC experienced difficulty in securing credit for this service when seeking employment. This deficiency was discovered by Colonel Rice in the midst of her own separation. When informed that no official proof could be given her of her fifteen months' WAAC service, she returned to G–1 Division, wrote and processed a corrective circular, and came back, bearing a certified copy, to complete her discharge. Five necessary special notations for women were discovered to be missing. Again, it was not possible to remedy these omissions in time to assist many women.[48]

Women returning from overseas appeared especially in need of some preparation for what awaited them. Wacs from the European and Mediterranean theaters were reportedly startled by the attitude of the civilian population toward Wacs, and by the accommodations offered troops in the United States, which were far less favorable than those overseas. Colonel Boyce's office therefore devised a plan whereby trained WAC convoy officers met and accompanied each returning group, and gently broke the news about life in the United States.[49]

In spite of minor difficulties, confusion, and lack of counseling, most Wacs, like the men, had little trouble in surviving the brief passage through separation centers. All Wacs reverted to inactive status, since Congress had authorized Reserve status only for men and Navy women. Colonel Boyce's office considered a survey of these WAC veterans, such as had been made for men, in order to discover how the separation process might be improved, but she was informed by Information and Education Division, which now had only a small staff, that such a plan for women would encounter "resistance," and at any rate survey results would be too late to assist the Army in processing women.[50]

Veterans' Administration Policy

To evaluate further the results of the demobilization process, the Veterans' Administration in May of 1946 undertook a WAC survey as a part of its survey of male veterans. As expected, it was found that women experienced much the same readjustment difficulties as enlisted men, plus a number of their own. Women were found to be taking jobs more slowly and in smaller proportionate numbers than men. Although 89 percent had been working before enlistment, only about half were found, three or four months after discharge, to be employed. The remainder were housewives, students, job-seekers, or "just resting." Even when they took a job,

---

[47] (1) TWX, TAG to all SvCs, SPGAT, 11 Sep 45, re TWX to same, 7 Sep 45. WDWAC 370.01, and WAC 370.01. (2) Memo, G–1 for Chairman, WD Printing Bd, 14 Dec 45, sub: WD Pamphlet 21–4a, Dec 45, WAC Supplement to Going Back to Civilian Life. WDWAC 300.6. (3) D/F, G–1 to TAG, 20 Dec 45. WDWAC 461.

[48] Observed by author. Also D/F, G–1 to TAG, 12 Dec 45. WDGAP 220.8 WAC, in WDWAC 220.8.

[49] (1) WD Memo 600–45, 23 Aug 45. WDWAC 320. (2) D/F, G–1 to CG ASF, 24 Oct 45. WDWAC 210.31. (3) Memo, Convoy Offs to Stf Dir NYPOE, 29 Dec 45. WDWAC 319.1. (4) Memo, Dep Dir for Dir WAC, 4 Jan 46. WDWAC 319.1.

[50] (1) Memo, Maj Alice Knight for Dir WAC, 14 Dec 45, with incls; (2) M/R, Col Davis, 19 Dec 45. WDWAC 292.

women showed almost twice as great a tendency as men to leave it. Only 22 percent of women went back to their former employment, although twice as great a percentage of men did so. Many of those women who did go back expressed dissatisfaction. To some extent the women's reluctance to go back to their old work seemed due to their desire to find work that offered the degree of responsibility learned in the service.

To a much greater extent than the male veterans, women had related their future plans to the skill they had acquired in the service, but only two in five employed women were able to use their service-gained experience on their new jobs. Others were prevented from doing so by the low salaries offered them, by unwillingness of employers to give credit for military experience, and by the refusal of civilian employers to hire women in unusual jobs if men were available. Those least likely to be able to use their skill were those trained in technical work usually thought of as men's jobs: radio operator, mechanic, aircraft specialist, and others. About the same percentage of women as of men had applied for readjustment allowances, and about the same percent had entered school. Fewer women than men were interested in loans to buy a home or to go into business.[51]

Army psychiatrists expressed fear that women's readjustment would be more difficult than that of men, since

Even more than men, these women have become unsuited to their former civilian environment because the change in their pattern of life was more radical. . . . Most of them have matured, have broader interests, and a new and finer sense of values.[52]

However, few Wacs reported worse effects than "nervousness and a feeling of strange-

ness, tiredness"; "lack of real concern for seemingly unimportant things"; "a failure of family and friends to accept me as a responsible individual." Some found themselves "lacking in initiative"; others, "too bossy." Possibly the worst generally reported result was "a lost feeling . . . lack of interest in former friends or environment . . . an inability to find work which seemed really vital."[53]

The returning female veteran also found that the jokes and stories on WAC morals had preceded her into civilian life. As one Wac put it, "I discovered that it is best not to mention my army career due to the unfortunate stigma attached to the WAC."[54] The head of the New York Veterans Service Committee, Mrs. Anna Rosenberg, reported: "Many [women veterans] have been disillusioned and discouraged by a cold reception from various women's groups."[55]

To combat such hindrances to readjustment, various plans were invoked. The National Federation of Business and Professional Women's Clubs launched its Servicewomen's Project, by which local club members assisted returning servicewomen in job counseling and placement. The Retraining and Reemployment Administration employed the former head of the SPARS, Capt. Dorothy C. Stratton, to insure that women were not overlooked in its mission of guiding civilian communities in reintegrating veterans and war workers. Still another government agency,

---

[51] *The Woman Veteran*, Research Studies MPR–2, 31 Apr 46, Rpts Contl Symbol PAB–7–S, by Research Serv, VA. Also correspondence, VA and Dir WAC, leading up to survey, in WDWAC 292, Mar–Sep 46.

[52] Margaret D. Craighill, M.D., "Psychiatric Aspects of Women Serving in the Army," *American Journal of Psychiatry*, Vol. 104, No. 4, October, 1947.

[53] Helen G. Brown, thesis cited n. 46.

[54] *Ibid.*, p. 56.

[55] *Washington Post*, editorial, January 24, 1946.

the U.S. Office of Education, requested its state offices to assist women veterans. Possibly the most extensive assistance came from the WAC's National Civilian Advisory Committee members, under a plan whereby a woman could obtain assistance in career planning by mailing a card to her service command advisory committee. Results were generally excellent, especially in the Second Service Command, where over a thousand women were assisted.[56]

The Veterans' Administration itself, as reorganized by Gen. Omar N. Bradley, was in a position to render greatest assistance, and therefore designated a returning employee, Colonel Brown, to act as adviser on women veterans. General Bradley directed that women be hired in policy-making jobs by Veterans' Administration local offices, "in view of the large number of women veterans who have served in World War II and the great number of widows or wives of veterans who are entitled to Military Preference." [57] General Bradley also obtained the services of the Army's senior woman medical officer, Colonel Craighill, to survey hospitals where women veterans were receiving care, and to prevent recurrence of previous difficulties.[58]

A Veterans' Administration survey showed that a considerable number of women veterans were refused recognition as such, not only by civilians and private employers, but even by government agencies, which were unaware that the women's services had legally been taken into the Army and Navy. Other agencies had apparently overlooked the women accidentally, although the combined strength of the various women's services had been around 370,000, between 2 and 3 percent of the armed forces. In other cases, the failure to recognize women as veterans was not accidental, as when one of the major veterans' organizations amended its constitution and bylaws for the purpose of excluding women from membership.[59]

Since former Waacs who had joined the WAC had no re-employment rights, the National Civilian Advisory Committee recommended that legislation be sought for their relief. The Army Service Forces nonconcurred on grounds that this would "create situations of great complexity" where employers had replaced Waacs with others on a permanent basis. Nevertheless, the legislation was finally obtained, although not until August of 1946, long after the last of the former Auxiliaries became eligible for discharge.[60]

Reserve Proposals

The majority of Wacs had returned to civilian life by the time the War Department arrived at the decision to request

---

[56] (1) Memo, SS Vet Pers Div for Dep Dir WAC, 25 Oct 45. WDWAC 080. (2) Memo, Mary-Agnes Brown, VA, for Dir WAC, 12 Sep 45. WDWAC 292. (3) M/R, 5 Jan 46. WDWAC 292. (4) Brookings Institution Rpt, cited by Dorothy C. Stratton, "Women After the War," *The Independent Woman*, October 1945. (5) Routing Slip, I&E Div for Dir WAC, 27 Nov 45, with atchd. WDWAC 292. (6) D/F, G-1 for TAG, 8 Sep 45. WDGAP 201.7. (7) Memo, ASF WAC Off for Maj Knight, 28 Dec 45. WDWAC 220.8.

[57] VA Serv Ltr to all Regional Offices and Cens, 17 Nov 45; and another, 29 Oct 45. Also, Ltr, G-1 to VA, 2 Nov 45, reply to VA Ltr, 26 Oct 45. WDWAC 292.

[58] (1) Ltr, Gen Bradley to The SG, USA, 28 Dec 46. (2) Ltr, Surg 7th SvC to SGO, 9 Feb 44. SPKSM 704.11 WAC, in SPWA 710.

[59] (1) *The Woman Veteran.* (2) Address by Lt Col Mary-Agnes Brown to American Vocational Association, 7 Feb 46. Copy in OCMH.

[60] (1) Comment 2, MPD ASF to G-1, to Basic Memo, G-1 for ASF, 28 Mar 45, sub: Recommendations of NCAC. SPAP 319.1 WAC (10-9-44). (2) PL 709, 79th Cong, 9 Aug 46. Published in WD Bull 26, 12 Sep 46.

that Congress allow reserve status to be offered to Wacs, as it was to men and to
Waves.[61] Reserve corps status had been
recommended to Colonel Hobby, soon
after V-E Day, by the General Staff's Reserve Policy Committee, which expressed
the desire to seek immediate legislation
"rather than to await the enactment of
enabling legislation when an emergency
was upon us." [62] Colonel Hobby gave
tentative approval to such legislation only
insofar as it concerned an officers' reserve.
She disapproved of an enlisted reserve,
and desired that even the officers' reserve
be limited to three women officers on
active duty in the War Department to
formulate policy, with all others on inactive status. To maintain the officers' reserve, she agreed to the eventual establishment of an ROTC system similar to the
men's. Any more extensive system would,
she felt, be uneconomical because of the
high attrition expected among female reserves by reason of marriage and mother-
hood, which would render many members
ineligible for recall.[63]

These ideas were at first endorsed by
Colonel Boyce when she succeeded Colonel Hobby at this point in the planning.
Colonel Boyce stated that "need does not
exist for the services or training of enlisted
women at this time." [64] Within a few
weeks, after repeated conferences with
members of G–1 Division, Colonel Boyce
was led to admit the possibility of an enlisted reserve. Her office also devised detailed schemes for a female ROTC, which,
it was pointed out, would be less costly
than the men's, since only six months'
basic training would be required, instead
of the two years needed by men. For the
men's advanced specialized courses, it was
proposed to substitute courses in hospital
administration, cryptanalysis, military ad-

ministration, and similar subjects.[65]

The War Department split into opposing groups when legislation to this effect
was proposed by the Reserve Policy Committee. When consulted, G–2, G–3, OPD,
and the Commanding General, Army
Service Forces, objected to reserve status
for women.[66] G–3 was willing to take wartime Wacs into an inactive reserve and let
it die gradually without replacements,
since "it may be politic" to make this gesture. In a recommendation quite similar
to one of twenty years before, these divisions proposed that "planning on this subject be carried out in the regular General
Staff Divisions without special provisions
of female personnel on duty in the War
Department for that purpose."

On the other hand, G–1, G–4, and the
Executive for Reserve and ROTC Affairs
favored full reserve status for women. G–1
offered the recommendation that the
WAC reserve system should parallel the
men's reserve system exactly. The Executive for Reserve and ROTC added:

It is recognized that women . . . will be
used in time of war; therefore it is deemed essential to have a nucleus which is available
in times of emergency. . . . To ignore the
women of the country might create an opposition to the Army.[67]

---

[61] Memo, JAG for MPD ASF, 30 May 45. SPJGA
1945/5434, in WDWAC 326.2.

[62] (1) Memo, Capt Stone for Dir WAC, 9 Jun 45,
and incls. WDWAC 326.2. (2) Memo, SPD for G–1,
29 Jun 45. WDWAC 319.1.

[63] *Ibid.;* Col Hobby's note and other M/R atchd.

[64] Draft of comment, Dir WAC to SPD, 23 Aug 45.
WDWAC 326.2.

[65] *Ibid.* Also, Draft of Memo for G–1, 5 Sep 45.
WDWAC 326.2.

[66] Following statements of opinion are all in M/R
with Memo cited n. 62(1) also atchd to proposed
Memo, SPD for CofS USA, 24 Sep 45. WDWAC
326.2.

[67] Memos cited n. 62(1) and n. 66. Also, Memo G–1
for SPD, 7 Jul 45. WDGAP 316.2 ORC.

The General Staff referred the conflicting opinions to Special Planning Division for preparation of a recommendation to the Chief of Staff.[68] Special Planning Division's final recommendation to the Chief of Staff was adverse. It was proposed that female nurses, dietitians, and physiotherapists be offered reserve status, but as for Wacs, the study concluded: "The awarding of Inactive Reserve commissions to present and former WAC officers is not considered a desirable or effective gesture of recognition." [69]

This recommendation had the somewhat peculiar effect of reversing the sentiments of the WAC staff as to the wisdom of a women's Reserve. Acting Director Woods pointed out that an inactive and unreplenished women's Reserve would cost exactly nothing, and that the deliberate omission of the WAC from this status, if it was to be awarded to every other women's service of the Army and Navy, could only be construed by the public as a condemnation of the WAC's wartime record. She noted that the using agencies—the Air Forces, Ground Forces, service commands, and overseas theaters—had not been allowed to comment, although they, having employed WAC personnel, were the only agencies in a position to assess the usefulness of the WAC. She added:

The Director WAC does not consider it her function to comment upon the Army's need, beyond pointing out that the usefulness of women members in a wartime army is no longer a matter of speculation. The WAC has made a record of service, either good or bad, during the three years of its existence. The War Department should evaluate that record, then plan and act accordingly.[70]

G–1 Division endorsed the WAC comments to the Chief of Staff, saying:

It is believed that such action in respect to the WAC would place the War Department in an untenable position at this time when every effort is being made to utilize the experience gained in the war. . . . The Corps represents an investment which should not be lost to the Army.[71]

This broadside was successful, but the results were more than the Office of the Director had bargained for. Planners were, as requested, directed by the Chief of Staff to get the opinion of the agencies that had employed Wacs, but the response of these agencies was to sweep the WAC into acceptance of a Regular Army Corps, instead of an inactive reserve, which was all that the Director had desired.

Plans for a Regular Army WAC

The recommendations received from the using commands on the inactive reserve proposal led the new G–1, General Paul, to direct Colonel Boyce to prepare an alternate plan for a small permanent force, to be either in the Regular Army or in a new type of active reserve. The Office of the Director complied, although expressing disfavor, saying that the Army would not desire such a group unless it was as efficient as in the past, which appeared impossible.[72]

Reactions to the plan revealed that foremost among the advocates of a Regular Army WAC was the Army Ground

[68] See D/F, Gen Porter, Dir SPD, for G–1, G–2, G–3, G–4, OPD, Ex Res and ROTC, 19 Jul 45. WDWAC 326.2.

[69] Memo, SPD for CofS, 24 Sep 45. WDWAC 326.2.

[70] (1) Memo, Dep Dir WAC for CofS through G–1, 1 Oct 45. WDWAC 326.2. (2) Personal Memo, "HHW" for Col Boyce, 14 Nov 45. WDWAC 319.1.

[71] Memo, G–1 for CofS through SPD WDSS, 15 Oct 45. WDWAC 326.2.

[72] Memo, Dep Dir for Dir WAC 26 Nov 45. WDWAC 326.2.

Forces, which not only replied favorably to the General Staff's inquiry, but imported from the European theater a staff of planners, including the former ETO staff director, Colonel Wilson. General Devers expressed surprise that no previous plan had been made to request legislation and that there was "some resistance to WAC planning at the War Department staff level." No less enthusiastic support came from the Army Air Forces under its new heads, General Spaatz and his deputy, General Eaker, who declared: "If I have anything to do with it, there will be a place for women in the Regular Air Force." [73] The Army Service Forces offered no such approbation; General Dalton stated that "in the event of an emergency, women specialists could be commissioned directly from civilian life to meet the demand." [74]

Considerable outside support for continuation of the WAC also began to appear from the American Association of University Women and other women's groups and from individuals like Mrs. Eleanor Roosevelt, who went so far as to favor universal military training for both men and women, saying, "While the men were receiving scientific training, women would be trained in dietetics, nursing, and the like, so they could serve in peace as well as in war." [75]

In conference with General Eisenhower, Colonel Boyce again urged that he announce only the Reserve plan, and postpone the Regular Army plan for later decision. Since demobilized Wacs were scattering rapidly, she favored a quick request to Congress for power to offer them Reserve status, after which the more controversial issue of a permanent Corps could be fought out at leisure. [76] General Paul

overrode this recommendation, fearing that Congress would consider only one bill. He therefore substituted a plan for a bill to ask simultaneous Reserve and Regular Army status, the adoption of which seemed to him by this time so certain that he informed a Senate committee of the plan. This was followed, on 5 February 1946, by the formal announcement to the Army that the Chief of Staff had directed the drafting of legislation "for the establishment of a Women's Army Corps in the Regular Army with concurrent Reserve Corps status." The same directive also provided for plans for an Army Nurse Corps and a Women's Medical Specialist Corps in the Regular Army and Reserve Corps. [77]

At once the expected delay and controversy descended on the Army, leaving the WAC's future uncertain. Public, Congressional, and military opposition were found to be so strong that General Eisenhower delayed issuing a public announcement to the press. When cornered by reporters on 5 March 1946, he stated that the question was "still under study," and when asked "No plan has reached you

[73] (1) AGF WAC Hist, Vol. I, p. 77; Vol. II, App. XXVII; see Ch. XVI, above. (2) Address by Gen Eaker at 60th OCS Grad Class, 17 Nov 45. WDWAC 352.

[74] Memo, Dir Pers ASF for Dir Plng Div ASF, 17 Dec 45. SPAP 326.2 WAC (12-5-45).

[75] UP release, 17 Oct 44, WDWAC 032.1, 1944; Washington Post, November 15, 1945; quotation from Washington Post, October 24, 1945.

[76] Memo cited n. 72.

[77] (1) Memo, Dir WAC for Gen Paul, 14 Jan 46. WDWAC 370.01. (2) Excerpt from Statement made by Gen W. S. Paul before Sen Subcom on Mil Affairs, 17 Jan 46. WDWAC 326. (3) Ltr, Gen Hodes, Asst DCofS, to WDGS, WDSS, maj comds, 5 Feb 46. WDGAP 326.2 Org Res Corps (7-12-45), in WDWAC 326.2.

yet?" he replied, "None has gone out of the War Department." [78]

None was, in fact, to go out of the War Department for another year, or to be voted on for still another.

The Interim

Meanwhile, the demobilization of the last 20,000 members of the wartime WAC entered its final phase, without benefit of a firm decision on the Corps' future. In order to slow departure, General Paul authorized, over Colonel Boyce's nonconcurrence, a volunteer program in which enlisted women were told that "General Eisenhower is calling upon the Women's Army Corps to remain in operation. . . . The Army is turning to the WAC for help in the manpower emergency." [79]

Response to the volunteer program was not enthusiastic. Although "without exception, headquarters personnel were anxious to retain Wacs," [80] the enlisted women showed a tendency to desire more specific information as to their eligibility for future careers if they remained, which could not be given them. Those able to keep more of their women included the hospitals, the Transportation Corps, and the Fifth and Seventh Army Areas. Very few—from none to fifty women—volunteered to remain with the Army Ground Forces, the Signal Corps, The Adjutant General, the Chemical Warfare Service, or the Ordnance Department.[81]

At the same time, also over Colonel Boyce's nonconcurrence, General Paul authorized a re-entry program to maintain Corps strength. While new recruits could not be accepted for lack of a training center, discharged Wacs were allowed to re-enter through regular recruiting stations.

In spite of all efforts, the Corps dwindled rapidly. Toward the end of 1946, the War Department permitted the departure of all men except those enlisting in the Regular Army, and all women except volunteers. At this time, with the departure of nonvolunteer Wacs, there remained of the wartime Corps only 8,461 enlisted women and 1,194 officers.[82] These women, interested in a permanent career, had already waited eighteen months since the end of the war for a decision. Another eighteen months of uncertainty awaited them. Colonel Boyce called upon WAC officers for "experienced advice and leadership that will carry our women through the waiting period," adding that "they have been good soldiers and have waited for definite word so they can plan their future. They do not understand why word has been so long in coming." [83]

With the decrease in size and the departure of many leaders, the Corps in a few months found most of its wartime advances swept away, and itself in a situation distressingly similar to that of the old Auxiliary in the worst of its early days. Supplies were scarce, and units in the field

[78] HR 4909, 79th Cong, 1st Sess, 5 Dec 45, A Bill To Provide for the Discharge of Members of Women's Reserves of Armed Forces. WDWAC 032.1. Also *Congressional Record*, same date.

[79] Mimeographed statement, sub: Mission. WDWAC 342 (1945–46).

[80] Memo, Dir WAC for G–1, 9 Apr 46. WDWAC 333.1.

[81] (1) D/F, G–1 to CofS, 1 Feb 46. WDGAP 370.01 WAC (1–4–46), in WDWAC 370.01. (2) Memo, Dep Dir for Col Boyce, 23 Jan 46. WDWAC 337. (3) Memo, Dir WAC for Gen Paul, 1 Feb 46, and another 25 Jan 46. WDWAC 342. (4) Memo, Dir WAC for G–1, 15 May 46. WDWAC 320. (5) Memo, Dir WAC for Dir P&A Div WD, 25 Sep 46. WDWAC 370.01.

[82] By tp from Maj Ruth E. Myers, Stat Br, G–1, 9 Nov 46.

[83] Message of retiring Director, Min, Stf Dirs, Conf, 26–28 Mar 47, Pentagon. WAC files, OCMH.

were for months unable to get either clothing maintenance or salvage. Job assignments reverted promptly to unmilitary duties in "service capacities" and as servants in civilian messes, quarters, and nurseries.[84] Applicants for re-entry "practically had to fight their way back into the Army,"[85] having been told at recruiting stations that male recruiters "did not know anything about the WAC," and to "go home and forget it."[86]

Director Hobby's minimum safety requirements vanished rapidly. Women were assigned in less than company units, without WAC officers in command. Because of the small numbers of Wacs, only the Army areas could now be required to have staff directors. Friction resulted as technical services again objected to supervision out of channels. All medical and psychiatric consultants for women left the Medical Department, and protective medical circulars lapsed. All specialists left the Bureau of Public Relations, and news stories again featured "khaki panties."[87] Policy powers were removed from Colonel Boyce's office and given to other General Staff sections, but numerous operating duties were returned to it, upon the abolition of specialist groups elsewhere—an approximation of the old WAAC system.[88]

Enough company commanders with previous experience could not be obtained, and none of the new Army area staff directors had served as such in wartime. Station commanders, many of whom had recently returned from overseas, were often unfamiliar with WAC administration. Some declared Army Regulations inapplicable, others refused to allow visits by WAC staff directors, and one moved a group of amazed WAC veterans to a floodlighted barbed-wire compound.[89]

Breaking with previous policy, General Paul returned small groups of Wacs overseas, where many served in units of no more than a dozen women without a com-

[84] (1) Two Memos, Dir WAC for Welfare Br P&A WD, 4 Oct 46, WDWAC 333.1; (2) D/F Manpower Contl GP&S Div to D/SSP, 17 Sep 46. WDGPA 421 WAC in WDWAC 421. (3) *Washington Post*, May 5, 1949, p. 20. (4) Ltr, Exec WAC to Chairman NCAC, 20 Sep 45, and incl. WDWAC 080. (5) Notes by author, Conf in O Dir WAC, 16 May 47. WAC files, OCMH. (6) Ltr, Dir WAC to all WAC Stf Dirs, 4 Sep 46. WDWAC 421. (7) WD Cir 281, 18 Sep 46, sec VII. (8) In WDWAC 421: (a) Memo, G–1 for Chief MPS Gp, 15 Apr 46, WDGAP 342.06. (b) Memo, G–1 Welfare Br for Gen Paul, 18 Apr 46, ref to Memo, SW for President of U.S., 4 Sep 45. (c) Ltr, Gen Paul to Gen Madison Pearson, 6 Sep 46. (d) Note, Sgt Grush to Dir WAC, undated. (e) Draft, Memo for President, undated.

[85] Memo, Dir WAC for Gen Paul, 7 Jun 46. WDWAC 342.

[86] Memo, Maj S. H. Herbert for Gen Paul, 27 Sep 46. WDWAC 342.

[87] *Washington Post*, February 3, 1949, p. 6. All in 1945–46 WAC files: (1) SGO Cir 1, 1 Jan 44; telephone call from Director WAC to author inquired whether provision re pelvic examinations had ever existed; telephone call from author to SGO ascertained that such SGO circulars were out of date. (2) Memo, Actg Dir BPR for Dir WAC, 17 Dec 45. WDWAC 320. (3) Memo, Dir WAC for WDBPR, 26 Dec 45. Abolition was by WDBPR Office Memo 1, 11 Jan 46. (4) Memo, Dir WAC for Lt Col D. J. Rogers, 3 Jun 46. WDWAC 320. (5) Memo, Maj Horak for Col Boyce, 4 Sep 46, same file. (6) Memo, Maj Herbert for Col Boyce, 1 Oct 46. WDWAC 333.1. (7) Memo, Dir WAC for Gen Paul, 27 Aug 46. WDWAC 210.31. (8) Memo, Maj Herbert for Col Boyce, 21 Jun 46, and Memo, Chief COAG for Col Boyce, 4 Sep 46, with note by Dir. WDWAC 210.31. (9) Memo, Col Boyce for Gen Paul, 30 Aug 46.

[88] (1) Memo, Dir WAC for Manpower Gp P&A, 12 Apr 46. WDWAC 210.3. (2) Memo, Dir WAC for Gen Henry, 14 Aug 46; reply, Brig Gen Morris R. Nelson, 15 Aug 45. WDWAC 210.31. (3) Memo, P&A Div WD for its Gps and Dir WAC, 27 Sep 46. WDGPA 320 WAC. (4) Memo, G–1 for DCofS, 2 Oct 46. WDGPA 320 WAC, in WDWAC 320. (5) Memo, Asst DCofS for P&A, O&T, SS&P, PRD, and I&E Divs, 14 Oct 46. WDGSA 320 (9–26–46) in WDWAC 320. (6) Memo, Dir WAC for G–1, 3 Apr 46, and reply, 9 Apr 46. WDWAC 300.3.

[89] All in 1945–46 WAC files: (1) G–1 Memo to AAF, AGF, ASF, and all Admin and Tech Servs, 16 May 46. WDGAP 320 WAC, in WDWAC 320. Also

pany officer.[90] In another reversal of Director Hobby's policies, he offered promise of overseas service to re-entries, a move which produced a morale crisis and charges of a "dirty deal" from Wacs still in the United States.[91] Because of faulty screening by male recruiters at recruiting stations, these re-entries when shipped overseas brought protests of "inferior quality" from theaters. Shipments included epileptics, manic-depressives, women just court-martialed, "homosexuals, alcoholics, and promiscuous women."[92] To improve the shipments, Colonel Boyce asked General Paul to send one WAC enlisted woman to each Army area—a total of six women, as against the 4,000 specialists who had once managed WAC recruiting—but this request was disapproved by General Paul as "wasteful of personnel."[93] Eventually the re-entry program was discontinued after getting only 1,690 women, more than half of whom required quick discharge as undesirables.[94]

All such problems, although inevitable in the attempt to hold a small Corps during the chaotic days of Army demobilization, caused considerable uneasiness to the Director. She feared particularly that the wartime WAC's good record would be damaged and Congress alienated.[95]

Regular Army legislation, toward which WAC leaders looked to end the chaos of the interim period, progressed haltingly. Colonel Boyce's advice was not always accepted on provisions, nor was she kept in close touch with planning.[96] She had recommended that Colonel McCoskrie be assigned to G–1 Division to draft legislation, but the work was instead given to an officer with no previous knowledge of the Corps.[97] Her suggestion for simple legislation with complete integration, such as that drafted for the WAVES,

[90] (1) Stat Info on Strength, Distribution, Rotation, and Redeployment of WAC Pers in ET, 31 Oct 46. WDWAC 320. (2) Ltr, TAG to TIG, AAF, PMG, and SGO, 20 Aug 47. AGAM–PM 334 WDGPA. (3) DA Memo 20–30–2, 27 Oct 47, Investigations of WAC Pers. WAC files OCMH. (4) Ltr, Maj Herbert to Col Boyce, 17 Sep 46. WDWAC 320. (5) Series of TWXs; 26 Feb–20 Jun 46. WDWAC 210.31 and 320.

[91] Intervs with ASF WAC Off, 19 Apr 46, and former Stf Dir 3d SvC, 12 Apr 46.

[92] (1) Ltr, WAC Stf Dir Hq USAF China to Dir WAC, 28 May 46. WDWAC 320. (2) Ltr, WAC Stf Dir Hq First Army to Maj Herbert, 18 Jul 46. WDWAC 210.31. (3) Boyce request cited in personal ltr, Maj Herbert to WAC Stf Dir Sixth Army Area, 17 Sep 46, with incl ltr, 16 Sep 46, SGO to Letterman GH. WDWAC 320. (4) Ltr, WAC Stf Dir 2d SvC to Dir WAC, 10 Jun 46. WDWAC 342. (5) Personal ltr, Maj Herbert to WAC Stf Dir USFET, 19 Jul 46. WDWAC 210.31. (6) Memo, Maj Herbert for Col Boyce, 23 Sep 46. WDWAC 720. (7) Personal ltr, Maj Herbert to WAC Stf Dir Sixth Army Area, 19 Sep 46. WDWAC 320. (8) Ltr, Dir WAC to Hq Fifth Army Area, 16 Oct 46. WDWAC 320. (9) Memo, Maj Herbert for Col Boyce, 1 Oct 46, WDWAC 333.1. (10) Ltr, Lt Irene Scott, WDBPR, to Editor WAC Newsletter, 14 Jun 46. WDWAC 000.76. (11) Memo, Dir WAC for Chief OT Div WD, 1 Aug 46. WDWAC 352.

[93] (1) Memo cited n. 86. (2) Memo, Maj Herbert for Dir WAC, 2 Oct 46, with reply.

[94] (1) Memo, Dir WAC for G–1, 17 Jan 46. WDWAC 320.2. (2) TWX to all SvCs, 9 Feb 46, CM–OUT 96566, DTG–0920082, in WDWAC 342. (3) WD Memo 600–750–13, 3 Apr 47. (4) Memo, G–1 for TAG, 25 Feb 46. WDGAP 220.3 WAC (2–15–46), in WDWAC 342. (5) Memo, Maj Herbert for Lt Irene Scott, 19 Sep 46. WDWAC 320. (6) Ltr, Dir WAC to all Wac Stf Dirs, 11 Sep 46, re sec III, WD Cir 241, 10 Aug 46. WDWAC 421.

[95] Ltr cited n. 92(3).

[96] Memos cited n. 88.

[97] Memo, Dir WAC for Gen Paul, 19 Jan 46, sub: Col Frank U. McCoskrie. 1945–46 WAC file, unnumbered. Colonel McCoskrie asked the author to send him "the WAC files," to which he intended to devote a week's reading in order to familiarize himself with its past history.

D/F, G–1 to TAG, 8 Jun 46, and Comment 2 to D/F, P&A Div, to OCSigO, 16 Oct 46. WDGAP 320 WAC (6–13–46). (2) Rpt on TD to 1st and 2d SvCs by Dep Dir WAC, 26 Oct–1 Nov, 2 Nov 45, WDWAC 333.1. (3) Ltr, WAC Stf Dir Seventh Army to Dir WAC, 22 Jun 46. WDWAC 320. (4) Memo, Dir WAC for P&A, 7 Aug 46, WDWAC 201, and Ltr, TAG to Dir WAC, 14 Aug 46, AGPR–D–A–210.31.

WAF, and women Marines, was rejected. Instead, the draft legislation provided for a separate corps with separate grades, as in Auxiliary days. A separate promotion list was provided, on the ground that WAC officers "could not be transferred into the other Arms and Services." [98] Women officers were limited to one temporary colonel and no more than 10 percent lieutenant colonels, as against 14 percent lieutenant colonels and 8 percent colonels for men. [99] Because of these low ranks, weeks more of delay resulted as special retirement rules and predicted attrition schedules were worked out. [100]

In another reversal of wartime policy, direct commissions were authorized for civilian women, since no ROTC training was authorized for women. In still another reversal, the age limit for enlistment was dropped to 18 years, a move that Director Hobby had several times rejected as dangerous. [101]

In the spring of 1947, Deputy Director Hallaren stated, "We felt that if we do not get it [legislation] in this session, we might as well quit; women interested in planning a career will give up and go home." [102] By March, the legislation was at last believed satisfactory to the War Department and ready for introduction into Congress. At this time Colonel Boyce, who had been hospitalized since late January, elected to leave the Army and the Acting Director and former Deputy, Colonel Hallaren, assumed office on 5 May 1947 as the third Director WAC. [103]

Congressional Action

On 15 April 1947, the WAC Integration Act of 1947 was introduced in Congress, and eventually was approved unanimously on the Senate floor. Everything appeared favorable to a speedy passage. Endorsements had been received from almost all important women's groups, and a Gallup poll disclosed that a majority of the American public—a majority of men as well as of women— also favored peacetime status. [104] General Eisenhower in 1946 took the step that General Marshall had taken two years before, and wrote personally to field commanders to request their support. [105] These measures proved inadequate to prevent another year's delay. [106] During this time there ensued an attack from the same source that in wartime had crippled WAC recruiting: Army men and veterans, articles in soldier magazines, and letters to the editor. [107]

Representative Margaret Chase Smith said that she had been told that the opposition stemmed from "off-the-record statements" made to Armed Services Committee members by "duly authorized

---

[98] Notes by author at Mtg, O Dir WAC, 10 Dec 46, Col Hallaren presiding for Dir WAC, Gen Dahlquist for Army.

[99] Min, Stf Mtg, O Dir WAC, 10 Jan 46, Col Boyce presiding. WAC file OCMH.

[100] (1) Memo, Maj Herbert for Col Boyce, 16 Sep 46. WDWAC 320.2. (2) Notes by author, Conf at O Dir WAC, Col Hallaren presiding, 27 Nov 46.

[101] *Ibid.* For final form, see PL 625 (1948).

[102] Notes by author, Stf Mtg, O Dir WAC, 28 Feb 47.

[103] Min cited n. 83. Also Ltr, CofS to Col Boyce, 14 Mar 47. OCMH.

[104] (1) Letters and Resolutions dated from January through June 1947, and read into *Congressional Record* by Representative Edith N. Rogers on 21 April 1948, pp. 4813–14. Also notes by author, Stf Mtg, 31 Jan 47, Col Hallaren presiding. (2) Gallup Poll, 21 Aug 47, in *Washington Post* for August 22, 1947.

[105] Personal ltr, CofS to CGs Army Areas, 23 Jul 46; replies, 29 and 31 Jul and 1 Aug 46. WDGPA 342.06 WAC (7–17–46), G–1 files.

[106] Personnel Newsletter 9, 1 Sep 47. WAC files, OCMH.

[107] *Washington Post*, July 15, 1947, March 11, 1948, and many others; *Salute*, August 1947, "Thirty-year Girls."

officer representatives of the Navy Department." [108] Representative Dewey Short of Missouri stated, without revealing his informants, that, "as far as the high officers are concerned, and from major down to second lieutenant, and an overwhelming majority of the enlisted men, they are against the Corps." [109] Representative Leroy Johnson of California explained:

The sad part about this is that we have only heard from a few top bracket men in the Army, and in asking questions I found that there were many, many officers in the Army who are not sure that it is the right thing to do to make these women a part of the Regular Establishment. They have never had a chance to be heard. [110]

Although Representative Frances P. Bolton said, "It seems to me that we should know why the Armed Services differ so definitely from the heads of services," no committee member made this clear. A member noted, "There are several aspects to this bill that I do not care to discuss here publicly." One representative exclaimed, "If we could only discuss publicly on the floor of the House those things that we discussed behind closed doors!" [111] The anonymous opposition became so general that early in 1948 Secretary of the Army Kenneth C. Royall reopened the question before the War Council as to whether the armed services should continue to sponsor the legislation. After a study of the "contribution and performance" of the wartime women's services, the position of the heads of the services remained unchanged. [112]

On 23 March 1948 the House Armed Services Committee voted, 26–1, to pass only the Reserve part of the legislation. The one dissenting vote belonged to Congresswoman Margaret Chase Smith of Maine, the only woman member of the committee. [113]

Representative Smith offered an amendment to put the Regular Army provisions back in the bill. When this was defeated, she immediately offered another to limit the Reserves to 10 officers and 25 enlisted women on active duty for not more than two years at a time, stating that she intended to make sure that armed forces did not employ large numbers of women "just as you would Regulars without giving them Regular status." This amendment was also defeated, and the bill was passed by the House authorizing only a Reserve.

The matter now took on an especial urgency, with only two months remaining before the date in June of 1948 upon which the wartime Corps, as part of the Army of the United States, must be disbanded because of the expiration of legislative authority for its continuance. Whatever the opinion of the anonymous Army man, the heads of the several services in all of that spring's hearings rallied to the support of the bill in a display of strength unprecedented in Corps history. Those who personally appeared before the armed services committees included Secretary of Defense James V. Forrestal, Generals Eisenhower, Bradley, Paul, and Brig. Gen. George Ellis Armstrong; Gen. Hoyt S.

[108] *Congressional Record*, 6 Apr 48, p. A2241.
[109] *Congressional Record*, 21 Apr 48, p. 4831.
[110] *Congressional Record*, 8 Apr 48, p. 4369.
[111] Both in *Congressional Record*, 21 Apr 48.
[112] Tentative Agenda, Mtg of War Council, 10:00 A.M., 20 Jan 48. Composition: Secys Royall, W. Stuart Symington, and James V. Forrestal; Gens Eisenhower, Spaatz; Admiral Louis E. Denfeld. Copy in WAC files, OCMH.
[113] By tp call, O Dir WAC to author, 23 Mar 48, and *Washington Post*, 24 Mar 48. Also *Congressional Record*, 6 Apr 46, pp. 4233–34. Full debate is in *Congressional Record*, 21 Apr 48, pp. 4806–34. See also *Washington Post*, April 27, 1942, for reporters' impressions.

Vandenberg and Brig. Gen. Dean C. Strother; Admiral Louis E. Denfeld, Vice Adm. Arthur W. Radford, Rear Adms. Herbert L. Pugh, Walter A. Buck, and Earl E. Stone. General Eisenhower stated:

When this project was proposed in the beginning of the war, like most old soldiers, I was violently against it. I thought a tremendous number of difficulties would occur. . . . Every phase of the record they compiled during the war convinced me of the error of my first reaction.

In tasks for which they are particularly suited, Wacs are more valuable than men, and fewer of them are required to perform a given amount of work. . . . In the disciplinary field they were, throughout the war, a model for the Army. . . . More than this, their influence throughout the whole command was good. Carefully supervised, presenting a picture of model deportment and neatness, their presence was always reflected around a headquarters in improved conduct on the part of all.

In the event of another war, which would be even more truly global than the last in its effects upon the entire population, it is my conviction that everybody in this country would serve under some form of call to duty. . . . I assure you that I look upon this measure as a "must". . . . You are at perfect liberty to quote me privately and publicly in this matter.[114]

General Eisenhower strongly opposed the substitution of Reserve for Regular status, adding:

The history of the Army shows that . . . there was tremendous resentment on the part of line officers originally when surgeons were given rank and called colonels, etc. . . . We have long since outgrown that and I believe that type of argument no longer has any validity.

Appearances were also made by the current heads of the various women's services, and statements were submitted by former Director Boyce and by various

women's groups including the WAC's National Civilian Advisory Committee. The wartime WAC leaders—Colonels Hobby, Bandel, Rice, Woods, Goodwin, Davis, and Strayhorn—were not asked to testify or to submit statements; the same was true of the wartime heads of the WAVES, SPARS, and women Marines. When privately approached by members of Congress to inquire whether such an invitation should not be issued by Congress, since it had not been issued by the armed forces, the wartime WAC leaders discouraged such action. While personally uninterested in peacetime service, most did not feel justified in barring it for any women who wished to remain. More important, they feared that their opposition to peacetime service might mistakenly be construed as a condemnation of the WAC's wartime record, or of future service by women in national emergencies.[115]

In the following weeks, the Senate stood firm in its earlier approval of Regular Army status. Before the voting, the House put up a final fight on what appeared to be the basic point of opposition—the fear that women would command men. One member, a Navy veteran, stated:

There is not a member of the House Committee on Armed Services who has not received a telephone call or a call in person from enlisted men objecting to the idea of having to take orders from a WAVES officer.

Another stated:

I heartily concur in all of the laudatory remarks. . . . But . . . what we are asked to approve today is an organizational change in the structure of the Armed Services which is as extreme and far reaching as any ever con-

---

[114] House Com on Armed Servs, *Subcommittee Hearings* on S. 1641, 18 Feb 48, incl Ltr, CofS to Chmn HR Com on Armed Servs, 30 Jan 48.
[115] Intervs, 1949–50.

templated by any nation. If we approve this conference report, women will become an integral part of the Armed Forces of the United States in peacetime for the first time in our history.

After a final struggle in which it was necessary for the sergeant-at-arms to close the doors and secure absent members, a vote was taken on 2 June 1948 which— 206 to 133, 91 not voting—placed women in both the Regular services and the Reserves.[116] On 12 June 1948, upon the President's signature, the measure became law.[117] The wartime Women's Army Corps, expiring in the same month, bequeathed some 2,000 of its former members to the Regular Army WAC.[118]

---

[116] *Congressional Record*, 2 Jun 48, pp. 7052–57.

[117] PL 625, 80th Cong, 12 Jun 45.

[118] By tp from Maj Ruth Myers, Stat Br G–1, 10 Nov 50. Some 5,500 Wacs remained in June; some 2,000 former Wacs (AUS) enlisted in the WAC (RA), chiefly from these women but partly from those returning from civilian life. Legislation provided for retention of women until integration could be effected.

CHAPTER XXXVII

Evaluation and Recommendations

Neither the cost nor the worth of the wartime Women's Army Corps, Army of the United States, was ever officially assessed. Few of the Army's operating agencies, fiscal, procurement, or otherwise, kept a separate Corps accounting or a separate total of expenditures. From the viewpoint of achievement of full integration, there was no reason why expensive separate accounts should have been maintained; even if they had been, there would have been no objective manner of weighing them against that intangible—performance.

Cost to the Army

For the information of Congress, the General Staff, in its postwar planning, compiled a chart of the estimated relative cost of male and female soldiers under "normal" conditions.[1] This summary made clear that there was no reason why a woman soldier should cost as much as a man. Aside from the considerable saving of food, the major economy in the use of female personnel consisted in the lesser number of dependents or persons legally entitled to be considered dependents, with resulting savings not only in wartime allotments of salary but also in dependents' quarters, travel, and other costs. Since combat training could be omitted, the re-

quired training time was also shorter and less expensive, particularly when, in wartime, numbers of older women already possessing needed civilian skills chose to enter. Under normal conditions, and if the estimates to Congress held true, it appeared that the wartime Army of the future could save itself at least $7,700,000 per year for each 100,000 women substituted for an equal number of male non-combatants.

In addition, if the estimates of commanders such as Generals Eisenhower, Eaker, and Devers were correct, the savings could be doubled by the use of only 50,000 women to substitute for 100,000 men in jobs in which women appeared to excel. In testimony before Congress every authority almost without exception stated that in such work one woman had in wartime offices replaced at least two men and possibly more. Such double savings, however, would apply only to part of the possible replacements. If it was necessary to extend the use of women to motor transport and mechanical jobs, no better than one-for-one replacement could be expected, while further extension to work in

---

[1] See accompanying chart. O Dir WAC, printed in House Com on Armed Services, *Subcommittee Hearings on S. 1641*, HR Rpt 238, 18 Feb 48.

AVERAGE COST ESTIMATES ON ENLISTED PERSONNEL

Per person per year

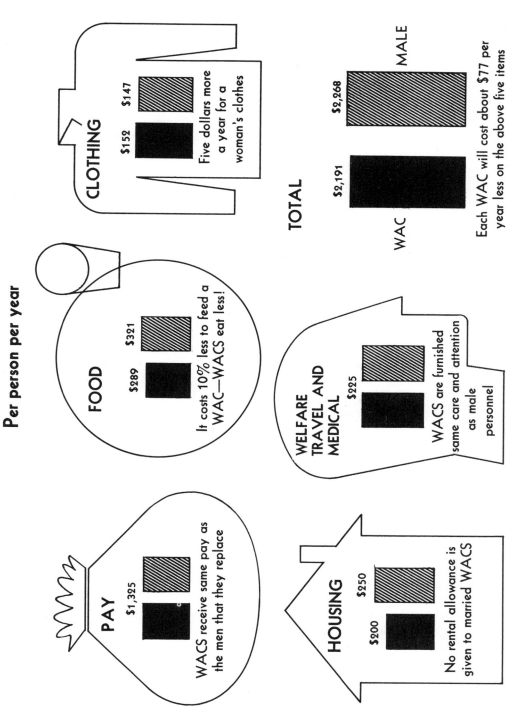

CLOTHING

$152 $147

Five dollars more a year for a woman's clothes

FOOD

$289 $321

It costs 10% less to feed a WAC—WACS eat less!

PAY

$1,325

WACS receive same pay as the men that they replace

WELFARE TRAVEL AND MEDICAL

$225

WACS are furnished same care and attention as male personnel

HOUSING

$200 $250

No rental allowance is given to married WACS

TOTAL

WAC $2,191   MALE $2,268

Each WAC will cost about $77 per year less on the above five items large messes and as hospital orderly would require two women for one man, thus canceling the earlier savings.

Such estimates gave no clue to the actual cost of the wartime WAC, which had never operated under "normal" conditions. The Corps as a whole had been the victim of the expensive experiments inherent in any new organization. It had accumulated stocks of unusable misfit clothing; it had spent money on early ill-planned recruiting schemes, with ill-chosen slogans and personnel, and aimed at unrealistic goals; it had opened and promptly closed large training centers for recruits who never appeared. It had also required incalculable man-hours of the time of experienced Army staff officers, from the Chief of Staff downward to every headquarters and station commander, which could not be reckoned in dollars and cents. Whether or not the expense of such an experimental stage was recompensed by even the most superlative efficiency in its members was a question difficult to answer. However, if later wars required total mobilization, and if the organizational lessons of World War II were not forgotten, the experiment had obviously been a useful and necessary one.

Recommendations for the Future

Although no WAC or Army authorities left detailed studies as to the means by which successive mobilizations could avoid the major causes of expense or difficulty in World War II, their general recommendations could to some extent be pieced together from speeches, separate staff studies, historical accounts, and lists of incomplete projects.

General Paul, the postwar head of G–1 Division, was the only man on the General Staff level to leave a formal recommendation. He stated that five problems "must be solved in order to effect a sound and complete utilization of women." Two of these had, he believed, been solved by Regular Army legislation: the "lack of prior planning" before an emergency occurred, and the "lack of an organized nucleus within the military establishment on which to build." Two others concerned what was generally now recognized by administrators of women: that women's jobs were more important to them than any other factor in their environment. General Paul therefore stated that the Army must not again be guilty either of "failure to evaluate civilian training and experience" or of "reluctance to utilize women in Army jobs formerly held by men." Finally, he noted the effect of unfavorable Army attitude on all echelons, resulting from "failure to orient key male personnel as to proper utilization of women in the Army." In spite of these past problems, General Paul was confident that they need not be repeated. In any case, he concluded:

Experience of World War II proved that women play a vital role in the military effectiveness of any nation. And American women, through their services in the Women's Army Corps, showed that, contrary to dogmatic opinion, the previously untapped potentiality of womanpower could be directed into the channel of personnel power with positive results. The record shows that their contribution erased any doubt as to the ability, adaptability, and stability of American women in time of national crisis.

As to continuation of this wartime performance in the peacetime Army or any future wartime Corps, only one immediate question occured to General Paul, which he called, "the question that pops up in anyone's mind—Would you be able to get the type of womanhood you want?" [2]

The final recommendations of Directors Hobby and Boyce were not so specific, being merely lists of unfinished business or other staff studies. It was noteworthy, however, that on several points there was general agreement between the views of both Directors, several major commands, and frequently General Paul or medical authorities. Points on which there was some agreement among several experts included the fields of Army opinion, women's jobs and housing, the caste system, the recruiting organization, and the proper employment of WAC advisers at all levels.

Army Attitude

On the question of Army attitude, both Colonel Hobby and Colonel Boyce agreed with General Paul in ascribing it a place of primary importance in the course of any future Corps. Colonel Boyce noted that "though improvement has come . . . this attitude is still not wholly corrected." She therefore recommended, for the future:

In any future organization for women, the War Department, through the Chief of Staff, should *at the outset* set forth to the Army the desire that the women shall be considered as full members of the Army and be accorded every courtesy and protection by all male members, commissioned and enlisted; and that all commanders be held responsible to prevent scurrilous comment and a negative attitude on the part of male military personnel toward the women within their commands.[3]

Women's Jobs

The Corps' entire history demonstrated that one factor above all others influenced women's morale, happiness, or discipline. This was, simply, correct job assignment and full-time work. Director Hobby had stated unequivocally at the end of the WAAC's first year: "That is the biggest single morale factor. If they feel that they have actually replaced a man, they feel that they are doing their job." [4]

An Army Service Forces survey in the last days of the war noted that job satisfaction would be essential "for the future utilization of women in emergencies," and that:

Satisfaction with her job is probably the single most important factor in an enlisted woman's evaluation of her role as a member of the Women's Army Corps, and, consequently, her general morale and adjustment in Army life.

Unlike men in the Army, who can display endurance and courage through hardships and combat, the women have only the work they do on their jobs to offer as evidence of their contribution to the war effort.[5]

From the viewpoint of mental health, General Menninger agreed that in the future more instead of less choice of jobs should be allowed a recruit: "We should attempt to mold and modify the program to . . . allow for specificity in assignment and an opportunity for expression of feminine . . . ability." [6]

Social Association

Subordinate in importance only to job assignment, both Colonels Hobby and Boyce listed the Army caste system as ap-

[2] All from Speech of Gen Paul at Comd and Gen Stf Sch, 3 Apr 46, p. II–8. WDWAC 350.001.
[3] Summary of Recommendations, Col Boyce, Dir WAC, 27 Nov 45. WDWAC 314.7.
[4] Speech, Dir Hobby. Stf Dirs Conf, Chicago, 15–17 Jun 43. SPWA 337 (6–1–43).
[5] Hq ASF, I&E Div Rpt C130, 7 Aug 45. OCMH.
[6] Menninger, *Psychiatry in a Troubled World*, p. 115.

plied to off-duty association of personnel of opposite sex, which Colonel Boyce called "the second strongest adverse factor in WAC morale." The Office of the Director, as well as Colonel Bandel in the Air Forces, continued to recommend that the only restriction be "the simple rule followed in most business offices"—that supervisors not date employees. Colonel Boyce also suggested that "an All-Ranks Club be established as an Army-wide custom, thus solving the problem for male Army personnel, Army Nurse Corps, and WAC officers and enlisted." The Medical Department's General Menninger endorsed this as a very practical recommendation and advised that the War Department publish a policy asserting that the laws of natural selection should govern off-duty associations between male and female personnel.

Even in the few cases, such as that in the European theater, where WAC advisers favored application of the caste system to social engagements, all without exception agreed that some Army-wide policy should be published, comparable to the Navy's publication. Colonel Boyce noted that "the absence of any announced policy by the War Department led to inevitable and unfortunate inequality in handling this problem . . . whatever is decided as the policy, it should be announced at the War Department level." [7]

While it appeared that the problem would be less evident among peacetime personnel, who enlisted in full knowledge of the system, wartime WAC leaders were unanimous that it would be unwise ever again to attempt to form a large women's corps, particularly if women were drafted, without such an announced policy. Army men were ordinarily surprised to find this problem given such a high place in the list,

yet all recorded comments of enlisted women were to the effect that "the whole experience was degrading and humiliating . . . I would not re-enlist for any amount of money unless the caste system is abolished in its entirety." [8] Regardless of conflicting explanations of why this attitude should be held so strongly by American women, the fact was that it did exist, to a degree that could not safely be discounted.

Housing

In the matter of housing, all WAC authorities agreed with Colonel Hobby's final report, which noted the need for a distinction between housing for transient troops and that for permanent employees. Colonel Boyce's final statement on the matter added that, if the War Department wished to attract a Corps of women of high ability, it would be obliged to provide "suitable living standards . . . a greater degree of privacy than the open barracks of the past war, and . . . heating systems which would not necessitate the stoking of coal stoves by women." Colonel Craighill's medical reports invariably attributed tension and exhaustion among Wacs and nurses in large part to the lack of privacy. Colonel Bandel's final observation, concerning Air Force experience, was:

From the standpoint of hindsight . . . it would seem that one of the major aspects of the WAC program which might have been improved, in the initial planning stages, was the housing program. . . . Field experience indicated that drab or flimsy wartime hous-

[7] (1) Summary cited n. 3. (2) AAF WAC Hist, p. 96.
[8] Ltr, Mrs. J. S. to Dir WAC, 19 Mar 46. WDWAC 095. This is typical of thousands of similar letters discovered in WAC files of every command.

ing had a greater effect on WAC efficiency and morale than anyone had anticipated.

Except for Colonel Craighill, none of these advisers applied such remarks to women overseas or otherwise transient in residence. It appeared that the problem would be less conspicuous in peacetime when all troops occupied more or less permanent housing, but in another mobilization a careful distinction was obviously required between those Wacs who could be considered transients and those who, in several years at one station, would benefit by housing comparable to peacetime Army quarters or civilian women's dormitories.[9]

The Uniform

Plans made by The Quartermaster General indicated that revision of the uniform would incorporate wartime lessons. The various uniforms worn by Wacs and nurses were scheduled for standardization to permit a common and simplified procurement. Work items needed by Wacs were added or retained: summer and winter slacks, a summer work dress, and adequate cold-weather clothing. The off-duty dress was temporarily dropped from peacetime issue, as civilian clothing could be worn off duty.

The only reversal of a wartime advance came in the matter of uniform color. From preplanning days, the Director's Office had successfully vetoed The Quartermaster General's ideas for a non-Army color for women's uniforms; the frequent wartime suggestions that the WAC uniform be changed to another shade had been rebuffed "in view of the fact that the WAC is a part of the Army." In 1946, the Office of The Quartermaster General returned to the attempt with a design for an apple-green uniform with a pale green shirt, intended to be more becoming and attractive to women. Although the WAC staff protested that "women's uniforms in general should be of the same material, color and design as that prescribed for men," The Quartermaster General proceeded with field tests, and finally abandoned the project only after receiving discouraging comments from enlisted women. A short time later, the Quartermaster Corps made a more successful attempt; another version was produced in another non-Army color, a grayish taupe model by a famous designer, cut with Peter Pan collar and general nonmilitary lines. Other services—the WAF, WAVES, and Women Marines—continued to employ regulation tailored designs.[10]

Recruiting

All WAC authorities affirmed the need for special recruiting methods and standards for women. Colonel Boyce wrote:

The costly and unsuccessful experiments in WAC recruiting indicate that regular R&I methods are completely unsuccessful with women. Recruiting policies for women require a special technique and approach and their establishment should be considered as

---

[9] (1) Memo, Dir WAC, for CofS through G-1, 11 Jul 45. WDWAC 319.1. Forwarded by Summary Sheet, Gen Henry, G-1, for CofS, sub: Final Rpt on WAC by Col Oveta Culp Hobby, Retiring Dir, 10 Sep 45. WDGAP 319.1 WAC (7-11-45). (2) Craighill SWPA Rpt. (3) AAF WAC Hist, p. 93. (4) Memo, Col Boyce, Dir WAC, for Welfare Br G-1, 12 Apr 46. WDWAC 334. (5) Rpt by Dir WAC, 27 Nov 45. WDWAC 314.7.
[10] Section on uniform from: (1) Ltr, OQMG to Mr. L. Margrave, 9 Jun 44. SPQRD 095, in WDWAC 095. (2) Comment 2, P&A Div WD to D/SSP, 30 Sep 46. WDWAC 421. (3) Bull, *Women's Uniforms, ANC-WAC,* 10 Apr 46, by R&D Br, OQMG. WDWAC 421. (4) M/R, 16 May 46, Mtg in O Dir WAC. WDWAC 421. (5) M/R, 12 Sep 46. WDWAC 400.34.

one of the primary functions on which the heads of the Women's Services should advise.[11]

These views were not concurred in by the postwar Adjutant General's Office. The early days of 1943, once viewed with alarm as the time of an influx of unassignables, were now cited as evidence of the superiority of a merger of WAC and Army recruiting, since the numerical intake had in those days been at its peak. As a result, the regular recruiting organization was employed for WAC recruiting. The WAC advertising account, as part of the Army account, was returned to the firm that had originated the slogan of "Release a Man for Combat." The recruiting program nevertheless profited from wartime lessons by setting high standards, and by warning that "Commitments made to the enlistee must be conscientiously carried out; no false promises."[12]

Both Directors were of the opinion that civilian women advisers such as the National Civilian Advisory Committee had been of great value to recruiting. Colonel Boyce noted: "The interest of the members of this Committee greatly enhanced the prestige of the Corps nationally and locally."[13]

Standards

Most wartime officers with experience in administering Wacs agreed that high enlistment standards—mental, physical, educational, and moral—were utterly essential to successful replacement of men in the type of noncombat work open to women and within their strength. General White noted later, "The biggest mistake we ever made was in briefly dropping our standards for numbers. Daytona Beach was the most convincing lesson

about that. From then on I bitterly opposed lowering standards."[14]

In spite of the fact that WAC enlistment standards had been higher than those of the Army, most authorities believed that they should have been even stricter. Colonel Boyce later commented that many Corps problems "would not have existed or would have been minimized" by constant and strenuous screening at the recruiting level, the basic training level, the officer candidate level, and before overseas shipment.[15]

Provision for Troop Officers and Cadre

Almost all final recommendations by WAC staff advisers cited the need for better provisions to make troop work more attractive to women leaders, and for better training for those engaged in it. Colonel Hobby, upon her departure from the Corps, called for advanced training schools not only for troop officers but for enlisted cadre, with emphasis on the medical, social, recreational, psychological, and disciplinary problems of women.

The Air Forces and the European theater also suggested an allotment of cadre grades to each station if the presence of a WAC unit did not decrease the number of men's units. The European theater added:

The major problem arising from assignment of WAC personnel to existing tables of organization has been in securing commensurate grades and ratings for cadre. In many

---

[11] Col Boyce, Summary of Recommendations, 27 Nov 45. WDWAC 314.7.

[12] (1) "Outline of TAG Organization," speech by Col Wright to Stf Dirs Conf, Jun 46. Notes by author, OCMH. (2) Summary, WAC (RA) Rctg. OCMH.

[13] Ltr, Mrs. Westray Battle Boyce Leslie to OCMH, 2 May 51.

[14] Interv, 5 Jan 51.

[15] Ltr cited n. 13.

instances it has been difficult to promote or even secure cadre personnel.[16]

The recommending agencies were of the opinion that the best female officers and enlisted women would not be attracted to troop duty as long as cadre grades were not provided for the WAC unit on the same terms as formally activated Army units. Colonel Bandel also recommended that the WAC officer candidate school be reserved for troop officers and that other women specialists be appointed in other arms or services.[17]

All wartime WAC and Air WAC advisers without exception agreed that it was essential to retain the system of permitting assignment of enlisted women only to units of company size commanded by women officers. Where this precaution had been neglected, WAC health, morale, discipline, and supply had invariably suffered, and necessary provisions of all sorts had been omitted. At least one full-time company commander, and at least one or two part-time junior assistants were stated to be the irreducible minimum for enlisted women's well-being.

Need for Staff Advisers

Although all WAC recommendations stressed the essentiality of female company officers, more question existed as to whether, in the future, female advisers like the wartime staff directors would be needed in the headquarters of major commands employing Wacs. Colonel Bandel noted that the question of what advisers would be required several decades in the future "can not be answered at this time," but that specialists would probably be needed "so long as a condition exists, as it did in World War II, in which women

represent only about three percent of the strength of any command."[18] Colonel Goodwin stated:

I believe that it will be absolutely necessary to have women staff advisers in future emergencies. I found that in all commands where the Staff Director was ignored, enlisted women were assigned to poor jobs and less than full utilization resulted.[19]

The pattern of WAC history in World War II showed that, in those commands that did not employ a staff director, problems arose—not merely occasionally, but invariably—to a greater degree than in commands that made use of such an adviser. Inferior results were also noted in commands that did not ordinarily give the staff adviser's recommendations the weight normally given to an Army special staff member.[20] Colonel Boyce gave her opinion that the time had not yet arrived when commands might safely dispense with a female adviser, even though her duties would gradually decrease, and that "in the utilization of women certain safeguards are essential for the protection of their health and well-being."[21]

The parallel example of industry offered strong support for the theory that the use of women staff advisers was not an interference with command but an assistance to it, and merely common sense in personnel management.

War Manpower Commission officials stated, during the war, "Employers can save themselves all sorts of trouble if they

---

[16] See Ch. XVI, above; also ETO Bd Rpt, Vol. II, App. 1, p. 10.
[17] AAF WAC Hist, pp. 85, 94.
[18] Ibid., p. 96.
[19] Interv and comments on draft of chapter, 2–4 May 51.
[20] See Chs. XVIII and XXII, above.
[21] Remarks of Dir WAC at Conf of Overseas Theater G–1s, 15 Oct 46. WDWAC 337 A–S.

will hire the best woman supervisors they can find, and give them enough authority in the plant to make their orders stick." Industry discovered that it lost women workers when it did not have women supervisors. Women supervisors proved able to prevent resignations and absenteeism by giving understanding attention to problems of home conditions, shopping hours, recreation, morale, and illness, and by securing clean washrooms, cafeterias, and labor-saving devices that maintained women's efficiency. Officials concluded that "a female personnel director for women, with common sense and efficiency, is the important catalyst." [22]

The Office of the Director

Many of the same conclusions appeared to be generally held concerning the need for a WAC director on the General Staff level. While the duties of that office would evidently decrease as women's needs were catalogued and provided for by Army Regulations, and as specialist groups in other offices were re-established and became capable of taking over operating details, there appeared to exist a continuing need for a nerve center to detect problems and disseminate latest advancements.

The precedent of the British and Canadian women's services likewise indicated a continuing need, not merely for a woman adviser located somewhere in the headquarters, but for an Office of the Director. In the Canadian Women's Army Corps, the experiment had actually been made of abolishing the office and assigning the director as an assistant adjutant general, a position equivalent to that of Assistant G–1 in the American General Staff, but after some months it was found necessary to re-establish an Office of the

Director.[23] A similar conclusion was reached by the American WAVES.[24]

The Unification Issue

The trend of all postwar studies was toward recognition that unification of the women's services was desirable, with one female adviser in senior rank at the highest level. Proposals for unification of the armed forces therefore met with strong support from women advisers. The European theater's final board report suggested that, at any headquarters level, there be one top adviser for Wacs, nurses, and civilian female employees, so that similar rules and equal consideration might be given all groups as to medical care, recreation, housing, and other matters of well-being.

The Robinson report to the War Department in 1946 recommended that a special adviser for women's affairs be appointed to advise the General Staff on matters pertaining to all female military personnel. Unification appeared even more desirable for women's services than for men's, in view of the smaller size and generally closer-knit nature of the groups, which made them especially sensitive to jealousies and lowered morale in cases in which better uniforms or housing, or more lenient discipline, discharge, or other rules, were seen in one group only.[25]

While medical and nursing groups had always remained aloof to any such unifica-

[22] "The Margin is Womanpower," *Fortune*, January, 1943.

[23] Draft of WAC Hist, 14 Nov 45, incl note. WDWAC 314.7.

[24] WAVES Hist.

[25] (1) Memo, Dir WAC for Plng Br, G–1, 13 Feb 46; (2) Memo, Dir WAC for Gen Paul, 21 Feb 46; (3) Memo, Dir WAC for Gen Paul, 4 Jun 46, re WD Cir 5–1, 27 May 46; (4) Memo, Dep Dir to Plng and Policy Co-ordination Br, G–1, 16 Aug 46. WDWAC 320.

tion, the four enlisted women's services of the Army, Navy, Marine Corps, and Coast Guard had in fact for most of the war acted in a unified manner insofar as their directors were able to achieve it. A telephone conversation between Colonel Hobby and Capt. Mildred McAfee of the WAVES gave some indication that they were at times in advance of their parent services in this respect:

Capt. McAfee: This is certainly something that had better be joint.
Col. Hobby: It would be terrible if it were any other way. . . . I wonder if it might not be well if we got together informally and agreed to something before we brought the men in?
Capt. McAfee: I think that's a smart thought.[26]

Nevertheless, the chief of the Bureau of Naval Personnel admitted that the Joint Policy Committee of the Women's Reserves, a subcommittee of the Joint Army-Navy Personnel Board, did not work as well as the women desired because of the "stubborn autonomy" of the parent services.[27]

Unhappily for women's efforts in this respect, the trend of the parent services was towards greater compartmentalization rather than unification. With the "unification" of the Air Forces, the Air Wacs became the WAF, with their own distinctive uniform, and headed by a director in the rank of colonel. The trend was increased by the determination of the Medical Department to achieve autonomy in its women's corps. In addition to the Army Nurse Corps, the Medical Department secured legislation for the separate Women's Medical Specialist Corps, composed of female officers commissioned as dietitians, physiotherapists, and other medical specialists. This corps, although

small, had equal status with the Army Nurse Corps and WAC, and was also headed by a colonel.

There seemed to be no very good reason, if this trend continued, why separate women's corps would not be formed by all the arms and services—a Women's Transportation Corps, Women's Quartermaster Corps, or Women's Signal Corps—each with its own director and its own regulations and policies. In fact, upon the analogy of the Medical Department, there seemed no reason why a service such as the Quartermaster Corps should not have two or more independent women's corps, such as the Women's Food Management Corps and the Women's Supply Corps. However, the recommendations of all women advisers were against such development of special corps for women and in favor of full integration into existing Army groups.

The Question of Conscripting Women

Although some Army leaders, like General Eisenhower, expressed the view that total mobilization would be required in future emergencies, none became more specific on the implied necessity for drafting womanpower. Testimony before Congress made quite clear that the Army did not consider the establishment of a peacetime women's corps to have any necessary connection with drafting women, which would be a matter for future and separate consideration by Congress in time of mobilization.

The precedent of British and other services indicated that, when and if such a proposal reached a legislative body, it

---

[26] Tp Conv, Col Hobby and Capt McAfee, 5 Mar 45. G–1 312–312.9, Drawer 6, DRB AGO.
[27] WAVES Hist.

would not come from the armed forces, which might encounter more bitter opposition, but rather as a part of a wider program of national mobilization, civilian as well as military. The first step would apparently be a mere registration of women, as a guide to planners concerning available skills, age groups, mobility, and other factors in the allotment of womanpower. Such a proposal had been recognized by World War II planners as the least controversial of several alternatives, and later had been tentatively endorsed by President Harry S. Truman. At a news conference in 1950, Mr. Truman told reporters that, in the event of an emergency, it was his belief that the government should require national registration of women for defense and industry.[28]

Should the emergency continue, British precedent indicated that the next step would not be the extension of military selective service to women, but rather their forcible direction into industry, farm work, and other vital civilian occupations. Since women who volunteered for military service were of course exempt from such a labor draft, the armed forces would possibly be assured a supply of female recruits as considerable as that which the British had received under like circumstances. This phase of mobilization offered a possible advantage to the armed services in that they would be able to pick and choose, taking only women of intelligence and needed skill. On the other hand, the Army prospects had to be considered in the light of the fact that, under such a voluntary system, British women had flocked in needed numbers to the WRNS and WRAF but not to the ATS, which required more personnel and had a reputation for menial work.

The final stage of such a mobilization,

as reached by the British in World War II, was the actual drafting of women into the armed forces. The Army's earlier draft plans, made on two occasions in World War II, indicated that exemptions for women would be more lenient than those for men, with the less mobile women, and those with children and home responsibilities, going instead into local industry. These plans had indicated no intent by the Army to take any women whatever from essential industry, agriculture, government, or their husbands and children. As long as fewer women than men continued to be required by the armed forces, it would obviously be to their advantage, as well as to the nation's, to use only highly selected, mobile women without dependents. It was of course uncertain whether the Army would be able to convince the highest manpower agencies that it should not be obliged to take women in the lowest AGCT grades, since they could not replace men one-for-one on unskilled heavy work or be sent into front-line combat units.

In some respects, the advantages of a draft over the voluntary enlistment system would be considerable. Without a draft, the armed forces could not expect, by wartime precedent, to plan on a women's corps of any great size. Greater expansion plans founded on voluntary recruiting had not only failed in World War II, but had involved the Corps in expensive miscalculations in clothing, housing, officer strength, and other allotments. The competitive expense of recruiting had also become so high that it appeared unthinkable for the armed forces and industry to enter another such contest against each other, with each spending tremendous sums on recruiting and advertising, and at times

---

[28] Washington *Times-Herald*, May 5, 1950.

attracting women who more properly should have used their skills in some other agency. It was also obvious that, without selective service, the Army would have difficulty in establishing firm and predictable schedules for the inflow of womanpower into basic and specialist training, and its allotment among various commands and overseas theaters.

Another likely advantage of such a selective service system would be the avoidance of recruiting commitments as to job or station, with resulting better morale among malassigned women. Classification surveyors noted that "the main problem in adjustment of women to the Army arose through conflict between the inductee's conception of the treatment to be accorded her and the actual Army situation." [29] From the viewpoint of mental health, General Menninger commented:

The whole problem of motivation for enlistment into the WAC raises the question of the disadvantages of voluntary enlistment for women . . . not alone for military duty but for assignment to civilian work. The British had fewer problems when they ceased to have a volunteer organization. . . .[30]

On the other hand, a drafted corps of considerably larger size would also encounter problems unknown to the wartime WAC, and might be in danger of disappointing using agencies who expected it to meet the World War II level of performance. British precedent indicated that, to the exact extent that the Army was obliged by civilian manpower agencies to be unselective about its womanpower, it would meet increased problems of efficiency, health, discipline, illness and attrition rates, and morale.

For this reason, wartime WAC experts such as General White expressed a hope that it would never be necessary to draft women, believing that the second or civilian-draft phase would be more advantageous in permitting selectivity. As an alarming precedent it was noted that, for men under Selective Service, Congress repeatedly forced cutting physical and mental standards below the limits proposed by the Army.[31]

In the opinion of some authorities, the second phase would also provide adequate numbers of women. The former Deputy Director, Colonel Rice, in a last interview before her death, informally expressed the idea that paper plans in World War II for use of a million or more women had been unrealistic, and that the wartime WAC had actually come close to the limits of efficient replacement. Instead, she believed that the next war's dangers would fall on the home front, and that the majority of women could most profitably be used in civil defense activities.[32]

In addition, wartime WAC leaders pointed out that under a system of selective service for women, there would be increased opportunity for neglect of or damage to the needs of a minor group, which were easily overlooked in any case. Most improvements in the Corps in World War II, such as that in the uniform, in medical specialization, in measures to change public and soldier opinion, and in correction of unmilitary assignments, had been undertaken solely because, without them, it became increasingly difficult to get recruits. Without the pressure of public opinion and of womanpower shortages, it appeared unlikely that the skilled specialists of World War II would ever have been

---

[29] Rpt of Survey Team, Southern Area, 8 Nov 43, in Hist of O Dir Pers ASF. OCMH.
[30] Menninger, *Psychiatry in a Troubled World,* p. 108.
[31] Interv, Oct 48.
[32] *Ibid.*

assigned to The Quartermaster General's Office, The Surgeon General, the Bureau of Public Relations, and dozens of other staff sections. It was doubtful whether, without such specialists and without any need to attract recruits, every command would provide as good care and attention to the peculiar needs of the minority as had been enforced in wartime.

Report of the Hoover Commission

This last possibility led directly to the most considered statement ever made by wartime WAC leaders as to the final issue at stake, and the possible dangers to be avoided, in the employment of woman-power by the armed forces. In mid-1948, former Director Hobby and other wartime women's leaders were called to testify before the Commission on the Organization of the Executive Branch of the Government, better known as the Hoover Commission. Since peacetime heads of the various women's corps were not so summoned, the committee report was not in every respect agreeable to them. It represented, however, Mrs. Hobby's only formal testimony of any sort upon the lessons of the wartime experiment.[33]

Minor and preliminary comments of the report were not startling, being generally in line with accepted opinion. It was noted that in spite of advancements "the place of women in the armed services is not completely secure," and that since women's morale depended so largely upon public and soldier opinion, a special information program designed to improve this should continue to be provided. As for women's jobs, caution was given against "the tendency to use women in the services as additional personnel in jobs that could have been filled by civilian employees."

The opinion was expressed that women should never be assigned in units of less than 50, and preferably not smaller than 200 or 300—an increase over the previous wartime size, and one that seemed useful to insure economy in the necessary provisions for a minority.

However, the report's most important conclusion concerned the Corps' greatest single dilemma—the need for modification of some Army rules and procedures for fullest protection to women's well-being. In business and industry, standards of production and well-being had often been set up with consideration of the needs of both sexes, but all armed forces rules and operations had naturally for centuries been worked out for men only, and there was a tendency to look on any modifications as favoritism or special privilege. Modifications also might damage the morale of enlisted men, and could thus be approached, if at all, only with the greatest caution. On the other hand, the only other alternative was for the women to make the entire adjustment to men's standards of rougher dress, decreased modesty or need for privacy and cleanliness, more strenuous sports and recreational interests, a single standard of morality, and different opinions concerning drinking, sex, and conduct in general. While there was no doubt that in time women could and would successfully make this adjustment, the responsibility for such masculinization of the American woman was one for which wartime leaders did not care to assume responsibility. General Menninger noted that, from the psychiatric standpoint,

[33] Entire discussion from: Report of the Commission on Organization of the Executive Branch of the Government, November 15, 1948, Vol. III, Sec. XIV. OCMH.

greater instead of less difference was desirable:

In the event of another emergency, more consideration should be given to the problems of the women in the Army—their protection from ruthless male officers in their environment, their personal needs. . . . Such steps would greatly improve their . . . mental health.[34]

It was evident, however, that less, instead of more, attention to these matters would be likely in future emergencies, particularly under selective service for women. It was also noted that peacetime policies were set increasingly in the direction of elimination of wartime safeguards, although every such loss meant some change in the traditional social, cultural, and moral standards of women in national life.[35] With the peacetime abolition of most specialist groups in The Surgeon General's Office and elsewhere, it appeared doubtful whether the well-being of women in the Army could be given care equal to that normally given men.

The commission's report therefore concluded:

The whole subject of the use of women for war must be studied against the background of the American philosophy. The proper utilization of women in the Armed Services and elsewhere for war purposes can undoubtedly aid military efficiency and the national effort. This factor of increased efficiency must be weighed against a break with the philosophy of the past and the possible dangers of too great a growth of militarism. Many of the steps proposed to this committee—among them, the compulsory utilization of women—undoubtedly would increase military efficiency, but at the same time all of them collectively and some of them individually would greatly increase military influence in the United States and, over a period of time, might tend to set the national thinking in a military mold. . . .

The utilization of women for war, if improperly developed, has certain dangerous implications to our way of life. This subject deserves the most careful and cautious study.

The Final View

In retrospect, many of the difficulties that had appeared incomprehensible to the WAC's leaders and its members were at last explained by the realization that the Women's Army Corps had passed through the natural evolution of any new cultural phenomenon: the mistakes and experiments, the blind opposition of opponents of change, the enthusiasm of a pioneering minority, the slander by the less venturesome majority, the gradual adjustments, the eventual success partially nullified by the exhaustion and departure of leaders and the bewilderment of followers—all might equally well have applied to the history of the flying machine, the forty-niners, or the American Revolution. The chairman of the WAC's National Civilian Advisory Committee, Mrs. Oswald Lord, wrote later:

These women were pioneers. Many of us wondered if the American sense of adventure and steadfastness had died with their grandmothers. . . . I know now that the American woman of today can "take it" as her grandmother did. With her sense of humor unimpaired, she has pioneered in a new field and has done her job well.[36]

All agreed on one thing. The Women's Army Corps, Army of the United States, World War II, had been a new thing un-

---

[34] Menninger, *Psychiatry in a Troubled World*, p. 120.

[35] M/R, 17 Apr 46, sub: Presentation of Army Postwar Policy for Female Pers at Joint Army-Navy Pers Bd, 17 Apr 46; sent by G-1 to Col Boyce. WDWAC 326.

[36] Article in *New York Times* by Mary P. Lord, September 2, 1945.

der the sun. Its three crowded wartime years had passed too quickly for evaluation, and too roughly for appreciation, but once over, its thousands of members and its Army sponsors realized that they had been part of a phenomenon that they would not have missed. In a world where new frontiers had been hard to find, they had found one; in an age where pioneers and their problems were a memory, they had been pioneers. They might, like the forty-niners, shrink from thought of repeating such a passage, but it would be the prized memory of any lifetime.

Appendix A

[NOTE: The apparent discrepancies between strength figures and those for accessions and separations are due in part to the time lag needed for the former to catch up with the latter and in part to the confusion that attended the period of conversion from WAAC to WAC. Also, as has been noted on several occasions in the text, there are discrepancies between current WAAC/WAC figures, which were all that were available for planning at the time, and the final figures of the Adjutant General's Office.]

TABLE 1—STRENGTH OF THE WOMEN'S ARMY CORPS: JULY 1942–DECEMBER 1946

| End of month | Total | Officers | | Enlisted | End of month | Total | Officers | | Enlisted |
		Commissioned	Warrant				Commissioned	Warrant	
1942					**1944 (cont'd)**				
July	728	1	0	727	October	89,014	5,900	20	83,094
August	1,811	432	0	1,379	November	90,519	5,908	25	84,586
September	3,697	775	0	2,922	December	90,191	5,852	26	84,313
October	6,383	999	0	5,384					
November	9,920	1,319	0	8,601	**1945**				
December	12,767	1,545	0	11,222					
					January	92,465	5,837	26	86,602
1943					February	93,976	5,856	27	88,093
					March	96,859	5,795	27	91,037
January	21,582	1,789	0	19,793	April	99,288	5,717	29	93,542
February	34,049	2,052	0	31,997	May	98,935	5,808	32	93,095
March	44,530	2,501	0	42,029	June	96,557	5,733	44	90,780
April	51,465	3,160	0	48,305	July	94,330	5,827	56	88,447
May	56,164	4,212	0	51,952	August	90,779	5,752	55	84,972
June	60,243	4,917	0	55,326	September	86,541	5,694	60	80,787
July	61,403	5,457	0	55,946	October	77,228	5,548	55	71,625
August	50,603	5,067	0	45,536	November	62,969	5,397	42	57,530
September	51,268	5,430	0	45,838	December	43,813	4,682	27	39,104
October	53,894	5,428	0	48,466					
November	56,945	5,835	0	51,110	**1946**				
December	57,731	5,856	0	51,875					
					January	35,947	3,918	27	32,002
1944					February	29,801	3,409	27	26,365
					March	26,263	2,763	26	23,474
January	61,355	5,866	0	55,489	April	23,558	2,330	19	21,209
February	63,942	5,861	0	58,081	May	21,679	2,024	14	19,641
March	67,215	5,841	4	61,370	June	18,510	1,793	18	16,699
April	68,801	5,834	4	62,963	July	16,693	1,503	9	15,181
May	73,435	5,851	7	67,577	August	14,371	1,413	7	12,951
June	77,152	5,855	10	71,287	September	13,773	1,361	8	12,404
July	79,239	5,868	15	73,356	October	11,015	1,304	5	9,706
August	83,755	5,907	18	77,830	November	10,264	1,256	5	9,003
September	86,351	5,930	20	80,401	December	9,655	1,189	5	8,461

Source: U.S. Dept of Army, AGO, Strength Accounting Branch, Strength of the Army (STM-30), 1 December 1946, 1 July 1948, and 1 January 1949.

TABLE 2—ACCESSIONS OF PERSONNEL IN THE WOMEN'S ARMY CORPS: 1942–1946 [a]

Period	Total	Officers	Warrant Officers	Enlisted	Period	Total	Officers	Warrant Officers	Enlisted
Total . . .	150,551	7,071	45	143,435	1945	15,566	429	18	15,119
1942	22,055	1,390	0	20,665	January	2,495	0	0	2,495
					February	3,287	51	2	3,234
1943	67,992	4,858	0	63,134	March	3,811	2	0	3,809
					April	2,177	0	3	2,174
January	10,736	315	0	10,421	May	1,227	100	6	1,121
February	12,589	319	0	12,270	June	1,131	4	0	1,127
March	11,930	466	0	11,464	July	670	95	0	575
April	7,284	812	0	6,472	August	674	85	5	584
May	5,181	1,117	0	4,064	September	2	1	1	0
June	3,822	518	0	3,304	October	3	2	1	0
July	3,041	641	0	2,400	November	89	89	0	0
August	97	97	0	(b)	December	0	0	0	0
September	2,953	213	0	2,740					
October	2,486	126	0	2,360	1946	3,471	48	1	c 3,422
November	4,627	147	0	4,480					
December	3,246	87	0	3,159	January	0	0	0	0
					February	4	0	0	4
1944	41,467	346	26	41,095	March	248	0	0	248
					April	627	0	0	627
January	3,199	0	0	3,199	May	360	0	0	360
February	3,573	63	0	3,510	June	203	1	0	202
March	3,647	34	4	3,609	July	211	0	0	211
April	3,989	2	2	3,985	August	530	1	0	529
May	3,727	31	3	3,693	September	426	0	0	426
June	3,762	35	4	3,723	October	427	0	0	427
July	3,624	32	6	3,586	November	250	3	0	247
August	3,411	46	3	3,362	December	185	43	1	141
September	3,743	0	2	3,741					
October	2,981	20	2	2,959					
November	3,452	69	0	3,383					
December	2,359	14	0	2,345					

[a] Most of the officers and warrant officers shown are also included in the enlisted column since virtually all were commissioned after enlisted service.

[b] Because of the conversion from WAAC to WAC, AGO records showed no new accessions of enlisted Wacs and recorded 41,177 WAAC personnel enlisting in the WAC. The August 1943 figure in Table 1 includes Waacs who did not enlist in the WAC until later.

[c] Data for 1946 represent re-enlistments in Army of the United States.

Source: U.S. Dept of Army, AGO, Strength Accounting Branch, Strength of the Army (STM-30), 1 February 1948, as revised by AGO.

TABLE 3—WAAC PERSONNEL STATISTICS

Strength (As of 31 July 1943)	Number
On active duty	60,905
Inactive duty	2,341
Separations	4,327
Total enlistments	67,573

Marital Status (Through May 1943)	Percent
Single	70
Married	15
Widowed, separated, or divorced	15

Dependency	Percent
Without dependents	83.3

Age (Officers and EW)	Percent
Under 25	40.9
25–29	27.6
30–34	14.3
35–39	9.5
40–44	6.4
45 up	1.3
Average age	27.9 years
Median age	25.24 years

Education	Percent
Grammar School	8.3
High School, not graduated	24.0
High School Graduate	41.9
College, not graduated	16.1
College Graduate	8.8
Postgraduate	.9

Civilian Occupation	Percent
Professional and managerial	14.4
Clerical and sales	44.9
Service	16.8
Agricultural	.3
Skilled, semiskilled, unskilled manufacturing or factory work	17.3
Uncoded	6.3

Applicants	July–Oct 1942	Nov 42– Jan 43	Feb–Mar 1943
Applications requested	75,000	122,386	113,213
	Percent	Percent	Percent
Percent of above filed	30	30	35
Percent of number filed found acceptable and asked to report for interview	60	75	93

Applicants—Con.	July–Oct 1942	Nov 42– Jan 43	Feb–Mar 1943
Percent of interviewees enrolled	65	93	70
Percent of enrollees 25 years or under	40	50	45

Completed Training	Number	Number	Number
Officers	1,127	621	1,430
Basics	2,477	8,796	31,617

Sent To Specialist Schools	Number	Number	Number
Administrative	39	526	5,822
Bakers and Cooks	65	512	1,753
Motor Transport	13	565	926
Discharged	29	166	891

AGCT Distribution (Sample of 1,400 of each race)	Percent Antici- pated	Number Actual White	Number Actual Negro
I	7	5	0
II	24	38	6
III	38	42	28
IV	24	13	39
V	7	2	27

Army Jobs (28,451 in field, May 1943)	Percent
Administrative and Office	64.4
Technical and Professional	13.6
Drivers	6.6
Food Service	5.6
Communications	2.7
Mechanical, Trade, and Manual	2.7
Supply and Stock	2.6
Radio	1.8

Rank as of 1 April 1943	Number
1st Officer	253
2d Officer	705
3d Officer	2,175
Chief Leader	14
1st Leader	127
Technical Leader	24
Staff Leader	180
Leader	1,299
Junior Leader	4,513
Auxiliary 1st Class	6,690

Source: (1) Info on WAAC, Dir's personal book of statistics. 1943 WAAC files, unnumbered. (2) WAAC Pers Statistics, 6 Sep 43. 1943 WAAC files, unnumbered. (3) Plng Proj 10, 7 May 43, Analysis of AGO Machine Records. WAAC Plng Serv file. (4) Plng Proj 5, May 43. WAAC Plng Serv file.

TABLE 4—STRENGTH OF WOMEN'S ARMY CORPS IN CONTINENTAL UNITED STATES: MAY 1943–DECEMBER 1946 [a]

End of Month	All Commands			Army Air Forces			Army Ground Forces		
	Total	Officers	Enlisted	Total	Officers	Enlisted	Total	Officers	Enlisted
1943									
May	55,858	4,187	51,671	6,424	168	6,256	1,070	16	1,054
June	59,926	4,884	55,042	10,415	362	10,053	1,154	21	1,133
July	60,466	5,407	55,059	13,732	454	13,278	1,138	19	1,119
August	49,130	5,002	44,128	12,231	594	11,637	757	23	734
September	49,457	5,361	44,096	15,486	1,160	14,326	817	25	792
October	51,711	5,336	46,375	16,386	1,395	14,991	1,033	70	963
November	54,323	5,735	48,588	17,702	1,616	16,086	1,050	73	977
December	54,625	5,705	48,920	17,840	1,758	16,082	1,190	82	1,108
1944									
January	58,254	5,709	52,545	19,628	1,776	17,852	1,387	94	1,293
February	60,513	5,699	54,814	20,809	1,803	19,006	1,461	103	1,358
March	63,102	5,615	57,487	22,144	1,901	20,243	1,681	120	1,561
April	63,925	5,449	58,476	23,760	1,888	21,872	1,777	119	1,658
May	66,085	5,365	60,720	25,368	1,832	23,536	1,893	118	1,775
June	68,439	5,314	63,125	27,202	1,841	25,361	1,982	117	1,865
July	70,433	5,294	65,139	29,336	1,848	27,488	2,054	115	1,939
August	73,268	5,255	68,013	29,802	1,836	27,966	2,078	111	1,967
September	74,329	5,243	69,086	31,076	1,723	29,353	2,077	115	1,962
October	75,599	5,157	70,442	32,172	1,658	30,514	2,119	111	2,008
November	77,244	5,145	72,099	32,970	1,654	31,316	2,094	109	1,985
December	76,374	5,023	71,351	33,361	1,641	31,720	2,064	103	1,961
1945									
January	78,183	4,987	73,196	33,982	1,639	32,343	2,035	103	1,932
February	78,430	4,963	73,467	33,829	1,625	32,204	1,990	103	1,887
March	80,899	4,873	76,026	33,669	1,607	32,062	1,944	104	1,840
April	83,246	4,797	78,449	33,238	1,622	31,616	1,912	111	1,801
May	82,062	4,787	77,275	33,050	1,686	31,364	1,958	110	1,848
June	79,612	4,740	74,872	31,505	1,660	29,845	1,933	114	1,819
July	77,295	4,681	72,614	30,490	1,610	28,880	1,924	111	1,813
August	74,888	4,613	70,275	28,394	1,489	26,905	1,858	120	1,738
September	71,777	4,607	67,170	26,750	1,367	25,383	1,836	117	1,719
October	66,220	4,582	61,638	24,233	1,293	22,940	1,616	107	1,509
November	56,454	4,707	51,747	17,365	1,252	16,113	1,403	99	1,304
December	39,351	4,119	35,232	9,851	973	8,878	1,109	77	1,032
1946									
January	31,872	3,401	28,471	8,392	658	7,734	678	61	617
February	26,487	2,909	23,578	7,026	488	6,538	532	49	483
March	23,426	2,279	21,147	6,365	399	5,966	494	45	449
April	21,399	1,911	19,488	6,041	362	5,679	384	41	343
May	19,592	1,667	17,925	5,777	324	5,453	244	31	213
June	16,719	1,479	15,240	4,975	287	4,688	217	25	192
July	14,991	1,280	13,711	4,165	254	3,911	189	19	170
August	12,564	1,128	11,436	3,597	228	3,369	173	21	152
September	11,273	970	10,303	2,787	202	2,585	158	20	138
October	8,215	909	7,306	2,003	169	1,834	96	16	80
November	6,920	848	6,072	2,085	160	1,925	122	29	93
December	6,313	758	5,555	2,146	150	1,996	106	14	92

[a] Distribution indicates commands to which personnel were regularly assigned. Does not reflect attached strength. Waacs were attached to AAF and other commands beginning September 1942; Auxiliary status precluded direct assignment until May 1943.

[b] Defense commands consolidated with service commands 31 March 1946.

TABLE 4—STRENGTH OF WOMEN'S ARMY CORPS IN CONTINENTAL UNITED STATES: MAY 1943–DECEMBER 1946 [a]—Continued

Army Service Forces			War Department Groups			Defense Commands			End of Month
Total	Officers	Enlisted	Total	Officers	Enlisted	Total	Officers	Enlisted	
									1943
44, 999	3, 859	41, 140	1	1	0	3, 364	143	3, 221	May
44, 391	4, 337	40, 054	107	15	92	3, 859	149	3, 710	June
41, 389	4, 749	36, 640	104	15	89	4, 103	170	3, 933	July
32, 799	4, 176	28, 623	114	18	96	3, 229	191	3, 038	August
31, 913	4, 094	27, 819	466	34	432	775	48	727	September
33, 055	3, 785	29, 270	490	43	447	477	43	704	October
34, 569	3, 979	30, 590	401	36	365	601	31	570	November
34, 387	3, 782	30, 605	641	55	586	567	28	539	December
									1944
35, 969	3, 743	32, 226	705	69	636	565	27	538	January
37, 051	3, 687	33, 364	740	83	657	452	23	429	February
38, 375	3, 475	34, 900	816	116	700	86	3	83	March
37, 516	3, 317	34, 199	872	125	747	0	0	0	April
37, 873	3, 288	34, 585	951	127	824	0	0	0	May
38, 379	3, 228	35, 151	876	128	748	0	0	0	June
38, 113	3, 204	34, 909	930	127	803	0	0	0	July
40, 417	3, 179	37, 238	971	129	842	0	0	0	August
40, 144	3, 277	36, 867	1, 032	128	904	0	0	0	September
40, 177	3, 260	36, 917	1, 131	128	1, 003	0	0	0	October
41, 149	3, 260	37, 889	1, 031	122	909	0	0	0	November
39, 867	3, 155	36, 712	1, 082	124	958	0	0	0	December
									1945
41, 074	3, 129	37, 945	1, 092	116	976	0	0	0	January
41, 515	3, 111	38, 404	1, 096	124	972	0	0	0	February
41, 165	3, 039	41, 126	1, 121	123	998	0	0	0	March
46, 950	2, 944	44, 006	1, 146	120	1, 026	0	0	0	April
45, 910	2, 873	43, 037	1, 144	118	1, 026	0	0	0	May
45, 027	2, 840	42, 187	1, 147	126	1, 021	0	0	0	June
43, 713	2, 833	40, 880	1, 168	127	1, 041	0	0	0	July
43, 484	2, 872	40, 612	1, 152	132	1, 020	0	0	0	August
41, 408	2, 941	38, 467	1, 783	182	1, 601	0	0	0	September
38, 785	3, 022	35, 763	1, 586	160	1, 426	0	0	0	October
36, 251	3, 215	33, 036	1, 435	141	1, 294	0	0	0	November
27, 218	2, 945	24, 273	1, 173	124	1, 049	0	0	0	December
									1946
21, 944	2, 570	19, 374	857	111	746	1	1	0	January
18, 172	2, 274	15, 898	756	97	659	1	1	0	February
15, 892	1, 741	14, 151	675	94	581	(b)	(b)	(b)	March
14, 156	1, 413	12, 743	818	95	723	(b)	(b)	(b)	April
12, 922	1, 225	11, 697	649	87	562	(b)	(b)	(b)	May
c 10, 932	c 1, 047	c 9, 885	595	120	475	(b)	(b)	(b)	June
c 10, 111	c 914	c 9, 197	526	93	433	(b)	(b)	(b)	July
c 8, 321	c 794	c 7, 527	473	85	388	(b)	(b)	(b)	August
c 7, 987	c 668	c 7, 319	341	80	261	(b)	(b)	(b)	September
c 5, 894	c 648	c 5, 246	222	76	146	(b)	(b)	(b)	October
c 4, 512	c 586	c 3, 926	201	73	128	(b)	(b)	(b)	November
c 3, 846	c 511	c 3, 335	215	83	132	(b)	(b)	(b)	December

c Army Service Forces (formerly Services of Supply) discontinued as of 11 June 1946 with reorganization of War Department (see War Department Circular 138, 14 May 1946). Figures shown for June–December 1946 are for administrative and technical services and headquarters of armies and army area troops.

Source: U.S. Dept of Army, AGO, Strength Accounting Branch, Strength of the Army (STM–30) and predecessor reports for respective months. Figures for July 1942–April 1943 are omitted because the early misunderstandings concerning WAAC status made them unreliable.

TABLE 5—WOMEN'S ARMY CORPS ENLISTED PERSONNEL IN ARMY AIR FORCES, CONTINENTAL UNITED STATES, BY MILITARY OCCUPATIONAL SPECIALTY: 31 JANUARY 1945

Specialty	Number of SSN's	Personnel	
		Number	Percent Distribution
Total	489	30,430	100.0
Administrative	20	14,011	46.0
Supply	10	1,364	4.5
Medical	12	1,879	6.2
Photographic	5	972	3.2
Weather	3	242	0.8
Airplane Maintenance	16	617	2.0
Aviation Specialist	5	656	2.1
Air Crew	1	20	0.1
Radar Operator	1	5	(a)
Armament	4	51	0.2
Vehicle Operator	3	1,628	5.3
Auto Mechanic	4	82	0.3
Radio Operator	7	301	1.0
Radio Mechanic	5	359	1.2
Wire Communications	4	650	2.1
Utility Construction	11	169	0.6
Duty [b]		5,726	18.8
Miscellaneous [c]		1,698	5.6

[a] Less than 0.05 percent.

[b] Includes 80 percent on-the-job trainees, newly recruited, and undergoing 90-day period required for AAF SSN. Estimated that these would be distributed into listed job groups according to the same ratio as other women. Remainder of Duty group includes messengers, duty sergeants, and other miscellaneous groups.

[c] Includes chiefly Food Services, also Chemical, etc.

Source: Extracted from list shown in "Strength of AAF Personnel in WAC within Continental U.S. by Command, SSN, and Race." SC–PS–123 (AAF Office of Statistical Control). Does not agree with AGO figure, Table 4, because of different reporting system.

TABLE 6—WOMEN'S ARMY CORPS OFFICER PERSONNEL IN ARMY AIR FORCES, CONTINENTAL UNITED STATES, BY MILITARY OCCUPATIONAL SPECIALTY: 31 JANUARY 1945

Specialty	Number	Specialty	Number
Total.	1,541	Radar Filter Officer	5
		Medical Register.	4
Administrative	412	Claims Officer	3
Company Commander	263	Legal Officer	3
Military Personnel Officer.	128	Vocational Education Officer	3
Adjutant	102	Aerial Photo Officer	2
Mess Officer [a]	70	Automotive Maintenance Officer.	2
Special Services Officer	68	Ground Safety Officer	2
Supply Officer [a]	43	I M Supply Officer	2
Technical Supply Officer	40	Operations Officer	2
Administrative Inspector	40	Parasitologist	2
Civilian Personnel Officer	38	Psychologist	2
Finance Officer [a].	33	Publications Officer	2
Classification Officer	29	Sales Officer	2
Priorities and Traffic Officer	27	Security Officer	2
Executive Officer.	25	Training Arts Officer	2
Statistical Officer.	19	Aircraft Maintenance Officer	1
Personal Affairs Officer	19	Air Traffic Service Officer	1
Personnel Staff Officer	13	Communications Officer.	1
Photo Interpreter [a].	13	Cryptographer	1
Passenger Transport Officer	12	Cryptographic Security Officer	1
Postal Officer	12	Fighter Interceptor Controller.	1
Training Officer	12	Inspector General	1
Intelligence Officer	11	Judge Advocate	1
Information and Education	9	Operations and Training Staff Officer	1
Instructor.	9	Ordnance Supply Officer	1
Motor Transport Officer	9	Personnel Equipment Officer	1
Historian	7	Petrol Supply Officer	1
Combat Liaison Officer	6	Salvage Officer.	1
Message Center Officer [a]	6	Signal Supply Officer	1
Physical Tng Officer	6	Student.	1
Bacteriologist	5		

[a] Two SSN's assigned to this Military Occupational Specialty.

Source: Extracted from list shown in "Strength of AAF Personnel in WAC within Continental U.S. By Command, SSN, and Race." SC–PS–123 (AAF Office of Statistical Control). Does not agree with AGO figure, Table 4, because of different reporting system.

TABLE 7—STRENGTH OF WOMEN'S ARMY CORPS IN OVERSEAS THEATERS: 1943–1946

End of Month	All Overseas Theaters			Africa and Middle East			China, Burma, and India			European		
	Total	Officers	Enlisted	Total	Officers	Enlisted	Total	Officers	Enlisted	Total	Officers	Enlisted
1943												
January	200	10	190	0	0	0	0	0	0	0	0	0
February	201	10	191	0	0	0	0	0	0	0	0	0
March	201	10	191	0	0	0	0	0	0	0	0	0
April	274	18	256	0	0	0	0	0	0	2	2	0
May	306	25	281	0	0	0	0	0	0	13	8	5
June	317	33	284	0	0	0	0	0	0	19	12	7
July	937	50	887	0	0	0	0	0	0	595	33	562
August	1,473	65	1,408	0	0	0	0	0	0	595	33	562
September	1,811	69	1,742	0	0	0	0	0	0	1,027	41	986
October	2,183	92	2,091	0	0	0	3	1	2	1,031	42	989
November	2,622	100	2,522	0	0	0	10	2	8	1,172	46	1,126
December	3,106	151	2,955	12	2	10	50	4	46	1,203	78	1,125
1944												
January	3,101	157	2,944	12	2	10	49	4	45	1,203	78	1,125
February	3,429	162	3,267	12	2	10	49	4	45	1,560	87	1,473
March	4,113	230	3,883	12	2	10	49	4	45	1,710	126	1,584
April	4,806	389	4,487	12	2	10	49	4	45	2,271	171	2,100
May	7,350	493	6,857	12	2	10	50	5	45	3,687	222	3,465
June	8,713	551	8,162	254	6	248	50	5	45	4,715	251	4,464
July	8,806	589	8,217	253	5	248	49	5	44	4,781	287	4,494
August	10,487	670	9,817	253	5	248	123	10	113	4,962	297	4,665
September	12,022	707	11,315	253	6	247	211	12	199	5,425	310	5,115
October	13,415	763	12,652	252	6	246	322	13	309	6,165	346	5,819
November	13,275	788	12,487	252	6	246	325	14	311	5,799	361	5,438
December	13,817	855	12,962	252	6	246	326	16	310	5,931	348	5,583
1945												
January	14,282	876	13,406	290	9	281	324	15	309	5,984	354	5,630
February	15,546	920	14,626	292	9	283	344	16	328	6,645	378	6,267
March	15,960	949	15,011	310	13	297	334	16	318	6,892	430	6,462
April	16,042	949	15,093	305	12	293	331	15	316	6,938	424	6,514
May	16,873	1,053	15,820	302	13	289	325	17	308	7,530	470	7,060
June	16,945	1,037	15,908	294	13	281	328	15	313	7,771	490	7,281
July	17,035	1,202	15,833	266	14	252	310	12	298	8,316	609	7,707
August	15,891	1,194	14,697	258	14	244	294	11	283	7,826	657	7,169
September	14,764	1,147	13,617	245	14	231	289	13	276	7,746	667	7,079
October	11,008	1,021	9,987	5	4	1	268	12	256	5,766	598	5,168
November	6,515	732	5,783	4	4	0	135	10	125	4,089	449	3,640
December	4,462	590	3,872	4	4	0	83	8	75	3,264	393	2,871
1946												
January	4,075	544	3,531	0	0	0	110	10	100	3,109	379	2,730
February	3,314	527	2,787	2	2	0	128	6	122	2,653	344	2,309
March	2,837	510	2,327	1	1	0	91	6	85	2,109	312	1,797
April	2,159	438	1,721	1	1	0	79	7	72	1,680	262	1,418
May	2,087	371	1,716	0	0	0	136	8	128	1,476	212	1,264
June	1,791	332	1,459	0	0	0	133	9	124	1,526	201	1,325
July	1,702	232	1,470	0	0	0	109	9	100	1,476	113	1,363
August	1,807	292	1,515	0	0	0	117	7	110	1,448	124	1,324
September	2,500	399	2,101	0	0	0	118	8	110	2,147	263	1,884
October	2,800	400	2,400	0	0	0	123	8	115	2,168	248	1,920
November	3,344	413	2,931	0	0	0	116	8	108	2,152	244	1,908
December	3,342	436	2,906	0	0	0	116	8	108	2,140	267	1,873

[a] Consists chiefly of personnel assigned to U.S. commands but on temporary or recurring duty overseas. Includes personnel en route from United States to theaters and small numbers assigned for short periods to Northwest Service Command and Caribbean Defense Command.

[b] Audited strength reports apparently incomplete. Other sources indicate total strength of 36 (11 officers and 25 enlisted women).

TABLE 7—STRENGTH OF WOMEN'S ARMY CORPS IN OVERSEAS THEATERS: 1943–1946—Con.

Mediterranean			Pacific			Other [a]			End of Month
Total	Officers	Enlisted	Total	Officers	Enlisted	Total	Officers	Enlisted	
									1943
200	10	190	0	0	0	0	0	0	January
201	10	191	0	0	0	0	0	0	February
201	10	191	0	0	0	0	0	0	March
199	11	188	0	0	0	73	5	68	April
272	16	256	0	0	0	21	1	20	May
295	18	277	0	0	0	3	3	0	June
283	15	268	0	0	0	59	2	57	July
338	16	322	0	0	0	540	16	524	August
784	28	756	0	0	0	0	0	0	September
776	30	746	0	0	0	373	19	354	October
1, 157	44	1, 113	0	0	0	283	8	275	November
1, 461	57	1, 404	0	0	0	380	10	370	December
									1944
1, 800	61	1, 739	32	7	25	5	5	0	January
1, 800	61	1, 739	b 4	b 4	b 0	4	4	0	February
1, 754	58	1, 696	157	16	141	431	24	407	March
1, 732	66	1, 666	157	17	140	655	129	526	April
1, 864	95	1, 769	654	128	526	1, 083	41	1, 042	May
1, 937	95	1, 842	1, 035	152	883	722	42	680	June
1, 897	96	1, 801	1, 419	163	1, 256	407	33	374	July
1, 928	99	1, 829	1, 421	169	1, 252	1, 800	90	1, 710	August
1, 905	99	1, 806	2, 643	211	2, 432	1, 585	69	1, 516	September
1, 991	104	1, 887	3, 745	243	3, 502	940	51	889	October
1, 620	90	1, 530	3, 384	231	3, 153	1, 895	86	1, 809	November
1, 576	87	1, 489	4, 343	278	4, 065	1, 389	120	1, 269	December
									1945
1, 569	89	1, 480	4, 712	339	4, 373	1, 403	70	1, 333	January
1, 547	86	1, 461	5, 262	356	4, 906	1, 456	75	1, 381	February
1, 652	89	1, 563	5, 237	333	4, 904	1, 535	68	1, 467	March
1, 608	89	1, 519	5, 173	328	4, 845	1, 687	81	1, 606	April
1, 503	86	1, 417	5, 011	337	4, 674	2, 202	130	2, 072	May
1, 418	85	1, 333	5, 068	329	4, 739	2, 066	105	1, 961	June
1, 200	74	1, 126	4, 856	347	4, 509	2, 087	146	1, 941	July
969	64	905	4, 705	342	4, 363	1, 839	106	1, 733	August
769	44	725	4, 285	321	3, 964	1, 430	88	1, 342	September
224	36	188	3, 605	295	3, 310	1, 140	76	1, 064	October
179	34	145	1, 287	136	1, 151	821	99	722	November
95	8	87	486	131	355	530	46	484	December
									1946
8	8	0	368	114	254	480	33	447	January
8	8	0	124	124	0	399	43	356	February
8	8	0	139	135	4	489	48	441	March
8	8	0	117	115	2	274	45	229	April
7	7	0	105	102	3	363	42	321	May
7	7	0	86	86	0	39	29	10	June
7	7	0	84	84	0	26	19	7	July
6	6	0	75	75	0	161	80	81	August
7	7	0	76	71	5	152	50	102	September
64	8	56	230	95	135	215	41	174	October
62	6	56	436	101	335	578	54	524	November
157	11	146	609	106	503	320	44	276	December

Source: U.S. Dept. of Army, AGO, Strength Accounting Branch, Strength of the Army (STM–30) and predecessor reports for respective months.

TABLE 8—DECORATIONS AND AWARDS MADE TO THE WOMEN'S ARMY CORPS: 7 DECEMBER 1941–30 JUNE 1947 [a]

Type of Award	Total	Continental United States	Pacific and Far East Commands	U.S. Forces in China	U.S. Forces in India-Burma	European Command	Mediterranean Theater of Operations	U.S. Forces in Africa-Mid-East
Total	639	41	105	21	10	314	145	3
Original	633	40	105	21	10	311	143	3
Oak-leaf Cluster	6	1	0	0	0	3	2	0
Distinguished Service Medal . . .	1	1	0	0	0	0	0	0
Original	1	1	0	0	0	0	0	0
Oak-leaf Cluster	0	0	0	0	0	0	0	0
Legion of Merit	62	33	5	2	1	8	10	3
Original	59	32	5	2	1	7	9	3
Oak-leaf Cluster	3	1	0	0	0	1	1	0
Soldier's Medal	10	5	4	0	0	0	1	0
Original	10	5	4	0	0	0	1	0
Oak-leaf Cluster	0	0	0	0	0	0	0	0
Bronze Star Medal	565	2	96	19	9	305	134	0
Original	562	2	96	19	9	303	133	0
Oak-leaf Cluster	3	0	0	0	0	2	1	0
Air Medal	1	0	0	0	0	1	0	0
Original	1	0	0	0	0	1	0	0
Oak-leaf Cluster	0	0	0	0	0	0	0	0

[a] Does not include Purple Heart or Army Commendation Ribbon.

Source: War Department, Decorations and Awards, HTM–14, Prepared by Strength Accounting Branch, AGO, under direction of Statistical Division, Office of the Army Comptroller, OCS, 30 June 1947.

TABLE 9—PERSONNEL DISCHARGED FROM THE WOMEN'S ARMY CORPS BECAUSE OF PREGNANCY: 1942–1946

Period	Total	Officers	Enlisted Women	Rate per Thousand per Month [a]	Period	Total	Officers	Enlisted Women	Rate per Thousand per Month [a]
Total . . .	11,402	465	10,937	4.0	*1944* (cont'd)				
					September	416	24	392	4.8
1942.	19	3	16	0.5	October	385	12	373	4.3
July	0	0	0	0.0	November	391	20	371	4.3
August	0	0	0	0.0	December	440	19	421	4.9
September	2	0	2	0.5	*1945*	5,923	232	5,691	5.7
October	2	1	1	0.3	January	546	15	531	5.9
November	2	0	2	0.2	February.	372	17	355	4.0
December	13	2	11	1.0	March	551	25	526	5.7
1943	815	49	766	1.4	April	473	23	450	4.8
January	14	0	14	0.6	May	489	27	462	4.9
February.	31	3	28	0.9	June.	655	22	633	6.8
March	50	0	50	1.1	July	687	31	656	7.3
April	57	5	52	1.1	August	504	22	482	5.6
May.	106	2	104	1.9	September	560	23	537	6.5
June.	95	7	88	1.6	October	444	13	431	5.7
July	150	5	145	2.4	November	332	5	327	5.3
August	42	12	30	0.8	December	310	9	301	7.1
September	43	2	41	0.8	*1946*	857	5	852	3.7
October	42	4	38	0.8	January	270	1	269	7.5
November	78	5	73	1.4	February.	95	1	94	3.2
December	107	4	103	1.9	March	71	0	71	2.7
1944	3,788	176	3,612	4.1	April	44	0	44	1.9
January	135	9	126	2.2	May	149	0	149	6.9
February.	175	10	165	2.7	June.	40	0	40	2.2
March	231	5	226	3.4	July	45	1	44	2.7
April	278	9	269	4.0	August	51	0	51	3.5
May.	280	13	267	3.8	September	31	1	30	2.3
June.	441	15	426	5.7	October	23	0	23	2.1
July	261	22	239	3.3	November	20	0	20	1.9
August	355	18	337	4.2	December	18	1	17	1.9

[a] Computed on the basis of month-end strength. Averages shown for periods are weighted arithmetic averages; geometric averages would be somewhat lower.

Source: U.S. Department of Army, Administrative Services Division, AGO.

TABLE 10—PERCENT DISTRIBUTION OF WAC AND MALE PERSONNEL IN THE U.S. ARMY, BY GRADE: DECEMBER 1942–DECEMBER 1946

Grade	31 Dec 1942	1943		1944		1945		1946	
		30 Jun	31 Dec	30 Jun	31 Dec	30 Jun	31 Dec	30 Jun	31 Dec
Commissioned Officers									
WAC	12.1	8.2	10.1	7.6	6.5	5.9	10.7	9.7	12.3
Male	6.8	7.6	8.4	8.8	9.3	9.5	13.9	13.0	11.3
General Officers									
WAC	0.0	0.0	0.0	0.0	0.0	0.0	0.0	0.0	0.0
Male	(a)	(a)	(a)	(a)	(a)	(a)	(a)	(a)	(a)
Colonel									
WAC	(b)	(b)	(b)	(b)	(b)	(b)	(b)	(b)	(b)
Male	0.1	0.1	0.1	0.1	0.1	0.1	0.3	0.5	0.5
Lieutenant Colonel									
WAC	0.0	0.0	0.0	(a)	(a)	(a)	(a)	0.1	0.1
Male	0.2	0.3	0.3	0.3	0.3	0.4	0.7	0.9	1.0
Major									
WAC	0.0	(a)	0.1	0.1	0.1	0.2	0.4	0.6	0.7
Male	0.5	0.5	0.6	0.7	0.8	0.9	1.5	1.5	1.5
Captain									
WAC	0.2	0.5	0.8	0.8	1.0	1.1	2.6	3.6	5.2
Male	1.3	1.4	1.7	1.9	2.2	2.4	4.2	3.6	3.4
First Lieutenant									
WAC	0.8	1.3	2.3	2.8	2.9	3.8	6.5	4.4	4.9
Male	2.0	2.1	2.4	2.6	3.0	3.6	5.2	4.7	3.8
Second Lieutenant									
WAC	11.1	6.4	6.9	3.9	2.5	0.8	1.2	1.0	1.4
Male	2.7	3.2	3.3	3.2	2.9	2.1	2.0	1.8	1.1
Warrant and Flight Officers									
WAC	0.0	0.0	0.0	(a)	(a)	0.1	0.1	0.1	0.1
Male	0.2	0.3	0.4	0.5	0.7	0.7	0.8	0.5	0.4
Enlisted Personnel									
WAC	87.9	91.8	89.9	92.4	93.5	94.0	89.2	90.2	87.6
Male	93.0	92.1	91.2	90.7	90.0	89.8	85.3	86.5	88.3
Master and First Sergeant									
WAC	0.1	0.4	0.7	0.5	0.5	0.6	0.8	1.2	2.6
Male	0.9	1.0	1.1	1.2	1.4	1.4	1.4	2.5	3.3
Technical Sergeant									
WAC	0.0	0.1	0.3	0.4	0.5	0.7	1.2	2.1	3.9
Male	0.9	1.1	1.5	2.0	2.4	2.6	2.1	2.0	2.6
Staff Sergeant and T/3									
WAC	0.0	0.6	1.9	2.3	3.1	3.8	5.2	7.9	14.6
Male	3.7	4.2	5.0	5.9	6.9	7.5	6.4	4.5	5.2
Sergeant and T/4									
WAC	0.2	4.3	10.0	9.9	11.0	12.0	17.5	24.8	32.0
Male	7.6	8.7	10.6	11.1	12.2	12.8	12.5	8.1	7.7
Corporal and T/5									
WAC	1.9	12.8	22.3	18.7	18.3	21.2	35.1	37.5	25.5
Male	12.4	15.2	16.6	17.1	18.7	18.8	18.6	14.5	14.3
Private First Class									
WAC	0.0	18.0	19.1	17.7	17.0	25.0	19.0	13.6	7.4
Male	13.5	19.1	19.0	19.0	19.4	27.5	24.6	25.4	24.6
Private									
WAC	85.7	55.6	35.6	42.9	43.1	30.7	10.4	3.1	1.6
Male	54.0	42.8	37.4	34.4	29.0	19.2	19.7.	29.5	30.6

a Less than 0.05 percent.
b The Director was the only woman in the WAC holding the rank of colonel.

Source: U.S. Department of Army, AGO, Strength Accounting Branch, Strength of the Army (STM–30), respective months.

TABLE 11—STRENGTH OF NEGRO PERSONNEL IN THE WOMEN'S ARMY CORPS: 1943–1946 [a]

End of Month	Total		Officers	Enlisted
	Number	Percent of Total WAC		
1943				
March	2,532	5.7	65	2,467
June	3,161	5.2	105	3,056
September	3,012	5.9	105	2,907
December	2,805	4.9	103	2,702
1944				
March	3,175	4.7	115	3,060
June	3,506	4.5	117	3,389
September	3,766	4.4	121	3,645
December	4,040	4.5	120	3,920
1945				
March	3,902	4.1	115	3,787
June	3,849	4.0	117	3,732
September	3,738	4.3	105	3,633
December	1,690	3.9	80	1,610
1946				
March	786	3.0	32	754
June	673	3.6	15	658
September	279	2.0	15	264
December	372	3.9	9	363

[a] Negro strength is based on personal statements at time of entry into active service. Does not necessarily include personnel of other races with Negro blood.

Source: U.S. Dept. of Army, AGO, Strength Accounting Branch, Strength of the Army (STM–30), 1 January 1949.

TABLE 12—ENLISTED PERSONNEL SEPARATED FROM THE WOMEN'S ARMY CORPS: AUGUST 1942–DECEMBER 1946 [a]

Period	Total	Death (Non-battle)	Reassignment		Honorable Discharge				Dishonorable Discharge	Discharge Other Than Honorable [d]
			Commissioned Officer	Warrant Officer	Medical [b]	Inaptitude or Unsuitability	Demobilization	Other [e]		
Total	137,209	160	7,833	39	22,324	1,322	43,093	61,155	71	1,212
1942	1,659	0	1,536	0	63	5	0	47	0	8
August	431	0	428	0	2	0	0	1	0	0
September	381	0	368	0	6	0	0	7	0	0
October	344	0	331	0	6	0	0	7	0	0
November	258	0	231	0	15	2	0	9	0	1
December	245	0	178	0	34	3	0	34	0	7
1943	26,079	29	5,005	0	4,263	53	0	16,427	0	302
January	377	1	313	0	28	2	0	27	0	6
February	483	1	320	0	98	4	0	48	0	12
March	963	1	486	0	314	4	0	135	0	23
April	1,310	4	663	0	413	5	0	205	0	20
May	1,973	3	1,130	0	536	4	0	268	0	32
June	1,693	1	673	0	604	8	0	347	0	60
July	1,695	1	528	0	677	10	0	428	0	51
August	e 14,310	4	252	0	348	11	0	13,664	0	31
September	1,844	6	203	0	506	1	0	1,098	0	30
October	430	4	127	0	235	0	0	51	0	13
November	513	1	162	0	253	1	0	80	0	16
December	488	2	148	0	251	3	0	76	0	8
1944	10,582	46	485	23	6,706	291	0	2,684	28	319
January	335	3	0	0	273	7	0	46	0	6
February	502	1	58	0	344	9	0	82	0	8
March	604	0	34	4	452	5	0	93	1	15
April	648	4	1	1	476	7	0	137	2	20
May	710	7	31	4	472	10	0	168	0	18
June	1,177	7	85	4	742	24	0	289	3	23
July	603	6	19	3	395	9	0	147	3	21
August	1,062	5	44	4	640	32	0	296	5	36
September	1,118	5	3	2	713	39	0	311	4	41
October	1,143	1	98	1	687	39	0	285	4	28
November	1,313	3	98	0	687	58	0	417	1	49
December	1,367	4	14	0	825	52	0	413	5	54
1945	67,105	71	697	16	10,013	896	22,582	32,238	41	551
January	1,524	8	55	0	899	49	0	442	3	68
February	1,108	3	59	1	615	45	0	330	5	50
March	1,670	6	8	0	950	78	0	536	1	91
April	1,351	10	40	2	761	61	0	428	5	44
May	1,530	0	119	2	812	74	38	441	3	41
June	2,811	18	96	4	977	88	145	1,431	6	46
July	3,828	15	54	4	1,128	147	233	2,172	10	65
August	3,187	4	101	1	935	97	477	1,525	2	45
September	5,154	4	4	0	808	59	1,871	2,374	2	32
October	9,160	1	23	2	812	100	4,040	4,142	2	28
November	16,013	2	131	0	716	60	8,227	6,845	1	31
December	19,769	0	7	0	600	28	7,551	11,572	1	10
1946	31,784	14	110	0	1,279	77	20,511	9,759	2	32
January	8,166	0	15	0	264	23	2,950	4,909	0	5
February	4,135	0	15	0	152	7	2,464	1,489	1	7
March	3,355	1	2	0	179	10	2,067	1,093	0	3
April	2,104	2	19	0	140	7	1,337	593	1	5
May	1,580	4	15	0	148	7	872	533	0	1
June	1,972	0	2	0	82	6	1,460	420	0	2
July	3,067	3	1	0	87	5	2,663	305	0	3
August	1,873	0	0	0	73	6	1,577	213	0	4
September	933	1	1	0	33	1	805	90	0	2
October	3,206	2	0	0	42	2	3,104	56	0	0
November	1,021	0	2	0	34	0	960	25	0	0
December	372	1	38	0	45	3	252	33	0	0

[a] Separations from November 1943 through June 1945 are based on month of processing. Other months reflect actual month of occurrence. Figures shown do not include the number dropped from the rolls because of AWOL and desertion.
[b] Includes certificate of disability, pregnancy and likelihood of early recurrences of incapacitating symptoms.
[e] Includes minority, dependency, hardship, marriage, national health, safety, or interest, and others. Includes 14,199 separated at their request during August–October 1943, due to conversion to WAC.
[d] Includes undesirable habits or traits of character and misconduct.
[e] Excludes 41,177 WAAC enlisted personnel re-enlisting in the WAC during August 1943.

Source: U. S. Dept. of Army, AGO, Strength Accounting Branch, Strength of the Army (STM–30) 1 August 1949.

TABLE 13—OFFICERS SEPARATED FROM THE WOMEN'S ARMY CORPS: SEPTEMBER 1942–DECEMBER 1946 [a]

| Period | Total | Death (Non-battle) | Honorable Discharge | | | | | Dishonorable Discharge | Discharge other than Honorable[c] |
			Resignation	Demobilization	Physical Disqualification	Pregnancy	Other[b]		
Total	5,622	21	29	3,602	262	465	1,219	3	21
1942	5	0	0	0	0	3	2	0	0
September	1	0	0	0	0	0	1	0	0
October	1	0	0	0	0	1	0	0	0
November	0	0	0	0	0	0	0	0	0
December	3	0	0	0	0	2	1	0	0
1943	479	7	1	0	55	49	349	0	18
January	0	0	0	0	0	0	0	0	0
February	3	0	0	0	0	3	0	0	0
March	4	0	0	0	1	0	3	0	0
April	5	0	0	0	0	5	0	0	0
May	8	1	0	0	1	2	4	0	0
June	15	0	0	0	2	7	5	0	1
July	17	0	0	0	5	5	6	0	1
August	205	0	0	0	2	12	188	0	3
September	191	0	0	0	36	2	140	0	13
October	9	2	0	0	3	4	0	0	0
November	13	2	0	0	4	5	2	0	0
December	9	2	1	0	1	4	1	0	0
1944	288	5	8	0	70	176	28	0	1
January	20	0	0	0	7	9	4	0	0
February	15	1	2	0	2	10	0	0	0
March	16	0	0	0	9	5	2	0	0
April	20	2	0	0	6	9	3	0	0
May	24	1	0	0	9	13	1	0	0
June	23	0	0	0	3	15	5	0	0
July	28	0	0	0	4	22	2	0	0
August	21	0	1	0	2	18	0	0	0
September	27	0	1	0	1	24	1	0	0
October	20	0	0	0	5	12	3	0	0
November	35	0	0	0	11	20	4	0	0
December	39	1	4	0	11	19	3	0	1
1945	1,545	6	19	963	103	232	218	3	1
January	28	0	1	0	9	15	3	0	0
February	31	0	4	0	5	17	5	0	0
March	45	0	2	0	15	25	3	0	0
April	50	2	7	0	11	23	5	1	1
May	39	0	2	1	2	27	7	0	0
June	39	1	1	3	7	22	5	0	0
July	58	0	0	11	6	31	10	0	0
August	83	1	0	35	14	22	10	1	0
September	71	0	1	30	10	23	6	1	0
October	162	2	1	114	10	13	22	0	0
November	325	0	0	273	4	5	43	0	0
December	614	0	0	496	10	9	99	0	0
1946	3,305	3	1	2,639	34	5	622	0	1
January	810	1	0	634	6	1	168	0	0
February	461	0	0	317	7	1	136	0	0
March	462	0	0	363	0	0	98	0	1
April	332	0	0	263	3	0	66	0	0
May	314	1	1	277	2	0	33	0	0
June	235	0	0	209	4	0	22	0	0
July	187	0	0	161	3	1	22	0	0
August	144	0	0	128	2	0	14	0	0
September	128	0	0	101	4	1	22	0	0
October	66	0	0	52	2	0	12	0	0
November	62	0	0	44	1	0	17	0	0
December	104	1	0	90	0	1	12	0	0

[a] Includes data for 47 WAC warrant officers.
[b] Consists chiefly of personnel released as surplus officers or relieved at own request.
[c] Includes undesirable habits or traits of character and misconduct.

Source: U.S. Dept of Army, AGO, Strength Accounting Branch, Strength of the Army (STM–30), 1 August 1949, and unpublished work sheets used in compiling this report.

Appendix B

Excerpt From Report on British Women's Services

Virtue has no gossip value. It has been one of the tasks of your Committee to form some conclusion as to why the Women's Services have incurred so much criticism. Anyone who has visited a Service camp and has watched the auxiliaries at work and at play; who has noted their trim and soldierly bearing, their good discipline and high spirits, can only marvel at the unfriendly comments often current. A reasoned judgment in this matter is not easy. . . .

The British, though they fight when called upon to do so with unfaltering courage, are not a military race. They cherish a deeprooted prejudice against uniforms; consequently a woman in uniform may arouse a special sense of hostility, conscious and subconscious, among people who would never give two thoughts to her conduct as a private citizen. . . . Further, though the service rendered to their country by the women is generally recognized, there are exceptions and critics. . . . Strictures from soldiers, sailors, and airmen, small minority though they may be, carry weight out of proportion to their numbers. . . .

For the ATS, we have been supplied with detailed figures on discharges for pregnancy which prove conclusively how little truth there is in the rumor regarding illegitimate pregnancy in that Service. There are in the ATS large numbers of married women and the pregnancies of these women are often, no doubt, carelessly confused with those of the single women. The pregnancy rate for married ATS women . . . for the first five months of this year ranged from 15.5 to 17 per 1000. . . . The *pregnancy* rate among single ATS personnel is 15.5 per 1000 per annum. The illegitimate birth rate among the civilian population groups from which the ATS are recruited is approximately 21.8 per 1000 per annum . . . it is clear that if comparable figures could be arrived at the gap would be wider. . . . Furthermore a number of single women come into the Forces already pregnant . . . the percentage of single women discharged for pregnancy who were pregnant before entering the ATS ranged from 18 to 44 percent. . . . We can therefore, with certainty, say that the illegitimate birth rate in the Services is lower than the illegitimate birth rate among the comparable civilian population.

. . . The Women's Services today represent a cross-section of the population and all types and standards are represented among them. . . . Unfortunately gossip mongers never stop to reflect on such abstract and unpicturesque details as incidence and ratio which would reduce the stories they put into circulation to their just proportion. Allegations of general immorality in a camp, when investigated, resolved themselves into one or two cases which, in the course of gossip, have multiplied times over. And the same applies to charges of drunkenness.

. . . Loose behavior, when it occurs, is not necessarily the product of service life: it is introduced primarily from without. Service life, with its discipline, work and good comradeship, generally puts the relations of men and women on a healthy and normal basis.

We can find no justification for the vague but sweeping charges of immorality which had disturbed public opinion, and in this we are supported by representatives of the various welfare organizations and the Chaplains who are in constant touch with the girls. . . . Promiscuous conduct in the Women's Services is confined to a small proportion of the whole. . . . Your committee can only deplore the irresponsible conduct of persons who, without any first hand knowledge, are content to damage the war effort by malicious or careless talk derogatory to the forces of the Crown. These tales are deeply wounding to auxiliaries. . . . Further, slanderous gossip has a very adverse effect on recruiting.

It is not without interest to note that in 1918 wild and fantastic tales were in circulation about the immorality of the W.A.A.C.s in France; tales almost identical in substance with those current. . . . A Commission of Enquiry which visited France reported that apart from some cases of misconduct, the charges as generalizations were mischievous and false. Then as now, a vast superstructure of slander has been raised on a small foundation in fact.

—Report of the Committee on Amenities and Welfare Conditions in the Three Women's Services, presented to Parliament by command of His Majesty, 5 August 1942, pp. 49–52.

Appendix C

A Summary of Controversy on Legal Status of WAAC

After the conversion of the WAAC to the WAC in September 1943, numerous questions continued to arise concerning the Auxiliary Corps' legal status.

WAAC service was eventually counted by the Army toward the points required for demobilization, and in computing accrued leave. Under legislation existing at the time of the conversion period, it was not possible to go further and count it toward longevity pay and the various benefits of the GI bill such as educational rights.[1] Congress did recognize the WAAC service in two further ways: it had already granted medical, hospital, and domiciliary care under the auspices of the Veterans' Administration to former Waacs; and in early February 1944 it shortly added legislation to give mustering-out pay to those Waacs who had been discharged for disability.[2]

Director Hobby shortly proposed that the War Department recommend to Congress that service in the WAAC be counted as military service for all purposes. She stated, "Such legislation would give recognition to the fact that from a practical standpoint members of the WAAC were regarded by the War Department as military personnel."[3]

The matter dragged on for some eight months without decision by the War De-

partment. It appeared that Congress might be favorably disposed to such a request, since certain members were experiencing considerable pressure from various constituents including American Legion posts, and several members of Congress asked the War Department to take action in the matter.

In the fall of 1944 one member of Congress actually introduced a bill to provide educational benefits for members of the WAAC and the Merchant Marine. Colonel Hobby favored this plan, but the Legislative and Liaison Division disapproved of Colonel Hobby's proposal and of the legislation, and was upheld by G–1 Division and the Secretary of War.[4] Said the Secretary:

The fact remains that the legal status of the members of both groups has been that of

---

[1] M/R, undated. WDWAC 292 (1945–46).
[2] (1) PL 10, 78th Cong, 17 May 43, in WD Cir 103, 1943. (2) PL 225, 78th Cong, 3 Feb 44, in WD Bull 3, 10 Feb 44.
[3] Memo, Dir WAC for G–1 WD, 26 Feb 44, sub: Proposed Legislation Relative to WAC. SPWA 314.7 (2–26–44) E, sec 5.
[4] (1) Ltr, Senator Theodore G. Bilbo to Dir WAC, 26 Oct 44, re Mrs. Margaret Fogarty. WDWAC 095. (2) Memo, Exec WAC for Leg and Ln Div, 20 Jun 45. WDWAC 242.12. (3) D/F, Leg and Ln Div, for Dir WAC, 9 Nov 45, sub: Lt Marie Simon. WDWAC 292.

civilians. . . . The proposed grant would establish a precedent for granting other veterans' benefits to the same and other groups of persons whose service was that of civilians. In the present war, such groups include, among others, certain contractors' crews; civilians serving on Army transports; civilian pilots of the Air Transport Command; civilian instructors of the Air Forces; war correspondents; personnel of the Army Specialists Corps, Civil Air Patrol, and the Women's Auxiliary Service Pilots; and certain personnel of the Red Cross.[5]

Director Hobby continued to protest this decision, pointing out that there were two differences in the WAAC and all of the cited groups: (1) the Corps had later been brought into the Army as a group, and (2) its members had received, not the larger salaries which supposedly recompensed the Merchant Marine and all others for their civilian status, but the mere $21 a month (later $50) of the Army men. They had also been obliged to live in barracks and under military restrictions not encountered by any other such group. Her proposals were disapproved and, ironically enough, she was blamed by the public for the War Department's action; a former member of the Corps wrote her:

God frowns on such things, especially in a democratic country, and he frowns on those who are in power to change it and don't. . . . Before you leave office have this cleaned up and your conscience will be cleared.[6]

Director Hobby was unable to secure approval before her departure, and neither was the second Director, after the end of the war. At this time three bills were introduced in Congress: one to give military benefits to all Waacs, one only to Waacs discharged for disability, and one to count WAAC service toward longevity pay of its members who had joined the WAC.[7] For at least the last proposal, the second Director could marshal strong support, since credit toward longevity pay had been given to Army nurses for their civilian contract service, to female dietitians for their earlier civilian service with the Army, to members of the Officers' Reserve Corps for the time during which they had resigned commissions to serve with the American Volunteer Group in China, and to numerous others including the National Guard and Reserves. However, the War Department again disapproved all proposals, saying:

There is no policy in the War Department more soundly fixed or more historically adhered to than that the Department should oppose the inclusion of civilian groups within the special class of the military group in the matter of eligibility for benefits. . . . As for the citation of the cases of Medical Department female personnel service being included as military service, since a statute of 1802 . . . nurses and surgeons have been closely associated with the military forces in their peculiarly military status. . . .

On only one such matter was legislation enacted. After Congress passed legislation granting re-employment benefits to members of the Merchant Marine, the War Department sponsored and obtained legislation to give the same to former Waacs who had joined the WAC, and who otherwise lacked the re-employment benefits of those who had joined the WAC direct from civilian life.[8]

[5] This and WD statement below quoted in memo, Col. D. M. McConnell for G–1 WD, 4 Apr 46, sub: Recognition of Serv in WAAC, with incls. WDGAP 324.5, in WDWAC 324.5,
[6] Ltr, Miss D. Anderson to Dir WAC, Sep 44. WDWAC 095.
[7] HR 2713, HR 1405, and HR 4569.
[8] (1) Memo, Dir WAC for G–1 WD, 6 Aug 45. WDWAC 292. (2) Memo, same, 7 Aug 45. (3) PL 709, 79th Cong, 9 Aug 46, in WD Bull 26, 12 Sep 46.

Appendix D

A Summary of WASP Controversy

On 6 April 1943 the Chief of Air Staff, Maj. Gen. George E. Stratemeyer, sent a memorandum to G–1 Division, War Department General Staff, "Women's Pilot Training Program." In this he recommended that as soon as the WAAC was put in the Army by Congress, the new WAC begin to recruit flight officers and commissioned pilots for direct appointment and assignment to the AAF. By covering indorsement, 17 April 1943, WAAC Headquarters concurred and recommended that necessary modifications be made in WAAC Regulations to suit the AAF's specifications.[1]

AAF WAC leaders later agreed that no especial difficulty would result, since there were only about 800 Wasps, roughly one third of the number of Air WAC recruits the AAF absorbed monthly; and the group would have no special needs, except needs as women, which would be met by the WAC organization, or needs as pilots, which would be met by the regular pilot-training authorities.

In the next two months the AAF reversed its decision. In June 1943, Gen. Henry H. Arnold sent a memorandum to General Marshall, undated, "Incorporation of Women Civilian Pilots and Trainees into AAF." General Arnold opposed putting pilots in the WAC because of the "need for undivided administrative and functional control which would not be possible if the WAAF was serving two masters, i. e., the WAAC and the AAF." A reply from G–1 Division, 20 June 1943, opposed the establishment of a separate Corps of women pilots on the grounds that "We have endeavored to keep the women's organization as simple and flexible as possible," and that it would be wasteful to have two women's corps.[2]

General Arnold's change of opinion was closely related to the fact that Miss Jacqueline Cochran had been appointed Director of Women Pilots on June 28, and was opposed to enrollment of women pilots in the WAC, preferring a separate corps headed by a female colonel similar to the WAC, WAVES, SPARS, and Marine heads.[3] This the War Department steadily opposed, since there were no separate corps for male pilots and all other male Air Corps officers. Nevertheless, on 20 September 1943, a bill was introduced in Congress by Representative John M. Costello to militarize a separate WASP. This ran into trouble because the AAF by this time already had a surplus of pilots. It was defeated in June of 1944, and Congress recommended that the WASP be abolished. Miss Cochran still opposed placing

[1] SPWA 314.7 (1–7–43) (1) sec 1.
[2] SPWA 324.5 CAP (3–25–43).
[3] Hist Recs Rpt 319, History of the Air Transport Command: Women in the Air Transport Command. USAF Hist Div.

the group in the WAC, and preferred instead that it be inactivated, which it was, in December 1944.[4]

Many members of the WASP wrote and came to Washington to see members of the Air Staff and members of Congress to beg that they be taken into the WAC, assigned to the AAF, and thus given military status, and later veterans' benefits. This matter was presented by the Air WAC Officer to the Air Staff for a policy decision. The decision was made that women pilots would not be commissioned in the WAC. The Commanding General, AAF, felt that in view of Congress' decision such subterfuge would be extremely poor diplomacy in Congressional relations. All inquiries were therefore answered to the effect that members of the WASP could, if qualified, enlist in the WAC for duty with the AAF, but that they would not be assigned as pilots, or promised flying duty of any sort, or commissioned unless they qualified as other Wacs did through selection by officer candidate boards, or allowed to pilot planes even if they were commissioned.

---

[4] *Ibid.*

Appendix E

(See Chapter XXXII.)

Course Content

Hours Devoted to Training

Course	WAC	1944 Men
Total	288	288
Indoctrination	15	0
Articles of War	9	} 5
Military Customs and Courtesies	12	
Safety Measures	4	2
Organization of the Army	10	2
Safeguarding Military Information, and Military Censorship	6	2
Army Orientation Course	18	6
Care of Clothing and Equipment	5	4
Interior Guard Duty	4	4
Map and Aerial Photograph Reading	10	10
Chemical Warfare	8	8
Recognition and Defense against Aircraft	5	4
Personal Hygiene and Military Sanitation	10	[a] 4 [b] 2
Social Hygiene	6	[c] 3
First Aid	11	7
Administration	14	0
Supply	6	0
Drill	30	17
Physical Training	30	20
Tests and critiques	10	6
Inspections	12	5
Ceremonies and Parades	12	0
Processing	11	0
Makeup and Review	30	24
Combat Courses	0	153

[a] Malaria Control.
[b] Sanitation only.
[c] Including Personal Hygiene.

Source: Men: MTP 21–3, 1 May 44, cited on p. 38 of "Unit and Replacement Training," ASF MTD. OCMH.
WAC: ASF Hist of WAC Training, p. 77–78.

Clerks Course

Course	Hours
Introduction	4
Organization of the Army	10
Touch Typing	80
Correspondence and Filing	35
Company Records and Reports	35
General Information	15
Military Discipline	8
Personnel Administration	30
Finance	21

Source: ASF Hist of WAC Tng.

MTP 35–10, Cooks Course, 1 July 1944

Course	Hours
Introduction	1
Mess Management	28
Meat, Fish, and Poultry	19
Fruit and Vegetables	6
Miscellaneous Foods	18
Baking	10
Dehydrated Foods	8
Field Cooking	6
Practical Cooking	192
Makeup, Review, and Tests	32
Physical Training	40
Close Order Drill	16
Army Orientation	8

MTP 35–10, Motor Vehicle Operators Course, 1 July 1944

Course	Hours
Elementary Driving Training	30
Motor Pool Administration	6
Engine	36
Chassis	30
Preventative Maintenance and Inspection	40
Administrative Dispatch Driving	36
Convoy Driving	68
Vehicle Recovery	24
Blackout Driving	16
Decontamination	2
Makeup and Review	32
Physical Training	40
Drill	16
Army Orientation Course	8

Medical and Surgical Technicians Course
(C–1 to MTP 35–10)

Course	Hours
Anatomy and Physiology	35
Emergency Medical Treatment	35
Hygiene and Prevention of Disease	28
Public Property	3

MEDICAL AND SURGICAL TECHNICIANS COURSE—Continued

Course	Hours
Ward Procedures	67
Mathematics and Materia Medica	24
Ward Management	6
General Hospital Procedures	58
Close Order Drill—½ hour per week	
Physical Conditioning—15 minutes per day	
Army Orientation—1 hour per week	
Makeup and Review—26 hours	

MEDICAL CLERKS COURSE
(C–1 TO MTP 35–10)

Course	Hours
Introduction	3
Organization of the Army	4
Organization and Administration of General Hospitals	7
Touch Typing	60
Correspondence and Filing	25
Company Records	14
Medical Boards and Reports	48
Personnel Administration	20
Finance	11
Military Discipline	3
Company Supply	6
Medical Supply	15
Machine Operations	6
Commandant's Time	12
Makeup, Review, and Tests	36
Physical Training—15 minutes per day	
Army Orientation—1 hour per week	
Drill—½ hour per week	

OFFICER CANDIDATE COURSES
(BY HOURS)

	WAAC (6 weeks)	WAC (12 weeks)	Men's Schools, 1943 AGO	JM	MA
Military Customs and Courtesy	4	10	3	4	6
Courts and Boards	14	39	[a] 36	[b] 14	[b] 25
Care of Clothing and Equipment	2			6	3
Defense Against Chemical Attack	4	6	4	4	24
Defense Against Air Attack and Camouflage	3	5	(3)	(8)	(3)
			2	9	4
Map Reading	8	16	20	33	26
Methods of Training	8	20	5	[c] 21 / [d] 19	[c] 19 / 13
Organization of Army	5	25	10	4	18
Leadership	10	12	3	3	2
Mess Management	20	20	5	4	6
Supply (Property Accounting)	15	16			
Company Administration	55	44		57	79
Interior Guard	2		4	9	2
Current History and Army Orientation	6	16	4	24	2

Officer Candidate Courses—Continued

	WAAC (6 weeks)	WAC (12 weeks)	Men's Schools, 1943 AGO	JM	MA
Classification	4	11			
Morale and Special Services	3	e 7			
Military Sanitation					
First Aid	5	14	4	23	36
Personal Hygiene					
Drill	30	36	78	40	49
Physical Training	24	59	47	27	12
Inspection and Ceremony	24	36	f 17	f 47	f 10
Commandant's Time	18	44			
Total	264				
Orientation		1			
Public Relations		6			
Duties and Responsibilities of An Officer		20			
Administrative Problems		20			
Recruiting		5			
Public Speaking		32			
Duties of a Staff Officer		14			
Procedure in a Military Office		7			
Signal Communications.		5	2	2	4
Makeup and Review		10			
Testing		12			
Total		578			
Combat Orientation			4		5
Defense Against Mechanized Attack			2	5	2
Malaria Control.			4		3
Marches and Bivouacs			26		17
Military Subjects (Miscellaneous)			41	290	36
Processing			20	10	
Tent Pitching.			2	9	5
Weapons Training.			38	92	
Total Common Subjects			384		
Total Technical			416		
Total			800		
Identification (of aircraft, etc.)				4	1
Information and Educational Activities.				17	
Motor Transportation				28	13
Total Common				813	
Total Technical				218	
Total				1,031	
Command of Negro Troops					1
Chaplaincy					1
Personal Adjustment Problems					1

a Military Law.   d Training Management.
b Law.   e Morale only.
c Instruction.   f Inspection only.

Source: This comparison is compiled from ASF Hist of WAC Tng and ASF Hist of OCT. An accurate comparison is impossible, since men's subjects listed under Miscellaneous or Technical were at times comparable to WAC subjects which appear to have no parallel, such as Administrative Problems.

Cadre Training Course

Course	Hours
Close-Order Drill	10
Physical Training	10
Leadership Qualities	12
Company Administration	28
Military Customs and Courtesies	3
Methods of Training	12
Supply	12
Army Orientation	2
Makeup and Review	3
Inspection	4

MTP 35–1, Unit Training Program for WAC Units in Field, August 1943

Required courses

Drill	½ hour each week
Physical Training	1¼ hour each week
Inspection	½ hour each week
Military Customs, etc.	2 hours every 3 months
Preventive Medicine	2 " " 6 "
Personal Hygiene	2 " " 6 "
Articles of War	1 " " 6 "
Safeguarding Military Information	1 " " 2 "
Disciplinary Procedures	2 " " 6 "
Orientation	6 " upon arrival

Suggested additional courses

Defense Against Chemical Attack	Army Orientation
Defense Against Air Attack	Current Events
First Aid	Technical and professional courses: typing, shorthand, language, etc.
Care of Clothing and Equipment	On-the-job Training

MTP 35–2, Mobilization Training Program for WAC Detachments in the Field, 15 October 1944

Required courses

Drill	½ hour each week
Physical Training	¼ hour 5 days a week
Army Orientation	1 hour each week
Social Hygiene	2 hours every 6 months
Personal Hygiene	1 " " 6 "
Control of Communicable Diseases	1 " " 6 "
Personal Adjustment	1 " " 6 "

Suggested additional courses

First Aid	4 hours every 6 months
Military Customs and Courtesy	2 " " 6 "
Safeguarding Military Information	2 " " 6 "
Organization of the Army	2 " " 6 "
Defense Against Chemical Attack	2 " " 6 "
Defense Against Air Attack	2 " " 6 "
Military Law	2 " " 6 "
Map and Aerial Photograph Reading	4 " " 6 "
Army Administration	2 " " 6 "
Drill (additional)	5 " " 6 "

Bibliographical Note

The materials for a history of the Women's Army Corps in World War II are widely scattered. Unlike the histories of some units and campaigns, the history of the WAC must cover most of the areas of the world—-Europe, North Africa, the Middle East, Southeast Asia, and the Southwest Pacific, as well as the three major commands in the United States—the Army Air Forces, Army Ground Forces, and Army Service Forces. Unlike the histories of technical services, it must tell the story of Wacs employed in not one but almost all branches of the Army.

During a good part of its wartime existence, the Corps had no centralized files to which automatically came all memoranda and other papers concerning the Corps. For the first year of its existence, as a separate Auxiliary, the WAAC had its own historian, 1st Lt. Virginia Smithson, and maintained complete records, as a project of the WAAC Control Division, which had hoped the material could "be referred to 20 to 30 years from now and a new women's organization built up on the experience we have learned from this experiment." Collections had been made of Army, WAAC, ASF, and AGO regulations, printed legislative records, headquarters policies, and other documents pertaining to the WAAC, and it was intended that the historian would set each WAAC company to collecting historical materials.

After conversion of the WAAC to full military status in the summer of 1943, however, work on the WAAC history was stopped, no separate historical program was permitted, and the WAAC files at the Office of the Director were broken up and scattered. From September of 1943 on, there were no centralized WAC records, and companies in the field did not forward any historical materials to headquarters.

Responsibility for keeping historical records was delegated to the various commands to which Wacs were assigned, but at the end of the war it was discovered that few Army commands had prepared any final record of their scattered and often tiny WAC minorities. In particular, it was impossible to obtain from Army histories, published or unpublished, the data on which the future planning for the efficient employment of women must be based. The present study, when commissioned, was thus handicapped by a late start, at a time when records and files were already intermixed with those of Army commands over four continents, and when many Wacs had already returned to civilian life.

The Women's Army Corps was created in wartime, and ran its course during months when the Army's primary mission was combat, not research. The WAC was not regarded by the Army as an experimental group on which it could collect valuable data, much to the disappointment of civilian agencies desirous of obtaining complete statistics on the WAC.

The lack of wartime field studies has made necessary a rather heavy documentation, since a chapter cannot be based on a single field study, or several, but must

ordinarily be based on previously un-
worked files and be laboriously footnoted
with hundreds of separate letters and
memoranda.

Primary Sources

The bulk of materials on the history of
the WAAC and WAC is in the WAAC–
WAC files, now in the G–1 Area, Depart-
mental Records Branch, Adjutant General's Office (DRB AGO), under several
file designations:

WA   : before 9 March 1942
SPWA   : 9 March 1942–29 February
          1944 (the period during
          which the WAAC–WAC
          was under the Army Service
          Forces)
WDWAC: 1   March   1944–(after   the
          WAC's transfer to G–1 Divi-
          sion of the War Department
          General Staff)

This collection contains the WAAC historical files (a series of looseleaf notebooks), the WAAC planning files (of Miss
B. Eugenia Lies and other consultants),
the WAAC Planning Service files, the
stayback files of Lt. Col. Gilman C. Mudgett, first WAAC Pre-Planner, and of Lt.
Col. Harold P. Tasker, as well as Colonel
Tasker's personal files.

At the same location are the *Hobby files,*
formerly at the Office of the Director,
WAC, comprised of Director Hobby's personal files and of the WAAC Daily Journal—the latter consisting of a manila
folder labeled "Staff Conferences for the
Period August–October 1942," and two
loose-leaf notebooks (Volumes I and II)
for the period November 1942–August
1943.

There is also a small file of WAAC–
WAC material, cited as *WAC files, OCMH.*
This material was collected by the author
during research for this volume and is filed
at OCMH as supporting documents. Some
material on the Wacs in the Army Air
Forces is at the U.S. Air Force Historical
Division, Air University, Maxwell Air
Force Base, Alabama. Some papers concerning the WAAC–WAC under the Army
Service Forces are in the file of the Director of Personnel, ASF, Special Collections,
DRB AGO. Also useful were the files of
the Chief of Staff, and General Marshall's
personal files, made available to the
author by his secretary.

For all other information on the WAC,
it is necessary to go directly to the files of
the command, branch, or theater concerned, as indicated in "Secondary
Sources," below.

Materials on the plans for the use of
women in the Army before World War II
are to be found principally in the War Department collection in the National
Archives, and in the G–1 files at DRB
AGO.

Secondary Sources

The secondary sources for a history of
the WAC consist principally of manuscripts prepared by the historians of various WAC units, or by historians of other
branches of the Army that employed
Wacs. These histories are of uneven
quality and degree of thoroughness of coverage. The story of Wacs in the Army Air
Forces, for instance, is thoroughly covered
in Lt. Col. Betty Bandel's history, The
WAC Program in the Army Air Forces,
while the corresponding manuscript for
the Army Service Forces consists of a ten-
page summary. The history of Wacs in

some services and branches—for example, the Chemical Warfare Service—was not recorded in detail, because of the secrecy of the work that Wacs performed. In other cases, material on Wacs quite probably exists in uncatalogued files of various commands and theaters, but obviously it was not possible for one writer-researcher to sift through all Army records for such material.

Army Air Forces

The WAC Program in the Army Air Forces, a 97-page typescript prepared in November of 1946, by Colonel Bandel, the Air WAC Officer, represents a summary of material then on file in the Air WAC Division, Headquarters, AAF. Copies are now on file at the Office of the Chief of Military History and at the U.S. Air Force Historical Division, Air University, Maxwell Air Force Base, Alabama. This study is cited in footnotes as *AAF WAC Hist.*

The history of Wacs in the Air Transport Command is partly covered in two manuscript studies: History of the Air Transport Command: Women Pilots in the Air Transport Command, and Historical Records Report 315c, Wacs in the European Division, Air Transport Command, both on file at the U.S. Air Force Historical Division. Most of the latter appears to be the work of Pfc. Mary E. Asseltyne of the Historical Unit. Information on Wacs in the Air Forces in Europe is contained in the History of the U.S. Strategic Air Forces. Statistics on Wacs in the Air Forces are found in the AAF Statistical Digest, World War II, prepared by the Office of Statistical Control, Headquarters, Army Air Forces.

Army Ground Forces

The history of Wacs in the Army Ground Forces is told in The WAC in Army Ground Forces, World War II, prepared by the AGF WAC Officer, Lt. Col. Emily E. Davis. It consists of two bound volumes of typescript: Volume I, Summary of WAC Program in the AGF (87 pages), and Volume II, Copies of Documents Cited (28 documents). This study is now on file at OCMH, and the documents that compose Volume II are on file in Folder "WAC" in the AGF files, Special Collections, DRB AGO. It is cited in footnotes as *AGF WAC Hist.*

Army Service Forces

Unlike the AAF and the AGF, the Army Service Forces did not prepare any history of its WAC program at the end of the war, because of its objections to separate statistics for women. The only document resembling a history is a ten-page summary entitled "Distribution, Versatility, and Excellence of Wacs Serving With Army Service Forces," which was prepared by the ASF WAC Officer, Lt. Col. Katherine R. Goodwin a year before the end of the war. It is now on file at OCMH and is cited in footnotes as *ASF WAC Summary.*

Also at OCMH are: (1) History: Office of the Director of Personnel, Army Service Forces, 20 July 1942–1 September 1945, prepared by Maj. Margaret Perry. (2) History of Military Training: WAAC/ WAC Training, Army Service Forces, prepared by Maj. Lavinia L. Redd, WAC, 5 February 1946, cited in footnotes as *ASF Hist of WAC Tng.*

Theater Histories

North African and Mediterranean Theaters. No history of the WAC in the North African or Mediterranean theaters was written, but material on this subject has been found in the History of the Mediterranean Allied Air Forces, December 1943–1 September 1944, by Headquarters, MAAF, and in the WAC Redeployment Summary, a memorandum from the WAC public relations officer, Headquarters, MTOUSA, for the WAC Group, War Department Bureau of Public Relations, 12 September 1945. The most important materials on the WAC in North Africa and the Mediterranean are in the WAAC–WAC files and in a collection of important theater memoranda in the personal possession of Lt. Col. Dorothea A. Coleman, WAC Staff Director, North African Theater of Operations, cited as *Coleman file.*

European Theater. The European theater was the only overseas theater that attempted any final written evaluation of its WAC program. This was Report of the General Board, U.S. Forces, European Theater, "Study of the Women's Army Corps in the European Theater of Operations," (G–1 Section, Study 11), a three-volume mimeographed study, on file at OCMH, cited in footnotes as *ETO Bd Rpt.* The members of the board were Col. Charles VanWay, Jr., GSC, Lt. Col. Anna W. Wilson, WAC, and Capt. Martha Selvik, WAC. The Historical Section, Headquarters, European Theater of Operations, prepared a manuscript, History of WAAC–WAC in ETO, 1942–44, a copy of which is at OCMH, cited in footnotes as *ETO WAC Hist.*

Middle East Theater. Unusually complete historical reports were brought back from the Middle East theater by Dr. T. H. Vail Motter, of the Middle East Section, OCMH. These are: (1) Historical Data, WAC Detachment, Middle East Service Command, Camp Huckstep, 11 September 1944, by Lt. Jane A. Riebesell, WAC Historical Officer, with appendixes for July, August, September, and October of 1944, cited as *Unit Hist Camp Huckstep.* (2) Historical Review, WAC Detachment, Cairo Military District, 28 August 1945, cited as *Unit Hist Cairo Det.* The last thirteen pages pertain to the WAC Unit at Camp Huckstep, September 1944 to April 1945. (3) Summary: WAC AMET [Women's Army Corps in the Africa–Middle East Theater], prepared for Dr. Motter by Sgt. Birdie Weisbrod, June 1945, based on files of the G–2 Historical Section, AMET, and cited as *WAC AMET Summary.*

Southeast Asia Command. No records of the WAC in this area were found, with the exception of a memorandum from Maj. Margaret D. Craighill for The Surgeon General, 6 April 1945, on medical and social conditions of women in military service in Ceylon, now on file at the Historical Division, Surgeon General's Office.

China–Burma–India Theater. The report on the China–Burma–India theater is the best documented of all overseas theater reports, since the entire files of the WAC sections of the theater headquarters were brought back to the United States by special courier and deposited in G–1 Division of the War Department General Staff, at the Office of the Director, WAC. These are bound in several indexed folders, referred to as *CBI WAC files.*

There are also two official reports on the WAC in the China–Burma–India theater: (1) A report by AAF headquarters, India–Burma theater, to The Adjutant General, in answer to a Congressional inquiry, on Wac health and living conditions in the India–Burma theater, 5 July 1945, now in the WAC files, cited as *AAF IBT Rpt.* (2) A report by Maj. Margaret D. Craighill to The Surgeon General, 30 March 1945, on medical and social conditions of women in military service in the India–Burma theater, cited as *Craighill IBT Rpt.* Some information on the WAC is also contained in the History of the India–Burma Theater, 25 October 1944–23 June 1945, prepared by the CBI Section, OCMH.

Southwest Pacific Area. No official history of the WAC in the Southwest Pacific theater has been written. Because of differences of opinion in the records, research has been carried to the unit records level, although time and facilities did not permit this to be done for other theaters. Besides thirty folders of theater files now at Field Records Division, Kansas City Records Center, Kansas City, Mo., the account of the WAC in the Southwest Pacific is based on the following reports: (1) The *"Griffith Account,"* an unsigned, undated typescript presented to the author by the War Department Bureau of Public Relations. Authorship of this document is reliably attributed to Capt. Velma P. Griffith, WAC Public Relations Officer, Southwest Pacific Area, who was an eyewitness to many events described therein, and who had access to theater WAC data. It is in agreement with other accounts and offers a valuable narrative of experiences of WAC detachments, although not employed as an authority for statistics or policy. (2) *WAC Draft AFPAC Reply,* draft prepared by the WAC Staff Director, Army Forces in the Pacific, in response to a War Department request for an investigation of WAC conditions in the Southwest Pacific.

This draft was approved by the WAC Staff Directors, Army Forces in the West Pacific and Far East Air Forces. It contains much material deleted by Headquarters, AFPAC, from the final version of the report. (3) *AFPAC Reply,* the official report, based on the above draft, from Headquarters, U.S. Army Forces in the Pacific, to The Adjutant General, 1 November 1945, on WAC personnel in the Southwest Pacific Area. (4) *Boyce Rpt,* an official report by Col. Westray Battle Boyce, Director WAC, to the Chief of Staff, USA, on her visit to WAC personnel in overseas theaters. (5) *Craighill SWPA Rpt,* a memorandum prepared by Major Craighill on medical and social conditions of women in military service in SWPA. Attached is a list of interviews with more than 200 individuals in SWPA, including chief nurses, WAC detachment commanders, hospital commanders, Army commanders, inspectors; also a table of comparative rates of medical evacuation for Wacs and Nurses, 1 July 44 to 1 April 45. (6) Approximately twenty-five interviews between the author and persons who had been in the Southwest Pacific Area during the war, and comments by some of them on Chapter XXII:

Theater Authorities:

Baird, Col. Harry H., wartime G–1, USAFFE until 1 June 1945; interview and written statement, 29 July 1948; comments on chapter, 23 April 1951.

Campbell, Brig. Gen. William F., Chief Quartermaster, USASOS; interview, 24 July 1947.

Davis, Col. Merle H., Deputy Chief Ordnance Officer, USASOS, Chief Ordnance Officer, AFWESPAC; interview, 24 July 1947.

Denit, Brig. Gen. Guy B., Chief Surgeon, USASOS; interview, 24 July 1947.

Dunn, Lt. Col. Charles, Personnel Policy Board (SWPA Replacement Study), Office of the Secretary of Defense; interview, 13 August 1947.

Ginsburgh, Col. A. Robert, G–1 and G–3, USASOS; interview, 25 July 1947; comments on chapter, 13 August 1947.

WAC Advisers:

Brown, Lt. Col. Mary-Agnes, Staff Director, SWPA and AFPAC, March 1944–May 1945; interview, June 1945 and 5 June 1947.

Costello, Dorothy Pat, a sergeant at AFPAC headquarters; interview, 4 August 1948.

Foushee, Capt. Fay, Transportation Corps, USASOS; interview, 27 July 1947.

Galloway, Lt. Col. Mera, Staff Director, AFPAC, September 1945–1946; interview, 6 November 1946; comments on chapter, 22 May 1951.

Gardiner, Maj. Annie V., Staff Director, WESPAC, September 1945–January 1946; interview, 22 July 1947.

Kelly, Maj. Charlee L., Assistant Staff Director, SWPA and AFPAC, 1944–45, and Acting Staff Director, May–September 1945; interview, 28 July 1947.

Kersey, Maj. Mary L., Staff Director, FEAF, October 1944–December 1945; interview, 23 July 1947; comments on chapter, 21 April 1951.

Letallier, Capt. Jeanne, IG Section, USAFFE; interview, 9 January 1946.

Shields, Capt. Rita, Ordnance, USASOS; interview, 27 July 1947.

War Department WAC Advisers:

Boyce, Col. Westray Battle, Director, WAC, July 1945–May 1947.

Craighill, Lt. Col. Margaret, MC, SGO.

Ludwigsen, Maj. Marjorie, Staff Inspection Section, Air WAC Division, Headquarters, AAF.

Theater Historians:

A draft of Chapter XXII was the subject of a seminar at which were present Colonels Brown and Ginsburgh and members of the Pacific Section, Historical Division, SSUSA (later OCMH), including Dr. Louis Morton, Mr. Samuel Milner, Capt. Robert Ross Smith, and Maj. Nelson L. Drummond, Jr., who furnished written and oral comments.

Wacs in the Technical and Administrative Services

None of the technical or administrative services prepared any final summary of its employment of Wacs. The nearest approach to such a survey is the typescript Narrative History of the Military Personnel Branch, Office of the Chief Signal Officer: Activities in Connection with WAAC or WAC Personnel for Signal Corps Duty, October 1943. The Office of the Chief of Chaplains included a section, "Ministrations to WAC," in its official history, Military History of the Second World War: The Corps of Chaplains. A chapter of the history of the Hampton Roads Port of Embarkation is devoted to the activities of the Transportation Corps Wacs.

Other Women's Services

The WAVES

No official history of the WAVES has ever been published. There is on file at the Office of the Director of Naval History a manuscript, First Draft Narrative, U.S. Naval Administration in World War II: Bureau of Naval Personnel, Women's Reserve, 18 January 1946, cited as *WAVES Hist.*

The Army Nurse Corps

Comparisons with the experiences of the Army Nurse Corps are based upon: (1) Organized Nursing and the Army in Three Wars; a Political and Administrative History of the Army Nurse Corps, by Mary W. Standlee, Walter Reed Hospital, in collaboration with Florence A. Blanchfield, R. N., Col., ANC, a copy of which was furnished the author in manuscript. (2) A pamphlet, *The Army Nurse,* published by the Army Nurse Corps.

The British Women's Services

Comparisons between American and British women's services are based principally on a 58-page pamphlet, *Report of the Committee on Amenities and Welfare Conditions in the Three Women's Services,* presented to Parliament, August, 1943, printed and published by His Majesty's Stationery Office. Other information is contained in D. Collett Wadge (ed.), *Women in Uniform* (London: S. Low, Marston [1946]).

List of Abbreviations

A–1	Assistant Chief of Air Staff for Personnel
A–4	Assistant Chief of Air Staff for Matériel
AAA	Antiaircraft artillery
AAB	Army air base
AACS	Army Airways Communications Service
AAF	Army Air Forces
ACofAS	Assistant Chief of Air Staff
ACofS	Assistant Chief of Staff
AFHQ	Allied Forces Headquarters (North Africa)
AFPAC	Army Forces in the Pacific
AFWESPAC	Army Forces in the West Pacific
AG	Adjutant general
AGCT	Army General Classification Test
AGD	Adjutant General's Department
AGF	Army Ground Forces
AGO	Adjutant General's Office
AMET	Africa–Middle East Theater
ANC	Army Nurse Corps
AR	Army Regulations
ASC	Air Service Command
ASF	Army Service Forces
Asgmt	Assignment
ASTP	Army Specialized Training Program
ASW	Assistant Secretary of War
ATC	Air Transport Command
ATS	Auxiliary Territorial Service
AUS	Army of the United States
AWS	Aircraft Warning Service
AWVS	American Women's Volunteer Services
Bd	Board
Bn	Battalion
CBI	China–Burma–India theater
Cbl	Cablegram
CDD	Certificate of Disability for Discharge
Cen	Center

CFTC	Central Flying Training Command
CG	Commanding General
CIC	Counterintelligence Corps
CID	Criminal Investigation Division
CinC	Commander-in-chief
Cir	Circular
Classif	Classification
CM–IN	Classified Message sent into Pentagon
CM–OUT	Classified Message sent out of Pentagon
CO	Commanding Officer
Co	Company
Cof	Chief of (in combinations)
CofS	Chief of Staff
CofT	Chief of Transportation
Com	Committee
Comd	Command
Comdr	Commander
Comdt	Commandant
Comptr	Comptroller
Conf	Conference
Contl	Control
CSigO	Chief Signal Officer
CT	China Theater
CWS	Chemical Warfare Service
DCofS	Deputy Chief of Staff
Def	Defense
Dep	Deputy
Det	Detachment
D/F	Disposition Form
Dir	Director
Div	Division
DRB AGO	Departmental Records Branch, Adjutant General's Office
EDC	Eastern Defense Command
EFS	Extended Field Service
EM	Enlisted men
Engr	Engineer
Enl	Enlisted
Enlmt	Enlistment
ESCTC	Eastern Signal Corps Training Center
ETO	European Theater of Operations
ETOUSA	European Theater of Operations, U.S. Army

EW	Enlisted women
Exec	Executive, executive Officer
FA	Field Artillery
FEAF	Far East Air Forces
FEASC	Far East Air Service Command
Fin	Finance
Fld	Field
G–1	Assistant Chief of Staff for Personnel
G–2	Assistant Chief of Staff for Military Intelligence
G–3	Assistant Chief of Staff for Operations and Training
G–4	Assistant Chief of Staff for Supply and Evacuation
Gen	General
GO	General Orders
Gp	Group
GS	General Staff
HD SSUSA	Historical Division, Special Staff, U.S. Army
Hist	Historical
HR	House of Representatives (before bill numbers)
HRPOE	Hampton Roads Port of Embarkation
IBT	India–Burma theater
I&E	Information and Education
IG	Inspector general
IGD	Inspector General's Department
Ind	Indorsement
Insp	Inspection, inspector
Int	Intelligence
Interv	Interview
IOS	Intermediate Officer's School
IPD	Industrial Personnel Division
JA	Judge Advocate
JAG	The Judge Advocate General
Leg	Legislative
Ln	Liaison
Ltr	Letter
MAAF	Mediterranean Allied Air Forces
MAT	Mental Alertness Test
MC	Medical Corps

MD	Medical Department
MDW	Military District of Washington
Med	Medical
MI	Military Intelligence
MID	Military Intelligence Division
Mil	Military
Min	Minutes
MIS	Military Intelligence Service
MOS	Military Occupational Specialty
MPB	Military Personnel Branch
MPD	Military Personnel Department
M/R	Memo for Record
Msg	Message
MT	Motor Transport
M/T	Manning Tables
MTD	Military Training Division
Mtg	Meeting
MTO	Mediterranean Theater of Operations
MTOUSA	Mediterranean Theater of Operations, U.S. Army
NAACP	National Association for the Advancement of Colored People
NATO	North African Theater of Operations
NATOUSA	North African Theater of Operations, U.S. Army
NCAC	National Civilian Advisory Council
NYPOE	New York Port of Embarkation
O	Office (in combinations)
1st O, 2d O, 3d O	First Officer, Second Officer, Third Officer
OC	Officer Candidate
OCMH	Office of the Chief of Military History
OCofOrd	Office, Chief of Ordnance
OCofS	Office, Chief of Staff
OCS	Officer Candidate School
OCSigO	Office, Chief Signal Officer
Off	Officer
OPD	Operations and Planning Division, War Department General Staff
Opn(s)	Operation(s)
OQMG	Office of The Quartermaster General
Ord	Ordnance
Orgn	Organization
OSS	Office of Strategic Services
OTI	Office of Technical Information

OWI	Office of War Information
OWM	Office of War Manpower
P&A	Personnel and Administration
Par	Paragraph
Pers	Personnel
PL	Public Law
Plng	Planning
PM	Provost marshal
PMG	Provost Marshal General
POE	Port of Embarkation
PRO	Public Relations Officer
Proj	Project
QM	Quartermaster
QMC	Quartermaster Corps
QMG	The Quartermaster General
Rctg	Recruiting
Rec	Record
Reg	Regulation
Rep	Representative
Repl	Replacement
Reqmt	Requirement
R&I	Recruiting and Induction
RPB	Recruiting Publicity Bureau
S	Senate (before bill numbers)
Sch	School
SEAC	Southeast Asia Command
Sec	Section
Serv	Service
SFPOE	San Francisco Port of Embarkation
SG	Surgeon General
SGO	Surgeon General's Office
SHAEF	Supreme Headquarters, Allied Expeditionary Force
SigC	Signal Corps
SigO	Signal Officer
SN	Secretary of the Navy
SO	Special Order
SOS	Services of Supply
Sp	Special
SPARS	Women's service in the U.S. Coast Guard
SPD	Special Planning Division

SPOBS	Special Observer Group (American Mission in Britain)
SS	Selective Service
SSN	Specification Serial Number
SSUSA	Special Staff, U.S. Army
Stat	Statistical
Stf	Staff
Sub	Subject
Surv	Survey
SvC	Service Command
SW	Secretary of War
SWPA	Southwest Pacific Area
Tab	Table
TAG	The Adjutant General
TC	Transportation Corps
T/E	Table of Equipment
Tech	Technical
Telg	Telegram
TIG	The Inspector General
Tng	Training
T/O	Table of Organization
Tp	Telephone
USAF	U.S. Air Forces
USAFBI	U.S. Army Forces in the British Isles
USAFFE	U.S. Army Forces in the Far East
USAFI	U.S. Armed Forces Institute
USAFIME	U.S. Army Forces in the Middle East
USAFPAC	U.S. Army Forces, Pacific
USAFWESPAC	U.S. Army Forces, West Pacific
USASOS	U.S. Army Services of Supply (Southwest Pacific)
USFCT	U.S. Forces, China Theater
USFET	U.S. Forces, European Theater Redesignation of ETOUSA after 1 Jul 45.
USMA	U.S. Military Academy
USN	U.S. Navy
USO	United Service Organizations
USSTAF	U.S. Strategic Air Forces (in Europe)
VA	Veterans' Administration
WAAC	Women's Army Auxiliary Corps
Waac	A member of the WAAC
WAAF	Women's Army Auxiliary Force (proposed name for WAAC)

WAAF	Women's Auxiliary Air Force (British)
WAC	Women's Army Corps
Wac	A member of the WAC
WAF	Women in the Air Force
WASP	Women Air Service Pilots
WAVES	Women Accepted for Volunteer Emergency Service (the women's service in the U.S. Navy)
Wave	A member of the WAVES
WCT	Women's Classification Test
WD	War Department
WDBPR	War Department Bureau of Public Relations
WDC	Western Defense Command
WDGS	War Department General Staff
WFTC	Western Flying Training Command
WIRES	Women in Radio and Electrical Service
WMC	War Manpower Commission
WO	Warrant Officer
WPD	War Plans Division, of the War Department General Staff
ZI	Zone of Interior

United States Army in World War II

The multivolume series, UNITED STATES ARMY IN WORLD WAR II, consists of a number of subseries which are tentatively planned as follows: The War Department, the Army Air Forces, The Army Ground Forces, The Army Service Forces, the Defense of the Western Hemisphere, The War in the Pacific, The European Theater of Operations, The War in the Mediterranean, The Middle East Theater, The China–Burma–India Theater, Civil Affairs, The Technical Services, Special Studies, and Pictorial Record.

The following volumes have been published or are in press:*

The War Department
Chief of Staff: Prewar Plans and Preparations
Washington Command Post: The Operations Division
Strategic Planning for Coalition Warfare: 1941–1942
Global Logistics and Strategy: 1940–1943

The Army Ground Forces
The Organization of Ground Combat Troops
The Procurement and Training of Ground Combat Troops

The Army Service Forces
The Organization and Role of the Army Service Forces

The War in the Pacific
Okinawa: The Last Battle
Guadalcanal: The First Offensive
The Approach to the Philippines
The Fall of the Philippines
Leyte: Return to the Philippines
The Seizure of the Gilberts and Marshalls

The European Theater of Operations
The Lorraine Campaign
Cross-Channel Attack
Logistical Support of the Armies (Volume I)
The Supreme Command

The Middle East Theater
The Persian Corridor and Aid to Russia

---

*The volumes on the Army Air Forces, published by the University of Chicago Press, are not included in this list.

Index